Defeat and Division

Defeat and Division launches a definitive new account of France in the Second World War. In this first volume, Douglas Porch dissects France's 1940 collapse, the dynamics of occupation, and the rise of Charles de Gaulle's Free France crusade, culminating in the November 1942 Allied invasion of French North Africa. He captures the full sweep of France's wartime experience in Europe, Africa, and beyond, from soldiers and POWs to civilians-in-arms, colonial subjects, and foreign refugees. He recounts France's struggles to reconstruct military power within the context of a global conflict, with its armed forces shattered into warring factions and the country under Axis occupation. Disagreements over the causes of the 1940 debacle and the subsequent requirement for the armistice mirrored long-standing fractures in politics, in society, and in the French military itself. Douglas Porch shows how efforts to reconstitute French military power crumbled into Vichy collaboration, de Gaulle's exile resistance, Alsace-Moselle occupation struggles, and a scuffle for imperial supremacy.

Douglas Porch is Distinguished Professor Emeritus and former Chair of the Department of National Security Affairs at the Naval Postgraduate School in Monterey, California. His previous books include *Counterinsurgency: Exposing the Myths of the New Way of War*, *The Path to Victory: The Mediterranean Theater in World War II* (published in Britain as *Hitler's Mediterranean Gamble*), *The French Secret Services: From the Dreyfus Affair to the Gulf War*, *The French Foreign Legion: A Complete History of the Legendary Fighting Force*, *The Conquest of the Sahara*, *The Conquest of Morocco*, *The March to the Marne: The French Army 1871–1914*, *The Portuguese Armed Forces and the Revolution*, and *Army and Revolution: France 1815–1848.*

ARMIES OF THE SECOND WORLD WAR

This is a major new series of histories of the armies of the key combatants in the Second World War. The books are written by leading military historians and consider key aspects of military activity for each of the major powers, including planning, intelligence, strategy and operations. As with the parallel Armies of the Great War series, military and strategic history is considered within the broader context of foreign policy aims and allied strategic relations, national mobilisation and the war's domestic social, political and economic effects.

A full list of titles in the series can be found at:
www.cambridge.org/armiesofworldwarii

Defeat and Division

France at War, 1939–1942

Douglas Porch

CAMBRIDGE
UNIVERSITY PRESS

CAMBRIDGE
UNIVERSITY PRESS

University Printing House, Cambridge CB2 8BS, United Kingdom

One Liberty Plaza, 20th Floor, New York, NY 10006, USA

477 Williamstown Road, Port Melbourne, VIC 3207, Australia

314–321, 3rd Floor, Plot 3, Splendor Forum, Jasola District Centre, New Delhi – 110025, India

103 Penang Road, #05–06/07, Visioncrest Commercial, Singapore 238467

Cambridge University Press is part of the University of Cambridge.

It furthers the University's mission by disseminating knowledge in the pursuit of education, learning, and research at the highest international levels of excellence.

www.cambridge.org
Information on this title: www.cambridge.org/9781107047464
DOI: 10.1017/9781107239098

First published 2022

Printed in the United Kingdom by TJ Books Limited, Padstow Cornwall

A catalogue record for this publication is available from the British Library.

ISBN 978-1-107-04746-4 Hardback

Contents

Figures

Maps

Abbreviations

AAA	Anti-aircraft artillery
AC	Armistice Commission
ACC	Allied Control Commission
ACI	Advisory Council for Italy
AD	Armored Division
ADD	Amis de Darlan
AEF	French Equatorial Africa
AFAT	Auxiliaires féminines de l'armée de terre
AFHQ	Allied Forces Headquarters
AFN	Afrique française du nord/French North Africa
AMGOT	Allied Military Government of Occupied Territories
AOF	French West Africa
AS	Armée secrète
Ast	Abwehrstellen
ATS	Auxiliary Territorial Service
Bat d'Af	Bataillon d'infanterie légère d'Afrique
BCRA	Bureau central de renseignements et d'action
BCRAA	BCRA Algiers
BCRAL	BCRA London
BCRAM	BCRA Militaire
BDM	Bund Deutscher Mädel
BDS	Befehlshaber der Sicherheitspolizei und des SD
BEF	British Expeditionary Force
BFL	Brigade française libre
BFO	Brigade française libre d'Orient
BIA	Bataillon d'infanterie aéroportée
BM	Bataillon de marche/bataillon médical
BMA	Bureau des menées antinationales
BMC	Bordel militaire de campagne
CAD	Civil Affairs Division
CAF	Corps d'armée français
CCFA	Commandant en chef français en Allemagne

CCS	Combined Chiefs of Staff (US and UK)
CCZN	Comité de coordination de la zone nord
CDL	Comité départmental de libération
CDM	Camouflage du matériel
CDN	Comité de défense nationale
CEF	Corps expéditionnaire français en Italie
CEFEO	Corps expéditionnaire français d'Extrême-Orient
CFLN	Comité français de libération nationale
CFT	Corps féminin des transmissions
CGM	Commandment des goums marocains
CGT	Conféderation générale du travail
CIGS	Chief of the Imperial General Staff
CLI	Corps léger d'intervention
CLL	Comité local de libération
CNF	Comité national français
CNI	Commissariat national à l'Intérieur
CNR	Conseil national de la résistance
COMIDAC/ COMAC	Comité d'action en France
COS	Chief of Staff
COSSAC	Chief of Staff to Supreme Allied Commander
CP	Command post
CPDN	Comité permanent de la Défense Nationale
CRA	Centre de ralliement et d'accueil
CRS	Compagnies républicaines de sécurité
CSAR	Comité secret d'action révolutionaire (Cagoule)
CSDN	Comité supérieur de la Défense Nationale
CSTM	Commandant supérieur des troupes du Maroc
CSTT	Commandant supérieur des troupes de Tunisie
CUAR	Comité d'Unité d'Action Révolutionnaire
CVF	Corps des volontaires françaises (female volunteers for la France libre)
DAA	Détachement de l'Armée de l'Atlantique
DAF	Deutsche Arbeitsfront
DAL	Deutsch-Arabische Lehrabteilung
DB	Division blindée/Armored Division
DBLE	Demi-brigade de la légion étrangère
DCA	Défense contre aviation
DCr	Division cuirassée de réserve
DFL	Division française libre
DGSS	Direction générale des services spéciaux
DI	Division d'infanterie

DIA	Division d'infanterie algérienne
DIC	Division d'infanterie coloniale
DIM	Division d'infanterie du Maroc
DLM	Division légère mécanique
DMC	Division de marche de Constantine
DMI	Division motorisée d'infanterie
DMI	Division de marche d'infanterie
DMM	Division marocaine de montagne
DMN	Délégué militaire national
DMR	Délégué militaire régional
DMZ	Délégués militaires de zone
DSM	Direction de sécurité militaire
DSPG	Direction du service des prisonniers de guerre
DSS	Direction des services spéciaux
EAC	European Advisory Commission
EMDN	État-major de la défense nationale
EMFFI	État-major des Forces française de l'intérieur
ESG	École supérieure de guerre
FAF	French Air Force
FAFL	Forces aériennes françaises libres
FANY	First Air Nursing Yeomanry
FEC	French Expeditionary Corps
FFC	Forces françaises combattantes
FFI or "fifis"	Forces françaises de l'intérieur
FFL	Forces françaises libres
FFO	Forces françaises de l'Ouest
FG	Feldgendarmerie
FL	La France libre
FN	Front national
FNFL	Forces navales françaises libres
FTP	Francs-Tireurs et Partisans
FTS	French Training Section
Gestapo	Geheime Staatspolizei (secret police)
GFP	Geheime Feldpolizei (Wehrmacht secret field police)
GHQ	General Headquarters
GMR	Groupe mobile de réserve
GPRF	Gouvernement provisoire de la république française
GQG Air	Grand Quartier Général Air
GTL	Groupement tactique de Lorraine
GTM	Groupement de tabors marocains
HC	High command
HCM	Hôpital chirurgical mobile

HJ	Hitlerjugend (Hitler Youth)
HQ	Headquarters
HSSPF	Höherer SS- und Polizeiführer (senior Nazi Party official in command of SS, Gestapo, or police units)
HUMINT	Human Intelligence
ID	Infantry Division
IPS	Instruction personnelle et secrète
IS	Intelligence Service
ISU	Italian Service Units (Italian POWS in Allied service)
JAG	Judge Advocate General
JCS	Joint Chiefs of Staff
JRC	Joint Rearmament Committee
KHD	Kriegshilfsdienst (female auxiliary service)
KDS	Kommando der Sicherheitspolizei und des SD
KG	Kriegsgefangener (POW)
KIA	Killed in action
LCA	Landing Craft Assault
LCP	Landing Craft Personnel
LFC	Légion française des combattants
LRDP	Long Range Desert Patrol
LSH	Landing Ship Headquarters
LST	Landing Ship, Tank
LVF	Légion des volontaires français contre le bolchévisme
MBE	Member of the British Empire
MBF	Militärbefehlshaber in Frankreich (Commander of occupation forces in France)
MEW	Ministry of Economic Warfare
MI5	Military Intelligence 5 (counterintelligence, UK)
MI6	Military Intelligence 6 (or SIS, foreign intelligence, UK)
MOD	Ministry of Defence (UK)
MIA	Missing in action
MO	Medical Orderly
MP	Milice patriotique
MP	Military Police (US)
MSR	Mouvement social révolutionnaire
MMLA	Mission militaire de liaisons administratives
MUR	Mouvements unis de la résistance
NAAFI	Navy, Army, Air Force Institutes
NAP	Noyautage des administrations publiques
NARA	National Archives and Records Administration

NATO	North Atlantic Treaty Organization
NKVD	People's Commissariat of Internal Affairs (USSR)
NS	National Socialist
NSDAP	Nazi Party
NSKK	Nationalsozialistisches Kraftfahrkorps (National Socialist Motor Corps)
OBW	Oberbefehlshaber West
OCM	Organisation civile et militaire
Oflag	Offizierslager (POW camp for officers)
OG	Operational Group
OKW	Oberkommando der Wehrmacht
ORA	Organisation de résistance de l'armée
Orpo	Ordinary police (German)
OSS	Office of Strategic Services (US)
OVRA	Organizzazione di Vigilanza e Repressione dell'Antifascismo (Italian secret police)
PCF	Parti communiste français
PCR	Radio receiver
PCT	Poste central de tir
POW	Prisoner of war
PPA	Parti populaire algérien
PPF	Parti populaire français
PR	Propagande révolutionnaire
PTSD	Post-traumatic stress disorder
PTT	Postes, télégraphes et téléphones
PWE	Political Warfare Executive
Pz	Panzer (tank)
Pz.Kpfw.	Panzerkampfwagen (tank)
RAA	Régiment d'artillerie d'Afrique
RAD	Reichsarbeitsdienst (Reich Labor Service)
RAF	Royal Air Force
RCA	Régiment de chasseurs d'Afrique
RCP	Régiment de chasseurs parachutistes
RDF	Radio Direction Finding
RI	Régiment d'infanterie
RIC	Régiment d'infanterie coloniale
RNP	Rassemblement national populaire
RP	Resistance point
RPF	Rassemblement du peuple français
RSHA	Reichssicherheitshauptamt (Reich Main Security Office)

RTA	Régiment de tirailleurs algériens
RTM	Régiment de tirailleurs marocains
RTS	Régiment de tirailleurs sénégalais
RTST	Régiment de tirailleurs sénégalais du Tchad
RTT	Régiment de tirailleurs tunisiens
SA	Sturmabteilung (Nazi party paramilitary wing)
SACMED	Supreme Allied Commander Mediterranean
SANA	Section automobile nord-africaine
SAQJ	Service algérien des questions juives
SAS	Special Air Service
SBD	Scout Bomber Douglas
SD	Sicherheitsdienst (security police)
SDPG	Service diplomatique des prisonniers de guerre
SEAC	South East Asia Command
SFHQ	Special Forces Headquarters
SFIO	Section française de l'internationale ouvrière (French Socialist Party)
SGDA	Secretariat général de la défense aérienne
SGJ	Sécrétariat général à la Jeunesse
SHAEF	Supreme Headquarters Allied Expeditionary Force
SHD	Service Historique de la Défense
SIGINT	Signals intelligence
SIM	Servizio informazione militari
Sipo	Sicherheitspolizei (security police)
SMERSH	Red Army Counterintelligence (from 1942)
SIS	Special Intelligence Service (MI6)
SNCF	Société nationale des chemins de fer français (French railways)
SO	Special Operations
SOE	Special Operations Executive
SOF	Special Operations Forces
SOL	Service d'ordre légionnaire
SR	Service de renseignement
SRA	Services de renseignement et d'action
SS	Schutzstaffel
SSA	Section sanitaire automobile féminine
SSM	Service de sécurité militaire
ST	Surveillance du Territoire
STO	Service du travail obligatoire
TOE	Table of Organization and Equipment
USAAF	US Army Air Forces
USMC	United States Marine Corps

USN	United States Navy
VP	Volontaire de place
WAAF	Women's Auxiliary Air Force
WAC	Women's Army Corps (US)
WAKO	Waffenstillstandskommission (German armistice commission)
WRNS	Women's Royal Naval Service (UK)
WS	Winston Special
ZOAN	Zone d'opérations aériennes nord
ZOF	Zone d'occupation française

Introduction

Despite a frequent tendency in the writing of the history of war to focus on a legend of a victorious general, or to view a decisive battle as a validation of national exceptionalism, Carl von Clausewitz posited the idea that in war, no result is ever final. In the event, the record of soldiers (and civilians, in this case, to be sure) in their variety who constitute the character of an army in a state and society or within the international system of alliances and coalitions becomes obscured or risks being condemned to caricature. In this regard, the story of any army in war and that of its soldiers comprises vastly more than simply the account of a single battle, for armies often pass through a cycle of victory, defeat, and regeneration, and new purpose. War – and in the case of France, occupation – also places societies under strain, pushes them into uncharted regions which require a new vocabulary and an altered language to express the misery, pain, humiliation, and bewilderment over a sense of altered certainties and shattered convictions. This generalization is especially germane to the story of the French Army and its soldiers and civilians in defeat and victory as a feature of the French nation and its role in Europe and beyond since the seventeenth century, themes which have been the subject of this author's scholarship for fifty years. In this regard, the French Army in the whole of the Second World War, its prelude and its aftermath, is a story that deserves a clear rendering in its extraordinary detail and complexity – the purpose of these two volumes.

The task to offer a comprehensive account of France for the Cambridge University Press series on Armies of the Second World War poses a significant challenge of chronology, cause and effect, and judgment, as well as the effort to cut through the myth, legend, and prejudice that too often characterize popular perceptions of France at war. This task starts with the fact that France's participation in the war, from say its prelude in 1936 through 1939 and onto the spring of 1945, fails to fit the pattern that might be said to adhere to such other major belligerents. Instead, the standard story of France in the Second World War as it now stands is segmented into distinct and often disjointed episodes, beginning with

Anglo-French appeasement of the 1930s, transiting through the Phoney War in 1939–1940, and culminating in the stunning and humiliating "strange defeat" of May–June 1940. This by itself has inspired several generations of robust and evolving historical forensics which of late have invited counterfactual speculation about alternative outcomes, in themselves often linked to the neurotics of decline via a cult of the past, and the nostalgia, even sentimentality, that has come to characterize much popular history of the Second World War. These will be dealt with in the conclusion to volume two of this work. At this point, the English-speaking scholarship of France's post-1940 presence in the war is largely reduced to cameo appearances of little explanatory power here and there such as Operation Torch, the November 1942 invasion of French North Africa, and the breakthrough at Monte Cassino in May–June 1944, spearheaded by the *Corps expéditionnaire français*. Here legend often obscures the truth visible in the best and most recent scholarship that breaks with fads, sentimentality, and a seemingly insatiable need to transform common men and women into heroes. This trend has been most apparent in France in a movement often referred to as "The French Resistance," more as a myth at the time and since, spontaneously generated inside the country to assume a vital role in the crumbling of the Occupation. While interesting as a phenomenon of wartime society in the face of Axis Europe, as well as the dictates of national reconstruction in the Fourth and Fifth Republics, internal resistance offers little more than a footnote to the war, although heavily romanticized at the time and since as the "Armies of the Shadows," and other melodramatic renderings. In addition to my work of 2013 on the ill effects of counterinsurgency in Western democracies, this work also aspires to demonstrate how this "resistance myth" laid a foundation, both intellectual and institutional, for the post-11 September 2001 craze for special operations as the highest expression of military organization and the sublime form of grand strategy.[1] The year 1944 witnessed the Liberation of France by Anglo-American armies, with Charles de Gaulle taking power in a flamboyant and highly mythologized manner during the August deliverance of Paris, leaving the final conquest of Germany to British, US, and Soviet armies – this is at best an incomplete misperception which this work attempts to correct in detail.

This customary fragmentation of France's Second World War story is, in my view, both inaccurate and, given the impressive expansion of especially French-language current research little known in the United States or the United Kingdom on the many aspects of France at war, also obsolete. Far too much attention is given to the legends of 1940 as the opening shot of the war in the West which established Axis domination of the European Continent, agonizingly reversed at enormous costs of suffering and death over the next five years. In this view, for France and the West, the 1940 battle of France became the war's culminating event, serving in the shadow of the Cold War as a sort of a cautionary lesson, along with the perils of appeasement, of the requirement for moral rearmament. Nonetheless, the 1940 armistice does not transform France into mere bystander and suffering victim of that war's larger course of events. In fact, like the other Allied powers who experienced initial battlefield setbacks – Great Britain, the Soviet Union, and the United States – France struggled to reconstruct its military power within the context of a global conflict. However, the nation and its army faced numerous handicaps, beginning with the fact that the armed forces were broken into warring fragments, while the country was occupied by Axis forces, which made reconstitution and renewing the fight doubly difficult. Unlike the other major Allied nations, Vichy French and Free French offered very different diagnoses of the causes of the debacle determined by ideology and long-standing frictions in politics, society, and the army itself, on what form France's military rehabilitation should take, and to what political and strategic ends French military power should be directed. Much of France's army of 1940 was incarcerated as POWs in Germany, so that military strength must be refashioned largely from the manpower of France's underdeveloped colonial empire, or internally from a civilian *levée*. This process forms a central part of this work and it is a story poorly understood in the English-speaking world.

These two volumes aspire to correct the skewed periodization and a distorted emphasis on the heretofore distinct episodes or ancillary events that compose France's wartime storyline, one that operated in many domains little prone to the customary chronology and cause and effect. This work breaks new ground to unify the many disparate realms of the conflict and the institution of the French military broadly defined, the French nation in its fractures, and the many fields in which French soldiers, sailors, and civilian resisters proceed over a longer period of time than as found in conventional histories on the topic that pivot too much on the early summer of 1940 and suddenly burst again into view in June 1944. This study goes beyond the "decisive battle" military history literature with its focus on "the Fall of France," to establish a narrative sweep of France at war within the international system, in Europe, Africa, and beyond, to include society and the respective political camps so central to French life and identity. Plainly, the story conceived in this more expansive and variegated framework does not finish in the newsreel scenes of the dining car at Compiègne in which figures in *Wehrmacht* field gray dwarf the handful of French officers. Rather, these books seek to address the military and the war in its totality, to follow France's post-June 1940 attempts to regenerate military power in its many guises and across political divisions, both at home and in the empire. These volumes follow the fate of soldiers in their diversity as they proceed through the years after June 1940, most of which has received entirely too little attention in the Second World War's grand chronicle. This work is also attentive to the full variety of France's wartime experience, seeking to incorporate those omitted from traditional descriptions of the war – POWs, women, civilians-in-arms, colonial subjects, foreign refugees – and to recall that much of the Second World War was fought outside of Europe, and by many non-European peoples. The simple fact is that France did not exit the war with the signing of the June 1940 armistice. But the effort to reconstitute French military power crumbled into Vichy collaboration, Alsace-Moselle occupation struggles, the mobilization of French North Africa, and the endeavors – some might say the antics of Charles de Gaulle as seen by skeptics in the year 1941 or 1942 – of "the squatter on the shores of the Thames," a man who appeared somewhat incongruous to Churchill and FDR, but who in France was perceived as noble, and of the French in exile within the Anglo-Saxon alliance.

1 France in the Age of Total War

As the revisionist powers shifted the European security order in the years after 1933, the public assigned blame to the imperfect peace signed with Germany on 28 June 1919 at Versailles, followed by treaties signed with Austria at Saint-Germain, and Hungary at the Trianon. Summing up the century, *The Economist* condemned the Versailles agreement as "the final crime ... whose harsh terms would ensure a second war."[1] As Canadian historian Margaret Macmillan notes, however, Hitler did not go to war in September 1939 because of the Versailles Treaty, although the burden of sole war guilt, disarmament, reparations, and occupation in the pact furnished a legend of martyrdom under the swastika. Though defeated on the western battlefields in the summer and fall of 1918 and temporarily immobilized by the revolution in 1919, a Germany that had internalized many of Erich Ludendorff and Walter Rathenau's principles of policy and strategy remained exceptionally powerful in Europe – a fact that became obvious after the stabilization of 1924 and Gustav Stresemann's reintegration of Germany into Western Europe in the years thereafter. The Great War had unleashed too many forces in the European system and radicalized the domestic politics of Central and Eastern Europe, to say nothing of a Western Europe exhausted by war, to be contained by the precarious post-war international collective security scaffolding erected in Paris's royal suburbs. In the wreckage of the Hohenzollern, Austro-Hungarian, and Ottoman empires and elsewhere, Woodrow Wilson's "national self-determination, that noble ideal, produced dreadful offspring when it was wedded to ethnic nationalism." The architects of the Versailles peace – Wilson, Clemenceau, Lloyd George – soon passed from the diplomatic stage as the disorder of an incomplete peace manifested itself in the discord of the victors and the unbroken will to fight of the vanquished. In November 1919, the US Senate refused both to ratify the agreement and to join the League of Nations, and gutted the Covenant of the League. Consequently, the League's concept of collective security proved unable to meet the dangerous effects of the failing peace once the Great War's victors surrendered the initiative in the decade of the 1930s.

Nor could French statecraft of alliance and containment in Western and Central Europe endure without ample backing from the Anglo-Saxon victors and in the face of German, Italian, and Soviet power. This American defection from European security in anything but a disjointed commercial role compounded the discord among the victors. (The Dawes and Young plans as well as the fairyland diplomacy of forbidding war had been underpinned with petty fogging macroeconomic ideas of balanced budgets and the reparations puzzle.) This disarticulation of statecraft deprived the post-Great War security order of many of the tools required to deal with large and difficult questions of national minorities in new nation states and the inevitable revival of aggression and militarism in Central Europe in a new style of diplomacy and conflict which makers of statecraft in the 1920s could only poorly answer in policy and strategy.[2]

By far the largest and most challenging Great War legacy in an epoch that came to be described by Ludendorff's term total war confronted civilians, soldiers, diplomats, and policymakers with this question: "whether and how modern war among highly industrialized nations was still possible as an instrument of policy." The destructive capacities of all-azimuths propaganda for boundless war goals, bombing aircraft, long-range, high-explosive artillery, poison gas, and submarine torpedoes exceeded the limited political objectives on a mid-nineteenth-century model that war was meant to achieve – these had been quickly swept aside by warfare on a scale that obliterated the traditional roles of armies, generals, admirals, combatant societies and ministries and courts to give some coherence to combat. "Warfare had become total war, affecting all aspects of the social and political life of the belligerents."[3] From the moment that he had been named Hindenburg's chief of staff in 1916 in the advent of the Third Army Supreme Command, Erich Ludendorff "became an advocate of 'what may be called a technical dictatorship for the purposes of the conduct of mass warfare' or what we more commonly call a technocratic rule," writes Michael Geyer. Ludendorff's concept of total war sought to harness the political, economic, and social dynamic of the nation to "engulf all of society in an ever-expanding machine of violence." Needless to say, Ludendorff's "total war" concepts reconfigured civil–military relations in Germany in a manner that the makers of peace struggled to comprehend fully in 1919, but which Ludendorff spent years enumerating in his incessant publications until his death in 1937. "Machine warfare was fought best by soldiers fortified by propaganda and backed up by an ideologically unified nation." Clausewitz's view of war as a political act became the first casualty of Ludendorff's "expanding and escalating the use of force" in which strategy was reduced to a form of social and technocratic mobilization as embodied in the second industrial revolution and the union of general staff and heavy industry management. This became reflected in escalating war aims via the *Vaterlandspartei* on the need to "purify" one's own society as a prelude to dominating that of the enemy. In Ludendorff's total war vision, soldiers no longer employed their expertise to achieve limited foreign policy objectives while containing inevitable losses. Hitler and the National Socialists eagerly took up Ludendorff's vision of "national purification through conquest or, as we have called it apocalyptic war ... [as] the first step in creating a new German master race ..."[4]

In his second book of 1928 and in his first meeting with the heads of the military in February 1933 once he became chancellor, Hitler expounded his view not only that war offered a feasible option for Germany, but also that war offered a way of life central to national socialism and the party-state regime that emerged in 1933, and the only way to realize his vision of achieving national purification. Unlike Hitler and his disciples, most European military and political elites had no desire to re-experience Great War traumas.[5] This anxiety was especially the case in the France of the Third Republic, for which national survival had been purchased in 1914–1918 at the exorbitant cost of 1,300,000 casualties and the occupation of ten of France's most productive departments.[6] "There was no fundamental disagreement in France between military leaders and politicians or diplomats in the principles of French security policy during the inter-war period," concludes the German scholar of inter-war militaries and keen observer of the skepticism of professional soldiers about Nazi ideals of total war Klaus-Jürgen Müller. "Generally, accord and accommodation rather than dissent characterized the relationship" between soldiers and political leaders in France.[7] That "accord and accommodation" centered on the Third Republic's "traditional military credo" of a fortified eastern border, foreign alliances, and universal conscription.[8] While such policy may have created a temporary French dominance on the continent in the 1920s, by the 1930s European diplomacy encountered several limitations. First, with the epoch of the dictators at hand and with enduring generalized disarticulated policy in Paris, London, and Washington D.C., three of Europe's five major powers sought to overturn the post-Great War status quo. Mussolini's Italy and Hitler's Germany were states ideologically committed to war, that, on the model of Soviet Russia, sought to deploy diplomacy to divide their enemies and better to position themselves for conflict when the time came to initiate it in what in the twenty-first century is called hybrid war, but was just as prominently a feature of totalitarian statecraft in this period of unrelenting conflict, subterfuge, mass persuasion, and intimidation. As early as 1933, Britain's ambassador to Berlin, Horace Rumbold, perceptively noted that Hitler's ultimate aim was the "creation of a militarized 'racial community' capable of waging wars of conquest." Nazism was "an ideology of war" in which "peace was regarded merely as preparation for war."[9] In equally significant measure, Stalin's outlook, driven by a Marxist-Leninist belief that war was an inevitable product of capitalist conflict, was more opaque. While Moscow was not looking to ignite a war, nor, plainly, was it committed to upholding the status quo hammered out at Versailles and its ancillary treaties. The Soviet dictator's conviction that the USSR was "encircled by enemies," i.e. especially the Poles and the Japanese, was confirmed in his mind by the Anti-Comintern Pact signed between Germany and Japan in 1936, which Mussolini joined the following year. Soviet intelligence bombarded Stalin with reports which nourished his paranoia. Meanwhile, the Commissariat for Foreign Affairs, which might have offered a corrective, became a central target of Stalin's Great Terror from 1934 onwards. Those experienced and sometimes sensible Soviet diplomats with actual knowledge of the outside world were sidelined, arrested, and an estimated 20 percent of them were executed as the terror took hold in the late 1930s. Many critical Soviet diplomatic posts went unfilled. For Stalin, the fact that European powers had launched rearmament in the 1930s meant that they sought to acquire the "means by which to re-divide the world." Peter Jackson notes that for the Soviet Leader, diplomacy offered "a tool to help ensure that 'inevitable war' would take place under conditions favorable to the USSR."[10]

Burdened with the long-haul impact of the war on their empires and domestic politics and economy, Britain and France remained the two status quo powers, and French pre-war diplomatic efforts focused on replicating the *entente* of 1914–1918. As the horizon darkened as the 1930s unfolded, this task would prove an elusive and often frustrating one for Paris for several reasons of domestic and international character as well as concerning military affairs. First, the long shadow of the Great War and the Depression disinclined the leadership and populations of both countries to contemplate an encore against Hitler, especially as rearmament with mechanized weapons would undermine economic recovery. This hesitancy was accentuated in London by the conviction of anti-Soviet conservatives especially, that Britain had made a grave strategic error in joining the Grand Alliance with France and Russia in 1914. From this classic balance-of-power and maritime perspective, as a naval power backed by a vast empire, the question of who dominated the continent was not an issue worth the sacrifice of significant amounts of British blood and treasure. Seen by the lights of the twenty-first century and not that of the year 1935, at the time of the Anglo-German naval treaty which scuttled the Versailles disarmament clauses that had not already been scrapped, such arguments are easily refuted. And, indeed, "British strategy underwent a remarkable evolution" in the wake of the September 1938 Munich Conference, by not only abandoning a policy of "limited liability" on the Continent, but also subscribing to the French thesis that the security of Western Europe and that of Eastern Europe were linked, and demanded once more a continental commitment with ground and air forces if war came.[11]

A second problem for Neville Chamberlain, Britain's Chancellor of the Exchequer since 1931 and Prime Minister from 1937, was an acute awareness that mobilization for a "people's war" would require, in the words of Labour intellectual Harold Laski, a "socialist reconstruction, national and international." Such a "new world order" would propel the United States and perhaps the Soviet Union into the first rank of nations, severely debilitate the British economy, and possibly witness the dismantling of colonial empires that would diminish Britain's international status and require a remake of British identity. Chamberlain's compromise in the defense realm was to focus on the modernization of the Royal Navy and the Royal Air Force (RAF). "Chamberlain thus fiercely opposed proposals for a large-scale expansion of the army," notes Talbot Imlay, out of "fear of the financial, industrial and political price of creating a mass army." He recognized that mass mobilization "risked transforming the balance of industrial and political power in Great Britain."[12] Rather than lay the groundwork for a "people's war," the British Prime Minister opted to preserve the British army basically as a diminutive, regimentally structured colonial constabulary that was outclassed by the rapidly modernizing *Wehrmacht* and even the Soviet Army. The RAF, destined primarily to shield the British Isles from air attack, and the Royal Navy became the pillars of Home defense. But as Whitehall began to worry that French resolve might falter in the face of a resurgent Germany, from early 1939, the British army belatedly began to garner attention. But this effort became a forward deployed contingent – the BEF – which the *Wehrmacht* routed in the Spring 1940 campaign that resulted in the Fall of France.[13]

France's post-1919 security was anchored in "collective security," a mesh of conventions and arms control and arbitration arrangements based on the Covenant of the League and the Little Entente that pivoted on Central European nations whose ambition could not match their limited means. Naval conferences at Washington in 1922 followed eight years later by that in London sought to prevent a naval arms race. If diplomacy of security failed, then sanctions could be imposed on the offending party through the League of Nations. Collective security came under pressure, however, first when Japan started a war in Northern Asia in 1931, and, later, when Germany stormed out of the Geneva disarmament conference in October 1933, and along with Japan, left the League, followed by Italy four years later. This collapse of collective security and the strategic answers of the period 1919–1935 challenged France to come up with new ways to manage its security.[14]

The centerpiece of post-Great War French diplomacy had been the 1925 Locarno agreement, which guaranteed the western frontiers of France, Belgium, with which France struck a military alliance, and the Germany of Gustav Stresemann in the few placid years of the Weimar government. In an attempt to extend Locarno eastward, Paris concluded a military alliance with Poland. The Quai d'Orsay also negotiated supplementary political treaties with Czechoslovakia, Yugoslavia, and Romania. These arrangements were sometimes disparaged by critics as "illusions of pactomania" which added up to something far less than an "eastern alliance system" equivalent to that with Russia in 1914. For starters, none of these countries provided a military or economic counterweight to Germany as the military power of the latter revived by 1935–1936. Nor were they predisposed to operate in concert. The Poles and Czechoslovaks in particular were at daggers drawn over Silesia, to which they both laid claim. For the decade from 1925, French diplomacy sought to extend Locarno eastward to entwine Germany in a European-wide security system underwritten by London and Paris. Paris' goal became to integrate both Great Britain and Germany into a multilateral mutual assistance regime to commit London to defend France and her eastern alliances. Unfortunately for France, London initially viewed France's diplomatic flirtation with these weak and mercurial Central European states as an alibi to shun a resurrection of the *entente*. French statecraft was dealt a blow in 1934 when Warsaw signed a pact with Berlin, more or less directed against Stalin, but at the expense of the French Little Entente. German statecraft was also active in Belgrade. While some British diplomats recognized Hitler's bellicose intentions early on, London believed that the best way to contain Germany was to persuade Berlin to curtail rearmament. The Anglo-German naval agreement of 1935, which sought to limit the tonnage of a growing *Kriegsmarine*, offered an example of this approach and symbolized the crossed purposes of policy among the victors of 1918–1919 in the changing European order.[15]

Given that the aim of Europe's revisionist powers was to capsize the diplomatic order established at Versailles, Saint-Germain, and Trianon, by 1935 if not before, the incoherence of France's diplomatic encirclement plan would have left Cardinal Richelieu red-faced with embarrassment could he have caught sight of it from heaven. The urgencies for

Anglo-French diplomacy became to act in concert to deter and ultimately to destroy the German and Italian regimes. This strategy required diplomats to develop an accurate assessment of the long-term intentions of the revisionist powers, formulate a coherent strategy for coalition-building, and finally convince their political leaders to accept the risks of war with sufficient armament and at huge cost. This policy was easier said than done, as diplomats disagreed on the hostile intentions of the revisionist powers that continued to talk peace as they rearmed and embarked on campaigns of conquest. They also evinced a stubborn reluctance to jettison a decade-long policy of collective security to which many were personally and professionally committed. The 1935 Abyssinian crisis found French diplomats divided over how to appease Mussolini while supporting London's Mediterranean interests. France's ambassador to Berlin, André François-Poncet, argued through 1936 that like previous German statesmen, Hitler merely sought to have Germany acknowledged as a great power. In any case François-Poncet opined, despite an aggressive rearmament program launched in 1932, the German public's aversion to war would act as a powerful constraint on Hitler's actions. The 1938 Czechoslovak crisis again produced policy cacophony at the Quai.[16] Therefore, in part because France's diplomatic sentinels failed to agree before the September 1938 Munich meeting that Hitler and Mussolini constituted a clear and present danger, the evolution from the "collective security" of the 1920s into a more robust posture of confrontation proved a slow and erratic one. Given that the Quai d'Orsay did not speak with a common voice, no doubt out of impatience with the measured pace of diplomatic practice, and to circumvent possible obstruction from career officials, some leaders like Pierre Laval and Chamberlain preferred to deploy personal summitry in their dealings with the Italian and German leaders. The resort to individualized diplomatic initiatives enshrined in news reels and illustrated newspaper photos further diminished the influence of the Quai on the evolution of French foreign policy.[17]

Appeasement

The diplomacy and strategy of the 1930s in France are too prone to clichés that little explain the cause and effect of events nearly a century ago. The exact meaning of the term appeasement has proven elusive, especially as it was little used in the 1930s when it came to characterize the foreign policies of France and Great Britain, and because its definition evolved over time. With a view to the classic phrases of diplomacy as used in the eighteenth and nineteenth centuries, the British American historian Paul Kennedy defined appeasement as: "the policy of settling international [or for that matter domestic] quarrels by admitting and satisfying grievances through rational negotiation and compromise thereby avoiding the resort to an armed conflict which would be expensive, bloody, and possibly very dangerous."[18] In the context of 1930s Europe, in which new forms of diplomacy and strategy connected to the totalitarians and the ill effects of total war, appeasement sought the avoidance of war by allowing Hitler to remedy peacefully the perceived errors and conditions of the Versailles pact in the hopes that German aspirations could be accommodated within a system of collective security with an anti-Soviet bent.[19] In the aftermath of Munich in the summer of 1938, however, appeasement increasingly became synonymous in the popular mind with surrender as the pace of German aggression only accelerated. The American historian Gaines Post argues that British practitioners of appeasement in the 1930s saw it as a theory of deterrence, which combined "conciliation with demonstrations of military force, the will to rearm, and international solidarity against aggression." What made appeasement divisive was that policymakers disagreed on where the emphasis was to be placed – constructing alliances, international sanctions, or threatening military action.[20] Even before Munich and its aftermath demonstrated that Hitler could not be placated, appeasement in France was also grasped by makers of policy as a way to buy time for rearmament.[21]

Preference in high places in Paris and London for a policy of appeasement was reinforced by several factors: the logic of France's financial and trade policies; economic frailty and fear of capital flight; rearmament problems linked to industrial renovation; and the tortuous and fitful process of French military modernization in the technical and doctrinal realms.[22] In the wake of the Popular Front government (1936–1938), there was also a fear among conservatives especially that a war requiring mass mobilization would challenge their hold on government and perhaps even pave the way for communist revolutions throughout Europe.[23] One had merely to look over the Pyrenees into Spain to see what horrors bulked at the moment in the years 1936–1939. Indeed, the period of the Popular Front coalition of socialists and Radicals, one supported by the French Communist Party (PCF), had traumatized many French officers. Despite *Deuxième Bureau* reports to the contrary, Weygand and other French generals firmly believed that the French communist party (PCF) had seized the opening of progressive government to infiltrate the army to lay the groundwork for a vast upheaval to be joined by a fifth column of left-wing Spanish, Italian, and Jewish refugees in France.[24] This helps to explain Weygand's practically hysterical pronouncements in the midst of the June 1940 retreat that PCF leader Maurice Thorez had seized power in Paris, when in fact the French communist leader was

1,500 miles away in Moscow.[25] And while Weygand plays down this incident in his memoirs, he was hardly alone – French naval chief Admiral François Darlan, Marshal Philippe Pétain, Generals Huntzinger, Héring, Voiriot, chief of the general staff for the Paris region, and his commander General Prételat, and no doubt others, also diverted troops to deal with an expected fifth column insurrection as German soldiers closed in on Paris. Not for nothing in a world of conservatives in the Third Republic did fear of communist insurrection border on paranoia among elements in the French army, one spawned by the Commune of 1871, and reinforced by 1917 in Russia, which many erroneously believed had triggered the French army mutinies of that year. The PCF had been active in protests of the 1920s against the Ruhr occupation of 1923–1924, and against colonial wars in Syria and the suppression of an uprising by the Rif of Morocco in 1925. Officers feared that the strikes that accompanied the 1936 Popular Front election were a prelude to a communist insurrection. This chronic obsession in the upper reaches of the French military with popular revolution was brought to the surface in the defeat, despite *Deuxième Bureau* assurances that the PCF-sponsored "*appareil militaire*" had failed miserably in its program to create cells and propaganda in the barracks.[26]

Scholars have traditionally linked appeasement to public opinion in the Third Republic and beyond among millions for whom war only meant catastrophe. In its primal form, appeasement was viewed as a policy manifestation that reflected a reluctance of the French and British populations to repeat the horrors of the Great War. In this way, "decadence" historians link France's 1940 defeat to a collapse of popular morale. Those scholars disinclined to accept this verdict view the evolution of popular morale as simply one factor that influenced French strategic choices in the 1930s. As public opinion gradually acknowledged the inability of a policy of appeasement to modify Hitler's aggressive behavior, political leaders were able to adopt a firmer stance against Axis aggression. In other words, resistance to German – and Italian – bellicosity increasingly in 1938–1939 became a source of popular unity, rather than a divisive policy imposed upon war-averse populations. This shift set up a post-war debate between those who like Churchill or de Gaulle had opposed appeasement as a policy failure and others like Chamberlain, Halifax, Bonnet, Flandin, Laval and so on who justified appeasement as the West's best option in the context of international and domestic political constraints in the rigors of the failure of collective security in the 1930s.[27]

From the advent of the Popular Front in 1936 to the aftermath of the Munich agreement of September 1938, appeasement enjoyed widespread popular support in France, perhaps best symbolized by the scenes of Jean Renoir's 1937 film *La Grande Illusion*, which highlighted the shared humanity of combatants and the idiocy of war. Even though he intensified French rearmament, Leon Blum's foreign policy still sought to reconcile with Germany even as it pursued Berlin's containment.[28] "One can hardly avoid the conclusion that France's grand strategy – conclusive as it was in itself – was wholly inconsistent with her alliance policy," concludes Müller.[29] Knowing that France lacked the economic and military reach to court allies in Eastern, Central, and Southeastern Europe, the Republic's long game, which de Gaulle mischaracterized as limited to "*la stricte défense du territoire*,"[30] was to keep its maritime flanks open, rely on a *repli imperial* – that is, fall back on the colonies[31] – and offer the Hexagon to Great Britain and eventually the United States as a continental bridgehead. This strategy symbolized a Julian Corbett-like vision of sea power as an enabler and sustainer of land warfare suited to a world war of indeterminate duration. Although the General was to embrace it in the aftermath of defeat as a justification for rejecting the armistice, it was not a strategy which in the mid 1930s was designed to appeal to a continentally oriented soldier like de Gaulle, suspicious of "les Anglo-Saxons," with little faith in the steadfastness of the French people, and who conceptualized the coming conflict as the latest mechanized installment in a perpetual Franco-German clash, as did Vichy and initially the resistance.[32]

Appeasement comprised several assumptions of diplomacy of dubious strength and high contingency. First, those who extended a pen to Hitler's hand reasoned that modest adjustments to Versailles would reconcile the Third Reich to life within a European collective security system that somewhat extended the international order of 1919. The risk was that, by embracing it, France and Great Britain surrendered potential strategic "opportunities" in Eastern and Central Europe that were catapulting out of the grasp of persons in London, Paris, and Geneva. The revision of policy to abet Berlin allowed Hitler to make time work for him with his march of conquest at home and abroad, to accumulate political victories. The Führer simultaneously acquired economic and financial assets, say in the Rhineland and in Austria, to boost German rearmament, and to undermine a "long war" French strategy of containment and blockade. Furthermore, Anglo-French "power, prestige and honor" evaporated as potential allies, especially Czechoslovakia, were sacrificed one by one to Hitler until appeasement assumed a "mythic status as a foreign policy of catastrophic failure."[33] French leaders associated with the policy – Blum, Daladier, Laval, Bonnet, and Gamelin, among others – subsequently justified their embrace of appeasement at Riom and elsewhere by pleading that it offered the best option given the flawed system of Third Republican governance, French military and economic weakness, and a strategic environment infarcted by international, national, and left–right ideological crossed purposes. The fallback was that, if all else failed, appeasement bought time to rearm. Unfortunately, given France's, and Europe's, fraught political environments, these calculations resulted in an uncoordinated response to Hitler's challenges in the years 1935–1939.

The fundamental miscalculation of appeasement is that almost everyone, including the Germans, totally – even willfully – misread, that is, underestimated, the radicalism and violence of Hitler and those in his corps of paladins such as Goebbels, Himmler, and Ribbentrop, believing that his ambitions could be contained in a European system that remedied the most obvious inequities of Versailles from Berlin's perspective. Until the March 1939 occupation of Czechia beyond the Sudetenland, the greatest risk of appeasement in the eyes of most European diplomats was that Hitler would seek to incorporate all Germans in Central Europe and beyond into the Reich. But Hitler's geostrategic and moral outlook was based on "race," not some tweaking of the balance of power or the realization of a nineteenth-century pan-Germanist project aborted by Otto von Bismarck's common sense from 1848 until 1879 that a Greater Germany would rupture a sound European order. According to Hitler's plan, the continental triumph of German racial imperialism as the basis of world power would mean that many nation states would cease to exist, while others would survive as German satellites according to their eugenic destiny. Perhaps, granted the generalized reign of Colonel Blimps and his French counterparts in the years 1919–1935, one could only poorly ask of Europe's inter-war leaders to radicalize their outlooks, imperial values, and diplomatic agendas effectively to counter Hitler's racist, destructive, and diabolical scheme that was less clear to many confused contemporaries, and took on a coherence later than certain persons in the twenty-first century can poorly comprehend.[34]

A dissenting opinion holds that: "French decision makers were provided with a reliable interpretation of the long-term objectives of Nazi foreign policy . . ." as writes Peter Jackson. Unfortunately, the *Deuxième Bureau* rather discouraged the inclination of French leaders to act preemptively because of "a penchant for exaggerating the productive capacity of the Reich's armaments and aircraft industries; and, following from this, a tendency to overestimate German military preparedness."[35] Also, because foreign intelligence in France was controlled largely by the military, not surprisingly, it focused primarily on information of interest primarily to commanders, like the German order of battle, doctrine, weapons systems, and the like. In this aspect, every German who wore a uniform, and in the years 1936–1938, this number of men and even some women in uniform grew steadily, was then counted as a combat-ready soldier. Second, various "filters" were applied to information before it reached decision-makers. While filtering – "sterilizing" or even politicizing – information as it passed through various echelons in the hierarchal chain is a problem for all intelligence services and political systems, it was particularly acute in France with its history of civil–military distrust, especially on the left. Inter-ministerial infighting could offer different foci or interpretations of information, most notably in this period of discord between the Ministry of Defense and the Quai. No intermediate organization such as Britain's Joint Intelligence Committee existed in France to collate, evaluate, and summarize information, or to resolve differences of interpretation or perspective. In theory, this problem was eased somewhat because Édouard Daladier, in command of multiple ministerial portfolios, had access to intelligence on the state of German military preparedness since 1932 when rearmament had indeed begun with the Kurt von Schleicher cabinet.[36]

A final and classical problem became what to do with intelligence once it reached cabinet level. It must not be overlooked that from 1936 the Popular Front gave a huge impetus to French upgrades in military affairs, based in large part on reports of German rearmament. But in general, French cabinets were multi-party coalitions of convenience, inadequate forums for policy discussion, much less for policy formulation. Gamelin confessed that he and Daladier were reluctant to share intelligence with a cabinet that included people like the notoriously appeasing Foreign Minister and serial leaker Georges Bonnet.[37] Otherwise, ministers were largely free to draw their own conclusions about the gravity of the Nazi menace, based in large part on their personal proclivities, or the attitudes of their party or faction. Therefore, responsibility for French military unpreparedness in 1940 cannot be laid at the feet of French intelligence alone. Politicians and the French public were divided on how to react to German rearmament and to Hitler's aggressive foreign policy. Several considerations other than intelligence reports shaped the French response, among them alliance politics, economic limitations, and public opinion.[38] Some important French leaders also clung to hopes that appeasement would eventually satisfy Hitler's ambitions short of war.

French military planners, meanwhile, assumed a defensive hunker, which would make it impossible to combine diplomatic initiatives in Central Europe with the threat of force. That France and Great Britain emerged on opposite sides of the Abyssinian crisis, triggered by Mussolini's 3 October 1935 invasion of that country, was largely the fault of French foreign minister Pierre Laval, "the epitome of Third Republic chicanery" charges Robert Paxton.[39] A lucrative Paris law practice and a regional media empire made Laval one of France's richest men in the inter-war years. His stance as a pragmatist willing to work with left and right, joined with a reputation as a political fixer, saw Laval assume the premiership for the first time in 1931. Unfortunately for France, Laval's domestic political skills, which French historian Jean-Baptiste Duroselle judged to have been "more cunning than competent," transitioned poorly into international affairs when he was named to head the Quai d'Orsay between October 1934 and February 1936. In fact, Duroselle credits Laval with being the major architect of what he condemns as the inconsistent French diplomacy of the 1930s.[40]

As French foreign minister, Laval feared that London-sponsored League sanctions on Italy imposed in the wake of Mussolini's Abyssinian incursion would shove the Italian dictator into the arms of Hitler.[41] But Laval genuinely admired Mussolini, with whom he shared Anglophobia and "*une certaine vulgarité.*" He was also encouraged by right-wing French intellectuals who, in keeping with a French conservative vision of creating a "Latin bloc" by conjoining the policies of France, Italy, and Spain, trumpeted Italy's action in Africa as a spirited expansion of Western culture and demonstration of imperial "vitality."[42] A rapprochement with Mussolini would excise the ideological component from France's differences with fascism, and allow Paris to focus on the Communist menace.[43] However, Laval's attempts to appease Mussolini only succeeded in alienating London, and did nothing to impede the Italian dictator's slither toward Hitler.[44] British deputy foreign minister Anthony Eden, already concerned that growing social and political unrest in France that peaked in the February 1934 riots outside of parliament might make Paris an unreliable partner, saw Laval's initiative as a direct threat to London's critical Mediterranean–Red Sea link to its East of Suez empire. As a consequence, Eden threatened to withdraw London's military commitments to France under the 1925 Locarno agreement. Rather than choose between London and Rome, Laval's temporization and absence of clear objectives had sabotaged League-based collective security, and launched France's slide toward appeasement and international isolation.[45]

As an encore, Laval negotiated a mutual security agreement with Stalin. But as Sean McMeekin notes, it contained "no binding military clauses whatsoever. It was all provocation and no deterrence," and actually served Hitler as an excuse to remilitarize the Rhineland in March 1936. In this reading, France's failure to seal a Soviet alliance was no "missed opportunity," because Stalin had no interest in "collective security," but sought to overturn Versailles, weaken capitalist regimes, and expand communism globally.[46] So, while in the long run, Allied strategy against the Axis that combined long war with peripheral operations and economic blockade was successful, in the short run it was condemned to failure because Stalin's participation was arguably *the* key element that would have allowed such a strategy to succeed.[47]

In the short run, however, Laval's initiatives locked France into diplomatic purdah as warnings of remilitarization of the Rhineland began to circulate in the summer of 1935. The timing of Hitler's announcement to coincide with a bitter and divisive French election and concerns over a sliding franc helped to guarantee a muted response from Paris. In the event, the *Deuxième Bureau* reported that the French military was superior to that of Germany at the time, although it appears that French commander-in-chief Maurice Gamelin (Figure 1.1) failed to share those

Figure 1.1 French army commander-in-chief Maurice Gamelin.

evaluations with his political superiors.[48] Rather, the army staff conflated SA (*Sturmabteilung*, the paramilitary wing of the Nazi Party), police, and labor corps units to report a figure of 295,000 German troops organized in twenty-one to twenty-two infantry divisions.[49] Memories of a calamitous 1923 Franco-Belgian occupation of the Ruhr remained fresh, so that both the Quai and the Finance Ministry, which feared that a crisis in the Rhineland would trigger a run on the franc, urged restraint.[50] Eager not to let the crisis go to waste, however, Gamelin tried to use the Rhineland as an opportunity to create an "Anglo-Franco-Belgian bloc whose massive solidity would be compensation for the loss of the Rhenish 'no man's land.'" In the event, he desperately miscalculated the international response according to his biographer.[51] Gamelin's effort to reconstruct an Anglo-French security cooperation, that Laval had significantly impaired, spoke volumes about political and administrative confusion in the Third Republic, the flaccid nature of civilian control of the military in France, and Gamelin's naive, if not ignorant, grasp of European affairs. Communications between London and Paris were at best perfunctory during the crisis. Belgian King Leopold worried that war would fracture his country, already deeply divided along political and linguistic lines. He therefore retreated into a Swiss-style neutrality minus the Alps. The only international support that France gained for intervention came from Poland, the very last country whose support Gamelin sought to court.[52] The service chiefs became fixated on French weakness and the definitive alienation of Great Britain, whose hoped-for rearmament became the object of their daily devotions.[53]

Eugen Weber notes that the French Commander-in-Chief, "brilliant but incapable of initiative" even when he commanded superior forces,[54] had made no plans to counter the Rhineland reoccupation because he was convinced that the government would accept it as a *fait accompli* in any case. But to solidify French inertia, Gamelin told the caretaker government of Albert Sarraut that a military response would require "all or nothing" total mobilization, precisely because he did not wish to act, and so supplied yet another alibi for inaction to his civilian bosses. Gamelin sought to postpone skirmishes that might derail his long-term rearmament plan. But in his defense, neither political nor popular support existed in France for a military response.[55] Nor did Blum seek to stir up the pacifist wing of the Socialists (SFIO) led by his party rival Paul Faure, and so cautioned against unilateral action, which telegraphed a message of foreign policy faintheartedness for the soon-to-organize Popular Front.[56] For the French public, the construction of the Maginot Line, which became a viable defensive barrier on the Franco-German frontier by 1936,[57] induced a false sense of security. The perspective of London and Paris putting their differences aside for a concerted opposition to the Rhineland remilitarization, which came on the heels of Germany's 1935 reintroduction of conscription in flagrant violation of Versailles, might have caused the German dictator to behave more cautiously, at least in the short term.

But this is mere speculation. More likely, as Gamelin feared, an invasion of German territory would turn into a rerun of the costly *Ruhrkampf* of 1923 that had found the French battling German popular resistance organized in a "national unity front" that resulted in 122 German deaths. An upstart Adolph Hitler had manipulated the Ruhr occupation to condemn Weimar as acquiescent to Allied demands. In the view of Ernest May, any Anglo-French attempt to counter the 1936 German reoccupation of the Rhineland would have rebounded to Hitler's advantage, rather than provoking his overthrow.[58] A French invasion would unify Germany, allow Hitler to play the victim both at home and abroad, further isolate France, and threaten to undermine France's already fragile finances.[59] On the debit side of the ledger, however, the remilitarization of the Rhineland was a blow, because it took away France's military buffer, tanked French prestige in Central Europe, and delivered the *coup de grâce* to Locarno and collective security.[60] The subsequent construction of the Siegfried Line made it more difficult to aid France's allies in the east. Brussels reclaimed its "independence" by renouncing its military alliance with Paris, which would further complicate French war planning. Paris' choice in the wake of the Rhineland remilitarization was to accept German hegemony in Central Europe or finalize a military pact with the USSR.[61] France did neither. By failing to take the initiative in the Rhineland, France had telegraphed the message that it was no longer a great power, which accelerated the perception of French "decadence."[62]

Of course, the revisionist argument is that French inaction over the Rhineland simply confirmed what was already obvious.[63] Nevertheless, Leon Blum inherited this diplomatic "landscape of ruins"[64] when his Popular Front government took power in May 1936. Historians have painted a largely sympathetic picture of Blum, who is most remembered in the popular mind at least for the introduction of the forty-hour work week and two weeks' paid holiday which the French have subsequently embraced and expanded as a sort of civic entitlement. But for those of his era, Blum became at best an incomplete, even a timid, reformer. Simultaneously, he was reviled unfairly in the French military and on the right as "the man of Stalin."[65] A Jaurès protégé of great intelligence, charm, and sophistication, even elegance, Blum stood out from a cast of Third Republic politicians who "were scarcely pleasant company," in the view of conservative journalist Henri Géraud, who wrote under the pseudonym Pertinax, and whose job it was to cultivate them. "Surely no one would ever have thought of entertaining them had not their government position made them temporarily interesting." In this crowded political field where intelligence rarely combined with character, nor decency with decisiveness, Blum stood out as "a man whose conversation was broad and subtle, a man of transparent honesty and charming manners. As a human being, he attracted one's respect and friendship."[66] Unfortunately, the very qualities which made Blum such a refined and agreeable dinner companion worked to undermine his effectiveness as a political leader. Blum's quaint views on the primacy of morality in politics, the value of conciliation and compromise, and his desire to achieve justice through social reform made him in the view of one of his biographers, Jean Lacouture, "an anachronistic figure ... not perhaps a man for the time of assassins."[67] A Jew of Alsatian origin whose parliamentary career only initiated at the late age of forty-seven, Blum was an outsider who underestimated the corrosive forces of his era. He always saw himself as a placeholder, a politician *malgré lui*, an amateur who preferred writing poetry to mapping plans to thwart Hitler, confront Europe's – and France's – often venomous antisemitism, or deal with the ruthless scheming and unceasing policy shifts of the PCF. Gamelin, who fancied himself "the personification of the educated soldier" with interests in art, history, and Bergsonian philosophy, privately disdained Blum as "a bogus or sham intellectual."[68] Blum's formidable intellect, more inclined to analysis than action, became a handicap, while his preference for temporization and compromise often translated into indecision. Vacillation was in part forced on him by the fact that his socialists – the SFIO – were bitterly split between anti-fascists and pacifists.[69] Party divisions restricted Blum's foreign policy agenda to "pious aspirations" based on collective security and disarmament which the Abyssinian crisis followed by the Rhineland reoccupation had rendered obsolete, but which many on the left continued to embrace through the Munich crisis of September 1938.[70]

In many respects, Leon Blum was unlucky. For no sooner had the Rhineland crisis receded and the wildcat strikes that had greeted the advent of his Popular Front government begun to dissipate than civil war broke out in Spain in July 1936. The Spanish Civil War became the central foreign policy conundrum of Blum's premiership, which arguably he mishandled by taking counsel of his fears and seeking consensus rather than providing leadership.[71] Faced with a divided cabinet and Senate opposition which reflected a lack of popular support for intervention except among communists and a knot of anti-fascist socialists eager to satisfy Madrid's plea for arms, Blum settled on a policy of non-intervention worked out by his Foreign

Minister, Yvon Delbos, which he preferred to call "non-interference."[72] But apparently struck with a "guilty conscience," he turned a blind eye to a secret program to funnel arms to the Republicans worked out by several of his associates. This typical Blum temporization benefited no one: too few French arms trickled into the Iberian Peninsula to tip the military balance against the torrent of Italian and German aid. But when news of the arms shipments leaked, the French right, which denounced the Spanish Republic as a communist front, erupted with righteous outrage. The news also irritated some of his Radical Party allies led by Édouard Daladier, who complained of his "relaxed non-intervention."[73] Meanwhile, those on the left of his coalition, including the communists and most Radicals and Radical-Socialists who supported the Spanish Republicans, not to mention the British Labour Party, saw Blum's backtracking as a spineless betrayal of Madrid.[74] Nevertheless, Blum remained convinced that non-intervention had prevented the outbreak of a general European war in 1936–1937. But more importantly, in his view non-intervention avoided a possible military *coup* or even a civil war in France, and kept the Popular Front from fragmenting. Duroselle cites Blum's muddled Iberian policy as more evidence of the immobility and paralysis of French diplomacy.[75] Writing in a period when "decadence" held the historical high ground, another of Blum's biographers, Joel Colton, also considered Blum's failure to aid the Spanish Republic "the most serious miscalculation of his government out of the misconceived notion that totalitarian dictatorships would honor agreements they had signed and that peace and the Spanish Republic could both be saved."[76] The Spanish episode made Blum appear simultaneously indecisive, naive, and stubborn by clinging to a failed policy. Abroad he was perceived as insincere – even duplicitous – which reinforced France's reputation as an unreliable diplomatic partner.[77]

Blum's foreign policy goal was to strike a triple alliance between France, Great Britain, and the Soviet Union. One view is that Blum's greatest foreign policy failure, one that overshadowed his limp response to the Spanish Civil War and in part shaped it, was not to have solidified a military pact with Moscow. But this was to prove a bridge too far – of the Popular Front's supporters, only the PCF, whose goal was to make French foreign policy Moscow-friendly, was keen to bolster ties with the USSR. The Socialists and Radicals remained suspicious.[78] Furthermore, prospects of a Franco-Soviet military pact reinforced the view on the right that the February 1936 electoral triumph of the Spanish Republicans, followed by the victory in May of the French Popular Front, signaled Moscow's creeping influence in Western Europe. Meanwhile, on the left, many European intellectuals muted their criticism of communism, interpreting events in Spain and France as evidence that Stalin supported the spread of democracy. This produced a backlash among "the enemies of the Popular Front [who] presented it as a conspiracy of the Communist International to rule the world," writes Timothy Snyder. "European public opinion was so polarized by 1936 that it was indeed difficult to criticize the Soviet regime without seeming to endorse fascism and Hitler. This, of course, was the shared binary logic of National Socialism and the Popular Front: Hitler called his enemies 'Marxists,' while Stalin's opponents were 'fascists.' They agreed that there was no middle ground."[79]

The Gaullist Jean-Louis Crémieux-Brilhac blasted the French right for sabotaging a potential Franco-Soviet alliance by linking it to the threat of "the internal enemy."[80] But they were not alone. In this fractious political environment, Blum would have had to overcome considerable opposition in the Quai d'Orsay, the French military, and his Popular Front Radical Party partners, not to mention in London, to have inched closer to Moscow. Critics complained that Moscow might invoke the March 1936 Franco-Soviet Treaty of Mutual Assistance to draw the French and other Locarno signatories into a war for Soviet interests. Largely due to French prevarication, preliminary Franco-Soviet staff talks initiated by Blum in 1936 had collapsed by May 1937.[81] Stalin's show trials of alleged traitors in the service of foreign intelligence agencies, begun in August 1936, spread to the Soviet military from late June 1937, where they eventually claimed eight senior military commanders, about half of the Red Army generals, and countless others. In the shadow of Stalin's purges, Gamelin complained that while he had always favored a Franco-Soviet alliance, the case for the USSR as a reliable military ally became more difficult to make in the Quai and the Defense Ministry, whose diplomats and soldiers were inclined toward distrust of their Soviet counterparts in any case.[82] The only reliable army east of Germany, in Gamelin's opinion, was that of Poland.[83] But this appears to offer yet another Gamelin alibi for inaction.

From a strategic perspective, Hitler was not going to launch an attack on France before he had neutralized Stalin with the August 1939 Nazi–Soviet Pact.[84] So while some French and British leaders, including Daladier, Bonnet, and Halifax, recognized that it was necessary to prevent a Nazi–Soviet covenant, they took no positive steps to preempt it with an Allied–Soviet arrangement. This was in part because Chamberlain and others insisted that a debilitated Soviet military could offer no effective military assistance. But whatever the weaknesses of the Red Army as revealed in Finland in November 1939 and in the early stages of Barbarossa from June 1941, its potential was superior to the diminutive, poorly armed, undertrained, and indifferently led force that Great Britain reluctantly mustered for France in 1939–1940. Furthermore, conventional wisdom held that a deal between bitter ideological and political adversaries like Hitler and Stalin could never happen,[85] a fatal strategic miscalculation as it turned out. So, while the Franco-Soviet pact came to be regarded in Paris as a hollow agreement, Hitler nevertheless invoked it as an excuse to remilitarize the Rhineland in March 1936, and to lay the foundation for the November 1936 Anti-Comintern Pact between Germany and Japan, as part of Berlin's strategy to distract Moscow from European commitments.[86]

These setbacks left Paris to juggle its interests between those of London and the toxic antagonisms of the Central European states. If the Balkans were Europe's Orient, Central Europe was its purlieu, a site of ancestral hatreds, disputed boundaries, and opportunistic conventions. As has been noted, France had bilateral treaties with the so-called *Petite Entente* – Romania, Yugoslavia, and Czechoslovakia – a full military accord with Poland, and a pact with the USSR. Yet, Paris' ability to operationalize these agreements was complicated by the situation on the ground. Romania and Hungary were in a spat over Transylvania. Paris considered Warsaw's prime minister, Józef Beck, unreliable after he signed a ten-year non-aggression pact with Germany. Poland was also at odds with Czechoslovakia, which had concluded a mutual assistance agreement with Moscow. Poland was unwilling to allow Soviet troops onto its territory. While Romania might permit Soviet overflights, Paris was unclear how Soviet forces could be deployed to help Czechoslovakia.[87] Romania and Yugoslavia refused to back France over Czechoslovakia so as not to alienate Germany and Italy. Yugoslavia had signed a non-aggression pact with Italy in March 1937, which effectively ended the Petite Entente. As Julian Jackson notes, this complexity robbed the Popular Front of a workable foreign policy.[88]

Paris' problem was that reliance on Central European states to contain Germany was a non-starter. From the unification of Germany in 1871, and certainly from 1918, it was clear that Central Europe would be dominated by Germany or Russia, not France, with or without de Gaulle's proposed 100,000-man armored force. Furthermore, Paris lacked the military, diplomatic, and economic clout to align interests among disputatious governments who legitimized themselves by picking quarrels with their neighbors. David Kaiser has demonstrated that no basis existed for a quid pro quo between France and potential allies in Central and Southeastern Europe. In the first place, these countries needed weapons for defense, which Paris simply could not supply because from 1936 it was preoccupied with defense industry nationalization and reorganization to rearm its own forces. There was also a fear that arms shipped to the east would be lost should Germany overrun Central Europe.[89]

Second, potential European allies had no way to secure loans for weapons except through agricultural products, mainly timber and cereals, or in Romania's case refined oil, that France could not accept because it was bound by imperial preference. For this reason, the Agriculture Ministry repeatedly blocked trade concessions to Danubian states because they would have contravened preferences for agricultural products from the Maghreb and Indochina especially, or competed with domestic production. The Quai, and the ministries of agriculture and finance, had different priorities, which "the medley of politicians pulling against one other" in a carousel of cabinets was powerless to resolve.[90] Third, Central and Southeastern Europe was dominated by German trade interests which the French were too weak and too distant to displace. Berlin bound up Eastern Europe with trade deals that gave arms for agricultural products that guaranteed Hitler a steady supply of raw materials and made these countries economically dependent on Germany.[91] As a consequence, France's failure to react to Hitler's March 1936 reoccupation of the Rhineland, combined with its inability to supply much-needed arms, convinced policymakers in Poland, Romania, and Czechoslovakia that France was not a dependable partner. Fourth, London, whose cooperation Paris prioritized, opposed France's entangling commitments in Central Europe. French acquiescence to Hitler's reoccupation of the Rhineland was done with an eye to gaining British support. But, for the countries of Central Europe, it showed just where Paris' priorities lay.[92] For all of these reasons, some important French policymakers believed that Central Europe invariably would slip into Germany's grasp without war.[93] So, with a dearth of viable strategic partners in the short run, and faced with the growing momentum of German rearmament, France had no choice but to rearm.

Rearmament

One of the strongest rebuttals to a "decadence" school of post-war historians, whose dean was Jean-Baptiste Duroselle, has been to highlight the significant effort at rearmament carried out by the Popular Front, even at the price of sacrificing the left's social agenda as well as some of its pacifist principles. The social costs of rearmament were also high. The surge in production quotas required an increase in workplace discipline, which meant rolling back some of the signature Popular Front achievements like the forty-hour week, paid holidays, pay rises, and the right to strike. Having at first tried to sabotage rearmament by capital flight, according to French historian Robert Frankenstein, the business class then turned it to their advantage by invoking the production crisis to reverse worker gains surrendered in 1936–1937.[94] The demands of rearmament returned the upper hand in the workplace back to the bosses and foremen, who were eager to avenge the indignities suffered and reverse the concessions made during the explosion of strikes and factory occupations that had occurred in the wake of the May 1936 Popular Front electoral victory. As the pace of rearmament quickened, foremen could require workers to labor up to seventy-two hours a week, suppress days off, impose night work even though workers had no way to return home once their after-hours shifts ended, and enforce strict discipline on the assembly lines.[95] Furthermore, devaluation and inflation eroded workers' pay raises awarded in 1936.

In many respects, Blum was simply expanding a rearmament program begun even before the remilitarization of the Rhineland triggered a widespread acknowledgement that France must take significant steps to increase the security of the Hexagon. Georges Leygues, navy minister for most of the years between 1925 and 1933, had launched an ambitious naval rearmament program which by 1939 found France in possession of what came to be called "*la belle flotte de Darlan*," although wartime French naval chief and sometime Vichy chief minister Admiral François Darlan became the fleet's heir rather than its progenitor. The French navy was superior to either the German or the Italian fleet. Conceptually, it offered an infinitely more rounded and capable armada than had the disparate flotilla that had constituted France's navy in 1914.[96] Money had been voted for what became known as the Maginot Line in January 1930, and construction continued until 1939, although it remained a work in progress. As army chief of staff in the early 1930s, Weygand's modernization plans that included motorization for part of the infantry and cavalry, as well as money for training and maintenance, had been curtailed in the 20 percent slash in government expenditures ordered upon the simultaneous 1932 arrival of the Depression and the *Cartel des Gauches*, a governing coalition devoted both to disarmament and to a balanced budget.[97] In April 1934, Foreign Minister Louis Barthou initiated a muscle up in the wake of the collapse of collective security.[98] At the end of 1934, Germany reintroduced conscription, and on 1 March 1935 announced the birth of the *Luftwaffe*. In the four years between 1934 and 1938, French military expenditures doubled.[99] Rearmament was sequenced by service: in 1935, the French air force attracted the bulk of the modernization funds. The following year, Blum refocused rearmament back to the army in the wake of the Rhineland remilitarization. From 1938, the air force again became the beneficiary of France's military upgrade.[100] As has been seen, the navy got the jump on rearmament from the 1920s. But it was largely excluded from this late-1930s sprint to war readiness, which in the view of Robert Frankenstein may help to explain the subsequent "admiralization" of Vichy.[101] François Cochet argues that the French did not lack funds for rearmament. Even with the budget cuts in the wake of the Depression, "special funds" were often voted to make up for shortfalls. In constant francs, the French spent more on defense in 1938 than they had in 1913 in the midst of the so-called "Nationalist Revival."[102] But at this point, France's rearmament surge ran aground on a sequence of reefs – financial, industrial, organizational, doctrinal – familiar shoals well marked on the charts of French military modernization.

Blum opted to finance rearmament through loans, because he feared that new taxes on consumption might erode popular support for a military buildup. Borrowing carried two risks, however: first, the Popular Front would have to go hat-in-hand to the people with capital, which meant the Bank of France. Second, the holders of capital in France knew that rearmament meant devaluation. The threat of devaluation would lead to capital flight, while lowering the value of the franc would trigger inflation.[103] Jonathan Kirshner is not the first scholar to argue that, while monetary orthodoxy did not cause the defeat of France, the stranglehold of orthodox financial policies suffocated the French economy and made French military modernization more difficult to achieve. The financial community was capped by the Bank of France, known as the Bastille of French financial policy, for which there would be no 14 July 1789. The Bank's governors and regents favored the interests of their shareholders and supported monetary orthodoxy at the expense of all other national priorities, including security. Because the Bank fixed the discount rate, it could severely limit the government's ability to borrow. The Bank's insistence on the conversion of the franc into gold at the 1928 level "not only prolonged the Depression but also sapped the strength and assertiveness of French foreign policy," Kirshner argues.[104] French industrial production lagged significantly behind that of Great Britain and Germany, while the requirement for a balanced budget delayed and complicated the modernization of France's military arsenal.

While the Popular Front abandoned the balanced budget to launch rearmament, their cabinets remained "prisoners of the capital holders."[105] As with many Popular Front initiatives, Blum's reform of the Bank of France was timid, ineffective, and only served to annoy financiers who continued to export their cash, whether out of prudence or from a deliberate desire to sabotage Popular Front initiatives is open to speculation.[106] Rather than nationalize and reorganize the Bank of France into a central credit agency for the government and for French businesses in need of funds to restructure and modernize, Blum merely tinkered with its governance structure.[107] Financial orthodoxy hurt French security in three ways: first, it sapped the strength of the economy as a whole because interest rates ranging between 9 and 12 percent discouraged investment. Poor economic performance eroded France's industrial base and delayed rearmament. Second, deflationary policies contracted government revenue, pressured budgets, slowed the modernization of defense industries, and led to cuts in defense spending. Finally, fears for the fragility of the franc conditioned the assessment of foreign policy choices and inhibited French leaders from rising to the challenge in crises.[108]

Kirshner insists that fear for the stability of the franc contributed to France's failure to act in the Rhineland and to Paris' futile effort to resuscitate the corpse of collective security in the face of Hitler's provocations. The ideas of John Maynard Keynes and Franklin Roosevelt's resort to deficit spending to finance the New Deal were viewed in France's conservative Finance Ministry as "Anglo-Saxon" monetary heresy that ran counter in both culture and economic theory to France's attachment to the gold standard. Budget-busting rearmament programs from 1936 created runs on the franc, led to repeated devaluations, and eventually toppled the Blum government in June 1937.[109] Weapons ordered as part of Blum's rearmament were delayed after Blum fell in June 1937, and his successor Camille Chautemps and Finance Minister Georges Bonnet again cut defense spending to balance the budget, which pushed back some new weapons and aircraft into 1939.[110]

Nor did France's leaders appear to understand the consequences of dumping buckets of cash into a dysfunctional arms procurement system anchored in France's antiquated industrial structure. French industry had suffered from a lack of capital to restructure and modernize, so that machine tools were twenty years old on average, compared with seven in Germany. Paris briefly considered creating an armaments ministry in 1938, but postponed the idea until September 1939 when it was set up under Raoul Dautry, "a first-rate engineer, thoroughly accustomed to large-scale planning and operations, a man of exemplary patriotism," according to Pertinax.[111] And while some historians hail Dautry's call-up as a sign of the dynamism of the Third Republic's ramp up for war,[112] in fact, Dautry's nomination offered an eleventh-hour Hail Mary in the face of the utter failure of French industry to meet its production quotas under Daladier's laissez-faire approach to war planning.[113] In the event, Dautry would face a "task ... of Herculean proportions."[114] In fact, the delays, absence of planning, a shortage of investment capital, and the transition from peace to a wartime footing meant that France's armaments surge was late, and lacked a clear structure and set of priorities. By

1938, French industry was working at full throttle to increase military weapons by 50 percent and munitions by 100 percent. Premier and Defense Minister in 1938 Édouard Daladier focused on production quotas but neglected the macroeconomic infrastructure to support them. Non-ferrous metals, coal, petrol, shipping, SNCF rolling stock which had suffered from lack of investment, and so on were all lacking. Despite the obvious production bottlenecks and shortfalls, only in the spring of 1940 after the high command had presented the government with a revised program of armaments requirements that called for a tripling of industrial capacities did France dispatch a special mission to the United States to tap into US industrial potential, a long overdue step.[115]

Rearmament and the Air Force

If the challenges of upgrading the French army were serious, those in the French aircraft industry bordered on catastrophic. The 1930s dawned on a French air force whose Great War glories had receded into the mists of wistful memory. An air ministry was created only in November 1928 over the vehement objections of the army and navy, while in that year air force personnel abandoned army khaki for a dark blue uniform uncomfortably similar in tone to that of the navy. Although air bases replaced the old aviation regiments, only in 1932 did the army agree to cede control over their air units on condition that they would be reorganized into tactical support groups. For its part, the navy categorically refused to release its planes. A July 1934 law made the air force an independent arm. However, emancipation from the army was conditional, for in wartime, the air force would provide defensive cover for mobilization and then shift to "cooperation" with the ground forces under the theater commander, invariably an army general. This "bastard" compromise, based on an outdated 1914 idea of "mobilization," stymied the development of a strategic air concept in France. Furthermore, the newly independent air force had to evolve an air doctrine, define a structure, construct a balanced inventory of aircraft, and then brawl with sister services over budget.[116]

The new French air force produced Plan I, which called for the production of 1,360 front-line aircraft in three years, along with air bases, arms, munitions, radios, and spare parts. But here the problems began, because France had no modern prototypes to build, only outdated 1920s designs. Worse, unlike Germany, which created an industrial infrastructure before it begun building planes, France simply dumped orders on a French aeronautical industry which offered an ill-organized hotchpotch of antiquated companies, backed by a tangle of subsidiaries, sub-contractors, and small

Figure 1.2 Air Minister Pierre Cot with his chief of staff and future resistance hero Jean Moulin. While Cot is credited for having nationalized and rationalized the French aircraft industry, in the process creating Air France, his attempts to reform the French air force met resistance. He and Moulin were outed for smuggling arms to the Spanish Republic in 1936 and forced to resign.

artisans clustered around Paris. As a result, the 1935 bump in the air force budget resulted in the delivery of only 500 aircraft.[117]

In June 1936, Blum named Radical politician Pierre Cot (Figure 1.2) to head the Air Ministry. On the surface, Cot seemed an inspired choice. A stout advocate of air power, Cot believed that a proliferation of aero clubs and what was called *aviation populaire* would create a grass roots constituency for French air force expansion. He had also engineered a shotgun consolidation of several independent airlines threatened by a withdrawal of their state subsidies into Air France. Cot arrived at the Air Ministry in the Boulevard Victor with a reputation as an advocate for Italian air theorist Giulio Douhet's vision of a strategic bomber force acting independently of other services. But French air doctrine remained in limbo because the French air force had yet to form an air staff or an Air War College, which welcomed its first class only in 1937.[118] In fact, after serious clashes in 1937 with army commander-in-chief Gamelin, who threatened to create his own army air corps, Cot conceded the requirement for air support of land forces, and so weighted his air program toward medium bombers.[119]

Cot's major challenge was to oversee the nationalization of 80 percent of France's aeronautical industry voted by parliament in August 1936. These air factories were also to be decentralized and relocated beyond German bomber range in Brittany and the Southwest. At the same time, parliament authorized the creation of a great air fleet to be built by 1941, that would include ground support units, an independent bomber force, anti-aircraft units, and paratroops. Blum and Cot bet that nationalization would allow the industry to concentrate on the production of a limited range of models and coordinate the production of guns, landing gear, propellers, motors, and other accouterments with that of air frames, something that was not invariably the case. A combination of this relocation process and a shortage of funds meant that in 1937, French aircraft production virtually zeroed out at a time when the *Luftwaffe* was expanding at a rate of 300 new planes a month. Not surprisingly, the stagnation of French aircraft production and an absence of modern prototypes seriously impacted the morale of the air force.

Nor did Cot's notoriously progressive opinions reconcile the air staff to their civilian boss. Cot was a strong advocate of a Franco-Soviet alliance, in part because he had been favorably impressed by the quality of the Red Air Force during a visit to the Soviet Union in 1933, especially with its airborne forces. He even went so far as to propose that France combine its air force with those of the USSR, Britain, and Czechoslovakia into a vast air fleet to overwhelm those of Germany and Italy, a proposal that allowed his enemies to denounce him as naive, unpatriotic, even defeatist.[120] Cot's pro-Soviet sympathies appeared confirmed when the cover was blown on the Popular Front's clandestine scheme to smuggle arms to the Spanish Republic, spearheaded by Cot and his chief of staff and future resistance hero Jean Moulin. This collapsed what remained of Cot's credibility in the air force, which had attracted a large number of right-wing officers, and with many leaders of the aeronautical industry. His critics claimed that in his preoccupation with reorganizing the air industry, Cot had neglected recruitment and training. Howls of protest ensued when Cot forcibly retired 400 air force officers who had exceeded the retirement age, a regulation habitually ignored in the services according to Pertinax. Indeed, the right-wing journalist speculated that anyone visiting 4bis Boulevard des Invalides, the army's peacetime headquarters, might easily have concluded that General Methuselah was in command.[121] Faithful to the spirit of *plus ça change*, identical complaints had been voiced in 1914. However, when Cot subsequently elevated 400 NCOs to officer rank, he was accused of fomenting a Masonic hijack of the air force. Indeed, to be labeled an "*officier Pierre Cot* " invariably translated into forced retirement in the summer of 1940.[122] This friction in the air ministry caused Cot to cocoon himself with a small staff of trusted advisors. The fact that he seldom convened the *Conseil Supérieur de l'Air* basically marginalized the air staff from consultations on air doctrine, air force organization, or input on new models.[123] So toxic was Cot's reputation that de Gaulle, desperate for any warm body to staff his nascent Free French movement, refused to enlist the former air minister when he appeared in London in 1940.[124]

Nationalization of the French aeronautical industry had simply extended the production of obsolete models, so that by 1937 the French air force was in crisis. "You have no modern aircraft and you are not capable of producing one," Chamberlain complained to French Premier Camille Chautemps and his Foreign Minister Yvon Delbos during their visit to London in the autumn of 1937. On his return to Paris, Chautemps' enquiries made him realize that the British Prime Minister was far better informed about the state of the French air force than was he.[125] When Daladier was told in 1938 that France's 35,000 aeronautical workers produced only 40 planes a month while 80,000 German workers turned out 400 planes every thirty days, he declared the situation "humiliating." At a secret meeting of War, Air, and Navy committees of the Chamber and Senate, Daladier conceded that France was falling behind Germany in numbers and quality of aircraft.

When Radical-Socialist deputy Guy La Chambre was enlisted by Chautemps to head the Air Ministry in January 1938, he immediately realized that he had inherited an air rearmament program that was seriously over budget while simultaneously under-performing. Pertinax characterized La Chambre as a Daladier flunky ignorant of air issues who allowed himself to be bullied by Ministry bureaucrats in the habit of cutting their own contracts with private suppliers with a minimum of oversight.[126] Nor was La Chambre popular among his fellow parliamentarians, who accused him of inflating air production figures for political purposes. In the wake of the French air force's abysmal performance in

1940, La Chambre's optimistic assessment of French air force combat power delivered in the critical meeting of the *Comité permanent de la Défense nationale* (CPDN) of 23 August 1939, that took the decision to declare war should the Germans invade Poland, was considered criminal dereliction of duty. Historians treat La Chambre more sympathetically, however. The new Air Minister's close links with Daladier, combined with an acknowledgment in parliament that the French air force was in dire straits, helped La Chambre to push forward a crash program of air modernization.

La Chambre chose Air Force General Joseph Vuillemin to head his new force. A rugged, even taciturn, veteran of the First World War and of bladder-busting endurance flights across Africa in the inter-war years, Vuillemin was no *homme à dossiers*, but a pilot's pilot. Sir Edward Spears, who in the company of Churchill encountered Vuillemin on 1 June 1940, at Villacoublay airfield southeast of Paris, described him with schoolboy-like malice: "He looked what he in fact was, a pilot of the last war who had gone to seed. N.C.O. was written all over him. Rather fat, rather pasty, bursting out of a uniform several sizes too small, which is a common failing of both French airmen and sailors, his bovine blue eyes had the same expression of rather hostile bewilderment to be observed in oxen as they watch the trains go by." Former Foreign Minister Yvon Delbos confirmed to Spears that Vuillemin "is quite inadequate. *Pas à la hauteur*."[127] Pertinax believed that Vuillemin was able to function as air chief only because Gamelin supplied him with a competent chief of staff.[128] But in 1938, Vuillemin was able to convey to his new civilian boss the poor state and abysmal morale of the service he had been selected to oversee.[129]

La Chambre realized that aircraft were being ordered with minimal input from the air force command to insure that they corresponded to a general concept of air defense. One of La Chambre's first acts was to reorganize the *Conseil supérieure de l'Air* with the mission to define an air policy and the prerogatives of the air chief Vuillemin.[130] La Chambre also realized that, despite alarming intelligence reports about the dramatic evolution of the German and Italian air forces, and technological progress which had practically doubled the speed of fighters, the French air force continued to fill its inventory with obsolete planes that were technologically three years behind German and Italian models. Furthermore, the man-hours required to build a plane had jumped from 2,000 to 15,000–20,000 a month, even 40,000 for larger bombers.

Vuillemin riveted the attention of those present at a 15 March 1938 meeting of the CPDN, when he predicted that, should war break out, the French air force would be obliterated within two weeks. La Chambre scrapped the previous failing rearmament plans in favor of Plan V, which envisioned a three-phase overhaul that would prioritize fighters to give the air force 2,617 front-line planes and 2,122 reserve aircraft by March 1941, earlier if possible, with fighters as a priority. The air force would expand from 55,000 to 83,000 personnel, while new factories would be built for an aeronautical industry that would expand from 50,000 to 80,000 workers by the end of 1938. The Air Force was given 30 percent of the defense budget to realize these goals. This did not sit well with Gamelin, nor with Darlan, who had his own naval rearmament priorities.

La Chambre, aided by his chief engineer Joseph Roos, sought to breathe energy into the French aeronautical industry. Unfortunately, Plan V encountered many of the same problems as had its predecessors: outmoded plant that could not be refitted before January 1939; an absence of skilled workers to augment the workforce on short notice; a lagging French metallurgical industry; delays caused by disputes over prototypes; each new model required many months of adaptation and numerous modifications; and so on. He tried to borrow methods from a successful British model of RAF modernization. In April 1938, La Chambre commissioned a French senator to initiate negotiations to purchase up to 1,000 US fighters and spare parts. By the armistice, 980 US-manufactured planes were in French service, some of which were enlisted in the battle for France, where they proved generally superior in performance to French planes.[131]

Like its failed predecessors, Plan V initially proved disappointing – on 1 April 1939, only 433 of the first tranche of 1,878 planes had been received. The good news was that aircraft production had increased from 40 planes a month in 1938 to 300 by the outbreak of war in 1939. By hiring females, the aircraft industry numbered 180,000 employees by December 1939, each working on average fifty-four hours a week. But the air force was not scheduled to receive its full inventory of planes until March 1941, and in the interim, those bought in the United States could not fill the gap. France's crash rearmament program was cut short of its goals by the invasion.[132]

Counting available aircraft is a perilous enterprise. Nevertheless, when war broke out in September 1939, the French air force listed an inventory of 2,227 planes, up from 533 in 1938. This was a significant production achievement given France's relatively small and antiquated industrial base. By 10 May 1940, the French air force counted 4,807 combat aircraft, of which 1,972 were stationed in France. Of these, 686, or 28.7 percent, were "unavailable," a normal maintenance rate according to historian of the French air force Patrick Facon, in part because France lacked aircraft repair centers, while the transition of an aircraft from factory to front line proved a glacial process. La Chambre was later criticized because French bombers – the Bloch MB.200 and 210, the Potez 540, and the Amiot 143, a true antique – were considered so slow and poorly armored that they could only sortie safely at night. Many commanders hesitated to order France's lumbering bomber force to undertake what were in effect suicide missions. Nevertheless, in May 1940 French bombers were forced into a sacrificial and largely futile daylight attempt to pinpoint bridges the *Wehrmacht* had thrown across the Meuse around Sedan. Also, reports from the Spanish Civil War demonstrated the value of dive and low-level bombing in support of land operations, although France's defensive doctrine discouraged the integration of these techniques into French air tactics.[133]

When obsolete aircraft are subtracted, Facon arrives at a figure of 1,013 French front-line aircraft. In addition, 416 British aircraft were dispatched to France in September 1939 out of the RAF's inventory of 1,873 planes. This Allied air fleet was aligned against 5,104 front-line *Luftwaffe* planes, of which around 3,500 participated in the Battle for France, handing the Germans a 2.5-to-1 aircraft advantage by Facon's calculations. Karl-Heinz Frieser counters that numerical and technical superiority of the *Luftwaffe* was yet another myth generated by the Fall of France. The Bloch 152, Dewoitine 520, and Curtiss Hawk fighters, not to mention the RAF Hurricane and soon to become legendary Spitfire, were every bit the equal of the renowned Me 109. Rather, German air superiority was achieved by *Luftwaffe* tactics that threw even reserve aircraft into mass strikes, while the Allies retained too many of their combat aircraft on air fields well to the rear or in Britain to preserve them, in keeping with their long war of attrition strategy.[134] But while Allied air tactics certainly proved ill-suited to parry the all-out *Luftwaffe* assault of May–June 1940, serious numerical disadvantages and technical deficiencies persisted in the French air force. France's inventory was heavy on fighters. But many "new" fighters were older models that the French continued to produce in the hope that later they could be retrofitted with more powerful engines. The Dewoitine 520 was still in prototype phase in the Phoney War, causing the French to rely on the 1937 Morane-Saulnier (MS) 406 fighter, outclassed by the Me 109E, the Curtiss H-75A, only slightly more agile than the MS 406, and the totally antiquated Dewoitine 510. French reconnaissance aircraft led by the Mureaux 115 were airborne artifacts, so slow that even the notoriously sluggish Stuka (Ju 87) might sprint past them.[135] The French air force was also handicapped by a severe shortage of experienced pilots and support personnel. But pilot attrition also became a problem in the *Luftwaffe* as the campaign advanced. And while the pre-war assumption was that the air force would support ground operations, the French lacked ground assault aircraft or a doctrine for their employment. Nor had they practiced air–ground support operations before the war. France's fighter command and anti-aircraft defense were grouped under the same inspectorate. As a consequence, neither was well served, especially as anti-aircraft defense was the province of the army, that manned it primarily with reservists. The French had some excellent anti-aircraft guns, and were even given some British radar systems. But they had only 1,200 guns, mostly 1897 model 75 mm pieces adapted for air defense, compared with 9,300 20, 37, and 88 mm pieces in the German inventory. French air defense was also hampered by a reliance on telephone communications run through the Post Office (PTT), which required everything short of depositing another "*jeton*" (token) in the coinbox to get an aircraft vector. This was a situation that Phoney War improvization could not repair.[136]

Rearmament and the Army

Crémieux-Brilhac insisted that France's industrial mobilization was a measured success, especially when compared with that of Germany, which encountered many of the same problems of crash rearmament and lack of raw materials as did France, but had surmounted them less successfully. Indeed, Germany's *Blitzoperationen* or *Blitzfeldzügen* (lightning war) concept, according to Frieser, evolved only gradually, and "signifies an attempt to turn strategic necessity into operational virtue against the background of shortages in economic resources."[137] By August 1939, a French armaments industry that had consisted of networks of small workshops with aging machine tools had been transformed into a modernizing industrial establishment able to produce enough tanks to organize three light mechanized divisions, four heavy armored divisions, 6,500 anti-tank guns, 7,000 mortars, and so on.[138] The problem with this more upbeat revisionist assessment is that there remained significant shortfalls both in quantity and in quality in France's military arsenal. Many of these "new" weapons were simply Great War upgrades and adaptations. Also, as de Gaulle pointed out, French rearmament merely served to reinforce an archaic military system rather than modernize and revitalize it.

As with the French air force, the modernization of the French army stumbled on the absence of a coherent doctrine, especially on the role of tanks in modern warfare. One view is that the mid 1930s found the French military "timid and unenterprising"[139] at the very moment when German rearmament accelerated. There is some truth to that accusation. Each arm tenaciously defended its doctrinal viewpoints and budgets. In semi-retirement, Pétain's dead hand limited military reform. France's First World War hero wrote the preface for General Louis Chauvineau's 1939 treatise *Une Invasion est-elle encore possible?* In the process, he gave the official blessing to Chauvineau's main argument that artillery, anti-tank guns, and mines offered an effective counter to independent tank divisions, whose claims for effectiveness owed more to Jules Verne than to Heinz Guderian. The problem with Chavineau's argument was that anti-tank guns and mines were poorly adapted to mobile warfare and in short supply in a French army incapable of organizing an effective counter to German mobile tactics. Daladier's *laissez-faire* approach to his ministerial duties and decentralized organization of rearmament, combined with Gamelin's placatory command style, failed to impel the French army's "feudal powers" to evolve an agreed role for tanks. But to be fair, motorization and mechanization met resistance in many armies in the 1930s, including the *Wehrmacht*, where Guderian's 1937 book *Achtung Panzer!* encountered similar skepticism.[140]

But as de Gaulle's *Vers l'armée de métier* testified, there was no shortage of reorganization schemes in the French army, nor ideas about how to coordinate land and air forces. Hardly had hostilities ceased in 1918 than debates flared in French ranks about the role of armor in modern combat. In 1919, General Jean-Baptiste Estienne, an innovative artillery general who had commanded tanks in 1917, proposed the creation of an "autonomous tank army" with accompanying infantry and artillery in tracked vehicles and with tactical air cover. As has been seen with de Gaulle's analysis, the spread of popular pacifism, the Third Republic's political muddle, and the cultural pessimism that gripped conservatives in France in the 1930s were reflected in the requirement for mechanization.

In systems of democratic civil–military relations, austerity combined with a sense of national decadence and peril within a total war culture typically generates military propagandists for a particular strategic ideal.[141] Not surprisingly, the politically reactionary Weygand had been in the modernization vanguard when he proposed the creation of seven motorized infantry divisions in October 1933. French tank production was hindered by many of the same problems that slowed air force modernization – bureaucratic disputes over prototypes; an antiquated, artisan-based industry lacking modern mass production techniques; and an absence of understanding of the larger economic requirements of armaments production among them.[142] In the 1930s, Generals Gaston Billotte and Pierre Héring were in the forefront of promoting the use of tanks in the French army. During his tenure of command from January 1930 until January 1935, Maxime Weygand had laid the foundation for a *Division légère mécanique* (DLM) built in 1938 around the SOMUA S35 tank, the French equivalent to the *Panzerkampfwagen* III (Pz.Kpfw. III), considered by many the best battlefield tank in 1940 because of its superior mobility, firepower, and armor.[143] In December 1938, the *Conseil supérieur de guerre* approved the creation of two heavy armored divisions (AD) called *Divisions cuirassées de réserve* (DCrs). Military reviews brimmed with articles on mechanization, motorization, and proposals for tank doctrine. The role of tanks was the subject of debates in the parliamentary army committee and the *Conseil supérieur de guerre*, and of lectures at the French War College.

When war broke out in 1939, France had one of the largest tank forces in the world. This was because from 1936, when it became obvious to everyone that the Germans could simply swing around the flank of the Maginot Line, the French army began to produce tanks in impressive numbers, many of them technically excellent. The rapid destruction of Poland revealed the utility of armor, so that by May 1940, the French order of battle counted three DLM and four DCrs uniting 960 of France's 2,900 tanks.[144] These included the *7ᵉ Division d'Infanterie Mecanisé* and the *2ᵉ Division Légère Mécanique*, both of which approximated a panzer division, as well as an armored group designed for breakthrough operations.[145]

The problem of the tank in the French army was that their tactical role remained a source of doctrinal contention among the different arms. Most armies came up with a main battle tank and built their doctrinal concepts around that – the Pz.Kpfw. III and IV for the *Wehrmacht*; the British Valentine; the American Sherman by 1942; and the Soviet T-34. However, given the fragmentation of the French high command with their entrenched loyalties to their respective arms and services, reinforced by the inability or unwillingness of Daladier and Gamelin to override the powers of the inspectors general, each arm developed its own prototype designed to fill a tactical niche. In 1936, Gamelin had proposed a light mechanized corps of three divisions, but the *Conseil supérieur de guerre* scaled back his concept by half, largely due to opposition by the Inspector General of Cavalry, Robert Altmayer, who argued that the horse still had a role to play on the modern battlefield, a retrograde but realistic view.[146] Those who, like de Gaulle, believed the tank to be a breakthrough weapon, favored a relatively robust *char de combat*, which in the French context translated into the Char B1bis and the various spin-offs like the SOMUA S35. The Char B1bis was a 31.5 ton colossus that carried thick armor, and packed a hull-mounted 75 mm gun and a 47 mm turret gun. The manufacturer Renault upgraded the engine to increase speed but neglected to enlarge the fuel tank, which limited operations to five hours maximum. It was also difficult to maneuver as the tank commander had both to man the 47 mm gun and operate a radio. Only 162 of these *chars de combat* existed in 1939, organized in four battalions. De Gaulle's complaint was that these should have been grouped in independent divisions, an idea that was studied, even approved, but applied incrementally by Daladier, perpetually at sea in his ever-proliferating ministerial dossiers. Only 25 percent of French tanks were actually grouped in the armored divisions that were formed in January and April 1940.[147]

Unlike the *Wehrmacht*, which created a *Panzerwaffe*, the French army never fostered a true armored arm. French tanks had three problems, beginning with the fact that doctrine for the DCrs stipulated their use within a methodical battle concept.[148] Half of the French tanks were employed in an infantry support role. "In short, tanks should accompany the infantry, *but the infantry didn't know how to use them*," concluded a 1941 report. "Or they will embark upon the D.C.R.s (DCrs) whose organization and training was embryonic. Fantasy in the way they were commanded. Casualness and fantasy in the way the tanks were sometimes used was completely unjustified."[149] The DCrs' "late formation and lack of preparation was a direct consequence of the French army's inability to understand the extra dimension mobile armor added to the battlefield," concludes Robert Doughty.[150] The DCrs lacked adequate doctrine, matériel, logistical and mechanical support, and motorized infantry to support attacks, as de Gaulle's experience with the improvized 4e DCr was to prove in May 1940. The army never massed tanks to achieve power and surprise in counterattacks, but was more likely to scatter them in blocking positions or to order sacrificial attacks by outnumbered and outgunned units. As a result, "improvization reigned."[151] The cavalry created its own version of an armored division in the *division légère mécanique de cavalerie* (DLM). But French methodical battle doctrine constrained their role, so that, "incapable of leading prescribed counterattacks, they found themselves rapidly tested, broken up, and reduced to infantry support," by an army obsessed with reconstructing solid fronts, concludes Gérard Saint-Martin.[152]

The three light armored divisions (DLMs) were to fight in front of or on the flanks of the main action, in *couverture* (frontier defense) and exploitation in the grand cavalry traditions. The infantry argued that their undertrained and vulnerable soldiers required a firepower upgrade. This referred back to Estienne's original idea that tanks best served as mobile artillery and tracked machinegun nests, a view, with the addition of engineers and "tank destroyers," not too far removed from the idea of "combat commands" developed in the US Army in the 1930s and imposed on the French army by the Americans in 1944–1945. Unfortunately, the technology failed to match the tactical vision, because it resulted in the mass production of the Renault R35, basically a Great War upgrade armed with a 37 mm gun that packed a pitiful punch. These were by far the most numerous tanks in the French inventory. Infantry tanks also proved to be slow, vulnerable when pitted against heavier German models, and scattered in penny packets across the battlefield. And like all French tanks of the era, they lacked radios, their radios were insufficiently powerful, or their radios worked only in receive mode. This meant that tactical movements were difficult to coordinate and intelligence could not be shared. A final problem was that the small gas tanks already mentioned, and the lack of a jerry can system like that developed by the Germans, limited their operational range. This was worsened by *Luftwaffe* dominance, which allowed German aircraft to target French supply convoys. Neither were French soldiers offered adequate time to train on tanks, nor were French generals educated on how to concentrate them to achieve maximum effect. Instead, they scattered them in independent battalions to be mauled by panzer divisions, for which the French tanks were a vulnerable prey, especially after they ran out of petrol.[153]

The Artillery

Not surprisingly, in the shadow of de Gaulle's prophetic *Vers l'armée de métier* and the Panzer triumphs of May–June 1940, scholarship on the French army in 1940 has tended to bypass the role of French artillery in the debacle. Since Napoleon at least, the artillery had been regarded as the French army's pride. That of 1940, however, had accumulated numerous deficiencies, beginning with the fact that most of its guns were of mothballed Great War vintage or design that lacked both range and mobility. French artillery officers criticized the nationalized French armaments industry for its inability to produce "interesting" guns such as the 20 mm Oerlikon, 25 mm Hotchkiss, 40 mm Bofors, 60 mm and 81 mm Brandt mortars, Schneider 105 mm 1936S, British 94 mm caliber 25 pounder, and so on.[154] But what French foundries did produce was interesting enough for the war that the French army intended to fight. Artillery doctrine was conceived for static warfare – distributing defensive barrages in front of the principle line of resistance from shallow strongpoints, or supporting counterattacks, which in 1940 were easily broken up by *Luftwaffe* intervention and German artillery barrages.[155]

French heavy field pieces like the 105 mm and 155 mm guns had in common the fact that they were cumbersome, fragile, and lacked range.[156] They were also slow to reach the battlefield: "Our artillery suffered terribly from a lack of transport," Captain Tulous remembered in 1942. "For the most part, our heavy artillery was pulled by old tractors from the 14–18 war which could travel at 6–10 kmh ... The canons arrived with 1, 2, 3 days' delay ... Nine times out of ten, the Germans generally got there first."[157] Inadequate numbers of field pieces combined with their lack of range compromised artillery support, especially as divisional artillery in 1940 was tasked to cover fronts of 15–30 kilometers. To defend this much ground, groups had to be "articulated" – that is, broken up, dispersed, and hence in the process they became more difficult to coordinate because of poor French communications. In 1940, an artillery battery might be located up to 10 kilometers or more from its group command center – the *poste central de tir* (central fire control post or PCT). Nominally, the PCT filtered requests for fire support that came in via telephone, and allocated it according to what it determined to be the most lucrative or urgent targets. The PCT was the quintessential static front system, where terrain had been mapped, distances calculated, sounding devices had pinpointed enemy batteries, and spotter planes could issue warnings and corroborate fire support requests. In a war of movement fought over unfamiliar terrain for which maps were lacking, with the tactical situation constantly changing, where telephone wire had to be frequently unrolled and recovered lest it be lost, where French spotter planes became choice prey even for slow-moving Stukas, PCT control was guranteed to break down early and often.[158] The first problem was the phones, which, Captain Paul Gail complained, "were old and in poor condition. The distances between the group and the batteries were too far, which made laying double lines impossible. The lines were too fragile, and constantly cut by shells." As an example of the slow reaction time of this bureaucratized and overly layered system, on 31 May 1940 between 08:00 and 09:00, Gail, commander of an anti-tank battery with the 68ᵉ DI, observed at 2 kilometers German infantry crossing the Bourbourg Canal at Dunkirk on boats with their mortars, "without being bothered by anyone." As his 75 mm guns lacked range, Gail requested an artillery strike by heavier batteries. "But it was only the next day that the 1st section of the 4th battery, at the request of the infantry and with the accord of the group commander, unleashed a barrage." By which time the Germans had long crossed the canal and moved on.[159]

Anti-tank guns, though better, also had their shortcomings. The 75 mm cannon had formed the backbone of the French artillery since the late 1890s. Rustic, serviceable, with a 1,200 meter range, able to fire four rounds a minute, by 1940 several generations of the 75 mm guns encumbered France's artillery inventory, where they had been demoted largely to an anti-tank and anti-aircraft defense role. While the more modern 47 mm and 25 mm anti-tank guns commanded a fan base, units generally were allotted only half the regulation number. Also, because of poor training and poor intelligence due largely to lack of radios, or failure to use them, these guns were too often positioned where Panzers could avoid them. While praised for its power and accuracy up to 800 meters, the 47 mm was cumbersome, slow to unlimber in a surprise attack or to displace to follow the battle. Its sites were constantly thrown out of alignment. But above all, a *division* was allocated only six of them![160] The 25 mm guns was effective against light tanks, but a shell fired by one of them simply ricocheted off the armor of Pz.Kpfw. IIIs and IVs unless by chance it struck just beneath the turret. Overall, the 25 mm gun was considered unstable and difficult to tow.[161] The fact that the medium and light artillery was largely horse drawn both devoured personnel and made it especially exposed: "Under air bombardment, horses escaped, became crazed, and made marvelous targets for assault aviation," read a post-1940 report. Tanks could move much faster than could the horse drawn 75 mm, 47 mm, and 25 mm cannons reposition to defend against them.[162] "Now, with thirty or so 75s and 47s for a ten-kilometer front, every (enemy) tank attack is bound to succeed," complained Gail.[163] While important for every arm, a preponderance of ill-trained reservists disproportionately affected a technical service like the artillery. Batteries staffed by a school master or the village *boulanger* were clueless about how to deploy for maximum effect. This especially impacted the combativeness of "B" divisions.[164]

A post-war report listed an absence of mortars, sub-machineguns and anti-aircraft artillery (AAA or, in French, DCA) as France's greatest deficiencies, together with a lack of tanks and air cover. Given the feebleness of the French air force, one would have thought that the question of air defense and radar would have been given a high priority in France as it was in Britain, even under appeaser-in-chief Neville Chamberlain. Instead, French AAA consisted mainly of 1,200 1897-model 75 mm canon on fixed mounts, incapable of hitting planes flying at 4,000 meters or above, or, in many infantry units, Hotchkiss machineguns. Documents prepared for the April 1942 Riom trials claimed that the army needed at a minimum 7,000 anti-aircraft guns in 1940. Nor, like anti-tank guns, did the AAA have sufficient munitions. This compared unfavorably with 9,300 German AAA batteries that included the redoubtable 88 mm guns. Newer model anti-aircraft guns were coming on line when war broke out. Not that they would have been used more efficiently: Franco-American and Stanford University alumnus Michel de Cazotte, designated anti-aircraft officer for his reserve infantry regiment, was dispatched on a course that consisted of three days' exposure to what were, even for an educated man whose specialty was finance, incomprehensible mathematical formulas. On his return, the best he could do was to show his fellow officers how to adjust the site of a Hotchkiss machine-gun pointed skyward, the only air defense allotted to his B division, made up principally of Breton peasants. "This, as ever, was a success, especially with the Artillery officers who, no doubt, had rarely to deal with anything so ridiculously small. Somehow I got through [my presentation]." But practice proved less successful: "Several weeks before (the German offensive), on the dunes near Dunkerque, a plane, flying slowly about 500 meters altitude, had drawn a target streamer back and forth above all the machine-guns of the regiment, [some fifty Hotchkiss guns, I guess] reunited, and all firing at once. Out of a thousand shots fired, I think only five or six reached the streamer. I had therefore but little confidence in the results that could be obtained by only one or two guns. Of course, there is such a thing as a lucky shot. It was certainly the duty of my D.C. A. unit to open fire nonetheless."[165]

Furthermore, control of AAA became a source of inter-service rancor. The French air force not only wanted to fly all aircraft. It also claimed a monopoly on shooting them down. A post-war letter complained that the army and the air force fought for control of the AAA like two divorcing parents squabbling over custody of their only child. As a result, the air defense troops became the army's waifs and strays, understrength, always on alert, and manned mainly by "the scrapings from the depots of every arm."[166] Here was another problem that Daladier should have prioritized but apparently neglected. For some French infantry units, air defense consisted of a pair of machineguns bolted together. Historians have generally concluded that the *Luftwaffe*'s air dominance was an important, but not decisive, element in France's defeat. But it is certain that being constantly strafed and bombed from the air, without the ability to reply, hardly bolstered French morale, nor that of the horses upon which they depended for mobility and logistics. "The absence of French anti-aircraft artillery had a very depressing effect on the morale of the troops [at Dunkirk]," Colonel Bernadin Raugel reported in the wake of the French surrender. Air attacks were particularly feared as French troops lacked picks and shovels to dig trenches.[167] As has been alluded to, a few bombs produced chaos in largely horse-drawn French supply convoys, severely disrupting logistics, contributing to the inability of the army to move artillery quickly to threatened sectors, and to a growing crisis of munitions and other logistical lacunae in front-line units. In the aftermath of defeat, the now largely grounded French air force grabbed control of air defense and turned it against Allied planes bombing targets in France.

Which is why the French army required radios, an item on which they spent barely 0.15 percent of their defense budget. French military opinion was hotly divided over the question of radios, as over most innovation. François Cochet attributes the French army's aversion to radios to two factors. The first was a "resistance to modernity" in an army that preferred the tried and true methods of runners, carrier pigeons, flares, or flags, even if tank commanders under fire had to stick their heads out of the turret to wiggle their pennants, and runners were nailed to the ground during artillery bombardments. The second was a concern for communications security, which bordered on a phobia.[168] Indeed, during the *drôle de guerre*, the army applied a radio blackout, because the high command did not want to reveal their order of battle to eavesdropping Germans. This especially riled the British, because the interdiction kept them from fully testing and adjusting their command-and-control system. Radios were treated as a backup system in case field phones or dispatch riders failed, which is precisely what happened in May–June 1940.[169] With French infantry and their supporting artillery spread out over extended fronts in 1940, it became difficult if not virtually impossible for even a battalion commander to control and maneuver his force in dynamic combat conditions, especially in broken terrain.[170]

And to be fair, a disappointing inventory of French army radios kept carrier pigeons in business – indeed, when a post-war report insisted that "the pigeon conserves its great utility," it was not referring to that bird's undoubted culinary properties.[171] A few radios got passing marks. But most French army radios were cumbersome, they lacked range, their batteries quickly depleted and were difficult to recharge, and they fritzed out with frustrating regularity. Transmission trucks festooned with large and visible antennae allowed the Germans through sight and radio direction finding (RDF) to pinpoint French regimental and division headquarters, around which clustered all sorts of ancillary services like telephones, field hospitals, supply depots, PCTs, and so on, which made them choice targets for artillery or Stukas.[172] For Second lieutenant Chevalier, radio offered "a weak and unpredictable solution that requires considerable personnel. The requirement to man it permanently is very fatiguing, but it is susceptible to considerable improvements."[173] The tradeoff, of course, was that a lack of radios "explains the vacuum of intelligence in which our infantry lived. It could transmit intelligence only with difficulty," read a post-war evaluation. "Neither the organization, nor the armament, nor the means of liaison were adapted to this form of (mobile) combat. If one adds to this *the frequent absence of intelligence on the enemy*, then we understand why our infantry was routed."[174]

Revisionists correctly warn against overstating an image of a backward French army pitted against a modern *Wehrmacht*, which Frieser describes in the spring of 1940 as a "semi-modern" force spearhead by an elite vanguard of 10 panzer and 6 motorized infantry divisions, behind which trudged 141 "rather old fashioned," poorly trained, largely horse mobile divisions armed "with inferior equipment."[175] Therefore, the argument continues, French failure cannot be pinned exclusively on a lack of modern weaponry and motorization that a "decadent" Republic failed to supply, although this certainly played a role. At the same time, it is not difficult to detect the portents of a German "strange victory," given that many French tactics, practices, and procedures were engraved in 1918 and largely unrevised in the face of the changing conditions of mobile warfare in the 1930s, which in turn shaped the type of armaments that the French military ordered, or maintained. By adopting a defensive strategy in keeping with their extended conflict scenario and controlled battle concept, the French amplified their weaknesses – they had to be strong everywhere, while an offensive-minded *Wehrmacht* could concentrate its most proficient elements against those French troops least prepared to withstand the shock of surprise and innovative methods.[176] The result was that a precipitous retreat in 1940 led to the rapid disorganization and disintegration of the army.

For these reasons, de Gaulle complained that the rearmament budget voted in 1936 merely "completed the existing system, it did not modify it."[177] Robert Frankenstein concluded that France's entire rearmament effort had served for naught. It disorganized France's industrial production, unsettled state finances, and delivered an inventory of poorly conceived, largely antiquated weapons to a French army that did not know how to employ them or, in the case of the navy, simply turned them against the Allies or sent them to the bottom of Toulon harbor.[178] "After spending billions and billions, the army mobilized without aviation, with few anti-tank guns, and not even able to provide complete uniforms for its personnel," complained a disgruntled reserve captain.[179] It may be argued that France's rearmament effort actually benefited Berlin more than the Allies – in the aftermath of defeat, German and Italian forces were allowed their pick of French tanks and planes, while French industry and skilled workers were harnessed to the Reich's war-making effort.

The French High Command

Upon assuming the portfolio of the air ministry in January 1938, Guy La Chambre had recognized multiple problems, beginning with the fact that the government did not have an overall national defense plan coordinated with the three services, with budget allocations to match. Nor did the French military have a coherent command structure able to define a national defense architecture and a joint services combat doctrine.[180] Blum had created a *Comité permanent de la Défense nationale* (CPDN) in June 1936, which helped to put some order into a disjointed defense policy-planning structure. A 1938 law directed that in wartime the general conduct of the war would be laid down by the cabinet and the *Comité supérieur de la Défense nationale* (CSDN). No supreme command existed in peacetime, and Daladier and Gamelin resisted efforts to create one because it might have short-circuited their extemporized *modus operandi.* In the meantime, the peacetime structure of the high command was less precise.

Rearmament fell under the purview of the CSDN, which answered to the premier, not to the minister of defense.[181] The fundamental problem of rearmament was closely tied to fragile French civil–military relations and to the evolution of Third Republican governance in the 1930s. The ascendant personalities who rose to prominence during the Great War and who dominated the post-war decade – Clemenceau, Barthou, Tardieu, Poincaré, Maginot, Leygues – gave way to a new generation of "system politicians" – political fixers able to maneuver within a complex multi-party system, exemplified by Daladier, Laval, Bonnet, Reynaud, and so on.[182] This contributed to drift and indecision in foreign and defense policy. While this does not let French officers off the hook, it certainly tests Philip Nord's assertion that the French military's operational and tactical dysfunction was somehow self-generated, unrelated to the political system that governed it and the society from which it sprung.[183]

War is certainly fought by armies, but also by societies, which impact each other in reciprocal ways. While it is certainly true that military organizations generate their own cultures, these are not unrelated to their political and social context, which determines the selection of the high command, the structure of the forces, funding, length of service time, disciplinary norms, even operational and tactical disposition. The Third Republic had evinced a distrust of strong, unified military leadership dating at least from Boulanger in 1889 and the Dreyfus affair at the turn of the twentieth century. As a consequence, the war and defense ministries were characterized by administrative muddle, petty intrigues, and a proliferation of bureaus and study groups whose role in producing a coherent vision of defense often went undefined. The corporate culture at the summit of the French military determined that, while senior officers groused in the mess about the Republic, they carefully cultivated influential politicians – indeed, had they not done so, they would never have arrived at senior rank. The labels of "right" or "left" were assigned in a French political context based on an officer's religious habits, offensive or defensive preferences, and party links. François Darlan's father had been a staunch republican, a Freemason, and served as minister of justice. This opened doors to influential political contacts and allowed him to run the navy as his private fiefdom through a patronage network known as *les Amis de Darlan* ("friends of Darlan," abbreviated as ADD). Throughout the 1930s, airmen and soldiers had been at daggers drawn over the independence of the French air force, air doctrine, and control of air defense. Like any bureaucracy, arms and services defended their interests and promoted their most articulate and talented officers to advocate for them. Budgets became battles for professional prominence, even survival.

At the top, the army high command separated into First World War legacy "houses," or satrapies of arms and services that defended their prerogatives, doctrinal concepts, weapons systems, and budgets with the tenacity of the Foreign Legion at Fort Zinderneuf. These fraternal networks were critical in promotions and assignments. "High French army circles remind one too often and too vividly of some club, or caste, insufficiently open to the outer world," opined Pertinax. "It can hardly be gainsaid that the officers trained by Joffre and Foch, and, to a lesser extent, those trained by Pétain, enjoyed, between 1920 and 1940, the privileges of a sort of apostolic succession. In practice, the ruling set in the Army was largely recruited by 'co-optation' under a self-perpetuating system, with all dissenters being deliberately hindered in their careers and persecuted."[184] American journalist A. J. Liebling confessed that reporting on French generals could be compared to "a hobby without apparent charm," like train spotting.[185]

Generals also acquired political labels based on their networks, connections, and religious habits. The cavalryman Weygand's professional reputation flowed from a belief that he was privy to the "secrets of Foch." His well merited status as "*de droite*" (right-wing) resulted from his proclerical opinions, his daily attendance at mass, his irascible and very public hostility to parliamentary oversight, his antisemitism, his obsession about communist conspiracies, and his preference for offensive warfare.[186] Because he was casual about his religious duties, was associated with the strategic defensive, and enjoyed a reputation for quelling the 1917 French army mutinies with understanding and restraint, Pétain was mistakenly believed to be safely republican. As a protégé of Joffre and Daladier's man, Gamelin was "de gauche," while his deputy and rival Georges was viewed as "de droite." First Army Group commander Billotte was close to the Radical Party, and so "de gauche."[187] De Gaulle had belonged to Pétain's circle until rusticated in 1938 for insubordinate behavior. Quite apart from the fact that he was a practicing Catholic, the modernization through mechanization proposed by de Gaulle challenged the republican *levée en masse*, because it incorporated military professionalization, mechanization, and strategies of preemption. The German Blitzkrieg offered an "optimization of force" that allied technocracy and ideology into a strategy of National Socialist warfare. It encouraged competitiveness in operational planning and risk taking on the battlefield that "fitted into a system that honored success in the pursuit of conquest."[188] France's *levée en masse* offered a system of civilian control built around infantry armies composed overwhelmingly of reservists, one that kept the high command on a short leash, discouraged operational adventurism, and circumscribed the escalation inherent in the German system. Modernization was seen as antithetical to casual Third Republic practices, whose imposition would require a much more authoritarian agenda and professional mindset.

In terms of their actual political outlook and disposition, all of these men could be categorized as conservatives, and their anxieties and rivalries were at root personal and professional rather than political. Nevertheless, as Paxton points out, the porous frontier between professional and political interests made the army's apolitical tradition a precarious one. Senior officers, their chiefs of staff and subordinates, were frequently obliged to play in the political arena for corporate or personal reasons. This history of having a hand in the formation of defense policy, central to the existence of the Republic and of France, combined with a view evident in de Gaulle's *Vers l'armée de métier* that defense policy was a mere extension of social policy. A melding of the professional with the political would facilitate, even put momentum behind, a shift of army support to Vichy. For these reasons, civilian control of the military in France had always been contingent, especially in the empire, where soldiers and governors, well out of view and quick to complain of the apathy or ignorance of Paris in imperial matters, had a habit of formulating their own rules.[189] As would be seen in June 1940, despite the solidly Republican and even Popular Front credentials of a number of senior generals, civil servants, imperial officials, and parliamentarians, few rallied to the Republic's defense.

However, in the run-up to war, this intermixing of corporate hierarchies and political connections merely served further to fragment the French military command, muddle coherent planning, and hinder the evolution of a realistic strategic vision with an operational doctrine to match. Arguments over strategy were folded into budget battles linked to domestic politics, which organs of mass persuasion spun as a clash between the ideals of military professionalism – *esprit de corps*, honor, the enduring principles of war – pitted against the requirement for "economies" and a democratic urge to circumscribe military pretention, ambition, and excess thorough austerity. In this atmosphere, strategy formulation could occur only in a negative sense. Finally, when combined with "methodical battle" doctrine, Gamelin's aloofness, a tradition of château generalship, and the "politicization" of the high command created an atmosphere of professional detachment at the top. The sense that the French army was administered rather than commanded filtered down the ranks. This discouraged initiative and any sense of "esprit tactique" on the battalion and company level.[190]

Civilian anxiety about the reactionary political opinions of the officer corps resurfaced as Weygand's tempestuous four-year tenure as army commander drew to a close in January 1935. The odds-on favorite to replace Weygand was Alphonse Georges, a man favored not only by the outgoing commander but also by the majority of the fifteen generals and marshals who peopled the *Conseil supérieur de guerre*. In Algiers in 1943, when Georges was brought in to strengthen the team of American-sponsored General Henri Giraud, both Robert Murphy, American Minister in North Africa in 1943, and his British counterpart, Harold Macmillan, were inclined to agree with de Gaulle's assessment that Georges was an aged reactionary who numbered among the French army's "great number of incompetent and outmoded officers."[191] But that view was colored in part by Georges' association with the defeat of 1940. In 1935, Georges was viewed as a "straight shooter" – "*Saint Jean bouche d'or* " became Foch's nickname for him, suggesting that while Georges could be depended upon to speak his mind, he was also something of a loose cannon. Gamelin complained that Georges "spoke loudly and often." But he, too, thought Georges honest until his deputy commander testified against him at Riom. "The double game is obviously a contagious disease," Gamelin concluded in a bitter reference to Vichy's post-war defense that its apparent collaboration with the Germans actually constituted a cleverly thought-out strategy of "resistance."[192] Pertinax believed that while Georges lacked Gamelin's intelligence, he possessed a better character, and was much more attuned to the need to incorporate aviation into French doctrine, to motorize, and to integrate armored divisions into the French order of battle than was Gamelin.[193] He was also considered safely "Republican," although he frequently complained of government weakness.[194] But the war minister in 1935 was Gamelin's good friend and classmate at the *Ecole supérieur de guerre* General Louis Maurin, an artillery officer who viewed calls for armored divisions as a nefarious plot to reduce the battlefield prominence of his *artiflots* – French military slang for "gun bunnies" and "twelve-mile snipers." Maurin chose Gamelin on the pretext that Georges was still suffering from the wound he had received in Marseilles in October 1934 while riding in a procession next to Alexander I of Yugoslavia and Foreign Minister Louis Barthou, both of whom died at the hands of a Bulgarian assassin.

While the appointment of Georges may not have changed the outcome in May–June 1940, it might have limited the dimensions of the catastrophe, Georges' biographer speculates, because Georges objected to the Dyle–Breda Plan imposed by Gamelin. Furthermore, unlike the Olympian and softly sycophantic Gamelin, Georges was genuinely popular in the army, and was also a good friend of Churchill. But even Georges' admirers were forced to concede that he was more respected as an administrator than as a strategic visionary. Georges' limitations included a lack of imagination, a relaxed command style, and a tendency to "conform with the mold and habits of military society," rather than fight his corner in the operational and strategic debates of the day. If Gamelin is to be believed, Daladier had no confidence in Georges because he had not commanded in battle, and wanted to replace him with First Army commander Gaston Billotte, an advocate for heavy tank divisions. But Gamelin convinced Daladier that to replace Georges as commander of the northeast theater would alienate Georges' many army friends. It proved a poor decision – in 1940, the stunning speed of German operations caught Georges completely by surprise to the point that he literally dissolved into tears.[195]

Gamelin's career had been nothing short of brilliant. From a military family with roots in Alsace and Lorraine, he had graduated *Major* – first – in his 1891 Saint-Cyr class, and a bare seven years later ranked runner-up in his class at the prestigious *École supérieur de guerre* whose alumni were destined to populate the army's senior ranks. As a member of French commander-in-chief Joseph Joffre's staff in 1914, Gamelin was cited as one of the major architects of the miraculous French victory on the Marne in September. His time as Joffre's aide-de-camp, that culminated in Joffre's removal as commander-in-chief at the end of 1916, taught Gamelin the value of nurturing political contacts. Unlike Weygand, who spent the entire war on Foch's staff, Gamelin served with distinction in the trenches of the Great War in charge of a battalion, then a brigade, and finally from April 1917 to the war's end at the head of the 11th Infantry Division. Post-war, he had quashed the Druze Revolt in the Levant in 1925–1927. He returned to a corps command in France and subsequently ran the Army general staff when Weygand was promoted Inspector General of the army in 1931. However, relations between the two men quickly deteriorated with the 1932 victory of the "enlightened internationalists" of the Cartel des Gauches. While Weygand's fabled feuds with the government were well advertised, Gamelin sought to sooth and temporize with left-of-center politicians like the socialist Joseph Paul-Boncour and Radical Maurice Sarraut. At the same time, he had to unite the French armed forces riven by inter-arm, inter-service, and personal rivalries in the face of a deteriorating international security environment, sclerotic budgets, and a parade of left-leaning governments led by men whom the vast majority of officers viewed as at best pale patriots, if not outright traitors.[196]

While Blum found Gamelin "intelligent but limited," his commander-in-chief helped to quiet an officer corps profoundly disturbed by the Popular Front's support of the Spanish Republic and the diplomatic outreach under the influence of Pierre Cot and Yvon Delbos toward Eastern Europe. Gamelin also quietly prepared a military response lest the explosion of factory strikes of May–June 1936 that greeted the Popular Front election turn insurrectionary, revealing a paranoia about the working class that contributed to the decision for armistice in 1940 and bled into military distrust of the French Forces of the Interior (FFI) and *l'amalgame* in 1944–1945.[197] In the process, Gamelin acquired the reputation of an unexciting but reliably "Republican" general who was adroit, nuanced, prudent, conciliatory, and pragmatic, sometimes to the point of sacrificing principle to expediency.[198] After Gamelin lost the battle for France, it became almost mandatory in retrospect to log an unflattering verdict. Fonvieille-Alquier complained that Gamelin's "lack of dash, his nervous jump and blinking eyes when the flash of the photographer's bulb was near to him, his awkwardness when he reviewed some unit or decorated one of his subordinates in front of the troops ..." made him resemble "a civilian dressed up as a soldier." His "fixed determination not to annoy and never to displease" might have made him a notable chief of staff under a dynamic commander.[199] Others agreed that while Gamelin projected the image of the self-effacing bureaucratic operator, he seldom made eye contact in meetings, while rubbing his hands together as if devising alibis and building escape clauses into every proposition so as not to compromise himself.[200] British General Edmund Ironside, who met Gamelin during the Phoney War, was surprised by his dyed hair and frustrated by his complacency, his wishful thinking that the German population would overthrow Hitler, and his stubborn reluctance to initiate combat.[201] In the autumn of 1939, A. J. Liebling interviewed the diminutive, rosy-cheeked French commander with his "Flemish head" and an optimistically upturned white moustache. The décor in Joffre's old study in the *École Militaire* which served Gamelin as an in-town office was straight-up Petit Trianon. After listening to Gamelin's confident bromides about French military preparedness, Liebling concluded that the French commander-in-chief seemed "like a somnambulist jauntily strolling off a roof."[202] André Beaufre, who served on Gamelin's staff in 1939–1940, found his commander uncommunicative, a "little man ... more professor than general, manifestly out of his depth," a temporizer who found it difficult to take the most simple decision.[203]

Gamelin's biographer, Martin Alexander, insists correctly that the French commander-in-chief has shouldered the burden of a defeat that should be more widely distributed. Gamelin's achievement was that he had helped to guide French rearmament and craft a long-war strategy against the Axis that, as the revisionist argument goes, plotted a strategic course that would eventually result in an Allied victory. Nor should the fact that Gamelin was not a "fighting commander" be held against him. Rather, the argument goes, Gamelin may be viewed as someone who was in the vanguard of the emergence of the strategic chief-of-staff with a firm grasp of the political dimensions of conflict, a category of senior leader who would come to the fore in the Second World War.[204] The counter-argument is that Gamelin was no Marshall, a man firmly in command of the US Army who had the full confidence of Franklin Roosevelt, with his little black notebook in which he wrote down names of talented officers to promote like Dwight Eisenhower. Nor was he an Allen Brooke, King, Dill, or Portal, solid characters all in the *avant garde* of modern pol-mil command trends who served strong political leaders who understood how to deploy a military instrument to political effect. Rather, Gamelin was the product of an older tradition of French political culture prevalent in an insecure Republic where memories of Bonapartism, Boulangism, and a soon-to-be-realized resurrection of the anti-Dreyfusards at Vichy set French civil–military relations on edge. But if the old adage holds that a nation gets the generals it deserves, Gamelin was perfectly suited to the mature Third Republic. His diffidence toward politicians sought to allay suspicion and insulate the army against political meddling. The flip side was that he proved to be a weak commander who never gripped his army, and never curtailed the power of the innovation-resistant arms inspectors, channeled the armored debates toward resolution, or forced a cohesive doctrine upon the army. While responsibility for the defeat of 1940 may have been widely shared, and the Maginot Line was something that, for better or worse, he inherited, the Dyle–Breda Plan was Gamelin's baby. Nor did he take the elementary precaution of maintaining a strategic reserve that might have staunched the German breakthrough at Sedan long enough for the French to stabilize the situation.

However, in Alexander's eyes, Gamelin's real shortcoming lay with his failure "in transforming or sufficiently remodeling the ideology of the French military cast." For in May–June 1940, the *Wehrmacht* merely galvanized a French civil–military crisis that permitted Pétain and Weygand, joined by "the nation's military and administrative elites," to back-stab the Republic.[205] Unfortunately, how Gamelin was to effect this change in the French military's stubbornly anti-republican culture with its deep-rooted sense of grievance is unclear. First, Gamelin represented the quintessential French military insider, a man comfortable in a pol-mil arrangement that had rewarded him handsomely. This in itself made him an unlikely candidate to spearhead a radical remodeling of French military culture. Second, attempts to make the army officer corps more "Republican" before the First World War by manipulating promotion to favor Masons and non-practicing Catholics had served only to foster division, resentment, demoralization, and a public backlash.[206] As has been seen, Cot's attempts simply to retire 400 superannuated air force officers provoked a tsunami of protest and accusations of political favoritism in a freshly created service that lacked the antiquity, entrenched traditions, or customs of the French army, but which subsumed in full measure the French military's wariness of the left and resentment at civilian meddling. After November 1942, the CFLN/GPRF, followed by the Fourth Republic, discovered that purges of compromised officers from the French military or police were checked by the need for commanders, technicians, and gendarmes to keep order in France and secure the empire. Staging a successful campaign to "republicanize" the armed forces in the polarized environment of the 1930s, in the face of German rearmament, with conservatives vocal in parliament and in the press, would have further roiled French civil–military relations at a critical period in France's rearmament effort.

Given these conditions, Gamelin sought to manage French civil–military relations rather than reorder them. He became the ideal commander-in-chief for the "system politicians" of the late 1930s, above all Daladier, who had no confidence that France alone could contain Hitler and who feared with justification that the Republic's soldiers might slip the leash of civilian control. American historian Ernest May surmised that Gamelin spent so much time massaging the insecurities of the Third Republic politicians that he paid too little attention to the Germans, a charge that Alexander believes exaggerated. But it is clear that Gamelin's pessimistic appraisals motivated in large part by his desire to keep his long-term rearmament strategy on track stamped a military imprimatur onto the politicians' disinclination to act.[207]

The revisionist attempt to shift the blame entirely onto military shoulders and so exonerate the Republic's role in the debacle overlooks the complexity of France's civil–military arrangement. A January 1938 decree named Gamelin Chief of Staff of National Defense, a high-sounding title that in fact carried only a small staff and no power to "command" the three services, only the ability to "coordinate" budgets, procurement, training, promotion, and peacetime policies at the behest of the *Comité de guerre*. This continued a command vacuum at the top of the services that Reynaud had condemned in 1936 when he called the position of French commander-in-chief "a label stuck on an empty bottle."[208] Williamson Murray and Alan Millett called the French high command "a nightmare organization" with little control and no coherent program.[209] But even if it did little to modernize French defense, this organization suited both the Third Republic's politicians and the service barons. When Gamelin was named Chief of the General Staff of National Defense and Commander-in-Chief of the Land Forces, he claimed to have asked what powers exactly did this entail, only to receive evasive answers. The navy and air force committees in parliament opposed extending the chief of the general staff's authority over their services, while no one wanted to strengthen Daladier's position by ceding too many powers to his acolyte.[210] But it soon became clear that while French soldiers complained bitterly about the dispersion of command authority imposed by a paranoid Republic, the men on horseback managed to concoct their own bureaucratic impediments based on personal animosities or inter-arm rivalries.

Gamelin was flanked by two deputies – Georges was deputy commander-in-chief designated to direct "the north-eastern theater of operations" on the outbreak of war, while Louis Colson operated as Army chief of staff. Henri Dutailly notes that this command "triumvirate" might have worked had it operated as a team. But this was the French army, after all, where it was said that lieutenants are friends, captains are comrades, majors are colleagues, colonels are rivals, and generals are enemies.[211] Gamelin's "assistants" had been installed, mainly at the machinations of Weygand, as a check on command authority. Ever the consummate bureaucratic politician, Gamelin found workarounds. The French commander refused to allow his deputy Georges to choose his own staff, and busied him initially with a rewrite of doctrine. The result was the "*Instruction sur l'emploi tactique des grandes unités*" of 12 August 1936. It was criticized post-war as too defensive, out of touch with modern combat procedures, heavy on motorized reserves and anti-tank guns, both in short supply in the French army of 1940, but light on air support and armored units.

Declared "*chargé de mission*," Georges was also dispatched to carry out inspections of this and that, often in the colonies, which kept him absent from Paris for long periods. These peripheral tasks intentionally assigned by Gamelin kept Georges on the road and little prepared him for his role as wartime theater commander. This was especially worrying as, wounded in 1914, Georges had spent the remainder of the Great War serving on the staffs, first of General Maurice Sarrail, who commanded the Balkan front from Salonika, and then on Foch's staff, rather than in combat commands.[212]

As Army chief-of-staff, the French army's principal evangelist of the Maginot Line and of defensive strategy, and a bitter opponent of a Soviet alliance, Colson stifled Gamelin's admittedly fitful flashes of initiative or imagination.[213] The French commander-in-chief's power was further diffused in a myriad of committees and staffs. While Georges recognized the need for armored units and to bring the three services under a single authority, one consequence of this intentionally diffuse French command system was that no single vision for the "Air–Land Battle" evolved, because the *Comité de guerre*, responsible for coordinating the three services, remained remiss in its duties. Gamelin complained that decisions were taken in cabinet or in obscure, often ad hoc, committees that kept no minutes – a standard practice in Third Republic governance that included the cabinet – without input from the general staff. Georges was aggrieved that Gamelin neglected to consult him on many of the major defense decisions.[214] The *Comité de guerre* and the *Comité permanent de Défense nationale* failed to articulate goals and define the powers of command. The services seldom consulted with each other, or with the Quai.

Inter-service rivalries were also sharp. According to Pertinax, Gamelin "exasperated" navy chief François Darlan, "and the Admiral never missed an opportunity to do the General a bad turn."[215] In any case, the proud admirals cracking lobster claws in their ward rooms, sheltered by a powerful parliamentary lobby, and under the iron thumb of Darlan, "hardly a man bothered by scruples," had no intention of taking orders from a five-foot, four-inch-tall trench digger with dyed hair.[216] Not only was the navy's sense of inter-service superiority secured by the technological conceit that de Gaulle was keen to appropriate for his *armée de métier*, but also this sense of exclusivity was heightened by the fact that the naval officer corps was dominated by the devout progeny of the provincial aristocracy, or families with aristocratic pretentions, recruited heavily from France's conservative Atlantic seaboard. From the moment they entered *l'École navale* – nicknamed *la Borda* after the series of ships so named and anchored in Brest harbor that had served as the original

Figure 1.3 November 1930. The Minister of the Navy reviews cadets of the French naval academy in Brest "where a confusion is deliberately maintained between a professional and a spiritual elite."

school – naval cadets were inculcated with the idea that they belonged to "a scholarly, and soon to be military aristocracy." As Thomas Vaisset notes: "This instruction finds its natural extension on religious grounds where a confusion is deliberately maintained between a professional and a spiritual elite. [The academy's commandant is called the "Pope."] The junction between the two operates in the ethical domain, especially around 'the morals of duty [that] furnish the link between religious and secular morality.'" (Figure 1.3).[217]

From there, it was a small step to view naval service as a religious vocation, and the man-o'-war as a sort of iron friary adrift in the sea's immensity. "It's the separation from land, the union of everyone from the commander to the lowest sailor, to reach for the same goal." This marriage of machine and monastery, the synergy between technology and spirituality, provided the classic interface between naval service and Catholicism, "because it allowed the exaltation of an ethic founded on selflessness, the cult of obedience, and service as the pinnacle of sacrifice." Service to France under God's watchful eye coupled the anchor inexorably with the cross. La Borda reinforced a very "Catholic-centric" concept of French identity taught in parochial schools, in which "eternal France" transcended the Republic. "Civism and Catholicism formed the basis of the social relationship."[218] This paved the way for the so-called "admiralization" of Vichy, when Cardinal Liénard, Bishop of Lille, famously quipped during the occupation that he feared he might soon be replaced by an admiral.[219]

This nautical narcissism was popularized by the inter-war writings of Commandant Paul Chack, who divided the world into "the living, the dead, and those who go to sea." French naval officers reveled in an imagined moral and spiritual ascendency conferred by lives lived in a pure medium, sheltered from the corrupting influences of politics and civilization, which they left behind when they cast off. This institutional self-righteousness seemed harmless enough so long as it remained confined to the bridge and la Borda passing out parades. But with the collapse of the Republic, these views, exaggerated and radicalized by the social and professional isolation of the inter-war years and the conviction that the navy endured as the last repository of France's moral and spiritual values that made sailors superior to the decadent citizens they defended, were to have political consequences. During the Occupation, French naval officers felt that, as one of the few healthy elements in French society, they must seize the wheelhouse of France's renewal through the National Revolution. But with little real-world experience, they tended to view political leadership as being akin to shouting orders from the bridge in a storm, to a crew drilled instantly to obey. For these reasons, naval officers were to become what Jean-Baptist Bruneau calls the sorcerer's apprentices of Vichy.[220]

In this atmosphere of bureaucratic muddle, political rancor, and the French military's condescending sense of moral superiority, "civilian control of the military" was a qualified term. Daladier's elusive bonhomie suggested that he was distracted by issues far removed from national defense, and unwilling or powerless to break down armed service parochialism. As Lord of Defense Improvization, Gamelin was harried, rushing from meeting to meeting.[221] The British attaché reported that France's MOD was just a glorified "committee" that merely "coordinated solutions of certain definite problems." Alexander notes that this convoluted and improvized command structure handed sweeping responsibilities to the French commander-in-chief while it hobbled his powers to execute them.[222]

Conclusion

As international conditions in Europe grew more complex, France was in a poor posture to surmount them. In the front line against a populous, powerful, and rearming Germany, led by the bombastic and belligerent Hitler, Paris' most obvious international option was to revive the pre-1914 alliance with Russia. However, although ratified, the Franco-Soviet Mutual Assistance Pact of May 1935 was never applied for a variety of reasons: the death of Louis Barthou who had negotiated it; suspicion of Stalin and the PCF – "the party of a foreign power" – on the right and in military circles; the Moscow purges which allowed those opposed to a Soviet alliance to argue that it was militarily worthless, especially as the smaller Eastern European powers would never allow Soviet troops on their territory; and the preference in the Quai to seek a détente with Germany, or an alliance with Great Britain, rather than to trust Stalin, who admittedly was entirely untrustworthy as the August 1939 Molotov–Ribbentrop Pact was to prove.[223] Gamelin's strategy was to build up an impregnable defense of the Hexagon, mount an economic blockade of Germany, and fight a war on the periphery – *la guerre ailleurs* – until the enemy was enfeebled and the Allies had amassed enough military power to take the offensive.[224] This left as potential alliance partners a constellation of quarreling Eastern European nations, or Great Britain, in the hands of conservatives whose policy until 1938 was one of "limited liability" in a continental conflict.[225]

This situation required France to rely at least initially on its own military forces. One of the arguments of post-war historians was that the Third Republic, and in particular the Popular Front, did little to shore up French defense. In fact, that was not true. The Maginot Line had been constructed to assuage civilian anxiety to protect the northeastern frontier, not because the French army stood unanimously behind it.[226] And while the Maginot Line had absorbed a large share of the defense budget in the 1930s, the Popular Front had expended a great deal of money to modernize the French air force and create one of the world's largest tank armies, despite the risk of capital flight, inflation, and the sacrifice of much of the social agenda of the French left. But defense modernization hit two snags. The first was a lack of government-directed coordination, which joined outmoded plant and industrial practices to put ambitious production quotas out of reach. The second was that this armament upgrade was bestowed on a multifaceted, Balkanized military organization whose leadership lacked a coherent defense vision for inter-arm and inter-service cooperation. Yet, after two years spent at the French staff college, Major Ralph C. Smith reported to his US superiors in August 1937, that:

> the French military doctrine is essentially conservative ... in harmony with the national policy as a nation that does not seek territorial expansion but desires to

> preserve what it has and to maintain the status-quo ... the situation that is ever uppermost in their minds is an attack on their territory by Germany ... After two years close contact with their methods, I feel that they have a good army, trained in a system that is adapted to their needs. Their doctrine is not suitable in its entirety for American purposes. But I think we can profitably consider their respect for the defensive power of an enemy in position.[227]

It was with a military force that was modernizing, in a piecemeal and improvized way, that France plunged into war.

2 From Phoney Peace to Phoney War, 1938–1940

The year 1938 is usually viewed as the critical year when France might have acted to galvanize Europe to organize a collective resistance to the *Anschluss*, Hitler's annexation of Austria in March, followed by his intrigues to split off the German minority in Czechoslovakia's Sudetenland. That would prove hard to do, however. As Talbot Imlay demonstrates, the international events of 1938 would nudge the foreign policies of France and Great Britain in opposite directions. British Tories increasingly worried that France might slip into appeasement, thus sabotaging Britain's strategy of limited liability on the Continent. This caused Whitehall gradually to shift Britain's defense focus away from the basically self-protective capabilities of the RAF and Royal Navy, and back to the army. Lacking an anti-fascist core, the French Right increasingly practiced a "selective pacifism" which contemplated war only against communist threats. As evidence to support this thesis, they needed only to point to the unique enthusiasm of French communists for belligerence that would only benefit Moscow. Meanwhile, the historic "*pacifisme intégral* " of the Paul Faure faction of the socialist SFIO was embraced as an antidote for war, an ambition that they shared with the vast majority of the French population at the time. In these circumstances, news in March that German troops had marched into Vienna and that Austria had been annexed into the greater Reich met with general indifference in France.[1]

Hitler's subsequent campaign to "rescue" the German minority in Czechoslovakia likewise elicited a flaccid response from Paris, even though it was apparent to even the ill-informed following the *Anschluss* that Czechoslovakia was Hitler's next target. This was in great part because a pivotal meeting of the *Comité permanent de la Défense nationale et de la Guerre* (CPDN) on 15 March 1938, presided over by Daladier, had pessimistically concluded that the German army and air force had surpassed those of France in strength, that France's Eastern European allies were disunited and impossible to assist in any case without their acquiescing to Soviet use of their national territory, and that appeasement governed in London under Chamberlain and Halifax. Blum's last pre-war government, which had been in office for less than a month, crumpled, which effectively terminated the Popular Front experiment. In April 1938, Blum was displaced as premier by the Radical Party Leader and his Foreign Minister, Georges Bonnet, an unreconstructed appeaser and former ambassador to the United States distinguished by his inability to speak a word of English and his antipathy toward Franklin Roosevelt. This government would endure until March 1940. The road to Munich yawned wide.[2]

"*Le Moment Daladier*"[3]

Although Daladier took the *Anschluss* as a signal that France must accelerate rearmament and solidify the British alliance,[4] he remains among the most contentious of the late Third Republic's constellation of controversial public figures. Pertinax accorded Daladier prominence of place in his boneyard of French "gravediggers." For a French public in search of scapegoats, and an outside world sifting for explanations, Pertinax's 1943 book written from American exile personalized and paved the way for the "decadence" explanation for France's ignominious 1940 collapse. While conceding that Daladier had an unimpeachable Great War combat record, and was educated, intelligent, incorruptible, diligent, modest, and capable of self-criticism, he was in Pertinax's view "weak and irresolute."[5]

Daladier's biographer Élisabeth du Réau struggles to amend Pertinax's unflattering portrait of the French Premier as a "man without a compass."[6] By the time he became War Minister – that is, minister of the army – in 1932, and subsequently presided over France's three services as Defense Minister, a post that he occupied almost continually from 1934, the young Dreyfusard firebrand of the 1920s, who had sought to energize the Radical Party and confirm it on a leftward course, had metamorphosed into the late Third Republic's quintessential opportunist, a skittle sliding along the linoleum floor of French public opinion.[7] In power, Daladier piloted the ship of state through the shoals of a fissiparous French parliament, rather than attempt to reinvigorate that body as an effective tool of government. And in truth, any demonstration of energy would have been inconsistent with his reputation as a political chancer lacking an ideological core, who confused French opinion with his shillyshally, and who resolutely refused to delegate responsibility.[8] Daladier's public image suffered from his mundane, untidy, even taciturn appearance. With a ubiquitous cigarette dangling from his lips, his rumpled jacket hitched back so that he could lock his thumbs into the armholes of his waistcoat, Daladier exuded an aura of bovine self-satisfaction, "the smell of the stables" as senior politician Joseph Caillaux unkindly said of him. In international gatherings especially, the charisma-challenged Daladier's diminutive stature, absence of eloquence, chain smoking, fondness for drink, and undistinguished "peasant" face might easily have caused participants to confuse him with the under butler in an unfashionable country house. His appearance and manners mortified the Quai's proudly patrician *corps diplomatique* and caused some foreign leaders and commentators to dismiss him as inconsequential. Nevertheless, despite his dearth of charisma, Daladier stood as a political Maginot Line against criticism of the high command, whether from Popular Front socialists or the critiques of Charles de Gaulle as amplified by Paul Reynaud.[9]

In Daladier's defense, du Réau emphasizes the parliamentary and institutional, not to mention international, constraints under which he labored. From the time he returned as Premier in April 1938, until ousted largely through the machinations of Pierre Laval in March 1940 and replaced by Paul Reynaud, Daladier arguably became the most popular French politician since Clemenceau. Backed by an overwhelming mandate from the French parliament, the "Bull of the Vaucluse" imposed a unity of sorts on a schismatic Radical Party, kicked the PCF to the sidelines, which *de facto* terminated the Popular Front experiment, staunched the hemorrhage of France's gold reserves, and, beginning in November 1938, enforced discipline in a strike-addicted French workforce. In this way, Daladier demonstrated, as Franklin Roosevelt was to do in the United States, that one could mobilize for a "people's war" without ceding political power to the trade unions and progressive politicians. Daladier's Jacobin energy is credited with lifting French resolve and psychologically preparing the population for war.[10]

But there the French Premier's resemblance to the American President ended. Imlay faults Daladier for relying on "the magic of the market," rather than centralized defense planning, to spearhead France's rearmament.[11] Du Réau concedes that Daladier was out of his depth in strategy formulation. He folded at Munich in part to steady the French financial market, only tinkered with the creation of armored units so as not to upset the "feudal powers" in the French general staff, and failed to mandate a modernization of French army and air force doctrine. His management of French diplomacy was characterized by a similar *laissez-aller*. The French Premier wanted to convert the Franco-Soviet Treaty of Mutual Assistance ratified in February 1936 into a full-blown military alliance. But he allowed British and Polish concerns, Laval's effective sabotage of the agreement by placing constraints on its application, as well as Right-wing opposition in France, to delay this goal until pre-empted by the Nazi–Soviet Pact in August 1939.[12] Nor did the "War committee" that Daladier had created in 1938 actually meet, all of which badly impeded the upgrading and restructuring of industrial plant, the modernization of French weapons systems, and increasing the volume of production.[13]

For a nation that cherished recent memories of vigorous wartime leaders like Clemenceau and Raymond Poincaré, Daladier seemed to personify the "inertia of the army and the nation" in the 1930s. While some historians protest the difficulties of making connections between army, society, politics, and the defeat of 1940, the systemic if anecdotal links are hiding in plain sight.[14] Daladier's "sluggish temperament" helped to explain his retention of Gamelin as commander-in-chief of French forces, and his toleration, even encouragement, of administrative confusion in the Defense ministry.[15] Meanwhile, his duties as Premier and eventually Foreign Minister increasingly distracted him from defense issues.[16]

Paul Reynaud, who succeeded Daladier as Premier in March 1940, faulted his predecessor for opposing an alliance with the USSR, and for rallying his Radical Party to shield Gamelin from dismissal. In Reynaud's opinion, Daladier's blindness to the defects of the French military amounted to dereliction of duty, especially in the wake of Germany's lightning April 1940 occupation of Norway. Reynaud attributed the Defense Ministry's "victory without battle" complacency to Daladier's naive fantasy that the besieged German economy would magically implode, or the German people under the iron thumb of the Gestapo would rise up and overthrow Hitler, without the requirement of an Allied attack.[17] Unfortunately, Daladier's "wishful thinking" was widely shared across a broad spectrum of French government and society during what came to be called the *drôle de guerre*. Gamelin for one seemed unwilling to go beyond mobilization and *Sitzkrieg*, in the hope that Italy would stay out of the war.[18] But the consequence was that Daladier overestimated Poland's ability to resist, never ordered the high command to carry out an offensive against Germany in September 1939, and kept his serious doubts about Gamelin's Dyle–Breda Plan to himself. Nor did he force his commander-in-chief to reinforce the Ardennes front, even though the vulnerabilities of this French defense hinge had been pointed out at least since 1938, and some might argue since 1870.[19]

But it was Daladier's sell-out of France's Czech ally in September 1938 that remains his most disturbing legacy. To be fair, Daladier had plenty of company, including his appeasement-minded Foreign Minister Georges Bonnet.[20] Nor was the High Command keen.[21] Without consulting with the French, Chamberlain held a face-to-face meeting with Hitler, first at Berchtesgaden on 13 September, and later on 22–23 September at Bad Godesberg. Although Gamelin remained reluctant to fight, France ordered a partial mobilization on 24 September, a dress rehearsal that proved an administrative shambles, visible confirmation that the French military was ill-prepared for war.[22] Blackouts were imposed, names of train stations were removed, and the windows of railway carriages tinted blue. However, war tensions subsided on 30 September 1938, when Chamberlain agreed that any areas of Czechoslovakia whose population was more than 50 percent German-speaking could be attached to the Reich. This effectively surrendered 30,000 square kilometers containing a million Czech inhabitants to Hitler. Daladier and Bonnet acquiesced, as did Blum, who muted the anti-fascists in his party. The French parliament minus the communists and two renegade deputies passed a vote of confidence in the Daladier government on 4 October.

It is possible that French intelligence estimates that the Germans could field and equip a million-man army of 120 divisions, as well as reports that the partially finished Siegfried Line constituted a powerful obstacle, contributed to Daladier's diplomatic retreat. Also, the pessimistic assessments of Air Minister Guy La Chambre and Air Force chief Joseph Vuillemin of the fortunes of a French air war should hostilities break out helped to sway Daladier's decision. Vuillemin's report was based on his summer tour through *Luftwaffe* bases guided by none other than Hermann Göring, who put the latest Stukas and Messerschmitt Bf 110 fighters through their paces. Both La Chambre and Vuillemin told anyone who would listen that, should war erupt, the French air force would be annihilated in fifteen days.[23] This sense of panic showed that both civilians and soldiers labored under an inferiority complex that even accurate intelligence could not have dispelled.[24] Indeed, while he regretted that Chamberlain had walked into a "trap" at Munich, Daladier concluded that his lack of armored forces, the weakness of the French air force, and the realization that the British army was far from prepared to shoulder its share of a war's burden made it prudent to jettison France's Czech ally.[25] There were also concerns in 1938 about France's financial stability, the ability of the French economy to withstand a long war, and distrust of the Soviets.[26]

The political price was high, however, as the abandonment of Czechoslovakia significantly diminished France's moral authority and diplomatic clout.[27] The Munich conference, from which he had been excluded, confirmed Stalin's view that the capitalist powers had tacitly encouraged Germany to expand eastward. This meant that "anything short of an offer of a full military alliance by France and Britain would be refused out of hand," by the Soviet dictator. But because Paris and London were unwilling to commit to "full reciprocity" on defense, the Soviets would explore rapprochement with Berlin.[28] At a stroke, the allegedly solid scaffolding of France's "long war strategy" came crashing down.

The post-Munich sense of reprieve that swept France soon gave way to the realization that the sacrifice of Czechoslovakia had been a catastrophe. Only 57 percent of the French population had approved of the Munich accord at the time. Blum, who on 30 September had welcomed Munich, confessed that he was "torn between cowardly relief and shame."[29] Practically every French party had split over Munich between pacifists and anti-fascists. France suddenly realized that the handover of an ally with its thirty-four divisions to Hitler meant that Germany could now muster more divisions than could France.[30] It was a poignant reminder of a decline of French prestige and that a "fundamental alteration" of France's relations with Eastern Europe had occurred.[31] This triggered a shift of perception in London, where British leaders wondered if France were sufficiently united to go to war – Churchill thought France "corrupt, divided, floundering, without compass" in the wake of Munich.[32] Chamberlain claimed to be exasperated by French ministerial instability and the "pseudo-Communist government" in France.[33] The fact that ministerial instability obliged French politicians to be more attuned to public opinion than were British governments was not necessarily reassuring. In the wake of Munich, Daladier concluded that a more robust foreign policy offered a vehicle to unify French public opinion.[34]

France's post-Munich mood has been a subject of considerable debate. Duroselle insisted that, having finally convinced Britain to commit to the containment of Hitler, Paris simply allowed London to dictate the pace of events as Frenchmen stumbled unenthusiastically toward war: "For this pacifist people, war itself was the first defeat," he opined.[35] Imlay believes that France's diplomatic mood swing signaled the perception on the French right that time was not on France's side. This would cause French strategy to become increasingly "reckless" – that is, eschewing direct confrontation with Germany in favor of peripheral operations that also targeted Moscow, like plans for attacking Baku or confronting the USSR in Finland.[36] In any case, France's wake-up call had come too late. Not only had Hitler's reoccupation of the Rhineland, French non-intervention in Spain, the *Anschluss*, and the failure to seal an alliance with Stalin, confirmed by Munich, liquefied France's diplomatic credibility, but also appeasement had severely curtailed France's ability to marshal a coherent military response from 1938.[37] "Buying time" through the postponement of war, which had constituted the foundation of French grand strategy, had only threatened to make war more terrible when it finally and inevitably arrived.

Revisionists counter that this view reads history backwards from a defeat that gave France "an aspect of tragic mediocrity" that makes the Fall of France in 1940 and acquiescence to the Vichy regime appear practically preordained.[38] Rather, in the revisionist canon, the September 1938 Munich conference represented a pivot, when French policymaking suddenly began to reflect France's material and psychological preparation for war, as France's leaders realized that Hitler would have to be fought sooner rather than later.[39] Lingering doubts were dispelled by *Kristallnacht*, launched on 30 November 1938, after a Polish Jew, Herschel Grynszpan, murdered the third secretary of the German embassy in Paris. This sent a strong signal that the assumption that Hitler could be convinced to operate within a modified collective security system was delusional.[40] Although "war anxiety" persisted, an estimated 70 percent of the French now supported resistance to Hitler.[41] "On the eve of war, France was characterized not by defeatism but by sober realism," concludes Richard Vinen.[42] Munich had delivered such a shock precisely because the French realized that they had come within a hair's breadth of initiating a war that their military was totally unprepared to fight.[43]

Sensing that the majority of French people were "morally prepared for war," Daladier moved toward popular mobilization, extending the working week and accelerating rearmament. A *Commissariat general à l'information* directed by playwright Jean Giraudoux was created to counter pacifist propaganda. Daladier decreed a reorganization of regional military commands, allowed conscripts to be retained after their period of mandatory service had expired, cracked down on espionage, and reformed electoral laws. He traveled to Nice, Corsica, and Tunisia to defy Mussolini's November 1938 irredentist claims on those territories.[44] Parliament was circumvented to the point that Blum complained that Daladier had installed a dictatorship.[45] He also worked to tie in his British ally, feeding Chamberlain intelligence reports that the Germans were preparing plans to invade the Low Countries. Under Daladier's direction, Gamelin proposed a Supreme Allied Military Commission to direct war strategy. He instructed La Chambre to buy 1,000 fighters from the United States. In this way, the revisionist view is that Munich both brought the inter-war years to a close and exposed the final illusions of popular pacifism. From now on, the state of the army, the shortcomings of the French air force, the fear of financial catastrophe, Britain's reluctance to embroil itself in a continental war, and opposition in France to a Soviet alliance were subsumed in the growing popular realization that war had become unavoidable.[46] "Having narrowly escaped war, French public opinion realized that it must pull together or perish," concludes Daniel Hucker.[47] Paris went to war at the right time with a population united against the German threat, with an army that was numerous and adequately armed, and with a British ally that, having been assiduously courted, now finally stood at thc altar. In other words, all the pieces for a successful "long war" strategy were in place.

Realizing that war was now imminent, Daladier executed a convincing display of "*virilité*," a deceptive pantomime perhaps, but one that generated "a palpable resurgence in French national resolve in the first six months of 1939."[48] The government's center of gravity shifted back to the center right, with the anti-appeasers Paul Reynaud, Georges Mandel, and Jean Zay included in Daladier's new cabinet, while those who had been fence sitters – La Chambre, Chautemps, Campinchi, and Daladier himself – now committed to preparing France for war. Bonnet was retained as foreign minister, but his appeasement-tinged *dégagement à l'est* was neutered, as the fruits of appeasement became ripe for harvest. On 16 March 1939, the parts of Czechoslovakia that Chamberlain and Daladier had neglected to surrender the previous September came under Hitler's control, with German occupation of Bohemia and Moravia as a *Reichsprotektorat*, and the establishment of Slovakia as a client state. Six days later, against a background of the contrived clamor of a German minority demanding reunion with the Fatherland, Lithuania ceded Memel to Hitler, who theatrically and symbolically sailed into this former outpost of the Teutonic Knights on the bridge of the pocket battleship *Deutschland*.[49] On 7 April, Mussolini invaded Albania, ostensibly to protect King Zog from Yugoslav aggression. On 28 March, Madrid fell to Nationalist forces, catapulting a first installment of half a million Spanish Republicans across the Pyrenees with more to follow. They were directed to *camps de concentration* that temporarily set the international standard for minimalist comfort.

By early 1939, French strategy was steaming toward the rocks. Paris had managed to draw in Great Britain. But Britain's minuscule army did not compensate for a barrier in Central Europe. Suddenly, as everyone realized that Munich had been a disaster, a pact with Stalin became imperative.[50] In a marathon speech delivered on 28 April, Hitler denounced the 1934 German–Polish treaty. Two days later, Stalin had proposed a military alliance against Germany. An Anglo-French negotiating team set out by sea for Leningrad. But while the narrow escape from war at Munich had made the French public willing at last to accept a Franco-Soviet Alliance,[51] Stalin had begun to explore other options.

"That the west would favor a German–Soviet war, and might even lend support to Germany's fight, was a constant component of thinking in the Kremlin," concludes Ian Kershaw. The Soviet leader viewed the Anglo-French retreat at Munich as evidence that they would not stand up to Hitler, and took the relatively junior diplomatic status and evasive tactics of the Anglo-French delegation as an indicator of a lack of commitment.[52] As negotiations dragged on from May to August, Stalin demanded from the Allies the right to intervene in Finland, Romania, Poland, and the Baltic states to prevent "indirect aggression." These new demands might have been a stalling tactic while he cut a better deal with Hitler. But had France and Britain gone to war over Czechoslovakia, at least they would have been guaranteed Soviet neutrality. Hitler would have been foolish to launch an attack against France and Britain before he had secured an agreement with Stalin. Stalin calculated that concessions from Germany would allow him to build a buffer in Poland and the Baltic and give him a few years of peace to prepare for war. In the meantime, the plundering of Eastern Europe combined with Soviet supplies to play a vital role in fueling Germany's war effort until June 1941.[53] It made peripheral operations calculated to weaken Germany and win the war quickly useless so long as Stalin held the back door to Eastern Europe ajar. But that only encouraged schemes pushed by the French right to attack both Germany and the USSR.[54]

Although fascist sympathizer Marcel Déat expressed a disinclination to "die for Danzig," his appeal for peace fell flat amidst a growing popular acceptance that appeasement carried out from a position of weakness was bound to fail.[55] The cascade of crises served to convince the most war-averse Frenchmen that the German dictator had played them for fools. Those who weeks before had argued that Czechoslovakia was impossible to defend now began to talk enthusiastically about creating an Eastern Front. Suddenly, intelligence reports became more upbeat, more optimistic about France's chances of success as they enumerated the weaknesses of the German economy, Germany's lack of raw materials, which would only become worse with an Allied blockade, and the doubts, even defeatism, of the German population. Hitler's intentions were now clear, so that France must make a stand or lose face.[56] In this way, intelligence underpinned a new "appeasement lite" strategy of "victory without battle." Détente with Germany became a dead letter. Daladier frequently took to the radio to emphasize the importance of national unity and the benefits of the empire for French productivity and defense. The Premier's popularity soared, as pacifism of left and right withered. While reporting that Germany was rearming, intelligence also emphasized German economic and financial vulnerabilities in a long war as a basis for strategic planning.[57] Daladier's critics counter that this show of resolution was merely empty bravado by a man who was politically isolated, indecisive, and frequently in his cups.[58]

Germans and Italians boycotted the 1939 *tour de France*. The annual 14 July parade featured British troops marching down the Champs-Élysées before a large and enthusiastic crowd. August brought news that the Germans and Soviets had signed a commercial agreement. Two days later, tripartite military talks between Britain, France, and the USSR were suspended after Stalin cut a secret protocol with Hitler to partition Poland. News reached Paris on the night of 22 August that German foreign minister Joachim von Ribbentrop would arrive in Moscow on the next day. On 23 August, Foreign Minister Bonnet requested a meeting of the *Comité permanent de la Défense nationale*, which assembled that afternoon in Daladier's rooms in the War Ministry on Paris' rue St. Dominique. The Nazi–Soviet Pact was a disaster for France, which desperately needed a second front.[59] News that Paris had squandered yet another diplomatic opportunity by allowing the Franco-Soviet agreement to expire through neglect unsettled the August holidays and triggered a call-up of reservists. Censorship of the press was tightened, while arrests of communists intensified. Bonnet forcefully requested the withdrawal of France's guarantee to defend Poland under the 21 February 1921 Convention, insisting that neither Moscow nor Bucharest would underwrite Anglo-French intervention. But events had moved on. Showing the resolve that had begun to take hold of British foreign policy, Chamberlain insisted that while the Allies had never agreed to go to war over Czechoslovakia, they were obliged by treaty to defend Poland. A desperate Bonnet proposed that Italian Foreign Minister Galeazzo Ciano arrange another international conference *à la* Munich.[60] But Ciano knew from early August that Hitler intended to go to war. He had also received advanced warning of the Nazi–Soviet Pact on 12 August. Given what he knew, at this stage Ciano's priority became not to prevent war, but to convince his father-in-law Mussolini to withdraw from the Pact of Steel before Italy became engulfed in a world war that it was woefully unprepared to fight.[61]

While his critics might remain unconvinced by Daladier's leadership style, no one could argue that he did not try to lead in his own way. The French Premier doubted that Hitler would keep his word. At this oft-referenced 23 August meeting of the CPDN, both Gamelin and navy commander François Darlan assured the ministers that their services were "ready" for war.[62] For his part, Guy La Chambre insisted that the air force had "made great progress" and that France's decision for war should not turn, as it had in 1938, on its relative inferiority in the air.

France would adopt a defensive air cover to protect mobilization. In six months' time, he insisted, the French air force would draw equal to the *Luftwaffe* in numbers of fighters. Both Gamelin and La Chambre would have to defend these confident prognostications in 1942 before the court at Riom. Anxious to avoid specious pronouncements, air force commander Vuillemin listened in silence to what he considered to be his minister's fantasy scenario. He subsequently prepared a memo for the record that underlined the superiority of the *Luftwaffe* and was intended to separate himself from what he believed to be the Air Minister's reckless optimism. Daladier's clinching argument was that the Allies could not allow Germany to gain control of the resources of Poland, Hungary, and Romania, which would compromise the Allied blockade. He declared that France must respect its agreement with Poland.[63] On 26 August, Berlin ordered a general mobilization. On the night of 27–28 August, Warsaw too went on a war footing. On 1 September, German troops invaded. On 2 September, the Senate and Chamber, including PCF delegates, met and listened to the case for war. But Daladier lacked enough confidence in the outcome to allow the two chambers to vote except to approve seventy billion francs in supplementary credits for war. Following London's lead, on 3 September 1939, France declared war on Germany.[64]

"This Derisory and Half-Hearted War"[65]

While it appeared on the surface that France had recovered its nerve, abandoned appeasement, and settled on war, Élisabeth du Réau argues that the spirit of appeasement in the guise of "victory without combat" hovered over the 23 August meeting of the CPDN. In other words, you could take Daladier out of Munich, but it was more difficult to take the Munich out of Daladier. While Nord asserts that "Daladier was ready to take the fight to Hitler in a way that Chamberlain never was,"[66] it was rather more a case of "*Messieurs les Anglais, tirez les premiers!*" The foot-dragging on 3 September 1939 was Daladier's – Chamberlain's declaration of war forced Daladier to give up on his hopes for mediation and follow suit.[67]

Other authors contend that, despite a lack of combat, the Phoney War should be treated as an episode in its own right rather than a prolongation of Appeasement, and not one in which defeat was foreordained.[68] As Martin Alexander has noted, the argument that Allied economic superiority would win the war without battle, like the entire "long war" strategy, was anchored in a perception of Allied military weakness.[69] Neither leader appeared eager to go *mano-a-mano* with the *Wehrmacht*, much less the *Luftwaffe*. And this despite the fact that Hitler's blitz into Poland had taken the German population by surprise. The *Wehrmacht*'s best units were in Poland, leaving only thirty-two divisions to defend an incomplete Westwall against which Gamelin might have massed eighty-four French divisions. The German conscript classes between 1919 and 1936 remained to be trained. The German tank inventory at this stage consisted mostly of small *Panzerkampfwagen* (Pz.Kpfw.) Is and IIs – indeed, specialists debate whether the Pz.Kpfw. I, originally designed in 1932 as a training vehicle, with light armor and just two machineguns as armament, should even qualify as a tank – while Berlin struggled with a munition crisis. This was the moment that France enjoyed a crushing superiority in both men and tanks, while the *Luftwaffe* was diverted to the skies above Warsaw. But rather than seize upon these fleeting advantages, Gamelin intended to take no action to defend Poland beyond acquiescing to mobilization. To be fair to Gamelin, Daladier, having honored the letter of the Polish pact while ignoring its spirit, had no desire to prod his service chiefs into action. Nor was London keen. *Au contraire*, when the first inter-Allied summit met on 12 September, the two premiers agreed that they could no nothing for Poland.[70] It is difficult to escape the conclusion that appeasement and ducking combat had become normalized behavior in the Allied leadership. And this even as the leaders of Germany, Italy, and the USSR redefined the normal parameters of international diplomacy. As May concluded, at this stage of the war, the Allied leaders grasped at any straw to shore up their hope that the war could be won without the need for combat.[71]

Mobilization

At the outset, Daladier failed to reassemble a 1914-style *union sacrée* behind a governing coalition that had shifted to the right in 1938–1939, in the midst of an "accelerating crisis in French domestic politics." Resistance to Germany followed by the Nazi–Soviet Pact had shredded the Popular Front. Unable to decide whether the main threat came from Germany or Russia, and reluctant to embark on total war, the right placed its hopes in deterrence, even though much of the political and military elite distrusted their own population.[72] A robust view held that the new generation, with schoolteachers in the lead, was defeatist. Many conservatives, led by those in the army, feared that the working class incubated "*l'ennemi intérieur*" in the form of a PCF "fifth column."[73] A grim Great War memory of victory gained through exhaustion and catastrophic casualties hovered over mobilization. The French public remained acutely conscious of the horrific sacrifices of the Great War, and fearful that France lacked the capacity to rescue Europe from Hitler. The great wellspring of popular resilience that had sustained the nation in 1914–1918 had been exhausted. The fact that German power had resurged barely four years after Hitler's seizure of power, shattering Europe's collective security system and dealing a string of diplomatic setbacks to Paris, offered proof that France was no longer a great power.[74] While it is difficult to generalize about the differences in popular morale in France in Britain, from the late 1930s the British Foreign Office and cabinet began to doubt France's ability to resurrect a *union sacrée*. Even before Munich, Churchill, who maintained many friends among senior French soldiers and politicians across the political spectrum, worried that political divisions, even hatreds, ran deeper in France, and politicians were less willing to cooperate in the national interests than in Britain. This would make it more difficult for France to rally in the wake of Dunkirk.[75]

Nothing preordained the failure of the *levée* had it been better managed. This post-1940 interpretation of defeat imbued of cultural pessimism and a mirror of Nazi Blitzkrieg propaganda that featured long lines of French POWs and fleeing civilians in the incongruously brilliant summer sunlight, and not just on the right, was that the explanation for France's 1940 debacle was generational – the soldiers of Sedan in 1940 were not those of Verdun in 1916. Like 1870, the debacle of 1940 was so unimaginable that it generated a crisis of masculine confidence, even of national identity.[76]

The *levée en masse* was launched on 3 September. Reacquaintance with the military life from September 1939 came as a shock, which gave France's citizen soldiers every reason to be upset. Call-up instructions recommended that reservists bring three or four days' worth of food, which most ignored. This understandably caused lots of grumbling among hungry soldiers.[77] A post-war report conceded that despite several partial mobilizations since 1936, the 3 September order for general mobilization caught the army completely flatfooted – officers were unfamiliar with their duties. Meanwhile, reserve orderlies, secretaries, guides, etc. who were to report immediately to help organize reception centers were delayed by the requirement to hand over their requisitioned personal vehicles, or had been reassigned, or designated as "*affectés spéciaux*" holding essential jobs, and so exempt from the call-up. As a consequence, reception centers were understaffed while the influx of reservists overwhelmed units.[78] Barracks lacked beds, and reeked of bad food and "unspeakable" latrines. Incorporated at Laval on 16 September 1939, Jean-Louis Crémieux-Brilhac joined a parade of recruits who shuffled single file below the first-floor windows of the local barracks – from the first window came a cascade of faded *horizon bleu* jackets. A second window disgorged trousers, while from the third streamed a cornucopia of leg wraps – the famous *bandes molletières* that consisted of two ribbons of cloth that wrapped the calf from the ankle to the knee, handy for absorbing moisture and lodging eating utensils, but otherwise useless. Clutching the elements of their "new" uniform, inductees then plucked a helmet from a pile in the corner of the barracks square. This single, ill-fitting uniform had to serve until they could have their uniform tailored on their first leave. Since the army lacked 150,000 pairs of trousers and 600,000 pairs of boots, many marched for months in their civilian trousers and footwear. The complaints were that French uniforms were both uncomfortable and impractical – too hot in summer, and not warm enough in winter. Backpacks were so awkward that soldiers often jettisoned them in combat, along with gas masks. French rifles were too heavy, with a rate of fire vastly inferior to the many sub-machineguns carried by the Germans. "It is surely possible to reduce the amount of material carried by the infantryman to allow an increase in the allocation of munitions," concluded a post-1940 report.[79]

Following a perfunctory medical examination during which everyone stood around naked and self-conscious, soldiers selected a spot to sleep on top of straw scattered on the floor. Since the army lacked 350,000 blankets, many would find the frigid winter nights particularly uncomfortable. The best-organized centers could get their soldiers clothed and on the road within three days. But elsewhere, reservists simply sat around for days waiting to be given a uniform and an assignment. "They went drinking with their relatives or friends," complained 1932 Saint-Cyr graduate Lieutenant Gaston Claude Vuchot. "After that, it was difficult to reintegrate them into the barracks and regain control."[80] Michel de Cazotte rushed home from a family holiday in Switzerland to report to his unit at Vitré in Brittany. His regiment was "obliged to quarter [the men] all over the town in barns and similar structures, each barn housing a small group of men, supposedly under the responsibility of a non-comm. The officers were billeted in private homes, which sounds very grand, but was in fact not much better." Many of the men simply hopped on their bicycles and peddled home to spend the night there, or disappeared into cafes. Later, when his unit, whose title suggested a North African provenance, was shifted to the front, "the town which had been dreading our invasion was surprised to find us congenial. They had feared all sorts of looting by wild North Africans, and found instead that we were quite well-behaved Bretons, who, though frequently drunk, were neither noisy nor destructive."[81]

Jean-Paul Sartre ran the switchboard for a meteorological unit that had requisitioned a hotel which had "an odor of neglect and slow decay very characteristic of evacuated dwellings."[82] Only when as a POW

Crémieux-Brilhac was temporarily housed in a new German caserne with showers, hygienic latrines, and flea-free beds did he realize how badly French soldiers were treated by comparison.[83] Oscar Fallek, mobilized eighteen months after he had completed his regular military service, was paired with another reservist and simply deposited in the Ardennes forest where the two men spent ten miserable months monitoring a network of microphones and small "seismographs" that allowed "mathematicians" in the rear to pinpoint the location of German batteries. Most of their time was spent gathering wood to stay warm in the freezing winter of 1939–1940, and making a rudimentary shelter of their own construction more weatherproof, as the army lacked 415,000 tents. Nor was Fallek alone, as local peasants complained that the army devastated forests for firewood. They also had to buy their own raincoats because the army had failed to issue them. From time to time, a corporal would appear to drop off rations.[84] At Metz, thirty-six-year-old journalist and cineaste Georges Sadoul washed in the mornings out of a bucket of water fetched from a well. Within days, his uniform, like those of his fellow soldiers, was full of lice, "that survive two hours cooking in the wash."[85] Packages from home, surreptitious and against regulations visits of wives at the front, the revival of the Great War institution of *marraines de guerre* (war godmothers), and classes or schools encouraged to "adopt" soldiers resulted in an influx of scarfs, socks, even boots and shoes to supplement inferior army-issued footwear which absorbed water like a sponge.

There was nothing particularly "colonial" about the 57th Colonial Infantry Regiment (RIC) in which Lieutenant Vuchot commanded a company. But its appearance was indeed exotic. Made up of Pyrenean peasants, it had been the last unit to be kitted out by its mobilization center. As a result, most of his soldiers still wore their civilian trousers, had string for rifle slings, "and their requisitioned automobiles and wagons constituted a convoy worthy of the most shabby provincial circus ..." Vuchot reported. The entire regiment looked like a convention of "clochards," with an anti-martial attitude to match.[86] But in their defense, how did Vuchot expect his reservists to adopt a martial attitude when they did not even look like soldiers? For the future Colonel Dominique Magnant, a graduate of the *École polytechnique*, a chemical engineer in civilian life and a reserve second lieutenant of artillery in 1939, the paradox of the French army was how so many obviously talented and professional officers could preside over such a dysfunctional organization: "I quickly discovered the inability of the French army to accomplish its mission," he remembered. "There is at the bottom an extraordinary incompetence, which is difficult to explain because everyone that I met in the army, my colleagues and above all my superiors were beyond criticism. Everyone did his job to the best of his ability. But there was on one hand a lack of organizational ability on the general staff, a failure to evaluate the potential enemy, a lack of support or incomprehension on the political level."[87]

The problem of armies in expansion is one of management. This is the domain of the staff officer. In the aftermath of the 1870 debacle, in 1876 the French army had replicated the Prussian staff system, whereby staff officers were recruited by competitive examination among lieutenants and captains with at least five years service, and sent for a two-year course in the *École supérieure de guerre* (ESG). After graduation, their careers were fast tracked, alternating between command and staff assignments in the different arms. The purpose was to give the army's intellectual elite a foundational apprenticeship in inter-arm planning and command to prime them for senior responsibilities. However, the men produced by this system had their weaknesses as well as their strengths. During the Great War, Count Harry Kessler compared the Prussian staff officers "exalted over the frontline officers" to "the Roman higher clergy [who] have turned war into a great bureaucratic business enterprise."[88]

The French army managed to replicate its Prussian model all too well. As Eugenia Kiesling notes, while the ESG imposed high admission standards, its curriculum was narrowly technocratic and its alumni too few adequately to administer a *levée*.[89] André Beaufre, who attended the ESG in the late 1920s, categorized it as "a good secondary school for the General Staff, with occasional sorties into the '*Supérieur.*' But above all, the shortcomings of the School sprang from the teaching of a restricted doctrine in which tactics, basically one-sided, were made to appear like a quantity surveyor's estimate . . . troops, ammunition, stores, casualties and time equated with the number of kilometers involved." The curriculum "failed to consider war as a whole, and even less to consider the problem of strategy," a subject on which Beaufre was later to publish an important book, which was simply viewed as the "handmaiden of tactics."[90] One consequence, as de Gaulle argued in *Vers l'armée de métier*, was to contribute to the disconnect in France between foreign policy, strategy, and military organization.

Some revisionists argue that the French army's performance in 1940 has been judged too harshly. The 1930s was not a prime time for defensive strategies, that appeared powerless to stop Hitler. And which army performed any better against the *Wehrmacht* and the *Luftwaffe* in the opening years of the Second World War? Nor must one factor out context: economic retrenchment, nationalist atavism that complicated international cooperation, and popular aversion for a repeat of Verdun that debilitated the *levée*. And French civil–military relations, if not entirely poisonous, were nevertheless toxic. Officers complained that political intervention in promotion and other institutional decisions fragmented the unity and undermined the morale of a nominally "apolitical" officer corps, which complicated their defense tasks. So, it seems unfair to put all of the responsibility for the defeat squarely on the shoulders of the French army.

One advantage of fighting incremental battles would have been to identify and eliminate under-performing commanders. This method allowed Churchill to clean house after Dunkirk, and served the British and Americans well in North Africa. Joffre, of course, had famously transferred 162 under-performing French generals to Limoges and other southern garrisons in the autumn of 1914. In contrast, Cochet categorizes Gamelin's purges during the Phoney War as Limoges lite – of seven corps commanders transferred, three were promoted. Likewise, of thirty-three reassigned division commanders, eleven were promoted to corps command, while one died of natural causes. Most of those thanked for their service and sent home were B division generals, some of whom had been summoned out of retirement in any case. Probably the most egregious case was that of Second Army commander Charles Huntzinger, who was retained in command even after the weaknesses of the Second Army's defenses at Sedan were reported by several sources. But such were Huntzinger's political connections and aureole of effortless professional success that blame for the Sedan breakthrough dropped on the hapless whistleblower André Corap, commander of the Ninth Army. Huntzinger's reputation as "*un diplomate et un mondain*," meant that in June 1940, de Gaulle would recommend him to Reynaud to replace Weygand as commander-in-chief.[91]

One of the consequences of poor management was that France's national mobilization plan proved to be "an empty shell" that repeated many of the mistakes of 1914, was costly to the manufacturing sector, relied on the notorious "*système D*" ("muddle through"), and convinced most that ordinary Frenchmen would again shoulder the burdens of war to the profit of *embusqués* (shirkers) and well-connected "string pullers."[92] The army seemed particularly ill-organized to absorb so many men at such short notice. Statistics vary, but according to du Réau, of five million Frenchmen between the ages of twenty and forty-eight eligible to serve, only 2,775,000 were in uniform by the spring of 1940.[93] Like every large conscript army in the Second World War, that of France was in reality two juxtaposed organizations, one regular, the other reserve. It counted 35,000 regular officers, about one-third of whom were graduates of Saint-Cyr or the *École polytechnique*, the rest either former NCOs or reserve officers who had been assimilated into regular status. While there were some relatively young stars who would rise to prominence during the war like Juin, Béthouart, de Lattre de Tassigny, Delestraint, de Hautecloque, and Koenig, too many regulars were aging Great War veterans known in the army as "*vieux cons*" (old farts). While a generally conservative lot overall, few career officers below the very senior ranks were actively political. They grumbled about the Third Republic in large part because it had presided over a decline in military prestige and standard of living to the point that many, perhaps even promising officers, had abandoned a military career. Those left often felt socially isolated, "*déclassé*," and consumed by administrative routine, a condition reinforced by Phoney War inactivity.[94]

When he became vice-president of the Council of Ministers and held the defense portfolio between February 1941 and April 1942, Admiral François Darlan was struck by the decentralization of army structures, the divisions between staff and line and arms and services, and the distance between officers and their soldiers that characterized the French army. However, when he tried to "navalize" the Vichy army by centralizing budget procedures to break down inter-arm rivalries, reduce staffs by 20 percent, increase command time for staff college graduates, and force officers to spend more time with their soldiers – for instance, dining in the mess rather than returning home to spend their two-hour lunch breaks with their wives – to create a "crew spirit," his reforms were rejected as undue maritime meddling in time-honored army practices.[95] The slackness of army command methods appalled reservist Dominique Magnant in 1939. "I was frightened not by the Germans, but by the ... negligence of some [French] officers. No one forced them to do their duty." The army's "*train-train quotidien*" (daily routine) mentality was on full display when, on 10 May 1940, Magnant's artillerymen were obliged to break into the artillery park and magazine because the officer in charge was on leave in Paris and no one could find the key. The equipment was in terrible shape. Many of the gun tractors, relics of 1918, failed to work. They tied their guns to the truck hitches with rope. It took several days to tow them to the front. "It was impossible for this to happen and the superior officer didn't know about it," Magnant complained.[96]

These regulars were joined by 80,000 reserve officers, around 45,000 of whom in theory were integrated into units in a ratio of three reserve officers to two career officers. In fact, regular units were often reluctant to part with the best combat officers, and might simply send spare staff officers and NCOs to B divisions.[97] Some reservists recalled to serve in the artillery or engineers were men at the top of their professions, like Magnant. Others, like the Californian Michel de Cazotte, placed in charge of a machinegun company in a B regiment, knew nothing about machineguns, nor was he prepared to manage fifty-six horses, "who show their teeth and snarl when I go by." Furthermore, de Cazotte found it wise not to ask too many questions about where his surly mechanic found spare parts and gasoline to keep the requisitioned company truck running.[98]

Fully 35,000, mainly older officers or fathers of families, whose military knowledge had atrophied or was out of date, were assigned to oversee depots and work sites, or settled in what was expected to be a quiet front like the Ardennes. Of these, 5,700 were soon judged to be professionally deficient and were sent home before 10 May 1940. Teachers figured prominently among reserve officers and NCOs, in part because "*préparation militaire*" was included in their normal school curriculum.[99] Vichy later tried to assign them blame for the catastrophe, as well as Freemasons, communists, and pacifists, who it claimed were also prominent among reservists. The fact that reservists had no secure status either at the front or at home offered one more indication that the national solidarity that supposedly underpinned the *levée* was lacking in France. In September 1939, Aspirant Crémieux-Brilhac was sent to Saint-Cyr, then in the shadow of Versailles, as part of the army's ultimately unsuccessful crash program to rectify its striking deficit of young subalterns. While he admitted that he was "very suspicious of the traditional army," he was impressed by the military academy, which resembled an English public school that combined discipline with an open, intelligent education. Still, he noted that there was little contact between regular cadets and the short-course reservists like him.[100]

Morale and increasingly discipline proved difficult to encourage and sustain in an army and population for whom, Sartre believed, the French officer corps had surrendered its "priestly infallibility" in the Great War. "The men nowadays no longer have the religious trust in the generals," he opined. "I've never heard anybody mention Gamelin here. Never – not even to say something bad about him. He doesn't exist at all."[101] The view of professional soldiers was hardly more positive. Although Beaufre viewed Gamelin as detached, rational, and with a highly intellectualized approach to war, the word among staff officers indoctrinated to believe that their mission was to shield the army from politicians was that he "has no guts."[102] Supremely Paris-centric, Gamelin personified the spirit of château generalship. A bishop *manqué*, the French commander-in-chief lacked energy and charisma, was a poor trainer and motivator of troops, and not a hands-on boss – in short, a general tailor-made for Daladier and the Phoney War. His infrequent visits to the front set a bad example for other senior officers, and telegraphed to the troops that army leadership declined to share their hardships.[103]

Reservists and conscripts viewed the regular military as a separate caste with their own hierarchies and puffed sense of self-worth: "In the artillery, like in the cavalry, they believe they are a superior species," Georges Sadoul grumbled. "You should hear how they speak of infantry officers, '*Bobosses*' [a pejorative term for infantryman] as they call them."[104] Sartre agreed: "Wherever I've gone, I've found the same hatred of officers: a restrained but profound hatred." This had nothing to do with doctrinaire anti-militarism, Sartre believed, but sprung from the silly punishments that officers inflicted as well as from the "always scandalously bad" organization of the French army which added to the deep resentment in the ranks and for which officers in their view bore responsibility. "[The soldiers are] always talking about bumping off their officers. None of them will do so of course; but the striking thing is that it isn't said mutinously, with clenched fists, but in a leisurely conversational tone, as something that goes without saying ... More than anger, they feel contempt for them."[105] Sartre and Sadoul were older reservists serving in support units. Nevertheless, many combat units were freighted with mature reservists who, like Sadoul and Sartre, would nevertheless find themselves swept up into combat in May–June 1940.

The NCO corps remained the French army's glaring weakness. Regular NCOs got passing marks in 1940. But, like many regular officers, they were too often shunted into desk jobs in "a heavily administered army."[106] Reserve NCOs usually counted effectively ten months of active service and had no command experience. "They lacked serious military training, initiative, energy, and aptitude for command," read a 1941 report.[107] Yet when the morale crisis hit in the winter, encouraged by the dual sentiments that their superiors had no idea what they were doing, and that as a consequence they simply wasted the soldiers' time, it fell to reserve NCOs to enforce discipline.[108] Rather than see themselves as vital links in the chain of command, however, many were too close to their troops, with whom they identified. Sartre recorded that his sergeant experienced "fitful bouts of heroism" and then just wanted to get the war over with. Everyone became consumed by the pointlessness of the war – "what am I doing here?"[109]

It is true that the German army, whose expansion only began in 1935, also lacked a sufficient number of NCOs.[110] But the *Wehrmacht* had advantages denied to the French army that included a tradition that accorded social status and respect to the military; a more solid training regimen; and, thanks to the defensive posture, when not passivity, of Daladier's long-war strategy, the *Wehrmacht* was free to create an operational/tactical mismatch. The *Wehrmacht* also enforced discipline with draconian ferocity backed by the Nazi security apparatus.[111] "'Punishment in the French Army is a thing of the past' – my young friends of the fighting formations said on more than one occasion," Marc Bloch recorded. "The generalization is, no doubt, crude, but there is more than a grain of truth in it." In Bloch's view, the acceptance of discipline should be, in the spirit of the original *levée*, both an extension of civic virtue and "an expression of the professional conscience." But those officers in command who combined "high-mindedness" with the "virtues of humanity" were in short supply. Instead, the atmosphere that reigned in the French army combined bullying with slackness.[112] It is difficult to imagine that Sadoul's many descriptions of soldierly indiscipline and insubordination in the French army during the Phoney War, even if exaggerated by his politics and recalcitrance, would have been tolerated for a moment in the *Wehrmacht*.

"Boredom without Grandeur" – Surviving the Phoney War[113]

It was one thing for France to accept the requirement for war on the psychological level. It was quite another to devise a strategy and create a military instrument to harness popular resolve, and to devise a plan that matched ends to means. While in the view of some, France's "long war" strategy was the correct one, it is equally possible to interpret France's post-September 1939 strategic posture as a sequence of improvizations, compromises, prevarications, confusion, and postponements, all lent a superficial coherence by a strong dose of wishful thinking which at times slipped into delusion. Strategy identifies goals, and accumulates resources to achieve those goals. Strategy should not be passive, but integrates both offensive and defensive components to achieve those ends. "Even the weakest party must possess some way of making the enemy conscious of its presence, some means of threatening him," Clausewitz advised.[114]

On the military level, a successful strategy incorporates the operational and tactical capability to realize the strategic plan. For a French high command that remained locked into a Great War mindset, the *levée en masse* would render a continuous front inviolate as the war unfolded by stages.[115] Military leaders and politicians calculated that a defensive stance adopted by a French nation mobilized in a *union sacrée* would act as a deterrent and put time on their side. The trick would be to make this time work for them.[116]

One reason for this was that strategy requires popular buy-in, the "people" leg of Clausewitz's "paradoxical trinity" which in the Prussian philosopher's view supplied "primordial violence, the mobilization and commitment ..."[117] Cochet argues that the mobilized soldiers fully expected to be thrown immediately into combat. He even suggests that had Gamelin attacked the thin shield of divisions left on France's frontier during Germany's invasion of Poland, one might even have witnessed the collapse of German morale. But when nothing happened, French soldiers began to question the reason for their mobilization – France had not been attacked, but was safe behind the Maginot Line, they reasoned. They had been separated from their families and their lives capsized only to sit around like workers on the dole. The population also began to wonder if the government even had a strategy.[118]

Called up in November 1938, Lithuanian Jew and naturalized Frenchman Roman Kacew noted that "the 'class' that was thus incorporated distinguished itself by its lack of enthusiasm and its profound conviction that the events of '40 would become entirely explicable, that one was being forced to participate in a 'stupid game.'" His mother was the only person among the parents and well-wishers who swarmed the train station to send off their sons waving a tricolored flag. "You can tell she's not French, that one," said a boy standing next to him.[119] While Aspirant (officer candidate) Crémieux-Brilhac had admired the crash training he received at Saint-Cyr in September 1939, the reason for the war was never made clear: "There's a war. We fight. What was curious was this absence of any discussion of what was at stake and the reality of what the Nazis represented," he remembered. In the New Year, he found the platoon of Breton conscripts in the 47th Infantry Regiment at Rennes, to which he was assigned, to be perfectly willing soldiers, if inordinately fond of cider and *gnôle*, a home-brewed *eau-de-vie*, and astonishingly unfit for country lads. However, already upset at being called up at harvest time, they were clueless about why France had declared war over some event in Central Europe. Indeed, even the better informed questioned the logic of going to war to defend Warsaw that a year previously had declined to support its Czech neighbor. France had not been invaded as in 1914. For many soldiers, the entire effort seemed to lack a national or ideological purpose, less alone a logic. This would translate into inertia, lack of effort, and an attitude that "it's not our war." Even Daladier noticed the "malaise" that seemed to have gripped the French army as the autumn turned to winter.[120] "[The soldiers] weren't sustained by any patriotic or ideological ideal," Sartre complained. "They didn't like Hitlerism, but they weren't wild about democracy either – and they didn't give a bugger about Poland. Into the bargain, they had the vague impression of having been tricked ... they had no impatience for victory, simply a profound desire for 'it all to end.'" (Figure 2.1).[121]

As everywhere in France, mobilization had hit civil society hard. Municipalities saw mayors, municipal councilors, and teachers

Figure 2.1 The Sitzkrieg. "They had no impatience for victory," wrote Jean-Paul Sartre, "simply a profound desire for 'it all to end.'"

disappear into the army. The countryside inopportunely emptied of its men and horses at harvest time, leaving women alone to manage the farms. Prized family sedans were requisitioned. Few shed tears when the local PCF headquarters were closed and documents seized, in accordance with parliament's 26 September 1939 ban on organizations affiliated with the Third International. Whether anyone took note of the 4 October desertion from the army of PCF leader Maurice Thorez is not recorded. By April 1940, he was broadcasting from Moscow. Citizens were also encouraged to report communists and "defeatists" to the police, so that 3,400 were arrested throughout France by March 1940. Able-bodied adults and school children dug trenches and practiced air raid drills. Mobilized soldiers began to receive letters from wives complaining that cooking oil and coffee were in short supply. As the Phoney War progressed, the lists of unobtainable items lengthened. From February 1940, queues formed at town halls to collect ration cards. But this did not stop galloping inflation that increased prices by as much as 37 percent by the New Year, and resulted in a shortage of provisions and clothes. The buying power of soldiers' pay collapsed, and the allocations paid to their families were no longer adequate. In this way, the black market was born. Blackouts enforced by air raid wardens were imposed from April 1940.[122]

While some historians praise the government's "long war" strategy, du Réau argues that the French public never understood that the government even had a strategy. "Long war" conveyed a message of delayed war, postponed war, even no war. The inactivity of the "Bore War" came as something of a letdown following on the heels of the French public's post-Munich resolution to confront Hitler. Paris simply resumed a pattern of inaction which had "profoundly degraded France's image" in the 1930s, and allowed the *Munichois* to linger on the fringes of policymaking.[123] The government and the high command produced no incremental success that might have inflicted a defeat on Germany and caused the French to take ownership of the war, much as the Battle of Britain later helped to rally the British population behind the war effort.[124] By the autumn of 1939, Paris and London had settled into a routine of leisurely procrastination. The "long war" strategy might have a rationale: avoid casualties, buy time for training and rearmament, preserve cash reserves, allow troops to come on line, and permit the "blockade" to bite.[125] However, this strategy had several problems, beginning with the fact that it was anchored in several erroneous assumptions. At the top of the list was the belief France could actually parry an initial German attack with minimal British support. Second, that the war would remain localized,[126] because the Royal Navy deployed as a deterrent in the Mediterranean and in Singapore would keep Italy and Japan neutral. Third, the war would then kick into a second phase that would see the Allies mobilize resources faster than could a "blockaded" Germany, thanks to their colonies and access to neutral trading partners. Allied governments never offered a rational, war-winning approach to Allied peoples, who were left to make of it what they could.

But the High Command had every reason to proceed with caution. France lacked demographic depth. While Pertinax complained that many French generals were too old and unfit for service, privates in their forties were common, while four years remained before fifty-three-year-old army reserve Captain Marc Bloch would age out of his rank *in a combat unit.*

Only with difficulty could France scrape together enough troops for 79 infantry, 3 cavalry, and 2 light mechanized divisions, and man 23 fortified sectors, while exempting up to 700,000 specialists and skilled workers as "*affectés spéciaux*." It was already clear to the High Command that combat losses would be difficult to replace. Half of the mobilized were designated for support functions – Army medical services alone required 60,000 men, not to mention 70,000 supply troops to run 275 depots in France and 83 in North Africa. Railway troops were needed to drive and support 100,000 trains, units were needed to build fortifications, guard POWs, and for postal control – the list is virtually endless. The infantry was short 9,570 officers on mobilization, while the artillery counted 4,100 vacancies. Young officers were in short supply. Hence a crash program to turn out 33,400 "aspirants" put in place in October 1939, of which Crémieux-Brilhac had been an early beneficiary. But less than a third of these had undergone perfunctory training by the outbreak of war.[127]

Indeed, given the cratering of French demography, the colonies were expected to make a considerable contribution to France's defense. Plan E devised in 1937 optimistically foresaw the conscription of 300,000 soldiers and 200,000 workers, to include 127,000 Indochinese and 250,000 from West and Equatorial Africa (AEF).[128] A vigorous propaganda campaign was launched to encourage indigenous volunteers. Nevertheless, propaganda failed to generate much enthusiasm, for several reasons, headed by memories of Great War sacrifices retailed by "*anciens combattants*," as well as unfavorable conditions of service. The biggest hurdle to recruitment, however, was the high percentage of "waste" – those rejected as unfit for military service because of malnutrition, epidemics, or some infirmity – as high as 65 percent in AEF and 75 percent in the Western Sudan.[129]

The assumption that the Allies could amass superior resources was underwritten by the belief that the blockade would bring Germany to its knees. In the view of the Treasury in London, Berlin would be forced to borrow to sustain the war, which would rapidly force it into bankruptcy. For its part, British intelligence failed to calculate that Germany continued to operate on a peacetime economy and had at its command all the resources of Poland, Czechoslovakia, Scandinavia, and Austria, as well as those of the USSR thanks to the Nazi–Soviet Pact. Allied guarantees extended to Romania and Greece failed to deter German and Italian aggression. Allied weakness eventually stimulated Japanese acquisitive interest in the Far Eastern and Indian Ocean empires of both nations.[130]

Allied "long war" strategy became hostage to contingency, and undercut by "fog and friction," poor net assessment, and wishful thinking. Several elements intervened to muddle strategic clarity on the Allied side. Rather than create a wartime government of all parties as Premier René Viviani had done in August 1914, Daladier simply reshuffled his cabinet on 13 September 1939, retaining some of the most notorious *Munichois*. This unwieldy, factionalized French cabinet under the Premier's "congenitally weak" leadership failed to coalesce around a plan, or even to define France's war goals.[131] The assumption that Polish resistance would endure until the spring convinced Daladier and Gamelin that they would have time to prepare French forces for conflict. As a result, they passed up the opportunity to take advantage of France's temporary numerical superiority to attack Germany, gain incremental success, blood the troops, and steady morale. The problem was that the neutrality of Belgium and Luxembourg reduced Gamelin's attack options to a 180-kilometer common Franco-German frontier between the Rhine and Luxembourg, much of it covered by the Maginot Line. The result was a reconnaissance in force into the Saar rather than a significant offensive designed to divert German troops from Poland. Six villages already evacuated but heavily mined and booby-trapped by German troops and around thirty POWs, mostly messenger runners, were seized in an operation that kicked off on 9 September. Because the Germans had not really contested the French advance, and no German tanks or planes put in an appearance, the French command was understandably reluctant to draw any firm conclusions from the operation. However, within a week, French infantry was "reorganizing" its positions, after getting a failing mark for lack of command initiative in tactical units, "too much rigidity" in their dispositions, failure to use terrain effectively, absolute "repugnance" to enter wooded terrain where "they did not know how to advance," and a tendency for the platoons to coagulate around the machinegun rather than advance by squads.[132] A follow-on operation scheduled for 22 September was canceled as Polish resistance collapsed.[133] Obviously, the command recognized that they had plenty of work to do to whip the army into shape for real combat.

There were also other reasons to delay the initiation of combat: the need to even out the quality between A and B divisions; the requirement for French industrial mobilization to keep pace with expanding military needs; the diminutive size of the BEF due to Chamberlain's rearmament prioritization of the Royal Navy and above all the RAF; the paucity of French and British armored units; the (hoped to be temporary) weaknesses of the French air force; "black legend" fears stoked by Interior Ministry reports that the PCF planned to sabotage industrial mobilization and undermine military morale; strategic confusion revealed with the November 1939 Soviet invasion of Finland over who the enemy actually was; a flawed military plan; faulty intelligence; underestimation of the enemy ... the list is endless.[134] Paris was reluctant to initiate a strategic bombing campaign, or follow Churchill's plan to drop mines into the Rhine River that might trigger a retaliatory *guerre aérochimique*.[135] With tiresome persistence, bedwetters like Bonnet continued to plead for an international conference *à la* Munich. This caused Daladier, at Reynaud's prodding, to shift Bonnet to justice and assume the foreign affairs portfolio, along with Defense, War, and the premiership.[136]

Savvy political leaders like Winston Churchill and Franklin Roosevelt realized the link between military action and popular morale, that one had to spar with the enemy early and often even if not fully mobilized for the main event – Mers-el-Kébir, Dakar, the Battle of Britain, attacking the Italians in Cyrenaica, Coral Sea, Midway, Guadalcanal, and Torch were meant to offer auditions, provide incremental success, gain strategic advantage. In Phoney War France, inaction also caused immense frustration. Darlan complained that the government's procrastination offered proof of an absence of any "*esprit de guerre*."[137] Cochet argues that the population and the soldiers would have bought into a "long war" strategy that defined clear war aims and rationalized the strategy of postponing combat. This did not happen, he believes, because "the true French strategy had nothing glorious about it."[138] Indeed, guarantees to Poland joined failure to intervene in Spain or Czechoslovakia as just another faithless French promise, insists Berkeley Professor Anthony Adamthwaite.[139] As a result, mobilized soldiers and the population were left in ignorance, "without other possibilities other than submission, depression, or imagination," concludes Cochet, which with defeat morphed into "treason."[140] Continued parliamentary shenanigans and backbiting, unbecoming and unpatriotic in the shadow of mobilization, sullied the sanctity of national sacrifice and stoked cynicism about the political leadership and doubts about the political direction of the war.[141] Postponing military engagement permitted political opponents of the war – pacifists on the left and "neo-pacifists" on the right – to linger in the war's wings, biding their time, according to French historian François Bédarida, while anti-war politicians like Laval and Flandin kept defeatism alive as a political option.[142] Daladier tried to show energy by persecuting communists and dissolving PCF-led municipal governments. Courts dished out fines and jail terms for "defeatism," which usually involved the town drunk shouting "Vive Hitler!" at bar closing time. Meanwhile, Daladier had rewarded the Phoney War's most notorious defeatist, Philippe Pétain, with the Madrid embassy in March 1939, where he could schmooze with his Rif War buddy Francisco Franco.[143] Hardliners began to criticize the French Premier for mobilizing the nation and then ordering "stack arms."[144] "Do you plan to keep them one year, two years, three years in the ranks?," the aging former premier and supporter of appeasement Joseph Caillaux chided. Daladier and Gamelin dared not acknowledge that they planned no major operations before 1941.[145]

But what was the alternative? "When arm-chair strategists complained of inaction," wrote Liebling, "all anyone had to say was 'Nivelle' to shut him up."[146] "The situation is so stationary that every now and then some people wish it would change," Sartre noted in his diary on 20 December 1939. "But then, suddenly reflecting that if it changes we'll be fired at, they recant their incautious words and declare for the status quo. Whereby someone else retorts that the status quo condemns us to stay here and grow old. Then everybody talks about something else. The problem is a very awkward one; in the meantime, the days go by, unhappily."[147] As Christmas approached, the High Command worried that soldiers were becoming complacent in the armed inactivity of "*Sitzkrieg*." Rather than actually get on with the war, however, it recommended that units try to "simulate the front" in their garrisons by creating "forward positions, where each company could take turns becoming accustomed to living a contact mission in all its forms . . ."[148]

Meanwhile, public opinion rationalized the "long war" strategy with the supposition that if Hitler were left to "stew in his own juice," the German people would realize that they could not win the war and so overthrow him.[149] According to Crémieux-Brilhac, Hitler had a contrary read on Allied inactivity – the passivity of the Allies, especially while the Germans were absorbed in the conquest of Poland, helped to convince the German dictator that France and Britain were decadent nations lacking the stomach for a fight.[150] He also concluded that time favored the Anglo-French, so that he must strike west as soon as possible.[151]

Given the weak rationale for the war in the popular mind, a lethargic "long war" strategy, and the anxious and unrelieved tedium of the Phoney War, France required a well-crafted program of popular indoctrination to explain why the Allies could not continue to tolerate Hitler's serial aggression and sell the strategic rationale for delaying combat. From July 1939, this task fell to the General Commission for Information under the direction of Jean Giraudoux. In many ways, Daladier's logic for appointing the celebrated French playwright to this key position was impeccable – he wished to avoid a repeat of the excessive claims of Allied propaganda about German atrocities in the Great War. The struggle against totalitarianism made no sense, the French Premier reasoned, if the Republic replicated Goebbels' methods of falsehood, deception, and bluster. The fact that Daladier was also reluctant to censor print and broadcast media, while perhaps laudable, meant that the French came late and poorly equipped for a propaganda war that Axis zealots had been perfecting for almost a decade. Daladier's anemic approach deemphasized the political and existential dimensions of a war against Hitlerism that was supremely political.[152]

Given the failure of the French government to define war aims or to come clean on their long-term strategy, it came as no surprise that Giraudoux and his pick-up team of "resting" actors, hack journalists, retired officers, and superannuated diplomats assembled at the Hôtel Continental on Paris' rue de Rivoli were seriously outclassed in their propaganda duel against Goebbels, "the prize-pupil of a Jesuit seminary [who] created a system of propaganda, ironically styled 'public enlightenment,' which successfully persuaded a people to believe that black was white."[153] To be fair to Giraudoux, it was very difficult to retail a rationale for a wartime strategy that the Allied governments seemed incapable of defining. But Giraudoux also imported his own encumbrances to this war of words. Fascinated by German culture, the French playwright simply could not wrap his mind around the concept that the war represented a conflict of good versus evil. From his cultural perspective, Germany was a nation peopled by musicians, philosophers, and poets. Hitler was an aberration. Giraudoux's radio homilies delivered in dated, intellectualized prose framed the war as a tragic misunderstanding. Otherwise, the repetition of insipid patriotic clichés like "heroic poilu," "sacred soil," and "accursed Boche," brought pleas from front-line soldiers for relief, while a skeptical French public increasingly treated these stiff official broadcasts as a joke. "Giraudoux and his kind were not made for taking serious things seriously or talking about them in simple, accessible terms," concluded Weber.[154] By November, the war had been relegated to the back pages of the newspapers. A. J. Liebling noted that talk filled a deceptive calm and approximation of peacetime life that put everyone on edge: "'operations' as small as the shooting of an enemy messenger dog" were regularly reported.[155] With official censorship, "[news]papers are so stupid, nobody reads them, though we buy them out of habit," Sartre recorded. "What we are thinking, for the moment, can be summed up in a single word, nothing."[156] The inability of either Allied government to frame the war as an ideological or national contest, to explain what Nazi Germany represented and why its "Total War" doctrine posed a threat to France, combined with the inaction of the Phoney War, impacted morale, especially in the critical winter months of 1939–1940 (Figure 2.2). In keeping with his attitude of Olympian detachment, Gamelin believed that morale-boosting propaganda was not the job of the army, beyond warning the troops about the risks of German espionage.[157] But all this did was to spark a "boomerang" wave of spy

Figure 2.2 "We'll win because we're stronger." French Phoney War propaganda was criticized for "an absence of any discussion of what was at stake and the reality of what the Nazis represented."

mania.[158] This "wait without glory" combined with "the incomprehension for the reasons that France was at war is the second element that undermined morale," concludes Cochet. "It is possible to identify there a major defeat of the military command but also of the politicians. Neither of these two centers of decision managed to convey to the soldiers, nor to the civilian public opinion, the values and the reasons to fight Nazi Germany, and the means deployed to win." The assumption was that, once fighting broke out, morale would somehow miraculously surge, which encouraged complacency in the hierarchy.[159]

But the reason for the message vacuum was that French politicians were divided on the nature of the war, on its goals, and on the best strategy to achieve them. To the historic pacifism of a section of the left was added the reluctance of the right, focused on combating communists, to launch an ideological crusade against Nazism.[160] In the vacuum of a serious campaign of propaganda and information, rumor ran amok, a favorite being that a "*paix blanche*" (compromise peace) was going to be arranged before any shots were fired.[161] Frenchmen tuned into the BBC or to the "Stuttgart Traitor," French journalist, antisemite, and Nazi sympathizer Paul Ferdonnet.[162] Julian Jackson acknowledges that

BBC broadcasts at this stage of the war were equally predictable, patronizing, and dreary. This sent many Britons to Radio Hamburg and William Joyce, a former member of Oswald Mosley's British Union of Fascists popularly known as Lord Haw Haw, in their search for comic relief.[163] Unlike the British, however, the genetically skeptical French did not tune in to Radio Stuttgart for giggles. Rather, they saw it as a "civic reflex," a protest against Daladier's dithering, the sentiment that the government was hiding something, and that Giraudoux's team in the Hôtel Continental took them for fools. And nothing was worse in the French mind than to be taken for a "con" (a stupid person). Radio Stuttgart spoke in a popular vernacular that was simply more accessible, convincing, and entertaining than was Giraudoux, who elevated propaganda into a sort of academic discourse. In this way, the communication contest waged between Giraudoux and Stuttgart was likened to "the flute versus the trombone."[164] By spring 1940, even Gamelin had woken up to the fact that troop-generated rumors and myths had flourished in the information vacuum and because of Radio Stuttgart's assurances that Hitler only wanted peace. Army action to counter the winter morale crisis on the unit level by officer-led "*causeries*" (chats) based on talking points supplied by Giraudoux's shop modeled on programs used in the Great War proved too little too late.[165]

Industrial Mobilization

One of the handicaps that revisionists assume by rationalizing 1940 as a contingent military event divorced from the broader society and politics of the late Third Republic is the confusion and inadequacies of French industrial mobilization for war. Proponents of the case for contingency advance three arguments. First, they claim that historians confuse the interests of organized labor with the success of French armaments production. Second, they cite Raoul Dautry, "a senior civil servant of exceptional organizational abilities," named Minister of Armaments in September 1939, as evidence that an allegedly "decadent" republic was capable of a remarkable effort. Finally, they argue that French rationalization basically paralleled that of Great Britain, whose relative success in armaments production "was a matter of degree, not of kind."[166] And indeed, one of the benefits of mobilization was that France at last acquired an industrial policy.[167] Nevertheless, despite the praise lavished on the French rearmament effort, industrial mobilization was less advanced than it might have been on the outbreak of war for several reasons, beginning with the fact that Daladier had failed to create an armaments ministry in 1938 and to "premobilize"

French industry for the war effort. Du Réau in particular contrasts Daladier's failure to gear up French industry for war unfavorably with the efforts, for instance, of American President Franklin Roosevelt.[168]

The British decision to work with the trades unions to increase output as opposed to a more adversarial approach in France is seen as irrelevant to the outcome in 1940. However, this decision was bound up with two radically different approaches to war production – a British preference for central planning, as opposed to a more laissez-faire French philosophy. It was also tied to a fear in France's managerial and military classes "of the revolutionary consequences of a possible war," which underpinned a preference in high circles for "appeasement to resistance" in France.[169] It is certainly true that defense workers found no reason to look back on their experience as a happy one, especially as French policy passed many of the costs of war on to the work force.[170] Having secured decree powers in April 1939, Daladier used them to speed up rearmament, impose strict discipline in the workplace, and crush strikes with heavy-handed police tactics and conscription of troublemakers, to the applause of a French public who welcomed the return of *l'autorité* to prepare the country morally for war.[171] But the point was that, by siding "with industry against organized labour," Daladier had ensured "that rearmament would continue along laissez-faire, economic liberal lines." As a result, with "little co-ordination or direction," Daladier's war economy featured a free-for-all competition for limited manpower and resources between the military services and various sectors of the economy.[172]

While British armaments production increased significantly from 1939, Imlay concedes that "the link between co-operative industrial relations (in Britain) and rising war production" is difficult to establish because a shortage of skilled labor affected both countries. "Nevertheless, it is hard to believe that the course of industrial relations did not contribute positively to rising [British] output."[173] In France, while mobilization may have focused industrial policy, it also transformed the shortage of skilled labor and engineers, already critical, into a crisis. "With the state abnegating responsibility in the economic realm, inefficiency and chaos resulted," concludes Imlay, as industry and the armed forces became locked into a "free-for-all" for scarce manpower and raw materials.[174]

This was at least in part because the French military had a voracious appetite for artisans and men with technical skills – 40 percent of French reserve engineers were allocated to the artillery, for instance. Engineer units, the navy, and the air force all clamored for engineers, machinists, and mechanics. Armored battalions required that 20 percent of their troops be metal workers.[175] This translated into critical manpower shortages in industry – Renault, for instance, complained that a dearth of skilled workers meant that they could fill only 30 percent of their orders. Dautry announced that he needed two million workers in the factories. Daladier had allowed for 300,000 "*affectés spéciaux*" exempt from military service, a number later raised to 500,000. But Dautry complained that this number was never attained because the military out of spite refused to release any soldier who belonged to a trade union, which most skilled workers did. In February, several thousand Great War veterans were shifted to armaments factories. But they soon protested their insalubrious housing, long shifts which might end in the wee hours of the morning when public transportation was no longer available to get them home, and a monotonous diet of horse and macaroni and cheese.[176] Crémieux-Brilhac offers a more positive assessment of French industrial mobilization. Germany, too, he notes experienced problems in its industrial and military mobilization mainly due to heavy-handed bureaucratic oversight and an absence of central planning. From this perspective, France's accomplishment was remarkable, given the artisan structure of many industries, which had to be totally transformed, and the smaller size of the industrial base in a country with 60 percent of the population of Germany.[177] Unfortunately, Germany fought the first two and a half years of the war with a peacetime economy. This only changed from February 1942, when Albert Speer became Minister of Armaments on the death of Fritz Todt.[178] Daladier's procrastination also revealed him to be a complete innocent when it came to the macroeconomic context required for industrial mobilization. For this reason, Raoul Dautry faced an uphill battle to organize his new ministry into six departments managed by recruits from the SNCF and the *École polytechnique*, and pull together stocks of coal, petrol, and non-ferrous metals, buy new machines for the factories, rolling stock for the railways, and so on. French industrial capacity had topped out in 1938, and production had actually suffered because of payment delays, inflation, and lack of machine tools. On 10 September 1939 Finance Minister Reynaud had imposed exchange controls to block cash from fleeing the country.[179] "In fact, by early 1940, disappointing production figures, dwindling financial resources, and the sharpening perception of a disgruntled workforce fostered the impression among French leaders that the war economy was not working," concludes Imlay. Nor, had the Republic managed miraculously to survive Hitler's May–June 1940 onslaught, would Daladier's market-based approach to armaments production and manpower allocation have been able to sustain a prolonged war.[180]

"La dépression d'hiver"

Thus, the problem for the *levée* as a strategy and not merely a deterrent was that the ersatz war of 1939–1940 offered a pointless and demoralizing tedium that seemed to strip the war of purpose and thus heroism and sacrifice of its context. In these conditions, it was only a matter of time before "*le cafard de l'attente*" ("the doldrums of waiting") began to impact troop morale, creating what Cochet calls "*la dépression d'hiver*" that was to last until spring.[181] The morale crisis was the product of grievances and frustrations that accumulated in an idle army as it entered the exceptionally cold winter of 1939–1940, beginning with low pay, slow postal service, absence of leave, inadequate uniforms and equipment, and a feeling that no one was in charge, or had any clue what they were doing. To control the crisis, older reservists busied soldiers with fatigue duties, while training took a back seat. Postal censorship revealed the age-old preoccupation of soldiers with wives and girlfriends abandoned at home, who complained that their family benefits and child allowances were devoured by inflation. The mail invariably arrived late, the food was copious but insipid, and leave only began to be granted from the end of November. At least there was plenty of acidic wine for troops at the front. Until December, however, morale remained high, especially in elite units and in those garrisoning the Maginot Line.[182]

What Cochet sees as spontaneous soldier protest against their treatment by both the government and the army took several forms.[183] To the army's chagrin, wives began to take up residence in towns close to their husbands' garrisons, bringing with them supplements of clothing, cash, food, and comfort. While unauthorized spousal visitations were hardly a new phenomenon, and had been fairly common in the First World War, they definitely contravened the hierarchy's interpretation of disciplinary norms. The army cracked down – in February 1940, General Billotte ordered raids on Lille hotels to roust out soldiers sleeping with their wives.[184] In Bloch's view, the military logic that "the legitimate intimacies of married love" undermined morale while a leap in the local brothel bolstered it demonstrated a "caste prejudice" among those at the summit of an army that little appreciated that they commanded citizens who had been forced to abandon their families to defend their country. The prohibition on spousal visits was deeply resented by the rank and file,[185] who reacted to this and accumulations of other frustrations and absurdities by acts of disobedience signaled by failing to salute officers or extend the normal military courtesies to their superiors. As Cochet notes, this was not the peasant army of 1914–1918. It was older, married, more urban, demographically fragile, and largely unchaperoned by professional cadres who were frequently shunted into administrative jobs. As a consequence, it was led on the unit level largely by reservists, unsure of their military knowledge and status, and so engaged in a constant renegotiation of the parameters of discipline with their subordinates.[186]

Liebling was tipped off by an acquaintance that "the army was rotten because the officers were afraid to work the men hard; energetic officers were curbed by their superiors, who lived in fear of politicians."[187] This offered an example of what Cochet categorizes as the "civilianization" of the army during the Phoney War. Gamelin set the tone by not wanting to appear too military so as not to alarm the politicians. Crémieux-Brilhac and Cochet agree that regular officers were acutely aware that the French public laid the blame on them for the Great War slaughter, and so felt the pressure to "spare precious French blood" and not push troops too hard.[188] Sartre reported that soldiers rebelled when they believed that officers were being too demanding.[189] It was not that French soldiers were defeatists. But one result of the absence of urgency that reigned during the Phoney War was that the B divisions especially, that made up a quarter of French strength and were destined to absorb the brunt of the opening German attack, lacked the physical, technical, and psychological preparation to withstand the initial shock of war.[190]

Given this lack of direction and purpose, the mobilized of 1939 longed to escape. "Why don't they send us home, because we do nothing, precisely because there's nothing to do?" was a constant refrain in Georges Sadoul's company. "Thus, to judge by the microcosm that makes up our barracks, the soldiers hate their leaders and hope for peace. Perhaps, we have an exceptionally bad attitude ... but it seems that our case is not an isolated one."[191] In short, in the eyes of many soldiers forced to endure nine harsh winter months of Phoney War, mobilization was no longer considered "an expression of individual freedom" associated with citizen "volunteers" as in the *levée*'s original script.[192] Nor was this limited to the French. CIGS General Sir Edmund Ironside believed that "perhaps the most dangerous thing of all is this idea amongst so many people that this war can be won without battle and that we are not going to have any casualties. Are we going to win the war and destroy the Bosche [sic] power without fighting, just by proving to the Bosches that they cannot win? I very much doubt it, and it is going to be very hard for [General Lord John] Gort to order his men to attack."[193]

A third manifestation of the morale crisis was drunkenness. While excessive consumption of alcohol was often blamed on France's powerful wine lobby, alcoholism was a serious problem in inter-war France. Crémieux-Brilhac found it necessary on training exercises to march at the rear of his section of the 47th Infantry Regiment to keep his Breton conscripts from peeling off into cafes.[194] Volunteers on railway platforms ladled hot wine laced with sugar, cinnamon, and – legend maintained – bromide to suppress sexual desire, out of steaming cauldrons, to soldiers in transit. This campaign to sabotage the message of the *Ligue nationale contre l'alcoolisme* and have the government buy up the excess wine production of the southwest was the work of the "*Œuvre du vin chaud au soldat* " (The Soldier's Hot Wine Charity). This patriotic enterprise was the brainchild of the deputy mayor of Béziers, head of the wine-growers association, and chair of the "drinks committee" of the Chamber of Deputies, Édouard Barthe. Thanks to Barthe's indefatigable promotion of wine as a "hygienic" beverage that "gives (the soldier) courage," by the spring of 1940, 2.5 million liters of this paint-thinning liquid – one-quarter of national production – had been loaded into tanker cars and railroaded daily to the front, to be distributed in mess halls and canteens whose ostensible purpose was to keep French soldiers out of France's record-breaking number of bars. By March 1940, complaints by officers and doctors that alcohol in such quantities was undermining the discipline and fitness of the French army caused Premier Reynaud to forbid the sale of alcohol to soldiers on Tuesdays, Thursdays, and Saturdays. But soldiers simply stocked up for "dry" days, or could always find a compliant farmer to sell them cider or the local *gnôle* (hooch).[195] Alcohol probably also contributed in no small measure to the growing number of brawls between *biffins* and Tommies, who counted five divisions by Christmas. British soldiers generally kept to themselves, marked out their own "pubs," or traveled in groups to Reims.[196] Attempts to make soldiers of the two nations sit together in entertainment venues only seemed to intensify their mutual antipathy. The French resented the twenty-five francs a day allowance paid to British soldiers, their Players cigarettes, and the fact that their duties seemed limited to manning anti-aircraft batteries.[197] Even the normally cosmopolitan Marc Bloch complained that the British soldier "is, by nature, a looter and a lecher," and treated the French as if they were a lower species of Punjabi house boy. The lack of a sympathetic *entente* between soldiers of the two nations contributed to the distrust and breakdown of morale at Dunkirk in May–June 1940, in his view.[198]

But, Bloch to the contrary, in the looting category, French soldiers bested the British hands down. The pillage of evacuated houses and farms in frontier regions constituted a fourth manifestation of the morale crisis. Following evacuation plans created in 1935, and updated during the Munich crisis, on 2–3 September, 374,000 Alsatians and 227,000 Mosellans, each allowed 30 kilos of baggage and four days' worth of rations, were evacuated by rail and scattered in towns and villages in the center and southwest of France. Another 100,000 left voluntarily, along with their prefectures, factories, teacher-training colleges, schools, and even the University of Strasbourg, which was installed in Clermont-Ferrand. Strasbourg was a ghost town, while Metz – the "capital of the Maginot Line" – lost half its 70,000 inhabitants. When the armistice was declared in June 1940, between evacuation and mobilization, roughly 40 percent of Alsatians were no longer residing in the province.[199]

Dispatched to Metz in early September 1939, Sadoul found that most of the shops and restaurants had been boarded up, while the stained glass windows of the Metz cathedral had been removed. Ordered out of their houses with no transportation provided, evacuees crowded the roads, the women dipping their swollen feet in small streams. At night, everyone slept where they could.[200] Liebling found Strasbourg "incredibly sad ... emptied of life." Customers for goods displayed in shop windows had evacuated, while beer mugs remained on tables where regulars had left them on 3 September.[201] Ironside, who visited Strasbourg in January 1940, was struck by the empty streets occupied only by a few gendarmes. "An occasional woman coming back escorted by a gendarme or two with perhaps a handcart to fetch her things."[202] Pigs and chickens roamed deserted Alsatian villages, while cattle stood abandoned in the fields. The army bought their horses, but urbanized French soldiers, generally novices in the art of horse care, then neglected them. Within two months, they became useless, a considerable handicap for a horse-reliant army. De Cazotte attributed high horse mortality to the frigid winter weather: "many caught pneumonia at Oostcappelle and died; others caught some other strange sickness and our Higher-ups were faced with the total destruction of the equine personnel, unless something was done to provide them with more comfortable quarters."[203] But Cochet sees the neglect of the animals on which the French army depended for mobility and logistics as an indication of the soldiers' "progressive disinvestment in the war."[204] Disinvestment morphed into resentment, and then into anger. French soldiers soon began to loot – because they took revenge on Alsatians whom they blamed for the war, believing them to be German sympathizers, and because they were idle, because discipline had slipped, and because officers turned a blind eye. Many reasoned that they should not endure discomfort when furniture and clothes abandoned by the local population were at hand to make their quarters more snug and habitable. According to Sartre, soldiers reasoned that it was only logical that they should loot houses that were slated for destruction in battle in any case.[205] In the absence of

Germans to fight, the local population became the enemy, the General Secretary of the Ardennes Prefecture complained.[206] The *Deuxième Bureau* warned Sadoul's unit that a quarter of Alsatians were not to be trusted, "which seems to me excessive and comes from a poor knowledge of the province."[207] Soldiers called Alsatians "*Boches*" or "*Alsacos*," and told them that they were not French. Alsatians "were packed off to the yokels of Limoges, the lowest of the low, backward, slow-witted, grasping and poverty stricken," Sartre recorded with more than a touch of Parisian condescension. "It has been confirmed that around Wissenbourg the French troops have looted everything."[208] Sadoul speculated that evacuated Alsatians "would all return as pro-Hitler."[209] While Nazi propaganda exploited the misery of the refugees, the experience of evacuation certainly did little to reinforce any sense of patriotic solidarity with *la grande nation.* Dumped in villages in the Massif Central and the southwest, where they were often housed in "catastrophic conditions" in barns and stables, with a daily indemnity of ten francs per adult and five per child under thirteen, "*les ya-ya*" were often resented by the local population, with whom they were barely able to communicate, and whose anti-clerical attitudes shocked the generally devout refugees. The prefects, mayors, and aid agencies scrambled to collect the basic implements and linens to set up a household, and to assure them that it was only "a temporary exodus."[210]

But they were hardly reassured by rumors that began to filter back that promises by Deputy Premier Camille Chautemps to place a guard on their abandoned houses, farms, and belongings were not being honored. Once leaves began at the end of November, Alsatian soldiers were allowed to visit the evacuated zone to retrieve some possessions. Some returned to their units in tears, with reports of smashed doors, emptied wine cellars, and vandalized shops. Sadoul maintained that soldiers on leave in Paris carried "various objects that must have come from the pillage of Alsatian villages."[211] The Prefect of the Moselle ordered the PTT to cease posting packages of goods looted by soldiers from evacuated homes.[212] The High Command reacted more slowly and with far less energy against this pillage, "unacceptable in an army of citizens," than it did against unauthorized spousal visits. Only in December, when Daladier ordered Gamelin to take action, was the plunder of Alsace curbed, by which time there was probably little of interest left to loot. Signs were posted promising the most severe penalties to looters. "And lo and behold, the war became a long tedium, a long wait, and the looted houses remain – shocking and indiscreet," Sartre wrote.[213] The retreat of May–June 1940 witnessed a resurgence of looting, both by soldiers and by fleeing civilians.[214]

The army was aware of the morale crisis. But the "long war" mindset led them to believe that they would have ample time to sort things out. And if not, actual combat would somehow miraculously lift army morale from its doldrums.[215] In the short run, however, the High Command reacted to the morale crisis and the erosion of discipline in several ways. The first was to lay blame on communist subversion. Already in October 1939, the government had arrested thirty-five PCF deputies. Jacques Duclos, "the eye of Moscow," disappeared into hiding, while Sergeant Maurice Thorez deserted in October, eventually to resurface in Moscow. Other vanished communists were condemned in absentia by court martial to significant prison terms. Known communist soldiers, especially those who worked in factories and belonged to communist unions, might be shifted to disciplinary battalions. In the spring, the army was ordered to draw up lists of those guilty of spreading "*propagande révolutionnaire*," short-handed as PR, in the ranks. Most communists in uniform kept quiet about their affiliation and did their duty, either out of patriotism or because they had been surprised, baffled, disoriented, and angered by the Nazi–Soviet Pact of August 1939. In the end, the units who filed the longest PR lists tended to be those with the most serious leadership problems.[216]

A second remedy for low morale was a crackdown on disciplinary infractions, with, as has been seen, uneven results. Third, the French stepped up to cushion the rigors of mobilization and dispel the "*déprime d'hiver*" by distracting the troops. Some restaurants offered free meals to soldiers. Popular artists like Maurice Chevalier and Josephine Baker toured with *Le Théâtre aux Armées*, where they enjoyed far more success than did performances by the *Comédie Française*, which battled with Giraudoux's propaganda broadcasts for the basement of troop popularity charts. Nevertheless, Sadoul complained that the best seats for performances were reserved for officers, so the troops could barely glimpse the stage.[217] "I'll tell you right off that the level of skits and songs were perceptibly lower than those at the Petit Casino in Paris," Sartre reported to Simone de Beauvoir in April 1940 after a visit of the army theater troupe. "They were the lowest of the low ... The women were, as they say here, 'rejects.' And the men, limited to those released from all military duty, were bald, obese or deformed."[218] Amateur theater groups proliferated in French units with time on their hands. Indeed, one reserve artillery captain, who complained that his B division never trained during the entire Phoney War because it was constantly shunted between garrisons, praised these artistic diversions as the only successful operation the French army seemed capable of executing.[219] Fourth, the command ordered troop rotations through the Maginot Line to give troops a taste of life at "the front."

The Maginot Line

No symbol more clearly encapsulated the futility, delusions, and waste of the Phoney War than the Maginot Line. Vast amounts of cash and significant numbers of troops were siphoned off to populate this marvel of defensive design. This Great Wall of France bequeathed a sense of false security to the population and to Allied soldiers. Of course, the Germans simply went around it, which in retrospect served to offer the Maginot Line as exhibit A in an indictment of Phoney War illusion and futility. But revisionists argue that forcing the Germans to circumvent this concrete obstruction had been the whole point. The Maginot Line protected vulnerable and economically vital frontier regions, some of which the Germans had overrun effortlessly in 1914; it limited German strategic options; it obliged a German attack to violate Belgian and most likely Dutch neutrality and hence invite international opprobrium; it justified and supported the forward defense concept inherent in the Dyle–Breda Plan; it substituted concrete for French blood that had been shed in 1914–1918; it projected a modernized and strengthened French defense image; and finally, it was perfectly compatible with the Jaurèsian version of the *levée*. For all of these reasons, the Maginot Line can be said to have served its purpose.[220]

Most visitors departed the Maginot Line impressed. Ironside's comparison to "an anchored man o' war" seemed entirely appropriate.[221] As in the navy, troops were organized into three "crews," one of which was always on "watch" in its tunnels and turrets. A sergeant explained to Sadoul that journalists were invariably offered a tour of "*l'ouvrage du Schiesseck*" near Bitche. Similar "*ouvrages*," or major fortifications each housing a battalion, existed every 3.5 kilometers, with an intermediate bunker sited every 600 meters. A network of underground concrete tunnels in each defensive position connected barracks, kitchens, refectories for officers and NCOs, magazines and store rooms, infirmaries and even morgues, chemical latrines, showers which were still rare in France, a water softening system, four diesel-powered generators that created a constant hum, a command post, and nine turrets housing machine-guns, mortars, and artillery pieces of various calibers which offered the last word in modern fortifications.

But beyond this showpiece installation, the Maginot Line offered a gloomy, sun-starved labyrinth of unheated concrete corridors. Service in the line was unpopular – future General Albéric Vaillant was forced to select the fortress artillery when his class ranking at Saint-Cyr failed to qualify him for the colonial army, which must have meant that he had failed calculus. But in Vaillant's opinion, NCOs in the Line were very professional and really knew the equipment. Each bay containing up to twenty-four soldiers – a mix of infantry, artillery, engineers, and communication troops – shared hammocks, and dined on folding tables set up in the corridors. Refuse bins were fixed high on the wall to prevent soldiers from relieving themselves in them. Because munitions conveyors often failed to work, soldiers, invariably swathed in overcoats against the penetrating cold, humped ammunition up narrow stairwells. Maginot Line inmates volunteered for any fatigue which would transpose them, however briefly, from their concrete warren into natural light.

But beyond the abysmal morale of the garrison, the Maginot Line had significant weaknesses. The water supply was linked to local springs, some of which dried to a trickle by June 1940. A post-war study also concluded that the personnel-to-weapon ratio was excessive given the Line's limited firepower, and led to overcrowding.[222] Many of the guns lacked range – a general problem with French artillery in 1940 – the turrets could turn only 60 degrees, while the minefields and barbed wire were inadequate and had constantly to be replaced or repaired when destroyed by German artillery, or even detonated by stray animals. A lack of searchlights facilitated German night attacks on some of the isolated firing cupolas. Strong points were armed with 50 mm mortars meant to defend against close-in attacks. "But loading them is rather dangerous," reported Lieutenant R. Weil. "Fuses should be placed without haste, and the shell is very dangerous especially when fired upright, as the firer – in the heat of combat – might drop and explode it." While lateral communications by telephone within a position were generally good, there was no link with higher headquarters in the rear. So, each bastion was isolated and on its own in combat. Also, in May–June 1940, the Germans targeted the switch boxes, fixed to the ground outside, "which were rapidly demolished," thus hindering communication even within positions.[223] During the fighting in May–June 1940, Vaillant noted that soldiers took the risk of going outside to listen to the radio bulletins to get the news and learn the progression of events. The gun turrets proved vulnerable to pounding, and any protruding barrels might be destroyed. Bombardment by heavy German artillery combined with smokescreens and the destruction of periscopes in the turrets served to blind the defenders. This would allow attackers backed by 88 mm batteries that constantly altered their position to approach the casemates from dead angles to fix explosive charges next to the turrets or push grenades through gun slits. "Cover" or "interval troops" were meant to guard the gaps between strongpoints and counterattack at the approach of the enemy infantry. But French infantry advanced slowly and hesitantly on foot, and their attacks might be thwarted by German artillery.

The fortification at La Ferté in the Montmédy sector of the Ardennes was taken on 18–19 May after the ventilation system failed. Refused permission to evacuate, 106 soldiers of the garrison died of carbon monoxide asphyxiation. This happened in part because La Ferté was not covered by heavy artillery.[224] As the situation deteriorated, on 13 June 1940, Weygand belatedly transferred interval troops to the Aisne to staunch the German breakthrough. This increased the dangers of venturing outside to bury the corpses of dead soldiers or even take out the rubbish. But the Germans seemed content to harass the various fortifications with heavy artillery fire or experiment with ground attacks rather than expend soldiers and ammunition when the war was being won elsewhere. Lieutenant R. Weil noted that the entrances to the various fortifications were above ground, not camouflaged and lightly defended, and so offered the best approach for an attacker, although the Germans never came that way. Adjutant Darchen reported that while his fort was heavily bombarded, it was never the object of an infantry attack. An after-action report complained with no apparent sense of irony that the "offensive spirit" atrophied in the Line's concrete casements. But the "defensive spirit" remained alive – Vaillant's fortification continued to resist until 22 June, although the corridors filled with smoke. A *Wehrmacht* platoon presented arms when they finally surrendered on 29 June.[225]

Part of the High Command's campaign to dispel the dip in morale during the winter was to rotate units into the Maginot Line as "interval troops."[226] Sartre was relieved when left out of a draft his unit sent into that "noxious cellar ... You've got to go down 95 steps underground. They have no electricity three hours a day. The rest of the time it's kerosene lanterns. All the officers eat in one room – all the men in another ... Apparently it reeks and it's damp."[227] Vuchot argued that the interlude spent by his Arriège reservists at "the front," "... confronted with a landscape emptied of the enemy," was actually counterproductive. "Above all [it] transferred to the men habits of laziness, insouciance, disdain for the utilization of terrain, without teaching them anything about observation, nor how to utilize their weapons. They nevertheless returned persuaded that they had rendered a great service to the Fatherland and were now entitled to certain rights vis-à-vis it."[228] Cochet argues that, despites its defensive benefits, the Maginot Line absorbed twelve of the eighty-three divisions serving in the Northeast Theater, which is certainly an underestimate. That many Maginot Line strongpoints surrendered without firing a shot also caused the garrison to be viewed as "the biggest shirkers of this war."[229] Indeed, when in November–December 1944 soldiers of the French First Army encountered the remains of the Maginot Line, they were amazed at the level of destruction of areas where the garrison had actually resisted German attacks.[230]

But life was not all gloom below ground. Liebling was invited to share Christmas Eve 1939 with a fortress artillery regiment manning the Maginot Line. During the autumn, the *popotier* (mess officer) had imposed fines for all sorts of bogus infractions and misdemeanors to purchase aperitifs, writing paper, and tobacco and create an extensive bar for the mess.[231] As a result, the aperitif was served from a drinks trolley groaning with an assortment of bottles. Once seated, the *popotier* announced the menu to shouts of derision and mock complaints. As dinner concluded, the Colonel led the regiment to midnight mass, after which the officers returned for a "supper" of consommé, oysters, foie gras, and champagne. "The battery departs!," shouted the Colonel as the plates were cleared. "At a walk!" The officers rapped their knuckles on the table. "Faster! At a trot!" "Faster! At a gallop!" The rapping promptly ceased at the call of "Halt!" After a second of silence: "First gun – Fire!" Glasses, bottles, fists slammed on the table. The second, third, and fourth gun were similarly discharged. Then the colonel shouted: "Fifth gun – Fire!" "There is no fifth gun!," the raucous cry went up. "Fire anyway," shouted the Colonel, the signal for the tables to be upturned as bottles and glasses shattered and skittled across the floor. The officers then staggered drunkenly to bed amidst the debris of the banquet.[232]

Training

A final mechanism to dispel the winter gloom was to order an extra dose of training. In theory, this was an excellent idea. Training offers a mechanism to build technical competence, unit cohesion, hone leadership and combat skills, and create self-confidence. Training allowed units to begin a maturation process and to overcome regional and class differences in the army by creating *esprit de corps*. Poor training had been the Achilles heel of the French army at least since 1928, when twelve months' service was introduced. In theory, every quarter a new batch of recruits appeared at the barracks gate to be trained by the company for four months, before being sent for a further two months of training on the battalion level. Advanced training then ensued for four months, while the final two months of service witnessed "field exercises." In fact, units became a churning jumble of soldiers with different levels of instruction constantly coming and going. Just as soldiers were ready for advanced training, a new batch of conscripts arrived to absorb the energies of the limited numbers of cadres. The usual distractions and diversions of military life – guard and kitchen duty, inspections, leave, sickness, fatigues, etc. – meant that soldiers often missed out on important training days, or simply rehearsed what they had already learned, like zigzagging across an open field, attacking the same village for the thirtieth time, or disassembling and reassembling the machinegun.[233] Pressure on training increased from 1936, when the "hollow years" of demographic shortfall caused many units to be understrength and placed even higher demands on fewer soldiers. The army also complained that they lacked the resources to offer refresher training for reservists who returned for annual duty. By the late 1930s, complaints abounded that French soldiers were clueless about how to use their weapons and that poor training had become flagrantly exposed in annual maneuvers.[234]

André Beaufre observed that the army rushed conscripts through four months of basic training, "and then everyone dissipated into one vast 'tail': cooks, orderlies, clerks, grooms, drivers, store men, etc. ... no battalion could put more than one full-strength company into the field – or at best two under-strength companies – and they never went into action properly trained. The hard core was either tied up in administration or in instructing raw recruits," who rightly concluded that they were wasting their time. Vuchot believed his Pyrenean peasants so discipline-averse and lacking in self-esteem as to be untrainable. When, in May 1940, the 57e RIC transformed into the *57e Régiment d'infanterie coloniale mixte Sénégalais*, many clamored to transfer to the pioneer corps, no doubt concluding that their amalgamation with African soldiers simply confirmed their cannon-fodder status. "Bottom line, most had no desire to fight," Vuchot concluded. "Rare were those who, at the moment of the transition of the corps into a Senegalese Regiment, didn't come into my office to ask for a transfer to the pioneer corps for multiple reasons [family – simply because they were married – age, even those who were thirty or less – minor infirmities]."[235] But *levée* mythology held that the Great War had been won by the reserves. "This transfer of interest from the regular Army to the conception of the national mobilized Army, together with the poverty of immediate resources, led to the worst kind of intellectual poverty, the bogus mystique of size for its own sake," Beaufre believed.[236]

In his memoirs, Gamelin implausibly claimed that the fact that some divisions were not training energetically and eliminating incompetent personnel was never brought to his attention.[237] But training was never high on Gamelin's agenda. And even when the French Commander ordered more training, he never energetically followed up to make sure that his orders were applied.[238] Had he done so, he might have realized that training was difficult to carry out because most of the army's reserve officers and NCOs had scant military knowledge to pass on to their subordinates. With mobilization, soldiers were increasingly diverted to dig trenches, employed to construct fortifications, or offered to farmers for agricultural work, all to the detriment of training.[239] The army's few training camps, at places like Le Vernet near Lyon, Larzac in the Massif Central, Coëtquidan in Brittany, which became home to the Polish army in exile, and a "concentration camp" originally set up for Spanish refugees and subsequently converted into a training camp at Barcarès near Perpignan, offered flat, bare terrain which did not replicate combat conditions. Training was also hindered by a lack of modern equipment like mortars, anti-tank guns, and mines, not to mention munitions. An after-action report for the *22e Régiment de marche des volontaires étrangers* recounted that "the men had hardly seen mortars and 25 mm cannon [anti-tank guns] – one cannon and two 81 mm mortars [existed] to train the three regiments in the camp. The 10th Company had only shot twice at 200 meters with automatic arms."[240]

The inclement and freezing weather of the winter of 1939–1940, the requirement to strengthen defensive fortifications in the Ardennes, a sense of lethargy that gripped the troops, and complacency in the High Command combined to limit training largely to drill and the occasional route march. Future resistance hero Pierre Brossolette, a captain of reserves whose battalion was assigned to guard GHQ at la Ferté-sous-Jouarre, described military life in the winter of 1939–1940 as "rain, absurdities, and gymnastics," punctuated by "punishments to hand out," a few firing sessions, marches in the rain, and "one exhausting night exercise." He spent most of his time reading novels, studying German, and bolstering the morale of his soldiers in an atmosphere of "defeatism *avant la lettre*."[241] Sadoul recorded that when training was mentioned, protests would erupt from soldiers, who would demand to be sent home. The one training session that he chronicled required the soldiers to rise at 6 a.m., in order to pile into trucks that took them to a forest where they were told to take up a position beside a frozen lake. They built a fire, talked, and then at noon someone appeared to announce that "*la manœuvre est finie*." A second training period scheduled for 30 December was canceled because of the cold. "Militarily speaking, we literally don't do anything," he wrote at the end of January 1940. "The training programs and lectures have been completely and definitively abandoned ... Talks, card games, and chess, an occasional walk occupies our lives." Someone would on occasion play an old piano in the corner of the room, but if he struck up *La Marseillaise* or *La Madelon*, "he receives a salvo of invectives."[242]

"You may ask what the men were doing all this time?," de Cazotte asked rhetorically. "Surely it would be impossible to keep on indefinitely refreshing them with warmed up military instruction. It was. After some feeble attempts, which met with only half-hearted cooperation, the military exercises were reduced to a minimum." De Cazotte did concede that, with the arrival of a new division commander in the New Year, many colonels were transferred and training was pursued with a vengeance. "A rifle range was rigged up, and the men had their first real chance to use their guns [rifles] since mobilization," he wrote. "The first results were shockingly bad, I am sorry to say, and so the exercises were frequently repeated with slightly better results."[243] That the 205th Infantry Regiment, part of the 71^{e} DI, would break at Sedan became entirely predictable, based on a training exercise in March 1940 that required infantry and tanks to take a hill. According to its colonel, the straggling was

> worse than in 1914 ... They approach the hill without a care in the world and rather than stop a little behind the ridgeline to mark the occasion, they advance, admirably profiling themselves in full view of the enemy – and after another fifty meters, stop on the forward slope in front of the enemy and start to fire, arranged like targets on a firing range – stupidly. I'm so "distraught" by all that that I prefer to stop the exercise altogether ... The tanks like the infantry were "lamentable" ... A sad state of affairs, but one must have the courage to say it: They don't have a clue about offensive tactics. This is the first time since mobilization that they have practiced an offensive maneuver with the company at full strength – and it showed. If they appear on the battlefield like that it would produce a frightening massacre. We have to start over patiently, slowly, point by point. These units need three months in a training camp to be capable of mounting an attack. That's the truth. This report, if severe, is not exaggerated. With me was the tank commander [a classy chap very serious], I had Major Chatelard of the 3rd battalion, and three or four officer observers. We were all absolutely of the same mind. This won't do. At all.[244]

But preparation for battle was the furthest thing from Sartre's mind: "It's purely a question of sleeping and eating and not being cold. That's all. One can hardly think of anything else ... We're exactly like animals. When I think that at this very moment there are people in the cafes or in restaurants, clean and in mufti, who will go to sleep in beds ... I can't imagine it happening to me."[245] French scholar of 1940 Robin Leconte argues that the lethargy, insouciance, pent-up resentment, and sense of futility of the Phoney War made the shock of combat all the more disorienting when it came: "The Phoney War especially was an event of great importance, reinforcing the incongruity that struck French soldiers so forcefully between 10 May and 25 June."[246]

Poor training, which contributed to a lack of professionalism and discipline, constituted a major post-1940 complaint: "An undisciplined infantry, poorly trained [the result of a lack of instruction during peacetime], many units having spent the winter in total inaction, that left them or imbued them with habits of laziness or insouciance, transformed them rapidly into a disorganized and disheveled horde," complained Colonel Desroche.[247] It is certainly possible to argue, as does Eugenia Kiesling, that of all of the French army's many shortcomings that contributed to the 1940 defeat, poor training and leadership counted as the most prominent.[248] It is equally true, however, that good tactics cannot redeem bad strategy. Gamelin's attempt at Riom to shift the blame for France's defeat onto his soldiers does not reflect well on his character, especially as soldiers fight best when the institution and its commanders put them in a position to succeed.

Revisionists point out correctly that the British army was no better trained than that of France, which is true, but misses the point. Only in March 1939, when Defence Minister Leslie Hore-Belisha announced that the Territorial Army (reserves) would be doubled, did the conservative government reverse years of hostility to the "Continental Commitment." Until then, the British army had treated the Great War as an aberration, an unfortunate, bloody, and never-to-be-repeated episode in British military history barren of lessons for the future. Five months after Chamberlain had vowed never to introduce conscription in peacetime, in April 1939 conscription was legislated "for home defence," in an effort to organize a continental intervention force of four divisions. This, in fact, was a down payment on a planned expansion to a thirty-two-division army, which came on the heels of Chamberlain's March 1939 guarantee to Poland, followed by those to Romania and Greece as a result of Mussolini's invasion of Albania. This was quickly upped to fifty-five divisions.[249] David Fraser writes that the British army arrived in France in 1939 "reluctant and dispirited ... soaked in the doctrine of the defensive, and sheltered behind the illusory safety of a great and expensive system of frontier fortifications" – the Maginot Line.[250] It also disembarked an undertrained, indifferently armed, and piecemeal infantry army. On the plus side, the BEF was well supplied with motorized transport, which, of course, only served to facilitate their scramble for the exits at Dunkirk and at Saint-Nazaire, and which they abandoned to the enemy on the beaches.[251]

The British army was unprepared for deployment to the Continent for at least four reasons. First, it was essentially a decentralized, regimentally based colonial constabulary whose main task was sovereignty operations. Second, the April 1939 application of conscription encountered no deep reservoir of men familiar with the fundamentals of military service, nor a large peacetime training infrastructure to draw upon. Above all, it lacked a core of officers with clear ideas of how to conduct a modern campaign combining air and mechanized forces. In the view of Fraser, leadership of territorial divisions was "flabby and defective," while the army lacked a tactical doctrine to train to.[252] Third, the British army had been intentionally neglected by Chamberlain in the pre-war years in favor of the Royal Navy and RAF. Finally, while Ironside groused about the low level of training in the British army, like Gamelin he did nothing to correct it.[253]

Crémieux-Brilhac concluded that this abridged and interrupted training regimen meant that, by May 1940, most French infantrymen knew how to fire a rifle and perhaps a machinegun, although familiarization was limited by the small number of firing ranges and a requirement to conserve ammunition. Many infantry divisions had never been introduced to an anti-tank or anti-aircraft gun, and had never seen an anti-tank mine, nor were they trained to react to air bombardment, in part because the 1936 combat doctrine was silent on anti-tank and anti-aircraft warfare, Crémieux-Brilhac maintained. For most soldiers, the day began with a formation, after which soldiers were left free to play cards, sleep, or drink wine. No doubt taking his inspiration from Alfred de Vigny's 1835 account of the *Servitudes et grandeur militaires*, Sartre labeled the French army's *drôle de guerre* routine as "boredom without grandeur."[254] In reality, it was more like POW practice. With time on their hands, a category of soldier emerged who became "retailers of discontent," according to Sartre, "'who aren't having the wool pulled over their eyes,' who are convinced this war is a clever trick played by the governments on their citizens . . . they bob about from one complaint to another, taking refuge from themselves in grievance."[255]

The *laissez-aller* of the Allied forces began at the top. A defensive doctrine combined with a "long war" strategy to infuse a passive attitude and feeling of inertia throughout the forces. "We think of maneuver, we discuss it, but we fear it," acknowledged Colonel Desroches.[256] For Ironside, Gamelin "shows very little desire to get a move on with the war." He evaluated the French commander's plan for possible operations in 1940 as "a very wooly piece of work . . . There is hardly anything but the most passive defensive . . . The French have no intention of carrying out an offensive for years if at all. There is none of that fire that animated them in 1914." That was because Gamelin "believes that the internal situation in Germany will explode. The wish may be father to the thought."[257] Gamelin's inaction can be explained in part as a stratagem to conserve his forces rather than see them frittered away in peripheral operations. But complacency had obviously infected some of his subordinate commanders. For instance, a main concern of Huntzinger, against whose Second

Army in the Ardennes the main German attack would fall, was that military preparations not disrupt agricultural activities. Therefore, he never asked permission from mayors and landowners to clear fields to create firing ranges. The artillery had few ranges on which to practice. Division-level exercises or maneuvers that combined air and ground forces were unknown. The 55e and 71e DIs holding the line around Sedan were particularly undertrained and lacking in anti-tank guns. Belated attempts to correct the paucity of defensive fortifications at Sedan and Mézières resulted in the construction of thirty-seven "rough and ready" bunkers lacking armored doors and camouflage, organized in shallow positions behind rudimentary anti-tank trenches.[258]

Ironside, who at a sprightly sixty in 1940 was eight years younger than Gamelin, found French generals "a bit old from our viewpoint."[259] The 55^{e} DI, commanded by a former native affairs officer of the colonial army who had been called out of retirement, was judged to be "hardly better than an untrained militia." The commander of the 71e DI was also considered too old for active combat command. Nor did Huntzinger verify that X Corps Commander General Pierre Grandsart, who commanded the Second Army's armored units, had a plan to counterattack should the Germans break through on the Meuse. In fact, Crémieux-Brilhac concluded that Huntzinger's missteps made defeat irretrievable, although military ineptitude failed subsequently to dent his reputation at Vichy.[260]

"A Vague Distraught Melancholy" – Military Leave in the *drôle de guerre*

The situation of "no war, no peace" did little to solidify a sense of mutual purpose and unity between front and the rear. The feeling that the nation had mobilized its soldiers for no purpose brought pressure on the government to grant fifteen-day leaves beginning in November 1939, "(called '*Permissions de détente*', or rest and relaxation leaves," remembered de Cazotte, "as if they weren't relaxed enough already!) When the first group returned another batch would be sent, and so forth. Officers would rotate in like manner."[261] Unfortunately, rather than improve morale, a visit to the rear merely allowed soldier and civilian to comprehend France's yawning civil–military divide. After spending all night on a train, Sartre disembarked at a military transit point in the Haute-Saône with other soldiers still wearing helmets, and with water bottle and gas mask fixed to their belts. Many also had fashioned walking sticks, and some even held a dog on a leash. The transit hub or "leave center" consisted of a collection of 30-meter by 8-meter wooden huts, nestled on a muddy plateau below a railway embankment. The men settled shoulder to shoulder on wooden benches illuminated by four naked light bulbs dangling from the ceiling. "*Plaisir d'amour*," Charles Trénay singing "*Ta main dans ma main*," and "unrecognizable scraps of tear-jerking music" crackled from loud speakers installed in each hut and on the roofs of most of them. An avuncular voice reminded "army personnel on leave" that the canteen was available only to those with their pink leave pass. But because the canteen was located an inconvenient twenty-minute walk away, few frequented it for fear of missing their train. The same voice eventually summoned them to board one of the color-coded trains for Paris or elsewhere. Although soldiers had already begun to loosen their uniforms, "what is striking, in fact, is that the men don't look as if they're enjoying themselves," Sartre noted. "They're calm and even a bit gloomy ... they appear reflective, as if it were both an undertaking and an ordeal. They seem not to be free from apprehension."[262]

The "vague distraught melancholy" detected by Sartre loomed because leave constituted a brief intermission in a larger event which they could not control. Leave was simply another "episode of war." They were frantic to commune with the familiar, not to waste a moment, but apprehensive in the knowledge that their days of freedom would quickly end. No one talked of the war, but it flowed over them like fate. Sartre found Paris a "bloodless" town drained of men. The blue lights and blackout curtains lent a practically erotic atmosphere, with cafes taking on "the clandestine look of brothels." A tour of the jazz clubs confirmed that they had lost their pre-war spark; Montmartre was "dead and desolate"; la Place Saint Charles in the 15ᵉ had "the gloomy vastness of some major road junction in the suburbs," and so on.[263] For Sadoul, Paris appeared both banal and "sinister." The war had not unsettled the capital's unperturbable normality. The "literary cafés" like the Café du Flore were filled with the same people, sitting at the same tables, sipping the same aperitifs, spouting the same nonsense. Social solidarity did not exist. Parisians remained consumers of security, indifferent, seemingly quarantined from the anxieties of conflict. A few refugee Polish officers strutted down the boulevards squinting with insolence through their monocles. He felt disconnected, alienated in a Parisian night filled with dark figures crowding into the metro, "their eyes closed, their faces drawn. A lugubrious people."[264]

The return from leave was ritualized with ballet-like choreography. A "slow, silent parade" of soldiers, the inevitable *bandes molletières* entwining their calves like faded shoots of ivy, moved onto the quay of the Gare de l'Est in the company of women "disfigured by the sleepless night, hastily clad ... All with the same red, dark-rimmed eyes." The soldiers would board the train, and this "strange social ritual" would be reenacted by a replacement cast of freshly bathed and shaved poilus who had taken advantage of their leave to tailor their uniforms or buy new ones, and shuffled onto the quay. Quietly tearful females clung to their arms and gazed at them "with a kind of ferocity." But the men had already departed mentally. They stared away, or at the other soldiers, in the realization that they were no longer "military personnel on leave" but men divested of their civilian identity, and with it went their power to plan for the future. Psychologically they had already returned to the barracks where they would be bullied, demeaned, and infantilized. They sat "silent and gloomy" in unheated carriages reading, sleeping, or just staring out of the window during the return trip. "I got the impression that they were all terrified of a spring offensive," Sartre noted in his diary. "That's what gave their departure that tragic aspect."[265] "Everyone generally returns [from leave] with a lower morale than when they left," Sadoul observed.[266]

That was because a war without combat failed to reinforce national solidarity, but instead revived and even exacerbated the political and social tensions of the 1930s.[267] The bonds between front and rear seemed brittle, tenuous, ephemeral. Reacquaintance with the civilian world left soldiers indignant about soaring prices and food shortages. They realized how little their army pay could buy. But above all, they came away with an impression that the population remained indifferent to war, even resentful of the soldiers impressed to fight it. Members of the military were not welcomed as heroes, the focus of popular gratitude, because mobilization without combat made the war seem like an abstract concept, relegated since October 1939 to the back pages of the papers. If this was not to be a real war, then why did France mobilize so many men? French soldiers were not under fire, in danger, nor did they seem to be providing any useful service. Rumor substituted for the failure of the government and the High Command to communicate – the war was going to end with a negotiated peace, the overthrow of Hitler, whatever. "I got the impression back there that everyone thought we were slackers," a fellow soldier told Sartre on his return from leave.[268]

For their part, reacqaintance with the rear deepened the bitterness of soldiers whose conditions of mobilization had already given them ample cause for discontent. A home stopover brought them face-to-face with a system that allowed "shirkers" and "string pullers" to wrangle cushy jobs in the rear. Peasants whose farms were abandoned complained of bureaucrats and factory workers exempted from service as "*affectés spéciaux*" (designated service). While this did not turn them against the war, they failed nevertheless to embrace it as an existential conflict, but experienced it as something more like a colossal inconvenience. They remained bitter at Daladier, at this "fucked-up democracy," and felt economically and socially insecure in a rural France in rapid transition to an urban society. The "long war" strategy may have made sense to Chamberlain, Daladier, and Gamelin. But, for many French soldiers, Germany was the ascendant power. France was economically and demographically exhausted. "We fought the last war standing up," Crémieux-Brilhac's battalion commander told him. "We're fighting this one on our knees. The next one we'll fight lying down."[269] Soldiers felt directionless, expendable. The result was that, "instead of saying 'It's *my* war' and trying to live it, they all take refuge from it in poses," Sartre observed. War forced people to measure their status in terms of petty privileges. "But instead of feeling glad that some people have had the luck or cunning to escape, they'd like to drag them all into the soup and drown together," he concluded.[270]

Crémieux-Brilhac cites *Deuxième Bureau* and postal control reports that concluded that army morale recovered in the spring. British liaison officers also passed on information to London about high French morale. From this perspective, the observations of older, educated, left-wing when not downright anti-militarist diarists like Sadoul and Sartre serving in rear echelon units should be taken with a pinch of salt. The French infantry especially was composed of rural recruits who were largely apolitical, who seldom read or listened to the radio, and who had been routinized by military discipline.[271]

On the other hand, it is perfectly possible to conclude that the morale crisis did not abruptly and miraculously lift in March 1940, as Crémieux-Brilhac admits. Why should it? Conditions that irked mobilized soldiers, which gave them the sense that the mobilization process was highly inequitable and that the nation did not stand behind them, did not suddenly evaporate with an improvement in the weather. British liaison officers who reported a resurgence of French morale were victims of a subterfuge by a *Deuxième Bureau* that had no incentive to alert their ally that many French soldiers lacked energy, and were passive, poorly trained, and upset by the inequities and privations of French military life. Nor was postal control willing to carry a bleak message of low morale to the High Command, even had they been equipped to do so. It is possible that Radio Stuttgart, or Radio Humanité and La Voix de la paix, two stations launched by Goebbels in December 1938, undermined French morale by spreading expectations of "victory without combat."

If, as Cochet argues, "patriotic renewal" in war is impossible without combat, the corollary would be that soldiers cannot fight successfully without morale, supported by the "passions" of the people. Although they came at it from different angles, this was the message of Clausewitz, Jaurès, and de Gaulle. Correlating the "mental attitudes" of civil society directly with combat outcomes may be regarded as hazardous. Desertion during the Phoney War, as in 1914, was negligible, as the attitude of most soldiers was that "We've got to finish with this."[272] At the same time, it might it be equally hazardous to imagine that the serious problems of French civil–military relations, tensions between cadres and conscripts, the army's lack of training, the complacency of French civilian and military leadership, and the lack of psychological preparation of the French population for war did not impact the outcome of the Battle of France.[273] Everyone underestimated the impact on morale of the shock of combat, especially in reserve units that were inadequately trained and led. When war actually came, it was simply easier for the individual soldier to "straggle" and shirk combat in the confusion of a war of movement than it had been in the trenches of the Great War, especially in reserve divisions. Therefore, a report that the morale of the 55ᵉ DI was "good overall" on the eve of combat in retrospect should have rung alarm bells in the rue Saint-Dominique.[274]

Speaking for the French artillery, Colonel M. Morel believed that "the prolonged stabilization killed the spirit of maneuver and initiative, abolishing training that is nevertheless indispensable and which one had the intention of emphasizing." Not enough men, not enough material, and no sense of urgency became his verdict on the Phoney War.[275] Viewed from this perspective, the Fall of France was no "strange victory" for the Germans. On 10 May 1940, the French army was primed neither physically nor psychologically for game day.

"The Dardanelles All Over Again" – the Narvik Expedition[276]

This "peacetime ambience" was suddenly shattered by the 9 April 1940 German invasion of Denmark and Norway. The *Deuxième Bureau* announced in its wake that "morale has recovered from its crisis" and that the army "will reclaim, at the proper time, all its combativeness and élan."[277] In fact, what eventually materialized as the Narvik Expedition, the first operation directly to match Allied forces against those of Nazi Germany, was to showcase many of the frailties of the Allies' long-war strategy, beginning with Ironside's observation that "We cannot convince the Germans they cannot win … by doing nothing."[278] For the British CIGS, the long-war strategy violated the first principle of warfare, that one must seize the initiative and hold it. Second, the failure of Paris and London to honor the pledge to Poland had neutral countries questioning whether the Allies would actually stand up to Hitler. Third, not only had military morale sagged in the Phoney War, but also the populations of

Britain and France were unnerved and put on edge by inaction. Fourth, it made proponents of a long-war strategy vulnerable to challenges by those who sought to accelerate events – and also to replace those in power – by promoting peripheral operations of questionable utility.

As the weeks of Phoney War inactivity lengthened into months, and "as the prospect of victory in a long war grew increasingly uncertain, French planners concluded that the Allies had to win a short war," argues Imlay. "By early 1940, France had abandoned a long-war strategy in favor of a short-war one." This shift resonated in Whitehall. "At work in this joint flight from strategic reality was a process of imitation . . . whereby British planners identified more and more with French views and concerns."[279] What Imlay labels as a "short war" strategy was really a preference for peripheral operations, driven in both countries by the realization that in the shadow of the Nazi–Soviet Pact, the Anglo-French "long war" strategy of blockade did not put time on their side. In France, the right's desire for action in the Balkans, against Baku, or in Finland targeted the Soviet Union rather than Nazi Germany, with which they had no ideological quarrel. In Britain, a desire for action was driven by Churchill, who faulted Chamberlain's dithering. A main stumbling block to the First Lord's ambition in the short run, however, was that options to attack Germany by sea appeared to be as severely restricted as were Gamelin's to attack Hitler on land.[280] In France, Reynaud, and eventually Laval, emerged as major critics of a strategy of procrastination championed by Daladier and Gamelin. "On the eve of the German blitzkrieg in the west," Martin Alexander concluded, "French war decisions were increasingly being shaped on grounds of private vendetta rather than strategic vision."[281] That strategic debate came to be defined by personalities is certainly true. However, behind it all was the feeling that time was no longer working for the Allies. In this way, the pursuit of peripheral operations was to cost the jobs of two prime ministers – Daladier and Chamberlain. And, if Paul Reynaud is to be believed, that of Gamelin as well.

So challenged, politicians and generals cast around for peripheral operations that would appease the clamor for action. But peripheral operations serve a constructive strategic purpose only if they contribute to victory on the main front. Governments handicapped by a peacetime mentality, overburdened by bureaucratic procedures, that seek to operate by compromise and consensus rather than select among difficult life-or-death strategic options, and are not versed in the finer arts of crafting strategy may find that choice difficult. So, imagining and planning a peripheral operation that does not divert resources from the main front and is strategically profitable offers a fifth conundrum. This in turn offers a sixth problem: competition among schemes for action can create mistrust among allies, as had been the case in the Great War. They may settle on a compromise informed by a heavy dose of wishful thinking and promising ephemeral success simply to sabotage some "madcap scheme" of their ally. All of these factors coalesced in the decision to send an expeditionary force to Norway in April 1940.

For all the criticism of the French cabinet and High Command, revisionists rightly point out that the situation in Britain was hardly more satisfactory. Chamberlain's cabinet was large, unwieldy, and stuffed with appeasers and men who by all rights should have spent their days slumped in a winged armchair at Boodles or the Reform Club, snoring beneath an open copy of *The Daily Telegraph*. This was rectified somewhat by the creation of an eight-man war cabinet, the apex of a series of committees formed to manage various dimensions of the war. Unfortunately, this group of men possessed a weak grasp of strategy-making and offered no overall guiding policy for the conduct of the war. Nevertheless, they proved very jealous of their prerogatives and so kept the service chiefs at arm's length. For instance, their deliberations that would eventually result in intervention in Scandinavia quickly descended to the operational level, where they were out of their depth, and hence unable properly to evaluate opposing opinions. The commitment of Chamberlain and his foreign minister Lord Halifax to the long-war strategy was not universally shared in the cabinet or the services. And this was because that strategy masked a belief among some that a war with Germany was neither one that Britain should engage in, nor one that it could win. This made the government vulnerable to manipulation by its most dynamic member, Winston Churchill. The chiefs of staff – Air Marshal Sir Cyril Newall, Admiral Dudley Pound, and General Ironside – received mixed reviews, but none of them laudatory about their mastery of the interface between strategy and policy. The same was true of their estimations of their opponents.[282]

All the more worry, then, when rumors filtered through from Paris of plots to create a Balkan front with divisions plucked from Syria or to bomb Soviet oil fields in Baku. This reflected a preference by the French right to attack the Soviet Union. By this time, London, and most specifically Churchill, was already considering the strategic possibilities offered by Scandinavia. The most promising option had been raised by the French at a 19 December 1939 meeting of the Supreme War Council. Fritz Thyssen was a steel magnate and early Hitler supporter, who, having fallen afoul of *Der Führer*, had fled to Switzerland. Deprived of Swedish iron ore, the exile Thyssen now avowed, the German economy could be brought to its knees. The Ministry of Economic Warfare appeared willing to credit Thyssen with unique insight, when it optimistically concurred that "a complete stoppage of Swedish exports of iron ore to Germany would . . . end the war in a few months."[283] It also accorded with French intelligence assessments that Germany lacked both raw materials and the ability to purchase them abroad, and would exhaust its petrol supplies in twelve to eighteen months. Thc calculation that blockade combined with mobilizing the resources of empire would lead to victory underpinned the logic of the Allies' "long war" strategy. Unfortunately, it also factored out the economic impact of the Nazi–Soviet Pact.[284]

The 29 November 1939 Soviet invasion of Finland had refocused possible peripheral operations on Scandinavia. On 19 December 1939, Daladier had proposed that the Allies break off relations with the USSR and seize the Russian-occupied Finnish port of Petsamo to introduce arms, supplies, and a force of 30,000 to 40,000 "volunteers" to bolster Finnish resistance. The wisdom of declaring war on Moscow when the Allies already had their hands full with Hitler was queried in London.[285] But Daladier sought to pose as the champion of Finnish resistance before his rival Reynaud could capture that accolade.[286] For his part, Chamberlain used the 5 February 1940 meeting of the Supreme War Council in Paris to sell a British plan to land a 100,000-man Anglo-French force at Narvik and then move overland along the railway line to seize Gällivare. Because the Gulf of Bothnia, the northernmost arm of the Baltic Sea, froze over in winter, iron ore mined in the northern Swedish town of Gällivare was shipped by rail to the Norwegian port of Narvik to be delivered via the fjord route to Germany by sea. The Allies retained the option subsequently to move on to Petsamo. That this 5 February meeting concluded in diplomatic harmony is attributed to the fact that important shortcomings of this plan were left unconsidered – among them, the impact of this diversion of troops and resources from the Western Front; the possibility that neither Norway nor Sweden would acquiesce to the invasion; and the impact of the German reaction to a plan anchored in best-case operational assumptions.[287]

Hitler's interest in Norway was tweaked from October 1939, when Admiral Erich Raeder expressed fears that a British takeover of Norway could function as a prelude to a Baltic incursion, a message reinforced in December when Norwegian National Unity Party leader Vidkun Quisling visited Germany. By February 1940, a specially created staff within the OKW had outlined a multi-service, corps-sized invasion plan that combined mountain and airborne divisions with motorized infantry units delivered by sea and air over four days against what was expected to be weak Norwegian army resistance. The British seizure on 16 February in

Norwegian territorial waters of the *Altmark*, which was transporting British seamen captured by the German pocket battleship *Admiral Graf Spee* before it scuttled off Montevideo in December 1939, helped to speed a 1 March Führer Directive for Operation *Weserübung*, expected to produce a peaceful occupation of Norway through complete strategic and operational surprise.[288]

Also, on 1 March, without consulting London, Daladier publicly announced that the French government stood ready to send 50,000 volunteers and 100 bombers to aid the Finns should they request assistance. On 11 March, the French ambassador informed Halifax that unless the Allies operationalized a plan, the Daladier government would surely fall. This forced a reluctant Chamberlain to announce that the British stood ready to help Finland, while the cabinet approved the Narvik operation, which also involved landings at Trondheim, Bergen, and Stavanger. The next day – 12 March – the Finns came to terms with the Russians. This put paid to Daladier's premiership, after Laval attacked him in a secret session of the Senate on 19 March for knowing neither "how to avoid war nor to prepare for it." Daladier resigned on 20 March, blaming British foot dragging over Finland for his demise. Anthony Eden believed Daladier's downfall the consequence of "those who were keeping an army of many millions in the field, with nothing to show for it but the dislocation of a nation's life." But in fact, the real issue for Laval and the appeasers was Daladier's failure to make nice with Mussolini.[289]

Reynaud's ascendancy to the premiership signaled a change of strategic direction at the top of the French government that made Allied cooperation hostage to French partisan politics. Reynaud was considered both a *belliciste* and a man of ambition. Measuring less than five feet tall, even the diminutive Gamelin threatened to tower over him. While Jean Lacouture compared Reyaud's face to the mask of a Japanese Samurai, others like Chamberlain were reminded of a fox, even a rodent. Reynaud had been born in 1878 into a wealthy textile family in Barcelonnette near the Italian border in the Mediterranean Alps. A law degree from the Sorbonne and a savvy marriage combined with a dry eloquence delivered in a radio-friendly metallic staccato voice to catapult Reynaud into the "Blue Horizon" chamber in 1919. His advocacy of tight budgets and a stable currency, together with his opposition to the Popular Front's forty-hour working week made him the darling of his wealthy Paris constituency that included the Paris Bourse. However, Reynaud established his political reputation by attacking three citadels of traditional power in France – the *Banque de France* that he blamed for imposing a financial orthodoxy that had suffocated French economic growth and delayed rearmament; the Quai for failing to seal a Franco-Soviet alliance; and finally, Gamelin and the general staff for their neglect of armored forces and stolid bureaucratic complacency. In Pertinax's view, Reynaud's strength resided in his alert, even brilliant mind able to mold abstract concepts into striking, accessible formulas. On 3 June 1940, Spears found Reynaud "caustic and funny," peppering his conversation with English phrases for Churchill's benefit. Nevertheless, despite Reynaud's fluent political oratory or perhaps because of it, he was considered slick rather than substantive. With no ideas of his own, he became "de Gaulle's megaphone." While Reynaud was often contrasted with his chief rival Daladier, in essential respects Reynaud was simply Daladier with a dictionary. For both men, relationships were transactional, not personal. Both were Rastignacs straight out of Balzac, ambitious provincial carpetbaggers, *arrivistes* trying to reinvent themselves as successful Parisian insiders. Many found Reynaud arrogant and detached, lacking intuition, flair, or discernment. "Reynaud's life was all fits and starts," Pertinax recorded. He was always rushing about, his head rotating as if on a swivel, spouting his latest platitudes in his grating nasal voice. His weaknesses were thought to be two. First, he lacked a solid political base that would have allowed him to pursue an independent war policy. Second, following his 1938 divorce, he surrounded himself with a "rotten set" of women led by Hélène de Portes.[290]

Indeed, the "rotten woman" trope, which in France dated at least from the *ancien régime* if not the Book of Genesis, reinforced the "decadence" lore of the Fall of France. The rivalry between Reynaud and Daladier played out in the very public competition between their respective *maîtresses en tître*, the Countess Hélène de Portes and Madame de Crussol. Each woman sought to muster influential allies into rival salons, where it was alleged that important contacts were made and political business transacted. For the Republic's critics, this feminization of French political life seemed reminiscent of the atmosphere of intrigue and scandal that had accompanied the demise of *l'ancien régime*. This was taken as evidence of a deficit of masculinity, as well as the corruption, sleaze, and "decadence" of a political milieu that resurrected a contemporary version of Louis XV's archetypal royal whores.[291] Pertinax for one was unimpressed by de Portes' salon that assembled derelict aristocrats, clapped-out politicians plotting for subministerial appointments, journalists in search of gossip, bureaucrats conniving for promotion, a scattering of English and American tourists at loose ends who believed that they had stumbled upon "*le vrai Paris*," and other scrapings of the French capital's governmental and artistic sub-strata.[292] De Portes' pro-Italian outlook caused her to be vilified as a sort of blackshirt Madame de Pompadour who intrigued to place defeatists in high government positions. Mythology requires that Reynaud's thirty-eight-year-old mistress be tall and vivacious.[293] But Sir Edmund Spears pronounced her "an unattractive woman ... She was certainly not pretty and quite certainly untidy, and her voice even in an undertone made one think of a corncrake muffled under an eiderdown." Spears was assured by Interior Minister Georges Mandel that de Portes' influence over Reynaud was "sinister," which seemed to be the prevailing opinion.[294] Ambassador William Bullitt, who was close to Daladier, told Roosevelt on 6 June 1940 that, "in the end [de Portes] will be shot." That became impossible when she died in a road accident near Sète as she and Reynaud attempted to flee to North Africa in June 1940. But even in death, rumors persisted that she was a Nazi spy and that the boot of the car in which she died was filled with gold bars, presumably meant to set up the couple in Algerine splendor.[295]

Reynaud, the wealthy, suave, well-connected Parisian lawyer who animated fashionable dinner parties like he sparkled in parliamentary debate, offered a stark contrast to his rumpled, ploddingly provincial rival Daladier (Figure 2.3). But despite his superior *savoir-faire*, Reynaud was "not a good craftsman on the lower plane of politics [because] he

Figure 2.3 Paul Reynaud and Edouard Daladier emerge from a ministerial meeting on 27 May 1939.

had no flair for backstage arrangement," as Pertinax noted. In short, Reynaud promoted his grand strategy cabaret before he had recruited a troupe and written the libretto. As a consequence, Reynaud inherited most of his rival's cabinet, including Daladier, whose retention as Minister of Defense became the *sine qua non* of Radical Party support for the new Reynaud government. Pertinax dismissed fully twenty-five of the thirty-five ministers who formed Reynaud's unwieldy new government as the same "shabby ministerial hacks, the flotsam of those two dozen cabinets which had mismanaged public affairs since [Raymond] Poincaré's departure in 1929 ... Worn-out, faded, discredited puppets." Reynaud kept the Quai for himself. The new ministry was approved by a majority vote of one, mainly because 111 Radical Party deputies abstained.[296] It was in this porous parliamentary punt that France poled into the gale force 10 of war.

Having gained the premiership on 22 March 1940 by demanding action, Reynaud need to score a rapid success. Barely four days in office, he began to press London to carry out the Norwegian operation and gain control of the Swedish ore fields, deliver an incremental success, and so enshrine Reynaud as the new Clemenceau, sprinting off the bench to win the rematch with Germany. But Reynaud's strategic appetite was not limited to Scandinavia. To appeal to the right's desire to take on the USSR, he also resurrected plans to bomb Baku and conspired with Churchill to propose sending British and French submarines into the Black Sea to attack tankers carrying Soviet oil.[297] It was activity for activity's sake, a show of energy, resolve, and action just so Reynaud could separate himself from the dithering Daladier, whom the new Premier took pleasure in comparing to the hapless Louis XVI. Chamberlain was almost pitched into a fit of apoplexy by the plethora of military projects spun off by the energetic French Premier and his British co-conspirator Churchill. Halifax predictably insisted that it was in Allied interests to preserve "a position of static warfare as long as possible." He preferred to put diplomatic pressure on Norway and Sweden to stop the export of ore themselves.[298] But Reynaud needed action to dispel grumbles that Paris had been dragged into the war by London's guarantee to Poland, and demoralized by parliamentary dithering. On 28 March, he flew to London to press Chamberlain to hasten the execution of the Narvik operation, because time was no longer working for the Allies. Churchill backed him in a 29 March meeting of the Supreme War Council, but not before Reynaud agreed to the First Lord's plan to seed German rivers with fluvial mines. People hardly noticed that the two countries also signed an accord to conclude no armistice or peace treaty with Germany "without a common accord."[299] But it was to become a major point of recrimmination once France sought to opt out of the alliance.

The retention of Daladier in the new cabinet jammed the signal being sent to London. On 1 April, Daladier mischievously convinced the cabinet to reject "Royal Marine," the codename for the Norway operation, over the issue of mining German rivers. But the press clambered for action, even though the Gulf of Bothnia would soon be ice-free, allowing the export of Swedish iron ore via the Baltic, and hence destroying the strategic rationale of Narvik operation. The 5 April 1940 found Churchill in Paris listening to Daladier's demands that he postpone Royal Marine, as the Service Chiefs assured the War Cabinet in London that they would have ample warning if the Germans planned to intervene in Scandinavia. In fact, they were unaware that Hitler had already met with his three service commanders on 1 April to go over the final preparations for Operation *Weserübung*. The Joint Intelligence Committee lacked both the heft to "connect the dots" and the analytical capacity seriously to challenge the Ministry of Economic Warfare's flawed assessment that severance of the supply of Swedish iron ore would bring the German economy to its knees. For to do so would have cast into doubt the Allies' long-war strategy and roiled the alliance. If the operation did not go forward, Reynaud might be toppled. So, the War Cabinet in London spent most of the meeting deciding how to handle press announcements of the operation.[300] When, on 7 April, German ships were reported to be on the move, Churchill and Pound surmised that it was a prelude for another Jutland and readied the fleet at Scapa Flow for a climactic naval battle at sea. Royal Marine never recovered from Churchill's miscalculation.[301] On 8 April, Allied mining of the waters off Norway began. There was almost a holiday atmosphere in London where ministers were confident that, while the Allies were quite prepared to divert men and resources from the Western Front, Berlin could not afford to be so distracted – Hitler had "missed the bus" Chamberlain confidently had declared to a Tory Party gathering on 4 April, which Churchill later categorized as an "unlucky" turn of phrase.[302]

On 9 April, *Weserübung* caught London completely flat footed and again set Anglo-French relations on edge. With dazzling speed and surprise, by 7 p.m. the Kriegsmarine had seized Norwegian ports from Oslo to Narvik, while German airborne forces captured key airfields that were rapidly occupied by the *Luftwaffe*. The king fled with his cabinet, to be replaced by Quisling as the new head of government. Within days, six German divisions had entered Norway via Denmark. Despite the impressive staff planning, inter-service coordination, and massive movements of men and matériel that *Weserübung* had required, the Allies had totally failed to see it coming – an ominous portent for the future.[303]

Landings at Trondheim, Namsos, Andalsnes, and Narvik, in the teeth of opposition from land-based German aircraft which British naval aviation was unable to suppress, telegraphed that the Allies were confused on the purpose of Royal Marine – rescue the Norwegians or cut off iron ore? France's contribution to the Scandinavian expedition included a naval flotilla transporting three "light divisions," largely a pick-up combination of Alpine chasseurs, a demi-brigade of Foreign Legionnaires, and a Polish brigade, to Narvik in the far north. On 13 May, French and Norwegian troops seized the village of Bjerkvik, 8 miles north of Narvik, which was only wrested from German hands on 29 May, five days after the Defence Committee had decided to tank the entire operation. Even before Narvik fell, Allied governments had begun to question Narvik's value. Carried out at the extreme limits of French logistical capabilities, Royal Marine had forfeited its strategic rationale, if it indeed ever had one. By the time the Allies gained control of Narvik, the evacuation from Dunkirk was under way. More importantly, it had all been a terrible waste – the Germans now had gained access to extensive iron-ore fields in Alsace-Lorraine and northern France.[304]

Nevertheless, the results of *Weserübung* were not entirely positive for Berlin, which lost practically its entire surface fleet, while creating a strategic vulnerability in Norway that required a garrison of around 400,000 German troops for the remainder of the war. In the short term, however, the Battle for Norway offered in its use of surprise and operational speed a curtain raiser for the Battle for France. Far from producing a "strange victory" on the Arctic Circle, the Germans had proven operationally and tactically superior to the Anglo-French in almost every category – strategic planning, joint operations, operational tempo, air superiority, intelligence, weapons and equipment, and so on. Although some German units had only been in existence for a few months, unit cohesion as well as standards of training, physical fitness, use of terrain, and combined arms cooperation proved superior to that of Allied units.[305]

Like the surrender of Finland, the Norwegian fiasco also reverberated in the corridors of government and did not bode well for Anglo-French military cooperation.[306] Desperate for a scapegoat, Reynaud unfairly turned his ire on Gamelin, who had opposed Narvik both as a dispersal of resources from the main front and as a waste of time because the Germans could import Swedish iron ore without having to go through Narvik. Like his British counterparts, the French commander-in-chief believed with some justification that the expedition was informed by no clear strategic vision but sprung from the political ambitions of two pretenders to premierships – Churchill and Reynaud. In the event, Gamelin deftly deflected the responsibility onto the British, who were in command, and Darlan, who had both enthusiastically supported the operation and coordinated the French naval contributions. "On that day, I decided to replace [Gamelin]," Reynaud remembered. In fact, Gamelin recounts that he had already offered to resign, but had been prevented by Daladier, who feared Gamelin's resignation would trigger a government crisis.[307]

In the event, Norway served Churchill's purpose because it provided a tipping point after months of mounting parliamentary impatience with Chamberlain. During a scheduled 7–8 May Parliamentary debate, "members in a high state of irritation and distress," Churchill recalled, pummeled and mocked Chamberlain for his policy of appeasement, for Munich, for the lack of the army's preparation, and for fumbling the Phoney War. Like Daladier, the Chamberlain government was not actually turned out. But the number of abstentions made it clear that Chamberlain had lost the trust of his Conservative Party. On 10 May he resigned as Prime Minister to be replaced by Churchill, ironically the Briton most responsible for the Narvik debacle.[308] "Our first defeat," Sartre scribbled when news of Narvik arrived. "Here, it's met with a kind of indifference. People say: 'Now the war will last ten years.'"[309] Ironside blamed the Narvik fiasco on the lack of trained troops in England, political influences which continually forced bad strategic decisions, and the "great ascendancy" of German airpower. "There is a lack of leadership all through," he lamented. "One thing is certain that we cannot attack until 1941, but shall we be given the time to train even for that?"[310]

Conclusion

In September 1939, France appeared to have "backed into the war" that its people feared and did not believe in, which compromised popular resolve from the beginning.[311] By declaring war on Germany, France and Britain were playing out of their league. Neither nation could any longer claim great power status. Philippe Burrin believes that France entered the war with fragile social cohesion, great psychological angst, deep political divisions, and an incomplete understanding of both the nature of the enemy and the capacities of France's British ally, while being "obsessed with the past and infused with self-pity."[312] Contemporaries like the future General André Beaufre believed that defeat simply confirmed a general lack of enthusiasm for war: "In France in 1940 the will for war, which had never been particularly strong, was completely shattered" by the military setbacks of May–June 1940.[313]

Peter Jackson offers a more positive spin on Paris' sudden show of resolve from 1938, by linking policymaking and the evolution of

France's material and psychological preparation for war, with the September 1938 Munich conference as the pivot. France prepared for war with a growing sense of popular resolve, and a leadership that realized that Hitler would have to be fought. From 1938, things seemed better – rearmament took off, labor unrest quieted, and London became committed to the continent. Intelligence assessments, while not entirely accurate, at least were not completely pessimistic. Unfortunately, the "long war" strategy adopted by French political and military leaders proved not so much a strategy as an absence of one, driven by a profound abhorrence of war on the left, and a desire to preserve the peace and the vestiges of France's great power status.[314] François Cochet argues that the complexity and multidimensional character of the Phoney War do not lend themselves to the drawing of facile conclusions, and that this pre-combat interlude should be separated from a narrative of defeat. "How do you motivate the soldiers when increasingly the civilian population seemed to lose faith in the war?," asks Cochet.[315]

Morale is not monolithic, but situational. National will has to be instrumentalized by leadership, focused by propaganda, and sustained by incremental strategic success. Cochet and Julian Jackson note that French morale was malleable, as indeed it had been in 1914.[316] War requires that combatants be socialized into military organizations, molded into fighting units, and have their sense of what Cochet calls "patriotic defense" renewed through combat.[317] In this way, the Third Republic squandered the Phoney War interlude by failing to prepare its troops and population adequately for the shock of combat to come, and instead played political games and chased peripheral operations like Narvik, whose premises were anchored in faulty strategic analysis, wishful thinking, the political ambitions of upstart politicians, and the need to shatter Phoney War torpor. So, the outcome of war in 1940 all came down to the ability of the French command to react adequately to strategic surprise, and to a more agile and technologically complete German model.[318] Given the negative reports on the state of readiness of French and British troops, and bottlenecks in the French armaments industry due to a lack of centralized planning, the prognosis was not good. In Imlay's estimation, even more threatening than fragile popular morale or lack of military preparation, was that, "With Reynaud's promotion to Premier, political divisions between and among the Left and Right combined to create an untenable situation . . . The *Union sacrée* was a hollow fiction."[319]

3 Case Yellow

> "The Principal Moral Elements ... are: the skill of the commander, the experience and courage of the troops, and their patriotic spirit."[1]

> "A successful unanticipated attack will facilitate the destruction of a sizable portion of the enemy's forces at a lower cost to the attacker by throwing the inherently stronger defense psychologically off balance, and hence temporarily reducing his resistance ... the numerically inferior side is able to take the initiative by concentrating superior forces at the time and place of its choosing, thereby vastly improving the likelihood of achieving a decisive victory."[2]

At the center of the explanations for France's fall in 1940 has been Gamelin's strategic miscalculation. The Anglo-French armies were surprised and wrong-footed at the outset of the campaign, and, given an operational and tactical system conceptually anchored in static defense, were poorly configured to recover. A Republic that had weathered the crisis of 1914 had been weakened by internal divisions. Its "system politicians" could no longer supply a robust leadership to inspire national resolve to continue the fight. The psychological resilience of the French population, hollowed out by inter-war pacifism and the Depression, before being lulled into Phoney War complacency, was suddenly thrown into a state of shock by unimaginable military setbacks that sent the Anglo-French armies reeling in retreat. The generals blamed the soldiers for a lack of fighting spirit, while the soldiers faulted the generals for trying to refight the last war.

Strategic miscalculation began with the Dyle Plan, that surged the French army's best divisions and the BEF into Belgium. This offered several advantages in Gamelin's mind: it would transfer the battlefield from northern France, deepen the distance for the *Luftwaffe* to attack, and incorporate what was expected to be twenty-two Belgian divisions numbering 650,000 men into the Allied order of battle. The addition of Belgian troops, and eventually Dutch divisions numbering 400,000 men, was important, Gamelin argued, because the British army was still building and lacked an armored division, which only began to disembark in France in May 1940 as Allied defenses crumbled. Without the Belgians, the Allies would be outnumbered. But also, Belgian fortifications along the Albert Canal and elsewhere were thought to offer a better defense option than did the open plains of northern France. From a political perspective, Gamelin speculated that Paris could not desert Brussels as it had Warsaw the previous September.

The decision to move into Belgium had several drawbacks, however, beginning with the assumption that the Germans would actually attack through Belgium. As noted previously, the Dyle Plan was complicated by the October 1936 declaration of Belgian neutrality. France would need an invitation to rush to Belgium's rescue, by which time much of that country might be overrun by advancing German forces. The dilemma for Belgian King Leopold was that a premature French entry would trigger the very German invasion that his policy of neutrality sought to avoid. But if he did not cooperate with the Allies, then assistance would be compromised. Belgian prevarication also caused considerable resentment among the Allies,[3] adding to the distrust and friction between Belgian, British, and French soldiers. Fortifications were particularly lacking between the Dyle and the Meuse, precisely the spot where Gamelin intended to make his stand. The Franco-British Supreme War Council discussed the issue on 22 September. Daladier and Chamberlain approved the concept of the Dyle Plan, so long as the Belgian army was mobilized and had taken defensive measures like inundations and erecting fortifications along obvious invasion routes between the Meuse and the Dyle.

The question became how much of Belgium to occupy. The optimum advance from a British perspective would be to the Antwerp–Namur line, the fall back being the Meuse–Dyle line. But the Belgians refused to initiate staff talks, while Generals Alphonse Georges, who would actually command the northeast front, and Georges-Maurice Blanchard, First Army commander who would lead the charge into Belgium, saw several risks in the Dyle Plan. With mechanization and motorization at a premium, the French army must cross France's northern frontier largely on foot, which would require ample time to reach defensive positions before the arrival of the more agile *Wehrmacht*. The risk remained high in their view that the French would be forced to fight an encounter battle with the Germans in central Belgium with inadequate air cover (Map 3.1).

Despite these objections from the two field commanders who would direct the fighting, on 15 November 1939, Gamelin signed the order

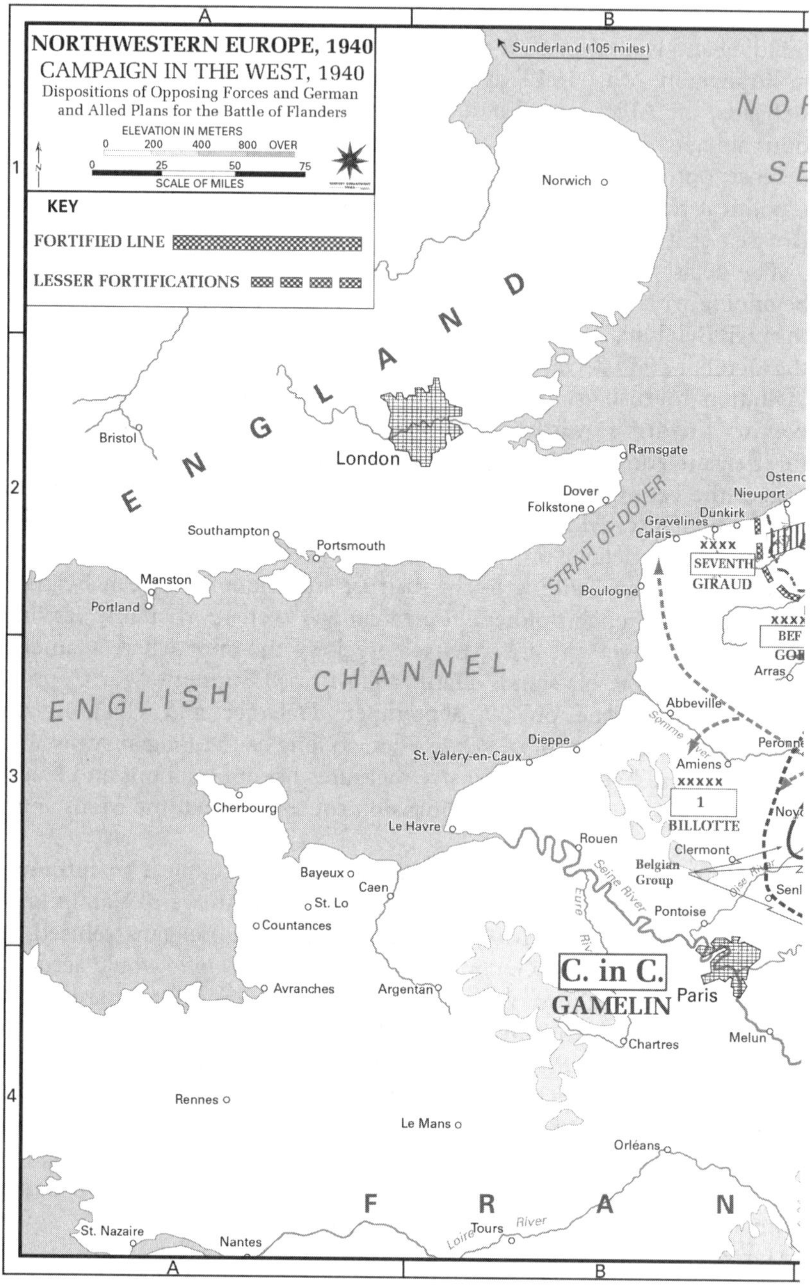

Map 3.1 Map of northwest Europe. West Point Atlas.

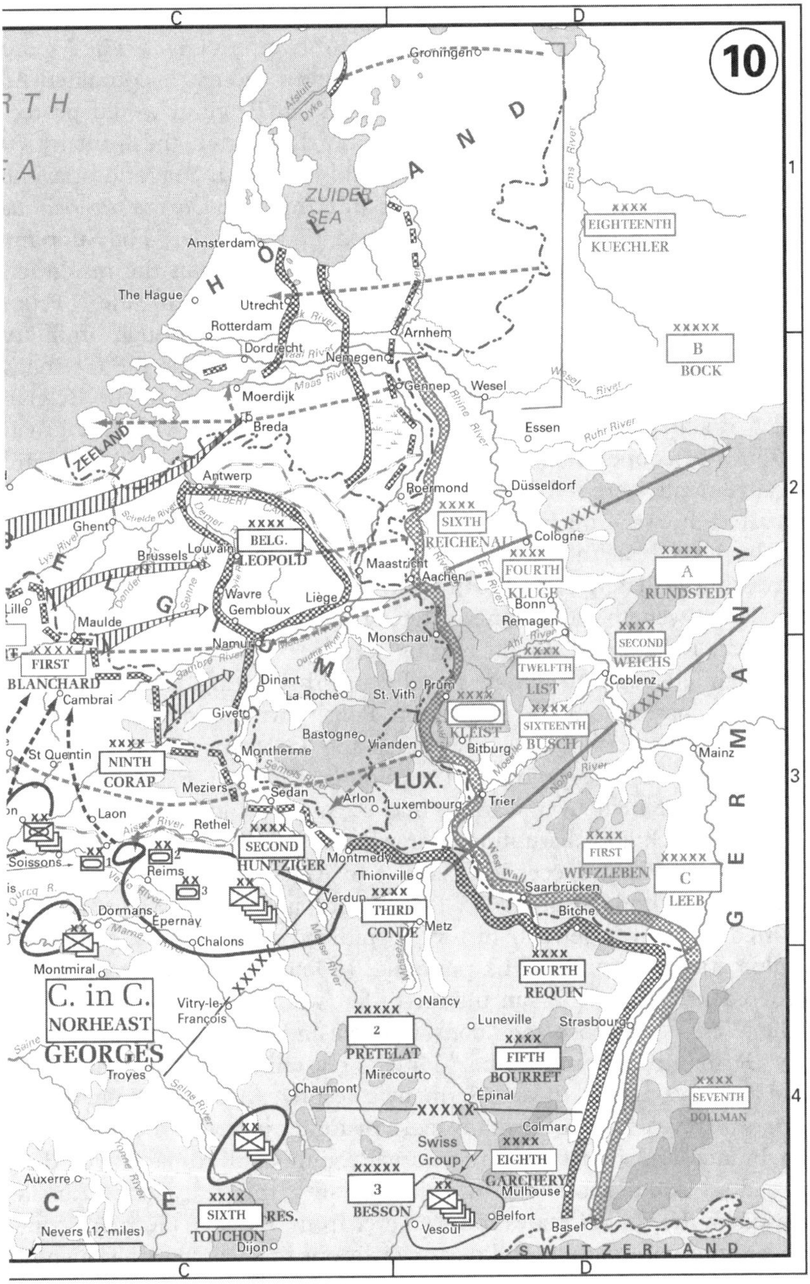
10
HOLLAND
ZUIDER SEA
Groningen
Afsluit Dyke
Amsterdam
The Hague
Utrecht
Rotterdam
Dordrecht
Nemegen
Arnhem
Moerdijk
Breda
Gennep
Wesel
Essen
ZEELAND
Antwerp
Roermond
Düsseldorf
Ghent
Brussels
Louvain
Maastricht
Aachen
Cologne
Bonn
Remagen
Lille
Maulde
Wavre
Gembloux
Liège
Namur
Monschau
Dinant
La Roche
St. Vith
Prüm
Coblenz
Cambrai
Givet
Bastogne
Vianden
Bitburg
St Quentin
Montherme
LUX.
Mainz
Meziers
Sedan
Arlon
Luxembourg
Trier
Laon
Rethel
Soissons
Reims
Montmedy
Thionville
Saarbrücken
Verdun
Metz
Bitche
Dormans
Epernay
Chalons
Montmiral
Nancy
Vitry-le-François
Luneville
Strasbourg
Troyes
Chaumont
Mirecourt
Epinal
Colmar
Swiss Group
Mulhouse
Auxerre
Belfort
Vesoul
Basel
Dijon
Nevers (12 miles)
SWITZERLAND
GERMANY
EIGHTEENTH KUECHLER
B BOCK
SIXTH REICHENAU
FOURTH KLUGE
A RUNDSTEDT
SECOND WEICHS
TWELFTH LIST
KLEIST
SIXTEENTH BUSCH
BELG. LEOPOLD
FIRST BLANCHARD
NINTH CORAP
SECOND HUNTZIGER
THIRD CONDE
FIRST WITZLEBEN
C LEEB
FOURTH REQUIN
C. in C. NORHEAST GEORGES
2 PRETELAT
FIFTH BOURRET
SEVENTH DOLLMAN
EIGHTH GARCHERY
3 BESSON
SIXTH RES. TOUCHON

Map 3.1 (Cont.)

that on news of a German attack would catapult Allied armies into Belgium to occupy a defensive line from Antwerp to Givet. The Meuse valley offered the best fallback position, even though it contained no man-made fortifications. An advanced line in Belgium would protect French industries concentrated in the north, shorten the front by 70 kilometers between the Maginot Line and the North Sea, and offer the best chance of incorporating the Belgian army. The *Comité supérieur de la défense nationale* (CSDN) concurred on 17 November. The Supreme War Council subsequently adopted without discussion the resolution that the Allies should move to the Antwerp–Namur line.[4] From November, only intermittent contact, mainly through military attachés, continued because the Belgians wanted to give the Germans no pretext to attack. Gamelin forwarded "suggestions" to the Belgian chief of staff General Raoul Van Overstraeten. In this way, the broad outlines of cooperation were sketched out. But details and command arrangements were left in abeyance. The Supreme War Council never revisited the issue during the Phoney War.

The Dyle Plan might have worked well enough had Hitler pivoted almost immediately from Poland and attacked west. But the truth was that Hitler went to war with no such plan because the Allied declaration of war over Poland had caught him by surprise. Nor were many German commanders eager to initiate hostilities with the Anglo-French, which they anticipated would far surpass the Polish invasion in complexity and intensity. Historians debate whether the German victory of May–June 1940 was the product of traditional German *Bewegungskrieg* – a doctrine of maneuver warfare that seeks to incapacitate the enemy through shock and disruption – or whether it was simply a desperate improvization that succeeded because of Allied strategic mistakes and tactical ineptitude. But the Fall of France had its origins in Hitler's twisted vision of German history, combined with a sense of fleeting diplomatic opportunity. His rambling 9 October 1939 memorandum ordered preparation for an offensive that would destroy the ability of "the West" to oppose the "consolidation and further development of the German people in Europe." Hitler's reasoning was that "the West" had always sought to thwart Germany's destiny. A quick diplomatic *tour d'horizon* revealed that Germany had a historic window to focus its forces on France and Great Britain before Belgium and Holland would be forced by London to abandon their neutrality, the treaty with "Russia" lapsed, or the United States could emerge from isolation. Germany could not endure a protracted conflict, especially one that would throw open the Ruhr to air attack. Therefore, control of the Low Countries was essential to deprive the Allies of air bases. He confidently boasted that German soldiers and commanders, as well as their weaponry, were superior to those of the French.

He ordered a two-pronged attack through Luxembourg, Belgium, and Holland. The "war aim" was the "annihilation of Anglo-French forces." The main weight of the attack would seek to cut off Antwerp and the Channel coast. While he was vague on the direction of the offensive, Hitler went into incredible tactical detail about how targets were to be attacked.[5] On 19 October, a plan known as *Fall Gelb* (Case Yellow) was completed. It had a strong north wing (Army Group B) that would attack in a westerly direction and a weaker southern wing (Army Group A) to protect its southern flank. A second version with a strengthened left prong was reviewed on 29 October. This contained the germ of what was to become the "Sickle Cut" maneuver of May 1940. The main thrust of the maneuver was directed at Sedan, the beginning of a shift in weight of the offensive away from Army Group B and the coast toward Army Group A and the center of the French line. But circumstance would determine which wing would be given priority. Over the objections of Generals Franz Halder and Walter von Brauchitsch, the army commander, that the German army needed to train its new recruits and that prospects for annihilating Allied forces were slim, Hitler ordered an offensive for 12 November. Its cancellation would be the first of what would eventually number twenty-nine postponements. This revised version of *Fall Gelb* still attacked on a broad front. German staff circles and Hitler regarded this plan in its essential outline as an unimaginative imitation of the 1914 Schlieffen Plan which would only produce the stalemate that Hitler sought to avoid. Case Yellow identified no real strategic objectives beyond conquering advanced bases in Belgium and northern France from which to attack Britain.[6]

In this way, the German invasion plan (Map 3.2) was still a work in progress when what became known as the Méchelen incident occurred. On the morning of 10 January 1940, a *Luftwaffe* reconnaissance aircraft, that had become lost in the fog covering the Rhine valley, crash-landed in a field at Méchelen-sur-Meuse, Belgium. One of its passengers was a Major Helmuth Reinberger, who carried the operation plan for the *7. Flieger-Division* that was to drop paratroopers near Namur during the planned 17 January attack. Although Reinberger attempted desperately to burn his incriminating documents, they were rescued by two alert Belgian border guards. Belgian intelligence collected the charred documents later in the day. The next day, Gamelin's personal representative in Belgium, Lieutenant-colonel Hautcœur, was handed a two-page résumé of the German document with no indication of how the information had been obtained. Gort and Churchill were also informed by Brussels. There

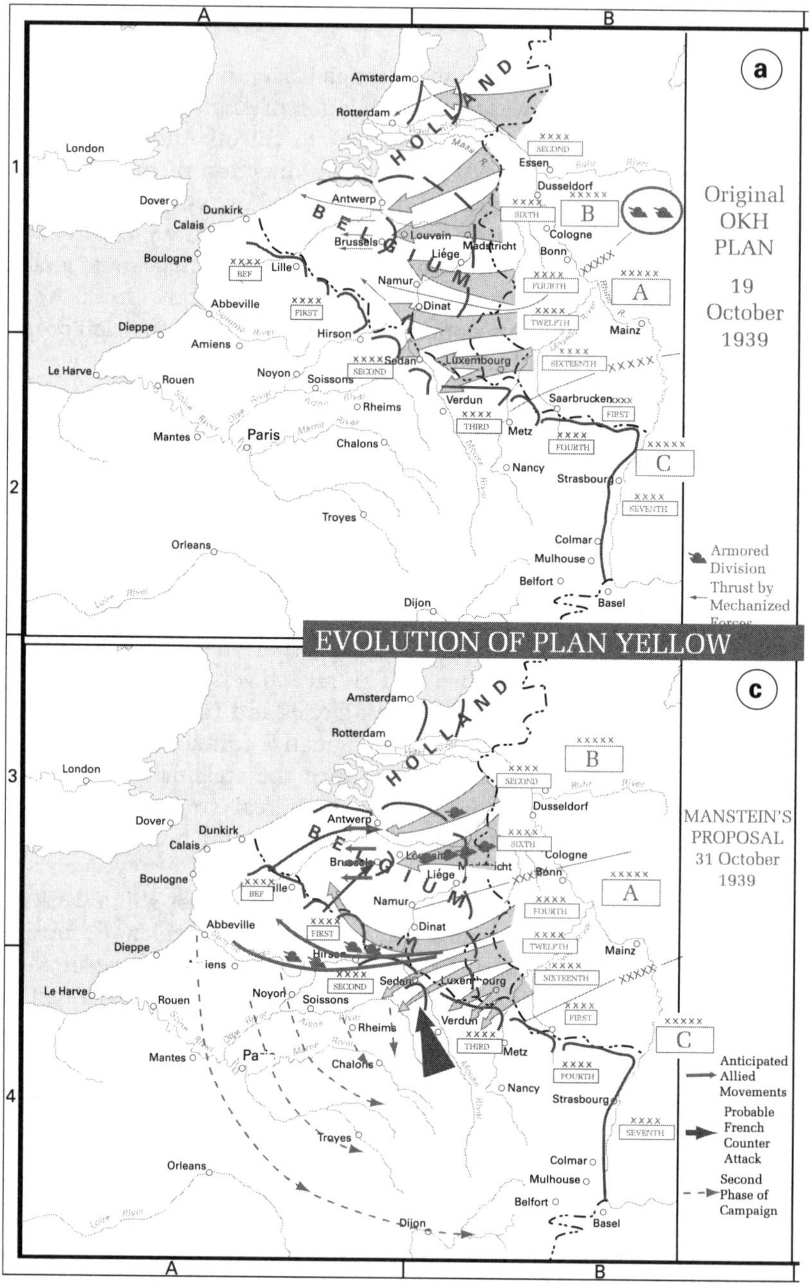

Map 3.2 Evolution of the German plan. West Point Atlas.

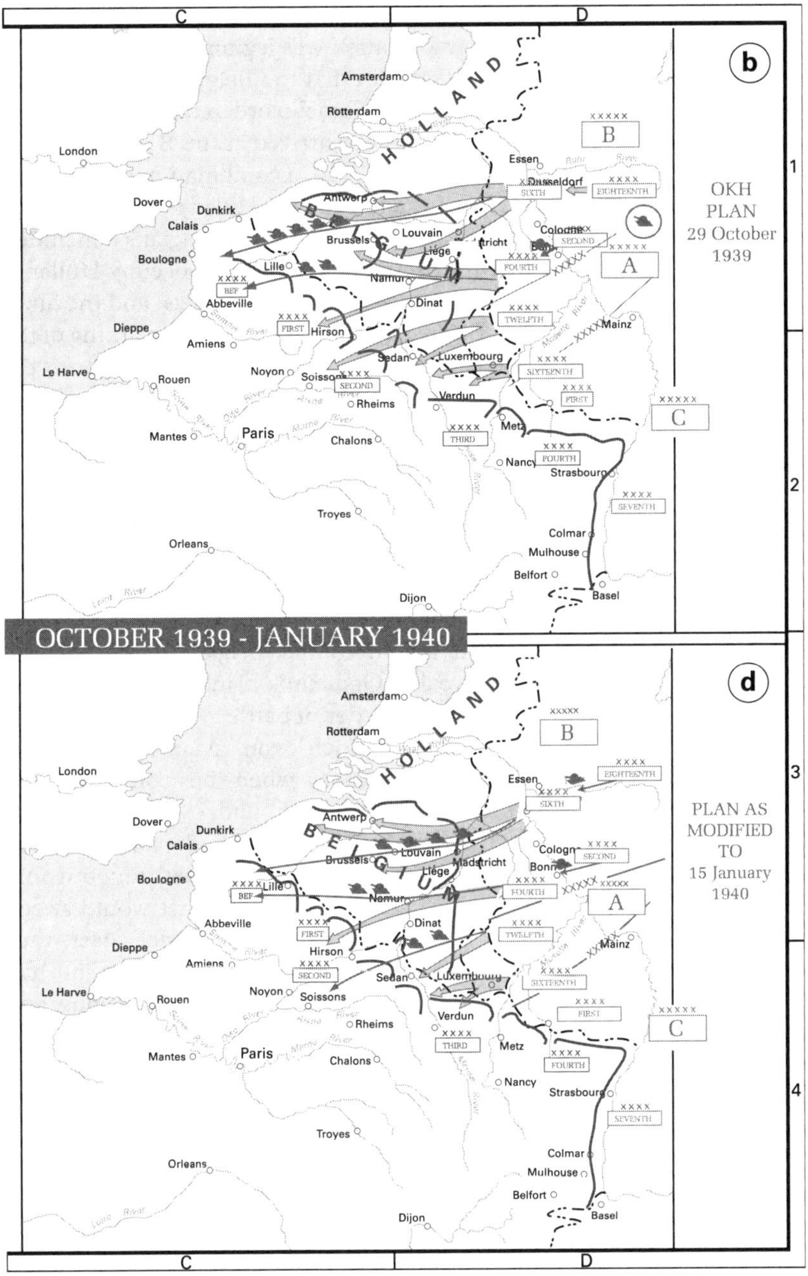
C
D
b
OKH
PLAN
29 October
1939
Amsterdam
Rotterdam
HOLLAND
London
Essen
B
Dusseldorf
EIGHTEENTH
SIXTH
Dover
Dunkirk
Calais
Antwerp
BELGIUM
Brussels
Louvain
Cologne
SECOND
Liége
Boulogne
Lille
Namur
FOURTH
A
BEF
Abbeville
Dinat
TWELFTH
Mainz
Dieppe
FIRST
Hirson
Amiens
Sedan
Luxembourg
SIXTEENTH
Le Harve
Rouen
Noyon
Soissons
SECOND
Rheims
Verdun
FIRST
C
Mantes
Paris
Chalons
THIRD
Metz
Nancy
FOURTH
Strasbourg
SEVENTH
Troyes
Colmar
Orleans
Mulhouse
Belfort
Dijon
Basel
1
2
OCTOBER 1939 - JANUARY 1940
d
PLAN AS
MODIFIED
TO
15 January
1940
Amsterdam
Rotterdam
HOLLAND
B
London
Essen
EIGHTEENTH
SIXTH
Dover
Dunkirk
Antwerp
Calais
BELGIUM
Louvain
Brussels
Cologne
SECOND
Liége
Madstricht
Bonn
Boulogne
Lille
BEF
Namur
FOURTH
A
Abbeville
FIRST
Dinat
TWELFTH
Dieppe
Hirson
Mainz
Amiens
SECOND
Sedan
Luxembourg
SIXTEENTH
Le Harve
Rouen
Noyon
Soissons
FIRST
C
Rheims
Verdun
THIRD
Metz
FOURTH
Mantes
Paris
Chalons
Nancy
Strasbourg
SEVENTH
Troyes
Colmar
Orleans
Mulhouse
Belfort
Dijon
Basel
3
4
C
D

Map 3.2 (Cont.)

was general disagreement among Dutch, Belgian, and French senior officers regarding whether the information was legitimate or a plant. On 14 January, Daladier informed Gamelin that the Belgians had agreed to a French advance into Belgium, which Gamelin ordered during the night of 14–15 January. However, Allied troops arrived at the Belgian frontier only to be denied entry. On 16 January 1940, a combination of snow and a feeling that surprise had been forfeited caused Hitler to agree to postpone the scheduled 17 January German attack. The Belgians concluded based on the document that the Germans intended to occupy Holland, and direct a two-prong attack, one prong through Brussels, and the other through the Ardennes on the Bastogne–Mézières axis. The warning of the Belgian attaché in Paris, General Maurice Delvoie, of the danger to the Ardennes also went unheeded, as did concerns of a parliamentary mission led by Pierre Taittinger about the poor state of French defenses in that region that were filed in early March.[7]

Méchelen produced a crisis mood among German planners. But its importance in the change of German strategy is contested. One version was that Hitler ordered Jodl to reimagine the entire attack on France emphasizing secrecy and surprise. But Hitler was already unhappy with *Fall Gelb*'s January reiteration. The most important consequence of Méchelen was that the Allied march to the Belgian border on the night of 14–15 January had revealed Gamelin's planned surge into the Low Countries, as well as the French order of battle along the Dyle line. This information armed General Erich von Manstein for his 17 February 1940 meeting with Hitler, when he convinced the German leader to catapult Army Group A under von Rundstedt through the Ardennes, to cross the Meuse at Sedan, to split the seam between the French Ninth and Second Armies. A breakthrough would be followed up by a "sickle cut" – a sharp right turn that would sweep behind the French advance into Flanders to the Channel coast, thus trapping the main Allied armies. Although the German command had studied Manstein's proposal and found it logistically challenging and vulnerable to French counter-offensives, the bravado of Manstein's vision appealed to Hitler's go-for-broke mentality. In the words of Karl-Heinz Frieser, the Manstein plan was "an operational-level act of desperation to get out of a strategically desperate situation."[8] The gamble consisted of pushing Panzer Group Kleist composed of five Panzer divisions divided into two corps supported by motorized infantry divisions – in all 41,140 vehicles including 1,222 tanks and 134,000 soldiers – along four narrow roads through the Ardennes forest. Guderian's XIX Corps directed its three divisions toward Sedan and the Second French Army, while XLI Corps under Reinhardt aimed for

Monthermé defended by the French Ninth Army. The XV Corps would cross the Ardennes further north headed for Dinant to protect the flank of the main attack. The potential for the attack to congeal into a vast traffic jam was high. To maintain secrecy, rehearsals were confined to *Kriegspiel* (war game exercises). Troops had to assemble rapidly at the start lines of attack to avoid detection. What is usually referred to as the Manstein Plan required tight traffic management, innovative logistics, especially the distribution of fuel via "jerry cans" carried by lorries that followed the vanguard, and sequencing of the arrival of units for attacks. Detection by the French air force, or the timely arrival of French reinforcements to strengthen the line on the Meuse around Sedan, might easily thwart it.

Deception was also a factor. To keep the Allies focused on Army Group B in the north, Admiral Wilhelm Canaris, chief of the *Abwehr* (military intelligence) coordinated a deception plan through radio broadcasts and false agent reports. *Fall Gelb* called for the *Luftwaffe* to be concentrated over the right flank for the first three days of the attack to throw the Allies off the scent. The sickle cut required the Germans to separate out the Panzers as independent tank armies accompanied by motorized infantry. In Poland, the *Wehrmacht* had been equipped mostly with light Pz.Kpfw. Is, usually not counted as a tank because it was armed only with two machineguns, and Pz.Kpfw. IIs. By May 1940, the *Wehrmacht*'s tank park counted 785 Pz.Kpfw. IIIs, 290 Pz.Kpfw. IVs, and 381 Czech tanks. It also had been able to increase its inventory of heavy artillery and heavy mortars, as well as replenish its ammunition stocks depleted in the Polish campaign. Unlike the Allies, the Germans spent the winter in intense training for their troops to correct the deficiencies noted in Poland, and to concentrate on challenges like river crossing and assaulting fortified positions. Nevertheless, many German soldiers had only a few weeks' training, while the army lacked experienced battalion- and company-grade officers. The bottom line was that in the spring of 1940, the German army was "semi-modern," outnumbered by the Allies in manpower, and inferior in tanks and artillery. Behind an elite vanguard of ten Panzer and six motorized infantry divisions, the remaining units were "rather old-fashioned," with inferior equipment and largely horse-drawn logistics. This explains why, during the "sickle cut" phase of the German advance from Sedan to the Channel, the vanguard units outdistanced their support. Indeed, the French were to surrender before a trailing edge of the German army's least modernized units could lumber onto the battlefield.[9] While it is true that, at this stage of the war, the Germans were still groping toward a doctrinal concept that would eventually be categorized, at least in the eyes of some, as *Blitzkrieg*, *Fall Gelb* can be seen as an updated and mechanized version of the elite storm trooper operational and tactical concepts that the Germans had applied in the final years of the First World War.

The Dyle Plan Becomes the Dyle–Breda Plan

The revisionist argument asserts that the Allies would have fared better in 1940 had the French High Command made a different strategic choice. While this may be true, insofar as they could hardly have fared worse, such counterfactual conjecture and wishful thinking deployed to bolster the contingent nature of the German victory is irrelevant.[10] What the historian is left with is a French military that was so operationally and tactically inept and out of date, and so poorly equipped and indifferently led, that even different force dispositions most probably would not have saved the Allies from defeat. Second, French military dysfunction was not merely a military problem, but a reflection of political and social conditions in France. These included a factious and mediocre political leadership, popular memories of the sacrifices of the Great War, a tenuous and fragile civil–military "social compact" enshrined in a Jaurèsian vision of the *levée en masse*, and societal divisions and differing values, all brought to a head by the seemingly pointless stasis of the Phoney War.

At the center of revisionist "what if?" alternatives lies Gamelin's decision in the spring of 1940 to modify his battle plan. While the Germans radically altered their dispositions in the late winter of 1940, Gamelin failed to reexamine the premises of his operational concept in the wake of the Méchelen incident. Ernest May argues that the failure to reevaluate the Dyle Plan was the consequence of two factors, one structural, the other political. Structurally, despite post-war claims to the contrary by some French intelligence officers, Gamelin was not tipped off about the alterations in the German order of battle by French military intelligence. This was because intelligence was neither a specialist arm in the French army, nor did it enjoy sufficiently high prestige invariably to attract staff college graduates. Intelligence was merely a staff activity overseen by one of the deputy chiefs. One consequence was that, unlike the German army, the French command system segregated intelligence from operational planning. Without knowledge of what the French command was planning to do, intelligence officers simply collected data on the German military and passed it up the command chain. The colonel commanding the *Deuxième Bureau* prepared intelligence reports, which were usually daily summaries of information devoid of context, unaccompanied by an evaluation of their significance, other than an assessment of the importance of the source. He exercised an editorial role to eliminate reports that were outliers or contradictory. But, unlike in the *Wehrmacht*, no senior general staff officer had the responsibility of assimilating intelligence reports, correlating them with French plans, and matching them against German intentions. "It is hard for intelligence officers ever to do their jobs well if they do not know who is making decisions in their own government or what those decisions are about," May concludes.[11]

In the post-war period, intelligence officers cited other problems, led by the fragmentation of the High Command, which translated into a divided intelligence apparatus – Gamelin at Vincennes; his chief of staff General André Doumenc at Montry some 15 miles away; Georges at La Ferté some 35 miles east of Paris; the cryptographers of the *Section du chiffre* were split between the Château de Vignobles about 35 miles north of Paris and the capital; and finally the Defense Ministry on Paris' rue Saint-Dominique. Liaison was via goggled motorcycle dispatch riders. Conferences called to interpret information or agree on bulletins to be distributed to the various commands meant that intelligence and staff officers wasted much time on the road. Officers complained that the fragmentation of the *Deuxième Bureau* meant that intelligence did not speak with a common voice, so that reasoned analysis was often lost in the wishful thinking, rumor, and "noise" of the Phoney War. Like the rest of the French army, the *Deuxième Bureau* was flooded with inexperienced reservists on mobilization. The declaration of war had cut French intelligence off from its most important agent in Germany, Asché (Hans Thilo Schmidt). The intelligence services struggled to come up with a coherent picture of German intentions precisely because the German plans were in flux. One result was a dozen alerts through the winter of 1939–1940, four or five of which emanated from French intelligence. While some of these alerts might have been based on credible information, when attacks did not subsequently materialize, *Deuxième Bureau* credibility took a hit.[12]

In theory, the defensive posture of the Allies should have strengthened the value of intelligence for Gamelin. In practice, however, while the French commander stood on the strategic defensive, he planned to execute a tactical offensive. Therefore, his focus was on applying his plan rather than becoming distracted by German intentions. In March, the French commander doubled down on his decision to fling his forces into the Low Countries. On his own initiative and over the vehement protests of Georges and First Army Group commander Gaston Billotte, on 12 March 1940, Gamelin decided to extend the French advance to Breda. This in his view would recoup Dutch divisions, while covering Antwerp and the mouth of the Scheldt. (Reynaud later argued that he too had opposed the plan, but Gamelin insisted that Reynaud had made no objections at the time.) For a man with a reputation as a cautious commander, Gamelin's battle plan incorporated uncharacteristic risks.[13] However, the Breda variant was meant to assuage British fears that Holland might become a base for air attacks on France and Great Britain, and to tie Belgium and Holland into the Alliance.[14] Occupying Holland would force the *Luftwaffe* to divide its aircraft, Gamelin argued. The downside was that the Breda variant required Giraud's Seventh Army to shift from a counterattack position between Rheims and Châlons-sur-Marne to the extreme left of the Allied line. Whether this decision guaranteed the success of the Manstein plan is open to debate – the basic problem was that Gamelin took the bait and put his head into the Belgian noose, thus ignoring the main thrust of the German attack. The move of the Seventh Army to the extreme left flank of the Allied position left Gamelin with a mere seventeen divisions – mainly unmotorized infantry divisions – in his general reserve around Rethel to cover the northern front. He could also have pulled some of the "cover troops" out of the Maginot Line had he wished. But the problem was not the lack of reserves – the French had enough troops to staunch the breach if they could get them there in time. While Giraud's Seventh Army was among the most "mobile" of French armies, it was undergunned, two-thirds of its poorly trained infantry were foot-mobile as in 1914, and its logistics was equine-dependent. French command-and-control was extremely underdeveloped, and the French were unpracticed in what later generations would call the "Air–Land Battle" – that is, coordinating infantry–armor–artillery–air operations. So, speculation that had Giraud's Seventh Army remained at Rheims, then France might not have fallen, and the Republic could have survived, constitutes an interesting but unconvincing counterfactual.[15] The important fact was that the troop density from Montmédy to the Rhine that included the Maginot Line was one division per 9 kilometers. Meanwhile, each of the seven divisions of Huntzinger's Second Army between Sedan and Dinant was responsible for a 25-kilometer front. The historical debate focused on the role of the Maginot Line has helped to obscure the inadequacy of French field fortifications. French doctrine and practice dictated that each infantry division front should organize around forty strongpoints, each armed with anti-tank guns. "Three-quarters of our strongpoints had only one anti-tank gun," read an after-action report. "Frequently, these strongpoints were attacked by more than 40 tanks. What could a single 25 mm gun do against that? They could knock out three tanks before being themselves destroyed in turn ... If we add that resupply of anti-tank mines and munitions was very difficult, one quickly sees why these small strongpoints created by our army were rapidly submerged by enemy assault waves." Nor was adequate artillery support or air cover available. The

French air force later complained that it was neither consulted during the decision for the Dyle Plan, nor informed about the Breda variant, which speaks volumes about a deficit of inter-service relations.[16]

The British, who numbered only ten infantry divisions by May 1940, with scant air cover, and who were subordinate to Georges as northeast front commander, deferred to Gamelin on war planning. Command relations appear to have been cordial enough. But attempts to encourage a sense of common mission between the populations of the two countries foundered on ancient prejudice and distrust. The French grumbled that while their ranks were replete with men in their forties and even fifties, the British were slow to mobilize. By the time the Germans attacked on 10 May, disagreements over strategy and arguments about burden-sharing had seriously frayed the civility of the *entente*.[17] The long-war strategy appeared to undermine Allied solidarity and dissolve rather than reinforce it.

Political distractions linked to growing impatience with "long war" passivity compounded the challenges of French intelligence. Pressure for action led to pressure for peripheral operations, which further diverted critical intelligence focus and resources. Scandinavia has already been discussed. Recalled from retirement to command forces in the Levant, in early April 1940 Weygand arrived in Paris to lobby for a Balkan front. Not only did this seek to replicate a Great War strategic distraction, but also, with impeccable timing, Weygand delivered his Balkan pitch just as the Germans surged into Denmark and Norway. Amid the anxiety of wresting an invitation from Belgium to permit an early entry of Allied forces, and with the commotion surrounding the fate of a Scandinavian expedition, Gamelin struggled to prevent further dispersion of his forces to far-flung theaters, while increasing the chances of success for his Dyle–Breda Plan.[18] *Deuxième Bureau* estimates about German deployment were flawed – French intelligence overestimated German forces along the Dutch frontier while underestimating those capable of attacking through the Ardennes. Above all, Gamelin was obsessed with taking the battle into Belgium. The Germans expertly camouflaged their intentions while the French telegraphed theirs at the time of Méchelen. French intelligence officers saw it as their duty to support the commander's intent rather than contest his assumptions. The conditions for strategic surprise were set.[19]

Sedan and the Ardennes

Des terres de malheur pour nos armes.[20]

The second German victory at Sedan in the space of seventy years was to launch three myths and legends about the Fall of France in 1940. The first was that the French army had been deserted by its air force, whose absence from the battlefield subjected French soldiers to a merciless pounding by the *Luftwaffe*, a claim the air force hotly disputed. The second was that the battle was lost by the indiscipline and defeatism of French soldiers, whose panic at Bulson near Sedan opened a gap that irrevocably compromised the French defense. A third was that the German breakthrough at Sedan initiated an unraveling that ultimately made the defeat of France all but inevitable. "The defeat of France was consecrated here," concluded Crémieux-Brilhac.[21] Like many myths, those surrounding Sedan contain a grain of truth. However, they fail to tell the whole story.

Indications that the Germans were on the move became apparent from 8 May. But as false warnings of attacks had punctuated the winter months, Gamelin saw no reason to put French forces on alert. Unnoticed by the Allies, at 17:00 on 9 May, the lead division of Panzer Group Kleist lurched forward from its assembly point on the Moselle River 40 kilometers southwest of Koblenz. A hard-hitting force that combined tank regiments, heavy and medium artillery, and accompanying infantry in lorries, plus support vehicles including fuel tankers and supply trucks, moved along three highways toward the Luxembourg frontier. The movement in total blackout along the tortuous roads that crossed the Eiffel Mountains required that drivers stay alert, which was often achieved by giving them a drug called Pervitine, a type of methamphetamine. For this reason, the logistical officer for the 1st Panzer Division, Colonel Johann Adolf von Kielmansegg, had ordered 20,000 pills to be distributed to German troops.[22] At 04:35 on the morning of 10 May, the concrete barriers that marked the frontier were cleared by engineers, allowing the column to cross the bridge into Luxembourg. By 07:45, the Germans had reached the Belgian frontier at Martelange. Special forces and infantrymen had been flown forward in small Fieseler Fi 156 (Storch) reconnaissance planes to seize key road junctions and bridges and cut communications. The advance was initially opposed only by bicycle-mounted Belgian *Chasseurs Ardennais* whose mission was to slow the attack before it met the main defense lines along the Meuse between Namur and Maastrich and the Albert Canal between Maastrict and Antwerp. Despite their light armament, taking advantage of destroyed bridges and prepared position, these troops put up one of the stiffest fights in the campaign, delaying the German advance by almost a day.

Under pressure of the German attack, the Belgians finally invited the Allies to cross their frontier (Figure 3.1). Allied bombers were dispatched to impede the German feint toward Holland and Antwerp. Problems of coordinating the various forces emerged immediately, while the solutions were hastily and unsatisfactorily improvized. The task of pulling together a defense of Belgium devolved to the First Army Group's commander, sixty-four-year-old Gaston-Henri Billotte. By French standards, Billotte was considered a conscientious, even innovative commander. Unfortunately, he lacked the seniority, adequate staff, and the mental toughness to coordinate independent armies whose commanders outranked him and who answered to their respective governments. In the end, as Georges' surrogate, he could command only French forces, which he sometimes did, altering their dispositions without informing Gort or King Leopold. Furthermore, the shortcoming exposed by the best divisions in the French army – a lack of infantry–armor cooperation, and only intermittent air cover – offered a sinister prognosis of how events might unfold elsewhere. Already by 15 May, unflattering criticism began to spread – Billotte was "temperamental," depressive, insecure, unable to

Figure 3.1 French troops lurch toward Breda in May 1940, a strategic advance ordered by Gamelin against the advice of most of his subordinate commanders.

handle the psychological pressure of command. Perceptive subordinate commanders quickly noticed the absence of a steady hand at headquarters. Within days of tolerating Billotte's command style that commingled agitation and confusion with bouts of depression, the British and the Belgians began to look to the exits – and the Germans had barely warmed up.[23]

On alert since 10 May, troops at Sedan had reinforced their positions with sand bags and put automatic weapons in place. Heavy artillery took up their assigned positions. The 5th Cavalry Division was dispatched into Belgium to impede the German advance, which was calculated to arrive no earlier than 15 May. They had traveled only 18 kilometers when they met the advancing *Wehrmacht* on the Semois River. Their horses proved no match for the German armored cars, which spewed a hail of machinegun bullets. Neither Ninth Army commander Corap nor Second Army chief Huntzinger appeared aware that the main German attack force was headed straight at them, even though French air reconnaissance reported considerable German forces advancing through the Ardennes carrying bridging equipment. The first wave of refugees began to filter south pushing bicycles and carts, or in cars, the vanguard of a human tsunami that would soon engulf the country. One of the myths of the defeat heavily promoted by the army was that these refugees were thoroughly infiltrated with a fifth column of German scouts who reported to follow-up German units the dispositions and fields of fire of French positions. However, an after-action report admitted that the French use of camouflage, especially for machinegun positions, was amateurish to the point that it forfeited surprise, and thus, "in that way, the spies who swarmed among the refugees were well informed about our fire plan."[24] South of the river, farmers transformed into drovers to evacuate with their livestock. By 12 May, Panzer Group Kleist reached the Meuse without encountering serious resistance. On that day, Sartre wrote to Simone de Beauvoir that rumors had filtered through that fighting had broken out in Luxembourg. "I'm unaccountably reassured," he told her. "No doubt because it's beautiful and it's morning. And besides, today's my day off."[25]

As the Germans approached on 12 May, French troops withdrew to the south bank of the Meuse. Throughout the night, French artillery peppered the growing number of German troops and armor that coagulated on the north bank before Sedan. Despite the unexpectedly rapid advance of what Allied air reconnaissance reported was a large armored force through the Ardennes, Huntzinger felt secure about Sedan, an overconfidence later cited as a major factor in the German breakthrough. While Huntzinger had no experience with armor, his job was the fairly straightforward one of holding the line of the Meuse. On this account, he had every reason for guarded optimism as the Germans closed in: the parts of the town north of the Meuse had been evacuated and the bridges blown. The Meuse formed a 60-meter-wide moat that meandered in front of a seemingly strong defense line established on the heights on the south bank of the river, backed by 212 guns in the X Corps sector. That the Sedan sector was garrisoned by the 55^{e} DI, a B-series reserve division, might be some cause for worry. The average age of its 6,000 or so infantrymen was thirty-five years old. The division numbered only 50 regular officers out of 450 in its command, and had few career NCOs. The 20-kilometer front for which it was responsible had steep wooded banks full of "dead angles" which would facilitate a German approach. Because Huntzinger thought a German attack was unlikely at Sedan, defense positions had received low priority until the last minute. The 2.5 kilometers of riverfront at Sedan were held by eight French infantry companies. Often cobbled together from different units, some of them only arrived in the night of 12–13 May after a punishing three-day march to occupy positions with which they were unfamiliar. In a March 1940 parliamentary report, the Taittinger committee had categorized French defenses at Sedan as "rudimentary" and "embryonic," without barbed wire, camouflage, or armored doors on the bunkers that could easily be infiltrated and attacked from the rear. "If we plan to resist on the Meuse," the Taittinger report concluded, "there is lots of work to do."[26]

Inspector of the infantry General Paul Gérodias echoed Taittinger in his 1941 analysis, asserting that the French positions on the Meuse would have been considered "precarious" even by 1914–1918 standards for several reasons, beginning with the fact that units were stretched too thin, there was too little barbed wire (not to mention anti-personnel and anti-tank mines), not enough anti-tank guns or anti-aircraft support, and reserves were inadequate, while the cadres were "of mediocre quality." In the face of new challenges like dive bombers and tanks, "the breakthrough was inevitable," Gérodias opined.[27] Huntzinger, who had dismissed the warnings of the Taittinger committee as alarmist, confidently calculated that the Germans would more likely try to cross the Meuse at Mouzon to the southeast and swing behind the Maginot Line. He therefore stationed his best troops there. Guderian, already gifted with strategic surprise, massed eight elite German infantry battalions and three engineering battalions supported by eight artillery groups against this derisory French defense line.[28]

Georges had begun to have an inkling that a significant force was approaching through the Ardennes. Corap had ordered the 18th ID, in reserve 65 kilometers south of the Meuse, to reinforce the Second Army. The 18th ID's two motorized battalions arrived on the morning of 11 May. Accelerating the arrival of the remaining seven foot-mobile battalions proved quite impossible. These divided the hike into three 25–30-kilometer stages. "It was very hot," recounted Gérodias. "The men, whose loads were lightened as much as possible by using battalion vehicles, were overloaded, impeded, and the forced march was punishing … 106 kilometers on foot in 52 hours for some units." The reinforcements filtered in on the evening of 12 May and the morning of 13 May. The plan was to have seven battalions hold a 20-kilometer front on the south bank, with two in reserve. In the end, only five battalions were in place when the German attack was launched on 13 May.[29]

At 07:00 on Monday 13 May, the *Luftwaffe* massed 1,000 planes in the skies over Sedan. Waves of Junkers Ju 87s, abbreviated to Stuka (from *Sturzkampfflugzeug* or "dive-bomber"), fitted with the so-called "Jericho trumpet," spent the day pummeling French positions with gut-wrenching, ear-splitting, morale-sapping bombardments that French anti-aircraft guns seemed powerless to discourage. While only 13 of 102 French divisions were judged to have adequate anti-aircraft artillery, the situation of 55^e DI, which counted only one anti-aircraft battery, was particularly precarious. Furthermore, the French artillery's effectiveness was limited, because its counter-battery techniques remained underdeveloped, especially once air reconnaissance which could reveal the position of German batteries was largely swept from the skies. Nor were the Second and Ninth Armies supplied with enough batteries dedicated to counter-battery fire around Sedan.[30] When combined with the artillery's sclerotic PCT system – the *Poste central de tir* or central fire-control post through which all requests for artillery support had to pass – it is little wonder that the artillery remained unresponsive to the German attack at Sedan.

"It seems that our artillery fire should have more effectively inhibited the arrival of tanks on the Meuse," read Gérodias' after-action report. "But on the morning of 13 May, our artillery was entirely under corps command, which delayed its intervention. It will only be late morning that the general commanding the 55e Division will obtain both complete control of division artillery and a sufficient allocation of ammunition. It is against this harmful and excessive centralization that one must react. An artillery commander who is so far away from the front cannot pretend to control the action of all of the artillery. Being so far away from the action, he will receive, if at all, insufficient and late intelligence on the evolution of the battle."[31]

In fact, in the wake of the June 1940 armistice Vichy's Armistice Army established a *Commission d'enquête sur les repliements suspects* (Committee for the investigation of suspicious withdrawals) to investigate the "evident failures of discipline, duty and honor, and more precisely the incidents of flight and presumed desertions." This investigative committee, considered so secret that its files were not opened to historians until 2013, identified a lack of artillery support as a first clue to infantrymen at Sedan that the artillery was withdrawing, a trigger that cascaded into mass panic at Bulson.[32]

The bomber force had been sent to cover the advance into Belgium, leaving only a thin fighter cover at Sedan. On the afternoon of 13 May, First Army Group commander Billotte belatedly reinforced air support for the Meuse sector. But by then the consequences of an absence of French air cover had become apparent. While historians have tended to downplay the importance of German air dominance in 1940, *Luftwaffe* attacks played an important role in helping to disorganize the French High Command and blind the French artillery, and sow chaos in France's horse-dependent mobility and logistics. The *Luftwaffe*'s medium bombers that targeted French command posts, railway yards, bridges, and logistical convoys stunned, disoriented, and helped to disorganize the defense, and threw French logistics into chaos. While *Luftwaffe* bombardments around Sedan had caused little damage, they not only rattled and exhausted the French defenders, but also destroyed many telephone links with the rear and indirectly contributed to the subsequent panic of French troops at Bulson. The *Luftwaffe* surge also created havoc in artillery parks, which meant that horse-drawn artillery could shift position only with difficulty. This complicated its ability to adjust a plunging fire into the Meuse River valley.[33] The French command had ordered radio silence for security reasons. The result was that not only did the French not know where the Germans were, but also these soldiers, scattered in penny packets in trenches and blockhouses, completely isolated from their command and from each other, were ignorant of what was happening on their flank, as well as out of contact with commanders in the rear.

Auftragstaktik – Mission Orders

In the middle of the afternoon on 13 May, the skies cleared as German artillery began a bombardment of French positions to cover assault engineers who pulled hundreds of inflatable dinghies toward the river. A few soldiers of the 10th Panzer Division managed to paddle across the Meuse to reach the opposite bank a kilometer and a half southeast of the Sedan. The main German effort was directed just to the west, where a prairie entirely denuded of defenses stretched for 2 kilometers. At this point, the Germans revealed the secret of their success – *Auftragstaktik*, or "mission orders." While French "controlled battle" doctrine and "order-based tactics" produced a top-down command system that deprived subordinate commander of initiative, German doctrine called for "leading through mission." This practice, which assigned maximum freedom of action and initiative to tactical commanders, had a long history in the Prussian military, dating to Scharnhorst and Gneisenau, implemented by the elder Moltke and emphasized by *Reichswehr* chief in the 1920s Hans von Seeckt. Von Seeckt's assumption was that the speed of motorized warfare would trigger a rapid unfolding of unforeseen circumstances that would devolve decision-making onto tactical commanders. In keeping with this philosophy, his goal had been to transform the post-Versailles *Reichswehr* into a *Führerheer* (army of leaders). The overwhelming nature of the German offensive came not from applying a pre-fabricated "*Blitzkrieg*" doctrine, but from mission command tactics that allowed German forces to move, adjust, and adapt. As will be seen, on the contrary, for a regimental or battalion commander to take the initiative within the French army's managed command structure risked causing a file to be opened by the *Commission d'enquête sur les repliements suspects*. Officers with no orders who acted on their own initiative courted charges of insubordination, especially if their decision resulted in a reverse, which alas was the fate of most French decisions.

"The French confirm all orders in writing," reported a US Army student at the *École supérieure de guerre* in 1937. "They use the telephone to speed things up, but they mistrust it. I honestly believe French is a harder language to transmit by telephone than English. It may be that their materiel is not up to our standards, but whatever the reason, they have more trouble in understanding each other over the phone than do our own people."[34]

Commanding officers with no orders, no news, no food, or no ammunition might be forced to absent themselves to go in search of all of the above, which might open them to accusations of desertion in the face of the enemy. Those in receipt of multiple, contradictory, even obviously out-of-date orders had to decide which to follow. Those who found themselves surrounded and out of means to resist might be forced to surrender their troops, an act technically punishable by death. Scrutiny focused on division commanders, that "transmission belt" of the army where strategic directives were conveyed to the operational and tactical levels, especially as the front folded, the situation became more fluid, and surrenders exceeded by far 1914 levels.[35]

In the early hours of 13 May, soldiers of Rommel's 7th Panzer Division had managed to cross a weir and gain a foothold on the south bank of the Meuse at the village of Houx, 4 kilometers north of Dinant. The French position folded after Rommel massed his tanks on the north bank to provide covering fire, and set houses downwind alight to provide a smokescreen, while he personally took command of an infantry battalion and crossed the river with the first wave of inflatable dinghies. Leading from the front, German company commanders were in the first waves of boats that crossed the Meuse at Sedan at 16:00 on 13 May. Guderian crossed with the assault boats of the second wave. A third crossing was made by Reinhardt's XLI Panzer Corps at Monthermé, 32 kilometers north of Sedan. By 17:30 in the evening of 13 May, German engineers began to construct pontoon bridges to the three bridgeheads established on the south bank of the Meuse.

Meanwhile, French commanders set up command posts well behind the front. French 55ᵉ DI commander Pierre Lafontaine was 10.5 kilometers away at Bulson. The X Corps commander General Pierre Grandsard was 21 kilometers distant in La Berlière, while Second Army chief Huntzinger redefined the concept of château generalship by remaining at Senuc, 45 kilometers away.[36] "From the 13th, in effect it became difficult to command," stated Gérodias. "To command, you have to know: know where the enemy probably is, which we never learned in time, but also know where our own troops are. Now, very rapidly all contact was lost with several of them, some regiments completely, which made it difficult if not impossible to make good decisions." A well-placed bomb on a command post, pre-identified by RDF or visually obvious from the air because of the presence of its large radio-transmission truck, a field hospital, and other accouterments of command, orphaned subordinate commands, which were left without orders or information. The French army's controlled battle concept crumbled largely because of the army's fragile field telephone-based communications systems (Figure 3.2).

The back-up of couriers were allocated only twenty-five motorbike dispatch riders per division. Because its motorbikes had failed to make their forced march to the front, the 18th ID had to confiscate motorbikes from the military police, which complicated road discipline. But the problems were greater still. In the trauma of Sedan, some commanders demonstrated little energy. Too many older or inexperienced reservists, or regular majors and lieutenant-colonels parked pre-war in "end of career" administrative positions, who had been assigned to B divisions in the "quiet sector" of the Ardennes, suddenly found themselves in the front line against Guderian and Rommel, which proved an unequal struggle. Several of them "disappeared for one reason or another," and had to be replaced. Unfortunately, according to Gérodias, the French army lacked a deep bench of competent company and field-grade

Figure 3.2 French soldier operating telephones at the front in 1940. French command-and-control quickly collapsed in the retreat due in large part to the lack of a robust communications system.

officers.[37] The result, the suspect withdrawals committee found, was confusion, not contingency:

1. The defensive organization was based on the postulate that the enemy would attack the RP (resistance point) only after a long delay.
2. Once the Meuse was crossed, surprise paralyzed all resistance.
3. One could not hear the fighting . . .
4. There was no request for artillery support on the 13th by the infantry of the 55^{e} DI . . .
5. At only 200 meters from a German column, the French machineguns did not fire . . .
6. The Germans who crossed the Meuse on boats were so relaxed that observers took them for French.
7. Panic-stricken deserters [were] everywhere.[38]

Once across the river, infantry from the elite *Großdeutschland* regiment operating in teams of six to eight men sprung from their inflatable dinghies and, under cover of smoke screens, sprinted toward the French defenses. "The troops of every arm were as ignorant of the details of how to use terrain in 1939 as they had been in 1914," read an after-action report. "Armaments were sited with no idea of camouflage, only to get a clear field of fire, without thinking that the weapon would be more effective if they had been concealed in a hedge, behind a wall, in a ditch, even if it impinged somewhat on the field of fire. Arms were therefore installed on the magnificent slopes facing the enemy, with no attempt at concealment. Others were installed out in the open, next to fortifications which screamed to be shelled." Most of the fortifications – small, concrete blockhouses – had been hastily constructed.[39] Thus, unhindered by barbed wire or anti-personnel mines, German infantry pushed hand grenades and explosive charges through the embrasures of the blockhouses dominating the heights. Individual German officers and sergeants led their men forward. Because the air bombardment had driven off covering French infantry, those attackers who had reached the south bank were free to approach the bunkers from dead angles or even infiltrate from the rear.

"The Meuse line had numerous blockhouses, but these were not impregnable," Gérodias admitted. "The hatches and the firing slits were demolished by artillery fire. The turrets were destroyed with grenades. It was also the case that to take out a bunker, one only had to obstruct the angle [of attack] with debris from bomb explosions."

French bunkers had been poorly sited, spaced too far apart to be mutually supporting, not staggered to slow and dislocate an attack until it reached the stop line. Nor did they have any way of communicating with each other or with their command. Smoke prevented French artillery from firing accurately on the attackers. Even well-organized batteries could be pummeled by German artillery or from the air, while Panzers simply infiltrated through the spaces between them.[40] The problem was compounded when the 4th North African ID was rushed into the breech at noon on 14 May: "The result has been proven repeatedly: this fresh force interceding in a line where everything is compromised can have no positive effect," insisted Gérodias. "It dissolved in contact with units already disordered and in retreat." This "disastrous" episode brought into question the entire French doctrine of "*colmatage*" (plugging the gap). The North Africans should have been bolstered by the newly formed 3e DCr (3rd Reserve Armored Division). Huntzinger had been slow to react on 13 May, and hesitated to order the 3^{e} DCr into battle on 14 May. In this way, the tanks only arrived on 15 May. Not surprisingly, a battle fought from tanks immobilized by lack of petrol "resulted in a disaster," which cost the division 100 tanks, although they appeared to have inflicted some serious damage on the Germans. Nor did a lack of French air cover help – while only a lucky Stuka strike could take out a tank, the concussion of bombs exploding nearby often immobilized the crews.[41] Those bunkers that held out could be bypassed by infantry and tanks in the manner of infiltration tactics worked out in the Great War, and left to following infantry to deal with. The stop line held no reserves for the counterattack. Soon, French infantry began to fall back through the artillery batteries sited 5 or 6 kilometers to the rear to announce that the Germans had crossed the river.[42]

At 3 a.m. on the morning of 14 May, Georges' headquarters was informed that the Germans had three lodgments south of the Meuse, which hurled the French commander into a state of near moral collapse. "The atmosphere was that of a family in which there had just been a death," remembered Beaufre.[43] For de Gaulle, whose view of leadership regarded it as "virtue" in the manner of seventeenth-century French playwright Pierre Corneille, "many things depend on the attitude of the command." While the solution to the breakthrough of a few German Panzer divisions was technically obvious, barely four days into the campaign, in his opinion, the French High Command had already lost its will to victory. Of course, de Gaulle had his own axe to grind. "So, the collapse of the system of doctrine and organization to which our leaders were so attached, undermined their resolve," de Gaulle asserted. In de Gaulle's view, at this point, "decadence" kicked in. "Suddenly, a sort of moral inhibition made them doubt everything and, in particular, themselves. From that point, centrifugal forces would soon reveal themselves: the King of the Belgians would envisage a surrender; Lord Gort evacuation; General Weygand, an armistice."[44]

Communications Failure

The French situation was critical but not yet hopeless. By 06:00 on 14 May, the first Panzers reached the south bank of the Meuse. The German bridgeheads south of the river were still shallow, and might have been eliminated by timely, even if improvized, counterattacks. It is at this point that some have speculated that had Gamelin not redeployed Giraud's Seventh Army to Breda in March 1940, France might have had a chance to staunch the breakthrough at Sedan. Unfortunately, the German onrush exposed a series of problems in French command-and-control that an army composed of mainly foot-mobile infantry was powerless to rectify, with or without a strategic reserve. Following methodical battle doctrine, the French were slow to organize a counterattack, laboriously assembling their artillery, infantry, and tanks, which inched north against an opposing tide of panicked soldiers moving south.

In these dynamic combat conditions, only those at the front could respond quickly, maintain a high operational tempo, and squelch panics. Unlike the French, the *Wehrmacht* had invested in radio communications to coordinate actions. Armored commanders had Panzer command vehicles equipped with long-range radios, unlike the heavy French ER 22, whose range was limited to 3 kilometers. The ER 40 used at the battalion level had an effective range of only 1,000 meters.[45] Each Panzer corps had a small command echelon equipped with radios. The Germans counted twelve times the number of radio operators as existed in the French army. This allowed the command post of Panzer Group Kleist, which moved thirty-four times in forty-six days, to coordinate movements, supplemented by 5,000 kilometers of telephone lines, and 2,500 kilometers of field cables laid by the signal communication regiment of the Panzer Group. Over this were sent over 3,500 radio messages. Compare this with the French, who had few radios and either could not use them because of imposed radio silence, or were deficient in technique due to lack of practice during the Phoney War.[46]

The absence of adequate radios was inexcusable, as in the Great War the French army had been in the forefront of the development of radio communications and training of "telegraphists" to operate them. Also, both civil aviation in France and the French navy made significant strides in developing communications in the inter-war years. As war approached, even the French air force proved willing to adopt British radar capable of identifying incoming planes 120 kilometers distant, but too late to deploy systems effectively. The *Société française radioélectrique* had the use of patents from Marconi, RCA, and Telefunken that could have been adapted for military use. However, the modernization of combat communications languished in the inter-war French army for several reasons, beginning with lack of research and development funding on radio communications. The Post Office (PTT) monopoly on communications in France stifled innovation. One result was that the military command believed that it could simply piggyback on PTT phone lines as a budget-saving measure. The absence of a signals branch in the French army meant that the case for the modernization of communications found no powerful advocate, especially in budget debates. Instead, signals were consigned to three "regiments" in the military engineers. Concerns about security, lest radio intercepts allow the *Abwehr* to sketch out a French order of battle, while justified, reinforced the reliance on telephones, and discouraged the embrace of new cryptologic methods and the training of operators to use them, presumably a concern in a short-service army that conscripted communists. Inter-war French maneuvers often showcased tracked vehicles with rollers for deploying and recuperating telephone wire, as if this technique were in the forefront of innovation. A doctrinal commitment to a static war of position added icing on the cake of a system that progressively appended strata of switchboards and kilometers of wire between the command and the action of battle, in the process reinforcing a tradition of château generalship.[47]

The failure to modernize field communications, one directly attributable to command complacency and institutional inertia, invariably led to a breakdown of battlefield command. This became a critical element in the meltdown on the Meuse in May–June 1940. The lack of heavy artillery and tactical air support for French infantrymen was also a consequence of the French army's communications collapse. Reliance on telephones required men to unreel, bury, and subsequently recuperate wire. Bombardment could cut wire and target the "*voitures téléphoniques*" that served as mobile switchboards. When, for instance, a forward observer battalion retreated near Dinant on 13 May 1940, it was forced to leave behind 19 kilometers of wire.[48] Communication problems metastasized throughout the army as considerable numbers of telephones and kilometers of wire were abandoned in the French retreat from the Meuse from 15 May.[49] "One should double the number of telephones and quadruple the kilometers of wire," asserted a post-war report.[50] "For starters, the telephone is hardly adapted to this type of war," read an after-action report for a heavy artillery unit. "Our telephone is too heavy, takes too long to install, is too precarious, too awkward and is not adapted to a war of movement ... In the artillery, which more than ever requires rapid and massive concentrations of firepower from common and precise elements, the only efficient and practical communication is through speaking. That's the only means that allows a constant and perfect liaison between those who observe and those who direct, and those who execute ... We only had a few radios, [which were] heavy and poorly adapted, few personnel trained to use them, few leaders who had any faith in the radio or who understood their possibilities."[51]

For this reason, French commanders fell back on motorcycle liaison. And when these dispatch riders failed to return, they looked for public telephones! On one level, this made sense because military and civilian communications had been intermingled by design. The problem was that commanders lost contact with their units as confusion spread. French soldiers became completely surprised by the sudden appearance of Germans in unexpected places. Unable to communicate and coordinate in an increasingly fluid situation, the French army on the Meuse began rapidly to decompose.[52] Spears noted that when the French government arrived at Briare in the Loire Valley on 12 June and took up residence in the Château du Muguet, it had to rely on a single civilian phone line, because the French army – inexplicably in his view – had failed to lay supplemental lines. "This made me realize, as much as anything else, the hopeless state of deliquescence of the French Army, the defeatism of the Staff, and Services that were not even trying," lamented Spears.[53] It may have been that by 12 June, the army simply had little wire left. While

French doctrine held that infantry determined the speed of operations, Guderian's organization was based on the Panzer, with infantry in armored half-tracked personnel carriers, reconnaissance units in armored scout cars, and artillery on self-propelled mounts, coordinated largely by radio communications. The Panzer and the *Luftwaffe* acted as "a pair of twins," with Stukas as "vertical artillery." In this way, the "Panzer force system" reflected a style of operational thinking which dated to Moltke. It allowed the Germans to produce a "motorized Cannae."[54] German tactical and operational advantages were so overwhelming, that keeping Giraud's Seventh Army behind Sedan would likely have provided no more than a speedbump.

"The Empty Sky"

At this point, the French air force might have intervened to prevent the German breakthrough at Sedan. In fact, no French complaint in 1940 was more prominent than that of "*le ciel vide*" ("the empty sky") – that is, the lack of French air cover over the battlefield. Gamelin included a no-show French air force in his *cahier de doléances* (book of grievances) of defeat. In a 1941 autopsy on the French army's collapse, General Gérodias, who had commanded the 29th Alpine ID in the "Weygand line" in June 1940, attributed the unraveling of France's defense first and foremost to "the surprise action of enemy aviation that often paralyzed [the action of the infantry], at least disorganized it, dislocated the framework in which it was to operate."[55] Former air minister Pierre Cot claimed polemically that only 357 French planes had been lost in combat, while 6,000 idled on French airfields when the Armistice was signed, charging that French air leaders were either "incompetent or traitors." French air commander Joseph Vuillemin's alibi was that the *Luftwaffe* enjoyed a crushing superiority over the French air force.[56] Not so, argues Frieser, who insists that the absence of French aircraft had nothing to do with the technical or numerical superiority of the *Luftwaffe*. The Bloch MB.152, Dewoitine D.520, and Curtiss P-36 Hawk, were "entirely equal" to the Messerschmidt 109, not to mention the Hurricane and the Spitfire. British bombers were better than most German models, with the possible exception of the Ju 88. Many German pilots were hastily trained, so deaths in flight accidents were frequent, which accounts for some of the 1,559 German planes lost in the Battle of France. German air superiority stemmed in part from doctrine, in part from the desperate nature of the Sedan gamble, and in part from poor French organization.[57]

Hitler wanted "no Verdun in the air," so *Luftwaffe* doctrine called for direct tactical and operational support of ground forces. During the first phase of *Fall Gelb* on 10–12 May, the *Luftwaffe* attacked French air bases, managing only to inflict "insignificant" losses. In some respects, the *Luftwaffe* attacks on French bases were a plus for the French, because they galvanized morale. The downside was that the French failed to retaliate by attacking *Luftwaffe* bases, freeing up more *Luftwaffe* aircraft for close air support, especially at Sedan, to escort German bombers, or to blunt Allied bombing runs.[58] Finally, during the race to the sea, the *Luftwaffe* sealed Guderian's flanks by attacking roads, railway junctions, supply convoys, and so on to keep the Allies from moving up reserves to attack the exposed flanks of the advancing German forces. To insure effective and timely air support, *Luftwaffe* liaison elements riding in staff cars and provided with radio equipment of a power and quality unknown in the French inventory accompanied advancing units. This allowed ground commanders to call in air strikes in as little as 45 minutes. Compared with the German system, French air–ground liaison was practically farcical – French ground troops could receive but not transmit messages to aircraft. Instead they were to communicate to pilots by deploying large geometric panels on the ground.[59] At best, an Allied request for air support might require six hours to execute, by which time the tactical situation would have altered completely.[60]

While one must be careful not to exaggerate the impact of *Luftwaffe* bombardment on French soldiers, it is certain that the *Luftwaffe* made a major contribution to the psychological dimension of the defeat. Marc Bloch writes that the "terror effect" of German bombing runs, and especially of Stukas armed with their screaming "Jericho Trumpet," far exceeded the physical damage they were able to inflict. They spread bewilderment, panic, fatigue, and despair among French units woefully underequipped with anti-aircraft artillery, and added another "surprise" which through accumulation kept the French High Command off balance.[61] While Bloch conceded that Stukas caused little damage, "the effect of bombing on the nerves is far-reaching, and can break the potential of resistance over a large area ... Under air bombing I was never able to retain anything like the same calmness [as under an artillery assault] except by making a very considerable effort of will ... The fact is that this dropping of bombs from the sky has a unique power of spreading terror. They are dropped from a great height and seem, though quite erroneously, to be falling straight on top of one's head ... the soldier cowers as under some cataclysm of nature, and is tempted to feel that he is utterly defenceless ... The noise is hateful, savage, and excessively nerve-racking ... which shakes every bone in one's body. It seems to crush the very air with unparalleled violence, and conjures up pictures of torn flesh which are only too horribly borne out in fact by the sights one sees."[62]

Jean-Jacques Arzalier noted that while much attention was given in post-war reports to human casualties, no one counted the impact of air attacks on horses, which formed the core of French logistics, and which died like flies, especially as a wounded horse was a dead horse.[63] An after-action report circulated in January 1941 conceded that while entrenched and well-led troops had little to fear from Stuka attacks, convoys in the open were thrown into complete disarray: "During the retreat to Lille, I saw convoys of horses and autos completely abandoned at the sight of enemy aircraft, creating irreversible traffic jams. Trucks had collided with each other blocking the road, horses without conductors, their harnesses inextricably tangled together, and in every direction." Furthermore, constant bombing sapped morale: "Exhausted and dazed, they are no longer in a state to fight."[64] "The great lesson," concluded Gérodias, "and it's not up to me, is that with limited productive capacity, it is better to manufacture fewer tanks and more planes so as better to maintain an equilibrium between the two."[65] The Germans, too, relied on horse-drawn logistics. But they were seldom unsettled by French aircraft and for the most part remained well to the rear of the fighting.

The French air force began from a different strategic, doctrinal, and operational vantage point. French air doctrine was informed by Douhet's view, perfectly logical in the Great War's wake, that the ground war would prove indecisive, so that the air force should be reserved for strategic missions. However, because of the technical inferiority of the French bomber force, a "profound personnel crisis" caused by a lack of technical specialists, and fear of *Luftwaffe* retaliation against French cities, French bombers were initially confined to limited night bombing runs. Attempts to use them against German advances in Belgium proved disappointing because of thick flak, the "deplorable state of the bombers," which were slow and lacked armament, and their inability to hit precision targets like bridges, especially when forced by flak to bomb from higher altitudes. Yet, the air force claimed that if bombers were not directed to the skies over Sedan on 12–13 May, it was because at that date the attention of Army command was still riveted on Holland and northern Belgium.[66]

The "long war" strategy dictated that the French air force preserve its aircraft by scattering them in airfields far from the front. While dispersion had helped to insulate French aircraft from preemptive *Luftwaffe* attacks, the tradeoff was the challenge of uniting them in sufficient numbers at the point of battle at opportune times. The air force fully expected to support the army. But doctrine had not yet been defined, tactics were a work in progress, and French planes were not adapted to a ground support role. The French lacked a system to allocate fighters between bomber protection, interception, and ground support. Therefore, the desperate improvization of the French air war offered a recipe for confusion and inter-service acrimony. By the seventh day of the Battle for France, the air war was lost, as was the one on the ground.[67]

Air support of land operations also suffered from a lack of method. No equivalent of a centrally controlled, joint army–air force command system of the sort worked out by the Germans existed in France. In what was known as the "watering can principle," French planes were distributed to army groups for specific days on a percentage basis and from there allocated to individual field armies. While a *Wehrmacht* commander had a *Luftwaffe* liaison at his side with a radio, a French tactical officer had to persuade his general to phone the commander of *les forces aériennes de l'armée* with a request to bomb an objective. This request was passed on to the *zone d'opérations aériennes nord* (ZOAN). If the request was approved, it was sent up to the air division, who pushed it to the air group. Needless to say, the ZOAN was overwhelmed with bombing requests from 10 May, and from 14 May it had to support both the Ardennes and the retreat from Belgium. Many French airfields consisted of a runway, a petrol pump, and a radio. As a result, many French squadrons simply sat on the tarmac and never received orders for action. Or, without radar guidance of the sort that benefited the RAF in the Battle of Britain, French fighters simply hurtled aloft in search of a target. According to some calculations, *Luftwaffe* squadrons averaged four sorties a day to 0.9 for the French.[68]

On 14 May, the Allied air forces belatedly massed 152 bombers and 250 fighters against the growing German bridgehead at Sedan. But although French bomber losses were extremely light in this instance, as had already been demonstrated in northern Belgium, outdated machines and horizontal bombing were ill-adapted to support the ground war. The Allies would have been forced to carpet bomb the sector to have any effect, which at this stage of the war they lacked the ability to do. Deficient in ground support technique, fighters were unable to ping Pz.Kpfws. Surprised by its unexpectedly high losses, the RAF suspended deep operations on 16 May. The French air force followed suit.[69] Nevertheless, Sedan had resulted in bad blood between the army and the French air force. One of the post-war myths, promoted principally by Gamelin at Riom, was that lack of air support had been the decisive factor at Sedan, a refrain caroled by a French Army chorale led by Weygand, Georges, and Corap.[70] Not surprisingly, this sent already wobbly inter-service relations into a tailspin. Air Force general and ZOAN commander François d'Astier de la Vigerie complained of the French army's terminal ignorance of air doctrine and air capabilities. At Sedan, the army envisioned the French air force performing as a "*corps de cavalerie*," that could be ordered to halt the German advance with repeated charges like the cuirassiers at Reichshoffen. Otherwise the air force was meant to compensate for the significant shortcomings of the French artillery and engineers. The French air force had not trained to attack ground objectives, nor did it have air-to-ground radios to allow it to coordinate this type of operation.[71] Indeed, it appeared as if the French High Command, having totally failed to anticipate a surprise attack through the Ardennes, to prepare adequately its defenses around Sedan despite repeated warnings about their vulnerability, to station first-class troops there, or to react in a timely manner to warnings of the approach of a large force via Luxembourg and eastern Belgium, now sought to divest responsibility for its complacency and incompetence onto the hapless FAF.

Bulson

Most problematic for revisionist interpretations of the Fall of France has been the panic of French soldiers at Bulson, which helped the enemy to break open the front at Sedan and pave the way for the "sickle cut" – Guderian's slice-up of French forces on his way to the Channel. Some French units certainly fought well. But elsewhere, unit cohesion collapsed and soldiers headed to the rear or surrendered wholesale. At the time, military excuses combined communist conspiracy with a metropolitan variant of martial race theory – the collapse was blamed on the fact that the 55^{e} DI was inadequately armed and counted only 20 regulars among its 450 officers, while the desperately understrength 71^{e} DI, recruited mainly from allegedly combat-averse and communist-influenced Parisian reservists, numbered only 10,000 of its normal complement of 17,000 soldiers.[72] Other explanations include poor training and leadership in these two reserve divisions, lack of air cover, absence of motorization and of anti-aircraft and anti-tank guns, inadequacies of "controlled battle" doctrine, poor communications, and the failure of the senior leadership to grip the situation among them – a virtually inexhaustible catalogue of shortcomings. Revisionists also complain that traditional narratives of the Fall of France skip quickly from Sedan, to Dunkirk, to surrender, omitting a stout French post-Dunkirk resurgence in early June on the Somme and the Aisne. The defense on the Somme–Aisne argument seeks to rebut the conventional view of British historian of 1940 Alistair Horne that the completion of the German conquest in June 1940 constituted a sort of leisurely mop up of French soldiers eager to surrender.[73] However, to strengthen their case, revisionists might do better to view the French panic at Bulson and "non-participation" in battle as a more generalized phenomenon of war common to conscript armies. This does not let the French army off the hook, but it does place its disintegration into a broader context.

By the afternoon of 13 May, the poorly trained and led soldiers of the 55^{e} DI, shaken by Stuka attacks, had begun to flee, first in small groups, and then in a mass panic, even before they had seen a German. The village of Bulson about 10 kilometers south of Sedan was soon filled with soldiers, most of whom had abandoned their weapons. Those who still retained them fired wildly in the air, claiming that German Panzers were just behind them (in fact, Panzers had yet to cross the river) and warning that everyone should "scram." Some soldiers had commandeered horses. Others carried suitcases full of items pillaged from farms evacuated barely forty-eight hours earlier. Artillery batteries that still retained their telephones spread the rumors of the German advance – they began to hitch up their artillery and take the road south, shouting to reinforcements marching toward the battle that the order was to fall back. Robin Leconte believes that, insofar as "the committee on suspicious withdrawals" was concerned, laying the blame for the panic at Bulson on the artillery, and more specifically on Colonel Poncelet's decision to order his heavy artillery to hitch up and retreat, was an attempt to circumscribe the investigation and divert blame for the collapse of the Sedan front from Huntzinger's command negligence. Having been assigned responsibility for the Bulson *sauve-qui-peut*, Poncelet committed suicide. "This senior officer [Poncelet] has expiated, by his death, his lack of composure," insisted a clearly relieved General Aimé Doumenc.[74] In fact, the causes of the panic at Bulson were more complex than anything Poncelet might have triggered by a premature retreat order. "The high command, who decided at Sedan to leave the population in place until the last minute, who mixed units and overextended the regiments along the front, seem responsible for the poor preparation on the Meuse sector," concludes Leconte.[75] Poorly trained and overstretched units failed to adjust to the sudden onset of combat that shocked them into a collective and highly contagious hysteria. At Vendresse, 20 kilometers south of Sedan, two officers confusing French tanks with Panzers reported the Germans' arrival to corps headquarters. Rumors of a fifth column, which persisted to the end of the campaign, began to circulate, infecting the entire army. Sartre, whose unit was stationed in Alsace, reported that "here there is lots of commotion. Spies first of all. They're all over the place, they're arrested in bunches and then a few are shot here and there ... Everybody has seen a spy, has been on the verge of nabbing him, and then of course the spy got away."[76] In fact, as Sartre suggests, some did not get away, as French soldiers executed civilians they claimed were parachutists, spies, or members of a German fifth column.[77]

In three-quarters of an hour, the panic had spread over an area 10 kilometers wide. If one unit gave an order to retire without permission of division HQ, this created a gap in the line through which the Germans might infiltrate. Germans suddenly began to appear in unexpected places, which produced a chain reaction of collapse and flight. Realizing their flank was uncovered, other units deprived of liaison might follow. Even division headquarters became infected with rumor. By 7 p.m. in the evening of 13 May, confusion reigned. Communications between the batteries and the division headquarters broke down, even as French soldiers continued to resist on the banks of the Meuse. The roads south were jammed with fleeing troops, artillery batteries, and supply trucks, which swept aside roadblocks set up by the military police. This was the moment to order a counter-offensive to restore the front. In January, Gamelin had stood up two armored divisions or *Divisions cuirassiers de réserve* (DCrs). When the Germans attacked, the French counted 1,761 modern tanks, although almost 1,000 of them were small Renault 35 "infantry" tanks, hardly more than tracked machinegun nests. The 1re DCr had been sent into Belgium, where it was destroyed at Namur trying to cover the XI Corps retreat. The 3^{e} DCr was in support at Sedan.[78] On 13 June, Pierre Billotte, son of the general, tried to push his tanks forward through "an uncontrolled panic beyond all reason" of artillerymen who were supposed to be supporting the 71^{e} DI. No officers were in sight. His tankers insulted the fleeing soldiers, only to receive the reply that the Germans were invincible. When orders finally arrived on 14 June, they were to retreat. His Char B1bis tanks ran out of petrol and he was captured (Figure 3.3).[79] "Scattered as 'stopgaps' on an 18-kilometer front, on line day and night, without maintenance, [the 3e DCr] was ruined before it was used as an armored division and it was almost impossible to reconstitute it as one," reported General Charles Delestraint, an armor officer called out of retirement in 1939 and future head of *l'Armée secrète* who was to be murdered at Dachau in April 1945.[80]

The situation for the French on the early morning of 14 May was serious but hardly irretrievable. The German footholds were shallow and eminently vulnerable to counterattack. But at this point, the French army revealed that it still operated on Great War time. On the evening of 13 May, 55^{e} DI commander General Henri-Jean Lafontaine was given two infantry regiments and two battalions of light tanks to mount a counterattack at Sedan. But the task of assembling adequate artillery and issuing the necessary orders was inhibited by poor communications and by the doctrine of *colmatage* – basically sealing off the breach. When Lafontaine's counterattack finally lurched forward at 6.30 in the morning of 14 May, it proved to be a ragged and ill-coordinated effort, as three of

Figure 3.3 While the circumstances of this photo are unknown, French tanks were often immobilized by a shortage of petrol and their crews forced to surrender.

France's armored divisions were fed piecemeal into the battle. Panzers that crossed the Meuse on pontoons in increasingly large numbers managed to get the best of French tanks whose small petrol tanks, cumbersome refueling system, and lack of radios quickly put them out of commission. On that day, panic infected the infantrymen of the 71e DI as well. Then 1,600 soldiers vanished to the rear in a flash. In all, 20,000 French soldiers are estimated to have bolted to the rear, disorganizing the Sedan sector until 22 May.[81]

For contemporaries, the take-away from Bulson was that the *levée* had been a catastrophic – even ignominious – failure. At Riom, Vichy's abortive attempt in early 1942 to pin the blame for the Fall of France on the politicians of the Third Republic, the panic at Bulson came to symbolize the public rot that underlay France's 1940 defeat – decadence, defeatism, cowardice, even treason. Unfortunately for Vichy, the work of the committee on suspect withdrawals pointed ineradicably to the fact that the defeat was triggered by strategic mistakes and military shortcomings, whatever its longer-term political or social causes. The committee "revealed rather the sense of powerlessness of soldiers mired in a campaign where everything became an insurmountable obstacle ... a fertile terrain for demoralization, despondency, even paralysis or a sort of *laisser-aller* toward the very end of the campaign," writes Leconte. While soldiers were eager to blame the Third Republic, "the truth was more concrete: the keys to the enigma of the defeat are to be found in the guts of the Battle of France."[82]

Unfortunately, Bulson became merely the opening act of a general disaggregation of the French army that featured a torrent of "individual lapses" – for instance, future Algerian nationalist leader Ahmed ben Bella, conscripted in 1939 and assigned to an anti-aircraft battery guarding Marseilles harbor, complained to his superior that every Frenchman on his crew had vanished at the appearance of Stukas. He came away from the experience with a *croix de guerre* and a conviction that French conscripts lacked the stomach for combat, a view that later informed his approach to the War of Algerian Independence.[83] On the whole, North African and especially Moroccan troops performed well, when properly led.[84] This was in part because three-quarters of the pre-war North African *tirailleur* regiments were made up of professional soldiers, often illiterate Berbers driven into the army by poverty rather than patriotism. While sons of well-off Muslims were encouraged to enlist in the Spahis, a cavalry regiment, Muslim peasants were largely confined to the infantry, lest access to artillery or tanks empower them to mutiny.[85] "Senegalese," a generic term the French applied to all sub-Saharan infantrymen, also came away underwhelmed with the performance of French conscripts.

Laqui Kondé, a Senegalese *tirailleur* whose unit was engaged on 23 May, remembered it thus: "We were always with the French. We were better than the Whites ... When the shooting started, they fled. They knew the region. We didn't, so we stayed. Our officers? They stood behind us saying: 'Stand up. We're going to win.' But the Germans were obviously stronger, so we paid no attention to them."[86] Gaston Vuchot recounted that "The Blacks showed the qualities and weaknesses that have been known for a long time. But many in their first battle in particular, terrorized by German artillery and air bombardments, had their nose in the dirt, and it was impossible to get anything out of them."[87] On the Somme in June, Captain Filet of the 21^{e} RIC reported that he had to point his pistol at several fleeing Senegalese to force them back into line. But once back in position, the Germans "had enormous difficulty to reduce the resistance of these last Senegalese, hidden in the cellars or in the corners of demolished houses, and they had to kill them one by one."[88] Indeed, a number of Senegalese and North African regiments and individual soldiers were cited in army orders.[89] Unfortunately, the sight of fleeing French soldiers, who often pillaged civilian homes and shops under the indifferent gaze of their superiors, surprised and shocked *tirailleurs Sénégalais* indoctrinated into the dogma of French invincibility.[90] Gamelin and the High Command generally interpreted the Bulson episode and the progressive unraveling of the French army in May–June as evidence of a societal failure that he could lay at the feet of the Republic, which the command was essentially powerless to counteract.[91] Vuchot, although at this stage of the war no great champion of the *levée en masse*, but who later in the war as "Commandant Noir" (Major Black) would join a Jedburgh team to reinforce the *maquis*, only to become fatally wounded in the reduction of the Colmar pocket in February 1945, was less convinced. Everyone, including his Senegalese, was demoralized by the weakness of the French artillery and the absence of air cover. But whether troops fought or fled depended on their leadership: "Where the leader [officer or NCO] disappeared, the soldiers faltered ... Where the man of rank stood firm, so did the soldiers. But nowhere did [one see] this intensity, this ferocious desire to advance whatever the cost that one saw in the enemy assault troops."[92]

Comparisons between the courageous performance of the *poilu* in the First World War and the implosion of the *levée en masse* in the Second have elicited various explanations, beginning with the generational differences that had underpinned de Gaulle's plea for a professional, highly mechanized army. Others would include the assertion that the trench warfare that characterized the Western Front in 1914–1918 did not impose on the individual soldier the isolation that was to characterize existence in the foxholes of the Second World War. But these explanations have their limitations – in the cauldron of Verdun or the Chemin des Dames, trenches might become a purely notional concept and the feeling of isolation and disorientation for a soldier frozen under bombardment in a shell hole was intense. Nevertheless, as Bloch noted, while being shelled in the trenches was unpleasant, one gradually adapted to it.[93] A third explanation was that France was actually attacked in 1914, while the fall of Warsaw and the subsequent *drôle de guerre* stripped the mobilization of 1939–1940 of purpose and of any sense that national survival hung in the balance. While Crémieux-Brilhac noted that most regimental officers fought with courage, he blamed the collapse at Sedan and Dinant on inept colonels and aged majors who abandoned their regiments and battalions on the pretext of reporting to headquarters to ask for orders. This dislocated the chain of command.[94] Leconte offers a different reading – while agreeing that many officers, especially in B divisions, did not meet the professional standards required, the dislocation of the command and a lack of liaison required majors and colonels temporarily to abandon their units to go in search of ammunition, supplies, and orders.[95] A fifth cause offered by Martin Alexander is that French soldiers did fight bravely, but that their resistance was sabotaged by an army whose doctrine and tactical concepts were out of date and vulnerable to the strategic surprise at Sedan.[96] In other words, the collapse at Bulson was top down, not bottom up.

All offer valid observations. But British sociologist Anthony King argues that soldier panics like that which infected the French at Bulson were "not an exception but an extreme case of a trend" that affected all Second World War conscript armies.[97] In fact, "non-participation" in battle was a problem famously and controversially identified and publicized by S. L. A. Marshall in his studies of the US Army in the Second World War. Marshall determined that citizen armies found it particularly difficult to generate unit cohesion and purpose around a common concept of masculinity and primary group loyalties, especially on modern, three-dimensional battlefields that combine mechanization, isolation, and the requirement to perform complex tactical maneuvers under fire. While Second World War militaries were able to generate enormous combat power, the main impulse among soldiers under attack is inertia. This had nothing to do with national character or regional recruitment, but is integral to the organization of modern conscript armies. Inertia had to be overcome through training, fostering unit cohesion, and the sort of lead-from-the-front command style displayed in German units crossing the Meuse. One could not animate the *levée* through the château generalship of Gamelin, Georges,

Huntzinger, and a High Command hunkered behind "controlled battle" doctrine. During the *drôle de guerre*, the French High Command had tried to reconcile a long-war strategy with "*la préservation du moral*," through creating "training schools" or rotating units through the "front lines" in Alsace. But this failed to prepare French soldiers adequately for the shock of combat when it came.[98]

Students of military cohesion emphasize that abstract notions of national mission and patriotism may meet skepticism in the front lines. But patriotism is the starting point in the development of loyalty, self-respect, pride, and a sense of honor that underpins the *raison d'être* of military service. The French *Réglement de l'infanterie* of 1940 stated that

> the moral force of the soldier has as its basis his faith in the grandeur and the destiny of the Fatherland, his conviction that he is fighting for a just cause, his confidence in his leaders and his comrades and a feeling of his own worth as a combatant. Patriotism is born in the family, it is developed in the school and encouraged in the barracks. It is the love of France, not only for its beauty and riches of its landscape, its intellectual and moral heritage and the glory of its history, but also for its radiance in the world.[99]

One view of the failure of 1940 was that inter-war pacifism broke the link between masculinity and nationalism. Marshall argued that when soldiers lose faith in their cause, for whatever reason, they are no longer willing to accept discipline. "If it can expect to receive quarter, the last reason for resistance has disappeared," he wrote.[100] Another explanation might be that "controlled battle" doctrine eliminated initiative *à la Auftragstaktik* from the script of battlefield success. For Crémieux-Brilhac, the psychological traumatism produced by a combination of the surprise and brutality of the German attack that paralyzed the High Command proved contagious, cascading downward through rumor to panic French troops on the Meuse. Demoralization was facilitated by a feeling of inferiority and abandonment, lack of preparation, and lack of faith in one's weapons. The German soldiers gained a moral ascendency in part because their uniforms and equipment seemed adapted to mobile warfare. In contrast, French soldiers came dressed in Great War legacy uniforms that were heavy, hot in the summer of 1940, and impractical, especially for soldiers expected to cover long distances on foot. Armed with rifles or carbines, and backed by a cumbersome machinegun, which they had seldom if ever fired, they felt disarmed before German soldiers with their light machineguns and maneuverable MG 34. This admiration for German equipment translated quickly into an inferiority complex among French soldiers, who became the walking symbols of yesterday's army. France did not succumb in 1940 because its uniforms and weapons were inferior. But it hardly improved the confidence of soldiers who were psychologically and physically exhausted, and "paralyzed in the face of soldiers whom they believed more battle hardened than they."[101] Regular units where officers enforced discipline were best able to maintain their cohesion. But they remained scattered in a sea of semi-trained and indifferently led conscripts and reservists, clearly rattled by the violence of the German onslaught.[102]

In the end, as an after-action report from the 15th Artillery Regiment concluded, simply too many things went wrong for the army to retain its cohesion under assault:

> In general, the personnel were demoralized by the immediate retreat which took on the character of a debacle [of the Ninth Army] in which they were caught up without having had a chance to become battle hardened. In this sense, for months many officers and NCOs would have liked to train, and to train their men by spending a few weeks in the front lines. Poor morale, lamentable dress, an absence of all offensive spirit was frequently reported. But placed in such brutally tragic circumstances, how could it have been otherwise with most men totally lacking any national and moral preparation? When in battery and supervised, the men held together. But in garrison, or during the retreat, their conduct became deplorable, and for many of them, a too large minority, it offered an unexpected opportunity to empty wine cellars and pillage abandoned houses. Disproportionate matériel force, morale shaken by air bombardment, a hopelessness that took hold after such an initial setback, can help to explain certain physical and moral lapses. Like many of the men, the officers themselves experienced low morale as they realized that a well-trained unit, commanded by a competent corps of NCOs, was not utilized, and frittered away. More than once, we prepared to defend positions, and as soon as everything was ready, we departed after hours of waiting in vain for orders and munitions.[103]

Marshall's measure of "non-participation" was the relatively low percentage of GIs who fired their rifles in combat. His conclusion was that this stemmed from a deficit of aggression. Critics of Marshall's methods countered that he had simply underlined the fact that most GIs considered the rifle to be inefficient and inadequate, especially when compared with automatic and crew-served weapons. But at the other end of the scale, "non-participation" might assume spectacular dimensions in the form of soldier panics sparked by the shock of combat among inexperienced troops who were poorly prepared and led. For example, the flight of British troops at Tretten during the Norway campaign, who, "yelling and screaming," ignored the direct orders from their officers to face the oncoming Germans, "had a depressing effect on the Norwegian soldiers who witnessed the behavior," one observer noted laconically.[104] Australian war correspondent Alan Moorehead became caught up in a panic during Operation Crusader mounted to relieve the siege of Tobruk in November 1941, triggered when

> about a hundred British trucks suddenly burst in in a whirl of dust. We looked up wondering … Then from another direction several hundred more vehicles, tanks among them, came flying pell-mell across the desert, racing past our stationary vehicles without stopping and covering us in great billows of fine sand. This was no organized convoy. The others got the idea at the same time as I did. As I raced back toward our trucks, Clifford and Busvine were already flinging the bedding, the cooking pots and our clothes into the back of the trucks. Everyone was packing at speed … One of our officers, shaving soap on his face, came over when he saw us packing and enquired with all the confidence of ignorance, "What's the flap? Ops will tell us if we have to get out." "Take a look at Ops," said Clifford briefly. The Ops crew was flinging aboard beds, maps, cases of food and everything they possessed. Another great swarm of vehicles rushed through the camp and now shells began to fall among them. It had been a bright morning but now the churned-up dust had blotted out the sun and visibility became reduced to two hundred yards or less. In this semi-darkness and confusion thousands of vehicles got hopelessly mixed so that men and vehicles of entirely different units travelled along together, and since many of the drivers had no orders they simply rushed ahead following anyone who would lead them … Twice we stopped and while men ran from one vehicle to another asking for orders and trying to find out what was amiss, more shell came over the horizon. We were being followed – and fast. So, the hue and cry went on again … Once when we paused on a rise – an odd collection of tanks, cars, lorries, light guns and command vehicles – a squadron of British aircraft came toward us flying low. Everyone ran to their places and the stampede began again. All day for nine hours we ran. It was the contagion of bewilderment and fear and ignorance. Rumour spread at every halt. No man had orders. Everyone had some theory and no one any plan beyond the frantic desire to reach his unit. … I came to understand something of the meaning of panic in this long nervous drive. It was the unknowns we were running away from, the unknown in ourselves and in the enemy. We did not know who was pursuing us or how many or how long they would be able to keep up the pursuit and whether or not they would outstrip us in the end. In ourselves we did not know what to do. Had there been someone in authority to say "Stand here. Do this and that" – then half our fear would have vanished. So, I began to realize … how important the thousand dreary routine things in the army are. The drill, the saluting, the uniform, the very badges on your arm that identify you with a solid machine and build up a feeling of security and order. In the moment of danger, the soldier turns to his mechanical habits and draws strength from them … These matters, I suppose, should have been obvious enough, but I personally only began to see them clearly during this ignominious retreat back into Egypt. I wanted badly to receive orders. And so, I think, did the others. It was a crestfallen and humiliated little group of men that finally felt its way toward the frontier wire fence as dusk fell. We found a gap in the wire and as we plunged through it with a feeling of relief – even a fence between us and the unknown pursuer was something – a British major came up in a truck and began to organize us and knock some sense into us.[105]

While significant in its strategic impact, Bulson was replicated in the wholesale surrenders of many Soviet troops in the summer and autumn of 1941, the stampede of GIs at Kasserine Pass in February 1943, or the capitulation of some green US divisions during the opening stages of the German offensive in the 1944 Battle of the Bulge. But these battlefield breakdowns could be passed off as "local incidents" explained by contingent circumstances – surprise, the confusion of battle, inexperience and lack of unit cohesion, a command rapidly surpassed by events, emotional fatigue caused by bombardment, an unfamiliar environment, and so on. In the case of the armed forces of the United States or the Soviet Union, they offered forgettable footnotes in a narrative of a rise to superpower status, submerged in the wave of "greatest generation" nostalgia.

However, for France, the panic at Bulson offered an exclamation point in a narrative of France's national decline – the unraveling of the front, the demand for an armistice, and all the humiliation that was to follow. "Strange victory" revisionists argue the *Wehrmacht*'s success in 1940 was contingent, even fortuitous, an "audacious raid" produced essentially by sixteen elite German divisions – ten Panzer and six motorized infantry – backed by the *Luftwaffe*, where exceptional leadership, even individual heroism, mobility, and efficient logistics were concentrated. The 1940 display of German military efficiency eroded over time. According to King, by 1942, the *Wehrmacht* began to experience the same problems of aged soldiers, poor training, "non-shooters," and even soldier panics on the Eastern Front that in the wake of 1940 had come to be seen as a uniquely Allied, and a notably Gallic, shortcoming.[106] Nevertheless, the *Wehrmacht* never ceased to fight, even as defeat loomed. John Ellis argued that panic in 1940 was not caused by demoralization, but had rather engendered it: the French soldiers "panicked and quit perfectly tenable positions, roads became hopelessly blocked as vehicles were abandoned and march discipline evaporated, and communications broke down … A hundred such failures quickly bred a thousand more, and these in turn gave rise to defeatism, despair and a fixed conviction that the enemy was invincible."[107]

The problem was that the French High Command never recovered from the German breakthrough on the Meuse. Henceforth, the sheer speed of events, their failure to grip the battle, steady their troops, to analyze and adapt to the success of German methods which depended on the tight coordination of tanks, artillery, and aircraft, logistical and transportation breakdowns, fatigue, poor communications, indecisive leadership, and lack of intelligence coalesced to sabotage a French recovery.[108] Therefore, the French failure in 1940 was systemic. And imagined counterfactual scenarios – like keeping Giraud's Seventh Army in reserve on the Meuse – that might have changed the storyline of the Second World War in the West and excised the "Vichy parenthesis" from France's sequence of Republican experiments belong to fantasy, not history. Nevertheless, Bulson defined the narrative of France's collapse, in the process tendering a judgment on the nature of French politics and national character. In the immediate wake of the Phoney War, Bulson became a symbol of a lack of national resolve, an implosion of French masculinity and pride, and the alibi for a French officer class that could reassign responsibility for defeat to the Third Republic and its signature strategic underpinning, the *levée en masse*. The panic at Bulson also gave Churchill his first inkling that France might fall.[109]

Belated RAF and French air force attempts to bomb the German bridgeheads on the Meuse were made ineffective by poor tactics, slow planes, small, hard-to-pinpoint targets, and considerable German flak, which translated into an 11 percent aircraft loss rate, unsustainable in the context of the French air force's "long war" strategy. By the night of 13 May, some of the reserves that Georges had ordered forward on 11 May began to arrive, most notably the 3rd Motorized Infantry Division (3ᵉ DIM) and the 3rd Armored Division (3ᵉ DCr) under General Jean Flavigny, considered an experienced tank commander. But, as usual, the French tried to direct the battle from remote positions in the rear and tanks were not placed under infantry command. One result was that liaison between infantry and tanks became so "precarious" that French tanks fired upon their own infantry when they attempted to counterattack. "So, the counterattacks were aborted because it could not have been otherwise," Gérodias reported.[110] When on 15 May the French attempted to seize the important crossroad at Stonne south of Sedan from the 10th Panzer Division, a combination of command errors and technical shortcomings compromised the French counterattack – disrupted communications, refueling problems, tanks slow to arrive and then thrown piecemeal into the battle, and so on. "Let's draw a final conclusion from this breakthrough on the Meuse," Gérodias wrote. "It illustrates the folly of trying to reestablish a position that is already completely demolished. When this happens, the only thing left is to fall back on a prepared position sufficiently far in the rear that is not only suitably fortified, but also is manned in advance by fresh units."[111]

Gérodias' advice was not followed, however, because even at this late date, Georges' assumption was that German troops in the Ardennes would try to outflank and swing behind the Maginot Line, or even launch a new offensive through Switzerland, a misperception that he and Huntzinger nevertheless clasped until it was far too late to recover. Gamelin and Billotte were still fixated on the events in northern

Belgium, even though it was clear that the Germans had made only weak attempts to impede the Allied surge north. On 15 May as Guderian pivoted west, Huntzinger abandoned defensive lines along the Chiers river, fearing that he would be encircled. Crémieux-Brilhac faulted Huntzinger's practically criminal complacency for the breakthrough at Sedan. By 26 May, the panicked Second Army commander was already urging Weygand to conclude an armistice.[112] Huntzinger's early advocacy of an armistice was to elevate his stock at Vichy, that rewarded his strategic prescience with the post of Secretary of State for War. Among other advantages, this placed him beyond criticism by the committee on suspect withdrawals. In this way, the alibi that France opted out of the war because its soldiers had failed to fight became an official dogma in Vichy, one incorporated into the decadence interpretation of France's collapse. At the same time, however, it is difficult to agree that the disintegration of the French army constituted a "strange victory," confined to a soldier panic at Bulson and to the complacency of Huntzinger and Corap. Systemic failures were pervasive, but difficult to document, because "I saw the order book of an army intentionally burnt," recorded Marc Bloch.[113] Once again, the Inspector General of the Infantry General Gérodias had hit the nail on the head – French generals had failed to command:

> During the first days of the battle, as during the entire campaign, too often the high command, rather than define the missions, issue orders, coordinate the liaison of subordinate units, limited themselves to repeating: "resist with no thought of withdrawal." This is really too simple a directive and they might often have done better. The High Command must direct the battle and not shed its responsibilities under cover of a facile formula easily enough said but in practice difficult to execute. They must also realize that they cannot issue orders repeatedly to the same troops to "die in place" without seriously undermining morale. The leader in the higher echelons must have sufficient character to take responsibility in these situations when the orders no longer truly match the situation.[114]

Responsibility for the collapse of the French position on the Meuse was shifted instead onto Huntzinger's neighbor André Georges Corap, whose Ninth Army had been assigned the sector adjacent to Sedan that ran downriver to Monthermé and Dinant.

"By the 15th, there wasn't much of a battle, just pockets of resistance here and there. Resistance invariably failed, outflanked and surrounded by an enemy that passed freely through the gaps." At best, the French were able to delay the German advance by a few hours. "And we kept repeating the same mistake," the report continued. "Confronted with this tide that arrives so rapidly, we will continue to feed in more or less fresh units. Might as well throw handfuls of sand on the beach in the face of the surge. So long as there is not a sufficiently high and continuous seawall, everything will be submerged."[115] Nor was Corap's withdrawal from Houx and Monthermé in the face of the advance of the German Fourth and Twelfth Armies well managed. The XI Corps commander Lieutenant-General Julien François René Martin was faulted when the 18e and 22e DIs took heavy losses as they attempted to withdraw in disorder. "For example, there is no doubt that had on 15 May [Martin] taken it upon himself to fix the axis of retreat and designate the points of assembly for elements that were scattered and incapable of serious resistance, the 18e DI would not have been destroyed on the battlefield but could have rendered appreciable services in the days that followed."[116] On 18 May, the general commanding the 1re DCr and much of his staff were surrounded and captured. Like Huntzinger's Second Army, Corap's Ninth Army had basically been annihilated. However, the main complaint against Corap was that his withdrawal had compromised the position of the French First Army to the west holding the Gembloux gap in Belgium. This crumbled the Allied position from east to west.[117]

General Henri Giraud assumed command of a Ninth Army that effectively existed only on paper. Less than a week into the fight, it was becoming apparent that the *levée* was on its last legs. By 16 May, the three separate German bridgeheads were joined into a 95-kilometer divot in the French line. A yawning gap had opened between the Ninth and Second Armies (Map 3.3). "Either they'll break through – which I don't expect at all – and we're screwed," Sartre wrote on that day. "Or they'll stop for a breather and the war of positions will begin again. In that case we'll probably see the leave-takers timidly reappearing. We must be patient, and above all tell ourselves that this proves that the German wants to be through with it before winter. So, the chances are good that we won't see the interminable three or four years of war that were first foreseen."[118] Bitter tank battles continued as Stonne changed hands several times. As "*colmatage*," it proved magnificent but irrelevant. On the 14 May, two groups of 155 mm artillery supporting the 5th Marine Infantry Division found that munitions, petrol, intelligence on potential targets, and above all orders were either late or never arrived at all. No liaison was established with groups they were meant to support. They finally opened fire on Germans trying to cross the Meuse at Dinant. "Three hours later, no serious resistance from the infantry . . . the group ordered a precipitous retreat." But outmoded Great War trucks capable of a speed of no more than 15 kilometers an hour, requisitioned civilian vehicles in poor mechanical condition, a lack of petrol, lack of infantry protection, air cover, and anti-aircraft artillery, poor use of 47 mm anti-tank guns, which were scattered about and withdrawn prematurely, and pre-Great War vintage machineguns, meant that they were overrun and forfeited most of their equipment.[119] The infantry complained that they were left on their own, with support from neither the air force nor their artillery, whose Great War schema had completely broken down in the confusion of mobile warfare.[120]

On 15 May, Generalleutnant Georg-Hans Reinhardt burst out of his incarceration at Monthermé and surged 60 kilometers to the west. By 17 May, Rommel had advanced for about 110 kilometers, outdistancing his infantry, artillery, and plodding logistics. *Panzergruppe* commander Paul Ludwig Ewald von Kleist fretted, but Guderian was not to be denied. The Panzers sparked panic among soldiers without anti-tank weapons, in makeshift defensive positions, and with inadequate cadres, and then carved up French divisions like so many Christmas turkeys.[121] In this way, the Fall of France brought to light institutional weaknesses in the French army that matched the underperformance of the French air force. What would normally have been a suicidal exposure of Panzers unprotected by infantry and artillery support became a triumphant advance because no organized Allied force remained in Guderian's path – Georges and Huntzinger had positioned their reserves to counter an imaginary German swing behind the Maginot Line. The Teutonic trap was beginning to slam shut.

"The Wounded Were Smiling" – De Gaulle Counterattacks

But it was not quite over. It was obvious that, just as Gamelin had stuck his neck into the Belgian noose, so Guderian had reciprocated by over-extending himself in his race to the Channel. The counter, as Gamelin had realized, was to mass "mobile forces" to attack the flanks of the German advance. But, given the escalating disaggregation of the Allied command-and-control in the wake of Sedan, combined with the fact that the French were largely clueless about how to deploy massed armored forces at this stage, what resulted were minor attacks, footnotes in the skid toward calamity, that would hardly merit mention in the history of the campaign except that some of them were carried out by a man who was soon to become famous. And as such, they aggregate into a pointillist counternarrative of heroic initiatives, foresight, and actions meant to rescue an otherwise dreary and inexorable debacle. On 11 May, Charles de Gaulle was named to command the 4^{e} DCr, which, as he noted, "didn't exist," but whose elements he was assured would gradually

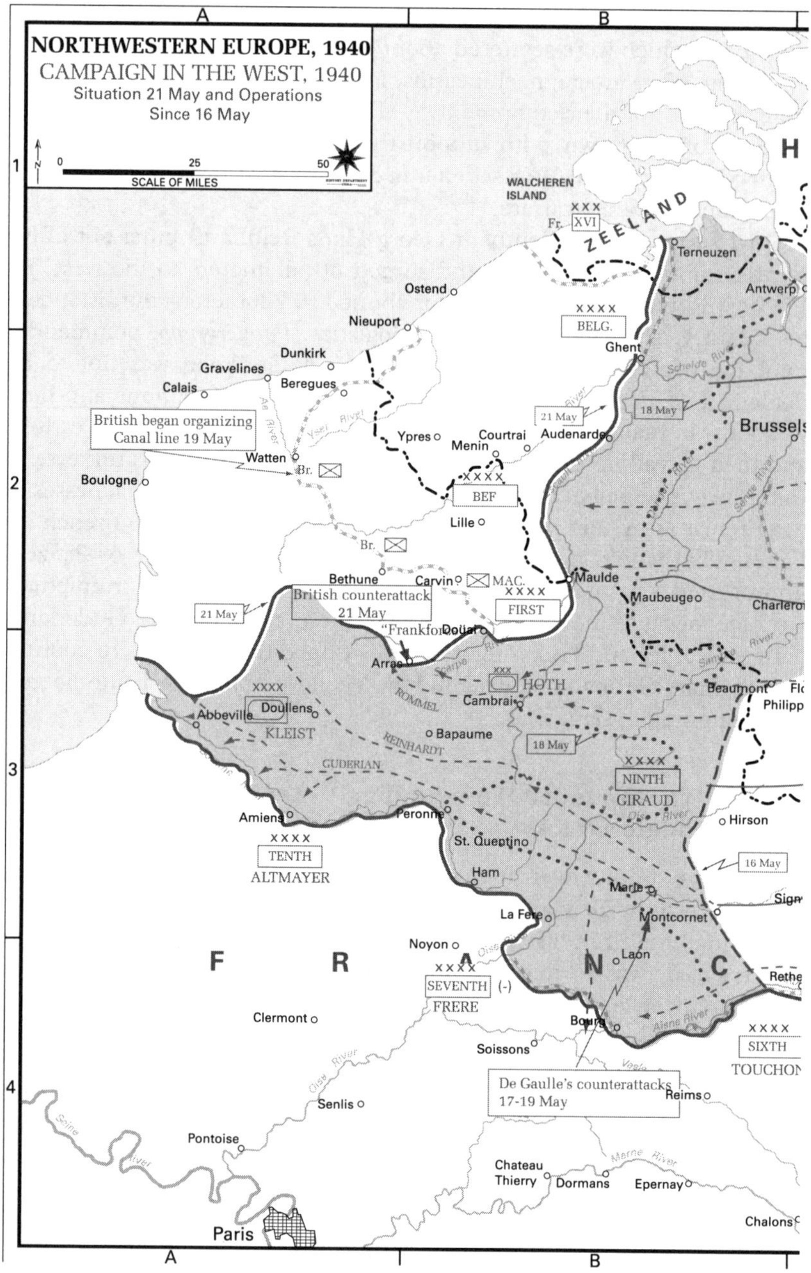

Map 3.3 Situation 21 May 1940. West Point Atlas.

12
HOLLAND
GERMANY
LUX.
Dordrecht
Moerdijk
Breda
Gennep
Goch
Wesel
Essen
Dusseldorf
Cologne
Bonn
Roermond
Maastricht
Aachen
EBEN EMAEL
Louvain
Wavre
Hannut
Liege
Monschau
Gembloux
Namur
Huy
Houx
Dinant
Marche
La Roche
St. Vith
Prum
Houffalize
Rochefort
Givet
St. Hubert
Bastogne
Bitburg
Vianden
Diekirch
Echternach
Trier
Libramont
Neufchateau
Revin
Montherme
Mezieres
Bouillon
Sedan
Bazeilles
Doneherty
Flize
Arlon
Carignan
Stonne
Virton
Longwy
Luxembourg
Saarburg
Montmedy
Longuyon
Merzig
Saarlautern
Saarbrucken
Verdun
Metz
Saareguemines
Pont a Mousson
EIGHTEENTH
KUECHLER
B
BOCK
SIXTH
REICHENAU
NINTH
BLASKOWITZ
A
FOURTH
KLUGE
SECOND
WEICHS
SIXTEENTH
BUSCH
TWELVE
LIST
SECOND
THIRD
C
LEEB
FOURTH
16 May
THE EIFEL
ARDENNES FOREST
PEEL MARSHES
ALBERT CANAL
C
D
1
2
3
4

Map 3.3 (Cont.)

assemble at Laon, a town whose twelfth-century cathedral rises out of the Picardy plain midway between Reims and Saint-Quentin. His unit would become part of the Sixth Army, whose task was to create a blocking position on the Aisne to keep the Germans out of Paris. He soon realized, however, that the Germans were dashing for the Channel coast, not Paris. What de Gaulle witnessed was the destructive passage of the very mechanized army that he had urged France to create in 1934 – a spearhead of armored divisions and motorized infantry, to which the *Luftwaffe* added a devastating layer of air superiority.

If de Gaulle's memoirs are to be believed, at this point he experienced an epiphany. The roads were jammed with refugees intermingled with French soldiers disarmed by the Germans and told "we don't have time to take you prisoner." It was clear that many French soldiers had been intimidated by their German opponents, who looked young, agile, and well-armed for modern war, to the point that some had surrendered without firing a shot to inferior numbers.[122] Furious at "the disdainful insolence of the adversary," de Gaulle vowed to continue the fight come what may. "The war begins infinitely badly. Therefore, it has to continue. There's plenty of space in the world. If I live, I will fight, where one must, as long as one must until the enemy is defeated and the national stain removed. That's what I could subsequently do. It was on that day that I resolved to do it."[123] De Gaulle biographer Jean Lacouture describes this celebrated passage as "the reflex of a slapped musketeer."[124] It was also the reflex of a skillful propagandist who, even before his historic broadcast of 18 June, sought to create a counternarrative of heroism and sacrifice kindled by a leader willing to defy tradition, take calculated risks, and challenge operational orthodoxy through tactical innovation, initiative, and imagination.

Between 15 May and 5 June, he commanded his 4e DCr in three attacks at Montcornet, Crécy-sur-Serre, and Abbeville, his only actual combat command of the entire war. But together, these skirmishes validated his operational vision, his composure under fire, and his leadership credentials. On 17 May, de Gaulle led what he describes as an "offensive reconnaissance" to Montcornet, 20 kilometers northeast of Laon, with a motley force of ninety-five tanks of mixed weights and armed with guns of various calibers. While de Gaulle gets high marks for his *coup d'œil* as a commander, Montcornet also showcased the limitations of his pick-up force – the lack of experience of his tank crews, mechanical difficulties, inadequate fueling capabilities, a lack of radios to coordinate attacks, and an absence of artillery and motorized infantry. Captain René Ribes, who commanded the 1st company of the 46th battalion of Char B1bis tanks, noted that his unit arrived at Montcornet guided only by a map taken from the Post Office Almanac after a "difficult" night march, "between a column of fleeing soldiers and one of refugees. We took our positions as best we could on completely unreconnoitered terrain." The attack kicked off at 04:15 in total darkness and a light fog in complete ignorance of the enemy's disposition. Five French tanks became lost and bogged down in swampy ground, which forced the others to travel single file for several kilometers down a road before they could deploy. De Gaulle ordered his force back to Laon after taking twenty-five casualties. Jean-Jacques Arzalier argues that while de Gaulle downplayed the significance of Moncornet, calling it an offensive reconnaissance in which he lost 200 men while inflicting numerous casualties on the enemy,[125] in fact, the costs were much higher: of 162 tanks committed, only 61 emerged intact, while 750 of de Gaulle's command were killed, wounded, or captured.[126]

Over the next forty-eight hours, de Gaulle attempted to restructure his new command to apply the lessons of Montcornet at Crécy-sur-Serre – his force numbered 150 tanks, 30 of which were Char B1bis heavy tanks armed with a 75 mm cannon in the hull plus a 47 mm gun in the turret, 40 were SOMUA S35 or Char D2 medium tanks with a 47 mm gun, and the remainder were diminutive Renault R35 "infantry tanks" with a derisory 37 mm gun and similar but faster Hotchkiss H39s. But *l'armée de métier* it was not. "It is true that, for the SOMUAs, each team was composed of a chief who had never fired the cannon and a driver who had not had four hours of driving." In a reprise of the 1914 "taxis of the Marne," his "motorized" infantry battalion was to be carried into battle in commandeered municipal buses. His artillery support was cobbled together from guns and support personnel out of weapons parks, and "many officers just met their men on the battlefield." Without radios, he depended on motorcyclists for communication with subordinate units, "and, above all, going to visit them." Transport, maintenance, and supply were lacking. "Nevertheless, this improvised outfit gave the impression of general enthusiasm," de Gaulle insisted.[127]

However, Gaullist gusto is decidedly absent from Captain Ribes' report of the 19 May battle: orders were "succinct" to the point of incomprehension, and intelligence was either non-existent or contradictory, while his company guided itself to Crécy using a large-scale Michelin map. On arrival, they were handed a smaller-scale map cut into two misaligned pieces, "which would be impossible to assemble," and which did not include part of the objective they were meant to attack. Nor did they know where friendly forces were located. At 07:00, a German reconnaissance aircraft buzzed overhead. The *Luftwaffe* appeared at the same time as did the French fuel trucks, and continued to harass them throughout the day, forcing tanks to disperse and making refueling an even more challenging proposition than usual. "And [the German planes] were never bothered, either by our air force or by our AAA," Ribes complained. German artillery had a field day. Ribes never detected any counter-battery replies from French artillery. Even when French tanks advanced, no infantry appeared to occupy the ground. The Germans closely followed the French withdrawal. Any tank disabled by mechanical difficulties or enemy fire, and its crew, became a German prize.[128]

Not surprisingly, de Gaulle's account is more upbeat. Despite the fact that German air superiority meant that tactical surprise was impossible to achieve, and German heavy artillery was lethal, the 4ᵉ DCr advanced, "head high. The wounded were smiling. Our cannon fired repeatedly," forcing a temporary German withdrawal.[129] He ignored Georges' retreat order that arrived in the middle of the afternoon of 19 May, because he was persuaded that, with a reinforcement of two more divisions, he could break through to link up with the armies in Belgium. But on 20 May, the same day that Maxime Weygand replaced Gamelin as commander in chief, he was forced to reposition, with the recompense of being promoted temporary brigadier. While Ribes, who by the time of writing of his report was serving in Vichy's Armistice Army, shared de Gaulle's vision for tanks, he questioned his former commander's tactical judgment: "These two operations during which a poorly trained unit was directed to undertake extremely difficult operations for which it was not prepared, without the slightest protection or support, that caused little damage to an enemy that shunned combat, caused significant losses: 18 of 34 tanks were missing at roll call south of Laon on the evening of 19 May."[130]

While de Gaulle would go on to make history, the French army came away from 1939–1940 with a failing grade in mechanized warfare. Like Montcornet, the attack at Crécy-sur-Serre had produced a "round trip" back to the start line for many of the same reasons – a lack of air support, too little motorized infantry to hold ground that the tanks had taken, and the fact that de Gaulle's vision for tank warfare outdistanced the capabilities of a French armored division in 1940. Delestraint categorized de Gaulle's actions as "glorious, brilliant *faits d'armes*, whose results, however, were disproportionate to the weakening of the division that resulted." Quite apart from tank losses, as part of the 4ᵉ DCr, the 10ᵉ Cuirassiers alone had lost 14 officers, 76 NCOs, and 476 soldiers. Undeterred by the carnage, on 29 May, de Gaulle set out to attack the German "pocket" at Abbeville on the Somme. Ribes complained that by the time the sixteen remaining tanks in his company reached Abbeville on 28 May, the men had been exhausted by repeated night marches – the B1bis traveled at only 10 kilometers an hour. Company commanders in the 4ᵉ DCr were called together at 13:30 on 28 May, and given verbal orders to attack at 17:00. The general concept of the operation was not explained, nor was any intelligence on the German positions offered. Units had to form the best picture they could by patrols, talking to the infantry or even to local civilians. Only fourteen of Ribes' sixteen tanks were mechanically in condition to participate. Nevertheless, in Ribes' opinion, de Gaulle's Abbeville attack succeeded because there was a general concept of maneuver, adequate artillery support, and the objective was the limited one of seizing the village of Huppy and taking many of the garrison prisoners. But the 28 May attack had failed to reduce the Abbeville "pocket" because it had been launched too late in the day. By 29 May when de Gaulle wanted to exploit his tactical success, the Germans had recovered from their surprise and reinforced their anti-tank defenses. French tanks sent to attack the Mont de Caubert south of Abbeville were greeted by 105 mm artillery fire at 2,000 meters, beyond their range of reply. At 1400, Ribes called over the radio for artillery support to take out the German anti-tank guns. That support only rained down at 2000. Three French planes had wandered over the battlefield at 1830, only to be chased away by a volcano of German flak. Ribes' crews were exhausted, having spent sixteen hours inside their tanks on 28 May, and a further twenty hours on 29 May, exiting only to refuel, to load munitions, and presumably to relieve themselves. Arzalier's verdict was that at Abbeville on 28 May under de Gaulle's direction, the 4^{e} battalion of *chasseurs alpins* lost 50 percent of its strength, while 80–90 of 180 tanks were lost.[131]

The French were learning the fundamentals of armored warfare on the fly – mass, surprise, artillery and air support, accompanying infantry to protect against ambushes by anti-tank guns, and to occupy the ground. But by that time, the 4^{e} DCr was used up – half of de Gaulle's tanks were out of action even before the Abbeville attack had been launched. Once again, despite some initial tactical success, de Gaulle was eventually forced to withdraw after losing around 300 men and most of his tanks. Delestraint concluded that the 4^{e} DCr's armored inventory – down to 74 tanks from a normal strength of 374, and half of those were diminutive Renault 35 "infantry tanks" – was insufficient to exploit a tactical success like that at Abbeville, and that it would take until the middle of June to refit the division for action again, provided it could get an infusion of new Char B1bis tanks. This suggests that the French were totally lacking the infrastructure to support an armored division – adequate tanker trucks, mechanics, recovery vehicles, and mobile motor pools to repair damaged tanks and get them quickly back into the battle. De Gaulle's *aller/retour* armored thrusts, required because he had no motorized infantry to hold ground he conquered, also meant that damaged or disabled tanks had to be abandoned rather than recovered and repaired. By the end of May, the 2^{e} DCr remained France's only armored division. But it too was so severely depleted that Delestraint declared it incapable of offensive action. While tanks continued to play a role until the end of combat, mainly covering the French retreat, Delestraint complained that French generals never understood how to mass tanks for an attack, and remained in "total ignorance" of the requirements for constant maintenance, so that they quite literally ran French tanks into the ground. "The opinion of all the commanders of tank units during this 39–40 war is that the few tanks that we had were badly deployed and often sacrificed." In part, this squandering of French tank forces followed inevitably from the fact that, from the beginning of the German offensive, French commanders were on their back foot, always forced to choose between bad options, "to play the last card." But the main reason was that the army had failed intellectually in the inter-war years to integrate tanks into a modern combined operations concept. And how could it be otherwise in the context of France's posture of strategic defense, which frittered away tanks in infantry support roles to "plug the gap?" "You can't change in the middle of a battle the mentality, the training of an army. One can't change the general concept based on defense and 'plug the gap' in poorly defended fronts … Tank warfare can't be improvized!"[132]

The significance of Montcornet, Crécy, and Abbeville in de Gaulle's retelling is that it was totally at odds with his cultural pessimism, and with his previous exultation of a professional military as superior to the citizens it defended. Once in command, his Olympian distrust of his own population infected with excessive individualism and "an anti-warrior psychosis" melted.[133] In short, in the wake of Bulson, de Gaulle paradoxically embraced the *levée*. If he could accomplish significant local tactical success with "an impoverished, weak, understrength, improvized, isolated" division, what might France have realized had it organized an elite tank army with the units already in the inventory, with an offensive mindset?[134] De Gaulle's experience as commander of the 4^{e} DCr encapsulated his paradoxical personality, a man who combined the futurist vision of H. G. Wells with the command flourish of Louis XIV. Concerned above all with the "prestige" of military authority, de Gaulle cut an imposing figure – tall, impeccably uniformed, wearing white gloves, he sought to lead through Olympian comportment and an air of unshakable confidence. The battlefield served as his stage. Exuding a regal poise, he refused to flinch as bombs fell, insisting that subordinates keep their distance so that he could remain visible to his men as he pirouetted from position to position. Unfortunately, charisma proved "the most fragile source of authority."[135] De Gaulle's "high mindedness" was unalloyed with "the virtues of humanity" that in Marc Bloch's view underpinned the *levée*.[136] This demi-person lifted from a Corneille drama, his emotions quelled in the pursuit of duty, treated his staff with "calculated brutality," addressed his subordinates in humiliating and sulfurous language, "irresponsibly" ordered one of his battalion commanders to undertake an attack whose only tactical dividend was to get people killed, and threatened to shoot a tank commander who ordered a temporary tactical withdrawal to refuel. Advice from his staff was unsolicited and unwelcomed – their job was to execute his orders unquestionably. This "egocentric" and "authoritarian" performance of late May, his indifference to casualties, offered an unpromising audition for *la France Libre*. And when the time came, no 4^e^ DCr alumni rallied to his banner – which is, however, "hardly ... significant" according to Julian Jackson, "since it was difficult for anyone to escape from France except with the most extraordinary resourcefulness"[137] – although several later joined the resistance. Opinions split on how his soldiers viewed de Gaulle's command methods – whether they secretly enjoyed seeing their officers humiliated, or if their Colonel's distant and overbearing demeanor simply constituted familiar officer behavior for most of them. Raoul Salan, commander of a Senegalese battalion in June 1940, remembered that his *5e Division d'infanterie coloniale* had loaned its white *22e régiment colonial* to Colonel de Gaulle for his attack at Abbeville on 28–29 May. As a consequence, most of them were killed or captured. "This sad episode made General de Gaulle unsympathetic to us," Salan recorded in his memoirs, although he insisted that it was Mers-el-Kébir that subsequently dissuaded him from joining de Gaulle in London.[138] As others, including Sir Edmund Spear's American wife Mary Borden-Turner were later to do, Lacouture traces de Gaulle's imperious comportment to a lacerating sense of humiliation – in this case at German insolence and disdain for French soldiers who meekly disarmed, and at a High Command that had rejected his ideas on armored warfare, and whose battlefield incompetence was on prominent display. He would demonstrate through his energy, courage, and self-control how to lead Frenchmen and how to fight using an armored division with success.[139]

Conclusion

While the German military was "modern," for Charles de Gaulle the *levée* lay like a dead hand on the French army and nation, stifling operational and tactical innovation, limiting the intellectual horizons of French officers, and hence constraining the foreign policy military planning options of French decision-makers. Nowhere were these limitations more apparent than in the French High Command, a highly politicized collection of elderly gentlemen who lacked the curiosity, expertise, and energy to integrate technology effectively into their operational and tactical systems, the intellectual flexibility to anticipate and react to strategic surprise, and the psychological resiliency to manage setbacks. They largely wasted the strategic breather of the *drôle de guerre*. French soldiers remained undertrained, and acquired scant knowledge about the latest weapons of war – tanks, anti-tank guns and mines, artillery and anti-aircraft artillery, and modern communications. Logistics were pre-modern, while tactical concepts, like methods of communication, remained mired in the trenches of the Great War. By the outbreak of the war, the French air force was rebuilding after almost two decades of neglect. Although French reconnaissance aircraft and bombers were slow and vulnerable, the air force had some excellent fighters, which nevertheless were poorly deployed, in part because they lacked a radar-vectored system of air defense to guide them. Aircraft were also held back from the front in keeping with a "long war" strategy. These frailties combined to allow the Germans to translate an operational surprise into a strategic walkover.

The panic of French reserve divisions at Bulson near Sedan on 13 May certainly did not help. But "non-participation" in battle was a fairly common phenomenon in most conscript armies. The remedies on the tactical level were better training to create unit cohesion, good leadership, and massive firepower. Because Bulson was not an exceptional event in warfare, it does not by itself offer evidence of French decadence. What made Bulson critical was its strategic consequences. That the French army and ultimately the Third Republic unraveled inexorably in the face of an easily anticipated tactical setback suggests the systemic fragility of France's entire political/military system. An account of May–June 1940 offers a cascade of poor decisions by Allied commanders, beginning with the Dyle–Breda Plan and its consequences. It is difficult to escape the conclusion that the Fall of France was more than a mere chronicle of bad luck and contingency. The "Blitzkrieg" may have been improvized as Frieser noted.[140] But the fall of France was no "strange victory." The arguments for contingency come down to imagining counterfactual scenarios – leaving the Seventh Army behind the Meuse, or Guderian turning east behind the Maginot Line rather than westward toward the Channel on 14 May, and for the German High Command slowing down the Panzer advance. "If only ..." Unfortunately, the German attack of 10 May 1940 laid bare the fragility of France's political–military interface.

As has been seen, French consensus over the viability of a long-war strategy had begun to erode from early 1940, if not before. Any effort made to transform Anglo-French armies into mobile, armored hard-hitting forces would no doubt have proved beyond the capacities of either army, especially in so short a time. Therefore, squatting in defensive positions with the goal of holding off the initial German onslaught was probably the best option open to the Anglo-French generals. However, war requires its participants to anticipate the unexpected. In the name of caution, the Third Republic's strategists, both military and political, denied the contingency of human affairs. Battle is not about applying a fixed methodology to the inert matter of war. War requires the creative interaction of two or more opponents. It creates its own milieu. Doctrine merely offers a guide, an initial game plan. Commanders require perception, imagination, and *coup d'œil* to adjust to the interface of violence. May–June 1940 offered a clash with an active German initiator, who seized the strategic initiative. It would be up to a reactive French High Command to reclaim it, as Weygand would attempt to do on the Aisne.

4 "Stand and Fight . . ."

"A Brilliant Second" – Weygand Takes Command

By the morning of 17 May, Paris was in a funk. To assuage popular anxiety, Reynaud added Pétain to his cabinet as Deputy Premier and Minister of Defense. Although this boosted the patriotic bona fides of his government and above all allowed him to give his archrival Daladier the boot, it would prove a pivotal blunder. On the same day, the French Premier compounded his misjudgment when he summoned Maxime Weygand (Figure 4.1) from the Levant to replace Daladier's discredited protégé "Gagamelin" as commander-in-chief. Weygand has attracted sympathetic Anglo-Saxon biographers, which is somewhat surprising as contemporaries gave him decidedly negative reviews. For the Third Republic, Weygand personified a civil–military rancor in jodhpurs. Any doubts were removed when his conduct during the June 1940 crisis practically amounted to a pronunciamiento to surrender. Although he conceded General Weygand's intelligence, Clemenceau had viewed him as a dyspeptic, priest-ridden intriguer, with links, it was rumored, with the shadowy *Cagoule.*[1] Pétain and authoritarian War Minister André Maginot had backed Weygand as Chief of the General Staff in 1930. Suspicious of his tepid Republican loyalties, parliament nevertheless had forced him into a humiliating public declaration of Republican fealty. Only the following year was Weygand named vice-president of the *Conseil supérieur de guerre*, the designated commander-in-chief in wartime, when Gamelin replaced him as the chief of the general staff. On Weygand's retirement in 1935, the two posts had been again combined under Gamelin.[2] Weygand's tenure at the head of the army had proven a tumultuous one that saw his plans for motorization sabotaged by Depression-era budget cuts, and the secession of the air force into an independent service. But above all, the political events of 6 February 1934 convinced him that he had to prepare both for the collapse of the French state and for war with Germany, while protecting the army from the anti-militarist attacks from the left. This experience reinforced Weygand's view that the army represented the

Figure 4.1 General Maxime Weygand, whose hostility to the Republic and fear that defeat would trigger a popular insurrection made him a prime proponent of an armistice.

best, most honorable portion of the nation that should be accorded popular respect and protected from attacks from anti-militarists. The army must assert its independence *vis-à-vis* a government that was slowly abdicating its power. According to Bankwitz, it was during his period as army chief that Weygand had concluded that the military's submission to civil authority should not be absolute.[3]

With France in crisis a decade later, Reynaud chose to overlook Weygand's violent temper, reactionary piety, contempt for politicians, obsession with an imaginary communist insurrection, and doctrinaire conviction that the army formed the pillar of the social order. Such was Reynaud's desperation in May 1940 that, rather than anticipate the risks of recalling Weygand in crisis conditions, his appointment to lead "this constellation of beaten men"[4] was hailed as Foch's reincarnation. "Small and slim, he seemed extremely young although he was actually over seventy," Beaufre remembered. "Elegant, well turned out, straightforward, amiable, but often abrupt and easily crushing, he generated immense energy and at the same time possessed astonishing physical flexibility."[5] Edgar de Larminat, serving in the Middle East at the time, attributed Weygand's willingness to take command of a battle already lost to an inflated sense of his own abilities, his disdain for Gamelin, and his self-perception as a "man of destiny," a category with so many pretenders in the summer of 1940 that the French military should have created a new rank to accommodate it.[6]

Offspring of *La Revanche*, Weygand displayed all the symptoms of unremitting Germanophobia. Anti-Dreyfusard by temperament and conviction, he bore the battle scars of the Third Republic's civil–military skirmishes. Service as Foch's Great War chief of staff anointed him with the infallibility of apostolic succession in the inter-war years. As army chief of staff and Inspector General between 1930 and his retirement in January 1935, he became an ardent – even acerbic – opponent of attempts by the Cartel des Gauches to slash his plans for army motorization. But Weygand was also victim of his own mordant personality and open contempt for Republican politicians. In this way, Weygand's politics exhibited what Richard Hofstadter later called a "paranoid style" characterized by a "sense of heated exaggeration, suspiciousness, and conspiratorial fantasy." While Hofstadter certainly did not have Weygand in mind, his description of a millennial personality fit that of France's recalled commander-in-chief, characterized by "the megalo-maniac view of oneself as the Elect, wholly good, abominably persecuted, yet assured of ultimate triumph; the attribution of gigantic and demonic powers to the adversary; the refusal to accept the ineluctable limitations and imperfections of human existence, such as transience, dissension, conflict, fallibility whether intellectual or moral; the obsession with inerrable prophecies ... systematized misinterpretations, always gross and often grotesque."[7]

Indeed, Gamelin's conciliatory attitudes and cooperation with Daladier when he succeeded Weygand in January 1935 were in large part a reaction to his predecessor's confrontational style that often had caused politicians simply to sidestep the process of civil–military consultation. Weygand lacked the diplomacy and patience to play the hand he had been dealt, to roll with the blows, to bargain for the most positive outcome, especially when dealing with a Republic that he associated with France's decadence and, to his ultramontane mind, its depravity. While one might certainly agree with Julian Jackson that Weygand harbored no ambitions to overthrow the Republic,[8] he reacted to setbacks with intemperance, which helped to win him chair 35 – Joffre's chair – among the "Forty Immortals" of the *Académie française*, where, among other things, he supported Franco after 1936, and wrote articles denouncing Republican schoolteachers and calling for a revival of "patriotic education."[9] By the time he was recalled at age seventy-three or thereabouts (Weygand's parentage remains a mystery and his birth year is disputed), the once smart cavalry officer, in Pertinax's telling, "looked like a retired jockey."[10] Spears recorded that Weygand's "parchment skin, tightly stretched over his Mongolian face, looked as if it would crack under the strain of his moving jaw." When he became excited and "was literally yelling," as was frequently the case during the month of June 1940, his "high-pitched broken voice" sounded like a concert of cats.[11]

While de Gaulle admired Weygand's candor and precision, and conceded that he had inherited on 20 May a desperate situation, the future chief of Free France complained that Weygand's military reputation had been puffed in the popular mind, conflated with that of Foch, for whom he had served as mere doorkeeper and office manager. He had never been more than "a brilliant second," a serial staff officer who had bypassed even regimental command in the course of his career climb. Recalled from four and a half years of retirement in 1939, he had spent the Phoney War inspecting sovereignty troops in the Levant and plotting to resurrect the failed Balkan strategy of the Great War. In de Gaulle's view, Weygand lacked the vision, charisma, and strength of character to lead. His conceptions of warfare were at least a generation out of date. He had no idea of the power of armored forces, of the strategic convergence "of alliances and seas," or of command as a confluence of vision, inspiration, and execution. Reynaud had handed Weygand responsibilities for which he was untutored and which he lacked the "outlook and above all the temperament" to perform. Once again, by choosing Weygand in its critical hour, the Republic, in de Gaulle's view, "had committed its habitual political error, which is called: the easy solution."[12]

Even Reynaud began to question Weygand's seemingly casual debut in his new job. The new commander-in-chief reached Paris from Beirut on Sunday 19 May at noon. He met with Reynaud and Pétain that afternoon. The next day he saw Gamelin, who explained his plan issued on 19 May to cut the "Panzer corridor" with coordinated attacks from north and south. Weygand appeared to accept the concept. However, he insisted that he must see firsthand the situation at the front and coordinate operations with General Billotte, First Army Group commander in Belgium. On paper at least, Billotte's command packed enormous power. It included the Seventh Army, now under Aubert Frère, the BEF under Gort, the First Army under General Georges Blanchard, the Ninth taken over by Giraud, the Second under Huntzinger, and the Belgians under Leopold III – in all, about one million Allied troops, most of whom were squeezed into the "Flanders pocket." Unfortunately, the situation in the Allied camp had become increasingly fluid – the Ninth and Second Armies had been virtually destroyed at Sedan. Giraud had been captured on 19 May in less than dignified circumstances while hiding in a barn, where he had been bagged by a German kitchen detachment brandishing spatulas and rolling pins. On 21 May at 7 a.m., Weygand flew out of Le Bourget for Béthune through sporadic German flak. Upon landing, he and his two accompanying staff officers were greeted by a disheveled soldier, who loaded them into the back of a commandeered Ford delivery van. They set out along roads clogged with refugees to find a phone in working order so that the commander-in-chief might actually make contact with his new command.

Weygand's plan envisaged Belgian forces holding a line along the Yser from the Scheldt through Ghent and Courtrai (Flemish Kortrijk) to Menin (Flemish Menen) to guard the western flank of an attack southward by the BEF and Blanchard's First Army toward Bapaume and Péronne. At the same time, the French Seventh Army under General Aubert Frère would pull together remnants of reserve divisions to attack northward. But to turn the elder Moltke on his head, no plan survives the first contact with one's allies. At Ypres he met a dispirited Leopold and his entourage of politicians and officers reluctant to abandon their positions and ammunition stores on the Escault and surrender much of eastern Belgium to the invader. Billotte, the army group commander, felt that Weygand's plan was too ambitious for the shaken French First Army to execute. Such was the confusion that Gort only reached Ypres in the evening after Weygand's departure. The British commander remained unconvinced by Billotte's briefing, and seemed to leave the meeting believing that the major effort would come from the south. In any case, Gort had his hands full defending Arras from Rommel. Billotte, the man tasked to coordinate Weygand's show, was badly injured in an auto accident on 21 May and died two days later without regaining consciousness.

In the event, far from clarifying the Allied situation, Weygand had spent two days wading against a tide of dispirited refugees and demoralized soldiers and their commanders whose headquarters had been turned topsy-turvy by air bombardment. Their campaign maps had huge white areas because they had no idea where their subordinate units actually were, much less the Germans, beyond the fact that the enemy seemed to be everywhere.[13] In Bloch's account, all was confusion in the Belgian pocket. "Officers whose job resembled mine never got any information at all about the enemy . . ." Nor did intelligence provide them "with what they should most certainly have known if they were to carry out their duties efficiently." The peacetime paperwork routines broke down in the fast-moving events in Flanders, where headquarters were in perpetual migration and staff officers got little sleep. Commanders lost track of their units, motorcycle couriers roared off never to return, while tactical units without orders from headquarters they failed to find simply followed the flow. Above all, the vaunted "experience" which had rationalized retaining a superannuated High Command proved powerless to cope with an unexpected, fast-moving, and to them unforeseen form of warfare. "Our war, up to the very end, was a war of old men, or of theorists who were bogged down in errors engendered by the faulty teaching of history," the historian Bloch believed.[14] The situation in Belgium had deteriorated rapidly to the point that, unable to fly back to Paris, Weygand had to be evacuated through Dunkirk on a French torpedo boat and landed at Cherbourg via Dover.

In Paris on 22 May, Weygand briefed his plan for Churchill, Reynaud, and other Allied officials and generals. But Weygand's scheme gradually unraveled as the BEF had its hands full at Arras and Gort had begun to contemplate evacuation. The Belgians were slow to readjust their positions in keeping with the overall Allied plan. By the afternoon of 23 May even Churchill had got the message and suggested that the BEF might be evacuated. Allied trust began to fray. Communications between Paris and the troops tapped in the Flanders pocket were sporadic. On 23 May, the British abandoned Boulogne without informing the French, who, having exhausted their munitions, surrendered it two days later. On the night of 23–24 May, the BEF began to withdraw toward the coast, failing to assist the Belgians who were under attack around Courtrai. In the mind of Leopold, this fully justified his 28 May request for a separate armistice. The Allied position in Belgium began to unravel as each of the commanders sought to insure the survival of his troops. Gort was convinced that the Belgians were about to crack. He also predicted that the French attack from the south would fail to materialize. And even if it did, it would lack the punch to break through. The British garrison at Calais was ordered to hold on to relieve pressure on Dunkirk. On the afternoon of 24 May, an embittered Weygand aborted his offensive, laying the blame on the British and the Belgians. Barely five days into his command, he delivered the first installment of what was to become a serial rant about the folly of France having gone to war.[15]

The only good news for the Allies was that the German advance had paused 15 miles west of Dunkirk. Why this was so subsequently became a subject of controversy. On 23 May, Gerd von Rundstedt sketched out the "close up" order because he feared that Weygand would attack the flanks of his "Panzer corridor." It was issued the following day over the protests of his corps commanders and the *Luftwaffe*. Taking credit for spectacular operational success while offloading failure onto Hitler became a popular post-war sport among surviving German generals. Hitler was culpable insofar as he rejected two pleas on 24 and 25 May to override his Field Marshal. Most Allied soldiers were still 100 kilometers from Dunkirk on 24 May, and the defense of the port was shallow. Two days later when the halt order was lifted, 28,000 British soldiers were already on their way to Britain as part of Operation Dynamo, and the defense of the port had stiffened. Various operational and logistical reasons were subsequently offered for an order that, from a German perspective, Karl-Heinz Frieser calls "one of the most serious mistakes of World War II." But in Frieser's view, the real reason was that Hitler sabotaged a potentially huge victory that might reflect well on the generals who had opposed his war in the first place. By allowing Rundstedt to pull up short of Dunkirk, the German dictator called the judgment of his generals into question. While it would be an exaggeration to say that the escape from Dunkirk of roughly 338,000 Allied soldiers lost the war for Germany, it was nevertheless a decisive turning point in German civil–military relations because power shifted in Hitler's favor and away from the General Staff. In Frieser's view, Dunkirk transformed Hitler into a warlord beyond the challenge of his knights.[16]

But if in retrospect the brief German stall before Dunkirk proved from Berlin's perspective a huge mistake, at the time it hardly appeared more than a tactical hiccup in the Anglo-French stampede toward annihilation. On 27 June, the British garrison at Calais capitulated. Among the POWs taken by the Germans were around 16,000 French and Belgian soldiers who, in Rommel's words "had not wanted to go on fighting" and instead cowered in cellars and houses.[17] On the night of 27 May, Leopold accepted unconditional surrender terms. Lack of coordination between Gort and Blanchard, Billotte's replacement as First Army Group commander, left 50,000 French troops trapped at Lille. These capitulated on the night of 31 May. On 29 May, French ships began to appear at Dunkirk to evacuate 5,000 French soldiers. The roads into Dunkirk offered a vast traffic jam of sleep-deprived soldiers, whose plight was made worse by blown bridges and the squeeze of advancing Germans. "The Army, as such, having ceased to exist," Marc Bloch plowed through the confusion of a town filled with soldiers searching for their units and officers burning their documents. Soldiers had commandeered lorries only to abandon them a few hundred yards further on. Military police "were clustered in ridiculous groups at every cross-roads." Dunkirk and the adjacent beaches were swathed in smoke from exploding shells and a burning oil refinery. The din was deafening – "the crashing of bombs, the bursting of shells, the rat-tat-tat of machine-guns, the noise of anti-aircraft batteries, and ... the persistent rattle of our own pom-poms." On that day, Churchill ordered that French troops were also to be evacuated by British ships. But the order was slow to be implemented, which meant that, in Bloch's retelling, "a sort of escape-hysteria had got hold of this mob of men. They were to all intents and purposes unarmed, and, from where they stood, packed together on the beaches, they could watch the English ahead of them already putting out to sea."[18]

The delay in evacuating French troops increased friction between the Allies as the window for evacuation was fast closing. In the last two days of the operation, the Royal Navy concentrated almost exclusively on evacuating French troops. This extraordinary feat was made possible by those manning Dunkirk's perimeter, who eventually exhausted their ammunition, then fled toward the port hoping to hop a ship. For many it was too late.[19]

"Our path led through the brickyard where elements from another Battalion of our Region [Brittany] were hidden," remembered Michel de Cazotte. "These men were completely disorganized. Some had thrown away their arms; a few had even tied white handkerchiefs to their guns. The situation arose, no doubt owing to the absence of any officer and to the news of our hopeless situation ... They tried hard to recruit more followers from my group, but to my great satisfaction, all said that where I went, they would go too. We marched in close formation through the whole crowd not losing one man. Threatening some of the most hysterical with my revolver, I was able to restore a semblance of order during our passage and the white flags vanished."

Unfortunately, the situation quickly deteriorated:

> The German attack began at dawn and we were able to hold out most of the morning. We were about as effective as the Chinese army in the Boxer days. We made some noise and looked fierce. Our armament was of course quite insufficient. We had nothing, but nothing, to stop a tank, and outside my lone machine gun, on a front of 500 yards, there was nothing else but rifles; each man having about 6 cartridges. In front of us the Herman Göring [sic] division.
>
> However, it was soon over. The fact that it hadn't ended more quickly only meant that the German advance was prudent.
>
> About the time when I was nearing the end of my ammunition for the Hotchkiss, by now red hot, I heard the Major pass the word down to me to cease fire. At the same time I looked up from the gun which I had been firing myself all morning, and saw a German soldier who had sneaked up on me from the right, unseen, pointing his Tommy gun at me, shouting: "Hände hoch!" He was only about ten yards off. Why he didn't kill me I'll never know. Anyway, Deo Gratis.[20]

For the only time in the campaign, the RAF and the French air force maintained a fitful air superiority. In all, Dynamo was a remarkable success – between 26 May and 4 June, 338,682 British and French troops were evacuated from Dunkirk. In all, 558,032 soldiers were evacuated to Great Britain by using other ports like Saint-Nazaire in Brittany, of which 368,756 were British and Canadian.[21] However, 30,000–40,000 French soldiers were abandoned at Dunkirk, largely because discipline broke down among the remaining French forces, who swarmed the jetty and prevented further evacuation. "Thus, it would seem that a breakdown in French Army organization, discipline, and morale . . . probably had more to do with this final tragedy – in which the real last-ditch defenders were left behind – than the peremptoriness often ascribed to the British," Eleanor Gates concluded.[22] Dunkirk left the Allies distrustful and divided. The British deeply resented the appalling French management of the campaign and the failure of French military leadership. The French grumbled about British disloyalty and lack of commitment to the battle. "If, for the British, the Dunkirk disaster could be accepted as the end of a bad beginning," concluded Gates, "for France it marked the beginning of the end."[23] Most of the 123,000 French troops evacuated at Dunkirk were reintroduced into France only to become POWs. The BEF escaped Dunkirk *sans* arms and equipment.

The air war began to collapse with the failure of land operations. Army requests for air support had resulted in bomber sorties being launched without fighter cover, with disastrous results. By 27 May, d'Astier refused to send bombers aloft unless fighter escorts were available. The *Grand Quartier Général Air* (GQG Air) estimated losses during May at between 649 and 704 planes, of which 429 were fighters, 100 long-distance reconnaissance planes, 75 spotter planes, and 100 bombers; 239 air force personnel had been killed and 124 wounded. It was clear that the French were losing aircraft and pilots faster than they could replace them. Nor did the GQG Air earn high marks for organizing a logistical and supply system for modern war – new planes rolling off the factory floor found no personnel to armor them, nor pilots to fly them to the front. Front-line units were short of replacement parts. Slow and vulnerable reconnaissance and spotter planes had paid a disproportionately heavy price, which was particularly tragic as the army had failed to use them to good effect, just as in 1914, in part because of a lack of radios. In early June, it was conceded too late that spotter planes should be handed over to army control. They were sent to bases in the rear to reorganize and ceased to play an effective role in the battle.[24] And while the French were very critical of the failure of the RAF to commit fully to the Battle for France, the British service sacrificed 1,029 planes and 1,526 men in

France, numbers more or less equivalent to French losses. The *Luftwaffe* lost around 1,300 planes in France.[25]

De Gaulle, who met with Weygand on 30 May, censured him for two reasons. First, the new French commander-in-chief had failed to follow de Gaulle's advice to mass France's remaining 1,200 tanks and scattered elements of armored units in two groups, one north of Paris, the other south of Reims, under the command of General Charles Delestraint, one of the French army's foremost proponents of armored forces. To this would be added two motorized infantry divisions, as well as double the regulation capacity of artillery support. In this way, the French army might have collected the means to attack the German flanks as the axis of the German attack turned south in the wake of Dunkirk. The second reason follows from the first – Weygand simply looked to exit the war. Crémieux-Brilhac declares Weygand "a Janus" who, already having decided that the war was lost, sought one final battle to recover the honor of the army, while on the political front he pressed a furious campaign for an armistice.[26] Weygand's defeatism sent a message that the war was winding down, one that gradually percolated through the echelons of command to the lower ranks, even before Pétain's infamous 17 June broadcast announcing that he would seek an armistice put the kibosh on what remained of French morale.[27]

Weygand had already raised the prospect of an armistice in a 25 May cabinet meeting, although at the time it was simply one of several alternatives discussed.[28] Nor, to be fair, was Weygand the first man to the lifeboats – after all, Reynaud had phoned Churchill on the morning of 15 May to announce that "we are beaten. We have lost the battle," although he claimed to be shocked when he learned that at General Headquarters talk of an armistice was already in the air. Reynaud complained that Weygand had wasted too much time from 19 May on his fact-finding reconnaissance, allowing a deteriorating situation to slip completely out of hand.[29] Spears believed that Weygand's vanity did not allow him to admit the shortcomings of his plan, so he blamed everyone else, especially the British, for his failure, a view supported by Crémieux-Brilhac.[30] For Eleanor Gates, Weygand's shortcomings as a commander were to persist in "schemes that had not the slimmest chance of success ... and by insisting on the primacy of French Command in the north long after it had ceased to exercise the initiative or control required by the situation ... Even allowing for the incompleteness of information available to him ... Weygand appears to have acted with a dangerous and almost inexplicable slowness throughout this crucial period." In the end, the irascible Weygand's command period only resulted in "further exacerbating the strained relations between British and French."[31]

"A National War"

Revisionists argue that the aftermath of Dunkirk coincided with an uptick in French morale and combat performance. Crémieux-Brilhac believed that Phoney War illusions and torpor had been blown away, and the trauma and shock of Bulson and the Meuse had subsided by June, so that the Battle for France finally became a "national war" for French soldiers.[32] One result was that when von Kleist opened a new phase of the German offensive with his two Panzer corps on 5 June between Amiens and Peronne, it met stiff resistance from "hedgehogs" that used 75 mm field guns as anti-tank guns to good effect. Sifting the shards of France's catastrophic defeat to find a flicker of redemption, early June witnessed a "Jacobin burst" of the sort that had characterized the original *levée*. "Early June 1940 merits a place in 'the story of French passions,'" Crémieux-Brilhac wrote. "It illustrates the persistence of patriotism and, even if it proved ephemeral, its energy." If French generals, thirteen of whom died in the course of the forty-day campaign, had proven to be unskilled and not up to the challenge of modern warfare,[33] the French army was basically sound at least on the "middle management" level, and French patriotism persisted, battered but intact in the face of the German invasion.[34] "French units fought tooth and claw in early–mid-June" Martin Alexander asserts, with something close to the *furia francese* of the original *levée*. "The battle for France after Dunkirk was a more even contest than admitted in the conventional historiography." To bolster the thesis of a patriotic renewal, revisionists cite expressions of soldierly resolve excerpted from postal censorship, French battle casualties, estimates of which have steadily declined in recent years, and "we won on my front" after-action reports of heroic and dogged defense of French soldiers in a clearly failing enterprise.[35] A further sustaining argument is provided by German battle casualties, which averaged 2,499 daily between 10 May and 3 June, and virtually doubled to 4,762 daily from 5 June to 24 June.[36]

Several factors might have contributed to this sudden – if admittedly ephemeral – *volte-face* among French soldiers, among them the destitution of some, but not all, of the least capable generals. As Cochet noted, compared with the scalpel that Joffre had taken to the French High Command in the autumn of 1914, 1940 witnessed a brief bout of Limoges lite that fell on mainly B-division generals. Nor did the sanctions invariably axe the most professionally culpable leaders. Bloch encountered one of them in late May at the headquarters of First Army commander General René Prioux near Lille, "the figure of a man slumped in a chair close to the door. Dull-eyed and gloomy, he sat there chewing innumerable cigarettes. He wore no badges of rank on his sleeve, and the personnel of the office pushed past him with no more consideration than they would have accorded to the lowest orderly. He was, in fact, a general of division who had been deprived of his command a few hours previously – for drunkenness, it was said, though with what justice I do not know."[37] That person was General François Picard, one of the French army's youngest high flyers and commander of the *1re Division légère mécanique* (DLM), a hard-hitting active service unit which constituted about the closest thing the French had to a Panzer division, equipped with SOMUA S35 medium tanks and Hotchkiss H35 light tanks, reinforced by AMD 35 Panhard 178 armored cars and AMR 35 tracked reconnaissance vehicles. In the vanguard of the Dyle–Breda scheme to bolster the Dutch army, Picard's command had been rebuffed and by 16 May had retreated to the contracting Dunkirk salient. Bloch encountered the distraught Picard on 24 May, as he awaited an exit interview with First Army Group commander General Georges Blanchard. And while the back story of Picard's dismissal initiated what was to become by far the most voluminous dossier treated by the suspect withdrawals committee, extreme fatigue rather than alcohol consumption appears a more likely explanation for any erratic behavior, real or imagined. Imagined, because Picard appears to have been the victim of a coup by a cabal of jealous and ambitious subordinates who, in the midst of combat upon which the destiny of the nation depended, capitalized on the elevation of Prioux, an ardent proponent of the continued relevance of horse cavalry on the modern battlefield, to sabotage and remove their avant-garde commander.[38]

Some French units had progressively adjusted to German tactics, while French soldiers were now less likely to panic when confronted by Panzers and Stukas. "Weygand's hedgehogs" devolved the battle onto the regimental, battalion, and company level officers where French leadership was more direct and hands-on, able to demonstrate "decisive fortitude and physical courage." Weygand's "hedgehogs" were also an attempt to exert the control of the cadres on a rapidly disaggregating soldiery, and to resuscitate the "controlled battle" concept, in which infantry and artillery were cooped together in the same enclosed space, to encourage greater communication and coordination. Major Vallette d'Osia recounted that his division in the "Weygand Line" never bothered to roll out their field telephone wire, but deployed an extra radio company and used motorcycle liaison.[39]

Furthermore, as Clausewitz predicted, combat casualties, etiolated logistics, and sheer exhaustion from a high operational tempo meant that the German offensive decelerated as it advanced. Also, by this time, the Germans had acquired a rather low opinion of French troops and might attack the "hedgehogs" head-on with insufficient caution, even dismissive arrogance, for which they sometimes paid a significant price.[40] New French divisions came on line: fourteen "light" infantry divisions, a colonial division, and three North African divisions, while Weygand belatedly began pulling thirteen "interval" divisions out of the Maginot Line. Some of the troops evacuated from Dunkirk and reintroduced into France through Cherbourg were also incorporated into the new defense scheme. This solution was "imperfect," Alexander concedes, but nevertheless "significant." And, to give Weygand his due, he locked French infantry divisions into their boxes with their artillery, ironically a sort of Jaurèsian defensive posture to maximize the strength of the *levée*. In addition, French fighters appeared more willing to take on a *Luftwaffe* that had lost 26 percent of its 4 May strength.

"Weygand's Hedgehogs" – 5–9 June 1940

Weygand's post-Dunkirk strategy to create defensive strong points along the Somme and Aisne Rivers was meant to slow down the German advance, stabilize the front, and eventually wrest the strategic initiative from the enemy (Map 4.1).[41] This should not be dismissed as a last, desperate attempt to avoid an inevitable defeat, revisionists assert. The French commander-in-chief explained the tactical concept to de Gaulle – a checkerboard of defensive boxes anchored in fortified villages facing 360 degrees with 75 mm field pieces used in an anti-tank role along a 600-kilometer front on the Somme and the Aisne rivers. According to Beaufre, the idea of a "Weygand Line" was suggested by General Aimé Doumenc, and embraced by Weygand with enthusiasm.[42] But in de Gaulle's telling, Weygand had little faith in his plan – if the British returned, if the RAF sent planes, if he could find arms for French forces evacuated from Dunkirk, "'then we might have a chance.' And the commander-in-chief added shaking his head: 'If not! . . .'"[43]

Some important contemporaries seemed to agree with Weygand's pessimistic prognosis. Reynaud expressed his discontent with what he believed to be Weygand's lack of imagination to Spears: "He has no ideas beyond fighting it out where the Army now stands and, if the front is broken through, allowing the different sections to stand their ground as long as they can. It is a simple strategic concept such as you might expect from a simple business man, a Director of Suez." (A reference to the fact that in retirement, Weygand had joined the board of the Compagnie de Suez.) Weygand's tactic was inspired by Pétain's defensive battle in Champagne in 1918. The idea was to deny the use of the roads to the

Panzers. "Above all things, should a unit find itself cut off from its neighbors it was not to withdraw but to fight on, holding up the enemy and endangering his advance. The utmost effort was to be made to deepen the zone of defense." This was vintage Great War strategy, which Spears doubted would work against an armored and mobile *Wehrmacht* that could simply bypass these strongpoints.[44]

And he was correct. Weygand's plan contained built-in conceptual flaws. Despite de Gaulle's advice to assemble his remaining armored forces, Weygand scattered them, in part because that is what French doctrine called for. The French army had lost a quarter of its strength between 10 May and 4 June, arguably its best troops – twenty-four infantry divisions, including six of the seven motorized divisions, two light cavalry divisions, and three light mechanized divisions.[45] Of its four DCrs, only one remained on paper – the 2^{e} – and its tank inventory had been severely depleted. The twenty-two divisions of the Belgian army had been destroyed, and of the ten-division BEF, only one infantry division – the 51st Highland – and part of an armored division remained on the Continent. They were joined by a British division and a Canadian division that arrived through Cherbourg and Saint-Malo. Weygand was down to sixty-six divisions, thirteen of them on the Alpine front. He was also slow to withdraw "interval troops," who were ordered out of the Maginot Line only on 13 June, almost a week after the Germans had smashed and outflanked his "hedgehogs." In all, the French Commander counted forty-three infantry divisions and three partially reconstituted armored divisions to cover a 225-mile-long front. Against this, the Germans could bring 104 divisions plus 19 in reserve. Their main attack force was organized into five armored corps, each containing two Panzer divisions and one motorized infantry division.[46] The French air force had showcased its technical and tactical backwardness, as well as its weak ground support capabilities. Nevertheless, d'Astier assembled 125 bombers and about 225 fighters. British enthusiasm for cooperating with the French was definitely on the wane. The RAF, which had lost 432 Hurricanes and Spitfires – 106 over Dunkirk – maintained only three fighter squadrons in France. Nevertheless, the RAF contributed thirty fighters and seventy bombers to support Weygand's defensive line.[47]

However, there are reasons to be skeptical of claims of a general French resurgence on the Somme and the Aisne, beginning with the fact that evidence suggests that it was in part deliberately fabricated. Spears for one questioned "moving and stirring tales of how the French infantry was resisting desperately, fighting back magnificently, making great ravages amongst the German armour, holding up the following infantry" retailed by French liaison officers about the "Weygand Line."[48] In the immediate

Map 4.1 Situation 12 June 1940. West Point Atlas.

14
HOLLAND
ZUIDER SEA
GERMANY
LUX.
SWITZERLAND
Groningen
Amsterdam
The Hague
Utrecht
Rotterdam
Dordrecht
Arnhem
Nemegen
Gennep
Wesel
Moerdijk
Breda
Essen
ZEELAND
Antwerp
Roermond
Dusseldorf
Ghent
Cologne
Louvain
Brussels
Maastricht
Aachen
B
BOCK
Wavre
Liége
Bonn
Maulde
Gembloux
Remagen
A
RUNDSTEDT
Namur
Monschau
Cambrai
Dinant
La Roche
St. Vith
Prum
Coblenz
Givet
Bastogne
Vianden
Bitburg
Peronne
St Quentin
Montherme
Mainz
NINTH
GUDERIAN
Meziers
Sedan
Arlon
Trier
C
LEEB
SECOND
TWELVE
SIXTEENTH
Luxembourg
Laon
Rethel
Montmedy
FIRST
Thionville
Reims
Saarbrucken
SECOND
Verdun
THIRD
Bitche
Dormans
Epernay
Metz
FOURTH
Chalons
FIFTH
SIXTH
Montmiral
Nancy
Vitry le Francois
Luneville
Strasbourg
4
HUNTZIGER
2
PRETELAT
Troyes
Chaumont
Mirecourt
Epinal
EIGHTH
SEVENTH
Colmar
Auxerre
Mulhouse
Nevers (12 miles)
Belfort
Vesoul
Basel
Dijon

Map 4.1 (Cont.)

aftermath of defeat, Weygand deliberately sought to publicize heroic French acts to deflect criticism of an army meant to occupy pride of place in Vichy's National Revolution. "It will not escape you that the publication of these heroic acts is meant to have a beneficial effect on the attitude of the country and to prevent the development of a campaign of denigration against the Army," Georges wrote to Blanchard on 6 July 1940.[49] In short, the generals settling in at Vichy deliberately sought to preempt and deflect well-deserved criticism of their strategic mistakes, operational backwardness, and command incompetence by planting stories in the press about heroic acts of French martial sacrifice.

Of course, Vichy's PR dilemma was how to rescue the reputation of "the army" and its High Command, while simultaneously blaming defeat on the cowardice and defeatism of French soldiers, or the neglect of French politicians. The High Command immediately realized that it would need to cloak the catastrophic performance of the French army and its High Command beneath a shroud of heroic actions. Not surprisingly, perhaps, in the wake of a defeat of such catastrophic proportions, with an estimated 1,800,000 French soldiers under German guard, Georges complained that repeated requests for heroic narratives to feed to the press had failed to materialize. Two weeks later, Vichy's Secretary of Defense repeated the request for "propaganda by precise acts" – almost a verbatim restatement of nineteenth-century anarchist Mikhail Bakunin's "propaganda of the deed" – along with officer casualty numbers, required in his view to squelch "a unhealthy propaganda that is spreading the legend that numerous French officers abandoned their soldiers." In August 1940, the war secretariat was still awaiting action on its requests for valiant battle anecdotes.[50] Vichy minted a new *Croix de guerre* for the 1940 campaign, which it distributed munificently. The army was inundated by a monsoon of *Légion d'honneurs* "*pour faits de guerre*" and *Croix de guerre*, in Crémieux-Brilhac's cynical view, in an attempt to show that the French army had "fought like lions."[51] In Sadoul's company, at the end of the campaign, only those who had been rabbit hunting had fired their rifles. Everyone handed back their packets of ammunition untouched. Of course, Sadoul was in a signals company. Nevertheless, it was announced that fifteen of them would be awarded a *Croix de guerre*. "Curious manner to decorate, after a defeat," he noted. "Generally, that might be done for the survivors of an infantry unit who had seen tough times ... But us!"[52]

One might easily have concluded that the brilliant ceremony organized by General Jean de Lattre de Tassigny on 1 August 1940 at Clermont-Ferrand – a large crowd assembled beneath tricolors snapping in the breeze, a press gallery, an impeccable march past a reviewing stand groaning with officers in dress uniform and white gloves – to pin the new *Croix de guerre* on soldiers of his Armistice Army 14^{e} DI was meant to celebrate a great victory.[53] Meanwhile, in the *Oflags* of Germany, officer POWs complained that those responsible for the defeat were rewarding themselves with promotions and decorations when in fact they should have been dragged before commissions of enquiry. The POWs, who made the real sacrifices, must content themselves with a dribble of recognition while surviving in dismal conditions.[54] Gamelin's former chief of staff, General Victor Bourret, found such ceremonies of the sort organized by de Lattre to be not only unprecedented but also positively embarrassing, even tasteless: "To declare a vanquished army the only healthy element in the nation, and to load it with compensation the abundance of which would have surprised even a victorious army," he complained after the war. "Never has one promoted, decorated, nor proffered so many honors." It confirmed the views of informed civilian opinion that the Armistice army, like its pre-war predecessor, was more focused on ceremony and public relations than on defending France. Even some on the right questioned how the French army could be both "beaten and covered with decorations."[55]

Archives are fragmentary. But assertions of a French military revival on the Somme and Aisne also invite skepticism because French military capabilities had deteriorated further after a month of battle. If Weygand was intent on populating the region with Zinderneufs-sur-Aisne, it was because the French defense had shot its bolt on the army and corps level, while the French air force focused on self-preservation in keeping with the now defunct long-war strategy. The DCr experiment had wasted away from attrition, misuse, and a lack of petrol. All of which severely narrowed Weygand's strategic options. Even when the troops were dug in, the same problems of lack of air support, a dearth of barbed wire, anti-tank guns, and mines, overly extended fronts, a cumbrous PCR artillery fire-control system, and an inability to communicate continued to plague them. On 5 June, Sadoul's company rolled out what was left of its telephone wire at Namps-au-Mont on the Somme southwest of Amiens. Units were completely mixed up and seemed to be randomly deployed. The château that served as headquarters had been thoroughly pillaged. "Behind us was an incredible field kitchen with chicken cages hanging off of it on all sides. A group of carrier pigeon troops." Initially Sadoul was encouraged – the division seemed to be holding its ground. Then at 10:00, they received orders to lighten their loads and prepare to retreat. They packed up their radio and placed it on a wagon. They soon became engulfed in a riptide of retreating soldiers and civilians, "the cohorts of defeat. There was a large number of horses, infantrymen, wagons, refugees. In a small wood, a huge traffic jam. Enemy planes circle overhead."[56]

"The Aisne and the lateral canal constituted a serious obstacle whose passage one must at all costs deny to the [German] infantry," Colonel M. Morel insisted in a generally positive assessment of the French revival on the Somme and Aisne. "The mass of the artillery must be able to fire over the entire front before, on, and beyond the river."[57] Unfortunately, French troops were no more able to prevent the Germans from crossing the Aisne on 8 June than they had been in defending on the Meuse in May, in part for the same reasons – the three battalions, which at full strength would have numbered roughly 2,400 soldiers, of the 170th Infantry Regiment at Vic-sur-Aisne had to defend a 13-kilometer front along the south bank of the river. A German reconnaissance plane, the invariable harbinger of attack, began its habitual languid orbit over French defenses on the afternoon of 7 June, untroubled by the French air force. On the morning of 8 June, mortars and artillery rained down on the 6th company, nominally 190 men but most certainly understrength by this point, responsible for a 3-kilometer-wide sector on the south bank. The Germans launched pneumatic boats and a few small fishing dinghies they had found on the north bank, which were capsized by a French machinegun. Two requests for artillery support went unanswered for unexplained reasons. But the artillery, too, had to cover large sections of front – for instance the 24ᵉ DI south of Amiens was assigned an 18-kilometer front that its divisional artillery had to support, much of it a dead ground of broken country with forests and villages. Communication problems persisted – the artillery, which depended mainly on telephones, had abandoned much of its equipment and wire in retreat, which might reduce means of communication between the infantry and its supporting artillery to runners and motorcycle dispatch riders. But the real problem, as Colonel M. Morel noted, was an overly centralized *Poste central de tir* (PCT) command system, which, along with poor communications, constricted the autonomy of commanders on the ground to respond to evolving tactical situations. Battery commanders also had to conserve munitions, whose resupply did not invariably follow the meanderings of the retreating troops. Morel sketched out a problem that was to preoccupy the suspicious withdrawals committee – why did so many French officers allegedly abandon their troops? Part of the reason was a perpetual search for supplies and ammunition: "Every evening a staff officer from the divisional artillery set out in search of munitions, and usually managed to find some," recorded Morel. The problem, concluded a separate post-war report, lay in actually distributing munitions to the batteries, because transportation, like target selection, was under divisional control. The ability of the artillery to support the infantry was also compromised by a lack of maps, so that it was virtually impossible to fix target coordinates. Reports of retreat find accounts of units guided by Michelin maps. But these were road maps, not topographical "general staff maps." Without maps, reports of air reconnaissance, or sounding devices to locate enemy batteries, the PCTs transformed into "calculation centers" to help the batteries determine the range of their targets. One advantage of Weygand's "hedgehogs" was that it allowed the French to reconstruct their PCT system. But this could only temporarily mask the fact that the army- and corps-level artillery had quickly become incapable of either distributing fire support or supplying munitions because the French army had virtually ceased to function at corps and army level.[58] Indeed, future resistance hero Major Vallette d'Osia noted that during 4–6 June, his division received only one order from the First Army, which was to hold in place, and finally joined the battle on 6 June on its own initiative. "Only on 8 June did Corps try to reclaim direction of operations by ordering a retreat, already almost impossible."[59]

With French command decision-making largely congealed, or irrelevant on the corps and division level, French positions rapidly unraveled on the Somme and the Aisne as on the Meuse due to the tactical initiative of small *Wehrmacht* units using infiltration tactics – hardly a surprise as, combined with *Auftragstaktik*, they had been the bedrock of German tactical doctrine at least since 1917. But "controlled battle" required an excessive centralization of command which condemned French commanders to linger in a stiff reactive posture.[60] As a consequence, the soldiers of the 6th company had only their rifles and a single machinegun to oppose twenty-six German infantrymen who plunged into the river and swam across. Enough reached the other side to neutralize the machinegun. Mortars silenced two other French machinegun nests. French troops were spread too thinly to counterattack, especially without artillery support. The Germans got enough troops across the river to attack the French stop line. These methods – reconnaissance aircraft as a prelude to heavy bombardment by mortars followed by improvized river crossings – were repeated at several points to give the Germans a lodgment on the south bank.[61] Meanwhile, because French infantrymen clutching their rifles waited in vain for a colonel ensconced in a PCT fire-control center kilometers away to order a battery to fire, they lacked the ability to counterattack effectively.

Luftwaffe dominance denied to the French critical intelligence on the position of German forces, and especially prevented the refueling of French tanks. "French tactics rested on aggressive defence and slowing down the German operational tempo," Alexander notes. The unraveling of the army on the Meuse and in Flanders and Dunkirk, together with the death in combat or capture of so many French flag officers, had disorganized the army- and corps-level commands. In a perverse way, this obliteration of the army's senior command echelons forced the French to decentralize command methods as infantry and artillery for better or worse were thrown back on their own resources and forced at last to cooperate. As both were now in the front lines of the hedgehogs, the need for forward observers and hence communications diminished as the artillery adjusted its sights on visual targets. Regulating the cadence of barrages might even be accomplished by whistles or by verbal commands. But German air superiority nevertheless helped to frustrate one of the main dimensions of Weygand's plan – its reliance on counterattack led by his remaining armored elements. While French tanks had proven superior to Pz.Kpfw. Is and IIs, which constituted three-quarters of the *Wehrmacht*'s tank inventory, the weaknesses of French armor persisted – commanders failed to concentrate them, their small fuel tanks gave them insufficient range, and a paucity of radios made armored movements difficult to coordinate and intelligence impossible to share. The French were surprised by the armor on the Pz.Kpfw. IIIs and IVs, which was thicker than had been reported by French intelligence. The StuG III self-propelled 75 mm cannon and 105 mm field guns blew holes in the Char B1bis, the heaviest French tank, while the outdated 37 mm gun on the Renault R35 proved no match for the high-velocity 37 mm cannon on the Pz.Kpfw. IIIs and the 47 mm cannon of the Pz.Jg. I, much less the 75 mm on the Pz.Kpfw. IV.

Nor were contemporaries as laudatory of the "hedgehogs" as some historians have been. This was in part because the strongpoint concept was not clearly communicated to subordinate units schooled in linear, phased warfare. "The development of barricades took on a considerable importance during the retreat and gave rise to an incredible diversity of dispositions, of which certain ones revealed the highest fantasy," read a post-battle autopsy. French positions were often organized according to the "lazy and easy solution" – that is, established on the forward slope, often in front of villages rather than incorporating houses into the defense. Anti-tank mines were available, but were underutilized because soldiers, including officers, were unaccustomed to them and even fearful of working with them. "The [anti-tank] battery had no personnel to lay out minefields, as everyone was needed to man the guns." Infantry officers often preempted captains in charge of the anti-tank batteries to plant mines and site anti-tank guns without cover or concealment in front of the "hedgehogs," on the mistaken assumption that the Panzers would approach along the roads and attack the strongpoints head on. This not only made these "points de resistance" visible at a distance, but also revealed their defensive fire plan. After-action reports pointed out that anti-tank guns should be manned by "choice personnel with particular characteristics: dexterity, sangfroid, decisiveness." Unfortunately, the best soldiers were too often skimmed out of the anti-tank battery for other duties. As a result, French anti-tank guns often fired prematurely at motorbikes or light vehicles, thus giving away their position. Vallette d'Osia complained that the defensive positions were overly extended, and incorporated a diversity of terrain, villages, and forest, which lowered troop density and made them difficult to defend. Above all, the "hedgehogs" lacked depth. Either the Germans overwhelmed defensive positions by massing up to sixty tanks to overpower a strongpoint, or "The tanks usually passed through the fields between the villages, to outflank and reach the rear."[62]

But according to an after-action report written from a POW camp in Germany, the entire "hedgehog" concept was "perhaps seductive in theory ... it is less so in practice, because the French soldier, when he sees the *Bosche* on his flanks or in the rear, he says we've been surrounded, without thinking that the enemy is in the same position. In reality, [hedgehogs] offer a poor man's defense," because there were not enough troops and artillery to cover all the positions. "When one doesn't have what you need to furnish the front, one says to the troops: 'It doesn't matter. Form a series of enclosed strongpoints, to fight in all directions and hold to the death.' If the enemy passes between the strongpoints, it's not important, so long as the strongpoints hold. Yes, but most of the time, a strongpoint that has been bypassed collapses!!"[63] Even Crémieux-Brilhac, who defended this early June phase of the campaign as evidence of a rebound of French morale, agreed that the appearance of a German soldier, even if he were a mere motorcyclist, to the rear of French positions set off a panic.[64]

The German tactic might be to probe these "defensive barriers" until they found a weak point to attack.[65] Then they would break into the first defensive line, and expand their foothold into the French defenses. The French would counter with quickly organized counterattacks from the "stop line" led by tanks. "But this is not an easy battle to manage," the after-action report conceded. "To do so, the command has to be well organized, units accustomed to working together, and liaisons quick and reliable." Unfortunately, this was not an accurate description of the French army in 1940, where a lack of communications and liaison was among the army's major weaknesses. Vague concepts in the regulations like "coordination" and "adaptation" simply diffused command responsibility. Orders, when they arrived, were criticized as verbose, imprecise, formulaic, and late. Initiative was discouraged among subordinate commanders by an overly centralized command culture, where orders were awaited like Moses descending with the tablets from Mount Sinai. Without doctrine, communications, and training, tanks and infantry failed to cooperate. Staffs regarded themselves as largely autonomous, and failed to liaise with neighboring units because they lacked radios and other means to communicate in any case.[66] French junior officers were discouraged from taking the "move-and-jab" *Auftragstaktik*-like counter-strokes that were fundamental to the defense of "Weygand's hedgehogs."[67] Unlike the Germans, "our cadres were too often timorous, hesitant, without audacity or initiative," complained Colonel Desroches. "Too many leaders were deficient . . . There was no desire to fight, a lack of professional competence, no concern to do good work, no enthusiasm, [just a desire] to get it over with as quickly as possible. Such soldiers were incapable of holding out, much less of vanquishing."[68] In other words, French operational and tactical concepts, and perhaps leadership and morale as well, were incompatible with the tactical initiative required to optimize the "hedgehogs."

While Weygand in theory thickened the center of his line to two divisions for 10 kilometers of front, the supporting artillery might have to cover double that distance. Artillery spotting declined to 1914 methods – direct observation by the batteries.[69] Besides, the French front repeated the error of being too shallow. By this time, the *Wehrmacht* smelled victory and often threw operational caution to the wind. Initially, Panzers tempted to attack the "hedgehogs" without artillery and infantry support might come away with a bloody nose. This taught them to return to more systematic attacks. "The German tactic consisted of attacking at selected points with a maximum of means [tanks, aviation], and then after having made a deep advance, turn back on the rear of units that had not been attacked, a procedure both economical and profitable for the attacker."[70] One advantage of attacks from the rear was that it might net French supply convoys. Colonel Robert Noirot-Nerin, who commanded the artillery for the 24^{e} DI strongpoint south of Amiens, conceded that "the horse-drawn supply convoys did their best. But their effort was clearly insufficient. Most of them fell into enemy hands on the 8th [June] when the enemy tanks coming from the west approached the rear of the division."[71]

Transport, reinforcement, and supply remained an insurmountable problem because of a reliance on horse transport, and because of poor traffic management. Traffic management seldom figures prominently in battle accounts. But it is certain that without meticulous traffic control, the German attack through the Ardennes would not have succeeded. Like every other dimension of their concept of operations, the French had expected to manage troop and supply movements behind a static front.

Unfortunately, units that became lost on the road, traffic jams at bottlenecks like bridges, or towns and villages, and the mixing of separate convoys became common in part because of the need to move at night, often with inadequate maps over unfamiliar roads. Without clear instructions or information, traffic control officers often sent units, soldiers searching for their units, and resupply convoys in the wrong direction. One officer described a scene of "automobiles and wagons going in the same direction with no order," which provoked tensions among officers to the point that some threatened to puncture the tires of vehicles that refused to give them the right of way. Disorder was transformed into chaos by the appearance of the first motorized German elements: "The first bursts of fire provoked a general panic which meant that all the vehicles [civilian and military] were abandoned on the spot."[72] While Stuka attacks may have been more noisy than destructive, their secondary effect was also to cause drivers to abandon their vehicles and flee into the countryside. They also spooked the horses, whose harnesses became irretrievably entangled in their panic to escape. Because the military police, like everyone else in the army, lacked vehicles, especially motorbikes, road discipline broke down: "Numerous elements strayed and sometimes became lost during the (approach) marches," read an after-action report from the *3e Division légère mécanique* operating in the Flanders pocket. "The principal reason resides in a lack of motorcyclists ... Only these vehicles allow orientation, surveillance of columns, and the transmission of orders during a march. One must point out that the very rare interventions of army road command were either ineffective or disastrous. Along the itinerary, mobile police must sort out traffic jams. This would have avoided the disastrous bottlenecks on the Lys and at the approach to Hondschoote. At intersections, fixed posts must orientate units toward destinations for which they have orders to proceed. It's not good enough simply to keep traffic flowing like in a fight."[73]

This road management confusion continued on the Somme and the Aisne in early June. Supply for the "hedgehogs" also suffered from the undermotorization of French forces. For instance, de Lattre grabbed all ninety of the supply vehicles allocated to the army corps for his 14e DI, and refused to release them, to the fury of the other units.[74] Major Vallette d'Osia explained that his division made a tremendous effort to assemble 2,500 vehicles to supply the Weygand line. However, the convoy that set out at 15:00 on 4 June along a single route to travel 140 kilometers to the Somme never arrived.

The misfortune was that 5 June saw the beginning of the German attack. Our column was taken apart by the aviation and the arrival of the infantry stalled by this action. The attack didn't end until toward 17:00 hours. Action by aviation on the roads continued to slow the movement of the troops in the night of the 5th–6th. On the morning of the 6th, the convoy was still 50 kilometers from where the division had hastily dug in, without food or munitions. At daylight, Army [command] gave the order to suspend all convoys and staff officers from the Division had to intervene and threaten to push through if necessary by force, to get to the units a few truckloads of munitions and a signals company. The rest of the convoy never arrived. Similar problems could have been avoided if the convoy had taken two or three separate itineraries which would have permitted the movement of the division in a single night.[75]

Barely two days after the Germans launched their 5 June attack, a huge breech had opened in the French left flank west of Amiens.[76] Strongpoints were not always organized for maximum defense, and lacked sufficient numbers of anti-tank guns, or they were badly sited. "The village of Grattepanche [south of Amiens] was seized by forty German tanks on 5 June at 8 o'clock despite the presence of six 75 mm cannon, because the defense was badly organized – far in front of the houses and with few trenches."[77] This may have been because the 75 mm cannons could not adjust for range, height, and distance fast enough to hit a Pz.Kpfw. III or IV speeding across a wheat field on the Somme at 40 kilometers per hour, and because of a lack of armor-piercing shells. Nor were there enough anti-tank guns in the French inventory, especially when the infantry had a tendency to requisition them to defend strongpoints. "You have to ask how, apart from weapons designed to defend a fixed position, can one counter a platform that is powerful, mobile, and strongly armored?," artillery Captain Convert wondered. "This inequality of force was particularly apparent on roads where columns were decimated by light tanks even before they could unhitch their guns."[78]

This was the beginning of a collapse of the French line west of Amiens where the 4th Colonial Infantry Division, attacked by the 7th Panzer Division, was responsible for a 22-kilometer front. With the French position unraveling, and fearing encirclement, on 6 June, in council with Georges, Doumenc, and General Antoine Besson, commander of the Third Army group, Weygand decided to withdraw. The retreat order went out on 7 June, a disaster in Beaufre's eyes because retreating soldiers were forced to abandon their equipment in their "hedgehogs." As at Bulson, the heavy artillery was the first to pull up stakes, in an attempt to preserve its guns from capture. Radio communication, which at last had achieved some measure of efficiency, slipped into silence as radios were loaded onto wagons, or fell into enemy hands. Thus, "the battle 'with no thought of withdrawal' had lasted forty-eight hours," Beaufre concluded.[79]

On 9 June, Rommel's Panzers, replicating the speed of the sickle cut, reached the Seine, rupturing General Altmayer's Tenth Army and cutting off the 51st Highland Division, which the French command had earlier refused permission to retreat to Rouen. The division surrendered on 12 June at Saint-Valéry-en-Caux after French troops also trapped in the Rouen–Dieppe pocket raised the white flag. At a stroke, Rommel bagged a further 40,000 Allied POWs. For the British, Saint-Valéry-en-Caux became Dunkirk without the heroic seaborne exodus. In the view of Beaufre, who accompanied General Headquarters on its quick-march migration to the south, by 9 June, "all hope was gone, the game was up, and nothing could save us."[80] From 10 June, barely a month after the Germans had crossed the Ardennes, the French army had effectively ceased to exist as a coherent force.[81]

The German Seventh Army pushed through the Maginot Line into Alsace, where three French armies were squeezed between Nancy and Belfort. French troops withdrew on the night of 10–11 June from their positions between Rethel and Montmédy. This made the defense of Paris untenable. The accretion of disheveled soldiers who had begun to appear in the capital from late May without their officers offered an initial disconcerting indication that the *levée* was imploding. At first, they were treated as deserters. But as their numbers increased, officials set up camps outside of the city so that the presence of an aggregation of disheveled and leaderless soldiers would not unsettle civilian morale. But officers driving south in civilian cars and soldiers scuttling home dressed in civilian clothes tipped off the population that the battle for France was not going well.[82] Hoping to get a cut of the spoils, on 10 June, as the French government fled Paris, Mussolini opportunistically declared war on France.

On 12 June, Weygand ordered a general retreat. Like previous French withdrawals, rather than designating large units to defend the road axes leading toward Orleans and the south, and retiring units by echelons to prearranged assembly and defensive points, with retreating units maintaining lateral contact to avoid being encircled, this quickly degenerated into another Bulson-like *sauve qui peut*. Captain Pierre Brossolette, a future resistance hero whose grave lies in Paris' Pantheon, complained that on 7 June the senior command which he and his men were meant to guard had fled without informing his battalion. This initiated "a humiliating and exhausting flight" of 60–70 kilometers a day, over highways congested with refugees, soldiers, horses, and mules, all under constant *Luftwaffe* attack, guided only by the maps on the back of PTT calendars. Soon Brossolette's battalion became strung out over 85 kilometers. By 25 June when the armistice was announced, he was south of Limoges.[83] "From 11 June [the beginning of the retreat] the artillery became very decentralized, few pieces, one or two at the maximum, few munitions, shooting 10 or 20 rounds," remembered Captain Fould.[84] Bridges destroyed by the *Luftwaffe* made every river an insurmountable obstacle for those headed south. From this point, GHQ became "just refugees on the road," according to Beaufre.[85] Officers struggled to keep their troops in hand, especially after the 10 June abandonment of Paris, which many soldiers took to signal a termination of their military obligation. In these demoralizing conditions, the appearance of the *Wehrmacht* produced for Martinet Duffreix, whose unit was overtaken on 8 June, a "moment of stupor! I was overcome by an immense lassitude. I put my revolver back in its holster . . ."[86]

Ironically, Crémieux-Brilhac rejects as calumny the oft-repeated charge that many officers abandoned their men, when in fact his platoon was captured on the Marne when his battalion commander fled in the medical officer's vehicle and the neighboring platoon vacated the field in haste without informing their neighbors, causing his unit to be surrounded.[87] "In effect, the Germans always attack in multiple places looking for the soft spot," writes Leconte. "If they hit upon a regiment or unit which has withdrawn prematurely, they infiltrate and outflank the [remaining] groups of soldiers one way or another from the breech." The result, once a unit realized they had been outflanked, might be a collective flight or surrender.[88] Crémieux-Brilhac also concedes that with Weygand's 12 June retreat order, units fragmented into leaderless groups, which contributed along with Bulson to the cowardly image of French soldiers of 1940. In a 27 September 1940 report, Captain Sébastien de Casalta complained that no action had been taken against two officers he had reported for deserting their troops on the battlefield. "Certainly, other cases are known. In the interest of discipline, I demand that all officers guilty of desertion be prosecuted."[89] By the end of September 1942, of 4,292 allegations of officer misconduct, the "*Commission d'enquête sur les repliements suspects*" had found fault in only 482 cases. What the commission's inquiries revealed was that, in the chaotic conditions of the retreat, officers most often became separated from their units when they went to the rear to search for a command post to receive orders, to establish liaison with neighboring units, or to seek resupply for units that had exhausted their ammunition and food. This was the case of Lieutenant colonel Montvignier-Monnet of the 205th Infantry Regiment, part of the ill-fated 71^{e} DI at Sedan. After thirty-six hours of combat south of Sedan, and having expended munitions and supplies, Montvignier-Monnet parked his exhausted men in a wood while he mounted a bicycle to go in search of division HQ. In the wake of the panic at Bulson, the military police manning a roadblock to intercept deserters were surprised to snag a solitary lieutenant colonel cycling down the road, and arrested him. While his division commander intervened to secure the Lieutenant colonel's release, the "affair Montvignier-Monnet" went up to army level and was considered worthy of an investigation by the commission. "The reality was that these incidents occurred out of negligence, and laisser-aller, rather than true flight in the face of the enemy," concludes Leconte.[90]

Combat units on the Aisne and Somme lost up to 10–20 percent of their officers killed or wounded. Officers in staffs or auxiliary or medical services without command responsibilities hit the road. In all, 41,000 officers eventually became POWs, or 50 percent of the French officer corps. One French general, headed to a POW camp in Germany, was evacuated toward Nancy: "We pass through a region where we fought every day. But you wouldn't think so! There were a few destroyed houses, some overturned cars, a few dead horses, but not a single human cadaver – when one compares it with 1914–1918, what a difference! The battle was always vicious and left visible traces on the ground. This time, really, our men didn't fight."[91] However, other explanations suggest that the disintegration of the army was a more subtle process; as cadres disappeared for one reason or another, units shattered or dissolved, requiring soldiers to take their own decisions.

But France's rapid implosion was not limited to the military, as the collapse of the army quickly contaminated civil society as gendarmes, mayors, sub-prefects, and prefects fled ahead of the *Wehrmacht* wave. Pillaging by refugees and soldiers began, all of which conveyed the message that the French government and society were in a state of meltdown. On 14 June, Rommel captured Le Havre and headed toward Cherbourg. Guderian attacked through Chalons-sur-Marne toward Besançon. Paris was occupied on 14 June, Dijon on 17 June, Nantes and Vichy on 19 June. Some French soldiers fought. But they were frequently dissuaded from resistance by mayors and citizens who, not wanting to see their towns become battlegrounds, hung out white sheets, prevented demolitions to set up defensive positions, and insisted that soldiers disarm (Figure 4.2).

After the war, high French casualty numbers were cited to underpin claims of a stout French defense. For instance, Pierre Pellissier declared in 1998: "An army that in six weeks counted 123,079 combat deaths isn't an army of deserters."[92] But in more recent years the high casualty figures cited by Pellissier have deflated to between 55,000 and 65,000, or fewer. In any case, French casualty figures in 1940 were far inferior to First World War casualty rates.[93] Mass surrenders of roughly 1.8 million POWs might offer an insight into the lack of will among French soldiers to fight. If one applies the same calculus as used by the British Eighth Army in 1942 to measure the ratio of those missing in action (MIAs) to

Figure 4.2 To avoid destruction, villages might display indications to the advancing Germans that they would meet no resistance.

total casualties, this means a whopping 96 percent of French "casualties" were surrenders. This is hardly surprising given the nature of a war of encirclement, and the rapid disintegration of the French army in May–June 1940. In 1942, the British Eighth Army would have taken that MIA figure as a measure of catastrophic demoralization and lack of leadership.[94] Because one is always dealing with snapshots of the 1940 campaign rather than with a comprehensive picture, casualty estimates especially for a military whose defensive capabilities rapidly deteriorated, and whose soldiers appeared increasingly incapable or unwilling to defend themselves, offer an unreliable indicator of fighting spirit.

Various explanations have been advanced for the high volume of POWs who surrendered in May–June 1940, surrenders that exceeded those of 1914, beginning with the classic generational decadence explanation. François Couchet suggests that the Great War left a profound cultural legacy that caused the succeeding generation to put limits on the sacrifices the state could ask of its citizens. The "blood tax" was at the top of their list.[95] This weakened sense of patriotic sacrifice was further accentuated by the deceptive inactivity of the Phoney War, which failed to prime French soldiers for the shock and surprise of combat. With inadequate training, too often French soldiers lacked the unit cohesion or the individual will to fight, especially when attacked by well-trained German soldiers who showed determination. German officers "led from the front," a leadership technique that yielded both tactical and psychological advantages in that they could staunch both individual lapses and collective panics of the sort that roiled the French defense.[96] Even many Great War veterans found the readjustment to combat, which brought bad memories flooding back, particularly stressful. To witness veterans break under air bombardment or throw themselves into roadside ditches, a look of terror on their faces, when a column of Panzers came roaring down the highway was particularly demoralizing.[97] This mentality of limited commitment kicked in when French defenses began to unravel. The future Colonel Dominique Magnant, a school teacher's son and self-professed pacifist who as a subaltern in the *310ᵉ Régiment d'artillerie colonial portée* was wounded in the foot and captured on 15 June, complained that officers and soldiers were fleeing to the rear: "They didn't have the least idea of their duty to stand and fight! Not the least idea!"[98]

A second, more prosaic explanation can be found in the army's failure to adapt to a war of movement, especially the lack of radios and motorization of French units. Telephones and land lines were abandoned in the retreat. Without radios, it became far more difficult to maintain the army's cohesion and to provide fire support to isolated units. When combined with "stand and fight with no thought of retreat" orders from a French High Command obviously bereft of ideas, the result was that French soldiers on foot, or trailed by a horse-drawn artillery and logistics, were overtaken and surprised by mechanized German units that often trapped and disarmed them on their way south or west, leaving the military refugees to be corralled by follow-up reserves. In this way, in May–June 1940, many would be surprised, bypassed, and captured.[99] For instance, Second Lieutenant Joseph Thirant's *159ᵉ Régiment d'artillerie à pied* stationed in Alsace was obliged to destroy four of its eight 155 mm guns when ordered to retreat to Belfort in June because they had no way to tow them to safety. His battery and several others were nevertheless caught by the Germans on 18 June and surrendered without firing a shot – artillerymen manning heavy batteries, expected to be well in the rear according to French linear concepts of battle, had been issued no rifles and machineguns with which to defend themselves.[100]

A third cause was extreme demoralization and hopelessness. Retreat, fatigue, hunger, and the breakdown of hierarchy and unit cohesion in many cases forced soldiers to grasp their own destiny, shed their uniforms, and take French leave. Even Marc Bloch, who had retreated to Rennes in Brittany, succumbed on 18 June when he spied a column of Germans 200 meters distant.

> Not a shot was fired. A number of French soldiers, including a few officers, just stood and watched ... I had long decided that I would take any step to avoid capture. Had I believed that I might, even now, be of the slightest use, I could, I hope, have screwed myself to the necessary pitch of courage to remain at my post. But now that all show of resistance had melted away, there was obviously no point in carrying on with my duties. Or, perhaps, I should put it this way: that it was more and more clearly borne in on me that the only manner in which I could continue to serve my country and my family was by escaping before the trap should finally be sprung.[101]

Nor was morale improved by tensions between soldiers and civilians, who blamed soldiers for their failure to defend the country, and who decried their indiscipline as they broke into houses to steal wine and civilian clothes. The most fantastic rumors circulated – peace had been signed, the Russians had invaded Berlin, and so on. In many areas, the "patriotic reflex" proved to be weak. Popular admiration for the Germans quickly surfaced – the Germans were "*serieux*," whereas French officers were denounced as "traitors." Many civilians sought to ingratiate themselves with the Germans, who, they hoped, would bring an end to the pillaging by French soldiers and restore order. In many places, the "patriotic reflex" against the invader was weak.[102]

To be fair to the French, large numbers of British soldiers also surrendered in 1940, the most noteworthy being the 51st Highland Division. But surrender occurs when a unit is surrounded with no chance to escape, and has exhausted its means of defense, as was the case of the men of the 51st when they were cornered against the sea at Saint-Valéry-en-Caux. In most cases, besides those garrisons left behind at Dunkirk, Boulogne, and other Channel ports, the French were not surrounded and retained the option to escape or fight on. But the link between demoralization and surrender, although contentious, caught the attention of British generals and even of Churchill in the Western Desert in 1941–1942, as they witnessed the percentage of "missing in action," compared with killed and wounded, climb steadily until it outstripped the surrender rates of

Germans and matched those of Italian soldiers in the *Panzerarmee Afrika* of 84 percent. As S. L. A. Marshall opined, in these conditions, if soldiers are offered the way out of a life-saving capitulation, they will be tempted to seize it. Morale cannot be separated from combat performance. "One fed the other," concludes Fennell.[103]

As suggested above, a fourth significant explanation is the expectation from surrendering soldiers that they will not be mistreated by their captors. The POWs' experience will be dealt with in the following chapter. However, German soldiers were quick to assure French soldiers that the war was over and that they would soon be released, which removed any reluctance among many French soldiers to down weapons, assuming that they still retained them. Finally, Pétain's 17 June broadcast, which gave the impression that an armistice was already signed, totally crumbled any residual will to resist. Sadoul gives a slightly different take, arguing that it was the evacuation of Paris that broke the morale of French soldiers. Pétain's 17 June broadcast stated his government's desire to achieve an armistice. But that is not what many soldiers heard. In fact, everyone had been impatient to hear Pétain's broadcast for some days: "So ... still nothing," Sadoul heard his officers say. "What are they waiting for? They're crazy! They don't realize the state of the French army ..."[104] If officers were done with the fight, who was left to spark a fire of resistance among the "other ranks"? Hungry and sleep-deprived soldiers began to search for scapegoats, raise white flags, pillage, get drunk, or simply sit down to await capture, which at least brought a sense of finality to the whole shambles (Figure 4.3).[105]

In eastern France, Marius Bailly remembered that columns of units still under arms, that had been bypassed by the fighting, took to the roads on foot, lurching forward for a kilometer or two, only to halt inexplicably. Officers had no information. They met stragglers on horseback or bicycle who retailed the wildest rumors. As they sat down to eat a meal prepared by their mobile field kitchens, suddenly: "A shot, raucous cries: '*Hände hoch!*' The Fritz are there. We expected them, but it was a surprise nevertheless. Everyone stood up, hands in the air ... It's done: we're prisoners." Roger Lanson explained that his unit stranded in the Vosges surrendered under the impression that they would be disarmed and sent home. Only too late did they realize that they had been "swindled." The 17 June broadcast marked the beginning of Pétain's betrayal of French soldiers. Yves Durand calculates that 50 percent of France's 1,800,000 POWs were taken between Pétain's 17 June broadcast and the actual application of the 22 June armistice on 25 June. If Bulson had witnessed a soldier panic, Pétain's misleading broadcast triggered the "mass surrender" of French units, many of which had not even fired a shot.[106]

Figure 4.3 French soldiers opting out of combat in 1940.

Surrender was not an option opened to Senegalese *tirailleurs*, who "never tried to flee. With our black skin, it would have been difficult." In fact, the *tirailleurs* experiment had taken a tragic turn. After hasty training, the largely illiterate African soldiers, with their superstitions and pidgin French, had been dispatched to the front, where they were "amalgamated" with a large number of young officers either straight from the bloated wartime officer promotions at Saint-Cyr or from other units without experience in commanding colonial troops. The consequences of understaffing, undertraining, and misunderstanding both linguistic and cultural undermined the combat value of the *tirailleurs* and soon led to an escalation of disciplinary problems. Accusations persisted that in 1940, several officers had abandoned their *tirailleurs*, and had even told them to surrender. German hostility to African soldiers, who were both feared and despised for their alleged savagery, dated from the Great War and the post-war occupation of the Saar. An unknown number of *tirailleur* POWs were shot out of hand by German troops, most notoriously at Aubigny in Burgundy and west of Lyon in retaliation for a stiff defense of the convent of Montluzin by the *25e Régiment de tirailleurs sénégalais* (RTS). Others were executed by the SS Division Totenkopf. White and black soldiers were separated and the Senegalese machinegunned. There also seem to have been executions inside Lyon, where *tirailleurs* were found hiding in the basement of the prefecture. Nor was Lyon unique. "They searched us. Pistols, wallets, pens, everything was confiscated. It's over. They ordered us to march under the amused gaze and insults of the *Boches*," remembered Captain Campos-Hugueney of the *44e Régiment d'infanterie colonial de marche sénégalais*. "It was the beginning of our captivity."[107] Jean Moulin's flight into resistance began when he refused to sign a paper inculpating African troops in the deaths of French civilians.[108]

On his drive from Tours to Bordeaux, Spears passed air force convoys, "their planes on enormous floats. Well-fed officers in touring cars led the way ... in which sat ladies whose ample proportions and commanding looks proclaimed them to be wives of senior officers." Towns were full of "idle, gaping soldiers. They were not in formations, just individuals in uniform, hanging about, evidently having been put down there and then forgotten ... How came it then that we were constantly told that all resources in manpower had been exhausted; that every available man had been thrown into battle? The answer seemed clear, the machinery of the Army had completely broken down."[109] Colonel Jacques Minart witnessed the French army disintegrate into "a dazed and worn out herd, units mixed together with service troops, hardly ten per cent retained their rifle. No automatic arms."[110] German soldiers were sometimes able to convince French soldiers to surrender without a fight, promising that they could go home. "The [Panzers] attacked with their hatches open, the crews wearing berets. This often caused mistakes that ended tragically for us. Some of them flew white flags or even tricolors [report of the 16e DI]."[111] Some soldiers simply waited for German troops to arrive in the belief that docility would make a good impression on their captors – in fact, the result was to invite disdain for men who seemed to have forfeited their soldierly honor and manly self-respect. Admonitions from commanders to resist until all resources were exhausted and to avoid capture were infrequent. French POWs rarely tried to escape, even though they were often left without guards.[112]

"A Harbinger of the End"

The 14 June occupation of Paris was a significant blow to French morale.[113] The evacuation of Paris also helped to disorganize a government that initiated an odyssey that eventually terminated in Bordeaux via the Touraine. The events that led France to exit the war are well known. In a critical 11 June meeting of the Supreme War Council at Briare, the Allies realized that their positions were incompatible – while Churchill argued that the fight must continue and that, at this point in the war at least, Germany could make no offer that would persuade Great

Britain to make peace, a spirit of defeatism had engulfed the French command. Weygand revealed himself as a French Ludendorff, eager to pin the blame for defeat on the government rather than the army.[114] He missed no opportunity to enforce his view that the war was lost and France must demand an armistice. He rejected Churchill's call for a Breton redoubt as impracticable given the disposition of French forces and the lack of resources – a contradictory position for a man who had believed that the Allies could create a maritime supplied redoubt at Dunkirk, noted Spears.[115] Not surprisingly, given the experience of the *francs-tireurs* and the Commune of 1870–1871, Churchill's proposal for guerrilla warfare was greeted with horror – Pétain insisted that such a strategy would bring on "the destruction of the country." The day before the government had decided to abandon the defense of Paris, which constituted "symbolically a harbinger of the end." The last French positions on the Seine and Marne crumbled the next day, and Weygand ordered a general retreat.[116] By this time, a furious Churchill had concluded along with the chiefs of staff that Great Britain must separate its fate from that of France. Even if the Allies managed to stabilize the front in France, Britain would be savaged by the *Luftwaffe*. The risk of continuing to dispatch British arms and men to the continent was to court defeat and surrender.[117]

Those looking to explain the Fall of France traditionally attribute it to several factors, beginning with a failure of leadership, one that pitted Weygand and Pétain against a handful of bitter-enders led by Reynaud. While it may be true that Weygand had no premeditated scheme to overthrow the Republic, he and Pétain became the main protagonists for an armistice. This should have been predictable given the man's outlook. In Weygand's universe, the army was the ultimate savior of the nation, whose "spirit" must be preserved at all costs to prevent France from succumbing to communist subversion. Never mind that the French High Command of 1940 had become a Madame Tussaud's of military mediocrity, a waxworks of bureaucratized leadership peddling an outdated doctrine and a flawed strategy, evincing no flair for command, and nurturing a smoldering resentment of parliamentary democracy which burst into flame in June 1940. In Weygand's view, the army could not be allowed to disintegrate or squandered in a misconceived and futile defense of a Breton redoubt. It must become the guarantor of internal order and the symbol of France's resurrection from the ashes of a decadent republic.[118]

At the root of the cabinet crisis which opened on 12 June lay the problem that Reynaud's strengths as a parliamentarian – the *bon mot* and rapid repartee which made him one of the Chamber of Deputies' star debaters and masked the fact that he was an independent with no significant party following – were ill-suited to the gravity of the moment. Reynaud was generally distrusted by his fellow conservatives as an anti-German "hardliner," which undermined his ability to create a consensus to continue the war.[119] Churchill's 16 June proposal of a Franco-British union was meant as a lifeline tossed to the French Premier to allow him to convince his cabinet to move to Algiers.[120] Yet, in a crisis, Reynaud proved an indecisive leader who allowed the pro-armistice faction, a number of whom he had recruited into his cabinet, gradually to gain the ascendency. Julian Jackson argues that the differences between a weak and pliant Reynaud and a stalwart Churchill have been overblown. Both men were political mavericks with a weak parliamentary base surrounded by defeatists. The difference was that Britain had not been invaded. The public mood in Britain eventually warmed to Churchill's defiant rhetoric as the Blitz gained momentum, more than Churchill's speeches firmed up British popular morale.[121] Gates, reflecting a more classic view of French defeat, wrote that Reynaud "yet lacked that inner core of confidence akin to religious fervor or mystical faith which alone enables a Churchill, a de Gaulle, a Clemenceau, or a Robespierre to inspire, to convert, to impose, and finally to triumph."[122] Imlay makes a more structural argument, that "French politics lacked an anti-fascist center." Whereas, in Great Britain, few Tories "if any subordinated their patriotic instincts to fears of losing power ... Defeating Germany remained the priority." Whereas in France the desire to continue the war was limited to the anti-fascist left, by June 1940 in Britain, the "appeasers" led by Chamberlain and Halifax had been eclipsed by Labour and dissident Tories who rallied behind Churchill to continue the war.[123]

Given a lack of consensus in a riven French political and military elite contaminated by defeatism, it would have required a Herculean effort to avoid an armistice. And in the eyes of many fellow cabinet members, military chiefs, and his British ally, the French Premier lacked the character, credibility, and following to exert that degree of leadership in a situation so fraught with danger for the nation. In crisis conditions, many viewed Reynaud with mistrust.[124] While Reynaud had tactical reasons to deceive his colleagues, in fact he undermined his position and confused the British who were trying to lend support to his refusal to seek an armistice. To be fair, neither Franklin Roosevelt nor Churchill had to deal with military leaders so inclined to push the boundaries of civilian control as were Weygand and Pétain – *autre pays, autre mœurs.* Reynaud discussed with de Gaulle the possibility of replacing Weygand with Huntzinger, who, despite his command catastrophe at Sedan, was thought, because of his experience in international missions, capable of taking a more global vision of the war than could his more parochial colleagues.[125] Too late, the French Premier realized that the entire point of Weygand's "hedgehogs" on the Somme and Aisne had been to preempt other strategic options.[126] This was possibly because he feared that Weygand would refuse to go quietly, that he might even orchestrate a coup against the government, or that Weygand's destitution would throw Pétain into opposition, which would scupper his government – the old thinking of a Third Republic politician who schemed to reorganize his cabinet as the country gurgled down the tubes. Spears, an acute if not always impartial observer of these events, wrote that Reynaud appeared to be "terrified of Pétain's resigning as he cannot face the prospect of governing in the face of the Marshal's and the Commander-in-Chief's combined and violent opposition."[127] But also, the French Premier inexplicably allowed his commander-in-chief to attend cabinet meetings, where he forced his case for an armistice in a theatrical and emotional manner, exceeding the bounds of his technical competency. What Reynaud seemed unable to recognize was that his commander-in-chief harbored a Hindenburg-like political agenda – shift the responsibility for the defeat away from the army and onto the government.[128]

Reynaud still commanded a cabinet majority on 12 June. But his arguments became wasting assets for several reasons, beginning with his lack of military expertise – Weygand belittled calls for a Breton redoubt or flight to North Africa and imperial resistance as civilian fantasy that ignored the logistical dimensions of modern conflict. Against the "fight on" crowd, who insisted that the Mediterranean constituted the new Marne, and that the empire, as an expression of national vitality, gave France manpower reserves and strategic depth, Pétain and Weygand countered with a Hexagonal strategy – the government could not abandon the French people to the occupation. The idea was irresistible under the circumstances: defeat was real, and had to be dealt with. To battle on from abroad required a leap of faith that few had the imagination or the gumption to make. For the French peasantry, the empire constituted an exotic, practically illusory concept – abstract, far-away realms valued primarily as places of exile for people "who had committed some kind of indiscretion."[129] France was "the land that doesn't lie." "To leave is to betray!" "It was an unequal fight," concludes Pierre Servent, "that of the real against the imaginary."[130] Slogans such as these masked the true agenda, which was to end the fighting and so preserve the army as the foundation for France's rebirth. Gates argues that Reynaud mishandled the famous 16 June proposal of union of the governments of Britain and France, which may have been a long shot in any case.[131] Technically, Reynaud's 16 June resignation was unnecessary as at the time a majority of the cabinet still supported him, no Chamber of Deputies existed to pass a vote of no confidence in the government, and President Lebrun favored a "Dutch solution" of declaring a ceasefire and then transferring the government abroad to continue the war. The counterargument is that military support for continuing the war eroded under Pétain's influence, while Laval had been actively unifying parliamentary opposition to Reynaud from 13 June. Churchill's calls to fight on proved counterproductive in an atmosphere of deep resentment against London, allegedly for dragging Paris into a war it was not prepared to fight. No foreign power like the United States offered to step in. Confusion reigned over the difference between a ceasefire and an armistice. The streets of Bordeaux teemed with refugees. In this atmosphere of "every man for himself," Reynaud resigned.[132]

Reynaud's exit allowed Lebrun inexplicably to name Pétain to head a new government, against the advice of Jules Jeanneney and Édouard Herriot, presidents of the Senate and Chamber, respectively. Both Lebrun and Reynaud believed that Pétain would find the German armistice conditions unpalatable and that Reynaud would reclaim the premiership in North Africa. On 17 June, Pétain announced that, "with a heavy heart, I must tell you today that fighting must cease." Not surprisingly, as a consequence French soldiers began to surrender in droves, which deprived France of the means to resist even had Hitler's terms been unacceptable.[133] Had Reynaud simply decamped to North Africa while still premier, any government organized by Pétain would have been illegitimate, and Reynaud might have played the role that de Gaulle was to assume. Unfortunately, in the view of Azéma and Wieviorka, "his ideas were stronger than his conduct." In the midst of a national crisis, Reynaud behaved as if he were dealing with just another ministerial rotation, thereby opening the door to Pétain.[134] Because Reynaud had resigned, the Vichy government was recognized diplomatically by forty countries.[135] "He was a bad picker of men – and women," was Spears' epitaph on Reynaud. "Not that his heart was in the wrong place or that he lacked nobility and courage. He did what he could, and, France having no Churchill, he was probably the best political leader she had."[136]

A second problem was that the French Premier anchored his main argument against the armistice in France's obligation to respect the 28 March 1940 alliance that precluded either government from concluding a separate peace. Memories of these fraught days have been shaped in large part by Churchill's powerful account, which invokes British resolve in the face of rising Gallic wavering and indecision. But as Julian Jackson notes, this offers a largely rear-view mirror interpretation inspired by

Churchill's defiant wartime rhetoric, the heroic conduct of the Battle of Britain, and a surge of British popular resolve. By the middle of June, long-standing French resentment against their British ally was intensifying – London had reintroduced conscription only as war loomed; had committed only ten poorly trained and armed infantry divisions to the defense of France, most of which bolted ignominiously through Dunkirk while the French held the perimeter. Finally, London's comprehensible insistence on reserving much of the RAF for defense of the home island while France's fate hung in the balance was perceived as the height of disloyalty. In the view of men like Weygand, France's grander sacrifices absolved it of any obligation toward Great Britain. On 12 June, he told Reynaud that "The country will not forgive you if, in order to remain faithful to Britain, you reject any possibility of peace."[137] On the contrary, by insisting on the integrity of the Alliance, Reynaud allowed Pétain to reframe the debate as a refusal to abandon the French people.[138]

This trending desire to capitulate was amplified by throngs of refugees who crowded into Bordeaux and whose piteous plight screamed for resolution. People were left in a state of shock as familiar social structures collapsed. Amid scenes of disorder and lawlessness, people instinctively blamed the government for what had come to pass. It made the cabinet vulnerable to calls for an armistice. As Robert Paxton notes, fighting on seemed to make no strategic sense. It even threatened France's existence, as the consequences would produce Guernica-like attacks on French cities, the use of poison gas, and a repetition of the Great War hecatomb. Survival required the restoration of order. Continued resistance could only benefit Stalin. The calculation seemed to replicate the logic of many French soldiers who surrendered to the *Wehrmacht*: if France ceased combat and behaved in a compliant way, it would benefit from more lenient armistice terms from Berlin, followed quickly by a peace conference.[139]

Frustrations focused on the 100 or so deputies who had followed the government south.[140] "Chautemps would have made a stone weep," Spears noted on 15 June. "He evoked in tear-drenched words the hungry people searching the countryside for food long since devoured by others, the exposure of children in the fields, the despair of the family whose car had run out of petrol, the motors thrown into ditches to clear the roads. It was very sad and very true."[141] In his 17 June radio broadcast, Pétain had announced: "In these dark hours, I think of the unfortunate refugees who, without resources, wander our roads. To them, I express my compassion and my solicitude."[142] Pockets of French troops gathered in Normandy, around Tours, and in the east between the Morvan and the Jura, where some fighting continued. But others began to pillage, even rape. Pétain's broadcast at 11.30 a.m. on 17 June that he had asked for armistice terms was greeted with popular relief.[143] Pierre Brossolette was shocked when his men cheered news of the armistice. "They don't understand what it means."[144] From Sadoul's perspective, 1940 was the antithesis of the *levée*, with some soldiers wishing openly to be captured, and everyone – soldiers and civilians alike – unanimous in rejecting Charles de Gaulle's appeals to fight on in June 1940, which met with no more success than had Rathenau's call for popular resistance in Germany in October 1918. "Soldiers and civilians have had enough. They want peace at any price," opined Sadoul.[145] Beaufre recounts that he was vaguely aware of de Gaulle's 18 June appeal for continued resistance. It "had our sympathy but at the time it seemed an easy way out and the least urgent of the matters in hand. The most vital task seemed somehow to drag the country out of the terrifying shambles into which defeat had plunged it."[146]

Retreat to a North African Redoubt

A strategic retreat to North Africa to continue the fight offered an option much debated by soldiers and politicians at the time, and by historians since. In June 1940, defeatists claimed that resistance from ill-prepared positions in North Africa, which had no industrial base and only one small shipyard at Bizerte in Tunisia, which was within range of Italian aircraft, amounted to folly. This view has found an echo among some historians, who argue that imperial resistance was a non-starter largely for technical and logistical reasons, but also because German, Italian, or Spanish intervention could have made the transfer of troops and matériel to North Africa from France problematic.[147] At the time, defeatists also argued that flight to North Africa would simply make them more dependent on "les Anglo-Saxons," while the French people and institutions would remain hostage to the Nazis and their French collaborators. Better cut the best deal they could while they still held a few cards – a fleet, an empire, and a more-or-less functioning government that could keep order and negotiate the parameters of the occupation. Curiously, Weygand's defenders give their man a pass on the fact that the armistice simply entrusted the army, and indeed the country, to a German leader whose total war philosophy held that defeated countries must be subjugated, if not made to disappear altogether. Who could have imagined, they say, that the United States would enter the war; that the Nazi–Soviet Pact could not endure; that Germany, especially after Narvik, retained no maritime capacity to invade Britain; that the industrial resources of the United States dwarfed those of the Axis; and that the German operational, tactical, and technological advantages on prominent display in

1940 were wasting assets? The answer is that Reynaud, Mandel, and ultimately de Gaulle, not to mention Churchill, insisted that the Fall of France was merely an opening battle in a greater world conflict, that once disarmed, France would be at Hitler's mercy, and that French national interests required France to commit its remaining assets to aid the British and eventually Americans in winning the war. But this required the courage to realize that the war had only begun, and the foresight to imagine a United States emerging from its isolation, the inevitable fracturing of the Nazi–Soviet Pact, and the eventual mastery and defeat of a seemingly redoubtable German military machine. It also required the continuation of a British alliance that had been discredited in the eyes of many – indeed, Spears admitted that by the middle of June, his British uniform made him a target of popular hostility. It also required Weygand and his fellow defeatists to lift their vision beyond the parochial perspective of France's culture wars. Not surprisingly, the argument for retreat to North Africa fell on the deaf ears of men who believed that Britain's surrender was only weeks, if not days, away, and that the Germans were invincible merely because they had just beaten an operationally and tactically rigid and poorly trained and led French army like a rented mule.[148]

In more recent years, a counterfactual school of French Second World War history has demolished the argument that in the summer of 1940, France would have been unable to transfer enough men and matériel to French North Africa (AFN) to continue the fight. With more foresight and fortitude, and a better appreciation of the strategic situation by the French leadership, more troops, aircraft, and supplies might have been evacuated to AFN in June–July 1940 to continue the struggle. This argument insists with reason that the Blitzkrieg was bloviated propaganda, not a military doctrine. While the German offensive in France had been spectacularly successful, it had come at high costs. At the very least, the German command would have had to pause their advance for two to three weeks to allow reinforcements and logistics to catch up. According to these calculations, the German offensive could not have restarted before 4–11 July, so that the *Wehrmacht* might have reached Marseilles at the end of July at the very earliest. This arrival might have been further delayed had the French army created defensive "pockets" around the major southern ports – Marseille, Toulon, La Ciotat, Sète – and at major road intersections like Toulouse. Transfers from France to North Africa had begun on 20 June. Given the port capacity in France and AFN, a "complete rotation" would have required a mere six days, which would have allowed a significant transfer of troops and matériel. Thirty to fifty planes a day were flying out of the factories in southern

France to AFN. US aid was already expanding, and with "*primes d'accélération*" (production bonuses) might have been increased more. The combined navies of France and Great Britain would have maintained a "crushing" superiority in the Mediterranean over the Italians, so that any attempt by the Italian navy to intervene to disrupt the transfers from France to AFN, or to protect Sardinia or Tripoli from an Allied offensive, would have resulted in a Mediterranean Tsushima. The *Wehrmacht* could not have deployed to Sicily in force before the end of 1940, because that island lacked air bases. Hitler could not fight an air war simultaneously over Tunis, Algiers, and Britain, while preparing for Barbarossa. With France still in the war, Franco would have even fewer reasons to make common cause with Hitler to attack through Gibraltar into Morocco. The fact that Germany did not possess the infrastructure to sustain a long war explains why Hitler jumped at Pétain's offer of an armistice, and fended off Mussolini's demands for war spoils at French expense because he wanted to do nothing to prolong France's participation in combat.[149] In this way, AFN had the potential to become the launch pad for French resistance from 1940, rather than after November 1942.

One of the main arguments against this counterfactual scenario – that AFN lacked the population to sustain a long war – does not stand up to close scrutiny. In 1939, 340,000 mainly Muslim soldiers with French cadres had garrisoned the three territories that together comprised the French Maghreb, which had supplied fourteen infantry divisions and five cavalry brigades on mobilization. On 1 March 1940, 70,000 had transferred to France, 100,000 remained in AFN, 23,000 were in the Levant, 2,000 in the navy, and 145,000 were designated as "*forces de territoire*," or sovereignty troops.[150] On 10 May 1940, eight North African divisions were at the front in France. In all, AFN contributed twelve infantry divisions and three cavalry brigades – in all 170,000 troops – to the defense of France in 1940. In the view of Levisse-Touzé, this hemorrhage of men across the Mediterranean, together with a lack of infrastructure for supporting an air force and a navy, had offered a main argument against fighting on from North Africa in June 1940.[151] At the very moment that Paul Reynaud was contemplating evacuating troops and supplies to form a North African redoubt, military traffic continued to flow from AFN to mainland France. But, as has been seen, France's problem in June 1940 had been a lack of will, not a lack of means. If AFN provided a springboard for the liberation of France in 1944, the strategic hinterland of the Maghreb also might have supplied a sanctuary for the survival of the Third Republic. On closer inspection, the claimed lack of manpower in AFN seems to be a red herring, since AFN was to dispatch a further 110,000 men to Italy in 1943–1944, and mustered 250,000 to land in

France in 1944. According to Julie le Gac, by 1944 the French *levée* in the colonies had raised an army of 630,000 men. Charles de Gaulle's "sword of France" was to be forged with African steel. The population in North Africa had been keen to fight on in 1940. One important reference point to support this thesis is that roughly 60 percent of the initial strength of what became the French First Army in the liberation of France in 1944–1945 consisted of Muslim soldiers.[152] Obviously, had the Third Republic decamped to AFN, the history of Second World War France might have looked very different. But this did not happen. Thus, denied "virtual history" wishful thinking, the historian must deal with the "tyranny of fact."[153]

Indeed, if a lack of political will among France's military and political leadership, not an absence of manpower, material, and infrastructure, ultimately sank those who argued for fighting on, this was in part because those who opposed war had hardly been eclipsed in the post-Munich period. Rather, they had temporarily gone to ground. From the perspective of the right and of a modernizing class of technocrats, Munich had simply revealed the obvious – that France was a second-tier power whose profound political divisions rendered it incapable of decisive international action. It reinforced their view that Paris should renounce its ambitions to play a major role in Europe, and fall back on the empire.[154] In their eyes, France's precipitous unraveling offered proof that they had been correct to oppose the war. On 13 June, pro-armistice Under-secretary of State and future Vichy Foreign Minister Paul Baudouin deliberately propagated a misinterpretation of Churchill's comments during a meeting of the Supreme War Council as a green light to France to request an armistice.[155] To these men, the German armed forces appeared invincible, while the exodus of unkempt French soldiers and civilian refugees in the last stages of despair and desperation constituted a potentially explosive social and political crisis. In this context, not only did Churchill's continued defiance appear to be so much hollow British bravado, but also these defeatists gradually reasserted themselves as it became apparent that the French public looked to exit the war, maneuvering in vintage Third Republic style to achieve an armistice. Thus, to imagine an alternative counterfactual scenario, however logical, speaks more to the neurotics of decline in the present via the cult of the past and nostalgia.

The defeatists also controlled the message. In the crisis of national identity caused by the rapid and unanticipated collapse of French arms, wistful appeals to family, religion, and renewal through a return to the roots of French tradition were evoked as a tactic to seize the momentum of snowballing popular despair in order further to isolate Reynaud. The diminutive and loquacious Premier cut a poor figure next to the dignified and revered Hero of Verdun and his co-conspirator who "possesses the secrets of Foch." Up close, Spears concluded that Weygand was nothing more than "a hysterical, egocentric old man."[156] But, in the popular mind, these military leaders represented integrity, courage, perseverance, authority, conviction, and the promise of a steady hand in a crisis. Defeatists in the cabinet turned a deaf ear to Reynaud's argument that an armistice would forfeit both honor and hope, deliver the French people as captives to the occupier, alienate France from the West, and invite British retaliation.[157] Spears found it incredible that the doomsayers seemed to believe "that if they stopped fighting they could just pay up and settle down with the loss of a province or so until the time came to recover them."[158]

But in the view of Pétain and Weygand, the Anglo-French alliance having failed, France could escape British tutelage, avoid the occupation of the entire country, and craft an independent policy. Moreover, the rump of the French army could be preserved as a bulwark of public order. Fear of civil unrest of the sort that had accompanied France's defeat in 1870 was integral to right-wing anxieties of national decline, to the point that, for them, popular rebellion sparked by defeat was to be more feared than foreign occupation. Weygand warned the council of ministers that the collapse of discipline in the army portended a complete breakdown of public order should an armistice not come into force. Indeed, the swell of refugees and leaderless soldiers invited comparisons with Petrograd (Saint Petersburg) in 1917. Already, during a cabinet meeting on the night of 13 June, Weygand had dramatically announced that the communists had seized power in Paris, disarmed the police and the Republican Guard, and cut telephone communications. A simple phone call to the Paris Prefect of Police immediately exposed Weygand's claim as a blatant fabrication crafted to stampede the cabinet into an armistice. However, rather than appearing chastened, Weygand doubled down on his "campaign of intimidation," by launching into a harangue against the government for having abandoned Paris in the first place, and denouncing suggestions of fighting on from the colonies as "absurd and odious." He then stormed out of the meeting after having proclaimed that the ministers should all be arrested. Pétain followed Weygand's curtain raiser by vowing never to "desert" the French people. This episode should have triggered Weygand's immediate ouster as commander-in-chief. Unfortunately, but entirely in character, Reynaud's riposte was anemic, and decisions were postponed while the government decamped to Bordeaux.[159]

Where were those who would defend the Republic? If a monarchy requires monarchist personnel, republicans needed to step up to defend the republic.[160] Indeed, the dismemberment of the legal government under the scalpel of Pétain, considered a "Republican" general and by his own definition "apolitical," constituted Charles Maurras' "divine surprise."[161] Geography increasingly became a factor as the government's retreat southward scattered, disorientated, wore down, and isolated the bitter-enders, while disrupting the normal cabinet deliberations. According to Lacouture, Churchill hoped that François Darlan would sail his fleet to North Africa and fight on – in retrospect, a totally fantasist expectation. But because Darlan stood out from the reactionary, Catholic naval hierarchy, looking to the French Admiral to play "the man of destiny" did not seem so farfetched at the time. His father had been a Freemason, a Dreyfusard and "progressive republican" politician, whose Radical Party contacts helped to account for Darlan's meteoric career rise under the watchful eye of naval minister Georges Leygues and Albert Sarraut, twice premier in the early 1930s. But in the event, Darlan disappointed, some believed because of his profound Anglophobia, or because Pétain promised to place him at the center of power at Vichy. Declaring that "the fleet separated from its bases and shipyards is useless," Darlan shared the prevailing view that "England will be finished in a few weeks. And you know, in our Fatherland's misfortune, we don't have the right to separate the fleet from the nation."[162] Those who had engineered "*la belle flotte de Darlan*" in the inter-war years, whose strategic rationale was to keep open France's links to the colonies, had neglected to create a significant shipyard at Mers-el-Kébir, Casablanca, or even Dakar. While this must constitute a significant strategic oversight, given the political mood in 1940 and the desperation of military leaders to scapegoat the Republic and the French people for the defeat, it would have made little difference to the decision to capitulate.

Abdication of leadership in the Hexagon threw the decision to fight on to France's colonial administrators. Again, on paper this looked to be a good bet, as several of the colonial governors, high commissioners, and military commanders were Popular Front appointees. Furthermore, organizing a North African redoubt had seemed within the range of possibility, although it would have taken a team of more independent-minded and energetic functionaries than the crop in charge of the French empire in 1940. Charles Noguès, Resident General in Morocco, held the key. "*Un officier de grand style*" and "*rassembleur de l'Empire*," with a reputation as a suave diplomat who maintained friendly relations with the British, he might have kept France in the war. Noguès commanded considerable forces and controlled a strategic shoulder of Africa with a major port at Casablanca. In the view of Robert Belot, all Noguès had to do was give the word and Boisson in French West Africa; Mittlehauser, commander-in-chief for the Middle East; Puaux, High Commissioner for Syria and Lebanon; Legentilhomme in Djibouti; Resident General for Tunisia Peyrouton; and High Commissioner in Indochina Decoux most probably would have followed suit.[163] Many, including de Gaulle, had hoped in 1940 that the then sixty-four-year-old Noguès, who also since 1938 doubled as commander-in-chief of French forces in AFN, would spearhead a movement for North African resistance. Noguès personified the success of the Third Republic's social engineering project to promote class mobility and populate the top echelons of French government and administration with an intellectual elite. A country boy from the Pyrenees, Noguès had managed nonetheless to graduate from the elite *École polytechnique* into an artillery commission. In his jodhpurs, braided kepi, a Sam Browne belt that corseted his heavily decorated tunic, and clutching his signature riding crop, Noguès exuded the stylish look of a congenial country squire, rather than a rough-cut officer of *l'armée d'Afrique*. Well-spoken and urbane, his salt-and-pepper hair and jaunty moustache framing a handsome face, Noguès was just the sort of eye-catching officer the legendary Moroccan Resident General from 1912 Hubert Lyautey had enlisted to populate the front office of the Rabat Residency. Furthermore, Noguès' Republican *bona fides* had been buttressed by his marriage to the daughter of the Third Republic's most successful foreign minister and architect of France's pre-1914 Entente cordiale with Great Britain, Théophile Delcassé.

On 17 June 1940, Noguès had invited Weygand to join him in Morocco to continue the war – and the Republic – at Great Britain's side. While the most battle-worthy divisions and equipment had been dispatched to France, by some accounts, there still remained the possibility of raising up to 400,000 troops, including native auxiliaries, in AFN.[164] The French navy was largely intact and much of it concentrated in the Mediterranean, or could steam there quickly from Brest and other Atlantic ports. Significant material and numerous aircraft existed in southern France that might have hopped to AFN. Noguès also had support from a significant population of military veterans in North Africa, both European and Muslim, as well as the British, who dispatched Lord Gort and Duff Cooper on 26 June to encourage him to resist. Pétain was not a particularly popular figure in Morocco, where resentment over his role in the 1925 ousting of then Resident General Hubert Lyautey in the midst of the Rif War lingered. (Indeed, Pétain's role in Lyautey's defenestration had initiated de Gaulle's disenchantment with his then professional mentor.) Noguès also feared both that an armistice might trigger indigenous unrest and that AFN might be parceled out between the Italians and the Spaniards, who had taken advantage of France's defeat to occupy the international city of Tangier on 14 June. Noguès had even sent officers to France on 18–22 June to begin collecting matériel to ship to North Africa to continue the struggle. Therefore, although in his memoirs Alphonse Juin insisted that collecting enough troops and matériel in AFN would have been difficult to organize, public opinion, both French and Muslim in AFN, would have backed continued resistance; significant matériel might have been transported from stocks in southern France; considerable airpower could have been concentrated there; the High Seas Fleet home ported at Toulon together with the merchant marine could easily have reached North and West African ports and eventually could have been maintained and upgraded with the support of Great Britain and especially the United States; and finally, the Axis lacked the means at once successfully to invade AFN in 1940 and sustain an air assault on Great Britain.[165]

But 1940 required men of decision. And Noguès was a trimmer, who had no intention of defying whatever decision was taken in France. While Juin opined that Noguès had found no support to fight on in AFN, Levisse-Touzé insists that, on the contrary, Noguès' offer to host an emigration of the Republic to AFN emerged from a fear that failure to prolong resistance might provoke a popular uprising in AFN. At the same time, the empire was built on a foundation of hierarchy and stability. Any hint that the metropole was divided would send tremors down to the village level in the colonies. Noguès had proven reluctant to play midwife to a government of refugees and renegades "without a mandate," like those deputies on the *Massilia* which cast anchor at Casablanca on 24 June 1940. Weygand dispatched General Louis Koeltz to AFN to explain Hitler's surprisingly lenient armistice terms, although Hitler's leniency was calculated to divide the Allies and convince France to exit the war. All the insecurities that lingered from fears of a popular rebellion in France, the lack of an industrial infrastructure in AFN as a basis to continue the war, and the fear of an invasion of AFN by nine Italian divisions in Tripolitania, not to mention more in Sardinia and Sicily, possibly facilitated by roughly 120,000 settlers of Italian origin mainly in Tunisia and eastern Algeria, combined to scupper talk of resistance. The 76,500 Spanish residents principally concentrated in Oran in western Algeria might become a Fifth Column for the 100,000 troops concentrated in the Spanish zone of Morocco.[166] In these circumstances, Noguès took counsel of his fears: the specter of an invasion of Spanish troops supported by German paratroops; the impossibility of British or American help in the short term; the certainty that London's surrender was inevitable, perhaps mere days away; and pressure from his defeatist colleagues in France combined to douse any faint embers of Noguès'

Republican resistance. He echoed Pétain's capitulatory cant that "one doesn't defend the country by leaving it." Noguès arrested the refugee deputies aboard the *Massilia*, at a stroke catapulting an unknown temporary brigadier who had fled into British exile into the leadership of the resistance. With the exception of the Governor-General of Indochina, General Georges Catroux, and Félix Éboué in Equatorial Africa, France's imperial proconsuls acquiesced to the Republic's overthrow. Meanwhile, defeatists led by Weygand, Pétain, Chautemps, and Laval assembled in Bordeaux with their baggage of Anglophobia, antisemitism, moral confusion, and confidence that France could opt out of the conflict with fewer consequences than if it remained engaged. France's imperial proconsuls were not men of character, in Larminat's view, but opportunist bureaucrats and soldiers who were fundamentally defeatists and quickly overwhelmed by events. Following orders from Bordeaux constituted their safest option. In this way, legalism, a strict, when not suffocating, notion of military discipline, and the Pétain myth smothered the will to go on fighting, concludes Belot.[167] For this reason, de Gaulle "didn't pick London by chance," Levisse-Touzé concludes.[168]

Conclusion

Whether the "Fall of France" was the result of the divisions and ambivalence of French society toward the war and the ideological divisions that fractured Europe, reflected in the choices made by political decision-makers and by a lack of popular will to defend the nation, or was the result of contingent factors, has sparked a complex and continuing debate among historians that will be addressed in this book's conclusion. The Vichy regime sought to shift the blame for an extraordinary and unforeseen collapse in the space of a mere six weeks of a major power, when confronted by what French historian Jean-Pierre Azéma categorized as "an audacious raid" by sixteen German divisions, onto the shoulders of the Third Republic's politicians and a lack of fighting spirit of French soldiers.[169] Indeed, so dysfunctional was France's military machine, so out-of-date and overwhelmed were French military leaders, so quick for whatever reason were many French soldiers to opt out of combat, that a "strange victory" assessment of the *Wehrmacht*'s triumph is difficult to embrace. The "Blitzkrieg" may have been improvized as Frieser noted,[170] and France's defeat was certainly not preordained. Nevertheless, France's breathtaking military collapse followed by the armistice casts doubt on "contingency" scenarios that seem to have conjured counterfactual speculation among some historians.[171] Unfortunately, the German attack of 10 May 1940 laid bare the fragility of France's political–military interface.

Revisionists rightly insist on viewing France's collapse within an Allied context. Julian Jackson reminds us that British morale during the Phoney War was as delicate as that of the French.[172] However, Talbot Imlay insists that structural differences between the two countries were critical. In France, "the Right was increasingly prey to pacifism and anti-communism," while "the Left was divided and isolated."[173] In contrast, according to Richard Toye, in Britain, "there was no popular movement in favor of peace, although the mood was one of resignation as much as of steely determination" in the wake of Pétain's 17 June 1940 armistice announcement. The sentiment in Westminster in June 1940 was to drive Chamberlain, Halifax, and other appeasers from the government. Churchill's desire was to keep fear of invasion high, because this stimulated British resolve. His "Finest Hour" speech delivered to parliament on 18 June – the same day that de Gaulle via the BBC called on the French to fight on – met with such enthusiasm that he repeated it on the radio.[174] These structural differences between France and Britain in June 1940 were critical: "In May 1940, Britain possessed a broad-based coalition government committed to Germany's defeat and an economy that, structurally speaking, was prepared for the long war that beckoned. France, by contrast, had neither a stable parliament majority behind the war effort against Germany nor an economy capable of meeting the demands of modern industrial war. Britain, in short, met the test of war better than France."[175]

For this reason, the Third Republic's leadership, or at least most of it, chose to opt out of the war, while Britain elected to continue in a conflict in which few, least of all at Bordeaux, rated London's chances of survival favorably. The British army had proven incontestably unprepared for a major ground campaign on the continent. But the Chamberlain government had invested in significant expansion and modernization of the Royal Air Force and Royal Navy, which proved critical to Britain's post-Dunkirk survival. Richard Toye concludes that British public opinion warmed to Churchill's defiant rhetoric, probably because it coincided with success in the Battle of Britain.

To flip the question, what would an Allied "victory" have looked like, and what would it have taken for Anglo-Belgian–French military forces to have produced one? Missed-opportunity mythology argues that different choices would have produced different results: formalize the Franco-Soviet pact; reform the Bank of France to finance rearmament; call Germany's bluff in 1936 or 1938; create heavy armored divisions; reform and modernize the French air force and update French army doctrine;

shake Phoney War lethargy and create "patriotic renewal" by attacking Germany from the get-go in September 1940; eschew the Dyle–Breda Plan to keep Seventh Army in reserve; find better, more modern generals; kick Pétain out of the cabinet and fire Weygand as commander-in-chief; transport the leadership of the Republic to North Africa and fight on; and so on – not only "what if?" but "if only." The multiple outcomes of "counterfactualism" when applied to 1940 are as endless as they are improbable.[176] The question became: what were the options for France going forward, as a German-imposed "New Order" settled on Europe, alongside the growth of "resistance," both external in the form of Charles de Gaulle's *France libre*, and internal, as a growing section of the French population rejected occupation and Vichy's collaboration?

5 "The War Is Over for Us"

La crise du masculin

The 1,800,000 or so French soldiers who surrendered confronted France with a catastrophe on multiple levels. The mass round-up of French soldiers who often had not even fired their weapons, and who allowed themselves to be marched off into captivity, offered a national humiliation that translated into a psychological crisis. French POWs bore witness to a society drained of military energy, devoid of political leadership, and exhausted by the perpetual demands of national grandeur. Half of the POWs were married, while 39 percent had children. That meant at least 800,000 wives were left at home to fend for themselves through the significant economic and social challenges of the Occupation. Politically, Vichy's betrayal of the very soldiers whose "honor" it vowed to uphold constituted its original sin, as hundreds of thousands of POWs and their families clung to Pétain's promises that he would work to liberate them. Control of 1.8 million French soldiers gave Berlin the whip hand in its dealings with its French client state, which helped to shape Vichy's politics of collaboration. Collaboration discouraged escape attempts, while the Germans freed French POWs only when it was in their interest to do so, which is one reason that only around 5 percent of French POWs managed to escape. The fact that many POWs who simmered for five years in *Offizierslager* represented France's intellectual, technical, and managerial elite also served as an insurance policy against a French revival, because it deprived the external and internal French resistance of both numbers and competence. The economic benefits to Germany were also considerable, as skilled workers and farmers who provided the backbone of France's industry and agriculture transitioned through *Stalags*, *Kommandos*, and other conscript labor arrangements like the *Service du travail obligatoire* (STO) to the benefit of Germany's war economy.[1]

French scholar Fabrice Virgili recounts the story of Marguerite Gonnet, department chief for the resistance group Libération-Sud, who, when asked by her military judge how she, as a mother of nine children, could be so irresponsible as to take up arms, replied: "Simply, mon Colonel, because the men dropped them." By some estimates, as many as thirty-five million people were categorized as POWs during the Second World War. And yet, until fairly recently, their removal from the battlefield also made them *hors de combat* for serious war history, leaving their story to be mythologized in Colditz-like sagas of POW resistance or sensationalized as in the forced repatriation of Soviet POWs from the West in 1945.[2] For France, the long lines of POWs in 1940 simply confirmed what Virgili calls France's "*crise du masculin*," which had asserted its grip during the inactivity of the Phoney War. Maurice Chevalier's "*excellents soldats*," who "march in step" and "only want to be left in peace," had failed to defend the nation. POWs have an insecure position in military lore, because, by surrendering, they forfeit their status as fighting soldiers and so remove themselves from the perils of the battlefield. Because the POW experience is usually confined to a minority, it can be explained away by contingent circumstances or bad luck – green units that were poorly trained or badly led; soldiers surprised, surrounded, and out of ammunition; those wounded or seized while unconscious as de Gaulle had been at Verdun in 1916; pilots shot down behind enemy lines; and so on. However, by capitulating *en masse* in 1940 and marching willingly into incarceration, failing to escape when they had the opportunity, the humiliation of POW status transferred to the French nation, a national disgrace to be redeemed by the myth of the Resistance.[3] This in turn was to create a post-war "memorial" crisis. Pétain's POWs alibi was that wholesale captures occurred because, "It was by clinging to the soil of France that they fell into the hands of the enemy," presumably a slap at de Gaulle and the men of *la France libre* who scuttled to England rather than stay and surrender like true patriots. He then sought to exploit the plight of French POWs to create a sense of social solidarity, bolster regime approval, and justify Vichy's collaboration with Germany – indeed, the regime's *raison d'être* – as a requirement to secure the release of French POWs. Guilt and a deep sense of inadequacy made French POWs in Germany "particularly receptive to Vichy's propaganda." Furthermore, Vichy misinformation about POW conditions in Germany, and the popular view that POWs had been solidly pro-Pétain, also complicated their post-war reintegration into France's war memory, because it made them resentful at their often frosty reception at home and increased their sense of victimhood.[4] This was because France was left to grapple with the place POWs, who many believed had failed the nation, should be assigned in France's firmament of villains, heroes, and victims, that included resistance fighters, *la France libre*, *l'armée d'Afrique*, work, racial, and political deportees, and the suffering of the

French population at large under foreign occupation and war. Ultimately, it impacted France's international diplomacy especially under Charles de Gaulle, as well as French popular memories of the Second World War in general.

Captivity might begin with POWs struck with rifle butts or poked with bayonets. On 11 June, Crémieux-Brilhac's section of Bretons was surrounded on the Marne, after the platoon on their right took off leaving their backpacks behind, and the battalion commander decamped in the medical officer's car. "I never saw anything so depressing ... really depressing," he remembered. Despite the fact that he had barely fired a shot, Vichy awarded him the *croix de guerre* nonetheless because it had to show that French soldiers had "fought like lions." The new prisoners were searched several times, some of their most personal possessions pocketed by their captors. Officers were culled and led away, on occasion after having been assured by a German soldier of rank that they would be treated as "*braves soldats*." Surprised by a German "mechanical armada" at 07:00 in the morning on 7 June near Rethonvillers, near Arras, Richard Bennaïm's alpine company was thrown into complete panic. "From several meters away, we heard a guttural "Halt!" Three Germans in helmets armed with sub-machineguns advanced on us. Our response was to throw ourselves on the ground. Their fusillade began, terrible and murderous." His French squad rose and tried to flee. "Plessis kept crying, 'Mother!' ... I proposed that we shout, 'Comrades!' And Plessis immediately stood up like he was crazy and waved a white handkerchief and screamed: 'Comrades, comrades!' To which the Germans replied: 'Schnell!' and barking other words that we didn't understand, but we knew that we had to move quickly. Not one of us ever fired his weapon. We were immediately searched. My legs shook ... A plane flew low overhead. The eyes of the German who captured us twinkled with joy. His precise features would be engraved on my memory for a long time."[5]

Surrender came as a shock for which few soldiers were psychologically prepared. The first reaction to becoming a *Kriegsgefangener* or KG was surprise. "I had never, even remotely, considered this possibility," remembered Michel de Cazotte. "Killed, yes! Or wounded; that was a reasonable supposition; but, to be taken prisoner! That had never entered my mind." Most French POWs were intimidated, embarrassed, even overawed by their guards – young, agile, physically fit, well-armed, but few in number, who assured them that the war had been the fault of Jews and the English, and that the Führer would soon release them. "Some of us wept, others raged, while the slightly wounded sought bandages and disinfectants," de Cazotte recounted. "Many, I suppose, were secretly relieved to find that the storm had passed them over."[6] Crémieux-Brilhac had already been impressed by the *Wehrmacht*, whose soldiers were disciplined and well trained, who sang while they attacked, and who fired tracer bullets, which the French had never before seen. German vehicles and bridging equipment exceeded in numbers and quality anything in the French army's inventory. German uniforms and equipment were practical and efficient, designed for an army on the offensive. Only later did Crémieux-Brilhac encounter German second-echelon troops trudging behind their sturdy four-wheel wagons pulled by horses and mules. French soldiers meanwhile were stripped of their weapons, a symbolic divestment of their martial status that confirmed a defeat so rapid and humiliating that they now incarnated the dishonor of the French army. For observers, their abandoned weapons offered evidence of their cowardice and lack of fighting spirit. They loitered apprehensively and self-consciously in dirty, torn uniforms, a mismatch of ill-fitting Great War surplus, knitting from home, the ridiculous and constantly unraveling *bandes molletières*, and for many civilian footwear and even trousers. Only the khaki color of their Adrian helmets with a high central ridge distinguished them from firemen, police, or indeed "blue horizon" soldiers of the previous war. Overloaded backpacks and long overcoats crisscrossed with straps at the end of which dangled a gas mask, a canteen, and leather pouches stuffed no doubt with cartridges and other indispensable impedimenta presented the very picture of "a static combatant."[7]

The thirsty wait by the roadside in the boiling sun of the summer of 1940 could seem interminable until, eventually, a young German NCO would arrive, order them into ranks of five, and then shout, "*Links alle!*" an order that would become familiar over the next five years. Marches could seem interminable for men who were famished, already exhausted, even wounded. Many soldiers who had thrown away their helmets, or had had them taken, grabbed hats, often women's hats, out of houses along the route of march as protection from the blistering sun, which lent to these POW processions a comical, even effeminate appearance.[8] Those captured in the "Belgium pocket" were force marched toward Germany immediately. The large paving stones common on roads in Belgium were especially hard on the feet. De Cazotte complained that unlike the French army that halted for ten minutes every hour on the march, the Germans simply pushed relentlessly on to their destination.[9] Some POWs fell by the wayside, only to be kicked, even shot by the guards. Dominique Magnant, who had been partly schooled in Zurich and so spoke fluent German, complained to the young officer in charge of his POW column that many men were unable to keep up with the relentless pace for another 50 kilometers until they reached Romilly. The German officer interpreted this objection as "rebellion" and ordered the guard who had been trailing the column on a bicycle to shoot him, and then walked off. As the column of POWs parted around the pair and shuffled down the road, the guard, who had obviously exploited his unsupervised rearguard position to visit several wine cellars, mumbled drunkenly that his rifle did not work, and wobbled off on his bicycle. Magnant rejoined the column.[10]

In towns and villages, populations intimidated by the Germans, and unsure how to behave, simply stared, or sheepishly tendered a piece of bread, or a glass of cider or water, which invariably provoked a shameless rush of captives. Sometimes their German guards took pity, offering a portion of their rations. More often, their sensibilities dulled by a combination of contempt and the sheer volume of captives, for which the Germans were totally unprepared, the reaction of the guards oscillated somewhere between indifference and violence. Joseph Brun remembered that in one Belgian town, the inhabitants threw bread down on them from upper story windows, until the guards opened fire. At night, the prisoners might be shut up in churches, a machinegun pointed at the door, in town halls, barracks, schools, farms, cinemas, jails, or stables, or simply parked in a field. A light soup might be served to those willing to queue for 30 minutes or more. Any water spigot came under immediate and sustained assault.[11] Magnant's POW cohort was parked on an island in the Seine near Romilly and fed moldy bread the Germans had captured in a French supply convoy. When combined with the river water they were forced to drink, diarrhea soon infected everyone in the column.[12]

This period immediately following capture in France offered an optimum time to escape (Figure 5.1). Initially, troops in western France noticed the "indifference" of their German captors, who disarmed them and told them to go home. Some French soldiers, who went into the bag at Cherbourg on 19 June, shed their uniforms. Dressed as peasants, they might put a pitchfork on their shoulder, and hit the road. By jettisoning their arms and uniforms and self-discharging from the army, they put the war behind them, and with it the risks of combat and death, to reconvert to civilian life. Those who looked to fight on were few. On 22 June, Thierry d'Argenlieu, both a lieutenant-commander in the French navy and the man who, as Father Louis de la Trinité, doubled as the *supérieur provincial de Paris* of the Carmelite monks or Carmes, was loaded into the back of a lorry that joined a convoy of POWs headed south down the Cotentin Peninsula towards Saint-Lô. He took advantage of a rest stop to strike out across a field toward the coast, determined to find a fisherman to take him to Jersey and from there to catch a "liner" to England. He had never heard of de Gaulle, although he would soon become one of Free France's most zealous proconsuls. His reasons for escape were both personal and

Figure 5.1 French POWs being marched toward Germany 1940. Most later regretted that they had passed up this opportunity when they were lightly guarded to escape.

ideological: "I would never have dared to greet my dear mother, alive and in good health, while the enemy occupied two-thirds of France," he confessed in 1941, "and this enemy is the bitter enemy of Christian civilization ... I will never submit, alive, to today's victor."[13] Apparently, Madame d'Argenlieu was a pretty formidable character, who had dispatched five of her seven children into religious orders. The remainder of the column, minus Thierry d'Argenlieu, continued on foot to Saint-Lô, where a local school teacher recorded their arrival: "The most horrendous thing in the war, more moving than the arrival of the Germans, was the passage of ten to twelve thousand French prisoners down the route de Carentan, exhausted with fatigue," she wrote: "... there were infantrymen dressed in khaki, wearing old dirty horizon blue, aviator officers with their braided kepis, many sailors also, and numerous negroes."[14]

The garrison in the Maginot Line was kept under light surveillance as they tidied up under German supervision. "The German occupation in the region was more or less non-existent," reported Adjutant Darchen, who took advantage of a trip to town to catch a train to Metz, then Paris, and from there to the Demarcation Line, which he crossed on foot in a wood.[15] But after the 25 June armistice went into effect, German surveillance tightened. Pierre Billotte, son of the French First Army Group commander who had died in 1940, was captured near Sedan when his tank exhausted its petrol. As a POW, he became paralyzed by "the complex of humiliation that overwhelmed me since the Battle of France."[16] The French colonel in charge of the transit of de Gaulle's future son-in-law Alain de Boissieu, captured on 12 June, to *Offizierslager* or *Oflags* in Germany, required all in the POW group to pledge their word of honor that they would not attempt an escape, insisting incorrectly that evasion contravened military regulations. De Boissieu nevertheless broke the lock on the train carriage carrying them to captivity in Germany, but was too exhausted to jump out and run.[17]

De Cazotte admitted that to slip free of the crocodiles of POWs winding through forests, often with only a single German soldier leading the column, would have been no problem. But he was prevented from doing so by a combination of hunger, fatigue, and "a friendly German attitude ... assuring us that the war would be over in a few weeks, and that our detention was purely a temporary measure. We would all be home in 6 weeks or so – so, what was the use in taking unnecessary risk? Thirdly, there was the natural desire to stick together among friends under uncertain and hostile circumstances. Besides, our Major frowned upon the idea. All this accounted for our docility with which we allowed ourselves to be led through Belgium. Only later did we bitterly regret the chances that we had passively let go by."[18]

Magnant's column, which he estimated at around 1,000 POWs, was guarded by a diminutive contingent of a dozen Germans under the command of a young officer, all made trigger-happy out of fear of a POW revolt that would overwhelm them. That the rebellion never materialized sprang from the fact that the POWs were too tired and humiliated to react. Magnant arrived at his decision to escape only after several days. Yet, when he tried to find an associate to join him – indeed, a reluctance to attempt a solitary flight seemed to impede escape attempts throughout the war – he found no takers. "What's the point? The war's over. England will be invaded in eight days. Why risk being shot? We'll be sent home in trains." He finally identified an escape partner in a man who was burning to get home to Bordeaux to divorce his wife. Their trek through France on foot was hardly facilitated by people who refused to give them civilian clothes or a mayor who declined to provide civilian identity cards, all because they feared complications with the Germans. Calculating that occupied Paris was too dangerous, in July, Magnant and his escape partner crossed the Loire hidden in the back of a wagon, and split once they traversed the

Demarcation Line – one headed to Bordeaux and divorce, while Magnant sought refuge with his wife's family in Grenoble.[19]

Fear of denunciation was no mere fantasy. Throughout the war, escaped POWs, who returned to the occupied zone after effecting improbable escapes and enduring harrowing journeys, were subjected to arrest and reincarceration in Germany, sometimes as the result of denunciations from other French people, who were not always happy to see them. For instance, after returning to his home at Soulles in La Manche after an escape, René Laisney "pretended to report to the *Kommandantur* at Saint-Lô, out of fear of being denounced" by his neighbors.[20] While much has been made of the grief of marital separation, which was real, some women must have viewed the disappearance of their husbands on mobilization and even into POW camps with a certain measure of relief. Louis Even managed to escape to his home in Vauville in La Manche only to be denounced by his wife to the Germans, who recaptured him.[21] Jewish POWs ran special risks in abandoning Geneva Convention protections: "I am deeply pained to say that after an audacious escape from captivity, so brave as to be almost suicidal, and a successful return to France, Captain Lautmann, being Jewish, was seized by the Germans, nearly a year later, and executed as a hostage," de Cazotte recorded in his memoirs. "It was a great loss to his country, for minds such as his are rare and far between."[22]

Following capture, the POW migration settled in temporary homes, phase I of capture that François Boudot calls "*la mise en place*" or "settling in." For Corporal Jacques Perret, this was a tent city – three men to a tent – in a field surrounded by barbed wire.[23] Father Alexis Canu's temporary "home" became the Bellevue barracks at Saint-Lô, which he reached on 22 June after an exhausting five-day hike from Sainte-Mère-Eglise, his place of capture, right behind what four years later was to become Utah Beach, where the *2e Division blindée* under the soon to become legendary General Philippe Leclerc would splash ashore. The new arrivals scrambled to find a space among around 8,700 POWs crammed into a barracks built for 3,000 soldiers. His became a small rectangle under the barracks roof. The next day, a Sunday, following 8 a.m. muster, priests in the ranks said mass in the barrack square. A quick look around revealed that this was not a young group. With an average age of just under thirty, roughly 60 percent of POWs were husbands, fathers, and breadwinners. It was not surprising, then, that their absence would have a significant impact on French society.[24] Bean soup was served at noon, and again at 6 p.m. with a small ration of meat and bread. By 1 July, rations were supplemented by the many families who had discovered that the Germans were concentrating their captured sons and fathers at Saint-Lô's Bellevue barracks, in the middle school, the Catholic Institute in Agneaux, and the stables of the extensive stud farm. So large and pressing did the crowds become at the Bellevue barrack gates that the Germans strung barbed wire and eventually organized spaces for visitors, who were allowed a weekly 30-minute visit with their incarcerated family members. What they saw was hardly reassuring – a disheveled, dirty, morose, listless group of men dressed in a mix of uniforms and civilian attire who spent their days lounging around the barrack square.[25]

To soften the routine of three daily musters and soup, "POW society" was already beginning to organize. If not quite a forerunner of Club Med, leisure management became the focus – football teams, musical groups, masses, theater, gambling, and auctions were organized. Those with the skills to survive in these beehives of confinement began to manifest themselves – caricaturists, carvers of walking sticks (a popular favorite), and makers of assorted trinkets did a booming business, as did thieves, black marketeers, snitches, and those who sucked up to the guards. Unlike the Phoney War, however, the expectation was that the POWs would soon be liberated. In August, those with an agricultural background – about one-third of the POWs – were formed into work details to be dispatched to farms throughout the department of La Manche. Mayors were held responsible should they escape, and fines were imposed. A German soldier cycled among the farms every other day to take attendance. But the numbers on these work details could be inflated by bribing guards – Canu recounts that a twelve-man work detail might balloon to forty bodies if the sentinels were offered adequate incentives. For this reason, the Germans never knew for sure how many POWs were on "furlough" at any one time. In fact, the routine for POWs at this stage of captivity was a pretty liberal one. Work details of indeterminate size and composition were dispatched daily beyond the barrack walls. A little cash thrust into the right hands allowed POWs to visit wives installed in Saint-Lô's hotels.

A visit to town allowed POWs to get a preview of what life under occupation would be like. The entrances to Saint-Lô were covered by anti-tank barriers manned by a hefty guard. Walls were placarded with the latest decrees and instructions in German and French directed at the population. Identity checks, at once frequent and unannounced, became a new fact of life, especially at the train station. In Agneaux, the dark stone walls of the Catholic Institute, like all public buildings, had received a coat of khaki paint. Students and professors were expelled, and their classrooms occupied by 2,200 POWs captured at Cherbourg. The mayor hastily dismantled the 1914–1918 *monument aux morts* which depicted a *poilu* with his foot posed on a coal scuttle helmet. It was briefly hidden in the town hall, until the Germans discovered and destroyed it. In town, the Germans had their pick of the housing. At the very least, families and hotels were obliged to accommodate the unwelcomed visitors. POW work details dispatched into the countryside found that the occupiers had requisitioned villas, holiday camps, even entire villages along the coast, much of which was now declared a *zone interdite*. The population was pressganged to dig anti-invasion trenches, erect radar towers and so on. Fishing was limited to 3 kilometers from the shore. *Wehrmacht* squads descended on farms to requisition horses and cattle, the first in a list of items that would grow to include hunting rifles, radios, tires, batteries, copper, and tin. Ration tickets, and with them seemingly endless queues for provisions, appeared in September. Both would become a feature of French life until 1946.[26] By 1943, a ration ticket purchased 1,200 calories a day.[27]

Medical professionals – doctors, dentists, pharmacists, and medics – railway employees, gendarmes, and police officers numbered among the POWs released in August in accordance with Article 29 of the 1929 Geneva convention, which allowed the release, exchange, or repatriation of non-combatant troops, members of the medical corps, or chaplains, together with seriously ill and wounded combatants. On 2 September, officers departed for Germany – not a good sign. As a consequence, POWs at Bellevue barracks now fell under the command of the senior NCO, an adjutant. September also saw the departure of many "indigenous" POWs, some of the 69,000 held by the Germans, most of whom were scattered in *Frontstalags* and *Arbeitskommandos* throughout France to be used as laborers.[28] By the end of September, the foundations of a "POW civilization" were created as inmates organized a library, a mess, a recreation room, a store, a theater, and a mailroom.[29] Things took a turn for the worse from 20 October, however, when the Germans discovered the secret back door by the latrines that had facilitated unauthorized visits into town as well as a considerable number of escapes. But as the Germans by that time had established individual files, some of the POWs could be recaptured at home. In retaliation, furloughs were suspended, the library and the theater closed, and the barracks square placed off limits after 1830 – German time, of course, now applied throughout France. A daily session of two hours of obligatory physical exercises was imposed on the POWs to "re-establish discipline." On 22 October, the French NCOs were assembled. Fifty were chosen as "police," issued yellow armbands, and told that they would be held responsible for the conduct of the men. This did not stop escapes, however, which Canu estimated averaged two a day, even after a German guard who notoriously took cash to look the other way was busted.[30]

As Yves Durand notes, the supreme irony – and subsequently the great regret – of many POWs was their failure to *filer à l'anglaise* during this period between capture and departure for Germany, which might be any time between July 1940 and February 1941. The Germans were overwhelmed by the numbers of French soldiers who surrendered. A census was a moving target at this early stage. The *Wehrmacht*, busy securing its new territory, had few troops to spare as guards. As the Saint-Lô experience demonstrates, it was relatively easy to slip away while on a work detail, fail to return from furlough in town, bribe a guard, or simply walk out the unguarded back door of the barracks. Nevertheless, Durand estimates that only 225,000 POWs seized the opportunity to escape while still in France, or roughly 12.5 percent of captives. Azéma's more recent work judges the number of escapees to have been a mere fraction of that number.[31] In any case, a requirement for more intense surveillance and the prospect of a benefit to the German war economy initiated a transfer of POWs to the Fatherland.[32]

Several reasons are advanced for the limited recourse to escape. De Boissieu believed that escape-discouraging rumors were intentionally planted by the captors: "Germany can't keep two million French as POWs, so they'll liberate you before Christmas." Or "The invasion of England will happen in a few weeks. As soon as England signs an armistice, you'll be let go." After Mers-el-Kébir and the failed Anglo-Gaullist attack on Dakar in September 1940, "The requirement to defend the empire means that active duty cadre will be sent out to do that." "The Germans won't get collaboration by keeping the POWs," became received wisdom after the Hitler–Pétain meeting at Montoire in October 1940.[33] In Sadoul's unit, NCOs tore off their stripes on the rumor that captured NCOs would be kept prisoner while conscripts would be released. "But the soldiers said: 'if only we were made prisoners, the war would be finished for us. And tomorrow, peace would liberate us.'"[34] Once the Germans put French officers and NCOs in charge of discipline, escape became a French disciplinary infraction equated with desertion, not a blow against the enemy. Some captives failed to escape because they feared reprisals against their families, or against other POWs. As has been seen, denunciation by French snitches remained a risk. The desire to remain in a legal status was inculcated into French society. Why imperil one's future and put oneself in legal limbo when the POWs would soon be released? But, in Durand's view, the reasons for the lack of escape were psychological – "patriotic humiliation accompanied this profound sentiment of defeat." The Germans appeared young, well-armed, and invincible. The dishonor of many who had surrendered without fighting – around half by some calculations[35] – in this way contributing to the national debacle, made them too ashamed and demoralized to escape. The passivity of French POWs also may have influenced the attitude of the Germans toward them. Some studies suggest that if POWs could convey a "hyper-masculine" impression, then their captors would treat them with more respect. This was obviously not the case with French POWs.[36]

The accusation of generational failure impacted the psychology of the captives. Like reservists, POWs occupy an ambiguous status in a military firmament anxious about the morale and commitment of its members. While still considered soldiers and protected by the Geneva Convention, POWs were no longer armed combatants. The popular sentiment that the *levée* of 1940 had failed the nation, and so revealed themselves as unworthy of their fathers of 1914–1918, not to mention 1793, accompanied the national meltdown of 1940. De Gaulle shared this view: when Pierre Billotte appeared in London in 1941, after a harrowing escape from a German *Stalag* via the USSR, de Gaulle seemed ready to court martial him: "How the devil did you become a prisoner?," the Free French leader challenged. Billotte pointed out that while he had indeed been captured at Sedan, at least he succeeded in escaping, an allusion to de Gaulle's failure to do so in the First World War.[37] As Gayme points out, de Gaulle nurtured a "barely disguised contempt" for POWs, who reminded him of his incarceration in Germany from 1916–1918, as well as of the defeat of 1940. He also reviled them because Vichy manipulated POWs both as a policy and as a propaganda tool against calls by the Gaullists for continued resistance. In de Gaulle's view, POWs became non-combatants at a time when the nation – and Free France – desperately needed them.[38] Nor was de Gaulle an outlier: Richard Bennaïm returned to France in October 1941 after having gained a medical repatriation from Germany by feigning an illness. "I expected to be welcomed, if not as a hero, at least as a defender of those who had stayed at home during the war ... Well no. In the train, a nasty character in his forties with an unpleasant face and a gimpy leg, wearing a beret tilted to one side, spit out after obviously cogitating for a while: 'You didn't know how to fight, you've dishonored the French army.' The worst was that almost everyone in the compartment joined in adding: 'You are fed and housed to do nothing while the rest of us are rationed ...' Only an old woman stood up and said to the nasty character: 'You should be ashamed ... My son is a POW. Where were you, while everyone else marched off to be killed?' The nasty chap stammered something about the Germans and concluded by hitting his thigh with his fist and pointing his finger at me: 'It's not with soldiers of this caliber that we would have won the war.' ... I didn't say anything, pretending to gaze at the passing countryside. But this incident

Figure 5.2 A young woman reading a newspaper article under the headline "No! Those under twenty are not among the vanquished." Unlike their predecessors in 1914–1918, the "generation of 1940" was viewed as defeatist.

troubled and remained with me, above all because I would discover with alarm a certain France deeply infatuated with a victorious Germany, looking for scapegoats everywhere ... With the Jews eliminated, now it was the POWs responsible for the defeat."[39]

The contrast with the Great War was only relative, however (Figure 5.2). Roughly 600,000 French soldiers had been captured during those four years, mostly in periods of a fluid front in 1914 and again in 1918. While Great War French POWs had been romanticized in films like "The Grand Illusion," like victims of what was diagnosed at the time as "shell shock," they lived under a cloud of popular mistrust and suspicion of deliberate surrender to escape the perils of the battlefield.[40] Initially denied medals, back pay, even their name listed on village *monuments aux morts* had they died in captivity, their combatant status was acknowledged only belatedly and grudgingly.[41] Indeed, the fact that de Gaulle had been captured at Verdun, and spent the last years of the Great War as a German POW, constituted yet another humiliation for a man who incubated the shame of

1940. French POWs of 1940 were derided as "knights of the white flag," "soldiers with their rifle butts skyward" – an accusation that signified at once insubordination, subversion, and cowardice – and were denied access to veterans' associations.[42] But others, and not just on the left, noted that in 1940 morale collapsed at the point when the German Blitzkrieg laid bare the incompetence of a French military leadership unable to deal with what, in effect, had been a giant raid.[43] In this way, POWs dwelled firmly in the tradition of equivocal popular attitudes and a lack of secure recognition as soldiers, either at the front or at home. At best, they might be viewed as victims. They were certainly not treated as heroes. Shamed and humiliated, these freshly captured soldiers felt powerless to act, shouldering the responsibility for and the shame of defeat, as the nation dissolved around them.[44]

The Myth of Châlons-sur-Marne

In the middle of November, the first draft of "other ranks" lodged at Bellevue barracks was marched to the Saint-Lô train station. The POWs remained unsure of their destination, although civilians on their route of march warned them that they were headed for Germany. Nevertheless, the absence of official information witnessed "a prodigious renewal of oral tradition" in a time-honored military practice of attempting to make sense of calamitous or seemingly random events, or in search of consolation for misfortune.[45] One result was that, even at this stage of captivity, rumors of imminent release remained robust. "Just to leave the camp, to move, to take the train, seemed to put us on the way to the end of our miseries," remembered Jacques Perret. Everyone had an opinion on their destination. The prevailing view in Perret's group seemed to be Versailles. "I remember that a large artilleryman from Toulouse who had a slightly crazy look grabbed me by the button of my jacket: 'I swear to you. You hear, I swear on the head of my mother that we're going to Châlons.'" According to Boudot, the "myth of Châlons-sur-Marne" as a staging camp for the release was widespread among POWs.[46] At this stage of captivity, the guards were still relatively easygoing. POWs were loaded into boxcars that contained a fairly comfortable thirty men. The doors to the cars were even left open, making it relatively easy to escape had anyone bothered, which, according to Durand, none did. But this relaxed regime did not last. Soon fifty POWs or more were crushed into a single boxcar lacking even straw on the floor. Red Cross women were forbidden to bring them food. Doors were slammed and bolted. Many remembered this trip as the Calvary of their captivity. The railway cars might become intolerably hot, causing the soldiers to suffer horribly from thirst. Many even struggled to breathe in the crush of bodies and the stench of urine and feces. Once a day, these trains stopped in the middle of the countryside where the POWs were lined up so that they could relieve themselves. But most had already soiled their clothes. After barely five minutes, the guards forced this reeking, dehumanized mass back into the wagons with guttural cries and a liberal use of rifle butts.

Crémieux-Brilhac remembered his morale-shattering arrival at Trier. The POWs were herded under armed guard through streets festooned with Nazi banners, past men drinking beer on café terraces or women who averted their gaze. Sometimes, children threw rocks at them or gangs of Hitler Youth might assemble groups of citizens to taunt and jeer. But mostly, the German population had grown indifferent to an unending gush of disheveled French POWs, who resembled convicts rather than soldiers. "I can assure you," remembered Crémieux-Brilhac, "it's very depressing to be paraded without arms or helmet, exhausted, unshaven in front of these civilians ..." He noted, however, that the officer POWs were temporarily housed in German army barracks which, new and complete with showers, were positively luxurious by French army standards. He took this as an indication of the higher popular esteem enjoyed by the German army, compared with that of France.[47] *Stalag* XIID, a sorting camp for POWs sent to Germany, offered an inhospitable enclosure of barbed wire and guard towers. In retrospect, it was comparatively comfortable. De Cazotte's transit camp at Nuremberg had "ample washing facilities ... and a shower and a shave raised our spirits considerably. The food seemed to us to be very strange and not very copious, but at least there was something to eat." The inmates were free to wander within the barbed wire. He noted that the POWs had become a local tourist attraction for groups of SS, Brown Shirts (SA), Nazi "*Parteigenossen*" (party members), and even Gestapo, all festooned with their red, white, and black armbands. "They looked us over coldly as if we were animals in a zoo, barking away in their guttural speech among themselves. All had apparently well dined and were smoking vile cigars. The impression was not pleasant." Nor were the guards particularly friendly. Some POWs had even worse surprises – Gendarme Maurice Codingnon and thirty-three other French POWs were mixed with a contingent of Spanish Republicans and delivered to Mauthausen in Austria to be abused by SS guards.[48]

Many POWs entered a period of self-doubt. In Perret's view, captivity was "a very large machine" into which POWs were fed like "raw material" to be "delivered, washed, stamped, and distributed throughout Brandenburg to meet the orders. The most disturbing part of this handling of the crowds is its efficiency and premeditation."[49] This quasi-industrial process merely confirmed in the minds of many POWs the scale of the French defeat. Not only were they defeated soldiers in torn, dirty battledress, but also they might come to believe that they were an inferior form of humanity, overwhelmed by a superior civilization, one better armed and organized, whose characteristics seemed to de Cazotte to include "tenacity, perseverance, and thoroughness." From inside the camp, the idea of collaborating with a people who appeared disciplined, modern, and dynamic might appear attractive. But de Cazotte concluded that such ideas were quickly discouraged by German attempts to separate out Bretons and Corsicans in a futile effort to create divisions among the POWs, and by the irrepressible arrogance of their captors.[50]

New arrivals were divided into groups of 300–400, and dispatched to *Durchgangslager* or *Dulags* – temporary camps for enlisted POWs scattered throughout Germany, Poland, Austria, and Alsace-Lorraine. At this stage, *Dulags* might be disaffected buildings, or hardly more than tents in a muddy field, that POWs were meant to transform into more permanent and standardized *Oflags* and *Stalags*. The POWs were again searched, then taken to the delousing facility to be stripped, their clothes put in bags to be steamed. They then submitted to a ritual that was to become standard in camps in the East – all body hair was shaved before POWs were deloused, showered, painted with disinfectant, and then reunited with the bag containing their steamed apparel. They were fingerprinted and photographed with their POW number hanging from a wooden bar. Their identity tag with their matriculation number was registered in the central POW files at OKW in Berlin.[51]

Life for enlisted and NCO POWs might prove to be significantly harsher than that for officers, but was just as replete with ambiguities. *Stalags* quickly became simply administrative centers where only 5 percent of enlisted POWs were retained as medical personnel and for administrative tasks. The Germans employed POWs as secretaries or *Schreiber* to register and maintain records on POWs, track assignments to and transfers among *Kommandos*, distribute millions of letters and tens of thousands of Red Cross packages, schedule medical visits with the camp doctor, arrange transport for those eligible for repatriation, and so on. A certain number of tradesmen – cobblers, tailors, and so on – also inhabited the *Stalags*.[52] Unfortunately for the French, some of the 200,000 French-speaking Belgian POWs who arrived first in the camps had snapped up many of the administrative posts to avoid being sent to a *Kommando*. This initiated the stratification and fragmentation of the POW community that Vichy propaganda continued deceitfully to insist was a strong, organic society where social classes mingled in contemplative, monastic-like harmony. POW life was marketed to the French public as an enriching journey of self-reflection and discovery from which POWs would emerge with a strengthened sense of civic responsibility.[53] Those who managed to corral a job in a *Stalag* – most of them NCOs – were deeply resented as *planqués* (those with cushy jobs) by the other POWs.[54] As the war progressed, *Stalags* and even some *Kommandos* became active centers in the growing black market for coffee, petrol, clothes and fabric, leather, tobacco, metal, spirits, and other increasingly scarce commodities. For instance, French soldiers working at the reception center for Red Cross packages just outside of Berlin at Falkensee – *Stalag* IIID, known as the "Louvre du Falckensee" (*sic*) – were reported to be transferring large sums of money to their families in France from the proceeds of selling the contents to German civilians.[55]

The 1907 Hague Convention allowed enlisted POWs to work in non-military activities. Article 27 of the Geneva Convention added that NCOs could not be forced to work except in a surveillance or administrative capacity. This should have been enforced by the "protecting power." However, on 16 November 1940, Vichy supplanted the United States in this role. As a defeated regime desperately in need of concessions from the occupying power, Vichy lacked the leverage, the incentive, and the diplomatic status required of the "protecting power" to enforce Geneva rules. Initially, ignorance of the conventions concerning POWs meant that most of the 130,000 captured French NCOs acquiesced when the Germans sent them to harvest crops. But once they became aware of their POW rights, many refused assignment to *Kommandos*. Judging from reports, the Germans probably tolerated this until the spring of 1942 when Barbarossa stalled and the Germans needed to add all enlisted POWs, including NCOs to the workforce. From this moment, reports on camp conditions invariably contained a category of "NCOs resistant to work" – that is, NCOs who invoked their Geneva rights not to be assigned to a *Kommando*. Having no legal stick to force them to work, the Germans might offer promises of better food and conditions. They might even appeal to their patriotism: "Lately, the German authorities have told these NCOs that Marshal Pétain has expressed a desire to see them work," read a 19 March 1942 report. "The NCOs replied that they would willingly comply with the Marshal's desires, if the direct order to work was transmitted from Marshal Pétain." But it appears that German patience with work-shy French NCOs hit its limits in the spring of 1942. "NCOs resistant to work" would see their rations cut, and be incentivized in other ways limited only by the sadistic imagination of camp guards. For instance, they might be forced to do physical exercises while wearing "clogs" (large wooden shoes) literally until they dropped, only to be "forced to stand up and continue by being cudgeled." German doctors would refuse to allow them to report to sick call, and so on. And it worked: "after several months of passive resistance, all of the NCOs agreed to work to avoid bullying: [abolition of rest periods, exercises, etc. . . .]," a 19 March 1942 report stated, often after they were offered a job in their trade.[56] Ironically, the German government filed a formal complaint through the Swiss to the Americans in 1943, when they received reports that the French were cutting rations and forcing German POWs in Morocco to perform punishment exercises. But early in the war, neither the British nor the French held many German POWs, and so had little leverage with the government in Berlin, who they concluded only applied Geneva protections when it suited them and they could obtain some advantage.[57] The pro-Vichy *Trait d'union*, a newspaper sent to families of POWs, lied that those who refused to work were preventing the release of more POWs. Others were threatened with "deportation" – the euphemism for *Stalag* 325, the punishment camp at Rawa-Ruska in Poland, which began life as an internment camp for Jews.[58] Kobierzyn near Cracow, officially known as *Stalag* 369, opened in June 1942 as a punishment camp for enlisted French, Dutch, and Belgian POWs often caught in escape attempts. Originally designed for 5,000 POWs, some estimates put the population at 17,000. Facilities were rudimentary – one stove per barracks, often insufficiently supplied with coal, inadequate food – and treatment oppressive – inmates searched four times a day, forced to sleep on boards, and allowed only one shower per month.

The most inventive torture might have been that inflicted on 200 NCOs who "resisted" work at *Stalag* IIA at Neubrandenburg in April 1942, and who as a consequence were thrown into the Russian POW camp. Altogether, the Germans captured around 5,700,000 Soviet soldiers during the course of the war, over half of whom perished in captivity.[59] Although the French were given their own compound, the view from the barracks windows, and probably the stench, was intimidating. René Saugenie from La Bochellerie in the Dordogne described the conditions he witnessed among the Russians: "they are two to three thousand – lots of deaths. Collective pits containing 300 cadavers where the corpses are thrown in completely naked. Among the Russians, there's no camaraderie. They steal from each other, eat garbage, hide the corpses to collect the rations of the dead. On work details they eat grass or wheat kernels. There are lots of female soldiers who have given birth. The French POWs with German permission collect condensed milk they receive in their [Red Cross] packets, to feed the Russian babies in the *Stalag*." The appalling hygiene of Russian camps spawned typhus, which soon spread to French POWs. A POW escaped from a *Stalag* near Furstemberg complained that "The Russians crawl through the wire at night to ask for food from the French camp," bringing disease with them.[60]

Having failed at war, "the masculine activity par excellence," defeated, disoriented, corralled, transported to a foreign land, and scattered in *Oflags*, *Stalags*, and *Kommandos*, POWs needed to rebuild their masculine identity to regain their self-respect, argues Luc Capdevila.[61] This would prove difficult, because to the epitaph of "knights of the white flag" was added that of *cocu* (cuckold), for concerns about spousal fidelity became yet another torture in lives over which POWs had lost control. While Vichy propaganda celebrated POWs as an expiation of the nation's sin, and awarded their forsaken wives' iconic status in Vichy propaganda, the reality was that wives and their families were left to survive in the midst of food shortages, rationing, and rampant inflation, and with an inadequate income. Their conduct fell under intense public scrutiny, subject to gossip and even denunciations for any behavior that hinted at a lack of modesty or infidelity. This was a reprise of the theme identified by Julian Jackson that emerged in the Great War and persisted into the inter-war years of "the unfaithful wife," who manufactured defective artillery shells during the day while pursuing illicit affairs at night, while her husband faced death at the front. The *poilu* who returned in 1919 had viewed the liberated women of the 1920s, with their short skirts, bobbed hair, and newfound sense of independence, almost as an affront. This only deepened in the aftermath of the 1940 defeat, which had ended the binary world of 1914–1918, or even of Phoney War, divided by a trench barrier or beyond the Maginot Line, with the enemy imagined but invisible on "the other side." Suddenly, the enemy was among them, "large men, well built, with their tough faces and their harmonious voices," in the description of Irène Némirovsky, impeccably uniformed, flush with inflated currency, and luxuriating in the aura of victory. In comparison with their conquerors, Frenchmen seemed diminished and undernourished. Quickly, these German soldiers surrendered their anonymity, as they offered a helping hand to women whose tasks traditionally were limited to looking after the children, the animals, and the washhouse. They acquired names often of the French person or his profession with whom they billeted: "Fritz de Durand, Ewald the Blacksmith, Bruno des Angelliers."[62] Wives of POWs were isolated, often in precarious financial straits. Some no doubt sought a protector, who might deliver favors or income, and help on the farm or in the shop. Some might even be looking for adventure. Poverty and separation may have forced some wives of POWs to join the 80,000–100,000 streetwalkers the Germans estimated to be active in Paris alone. A doctor in the Loire valley reported that "minors, wives of POWs, mothers of small children are causing a veritable scandal" by going out with German soldiers, whose departure in 1944 left a between 50,000 and 70,000 offspring in their wake.[63]

Darlan allegedly latched onto the popular suspicion that unsupervised POW wives were responsible for the explosion of prostitution that hit France during the occupation as a tactic to force an increase in allowances for families of POWs. A 2 April 1941 law took aim at divorce, considered a symbol of Republican individualism and an embryo of national decline.[64] In December 1942, a Vichy law instituted severe penalties for adultery committed with a POW wife to "protect the dignity of the home." Nor could wives of POWs seek a divorce unless they had been married to their POW husband for at least three years.[65] As Capdevila notes, as the war wore on, these soldiers already "vanquished by the enemy" would be "forgotten by their country, abandoned by their family, without news of their children," more connected with the German society in which they lived and worked than with their own country.[66]

Meanwhile in Germany, sexual relations between POWs and German women were strictly prohibited by Göring on racial grounds. French POWs caught in flagrante might be sent to the disciplinary camp at Graudenz, where their existence was made intentionally harsh – according to an October 1942 report, 900 French POWs had been sent to Graudenz "for sentences varying from 2 months to 8 years for various reasons, relations with women, refusal to work above all." One German farmer who caught his daughter having sexual relations with a French POW obliged them to marry – one assumes that Göring was not invited to serve as best man. "His repatriation would avoid lots of problems," Major du Pavillon helpfully suggested to the war secretariat at Vichy. Roughly 80,000 French women, mainly working-class girls attracted by the high salaries, also volunteered to work in Germany, a number of whom became pregnant. Pavillon also noted that "French female workers seldom work in factories, but frequently elsewhere. They 'patronize' Germans, Italians and French – price 5 to 10 marks – the prisoners pay in chocolate." All of which created a narrative that associated French female sexuality with treason – "*putain et collabo*" (whore and collaborator) – that exploded in "*les tontes*" or head shavings, at the Liberation. But the number of French women who traveled to Germany for adventure or income is seldom referenced. Ironically, the Germans distrusted these French women, who they believed facilitated French POW escapes.[67]

But if French reports are to be believed, it soon became apparent that not all German women were willing to comply with the *Luftwaffe* Chief's "no sex until we've won the war" edict. The *Service d'accueil et d'information auprès des prisonniers de guerre rapatriés en gare de Mâcon* noted that

French POWs had enthusiastically embraced Vichy's policy of collaboration, when sentences of "2, 4, 6, 8 years were being handed down to 'many,' [presumably enlisted French prisoners] for having sexual relations with German women. The sentence is proportional to the social situation of the woman, and if she is married or unmarried. A prisoner Levreur was given 8 years for having impregnated a mother and her 2 daughters!!! German women often seek out relations with the prisoners. A piece of chocolate helps relations along. The women who are caught or denounced are also punished – the rumor is that children with a POW father are killed."[68] Whatever were the Master Race custodians thinking when they exported Deutschland's breeding-age males to be butchered in exotic locations, while importing *Untermenschen* proxies? If France was occupied by a foreign army, so was Nazi Germany after June 1940. In this way, the 1940 Franco-German armistice became a sort of exchange-of-forces agreement. If the Liberation found "Fifis" (a derogatory contemporary term for *Forces françaises de l'intérieur* or members of the resistance – FFI) shaving the heads of French "horizontal collaborators," some *Wehrmacht* survivors no doubt returned at war's end to a few surprises, rather like Maria Braun's husband Hermann in Rainer Werner Fassbinder's 1978 film. Levreur symbolized the POW cuckolds' revenge, the retribution of the defeated, the insemination of German women as a patriotic act. Who needs to escape when one can subvert the Master Race from within, and have fun doing it? Levreur and his ilk deserved their own category of resistance medal – the "knights of the white flag" recouped their masculinity via Red Cross chocolate and fraternization. On the other hand, Boudot cautioned that the "myth of Don Juanism" was deliberately cultivated by POWs and should be taken with a bag of salt.[69]

Maintaining sufficient stocks of chocolate might pose a significant problem for POWs, however. Unlike the lucky few who remained in the *Stalags*, POWs scattered in *Kommandos* throughout the German economy might only intermittently receive Red Cross food parcels from their families, especially if their contents were being auctioned off at the "Louvre du Falckensee" and similar distribution points. POWs subsisted in theory on a daily diet of 1,350 calories, made up of Ersatz bread, tea brewed from diverse plants, and meat and margarines of indeterminate origins. However, an October 1941 a report noted that while those assigned to agriculture work were sufficiently fed, those on road works and in mines were seriously undernourished. Furthermore, their clothes were worn out and a "point system" that allowed replacement clothes was clearly inadequate.[70] But most POWs were not averse to working, because, as noted, they were paid.[71] By 1942, reports abound with complaints of poor nourishment for *Kommandos* working in factories – "a liter of soup a day. No potatoes. 200–300 grams of bread."[72]

Officers, who were not required by Geneva Convention rules to work, now had a chance to become familiar with what for most would be their homes for the next five years. De Cazotte's *Oflag* IVD, a converted *Wehrmacht* training camp, offered a rectangle defined by three layers of barbed wire, with guard towers at regular intervals equipped with searchlights and machineguns, supplemented by guard rounds outside the wire. Crémieux-Brilhac was particularly incensed that none of his fellow inmates protested when the Germans quarantined six Jewish officers in a separate barracks with no electricity. Crémieux-Brilhac had sought without success to convince the "*homme de confiance*" – at first appointed by the Germans, and subsequently elected by the inmates as their contact and spokesman with the Germans and with Vichy's POW service – "a superb officer of zouaves," that as racial categories were not recognized in French law, he was under no obligation to supply his captors with a list of Jewish POWs. That of course would change under Vichy. Nor did the other officers even bother to visit their quarantined Jewish colleagues. The only thing that saved Aspirant Crémieux from a similar fate was his transfer to a *Stalag*.[73] In fact, it became standard procedure to segregate Jewish officers. However, attempts to make them wear yellow stars were abandoned after Red Cross protests that this violated the Geneva Convention. The "fates of Jewish POWs always depended on those who shared their German captivity," notes Aron Shneyer, a specialist on Soviet Jewish POWs.[74] At Lübeck, French officers showed their solidarity by attending Jewish religious services and protesting the yellow star. Shneyer also cites an instance when French POWs assigned to a mine *Kommando* threatened to strike if two Jewish soldiers were punished.[75] Hardly had Richard Bennaïm been captured, than a German officer circulated among them: "He asked calmly, almost in a friendly tone: 'Are there any *chuifs* among you? Are there any *chuifs*?' Not a hand went up." However, he took the precaution of tearing the first two pages out of his pay book that listed the name of his parents. He recorded his name as Benin, a Catholic from Nice. Nevertheless, fear of being exposed as a Jew by a snitch in his *Kommando* steeled his decision to escape.[76] In general, the *Wehrmacht* respected the Geneva rights of Jewish soldiers captured with the French, British, Yugoslav, and even Polish armies. However, as many as 100,000 Soviet Jewish POWs were rooted out among the millions of Soviet POWs and murdered.[77] POWs from Alsace-Moselle were offered their freedom if they signed a "declaration of German origins," which was not a great option as it became a fast-track to the Eastern Front after June 1941. Bretons and Corsicans were initially segregated in the expectation that they might succumb to nationalist propaganda, without result.[78]

At this point, the realization that they had passed up golden opportunities to bolt, while poorly guarded in France, simply deepened the POW's malaise and sense of inadequacy. After the war, many French people found it hard to imagine why POWs remained five years behind barbed wire without escape – Evelyne Gayme puts successful POW escapees at 32,000 or 4.37 percent of the POW population. Although if the reports of the *Service d'accueil et d'information auprès des prisonniers de guerre rapatriés en gare de Mâcon*, which interviewed returning POWs, are to be believed, many more apparently tried. Robert Salmon, who escaped his *Oflag* to join a resistance group on his return to France, noted that, "We were at least 800 officers. I asked around but only on the third day did I find a guy who showed the slightest intent in beating it. And I met many people not unhappy to go to Germany."[79] Of course, the obvious retort was: why had the vast majority of French men and women tolerated Vichy for four years, and even collaborated with it? After all, occupied France had transformed into a vast *Kommando* where the population labored and was starved for the benefit of the occupier. Why had so few chosen to resist?[80] POW escape carried few real risks, Gayme maintains. The Germans expected the French to attempt escape, so that unsuccessful escapees were merely collected by the police or border guards and returned to their camps to be punished with a few days in the cells. Once POWs were transferred to Germany, escape simply became more difficult.[81] This was true for several members of Bennaïm's *Kommando*, who walked out of their Bavarian village easily enough in March 1941. However, they were picked up by German police near the Swiss border and simply returned to their employers, rather than punished.[82]

Escape proved more difficult for officers incarcerated in *Oflags*, agreed the future Colonel André Perrin, who was captured in the Maginot Line and in 1943 finally succeeded in fleeing Lübeck on his thirteenth attempt. For Perrin, the relatively few escapes could be blamed on a lack of an "*audace d'évasion*" (boldness to escape) in most French POWs, who, having survived 1940, were not keen to rejoin the war. In his view, officers simply found excuses to sit tight and wait out hostilities.[83] However, the quintessential obligation of a captured soldier was to attempt escape. Aspirant Crémieux, who resolved to flee his *Oflag* at all costs, was appalled at the "submission and passivity of French officers ... Their reaction was that the armistice couldn't be signed quickly enough so that they could return home. I can't say that there was the least sense of indignity among these officer POWs. What upset me was that subsequently they so quickly accommodated to their situation."[84]

The simple truth is that POWs of most nations elected patiently to await liberation behind barbed wire, not just the French. And most of those who tried to escape were unsuccessful. For instance, some version of a 1942 report from *Stalag* IIID at Berlin, "Escapes: 10 a day on average. But very few succeed," could have been multiplied across the spectrum of *Stalags* and *Kommandos*, perhaps less so at the tightly supervised *Oflags*. According to Perret, who succeeded on his third escape attempt in 1942, this was because escape required a combination of preparation, luck, and "the psychology of a gambler."[85] Those escapees who were caught and returned to the *Oflag* were interrogated by their fellow inmates to discover what went wrong – POWs might be picked up trying to purchase a train ticket without an *Ausweis* (identity card or pass), at a checkpoint on a bridge over the Rhine, trying to cross the border, or simply walking down a country road. Was it better to get lost in the crowds, or hide out and move overland at night? With each successful escape from his *Oflag*, de Cazotte noted that the Germans closed off that option, so that flight became progressively more difficult – hiding under refuse being evacuated from the camp; masquerading as an orderly taking food to a work party beyond the wire; cutting and crawling under the wire at dusk before the searchlights had been turned on or as the guard mount was rotating; putting on a German uniform and shouting preemptively at the gate guards (only recommended for fluent German speakers); substituting a dummy during roll call or during a fatigue duty outside the camp so that escape would go undetected for at least twelve hours, and so on. In de Cazotte's *Oflag*, a 15-meter expanse of white sand defined by a guardrail was laid out inside the wire to designate no-go areas for POWs, "under pain of being fired upon," after an inmate successfully slipped under the wire at a place where it crossed a depression. After what de Cazotte qualified as "some sensational tunnel escapes," "microphones were buried in the earth at short intervals around the camp so that the guards would, at once, learn of any mole-like activity on our part." This meant tunneling even deeper to avoid detection, which increased exponentially the degree of difficulty. In July 1942, 147 French officers were captured at *Oflag* IVD at Elsterhorst, when they put a tunnel through the latrines, only to discover that the Germans had moved the sentinel line beyond the point where the tunnel emerged.[86] German guards might also confiscate empty food tins or crates that brought in "biscuits Pétain" that inmates used to shore up tunnels. Solitary escapes violated the ethos of camp solidarity, while plans for mass evasions were invariably betrayed by a "rat."[87]

In fact, "rats" may have seen themselves not as traitors, but as civic-minded individuals who sought to avoid the collective reprisals that invariably fell on the remaining POWs in the wake of an escape. Guards prolonged roll calls or called "*Blitzappel* " – surprise formations to clear the barracks so the guards could inspect for evidence of escape preparation, like traces of subsoil, food stashes, maps, or reserves of Reichsmarks. At the very least, this meant increased barracks inspections, during which inmates might be forced to move all of the beds and tables to the middle of the room so that guards could rifle through POWs' belongings, confiscate foodstuffs, and check for tunnels. Prolonged roll calls in the dead of winter, suspension of food parcels, and so on were weapons that the camp guards regularly deployed as punishment for an escape attempt. When officer POWs complained that guards were using these "inspections" to steal their cigarettes and chocolate, they were admonished for insulting the honor of the *Wehrmacht*.[88] But this provision war eventually gave way to a compromise that allowed the officers in de Cazotte's *Oflag* to create a central food reserve, and even to cultivate their own garden plots, fertilized with waste from the latrines. But increased inspections did not exhaust the repertoire of deterrents available to camp guards: in February 1942, the Germans declared that for every successful escape, an officer would be removed from the list of those designated for medical repatriation and the relative freedom enjoyed in some *Kommandos* would be curtailed.[89] That gave officers on the medical repatriation list every incentive to tip off their captors about escape plans.

Serial officer escapees and other "undesirables" might be transferred to Colditz or, from the summer of 1942, to *Oflag* XC at Lübeck, whose official name in French translation was "*Camp international politique et de représailles*." On the other hand, assignment to *Oflag* XC might be purely arbitrary, or at least appeared to be so – when Lieutenant Krugell demanded in writing to know why he had been transferred to *Oflag* XC from his previous accommodation, the following reply came back: "The camp commander and the *Abwehr* [military intelligence] judge that you are too dangerous for your comrades. Also, the camp that you will join is better guarded." The report lists only four French officers sent to *Oflag* XC for attempting escapes, and two for counterfeiting false papers and "corruption of a sentry." The sons of Stalin and of Léon Blum counted among *Oflag* XC's distinguished guests in 1942.[90] According to his biographer, Braudel was sent to Lübeck because of his "Gaullism," detected by German censors reading his correspondence with fellow historian Lucien Febvre.[91] In mid 1942, *Oflag* XC was shared by about 200 French enlisted men sent to work in the camp, as well as significant contingents of Belgians, Poles, and Yugoslavs, all considered enemies of the Reich because, according to the welcoming address by the camp commandant, they were communists, anarchists, and anti-German. He might have added Jews, because eighty-two French Jewish officers are listed by name in the summer of 1942. Ironically, *Oflag* XC was being organized at the very moment when Vichy, too, was beginning to worry that POW camps were becoming incubators of "undesirables" – such as communists, Gaullists, and Breton or Corsican autonomists. Vichy established its own network of camp snitches to report officers whose adulation for the Marshal fell short of fawning.[92]

A second challenge became what to do once a POW got beyond the camp wire. As many POWs were parked in camps in the East, and the Swiss frontier was heavily fortified and guarded, a trek across Germany to France offered a long and hazardous route to those who spoke no German, and had no civilian clothes, maps, identity papers, or an *Ausweis*, although camp forgers became particularly adept at providing these. For this reason, before June 1941, some, like Pierre Billotte and Crémieux-Brilhac, successfully attempted a snowy exit via the Soviet Union. The reasoning was that once the Germans discovered that their POWs had gone missing, they would assume that they had fled west, not east. Success required a lot of luck – their Alsatian companion charmed the young female ticket agent into selling them a railway ticket to the frontier even though they could produce no *Ausweis*. Crossing the Lithuanian border into a USSR in the grip of Stalinist paranoia offered its own set of challenges. Indeed, enquiries as to the fastest way to the Soviet border provoked looks of astonishment from Balts incredulous that French POWs sought to swap a perfectly serviceable *Oflag* for the warmth of Soviet hospitality. Alain de Boissieu crossed a frozen river in a snowstorm. But rather than being welcomed with opened arms, the Soviets assumed he was a German spy. They shaved his head and tossed him into filthy cells so crowded that the mostly political prisoners had to take turns lying down to sleep. This became a standard experience of a handful of French officers who fled east, only to be assimilated with "enemies of the people," and interrogated, often brutally, by suspicious NKVD officers, and ratted on by French communists in their camp.[93]

In theory, escape was easier for enlisted POWs scattered in *Kommandos*, which increasingly were left unguarded as the Germans mustered every available man for the Eastern Front or North Africa. Perret recommended civilian clothes, food, money, and convincing civilian identity papers as essential accouterments for a successful escape. One also needed a knowledge of escape routes. One source from September 1942 was French civilian workers, who began to arrive in Germany as part of a program called "*la Relève*" – a 1942 Vichy scam marketed as a bonding experience between French workers and their POW brethren that "exchanged" three civilian workers for a repatriated

POW, who could return to his wife and children.[94] *Oflags* and *Stalags* had their forgers and tailors, who would dye and otherwise transform military uniforms. Perret indicated that one might acquire forged papers in shady Berlin cafes, "these doubtful milieus where foreigners mixed with Germans."[95] Indigenous soldiers parked in camps in *Frontstalags* and *Arbeitskommandos* in France were more likely to flee: "500 escapes around Poitiers in a year," read a July 1942 report. "Above all the North Africans. They are the kings of escape ... They leave sometimes 20, 30 from the camp at night or while on a work crew," read a July 1942 report. "We recapture few of them [one out of twenty perhaps]. Punishment: a month in prison."[96] Muslim POWs had a special incentive to escape. Not only were they in France, but few had contact with their families. Letters to North Africa had to pass through the censor in Bordeaux. Many of their families lived in remote *douars*. If they heard from them at all, the news was about failure to receive their promised military indemnities and other hardships of life in food-starved AFN.[97]

By 1943, Germany thronged with involuntary "guest workers" and POWs, so that one more poorly dressed, polyglot person wandering the roads might attract little notice. When de Cazotte's *Oflag* finally hit the road as the Soviets closed in in 1945, "it was clear why an escapee could safely travel in this country," he wrote. "It was full of laborers, forced or voluntary, representing nearly every European nationality. Strange tongues were to be heard in nearly every village. Men could pass dressed in army pants and civilian coats or vice versa; the army clothes being of every conceivable cut and color. How could anyone keep track of this mixed circus? It was obviously impossible." The Italian and Soviet POWs looked to be in particularly bad shape.[98]

It is difficult to quantify the escape phenomenon. Reports from the "*Service d'accueil et d'information auprès des prisonniers de guerre rapatriés en gare de Mâcon*" list multiple escape attempts, most of them thwarted, with the fugitives recaptured and returned to camp. For instance, in April 1942, *Stalag* IIA at Neubrandenburg described escape attempts as "pretty frequent, 15% to 20% in the camp," which had caused a tightening of security.[99] But much of this information was based on hearsay and rumor, which repatriated POWs may have passed on to inflate a "resistance" image of POWs. Punishment was also a deterrent. If unsuccessful officer escapees might be given a few days in the cells or transferred to more restrictive *Oflags*, enlisted POWs caught while trying to reach the border could be assigned to disciplinary *Kommandos* where life was made very unpleasant indeed. For instance, Sergeant Gaston Portenx's failed escape attempt resulted in a sentence to a disciplinary *Kommando* at Hohenfels near Nuremburg, where "800 prisoners [Jews, recaptured escapees] worked on road construction during the winter, above all on snow removal. One team was ordered to remove snow along a 30-kilometer road so that a German colonel who was commanding an *Oflag* for Serbs could go hunting."[100] Escapees might also be shot, as happened to Adjutant Menuier, a professional soldier and "father of a child, escaped, recaptured, was killed by a sentinel ... returned to the camp with two bullets in his chest."[101] In April 1941, *Unteroffizier* Schmitt, deputy commander of the Burbinger *Kommando*, who had promised to kill the next man who tried to escape, apparently kept his word when a lorry delivered the body of an escapee to the camp.[102] Some POWs lived in hope of repatriation for health or family reasons, or because they had an inside track with the *Service diplomatique des prisonniers de guerre* (SDPG) or friends at Vichy. Richard Bennaïm gained repatriation in October 1941 by inserting an irritating powder into his eyes so that he could no longer work. Some might have been too ill or weak to escape – for instance, typhus arrived with the influx of Soviet POWs from the summer of 1941, which eventually sickened French POWs as well. Successful escape was a long shot in any case. France teemed with Germans, collaborators, and vindictive neighbors. So, reaching home did not necessarily mean that one was home free.

For all these reasons, it would be misleading to argue that a lack of will, rather than the degree of escape difficulty, offers the most plausible explanation for the relatively low rate of POW escapees of all nations. Why this was so can be judged only by informed speculation as it is difficult to generalize about the individual experiences of 1.8 million or so French POWs, all in different circumstances that constantly evolved with the course of the war, where the attitudes of their guardians ran the spectrum from indulgent to brutal. It is possible that enlisted POWs, at first viewed as trophies of a Nazi victory, ceased to see themselves as combatants as they transitioned out of military detention to a farm or shop in a provincial town and might simply be required to report to a German police station with decreasing frequency. The presumption is that they were least likely to view escape and resumption of combat as a military duty, especially as the armistice had taken France out of the war. They became isolated individually or in small groups, assumed productive civilian tasks, and intermingled with the German civilian population, with whom many came to identify and sympathize. This established human relationships, even romantic attachments, as some might reclaim masculine roles in a country increasingly under siege, populated by the old, and by women and children, where everyone was now a victim, that broke down the Manichean simplicity inherited from the war.[103]

"Escape, then, was an élite and minority activity – and even then, one resorted to only by those who temperamentally found the tedium of confinement intolerable," concludes Joan Beaumont, speaking of the British POW experience.[104] Most POWs were simply too busy surviving to look to escape. "The first duty of a prisoner," Perret insisted, "is not to die of hunger."[105] That one should believe otherwise was in part a product of post-war conditioning – what British historian S. P. Mackenzie calls "the Colditz Phenomenon," a portrayal of British POWs spending their incarceration digging escape tunnels while baiting and "outwitting the Hun." Marketing a saga of steadfast and heroic captives became a veritable "industry" in post-war Britain, with books and a popular television series.[106] But the reality was that the chances of an escaped British POW reaching Blighty were virtually nil. The alleged passivity of French POWs joined the armistice as another "verdict on France" which served to showcase British heroism in comparison. Indeed, Bennaïm noted that in his immense, multinational *Stalag* in August 1941, "In contrast to the British who were united by a formidable solidarity, most of the French were individualists and thought of nothing else but to complain about their lot and to return home, in a total indifference to others and even of the war's outcome. The English in contrast displayed an attitude of pride and faith in their government. They shaved and combed their hair every day, while most of the French really went to seed."[107]

In post-war France, a successful escape offered an entrée into the POW as resister narrative, which was most aggressively promoted by future French president François Mitterand, himself an escaped POW. But that came later. At the time, even successful escape was neither encouraged by Vichy nor honored in France. In March 1942, Adjutant Jacques Ragu complained that, although by escaping he had accomplished "the act of a soldier," he arrived in France dressed in clothes given him by people in Lorraine, without papers or ration cards, unable to find employment or visit his family in the occupied zone, and lived in constant fear of denunciation.[108] Fugitive POWs found it prudent until November 1942 to reach the so-called *zone libre*. But increasingly Vichy turned a cold shoulder to escaped POWs, as André Perrin discovered when he appeared in Vichy in 1943. This combined with the November 1942 German occupation of southern France to make North Africa the best sanctuary.[109] But reaching North Africa via Spain offered an additional series of challenges. All of which made successful escape a long shot. And as de Cazotte noted, over time the "fraternity of the camps" fragmented along the usual French political cleavages between pro-clerical and secular officers, stirred up in de Cazotte's view by graduates of the "detestable" normal schools. However, it was only when these more "secular"

POWs began to challenge the *Cercles Pétain* and priests for camp leadership, printed anti-collaborationist tracts, and gave lectures whose anodyne titles camouflaged a very subversive message that POWs might lay claim to any activity that qualified as "resistance."[110]

For this reason, passivity behind the barbed wire was neither a particularly French phenomenon, nor was it confined to the "decadent" generation of the Second World War. British military psychologists in the First World War had identified what they termed "barbed wire disease," which they classified as a form of "neurasthenia" "characterized by mental exhaustion, irritability, intellectual instability, loss of concentration and disturbance of memory . . . caused by confinement and monotony, accentuated by 'sexual deprivation' and lack of privacy."[111] These observations were expanded from 1943, when a pilot study of British POWs, part of a group of 5,000 exchanged British, Commonwealth, and American noncombatant troops, discovered them afflicted by a sense of guilt, inferiority, and inadequacy, shocked by changes that had occurred at home during their incarceration, and by a general feeling that life had passed them by. Those POWs who had manage to escape displayed high levels of anxiety and aggression. Those who survived best behind barbed wire were those like priests and doctors who could continue to perform "productive work."[112]

The interior of de Cazotte's *Oflag* was divided into "blocks" of wooden barracks with dormitories containing three-tiered pine board frames that served as beds. Each officer was issued a sheet and two blankets, and a mattress filled with straw or wood shavings. Soon officers put up cardboard or newspaper partitions, even blankets, around their bunk for privacy, and eventually the dormitories themselves became divided by partitions into separate rooms. A center space contained a large table and chairs where inmates sat, ate, or read. At the end of each barracks was a washroom with troughs and cold water taps for washing clothes or minimal hygiene. Administrative buildings, guard quarters, a jail that frequently hosted aviators who had a particularly difficult time adjusting to incarceration, a latrine block that offered minimal privacy, and a building with a tall chimney which housed the showers – POWs in de Cazotte's camp were entitled to one every fifteen days, but soap was scarce and hot water rationed – and a delousing facility finished out the camp. Eventually one of the barracks was designated as a chapel. All of this was arranged along a single street, itself lined with barbed wire with passages at various intervals, which the inmates baptized "Hitler Strasse." An infirmary ensconced in its own wire enclosure stood separately from the main camp, which seems to have been fairly standard in camp layouts. Beyond, the monotonous Silesian plain, bedded with sugar beets and rutabaga, extended toward the horizon until it melted into somber forests of spruce and pine.[113]

The most remarkable thing about *Oflag* incarceration, de Cazotte noted, was that direct contact between the POWs and their German captors was normally limited to two daily musters. Morning roll call occurred at 7 a.m. in summer, 8 in winter. Officers stood at attention in a square behind the latrines in groups of 100 to be counted by two *Feldwebels*, who moved in front and behind each group, and then reported to the controlling German officer. Observant POWs noticed that the *Feldwebels* counted the ranks, not the individual POWs. So, inmates would fashion dummies out of broomsticks. In winter, when everyone had hats or hoods, and with collars of coats pulled up, dummies could mask the escape of POWs for up to two days, Alain de Boissieu reckoned.[114] If the numbers appeared correct, the block commanders saluted the German officer, and the formation was dismissed. "Supposedly we were to be properly dressed for these roll-calls, but very soon, our martial appearance left much to be desired," remembered de Cazotte. In fact, the Germans kitted out POWs in all sorts of captured uniforms, or even *Wehrmacht* surplus. Therefore, turning out smart for parade was not a high priority, especially in −20 °C weather. After formation, a handful of dejected, ragged Polish enlisted POWs who resided in their own enclosure on the other side of Hitler Strasse filed off to work in a nearby lignite mine, their marching song a dirge punctuated by the barking of *Feldwebels*. But they were eventually shifted elsewhere to make room for more French officer POWs, who continued to arrive, which eventually brought their *Oflag* population to 5,000.[115]

Initially, conditions in the *Oflag* were barely above a survival level. Food was delivered in large vats by French and North African enlisted POWs who worked in the kitchens housed in a separate building, and the officers distributed this food among themselves. A basic camp diet consisted of black tea in the morning, followed at noon by a ladle of rutabaga, cabbage, or, if the inmates were lucky, barley soup, which might contain a boiled potato, noodles, or small pieces of fried cod. At 14:00, a small snack of cheese, margarine, jam, and sausage might be served. Dinner consisted of 250 grams of black bread and a small slice of sausage at 5 o'clock after evening roll call. In their early days of incarceration, most officers lost a considerable amount of weight as well as strength. Medical care provided by the camp doctor, also a POW, proved to be as minimalist as was the diet. After conversation, an exchange of rumors, reading, a visit to the latrines, officers settled in bed to read by the light of a homemade grease lamp. They cast a nocturnal look at family pictures, and wrote RAS – "*rien à signaler*" (nothing to report) – in the day's box on their calendars.[116] Lights went out at 21:00.

But conditions improved after the first six months, during which the Germans had been forced to improvize to accommodate the unexpected arrival of large numbers of Frenchmen. *Oflag* existence, while monotonous and uncomfortable, was hardly arduous or life threatening by Second World War standards, except when Allied bombers appeared overhead. There were no shelters at *Oflag* XC, so that POWs were simply forced into barracks during air raids. A Polish officer was killed by a stray bomb in April 1942 during a bombing raid on Lübeck, and one of the camp buildings burned to the ground: "no prisoner tried to put out the fire." The Germans installed anti-aircraft guns around the camp, which probably suggested to the Allied air forces that it was an important target.[117]

De Cazotte noted with a certain pride that POW energy was expended principally in making camp conditions more livable, beginning with the quality of the cuisine: German cooks were replaced by French POW chefs under the supervision of a reserve officer who had been a maître d'hôtel in civilian life. At least this improved the flavor of the rutabaga soup. The arrival of Red Cross parcels sent by the families of POWs also increased the possibilities of a culinary upgrade – each officer was officially allowed two 5 kilo parcels monthly, but by forging official labels, with the connivance of French POWs working in the parcel distribution office, and bribing German guards with part of a sausage or bar of chocolate, a considerable contraband of multiple monthly parcels weighing up to 20 kilograms developed in *Oflag* IVD. De Cazotte's barracks even did a brisk business in homemade gin produced from fermented pumpkin jelly.[118]

Conditions at Lübeck appear to have been more Spartan. Like *Oflag* IVD, officers dined in "*popotes*" or messes, each of about twenty officers, who combined the contents of their Red Cross packages. These "popotes" became like families as well as an economic unit. Similar conditions might prevail in *Kommandos*, where soldiers grouped together and developed tight friendships to survive. This also discouraged escape attempts, because flight was viewed as a betrayal of group solidarity.[119] Because packages from France might contain contraband items – maps, money, or lists of contacts should one want to make an escape – they were diligently searched by German guards, "who desire to keep their good assignments and not risk their hides on the Russian front."[120] At Lübeck, tinned goods had to be opened in front of the guards, and the contents poured into a mess tin, after which the guard confiscated the tin, lest it be fashioned into a tool for digging tunnels. Each "popote" constructed its own brick stove, so they could concoct their own meals rather than depend on the camp kitchens. The greatest problem was the lack of wood or coal, a situation that might be remedied by giving the guard a few cigarettes to fetch some combustible material. Each "*popote*" also had its own garden, for which the "*popotier*" or mess officer was responsible in season. But Lübeck appears, in 1942 at least, to have redefined the concept of frugal dining.[121]

Red Cross inspections were suspended on Hitler's orders from May through October following General Henri Giraud's daring April 1942 escape from Königstein Castle near Dresden.[122] But officers continued to receive full pay, and more or less adequate rations once Red Cross packages arrived, and were not required to work outside the camp as were NCOs and enlisted soldiers, who regarded officers as *planqués*. In Germany, many French officers lived a life of relative leisure, paying enlisted POW orderlies in camp-issued marks to wash their clothes and clean their spaces. Camp economies were run largely on a barter system, with American cigarettes as the gold standard.[123] The exception was Gaullist POWs, who were not paid initially. At least these Gaullists had survived – reports reached London in the spring of 1941 that the Italians were executing FFL POWs in North Africa on the pretext that they did not represent a legal state as defined by the 1929 Geneva Convention. It is possible that the French abused some of the 43,000 Italian POWs who fell into their hands in Tunisia in 1943, refusing to acknowledge Italy's "co-belligerent" status after September 1943, and as a method to demonstrate to the indigenous population of AFN that Italians were "inferior white men." One result was the mass escape of Italian POWs in North Africa from French camps into the relative benevolence of US-run POW camps.[124]

Nor were these camps intellectual wastelands. On the contrary, *Oflags* contained a significant percentage of France's professional and technical elite, which starved both Vichy and Free France, not to mention the post-November 1942 French Army of Liberation, of considerable talent. Various schools and universities sent books to populate camp libraries.[125] Artillery Lieutenant Fernand Braudel even managed to outline his magisterial *The Mediterranean and the Mediterranean World in the Age of Philip II* from memory while incarcerated in Lübeck. Indeed, some have even suggested that the experience of war and captivity actually informed his approach to the study of the past.[126] Camps were culled for university professors and other specialists to give lectures on a scientific or literary topic. An art or sculpture class might occupy the morning. In *Oflag* IVD, a notary from Beauvais hosted Saturday afternoon discussions with proper crockery, napkins, cakes, milk, lemon, and various brands of tea, which invariably featured a camp celebrity as speaker. Mess groups organized dinners with a featured guest presenter. Municipal, regional, and even professional associations of POWs, often linked with an "amicale" of wives, families, and friends at home, might meet before Sunday mass to exchange news, keep up with changing regulations affecting their particular profession, and maintain morale. Senior officers in a "Professional Officers Club" spent their meetings arguing over the causes of France's defeat and providing career advice for their younger professional colleagues, which would be completely out of date in the radically altered circumstances of the Liberation. There was even a fishermen's club, where avid anglers met to exchange sagas of fishing expeditions whose catches became grander with each retelling. After June 1941, officers from the army's cartographic service produced detailed wall maps of Russia, and eventually other theaters, so that POWs could follow the progress of the war. So long as Germany was on the offensive, German officers regularly stopped by to consult the maps. However, once the Fatherland's long retreat began, the camp commandant declared the POW map room off limits to *Wehrmacht* personnel, although they frequently consulted it on the quiet. Camp loudspeakers broadcast *Wehrmacht* news bulletins at noon, translated by German-speaking French officers. Officer POWs also had access to German newspapers and French publications from the *zone occupée*. Camp newspapers were also printed under the rubric "*au service du Maréchal*," all supervised by the *Sonderführer* – a specialist in propaganda or with linguistic skills who was given oversight responsibilities. Unauthorized papers might be smuggled in, or news secreted into Red Cross packages. Some barracks even rigged up clandestine radios to follow the progress of the war.[127]

But there is no denying that incarceration was a relentlessly demoralizing experience, for which everyone devised their own coping mechanisms – religious fervor, sexual obsessions, black humor, anger, or seeking solace in rumor. Sports offered a particularly popular form of distraction, with football and fencing in the lead, which often drew the guards as spectators. Chess and bridge competitions attracted a more highbrow audience. Cazotte noted a religious revival in his *Oflag*.[128] Priests among the POWs organized choirs to accompany mass. Many found an outlet in camp theater productions, playing in one of the camp's many musical groups, or organizing gala evenings that might require that everyone appear in costume to be entertained by vaudeville acts, a jazz combo, and spoof Parisian fashion shows. Those of a particular arm might host an evening – de Cazotte remembered "Cavalry night" as an especially chic event. Dressed in their best uniforms, everyone consumed an admittedly indifferent meal nevertheless served in style by liveried orderlies, while the theater group's usual cast of female impersonators appearing in *décolleté* crooned "Franklin D. Roosevelt Jones," and other decadent songs accompanied by the music of the *Oflag* dance band (Figure 5.3).[129]

Figure 5.3 *Oflag* cabaret. Female impersonators were in great demand.

Without a doubt, survival in *Oflags* required patience, stamina, imagination, and an "extraordinary ingenuity." It was a world where the odd-job man, the tinkerer, the artisan, and the craftsman were king.[130] Some inmates with technical backgrounds crafted replicas of the Eiffel Tower or even clocks that kept perfect time out of empty food tins using weights and string. But this resourcefulness, fortitude, and the odd prank played on the guards hardly constituted heroism. Such was de Gaulle's caustic "Why not hairdressers?" verdict when escaped POW Sergeant Mitterand tried to convince the General to recognize POWs as a "resistance" group. That mantel might fall on those few who attempted to escape. But for de Gaulle especially, and military purists in general, to pin a *médaille de la resistance* post-war on the chest of the *Oflag* bridge champion or a troop of female impersonators, or awarding it to Levreur for patriotically impregnating multiple German females, while perhaps above and beyond the call of duty, stretched the definition of "resistance." The battle even to award former POWs a *carte de combattant* in post-war France, one spearheaded by Mitterand, became a bitter and hard-fought one that was only resolved administratively for the POWs in 1949.[131]

In essence, *Oflags* merely prolonged Phoney War ambiguities. "Although we had escaped the bloody arena of battle," de Cazotte opined, POWs remained combatants who through capture had surrendered their military dignity. For five long years they existed without privacy, in barracks that were freezing cold in winter, flea- and lice-infested in summer, with medical care provided by POW doctors and dentists without proper equipment or medicines, corrected by haughty German officers of equal rank on their deportment and ordered about like conscripts by snarling *Feldwebels*. Camps became a front without a rear, where POWs existed, suspended in a constant anxiety about their wives and families, and were on occasion abandoned by them – a disaster because it meant the end of food parcels. Above all, in the camps one lost control over the future. "The sinister Silesian plain yet surrounded us with the menace of long suffering misery, disease or starvation perhaps, and ever present we sensed around us the grim specter of death."[132]

Although de Cazotte's memoir had no deliberate political agenda, it falls into a category of war literature that aims to socialize in the popular mind an image of the "fraternity of the camps" as an extension of the "fraternity of the front." It portrays POWs as a strong, organic community bonded by suffering and a Vichy-inspired spirit of "Obey and Serve."[133] POW social activities, pranks played on slow-witted guards, and escape attempts were not mere amusements, attempts by POWs to pass the time and make the best of a bad situation. They are presented as the transfer of the camaraderie of the front to the POW barracks, to maintain morale, continue the fight, and convey French intellectual vitality, resilience, and resourcefulness in adverse circumstances. Camps were presented as a prolongation and intensification of the military as the quintessential national melding pot, where social classes intermingled and ideologies were subsumed in an *union sacrée* behind barbed wire. In fact, the stratification of the camps was immense in a myriad of ways – between *Oflags*, *Stalags*, and *Kommandos*, between *planqués* and those forced to work, between those who had "*un bon petit commando*" or who dallied with the wife or daughter of the soldier at the front, and those in *Zweiglager* (satellite camps depending on a larger *Stalag*), who endured forced labor by day and Allied bombing by night. In these memoirs, inmates remain patriotic, sacrifice for each other, and are humanized and rehabilitated. Suffering in captivity was the equivalent of being wounded in combat. In this way, POWs sought to retain their warrior status, and jettison their negative image and sense of guilt at surrender. The POW remained a combatant, a resister, even though he had surrendered his weapons.[134] But this image of POW fraternity and solidarity in keeping with Vichy propaganda boomeranged on the POWs post-Liberation. The public perception saw the POWs as having experienced a relatively easy and risk-free war, practically *une vie de château*, and wondered what the POWs had to complain about when compared with the occupation endured by the French at home.[135] The behavior of the soldiers of 1940 had failed to meet the patriotic standards set by the *poilus* of the Great War, those of Second World War resistance heroes, and even those of the colonial soldiers who would blow open German defenses at Cassino in May 1944, and hold the line in Alsace in the harsh winter of 1944–1945, before storming the Rhine into Germany.

POWs as Propaganda

The "Colditz" image of the POW as a soldier who continued the war behind barbed wire became a hard sell in France, as they were disarmed, incarcerated, civilianized, and put to work to bolster the German war effort. The simple fact was that by signing an armistice to "preserve the army" and the social order, Weygand, Pétain, Huntzinger, and other soldiers had triggered the very Jaurèsian civilianization of the *levée* that they had sought to short-circuit. POWs who missed out on the occupation, and who remembered Pétain as a hero, found no place in the resistance myth, any more than did those who submitted to the *service du travail obligatoire* (STO).[136] By handing over the POWs, Vichy had put their fate in the hands of Hitler, who used the POWs as a cudgel to coerce Vichy collaboration. "So that France can live, it requires that the elite of [France's] youth, for the moment prisoners, can return, produce children, resume their industrial and agricultural activities, rather than remain inactive in German POW camps," read a 21 May 1941 Vichy report that sought to justify allowing the *Luftwaffe* into Syria to support a rebellion in Iraq against the British-installed regime.[137] As the war intensified, the Germans increasingly violated the Geneva protocols, insisting that the November 1940 Franco-German agreement allowing Vichy to manage its own POWs through the *Service diplomatique des prisonniers de guerre* (SDPG), better known as the "mission Scapini," superseded Geneva. This subjected POWs to the dangers of Allied air bombardments, which increased from 1941, especially as POWs were often denied entry into air raid shelters, thus making them human shields.[138] In this way, Pétain shattered the "social contract" between the armed forces, the state, and society. Indeed, a November 1941 report warned that many POWs were "beginning to believe that if the prisoners were not liberated *this was more the fault of France than of Germany*." (italics in original).[139]

To mask that reality, Vichy sought to mobilize POWs and their families behind the National Revolution.[140] POWs were transformed into a core validation in Vichy's message of redemption through suffering. Pétain's propaganda idealized *Stalags* and *Oflags* as monastic retreats from which POWs would emerge spiritually renovated, cleansed of their sins of defeatism and cowardice. On the New Year, each POW received a postcard bearing Pétain's portrait emblazoned with a *francisque* – the double-bladed axe that Pétain adopted as his symbol. "Prisoners, my friends and children," the Marshal's infantilizing message began, "I think of you with affection and I congratulate the noble courage you continue to demonstrate while awaiting the day when I will greet you on your return to the fatherland." Vichy propaganda aimed at POWs had to pass muster with a *Betreuer*, a German officer in each camp whose job was to oversee "cultural" activities with a goal of identifying collaborators and eventual converts to Nazism. Censored French newspapers reported that the conditions in which the POWs were kept were "acceptable." They were well fed and "correctly" clothed, while the German administration of the camps was "excellent."[141] At this early stage, even the future Gaullist Crémieux-Brilhac conceded that Pétain was respected by everyone in his *Oflag*. "We couldn't imagine that Pétain wasn't the best defender of French interests," he remembered, or that any solution other than an armistice offered a viable option. Only as Britain held out in the summer and autumn of 1940 did people begin to imagine an outcome other than an outright German victory and question France's decision for an armistice. But the Gaullists feared in 1945 that liberated POWs would return home as unreconstructed Vichyites hostile to the resurrected Republic.[142] In October 1941, Richard Bennaïm and his group of "medical evacuees" had to run a gauntlet of speeches, ceremonies, and reviews on their return to France, in which mayors and priests assured them: "You left behind a pagan and materialist country. Today as you return home thanks to the Marshal who gave the gift of his life to the country, you are going to rediscover a new France, where Christian values and those of the family have assumed their rightful place . . ." After being told to "respect the legitimate authority of our German friends," everyone stood at attention to sing "Maréchal, nous voilà!" "This pathetic comedy finished as the welcome committee distributed 1,000 francs and a travel voucher . . ." After a final medical examination, and dressed in a new uniform, they scattered.[143]

In fact, Vichy scrambled to recover from the debacle of the armistice, of which Article 20 stipulated that POWs would remain under German control until a peace treaty between Germany and France was signed. Germany's refusal to conclude a peace made Pétain vulnerable to charges of betrayal, which pushed Vichy toward collaboration, justified by Pétain on 31 October 1940 as a means "to lighten the weight of suffering of our country, improve conditions for our prisoners, and attenuate the costs of occupation." From this point, POWs were enlisted as weapons in Vichy's propaganda war. Vichy manipulated the anxiety of POWs' families, who saw the Marshal as their best hope of repatriating their husbands, fathers, sons, and brothers, to solidify support for Pétain. Postal censorship in the *zone occupée* reported in the autumn of 1941 that the only support for Vichy could be found among families of POWs. Indeed, one resister in Lyon remembered the rock-solid loyalty of POW families to Pétain as doing "enormous damage to Resistance. His hold over the families of prisoners of war was very strong."[144] But while POWs and their families were presented as being in dire need, Vichy did not do much to help them, beyond offering aid packages identical to those of 1914–1918. In fact, Vichy's efforts on behalf of POWs were hampered by administrative confusion. Several ministries – called "secretariats" under Vichy – organized POW sections. It was soon clear that the *Comité Central d'Assistance aux Prisonniers de Guerre* in the War Secretariat did not have a good handle on how many POWs, especially colonial POWs, were in German hands.[145] The winter of 1940–1941 found Vichy organizing the dispatch of food parcels, collecting money at galas and other events, or hiring the ever-reliable Maurice Chevalier to perform at the Folies-Belleville for the "*secours national du Maréchal*" (the Marshal's national charitable fund). But, by spring 1941, it had become clear that these measures were not working for at least four reasons. First, the war, and hence the captivity, was going to last. As a result, wives and families began to organize in the larger towns, which presaged greater popular pressure on Vichy to resolve the POW issue. Second, the government began to realize belatedly that the financial destitution of POW families had become critical, to the point that some POWs wives at least were forced to seek other sources of income and/or protection. Third, the morale of POWs bottomed out, as the realities of their incarceration, mixed with deep regrets at not having escaped early on when they had a chance, began to seep in. Finally, Vichy realized that their neglect of the POW issue opened them to criticism, even on the right.[146]

Already, on 28 July 1940, the Defense Ministry created the SDPG, whose immediate task was to take a census, create a registry of POWs, inform families of capture, and regularize their administrative situation. Two days later, Pétain appointed Georges Scapini to make contact with the Germans to regularize the status of the POWs. A blinded veteran of the September–October 1915 Champagne offensive, Scapini had taken advantage of post-war benefits offered to *grands mutilés de guerre* to master Braille, complete his studies in the Paris law faculty, and pass the Paris bar. Active in veteran's movements, he became president of the *Union des*

Aveugles de guerre (The Union of the War-Blinded). From 1928, Scapini represented Paris' XVIIe arrondissement in the Chamber of Deputies, where he sat with the nationalist right. From 1936, he became co-president with his friend Otto Abetz, future wartime German ambassador to France, of the *comité France–Allemagne*, dedicated to the rapprochement between the two former belligerents. In this capacity, Scapini twice met with Hitler, and with Ribbentrop on several occasions. Scapini's unimpeachable Great War record and his reputation as a right-wing pacifist made him an ideal fit for Vichy, which, in September 1940, named him Ambassador and head of the SDPG. His ambassadorial status made him the diplomatic equal of Abetz. Ambassadorial rank also allowed him to serve as the intermediary with the *Militärbefehlshaber in Frankreich* (MBF, or Military Commander in France) for questions relative to POWs still in France, and with OKW for questions of POWs in Germany. As such, he answered directly to Pétain. Paxton also sees Scapini's appointment as part of a drive by civilians to reclaim control of governance at Vichy from soldiers.[147]

For French POWs, Scapini's appointment would not be good news, because he embodied all of Vichy's ambitions and contradictions. Vichy's objective was to remold France through the application of the "National Revolution," which offered a domestic framework for collaboration. Different factions at Vichy emphasized those aspects of the program most congenial to their ideological outlook. But basically, the National Revolution sought to offer an antidote to French decadence. It proposed a "radically nostalgic agenda – Catholic, patriarchal, and pre-modern," promoted through corporatism, anti-parliamentarianism, antisemitism, and a rejection of class conflict and of cultural modernism.

Initially seduced by Scapini's bromides about Britain's imminent collapse and their pending liberation, POWs provided a captive, expectant, and initially receptive audience for Vichy indoctrination. When, from the spring of 1941, it became clear that POW repatriation was not on the cards, Scapini's mission expanded beyond visiting the camps to record complaints, and to represent them to the Germans. Each visit was to feature a speech praising the National Revolution and the Marshal's policies. From mid 1941, a "*cercle Pétain*" was to be created in each camp, each circle containing a "*groupe d'étude du rayonnement français*" (a study group for French influence) as well as a "Group for the study of the principles of the New Order," which became a running pro-Vichy seminar whose purpose was to praise Pétain and promote the "moralism" of the National Revolution, as well as its "technical focus." A "study group for practical relations" followed the evolution of Vichy legislation and cultural policies. These circles also doubled as intelligence agencies, reporting on the state of camp opinion. The goals of the National Revolution were to be explained in a series of talks, conferences, and camp newspapers. Shows featuring camp crafts – often crosses or sculptures in honor of the Marshal – were organized to demonstrate that vitality and morale remained high, along with a sense of contrition. Pétain's 25 April birthday was celebrated with parades, sports events, and a speech by *l'homme de confidence* delivered beneath an immense portrait of the Marshal. Oaths to the Marshal were taken in front of the flag. A celebration of the Marshal's birthday organized by the *Mouvement Pétain* was held in *Stalag* XVIIIA at Wolfsberg in 1942 before "the portrait of the Marshal, painted by a prisoner. The Stalag chorale, accompanied by the band, sang la Marseillaise. The Germans [officers and soldiers] stood at attention and saluted."[148] How effective these propaganda efforts proved among enlisted men scattered in *Kommandos* and *Zweiglager* is open to doubt. For instance, a report of October 1942 for the nearly 5,000 French POWs working in the "H. Georing (*sic*) factories" reported the "Pétain Movement – non-existent – in any case the prisoners are so tired once they have finished work that all they want is rest."[149] In the long term, associating the POWs with Vichy's National Revolution and collaboration, especially using them as the alibi for dispatching civilian conscript workers to France from September 1942, further tarnished the already-battered image of the "knights of the white flag" in France.

As the fortunes of war tilted toward the Allies, French heroism and recovery of masculinity found a focus in resistance, while labor, political, and "racial" deportees to Germany, not POWs, came to be seen as the war's principal victims. In this way, POWs emerged from the war bearing the stigma both of defeat and of collaboration, while serving as the excuse to victimize yet more young Frenchmen. Scapini's two major initiatives revealed that his primary mission was to facilitate the integration of French laborers to increase the productivity of Germany's war economy: *la relève* ("the relief" or "exchange") of September 1942 allegedly repatriated a POW for every three French volunteers who went to work in Germany; 90,747 POWs returned to France under *la relève*. Young men who resisted voluntary departure on *la relève*, and from February 1943 its conscript labor successor the STO, were vilified and their families threatened with reprisals because their selfishness supposedly kept a POW from returning.[150] While Scapini presented it as a scheme to substitute voluntary French civilian labor for POWs, *la relève* demonstrated that Scapini "was willing to go further in collaboration than was Laval in 1942," concludes Durand. *La relève* also proved immensely unpopular among POWs, who complained that the selection of returnees was left to the *hommes de confiance* who designated "*Cercle Pétain*" activists and those willing to do favors for guards. Some French people had volunteered for *la relève* in the mistaken belief that they would be taking the place of their POW family member. Those with political contacts at Vichy were also prioritized for release. Demoralization settled among those who concluded that they lacked political clout or fell outside those categories eligible for repatriation.[151] Post-1945, POWs faced the unjust accusation that they had experienced an easy war nestled in the arms of a lonely *Hausfrau*, while civilians at home had resisted while suffering strict curfews, Allied bombing, quasi-starvation, and deportations.[152]

Billotte grumbled that Scapini "contaminated the atmosphere" among POWs.[153] But he was simply implementing Vichy's policy of collaboration, with its confused message about where POW duty lay, and discouraged escape attempts. André Perrin complained that Scapini instructed the inmates of his *Oflag* that escape would "complicate Pétain's policy" toward Germany.[154] Vichy's emotional and psychological domination of French POWs progressively diminished from 1941 as these emasculated warriors in involuntary exile came to realize that they constituted expendable pawns to support Vichy's illusory strategy to increase French influence in Hitler's Europe. A May 1942 report noted that the "Mission Scapini: is disliked," for two reasons. First, "Having initially raised hopes of repatriation, their prestige is irrevocably destroyed by [favoritism]." Those with contacts at Vichy, even Scapini's former constituents, were selected for repatriation over men who should have been given priority because of their family situation or health. The second, larger point was that there was a growing rejection of collaboration. "The principle was accepted earlier. Now, it meets more and more hostility."[155] Marie Vassiltchikov, a White Russian émigré, who met Scapini during a September 1943 visit to Berlin "to negotiate the return of French prisoners-of-war in exchange for 'voluntary' labour," described him as, "a pathetic figure; blinded in the last war, he is always attended by an Arab servant, who acts as his eyes and describes everything going on around him."[156] POWs, like everyone else, were beginning to understand Vichy's fundamental contradiction – to survive, Vichy required a German victory. Like much of the rest of the French population, Vichy enlisted the POWs in that effort. Scapini became increasingly unpopular with POWs, who concluded correctly that he was a collaborator whose main concern was to ensure that POW labor helped to offset US support for Great Britain. The liberation of POWs would occur only with an Allied triumph. Scapini's visits merely served the purposes of propaganda and resulted in no improvements in conditions. "Furthermore, the [DSPG] delegates give the impression that they make no effort to try to understand the situation of the prisoner."[157] "These Scapini ceremonies are lamentable," a "senior officer" POW reported back to Vichy in 1941. "His tactlessness and inappropriate language mean that he is looked upon as a simple politician whose visits are compared to old-style political rallies. He doesn't know how to talk to POWs, whether active or reserve. He's a joke. His visits leave everyone depressed."[158]

POWs became hostages that the Germans dangled before Vichy, which danced to Berlin's tune without receiving significant concessions in return. Fifty-three percent of those POWs who were repatriated were sent home because they fell into categories that Geneva protocols required to be released. Vichy collaboration was not decisive for the return of POWs, although these repatriations were publicized by Vichy in cinema newsreels and elsewhere as the direct result of Vichy actions. For instance, Scapini was filmed welcoming medical evacuees presented as a triumph of Vichy diplomacy, when in fact the Germans had no interest in retaining men who had become a medical burden. In September 1942, Hitler liberated all POWs from Dieppe to show his gratitude for the fact that the local population had not assisted the August Allied "raid," but in fact helped to repulse it, according to Vichy. In short, the Germans liberated POWs when it was in their interests to do so, not because they were pressured by Vichy. Unlike other governments, Vichy propaganda encouraged French POWs to cooperate with the Germans. Assiduous at propagating Pétain's National Revolution, Scapini was slow to defend POW rights under the 1929 Geneva Convention which forbade employment of POWs in war-related industries. Nor did he press their complaints of dangerous working conditions.[159] General A. Lucien, the senior French officer in *Oflag* VIA, reported in February 1943 that Pierre Laval's call for Franco-German *rapprochement* had created "*un choc psychologique*" among his officer POWs, who now placed their hopes for liberation not in the Marshal, but in an Allied victory.[160]

Transformation

From December 1941, as Barbarossa stalled before Moscow and the perspective of a longer war loomed in Berlin, the decision was taken to transfer the more skilled French POWs from agricultural work to industry. Vichy propaganda was careful never to mention that rather than spend their days in cloistral contemplation of France's resurrection, POWs were set to labor on military projects like German roads, railways, and canals, and in mines, quarries, and factories, in violation of the Geneva agreements, but freeing up German men to fight the Allies. Some worked for large companies like Opel or Siemens, and in munitions factories which increasingly became bombing targets from 1941, all the while subsisting on a diet of rutabagas, cabbage, and beetroot.

The addition of French POWs to the workforce also offered a significant benefit for OKW, which charged a fee for leasing them out. Many French POWs worked hard to gain extra rations, free time, and the esteem of their employers, or just to demonstrate that the French were capable of hard work. Those assigned to farms often became the sole male presence in a society increasingly emptied of German men. The joke was that many German rural communities would soon elect French POWs as mayors.[161] The dilemma, of course, was that they were bolstering the German war effort. This was compatible with Vichy policy, however, whose collaboration was based upon an acceptance of Vichy's dependence on Germany and France's integration into a German-dominated Europe. In this way, POWs became hostages manipulated by Berlin to influence Vichy policy.

Many of those who feared that their chances of repatriation were slim as the war gained in intensity were no doubt tempted by "la transformation," Scapini's second initiative. Proposed in 1940 by Scapini, echoed the following year by Laval, and eventually applied in 1943, this program allowed POWs to "transform" their POW status into that of "free workers" in Germany.[162] By doing this, the Germans believed that they could squeeze more productivity out of their captives, and convert 30,000 POW guards into fighting soldiers. The selling point to the POWs was that they would receive a salary equivalent to that of a German worker, a certain percentage of which they were allowed to remit to their families, could take a two-week leave to visit France, could wear civilian clothes, would receive an *Ausweis* allowing them to move around certain restricted areas, and fell under police rather than army surveillance. It also ended the POW – i.e. military – status, which appeared as if it would go on indefinitely. There was also the possibility in some cases to reunite with one's wife, who might come to Germany on a one-year "spouse" contract. While an estimated 221,000 POWs, including some officers, elected to "transform," like the armistice, "transformation" offered another Vichy sell-out of its POWs, and a further step toward "collaboration." By "transforming," POWs surrendered their combatant status and hence Geneva and Red Cross protections. They were no longer soldiers at war with Germany, but civilians integrated into the German war economy. This meant that any escape attempt, or other irregularity like suspected sabotage at work, for instance, would be handled by the police or even the Gestapo.

Furthermore, Vichy promoted "transformation" to alleviate pressure from Berlin to conscript more French civilians for STO.

Transformation might be attractive to officers enticed with promises that they would work in an occupation that reflected their expertise. "Most of the officers didn't approve of these volunteers. Several incidents occurred at their departure: they were jeered. A French doctor refused to attend one of the officers sent by the factory to the *Oflag* to be treated."[163] One hundred and twenty officers at *Oflag* IIIC at Lübben, southeast of Berlin, volunteered to work outside the POW camp, obviously with the blessing of the senior French colonel, who lauded them as "Pioneers for a New Europe." Recruitment was done by a lieutenant, notorious as a camp snitch, who found them work as tramway drivers, in a local chocolate factory, and in other industries and shops around town. "[The lieutenant] has been thrown out the door more than once" by the other POWs. Another camp reported seventy volunteers, "Designers, engineers, photographers, cinema operators, several, above all teachers or former NCOs, accepted less glamorous offers as laborers, in agriculture, gardeners, farmhands, test drivers at Stettin. They all gave their word not to escape, looking to find in work wellbeing, a moral 'escape' from the barbed wire, better food."[164] But while they were liberated from camp confines, they might find themselves assigned to crowded quarters, encounter poor working conditions, and be fed the same inadequate rations as *Ostarbeiter* – conscript laborers from the East. The *Wehrmacht* had no rank equivalent to *aspirant* (officer candidate), and Vichy conceded that *aspirants* were not fully commissioned officers, which made them eligible for the *Kommandos*.[165] But the process seems to have been a gradual one – *Aspirant* Jean-Louis Crémieux, who later would add his resistance name of Brilhac, remained in his *Oflag* for several weeks after many of his contemporaries had been transferred, and escaped before he could be reassigned.[166]

Article 29 of the Geneva Convention stipulates that POWs cannot be assigned a task that they are physically unable to perform. Article 32 forbade assigning unhealthy or dangerous tasks. Many of these provisos were ignored. Ninety-five percent of enlisted POWs were dispatched to *Kommandos*, a fact carefully omitted from Vichy propaganda.[167] These varied from the satellite *Zweiglager*, which could number several hundred men, to a "bon petit *Kommando*," where discipline was relaxed, food was relatively plentiful, and the work not too hard. "I was never lucky with my commando," insisted Perret. "Always dirty or stupid work, while some were fortunate enough to be sent to small farms where they had plenty to eat and slept in real beds, often that of the farmer's wife; or sent to work in a suburban café, or with the local butcher or carpenter. I even knew one who worked as a horse trainer at the track in Karlsruhe . . ."[168]

According to Durand, half of the POWs were set to work in agriculture, 8 percent in forests and fisheries, 17 percent in mines, metallurgy, engineering, and chemical industries, and 11 percent in other industries. Seven percent worked in construction – often to build bomb shelters or repair bomb damage – and 3 percent in transport and communications. But these *Kommandos* were not necessarily stable. As the German industrial requirements skyrocketed from early 1942, and more POWs fell into German hands, French POWs considered more capable of skilled labor might be shifted to factories or construction, and be replaced by Russian or, after September 1943, by Italian POWs in agricultural work. Generally, POWs were assigned to tasks that they were qualified to perform as the Germans sought to optimize their efficiency. They were usually housed close to their place of work. Because German employers paid the *Wehrmacht* 5 Marks a day for each POW, they wanted them to work well, and usually did not mistreat them unless they refused to work, or were sent to punishment camps for some misdemeanor like escape attempts. POWs officially earned 84 *Pfennigs* (pennies) a day, which had the purchasing power of two glasses of beer. POWs were paid in camp script called *Lagermarks*, worth less than *Reichsmarks*, which they were in theory forced to spend in the *Kommando* store or canteen. But some living among German civilians, working skilled jobs or overtime, or trading on the Black Market might earn considerably more – up to 10 Marks a day. Perret insisted that the secret of survival in a *Kommando* "is to give the impression of activity without a noticeable result. Some were real artists in this endeavor . . . Rarely resting, never immobile, they nevertheless found that at the end of the day they had accomplished merely half the work of the laziest among us." One had to be especially careful, however, not to be accused of sabotage.[169]

POWs who opted to be "transformed" were usually those in relatively cushy situations who feared being sent to an industrial *Kommando*. By giving up their POW status, they kept their jobs and were treated like STO draftees. They were paid in real Marks rather than camp script, which they could remit to their families. Home leave was also a significant inducement, although when a considerable number from the first leave contingent failed to report for the return trip to Germany, home leave was discontinued.[170] These cynical compromises did not discourage Vichy from attempting to legitimize itself through its "protection" of POWs. Gayme estimates that 23 percent of French POWs were so "transformed" by June 1944, and 24 percent in January 1945. This "transformation" could occur against their will or even without their knowledge, when whole sectors like mining and other war-related industries saw their POW work force magically converted to civilian status.[171]

Outwardly, Pétain demonstrated solicitude toward POWs and their families by passing legislation favorable to POWs, and creating commissions of ex-POWs in the administrative center of each department. *La Maison du prisonnier* allegedly provided a service through which families could get information about their captive "dear absent ones" and send them packages through the Red Cross.[172] But increasingly, POWs and their families felt that not enough was being done by Vichy to support them. Family allowances were inadequate – 1,000 francs a month, worth about $20 in 1940, but not indexed to inflation, which was rampant, as food and clothes became scarce. Officers' wives received one-half to three-quarters of the pay of their POW husbands. One reason that Vichy contributed so little was that the armistice surrendered 58 percent of its budget to support the Occupation. This drove women into the workforce, or forced them to seek out male protection and support in other ways, especially as women under French law were treated as legal minors. Indeed, one of the functions of *La Maison du prisonnier* was to keep an eye peeled for adultery among abandoned spouses.[173] For families of POWs, war brought loneliness and hardship.

As the war wore on, the initial adulation for Pétain also ebbed among POWs, who increasingly refused to receive the collaborator Scapini during his visits to French *Oflags* and *Stalags* because he failed to stand up for their interests. Despite Vichy's sanctimony about Catholicism and spiritual renewal, many *Kommandos* never saw a priest. Scapini's position was compromised by the fact that it was difficult to press for the application of the Geneva Convention when Vichy was totally dependent on Hitler for its survival, and Vichy held no German POWs to use as leverage.[174] Scapini did manage to gouge a few concessions from the Germans, although these were usually included as addenda in the context of larger Vichy–Berlin protocols: in November 1940, fathers with four or more children became eligible for a *congé de capitivité* (POW leave) as a result of the 1940 Hitler–Pétain meeting at Montoire.[175] Sixty thousand or so veterans of 1914–1918 were also released. He also lobbied for indigenous POWs in Germany to be sent to camps in the south of France. But these were mere crumbs that Berlin could toss before a politically challenged Vichy to give an impression of flexibility, and more in Berlin's own interests than in those of France. After all, Berlin had all of occupied Eastern and Southern Europe to exploit for labor, millions of Soviet POWs whom they belatedly realized were more valuable alive than dead, and, from September 1943, over 700,000 surrendered Italian soldiers who were not covered by Geneva and so locked into slave labor. They also had a phobia about diseases brought by Africans, and so were happy to expedite them back to France, where they labored for the Todt Organization.

Scapini saw his basic job as insuring the link between POWs and their families, mainly through the *homme de confiance* or prisoner liaison. French POWs complained about lack of news from families, the absence of pay, and the lateness and inadequacy of family allowances. While French POWs were not starved to death as the Russians were initially, POW morale was undermined by the lack of warm clothes and sufficient food, especially as war conditions worsened. They complained that Red Cross inspections of the camps were perfunctory, and that inspectors were invariably accompanied by Germans so that POWs could not air their grievances without fear of retaliation. Brutality by guards was commonplace. Once Allied air raids began, the absence of shelters became an issue. Sub-Saharan and North African POWs were seen as expendable – 18,612 indigenous POWs had died by April 1944, many of tuberculosis.[176]

Conclusion

Of 1,800,000 POWs captured in 1940, 600,000 returned to France between 1941 and 1944. Vichy can take credit for 220,000 of these. "Senegalese" and some North African POWs usually were retained in France to slave for the Todt Organization. The remainder either escaped or were repatriated under the Geneva Convention because they were wounded or sick. Also, among the 600,000 POWs released by Germany were farmers, civil servants, policemen, officers and NCOs of North African and colonial forces, and technicians whose liberation was required by the Geneva Convention or that served German interests. "So, really, only the liberation of the veterans of the 1914–18 war can be counted as an unconditional success," concludes Yves Durand.[177] Although they viewed themselves as "victims of the debacle," POWs were expelled from French wartime memory because they failed to qualify for the heroic Resistance motif of the Liberation. On the contrary, they symbolized France's greatest defeat and hence personified France's crisis of national and masculine identity. They had proven "inadequate in some way" because they had allowed themselves be captured, and 95 percent of them had failed to escape, although the French border was often just kilometers away.[178] But also, they were shunned because they had been "Vichy's adored children" and so discredited along with collaboration. Nevertheless, the Germans were shocked in 1945 by the bitterness of the

French for the alleged poor treatment of French POWs and laborers in Germany. Because the popular image of the French POW was that of a man who had settled comfortably into local life, often substituting for absent German men, to the point that, in German eyes at least, French POWs came to be seen as the war's "spoiled children."[179]

6 "The Wisdom of a Great Leader"

France's defeat was the direct offspring of the military's intellectual and institutional inadequacies, shaped in part within the context of the *levée en masse*. However, France's acceptance of defeat – and its corollary the armistice – suggested a crisis on multiple political, social, and even psychological levels. A rout in a mere six weeks at the hands of an adversary France had conquered a quarter century earlier shattered the fragile façade of Phoney War concord. For France to have rejected the armistice would have required a sense of shared values, a feeling of national solidarity, a popular willingness to sacrifice, and an understanding of the true nature of the enemy. But several things intervened to keep this from happening, beginning with the fact that France and its military were too obsessed with the past and too infused with self-pity.[1]

On 17 June, the day Pétain announced that he would seek an armistice, he also offered, in a voice quavering with age and emotion, "the gift of myself to attenuate [France's] misfortunes." If, in the view of Burrin, the eighty-four-year-old Marshal of France seemed to "derive a morose satisfaction"[2] from defeat, it was because the national collapse allowed him to pose as the guardian of a people whose entire identity had been thrown into question. If the Third Republic had failed to grasp the revolutionary and mobilizing power of war to energize and unify the nation, in defeat, Pétain would conjure humiliation and contrition to forge a popular constituency for Vichy. The Marshal's curriculum vitae was tailored to his adopted role. A Jesuit-educated boy of Artois peasant stock, Pétain nonetheless was never more than a "seasonal Catholic," who late in life married a divorced woman – "It is not likely to have been a church wedding," Pertinax cracked.[3] He shared the anti-Dreyfusard sentiments of his turn of the century military milieu, and blamed nefarious Masonic influence for curbing his honorable but unremarkable pre-1914 career, a common professional alibi in the period for unexceptional performance. French commander-in-chief Joseph Joffre's decimation of the French High Command in the autumn of 1914 expanded Pétain's career opportunities. He distinguished himself in the Artois in 1915. But it was his command of the Second Army at Verdun in 1916 that made Pétain a household name in France. "The victory of Verdun – though the masses were conscious of its immense significance – would have lost some of its awe-inspiring power had it not taken on some distinct human shape, had it not been all aglow with the will, the intelligence, the wisdom of a great leader," Pertinax perceptively noted. Pétain personalized the anonymous, off-the-shelf heroes in the Great War trenches, where France's unknown soldier "was chosen as from a lottery of coffins." "Enshrining the unknown soldier called for enshrining that leader."[4]

Pétain's tactical method was to lay down lashings of artillery fire before an attack. This proved both a politically and a tactically shrewd technique for a conscript force whose natural inclination was to burrow as deeply as possible into the earth. Pétain's reputation for sparing the lives, and looking after the interests, of his citizen soldiers was enhanced by his deft handling of the 1917 mutinies that emphasized improved conditions of service over naked repression. He also issued a "Why We Fight" statement, something that the government had failed to do, explaining to the soldiers that despite the abdication of the Czar and the peace terms offered by the German government, "Germany alone is the obstacle to peace . . . all we ourselves do is to defend ourselves in the name of Liberty and to save our existence."[5] In this way, Pétain's Verdun victory joined his restoration of discipline in the French army in the wake of 1917 to cement his reputation as a soldier's general. "Thus, was built the legend of Pétain," Pertinax concluded. "The reflexes of the crowd produced it . . . The Pétain legend is like a fountain which collects in one single stream a host of rivulets and channels them into an artificial head."[6]

Pétain quelled the Rif rebellion in Morocco in 1925 by a combination of Great War firepower and a starvation blockade, in the process rejecting the signature light-touch colonial methods of warfare allegedly favored by Moroccan Resident General Hubert Lyautey. Indeed, the subsequent forced retirement of France's quintessential colonial proconsul alerted de Gaulle that his patron's natural reflex was to back-stab when it served his personal interests. The Rif War also offered an opportunity for Pétain to make the acquaintance of rising Iberian celebrities like Francisco Franco. His advocacy of a defensive strategy in the inter-war years reassured the left of his commitment to the *levée*. But his reputation as a "republican general" was a carefully crafted deception – he continued to view trade unions, schoolteachers, and Freemasons as agents of subversion, although it had been clear that peasant soldiers pushed to the brink of endurance by failed military leadership had ignited the 1917 mutinies, not subversive intellectuals. His close associates were regularly reminded that politicians "make me sick." As Henry Rousso points out, the entire Vichy regime was fashioned as a form of revenge against Leon Blum's Popular Front.[7] Nevertheless, Pétain had the discretion and the political savvy to maintain his distance from coup-plotting organizations like *la Cagoule*. His reputation as a pragmatist and a partisan of the Maginot Line gained him the trust of the left as well as of Reynaud. But in fact, Pétain was a man of order – frosty, impersonal, egotistical to the point of callousness – whose parched cynicism masqueraded as realism.[8]

Most aging military heroes might be content to bask in the warmth of a reverential public and slip into mellow senility. However, the years since Verdun had failed to soften Pétain's character, temper his Olympian self-esteem, or moderate his opinions, a distillation of traditionalist dogmas and platitudes from the officers' mess. De Gaulle's oft-quoted verdict on his former patron – "old age is a shipwreck" – is modified by most contemporary testimony, which concluded, as did de Gaulle, that egotism and lack of character, not senility, was Pétain's problem. Visitors found him alert, even vigorous, despite his age. But, when it served his interests, he could play possum: in 1942, US ambassador to Vichy and friend of Roosevelt Admiral William Leahy found Pétain to be a "tired old man," who in their interviews kept muttering, "I am a prisoner." He allowed either his Foreign Minister Pierre Flandin or his Premier from April 1942 Pierre Laval to speak for him. But the American ambassador concluded that this was a ruse to avoid serious policy discussion.[9]

Amidst catastrophe, Pétain had stealthily sought power by masquerading as a "republican," and hence a humanized military man. The reverence bestowed on him since 1916 had bolstered his perception of infallibility. Popular adulation offered incontrovertible proof that he personified the nation. He listened to others, and sometimes said things to please them, which might convey the impression of open mindedness, or vacillation. But he stubbornly embraced power's consequences as war and occupation revealed his strategic judgment to be criminally misguided and his policies immoral. In the face of an avalanche of evidence, he obstinately clung to his political choices even as their disastrous consequences unfolded. Only at the mention of de Gaulle's name might his composure liquefy – his face changed color as he spat scorn on "that viper" and "a stain on the honor of the officer corps."[10] De Gaulle reciprocated with withering acerbity that the "bitter caresses ... of military glory" had deepened Pétain's solitude and contempt for others. Secretive, cautious, suspicious, and prickly, Pétain's main purpose in life was to nurture his renown and armor his prestige. In the "extreme winter of his life," Pétain welcomed France's national disaster "as a sign of his elevation and the adornment of his glory."[11]

It is certain, however, that in the middle of June 1940, Pétain had taken the measure of the national mood, which embraced him as "a substitute for politics and a barrier to revolution," as Paxton notes. By the end of 1940, if not before, the logic that had underpinned the acceptance of the armistice – a short war, Britain's rapid capitulation, the looming threat of communist revolution, and the quick conclusion of a Franco-Axis peace that would liberate French POWs – had skipped from delusion to dishonor. But a Third Republic already delegitimized in June 1940 committed suicide when, at the direction of Pierre Laval, the constitution of 1875 was suspended on 9 July. The following day, Pétain was voted "full powers" to draft a new constitution by a vote of 569 to 80, with 17 abstentions. On 11 July, the Marshal proclaimed himself "Head of the French State," with the authority to carry out all executive and legislative acts, except declarations of war, without referring to the Assembly.[12] *Action Française* leader Charles Maurras' "divine surprise" proclaimed "la grandeur that emerges from our disaster," casting Pétain as "*l'homme providentiel*," a Christ-like figure who through the sacrifice of his person would redeem France's decadent past. Never mind that his public utterances consisted mainly of gloomy vapidities. They were received as Divine pronouncements because the "supreme catastrophe" had produced communal trauma and shared contrition. Lightning defeat had blown away a sense of security lent by the Maginot Line and deceptive Phoney War normality. Defeat reversed the verdict of 1918, shattered faith in the *levée*, humiliated the French army, and stigmatized a generation. For a disorientated nation suddenly gripped by "an immense collective fear," culpability, and a sense of abandonment, Pétain became the pivot of a new cult, "sent to us by the dead of Verdun ..."[13] Gaullist Diego Brosset believed that, "in their faith in Pétain, the French above all manifested a desire to obey an authority."[14] Indeed, detractors subsequently complained that Pétain made France pay the price for Verdun twice over.

When France's most glorious living figure announced that resistance must cease, a shattered and disheartened nation obeyed. France must "regenerate" through suffering. "A comparison with the 14–18 war does not favor the French of 1940," concluded Captain Paul Gail in the aftermath of the armistice. "Less guts than in the last war. Much less initiative. Lack of education, both general and military. In short, a *diminished race, undermined by alcohol, debased by the amoralism of public institutions, by public schools and all social life. A Nation to reconstruct, for whom the defeat was necessary.*" (Gail's italics).[15] The groundwork for resurrection was to be prepared by initiating France into "a phase of sorrowfulness and infantile shaming,"[16] to stabilize the regime and put the French population into a rehabilitative mood. The silver lining of

1940 for the anti-Dreyfusard military elite who dominated Vichy in its early months was that *Der Führer* had liberated them from the *levée*, with its inherent threat to the existence of the professional military and its potential for communist-led subversion.[17] Meanwhile, collaboration was expected to pay handsome dividends by positioning France to play an important role in Hitler's "New Europe." In this way, Vichy's National Revolution aimed at nothing less than to initiate a mental, psychological, and social restructuring of France.[18]

Vichy's ideological and cultural miscellany was lent coherence by the cult of personality centered on the Marshal, headlined by Vichy's mantra of "travail, famille, patrie" (work, family, fatherland).[19] In the wake of France's national identity crisis, the National Revolution held great appeal at least through 1942, and not just on the right. At once, it offered both an explanation for defeat and a formula for national renewal through the recovery of traditional and masculine values. Above all, Pétain's message seemed to be one of discipline and unity supported by the Church. Technocracy required virtue, purity, and a strong leader. Vichy was a reaction against the cronyism and disorder of the "Republic of pals." This is why its advent was hailed by most of the French military and civil service, who perceived democracy to be corrupt and inefficient, characterized by *laissez-aller* that suborned a rules-based order, and made it difficult for them to do their jobs. Technocrats, Radical Party "Young Turks" and neo-socialists, and some Christian Democrats initially were attracted to Vichy's promise of government efficiency through a rational and interventionist role in the economy for a French state liberated from Third Republic skullduggery.

Some enlightened conservatives like Jewish intellectual Raymond Aron assumed initially that Vichy's anti-Jewish laws had been imposed by the Germans. As professional soldier and resistance leader Henri Frenay noted, smitten by Pétain's prestige, officers of the Armistice Army were content to validate their "strongly reactionary" values behind a doctrine of "obedience to legality." Pétain's collaboration was rationalized as a "double game" deception to mask preparation for *la Revanche*.[20] However, as Burrin notes, that Vichy's mediocrity and ineptitude rivaled that of the Third Republic is hardly surprising, given that the Marshal's government retained *la troisième*'s most pliant officials and incompetent administrators. Meanwhile, Vichy's political and military leaders, overawed by Germany's military prowess and dependent on Hitler for their political survival, not only buckled to Berlin's demands but also jostled to anticipate them.[21] As a consequence, many talented technocrats, like Jean Monnet, would eventually transfer their loyalties to Fighting France via Henri Giraud. Even some army officers like Henri Frenay woke up in 1941 to the "tragic illusion" of Pétainism, which he called a "clever attempt at perversion, these campaigns of lies, these crimes committed beneath a veil of honor and the appearance of patriotism ... [these appeals] to obedience, to discipline to cover cowardice and treason."[22]

The collective sigh of national relief that greeted the cessation of hostilities had been encouraged by Pétain's assurance that the armistice would not only preserve the army, but also protect civilians caught up in the exodus. Nor, he insisted, was it "contrary to honor," which the French would discover was a very tactical concept for the old Marshal.[23] Few military men dissented. At a stroke, surrender became an "honorable" act. By ceasing to fight, soldiers capitulated as an army, "honorably" as a collective under orders from the political authority, not as individuals.[24] Numbered among the dissenters was Lieutenant commander Georges Thierry d'Argenlieu, for whom "the moral duty of the soldier is to continue the struggle out of fidelity to his military ethic." Those who downed arms because so ordered by a "legal" government, brought to power in effect by a coup d'état on 17 June, simply sought refuge behind a "facile obedience, a soothing balm for tender or timorous consciences."[25]

The request for an armistice – that is, a temporary truce that suspends military operations, meant as a preliminary step toward a peace treaty – also acknowledged that, in defeat, France was no longer a great power. Those republicans who calculated that Hitler's armistice conditions would prove unacceptable even to defeatists were quickly disabused. Hitler's strategy was to offer relatively soft terms to keep the fleet and the empire from defecting, and then coax Great Britain out of the war. General Charles Huntzinger, chief architect of the Sedan debacle and Pétain's choice to represent France at Rethondes (Figure 6.1), phoned news of Hitler's "concessions" to Weygand on 21 June, presented as if they had been the result of his superior negotiating skills. In fact, as Paxton notes, Hitler had drawn up the armistice provisions on 16 June, a day before Pétain's signature broadcast announcing that he would seek an armistice. Hitler's "concessions" merely signified that these heretofore great symbols of French sovereignty and international status were henceforth subsumed into the German empire, like the Poles of Silesia or the Czechs of the Sudetenland. At a stroke, a once-great colonial power transformed itself into a colony, first of the Germans, then of the Americans.

The armistice contained only thirty-five articles. It made no territorial or colonial claims. France was to be divided into occupied and unoccupied zones, with a demarcation line dividing the two (Map 6.1). Article 3 stipulated that in the *zone non-occupée*, misleadingly branded the *zone libre*, which covered about three-fifths of French territory, the Reich would

Figure 6.1 Col. Gen. Wilhelm Keitel reads out the conditions of the armistice at Rethondes, France, in the forest of Compiègne, 22 June 1940. On the left, Hitler; in the middle, Léon Noël, French ambassador to Poland; on his left, General Charles Huntziger. Also present are Grand Admiral Erich Raeder, Field Marshal Hermann Göring, Col. Gen. Walther von Brauchitsch, Rudolf Hess, Rear Admiral Maurice Le Luc, and foreign minister Joachim von Ribbentrop. Standing in the rear are Chief Adjutant Wilhelm Brückner and translator Paul Schmidt.

exercise "the rights of the occupying power." The French administration there would "collaborate" in a "*manière correcte.*" It allowed the French government to select an administrative capital in the unoccupied zone. After rejecting several potential locations, Vichy, France's leading spa town, with ample hotel space to accommodate the ersatz government's relocated ministries, was chosen as the new capital. When he first encountered Vichy in early 1942 after his escape from captivity in Germany, Sergeant François Mitterand described it as "an awful town [not disagreeable, not boring: ugly]. Nothing arrests your attention, in its voluminous and stupidly linear hotels, its villas pretentiously arranged according to the questionable tastes of overweight women. One should tear down these spa towns."[26] When Admiral William Leahy, Franklin Roosevelt's friend and the new American ambassador to France arrived in Vichy in January 1941, he encountered "A government that wasn't fully sovereign, in a small city that seemed

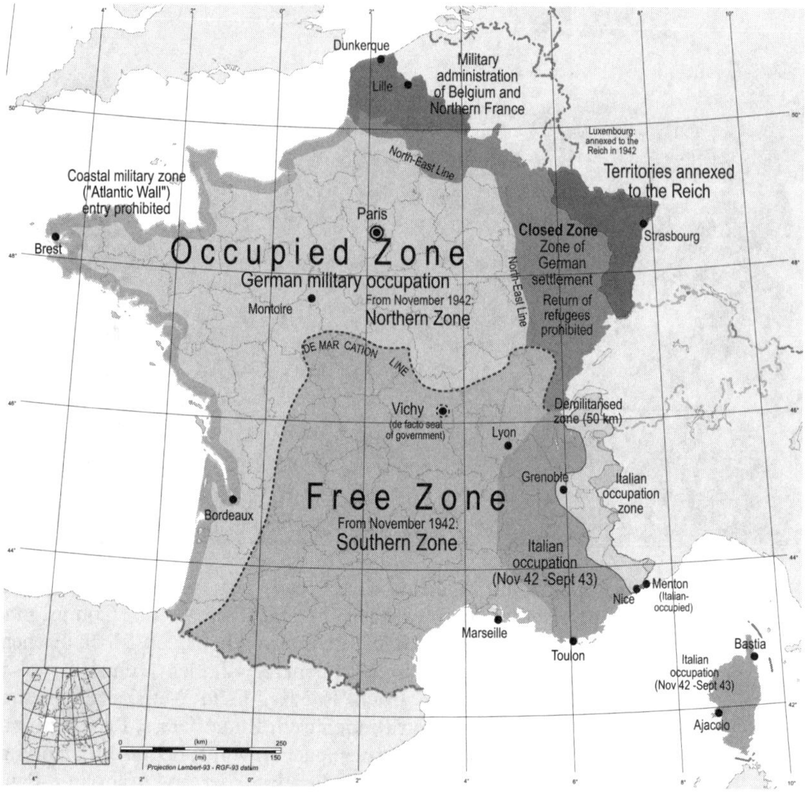

Map 6.1 Map of occupied France. Authors: Eric Gaba (map), Rama (zones). Data source: NGDC World Data Bank II. Wikimedia Commons, GFDL.

permanently on the edge of a nervous breakdown," in the words of Leahy's biographer Philipps O'Brien. "Vichy struck Leahy as part soap opera, part asylum, part tragedy in need of support and pity." All of France's shame and trauma of defeat, all of its insecurities, congealed in this small space.[27]

The Armistice Army

Even if the armistice confirmed France's decline to the status of a second-tier nation, Vichy nevertheless retained considerable military power, although much of it remained incarcerated in German prison camps or captive to the combat-discriminatory mindset of the Vichy navy. Article 4 required French forces to demobilize, except for those needed to maintain internal order. On 25 November 1940, an "Armistice Army," whose strength was fixed at 100,000 men on the French mainland, was approved. This number was imposed by the Germans to replicate the Allied imposition of the *Reichswehr* post-Versailles. It was to be composed of three-year volunteers from the unoccupied zone – requests to recruit in the occupied zone were rejected by the Germans. From Vichy's perspective, the purpose of the Armistice Army was to spearhead France's resurrection by bringing "public opinion into accord with the views of career officers." Vichy's traditionalist message would be disseminated "first within the army, then within the nation."[28] However, to sustain a 100,000-man strength level required the incorporation of at least 1,500 volunteers each month, a figure never attained, according to Paxton. For that reason, until 1942, the army continued to include soldiers from the last conscript classes mobilized for the war. Units were closely monitored by inspection teams from the German control commission to make sure that they contained no more than 4 percent officers and 12 percent NCOs.[29]

Historian of the French air force Claude d'Abzac-Epezy argues that, despite armistice restrictions, Vichy maintained a considerable force under arms. She reckons that the Armistice Army in France numbered around 95,000. To this could be added 60,000 gendarmes and 26,000 firemen who were included in army ranks, as well as *gardes mobiles* and *travailleurs coloniaux*. Depending on who one counts as "soldiers," North Africa was garrisoned by between 100,000 and 140,000, with similar numbers in the colonies. The Navy retained 60,000 sailors, while air force numbers were 80,000 in 1942, half of whom were in the AAA, which was transferred from the army to the air force in the wake of the defeat.[30] Vichy was allowed to raise a civilian conservation corps called *les Chantiers de la Jeunesse* meant to serve as a reservoir of volunteers, and create *écoles des cadres*, whose purpose was to build the character judged to be so lacking in French youth. Later, various paramilitary groups would also be raised to reinforce internal order, to include *la Légion des volontaires français contre le bolchévisme* (LVF), the dreaded and thuggish *Milice*, and a paramilitary police, the *Groupe mobile de réserve* (GMR).

However, rather than prepare clandestinely for *la revanche* as many of its supporters believed, Vichy's energies were directed into collaboration. The lesson of 1940, at least on the right, was that defeat had delegitimized the Third Republic,[31] in the process delivering the *coup de grâce* to a Revolutionary and Jaurèsian vision of the *levée en masse* as a dynamic association of the state, the regular army, and the citizen soldier in the common purpose of national defense. Conservatives blamed 1940 on "three generations of antimilitarist and antipatriotic lay school instruction," which had turned reserve officers into "skeptics" and eradicated all respect for authority among the troops. The *levée* had to be reconfigured to bolster a conservative order. With the professional soldiers in the vanguard of Vichy's National Revolution, the *levée* would prove challenging to resurrect on the basis of a Republican civil–military compact. So, what France would witness in the wake of the November 1942 dissolution of the Armistice Army would be an imperial mobilization directed by colonial soldiers, while within the Hexagon there would emerge a civilian *levée* as part of a European groundswell of resistance to Fascism. Absent an *union sacrée*, Charles de Gaulle would order the "amalgamation" of these competing *levées* from September 1944.

The *zone libre* was partitioned into eight military regions, each with its own infantry division, consisting of three infantry regiments, one cavalry regiment, and a horse-drawn artillery regiment whose gun calibers could not exceed 75 mm, plus an engineer battalion, and signals, supply, and police companies. Units in France were forbidden to include tanks, anti-tank guns, and anti-aircraft artillery in their arms inventories, and their munitions stocks were limited. Because infantry regiments were allowed only five automobiles and seven motorbikes, locomotion was mainly by bicycle, horse, and on foot – not much of a change from 1939–1940! But for Huntzinger, who replaced Weygand as *Ministre secrétaire d'état à la Guerre* on 6 September, armaments were secondary to building a "will to fight." To achieve this end, Huntzinger emphasized ceremony and sports competitions to create a taste for risk and adventure, group pride, and confidence which, through osmosis, this would invigorate the civilian population. But these goals would prove elusive for an army whose precarious inter-war prestige had completely flamed out in May–June 1940. Its mission allegedly was to maintain internal order in a country where *francs-tireurs* and Communards of 1870–1871 stubbornly failed to materialize in its brief lifetime. Some of its members naively believed that the armistice army's purpose was to defend Vichy from a German invasion of the *zone libre*, and to stash weapons and train to lead the *levée* in *la Revanche*. But apparently that thought never entered the heads of Pétain and his inner circle. As a consequence, Vichy fashioned a phoney army for a phoney regime.[32]

Eight thousand of the pre-armistice army's 30,000 regular officers were to be retained in France and North Africa. More interested in reinforcing tradition and in the spirit of *attentisme* ("wait and see"), Vichy's principal concern was to homogenize the officer corps rather than open it to innovation and fresh ideas, for which admittedly there was not much scope. A considerable number of regular officers remained in *Oflags*. Lowering the retirement age limit eliminated some older officers. Many non-combat posts – medical, logistics, military justice, and so on – were civilianized. Preference for retention went to Saint-Cyr graduates, while many reserve officers or NCOs who had converted to regular status were offered "armistice leave," which sent them home with reduced pay. The *Statut des juifs* (Statute on the Jews) of 3 October 1940 defined who was a Jew in the eyes of the French state and then excluded them from a range of positions in public service, liberal professions, and the officer corps, although the military services went beyond the *Statut des juifs* and excluded Jews from the NCO corps as well. In Algeria, Jews were forbidden to enlist in the military services, and excluded from the *Chantiers de la Jeunesse*. Jews were not considered French *de la souche* by Vichy, but rather addenda to the national community whose loyalties were tribal rather than national. This was not forced on Vichy by the Germans, but was self-generated and anchored in popular prejudice, no means confined to France. "Without any possible doubt, Vichy had begun its own anti-Semitic career before the first German appeared, and without direct German order," conclude Michael Marrus and Robert Paxton.[33]

"Secret societies" formed a particular obsession of Vichy, convinced that Masonic infiltration of the French state had formed a fifth column that had facilitated defeat. The "Masonic plot" had fused with the "Jewish plot" at the end of the eighteenth century as an explanation for the French Revolution among conspiratorially minded clerics, to be fleshed out and propagated in the nineteenth, gaining the imprimatur of several Vatican senior residents. A belief that a sinister "Judeo-Masonic plot" churned in the backstage of the Republic had become widespread in the French officer corps in the wake of the Dreyfus affair and the 1905 revelation that the War Minister, a Mason, had enlisted the Grand Orient de France to collect information on the political opinions and religious practices of officers. Conservatives accused Masonic lodges of fostering a parallel system of loyalty to circumvent and subvert the military hierarchy, undermine the army's essentially Catholic values, and hence destabilize French defense. Because many Radical Party politicians were also Masons, expelling Masons from the Armistice Army would also expunge the last residues of Third Republic subterfuge from the officer corps.[34]

Given the antipathy for the Masons on the French right, and the certitude that Masonic conspiracies and favoritism had hijacked and suborned the French state, hardly had *l'État français* come into existence than, amidst the turmoil of defeat and *exode*, it prioritized a 13 August law outlawing Freemasons. The German occupation of Paris on 14 June 1940 was followed by a descent on the Grand Orient de France and the Siège du Droit humain on the rue Jules-Breton in Paris' XIIIe arrondissement.

Unfortunately for the Germans, the Grand Orient's membership lists had been evacuated and destroyed during *l'exode*. An anti-Masonic fringe at Vichy led by Bernard Faÿ, an academic Americanist, royalist, professor at the prestigious Collège de France, and Director of the Bibliothèque nationale, maintained an almost cultic fascination for Masonic symbols and rituals. Faÿ was backed by Pétain, who, with his familiar penetrating wisdom, pronounced: "A Jew is never responsible for his origins, but a free mason always has a choice." With sparse documentation, it took Faÿ's *Service des sociétés secrètes* almost a year to reconstruct a list of Masons, much of it through denunciations, which was made public on 12 August 1941. Obviously, they had cast a wide net, assembling 170,000 names, 17,000 of which were published in the *Journal officielle*, when the actual number of masons in France was more like 60,000. The propaganda impact fell far short of Vichy expectations, however. A number of Vichy supporters, antisemites, and anti-parliamentary politicians and journalists were listed, among them Georges Dumoulin, a journalist at *Nouvelles continentales*, a German propaganda outlet in France. But the most surprising name on the list was Marcel Peyrouton, Vichy Minister of the Interior in September 1940, who until 1934 had been a member of the Grand Orient de France. As a cure for the army's problems, it must have come as a disappointment that masons were sparse among professional soldiers: 96 Jewish officers and 216 NCOs were forced into retirement, while the anti-Masonic decree netted only 135 officers, 10 of whom were generals, and 24 NCOs, mostly in support services. This rather mocked claims of nefarious "secret society" influence in the army, which had been dogma among conservatives since Dreyfus.[35]

For their part, ordinary French people discovered that, far from a dark conspiracy to pervert the normal functioning of government and undermine the Catholic religion, the lists included the friendly gendarme, the chatty postman, the school teacher who had coached their child through his exams, and the mayor for whom they had voted. Many on the list were long deceased, while others had never darkened the door of a Masonic hall. Their cover blown, some begged to be pardoned for *une faute de jeunesse*. The backlash was such that by November, Vichy was forced to create a commission to consider dispensations and exceptions, one which from March 1943, under the chairmanship of liberal jurist Marcel Reclus, who found the whole "secret society" concept a legal absurdity, did much to gut Vichy's anti-masonic measures of substance. In the end, around 3,500 were eventually fired from official positions for Masonic connections. Masons continued to meet clandestinely in France, and reorganized seventy masonic lodges across North Africa following Torch in November 1942, where anti-masonic legislation was not repealed until

December 1943. An estimated 2,000–3,000 Masons joined resistance groups.[36]

What this "transition army" was actually meant to transition to was unclear. One view is that the Armistice Army was a sort of "pre-resistance," in the form of arms caches and plans to make common cause with an Allied invasion of France's south coast in late 1942 or 1943. From 1942, several hundred of its officers joined the internal resistance or made their way to North Africa after November 1942.[37] But, as Paxton notes, the vision at Vichy was not to create an "army of leaders" in the style of the post-Versailles *Reichswehr*. Nor was it encouraged to prepare for *la Revanche*, which, until the Anglo-American invasion of French North Africa in November 1942, remained largely a Gaullist monopoly. The hypothesis that had informed the 1940 armistice lingered – that Britain would be defeated, France would sign a peace treaty with Germany, the POWs would be repatriated, and over time France could reclaim its standing because Hitler could not build his "New Europe" without France. Even when none of these predictions materialized, Phoney War thinking that the conflict's likely outcome would be "peace without a victor" lingered. In the meantime, the French military reveled in its pyrrhic triumph over the *levée*. Pétain had transferred responsibility for the debacle to the Republic, and so assuaged officially the army's sense of culpability and the humiliation. Order and hierarchy appeared to have been restored in France, that could now regenerate from within – the notion that France could be rescued from abroad by a claque of British-financed *émigrés* denied the cult of Pétain and "His Majesty the Soil." In this way, the Armistice Army became a sort of Marshal-centered sect, in which officer members surrendered "the individual conscience of free citizens." In their view, de Gaulle was a "dissident," an apostate, a mercenary, a deserter, and an outcast. "Blind obedience [to Pétain] had become, for the soldiers, the highest form of duty," concludes Belot.[38] Restored to the center of French decision-making, soldiers and sailors infiltrated France's civilian infrastructure, armed with the full powers of the 1939 State of Siege. More officers sat in Pétain's 12 July government than in any French government since that of King Louis-Philippe in 1832. Military men occupied the governorships of France's five most important colonial possessions. Eight officers became prefects, while Admiral François Bard occupied the prefecture of the Paris police for a year from May 1941.[39]

Not everyone was taken in by France's newly militarized profile. Without a constituency, held in low public esteem, limited in its mission, and closely monitored by the occupier, the Armistice Army's freedom of action was tightly circumscribed. French journalist Alfred Fabre-Luce, initially favorable to Vichy, likened the Armistice Army to a comic opera force composed of officers without soldiers who had switched out their tanks for "an insulting bicycle."[40] US ambassador Leahy, who attended a military review in early 1942, discovered that not only was Vichy having trouble finding volunteers to fill Armistice Army ranks, but also "the Marshal's 'army' looked like a convention of the Knights of Pythias. It was really pitiful. Here was a hero of World War I. He had commanded a great army. He had become Chief of State. Now he had nothing."[41] A June 1942 German evaluation of the Armistice Army noted that the lack of a war college had resulted in a shortage of staff officers, little training was done above the company level, and no arms or ammunition was available for firing practice. As a result: "The preparation of the units of the Transitional Army for combat [employment] corresponds to the lack of uniformity in training, but is sufficient to permit their employment for the quelling of internal disturbances."[42]

On 19 October 1940, Huntzinger gave strict orders that no resistance be offered should the Germans invade the *zone libre*. Indeed, the Germans were surprised when, during the tensions produced by Pétain's firing of Laval in December 1941, the Armistice Army took no defensive measures against a potential German incursion.[43] The army's task was to play its role in the rehabilitation of the French nation. Because France's defeat had been induced by the Third Republic's political divisions, weak leadership, and public demoralization, recovery would occur only when popular morale and confidence had been regenerated through Vichy's National Revolution. In the meantime, this "transition army" would keep France's military traditions alive and assure institutional continuity. For France's defeated soldiers, Pétain personified the army, and allowed military leaders at last "to be heard" in the corridors of power.[44]

But the price to be paid by the armed forces for gaining fleeting and largely illusory sway in a remaindered government would be high. Nor did it foreshadow the mentality and moral choices required for resistance participation. In the vanguard, Henry Frenay resigned his commission in January 1941, broke with Vichy, and later joined Jean Moulin's *Conseil national de la résistance* (CNR) formed in May 1943. He complained that while the anti-German sentiments of many officers initially drew them to Vichy, Pétain had abused their patriotism to convince officers that a clandestine national revival was being plotted beneath a subterfuge of Vichy collaboration. Although Frenay had recognized Vichy's scam from early 1941, it would take Torch, followed by the Axis invasion of the *zone libre* and the concomitant inertia of the Armistice Army to lay bare the full scope of Pétain's swindle. The final blow became orders from Vichy to surrender arms caches to the German and Italian occupiers, which many of Vichy's military backers naively had believed secreted to arm *la Révanche*. And even then, they excused Pétain with the alibi that he was a "prisoner." Frenay blamed this myopia on the "strongly reactionary" values of a French military milieu that inculcated "obedience to legality" and discipline over "the individual conscience of a free citizen." "For soldiers, blind obedience became the highest form of duty," he remembered. It was a culture that not only tolerated the occupation, but also encouraged a civil war in France because officers had lost the ability to question their values and examine the consequences of their choices. It was loyalty to the tribe over the nation, precisely the crime of which they accused Jews and Freemasons. Pétain was a fellow officer, one of them, and therefore his motives remained beyond reproach. Weygand and Huntzinger could not break out of this "legal framework" of obedience that required "total adherence" through an oath of loyalty to Pétain.[45]

Enlistment in the Marshal's cult was comforting, because it lightened the burden of defeat, while also absolving soldiers of responsibility for the debacle. Vichy promised a restoration of hierarchy and order, which in their view the Third Republic had subverted. A contrary view advanced by those officers who signed on to assist the November 1942 Anglo-American invasion of AFN argued that officers whose logic was anchored in an anti-republican sentiment failed to realize that military obedience was subject to conscience. Frenay came early to the view that France's allegedly "apolitical" military had descended into groveling adulation, a sentimental, even "fervent," allegiance to a political leader. By taking a personal oath of loyalty to Pétain, they were enlisting in a totalitarian process to transform the army into "a servile political instrument ... in which the duty of obedience is not necessarily compatible with patriotic duty." The Gaullists had identified immediately what Frenay called the "tragic illusion" of Pétainism, with its "shrewd attempts at corruption, its campaigns of lies, its crimes committed under a veil of honor and appearances of patriotism ... [these appeals to] obedience, to discipline to cover cowardice and treason." But the vast majority of officers remained persuaded that Pétain "was preparing an army of revenge in the shadows," and would be hard pressed to reconcile themselves to de Gaulle's treachery.[46]

As Julian Jackson notes, Pétain's problem was that increasing German pressure to transform France into a war economy and deliver Jews, combined with its need to repatriate French POWs to demonstrate the benefits of collaboration, had stripped Vichy of its independence.[47] While not all officers agreed with official Armistice Army passivity, especially in the face of Italian pretentions, even pro-Allied officers were wary about taking "premature action" against the Germans. From the beginning of the occupation, however, some officers had begun to secrete arms in anticipation of Liberation and a final showdown with the occupiers. Initially, Huntzinger had discouraged acts that might jeopardize the armistice. As a consequence, the vast bulk of French arms and munitions had been surrendered in 1940 – more even than the Germans had anticipated. Only in September 1941 did Huntzinger authorize the formation of a *compagnie camouflée de transport militaire* to defend Nice in case of an Italian occupation. But by then, Huntzinger was playing catch-up, for officers encouraged by General Jean-Édouard Verneau, Noguès' former chief of staff and, from August 1940, *Chef de la délégation des services de l'armistice*, had established secret arms caches throughout the unoccupied zone – indeed, when the Germans occupied the *zone libre* in November 1942, they were astonished to discover 536 arms depots. Many of them represented the initiative from July 1940 of Colonel Emile Mollard, who organized the *Camouflage du Matériel* (CDM) under the name of a phantom company, la société Étienne Dubourg registered in Marseilles. Trucks were hidden in the inventories of transport companies, known as "sociétés XV." However, when in November 1942 news of the Allied invasion of North Africa reached Vichy, some officers at least made preparations to shift to defensive fallback positions in the face of the German invasion of the *zone libre*. However, on 10 November, the *Ministre secrétaire à la Guerre* and army commander General Eugène Bridoux repeated his predecessor Huntzinger's order to offer no resistance to German encroachment. Of the two division commanders who disobeyed Bridoux's order, only Jean de Lattre de Tassigny was court martialed and imprisoned.[48] Captain Jean Vallette d'Osia fled into the resistance in December after refusing to deliver arms stocks to the Germans on the orders of the Prefect of the Haute-Savoie.

While these very ingenious labors were in retrospect presented as evidence to bolster the resistance credentials of the Armistice Army, Frenay pointed out that the army had no plan to use the cached weapons.[49] When it became apparent, on 9 November 1942, that German troops were massing to invade the *zone libre*, Pétain called a conference of his military command, including Weygand and Georges. No one suggested resistance to the Germans. In fact, Weygand professed not to know what the plan was to resist an invasion from the north. In the process, Pétain replicated Weygand's attempt to combine an anti-German spirit with a refusal to enter into dissidence.[50] There was a brief spasm of activity on 9 November, most notably the withdrawal of some units of de Lattre's 14th division toward defensive positions in the Corbières hills near Perpignan. But the order was rescinded on the next day, because to resist ran counter to Laval's policy of collaboration. Vichy officials, including Armistice Army leaders, also feared German reprisals and public unrest. To have offered armed resistance required acts of disobedience, to transgress the selective "neutrality" that underpinned Vichy foreign policy, and which violated the behavioral norms of the vast majority of the Armistice Army officers inculcated into a cult of obedience and Marshal worship. Weygand also feared that resistance would merely terminate in yet another ignominious surrender by the French army. Instead, until 19 November 1942, when Hitler ordered them to withdraw, Armistice Army units were deployed on the south coast to repel possible Allied landings. This was because Vichy still saw value in adhering to the armistice. "The fact that at least two of the eight Military Divisions [the 12th and 14th] received formal orders not to open fire [on the Germans], appears to demolish the legend that the Armistice Army General Staff attempted to mount an armed opposition to the Germans," concludes Paxton.[51]

Jean de Lattre de Tassigny proved to be the exception, although in many respects a surprising one. His taste for pomp, and a personality so flamboyant that he made Oscar Wilde seem like a wallflower, had already differentiated de Lattre from his intense, deferential, conventional colleagues. His conservative outlook and taste for political intrigue had made him an objective of parliamentary scrutiny in the wake of the antirepublican riots of February 1934.[52] Indeed, Pertinax remembered an argument over de Gaulle's proposal for a professional army that had erupted over lunch at his home in 1935 between Lieutenant colonels de Gaulle and de Lattre, at the time a member of Weygand's staff, so acrimonious that his wife complained that the two guests had transgressed the decorum of hospitality.[53] De Lattre's post-defeat enthusiasm for *écoles des cadres* (leadership schools), to bypass the deadening monotony of barrack life and repair the "decadence" of French youth, anchored him intellectually in the Vichy camp, although the sentiment that a "decadent" France must be revitalized was shared across the political spectrum. De Lattre's name was even placed in the running to replace Huntzinger at the Defense Secretariat. But de Lattre's star at Vichy had begun to dim after he fell out with Alphonse Juin over plans for the defense of Tunisia. And clearly resistance leaders had identified de Lattre as part of the "dissident" faction at Vichy, because in the summer of 1942 he had been approached by an emissary of Jean Moulin to head-up the *Armée secrète* (AS), the military wing of the resistance, an offer which he declined. While the German invasion of the *zone libre* in November divided the Armistice Army, it succeeded in pushing de Lattre into rebellion. But when on 11 November Vichy Secretary for

Defense General Eugène Bridoux reversed Armistice Army chief of staff General Verneau's order to take up defensive positions, de Lattre ordered his "division" to resist in any case. But three out of his four regimental commanders were prepared to buck their boss and "remain within the framework of superior orders." On 11 November 1943, de Lattre's command was terminated, and he was placed under arrest. He refused escape offers from the resistance, explaining that he was counting on justice from the Marshal. In fact, on 9 January 1943, the "Marshal's justice" rewarded him with a ten-year sentence for "treason" and abandoning his post. Stripped of his rank, de Lattre would spend the next ten months in prison in not too onerous circumstances – at least his guards continued to salute him. Rudolf Schleier, who replaced Otto Abetz as ambassador to France during 1943, and Krug von Nidda, the minister plenipotentiary at Vichy, numbered among those who had wanted to ship de Lattre to Germany out of fear that he might become the ring leader for a military coup against Pétain. And they were no doubt correct, because a failed escape attempt in May 1943 was followed by a successful one on 2–3 September. To her dying day, Madame de Lattre maintained that her husband had sawed through the bars of his cell, climbed down a rope, and then scaled the outer wall of the prison on a ladder provided by their son Bernard. Most believed this athletic exploit, which rivaled in drama the escape of Henri Giraud from Königstein Fortress in Saxony, was concocted to hide the complicity of de Lattre's jailers. Supplied with false papers by the resistance network Gallia, he hid out in the Massif Central until evacuated to London in a Hudson light bomber on the night of 16–17 October from a field north of Mâcon, and subsequently made his way via London to Algiers, where his junior at Saint-Cyr Charles de Gaulle rewarded him with the rank of *général d'armée*.[54]

Of course, it must be pointed out that the inaction of Armistice Army personnel fell squarely within the norm of the tens of thousands of French civil servants, police, businessmen, and bankers whose collaboration allowed a relative handful of *Wehrmacht* and Gestapo to control roughly 40 million French men and women, pillage the economy, deport Jews, and conscript workers for obligatory labor in Germany and France (STO).[55] Resisters, like Jean Moulin, Pierre Brossolette, and their ilk, were the exceptions, not the rule. Few weapons or vehicles from Armistice Army stashes ever found their way into the hands of the resistance. By the Liberation, many of these hidden weapons, like anti-tank guns, were out of date in any case, as they had been in 1940, and would have done little to increase the capabilities of the Armistice Army to resist the Germans, even had they been so inclined. Along with the CDM, the Armistice Army also created a *Bureau national des statistiques* to keep track of reservists to be called up at the Liberation. The *Chantiers de la Jeunesse* and a 20,000-man Polish resistance active in France were also to be mobilized to assist an Allied invasion of France's south coast, which was expected in early 1943. On paper, this mobilization was calculated to bring Armistice Army strength to 175,000 men organized in twenty-four small divisions. But most of those registered were First World War veterans. *Vichysto-résistants* refused to cooperate with Gaullists. The best-case scenario envisioned by Armistice Army revanchists would be a German evacuation of France, so that the mobilization could be carried out without interference, and the superannuated reservists assembled into divisions would enter Paris – perhaps on foot and clutching their disparate antique weaponry – but in triumph nevertheless.[56]

With the occupation of the *zone libre*, the vision of an army-led revival of France imploded, together with Vichy's sham sovereignty. A number of officers formed resistance organizations, or defected to existing ones like the ORA or the OCM. A few stiffened groups of *maquis*, who in the course of 1943 began to collect in the Alps and other remote regions. Around 1,000–1,500 officers by some estimates became *évadés de France* by scaling the Pyrenees to reach North Africa via Spain to enlist in the reorganizing French forces. For their resistance efforts, which continued after November 1942, both Verneau and Mollard perished in deportation. But the simple truth was that, by their refusal to disobey the Marshal, the army had ceded leadership of the resistance *levée* to civilians. The collapse of organized military resistance in the shadow of Vichy revealed the toxic influence of Pétainism on public opinion, and on the spirit of officers in particular.[57]

Resuscitating French Virility

In the wake of France's catastrophic defeat, conservative scolds jostled to offer remedies for France's generational dissipation. These experiments also drew inspiration from older French traditions of religious associations, *compagnonnage*, as well as the Scouting movement. Henry Dhavernas formed the *Compagnons de France* in 1940, an organization of Maurrassien inspiration which alloyed the ideals of the Boy Scouts and Catholicism, which Dhavernas believed inseparable.[58] Something called *écoles des cadres* – schools for leaders – became all the rage among muscular Vichy supporters, who envisioned a mechanism to harden and reinforce "salutary" military values and discipline among French youth, while evangelizing Vichy's National Revolution by inculcating leadership qualities and patriotic behavior. Under the charismatic Captain Pierre Dunoyer de Segonzac, the *École nationale des cadres de la jeunesse* was officially created at Uriage in the Savoie on 7 December 1940, out of a series of two-to-three-week short courses that had been initiated since September of that year. In the view of de Segonzac and his roughly twenty "apolitical" Catholic officer acolytes, 1940 had witnessed a collapse of national leadership at all levels – social, political, intellectual, and military. His *École des cadres d'Uriage* aspired to forge new elites trained in the "profession of leadership." The course was underpinned by a miscellany of military values, with the emphasis on honor, discipline, and "energy in action," the importance of the "team" under a "leader," a cult of initiative, improvization, service to others, critical thinking, and self-control. Initially, Uriage found favor at Vichy, and earned de Segonzac a *francisque* – a sort of Vichy equivalent of de Gaulle's coveted *compagnon de la libération* – as Pétain's special token of gratitude. One selected for the honor must swear that he was neither a Jew nor had ever belonged to a "secret society," and make "the gift of my person to the Marshal," *et voilà*, he was awarded a decoration that, like François Mitterand, he would spend the remainder of his post-war existence struggling to conceal. Uriage fell under the supervision of Georges Lamirand at the *Secrétariat général à la Jeunesse* (SGJ), a subsidiary of the *Ministère de la Famille et de la Jeunesse.* An engineer with a law degree, strongly influenced by Marshal Hubert Lyautey and social Catholicism, and active in the *Union sociale des ingénieurs Catholiques*, Lamirand had pioneered apprenticeship training for young workers in the inter-war years. One of the goals of the *écoles des cadres* was to provide a structure for France's unemployed youth and infuse them with "*l'esprit d'Uriage.*"[59]

Given his flamboyant personality, boundless energy, and temporary underemployment, Jean de Lattre de Tassigny too dabbled in Vichy's *école des cadres* industry, organizing around 100 students from the University of Strasbourg who had decamped to Clermont-Ferrand in 1939. De Lattre's experiment found a home at Opme, a dilapidated, quasi-moribund village on the plateau de Gergovie near Puy-de-Dôme in the *zone libre*, many of whose residents had emigrated to factory jobs in nearby Clermont-Ferrand. The project included the restoration of the local château, which the patrician de Lattre promptly requisitioned as his headquarters and seigniorial residence.[60] De Lattre's aspiration was that through communal living and dedication to a common enterprise, French youth would acquire the virtues of discipline, risk, initiative, and fortitude to persevere with a mission. For their part, team leaders would direct and inspire their subordinates in a way that reserve officers and NCOs in 1940 had clearly failed to do. At Opme, de Lattre's Alsatians shared in manual labor to rediscover "the traditions of peasant France." To add authenticity to de Lattre's rustic reenactment as well as protest his annexation of their village for his nostalgic vanity project, local bumpkins regularly paved the streets with cow manure.[61] The *écoles des cadres* idea would be revived by de Lattre on the Liberation when he served as the army's Inspector General, Chief of the Defense Staff, and Vice-President of the Supreme War Council – indeed, one of the criticisms of French army post-1945 basic training was that it simply recycled Vichy character-building drills from Uriage and Opme.

However, hardline collaborationists, who seized control at Vichy in the wake of Laval's April 1942 return to power, grew leery of the spontaneous proliferation of these loosely monitored and possibly subversive "leadership" experiments. Rather than a coordinated program shaped by a common philosophy, each *école des cadres* experiment reflected the idiosyncrasies of its organizer. Ideologically they became viewed as antiquated heirlooms of nineteenth-century social Catholic idealism, not institutions compatible with the demands of Hitler's "New Europe." In this spirit, these *écoles des cadres* came under increasing pressure to replicate totalitarian indoctrination practices believed better suited to an era of total war. This was particularly the view of Paul Marion, named general secretary of information and propaganda at Vichy in August 1941, whose ambition "to create a Frenchman of a new type" caused him to found a school of propaganda to rival Uriage, although it flopped. A combination over the course of 1942 of Laval's German-engineered rehabilitation, the institution of *la relève*, and protests by some French bishops in the summer over the deportation of Jews, followed by Torch in November, foreshadowed difficulties for Pétain and *La Révolution nationale.* While Georges Lamirand clung doggedly to his post as SGJ until ousted in March 1943, Laval's collaborationist Secretary for Education Abel Bonnard increasingly infused "*la politique de la jeunesse*" with new personnel determined to integrate proto-fascist organizations that would eclipse Uriage. Laval shuttered Uriage on 31 December 1942, and disbanded the SGJ a few months later. Threatened with arrest, de Segonzac vanished into the *Organisation de résistance de l'Armée* (ORA), eventually commanded an FFI region in the southwest, and joined the French First Army in the autumn of 1944.[62] De Lattre's trajectory from pillar of the Armistice Army to resistance followed a path similar to that of de Segonzac.

"Vichy's Best Idea" – *les Chantiers de la Jeunesse*

Probably no institution encapsulated what Eugen Weber called "the archaic dottiness of Vichy claptrap, all clean living and fuzzy thinking" more than the *Chantiers de la Jeunesse* (youth camps).[63] With conscription, which since the 1870s had marked the passage to manhood in

France, now outlawed, Vichy had to invent new schemes to "*viriliser la jeunesse.*" The *Chantiers* sought to inculcate twenty-year-old French males with "the joys of nature, spirit of sacrifice, and rewards of effort" by making them live rough for eight months.[64] They would emerge with a respect for authority that would lay the groundwork for military training and discipline absent in the 1940 *levée*. This youth community work scheme, initially called *Groupements de jeunesse*, offered a Vichy project to remove French youth from corrupting and politically noxious urban environments, and scatter them in small groups throughout French forests, where they could toughen up, invigorate their patriotism, acquire a team spirit, and reinforce their *francité* – a Vichy-invented fatuity for "a collective French identity." By some accounts, the *chantiers* came about almost by accident. On 2 July, Armistice Army chief of staff General Odilon Picquendar was at a loss about what to do with 100,000 men called up as part of the second half of the conscript class of 1939. These men had been ordered to report to their mobilization depots in early June, by which time many of the depots had been occupied by the *Wehrmacht*. De Gaulle had hoped to evacuate these depots to North Africa in June 1940 to form the nucleus of a reconstructed French military.[65] Some had reported as required, while prefects complained that others, "tattered, disarmed, without hope," wandered the highways, exacerbating the chaos of France's refugee crisis. Many could not return home because their families had been uprooted, or they were stranded south of the demarcation line. In any case, sending them home would only increase unemployment.[66] Weygand, and other army leaders in June 1940, feared the revolutionary potential of leaderless soldiers in the confusion of defeat *à la* 1917 Petrograd.

Because the Armistice Army was forbidden to incorporate conscripts, and because French generals were convinced that victory had been sabotaged by the lack of fighting spirit among their soldiers rather than by their own strategic miscalculations, compounded by antiquated and inept methods of combat, some at least in Vichy's hierarchy warmed to the remedy of assembling French youth into an organization that would revive the patriotism absent from a Republican school curriculum taught by pacifist professors, provide moral guidance, and inculcate a culture of physical fitness. Oliver Faron believes that de Lattre harbored ambitions to lead this youth experiment, but was eliminated from consideration because of his "explosive personality" – one of the descriptors habitually deployed to describe this man of unconventional tendencies.[67] De Lattre was also a man much attached to his creature comforts, so it is difficult to imagine him roughing it in the woods with a farrago of twenty-year-olds. If so, it was a godsend because, at the Liberation, the man Picquendar

Figure 6.2 General Joseph de La Porte du Theil visits a *Chantier de la Jeunesse* in Savoie.

eventually chose – General Joseph de La Porte du Theil (Figure 6.2), an artillery officer, graduate of the *École polytechnique*, and a leader in France's Scouting movement – was stripped of his civic rights and forced to defend himself against charges of collaboration. De La Porte du Theil proposed to Picquendar the creation of a youth organization in France and in Algeria, in which twenty-year-old French males would serve for eight months. The cadres would be recruited among officers and NCOs placed on "armistice leave." In this way, French youth could be subjected to military discipline, while administratively these youth camps would be run by the secretariat for education and so escape manpower restrictions imposed by the armistice. The idea was approved by the army chief at the time, General Louis Colson, who allegedly insisted: "We need a scout and a military leader rolled into one."[68]

While their origins were perhaps fortuitous, the impulse for the *Chantiers* was neither original, nor was it especially French, although the goals of the *Chantiers* were very much in keeping with the traditions and outlook of French military officers, and French conservatives generally. Mimicking trends in Britain and Germany, over 5,000 gymnastic, shooting, rowing, swimming, athletic, horseback riding, and football associations combining over 800,000 young men had popped up in France in the wake of defeat in the Franco-Prussian War. Predictably, these societies also became enmeshed in France's customary Church–State conflict,[69] as did the Boy Scouts, who found an enthusiastic audience in France when they arrived in 1920, especially among conservative Catholic laypeople and military officers, who embraced *le scoutisme* as a remedy for divisive Gallic individualism. Scouts numbered 72,000 in France by 1940, in troops most commonly organized around parish churches, when the German occupiers outlawed *les Scouts de France* in the *zone occupée*. Vichy tried to extend its control over the rump of the Scouts in the *zone libre*. Into this moral and institutional void of defeat stepped Joseph de La Porte du Thiel – Teddy Roosevelt in a beret, the French incarnation of "Buckskin Man," albeit gussied up in a *uniform de fantaisie* – who envisioned the *Chantiers* as filling a moral void left by German proscription of the Scouts, as well as providing spiritual uplift to France's urbanized youth. Similar educational experiments in inculcating "virility and unity" in youth were to be found in Franklin Roosevelt's Civil Conservation Corps (CCC), and in the German *Reichsarbeitsdienst* (RAD) created in June 1935.[70] So in this respect at least, the *Chantiers* might be viewed as a Gallic knockoff of the CCC, the *Hitlerjugend* (HJ) by way of the *Wandervogel* and Gordonstoun, a concept of virile education uprooted from the shores of Lake Constance after its Jewish founder and Christ Church, Oxford alumnus Kurt Hahn was arrested and expelled from Germany by the Nazis in 1933. The following year, Hahn recreated his "bogus Eton" – later nicknamed "Colditz in kilts" – "on the uttermost, extreme, uninhabitable sub-arctic fringe of barbaric Scotland."[71]

In this way, the *Chantiers* and other youth management experiments, like the *cœurs-vaillants*, *jeunesse de montagne*, and so on, were hardly unique to France. What made them special and as a consequence so difficult to integrate into the "memorial" legacy of the war in France was their context. The *Chantiers de la Jeunesse* proved no exception, in that they reflected General de La Porte du Theil's particular background as the son of an inspector general of *des eaux et forêts* (water and forests). Scattered in forty-three woodland camps, each grouping around 2,200 young men – the size, more or less, of an infantry regiment – in the *zone libre* and in Algeria, *Chantiers* inmates spent half the day in forestry work, which consisted mainly in chopping down trees to produce charcoal, a commodity in demand during the Occupation to fuel gas generator-powered (*gazogène*) vehicles. Otherwise, they attended lectures on subjects such as Lyautey's "*Rôle social de l'officier*," René de La Tour du Pin's "*fraternité chrétienne*," and on French history and institutions which reflected de La Porte du Theil's conservative views and reinforced Vichy's ideological nostalgia. Lectures on "*l'armée nouvelle*" – an ironic branding plagiarized from the title of socialist leader Jean Jaurès' 1911 work which called for French defense to be entrusted to a civilian *levée* – were meant to encourage *Chantiers* alumni to enlist in the Armistice Army, and following its abolition in the *1er régiment de France*, founded by Laval in July 1943. Although Armistice Army recruiting sergeants regularly dropped in, the *Chantiers* yielded few volunteers. De La Porte du Thiel also sought to assign basic military tasks to his recruits, like guarding bridges, to develop a taste for soldiering. But this was vetoed by Vichy. In many respects, the *Chantiers* resembled *Stalags* and *Kommandos* rather than an uplifting patriotic experience. Indeed, as early as August 1940, inmates referred to the *Chantiers* as "disguised German work camps." From 1943, the "disguise" came off, as *Chantiers* conscripts were corralled for the STO or labored for the Todt Organization on various defense projects in France. Recruits who failed to "get with the program" might be dispatched to *groupement 103*, a penal *Chantier* at Blida outside of Algiers. "That tells us a lot about how French North Africa was viewed at the time among elites in the hexagon," opines Olivier Faron.[72]

The Germans suspected that the *Chantiers* camouflaged an army reserve, and some historians have concluded that their main goal was military preparation. In fact Vichy's ambitions for the *Chantiers*, rather like for the Armistice Army, never seemed to extend beyond "*l'éducation de la race*" and unstitching several generations of damage inflicted on French values by the Republic's secularized school system.[73] De Lattre criticized de La Porte du Thiel's methods as "bad Boy Scouting" for the masses, which, beneath a "pseudo-military" ritual of bugles, flag raising, and marching, sought to rehabilitate French youth through – the manufacture of charcoal! For de Lattre, de La Porte du Theil's curriculum was more appropriate for pubescent, bourgeois Catholics than for rural and working-class young men.[74] The *Chantiers* were also designed to bolster the social control of an authoritarian regime that many in 1940 believed that France required. A major fringe benefit for Vichy was that postal censorship of *Chantiers* correspondence offered a window into public opinion. The philosophy and methods used by de Segonzac, de Lattre, and de La Porte du Thiel were remarkably similar. This helps to explain why the *Chantiers* became so difficult to slot into the post-war resistance/collaborationist dichotomy. French historian Henry Rousso condemned the *Chantiers* and their leader as "playing the same role as did overtly pro-German organizations."[75] Indeed, the *Chantiers* were frequently, if mistakenly, lumped with various Vichy-sponsored collaborationist paramilitary organizations, such as the *Légion française des combattants* (LFC), the *Service d'ordre légionnaire* (SOL), and the *Légion tricolore*, shading off into the notorious *Milice*.

At his 1947 trial, de La Porte du Thiel struggled to justify the *Chantiers* in the context of what in succeeding generations would come to be called the "Vichysto-résistant" narrative, defined by Azéma in 1997 as "those who were undoubtedly resisters ... nevertheless in the first instance having loyally served the Vichy regime, being anti-German, to the point of preparing *la revanche*." However, as Johanna Barasz points out, "The Vichysto-résistants bestowed upon themselves their own definitions of the Resistance and its contours, in which it would be extremely reductionist not to detect a bad faith justification."[76] Once the *Chantiers* became a holding pen for STO from 1943, desertions skyrocketed, so that cadres – e.g. French officers and NCOs on "Armistice leave" – accompanied *Chantiers* labor drafts to Germany to discourage escapes. So badly did discipline slide that the Germans complained that the *Chantiers* had become a danger for French internal security. Nor did "virilization" necessarily translate into "Maréchalization," as was the case in French North Africa where the Jewish-dominated Georges Gras gym club in Algiers bulked up to aid the Torch invasion, while Muslim Boy Scout troops in Algeria proliferated the mantra of nationalist leader Abdelhamid Ben Badis: "Arabic is my language, Algeria is my country, Islam is my religion."[77] Like colonial POWs in French *Frontstalags*, the *Chantiers* in France transitioned into labor reservoirs for the Todt Organization, in keeping with a shift in policy in Berlin which found it more profitable to keep French workers in France than to deport them to Germany. When de La Porte du Thiel protested the perversion of the *Chantiers* ideal, he was arrested by the Gestapo on 4 January 1944 and deported. The Germans shut down the *Chantiers* in June 1944, on their way out the door.

In his defense, de La Porte du Thiel claimed that the *Chantiers* should be considered part of the resistance for at least three reasons, beginning with the fact that they offered asylum to refugees from Alsace-Moselle. This was partially true, although many from Alsace-Moselle did not take advantage of a *Chantiers* sanctuary because they rightly feared German retaliation against their families. Nor could they count on the protection of a Vichy government willing to sacrifice Alsace-Moselle as the price of collaboration. Second, de La Porte du Thiel had never relieved the head of the *Chantiers* in French North Africa (AFN), Colonel Alphonse Van Hecke, a Belgian who had acquired French nationality through service in the French Foreign Legion. Van Hecke, who had early on lost faith in the

Marshal after Montoire, later became one of the "Group of Five" who plotted with US minister in AFN Robert Murphy to facilitate the Torch landing in November 1942. The *Chantiers* subsequently became an important reservoir of soldiers in AFN after Torch. For instance, Van Hecke personally organized the *7e Régiment de chasseurs d'Afrique*, in part out of personnel drawn from his North African *Chantiers*, as well as Jews, Spanish Republicans, Foreign Legionnaires, and others excluded from *l'armée d'Afrique*, to fight against the Germans and Italians in Tunisia in 1942–1943. Most of the *Chantiers* alumni were distributed around the various regiments and services in the expanding French forces after Torch.[78]

It was also true that the man who assassinated Darlan on 24 December 1942, Bonnier de la Chapelle, was a *Chantiers* alumnus, although the origins of that murky episode remain unclear.[79] Finally, de La Porte du Thiel insisted that his oral instructions frequently contradicted his written ones, a fairly typical collaborator defense in the post-war period, one deployed by Laval among others. His trial also revealed the persistence of the idea of reinvigorating France through the reeducation of its youth, even in the wake of occupation and Liberation. The witnesses for the defense included Henri Frenay, leader of the resistance group *Combat*, who praised the *Chantiers* as "Vichy's best idea" – a version of FDR's CCC that reduced youth unemployment, executed public works "in the general interests," and laid the foundation for military training. Others postulated that the *Chantiers* were a rich source of resistance recruitment. This was partly true in that the major impetus for the resistance phenomenon called *le maquis* was the imposition from September 1942 of forced labor schemes for twenty-year-old French males, for which the *Chantiers* might serve as a mere passthrough. But to see the *Chantiers* as a hotbed of revanchist sentiment would be a mistake. For these reasons, and because they did not really understand at this period the nature and extent of Vichy collaboration, the judges dismissed de La Porte du Thiel's case. In Faron's judgment, like so many actors at Vichy who began as anti-democratic idealists, de La Porte du Thiel became ensnared in "an infernal spiral, that of support for the schemes of the occupier that became increasingly manifest, and which were against the interests of the nation."[80]

The French Air Force and the Navy

Article 5 of the armistice required all tanks and planes to be turned over to the Germans. The paradox for the French air force (FAF) was that the armistice found it in better condition than it had been at the beginning of hostilities. While 70 percent of its front-line fighter inventory on 10 May had been destroyed and some squadrons had been decimated, between 10 May and 10 June, 1,042 new planes had been delivered – 599 fighters, 309 bombers, and 116 reconnaissance planes. The problem was that they were not combat ready. The FAF's personnel losses had been relatively light – 541 killed, 364 wounded, and 105 missing. But this represented 40 percent of its flight crews. Axis inspectors counted between 5,250 and 6,856 planes in the air force inventory in France and North Africa. While the top numbers were probably overestimates, d'Abzac-Epezy's contention is that, like the navy, the FAF had emerged relatively unscathed from the war.[81]

The problem became that by confiscating its planes, Article 5 deflated the FAF's stratospheric self-esteem. An image of the "Archangels of the Air" crafted by Saint-Exupéry and Joseph Kessel had immunized the FAF against the Third Republic's culture of decadence. Therefore, France's moral regeneration required the participation of pilots. But here the problems began, for a parade of army generals at the Riom trials (February–April 1942) and elsewhere loudly denounced a sky "empty" of French planes during the Battle of France, in stark contrast to the RAF, whose stalwart pilots in Spitfires and Hurricanes had bested the Blitz. Needless to say, this "empty skies" accusation put French pilots on the defensive.[82]

Article 8 of the armistice concerned the fleet, whose disposition was to be of great concern both to the Americans and especially to the British. The Reich declared that it harbored no ambitions to take over the French fleet, which was to be divided into three categories as follows. Certain ships would be designated to police French and imperial seas. Ships belonging to a second category of ship were to be returned to their home ports, some of which – Brest, Cherbourg, and Lorient in particular – were under German occupation, where they would be stripped of weapons and munitions, but maintained with skeleton crews in case they needed to be rearmed. Ships belonging to a third category, comprising 13 percent of the fleet, were to be mothballed at Toulon. Darlan's word that the French fleet would not be handed over to the Germans was hardly sufficient. Already, France had returned 400 captured *Luftwaffe* pilots to the Germans, and the French had failed to consult London on the conditions of the armistice as promised. London correctly surmised that Vichy had surrendered its destiny to Hitler.[83] Time would prove that Hitler repeatedly transgressed the conditions of the armistice, as well as of the Geneva conventions prohibiting use of POWs in war-related work. Having no faith in Hitler's promises and eager to demonstrate that the temporization of the Phoney War was well and truly ended, Churchill ordered Operation Catapult. A British Mediterranean squadron christened Force H under Admiral James Sommerville was ordered to neutralize French ships at anchor at Mers-el-Kébir, the port of Oran, on 3 July. Sommerville offered the French admiral, Marcel Gensoul, four options: sail to Britain, the United States, or the Caribbean, or scuttle. Martin Thomas calls the option of demilitarizing the ships – basically disarming the firing mechanisms of the main vessels, and sailing to the West Indies – "generous." These ships could be easily rearmed, and Fort de France offered a first-class deep-water harbor under the control of pro-Vichy Admiral Georges Robert, and so remained under Vichy jurisdiction. Gensoul did not reveal all of these options to Vichy, but rejected Sommerville's ultimatum, causing the British to open fire. Close to 1,300 French sailors perished, most of them when the battleship *Bretagne* exploded under a hail of British gunfire (Figure 6.3).[84] At Vichy and in French naval circles, the British action was denounced as a cowardly and disloyal act. Its operational benefits were minimal. But that was hardly the point of Catapult. While Churchill was certainly eager to minimize the naval threat to the UK, he also sought to demonstrate to the British people and American President Franklin Roosevelt that he meant to continue the war. Darlan's angry demand that France declare war on

Figure 6.3 Funeral for French sailors killed by the British at Mers-el-Kébir on 3 July 1940.

the British was overruled by Pétain, Weygand, and other defeatists in the government.

Historian of the French navy Thomas Vaisset argues that Mers-el-Kébir has been given far too much prominence in the history of Vichy, of the wartime French navy, and of Anglo-French relations. This happened largely because of post-war pleading by Darlan's chef du cabinet and later *Secrétaire d'état de la marine* at Vichy Admiral Gabriel Auphan. Auphan teamed up with his cousin, former head of naval medical services and a post-war *officier-archiviste* at the *Service historique de la marine* at Vincennes, Hervé Cras, who wrote under the pen name of Jacques Mordal. These "admiral-historians" claimed that de Gaulle's vituperative denunciations of Pétain had convinced Churchill to launch Catapult. Therefore, not only was de Gaulle ultimately responsible for the shedding of French blood, but also Mers-el-Kébir became the event that both impelled and justified Vichy's collaboration with the Axis, and activated the Anglophobia that was to transform the French navy into a central pillar of the Vichy regime.

Not only are Auphan's and "Mordal's" sources "specious," in Vaisset's estimation, but also Catapult crescendoed on 3 July, fifteen days after the armistice was signed. In one sense, Mers-el-Kébir did rescue the French navy from marginalization. Pleading that Vichy required a navy and limited air power to defend the empire, French negotiators at Wiesbaden persuaded the Germans to suspend the disarmament of the French fleet, much to the chagrin of the Italians, who sought to neuter French maritime power. The French navy had acquired a mission – protect the empire – which gave it limited independence and armored its loyalty to Vichy. On paper, it remained a strong force with four modern battleships, two cruiser squadrons, three destroyer squadrons, and numerous smaller vessels. But since the Vichy fleet remained under Armistice Commission control, and the fleet at Toulon ultimately scuttled in the wake of the November 1942 German occupation of the *zone libre*, the French navy was destined to join the Armistice Army and the empire as one of Vichy's – and France's – wasting assets. Darlan's desire to ease these restrictions which would allow him to confront the British blockade of the colonies pushed him toward greater collaboration with Berlin.[85] The irremediable rupture in Vichy–British relations occurred in the wake of the failed Anglo-Gaullist attack on Dakar in September. Catapult did not disrupt the monthly rate of defections of French sailors to the *Forces navales françaises libres* (FNFL) or to the Royal Navy. Most of de Gaulle's entourage agreed that Pétain's treason fully justified Catapult. Colonel, later General, Edgard de Larminat insisted that Mers-el-Kébir changed nothing because "Gaullists" had not become dissidents "out of love for the English." Jean-François Muracciole notes that by the end of August 1940, *la France libre* numbered 11,000 recruits.[86] The importance of Mers-el-Kébir was that the event was enlisted to "rehabilitate the choices" made by naval officers in the summer of 1940, and to bolster post-war pleading by erstwhile Vichy supporters that French strategy in 1940–1944 had been shaped by a tacit collusion between Vichy, that acted as the "shield" of France, and de Gaulle, who meanwhile became its "sword."[87]

Philippe Mason, the doyen of French naval historians, agrees that Mers-el-Kébir did not push Vichy toward collaboration. This had been made inevitable with Pétain's request for an armistice. On the contrary, the crisis created by Mers-el-Kébir showcased Vichy's clueless command of strategic realities – ". . . it is striking to note at Vichy that neither Laval nor Darlan understood the elementary repercussions of an aggressive attitude toward England," Masson writes. The new French government ignored several realities: that the "Anglo-Saxons" viewed the potential for the French fleet to switch sides in the conflict, voluntarily or under duress, as a threat; that Roosevelt supported Churchill, and had no intention of mediating between the French and the British; that Vichy was not only isolated, but was entering into diplomatic purdah; and finally, that, by choosing "neutrality," Vichy had placed AFN in the war's cross-hairs.[88] Indeed, even before the United States entered the war, in October 1940, Roosevelt dispatched the State Department's "French expert" Robert Murphy to Algiers as "Minister" and Roosevelt's "personal representative" to lay the groundwork for AFN's flip to the Allies.[89]

In the shadow of Mers-el-Kébir, Vichy realized that it had no good retaliatory options, and contented itself with a half-hearted air attack on Gibraltar and a request through the Control Commission at Wiesbaden to suspend military demobilization so as better to protect the empire, that was partially granted. As Paxton notes, the conclusion drawn at Vichy from the Catapult episode and its aftermath was that an energetic defense of the neutrality of the fleet and the empire offered the best strategy to keep both Axis and British forces at bay, and maintain a veneer of French sovereignty. The Anglo-Gaullist threat to the empire also allowed Vichy to gouge concessions out of the Control Commission in Wiesbaden. For instance, in the wake of Mers-el-Kébir, the Germans not only suspended the disarmament of the fleet but also upped the number of troops allowed in AFN to 120,000, with increased troop strength in sub-Saharan Africa, as well as armed with some military equipment more modern than that allowed in France.[90]

Mers-el-Kébir and the September Anglo-Gaullist attack on Dakar also rescued the FAF from extinction. Despite official rhetoric, as with the

Armistice Army, survival of the FAF as an institution took precedence over honor and morale. On 7 August, Hitler set FAF strength at 19,607 men for Metropolitan France, distributed across sixteen bases in the *zone libre*. Of these, 3,351 were soldiers. Another 7,439 "agents des services de l'Air" were civilians, although they wore uniforms. A further 8,797 formed a "provisional" force kept on active reserve because of Great Britain's refusal to surrender. The air force maintained 259 modern planes in the *zone libre*, and was permitted 500 aircraft and 21,090 men in the colonies. With Mers-el-Kébir, air force officers abandoned dreams of reentering the war on the Allied side. Mers-el-Kébir was the event that broke resistance to the armistice in the air force, and would pave the way for confrontations with the Allies.[91]

The FAF flew into battle nine times over the first two years of occupation, eight of them against the British.[92] Like the Armistice Army, it totally failed in November 1942. French air force personnel served as meteorologists, and in aircraft detection and logistical support for the *Luftwaffe*. French bases were made available to the Germans in May 1941 to support the Rashid Ali revolt in Iraq. Japanese long-range torpedo planes flying from air bases in French Indochina sank the British battle cruiser *Repulse* and the battleship *Prince of Wales* off Singapore on 10 December 1941. On 27 November 1942, the FAF was dissolved and the Italians and Germans divvied up the planes – mainly transports – between them. Two months later, the Germans resurrected a flightless FAF under tight *Luftwaffe* supervision, and created a railroad anti-aircraft section after November 1942 to shoot down Allied planes preparing the liberation of France.[93]

That the armistice, not Mers-el-Kébir, took Vichy down the path of collaboration and exploitation was apparent in its remaining clauses. French citizens were forbidden to take up arms against the Reich. Article 18 required France to pay the costs of the occupation, set at a stunning 400 million francs a day, raised to 500 million in November 1942 in part in punishment for scuttling the Toulon fleet. Article 20 stated that French POWs would remain in German custody "until the conclusion of peace," which, Vichy discovered, was like waiting for Godot. All German and Austrian refugees on French soil would be surrendered to Berlin. An armistice commission eventually established at Wiesbaden would monitor and regulate the application of the armistice, which would remain in effect until a peace was signed.[94] Without a Franco-German peace, the armistice could only be overthrown, not superseded.

No one knew in June 1940 what Pétain and Vichy would become. Both Britain and the United States continued to hope that someone with a more global, strategically grounded vision might slide Vichy loyalties toward the Allies. Like "decadence" or "resistance," "collaboration" was an elastic concept, not just in France but throughout wartime Europe, whose pliability was shaped by ideology, distance, whether a country were annexed, occupied, a satellite of the Axis, or a "neutral." Nor was "collaboration" a rigid concept, but might transition from involuntary "adaptation" to *force majeur*, through "cooperation" in the national interest, to outright treason and betrayal of one's own population. While "collaboration d'État" played out on an official level, "collaborationism" was a choice of individuals for reasons of politics or self-interest – even survival.[95]

France's defeat followed by Germany's partial occupation of France together with the retention of over a million French POWs actually served the goals of French conservatives assembled at Vichy, as it supplied the pretext to impose the "Révolution nationale," a conservative agenda inspired by Salazar's Portugal. But at the same time, "collaboration" also served as a whip that Berlin's ambassador Otto Abetz cracked to blackmail Vichy to do its will, by profiting from Vichy's sense of culpability, and from missteps, to force Vichy continually to prove its loyalty to the Reich by making new concessions which opened France to exploitation. Otherwise, Abetz threatened to do business with a shadow "counter-government" of ideological fascists in Paris, which he manipulated to enflame tensions between Paris and Vichy.[96]

Leahy quickly concluded that Pétain was a lost cause, and that Laval was Hitler's pawn. But Weygand, Darlan, and Giraud were all auditioned at various stages to engineer a turnaround in the Allies' favor. By signing the armistice on 22 June 1940, Pétain surrendered France to Hitler's mercies. This became inevitable with London's refusal to concede, which guaranteed the continuation of the war. In these conditions, Germany and Italy were in no rush to conclude a peace treaty with France. Otto von Stülpnagel, who commanded the *Militärbefehlshaber in Frankreich* (MBF), saw the line of demarcation which separated "free" and occupied France as the "bit" to control Vichy. One required an *Ausweis* to cross, and correspondence across the line was limited to formulaic postcards, while the occupiers could always shut down transit to punish Vichy, as in December 1941 when Pétain replaced Laval with Darlan as premier.[97] But Stülpnagel might have said the same thing about many of the armistice provisions, especially the retention of the POWs. Churchill's warning that France and its colonies could not escape the consequences of the war, especially if it became a platform for attacks on the UK, was ignored.[98]

Although Pétain rejected co-belligerence, with the armistice, France became an objective ally of the Reich. Pétain had linked Vichy's destiny to that of Germany because he knew that the victorious Allies would fail to perpetuate the Vichy regime. Pétain's goal was to actuate defeat to validate his political order, while sidestepping direct engagement in the global dimensions of the conflict.[99] Vichy offered the backing of the empire to seduce Hitler. Japan was allowed to install itself in Tonkin in return for a figleaf of recognition of French sovereignty. If French citizens were forbidden under the armistice to resist the occupation, plenty of them were enticed or coerced into supporting the Germans. The Oberg–Bosquet accord of August 1942, which committed the French police to enforcing Berlin's occupation goals in a "mutually beneficial" alliance against common enemies – "communists, Gaullists, and Jews" – was seen as a vehicle for Vichy to recoup some administrative autonomy in the *zone occupée* and "safeguard the unity of the French administration." But any pretense of Vichy independence collapsed with the invasion of the *zone libre* in November 1942. Vichy preferred to scuttle the fleet rather than steam to Gibraltar or Dakar. Abetz was recalled, and the Sipo/SD became Berlin's new interlocutor with the French police, whose cooperation became essential in quelling what the Germans anticipated correctly would become a swelling resistance in France.[100] With no cards left to play, Vichy had to accept the occupation of the entire country, and the loss of Alsace-Moselle and the "forbidden zone" in the north,[101] as well as the entry into the government of collaborationists in January 1944, and the increasing *fascisation* of the regime. Bousquet was replaced by Joseph Darnand as the police and *la Milice* lent muscle to the occupation, without which the roughly 2,500 German police in France, many of whom had been drafted out of local administrations, who had minimal counter-intelligence training, and who were saddled with multiple tasks, could hardly have functioned effectively. "France was converted into a bazar where, under the old Marshal's malevolent eye, the fruits of denunciation and plunder were for sale," writes Paul Sanders.[102] The Waffen SS established a French division. As Alsace-Moselle slipped under Reich authority, many of its citizens were forcibly enlisted into the *Wehrmacht* and SS, and conscripted to labor in Reich defense industries. French guest workers were pressganged to work in German factories, while those in France built fortifications to armor France against liberation, working to feed the German population and supply the Nazi war machine.[103]

Pétain cynically betrayed a French population which the armistice was advertised to "protect." French historian Pierre Servent views Vichy's slogan – Patrie, Famille, Travaille – as a cruel joke. Pétain betrayed his fatherland, he had no family, and his daily schedule consisted of a leisurely, work-shy routine, whose principal preoccupation became his luncheon menu. The magnificent aureole surrounding the Marshal offered only "a miserable envelope of an outdated glory that was hoisted, *faute de mieux*, up the flagpole of defeat." Pétain became just an old man dominated by egotism and reduced to dissembling. No lie was too brazen. This became apparent at Montoire, an obscure town in the Loire valley, where France's Great Savior had a fleeting encounter with Hitler on 24 October 1940, one of whose goals was to speed the replacement of the armistice with a peace treaty. To those ends, he announced, in a 30 October radio broadcast, that Vichy would "enter into the path of collaboration," as if playing nice with Hitler would soften *Der Führer*'s "total war" attitude toward France. But Hitler was preparing for Barbarossa and had no interest in concluding a peace with France, much less enlisting Vichy on the side of the Axis. And why should he? Hitler's goal was to keep France neutral so that he could pillage it.[104] Only when photographs of Pétain's handshake with Hitler at Montoire were published to an aghast public did the Pétain myth began to show fissures. But Pétain was too egotistical to realize his public relations mistake. Instead, he committed his immense prestige to a search for an accommodation with Nazi Germany, in the process collaborating with the occupier to transform France into a prison and reduce the French population to wretchedness.[105]

"*Contre-mémoire*" – Alsace-Moselle

The list of those sacrificed to Vichy collaboration is extensive. The abandonment of French POWs was quickly matched by the forfeiture of three of France's most iconic departments. The special place occupied by Alsace-Lorraine in French memory of the war as "victimized and romantic," was in part a carryover of Third Republic irredentism for the "lost provinces" surrendered to Germany by the 1871 Treaty of Frankfurt. From 1871 to 1911, the two provinces combining the three departments of the Haut-Rhin, thc Bas-Rhin, and thc Moselle had been designated the *Reichsland* (imperial state) of *Elsaß-Lothringen* (Alsace-Lorraine) and administered directly from Berlin. Apart from a few francophone pockets, mainly around Metz, "capital of the Maginot Line," the peasantry spoke German dialects. Integral to the French myth was that the inhabitants of Alsace-Lorraine longed to be reunited with their French motherland. For this reason, Alsace-Lorraine figured prominently in the imagery and propaganda of *la France libre*, whose dissidence was symbolized by the Cross of Lorraine. Philip Leclerc's "Oath of Kufra" sanctified Strasbourg Cathedral as the apotheosis of the reunion of the French national communion, which had been martyred to Teutonic barbarism.[106] Although only 4 percent of France's population was contained in the three departments annexed by Germany,[107] the narrative of Vichy's sacrifice of the population of Alsace-Moselle on the altar of collaboration both served the ends of Gaullist propaganda and provided an alibi for a population bitter that Vichy's alleged "shield" had failed to safeguard them. Instead, not only had France abandoned them in the Second World War, but also in the post-war period they would be doubly victimized when Paris accused and tried some *malgré-nous* ("against our will") – that is, the name assumed by "Alsace-Mosellans" forcibly incorporated into the German military services from 9 August 1942 – for war crimes committed while in German uniform.

The butcher's bill in Alsace-Moselle was also exorbitant – at the end of the war in 1945, an estimated 100,000 from Alsace-Moselle were repatriated to France from Germany. And these were merely the survivors – between 31,000 and 40,000 men, almost all of whom had perished on the Eastern Front, failed to return. Another 32,000 had been wounded, 10,000 of whom had been left severely disabled.[108] Many Alsatians who returned home in German uniform were stigmatized as "collabos," or worse. Indeed, Pierre Weisenhorn, a "*malgré-nous*," who represented his parliamentary district in the Bas Rhin between 1973 and 1986, discovered that among his parliamentary colleagues, the mention of Alsace-Lorraine invariably conjured up the horror of Oradour-sur-Glane, the signature slaughter of 642 French civilians on 10 June 1944 in the small village near Limoges, carried out by soldiers of the 2nd SS Panzer (Pz) Division "Das Reich," some of whom were Alsace-Mosellans.[109]

Alsace-Lorraine had not been mentioned in the June 1940 Armistice, because Hitler did not want to encourage Mussolini to claim Nice, Corsica, and Tunisia, and also because he did not want to incentivize France to continue the struggle.[110] But the ambiguous status of Alsace-Moselle in French eyes helps to explain why Vichy subsequently made no effort to protest the subsequent integration of the region into the Reich.[111] Vichy Prime Minister Pierre Laval famously described Alsace-Moselle to an American reporter as being "like the minor children of a broken marriage, who live sometimes with the father, sometimes with the mother, and place demands on one or the other through violence."[112] The French regarded Alsatians as bumpkins, and referred to them as "*les Ja Ja*" or "*Alsacos*," and by the late 1930s, some at least were ready to turn over the three departments to Hitler as a way of avoiding war. The irony was that Hitler was little interested in *Elsaß-Lothringen*, whose inhabitants were considered *Volksdeutsche* – that is, members of an ethnic German community – rather than *Reichsbürger* or *Reichsdeutsche*, and so were viewed as insufficiently assimilated into the ethos of the Fatherland. For instance, when Moselle native Marie-Thérèse Petitjean, whose first language was French, was incorporated into the "damned RAD" (*Reichsarbeitsdienst* – Reich Labor Service), her name was changed to Maria Theresa, and she was told: "According to your papers, you are a German of annexation. I hope that soon you will become a heartfelt one."[113] The certitude in the German army that these "Germans of annexation" made inferior soldiers had been buttressed by a high Great War desertion rate among conscripts from the province. For this reason, soldiers from *Elsaß-Lothringen* usually had been assigned to the Eastern Front, and from January 1916 were barred from any military occupation that gave them access to classified information. And although they were from 1940 reclassified as *Reichsdeutsche*,[114] *Elsaß-Lothringen* continued to top Germany's league table for deserters and refractory conscripts in the Second World War. Unfortunately, its percentage of war dead was also proportionately 6.5 percent higher than that for the rest of France.[115]

In Alsace-Moselle in 1940, over 700,000 people claimed to speak only a German dialect, and 800,000 were bilingual, while 200,000 peopled a francophone belt that stretched from southern Lorraine to include the city of Metz, into western Alsace.[116] Hitler shared the unflattering *Reichsbürger* opinion of the province's inhabitants. However, during a 28 June 1940 visit to Alsace in the company of the Gauleiter of Baden, Robert Wagner, Hitler declared that Germany would annex it. On 15 July 1940, customs posts were moved forward to the 1914 frontier, the railways attached to the German network, and the PTT absorbed by the Deutsche Reichspost, as Wagner moved quickly to integrate Alsace into the Reich economy. From October 1940, POWs from Alsace were liberated from *Stalags*, although most officers from the region remained in their *Oflags* because the *Wehrmacht* believed them unwilling to assimilate. Of those who had been forcibly resettled in France in 1939, roughly two-thirds had elected to return, either voluntarily or under threat of German reprisals. So as to violate neither the Armistice nor international law, for the moment Hitler recognized Alsace-Mosellans as French citizens and hence exempt from conscription into German forces. Nevertheless, along with Luxembourg, the region was administratively joined to Germany – the two departments of Alsace were attached to Baden, while that of the Moselle fell under the control of the Gauleiter of Saarpfalz, Josef Bürckel, and was integrated into a *Reichsgau* (administrative region) named Westmark including also the Saarland and the Palatinate.

An austere and fanatical Nazi of modest background, Wagner managed to convince Hitler that he could transform the *Volksdeutsche* of Alsace into proper Germans in five years. Hitler basically gave him a free hand to launch a program of "*Rückdeutschung*" – re-Germanization – in Alsace.[117]

Wagner's goal was *Gleichschaltung* – to bring the population of Alsace to "conformity." From July 1940, Wagner's *Aktion Elsaß* (Alsace initiative) decapitated Alsace's prefectural apparatus and replaced two-thirds of Alsace's mayors. One of the first acts of the new regime was to liberate autonomists incarcerated by the French, who, in gratitude, dutifully demanded that Alsace be incorporated into the Reich. Several were made *Kreisleiter* (district commissioners). The *Kommando der Sicherheitspolizei und des SD* (National Police and SD Regional Command) or SS security, known as the KDS, and the *Befehlshaber der Sicherheitspolizei und des SD* (Commander of the National Police and the SD), known as the BDS, installed themselves in Strasbourg and Metz with regional substations. Some of their personnel were chosen from those Germans who had been expelled from Alsace-Lorraine in 1919. Resistance in Alsace-Moselle was defined as a refusal to Germanize, a trait especially evident in the more Francophone Moselle. The list of potential infractions included listening to Swiss or British broadcasts, displaying the French tricolors ostentatiously, being disloyal to Germany, or even speaking French. Between 300 and 400 bilingual Alsatians were recruited by the Gestapo to serve as interpreters in France, to carry out interrogations, and to infiltrate resistance and POW escape and evasion networks to discover itineraries, the identity of "*passeurs*" across the reestablished frontier of 1871, locations of mail drops, and so on. On the liberation, around 8,000 Alsatians were arrested and interned for aiding the Nazi occupation. The Metz office of the Gestapo was reputed to be particularly efficient and brutal, quick to execute deserters, STO evaders, and escaped Soviet POWs who sought refuge in the forests of the Moselle. Anyone whom the Gestapo designated as a recalcitrant might be dispatched to the Natzweiler-Struthof concentration camp, located in the Vosges mountains 50 kilometers southwest of Strasbourg.[118]

German was declared the official language, so that speaking French as well as Alsatian dialects in *Elsaß-Lothringen* was viewed as a rejection of German culture and hence a form of resistance.[119] This offered an occasion for an auto-da-fé of French books and meltdown of Jeanne d'Arc statues, while Goethe supplanted Molière in theaters, and the names of streets and even towns were Germanized. Catholic schools were closed and the Jesuits expelled. All French associations were banned, along with that quintessential symbol of Frenchness – *le beret Basque*! Residents with French names were forced to Germanize them – when in September 1940 the family of Marthe Lefèbvre returned to their village of Herbitzheim in the Bas-Rhin from which they had been evacuated in September 1939, they learned that henceforth their surname was Schmitt and that, together with constant administrative harassment, they were no longer permitted to speak French.[120] In the name of "ethnic purification," Wagner expelled 25,000 Alsatian Jews, francophones, foreigners, and gypsies between July and December 1940, while another 100,000 Alsatians in France were forbidden to return or elected not to. In this way, Alsace shed 15 percent of its population. Bürckel's house cleaning proved even more brutal in the Moselle, where he aimed to retain only *Volksdeutsche*. The goods of those expelled were confiscated, and German settlers were invited to occupy the vacated houses and lands.[121]

In 1941, the two Gauleiters further tightened the screws on the population. On 22 March, the NSDAP was officially introduced as the principal watchdog on collaboration, and by June 1944 counted 25,000 adherents. The Nazi Party was to cap a panoply of paramilitary organizations meant to indoctrinate the population into German political ideology and prepare it for war. Nevertheless, the *Sicherheitsdienst* (SD) complained that the annexed population seemed impervious to Nazi propaganda, a reaction explained in part by the 1 May 1941 forced conversion of their francs into marks at half the 1939 official rate. Prices were also aligned with those in the Reich.[122] From February 1941, a mobilization began for those born in 1919–1928, initially for six months into the *Reichsarbeitsdienst* (RAD), a Teutonic version of the *Chantiers de la Jeunesse* but divided into male and female sections, under the Ministry of the Interior. Around 40,000–50,000 from Alsace-Moselle eventually served in the RAD. As with military service, inductees began at the *Musterungstag* or recruitment board. The Germans attempted to transform induction into a patriotic event, with officers from the *Wehrmacht*, the police, and the RAD seated behind tables in a room decorated with German flags and Nazi emblems. Conscripts for the army or RAD might be given a math quiz or a dictation to test their knowledge, before being asked to produce their birth certificates, diplomas, work histories, certificates from Nazi organizations, driving license, and so on. Then they were given a medical examination. Many Alsatians came armed with doctors' certificates diagnosing them with a particular ailment that should disqualify them for military service. However, rather than see this as a form of resistance, the Germans concluded that those from Alsace-Moselle suffered a high disability rate due to poor French hygiene. Conscripts classified as apt for combat were designated for one of the combat arms. Others might be declared fit only for the support services, for service in Germany only, or for civilian labor, or might be exempted from military service for a disability or employed in activities critical to the war effort like farming, transport, or in particular industries.[123]

The *Musterungstag* could be particularly humiliating for young women destined for the RAD, as they were forced to parade in "the costume of Eve" before a panel of German doctors. Florence Thomas from Strasbourg was "terrorized and humiliated by their eyes that scrutinized me from head to foot. They examined me, took a urine sample, then declared me fit for service. Since the war, I've had a hundred nightmares about the experience." Scattering the inductees from *Elsaß-Lothringen* throughout Germany among youth inculcated into a Nazi ideology in the HJ or BDM became a tactic to isolate them and hence discourage resistance. Upon incorporation, groups of Alsatian women, usually accompanied by a female member of the *Schutzpolizei*, known as the *Schupo*, were dispatched to camps inside Germany, where they formed an infinite minority of inductees. For most, it was the first time away from home, traveling across Germany in trains filled with soldiers returning from leave. In September 1943, Marthe Elles awakened with a start as her train suddenly screeched to a halt. Everyone jostled for the exits and bolted into the countryside where "there wasn't a tree or a bush to hide behind. The black night enveloped us, ripped by tracers in the sky. I shivered with cold and fear. After a brief moment that seemed to me an eternity, whistles blew, orders were shouted, and we immediately returned to the train."[124]

Upon arrival at the station, RAD inductees were met by a *Führerin*, a sort of female group leader, who led them to their camps, that were located in youth hostels, parish halls, or simply wooden barracks, usually situated in a very rural setting. After being issued an *Ausweis*, and pledging allegiance to Hitler and the Third Reich, they became *Arbeitsmädchen* and settled into an uplifting program of cold showers, gymnastics, drill, and work, often on farms, doing chores and babysitting the children of officers, or physical labor under Todt Organization supervision. Those with a good command of German might land a coveted administrative job. They were also given contraceptive shots, which would disrupt their menstrual cycle and cause them to gain weight. The evening was taken up with political indoctrination, which might consist of taking turns to read a few pages from *Mein Kampf* and everyone standing to attention to sing the "Horst-Wessel-Lied," the Nazi party hymn, followed by barrack chores and bed, often lulled to sleep by the low drone of Allied bombers in search of some German city to pulverize. Joséphine Marchal was sent to Germany with five Mosellans, none of whom spoke German, and because they were forbidden to speak French, could only communicate through gestures, "the height of ridiculous!" This was probably just as well because Marie-Thérèse Petitjean, dispatched in 1943 to Lager 2–28 at Wolfstein in the Palatinate, was warned by her father "to speak as little as possible." But after three generations of being sandwiched between two warring colossi, the inhabitants of the Vosges valleys had learned to keep their opinions to themselves. And caution was required among this sprinkle of French women required to determine who among the *Reichsdeutsche* were confirmed Nazis. "Lesson #1," counseled Marthe Elles, "Never talk politics." At the end of their training, they were sent out to work on farms, sometimes in the company of POWs from France, the USSR, or Poland. This allowed some to rediscover a family atmosphere that they had left behind in Alsace-Moselle.[125]

In October 1941, Wagner launched a vigorous campaign to drum up volunteers for the *Wehrmacht*. However, although recruitment posters were liberally plastered on every available wall, and Wagner promised employment for anyone who volunteered for the RAD, the *Wehrmacht*, or the SS, Wagner's campaign of *Gleichschaltung* seemed to have been received like a soggy *Flammeküche*, as only 20 percent of the population viewed the Reich favorably, which had translated into a mere 2,100 volunteers for the *Wehrmacht* and SS and 13,191 in the SA, some of whom were Germans living in the province. Seven hundred and fifty-nine Alsatians enlisted in the police in 1941, possibly as a way to avoid incorporation into the *Wehrmacht*.[126]

Heretofore, OKW had opposed extending conscription to *Elsaß-Lothringen* and Luxembourg because of a lack of enthusiasm for the *métier d'armes* in those provinces, at least in German service, especially among veterans of the French army. It was also likely that conscription might produce resistance that the *Wehrmacht* lacked the resources to repress. But above all, it was illegal, both in German and international law, a technicality that at this stage of the war the military at least still seemed to care about. German law of 1935 restricted military service to German citizens, while international law forbade them from impressing non-nationals into the army. But by early 1942, with victory elusive and casualties escalating, to leave 130,000 French men of military age in Alsace-Lorraine and 10,000 Luxembourgers – the theoretical equivalent of ten divisions – free to enjoy civilian pursuits seemed a waste of manpower. The issue came to a head at a meeting on 9 August 1942 at Hitler's HQ in Vinnitsa in Ukraine. Although it had been convened to configure an offensive aimed at Stalingrad, Keitel and high Nazi officials including Himmler, Ribbentrop, Borman, and others, as well as Gauleiters Wagner, Bürckel, and Gustav Simon, Gauleiter of the *Mosselland Gau* and Civil Administrator of Luxembourg, diverted the discussion to the issue of what to do with the recalcitrant provinces. After considering and rejecting a proposal to deport a further 20,000 "asocials" from the region, Hitler reluctantly was persuaded by the firebrand Wagner to extend conscription to these occupied territories. To overcome Keitel's objections that such a move was illegal, they discussed the possibility of applying a law of 4 September 1939 which allowed naturalization of foreigners who volunteered for service in the *Wehrmacht*. But forcing these men to volunteer would prove a brutal process, while the Hague Convention forbade the recruitment of the populations of occupied territories. Eventually a 9 July 1943 decree that would bestow provisional, revocable naturalization upon enlistment assuaged Keitel's legal qualms. Hitler eventually gave in to Wagner, even though he had doubts about the loyalty of those in the occupied territories, throwing the application of conscription into the laps of the three Gauleiters. Bürckel, still very much in an expelling mode, and Simon, who believed conscription "premature" in Luxemburg, applied the rule more flexibly than did the zealous Wagner.[127]

From the end of August 1942, Alsatians began to receive conscription notices. Flight offered one method of resistance opened to perhaps 2,000–3,000. But flight to where, and what was one to do even if the escape attempt were successful? And what were the likely consequences of failure? Already in 1941, young men with a premonition that conscription was only a matter of time had begun to vanish with the intention of reaching the *zone libre*. About 1,000 managed to enter Switzerland, most with the help of an escape network based in Mulhouse. Apparently unaware of this network or unable to pay for it, in April 1942, Georgette Luttringer attempted to flee Mulhouse with her brother-in-law for Switzerland. Unfortunately, they were snagged by customs officers and turned over to the Gestapo, who slapped her around before sending both of them to Schirmeck, a disciplinary camp in the Vosges Mountains established in July 1940 to discourage "resistance." By 1942, Schirmeck housed around 1,000 male and 400 female inmates, most nabbed while trying to escape. After a month at Schirmeck, Luttringer was turned over to the RAD, whose doctors found her so debilitated that they postponed her incorporation for a year.[128] Others sought to reach the *zone libre*, where they might enlist in the Armistice Army, where some units were 35–40 percent Alsace-Mosellan according to Eugène Riedweg, or attempt to reach AFN. But the disappearance of the *zone libre* in November 1942 and with it the potential asylum of the Armistice Army helped to discourage escape attempts, as did the archetypal German "forbidden zone" 3 kilometers deep along the Swiss and Spanish borders. Some demobilized Armistice Army soldiers and sailors were given false papers by local prefectures or police, because Vichy refused to issue them so as not to unsettle relations with Berlin. In March 1943, the CFLN passed on Vichy estimates of 12,000 *évadés* from Alsace-Moselle. After the war, 25,600 applied for a *carte de réfractaire* (absconder or truant status) for refusing to submit to German conscription.[129]

Undeterred, Wagner refused to back off, especially following Goebbels' post-Stalingrad speech summoning the German nation to total war. Wagner banned demonstrations and imported impressive numbers of police into Alsace along with the *Volksgerichtshof*, the tribunal normally reserved for treason trials and which would lurch into action against the perpetrators of the 20 July 1944 attempt on Hitler's life. Like STO in France, this forced potential conscripts, sometimes the young men of whole villages, to hide out or flee. The Germans executed some of those caught as "deserters." On 15 August 1942, Wagner announced that those who continued to defy the will of the state would be deported, which the following month translated to 290 people, some of them parents of young men who had failed to report for conscription. But as this failed to staunch the hemorrhage, on 1 October 1943, Wagner began to apply a policy of *Sippenhaft* – essentially "collective responsibility" – by deporting extended families of deserters, taken to include grandparents, siblings, wives, and children, to camps in Württemberg, Saxony, and Silesia, after confiscating their property. The idea was that deportees would remain in these camps without resources until they found work in Germany. While Wagner reported that 3,549 people had been transferred to Germany from Alsace in 1943, post-war records estimated four times that number. In all, Wagner mobilized twenty-one conscript classes between September 1942 and the Liberation. Perhaps taking his cue from opposition provoked by Wagner's call-up in Alsace, Simon in Luxembourg stopped with the class of 1920 – in any case, he counted a recruitment pool of only 15,500 men, compared with 200,000 in Alsace-Moselle. In the Moselle, Bürckel limited the call-up to only fourteen classes, which produced 30,000 soldiers as compared with 100,000 in Alsace, with the result that at the end of the war, Lorraine's KIA rate was far inferior to that of Alsace.[130]

Nor were women exempt from military service. Service in the RAD had not met much resistance because it required eighteen-year-old women to provide six months of essentially civilian farm labor or domestic service. However, on 1 October 1942, Berlin introduced *Kriegshilfsdienst* (KHD) or auxiliary military service for women, a follow-on from the six months' RAD. No sooner had Joséphine Marchal completed her RAD in October 1943 than she was unceremoniously packed off in an army lorry with four other women from Alsace-Moselle to an armaments factory to powder and assemble artillery shells without even being allowed leave to see her family. These factories were often unheated sheds and bunkers secreted in forests, and filled with a multinational workforce of

POWs and slave laborers required to work exhausting hours, although often sick with tuberculosis, scarlet fever, typhus, or diphtheria, not to mention *Pulverkrätze* – scabies brought about by allergy to gunpowder, which caused unbearable itching. Because the KHD was considered military rather than civilian labor, supervision was strict, especially for those from Alsace-Moselle, who were sent to a factory because they did not speak *Hochdeutsch* (High German). Simply exchanging greetings with a French POW or STO might result in a lengthy interrogation. Suspicion of sabotage offered a one-way ticket to a concentration camp. "We were seen as the Reich's bad citizens, saboteurs, at risk of disciplinary sanctions or worse, deportation. All five of us stayed very vigilant and looked out for each other." Inspections were frequent, and if the murmur of voices became too pronounced, a shout of "*Ruhe!*" (Silence!) rang out from the floor supervisor. When the pace of work slackened due to an absence of parts and powder, the women would be assigned to unload railcars filled with empty shell casings from Russia. Working constantly in the cold with little sleep eventually took its toll.[131]

Ironically, assignment to a combat unit was a reward reserved for boys and girls with a high school diploma and good German. This meant in the *Flak* or anti-aircraft units as a *Luftwaffenhelfer*, *Flakhelfer*, or *Flakwaffenhelfer*, but soon was expanded to include medical services, the Todt Organization, NSKK transport, *Frontarbeiter* (labor service), or *Landesschutz-Bataillone*. From September 1943, Wagner directed 2,600 high school students into the *Flak*, often straight out of the classroom, without even allowing some of them to say goodbye to their parents. The word quickly spread that Wagner was kidnapping children. As soon as the boys accomplished their *Flak* apprenticeship, many were directed straight into the *Wehrmacht*.[132]

Of course, assignment to the *Flak* put them in harm's way, subject to the full force of Allied bombardments. Marguerite Zimmerlin from Jebsheim, near Colmar, was detailed to a *Flak* unit at Nuremburg, where the women manhandled the searchlights in the middle of the airfield, while the males fired the batteries from the relative cover of the surrounding forest. "We heard the bombs whistling around us and our searchlight shattered from the bomb blast," she remembered of one raid. "The girls buried their faces in the sandbags. I still wondered how I survived that Hell ... That night, ninety percent of Nuremburg was destroyed."[133] From the autumn of 1943, KHD might also mean assignment to one of the military services, where women might be found in almost all non-combat positions, as well as in transportation, hospital, or administrative services. In fact, by late 1943, KHD might supersede RAD, as was the case of Marthe Elles who upon arrival in her RAD camp was sent straight to the North Sea coast for military training in the *Marinehelferinnen* (German equivalent of the WRNS). The same happened to nineteen-year-old primary school teacher Alice Meyer from Mulhouse, who in November 1944 was impressed to clean and rearm fighters at the *Luftwaffe* base at Schongau-Amlesch. "It did not require much technical competence," remembered Eugénie Biegert of Strasbourg of similar work she had to perform as an eighteen-year-old at Munich. "But it was very dirty: clean the motors, change the oil, change the munitions boxes, minor mechanical repairs. More, we had to help in digging the defenses around the airbase." Eighteen-year-old Lisette Baldensperger was assigned to Minotaurus, a gigantic five-story bunker near Schleißheim, where the room full of women sat with headphones to monitor the radios and track the vectors of incoming flotillas of Allied bombers, and then send out messages in Morse to direct *Luftwaffe* fighter interceptors. Unlike in the RAD or the ammunition factory, the well-educated young German women who worked next to her from Vienna and Munich proved quite eager to maintain their gymnasium French. But by the autumn of 1944, with German defenses crumbling, more were willing to take their chances with evasion. "The administrative chaos was such in Germany that the verification of papers became impossible," Eugénie Biegert remembered of the Third Reich's wheezing moments, as she and several comrades took advantage of an air raid to steal away. But destroying one's German uniforms and military identification to escape, and pretending to be refugees put on the road by Allied air raids, meant that one had no access to ration coupons and might find it hard to buy railway tickets. Returning to Alsace, which by October 1944 had become a battle zone, also posed the risk of being caught up in the fighting. Still wearing her *Wehrmacht* uniform, Émilie Schibény was captured by American troops during the Battle of the Bulge and thrown into a paddock with German POWs.[134]

As far as Alsace-Moselle was concerned, Vichy's defense that it acted as France's "shield" proved a total fabrication. Although well informed of events in Alsace-Moselle, Vichy's first protest about incorporations into the RAD occurred only on 27 October 1941. But like subsequent protests registered at Wiesbaden, and complaints passed on by Laval to Germany's Vichy Ambassador Otto Abetz, they were not made public but remained merely pro forma. Eager to collaborate with Germany, Vichy also felt that, as the French government was facilitating the recruitment of French volunteers for the German army – the LVF and the Division Charlemagne in particular, whose members also took a loyalty oath to *Der Führer* – to protest the incorporation of Alsace-Mosellans would appear illogical. Vichy treated those from Alsace-Moselle who refused to serve as "deserters from the German army." "It was the silence of Vichy that allowed Wagner to realize his meticulous plans for the Germanization and the Nazification of Alsace, of which military service in the *Wehrmacht* was only the crowning act," concludes Riedweg. And if Vichy failed to protest the incorporation of French citizens, why could OKW or the German Foreign Office object to its illegality? "It was Vichy's silence that handed over 130,000 Alsatians and Mosellans to the *Wehrmacht.*" Berlin realized that French protests were not serious, and so never bothered to reply. Those in the "lost provinces" saw it as a recurrence of France's 1871 sell-out.[135]

The "Unlikable Vanquished"

Philippe Carrard proposes that French memory of the Second World War should expand to include an "unlikable vanquished" category, with "the French who fought for Hitler" at the top of the list.[136] While the French were accustomed to foreigners and colonial subjects stepping forward to serve in French ranks, the specter of significant numbers of Frenchmen volunteering to serve in a foreign army came as a shock. For this reason, collaborators are dismissed in the Gaullist/resistance narrative of the war as a handful of criminal outliers and right-wing fanatics, whose numbers were fluffed by an unmoored, unprincipled, and generally apolitical assemblage of troubled souls who, in the confused circumstances of the war, simply made regrettable choices. One of these disoriented was Pierre Rostaing, a former colonial soldier who joined the *Légion des volontaires français contre le bolchévisme* (LVF) in 1942. Captured in April 1945 wearing an SS uniform while defending Berlin against the Red Army, Rostaing was subsequently told by a French army doctor who visited him in prison: "You made a bad choice. You should have been a resister."[137] This was the message of Louis Malle's 1974 film *Lacombe, Lucien,* that the choice between resistance or *la Milice* was an ideologically neutral one that turned on circumstance and self-interest. It offered great appeal in France's memory zone. According to Division Charlemagne veteran Christian de la Mazière, for most of his fellow soldiers, enlistment "was not a result of mature reflection, but rather a matter of impulse and anger which were part of the paradox of our particular adventure." Indirectly, this allegedly Wagnerian reflex was in itself self-serving, rationalizing in hindsight a decision taken several years earlier in a completely different ambience. It also let many collaborators off the hook by ignoring the "moral choice" of their decision to don the black uniforms of the GMR or the Waffen SS, or the blue of *la Milice.* It also offered plausibility to the post-war alibi of collaborators like de la Mazière that they knew nothing about Nazi atrocities, when, in fact, they helped to perpetrate them by persecuting and deporting Jews in France, torching Soviet and French villages and farms, and torturing resisters. "I was not able to accept the idea of collective guilt," de la Mazière rationalized. "Our commitment had been a purely physical one founded on some high ideas."[138]

After the war, former collaborators fashioned a "lost cause" literature of noble suffering by a misunderstood collection of idealistic and loyal warriors who enlisted in the German forces to build Europe and fight Bolshevism, "the enemy of all civilization." This helped to spin a Cold War campaign to rehabilitate the "clean *Wehrmacht* " as a collection of noble and honorable fighters led by brilliant generals like Guderian, Manstein, and Rommel, whose warrior ethic distanced them from Nazi atrocities.[139] Defiant "*je ne regrette rien*" memoirs like those of Rostaing and Bayle offer a counterpoint to the PCF myth of "*le parti des 75,000 fusillés*" ("the party of 75,000 shot") by presenting the Soviets as both backward and barbaric, people whose victories depended on US material support, who starved POWs, and whose attacks are described as costly human wave assaults by Asiatic hordes, evidence of communist indifference for the lives of their soldiers. The wholesale rapes of German women witnessed in 1945 by some French SS men and POWs are offered as evidence of the barbaric norms of both the Red Army and Bolshevism.[140] They evade moral responsibility by sheltering behind the technical legality that enlistment in the Nazi war machine had been permitted, even encouraged, by Vichy, while their motives, both personal and political, had been noble. Although those who served on the Eastern Front burned villages and terrorized civilian populations, ignorance of Nazi atrocities, "denial of responsibility," and a lack of repentance characterize their narratives. In this way, the "unlikable vanquished" attempted to assimilate themselves into French history's constellation of romanticized martyrs like the Cathars, Templars, *les grognards de Napoleon*, or Communards with their own gallant commitment, nostalgia, esprit de corps, and tragic destiny.[141] This collaboration category shades off to specialized paramilitary units like the GMR and *la Milice*, and then incorporates the opportunists who snitched for the Gestapo by infiltrating resistance groups, betraying Jews, or informing on their fellow citizens. And while it may be easy to dismiss these "unlikable vanquished" as historical anomalies, misfits, and outliers in France's wartime narrative – "a handful of criminals" – the fact is that around 40,000 Frenchmen had volunteered to wear a German uniform, not counting those conscripted from Alsace-Moselle, which, when combined with 30,000 or so serving with *la Milice* or the GMR in the summer of 1943, roughly equaled the number of FFL volunteers in the same period.[142]

Indirectly, the "Lacombe, Lucien" exoneration offers a proxy authentication for the Gaullist narrative that banished collaboration to a fringe of delinquents, opportunists, and idlers, and a class of gullible, immature, socially adrift young men, disoriented by Vichy propaganda and seduced by a wartime challenge to validate their masculinity and find a social niche. These weak characters – some perhaps seeking to escape STO – were attracted by the pay, the uniform, or the prestige and power of a weapon. In search of self-realization and a masculine identity, they embraced what appeared to them – at least initially– to be a sensational adventure. While there was nothing to admire about their choices, and while the majority seemed defiantly lacking in remorse, by classifying the taking up of arms even indirectly against France as a masculine fantasy impulse, even a miscalculation, they remained part of the nation, deserving of understanding and even pity, and eligible for rehabilitation. And why should they have a bad conscience, especially as the Cold War took shape? They were French nationalists fighting to save civilization, culture, and the West. They were *Versaillais*, not Nazis. They sought to buy time in the hope that things might change. This was the attitude of the post-war courts which freed most of these volunteers even before the amnesty of 1951.[143] The rehabilitation of the *Wehrmacht* and those who had served in it accorded well with a post-war enterprise of Franco-German reconciliation, town-twinning, and NATO, which sought to bind "the West" in a collective defense against Eastern hordes. Besides, the efforts of de Gaulle and the PCF to create a narrative of liberation through the French Resistance fell short of convincing. Novelists looking for heroic narratives of the war were virtually forced to turn to "the brave and heroic German soldier," who, like the French, was also a victim of the war. In this way, the image of "the good German" melds into that of "the good collaborator."[144]

But these French volunteers knew exactly what they were doing: "I am French," insisted thirty-three-year-old Adjutant-chef Rostaing, who with a record of military service in Africa and Indochina, hardly qualified as an impressionable adolescent. He admitted that he was bored, and had a taste for adventure, stating "I am anti-Communist. I am a soldier. I respond to the Marshal's call to defend France." Not to have enlisted in the LVF in his view would have been the act of a coward, a betrayal.[145] De la Mazière had grown up in a right-wing household, but found *l'Action Française* to be a fading anti-Dreyfusard artifact of dyspeptic right-wing journalists and intellectuals. Even as Allied armies closed in on Paris, he fled into the SS: "I was proud of the Hitler salute because it struck me as signifying a new start, and through it I entered an order of things where nothing was easy but where everything was more pure and honest."[146]

Taken as a boy to the 1936 Berlin Olympics by his parents, both physical education teachers, gymnasts, and members of the French Olympic delegation, André Bayle found that the "robustness and dynamism" of this Nazi theater alive with swastika banners, snappy uniforms, and exuberent crowds offered a release from dowdy, depression-era France. "The Hitler Youth and youth in general breathed good health and vitality," he remembered, and this primed the impressionable adolescent to embark on his SS adventure in 1943.[147]

So, these were no aimless, untethered, bored, clueless Lacombe, Luciens. This was an ideological war, and volunteers who fought it espoused an ideological commitment. France must become like Germany, not be liberated from it. Through their commitment and sacrifice, collaborationists sought to secure France's position in Hitler's Europe. This immersion in a "moral cause" defined a "purposeful life" – to spin in history's vortex, paddle in the comradery of combat, murder inferior peoples in a "total war" embrace, and in the process molt into "a new man."[148] Carrard's "unlikable vanquished" repudiated the Gaullist resistance myth. The French were not resisters, they were "*attentistes*" simply trying to survive, in the view of LVF/SS veteran Rostaing, "too cowardly to choose one camp or another."[149] "The 'Resistentialism' that I will discover on my return in 1946, could only make me smile . . .," declared Bayle, who had been allowed to enlist in the SS at age sixteen.[150] The one point on which the "unlikable vanquished" and de Gaulle would have agreed was that Vichy was managed by "a band of gutless old chickens."[151] But despite the defiant and frequently bombastic tone of these memoirs, and a fabricated post-war image of heroic, misunderstood warriors enlisted in a noble but tragic crusade, the military efficiency of these collaborationist units, as well as their morale, frequently hovered near zero.

Like resistance, collaboration in France was part of a broader European phenomenon unleashed by Barbarossa. But it also offered Vichy a backdoor opportunity to reconstruct a military force and ease the conditions of the armistice by assisting Hitler's ambitions, while maintaining a fiction of autonomy. In July 1941, Hitler reluctantly approved the creation of a volunteer French unit – the *Légion des volontaires français contre le bolchévisme* (LVF). This was a result of vigorous lobbying by France's right-wing collaborationist parties that included Doriot's PPF, Marcel Déat's *Rassemblement national populaire* (RNP), and Eugène Deloncle's *Mouvement social révolutionnaire* (MSR), which received Abetz's endorsement. According to American sources, Vichy contributed 10 million francs to set up recruitment bureaus in the *zone libre* under PPF auspices, with the goal of recruiting a force of 10,000–15,000 men who would receive basic training at the Borgnis-Desbordes barracks at Versailles, and in the *zone libre* at Guéret in the Creuse, before being dispatched for advanced training at Dęba in Poland under German supervision.

In January 1942, convinced that the *Légion Tricolore* – Vichy's stillborn attempt to revivify the LVF – would never see combat (the Germans refused to approve it), Rostaing had reported to LVF headquarters at Versailles' Quartier de la Reine to enlist, "drawn by my visceral anti-communism and love for France. All the arms, from infantry to cavalry, were to be found in this tower of Babel, where propaganda had sucked in thousands of men," he recorded. "Large, small, old men with white hair, youngsters who expanded their chests to make them look older than their fifteen or sixteen years. The corridors teamed with aristocrats who hoped to rediscover through the adventure of a skirmish, the glory of their ancestors. The mechanic or the postman from the northern suburbs, wearing the insignia of Jacques Doriot's PPF, dreamed of a marshal's baton quickly won between Smolensk and Moscow. The vanquished soldier of the Phoney War and the sinister defeat, offspring of the Popular Front of 1936, hoped for a revenge that would allow him to recover his honor, lost somewhere between the Ardennes and Bordeaux ... France never changes ... with the mix of juvenile enthusiasm and irritating skepticism."[152]

Despite the relatively high pay, in the view of merchant marine officer and LVF "Oberleutnant" Rémy Ourdan, this collection of volunteers, recruited mainly in Marseilles and Lyon, neither hothouses of French martial race theory, was "difficult and rather mediocre ... mostly made up of the unemployed or men of no defined profession, having generally a record of civil and sometimes military punishment, drawn by the pay rather than by any ideal," or to escape a sour marriage. The German medical inspection was at best perfunctory, allowing the incorporation of men over fifty-five and even some with a limp, totally unable to survive a rigorous Russian winter. On the other hand, many were simply too young, including three fifteen-year-olds allowed to enlist. Most of the NCOs had no notion of their duties. A number of them, especially those who belonged to the MSR (Cagoule) had prison records. The officer corps was commanded by "68-year-old Colonel Labonne." Actually Roger Labonne – a colonial soldier, First World War veteran, former French attaché in Ankara and, incidentally, member of the PPF – was a spry sixty-two. The LVF officer corps fell into a "geriatric but still mobile" demographic, with captains aged between forty-five and sixty-five, and lieutenants averaging between forty and fifty years of age. "With my 35 years, I can pass for a junior," boasted

Ourdan. Only one was a professional soldier, the others reservists, or, he suspected, men armed with forged military credentials pushed forward by Deloncle. "Many were promoted through the ranks and spent their entire career in the colonies. None come from a high social milieu. All have careers tarnished by more or less serious professional transgressions." In fact, the August 1941 ceremony to mark the sendoff of the first contingent to Russia saw a failed assassination attempt against the leadership that included Déat, Doriot, Fernand de Brinon, and Laval by one of the volunteers – a former *Camelot du Roi* Paul Collette. Collette's botched assassination was simply the most public of many acts of fratricide within the LVF. Like prison gangs, once in barracks, the various political factions competed to recruit adherents. As a result of animosities, whether political or personal, the rifle range became perilous territory. Nor was the fact that most recruits proved to be appalling marksmen a guarantee of survival, when a shot meant for an unpopular second lieutenant accidently killed a member of the PPF instead. Doriot buried the affair. But as several senior officers including Labonne were active PPF adherents, they must have considered taking out extra life insurance. RNP members were so terrorized of being shot by their political rivals that many preferred the cells to the firing range. Indeed, Cagoulard Eugène Deloncle declined to join the LVF out of fear that he might be snuffed by Doriot's henchmen.[153] Not surprisingly, the LVF merely reinforced German negative impressions of France and the French army. Ourdan suspected that the goal of Deloncle and Doriot was to create a politicized force to eliminate their political rivals rather than campaign for Germany, because some of the officers spoke openly of carrying out political assassinations and "cleaning up" Paris and AFN at the muzzle of a machinegun.[154] Indeed, the Germans never trusted the LVF, and placed their spy in the propaganda section to report regularly on events in the group.[155]

By this time the Germans had realized that many LVF volunteers were too old or unfit to campaign, and so rejected "at least forty per cent of them." Nevertheless, what was left hardly called to mind Napoleon's *grognards*, as fistfights between officers and enlisted men, and even assassinations of officers, punctuated LVF life.[156] In fact, American Minister in Algiers Robert Murphy reported, in January 1942, that the small numbers and poor quality of LVF recruits meant that "the role of the Legion was never more than negligible."[157]

The original idea was that these soldiers would wear French uniforms and fall under French command. However, as France was not at war with the Soviet Union, they were incorporated into the *Wehrmacht* as the two-battalion – with attached artillery and anti-tank companies –*Verstärktes*

Französisches Infanterie-Regiment 638 (Reinforced French Infantry Regiment 638). Although technically an understrength *Wehrmacht* regiment, their immediate commanders were French officers commanded by Labonne, under the supervision of a thirty-five-man German liaison detachment. While they were allowed to march behind the tricolor, wearing a German uniform proved a deal breaker for some volunteers. After training in Versailles and subsequently in Poland, on 30 October 1941, the LVF entrained for Smolensk, without being issued winter clothing.

At Smolensk, they were put in charge of 600 horses and 300 wagons, and told to march the roughly 400 kilometers to the front 35 kilometers west of Moscow over "roads covered with snow and ice." Many of the horses were in poor physical condition, less than 10 percent were shod for the ice, and nor were the traces capable of pulling heavy loads, like the regiment's two 155 mm artillery pieces. Several men died on the march, while others had to be evacuated and discharged. "Our men, mostly from the cities, had no experience with horses," complained Labonne. Two hundred reinforcements arrived, who had received no military training whatsoever. Attached to the German 7th Infantry Division, they were kept for fifteen days in the front lines outside of Moscow without winter uniforms despite the "terrible cold." The failure to take Moscow and the subsequent retreat was a blow to French morale. Reduced to 1,200 "barely armed" men by February 1942, they fought a defensive action between Vitebsk and Smolensk against a "Siberian division" whose troops moved on skis and motorized sleighs in temperatures that fell to −50 °C. Extracted thanks to the intervention of Panzers and the *Luftwaffe*, the 638th Regiment was withdrawn to Poland to regroup. Reports that by the spring of 1942 up to 1,000 of the volunteers in the "French Legion" had deserted to Soviet forces may have been exaggerated, but probably not by much.[158] It was "by the hundreds" that LVF soldiers were subsequently dismissed from service. Labonne complained that many discharged from the LVF had no money, and so began to commit acts of "looting" and "pillage" in Paris, imitating what "they had seen the *Wehrmacht* do on the steppe," and for which German military tribunals had them shot. One of those executed was Labonne's former chauffeur. Once discharged and in France, some LVF veterans were enticed into the SS, or the Gestapo.[159]

Newly returned to power, in June 1942, Laval officially converted the LVF, hitherto supported by private funds and Berlin, into an official Vichy-sponsored organization. But the LVF's main problem was that it constituted a "warren of political agitators and conspirators" under German control, not as Vichy had hoped, a French military force able to support Vichy interests by easing armistice conditions through its service.[160] By May 1943, the number of LVF volunteers had swelled to around 6,000, to include Foreign Legionnaires of various nationalities, as well as Spanish Civil War veterans, and even a sprinkle of Arabs and sub-Saharan Africans. "However, the French were considered among the worst of all foreign volunteer units serving with the *Wehrmacht*, and the LVF was destined to remain in anti-partisan duties for the remainder of its existence," writes Christopher Bishop.[161] Neither part of that statement was quite accurate. The LVF and its lineal SS descendants were massacred in main force confrontations on several occasions. And subsequent evaluations concluded that, despite its numerous shortcomings, the LVF was perhaps marginally more efficient than the French SS formations that succeeded it: "The former L.V.F. was commanded in French and maneuvered in a French manner. Its cadres were generally better, made up of several officers or by elements promoted from the ranks with combat experience." Those who subsequently commanded the French SS formations, however, "owed their rank to their political connections," read a post-war evaluation.[162] Professionally upgrading the LVF proved a virtually hopeless task, because it was in the grip of an old-boy political mafia that wanted to continue their "*belle vie*" (a reference to LVF officers having their way with Russian women), and because the Germans had no incentive to create a militarily efficient French force. Despite an intensive recruitment campaign that included sending 2,491 personal letters, the brief hope that at least 500 men from the Armistice Army, disbanded in November 1942, could be enticed into the LVF ended in "fiasco" when only twenty-six deigned to post a negative reply. Vichy determined that the attempt to attract Armistice Army veterans had failed for four reasons: the political opinions of the demobilized; a pronounced antipathy for the LVF; a repugnance to serve in a German uniform; and the tactlessness of the recruiting officers. Lieutenant Streit, assigned as one of the LVF recruiting officers in Nice, reported that "many contacted responded: 'if they want to send us to Russia, then mobilize us and send us officially.'" In January 1943, the LVF counted 91 officers, 390 NCOs, and 2,825 soldiers (Figure 6.4).[163]

Rostaing's LVF reinforcement entered Russia in the spring of 1943 on a troop train that never exceeded 10 kilometers per hour through what seemed interminable fir forests. Every few miles a blockhouse guarded a clearing where the trees had been cut back for a few hundred meters to clear fields of fire and frustrate ambushes. The locomotive pushed two flat cars loaded with sand meant to absorb the blast of mines. The debris of flatcars along the rail line suggested that mines posed a rather frequent hazard, which added to the sinister gloom of the seemingly limitless woodlands. The LVF was off-loaded in Byalynichy,

Figure 6.4 Parade of the LVF on the Champs-Élysées in 1943.

which Rostaing described as a large town in White Russia (Belarus) about 100 kilometers east of Minsk, constructed entirely of wood. The LVF troops were billeted in one-room windowless Russian houses, each heated by a stove, which one legionnaire described as little better than a "bad stable" in France. Initially at least, anti-partisan operations were not particularly onerous, and consisted mainly of patrolling between villages held by German troops.[164] This was because, surprisingly perhaps, the Red Army had proved remarkably unprepared to wage guerrilla war against the invading *Wehrmacht* after June 1941, for several reasons. Because partisan forces had operated against the Bolsheviks in Siberia and Ukraine during the Russian Civil War in 1918–1920, guerrilla warfare was viewed as a tactic to subvert the Soviet order, not defend it. Also, anyone who suggested before June 1941 that Moscow might be forced to wage partisan warfare on Soviet soil would have been branded a defeatist. Many of those with expertise in partisan warfare had perished in the Great Purges of 1936–1938, and the weapons caches to sustain a partisan war had been liquidated. Partisan warfare had been incorporated neither in Red Army doctrine nor in training, beyond use as "behind the lines" sabotage or intelligence missions.[165] As a consequence, a partisan movement on the Eastern Front, begun as *ad hoc* initiatives of local party and NKVD (People's Commissariat for Internal Affairs) officials, was slow to build momentum. Nor initially was much of the population enthusiastic about defending a brutal Soviet regime that, until late 1942 and Stalingrad, appeared incapable of delivering victory. Therefore, as in France, "wait and see" initially became the characteristic popular response to German invasion and occupation.

Unfortunately for them, SS *Einsatzgruppe* units, fueled by Nazi racism and anti-communist fervor and supported by regular *Wehrmacht* formations, began to subject the population to "criminal orders" that included hostage-taking, reprisals, and generalized terror. By late summer 1941, a nascent guerrilla movement had emerged, but lacked preparation, arms, and outside support. Moscow woke up to the need to have "partisan-diversion groups," but initially the NKVD, the Red Army, and the Party disputed control. Without firm directives, all three groups began to sponsor partisan experiments of varying effectiveness, which was to create a competition not unlike that which was to play out between the SOE, OSS, and BCRA to direct resistance action in France in 1943–1944. These groups were bolstered, when not supplanted entirely, by Red Army soldiers cut off by Barbarossa, and whose attacks on German forces, especially in the spring and summer of 1942, sparked retaliation against the local populations. Only in May 1942 did Moscow establish a Central Partisan Headquarters to recruit insurgents and coordinate their activities. But a significant difference was that, unlike the *maquis* in France, which burgeoned in the summer/autumn of 1943, the Soviet partisan movement had a strong regular military component, which resulted in "the effective professionalization of the partisan movement" in the Soviet Union. It also operated just behind the front lines to optimize coordination with conventional operations, not simply to carry out stand-alone missions. As it became increasingly clear from late 1942 that the USSR would not be defeated, even former collaborators began to join partisan groups to save their skins. By 1944, the Soviet partisan movement was "much more like a regular army in the enemy rear than the obviously amateurish movement of 1941," especially around Leningrad.[166]

Initially, however, the size, quality, and discipline of partisan forces was uneven, and as a consequence, so were their results. And, in fact, even though militarized, they were lightly armed and so unable to take on main force German units without incurring heavy losses. Therefore, the activity of Soviet partisans was usually limited to attacking collaborators and engaging in sabotage operations. Fortunately for the partisans, their opponents were overwhelmingly second-tier "security divisions," *Einsatzgruppe* (paramilitary "deployment groups"), *Luftwaffe* ground troops, and reserve divisions, deemed inadequate or unready for front-line service, or understrength "reserve" units.[167] Prominent too in anti-partisan operations on the Eastern Front were groups of German-recruited collaborators like the French LVF, who were joined by police units from the Baltic republics, as well as Hungarian, Romanian, and Slovak army units.[168]

In September 1942, Stalin issued Order Number 00189, "On the tasks of the Partisan Movement," laying out the concept of "people's war." Partisan tasks were defined principally as supplying intelligence on the location of German units through radios increasingly deployed at the front, attacking collaborators, and disrupting German logistics. This reinforced what was called the "War of the Rails," which had begun in July, and which, given the limits of Soviet airpower, was viewed as among the most effective of partisan activities, since it forced the Germans to concentrate enormous resources to keep their supply lines open, and prevented them from devoting troops to bringing in the harvest in the occupied territories in the East.[169] While one had to be watchful of mines on the road, and repair communications that the partisans were constantly cutting, at least for Rostaing's LVF reinforcement, the early summer of 1943 was characterized by a tacit "live and let live" agreement, whose terms apparently ruled out neither rape of local women nor theft of Russian horses.[170] Twice a week, peasants brought their produce into market, which was vital because the German army in the East was largely forced to "live off the land." Mounting guard on one of the bridges into town and taking their cue from French *ancien régime* practice, Rostaing's squad took their *dîme* (10 percent) of the eggs, milk, fish, fowl, or fruit. As no one complained, they figured that this was acceptable in local custom. At least, this allowed the LVF to eat well, supplemented by any carrier pigeons, which the partisans used to communicate, they could shoot. As Red Army summer offensives forced German troops to retreat, however, this "benevolent neutrality" ceased as peasants and their food disappeared from the market. So, the LVF sent out a few patrols to burn villages and plunder, which only temporarily improved their resupply situation. Supplies now had to arrive via horse-drawn transport, which offered the partisans lucrative targets and resulted in a few convoy massacres. The counter was to create and garrison smaller posts along the roads. But this scattered LVF strength, deprived them of offensive capability, gave the partisans more targets to strike, which they usually did at night, and allowed them further to strengthen their control over the population. So, LVF posts sat like armed atolls in a forested hinterland through which partisan bands moved and struck at will. The LVF leadership lacked aggressiveness, while replacements were slow to arrive: "That's the LVF," Rostaing complained. "Sentiment trumps efficiency while the enemy is ever showing himself more dangerous and entrepreneurial."[171]

Inspection reports confirmed Rostaing's analysis, pointing out that LVF *esprit de corps* was "pathetic," and even sending them regular French veterans would serve only to "contaminate" perfectly good soldiers. The fight seemed to have gone out of the LVF for several reasons: political quarrels; lack of faith in the mission; a creeping awareness that the LVF had been abandoned by Vichy and that promises had not been kept; and neglect of the families of legionnaires. "They are militia and not soldiers. Dressed in German uniforms, disavowed by their families, and abandoned by their government, they are denationalized," read a June 1943 report, which also called for a thorough purge, beginning with the officer corps. Second, it also recommended that the LVF be withdrawn from demoralizing anti-partisan duty, which had cratered discipline and morale, and, after serious retraining, be transferred to an active front.[172] But, given a lack of quality reinforcements and the fact that the increasingly stretched Germans, not the French, controlled the LVF assignments, this was unlikely to happen.

To put his detachment back on the offensive, Rostaing organized a "section de chasse" (hunting party) which, disguised as partisans, moved around on horse-drawn sleighs. They managed to take some partisans unaware or to infiltrate and disrupt ambushes. This was part of a larger German effort to constitute *Jagdkommandos* (hunter groups) dispatched on "encircle and destroy" operations that targeted villages, their crops, and livestock. But, focused on guarding lines of communications, neither in Yugoslavia nor in Russia were German troops numerous enough to sustain operations, nor could they kill enough guerillas to make their "encirclement" campaigns decisive.[173] Tipped off that the partisans were being supplied through an airfield in the forests, in October 1943, Rostaing's "hunting party" encircled the airfield but found no one. In fact, his "section de chasse" struggled to survive: "We chased many more chickens than partisans," he lamented. In the meantime, "walled up in their posts for month after month, the legionnaires drank: cognac, schnaps, and above all Samagonka (moonshine). This drink is more likely to destroy men than the partisans. This violent poison puts men in a torpor followed by sleep peopled by horrible hallucinations." While Rostaing admitted that the LVF had disappointed as a military organization, he blamed it in part on the tactics, but also on a lack of "an energetic leader. Now, he who commanded us for several months, Colonel Puaud, reminded me more of a recruiting sergeant than an officer conscious that he was leading troops in a campaign on the brink of hopelessness." A fifty-six-year-old former Foreign Legionnaire, Edgar Puaud was so weighted down with medals, both French and German, that he had become practically bulletproof. In June 1944, Laval would deny Puaud's request to throw the LVF into the fight against "terrorists" at the side of *la Milice*, for fear that he might conspire with Darnand to launch a coup d'état at Vichy. Despite his Great War combat record, Puaud only came once to Russia to inspect the LVF, instead remaining in France through most of 1943 giving speeches and raising recruits. While the command presence of this small, nervous man was disappointing, his attractiveness to the Germans was that he was a "strawman ... neither Doriot nor Darnand," and so would not enflame further the political divisions among these already-feuding French exiles.[174]

"Only during late 1943 and early 1944 when German occupation policy became even more brutal and a 'scorched-earth' policy was being adopted by German forces in retreat and facing defeat, did the civilian population *en masse* consider the risks of siding with the increasingly well organized and supplied partisans worthwhile," concludes Alexander Hill. Those who joined partisan groups often did so to escape being *Ostarbeiter*, the East European equivalent of STO, or because they wished to avoid having to justify their failure of patriotic engagement to SMERSH, Red Army counterintelligence, after the war. Although the war in the East was brutal, especially for civilians, partisans had advantages denied the French *maquis*. When pressured, partisan groups on the northern and central sectors of the Eastern Front could retreat deep into the forests, or even slip behind Red Army lines to rest and recover. Brutal German reprisals against civilians in the aftermath of partisan attacks adjourned the possibility for popular uprising in the German rear. During the battle for Stalingrad, which ended with a Soviet victory in February 1943, and the battle of Kursk in July 1943, partisan groups worked to sabotage German supply lines. The military effectiveness of Soviet partisans in terms of losses inflicted on the *Wehrmacht*, or the disruption of communications or destruction of supplies, was limited. Terrain and lack of enthusiasm for the Soviet regime limited the effectiveness of partisan units in Ukraine. Attacks on railways diminished in effectiveness as the Germans ran trucks in front of locomotives to detonate explosives, and better protected bridges. To counter this, partisans simply pulled up track. But damage was quickly repaired. Partisan losses were also high – over 10 percent – in part because their units, swelled with Soviet soldiers trapped behind the lines and refugee civilians, increasingly became harder to conceal, and because they were ordered to undertake missions which they were untrained and ill-equipped to execute. As a consequence, desertion appears to have been fairly high. But, by 1944, the *Wehrmacht* had few troops to spare for rear area security as even third-tier troops like the LVF were thrown into the front lines, and so had to confine their activity to towns and communication links, while insurgent recruitment spiked. The partisans were also given new tasks, like protecting populations from retreating Germans, and preventing the destruction of bridges and infrastructure to be used by the advancing Red Army. "The guerrillas' main *military* value during the Second World War," concludes Ben Shepard, "lies in the fact that they did eventually provide worthwhile, if uneven, support for Allied conventional operations."[175]

Conclusion

In its eagerness to conclude an armistice and put paid to the Third Republic, Vichy laid a bad bet – that it retained enough military force in the Armistice Army to maintain order in the *zone libre*, while its navy would maintain contact with the empire. Vichy calculated that Germany had won the war, and that Hitler would require French cooperation to realize his vision for a "New Europe." Britain's continued resistance and Churchill's sponsorship of Charles de Gaulle's *France libre* initially seemed ambient noise, except, of course, when de Gaulle and his British sponsor sought to suborn Vichy rule in the French colonies which symbolized sovereignty and legitimacy for each camp. But Pétain had entrusted France's future to Hitler's forbearance, so that Vichy had continually to prove its value to Berlin, by registering merely formulaic diplomatic protests as Hitler annexed Alsace-Moselle into the Reich and subjected French citizens in these three departments to a policy of Nazification and incorporation into Berlin's war effort. And if this were not enough, Vichy felt that it could not protest the violation of the rights of French citizens at a moment when Pétain blessed the campaign by three extremist French right-wing parties to raise volunteer French forces to fight for the *Wehrmacht*. The LVF experience is important for at least three reasons. First, it challenges the Gaullist "resistance" narrative, in that right-wing paramilitary groups were able to raise almost as many volunteers as was the FFL in roughly the first two years of the occupation. Second, rather than appreciate Vichy's goodwill gesture, the highly politicized and militarily inefficient LVF recruitment only invited Berlin's contempt for what counted as among the worst contingents in the German forces. Finally, the LVF experience in Russia also brings into question the military value of partisan warfare, one which would in 1943–1944 impinge on the role and scope of the French resistance and the *maquis*.

7 *La France libre*

In his second BBC address on 22 June 1940, Charles de Gaulle pointed out that France's request for an armistice was unique among the defeated nations.[1] In the view of French historian Jacques Sapir and others, too many senior political leaders and administrators were defeatists, as the French parliament's 10 July vote of "full powers" to Pétain was to demonstrate.[2] For many at the time, and for historians since, 1940 had simply confirmed France's great power decline, reflected in the division and demoralization of its people, economic stagnation, the dysfunction of its political institutions, and the failure of its military to defend the country. However, for de Gaulle and *la France libre*, 1940 had marked a chapter break, a contingent shocker rather than an enduring downgrade in France's international status. Unfortunately, for the moment, de Gaulle's quest to recoup French grandeur far out distanced *France libre*'s political clout and military capacities. Of course, one of the purposes of de Gaulle's rhetorical hyperbole and political intransigence was to allow his Free French movement to punch above its weight in the Alliance. While Gaullist historians like Crémieux-Brilhac view de Gaulle's 18 June 1940 call to arms as the founding act of the French Resistance, the simple truth was that *les forces françaises libres* (FFL) were never large. Even in July 1943 at the moment it "fused" with *l'armée d'Afrique* in the wake of Operation Torch and the Tunisia campaign, the FFL numbered between 50,000 and 60,000 combatants, or less than 2 percent of French forces at the time of the 1940 armistice. Furthermore, between half and two-thirds of these soldiers were impressed imperial levies.[3] As French historian of European resistance Olivier Wieviorka has noted, although de Gaulle was an iconoclast in so many ways, he thought very much in conventional military terms, and "limited himself to recreating, on the British archipelago, a conventional army" that would represent France, not serve as an auxiliary of Gallic exiles in His Majesty's forces. Military force gave him leverage, so that his priority was not to win a war whose outcome was in his view a foredrawn conclusion, but to deploy his diminutive legion to optimize France's post-war position. While he well understood the value of propaganda to build a popular base, the 18 June address had been directed at soldiers, politicians, technicians, and specialists out of whom he would forge first a movement, then an army, and finally a state. De Gaulle did not share Churchill's goal "to set Europe ablaze" through popular insurrection. Like Pétain and Weygand, he feared that a spontaneous, unstructured *levée en masse* held the potential to shred society, not rehabilitate and restore it.[4] De Gaulle may have been a revolutionary in many ways, but he was no Communard.

That few in the summer of 1940 would have forecast the ultimate triumph of Charles de Gaulle and *la France libre* is hardly surprising. Known in pre-war government circles as an intelligent if iconoclastic mid-career defense intellectual, de Gaulle was hardly a household name. But in June 1940, a vigorous, clairvoyant if relatively obscure temporary brigadier stepped into France's leadership void. Few heard what was to become his legendary inaugural BBC address, in which de Gaulle gave voice "to all those who refused by instinct or reason [to accept] defeat."[5] In that short speech, de Gaulle sought to shape France's future by summoning the spiritual power of its past. His fearlessness and brutal candor were perversely uplifting in an atmosphere shaped by pervasive panic. The 18 June address also encapsulated a condensed version of the unvarnished strategic assessment he had unsuccessfully retailed to generals and government officials at Briare and Bordeaux – France had lost an opening battle in a world war because "the German tanks, planes and tactics ... surprised our leaders ... Whatever happens, the flame of the French resistance must not and will not be extinguished." A rebound is possible, but in the Mediterranean, not on the Marne as in 1914. His goal was to "serve and save the nation and the State." The strategy linked to a scenario of victory required "the reappearance of our armies on the battlefield, the return of our territories to belligerence, the participation of the country itself in the efforts of its combatants, the recognition of foreign powers that France as such will have continued the struggle, in short, the transfer of sovereignty, beyond the disaster and procrastination (*attentisme*), to the side of war and, one day, of victory."[6]

While de Gaulle's prediction that a world war would eventually ally multiple nations whose combined power would overwhelm the Axis proved prescient, especially among a defeatist French elite for whom 1940 combined popular moral collapse with Allied abandonment, de Gaulle's vision for victory in 1940 appeared to fit awkwardly into French history and tradition. First, his call for "resistance" implicitly viewed the *levée* as composed of hierarchically organized conventional forces at a time when, by de Gaulle's own 18 June indictment, France's military leadership had totally discredited itself both professionally and politically. Furthermore, recruiting a military force would prove difficult in these early days. Muracciole notes that 80 percent of *les Forces françaises libres* (FFL) – that is, those who enlisted between 18 June 1940 and 31 July 1943 – were not "active citizens" in 1939, "which seriously undermines the vision of the (external) Resistance as an armed citizenry."[7] But it does boost an interpretation of "resistance in France" as part of a broader international phenomenon.

Second, the entire premise of de Gaulle's plan to liberate France from abroad met with opposition, even from people who rejected Vichy. In the wake of the 1940 armistice, even the cosmopolitan Jean Monnet advised the chief of *la France libre* that "it's not from London that the effort at resurrection must emanate ..."[8] But alternative venues for a revival of French fortunes were lacking, especially after most of France's imperial proconsuls rallied to Vichy. And even an internal Resistance would require an organization to coordinate and realize its aspirations, as well as an international representation to finance, supply, and impresario the coming struggle in France, and for France. But in this way, a snowballing boycott of de Gaulle by important armistice opponents revealed Free France's vulnerability to the Vichy indictment of the Gaullists as deserters, and the claim that the FFL formed an army of mercenary *émigrés* on English stipend. In this way, historical memory and legend became yet another impediment to rational decision-making in 1940 France. If Weygand feared the Commune's reappearance, so Republican opponents of the armistice hesitated to rally under the banner of a lanky brigadier with unproven democratic bona fides who resurrected the army of Condé complete with its English paymaster.[9]

A third problem for de Gaulle was that his grand ambitions were sustained by meager means. Indeed, the source for an October 1940 Vichy report on the nascent Gaullist movement recounted that his meeting with the Leader of Free France quickly degenerated: "One is for or against me. You follow me or not. Make your choice and give me your immediate response." This source claimed that de Gaulle's "lack of diplomacy" had almost wrecked his relations with the British, but that the people of London had given de Gaulle's forces "a warm welcome ... One felt that the propaganda in this sense was very well organized."[10] The process of transforming de Gaulle into a British propaganda asset was neither obvious nor easy in June 1940.[11] Britons were happy enough to wash their hands of the French, who most believed had not put up much of a fight. De Gaulle was unknown in London, as were the policies that Pétain would subsequently adopt. Most important, the question of the fate of the French fleet hung in abeyance, at least until Mers-el-Kébir on 3 July, after which Pétain severed relations with London. Nevertheless, the British cabinet proved eager to deescalate conflict with Vichy, especially over colonial issues. Until the end of the year, hopes persisted in Whitehall that London might still do business with "moderates" at Vichy.[12]

Policy began to shift from 20 July, when Minister of Information Duff Cooper suggested that while an isolationist "Britain alone" image might bolster popular resolve in the short run, given Britain's obvious military weakness, London should craft a message with more international appeal. This would expand the storyline beyond that of an Anglo-German conflict, and lay the groundwork for a global, and in particular Anglo-American, alliance whose objective would be to liberate Axis "vassal" states. In this context, Dunkirk should not be interpreted as the termination of the Franco-British alliance and Britain's decoupling from the continent, but rather as a transition to a global war strategy "in anticipation of a post-war settlement in which France would have a seat at the victor's table."[13] For this to happen, the armistice must be portrayed as a "betrayal" of a "victimized" French people by a "defeatist clique" led by the "dishonorable" Marshal. The regime must always be referred to as the "Bordeaux," and subsequently the "Vichy" – rather than the "French" – government, to strip it of political and moral authority. But by then, Cooper was preaching to the converted, because this was a viewpoint that the British press had begun to convey from the middle of June. In an attempt to lay a claim for the legitimacy of *la France libre*, de Gaulle, too, had emphasized the unconstitutionality and lack of popular support for Vichy and the continuity of the Anglo-French alliance in his BBC broadcasts of 18 and 22 June. The assumption of Vichy's illegitimacy was implicit in the formation on the French National Committee on 23 June, and in the 27 October 1940 Brazzaville Manifesto.[14]

The Prime Minister desired a symbolic French military presence to continue the war at Britain's side. On 27 June, Churchill acknowledged de Gaulle as "the leader of all free Frenchmen," thus linking him to British policy. Although this was followed by a 7 August agreement, the actual status of *la France libre* would remain "legally obscure" until somewhat clarified by the creation in June 1943 of *le Comité français de libération nationale* (CFLN), which was recognized by London merely "as having *de facto* sovereign rights over the territories which acknowledge its administration."[15] Public relations consultant Richmond Temple was engaged to promote and humanize "General de Gaulle and his armies of all free Frenchmen" to the British public through feature articles and photo shoots. This was part of a broader strategy to underscore the betrayal of the French people by Vichy defeatists, emphasize the continuity of the Franco-British alliance, and publicize de Gaulle's "France has lost a battle" mantra. Any reference to the Vichy government was prefaced by the adjective "makeshift," Pétain was "senile," and his ministers "treacherous," while Free France became "the real chivalrous France, as typified by those who have loyally chosen to join their destiny with ours." A quick book was published, whose central theme focused on de Gaulle's inter-war foresight in predicting the decisiveness of armored warfare. Churchill was especially keen that the Free French be depicted as comrades-in-arms and symbols of continuing Franco-British military cooperation. On 14 July, a ceremony was held before the statue of Foch in London's Lower Grosvenor Gardens, as a tricolor was raised over the Palace of Westminster. This "continuity" of the Anglo-French partnership is often overlooked, given the frequently acrimonious relationship that developed between Churchill and de Gaulle, and the requirement for the British Prime Minister to support the Leader of Free France in the face of President Franklin Roosevelt's distrust, even dislike, of the man. But the policy of Franco-British cooperation laid down in 1940 continued to be expressed through the Foreign Office, through the Special Operations Executive (SOE), created in the wake of Dunkirk to support an as yet non-existent resistance in France, by the Political Warfare Executive (PWE), and via military cooperation. This was because, in the opinion of Rachel Chin, "Rhetorically, Britain painted itself into a corner that made repudiation or replacement of de Gaulle very difficult." The result was that, despite some very stormy moments between their respective leaders, "cooperation" and "continuity" continued to frame Anglo-Free French relations.[16]

Finding soldiers for what would become *les Forces françaises libres* (FFL) became a problem. Of roughly 130,000 French sailors and soldiers marooned in Great Britain in June 1940, only a fraction volunteered to continue the war at the side of the British. There were several reasons for this low number, some of which have already been touched upon – a belief that the war was over; a desire to return home; a lingering reverence for the Marshal; the requirement to remain in a legal status; resentment against heavy-handed British behavior that included seizing French ships and interning French sailors; Mers-el-Kébir, which de Gaulle certainly believed had inhibited recruitment; the fact that the largely unknown de Gaulle lacked a democratic identity or legitimacy; or because some who might have enlisted had no way of reaching Britain, which explains the high percentage of Bretons – 39 percent of recruits for the Free French Navy (FNFL).[17] On 1 July 1940, Foreign Legion Captain Gabriel Brunet de Sairigné, marooned in Britain on his return from Narvik, briefly sketched the motives of those who joined *la France libre*: "Some don't lay down any conditions, and are ready to serve as privates in the British army. Others think de Gaulle's movement might bring some advantages. For those who think about things a little, the goal is to 'fire a final shot,' incidentally, if possible [hard to imagine in that moment], win the war with England, which will surely lift up France."[18] When Russian Jewish immigrant and naturalized Frenchman FAF Sergeant Roman Kacew, at the time in search of a *nom de plume*, heard de Gaulle's 18 June address, "my first reaction was a moment of rage because I had not thought of inventing this beautiful name fifteen years earlier: Charles de Gaulle, would certainly have pleased my mother, especially if I had written it with a single 'l.' Life is full of missed opportunities."[19]

De Gaulle's personality also slapped a dampener on enlistment. *France libre*'s Churchill-appointed minder General Sir Edward Spears noted that while de Gaulle could be "charming ... warm, generous ... as if another creature lay hidden in an ice-cold prison," his preferred "method" was "to freeze even his most devoted followers to a distance from which no sign could be made, no advice given, no suggestion offered ... Indeed, when he attempted a genial manner for social purposes, it was more disastrous in its effect than the more usual exhibition of supercilious dislike of his fellow men in the mass ..."[20] When he joined Free France in 1941 after escaping from an *Oflag* via a Soviet jail, Alain de Boissieu praised his future father-in-law's "rare intelligence," his "vast historical culture," his capacity for strategic analysis, his "inflexible willpower," and "his ardent faith in the destiny of France." But he also acknowledged that he "held mediocre and indecisive officers in complete disdain."[21] While de Gaulle certainly possessed strength of character and single-minded determination, he also had a "sense of being an outsider who must depend only on himself."[22] Fellow 1912 Saint-Cyr graduate General Antoine Béthouart, rotating through London from Narvik, where he had commanded the French contingent, was well aware of de Gaulle's "brilliant ... but difficult" reputation in the army, where, throughout his career, he had tried the patience of his commanding officers with a censorious arrogance that bordered on insubordination. He was also troubled that no major politician had rallied to de Gaulle. On 30 June, Béthouart informed his classmate that it was his duty to accompany his soldiers, very few of whom had elected to fight on with de Gaulle, back to France. He abandoned his contemporary sitting dejectedly in his small, sparsely furnished London flat looking the very figure of solitude. The news of Mers-el-Kébir, which reached Béthouart on his voyage to Casablanca, temporarily convinced him that he had made the correct decision.[23]

Not surprisingly, the personality of the leader of Free France offered a public relations nightmare, and guaranteed that Richmond Temple fully earned his fee. From a distance, de Gaulle's small head perched atop a towering frame made him look to some "like a simpleton." He seldom made eye contact, but "addressed his remarks to the horizon, passing over the heads and the understanding of his audience."[24] Nor did he necessarily improve upon closer inspection. A *tête-à-tête* with the leader of Free France might leave potential recruits with an impression of a haughty, taciturn, distant, impatient personality, a tall man in search of a balcony, or perhaps a microphone. Churchill perceived that, "Under an impassive, imperturbable demeanor [de Gaulle] seemed to have a remarkable capacity for feeling pain."[25] For him, *la France libre* was a movement that emerged from mourning. Enlistment into its ranks was a calling that required true piety and a sense of mission. But most French officers forced to make a momentous decision in the summer of 1940 to fight on from Britain or return to France were too preoccupied weighing the pros and cons of their choice to make allowances for de Gaulle's supercilious angst. When Captain Diego Brosset arrived at Gaullist HQ at Carlton Gardens in January 1941, having deserted the French military mission in Bogotá, he found his new boss "amiable and authoritarian," a man who "mixed realism with prophecy." While de Gaulle "is a leader … he is timid and doesn't win people over."[26] This "King in exile" demeanor fit the personality of a man who believed that "nothing great can be done without great men, and they are great because they have willed greatness. The most noble cause was to give glory to France, which he regarded not as simply a nation, or a race, but a person …"[27] But so detrimental to enlistment might a first-hand encounter with de Gaulle's imperious manner prove, that Free France's senior naval officer, Admiral Émile Muselier – himself no model of conviviality and nautical bonhomie – urged him to stop inviting potential officer recruits to lunch.[28]

Jean-Louis Crémieux, who in resistance became Jean Brilhac and who volunteered to join de Gaulle to escape a Soviet prison in the autumn of 1941, agonized during his voyage from Murmansk to Glasgow: "Hopefully he's not just a cavalry officer." When, upon his arrival in London in October, he mustered with other novice FFL recruits to be addressed by de Gaulle, he fully expected to be greeted "by the pompous words of a patriotic general." "I wouldn't say that he had charisma, because he was glacial," remembered Crémieux-Brilhac. He spoke in military language, "without great eloquence. But something sovereign. He was impressive … It was France who spoke: whatever difficulties or risks we had taken to join him were simply in compliance with military regulations, and henceforth together with him we were responsible for France. None of us could have imagined de Gaulle as a simple citizen." Nor was he alone in detecting in his new leader a sort of messianic providence – the man standing next to

Crémieux-Brilhac in formation whispered: "It's Charles XI!"[29] A member of de Gaulle's staff, Claude Hettier de Boislambert, found de Gaulle to be a demanding superior. Any order given was considered an order executed. De Gaulle virtually never took advantage of country houses that English friends placed at his disposal to relax on weekends. On the contrary, his staff must remain on the *qui vive* 24/7 because the General had an extraordinary, practically a mechanical, capacity for work. "There was an almost mystical side to de Gaulle," de Boislambert continued. "It wouldn't take much to say that he believed himself to be 'called' . . . In any case, he embodied 'France' – and he had the conviction that he was defending it, the intention to save it – with, or in spite of the French people."[30]

Pierre Brossolette, the brilliant Normalien and SFIO (Socialist Party) activist who joined de Gaulle in April 1942 to become, along with Jean Moulin, one of his principal architects and martyrs of the mobilization of the internal resistance behind the Gaullist movement, criticized de Gaulle's leadership style, which he believed contributed to the mediocrity of *France libre*'s headquarters personnel. In a personal letter written to his boss on 2 November 1942, Brossolette objected that the way de Gaulle treated subordinates, his rejection of criticism, and his refusal to tolerate debate on subjects declared taboo only resulted in "nothing but gratifying assent" from his staff.[31]

Indeed, the question becomes: why did anyone rally to Free France in the summer of 1940? According to Sadoul, de Gaulle's 22 June 1940 BBC address was badly received when his signals unit broadcast it on loud speakers in a small village in the Charente between Angoulême and the destined to become infamous Oradour-sur-Glane: "'Go ahead, fight you bastard! You have your butt in an armchair and you want others to go get killed. Dream on!' Those were the soldiers talking, but the inhabitants and the refugees agreed. The soldiers and civilians have had enough. They want peace at any price." Although Mers-el-Kébir had yet to occur, Sadoul believed that Anglophobia also played a role in the rejection of de Gaulle's call to resist.[32] When, on the morning of 19 June 1940, a friend he encountered in Toulouse asked the eighteen-year-old Louis Bacquier, "Are you a Gaullard or anti-Gaullard?," he had no idea what he was talking about. "It seems that there was this obscure general apparently full of good intentions, who spoke the night before on the London radio to call for a continuation of combat. He was called la Gaule or de Gaule . . . Therefore I was a gaullard before becoming Gaullist."[33]

Some of those who joined de Gaulle were no doubt propelled by patriotism. But patriotism had its limits as a recruiting tool when, in its first two years, only 18 percent of volunteers for *la France libre* were actually French citizens. The initial choice to join de Gaulle was not even political, as only gradually did the Gaullists define an agenda and Vichy come to denounce the Gaullists as subversives. Frenchmen who joined de Gaulle initially were "apolitical dissidents" engaged in a "pure revolt against defeat." However, those who had joined the Foreign Legion had already exhausted other options, like 983 of 1,619 legionnaires – many Jews and Spanish Republicans – from the *13ème Demi-brigade de la légion étrangère* (13ème DBLE), part of the Narvik force, who on 30 June enlisted in the FFL after listening to a speech by de Gaulle at Trentham Park. Another 300 former Spanish republicans refused to board the ship for Morocco at Barry Docks in South Wales, out of fear that the French would simply surrender them to Franco. Most would join the contingent of foreigners who would make up 16 percent of *les Forces françaises libres* (FFL), which is perhaps an overestimate.[34]

The cast of men who gradually assembled in London knew that they would either become celebrated, or be hanged. Thierry d'Argenlieu (Figure 7.1), who fled to Britain via Jersey, was conquered by de Gaulle's voice, which, having just arrived in Southampton, he first heard on a 26 June BBC broadcast. De Gaulle's "clairvoyant word" washed over this Carmelite father like a brilliant sermon for souls on the brink of spiritual and moral despair. For d'Argenlieu, the General's patriotism, his rejection of defeat expressed with authority in spare military language, "dissipated the shadows and darkness."[35] While Béthouart had elected to sail to Morocco with his men, he nevertheless encouraged Captain André Dewavrin, one of his *chasseur alpin* subordinates at Narvik, to follow his instincts. Under the code-name Passy, *École polytechnique* alumnus, sapper, and Saint-Cyr professor Dewarvrin would direct and develop de Gaulle's intelligence and special operations bureau, the BCRA, into a formidable organization to consolidate the Gaullist hold over the internal resistance. Literally sickened by the celebration in the mess at Vichy that followed Pétain's 17 June announcement that he would seek an armistice, diplomat and reserve Lieutenant Claude Bouchinet-Serreulles made the decision to desert. At La Rochelle, he met Jacques Bingen, wounded in Normandy while serving as a liaison officer with the 51st Scottish Division. Together, they caught a ship to Casablanca and then to Gibraltar and Britain. Bouchinet would head de Gaulle's civil cabinet, while Bingen initially would be directed to assemble a merchant marine.[36] Captain Pierre Koenig washed up in Britain among the Narvik refugees. Indeed, in the true spirit of the early Gaullists, he selected "Mutin" (Mutineer) as his *nom de guerre*. The journey of thirty-eight-year-old cavalry Captain Philippe de Hautecloque was more circuitous and displayed the considerable energy, resourcefulness, and

Figure 7.1 Carmelite Father and Rear Admiral Georges Thierry d'Argenlieu in London. Of the men who rallied to *la France libre* in the early months of the war, "[de Gaulle] allowed that there were only two," according to the diplomat Claude Bouchinet-Serreulles, "d'Argenlieu and Leclerc. The rest are unfortunates . . ."

focus that would become his trademarks under the Cross of Lorraine. Twice wounded, escaping German captivity not once but twice, he made his way across France, much of it on a bicycle. He crossed the Spanish frontier with a forged passport and caught a train for Lisbon. On 24 July, he arrived in Britain by ship. Colonel Edgard de Larminat, who defected from Syria to British-occupied Palestine in 1940 to join the Free French, avowed that de Hautecloque left "a strong impression" when they first met in Accra in August 1940, "for he was gifted with a very powerful magnetism. Charming, courteous, and lordly in his private relations, in action, he was the most fierce and tough man I ever encountered."[37]

Vichy initially dismissed the Gaullists as a having attracted no more than 5,000 to 6,000 recruits, among them "no senior officer, a few professional officers, and a dozen reserve officers."[38] This proved to be a generous overestimate – on 15 August 1940, Free France numbered 2,721 men, including 123 officers.[39] That was barely enough to muster a couple of infantry battalions, much less a political movement with a civil and military staff, an army and a navy, with aspirations to create an air wing. But that would be difficult to achieve, because even for the strong willed, reaching England in the summer of 1940 was highly difficult: stranded at Bordeaux-Mérignac, "a strange aerial Dunkirk," whose runway was chock-a-block with every French plane prototype produced in the last twenty years, a confusion of "distraught generals," air crews keen to evacuate their families, and civilians pushing cash on pilots to fly them to Spain, FAF Sergeant Kacew (later celebrated under his penname Roman Gary) searched in vain for an "owner" willing to fly him to England. "I say 'owner' because [the pilot] was sitting in the grass, next to his plane, with the air of a suspicious farmer protecting his cow." Unfortunately, "the English were unpopular," and requests to fly to Britain only brought threats of court martial for desertion, and even a beating at the hands of an adjutant-chef. Kacew was eventually evacuated to Meknès in Morocco, but found that planes were closely guarded and disabled, lest anyone seek to reach Gibraltar. Because he had spent part of his youth in Poland and spoke that language fluently, he managed to borrow a few pieces of Polish uniform and insinuate himself in a group of Polish troops evacuated from Casablanca to Gibraltar.[40]

Spears' American wife Mary "May" Borden declared de Gaulle's praetorians to be "sweet, silly officers" and predicted that they would prove useless in battle. John Stokes of the Royal Fusiliers, who participated in the Dakar expedition and would later serve as Spears' aide in the Levant, remembered that "the French mostly looked very unprepossessing – very poor specimens of manhood. But when they talk, all that changes."[41] In Philippe de Hautecloque, who took "Leclerc" as his resistance name, *la France libre* would acquire its single Staff College brevet. Only one flag officer initially rallied to *la France libre*, and he proved a controversial catch. Admiral Émile Muselier (Figure 7.2) enjoyed a reputation as a good sailor with an aggressive Great War record. He had also demonstrated considerable energy during the Fall of France, when he escaped Marseilles on an English collier to Gibraltar, where he rounded up French ships to sail to the UK.[42] Unfortunately, Muselier was also regarded as "a joke, an eccentric, at best an original character," writes historian of the French navy Philippe Mason, who embellished his sober naval blues with non-regulation baubles, with a reputation as a serial womanizer who was rumored to be an opium addict. Despite the fact that he had quelled a communist-inspired mutiny on his ship in the Black Sea in 1919,

Figure 7.2 De Gaulle reviewing French sailors in January 1941 with *France libre*'s controversial Vice-Admiral Émile Muselier in the foreground.

Muselier was labeled a "red admiral," a career-killing moniker in a reactionary French navy.[43]

For the staff at Carlton Gardens, Muselier was a loose cannon, a one-man upwelling of unsanctioned initiatives who seemed to thrive on conspiracy and intrigue. De Gaulle neither liked nor trusted Muselier. But *la France libre* required a symbol of naval support. De Gaulle was allegedly reluctant to depart London, because it would mean leaving Muselier in charge: "[de Gaulle] is afraid that he would do an enormous amount of harm." But Muselier proved difficult to offload. The Admiralty denounced as a "monstrous suggestion" Muselier's accusation that the shortage of sailors for the *Forces navales françaises libres* (FNFL) was caused by the British sending women to seduce French sailors in Britain into enlisting in the Royal Navy. "It is a deliberate lie on Admiral Muselier's part and I lost no time in telling General de Gaulle so," Spears recorded. "I explained that it was this sort of thing that made Admiral Muselier so obnoxious to us here."[44]

An undated report on Muselier by a Commander Roberts of the Royal Navy, probably written in January 1941, gave a more positive view of Muselier's achievements: he had organized a naval force of twenty-eight ships from scratch, and converted the old battleship *Courbet* at Portsmouth into a reception center for volunteers. Unfamiliar "with British character or with British methods," he was initially "inclined to be brusque and preemptory." But, recognizing that Britain confronted an existential threat, Muselier had adopted a conciliatory tone following the two "shattering blows" to recruitment and morale on 3 July in the British takeover at gunpoint of French ships in British harbors and Mers-el-Kébir. Roberts attributed most of the unflattering rumors about the French Admiral to Passy's *Deuxième Bureau*, which news of Muselier's arrest in January 1941 appeared to confirm. Commander Roberts also exculpated Muselier for the poor discipline among FNFL sailors and complaints about their unmilitary appearance, which he blamed on enforced idleness, which dampened the initial enthusiasm of recruits in the summer, the absence of a mission, and the fact that until the passage of the Allied Forces Act in January 1941, it was virtually impossible to court martial French sailors for disciplinary infractions. Roberts admitted that while at first he did not like Muselier, over time he recognized that "he has a strong character and a heart of gold."[45]

Roberts' charitable assessment was not shared at Carlton Gardens. Brosset found Muselier amiable enough, but volatile and "cunning," with a "bad character." De Boislambert complained that the Admiral did not clean up well. Beneath his moustache and heavy Levantine features, he always looked unkempt, "like a corsair who had fallen into a coal bin." Muselier's presence as the head of the FNFL nearly cost the loyalty of d'Argenlieu – the FNFL leader's scruffy appearance, his incoherent speeches to 10,000 to 15,000 French sailors interned at Aintree racecourse near Liverpool, and his disloyal comments about the Leader of Free France compromised recruitment. The Carmelite Father required a meditative withdrawal to the priory at Kensington to marshal the full measure of his Christian fortitude to remain under Muselier's command. "He's too imaginative, too emotional, too temperamental in his behavior to work with constructively on a regular basis," d'Argenlieu complained.[46] Muselier was not only the first flag officer to rally to de Gaulle, but also he would be the first to defy him, an act for which he was never pardoned. A latent tension festered between the Admiral, who treated the FNFL as his personal fiefdom, and the Brigadier, whose temporary rank had been rescinded by Vichy in the wake of de Gaulle's 18 June address. Some factious Gaullists, encouraged by Churchill, viewed Muselier as a way to control the confrontational de Gaulle. This tension over seniority was removed only when the five-star General Georges Catroux arrived in London in September and agreed to serve a dissident movement led by a man whom he outranked.

Muselier's most lasting legacy lay with his suggestion that *la France libre* adopt the Cross of Lorraine as the movement's symbol.[47] However, for the purposes of the war, Muselier's contribution to *la France libre* included the occupation at de Gaulle's direction of Saint-Pierre and Miquelon in December 1941, which temporarily elevated his stock at Carlton Gardens. Unfortunately, the seizure of these seemingly obscure islands in the North Atlantic announced a pattern of behavior by which de Gaulle would present his Anglo-American sponsors with an unwelcomed *fait accompli*, which contributed to sour relations between Roosevelt and de Gaulle.[48]

The Empire

To triumph, de Gaulle would have to appropriate Vichy's imperial bargaining chips by consolidating Gaullist authority over the empire. This ran counter to a policy of American appeasement of Vichy, while French mismanagement of the Levant threatened the interests of the British Empire and Middle Eastern stability. Insofar as Franklin Roosevelt doubted de Gaulle's commitment to democracy, the leader of *la France libre* also potentially threatened the American President's geopolitical vision for a liberal post-war order in Europe. So, de Gaulle's priorities became, first, to pursue his civil war against Vichy, and second, defend French interests from Allied encroachment. The defeat of the Axis would take care of itself.

Vichy was a colonial power, while *la France libre* aspired to become one as its only way forward. Virtually the only point of agreement between France's warring factions was that empire formed the cornerstone of French grandeur, and acted as a talisman against decadence, that the 1940 debacle had transformed into an obsession.[49] In August–September 1940, de Gaulle picked up some quick wins without the indigenous populations being much consulted in the matter. In most cases, the key factor that swayed the decision was the threat of a British blockade. The one exception was New Caledonia, where a popular movement favorable to the Gaullists did emerge, given a boost by the presence of an Australian warship in Noumea harbor. On 24 September, New Caledonia declared for de Gaulle. Elsewhere, Vichy was decapitated rather than subverted. In "*les trois glorieuses*" of 26–28 August 1940, the Gaullists snatched a hat-trick of acquisitions in French Equatorial Africa (AEF). On 26 August, the governor of Chad, Félix Éboué, a Freemason of Guyanese origins, simply announced a transfer of allegiance after consulting with Lieutenant-colonel Pierre Marchand, military commander of the territory, and Meharist Major Jean Colona d'Ornano, and confirming supplies and military support from British Nigeria. Éboué's logic was that an armistice signed under duress was not legally binding. He also feared that Vichy would sell out the colonies to the Axis. Camel corps officers in the north of Chad had simply slipped over the borders into Nigeria or the Sudan. Debates among the 469 European cadres in the *Régiment de Tirailleurs Sénégalais du Tchad* (RTST) were often "violent." A clear majority of French officers who had not witnessed 1940 were opposed to the armistice, in great part because they feared that it would rattle the colonial order. Thirty-two percent of the officers at Fort-Lamy elected to follow their battalion commander and the medical officer, as well as a smattering of civil servants, and exit Chad toward Vichy-loyal French West Africa rather than initiate civil war.[50]

Ostensibly, "the Chadian *cul de sac*" counted as the most backwater colony in AEF's constellation of undistinguished imperial acquisitions. However, it would soon acquire a strategic importance both because it abutted Italian-controlled Cyrenaica and the Fezzan, Vichy French West Africa (AOF), and because Fort-Lamy would serve as a vital link on the Takoradi air route. But strategic opportunities there waxed and waned with the advances and retreats of the British Eighth Army along the Mediterranean coast from 1940 until General Bernard Montgomery's victory at El Alamein in November 1942. By 1943, 5,000 planes had made this trans-Africa journey along the old Imperial Airways route, a lifeline that Churchill believed made the difference between survival and defeat of British forces in Egypt in the dark days of 1941.[51] Initially, Vichy was keen to retake Chad, but lacked the reach to dispatch an expeditionary army across the 2,000 desert miles that separated Dakar from Fort-Lamy.

At this stage of the war, the Gaullist insurgency was defined by improvization, audacity, and luck. Calculating that, with the exception of Gabon, AEF might be won over without the requirement for a military force, on 6 August, de Gaulle had dispatched an unlikely trio of persuaders composed of businessman and banker protégé of Jean Monnet René Pleven, Claude Hettier de Boislambert, a wealthy landowner from the Calvados and intrepid African traveler, and Captain Phillippe d'Hauteclocque, whose head was still bandaged from a wound received in Champagne, from London to Lagos. D'Hauteclocque adopted the pseudonym Leclerc, got a yellow fever shot, purchased some tropical kit at W. H. Gore & Co in London, and self-promoted to colonel to jawbone the Cameroon into the Gaullist camp on 27 August. The next day, Brazzaville, capital of the "Moyen-Congo," rallied to Colonel Edgard de Larminat, a much-decorated Great War veteran, who in 1940 was serving as chief of staff to the French commander in the Levant, Eugène

Mittelhauser. When Larminat protested the armistice, he had been placed under house arrest, from which he escaped and made his way to Africa via British Palestine. On 29 August, the governor of Oubangui-Chari (the modern-day Central African Republic), Pierre de Saint Mart, called a meeting to convince a handful of expats to switch loyalties away from Vichy. This left Gabon as the only holdout in AEF. Henceforth, from 29 August 1940, this insurrection against the armistice became officially labeled *la France libre*.[52]

This audacious sweep of AEF entered Gaullist lore as the epic birth of the movement. In 1942, Captain and medical doctor Paul Moynet wrote to de Gaulle that the Gaullists had captured AEF through a "military *coup d'état* . . . Nothing would have been possible in Chad without success in Brazzaville, and nothing was possible in Brazzaville without a force superior to that of [Governor] General [Louis] Husson."[53] Martin Thomas argues that the critical swing faction was in fact local businessmen who needed to export their products – palm oil, cocoa, timber, mahogany – often via Nigeria, to Britain, which was their main market. They opted for Free France for economic rather than political or ideological reasons. Those colonies that rallied to de Gaulle benefited from a 7 August accord that allowed de Gaulle's dissident movement to recruit in the colonies soldiers who would be paid by London, and that also guaranteed the colonial currencies and agreed to purchase any unsold commercial items. Vichy's hands were tied – they could not appeal to the indigenous population, who regarded the French administration as oppressive. Nor were these clean wins. While a colony might "rally" to *la France libre*, not all of the officers did, especially in Oubangui-Chari. Even the victors were divided over their attitudes to Pétain, over whether to oppose Vichy or the Axis, or to enlist with de Gaulle or British forces. Gabon experienced a minor civil war before it toppled to the Gaullists in November. To shore up his authority, de Gaulle quickly appointed officers who had rallied to him in London to top positions in AEF, led by Leclerc, who took command of the RTST. But, apart from a handful of raids into the Fezzan that culminated in Leclerc's capture of the Koufra oasis in early 1941, an exploit that would enter the lexicon of Gaullist mythology, most of the military action between 26 August 1940 and the first meeting with the Germans, at Ksar Rhilane in Tunisia on 10 March 1943, amounted to chastising African communities who fled French forced labor projects or who neglected to pay their taxes.[54] So, if indigenous Africans feared Vichy servitude, Free France would be accused of instituting "quasi-slavery" practices. Tensions within the indigenous communities, and between the local populations and their new Gaullist overlords, led to the Brazzaville conference in 1944 in an attempt to recalibrate the guidelines of France's imperial relationship. But Vichy was momentarily unable to exploit these divisions, beyond broadcasting threats of reprisal. An expedition to recapture the colonies would have required resources that Vichy found it difficult to muster, as well as authorization from the armistice commission in Wiesbaden. The appearance of a British fleet off Dakar in September also cooled enthusiasm in Vichy for expeditionary warfare. But London's tolerance for Gaullist colonial acquisition also had its limits, especially in the Foreign Office, where Lord Halifax sought a détente with Vichy, and was "unconvinced of the Free French movement's capacity to act as [the empire's] custodian."[55] The Royal Navy lacked ships effectively to enforce a blockade of those French colonies that remained loyal to Vichy. British dependencies like Sierra Leone and Gold Coast anticipated retaliation from Vichy-controlled AOF. Some feared with good reason that Vichy might invite into Dakar U-boats that would threaten the lifeline to Egypt via the Cape. But, "even if Free French claims to colonial popularity were discredited" by the failure of Menace, as Eric Jennings notes, one major consequence of this Gaullist colonial offensive was that in Free France's first two years, de Gaulle's army and the basis of his "sovereignty" would in fact be largely African.[56]

Fearing that a loss of colonies would increase Axis pressure for concessions, Vichy began to tighten control over its remaining territories. In Pondicherry on 9 September, Governor Louis Bonvin tipped the loyalties of *les comptoires des Indes* to the Allied camp basically because, surrounded by the British, he had little choice. Hesitation by colonial and naval authorities was a significant factor in Gaullist triumphs in New Caledonia and Tahiti, where the expat community was well aware that Vichy was in no position to protect them from the Japanese.[57] That would not prove the case in the West Indies, where popular opinion found its limits when demands by elected officials to continue the war at de Gaulle's side were checkmated by the Vichy loyalist Admiral Georges Robert. In the Middle East, appeals to remain loyal to Vichy mixed themes of race with those of discipline: "Dissidence is a very contagious disease for which the whites will pay in the end. Movements that do not respect hierarchy carry within themselves the ferment of dissolution."[58] Indeed, a major complaint against de Gaulle was that by spreading dissension in the colonies, he threatened to strip France of the foundation of its grandeur, deprive Vichy of one of its major bargaining chips with the Axis, and prod indigenous peoples to rebel against colonial governance. While Robert's action in the French Antilles had been ordered by Darlan, racist disdain for "an impressionable population, with limitless credulity for false news, a total inability to analyze events with detachment," also informed Robert's decision. The clincher, however, was a *pronunciamento* by the captains of the three ships under Robert's command at Fort de France to force their superior to declare for Vichy. The ringleader of this Antilles 18 Brumaire was Pierre Rouyer, captain of the *Jeanne d'Arc*, who tapped into the insecurities and anxieties of the pro-Vichy Békés – local white planters – to create a repressive state to preserve their social and economic preeminence. In the view of Gaullists, it also offered yet another demonstration of the "obstinate fanaticism of the Navy-state," that conjured up the specter of an American invasion to justify a state of siege mentality. As a reward for his loyalty, Rouyer was promoted to admiral in November 1940 and named in 1943 to command the naval base at Loirent, which contained major U-boat pens and a *Kriegsmarine* base in the Battle of the Atlantic.[59]

For "*Charles-sans-terre*," a tour of his newly acquired African domains, replete with military reviews, offered periodic spiritual uplift and restored faith in his destiny. De Gaulle's subordinates noticed that he actually appeared to be in a cheerful mood for once – "So, we keep going?," he chortled to Larminat.[60] Another plus for *la France libre* was the arrival in London on 17 August of General Georges Catroux (Figure 7.3), while de Gaulle was besieging Dakar. Opposition to the armistice had caused Vichy to bounce the sixty-two-year-old, five-star *général d'armée* from his post as High Commissioner in Indochina. While being repatriated to France, he had jumped ship at Singapore, and made his way to Britain with his redoubtable wife, considerable retinue of Siamese cats and Indochinese servants, and enough furnishings to fill a provincial château. A wealthy *pied noir* (North African settler) with a clipped moustache and close-cropped dark hair, Catroux enjoyed a reputation as a stylish, chivalrous dandy whose military cap tilted at a jaunty angle. Harold Macmillan, who would meet Catroux in Algiers in 1943, described him as "old – about sixty-three – *très fin*, *très souple*, and all that. A good diplomatist; a man of the world; with a very high standard of personal comfort; a French snob (princesses and all that) and yet broad, tolerant, liberal view of life. He is a sort of French Whig. I find him very easy to deal with and very agreeable. He speaks beautiful French – witty, subtle, but not overstrained phraseology."[61]

Like Brossolette, Catroux's initial encounter with *la France libre* in London failed to dispel his apprehensions. Not surprisingly, Muselier, who received him, left an unfavorable impression. Catroux took note of an "atmosphere of psychosis that weighed on *la France libre*." In the wake of the failure at Dakar, with de Gaulle's prestige in free fall and the General tramping the tropics to stir up support, Carlton Gardens bubbled with intrigue centered on suspicions that Muselier was preparing to supplant their leader in de Gaulle's absence.[62] Although a soldier, most

Figure 7.3 General Georges Catroux in Damascus with General Paul Legentilhomme, 26 May 1941.

of Catroux's Great War service had been spent as a German POW at Ingolstadt, where he had met de Gaulle, whom he admired personally. At Carlton Gardens, however, Catroux represented the quintessential "political general," whose battle ribbons had been won in committee meetings, in conference rooms, and in the stratosphere of France's imperial civil service. As a protégé of Georges Mandel (né Rothschild), associate of Clemenceau, Dreyfusard, hard-line anti-fascist, and Colonial Minister from 1938 to May 1940 and briefly Interior Minister in Reynaud's government, Catroux's Republican résumé failed to catapult him to the front of the queue at Vichy, which was reserved for defeated generals, appeasers, and nautical reactionaries. In fact, Catroux's sudden appearance in London caused *la France libre*'s *jeunesse dorée* rightly to suspect a Churchill-engineered coup. Diego Brosset would declare Catroux charming, but too old school to lead in a modern, mechanized war – not necessarily an immediate disqualification in a force that had no tanks but was in significant need of political counsel. In this way, he shared de Gaulle's view of Catroux as a representative of the French army's "discredited generation." But for British Tories like Macmillan and Spears, Catroux was just the sort of Frenchman that they could relate to: urbane, intelligent, courteous, cosmopolitan, a man of "immense self-control . . . he belonged to the comfortable world of good company and privilege," noted Spears, "and indeed there was something of the planter about him." Churchill wanted Catroux to supplant de Gaulle. But according to Spears, "[Catroux] felt that de Gaulle had created a strong position for himself in London," which he was loath to challenge. According to his biographer, Henri Lerner, the real reason was that Catroux had not entirely made up his mind to associate with this motley gang of Gaullist exiles. In the event, he accepted Churchill's offer to become French delegate in Cairo. Catroux subsequently flew from Cairo to Fort-Lamy on 18 October 1940 to meet with de Gaulle. In what Lerner calls one of the pivotal moments in France's wartime history, when the two men met on the runway, Catroux immediately broke the tension by saluting his junior de Gaulle: "*À vos ordres, mon Général!*"

In fact, Catroux's biographer believes that it was a lengthy 23 September interview with René Cassin, prominent jurist, French representative to the League of Nations until 1938, and future Nobel laureate, that persuaded Catroux to throw in his lot with *la France libre*. While de Gaulle and Catroux differed in temperament and method, over lunch with Éboué at Fort-Lamy, they realized their convergent vision. Catroux's opposition to the armistice had been based on his recognition of the global nature of the war and that it was his duty as a soldier to fight, not conform to a counterfeit Vichy conception of discipline. He was also convinced that Hitler would work to destroy France. Finally, as a colonial official, Catroux realized that the armistice threatened imperial stability, where French rule was anchored in the authority and prestige of racial hierarchy, not, as Vichy pretended, on indigenous sentiment and gratitude for French culture and beneficence. The armistice had also forfeited imperial and great power status, transforming France into "a protector incapable of protecting," the latest "dead god" of the Middle East. Finally, they agreed that *la France libre* must prioritize the Levant, which both men were convinced would become an Axis target sooner rather than later. For the moment, Catroux should carry on as French representative in Cairo with an ambassador's salary, as well as being remunerated by *la France libre* as commander-in-chief in the Middle East, which allowed him to keep the formidable Madame Catroux in the couple's agreeably luxurious lifestyle.[63]

Crémieux-Brilhac argued that Catroux reaped insufficient credit for his role in de Gaulle's ultimate triumph, where he played the adult in the room whose task was to smooth feathers ruffled by de Gaulle's glacial *hauteur*. By nature and profession a diplomat, Catroux believed de Gaulle far too inflexible and authoritarian, and frequently told him so. He failed to grasp de Gaulle's tactic of deploying intransigence to dramatize issues and force the British, who hated "scenes," to make concessions. Harold Macmillan, present in a June 1943 meeting in Algiers that brought together de Gaulle, Henri Giraud, and Dwight Eisenhower, from which de Gaulle left "evidently in a great rage," immediately twigged de Gaulle's tactic: "I think partly simulated (he is a good actor, and does his stuff well). Giraud left a few minutes later, dignified but flushed. Eisenhower seemed rather taken aback by de Gaulle's powerful personality (he had never seen him 'in action' before) but was otherwise unshaken."[64] As *la France libre* played mainly in the colonies in its formative years, Catroux's knowledge of the French imperium, especially of the Arab world, proved invaluable, although, as would be seen in Syria, the uncompromising de Gaulle and the temporizing Catroux were not always on the same page. Catroux believed himself to be a realist willing to prioritize alliance requirements over de Gaulle's unyielding ambitions for France. He corresponded directly with Churchill and Anthony Eden, who was Foreign Minister from early 1941, to deescalate tensions sparked by de Gaulle's recurrent tantrums. Catroux's flexibility and "desire to please" did not always sit well with *France libre*'s leader, who, on occasion, wondered if Catroux were working for him or for the British, and who whipped him back into line with peremptory telegrams. In the political line-up at *la France libre*, Catroux counted as a wet, who criticized neither Pétain nor Laval in public, and who clung to the unrequited dream he shared with Roosevelt, that Weygand might somehow convert to the Allied cause. But in his more temperate moments, de Gaulle realized that Catroux was "his most important war companion." However, Catroux's charm and flexibility were not shared by the thrice-married Madame Marguerite Catroux. In fact, the "wise but weak" Catroux and his gossipy and "ostentatiously elegant" wife became camp followers rather than converts to de Gaulle's uncompromising mission to restore France's grandeur.[65] Macmillan declared Madame Catroux, who quickly acquired the nicknames Mad Cat and la Reine Margot, "an interesting Edwardian survival," who surrounded herself with "guards of honour, Indo-Chinese servants, aides-de-camp, secretaries, and all the paraphernalia which the French adore." Although her husband had commandeered the best accommodation in Algiers, she "has pronounced the villa to be *effroyable*. She apologizes for the bad food, the indifferent service, the poor display of silver, the *mauvais goût* of the furniture, the second-rate wine – in fact, all is exquisite. She bosses everyone; she is a *mauvaise langue* . . . the luncheon was very recherché – exquisite food, exquisite women (mostly princesses) and a lot of bullying of the servants. Quite a relaxation." Mad Cat also thought de Gaulle an insufferable brute and lobbied indefatigably for her husband to take the reins of *la France libre*.[66]

Operation Menace

Although a brief aftershock coming on the heels of the seismic quakes of Dunkirk and the armistice, the September 1940 Anglo-Gaullist attack on Dakar – codenamed Operation Menace – was to reorder the early seemingly effortless expectations of the nascent Gaullist movement, as well as help shape its relationship with its British sponsor. The origins of Menace remain unclear, although one source believes that the "lobbying" of Churchill's friend and de Gaulle's minder Sir Edward Spears played a role.[67] Max Egremont insists that it was not de Gaulle's idea, although a January 1941 report insisted that the French leader "has several times asked that French forces be engaged as soon as possible to rally African colonies." An operation against Dakar appears to have been first discussed at 10 Downing Street on 31 July or 1 August, and subsequently at Chequers, the Prime Minister's country retreat, on 3 August.[68] In his memoirs, de Gaulle acknowledged that French West Africa (AOF) would prove a tough nut to crack for several reasons: imperial authority under Governor General Pierre Boisson, a staunch Vichy supporter, was more concentrated there; Dakar was a well-fortified base; while West and North Africa were closely linked.[69] Nevertheless, following the failure of French North Africa to rally, wining Dakar for Free France appeared vital to maintain the movement's momentum and credibility. Churchill pushed Menace for several reasons: he feared that a U-boat base in Dakar might threaten the Cape convoy route and complicate the Battle of the Atlantic. He was also keen to recoup Belgian and Polish gold reserves stored at Dakar. But above all, frustrated by a lull in the war, Churchill needed to take the offensive, show some gains somewhere. Dakar seemed to offer a target well within Britain's capabilities. With the Free French in the forefront, he could also escape the charge that London hoped to capitalize on France's weakness to expand its imperium.[70] Furthermore, the Gaullist land snatch of "*les trois glorieuses*" of 26, 27, and 28 August, when Chad, Cameroon, and the French Congo had in rapid succession defected to *la France libre*, convinced an imaginative Churchill that for "a large portion of the French officers, officials, and traders in all these territories . . . General de Gaulle shone as a star in the pitch-black night."[71]

Unfortunately, given the high stakes involved in Menace, the operation plan was badly conceived, poorly managed, and dogged by bad luck.[72] On 23 September 1940, a formidable British Task Force M commanded by Admiral Andrew Cunningham appeared before Dakar with its Gaullist elements in a show of overwhelming force, and summoned the garrison to rally to the Allied camp.[73] At this point, the bad luck kicked in, beginning with the presence of a French squadron dispatched from Toulon that, because of Force M's proximity, had sought refuge in Dakar, thus reinforcing the African stronghold's already formidable firepower with a top-up of French navy resolve. Second, the psychological impact of Force M's appearance before Dakar on 23 September was masked by a heavy sea mist that concealed the size of the British fleet. Appeals to the garrison to rally were rejected, and landing parties under a white flag were fired upon, which triggered a ship-to-shore artillery duel. A second attempt on 24 September only resulted in more inconclusive artillery duels and eight planes lost from the carrier *Ark Royal*, while three appeals to the population by de Gaulle went unheeded. Cunningham had a third go on 25 September, only to have HMS *Resolution* torpedoed while HMS *Barham* absorbed a shell from the battleship *Richelieu*, forcing Cunningham, with Churchill's permission, to call off the attack.

Not only had the failure of Menace dented the Royal Navy's reputation, but also de Gaulle's credibility had been struck a near fatal blow. The leader of *la France libre* insisted that while the garrison had wanted to rally to his movement, this had been thwarted by German pressure and his reluctance to ignite a civil war. AOF was not ready to rally to de Gaulle, who was seen more than ever as a pawn of the English. Dakar's silver lining for de Gaulle was that the French naval reinforcements at Dakar that helped to repel Cunningham had in fact been dispatched to prevent further defections in AEF by retaking Douala, capital of Cameroon, and so had been diverted from their primary mission. Given the line-up of forces at Dakar, even without the presence of naval reinforcements, it is unlikely that AOF would have rallied to de Gaulle. But silver linings were not at the top of the agenda aboard de Gaulle's flagship, the *Westernland*, where de Gaulle's mood was depressed, possibly even suicidal, as he considered throwing in the towel.[74] "The days that followed were cruel for me," de Gaulle admitted. In a sense, thrown together in the wake of defeat, d'Argenlieu became his confessor. The Carmelite monk recorded in his diary: "Suddenly, for the first time, abandoning his habitual distant and cold demeanor," de Gaulle admitted to d'Argenlieu, "If you only knew, Commander, how alone I feel." This became a foundational moment in the relationship between the two men, "the birth of a reciprocal fascination . . . The link that united the two was in its essence that of a feudal-vassal relationship. D'Argenlieu, the great devotee of Gaullism, offered his faith and homage to his sovereign."[75]

The negatives flowing from the setback at Dakar, both for Free France and for Churchill, seemed far out of proportion to the insignificance of the event, however. First, eager to extend and solidify loyalty to Vichy at Dakar, Weygand, Boisson, and Huntzinger toured from the middle of October to insulate AFN and AOF against further defections. Laval removed the High Commissioner in Lebanon and Syria, Gabriel Puaux, and in November replaced him with the more reliable General Henri Dentz, who had been Weygand's intelligence chief in the Levant, and whose military laurels included the surrender of Paris on 14 June 1940.[76] In AOF, Boisson launched a thorough purge of his colonial administration in the wake of Menace, and interned British residents. Named Delegate-general for Africa, Weygand ordered tightened surveillance and increased police powers to stamp down on any hint of Gaullist opposition. Vichy's *Deuxième Bureau* under Colonel Henri Navarre was to keep a sharp eye for signs of disloyalty. By October 1940, it had become obvious that Gaullist dissent in the empire had peaked. *La France libre* must find ways to operate in a climate that appeared, at least in the short term, to be increasingly unfavorable.[77]

A second consequence of Dakar was that the failure of Menace followed by the strengthening of Vichy's grip on the empire cast doubts on Free France's prospects. "Although the British were still treating him as a man with a future,"[78] Dakar highlighted the limits of de Gaulle's appeal among the French, and exposed as pretense his claim to speak for France, ironically in a way in which the bloodbath at Mers-el-Kébir had not, because Vichy control of AFN and AOF had firmed up.[79] The rebuff at Dakar did not just dampen Churchill's initial hopes that de Gaulle could summon a following in the colonies, where Vichy was clearly perceived as legitimate.[80] It also virtually dried up recruitment, much more than had Mers-el-Kébir, initiating the so-called "crossing of the desert" when so few recruits came in that *la France libre* was barely able to replace its losses.[81] Dakar also became a source of serious acrimony between Free France and its British promoters – de Gaulle complained that the operation might have succeeded had the British not allowed the French squadron through the Strait on 11 September. The Admiralty replied that denying French ships access to the Strait was neither practical nor desirable, and argued against Churchill's request in October 1940 to mount a second operation against Dakar.[82] Gaullists complained that Cunningham's head-on assault of the heavily fortified harbor was unimaginative and counterproductive, when a landing on an undefended beach at Rufisque might have taken Dakar from the land side as all the batteries were pointed seaward, and only the French navy was keen to resist.[83]

Third, Dakar brought down the curtain on the Churchill–de Gaulle honeymoon, and would draw the two leaders to the brink of divorce in the next months. It also began to put distance between de Gaulle and Spears. For starters, the British asserted that a lack of security consciousness among Free French participants had compromised Menace, an untrue but robust allegation. In fact, Menace had caught Vichy totally unawares.[84] But the view that the Gaullists were an intelligence sieve was to hurt relations throughout the war, and cause them to be cut out of operational planning. There were even hints that *la France libre* had been infiltrated by an agent, which provided the supposition underlying the Muselier affair of early January.[85] Security concerns were to stalk the Free French for the remainder of the war, giving Roosevelt another excuse for excluding de Gaulle from planning for Torch in 1942 and Overlord and Anvil two years later, when coordination with the French resistance was vital. The *Daily Telegraph* compared Dakar to Narvik, a shambles that made Britain appear less reliable to potential allies – e.g. the United States and the Dominions. The *Daily Mail* denounced Dakar as "the lowest depths of imbecility to which we have yet sunk," invariably compared it to Gallipoli, although the two operations bore little resemblance, and complained that once again, Dakar had showcased the amateurish British approach to war. Cruel caricatures of de Gaulle, blamed for dragging Churchill into the quagmire of French African politics, appeared in English papers. American Ambassador Joseph Kennedy, never a reliable guide to British public opinion, insisted that Dakar had wounded Churchill's popularity, and showcased the UK's weakness. American Army COS General George Marshall urged the President to keep war material at home to arm future US forces rather than export it to Great Britain where it would be frittered away.[86]

The failure of Menace also amplified mutterings in the Foreign Office and the Admiralty that *France libre* was a liability, and that a wiser policy would be to appease Vichy rather than risk alienating it. These fears were heightened by the Hitler–Pétain handshake at Montoire on 24 October. Halifax argued that if AOF and AFN shifted from neutrality to belligerence, then London would face serious strategic challenges. Negotiations opened in Madrid on 1 October between the British and French ambassadors with the objective of easing the naval blockade of France. George VI sent his compliments to the Marshal.[87] Appeasement of Vichy would also put British policy on the same page as that of the United States, where, if Lacouture is to be believed, Dakar had hardened Roosevelt's hitherto merely patrician distaste for de Gaulle into a posture of profound antipathy.[88] De Gaulle's denunciations of Vichy, which Roosevelt was assiduously courting, as an illegal pseudo-state simply pitched more fuel on that fire. Churchill began to see de Gaulle as an obstacle to winning over the French empire, and as an irritant in his relations with Washington. Halifax of all people complained that de Gaulle should restrict himself to military matters and stop behaving like a fascist dictator. Needless to say, this British attempt at realpolitik collided head-on with de Gaulle's anti-Vichy jihad. Churchill dispatched Catroux to Cairo to attempt to sway the French Levant. This made Catroux seem to be more a creature of Churchill than of Free France, so that de Gaulle at this stage remained wary of him.[89]

Above all, the failure to rally Dakar was a giant step in the radicalization of *la France libre*. Despite the fact that, fearing a repeat failure, Churchill initially refused to aid in the seizure of Gabon, de Gaulle pressed ahead, and with good reason. On 28 August, the governor of Gabon had declared for de Gaulle, only to be deposed by local French expats led by the Bishop, Monseigneur Louis Tardy. Libreville was hardly Dakar, defended only by the small dispatch boat *Bougainville* and the submarine *Poncelet*. However, the Hitler–Pétain handshake at Montoire on 24 October had caused Churchill to permit Royal Navy participation in the operation – depth charges dropped from a British biplane damaged the *Poncelet* and caused it to scuttle on 7 November off Port-Gentil. Forces under Major Pierre Koenig landed on 8 November. Barely recovered from his leg wound received at Dakar, d'Argenlieu reveled in the thought of steaming into Libreville harbor on the bridge of the Gaullist dispatch boat *Savorgnan de Brazza*, which sank the *Bougainville* on 9 November. Libreville, a modest but symbolic prize, surrendered that day. Three days later, on 12 November, Port-Gentil struck its flag despite firm orders from Vichy to resist to the last bullet. The garrison under General Marcel Tetu refused to rally to de Gaulle, and so were interned in AEF for the remainder of the war. The victory was marred somewhat when d'Argenlieu and Leclerc revved up the enduring army–navy scuffle over precedence in the colonies regarding who should be accorded the honors of victory, which foreshadowed a more caustic disagreement that was to have far more tragic consequences in Indochina in 1945–1946. Demonstrating his refined ecumenical sensibilities, d'Argenlieu ordered a Protestant officer to arrest the pro-Vichy Bishop Tardy, who retaliated by excommunicating *France libre's* Carmelite father. Fortunately, the Apostolic Delegate in the Belgian Congo intervened to restore d'Argenlieu's celebrity standing with the Deity.[90]

A New Elite?

The popular cliché held that the Gaullists were a conspiracy of minorities – "A handful of aristocrats, some enlightened Jews, and fishermen from the Île de Sein."[91] Emmanuel d'Astier de La Vigerie, who together with his two brothers attempted to replicate a French male version of the Mitford sisters, insisted that those who chose to join this snowball of dissent were "*des marginaux*" – fringe elements, non-conformists, wasters. In January 1941, Brosset certainly found de Gaulle's staff encumbered with "people who had nothing to lose: lots of Jews; very respectable people; more modest straightforward individuals." Jews were prominent in the upper echelons of *la France libre*, among them René Cassin, Maurice Schumann, André Manuel, Jacques Bingen, and Jean Pierre-Bloch in the BCRA, as well as Georges Boris and Pierre Laroque in the *commissariat national à l'Intérieur*, not to mention Aspirant Crémieux-Brilhac, still fairly junior but destined for a brilliant post-war career as a jurist and historian. But antisemites and holdovers from the anti-parliamentary right and *Action Française* also lurked on *la France libre*'s fringes. The administrative cohesion for this incongruent congregation was provided by its two-finger typist secretary Élisabeth de Miribel. While it is true that Free France attracted its share of non-conformists, led by Charles de Gaulle, Protestants and Jews were overrepresented at Carlton Gardens, as were Bretons in the FNFL. But, socially and politically speaking, many officers in Free France would have felt perfectly at home in a Vichy mess were it not for their rejection of the armistice.[92] The enigma of Free France in these early days was that it was an inexplicable enigma. It emerged from defeat, and was defined by what it scorned, not what it embraced. According to Belot, de Gaulle managed "to federate and represent a front of refusal characterized by its heterogeneity." Nevertheless, for many across the political spectrum and abroad, that *la France libre* was led by a soldier with no political past invited analogies to Bonaparte and Boulanger, and summoned fears of dictatorship. Some even seemed to believe that de Gaulle was a fascist, others that he was a communist, which demonstrates how difficult it was in these early days to situate him politically or to divine his intentions.

Muracciole argues that while, from its inception, *la France libre* grouped at its core an elite of middle-class, patriotic Frenchmen, the external resistance offered a remarkably eclectic gathering, an archipelago of dissent that would become increasingly heterodox as the Gaullists collected rebellious colonies, Vichy increasingly self-discredited through collaboration, and the external resistance became "a natural refuge for outcasts of the Marshal." Foreign legionnaires of the 13th Demi-brigade assembled for the Narvik expedition, many of them refugees from the 1939 collapse of the Spanish republic, made up almost a quarter of Gaullist recruits in the summer of 1940. The following year, the percentage had risen to almost a third on the heels of the Syrian campaign.

Recruits from *les comptoirs des Indes*, New Caledonia, and Polynesia mingled with *tirailleurs* from AEF. Indeed, if you wished to join Free France, it helped to live abroad, in the colonies and dependencies, or alternatively close to the Channel coast. The average age of these volunteers was 25.4 years, an average that continued to decline so that, by 1943, half of Free France's recruits were under twenty-three years old and a third under twenty-one. "The entire spirit of Free France and Gaullism resides in this apparent paradox," concludes Muracciole. An infinitesimal number of the estimated 32,000 French nationals (excluding foreigners and imperial subjects) who served in the FFL were peasants, and they were not defending the soil of France. In fact, initially Free France resembled the international brigades of the Spanish Civil War, or a polyglot, multiracial, heterodox version of the Prince de Condé's corps, rather than a revival of the citizen *levée*.[93] In contrast to the Gaullist notion of French resistance as an aristocracy of disobedience and audacity initiated on 18 June 1940, exemplified by its poster boy Philippe Leclerc, the *levée* analogy transitioned more easily to the internal resistance, which prided itself on representing all of the French people in "a community of suffering and combat," writes Géraud Létang. "While the FFL created an identity based on its superiority to the rest of the French, the combatants of the shadows on the contrary were proud to assemble clandestinely all the diversity of French society."[94]

Why *la France libre* formed a new elite was not immediately apparent. In an often overlooked 24 March 1942 address on Radio Londres, de Gaulle defined his movement as "a new elite, a combat elite ... men who know how to go forward without hesitation, without second thoughts, without calculation. In their action, as in their eyes, one sees the first signs of a new France. Henceforth, the destiny of our country depends on this audacious elite."[95] "The Free French are idealists," declared Larminat in 1943, because they refuse to accept defeat. "They proved it by deliberately accepting all the risks for an idea at the moment when the chances of success were the least likely ... They firmly believe that they are in communion with the oppressed and resistant nation."[96] *La France libre* linked its elite status to action. "The war will offer the opportunity to reveal those judged the most worthy to lift up France," notes Létang. A self-proclaimed elite defined by "action" and "collective disobedience" with its own chivalric order, *les compagnons de la libération*, certainly gave *la France libre* a distinct identity. It also served to bond those who worked at the head office in London with colonial exiles scattered in Chad, New Caledonia, and *les comptoirs des Indes*. Class differences also evaporated in the heat of "action." In fact, de Gaulle's "*politique du prestige*" was well adapted to the colonies, where "a scrupulous management of appearances" was a daily requirement because "together with the rifle and the cudgel, it was etiquette and all the bearing of deference that were mobilized to maintain the continuity of domination." Some colonies, like Chad, had flipped to *la France libre* for economic rather than for ideological reasons, but even more because the white elite realized that a Vichy–*France libre* civil war threatened to collapse their dominance over indigenous populations.[97] So, rather than act as a progressive and modernizing force, Gaullism superintended a reaffirmation of France's colonial identity and hierarchy, together with an intensification of indigenous exploitation.

A second challenge became how to realize de Gaulle's intertwined priorities: "In the vast expanses of Africa, France could in effect remake its army and reclaim its sovereignty," de Gaulle notes in his memoirs. Africa would give him a base; it would provide soldiers for his army, and bestow "territorial legitimacy" that would bolster his case for political recognition. It was in the colonies that de Gaulle could advertise his themes of resistance, republican legitimacy, and regeneration of constitutional government.[98] For de Gaulle, seizing the colonies also constituted an attack on Vichy's independence and legitimacy, a vital first step in restoring French sovereignty and democracy. But building political legitimacy and an armed force via the colonies also contained significant risks, for several reasons, beginning with the fact that *France libre*'s ideals were of little interest to the colonized, and might even be perceived as contrary to their interests. Hopes for even a modest liberalization and modernization of the French imperium from 1936 had collapsed with the Popular Front. This left indigenous nationalists in many colonies, but especially in Indochina and North Africa, increasingly persuaded that the French were not honest brokers. Second, because colonial control was vital for their sovereignty, legitimacy, and military power, both French camps prioritized "the Franco-French wars" over *la revanche*. Third, colonial tensions stoked the ambiguous relationship between *la France libre* and its British patrons, whose interests and methods often clashed. As a man of "the long nineteenth century," de Gaulle was primed to be suspicious of British aims. And British policy often served to reinforce those expectations: "[De Gaulle] links [his many] perplexities first to British obtuseness, then to British policy, and finally to British perfidy," wrote the British Consul-General in Brazzaville. "He will never be able to rid himself of the burden of distrust and dislike of Great Britain …" His tactic for dealing with what he saw as British double-dealing was intransigence, often expressed through disagreeable, even offensive behavior. This was in part a tactic, certainly. And while it sometimes worked, obstinacy and uncivil behavior guaranteed that the relationship between Churchill and de Gaulle frequently became tempestuous.[99]

The BCRA

The task of coordinating the internal and external resistance in France would fall to the *Bureau central de renseignement et d'action* (BCRA). In keeping with de Gaulle's military experience and vision, the BCRA was to serve as a *Deuxième Bureau*. The organization's inception is a well-known story. André Dewavrin, a tall twenty-nine-year-old with thinning hair, a graduate of the *École polytechnique* who on the outbreak of war was serving as professor of fortifications at Saint-Cyr, had joined the Chasseurs alpins as part of the Narvik expedition. After gut-wrenching reflection because he had left a wife and children in France, on 1 July he presented himself at Saint-Stephen's House, where, with indecent haste and minimal reflection, de Gaulle tasked Dewavrin to organize his Second (intelligence) and Third (operations) Bureaus. As Sébastien Albertelli records, de Gaulle's apparently impulsive appointment of a young, inexperienced officer of engineers to lead his intelligence section sought to preempt Muselier's effort to place a much better qualified and more senior naval captain at the helm of intelligence, because he did not want to depend on the navy for his contacts with France. This would spark a smoldering competition between Muselier, who created his own FNFL *Deuxième Bureau*, and the BCRA, that would kick-start the black legend of Free French intelligence as Passy's anti-republican "entourage," an "aerie of Cagoulards" which functioned as a "French Gestapo."[100]

Although Gaullist mythology maintained that there would have been no resistance without de Gaulle, in fact the Gaullist movement with its classic military *Deuxième Bureau* outlook and organization proved to be ill-equipped to stimulate or even capitalize on an internal resistance. Like other Allied intelligence services with no irregular warfare experience, the BCRA proved largely clueless about how to assess, stimulate, and operationalize a movement that spontaneously if slowly gained momentum. On the contrary, the BCRA proved a source of dysfunction within *la France libre*, one exposed early on by the "Muselier affair." Muselier never forgave Passy after Churchill personally ordered the Admiral to be arrested and imprisoned on fabricated charges that he had leaked the secret of Menace to the French air attaché in London prior to his repatriation to Vichy.[101] Although quickly freed and given a letter of apology after de Gaulle protested, the Muselier affair would have long-term implications for *la France libre*. First, as much as he resented Passy, Muselier remained convinced that the BCRA was a mere executor of a de Gaulle plot to jettison him, which contributed to Muselier's definitive break with *la France libre* in March 1942. The Muselier affair also served to reinforce de Gaulle's deep-seated ancestral Anglophobia. Given this mental schema, the Muselier affair made de Gaulle even more conscious of the precariousness of his position in Great Britain. Nor was his confidence in his BCRA, that he believed manipulated by the British, strengthened. *Au contraire*, he feared that Passy was being drawn unwittingly into a larger British conspiracy to steal France's colonies, the inception of a paranoia that was to explode during the Syrian campaign of the summer of 1941. Finally, the Muselier affair triggered a row with the British, the first of many that would roil Anglo-*France libre* relations: "De Gaulle is meanwhile said to be taking steps which are really tiresome and childish and show how extremely suspicious he is," wrote Sir Donald Somervell, the British Attorney General investigating the Muselier case, on 24 January 1941. "He is stated to have given orders that anybody in his Headquarters of English origin is to be dismissed at 48 hours' notice. He is in fact applying the Nuremberg laws to the English! I am going to have it out with him on behalf of M.I.5 who not only are comprehensibly resentful at his attitude but whose responsibility will become quite impossible if they have no contact with the French."[102]

De Gaulle's perception of the BCRA as a British Trojan horse within *la France libre* was strengthened by the necessary cooperation between the nascent Gaullist service and their far more experienced and better resourced British counterparts. Adopting Passy as his *nom de guerre*, most of Dewavrin's apprenticeship as *la France libre*'s intelligence chief took place under the supervision of Sir Claude Dansey, the pugnacious assistant chief of the Special Intelligence Service (SIS), whose intelligence career dated from the Great War. But in the best traditions of intelligence services, those of Free France and Great Britain, and later the US Office of Strategic Services (OSS), would frequently compete rather than cooperate in collecting intelligence and creating resistance and intelligence networks. It proved an unequal competition as the BCRA lacked the tools – a large London staff, agents, radios, an organization to counterfeit papers, air transport, cash, and above all experience – as well as the methods, effectively to execute its task without assistance. The BCRA's inherent advantage – knowledge of the operational environment – was diminished in part because of its composition of largely conservative *émigré* officers isolated from French civil society. This competition became a source of tension between Passy and his autocratic superior. Passy complained that de Gaulle seemed indifferent to the BCRA's lack of means. But also, the BCRA chief believed the increasing bureaucratization and outmoded military formalism that overtook *la France libre*, as new recruits were incorporated into its command structure, constricted the BCRA's operational flexibility and institutional development. Increasingly, Passy also realized that British assistance was not always disinterested, although he never replicated his boss' visceral distrust of the British in general, and their intelligence services in particular.[103]

Above all, the Allies and the BCRA had different goals – getting on with the war versus reestablishing a non-Vichy government in liberated France while avoiding civil war or an Allied occupation. Intelligence collection would become important, however, because intelligence served as political currency in *la France libre's* war for recognition and status. Unfortunately, the BCRA's energy was initially expended in a frustrated effort to introduce agents into AFN to seize control of military command and guide AFN into dissidence. When hope of an early conversion of AFN to the Gaullist camp faded, agents, some equipped with carrier pigeons, were infiltrated into France via fishing boat to establish the German order of battle and possibly sniff out plans for an invasion of the British Isles. But after a year and a half, the BCRA had little to show for its efforts – most of its networks had been penetrated and dismantled, while a prize agent, Lieutenant Commander Henri d'Estienne d'Orves, who had abandoned the French squadron interned at Alexandria to rally to *la France libre*, was betrayed by his radio operator and shot at Mont Valérien, a German execution site for resisters and hostages located on the western outskirts of Paris. By the summer of 1941, only one BCRA network was functioning in France, that established by Gilbert Renault, alias Rémy, and its intelligence product was modest. In fairness, despite their superior resources, in these early months of the war, MI6 and the Special Operations Executive (SOE) were also largely spinning their wheels in France. Nevertheless, many of the BCRA's problems were self-inflicted: an overly militarized approach to resistance; refusal to cooperate with a growing groundswell of resisters from the trades unions and the left generally; preference for contacts with officers from the Armistice Army and Vichy police, which would lead to betrayal as Vichy increasingly deepened its commitment to collaboration; antipathy to any form of popular mobilization and action that transgressed the BCRA's militarized concept of "resistance"; and the legitimate fear of involving civilians in actions that might provoke harsh reprisals. They were also hamstrung by de Gaulle's reluctance to fix *la France libre* politically in the republican camp until 11 November 1941.[104]

There were several tactical reasons for de Gaulle's hesitant embrace of France's republican traditions. Like many in his conservative milieu, he faulted a dysfunctional Third Republic for France's defeat. Also, Crémieux-Brilhac points out, in the beginning, *la France libre* was on the defensive, regarded even by many anti-Vichy French exiles as a diminutive expatriate conspiracy bankrolled by perfidious Albion, led by a headstrong "political general" who claimed to speak for France.[105]

Finally, the *raison d'être* of *Gaullisme de guerre* was to continue the war, not become bogged down in politics.

Nevertheless, *la France libre* began to lay the political foundation for a government with a global policy with the creation of the *Conseil de défense de l'Empire* at Brazzaville on 27 October 1940.[106] From November 1941, de Gaulle felt secure enough to take "a democratic turn," embracing "Liberty, Equality, Fraternity," the "motto of our mayors," as the device of *la France libre.* He installed a Jewish chaplain. From the spring of 1942, he increasingly incorporated men of the left like André Philip, Jean Moulin, and Pierre Brossolette.[107] But Gaullism only began to accentuate its republican bona fides in the wake of Torch, the November 1942 Anglo-American invasion of AFN. The infamous "Darlan deal," struck between the invading Americans and the collaborationist French admiral, would conjure fears that Franklin Roosevelt intended to ignore both external and internal resistance and impose a Vichy-lite government on liberated France through Allied Military Government of Occupied Territories (AMGOT). Stoking the not unfounded perception that the Anglo-American goal was to diminish France as a world power also offered a tactic to whip the internal resistance into line behind de Gaulle's leadership through his agents Moulin and Brossolette. The political contours would fully emerge from mid 1943 when de Gaulle asserted his leadership in North Africa through the *Comité français de libération nationale* (CFLN). Until then, according to Patrice Arnaud, *la France libre* was "fluid, without a concrete political project beyond the armed struggle against Germany and an assumed Anglophilia." Indeed, when the leader of the resistance network *Libération nord*, the SFIO syndicalist Christian Pineau, met de Gaulle in London in March 1942, he was shocked and practically offended, when de Gaulle condemned both the Third Republic and Vichy, with equal virulence. Gaullists were optimists who rejected Vichy's paternalistic gloom, and whose sense of "honor" diverged radically from Pétain's saturnine acquiescence to defeat. They were men prepared to defy legality, to take risks. In Piketty's view, the salient quality that united the men and a few women who rallied to de Gaulle was their "capacity to leave everything behind."[108]

While de Gaulle's wartime speeches projected an image of a commander eager to revitalize and energize the nation, his vision for France's future remained fixed in its past. De Gaulle had been raised with what Thomas Vaisset calls a "Catholicocentrique" concept of French identity, "in which the values unique to this religion are established as an indispensable condition to accede to the statute of French citizenship. This paradigm inextricably mixes France and God ... the fusion of civic morality and religion ... for them, civism and Catholicism form the bedrock of the social bond."[109] His crusade for national redemption was initiated in a spirit of penitence, and propelled by true piety. If his evocation of Jeanne d'Arc at Anfa, in January 1943, produced much mirth between Churchill and Roosevelt, the two leaders totally missed de Gaulle's point that, even in defeat – especially in defeat – France remained spiritually resilient. De Gaulle's mandate had not been bestowed by ballot count. France's historical leaders authenticated themselves by stepping forward in the nation's hour of need. The mere act of taking up arms to liberate France legitimized *la France libre*, while collaboration rendered Vichy counterfeit. But neither de Gaulle's "Gothic" outlook nor his "monarchical temperament" made him anti-republican, although many in his movement were. He saw the French Revolution with its "Declaration of the Rights of Man and of the Citizen" as central to French identity. It also allowed him to align *la France libre* with the political goals of the Western Allies, fend off accusations from Roosevelt that he lacked democratic aspirations, and brand Vichy as "anti-French."[110]

However, for men of de Gaulle's disposition, "Eternal France transcends the Republic," which was merely an episode in French history, not the French nation's defining characteristic. According to one of de Gaulle's staff officers in these early days, the leader of Free France saw only two men who entirely shared his outlook: "… Leclerc and d'Argenlieu and they alone. The rest are just unfortunates …"[111] France was to be redeemed by this spiritual elite, prodigies of faith and valor, not a brutish *levée* of insubordinate plebeians, global vagabonds, and the slurry of a wasting empire. If Pétain embodied the spirit of the peasantry defending the sacred French soil of Verdun, as its critics frequently pointed out, *la France libre* offered a reincarnation of the Prince de Condé's spurned *émigrés* and their imperial retainers who, having eluded the guillotine, would unshackle France from abroad. Apart from their aristocratic heritage and "Catholicocentric" visions, these three men were also ascetics who, in their truculent courage, appeared to welcome privation – even require it. But, while *la France libre* was never of one mind, it was small enough initially to reflect the personalities of its adherents. Among the factions, Vaisset identifies the "moderates" that included the Jewish jurist René Cassin, Muselier, and Catroux, who wanted to keep the doors to Vichy open. Larminat, Leclerc, Chad's Governor, General Félix Éboué, General Adolphe Sicé of the colonial medical corps, and d'Argenlieu he includes along with de Gaulle in the "fraternity of unswerving mystics."[112]

A traditional republican politician like Pierre Mendès France was predisposed to see the French people as described by Michelet as the engine and protagonists of history, who embodied the will to transform

France into both a nation and a democracy, the bedrock of "French exceptionalism." De Gaulle, on the other hand, saw the French people in their predisposition to fickleness, a spirit of division, and an inherent indiscipline as a nation of subversives, "to the point that the future of the State becomes a recurrent problem." For de Gaulle, the history of France offered a chronicle of existential crises in which the State could only be "reestablished and salvaged" by "an exceptional man." "From this, de Gaulle had a tenacious will to consolidate the nation by closing a parenthesis opened by the French Revolution. That is, by attempting to combine the principles of authority and hierarchy of the *ancien régime*, restored in an elective monarchy, with the inevitable modern requirements of popular consent."[113] This historically crafted crusade to restore French grandeur, rather than an appetite for personal power, underlay de Gaulle's authoritarian reflex, a dimension lost on "les Anglo-Saxons."

Defining Resistance

In January 1941, US Ambassador to Vichy William Leahy found that the "total defeat of the French Army has left the people with a sense of shame, helplessness, and loss of self-respect that inclines them toward any compromise with the Germans ..."[114] But, while most of the French felt overwhelmed and anesthetized by the shock of defeat, despite its tradition of Jacobin centralism – or perhaps because of it – France also nurtured a rich tradition of resistance. Historians have struggled to define and categorize something formerly called "the French Resistance." Debates about resistance with a capital R have swirled around its character, size, and impact. Indeed, what actually qualified as "resistance" became an issue even before the war was concluded. Imitating tradition, Gaullist mythology represented "the French Resistance" as a democratic and patriotic army of citizens who unanimously rejected defeat, armistice, and occupation – a reprise of 1793's *aux armes citoyens!* Founded, mobilized, and directed by Charles de Gaulle from 18 June 1940, structured and operationalized by his BCRA, the Resistance phenomenon erased the shame of 1940, the dishonor of the armistice, and the stain of Vichy collaboration as emblematic of France's decline into the status of a German satellite. Resistance also bestowed a national mandate that legitimized *la France libre*, that in July 1942 was renamed *la France combattante* (Fighting France), precisely to acknowledge a growing internal resistance. This allowed France to surmount the trauma of defeat and occupation and reclaim its international standing alongside that of the victorious Allies.

Knocked off balance by the 1939 Nazi–Soviet Pact, French communists had initially tried to use the occupation to reestablish *l'Humanité*, reclaim town and union halls, and create "popular committees" to agitate for better wages and working conditions. Only after June 1941 did they take their inspiration from 1917 Petrograd, to mobilize and maneuver "the Resistance" as a vehicle for a "National Insurrection" that would redeem and legitimize the PCF, and perhaps catapult it into power. But between an avenging army determined to liberate France from abroad and the PCF's storming of the Bastille redux, internal resistance offered a diverse menu of actors, motivations, strategies, and tactics of defiance. François Bédarida once defined resistance as "a clandestine action carried out in the name of the nation and of individual dignity by volunteers organized to fight the domination [and more often the occupation] of their country by the Nazi or fascist regime or one of its satellites or allies." So clandestine, in fact, was this action that German armaments minister Albert Speer famously claimed to have been totally unaware of it.[115] One salient problem with Bédarida's definition of resistance was that it excluded the external resistance, as well as what Olivier Wieviorka calls "résistance-mouvement," a "resistance outside of *la Résistance*" that although "ad hoc, fleeting, and limited" created "a climate of complicity for *la Résistance organisée*." From 1943, there also developed a *maquis* quite separate from structured resistance groups – that is, young men who fled into remote regions to avoid work conscription. Henri Michel, who pioneered Second World War studies in France, defined the Resistance "first as a patriotic struggle to liberate the fatherland. [It] is also a struggle for the liberty and dignity of man against totalitarianism."[116] But this, too, constricts the political and ideological heterogeneity of resistance in France.

Resistance eventually found its ideological roots in patriotism, antifascism, and humanist and republican values, reinforced by memories of 1870 and the Great War, and "*une profonde germanophobie*." But the initial problem with associating resistance with a republican *levée* was that popular sentiment held that democracy had lost the war. "A moral, social, political, economic regime abdicated in defeat," de Gaulle told the socialist Christian Pineau in March 1942. "Another is born and nourished by capitulation. The French people condemn both of them . . . Don't ask me to approve what I have condemned many times, a Republic without authority, a regime of parties." When Pineau objected that de Gaulle classified the Third Republic and Vichy in the same negative category, only reluctantly did de Gaulle promise to support a "new national and international order."[117]

In the war's opening years, *la France libre* had no lock on "resistance," whose numbers Muracciole estimates to have been "on the outside no more than 30,000 active militants at the end of 1942."[118] A widespread view held that France required an authoritarian and hierarchical regime that would stand up for French interests and rehabilitate French society. Pétain was France's quintessential patriot. The destitution of Pierre Laval on 13 December 1940, and the presence of the anti-German Weygand, were interpreted as evidence of Vichy's anti-collaborationist spirit, its "resistance." Therefore, between 1940 and sometime in 1943, it was possible to oppose the Occupation, hope for an Allied victory, and consider oneself a "resister" without being a Gaullist.[119] What later came to be called the *Vichysto-résistants* claimed that by hiding arms and, in the case of Vichy's *Deuxième Bureau*, tracking Axis agents and armistice commissions in North Africa, they were in fact defying "legality" in ways that allowed them to claim resistance status, while remaining loyal *Maréchalists*. Republican institutions and values had been discredited, while traditional political parties and trade unions had been thrown into doctrinal and moral disarray by the Nazi–Soviet Pact of 1939 and by the speed and totality of defeat. For the first two years or more of the occupation, most of the right lined up behind Vichy's National Revolution. For these reasons, popular resistance would have to emerge from civil society, not from the political classes or established institutions. Above all, it would have to grow in opposition to Vichy's "double game" of obfuscation.[120]

The justification for the armistice, the bedrock of Vichy legitimacy, was that it allowed France to conserve a vestige of independence as represented by the empire, the fleet, and what was ingeniously marketed until November 1942 as the *zone libre*. In de Gaulle's eyes, the armistice was more than a crime, it was a strategic error. While the Marshal might insist that his bicycle-mounted Armistice Army would secure the unoccupied zone, that Darlan would keep the fleet out of Axis hands, and that the colonies would not become a base for Axis aggression, in his view, Vichy's word was not to be trusted. In London in June 1940, speaking of their erstwhile superiors who were assembling in Vichy, de Gaulle had predicted to his Saint-Cyr classmate Antoine Béthouard: "You'll see, they're just a band of gutless old cowards."[121] The Paris protocols which channeled French support to Rommel in the Western Desert, the sell-out of French POWs and French citizens in Alsace-Moselle, STO and harnessing France's economy to the German war effort, that basically put the French people on starvation rations for German benefit and transformed them into targets of Allied bombers, would later vindicate de Gaulle's prophesy. But also, Vichy's political agenda and strategic interests depended on Hitler's sufferance when not his downright support. In Washington, diplomatic recognition of Pétain's government was grounded in large part in the fear that Vichy might surrender its assets – in particular Darlan's High Seas Fleet – to the Axis camp, but also in fears that de Gaulle's political ambitions for France were authoritarian rather than democratic.

Romain Durand described the resistance in North Africa that preceded the Allied landing in November 1942 as "numerous, multiform, poorly coordinated in the event, and which did not distinguish itself by its discretion," to the point that the Vichy *Bureau des menées antinationales* (BMA) considered it a negligible threat.[122] French historian of resistance Olivier Wieviorka notes that, while the BCRA and the British SOE played a decisive role in the development of European resistance and the coordination and implantation of its networks, the phenomenon itself was a spontaneous and unprecedented manifestation of civil society that emerged from the detritus of the Third Republic's eclipse, including of its political parties, trades unions, the Church, and the army.[123] As such, the phenomenon of resistance was so plural and diverse in its social composition and political aspirations, engaged in both conventional and unconventional operations, was constantly changing shape and shifting loyalties, that it is difficult to treat resistance as a "bloc." The only thing that united resistance groups was their shared belief that their sacrifice qualified them to spearhead and revivify a post-war renaissance of France. Unfortunately for them, they lacked the vision, skills, and numbers to realize their self-ascribed mandate, so that, on the Liberation, they were to be outmaneuvered and displaced by a resurgent French state and its largely discredited political institutions.[124]

Given the diversity of its structures, methods, and aspirations, scholars like Robert Belot, Robert Gildea, and Wieviorka interpret resistance as "a moral and individual reaction" against France's post-armistice situation, an "act of war" in defense of a certain idea of humanity.[125] This resistance gradually mobilized a cascade of individual choices whose salient characteristic proved to be its spontaneity. H. R. Kedward categorized resistance, as it emerged in the aftermath of defeat, as "a diffused and inchoate phenomenon, heavily dependent on variables in personality, politics and place."[126] Gildea is hardly the first scholar to point out that the resistance narrative became central to French identity, a therapy to palliate the trauma of defeat, occupation, and incipient civil war that gradually engulfed France as liberation approached.[127] By 1987, French historian Henry Rousso had categorized "resistencialism" – a term coined during the war and whose meaning evolved – as a deliberate process promoted by de Gaulle and the PCF that had sought to minimize the importance of Vichy and collaboration in favor of a narrative that associated the nation as a whole with a French Resistance.[128] Because resistance represented a collage of personal choices and often random – even "absurd" – acts of defiance, and because it was an international phenomenon with shared attributes that characterized the Second World War both in Europe and in Asia, it would be more accurate to speak not of "the French Resistance," but rather of "resistance in France."[129]

The fact that "the French Resistance" counted numerous foreigners among its ranks particularly irked de Gaulle, who sought to market an image of resistance as a national rejection of defeat and Vichy, rather than a collection of young men and some women, both French and foreign, drawn together by circumstance and conviction to oppose the Occupation. The fact that many resisters were Jews – French, North African, and foreign – linked resistance to the Holocaust and to a general European rebellion against Nazism, a far broader context than was de Gaulle's perspective of France's Thirty Years' War with Germany. Only 5 percent of those inducted into the sanctum sanctorum of the *Compagnons de la Libération* were foreigners.[130] Furthermore, the FFL relied heavily upon largely dragooned imperial subjects. Thus, de Gaulle's August 1944 claim that Paris "liberated itself" would offer an artful piece of nationalist invention that confirmed Bédarida's warning about the propensity for state-sponsored "mythologization" of the resistance phenomenon, and the requirement to separate history from "memory."[131] Nevertheless, there would have been no "French Resistance" without de Gaulle, although there would most certainly have been resistance in France, especially in the wake of Barbarossa. The leader of *la France libre* "federated the plurality of motivations," gave the resistance a face, ascribed purpose to its often disjoined, futile, even morally ambiguous acts, and conferred a legitimacy that it would never have otherwise achieved as a cacophony of competing leaders, organizations, political agendas, and strategies, whose activities would have amounted to little had they not been funded and coordinated by outsiders in the SOE and OSS.[132]

Assembling a fissiparous resistance in France under a Gaullist aegis also sought to establish the primacy in French memory of the external resistance composed of a clairvoyant leader, the continuance of a legitimate republic rather than the ersatz Vichy parenthesis, and the preservation of the regular French army. As Henry Rousso argued, the "man of 18 June" was meant to symbolize resistance while diminishing the role of political parties and competing resistance leaders. The primacy of a resistance myth that embraced the totality of the French *levée* also served a post-war political narrative that sought to erase the shame of 1940 and outsource Vichy collaboration to a claque of criminals, rather than to reflect wartime realities.[133]

For those French men and women who did not buy into the Vichy narrative, the quintessential question became, what could one do to "resist?" At least the "*Vichysto-résistants*" could claim to be actively preparing for *la revanche* by creating arms caches, training armistice army recruits, even hardening French youth in the *Chantiers* and *écoles de cadres*. For civilians, however, there was only a small margin to act because, north of the demarcation line, Germans were ubiquitous – they commandeered hotels and châteaus, and billeted their officers and troops in homes. Frequent parades and military concerts, which advertised their presence and dramatized their superiority, were meant to intimidate. Behind the uniforms, drum rolls, and parades of the occupying forces lurked the *Gestapo*, the *Abwehr*, the *Sicheitsdienst*, the intelligence service of the SS, and its security police, the *Sicherheitspolizei*. The French police collaborated with all of these. With the exception of the Nord and the Pas de Calais, and Alsace-Moselle, each department in the *zone occupée* hosted a *Feldkommandantur* (FK) with court martial authority, and each arrondissement a *Kreiskommandantur* (KK). *Feldgendarmes* of the German military police maintained checkpoints on roads and in railway stations. And that was simply the visible presence of occupation. At the time of Barbarossa on 22 June 1941, the logic of Occupation policy was colonization in the East, and collaboration in the West to get resources and harness the French population and industry to the German war effort. Initially, the German military administration in occupied France, the *Militärbefehlshaber in Frankreich* (MBF), followed a pragmatic policy of "maintain order and security," rather than spearhead an ideological crusade, in great part because they were too thin on the ground and so supervised and directed the French police upon whom they relied to keep order. Legend holds that German occupation policy became more brutal with the arrival of the *Sipo/SD*, the SS security police, in June 1942 under *Höherer SS- und Polizeiführer* (HSSPF) Carl Oberg. But Oberg's arrival signaled a stage in the evolution of German repression, rather than an abrupt crackdown.[134]

Unlike the Nazified *Sipo/SD*, which ultimately answered to Himmler through his deputy Reinhard Heydrich, the leadership of the MBF was generally made up of career Prussian officers in their late fifties. However, any impression of professional restraint was quickly dispelled by the fact that security policy was set by a group of young jurists, products of Nazified universities and court systems. In this way, the MBF's mental universe was shaped by nationalism, antisemitism, anti-communism, anti-Slavism, and hostility to other perceived threats that imperiled Germany's existence. This world view helped to lay a foundation for a ratcheting up of repressive policies in the German tradition of

Kriegsnotwendigkeit ("the needs of war") that prioritized military requirements over humanitarian ones. The MBF enjoyed a less ruthless reputation than did the *Sipo/SD*, which combined the *Sicherheitspolizei*, which included both the Gestapo and the *Kriminalpolizei*, and the SD under Himmler. The MBF operated initially largely through "administrative surveillance," which seemed to permit French officials a great deal of autonomy. However, it did have the authority to take judicial and police measures to protect German soldiers and property, and increasingly did so from August 1941.

Usually the *Abwehr*, German military intelligence, carried out investigations of resistance activity, and turned its findings over to the *Geheime Feldpolizei* (GFP), a plain-clothes adjunct to the *Abwehr*, to make arrests. However, from June 1940, the Gestapo, technically part of the *Sipo/SD*, was present in France, its operatives initially attached to the GFP, where they pursued resisters, communists, and Jews. The Gestapo also created field offices, and was well ensconced in the *zone nord* by April 1942, when Hitler allowed Himmler formally to take over police powers from the army of occupation. Nor did this shift in direction at the top mean a change in personnel, because the GFP and the *Orpo* (*Ordnungspolizei*, the "ordinary police," sometimes referred to as the *Grüne Polizei* because of the color of their uniforms, who performed various functions like policing railways, guarding internment camps and ghettos, frontiers and internal lines of demarcation, ferreting out resistance radios, and so on), were simply transferred to the *Sipo/SD*.[135] In the meantime, the *Abwehr* became part of a repressive apparatus that from 1941 had become very efficient in rolling up resistance networks, like that of the *Musée de l'homme*, while the *Geheime Feldpolizei* combed POW and internment camps looking for Spanish Republicans, 8,000–9,000 of whom were then deported to Mauthausen on the banks of the Danube, where only 35 percent survived.[136] MBF courts martial also lent a legal veneer to repression in the first months of the Occupation. MBF officers were in general pleasantly surprised by the willing assistance they received from French authorities for their repressive activities, such as the execution of hostages and deportation of Jews. This came in part because Vichy also multiplied the numbers of *tribunaux d'exception*, as it reinforced and centralized police power in the spring of 1941 under a *Secrétaire général de la police nationale*, as well as creating new organs of repression like the *Groupements mobiles de réserve* (GMR) that might request assistance by "*groups d'action*" of Doriot's PPF.[137]

Some MBF officers began to question the value of mass executions of hostages in retaliation for attacks on German soldiers that multiplied following the August 1941 assassination of German naval cadet Alfons

Moser in Paris' Barbès-Rochechouart metro station by Pierre Georges, the future "Colonel Fabien." However, their scruples were tactical rather than humanitarian. For these reasons, while much more ideological, the *Sipo/SD* complemented the MBF, rather than clashed with it. From January 1941, MBF arrests in France began to climb exponentially, while their courts martial, bypassing the French judicial system but under pressure from the *Oberkommando der Wehrmacht* (OKW) to act, began dispensing death sentences like free metro tickets. In August 1941, with no prompting from Berlin, the MBF initiated mass executions of French hostages, and pressured the French administration to act more aggressively against resistance attacks on German soldiers in France. From December 1941, the MBF advocated for the deportation of Jews and communists as a tactic of "preventative terrorism." Fearing that a tactic of mass executions was simply increasing resistance to occupation, to augment the effects of terror, on 7 December 1941, Hitler issued his "*Nacht und Nebel* " ("night and fog") directive. Henceforth, those convicted for "attacks against persons, espionage, sabotage, communist agitation, other infractions that troubled public order, [and sharing] intelligence with the enemy," simply disappeared, many into the Natzweiller-Struthof camp in the Vosges.[138] Oberg's arrival merely confirmed the radicalization of occupation policy. He did not propel it into a new, more repressive direction. MBF courts martial continued to function. They simply increasingly came to reflect policies transferred from the East, as *Jagdkommandos* were formed to break up growing *maquis* bands, every civilian was deemed a potential "terrorist," and "justice" accelerated. MBF tribunals were estimated to have condemned between 45,000 and 60,000 civilians to death, and deported 72,000 French and foreign Jews.[139]

This ubiquitous German presence in itself was a humiliation and a provocation for action.[140] "When I saw a German soldier, or a Vichy cop, I didn't want to hold a discussion," Louis Bacquier recorded. "I wanted to fight back ... We're all, over the course of years, confronted with one, two, three decisive rendezvous with life, with death. We meet with luck, or destiny. You don't want to miss them under pain of mediocrity."[141] But as a practical matter, it was easier to do "something" in the *zone libre*. But what? Guerrilla warfare was out of the question, because initially the SOE and BCRA had no way to train and arm civilian resisters. Besides, attempts to carry out even low-level operations would have been suicidal and invited indiscriminate retaliation. The margins within which to act at this early stage were very small. The impediments to reaching Great Britain and enlisting in the FFL were practically insurmountable. The dilemma of resistance was that the resisters needed to network to accomplish their many tasks. But multiplying contacts compromised security, which made them vulnerable to infiltration, detection, and arrest.[142]

For these reasons, the bargain basement price of entry into resistance might begin with a patriotic gesture, often an attempt to "reclaim symbolic space" by singing the Marseillaise, or placing flowers or hanging tricolors with a Cross of Lorraine on war memorials, or beneath statues of Clemenceau, as an expression of popular defiance.[143] Despite Monnet's objection that resistance could not come from without, it appears that de Gaulle's name did make an impression inside France early on, in the form of seditious inscriptions or scattering of leaflets in public areas. The British produced pictures of de Gaulle and dropped them over France, while de Gaulle's sister living in Saint-Étienne produced some old pictures that the resistance circulated. De Gaulle's name was first shouted in street demos on 11 November 1940. On 1 January 1941, people were encouraged to stay home from work for an hour as an act of civil disobedience. On 1 May 1942, citizens gathered at a republican monument at half past six in the evening. Actions planned for 11 November 1942 were postponed because of the German invasion of the *zone libre*. Resistance evolved into distributing leaflets, organizing protests against *la relève* in 1942 that transitioned the following year into compulsory labor (STO), and so on. These activities often involved women, who were particularly affected by the hardships of the occupation, and incensed by the call-up or arrest of a father, brother, or husband. To organize demonstrations and strikes was to come out into the open, be identified, and possibly arrested. Therefore, becoming a "resister" even through minor civic gestures required honest folk to break with "legality," to lie and dissemble, to acquire acting skills, to take risks, to live in solitude and fear, and to be prepared for arrest, deportation, and death. This was a difficult step for most to take. Under a yoke of repression and deprivation, even the reviled Third Republic became an object of wistful nostalgia in the popular mind.

In this way, the internal resistance began as a hesitant, spontaneous but somewhat confused, very amateurish collection of independent actors and entrepreneurs who had to create and grow their movements initially with little outside assistance. This quiet dissent would eventually evolve into what Gildea calls "Resistance with a capital 'R,'" usually among collectives of men and women of similar background and associations who began to take more active measures to help the Allied war effort: provide intelligence, help POWs or downed airmen to escape, organize protests – a specialty of Cécile Tanguy, wife of the man who would become the prominent resistance leader Henri Rol-Tanguy – or write propaganda flyers. Most resistance groups began as propaganda sheets and recruited professional journalists to produce clandestine newspapers to influence public opinion, and delegitimize Vichy by attacking Pétain from 1941. Anyone might print and distribute tracts or pass on information. Three people with a mimeograph machine, a paintbrush, and a bucket of paste might constitute a "movement." But because printing presses, mimeograph machines, and paper were controlled, decorating walls with Vs or crosses of Lorraine offered a more immediate emotional reward and mechanism to reclaim public space. But it was war by paintbrush. French resisters might be joined by outcasts whose ability to find a sanctuary was increasingly squeezed, like communists, Jews, and refugees. The requirements of a clandestine existence forced them to branch out into false papers, often acquired with the assistance of municipal employees – demobilization certificates, work permits, identity cards, drivers licenses, *Ausweis*, ration coupons, and so on.

But detecting and enlisting in a resistance network was neither easy nor obvious. Most groups formed initially around small, trusted clusters of people who knew each other, either professionally or socially. This was the origin of a small network centered on Paris' Musée de l'Homme organized from the summer of 1940, whose initial task was to facilitate the escape of colonial POWs incarcerated in France, mainly by wrangling medical diagnoses of tuberculosis or malaria, a network that initially enlisted SFIO activist and journalist Pierre Brossolette. It published five editions of its clandestine journal, *Résistance*, between 15 December 1940 and March 1941 before the *Abwehr* infiltrated and dismantled it. A second group was organized by Maxime Blocq-Mascart, an intellectual property lawyer. It eventually amalgamated other small groups into what evolved by December 1940 into the *Organisation civile et militaire* (OCM). Because of a significant recruitment among former officers, the OCM focused on intelligence collection, as did what became *Ceux de la Libération*, which passed on intelligence to the IS through the *Service de renseignements de l'Armée de l'Air*, which had its own networks of informers among reserve officers.[144]

Jean Moulin, *protégé* of Pierre Cot and Prefect at Chartres in 1940, not surprisingly had been cut loose by Vichy. Unemployed, Moulin had spent the next months reaching out to the leaders of the three principal movements that were in the process of organizing in the *zone libre*: Emmanuel d'Astier de La Vigerie, head of *Libération-Sud*; Henri Frenay, the chief of *Combat*; and Jean-Pierre Lévy of *Franc-Tireur*. By mid 1941, the framework for resistance in France was more or less defined: *Franc-Tireur*, *Libération-sud*, *Combat*, and *Témoignage chrétien* that had put down roots in the *zone libre* were more focused on propaganda and political action. In the occupied zone, *Ceux de la Libération*, *Défense de la France*, *Libération-nord*, *Organisation civile et militaire*, and the *Front national* more cautiously envisaged taking military action. A few organizations, like *Ceux de la Résistance*, would appear after 1941. These covered the political spectrum from *Libération sud*, on the left, to *Ordre civil et militaire*, on the right. Nevertheless, at the end of 1941, resistance in France remained "ultra-minoritaire" – small, fragile movements without means, politically and ideologically divided, but with the potential to contest the Vichy narrative and to strike in-country partnerships with *la France libre*.[145]

While de Gaulle's plan to rescue France from without battled the headwinds of diminutive resources, Vichy truculence, and Allied indifference, a new axis of advance had presented itself on 25 October 1941, when Jean Moulin strode into de Gaulle's office at Carlton Gardens. On 9 September 1941, Moulin had departed France armed with a false passport and reached London via Lisbon. The General named Moulin *délégué du Comité national en zone libre* and parachuted him back into France near Lyon on the night of 2 January 1942. Early efforts at channeling these civil society currents in France were largely unproductive because *la France libre* had no conception of what form popular resistance should take.[146]

While the dangers of participating in resistance activities were significant, for some the attractions of living a secret existence and assuming a false identity included living an adventure, establishing links of comradery, even intimacy, and a flirtation with heroism. But as the Occupation wore on, joining the resistance increasingly offered a gamble with death.[147] In May 1942, the communist-led *Francs-Tireurs et Partisans* (FTP) created an intelligence division. This divided into military, political, and counterintelligence sections when the FTP joined *Combat* and *Libération-Sud* in January 1943 to form the *Mouvements unis de la résistance* (MUR). They also developed *corps francs* to attack Germans or collaborators, although this remained a secondary role unpopular with the public because it invited indiscriminate retaliation, or organize workers to carry out sabotage in their factories or worksites, also a risky undertaking.[148]

Conclusion

Despite the disappointment of Dakar, in the six months since the Fall of France, de Gaulle's crusade had come a long way. By November 1940, its army had swelled to 19,679 soldiers, of whom 3,702 troops and 732 officers were "Europeans," the remainder composed of indigenous conscripts.[149] Arguably the setback at Dakar became a benefit, not least because, following the failures of Narvik and Dakar, it forced the Royal Navy to begin to develop a doctrine and techniques for amphibious assault, beginning with a communications ship to coordinate action across three dimensions of combat, which would become vital to Allied success going forward. Failure at Dakar hardened and focused the French exile movement, forced it to adjust to a long-war strategy, and obliged de Gaulle to elevate his vision, to calculate in a more strategic mode, to initiate the transition from a military organization with a political agenda into a political movement with an, albeit constricted, armed wing. The creation on 27 October 1940 of a *Conseil de la défense de l'Empire* composed of the Gaullist barons was a first step. The external resistance was now a legitimate territorial power with a name – *la France libre* – administrative responsibilities, a capital, money, Radio Brazzaville to broadcast its message free of Foreign Office censorship, a symbol in the Cross of Lorraine, guided and overseen in its colonies by a political body.[150] In the BCRA, it had an organization with the potential to structure and operationalize an as yet diminutive but inevitable internal resistance as Vichy's collaboration would progressively discredit it and the war would increasingly weigh against the Axis.

On the debit side, *la France libre* remained an insecure movement with a narrow if increasingly fanaticized base, factionalized between soldiers and civilians, between the various branches of the movement, torn between its civil war with Vichy and the compulsion to fight the Germans. Like its British SOE equivalent, its BCRA "interface" with the internal resistance was inexperienced in clandestine mobilization, without a strategy, and dependent on the British for resources. While its new African base gave *la France libre* a modicum of legitimacy, it was also a marginal territory that suffered from severe underdevelopment that would greatly constrain its contribution. While de Gaulle exhibited many noble qualities, even elements of true greatness, and had stamped his personality on his organization, his attributes were offset by an autocratic temperament and imperious behavior that exasperated allies and alienated potential supporters. Furthermore, at this stage in the war, Vichy was like a maturing spinster, past her bloom perhaps, but still commanding a dowry in the form of its High Seas Fleet and its control of the strategically important Levant, Dakar, and AFN, substantial enough to make her an object of courtship by Whitehall and Washington. Pétain also enjoyed patriotic prestige and credibility with a French population disoriented by defeat, most of whom had faith in his ability to secure the release of almost two million French POWs, and who were convinced that he was plotting "la revanche" against Germany.

Hence the ambiguity of British policy that continued to recognize Vichy while supporting de Gaulle, who insisted that he alone had the right to speak for France, guarantee French interests, and restore France's international status and grandeur. With the United States poised to enter the conflict, relations among the three allies would grow more complex.[151]

8 *"Grandi soldati"*

As the internal resistance groped toward mobilization and relevance, de Gaulle had to find a means to resuscitate France from abroad, a feat that Jean Monnet had predicted was unachievable. And certainly, the *levée* myth of the peasant soldier defending the Hexagon *à la* Verdun for the moment remained safely incarnate in the Marshal. In the wake of 1940, *la France libre* required a heroic narrative to authenticate its masculinity and advertise its fanatical pursuit of France's resurrection in contrast to the "gutless" leadership at Vichy, who unleashed a deluge of decorations upon the Armistice Army, abandoned the citizens of Alsace-Moselle to the Nazis, and handed over French citizens to bolster the German war effort. Therefore, *la France libre*'s campaign to resurrect France from abroad became an exercise in the romanticized revival of an aristocratic and racialized view of personal honor reaffirmed through overcoming adversity to achieve manhood. This view had been foreshadowed in *Vers l'armée de métier* – the exultation of the professional military as superior to the citizens it defended, and the belief that France's considerable deficiencies that included excessive individualism and "*une psychose antiguerrière*" could be salvaged by leaders of exceptional ability.[1] In a refutation of Monnet's skepticism, France's revival from without would be achieved by showcasing the soldierly ideals of honor and sacrifice, a code of brotherhood historically deployed on far-flung imperial battlefields, memorialized in *les compagnons de la libération.*

Unfortunately, the reality was that de Gaulle's territorial base in AEF had been acquired mainly by persuading expatriate elites to rally to avoid the financial ruin of a British blockade and an intramural conflict that would undermine colonialist supremacy. While the core of de Gaulle's disciples may have become fanaticized by the scandal and dishonor of the armistice, "join de Gaulle or starve" hardly offered a heroic rallying cry for national liberation.[2] The majority of colonial civil servants regarded *la France libre* as little more than a posse of pistol-waving hotheads in the pay of His Majesty's Government. While they remained loyal to Vichy in spirit, most civil servants were too indolent or snug in their privileges and pensions to surrender the comforts of colonial villas, retinues of servants, and sundowners on the veranda for the uncertainties and austerities of occupied France. The protagonists of *la France libre* would live, through the Liberation and into the post-1945 occupation of Germany, with the irony that they would rely on Vichy loyalists to manage their conquests. In the meantime, however, the failure at Dakar had advertised to its British sponsors *la France libre*'s military weakness and circumscribed political appeal.

De Gaulle required victories to establish a martial narrative to offset memories of the disaster of 1940 and legitimize the movement through a chronicle of heroic military sacrifice. As Jennings notes, without the seizure of Kufra in 1941, the invasion of the Fezzan in 1942, and the dogged defense of Bir Hakeim in the same year, minus the growing military reputations of Leclerc and Koenig earned on the battlefields of a world war, de Gaulle and *la France libre* would have cut a poor figure in comparison with de Gaulle's rival Henri Giraud in 1943.[3] But these backwoods "victories" marked mere skirmishes on the grand stage of a world war, and *la France libre*'s heroes were leaders of companies and brigades, not armies, whose reputations were puffed for the requirements of Gaullist propaganda. After deducting "sovereignty forces," *les Forces françaises libres* were able to align only four "*bataillons de marche*" – that is, stripped down mobile battalions – three made up of "Senegalese" recruited in AEF, a battalion of marine infantry, and a brigade of the Foreign Legion.[4] In fact, building an army even with the manpower resources of AEF – especially with the manpower of AEF – would prove a challenge. In the French martial race hierarchy, the "Senegalese" of AEF ranked as inferior to the "Senegalese" of AOF, not to mention Arab and Berber *tirailleurs* of *l'armée d'Afrique*. Leclerc did not think highly of his African troops, who could not reach their potential in part because they lacked European cadres, without which, Edgar de Larminat complained in December 1940, "their combat value will be considerably diminished." The dearth of white officers and NCOs impacted the FFL until its amalgamation with *l'armée d'Afrique* from September 1943, and beyond. Until then, *la France libre* found its leadership where it could. Despite the image of Free France as a Masonry of high-minded idealists determined to liberate France and restore its international status, Larminat pointed out that many of the officers and NCOs of the *Batallion de Marche 2* from Oubangui-Chari which would do battle at Bir Hakeim were white *colons* (settlers) from the same region: "professional hunters, farmers, woodsmen, gold prospectors who were rough characters." Often their soldiers had worked for them in civilian life as porters, on their plantations, as "boys," beaters on safaris, but also on forced labor projects or even as convicts punished under *le code de l'indigénat*, a harsh set of rules and restrictions developed in the 1880s that imposed slave labor penalties and conditions on French colonial subjects.[5]

The Cameroon and AEF provided slightly over half the recruits for the FFL until 1943. Calculations differ, but Eric Jennings put the figure of those who eventually served at around 27,000. However, this does not count the thousands of Africans impressed to build roads, work in mines and on plantations, and so on. The leadership complained that most of the recruits were not physically fit, lacked the education to fill even minor technical positions, and did not have a fundamental grasp of Western military norms and requirements, that made them difficult to train and assimilate. For instance, Leclerc reported the control and motivation of his African soldiers, who demonstrated "little aptitude for this form of modern combat," to be the most difficult aspect of the Kufra expedition.[6] This may explain why he felt obliged to take so many personal risks during the operation. Nor should any of these complaints come as a surprise, given the lack of investment by France in the colonies and its peoples, and the press gang methods of recruitment employed by *la France libre* to raise its small army. While all *tirailleurs* were described as "volunteers," whose motivation for enlistment encompassed a desire to learn the French language and acquire skills, as well as their need for the pay, most regarded military service as both a personal misfortune and an economic disaster.[7] In most places, "customary chiefs" chosen by the French designated recruits among those who failed to flee in time to the sanctuary of British Nigeria or who lacked the means to bribe their way out of military service. In a reprise of slave-raid tactics, Free French officials might execute "*rafles*" or round-ups in villages to net recruits, workers, and porters. By 1942, recruiting agents were authorized to offer a recruiting bonus of 50 francs. But locals called these men "jackals" since they employed coercion, threatened reprisals against families of recalcitrant "volunteers," or might simply sign up the recruit and pocket the bonus. Indeed, one of the ironies of *la France libre*'s crusade to liberate France was that Gaullist legitimacy required that the empire remain intact, firmly under French occupation, and subjected to a French colonial version of STO. René Cassin admitted to Éboué that *la France libre* squeezed AEF so hard that he feared the Gaullists would be accused of perpetuating quasi-slavery practices, which of course is precisely what they did. Military training camps were primitive. The FFL lacked weapons, equipment, and cadres, so their recruits might simply be assigned to forced labor projects, or abandoned in underemployment and idleness in imperial backwaters, where they took up with local women and might become discipline problems.[8] The food was insufficient and bad, which provoked many acts of indiscipline and even mutinies. Desertion was rampant. When officers lamented that their soldiers lacked initiative, the Afro-Caribbean Éboué replied that this was hardly surprising as racism reigned in the ranks, morale was low, and *la France libre* had done little to cultivate the "solidarity of empire."[9] Of course, to put the French situation in perspective, other multiracial armies such as those of Great Britain and the United States also discriminated against soldiers of color in their ranks and employed them in non- or quasi-military tasks.

East Africa

Although de Gaulle's new conquests had netted him a domain of six million Africans and 20,000 whites, Susan Travers (Figure 8.1) had concluded that AEF and the Cameroon were no Shangri-La. The daughter of a Royal Navy captain, Travers had spent part of her unhappy girlhood in the south of France, and the decade of the 1930s on the semi-professional tennis circuit, where mixed doubles translated into a competition played out in an *après-sport* regimen of parties, alcohol, and sex. With the outbreak of war in 1939, and all of the men in uniform, she had volunteered for the French Red Cross. Following a three-month-long nursing course at

Figure 8.1 Susan Travers.

Poitiers, Travers was dispatched to Helsinki as an ambulance driver during the Winter War. In early July 1940, the thirty-year-old Travers had caught a ship back to the Clyde, where she had volunteered to serve as a "nurse" with de Gaulle's exile movement, with the equivalent rank of sergeant, "at two-thirds a sergeant's pay," she noted. She went to the army and navy store near Victoria Station, bought a canvass bath and some tropical kit, and entrained for Liverpool, where she boarded the *Westernland* on a moonless night as German planes buzzed overhead. Travers was one of ten nurses, five British, five French and Belgian, who mustered on deck as de Gaulle came by to shake their hands: "'*Bonjour, merci de votre assistance.*' ... He didn't go out of his way to be friendly." Travers claimed to have been totally baffled by the Franco-French confrontation at Dakar, although her first patient was Thierry d'Argenlieu.

After stops in Freetown and Douala, which she admitted were "a long way from Cannes high society ... I'd never known such discomfort," Travers and two of the English women volunteers were sent to Brazzaville, "a depressing town on a plateau, its white-painted bungalows and their gardens sadly neglected and forlorn. All the colons living in the old French quarter seemed to dislike one another and, divided into rigid social cliques, were mainly pro-Vichy and anti-English." The town counted only three restaurants, while its commercial district was made up of small wooden stalls out of which Portuguese and Syrian merchants sold smoked catfish, lemons, oranges, coconuts, bananas, and other tropical products. Because there were few roads, most travelers boarded an antiquated train or traveled via riverboat, which was itself an adventure, because the boats invariably ran out of petrol and were swept down river until they grounded on a sandbank populated by high reeds, crocodiles, and swarms of mosquitoes. The two other British female volunteers quickly found secretarial jobs in the British consulate. But as Travers lacked typing skills, she was stuck with the Gaullists for better or worse.

Nor did Free France's newly expanded military force live up to de Gaulle's *Vers l'armée de métier* vision, much less appear capable of striking terror in the hearts of the *Wehrmacht*. Travers' roving eye settled on a battalion commander in the 13ème DBLE, Dimitri Amilakvari, a man with drop-dead "sparkling ... crystal blue eyes," who "oozed charisma," and spoke French with a charming Georgian accent. Her impression of the unit's commander, Lieutenant-colonel Magrin-Vernerey, alias Monclar, was less favorable. A "stocky, grey-haired man with combed-back hair and a disconcerting, swashbuckling air," Travers found Monclar to be "a terrifying little man," except when overtaken by bouts of uncontrollable hiccoughing which made it difficult to keep a straight face. Spears confirmed that Miss Travers had every reason to be terrified of Monclar, a "curious priest-like, bespectacled, soft-spoken . . . little man whose gentle violence was that of the cat . . . catapulted across the room at the sight of a mouse." He also had a sense of humor, although one lost on his British hosts – so shocked had they been after Monclar threatened to shoot two of his legionnaires who broke windows at Aldershot, that Parliament passed a law forbidding foreign armies from executing their own soldiers on British soil.[10]

Although as "La Miss," Travers would go on to assume quasi-iconic status in Foreign Legion lore, initially she was allotted a "beaten-up old Humber . . . quite the most exhausted-looking vehicle I had ever set eyes on . . ." and assigned to drive the medical officer (MO) of the Chadian troops, "a remarkable group of men from an Oubangui-Chari tribe who brought with them their own camp followers and even their own witch doctors." Nor did stealth seem part of their tactical lexicon: "Their noisy, dusty arrival was like that of a warrior tribe descending on a fort," she remembered. Each officer was assigned a batman, or "boy," who marched with saucepans and a frying pan "hanging on a string from his belt and clanging together to make an awful din." The British held this "army," and any British woman who would volunteer to serve in it, in barely disguised contempt. Her status with the French was equally ambiguous – the colonel commanding the Chadians banished her from the mess, so she dined solo. Indeed, one consequence for any middle-class women who volunteered to serve was instant *déclassement*. While the FFL, like most militaries, reluctantly solicited women "auxiliaries," females were viewed as a threat to good order and discipline. Officers sought out their company in dances and competed to sleep with them. At the same time, they were consigned to the sergeants' mess, and spent their days in the motor pool or with medical orderlies who resented them as unqualified, condescending, mattress fodder for officers. At least the MO's "boy" – the single person in Africa she actually outranked – helped Travers to turn the crank on the Humber each morning. But it was her job to master mechanics sufficiently to keep this scrapheap refugee in running order.[11]

Strategically, a campaign against the Italians in the Horn of Africa fit well into Allied plans. With the war stalemated in Northern Europe, Churchill's attentions had fixed upon Mussolini's Mediterranean over-stretch. During the summer of 1940, Italian forces commanded by the Duke of Aosta had imprudently seized border posts in the Sudan and Kenya, and, to Churchill's fury, forced the understrength and lightly armed garrison in British Somaliland to execute a reprise of Dunkirk in the Gulf of Aden. In early September 1940, General Rodolfo Graziani pushed his troops 80 kilometers into Egypt from Cyrenaica to Sidi

Barrani, where he promptly squatted. Meanwhile the *Regia Aeronautica* pummeled Malta. By November the Italian dictator's autumn offensive against Greece had congealed in the mountains of southern Albania. The British counterpunch began on 11 November 1940, with a daring Royal Navy raid that crippled the Italian fleet at anchor at Taranto, and so brought the battleship era in naval warfare to a dramatic end.

What the French referred to as the 6,500-strong *Régiment des tirailleurs sénégalais du Tchad* (RTST) was fragmented and dispatched in several directions. The battalion of Chadians and the 13ème DBLE, to which Travers was attached, departed with the British on a campaign to wrest the Horn of Africa from the Italians. Churchill's goals in ordering the campaign were two. First, taking advantage of Italian isolation south of Suez to eliminate the – on paper at least – considerable garrison of 250,000 soldiers. Second, and most importantly, he sought to remove Italian East Africa from the flank of Britain's vital sea routes to Suez from the Cape and from India. The Italian naval squadron composed of nine destroyers, eight submarines, and other vessels based at Massawa in Eritrea made the Gulf of Aden and the Red Sea a "combat zone." This meant that American cargo ships were barred at this stage of the war from sailing to Suez by Congressional "neutrality acts." This prohibition severely strained London's ability to supply the buildup of British forces in Suez and the Middle East. Churchill wanted the Red Sea cleared from that list.

The East Africa campaign was prosecuted "against nature." Heat, lack of water, distance, and a tormented terrain of Biblical dimensions offered obstacles far more formidable than did Italian forces that ran the gamut from one regular division through a rapidly descending hierarchy of units from Blackshirt militias to tribesmen armed with spears. Furthermore, their communications were an open book, as Bletchley Park had broken the Italian codes, which revealed deteriorating Italian morale and a near desperate supply situation. The British offensive consisted of two prongs: the first out of the Sudan under the command of General Sir William Platt contained the *Brigade française libre d'Orient* (BFO), which in the six months from January to May 1941 conquered Eritrea and Northern Abyssinia. A second column out of Kenya moved into Italian Somaliland, before turning north to seize Addis Ababa and join with Platt's force in the north. The Italians retreated to Keren, situated on a high plateau surrounded by mountains, in an attempt to block access to the port of Massawa on the Red Sea. Attacks on the heavily fortified Keren by the 4th Indian Division in early February were unsuccessful, which diverted Anglo-French attacks toward Kub-Kub. Assigned to the BFO, Travers found the countryside of deep gorges interspersed between

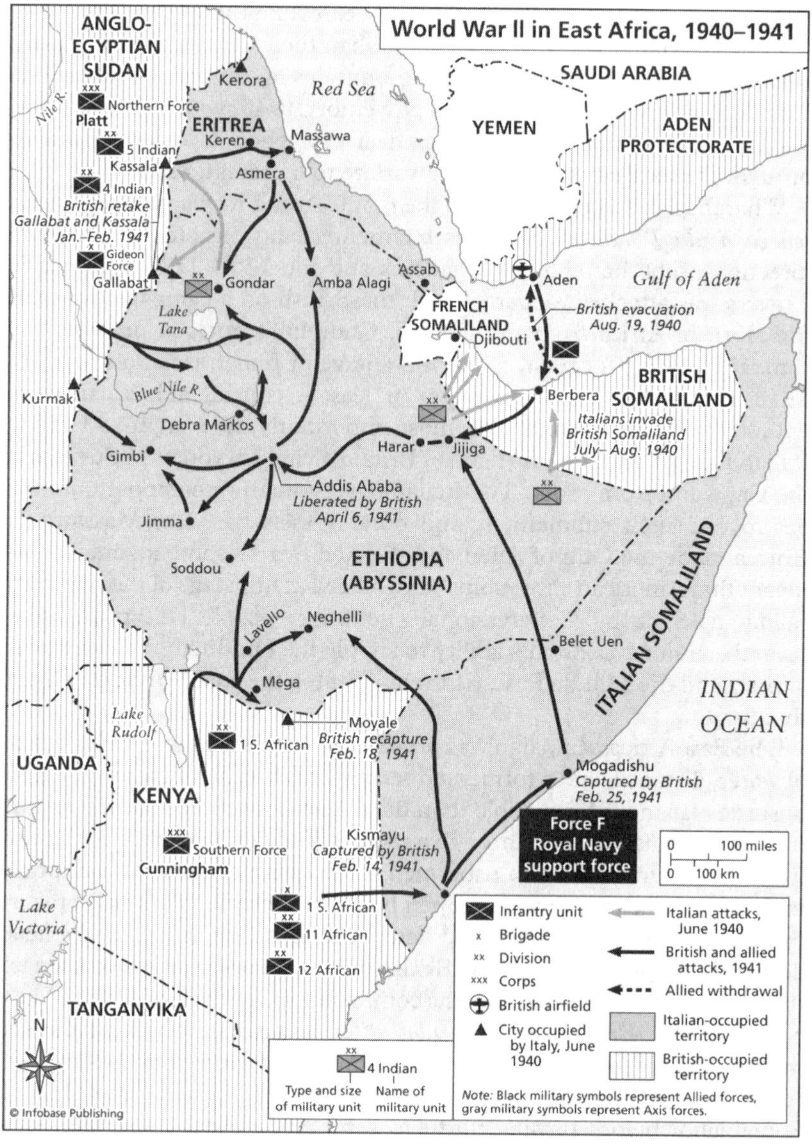

Map 8.1 The Campaign in East Africa – March 1941–November 1941. From *The Path to Victory: The Mediterranean Theater in World War II* by Douglas Porch. Copyright © 2004 by Douglas Porch. Published by Farrar, Straus and Giroux. Original source: Frank Martini, Campaign in East Africa and Middle East; *History of the Second World War: The Mediterranean and the Middle East II* by I. S. O. Playfair, Her Majesty's Stationary Office (HMSO).

precipitous ridges, and a high plateau covered with eucalyptus, both spectacular and exotic. Troops of baboons strutted alongside the road to Kub-Kub, which climbed to a 4,000-foot plateau. The Italians tossed grenades at the advancing Allies from the crest, but it did not save them. As Italian fortunes ebbed, some of the locally raised troops deserted, or turned on their colonial overlords, confusing the British about who they were actually expected to fight. The British began withdrawing troops even before the campaign was concluded. The Legion performed well at Keren, which was seized by Indian troops and legionnaires on 27 March 1941 after a battle lasting several days. As the Anglo-French forces pushed toward Massawa, with the French supported by British artillery, legionnaires took advantage of the fact that the Italians began surrendering in droves to replenish their stocks of weapons and grenades.

The countryside was littered with dusty, straw-roofed villages that whiffed of smoke and cow dung, occupied by friendly populations who welcomed the invaders with fascist salutes, which they believed a traditional Western greeting. Travers tried to keep her head down, maintain her vehicle with makeshift mechanics, not cause a fuss, but just become one of the boys. For amusement, she would go into the desert with some British officers to drink beer and throw grenades. While mixing alcohol and explosives is generally discouraged, opportunities for diversion were limited when the British army obviously forgot to pack the cricket bats? French operational shortcomings included an absence of reserves and a lack of radios, so that the French were obliged to communicate through runners. Fortunately, the concept of the counterattack seemed to have been omitted from the Italian field manual. Massawa fell on 8 April following a significant bombardment. BFO commander Colonel Magrin-Vernerey (Monclar) made his way into town, and entered Italian headquarters to take the surrender. The Italian commander, Rear Admiral Bonetti, threw his sword out of the window into the surf, declaring pompously that an Italian admiral never surrenders his sword. Fortunately, a legionnaire had taken note of its trajectory, waited for low tide, and waded in to retrieve it. Gabriel de Sairigné noted that the spectacle of the surrender of Bonetti and 11,500 Italian officers and soldiers, against 150 French casualties, 30 of them KIA, "would be very interesting if it were not comparable to what I observed in France on 18 June."[12]

As the Allies would often find to be the case in the Western Desert, Italian bases were extremely well provisioned, which made a welcome break from tins of British bully beef, jam and biscuits, and tea. The greatest lacunae of the campaign proved to be poor communications and erratic petrol supply. However, when, as a little reward for his legionnaires, Magrin-Vernerey organized a makeshift brothel staffed by locally recruited talent, the British became indignant. On 11 April, Roosevelt lifted restrictions on US merchant ships entering the Red Sea and the Gulf of Aden.[13] On that same day, de Gaulle ordered the formation of the 1st Free French Infantry Division (*1ère Division française libre* or 1ère DFL). The end of the East Africa campaign found the FFL with a strength of 5,713, of whom 1,513 were Europeans, including officers. As always, finding enough officers with armor experience – indeed, finding enough officers, period – hindered the development of an FFL armored force. The French could take territory, but to garrison it required enlisting local recruits.[14]

Kufra

On 2 December 1940, Leclerc was named military commander of Chad and ordered to make trouble for the Italians in Libya. Unfortunately, Leclerc's grand title masked the fact that he had few resources, and, like the rest of *la France libre*, depended largely on the British for supplies and support. For this reason, he chose Kufra (or Koufra), a fortified Italian base in Cyrenaica near the Egyptian border, as his objective because Muzurk, the capital of the Italian Fezzan, was too distant. While the Italian presence to the north posed no discernible threat to Gaullist-controlled AEF, Mussolini was on the menu in the winter of 1940–1941, and Leclerc wanted his slice, especially as the Italian dictator's declaration of war on France on 10 June 1940 was regarded as a treacherous and cowardly "knife in the back." Although a marine infantry battalion had been incorporated into British forces in the Western Desert from September 1940 to May 1941, de Gaulle and Leclerc sought to launch independent operations.[15] Attacking Italian Cyrenaica would exact a measure of revenge, and bring *la France libre* back into the war. It would also focus on an Axis enemy, rather than contribute another skirmish in the snowballing civil war against Vichy. Kufra arguably had some strategic value as an air link between Italy and Ethiopia, a possession that in any case the Italians were in the process of forfeiting in early 1941. It also anchored the flank of the British campaign in North Africa. The stiff, formal, aristocratic Leclerc also needed a dramatic mission to impose his authority over his notoriously independent Saharan troops. Finally, one cannot discount the historic Anglo-French competition for colonial space. De Gaulle might reinforce his political legitimacy, and counter Vichy charges that he was surrendering the French empire to the British, if he were able to expand France's imperial patrimony – even if it were only worthless sand.

However, opening a Saharan front posed multiple problems, beginning with geography. To seize Kufra, Leclerc must first get there. Spears found the capital of Chad, Fort-Lamy, "a strange and unpicturesque little town," where prisoners chained by the neck ceaselessly carried buckets from the Chari River to water the governor's "dreary garden."[16] In any case, Fort-Lamy was too distant from Italian territory to serve as a base of operations. Over 1,000 kilometers of desert separated Faya-Largeau in northern Chad from Kufra. The Kufra oasis had been seized by the Italians in 1931 as the ultimate capture in their long counterinsurgency campaign that began with the invasion of Tripolitania in 1915, to subdue a Senussi insurrection that opposed the Italian consolidation of Libya. In the process, the Italians had evolved Auto-Saharan companies – the *Sahariana* – that combined Fiat armored cars, camel-mounted infantry, and aircraft both for reconnaissance and for logistical and fire support. Their purpose was to control the local population, not fight pitched battles as adjuncts to conventional operations. The British in Egypt soon followed suit. In the 1930s, Royal Engineer Major Ralph Bagnold had experimented with the creation of "light car patrols" in Egypt, whose vehicles combined innovations like radiator condensers, low-pressure tires, and other techniques to keep vehicles sand-free and increase off-road mobility. Like the *Sahariana*, the purpose of "light car patrols" was territorial management. For this reason, law enforcement enlisted them for anti-smuggling operations on the Egyptian frontier and for use against anti-Zionist Arab insurgents in Palestine.

Recalled to active duty in 1939, Bagnold persuade British commander in the Middle East General Sir Archibald Wavell to revive, transform, and expand the light car patrols into what became the Long Range Desert Patrols (LRDP) for special operations use. The major role of the LRDPs in the context of Britain's Western Desert campaign of 1940–1943 was to operate as a reconnaissance and raiding force, to provide intelligence, and to distract and keep the Italians and Germans off balance while the British prepared conventional operations along the Mediterranean coast.[17] For *la France libre*, these raids had a political purpose – to gain legitimacy through military action and acquire territory. Often manned by hearty Antipodeans, each LRDP consisted of two officers and thirty men packed into eleven one-and-a-half-ton Ford or Chevrolet trucks, stripped of doors and windshields and supplied with enough petrol to travel 1,800 miles. Each vehicle mounted a machinegun, while each patrol packed four anti-tank guns and a 40 mm Bofors, as well as two 76 mm mortars. The various groups communicated among themselves and with their base through Morse, so as not to give away their locations. Their role was to plant mines, attack convoys and airfields, destroy supply dumps, and generally distract the enemy and keep them on edge.

On 11 January 1941, two LRDPs that included a French contingent led by future general and French commander-in-chief Jacques Massu raided Murzuk in the Fezzan to destroy three obsolete Caproni bombers on the ground. But they were unable to overcome the 200-man Italian garrison holed up in the fort. Unfortunately, the Murzuk raid cost the life of Lieutenant-colonel Jean Colonna d'Ornano.[18] A simultaneous raid on the Italian aerodrome at Tedjeré proved a failure. Tedjeré had been d'Ornano's pet project for some time, but the raid was led by Captain Maurice Sarazac. Without vehicles of the sort used by the LRDP, Sarazac was forced to rely on sixty-three camels to transport his force of three Frenchmen, twenty-five tirailleurs, and nineteen guides and drivers, who proved eminently unreliable. The force proved too small and too lightly armed successfully to assault the Italian post, which had possibly been alerted by a deserting camel driver. And after two hours of desultory firing, Sarazac was forced to retrace his steps through the desert. At least he proved conclusively that camels were poorly adapted for offensive operations.[19]

Although Kufra was less remote than Murzuk, it was still 800 kilometers northeast of the nearest French frontier post in Chad. One of a chain of frontier posts strewn along the border between Cyrenaica and Egypt, the Fort of El Tag, Kufra's main defensive position, was garrisoned by a light battalion of 327 mostly indigenous recruits armed with four 20 mm cannons, plus 21 heavy and 32 light machineguns. Kufra was also the base for the *Sahariana di Cufra*, several of whose officers had reputations as experienced desert fighters. The weaknesses of Kufra's defense included the following: an absence of indirect fire artillery; a flawed defense plan that depended on the use of mobile groups to harry attackers in the oasis, although the defenders lacked mobility; and the fact that El Tag was too small to accommodate its garrison.

Basing his raid on the LRDP model, Leclerc gathered a force of roughly 400 men, in an assortment of 60 vehicles in various conditions of mechanical reliability. Leclerc's force was plagued by a paucity of spare parts, tires that were practically bald, and a heavy-weapons arsenal limited to four machineguns, twenty-six sub-machineguns, a 75 mm gun, and four 81 mm mortars. Twelve Blenheim bombers stood by in support, as did several smaller planes. One Blenheim had taken valuable reconnaissance photos of Kufra and El Tag. But as long-range artillery to carry out a preliminary bombardment of Kufra that Leclerc ordered, the Blenheims proved virtually useless. Leclerc recommended that aviators gain some experience in motorized operations so as better to support them. But he seemed to have a difficult time understanding that air support had its limits in the desert, where sandstorms frequently grounded planes, navigation by map over featureless desert terrain offered a formula for disorientation, and bomb loads were dropped blind and on the fly. But such limitations might be lost on a French cavalry commander from an army that had developed no doctrine for coordinating land and air operations in 1940, and who believed that aviators, like horses, needed to be whipped into action. A British LRDP was also meant to take part in the Kufra attack. But on 28 January it had been detected by Italian air reconnaissance and by Italian direction finding after it imprudently broadcast its report by radio. This allowed the Italians to ambush it on 31 January. The LRDP turned back after a loss of three vehicles.

The expedition's first echelon departed Faya-Largeau in northern Chad on 26 January 1941, Leclerc in the lead with a motorized company. The bulk of the column followed a day's march behind. From Brazzaville, Larminat wired that the object of the operation was to "harass this post, and to hinder an eventual retreat of the enemy and to occupy the post if the enemy abandoned it. It is impossible to think of overwhelming Kufra. It's a solid, well-armed and provisioned fortress. And we would not have enough desert vehicles necessary to carry out such an action."[20] On 18 February, the column was intercepted by a *Sahariana* company. Despite having air support, the *Sahariana* departed after a brief skirmish, clearing the way to Kufra, where Leclerc instituted a siege, despite the fact that "the inferiority of our armament compared with that of the enemy was flagrant and serious," especially the absence of a heavy machinegun. The rough desert terrain had totally lacerated the boots of the men, and even the officers, whose feet were bleeding. Nor did his AEF tirailleurs show much "aptitude for modern combat," noted Leclerc. "Their reflexes are slow, they have neither a sense nor a taste for war that one finds among other indigenous races. They are incapable of initiative. With long and difficult training, one can impart some very basic combat reflexes. But unexpected situations seem to disorient them. Their worst habits disappear in part with experience . . ." and can be mitigated by strong European leadership. The greatest advantage for the attackers were his 81 mm mortars, for which the Italians had no counter. All the fighting was done by the European officers and NCOs, with the tirailleurs in a support role. Nevertheless, the Italian garrison felt abandoned, and failed to muster much resistance. On 28 February, the Italians asked to parley, and surrendered the following day. For the equipment-starved Free French, Kufra yielded considerable booty – four 20 mm canon, three light and eighteen heavy machineguns, a million bullets, and fourteen vehicles, at a cost of four killed and twenty-one wounded.[21] Having seized Kufra, the Free French were unsure what to do with it. On 23 March 1941, de Gaulle ordered that Kufra be garrisoned on the logic that he needed to hold captured territory as a bargaining chip. But the difficulties of finding troops to occupy the remote fort, much less supplying it, posed considerable challenges for an organization that was living from hand to mouth.

Kufra offered a skirmish so obscure that it hardly merited a footnote in the North Africa campaign, much less in the larger history of the war. However, according to Leclerc biographer Jean-Christophe Notin, it was Larminat who realized that the symbolism of Kufra far exceeded its actual military value. In a war that so far had featured Bulsons and Dunkirks as yet unredeemed by El Alameins and Stalingrads, Kufra provided an important step in publicizing FFL feistiness, while lifting Leclerc to *France libre* stardom. The official history depicts Leclerc impelling the hesitant Italians to surrender through force of will. "From the mythical Sahara, emerges a legendary cavalryman," whose fame quickly spread to *Oflags* and Armistice Army messes, according to the encyclopedic *Histoire militaire de la France*.[22] Radio Brazzaville puffed Leclerc's exploits, and de Gaulle knighted Leclerc as the thirty-third "companion of the Liberation," nine of whom were already KIA. He praised the Kufra operation – in reality a logistical nightmare of broken-down lorries, with victory won by achieving a psychological ascendency over a handful of isolated Italian officers – as "returning glory under the folds of the flag." Spears instantly spotted the hyperbole. "I liked Leclerc," Spears, the very soul of condescension, recorded in his memoirs. "He was disciplined, and his was the simple code and faith of a good cavalry officer. On matters of conviction, he would stand up even to General de Gaulle, as when his leader wished to discard the Cross of Lorraine on the national flag in favour of the plain tricolor and won. He was brave, and decisive, and prompt, very much the cavalryman; yet, likeable though he was, his real professional status was not much above that of second-in-command of a squadron."[23] Seven officers who participated in the expedition were promoted in what was subsequently baptized "the Kufra class." In August, Leclerc and Monclar joined de Gaulle as brigadiers *à titre temporaire*.

The legend, inculcated in the famous "Oath of Kufra" – "Swear not to stack arms until our colors, our beautiful colors, float above the Strasbourg Cathedral" – is also shrouded in myth. Notin believes that there was no oath at all but a statement of intent in a short, simple address delivered by Leclerc to his officers on 2 March that actually minimized Kufra as representing a very modest step toward the liberation of France. Indeed, Larminat categorized Kufra as "a stone pile of no interest," a strategic assessment with which de Gaulle, determined to grab the

Fezzan, not Cyrenaica, ahead of the British, agreed.[24] But the genius of the "oath" was to incorporate Strasbourg Cathedral – on the face of it a somewhat incongruous image in the middle of the Libyan desert – and by extension the "victimized and romantic" province annexed by Nazi Germany, into the canon of Gaullist irredentism. In fact, the evocation of Strasbourg Cathedral had resonance precisely because it was an image etched into the memory of every Third Republic school child, who was made to recite: "Never will the spire of Strasbourg Cathedral be erased from my horizon." Indeed, so omnipresent had Strasbourg become as a unifying symbol in the iconography of Third Republic France, that Leclerc's 1923 Saint-Cyr class had adopted in the traditions of that institution the extraordinarily oracular moniker, "Metz et Strasbourg."[25] Unlike Laval, willing to sacrifice Alsace-Moselle on the altar of collaboration, "martyred and patriotic" Alsace-Lorraine became a symbol of a mobilization against Nazism, the cathedral spire "the focal point of *la France libre*," and Kufra, a remote and desolate map coordinate, transformed into a Gaullist "place of memory."[26] In this way, an inconsequential skirmish ballooned into an act of major consequence for the purposes of propaganda. Nor would it be the last time that *la France libre*'s limited armaments would be unsheathed from the scabbard of legend. However, in the meantime, more important, more significant, and more politically complex battles remained to be fought.

Syria 1941

Events quickly conspired to reduce Kufra to a diminutive footnote in the tempestuous saga of *la France libre*, and in the seesaw war in the Eastern Mediterranean. Spears' biographer rightly called the 1941 invasion of Syria "a nasty campaign."[27] This was perfectly foreseeable, for at least three reasons. First, in the wake of Dakar, any face-to-face confrontation between the forces of Vichy and those of *la France libre* was destined to deepen animosities between the two estranged French factions. Second, the Anglo-*France libre* invasion of the Levant was an improvized and largely ad hoc operation carried out in the midst of policy confusion that only deepened mistrust between de Gaulle and Churchill. Third, at least a portion of the Syria garrison, still smarting from accusations flowing out of 1940 that the French could not fight, were determined to give a good account of themselves. In the process, Syria exposed some of the risks and limitations of de Gaulle's strategy of legitimizing *la France libre*, resurrecting France, and restoring French prestige and status through empire recuperation and mobilization, especially while depending on British sponsorship and support. Because de Gaulle needed to restore France's patrimony – including its imperial possessions – intact, or risk confirming Vichy accusations that *la France libre* was merely a mercenary English auxiliary force, Syria demonstrated how, in the mind of the distrustful leader of *la France libre*, "les Anglo-Saxons" presented a more immediate threat to the legitimacy of his movement and the restoration of French prestige than did the Axis.

Ever since the 1915 Sykes–Picot Agreement had divided the Middle East between them, the two powers had been at odds in the region. From the British perspective, the French had made themselves very unpopular by pushing their "Civilizing Mission," administering their mandates through a "condescending" and "mediocre" bureaucracy, and favoring Maronite Christians over the Muslims in a deliberate "divide-and-rule" tactic of governance. Blum had attempted to liberalize French policy by signing a transitional deal to independence with the parliaments of Syria and Lebanon in 1936. But this plan collapsed with the Popular Front. Even without the Fall of France, it was clear by September 1939 that the French days in the fractious Middle East were numbered. With the 1940 defeat, followed by food shortages that produced riots and strikes in Damascus, the nationalists viewed the mandates as moribund, and none of de Gaulle's invocations of French *gloire* were going to revive them. The British fear was that an anti-imperial attitude in the French mandate might prove contagious in British-controlled Palestine, the Transjordan, and Mesopotamia. In contrast to the doctrinaire French, the British viewed themselves as pragmatists, whose interests in the Middle East were limited to strategic position and oil, and who, unlike the French, were willing to grant local autonomy, as they had in Egypt with the 1936 Anglo-Egyptian treaty. However, in the Middle East, Britain was "a presence in search of a policy," under inadequate officials and a clumsy bureaucratic structure, with too much decision-making centralized in London. Furthermore, London had shot itself in the foot – if not the head – when Britain had invited Zionist immigration into Palestine, which forced the British occupiers into "a daily balancing act."[28]

That this tension was not foreseen is all the more surprising as both Churchill and de Gaulle had predicted that one day, Hitler would come after the Middle East. And indeed, the events leading up to the Syrian campaign seemed to suggest that very scenario. On 20 November 1940, Hungary joined the Tripartite Pact. In January 1941, General Ion Antonescu abandoned neutrality and invited German troops onto Romanian territory. Given the pace of Axis momentum, the British cabinet's strategic assessment in early 1941 erred toward pessimism – it noted growing evidence of German plans to invade the Balkans and

Greece, possibly also Turkey and the Middle East, with the goal of eliminating Britain's base in the Eastern Mediterranean. In January, *Fliegerkorps X* arrived in the Mediterranean. From bases in Italian-controlled Rhodes, the *Luftwaffe* began to attack British shipping, and to sow both magnetic and acoustic mines in the Suez Canal, seriously backing up traffic there, as well as in the harbors of Sollum and Tobruk. Malta and Benghazi came under regular bombing attacks. On 14 February 1941, the lead elements of Erwin Rommel's *Deutsches Afrikakorps* began to disembark in Tripoli. On 6 March, Mussolini launched a twenty-eight-division offensive against fourteen Greek divisions in Albania. By 28 March, King Boris allowed fourteen *Wehrmacht* divisions into Bulgaria against a promise of Greek territory in future. A nationalist uprising launched on 31 March 1941 in Baghdad brought Prime Minister Rashid Ali al-Gaylani, a member of the Muslim Brotherhood, which had cells throughout the Middle East, to power. Rashid Ali promptly called for German assistance. Operation Marita, launched on 6 April against a million-strong Yugoslav army, made *Fall Gelb* appear a slogging match by comparison. A week later, Rommel launched an offensive against British forces in Cyrenaica. Despite Wavell's overstretch in Egypt and Italian East Africa, Churchill ordered almost 60,000 British and Commonwealth troops to Greece, on the logic that, in the interest of British credibility, Athens could not be abandoned as Warsaw had been in 1939. But, by 14 April, the British were preparing for another Dunkirk in Greece, and six days later the Greeks requested an armistice. The Germans put the final touches on *Unternehmen Merkur* (Operation Mercury) – the invasion of Crete.

On 6 May, after discussions with Abetz, the opportunistic Darlan, seeing a chance to kick-start collaboration with Germany, allowed the *Luftwaffe* the use of French airfields in the Levant and released Vichy war stocks in Syria to support the Mesopotamian uprising. In return, Germany agreed to allow the rearming of a few destroyers and release 90,000 French POWs. At a stroke, Darlan ripped off the thin veil of Vichy neutrality, while putting Vichy's Middle Eastern territories at risk. This action also revealed how Vichy's requirement to recuperate POWs to demonstrate to a skeptical French public the payoff of collaboration had caused Darlan to throw open the empire to the Axis.[29] Five days later, in an effort coordinated by Dr. Rudolf Rahn, the German representative on the Italian armistice commission in Syria, 200 *Luftwaffe* personnel were installed on the airfield in Aleppo. On 12–13 May, 26 railway cars of French matériel departed for Baghdad, the first of three shipments that eventually included 20,000 rifles, 200 machineguns, 400 sub-machineguns, 5 million bullets, 56 aviation fuel trucks, and four 75 mm and eight 155 mm guns with munitions.[30] On 13 May, news arrived that *Luftwaffe* aircraft and some Italian planes had landed on Syrian airfields. Given that de Gaulle harbored a deep distrust of Churchill's designs on the French empire, from his perspective he was certainly taking a risk when he urged the British Prime Minister to invade the French Levant. But May 1941 found the Eastern Mediterranean in crisis. The Rashid Ali revolt looked as if it might spark a Hitler plan to invade the Middle East. On 14 May, Churchill ordered his C-in-C Middle East, Archibald Wavell, to intervene. British forces from India landed at Basra, while a second invasion was mounted through Jordan to reach Baghdad and restore order. By the end of the month, Bagdad was back in British hands, the deposed regent had been reinstalled on the throne, and the Germans had departed Syria.

But all the dominoes toppled by the Rashid Ali rebellion had yet to fall. Never one to let a crisis go to waste, de Gaulle flew to Cairo to press Wavell to invade Syria and Lebanon. He painted an optimistic picture of a Syrian garrison eager to transfer its loyalties to *la France libre*, supported by Spears who sent Churchill a report claiming that "seventy per cent of junior officers and NCOs are said to be inclined toward the Free French movement." Catroux argued that the appearance on the frontier between the two mandates of FFL troops flying the tricolor would rally the Vichy garrison.[31] Because the Rashid Ali crisis coincided with the German invasion of Crete on 20 May, Catroux made a plausible case that Greece and Crete would become Axis stepping stones to the French Levant, with the door held ajar by the Vichy French commander in the Levant, General Henri Dentz. In Jaffa, de Gaulle assembled 5,400 men into the *1ère Division légère française libre* (1ère DFL), which was in numerical strength more like a half division. Initially Monclar was placed in command. But when he balked at fighting his fellow countrymen in the Levant, he was replaced by Paul Legentilhomme, who, upon hearing of the armistice in June 1940, had abandoned his post of *Commandant supérieur* in Djibouti and defected to *la France libre*. Heaving a weary sigh, from 25 May, Wavell reluctantly began to scrape together troops from his overextended force for an invasion of the French mandates.

For Crémieux-Brilhac, the Syrian campaign offered "a civil war in a colonial décor."[32] But the implications of the Syrian campaign spilled beyond a mere Franco-French conflict. Operation Exporter was "an unhappy improvization," carried out in haste and confusion, with no one having the time to think through the implications of the invasion, or to plan for surrender and occupation. Acting in conjunction with Wavell and Sir Miles Lampson, British ambassador in Cairo, not de Gaulle, Catroux publicly promised independence to Syria and Lebanon on the

Egyptian model. Operation Exporter launched on 8 June with a scratch force of 34,000 British, Australian, Indian, and FFL troops under the command of Henry Maitland "Jumbo" Wilson, attacking out of Iraq, Palestine, and the Transjordan against a Vichy garrison of equal or even slightly greater numbers. But only 6,000 of the Vichy troops were metropolitan French. The remainder were Algerian and Senegalese, as well as local levies of Druze, a minority Shia sect. *Luftwaffe* planes flying from Greece and Rhodes at the extreme limit of their operational range bombed the oil pipeline terminal at Haifa. Hitler ordered the Armistice Army reinforcements to be brought by rail to Salonika. But the prospects for Vichy backups reaching the Levant were stymied by the presence of the Royal Navy, Turkish neutrality, and the reluctance of the Germans to transport French troops by air lest this roil Arab opinion. The Vichy French gave a good account of themselves in battle, especially against the FFL, and held their own for a while until Wavell rushed reinforcements from Iraq and Egypt (Figure 8.2). Susan Travers had been assigned to drive Legion colonel Pierre Koenig. While this was a huge promotion from chauffeuring the MO of the Chadians, who had been wounded in Syria, her old Humber 38 combined the disadvantages of stiff acceleration, faulty brakes, and a motor so deafening that the passengers remained unaware of approaching aircraft until bombs began to explode around them. Because the previous driver had died with the keys in his pocket, ignition required her to hotwire the vehicle by pressing together two wires in the steering column.[33] De Gaulle criticized Wilson's invasion plan, and his generalship, which he judged too hesitant. Above all, the British had failed to supply the FFL with trucks and tanks. On 11 July, with both Beirut and Damascus in British hands, the RAF commanding the skies, and his supplies exhausted, Dentz requested an armistice.

What should have been a happy outcome left de Gaulle embittered, because Exporter proved to be a successful military campaign imposed on a tangled political agenda. On 19 June, de Gaulle had laid out his armistice conditions in Cairo to Wavell, British ambassador to Egypt Miles Lampson, and Catroux, who assented.[34] In what Julian Jackson describes as a "very odd" move, de Gaulle then flew off to Brazzaville rather than linger to recruit among the Vichy garrison, possibly because he realized that the application of the armistice agreement, which allowed the Free French to recruit among Vichy's Syrian garrison, would prove unacceptable.[35] Churchill, the Foreign Office, and Wavell were eager to close down the Levant theater as quickly as possible, repatriate Vichy French troops, and concentrate resources on putting out fires elsewhere, especially in Egypt, where Rommel had blunted Wavell's Battleaxe Offensive of 15–17 June and forced him to retreat from the Halfaya

Figure 8.2 Free French Troops enter Damascus 27 June 1941.

Pass. Nor was London eager to push Vichy further into Hitler's arms. At this critical moment, de Gaulle departed on an unannounced walkabout to Brazzaville, and spurned Eden's request that he come to London to discuss the Levant. This did not burnish de Gaulle's reputation with either the Foreign Office, that interpreted de Gaulle's boycott as an attempt "to destroy the idea that he is under British tutelage," or Wavell, who believed that the leader of *la France libre* wanted to avoid being confronted with the fact that the French were immensely unpopular in the Levant. Cairo's fear was that Exporter would boomerang on the British in the form of a Rashid Ali-like uprising in Syria. Another bad-case scenario for London was that the Levant might become Hitler's Trojan Horse in the region. Given these imponderables, for London and Cairo the repatriation of a few thousand French POWs to Vichy seemed a small price to pay.

De Gaulle declared Catroux *Délégué général et plénipotentiaire au Levant*, with "all the powers and responsibilities of the High Commissioner of France in the Levant."[36] But in Spears' eyes, Catroux's limitations were on full display during the armistice negotiations and the surrender ceremony. Dentz declared that he was not authorized by Vichy to negotiate with representatives of *la France libre*. Whether because he was out of his depth, as Jackson believes, or because he had received instructions from London, Wilson skirted the issue by including Catroux in the armistice delegation, but did not allow him to sign the documents, which apparently would return Dentz to Vichy without being jailed, at least not immediately. In fact, de Gaulle's revenge would be served cold – Dentz would die in Fresnes prison in December 1945. What Catroux, and indeed the British Minister-resident for the Middle East, Sir Oliver Lyttleton, did not know was that Wilson and Dentz had negotiated a "secret protocol" in the Saint-Jean d'Acre agreement which banned all contact between Gaullists and Pétainists, confined *la France libre* spokesmen to using pamphlets, loudspeakers, and wireless communication, and allowed the Vichy French to depart with their weapons. This "farcical arrangement" incensed Lyttleton. It also put Catroux in the hot seat with de Gaulle.

But the political insensitivity of his conduct utterly escaped "Jumbo" Wilson, not rated among the sharpest tools in the British command shed. A bald man with a broad middle, who in a lemon-squeezer hat and Sam Brown belt resembled a pear-shaped scoutmaster, Spears compared Wilson to a large featherless owl. A Royal Green Jacket carried by a staff innocent of the political dimensions of the Syrian situation, but who, nevertheless, "hovered like mess waiters round the officers' table at guest night," Spears likened Wilson's inexplicable professional success to that of "a Montgolfier balloon levitated by hot air alone." Indeed, Wilson might easily have been taken as the model for the 1934 David Low cartoon character Colonel Blimp. Nevertheless, he was no pushover: he had "sharp claws when he chose and could be very caustic."[37] Wilson simply ignored Lyttleton's orders to give *la France libre* access to Vichy troops, using the excuse that he feared disorder. Both sides were embittered by casualties taken in a wasteful and superfluous campaign fought after the Rashid Ali revolt had been quelled and the *Luftwaffe* had departed Syria – 1,066 dead and 5,400 wounded for Vichy, while the British had absorbed 3,000 casualties and the FFL 627, of whom 156 were KIA. Among the wounded was a young American, John Hasey, who worked at Cartier's in Paris and had joined *la France libre* in London, who had his jaw shot off. Furthermore, on 22 June, Hitler had invaded the Soviet Union, which demonstrated that the Eastern Mediterranean was not, after all, a strategic priority for the Reich.

De Gaulle's immediate problem was that British generals led by Wilson declined to view Exporter as a fight to restore French imperial grandeur. On the contrary, the Arabs had welcomed the British as liberators. British specialists on the ground – whom de Gaulle dismissed as "Arabists" – who would have struggled to delineate the distinctions between Vichy and *la France libre*, found their ancestral stereotypes of Gallic querulousness and dysfunction reinforced. Because they were more numerous and powerful than the FFL, whom they regarded at best as mere auxiliaries, at worst as rebels, British soldiers shaped the peace without input from higher officials, especially Lyttleton, who sought to impose a more politically attuned settlement. But where distance, poor communication, bad liaison, distractions, insularity, and incompetence had led to misunderstanding, de Gaulle perceived conspiracy. Martin Thomas also suggests that the British may have been more lenient with the Vichy French out of embarrassment at the indiscipline of some Australian troops, who looted, and even mutilated the bodies of French dead.[38] De Gaulle flew to Cairo from Brazzaville, where he raged at Lyttleton, threatening to remove the FFL from British command. Brosset, who visited Vichy troops held at the POW camp at Latrum, found them hostile, blaming the FFL for shedding French blood. All of which he interpreted as a sign of a "bad conscience."[39] "Impossible to reason with most of them," recorded de Sairigné. "They won't pass judgment and 'follow their leaders.'"[40] In July, Travers chauffeured Koenig to the Legion mess in Beirut, where the Vichyites and *France libre* officers dined at opposite ends of the hall, neither acknowledging the presence of the other. Vichy troops were accorded the honors of war by Wilson and repatriated to North Africa, their view of *la France libre* as British mercenaries and traitors reinforced. Only 3,000 Europeans and 1,500 colonial soldiers in the Levant garrison remained behind with *la France libre*, which the British estimated numbered 9,336 troops in September 1941. De Gaulle's figures were considerably higher – 18,650 in the same month. The Arabs observed the "victory parade" in Damascus in stony silence.[41]

Not surprisingly in the wake of these events, de Gaulle's relations with the British dropped from cool to glacial, as he saw the Saint-Jean d'Acre accords as "pure and simple transference of Syria and Lebanon to the British." Formally speaking, that was untrue, although the post-invasion situation was complex. On 16 July, de Gaulle gave an interview to the *Chicago Daily News* during which he claimed that the British and German governments conspired to keep Vichy alive because it served their mutual interests, just the sort of intemperate provocation that set Churchill spinning and fundamentally transformed the relationship between the two men into one of mutual antagonism.[42] On 25 July, he signed an accord with Lyttleton that hammered out the arrangements for the civil administration of the Levant. With the title of commander-in-chief, *troupes du Levant*, Catroux and "la Reine Margot" settled into Beirut's Grand Serail, an immense palace, complete with the couple's servants, cats, and Louis XV furniture. Spears remained unimpressed: "[Catroux] is, however, incapable of organizing anything and entirely devoid of 'drive,'" he wrote. "His staff is farcical, comprising jejune officials who have found a haven of refuge in sleepy offices where nothing is ever planned much less carried out ... [de Gaulle] cannot trust him with anything really difficult or important."[43]

But Catroux's problems went deeper than a lack of drive and an ambitious, hectoring wife, although that was certainly part of it. For the Arabs, the French army had forfeited any residual prestige it still retained by being defeated by a multiracial and multinational British-led force. Furthermore, for the locals, the switch to *France libre* sovereignty offered a case of colonial *plus ça change*. Having promised independence on the eve of invasion, Catroux was forced by de Gaulle to backtrack and prevaricate, postponing elections that the nationalists were bound to win, lest Vichy accuse him of forfeiting the empire. De Gaulle adopted a legalistic position that, although Catroux had offered provisional independence, *la France libre* lacked the legal standing to terminate the mandate. De Gaulle's temper tantrums had forfeited any residual sympathy for him in Whitehall, which made it difficult for Catroux to coordinate Middle East policy through Spears. The French Plenipotentiary continued the tired and transparent French divide-and-rule ploy in the Levant of pitting Christians against Sunnis. Despite his reputation as a connoisseur of the Arab world, Catroux's choice of interlocutors was not always felicitous – he appointed a pro-French sheikh as President of Syria, and retained Vichy's choice as President of Lebanon. Disorder continued in a well-armed population that *la France libre* lacked enough troops effectively to police, and the French administration depended on deliveries of British food to keep the lid on a combustible situation. But often this only led to hoarding and rampant inflation. De Gaulle refused advice to wind up France's Middle East occupation and depart without validating Vichy accusations of imperial sellout. Rather, he forced Catroux and his successor from 1943 to cling doggedly to France's failing Middle East mandate, with a diminished crew of frequently disloyal civil servants. Roughly a fifth of France's colonial administrators departed for France in the autumn of 1941. But half stayed on without switching their loyalties from Vichy, while fewer than a third declared for *la France libre*. So, essentially, Vichy continued to administer the Levant in spirit, and some civil servants were supplying intelligence to Vichy right up to the liberation in 1944.[44] Unfortunately, the Levant offered an ominous preview of Gaullist overreach and muddle in Indochina in 1945–1946.

Spears' relationship with de Gaulle also fell casualty to Exporter, which revealed de Gaulle's priorities to be "the political future of the States under French mandates," rather than the war effort. Spears was named British minister to the paper republics in Lebanon and Syria. By August, he was publicly advocating de Gaulle's ouster. With 100 political officers who reported directly to him, he worked to undermine Catroux. He met directly with the Presidents of Lebanon and Syria without going through Catroux, basically sending a strong signal that he refused to recognize the French mandate. Catroux complained of Spears' "discourteous and threatening manner," while, from Cairo, Lyttleton reported to London that Spears "makes mountainous protests about molehill incidents that irritates Catroux." *La France libre* was too weak to stop Spears, and too insecure to show flexibility. De Gaulle continued to insist on the validity of the mandate, and that the empire was France, which accentuated the anachronistic colonialist dimensions of Gaullism in Arab eyes. Churchill refused to rein in his friend Spears. On 9 September, Churchill told the Commons that Britain "had no ambitions in Syria." But, as General John Bagot Glubb, better known as Arab Legion commander Glubb Pasha, pointed out, the paradox of British policy was that they could not both support Arab aspirations and accommodate *la France libre*.[45]

Not surprisingly, perhaps, Vichy failed to acknowledge that, by inviting the *Luftwaffe* into the Levant to aid the Rashid Ali revolt in Mesopotamia, they had forced Churchill's hand, and redefined their policy of "neutrality." Vichy also expressed some satisfaction with the performance of its forces in the Levant campaign. Apart from some of the irregular units, Vichy's army had fought well, inflicting severe casualties on Gaullist forces. Only an estimated 200 soldiers, mostly Foreign Legionnaires, and half a dozen officers had "deserted" to "the Gaullist felons." While conceding that the Gaullist forces had fought well, "the soldiers are dirty, undisciplined, don't salute their NCOs. At night, most are drunk – a pitiable spectacle for the French." Their officers were reduced to appropriating vehicles and arms from the Vichy French. Once it had been repatriated to AFN, Vichy estimated that the 32,000 strong "*Corps expéditionnaire du Levant*" could be used both to bolster the defenses of AFN and as a sort of mobile reserve to defend vulnerable points of the empire. Furthermore, these forces were inoculated against Gaullism. "The issue is settled: a divide exists between the French forces of the Levant, and the Gaullist troops."[46] Vichy might also derive some consolation from the fact that Syria would continue to roil British–Free French relations for the remainder of the war and beyond.

La France libre Transforms from a Military Rebellion to a Political Movement

Hardly had Syria been conquered than it was relegated to the back burner of the war, although it would again flare up as an issue between France and Great Britain in 1945. De Gaulle had emerged as the big winner in the Syrian campaign for at least three reasons. First, he had demonstrated that "legal" France had backed the wrong horse by allowing German access to the Levant. Second, he had added two more colonies to *la France libre*'s patrimony, in the process elbowing Vichy out of the Middle East. By permitting the Germans access to Syrian airfields, Vichy had narrowed Churchill's diplomatic options: "When you deal with Vichy, you deal with Hitler," de Gaulle had warned the British Prime Minister.[47] But it was not immediately apparent to Churchill, or to Roosevelt for that matter, that *la France libre* remained the only game in town as far as France was concerned. Syria narrowed Allied alternatives to de Gaulle. If ever the French army returned to combat, it could not ignore its Free French element. Politically and ideologically *la France libre* became more fervent, de Gaulle more coldblooded, and more resolved to triumph.

On 24 September 1941, *la France libre* took a further step in transforming from a military force into a "quasi-government" when it formed the *Comité national français*. In some respects, this shift was in part an accident, a spinoff of a battle in Carlton Gardens between de Gaulle and Muselier for control of the BCRA. But in the process, it demonstrated the ability of de Gaulle to turn the tables on those who sought to oust him from the leadership of *la France libre* and derail his crusade to restore France's political standing in the Alliance. The idea for an "executive committee" began as an attempt by Muselier and André Labarthe, formerly a close associate of Pierre Cot, who edited the publication *France*, to give more influence in *la France libre* to those volunteers who represented the left of the political spectrum. The idea of creating a committee to displace de Gaulle and possibly wrest control of the BCRA from Passy gained the support of Desmond Morton, a senior British civil servant and Churchill's personal assistant. Churchill justified an opportunity to "drown de Gaulle in a committee" with the argument that it would enlarge *la France libre's* base, and create a body with which the British government could negotiate. De Gaulle agreed, but turned the table on the plotters by refusing to accede to Muselier's demand to chair the committee and facing down the Admiral's threat to jump the Gaullist ship, while taking the FNFL with him. He also declined to name Labarthe to the committee. Once the committee had been created, de Gaulle then demanded that, now that *la France libre* had an executive authority that could legislate, as well as other services and appendages that replicated those of an established government, His Majesty's Government must recognize *la France libre*'s diplomatic status as equal to that of other governments in London exile. Realizing that he had been outmaneuvered, in a fit of pique Churchill forbade de Gaulle to leave the United Kingdom. But even the de Gaulle-averse United States made *la France libre* eligible for Lend-Lease aid in November 1941.[48] For these reasons, even before the November Anglo-American landings in AFN, 1942 had marked an important turning point in the war for *la France libre*. In December 1941, the United States joined the war and in February 1942, Washington officially acknowledged de Gaulle's control of AEF.[49] All he needed was a military victory to symbolize Free France's courage and indominable will.

Bir Hakeim

Until 1942, Gaullist forces had collected a few remote Vichy colonies, and participated in campaigns in East Africa and the Levant at the side of the British. But so far, they had failed to lay a glove on the *Wehrmacht*. That Bir Hakeim offered *la France libre* a Beau Geste moment was entirely appropriate, as the *13ème Demi-brigade de la légion étrangère* became one of the featured units in the engagement. Following the Syrian frustrations, the FFL had been pulled together as a "light motorized division," which was infantry-heavy, contained a single tank company, and whose artillery support came mainly from 25 mm anti-tank guns and 75 mm field guns, both already obsolete in 1940. Given these shortcomings, the British referred to it as the 1st Free French Brigade and gave it low priority for logistics and armament upgrades, a slight that many in the FFL regarded as intentional and which further encouraged their reluctance to assimilate to British military practice, but instead evolve "French" solutions. Judging by the correspondence, discipline was not as rigorous as it might have been among the almost 9,000 FFL troops serving with the Eighth Army, the second-largest foreign contingent after the 12,000 Greeks.[50] Uniforms and insignia were such a hodgepodge of mix-and-match that General Legentilhomme struggled to impose a modicum of uniformity on his heterogeneous command. By March 1942, the FFL numbered 18,390 troops scattered in those colonies that had declared for *la France libre* and in Great Britain. Only 6,356 were Europeans, however, the rest being native levies. Training remained a problem, because instructors and training camps, not to mention weapons and other normal accouterments of military life, were in short supply in Africa.[51] On

10 April 1942, *la France libre*'s War Commissariat in London conceded that the fluid strategic situation, the exile organization's requirement to defend AEF, the prospect of reclaiming other imperial territories from Vichy, and participation in future Allied conventional operations, not to mention the heterogeneity of FFL personnel, made it difficult to settle upon an operational model. Nevertheless, London ordered the creation of two infantry-heavy brigades, each provided with one 75 mm artillery battery, some engineers and transport, a mechanized reconnaissance squadron, and a tank company formed should the two brigades operate as a division. Yet, even by the standards of early 1942, this organizational schema did not have much mobility, and promised to be more effective in defensive operations.[52]

The British Eighth Army that the *1re Brigade Française libre* was to join had yet to acquire the swashbuckling allure that it would display from August 1942 under the authority of General Bernard Montgomery. "The fact was that the Eighth Army was not a European army anymore," wrote Australian war correspondent Alan Moorehead. "To a great extent it had become an overseas army, an army based not on London but on Cairo. For months and years it had been cut off from Europe, and in their isolation the troops had developed a complicated set of private habits, and even a slang language of their own."[53] Although the Eighth Army had bested Rommel in the Crusader Campaign of November–December 1941, thereby relieving the siege of Tobruk and pummeling the celebrated German commander back into Tripolitania, by the summer of 1942, the British force seemed to be experiencing a serious crisis of morale, which would impact performance in the Gazala or "summer" battle of 1942. Coming on the heels of the February 1942 surrender of 130,000 British troops at Singapore, the British command was particularly concerned by the growing percentage ratio of missing/surrendered to killed/wounded in Cyrenaica, a worry that stretched to Whitehall. Some historians have subsequently argued that the fluid, not to say chaotic, nature of the fighting in the Western Desert, and the poor quality of British anti-tank guns at this stage of the war, meant that British troops might frequently be put in a position where they had no choice but to surrender. But certainly, at the time and since, high surrender rates have been interpreted as a symptom of low morale, especially when corroborated by desertions and court martials, and evidence from postal censorship.[54]

The causes of this morale crisis were multiple, but were heavily influenced by the soldiers' views on the competence of their military leadership and the lack of progress of the war.[55] Part of the problem was that too many soldiers had been marooned for too long in the seesaw, inconclusive desert combat. The monotony of this gray, featureless, sand-blown landscape swarming with flies, that settled on eyes, buzzed up nostrils, and coagulated on plates and tea mugs, bleached morale. But more, British-led forces had faith neither in their weapons, nor in their tactics, nor in their commanders. The feeble 2-pounder/40 mm standard anti-tank gun in the British arsenal proved powerless against "face-hardened" Pz.Kpfw. IIIs and IVs beyond 500 yards. German tanks fired both armor-piercing and high-explosive shells, which bestowed upon them a dual-purpose role of both mobile artillery and anti-tank weapons, especially when backed by formidable 88 mm dual-purpose anti-tank/anti-aircraft guns. But German attacks usually involved the entire orchestra, not simply the chamber quartet as did those of the British. "You hear the German cannon five miles away," wrote Caleb Milne, an American Field Service ambulance driver in the Eighth Army. "Then the loudening whistle, overhead it becomes a mounting whine then a descending scale of nasty rushing through the air. It disappears over the next wall, one sees a sudden cloud of black smoke rise and then, curiously enough, the deafening roar is heard. Like the final fury it arrives seconds after the smoke ... My curiosity is satisfied on one point at last! There *is* time to review your entire life before the shell arrives, though I doubt if anyone thinks that concretely at such a time."[56] A drone of Stukas or Bf 109s might suddenly dart over a rise, their bombs instantly crashed, flashed, and sent up plumes of smoke mixed with fine sand that veiled the armored melee, "while the whine of guns and the delicate tracery of fire-bullets crisscrossed the sky."[57] All this translated into an absence of the concentrated firepower and organization required to take on Rommel's *Panzerarmee*.

Observing the Crusader battle from the rocks of the Tobruk escarpment, Alan Moorehead "saw [the enemy's] guns ranging on our forward tanks in the north and they stood like knockovers in the shooting gallery of a country fair. Like an endless chain of artificial ducks."[58] This German operational advantage in armor and artillery had accentuated the British tactical mistake of attempting to fight tanks with tanks, rather than letting anti-tank guns take care of tanks and sending their tanks after "thin-skinned" vehicles.[59] The German tactic was to create a well-camouflaged line of anti-tank guns anchored by the formidable 88 mm cannon that could disable a British tank at 2,000 yards, and draw British tanks into an ambush. The British were aware that this tactic was being used against them from Operation Battleaxe of June 1941. But little was done to prepare the army to counter it for several reasons, beginning with the fact that most British tanks were issued only armor-piercing rounds, which meant that they could only fight other tanks. Second, British anti-tanks guns were too feeble effectively to engage the Pz.Kpfw. IIIs and IVs.

For fire support, the British relied on the 25 pounder, roughly the equivalent of the German 88 mm, in the middle of the light artillery range between the 75 mm and the 105 mm. In Crusader, the 25 pounder was the best killer of German tanks. But the requirement to protect the infantry by splitting tanks and artillery batteries into brigade groups and "Jock columns" further fragmented the impact of British firepower, and reduced British mobility, which allowed the Germans to concentrate more firepower more quickly at chosen moments in the battle.[60] The medium Crusader tanks, rushed into production to replace the slow Matilda "I" (for infantry) tanks, were immensely unpopular in the Eighth Army because they were both mechanically unreliable and vulnerable to German anti-tank guns. These were gradually replaced by the Valentine and the American-built Grant tank from the summer of 1942. Although the Grant was slow, its popularity can be explained by its 75 mm gun mounted in a sponson and a 37 mm high-velocity anti-tank gun in the turret. This by the summer of 1942 would give the British something closer to tank parity.

Crusader had proven that fighting in the desert was a disorienting experience: "As far as I can see the landscape is dotted with little black specks, some moving, others stationary," wrote Milne. "It seems odd to think they are huge tanks and trucks and men. I am continually feeling like some busy ant going laboriously forward to some ant battle . . . out here [battles] seem puny and man-made." The few topographical reference points in a landscape "striped with long, low ridges of sand-ripple, bristling with gnarled shrubs, very gray-green," might be distorted by "heat-shimmer," or soften into a gauze of color and shadow that changed with the hour, "so you can imagine the trickiness of vision here."[61] In these conditions, commanders were often clueless about their own location, let alone that of the enemy. Driving, especially off road, was exhausting. In the featureless Western Desert, Travers had to navigate using sun compasses, or maps that were like reading naval charts, all while keeping a close eye on water, oil, fuel, and tire pressure. Air filters frequently clogged with sand in North Africa, and had to be cleaned.[62] Confusion was increased by the tendency of the British, German, and Italian armies to incorporate captured vehicles into their inventories. And if this were not disorienting enough, the smoke, dust, and debris of battle became mixed with periodic sandstorms, often serving to limit vision to a few dozen meters. All of this made German ambushes virtually impossible to detect until it was too late. The 738 tanks in the Eighth Army inventory at the beginning of Crusader had been reduced by about 600 – or 81 percent – by the end of the battle. British scholar Jonathan Fennell reports that the British carried out various partial studies on their high tank losses in the desert. The exact percentages varied, but by far the biggest tank killer in the British army in North Africa was mechanical breakdown, which might run as high as 50 percent. Because at this stage of the war the British lacked the German system of tank recovery vehicles and mobile repair shops, these tanks became lost to the fight. The other 50 percent was caused by an amalgam of 88 mm guns and lighter anti-tank weapons, the 50 mm cannon of the Pz.Kpfw. IIIs, and mines. The impact of the 88 mm, like that of the Stuka, was greater psychologically than it was in reality.[63]

Finally, a lack of systematic training in the British forces, especially in theater, undermined the ability to transmit and inculcate "lessons learned" from each action. This problem was accentuated by the fact that experienced units were frequently rotated out of the line to be replaced by regiments and even divisions newly arrived from England or India, that were totally unfamiliar with and unprepared for the conditions and fast-moving tactics of desert warfare. Officers on their way to the front were simply handed pamphlets that explained the latest German equipment and tactics, in the hope that they might find time to read them. Once at the front, the British often mixed and matched units into "composite battalions," brigade groups, Jock columns, and so on. And while this offered advantages of operational flexibility, it also prevented the formation of meaningful command relationships and standardized operational practices, among a diverse army made up of British and imperial soldiers, not to mention Poles, Free French, and other flotsam of Europe's defeated armies and desperate refugees. It also undermined *esprit de corps* in an army whose foundational unit was the regiment, whose fighting qualities were underpinned by regional pride and the special history and traditions of each regiment. New weapons, including tanks, were distributed to front-line units with little or no training on how to use them, much less a tactical and operational concept. This constant churning of units was matched on the leadership level, a spinning carousel of commanders, each more clueless than the last. Rommel would face six different British commanders in the Western Desert, each of whom had to deal with micromanagement of operations by Archibald Wavell and Claude Auchinleck from Cairo, not to mention the crack of Churchill's bombastic lash from London.[64]

The British were under no illusion that Crusader had put paid to the Rommel threat. By the end of April 1942, British intelligence intercepts began to suggest that he was preparing to advance in the Western Desert, possibly as early as May. British Middle East commander Auchinleck ordered General Neil Ritchie to arrange his Eighth Army into a blocking position anchored on Tobruk, the fortified harbor made famous the preceding year when the Australian Ninth Division had withstood a 241-day siege by Rommel. The calculation was that a defensive battle would negate the superior German maneuverability and firepower against scattered and undergunned British units that, even in Crusader, had handed a tactical edge to Rommel. It should also help to eliminate the command-and-control issues that made desert warfare in general and Crusader in particular so challenging. It should also in theory help the British to curtail their high missing/surrender rate by concentrating their soldiers in solid defensible positions. Richie's defensive arrangement consisted of seven brigade-sized defensive "boxes" echeloned in a V from Gazala on the coast 30 miles west of Tobruk, running inland for 45 miles south to Bir Hakeim, situated at the base of the V. The Gazala "box" on the coast 30 miles to the west of Tobruk was to be defended by South Africans, a second position, called Knightsbridge, by the British, the "box" called El Adem was to be occupied by Indian troops, and Tobruk by South Africans and British. This left the extreme southern position at the apex of an inverted triangle at a small Italian desert outpost at Bir Hakeim (Map 8.2) to be occupied by the FFL.

On paper, Richie's two-corps-strong position appeared impregnable. Gaps between the defensive positions were patrolled by 849 tanks, 316 of them new Grant tanks designed to match the speed and firepower of the Pz.Kpfw. IV, and sealed by mine fields. Ritchie also created a mobile force to counterattack any attempt by Rommel to penetrate his position. However, any veteran of the Maginot Line must have been gripped with a portentous sensation of *déjà vu*. Surprisingly, perhaps, two years after the Fall of France, a combination of minefields left uncovered by fire so that they could be cleared at leisure, counterattacking forces massed too far to the north to intervene in a timely manner, poorly trained British troops who had yet to master their new anti-tank guns, château generalship from Auchinleck in Cairo, and the ability of the Germans simply to circumvent the Gazala line to the south would offer the lead-from-the-front Rommel an opportunity to disaggregate Richie's position one "box" at a time.

For soldiers of the British 150th Infantry Brigade at Bir Hakeim, the sight on Valentine's Day 1942 of a motley convoy of ancient cars, rusty lorries, and requisitioned buses whose conductors had collected their ultimate fare at Piccadilly some months, if not years earlier, bouncing south along a stony track lined with burned-out tanks and broken-down lorries toward their outpost must have come as a relief. Susan Travers learned that a *bir* was a stone cistern for collecting rainwater. Rainstorms did periodically lash this desiccated sandstone rise, turning the ground to mud. But any trace of cisterns had long ago been erased by sand-blown

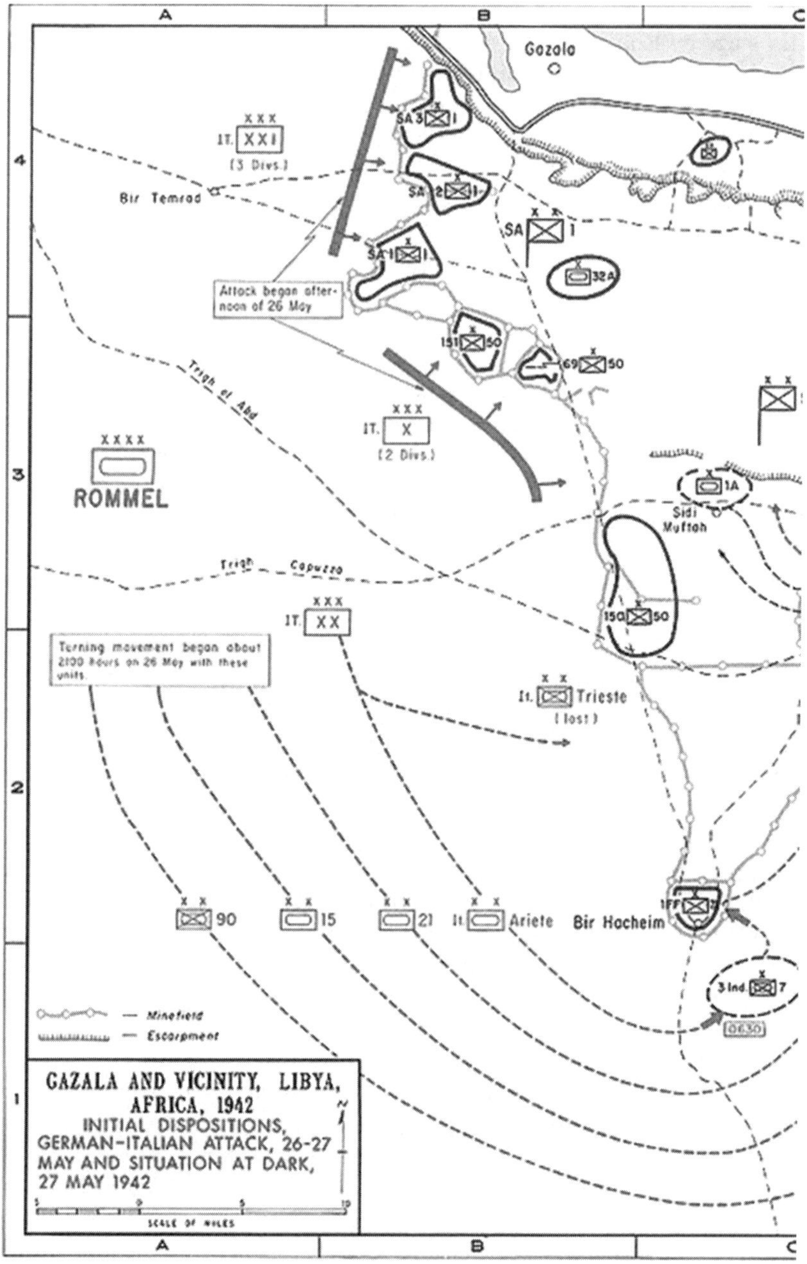

Map 8.2 Map of Bir Hakeim. West Point Atlas.

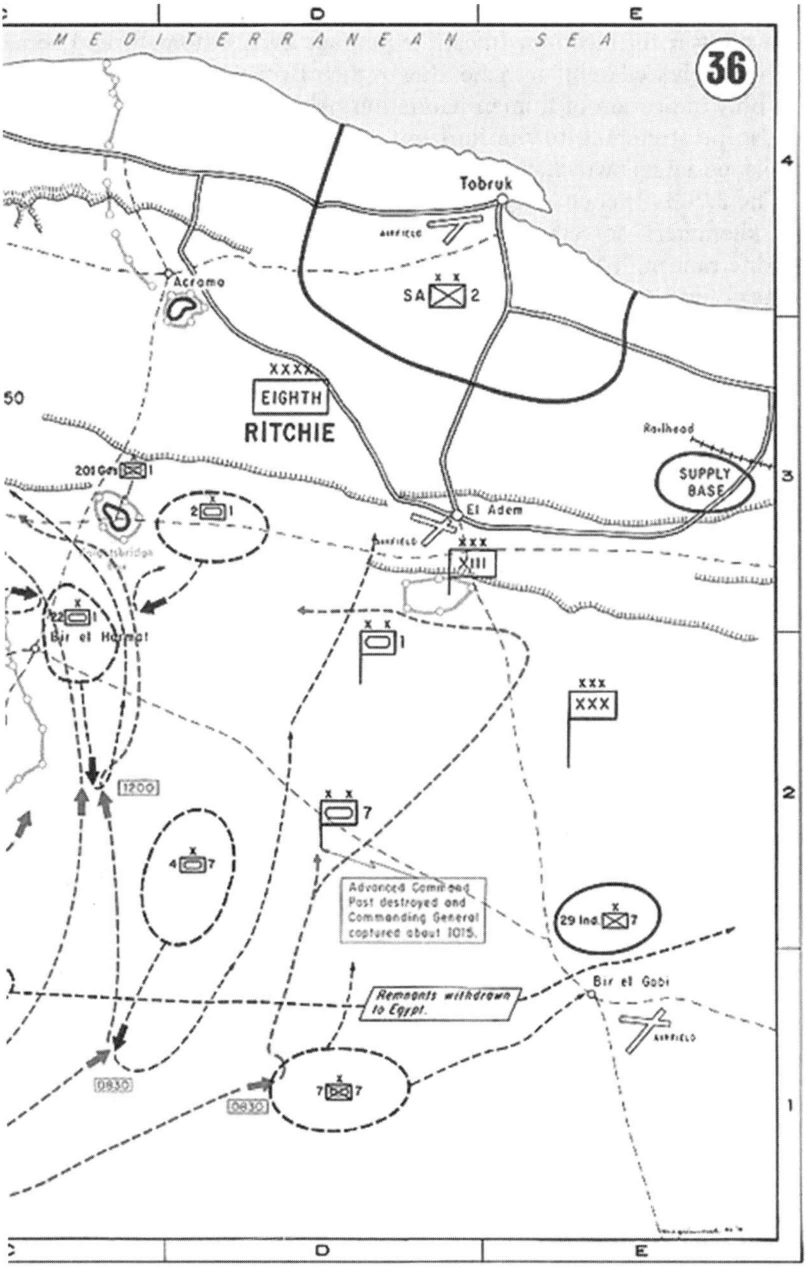
MEDITERRANEAN SEA
36
Tobruk
Acroma
SA 2
EIGHTH
RITCHIE
Railhead
SUPPLY BASE
El Adem
XIII
Bir el Hamat
XXX
Advanced Command Post destroyed and Commanding General captured about 1015.
29 Ind.
Bir el Gobi
Remnants withdrawn to Egypt.
1200
0830

Map 8.2 (Cont.)

gusts, sometimes clocked at 60 miles an hour. The crumbled foundations of a pre-war fortification, Italian or perhaps even Ottoman, and some "remarkably well built" trenches dug by their British predecessors offered the only indication of human habitation. Already, the featureless beige landscape stretching to the horizon, across which spiraled ochre dust devils, posed its own challenges of psychological adjustment.

The 3,703 "French" troops and Susan Travers settled into a polygon 16 kilometers in circumference located 65 kilometers from the Mediterranean. Their new position appeared to have been designed by some desert Vauban – an almost equilateral triangle, 4 kilometers on each face, punctuated by strongpoints, each held by a company armed with fifty-four 75 mm anti-tank guns captured in Syria, sited behind a "swamp of mines." Of necessity, the Free French had gained a reputation as scroungers. They also had no faith in the French 25 mm anti-tank gun or the obsolete British 2-pounder (40 mm), and instead had chosen the 75 mm as their main anti-tank weapon. This gave the FFL 1st Light Division more firepower than a French infantry division of 1940 or their British counterparts at Gazala. While the British had distributed no heavy artillery to Bir Hakeim, the garrison was supplied with twelve Bofors 40 mm anti-aircraft guns, manned by French marines. If need be, these could double as medium-range anti-vehicle guns. In this way, Bir Hakeim was able to to hold out for fifteen days, in the process destroying fifty-two Axis tanks and eleven armored cars.[65]

Inside the defense perimeter, soldiers dug their own slit trenches, covered by canvas or a roof of corrugated metal. "There is something dejecting to the human spirit, mine at least, to see a flock of men streaking across the land into a hole in the ground," Milne recorded.[66] The garrison resembled the clean-up crew from the 1931 Paris Colonial Exposition. Included was a battalion of marines from Tahiti, New Caledonia, and the Marquises; a company of North African tirailleurs who had rallied in Syria and were probably now lamenting a decision taken in haste; two battalions of legionnaires, German and Eastern European Jews and Spanish Republicans prominent among them; "Senegalese" *tirailleurs* from Oubangui-Chari, with their ubiquitous cooking clobber, officered by white *colons* and missionaries; an artillery regiment manned by black soldiers from AEF and Madagascar whose twenty-four 1897-vintage 75 mm guns mercifully had their wooden wheels replaced by tires following the Syria fracas, supplemented by two 25 pounders and seven 47 mm guns; some European settlers from New Caledonia; a company of engineers to lay minefields; a supply unit; and a headquarters company. The British army contributed a six-gun anti-aircraft battery and a liaison detachment.[67] And finally, the Hadfield–Spears "light surgical unit," whose official designation was *hôpital chirurgical mobile (HCM) 3*, with a contingent of French doctors, provided medical support. The unit had been formed courtesy of Spears' wife, the American novelist Mary "May" Borden, and her friend and fellow American Lady Frances Belt Hadfield, wife of British steel tycoon Sir Robert Hadfield. They had seen action in 1940, and had been shipped to Suez in May 1941, where they had been mobilized for the Syria campaign, much to the distress of Madame "Mad Cat" Catroux, who for unknown reasons objected to British nurses taking care of French wounded. HCM 3 had been sent to Tobruk, with a "Forward Theater," that included its Quaker male nurses and English female drivers known as Spearettes, detailed to Bir Hakeim.[68]

The new garrison spent the next weeks deepening minefields, adding additional trenches to protect against air and artillery attacks, gun pits, observations posts, and larger dugouts for command posts, not an easy feat in rock-hard ground. But the effort was effective – the Germans subsequently commented on the strength of the "fortress" and its skillful use of camouflage, as few of the defenses were visible above ground. Following British practice, Jock columns – combined-arms groups of motorized infantry, artillery, and armored vehicles developed by British Colonel Jock Campbell and replicated in the FFL by Larminat – patrolled outside the wire, linked by radio to command posts to detect and harass enemy reconnaissance parties or incoming attacks. Despite the obvious risks, duty with Jock columns offered a popular escape from the hard-scrabble task of chiseling holes into Bir Hakeim's rock-hard sub-soil.[69] The hospital, individual messes, and communications went under canvas. Travers' personal dugout was waist deep and about four feet wide, spacious enough to accommodate a camp bed, a folding chair/table, and a suitcase. But the blistering heat of day gave way to a cold so intense at night that she preferred to sleep in the back seat of her Ford wrapped in a sheepskin jacket. Latrines were dug in the middle of the position. Vehicles were parked in pits surrounded by sandbags. Mess times, announced by bugle blasts, produced little excitement because, if Bir Hakeim were nominally French territory, the cuisine remained emphatically *outre-Manche* – bully beef and rice served in a thin sand sauce, washed down by tea and condensed milk poured into enamel mugs, with dry-tack biscuits for dessert. At least the Indochinese cooks became adept at transforming these unappetizing ingredients into something almost edible, which meant that mealtimes invariably witnessed the fortuitous appearance of senior British officers "on inspection." Otherwise, the FFL settled into the southern apex of the Gazala line like the Eighth Army's orphan legion. Tanker lorries arrived from Tobruk with foul-tasting water that was transferred to individual units' water tanks on wheels – Jean-Mathieu Boris could not decide if the water's bitter taste resulted from the fact that it was desalinated sea water from Tobruk harbor, or because the tanker lorries alternately transported both water and petrol. Barbed wire was rolled out, 50,000 more mines were laid, circular holes dug, into which 75 mm guns were rolled, and positions for forward artillery observers established, linked by telephone wires to Boris' *Poste central de tir* (central fire direction post). As in 1940, he had a backup radio in case the wires were cut by Axis artillery fire. But it was often put out of commission by blowing sand. The occupational hazards of Bir Hakeim included heat, sunburn, which was punished like a self-inflicted wound, and the ubiquitous flies. At least, discipline was relaxed and a true front-line informality reigned.

All of this was commanded by forty-four-year-old Brigadier – the official after-action report refers to him as Colonel – Pierre Koenig from a mobile command post (CP) consisting of a Renault van that had been fitted with faux wagon-lit wood paneling in Aleppo. Sited in the middle of the position with tent flaps stretched like wings on either side, the ungainly CP appeared as if prepped to taxi down an imaginary desert runway for takeoff. Although his family origins were Alsatian, Koenig was a native of Caen in the Calvados. Having enlisted in April 1917 as a nineteen-year-old infantry private, he finished the Great War as a sub-lieutenant with the *médaille militaire*. However, brilliant military careers in the inter-war French army were not forged from battlefield promotions but rather networked through Saint-Cyr and staff college channels. Despite service with the chasseurs alpins and the Foreign Legion, and time spent as part of Catroux's staff in Marrakech, the outbreak of war found Koenig a captain buried in a somnambulant colonial posting. Along the way, he had married Marie Klein, who, according to Travers, was a wealthy divorcee with children. In February 1940, Koenig had volunteered to serve as chief of staff for Lieutenant-colonel Raoul Magrin-Vernerey, who would command the 13ème DBLE at Narvik. This merited promotion to major, and in June 1940 gave him the opportunity, after escaping from Brittany via Jersey, to rally in Great Britain with his commander and 1,000 or so legionnaires to de Gaulle. Koenig had joined the planning staff for "Menace" – the Dakar expedition – and when that miscarried, he played an important part in *la France libre*'s November 1940 takeover of Gabon, a role that merited a lieutenant-colonelcy and the title of military commander of Cameroon. But Koenig barely lingered in AEF before he became, in early 1941, chief of staff to General Paul Legentilhomme, commander of the *1ère Division légère française libre* with the rank of colonel. He continued in that position with Legentilhomme's successor Larminat. In April 1941, Koenig was named to lead his bosses' old command with the rank of brigadier. In this way, through meteoric rises not seen since the wars of the French Revolution and Napoleon, Leclerc and Koenig became the Wunderkinder of *France libre.*[70] "Tall and straight-backed with blue–grey eyes and a moustache, he was more authoritative-looking than handsome," remembered Travers, who had an affair with Koenig lasting several weeks after she had become his driver in Syria. "In his early forties, he was eleven years older than me and his hair at close quarters was greying slightly ... his manner towards me was much more soldierly, even rather stiff and formal on occasions ... The Colonel, I decided, wasn't a man who gave much away." While Travers found Koenig to be sophisticated and well-bred, he was nonetheless remote, and could be sharp, even cruel, at times. Despite the intimacy of their earlier relationship, at Bir Hakeim, Koenig was all business, "at his most militaristic, barking orders and directions," often at her. "He became reserved and moody ..."[71] The British preferred Koenig to the prickly Larminat, while their commander's bluntness and informality appealed to his soldiers, who nicknamed him "*le Vieux Lapin*" (the Old Rabbit).[72]

Rommel initiated the Battle of Gazala on 26 May in the midst of a sandstorm of moderate intensity with the earsplitting, combined-arms pyrotechnics that had come to typify his attacks, ones deliberately designed to disorient and intimidate the enemy. *Luftwaffe* flares and incendiary bombs preceded an attack of five Axis divisions, four of them armored, combining 10,000 vehicles. While the Italians struck at the middle boxes of the British position, the 15th and 21st Panzer Divisions and the 90th Light Division, organized on a 35-mile front, circumvented the flank of the Gazala line south of Bir Hakeim in what Rommel had christened the Great March. Travers remembered the moment when, just before dawn, she heard firing in the distance and noticed the sky light up to the north. Soon about eighty tanks rushed their position, firing indiscriminately, "the squeaking of their tracks adding to the fearful cacophony ..." "Numerous tanks are stopped by artillery and by mines," read the 27 May entry, a reference to an attack by the Ariete Division, which came in two waves from around 09:00, only to be met by mines and anti-tank guns. The few that got through "were violently taken apart." By 10:15, the ground before Bir Hakeim was littered with thirty-two M13 tanks. Groups of legionnaires and engineers fanned out to chase off their crews and render the tanks unsalvageable. "During this time, hundreds of vehicles passed by ceaselessly (south of Bir Hakeim) making an impressive racket." Some of them set off mines as they rolled past. Ninety-one Italians were captured, two of whom died before they could receive medical attention. All seemed surprised by the density of the minefields, which they had not anticipated on the back side of the position. These prisoners were joined later by a dozen other Italians in two lorries who inadvertently drove into Bir Hakeim thinking it had been successfully assaulted in the earlier attack. Patrols rounded up other POWs, including an Italian liaison officer. After the excitement of 27 May, Bir Hakeim lapsed into four days of relative quiet. On 28 May, a supply convoy of fifty vehicles replenished the diminishing stock of 75 mm shells, food, and water. In the evening, a mistaken RAF attack on Bir Hakeim caused Koenig to demand an adjustment of the bomb line. Patrols fanned out to capture lost or isolated Italian vehicles, and supplies and munitions were counted and reorganized, while the endless work of repairing broken telephone wires to forward artillery spotters continued.[73]

While Rommel's troops bypassed Bir Hakeim to the south, the Trieste Division was ordered to break contact between Bir Hakeim and the nearest "box," that of the 150th Brigade Group 13 miles to the north. But the Trieste Division became bogged down in the minefields, and was badly chopped up by counterattacking South African infantry backed by British tanks. Meanwhile, Rommel's main attack, directed at a "box" that the British had christened Knightsbridge, had smashed its way into the center of Richie's disposition, mauling three of the British brigades and briefly capturing the commander of the 7th Armoured Division, who stripped off his badges of rank and, masquerading as a common soldier, managed to slip away. However, when Richie counterattacked with his new US-supplied Grant tanks, with their 75 mm cannons, and 6-pounder anti-tank guns into what the British had nicknamed the "Cauldron" – the Germans called it the *Wurstkessel* (sausage boiler) – Rommel looked on as about a third of his armor was reduced to scrap.

By now, the combination of smoke from burning vehicles, and sand kicked up by explosives and carried by the wind had swathed the battlefield in a thick blue haze, through which careened ambulances, tanker trucks, supply lorries, and armor-recovery vehicles looking for tanks to salvage. Soldiers, with their heads swathed in towels against the blowing sand, struggled to breathe. The surviving British "boxes" were virtually encircled. But Rommel, too, had his problems – his "lead from the front" style meant that no one remained at headquarters to direct the battle, especially after his chief of staff and operations officer were killed. Supply problems continued to hinder his advance. Meanwhile, Afrika Korps commander Ludwig Crüwell had been captured when, in the confusion of battle, the pilot of his Storch observation plane mistook British troops for Italians and landed among them. Rommel had also assumed that the two most southern boxes in the Gazala Line, one of which was Bir Hakeim, would fall easily. The fact that they held out seriously overextended the lines of advance and supply for German forces that had to detour into the desert to bypass Bir Hakeim. Indeed, so confident were the British that Rommel this time had overextended his forces that on 28 May, barely two days into the battle, from Cairo Auchinleck prematurely broadcast victory congratulations to Richie.

While British and Axis troops duked it out in the Cauldron, the garrison at Bir Hakeim became largely spectators as Axis troops rumbled past their position beyond the range of their antiquated 75 mm guns. The kitchens closed, and everyone ate out of tins. But they supplemented their diet by launching raids on the parade of passing Axis convoys, targeting those of the Italians in particular because they carried hams, wines, preserves, and cheese. On 29 May, one patrol captured a German ambulance carrying thirteen wounded, while two other ambulances drove up to the position and surrendered along with their wounded soldiers. Patrols were returning with so many POWs that a barbed wire enclosure was constructed in the middle of the compound to hold them. Eventually, they were put to work building a landing strip. The work to repair broken telephone lines was constant. But by 30 May, there seemed to be a vacuum around the camp, and patrols were encountering only solitary enemy vehicles. From 08:00, Indian troops, some escaped from Axis captivity, others scattered by the battle for the British boxes, began to stumble into Bir Hakeim. Their numbers eventually reached 600, many of whom had not had water for three days. Koenig radioed the British command that these refugees were compromising his position. And if the British did not collect them, he would be forced to expel them back into the desert. As a convoy was assembling on 31 May to evacuate the Indians and 170 Axis POWs, 70 of whom were Germans with their 7 officers, it was attacked by six Junkers 88 light bombers, who managed to wound 42 POWs, 3 "Hindus", and 4 French soldiers. On that day, Amilakvari organized a "mobile column" with his legionnaires, who shot up four tanks and returned with four prisoners. On 1 June, an air attack took out an artillery piece, killing the crew, and destroyed an ambulance and two lorries, part of a series of air attacks that continued throughout the day.[74]

One morning the "box" was swarmed by Pz.Kpfw. IVs and Italian tanks, six of which survived the mines and reached the perimeter, from which legionnaires sprinted, clambering aboard to fire pistols and ram grenades through the gun slits. The POW pen established in the middle of the position was gradually filling up. Travers for one admired the spirit and bravery of the Italian soldiers, noting, however, that they were severely handicapped by poor equipment. At this point, the British command ordered all women out of the front lines, causing Travers and two

Spearettes to be evacuated to Tobruk, from where Travers promptly hitched a ride back to Bir Hakeim on a returning supply convoy.[75]

The battle which the British had mistakenly believed all but won on 28 May gradually began to tilt against them for at least three reasons. First, British commanders remained too passive. While Ritchie did attack Rommel on 30 May, he failed to concentrate his forces, so that the two sides merely traded tanks. For the most part, the British remained locked in their "boxes." Content merely to fend off Axis attacks, they ceded the initiative to Rommel. A second factor was that Rommel's supply problems were gradually sorted out. Finally, there was the arrival of Field Marshal Albert Kesselring, commander-in-chief South and nominally Rommel's superior, who nonetheless agreed to substitute for the captured Crüwell in an attempt better to organize Rommel's hitherto energetic but disjointed effort. By 1 June, the Got al Ualeb box held by the 150th Brigade to the north of Bir Hakeim had fallen, after a tenacious defense, to an all-azimuth attack backed by Stukas.

By 2 June, Bir Hakeim had become a *France libre* atoll awash in an Axis sea. For the Germans, the fall of Bir Hakeim would accomplish several things: destabilize the Gazala Line by removing its southern cornerstone, open up a pocket in the south, and secure the German supply line so that Rommel might realize his goal of attacking the Gazala Line from the rear. Rommel's investment of Bir Hakeim proceeded in three phases. First, 2–7 June, the enemy surrounded the position, and attempted probing attacks behind heavy artillery barrages. Then, 7–10 June, the bombardments became increasingly heavy and were often accompanied by combined infantry–armor attacks. Finally, Koenig ordered a breakout on the night of 10–11 June.

Daybreak on 2 June revealed considerable movement of enemy armored convoys as the 90th Light and Trieste Divisions had moved through the minefield to encircle Bir Hakeim from the east. At 10:00 on 2 June, a car flying a white flag brought two Italian lieutenants to the edge of the defenses. They were blindfolded and led into Bir Hakeim to deliver a proposal of unconditional surrender that allegedly came straight from Rommel himself. Koenig sent his compliments to their general but declined their offer. "*Grandi soldati*," the envoys commented as they saluted and departed. This was the prelude to a barrage of German 105 mm and 88 mm guns which Koenig's paltry 75 mm guns were powerless to answer. At noon, as a sandstorm raged, Rommel radioed in a surrender demand, which Koenig again rejected. The German commander followed up with an ill-coordinated attack by the 90th Light and Trieste Divisions which snagged on barbed wire, minefields, and fire from the 75 mm guns aimed at approaching tanks and infantry. The next day –

3 June – was when, according to the British official history, the *Luftwaffe* attack on Bir Hakeim began "in earnest." It followed a similar demand to surrender, this time conveyed directly from Rommel via two British officer POWs, which Koenig again rejected. The RAF attempted to defend the base from incessant and, for Travers, unnerving Stuka attacks that pockmarked the interior of Bir Hakeim and destroyed the hospital. Koenig dispatched raiding parties that netted fuel, water, supplies, vehicles, and POWs. At night, infantry patrols covered parties of sappers dispatched to repair and strengthen the minefields, of particular concern to Koenig as he lacked sufficient barbed wire to deter approaching infantry. Nevertheless, he calculated that he had enough ammunition and supplies to hold out for at least a week.

For the next two days, firing from 155 mm and 210 mm guns stopped only at night, and resumed at 6 a.m., unless sandstorms limited visibility. From dawn to dusk everyone except a few souls sent to repair telephone lines crouched in their holes, as a quantity of metal shards worthy of a Great War barrage exploded and ricocheted around the camp, and the glacis was swept with heavy machinegun fire, while black smoke from burning vehicles joined the plumes of dust kicked up by exploding shells to envelop the camp in a suffocating opaque haze. An attack on 6 June by elements of the Afrika Korps across open ground did not even reach the minefield before it was halted. French gunners fired 40,000 75 mm and 81 mm rounds at groups of infiltrating infantry, while overhead the RAF lost 70 fighter planes while trying to provide air cover for the base. On 6 June, Richie contemplated abandoning Bir Hakeim, but was dissuaded by Auchinleck in Cairo. Nevertheless, Koenig ordered all officers to make sure that their vehicles were in good repair. Outside the camp, British armored car units raided the German rear, disrupting the enemy convoys, and forcing passages for increasingly reduced resupply convoys into Bir Hakeim, which departed with the wounded. Nevertheless, the consumption of artillery rounds by the French was so great that Koenig ordered a slowdown in the firing to conserve shells. A German officer bearing a summons to surrender was given five minutes to depart by Koenig.[76]

The 7 June proved to be a relatively quiet day for the garrison – a light drizzle of artillery shells, a tank assault at 08:40 that was repulsed, and a single bombing run. However, resolved to end resistance at Bir Hakeim once and for all, on 8 June, Rommel personally led an attack on the vulnerable north side of the redoubt. Following an artillery duel during which the undergunned French were at a decided disadvantage, the *Luftwaffe* unleashed twenty bombers at the north side of the camp. No sooner had the sky cleared than a ferocious artillery barrage erupted: "The entire position seemed to be boiling around us, sand was projected into the air and it was a miracle that we survived," remembered Boris. One German battalion actually managed briefly to penetrate the perimeter before being driven back. But soldiers had to keep a low profile to avoid sniper fire. And the latest resupply convoys had delivered armor-piercing shells, useless against infantry attack. At 13:00, sixty Junkers overflew the camp, the prelude to an assault of tanks followed by infantry. By the end of the day, many of the French vehicles had been destroyed, supplies, especially water and medicines, were running low, and the Axis siege lines had tightened. The incessant bombardment had caused few casualties, but its effects were psychologically draining.[77]

The general feeling in the garrison, and in the German camp, was that, despite RAF support and one armored counterattack, the British command was more interesting in protecting its own supply lines than rescuing its French allies. But the British official history notes that on 8 June, the RAF flew 478 sorties over Bir Hakeim, the highest total for any single day in the desert war so far, while Hurricanes and Bostons dropped supplies to the garrison. Alas, air-dropped supplies were too few to keep the garrison fighting. The British, their hands full in the Cauldron, launched a weak diversionary attack that predictably fizzled. They had also directed four supply convoys through a gauntlet of minefields and Axis troops to the garrison, the last on 7 June. British units up to Eighth Army were also broadcasting messages of encouragement and praise. At the end of the day on 8 June, Ritchie issued a warning order to make preparations to withdraw on 10 June. It could not come too soon. The men, who had been reduced to one-quarter liter of water per day, saw their allocation raised to one and a half liters of water per man per day. Fifty-three soldiers lay wounded.[78] By the end of the day on 9 June, the French had virtually exhausted their ammunition and water. Only two of Boris' six 75 mm guns were still operational, and he was down to eight shells. But Kesselring was also growing impatient that the stubborn defense at Bir Hakeim had upset the German timetable. On 9 June, Rommel ordered up another unit of the Afrika Korps, and promised to lead the 10 June assault in person – unleashed behind three successive waves of bombers that dropped 131 tons of bombs, while artillery pounded the fortress. "At least 100 Stukas, accompanied by more than 100 fighters," de Sairaigné recorded. "The cloud of dust and smoke that the explosions project skyward is incredible."[79]

Koenig had preferred to sortie on the night of 9–10 June, but the British 7th Armoured Division could not muster the sixty lorries and thirty ambulances he had requested at the agreed rendezvous point on that night. At 18:00 on 9 June Koenig had called an officers' meeting to announce a breakout toward the west. A silent exit on foot was rejected because it would mean abandoning vehicles, heavy arms, and above all the seventy-seven wounded. Bir Hakeim was thoroughly cratered by shells. From 21:15 on 10 June, soldiers began quietly to load those trucks that were still operational. Travers prepared her automobile, in which she had little confidence, checking the oil and petrol, and cleaning the sand out of the carburetor. The night of 10–11 June was cold and moonless as the men assembled silently. Boris gathered his artillerymen from their slit trenches and dugouts, attached his two working 75 mm guns to a tractor, and took his place in a Bren carrier with a machinegun mounted on the front. Sappers cleared a 200-meter-wide path through minefields to the west of the perimeter. The exit, scheduled for 22:30, only got off at 00:15 on 11 June. Bren carriers, trucks, five ambulances carrying the most seriously wounded, and legionnaires on foot organized into two columns squeezed through the very narrow breach in the minefield behind the command car driven by Travers. Koenig stood in the rear seat, his head protruding through the roof hatch, and signaled directions to Travers with taps on the metal. They were followed by a convoy of vehicles to transport the wounded and tow the heavy equipment. Special lamps whose soft beams pointed down offered some light. A Bren carrier strayed off the path and set off a mine. This and the noise of the vehicles alerted the Germans, whose positions were closer than had been realized. "A flare went up," remembered Boris. "Nothing serious. Then there was a short burst of machinegun fire. We were still OK. But suddenly, firing broke out all around, a hundred flares shot skyward, tracer bullets filled the night sky, which it was difficult not to find beautiful." Crammed into the narrow passage and without radios to coordinate action, officers struggled to deploy their soldiers. Boris' battery commander took a sack of grenades out of the Bren carrier and set out to silence a nearby machinegun nest. He was never seen again. A spray of fire killed the machinegunner on the Bren carrier, and the two men standing next to him. Boris pulled a man covered with blood into his Bren carrier, only to discover that it was Colonel Masson, Koenig's deputy commander. They passed a Hadfield–Spears ambulance engulfed in flames. Trucks disabled by gunfire stalled in the middle of the escape corridor, making it impassable. Everyone stopped, not knowing what to do. Amilakvari's car hit a mine. But, unscathed, he first led a charge against the German guns, and then jumped into the car with Travers and Koenig. Travers drove around the stalled vehicles without headlights, bumping across the desert at 40 miles per hour as bullets slammed into the car. Other vehicles followed her lead. Groups of ten or fifteen vehicles dodged and swerved to find their own way past the strings of German machinegun nests, whose bullets punctured tires, holed radiators, and killed drivers. Only by sheer good fortune did Travers and her passengers cross the minefield and the German defense cordon unscathed. With firefights erupting all around them, she was totally disoriented, "and none of us seemed to have any idea which way we were going." Amilakvari shone a flashlight on his pocket compass and shouted directions. They were soon alone, but inadvertently drove into a laager of Panzers. Travers gunned the motor to escape, helped on her way by a pop of gunfire.

When dawn broke, the trio was alone in the desert silence. Having dissolved into knots of men and vehicles that sought their individual salvation, the garrison had dispersed or died in place. Unable initially to find the rendezvous point, Koenig feared that they had been the only escapees. Overwhelmed by a sense of shame, he talked of surrendering to the Germans, which angered both Amilakvari and Travers. In the late morning, they located the assembly point at Gasr-el-Arid, occupied by the British 17th Motorized Brigade, but empty of Bir Hakeim refugees. Travers took the car to the mechanic, who counted eleven bullet holes and expressed disbelief that it was still running. Gradually, however, other survivors began to filter in. "The English watched our Bren carrier arrive filled with bearded men, in torn, often bloody uniforms, who had only one word on their lips, 'water,'" Boris recorded. Travers remembered a joyous scene: "Everyone was laughing and crying and shouting all at once," excitedly exchanging stories about escaping in the confusion. By 19:00, fully 2,500 men had assembled (Figure 8.3). In the hours and days that followed, isolated vehicles found their way to the site, and other escapees were brought in by British patrols and search parties.[80]

The 90th Light Division occupied an abandoned Bir Hakeim at 06:45 on the morning of 11 June. That evening, CIGS Alan Brooke sent a messenger to de Gaulle in London informing him that Koenig and most of the Bir Hakeim garrison had reached Bir el Gubi and were out of reach of the enemy. "I thanked the messenger, saw him out, and closed the door," de Gaulle remembered. "I am alone. Oh! My heart beat with emotion, sobs of pride, tears of joy!" On 12 June, de Gaulle sent a message via General de Larminat: "General Koenig, know and tell your troops that the eyes of all of France are upon you and that you are its pride." The Free French stand at Bir Hakeim made global headlines, and gave Churchill a reason to congratulate de Gaulle, who was for once in excellent spirits. Both Boris and Travers were awarded the *croix de guerre*, while Travers was cited in corps orders.[81]

Before the breakout, French losses at Bir Hakeim had been a relatively light five officers and eighty-four soldiers killed, and seventy-seven

Figure 8.3 Soldiers of the 1ère DFL who escaped Bir Hakeim.

wounded. After-action reports established that a further 9 officers and 32 men were confirmed killed in the breakout, while another 9 officers and 116 men were wounded. Seven officers and 659 men were missing. A further 12 officers and 136 men had been taken prisoner.[82] Koenig had managed to lead 2,600 of a garrison of 3,700 men to safety, or around 70 percent of the garrison, but was able to salvage only 30 percent of their heavy weapons. The primary impediment had been the narrowness of the passage cleared through the minefield. When the Germans had opened fire, it had caused confusion and a huge traffic jam that was slow to untangle. However, given the need for surprise, which meant that the sappers could only begin mine clearing after nightfall, there had not been enough time to create a larger breach.[83] German Lieutenant Kämpf was nonetheless aghast at the multiracial and multinational composition of the 25 officers and 820 men captured at Bir Hakeim: "Red Spaniards, Swiss, Czechs, Poles, and Negroes – riff-raff of the worst kind," he reported, only 10 percent of whom were French. This meant that 22 percent of the garrison was captured, with another roughly 8–10 percent killed. These figures are approximate, but amount to a roughly 71 percent captured to KIA ratio, lower than the British ratio of 85 percent of missing/POWs to casualties in the period from 27 May to 4 August.[84] Italian foreign minister and Mussolini's son-in-law Galeazzo Ciano attributed the stout defense of Bir Hakeim to the fact that its garrison was made up of political refugees who feared execution if captured. Nor was this an idle reflection. On 12 June, Berlin radio announced that those captured at Bir Hakeim would be executed because they were not part of a "regular army." De Gaulle went on the BBC to threaten retaliation. Incensed that such a rabble could defy the *Wehrmacht* for almost two weeks, Hitler ordered that any German political refugees – that is, Jews – captured at Bir Hakeim were to be executed, a directive that Rommel refused to carry out.[85]

Following the "Oath of Kufra," Bir Hakeim rapidly transformed into the second great myth of *la France libre*. The fact that Bir Hakeim was a small incident in an otherwise catastrophic British defeat failed to deter the *Daily Mail*, whose account of the battle appeared under the headline: "VERDUN." The FFL's stalwart performance at Bir Hakeim stood out in a battle that showcased the "nadir of British generalship during the desert campaign,"[86] and probably a nadir of British morale, an unraveling that terminated in the fall of Tobruk on 21 June, with the capture of 31,000 POWs as well as immense stocks of matériel and precious petrol that allowed the otherwise resource-starved Afrika Korps to continue its offensive into Egypt. The triumph won Erwin Rommel a promotion to Field Marshal, a reward that the FFL believed justly deserved: "Rommel won the battle of attrition, thanks to the quality and number of his anti-tank defenses and his economy of force tactics with his tanks, that left him with superior tank resources for the final phase," declared the French after-action report.[87] One immediate consequence of Bir Hakeim was that French stock in the Eighth Army surged, as it completely changed the perspective of officers who had served in France in 1940.[88] Churchill, Alan Brooke, and Auchinleck credited Koenig's stand for buying time for the British to retreat into Egypt, a narrative spun by a British press eager to counterpoise the dual military calamities of Singapore and Tobruk. But whatever the tactical benefits of Bir Hakeim in salvaging in small measure the British army's otherwise battered reputation, the battle's symbolic importance was paramount. For once, the French were not fighting among themselves, but had turned their weapons against the Axis, led by Rommel no less. Jean Marin, Jean Oberlé, and Maurice Schumann broadcast stirring accounts of the "*rendezvous d'honneur* " in the desert for the BBC's French service, which had steadily been accorded more airtime, in the process making Koenig a household name. Abroad, Bir Hakeim rekindled embers of pride among Francophiles embarrassed and dispirited by the ignominious 1940 collapse. Congratulations poured in from foreign governments. In the Commons on 12 June, Churchill praised the FFL, most probably to deflect criticism of his wartime leadership in the shadow of yet another British battlefield collapse. Desperate for military victories of any sort to boost the legitimacy of what, on 13 July 1942, he had rechristened *la France combattante* (Fighting France), on the second anniversary of "the call of 18 June," de Gaulle praised the defenders of the desert outpost for casting "a ray of reborn glory" on a resurrecting France. The Albert Hall throbbed as the capacity crowd replied to his emotional tribute with fervently sung stanzas of the Marseillaise. Bir Hakeim offered a direct rebuke, first to the British who had abandoned the outpost, an accusation that German radio was happy to repeat; and then to Vichy, which had surrendered Alsace-Moselle, and that pretended to virilize French youth through the making of charcoal, and which would soon dispatch them to forced labor in Germany. Meanwhile, its feckless Armistice Army frittered away time in sports competitions and pretended to engage in "resisting" by secreting weapons it would subsequently surrender to the Axis. Finally, Bir Hakeim provided inspiration for a growing "*résistance-organisation*," which proliferated groups who adopted the name Bir Hakeim.[89]

Bir Hakeim also left the British gobsmacked, surprised that men who "symbolized indiscipline and the disdain of hierarchy" proved capable of such a stout defense.[90] Bir Hakeim's success was put down to the solid organization of the position, an active artillery based on an excellent defensive fire plan, the "courage, obstinacy, and imagination" of the troops, and Koenig's leadership. In the process, the British concluded that Bir Hakeim had been a thorn in the side of Rommel's communications, had attrited Axis forces, and had slowed and disjointed Rommel's offensive.[91] While the Free French always seemed raring to fight, their mongrel recruitment and slack discipline appeared to offer a permanent conspiracy against military order and hierarchy. Their air of entitlement, even insolence, turned notions of hierarchy, rank, discipline, and obedience on their head. They were an armed protest movement, not a classic military force. The defense of Bir Hakeim seemed to redefine the notion of obedience in ways foreign to the British army, or at Vichy for that matter. What the collaborationist newspaper *Je suis partout* denounced as "a gaggle of young thugs, unprincipled Jews, and mercenaries lacking pay and promotion" had scored an improbable moral victory.[92]

El Himeimat

Bir Hakeim would prove the Everest of *la France combattante*'s military reputation. The defense of the FFL "box" at Gazala had certainly offered a courageous and even skillful defensive stand by an ill-equipped contingent that contained few professional soldiers, against an Axis force whose commander and reputation stood at their apogee in the summer of 1942. Its aftermath, however, offered a demonstration of the frailty of de Gaulle's strategy of investing the aspirations and reputation of his movement, and his hopes of rescuing France from abroad, in the combat performance of a pickup force of imperial levies and foreign refugees operating in the ranks of a so-far bumbling and amateurishly led British army. Once GHQ identified a competent commander who forced the British army to return to the basics of soldiering; once attrition and the demands of the Eastern Front blunted the virtuosity of the Afrika Korps and the *Luftwaffe*, and forced Rommel into a desperate dance to fend off inevitable defeat; once the enormous manpower and material resources of the United States and the USSR kicked in, then the FFL's diminutive contribution to a vast Allied mobilization would fail to match even that of the once-despised Polish exile army, and position it only a notch or two above that of the Czechs.[93] In this way, de Gaulle's pretense that France remained a great power, expressed through frequently ill-mannered and ungracious words and acts, increasingly came to be viewed by Allied leaders as pretentions, lacking in gratitude, and a diversion from the primary goal of winning the war.

That *la France libre* failed to figure prominently in Allied strategic calculations was driven home in May 1942 with the British seizure of Madagascar. This was a knock-on effect of Vichy's invitation to the Germans to utilize Syria in 1941, which was to have considerable repercussions. While Roosevelt in particular still hoped to entice some French colonial officials to defect to the Allied camp with their territories, it was clear since Syria that Vichy "neutrality" was tottering toward the Axis, especially once Pierre Laval returned to the Vichy premiership in April 1942. Operations were envisioned by the Allies that would preempt Axis penetration of Vichy territories. Operation Torch – the 8 November 1942 invasion of AFN – would feature most prominently among them.[94] On 5 May 1942, a British force began the seizure of Madagascar *sans la France libre*, an operation triggered by information that Laval planned to allow the Japanese access to the island, similar to Vichy collaboration with the Japanese in Indochina.[95] An armistice signed on 6 November allowed the island to remain in French hands. Although sovereignty was surrendered to *la France combattante* in January 1943, de Gaulle saw Madagascar as a trial balloon by his British ally to try to run the island with a Vichy administration, foreshadowing Allied policy in AFN in the wake of Torch.[96]

The FFL now numbered two brigades (BFL). The 1[re] BFL had left most of its equipment and about a quarter of its strength at Bir Hakeim.

The 2^{e} BFL remained largely a phantom organization. As a result, the French had missed out on the first Battle of El Alamein, conducted by Auchinleck, that had halted Rommel's advance toward Alexandria and the Nile Delta. However, this victory did not rescue the Middle East Commander, who was replaced by Harold Alexander as C-in-C Middle East, while Bernard Montgomery assumed command of the Eighth Army. In the October Battle of El Alamein, Koenig's 1re BFL was attached to the 7th Armoured Division under General John Harding, which occupied the extreme southern end of the El Alamein line. Koenig was assigned a diversionary attack against El Himeimat, a fortified ridge rising 1,300 feet over the Quattara Depression that anchored the southern extremity of Rommel's defensive line. El Himeimat offered a test both for Koenig's BFL and for the Eighth Army. As solid as the FFL had proven in the defensive posture of Bir Hakeim, questions remained over the ability to coordinate a complex attack as part of an offensive operation.

A reconnaissance told Koenig that El Himeimat would prove a challenging objective. An approach march of 15 kilometers across a flat plain of soft sand could not hope to surprise the defenders, the 5th Parachute Battalion of the Folgore Division armed with mortars and heavy machineguns, and ensconced on the steep hillside behind two belts of mines. An assault on the butte by foot soldiers would require lashings of artillery. But as Montgomery's plan for the battle required that Rommel be convinced that the main British attack was coming on the southern end of the line, Koenig had no choice but to put on a convincing show.[97]

Koenig divided his brigade into four groups. Even the approach march, which set out at 19:15 on the evening of 23 October under a rising moon, accompanied by its British artillery observer, had hit difficulties, when many of its vehicles became stuck in sand and had to be towed out by British tanks. By midnight, as they cleared the minefield, they could hear artillery and see the pyrotechnics to the north. El Himeimat loomed ahead, illuminated by moonlight. Axis artillery opened up, causing several casualties. More importantly, radio contact between the two battalions was lost. The attack was launched at 03:50, the goal being to occupy the ridge line before daylight. Artillery explosions enveloped the Italian position. But the two-battalion FFL assault, advancing through a smoke screen, failed to follow the path cleared for them through the minefield. Instead, the French fanned out, became bogged down in sand, and set off mines as they came under heavy artillery fire. The infantry attack was poorly coordinated with its artillery support, a situation not helped by faulty radio communications. An Italian counterattack, led by eight captured Stuart M3 tanks, armed with 37 mm guns, revealed that either the French had failed to bring their anti-tank guns forward, or that their barrels were stripped. So, the artillery could not fire until the infantry retreated out of the field of fire. While the 1st Battalion had reached the objective by 08:00, the 2nd Battalion had failed to advance. At 09:25, Amilakvari called off the attack. Half an hour later, he was mortally wounded by a shell fragment to the head. By 14:00, the 2nd Battalion was back at the start line of the 1st Battalion. The *Dictionnaire de la France libre* concedes "complete confusion" but speaks of "heavy losses" in a "true Calvary." In fact, the two battalions with a nominal strength of 1,600 men combined counted only 23 killed and 100 wounded.

The next day, Koenig gave the officers a pep talk, telling them they had to work harder. A report written by Larminat tried to lay out the mitigating circumstances: El Himeimat had been heavily defended; the approach march was 15 kilometers through the sand; the Italian defenders were well dug in, backed by tanks and artillery, and so on. While Larminat insisted that the BFL had been given an "impossible mission" and had not been adequately supported by the 7th Armoured Division, who had run into their own problems to the north, the botched FFL attack on El Himeimat had left Monty unimpressed. French inadequacies included a failure to insure adequate liaison between the infantry and artillery support. Nor had the anti-tank guns accompanied the infantry attack. The newly crowned Hero of El Alamein and Rommel's conqueror concluded that the FFL was all puff and no fight. Along with an absence of soldierly skills, Monty blamed the failure at El Himeimat on a loss of nerve. The FFL could not participate in the pursuit of Rommel's forces in the wake of El Alamein in any case due to the lack of motorized transport. He relieved the Free French Brigade and consigned it to guarding airfields and recuperating abandoned equipment for the remainder of the North African campaign.[98]

Travers noted that, coming on the heels of Bir Hakeim, the failure at El Himeimat "was a bitter pill to swallow," both for *la France combattante* and for her personally. Travers had rightly been decorated for driving her *ménage à trois* to safety out of the desert at Bir Hakeim. But now, one of her lovers, Dimitri Amilakvari, lay dead. Her affair with Koenig had become public knowledge in Beirut to the point that even Italian radio sniggered about it in propaganda broadcasts. Never one to let a salacious scandal go to waste, la Reine Margot had alerted Koenig's wife in Marrakech about her husband's scandalous behavior, and suggested that she get to Cairo ASAP. Travers was sent "on leave" to Port Said and informed that *la France combattante* no longer required her services. To keep a close eye on her husband, Madame Koeing checked into

Shepard's Hotel, the favorite British watering hole in Cairo, described by Caleb Milne as "all red plush and very wide corridors. Outside a woman's orchestra plays waltzes, everyone is gay or weary, the four bars in the hotel are crowded and the clerks are busy being rude to the overflow." Travers became a temporary Spearette, until April 1943, when she rejoined the FFL in Tunisia, and picked up where she left off with Koenig.[99]

Conclusion

As 1942 inched toward closure, *la France combattante*'s prospects certainly appeared brighter than they had a year and a half earlier. The Soviet Union and the United States had joined the conflict, which merely confirmed de Gaulle's strategic assessment of 1940 that Vichy's bet on an Axis victory in a world war had been folly, as well as inimical to French interests. Resistance in France was growing. Jean Moulin had been dispatched to organize and harness it to *la France combattante*'s political agenda, and to define its missions. While de Gaulle's movement remained small, the FFL had demonstrated fighting resolve at Bir Hakeim, a small but symbolic step toward wiping away the stain of 1940. Vichy's deepening collaboration with Hitler helped to put *la France combattante* on firmer political footing, as de Gaulle had waylaid conspiracies against his leadership, imposed his personality on the movement, and gained a mastery of international politics. Although Churchill on occasion expressed deep irritation with the man, Foreign Minister Anthony Eden, for one, remained convinced that de Gaulle was France's only viable representative. Nevertheless, as de Gaulle realized, the Americans in particular posed a more immediate threat to the achievement of his goal of reasserting French grandeur and global influence than did either the Germans or Vichy. It would require all of de Gaulle's determination and political savvy to keep *la France combattante* from being relegated to one of the Second World War's obscure footnotes in the wake of Operation Torch – the November 1942 Anglo-American invasion of AFN.

9 France's North African Hinterland

In 1940, the prospect of fighting on from French North Africa (AFN), "the support base of the homeland," would have required a leap of imagination and a determination that most French politicians of the era lacked. North Africa was viewed as the Hexagon's strategic hinterland, a reservoir of soldiers whose fissiparous populations required vigilance and judicious management, at best suited to play a rear echelon role.[1] But this view of AFN had evolved gradually in the course of the nineteenth century. Under French rule, AFN would evolve into a complex overlay of tribes, cultures, and religions, where an exaggerated patriotism among settlers of French origin mixed with sub-national loyalties, virulent antisemitism, racism, the political disenfranchisement of Muslims, and, among much of the European settler population, ardent *Maréchalisme* motivated in great part by their insecure sense of "*francité* " (Frenchness).[2] This complicated the battle for post-Torch political supremacy fought out in AFN between the Gaullists and the American-sponsored followers of General Henri Giraud. While an Allied-liberated AFN might just be capable of organizing a martial races imitation of a *levée en masse*, an *union sacrée* lay beyond its capacities.[3] For all of these reasons, the Allies would discover that AFN was home to three umbrella populations, each splintered into micro-identities based on origins, region, and religion, which presented a significant challenge of political management, strategic direction, and military organization.

"An Unstable Equilibrium"

In 1940, settlers of European extraction in AFN numbered roughly one million people precariously afloat in an Arabo-Berber sea fifteen times their number. Tunisia had been absorbed by France as a protectorate in 1881, and Morocco followed suit from 1912. Although each was nominally ruled respectively by the Bey of Tunis and Sultan of Morocco, in effect both were steered by a Paris-appointed resident general backed by a panoply of French colonial officials and soldiers under Quai d'Orsay oversight.[4] Algeria had an alternative history, and consequently existed under another, although equally exceptional, statute. In 1848, the short-lived Second Republic ended Algeria's status as a colony and declared it an integral part of metropolitan France, at a stroke importing into French politics a panoply of political issues, including the citizenship status of those inhabitants of Algeria whose antecedents could not be traced directly back to the French mainland. Religious diversity joined cultural incompatibility and dissimilar levels and patterns of economic development and opportunity, not only within Algeria, but also between the two shores of the Mediterranean, to complicate the integration of Algeria into a coherent French national project. Unlike the protectorates of Tunisia and Morocco, Algeria was considered what Benjamin Stora labels as a "false model" of the French Republic, where life "was always intensely political, even more than in the South of France, and it was dominated by personal considerations and organized in clienteles."[5] The 1870 Crémieux Decree had naturalized Algerian Jews. An 1889 law hailed as "the birth of the European peoples of Algeria" automatically bestowed French nationality upon any person of European origin born in Algeria. At a stroke, the children of Algeria's substantial communities of Italian, Spanish, and Maltese immigrants, collectively known as "néos," became French. Muslim Arabs and Kabyles were denied citizenship and forced to live under an *indigénat* legal code, although a handful of Muslim *évolués* – that is, men of property and education – might have influence and standing within local communities. This created hybrid, multiple, and constantly churning Algerian identities, shaped by intense competition on the political and economic levels for "status" among the various communities.[6] Unlike metropolitan France, laws passed in 1898 and 1900 gave Algeria its own civil administration, legislative assembly, a financial delegation with the power to veto parliamentary legislation for Algeria, and a special budget.

The settler population of AFN also offered a combustible alloy of tribes and ethnicities that defied a binary identity of either "European" or "Muslim." Commonly referred to as "*pieds noirs*" – literally "black feet," an unflattering nickname whose provenance is disputed – settlers of European origin numbered 936,531, or 11.4 percent of the population of Algeria in 1940, including Algerian Jews who had been naturalized in 1870.[7] In 1940, the more common term used to describe the Europeans of Algeria was "Algerians," "North Africans," or "*français d'Algérie*" to distinguish them from Muslims – called "*indigènes*" or natives – but above all from "*les français de France.*" But the term "Algerian" was ambiguous. When Richard Bennaïm reported for sick call during his military service in the late 1930s, "the doctor asked my name and even before being concerned about my ailment, he said curtly: 'Where do you come from ... Algeria? Ah! You're an Algerian ... [by which he meant Jew] ... OK, consider yourself seen and treated.'"[8]

Ninety percent of "*français d'Algérie*" were town dwellers holding modest civil service posts or mercantile jobs. While a few ascended into the liberal professions and the "*gros colons*" – "the lords of the vines and wheat" – owned extensive land holdings and mining interests, the revenue of 72 percent of settlers in Algeria fell below the French average. This inferior economic status persisted even given the "colonial fourth" salary boost paid to non-Muslim teachers and other civil servants in Algeria.[9] Nevertheless, "*les français d'Algérie*" hardly formed a homogeneous block. "Status anxiety" and inter-communal friction played out particularly on the municipal level. French was the official, rather than the common, language of Oran and the Oranie of western Algeria, which was Spanish.[10] In 1936, 65 percent of Oran's 206,000 Europeans were Spanish, 41 percent of them naturalized. Spaniards imposed their own culture on Oran, which included bullfights, paella, the evening paseo, and religious processions. Oran in the 1930s was a hotbed of pro-Franco phalangists, and from 1941 right-wing political organizations and militias like the SOL, all nourished by AFN's virulent antisemitism.[11] Local hostility to "liberation" post-November 1942 caused GIs to refer to Oran as well as other towns in the Oranais as "little Berlins."[12] On the other side of the political ledger, Oran hosted numerous Masonic lodges, while the left-leading *Conféderation générale du travail* (CGT) in Oran counted 25,000 members, almost all Europeans. Oran had sent a significant contingent to fight with the International Brigades during the Spanish Civil War (1936–1939), and from the spring of 1939, ships from Spain began to disgorge thousands of refugees from that war, principally in Oran, most of whom were settled into internment camps in the interior.[13] Oran also hosted a large Jewish population, almost universally local bulwarks of Léon Blum's Popular Front. A popular saying held that in Oran one did business in French, swore in Arabic, joked in Spanish, and prayed in Hebrew.

If Spanish dominated the Oranais, not surprisingly, perhaps, the eastern Maghreb hosted a significant population of Italians and Maltese. In 1938, 2,700,000 people lived in Tunisia. Of 241,000 Europeans, 135,000 lived in and around Tunis. At 94,289, a largely rural population of Italians, engaged in producing mainly wine and olives, numbered almost as many as the 108,068 mainly urban French. While French and Arabic were the official languages of the Regency, Italian remained a common language, not only in Tunisia, but also in the Constantinois of eastern Algeria, where only 5 percent of the population were "*français d'Algérie*."[14] In 1926, Algiers counted 264,232 inhabitants, 60 percent of whom were "*français d'Algérie*," as well as two air bases, which would make it a prime target of the Allied invasion in November 1942.[15]

A further 126,563 "stateless persons" – mainly Spanish Republicans, East European Jews, and fugitives from Alsace-Moselle – had also flooded into AFN from 1939.

Historically, the deep divisions among Europeans in North Africa had been subsumed in a common "*pied-noir* " outlook and mindset, based on a feeling of being a dominant but insecure minority nested in a disenfranchised, sullen, volatile, and far more numerous Muslim majority.[16] Army and empire formed the twin pillars of AFN's stability, both of which had been called into question by the 1940 defeat, and subsequently by the Anglo-American invasion of November 1942. As a trans-Mediterranean frontier population, *les français d'Algérie* nurtured a sense of class and cultural inferiority vis-à-vis the mainland, of wounded self-pity and resentment that their patriotism and sacrifice went underappreciated in France. And this bitterness had a solid foundation – of 125,000 *français d'Algérie* mobilized in 1914, 22,000 had died in action, or almost one in five. The situation in the wake of 1940 simply reinforced the *pied noir* conviction that Algeria's sacrifice went unacknowledged and undervalued by the mainland: AFN dispatched twelve divisions to France in 1939–1940, composed of 2,575 officers, 9,730 NCOs, and 157,000 soldiers. Of these, 43 percent failed to return – 5,400 had died, while at least 67,400 had become POWs, which may be an underestimate.[17]

The French settler population in Morocco numbered 155,569 by 1936, 73,594 of whom lived in Casablanca. They were joined in the French zone by 23,414 Spanish, 15,645 Italians, and 11,878 "diverse" nationalities.[18] Meanwhile, their largely illiterate 5,898,222 Muslim counterparts also increasingly abandoned the countryside, for shantytowns that mushroomed around cities like Casablanca, Fez, Rabat, and Meknès, where at least they would not starve. Once in the cities, some turned increasingly toward Moroccan nationalism, spread through the mosques and new political organizations, which often focused on support for the Sultan's resistance to encroachments by the Residency on the Crown's prerogatives recognized under the March 1912 treaty which established the protectorate. Morocco's estimated 265,000 Jews huddled under the traditional canonic protection extended by the Sultan to *dhimmī-s* (protected persons), which decelerated, but failed to waylay, Moroccan Resident General Charles Noguès' inclination or ability to apply Vichy's antisemitic laws in Morocco (Figure 9.1).[19]

Apart from a small Muslim "*aristocratie de grande tente*," who collaborated with the French authorities to protect themselves from their own subjects and from the settlers, French colonization had proved an unmitigated disaster for Muslims. The French had seized all the *beylik* lands in

Figure 9.1 Moroccan Resident General Charles Noguès visiting the Zaër Tribe.

Algeria – that is, the best lands distributed under the authority of the Ottoman-appointed Bey of Algiers – as well as the lands of Muslim religious foundations and tribes that resisted French colonization. Muslims became "subjects" forced to serve the state, under the crushing conditions of the 1881 *code de l'indigénat* (native law code), which taxed their sheep, goats, and even their dogs, and legalized the requisition of Muslim labor for agriculture, mines, and infrastructure projects. A similar process of rural disenfranchisement and dispossession was instigated from 1913 in Morocco, where colonists scoffed up the best land and water rights, leaving indigenous farmers too impoverished to adopt modern agricultural methods. The progressive consolidation of large tracts of land by the "*gros colons*," a process facilitated by state loans, subsidies, and protective tariffs for the industrialized production of wine, cereals, and minerals for export to France, resulted in a 20 percent reduction in cereal production in Algeria in the face of an exploding population, which contributed to periodic shortfalls and even famines. Muslims were reduced to sharecropping, joining a proletariat of seasonal day laborers on what were in effect industrialized plantations, who were increasingly forced into shantytowns on the edges of cities, or emigration to France. Over time, nationalism would take root among this Muslim "*sub-prolétariat*," who took their political battles into the towns, where the fundamentals of their independence strategies were set.[20]

Although denied citizenship in Algeria, as the Great War approached, Muslims were subjected to conscription, which had provoked a serious rebellion in eastern Algeria in 1916. About 173,000 Muslims eventually served as soldiers in the Great War, in which around 25,000 of them perished. A further 119,000 men were requisitioned for war work in France, where permanent communities of North Africans took root in Marseilles, Paris, and the Nord. Muslim nationalism was kindled in France through contact with other colonial subjects, and in factories and mines where trade unions organized. In the hope of diffusing this as yet incipient but menacing desire for decolonization, in 1919 Clemenceau had created a "native" electoral college to vote for local Muslim assemblies. But this timid attempt to permit a degree of indigenous self-governance succeeded only in creating a second-tier level of Muslim officials deprived of real power but who incubated aspirations to citizenship status.[21]

Meanwhile, Muslim nationalism continued to progress in the inter-war years through religious and secular movements as well as the Muslim Boy Scouts.[22] However, this strong nationalist undercurrent in North African, obscured by the Vichy–de Gaulle wartime rivalry for imperial control, went unreported by the French press. But also, acknowledging Muslim nationalism challenged the certainty shared across the political spectrum that empire guaranteed France's status as a great power, offered a talisman against the "decadence" that allegedly permeated the Hexagon, and bolstered the settlers' fragile sense of their frontier mission.[23] Therefore, colonialist propaganda paradoxically allied a dynamic imperial vision of French power with an incompatible "colonial immobility." An official faith in "the moving fidelity of the indigenous population to the Mother Country" led to pronouncements that AFN stood ready to raise an army of half a million men to defend France. But while there was no Muslim popular uprising, the reality was that "veiled violence" became an endemic feature of Muslim–State relations. Yet flare-ups that might suggest underlying tensions could be dismissed by a pliant press or local officials as isolated events that had purely contingent explanations, or be attributed to the volatility and credulity of an infantilized Muslim population.[24]

A Sephardic population that had originally arrived in Phoenician ships, reinforced in the fifteenth century by Jews fleeing the Spanish Inquisition, constituted a smaller but significant demographic in AFN. The arrival of the Spanish diaspora had strengthened and refined the cultural and religious practices of North African Judaism and aligned it with mainstream Jewish rites. In 1830, the French invaders discovered a "nation" of around 25,000 Jews scattered throughout the Maghreb, made up mainly of small traders and artisans. That such a small and seemingly unimportant minority could provoke such violent reactions is somewhat perplexing. But, despite arguments that justified antisemitism in a North African context, its origins had more to do with imported French prejudices and racial insecurity. Two architects of the French conquest, Marshals Thomas Robert Bugeaud and Achille de Saint-Arnaud, had been virulent antisemites, who communicated their prejudices to *l'armée d'Afrique*, where accepted wisdom maintained that any consideration shown Jews would automatically forfeit cooperation among the Muslims, upon whom France relied for its soldiers. Unfortunately, *l'armée d'Afrique* became pretty adept at forfeiting Arab collaboration *sans* Jewish assistance.[25] From the 1830s, French Jews led by the *Consistoire israélite de France* initiated the "civilization" of their Algerian co-religionists. Laws of 1841 and 1842 gave jurisdiction over Jews in Algeria to French tribunals. In 1845, consistories were created at Algiers and Constantine.[26]

The assimilation of Algerian Jews received its major propulsion on 24 October 1870, when Adolphe Crémieux, Liberal jurist, Freemason, and Minister of Justice in the new Republican government, naturalized 34,574 Algerian Jews. This had accelerated the Gallicization of the Algerian Jewish community, which witnessed the elevation of many of their number through the French education system into the liberal professions, officer corps, and successful commercial classes, and onto municipal councils and other important community roles. These relatively affluent, assimilated Jews were sometimes referred to as the Ashkenazim of Algeria, while their less affluent co-religionists, especially in the Constantinois, remained culturally closer to their Berber roots. Algerian Jews became a visible, and, for antisemites especially prominent among status-hungry néos, deeply resented "sub-culture" in Algerian society, whose citizenship was perceived as a first step toward Muslim equality.[27] "Behind antisemitism," insists Benjamin Stora, himself a Constantinois of Jewish origins, "lay a fear of the 'Arab peril.'"[28]

In November 1940, although Jews in Algiers made up only an estimated 9 percent of the population, they included many prominent citizens.[29] Crémieux was rescinded by Vichy on 7 October 1940, an act that was interpreted as retaliation for Jewish support for Blum's Popular Front. But the revocation of Crémieux was part of a larger pattern of Vichy repression and exclusion that also targeted Gaullists and Spanish Republicans in AFN.[30] From 1940, Jews in Algeria faced worse discrimination than did those in the *zone libre* of Vichy France. The withdrawal of citizenship was followed in March 1941 by the creation of a *Commissariat général aux questions juives*, tasked with enforcing anti-Jewish laws that restricted the admission of Jews to schools and universities, and enforced policies like the "economic aryanization" announced from 2 June 1941, a vehicle to strip many Jews of their livelihoods and property. The following August, Weygand created a *Service Algérien des questions juives* (SAQJ), whose task was to stamp Jewish identity papers with the words "*juif indigène*" (indigenous Jew). A 3 October 1941 statute excluded most Jewish children from French schools.[31] A French version of the Nazi *Judenrat* – *l'Union général des Israélites d'Algérie* – was announced on 6 November 1942, inopportune timing from Vichy's viewpoint. Although the *levée* in Algeria had been divorced from citizenship since the Great War, Jewish veterans struggled to have their rights and pension benefits honored. Post-Crémieux, Jews were to be excluded from the *Chantiers de la Jeunesse*, while their military service was to be performed in the pioneer corps, which neither required the bearing of arms, nor conferred veteran status that might incite assertions of citizen rights. On the contrary, it meant breaking rocks in four specially designated internment camps in southern Algeria. The Vél d'Hiv round-up and deportation of Parisian Jews in July 1942 signaled that a similar fate stalked Jews in North Africa, especially were the Germans to carry out their widely anticipated invasion. Fortunately, they were trumped by the Anglo-American invasion of 8 November. Paradoxically, Vichy's anti-Jewish measures in Algeria put it in an unflattering posture when compared with far more tolerant policies in Franco's Spain, which welcomed Jewish refugees, and Italy that adopted the cause of Jews in Tunisia.

This complicated background meant that, by invading AFN, the Anglo-Americans were not simply "liberating" a portion of overseas France and its empire, and setting up a base for further Mediterranean operations, whatever their intentions. Rather, they would crash a complex political, social, and religious milieu where their collaborators – an incongruous coalition of conservative colonists, military men, and Jews in

Algeria eager to reclaim their citizenship status and, like the rest of France, their masculine identity – nurtured mutual distrust and pursued very different, even incompatible agendas. The prominence of Jews in the Algerine resistance on 8 November 1942 – 85 percent according to Sophie Roberts[32] – has prompted historians to question how far these resisters acted out of a desire to reassert their Jewish identity, or whether, as on the mainland, resistance was the reaction of outraged French patriotism. In either case, by disenfranchising a category of its citizens, Vichy helped to create a fifth column in AFN, much as racism, land appropriation, excessive taxation, and forced labor had predictably fostered the Muslim resentment which underpinned the appeal of Algerian nationalism. In fact, for Muslim nationalists, the revocation of Crémieux simply offered yet more evidence of France's casual disregard for legality, which made a Muslim quest for French citizenship a pointless ephemeral aspiration.[33]

From Weygand to Giraud – American Policy toward French North Africa

Franklin Roosevelt's strategic vision was informed by a Mahanian, navalist geopolitical optic in which sea power would drive the "engine of strategic possibilities." For this reason, as the United States entered the war in December 1941, the American President gave priority to the Mediterranean within a framework of a broader US and Allied "grand strategy." "Roosevelt understood that a U.S. victory required defeating the Axis powers while *simultaneously* preparing for a new world order of capitalist nations and free markets structured under the hegemony of the United States," Andrew Buchanan states. "In this context, a cross channel invasion of northern Europe in 1943 was not only risky, but would pass up opportunities to shape the emerging postwar configuration of southern Europe and the Mediterranean ... From this viewpoint it becomes clear that, far from being a diversionary theater or a cul-de-sac, Washington's intervention in the Mediterranean was an indispensable element in the overall process by which America's postwar hegemony in Europe and beyond was established." In this way, AFN was not an end in itself, but provided the gateway to the Mediterranean, and hence into Europe, that Roosevelt sought.[34]

In this reading, AFN was not an incidental Allied target, nor the Mediterranean an opportunistic theater into which a gullible US President was enticed by a Machiavellian Churchill, but fell squarely within FDR's geopolitical bull's eye.[35] It was in this context of strategic decision-making, argues Buchannan, that the role of intelligence and

Figure 9.2 Robert Murphy, American Minister in Algiers and *éminence grise* of Roosevelt's policy of "Vichy engagement."

resistance became important, rather than in its operational and tactical application. Robert Murphy proved an improbable actor at the center of the evolution of US policy on France, and conduit for information that would help to alter the course of the war, and certainly France's role in it. A Milwaukee publican's son, upon receipt of a bachelor's degree from Marquette University, Murphy had traveled to Washington, D.C. in 1916, where he was hired by the US Post Office and trained as a cypher clerk, before transferring to the State Department in 1921. His career at State advanced through the consular service in the inter-war years. While stamping visas hardly offered a fast track for diplomatic preferment, 1940 had found Murphy in Paris, at the side of Ambassador William Bullitt, whom Roosevelt faulted for lingering to "save" Paris, rather than track France's peripatetic government to Bordeaux and exert US influence to keep France in the war.[36] From September 1940, Roosevelt dispatched Murphy to Algiers with the title of "Minister."

General Antoine Béthouart, who would join Murphy's conspiracy to facilitate Torch, described him as "a tall blond young man, more

Europeanized that most Americans, more snobbish also – for which he would later be criticized – very direct [which was also a tactic, because his calculations were always very complicated, sometimes Machiavellian], with an apparently congenial personality."[37] Why Roosevelt's choice fell on an obscure, second-, if not third-tier functionary like Murphy is unclear, but at least has a rationale. Roosevelt was searching for a way to entice France back into the war on the Allied side. Policy on France was in flux, with Bullitt recalled under a cloud of FDR's disfavor, and Admiral William Leahy not yet appointed to represent US interests at Vichy. Preoccupied with congressional opposition to US entry into the war, the disposition of the French fleet, and fears that the Germans might seize Gibraltar, thus closing off a future Mediterranean strategic option, Roosevelt hoped to deploy information provided by Murphy to overcome obstructions erected by Cordell Hull, the former senator from Tennessee whom Roosevelt personally disliked but who was a critical political ally, whom he had named to run the State Department. For better or worse – mainly worse – Murphy had acquired a reputation during his four years in the Paris consulate as State's "French expert." That label would be contested by de Gaulle, who loathed Murphy, an antipathy that was reciprocated, especially after Murphy became the champion of de Gaulle's American-sponsored rival Henri Giraud.[38] "[Murphy] is a pleasant enough creature and amenable to kind and firm treatment," Murphy's British counterpart in Algiers, Harold Macmillan, noted in his diary in March 1944. "But he has neither principles nor judgment." Like Béthouart, Macmillan found Murphy to be an obsequious social climber, "flitting about like a Monseigneur in a Papal Palace" when American Secretary of State Cordell Hull visited Algiers in 1943. The fact that both Dwight Eisenhower and his chief of staff, Walter Bedell Smith, disliked Murphy would often put Macmillan in an awkward position, "and I have to be very careful about this."[39]

"The French Africa policy of the U.S. Government thus became the President's personal policy," Murphy recorded in his memoirs. Roosevelt's instructions to Murphy were to cultivate General Maxime Weygand, who served first as Vichy's defense minister, and from 6 September 1940 until his ouster at Berlin's insistence in November 1941, *Délégué général en Afrique française*. In his memoirs, Weygand claims that his goal was to reconstitute *l'armée d'Afrique* and prepare it for the resumption of combat, while in the meantime confounding the German and Italian armistice commissions.[40] To do this, he installed himself in the *Délégation générale* in Algiers, with a general staff and a secretariat of officers and senior officials led by Yves Châtel, who would be Algeria's acting governor general when the Allies landed in November 1942. The "Délégation" centralized a number of services that included signals, transport, Muslim military affairs, and postal and telephone control to keep an eye on public opinion, and the *Bureau des menées antinationales* (BMA) tasked with sniffing out "dissidence."[41] Weygand's fabled anti-German sentiments offered a principal reason why that incorrigible reactionary was wooed by the American President. But Weygand's Germanophobia did not make him pro-Allied. Rather, he saw his task as preserving the integrity of the empire against the depredations of both Axis and Allied camps.

"'You might even go to church with Weygand,'" a jocular FDR suggested to Murphy. "The President seemed to have exaggerated ideas of the bond existing between Catholics because of their religion." De Gaulle was "barely mentioned" in Murphy's discussion with the President. Nor could the new US "Minister" draw on institutional memory about AFN, as the State Department had added little to its regional files since Lieutenant Presley O'Bannon and his US Marines had stormed "the shores of Tripoli" in 1805. Murphy complained that US military intelligence, whose cooperation he required, was "primitive and inadequate. It was timid, parochial, and operating strictly in the traditions of the Spanish–American War" of 1899. It contained neither Arabic speakers nor any knowledge of shipping. For the US military, AFN might as well have been on "another planet." Only with the help of the Office of Strategic Services (OSS) Chief William Donovan and Admiral Leahy was he able to put together a team to work in AFN, led by "one of a kind, unique" Arabic speaker and USMC Colonel William Eddy, who was appointed naval attaché in Tangier. A virtually inexhaustible mine of misinformation, Murphy echoed the prevailing view of Weygand, and the conservative milieu that he obsequiously prowled, that responsibility for 1940 could be blamed on the defeatism of the Republic's political leadership, the "sullen apathy" of the French population, and the Communists. De Gaulle was a "forceful" but "obscure" and "distrusted" personality, with "dubious" political views, who could safely be ignored.[42] Murphy encouraged the happy thinking that underpinned the American President's illusions that Vichy could be enticed back into the war, by reporting that Weygand, with Pétain's tacit approval, was preparing French forces in AFN "for substantial military action against Germany and Italy." According to Murphy, all the French demanded in return was some economic aid and a promise that the United States would neither stir up the natives nor otherwise meddle in French colonial affairs. Although Murphy's missives were mostly fiction – indeed, *because* the "Minister's" reports offered an anthology of misinformation – "Measured by its delivery of the product that Roosevelt wanted, the covert operation in the Maghreb was a resounding success," concludes Buchanan.[43]

From Washington's perspective, Roosevelt's investment in Weygand seemed to make perfect sense. The salient characteristic of Vichy foreign policy resided in its ambiguity, summed up by the phrase "defense against whomever." Vichy's initial bet had been that neutrality best served French interests. Not surprisingly, as Hitler's demands became increasingly inconvenient, Vichy's leverage with Berlin dwindled, and its efforts to collaborate were rebuffed, Roosevelt's calculation was that France's – or at least Weygand's – allegiance might be swayed, and the fleet and the Maghreb prevented from falling into Axis hands, by assuring supplies of basic commodities to AFN. The precarious economic situation of AFN, in great part the result of French policy which had turned independent Muslim farmers into day laborers for industrialized, monoculture, export-oriented agriculture and mining, gave Roosevelt an opening. In fact, Weygand's readiness to accept US economic aid was based on his view that the biggest threat to stability in AFN was the economic misery of the Muslim population, that was exploited by "anti-French" groups to call for an end of French rule in AFN. The Maghreb depended on imports of sugar, tea, coffee, and fabric that were staples for the Muslim population that hovered on the cusp of destitution. Even with strict rationing, cereal production was barely adequate for North Africa, much less to send commodities to France, a situation made worse by the post-defeat influx of refugees into AFN. Not enough new land was cultivated, nor did severely depleted petrol stocks allow the harvesting and transportation of crops.[44]

In his December 1940 instructions to his new ambassador to Vichy, Leahy, Roosevelt emphasized that Pétain must understand that the United States would not allow Great Britain to lose the war. Furthermore, cooperation with Germany would result in the dismemberment of the French empire and the reduction of France to a vassal state.[45] However, for Roosevelt to imagine that he could sway Vichy policy with a dollop of aid,[46] or convince Weygand to carve out a US friendly satrapy in AFN, was at best optimistic, at worst delusional. After all, Hitler held the whip hand in the form of French POWs, control of the Demarcation Line, and the power of Axis Armistice Commissions in Wiesbaden and Turin, which by May 1941 had dispatched or recruited 652 inspectors in AFN, not counting *Abwehr* agents on the *qui vive* for secret arms caches, with their ability to disapprove troop transfers and shipping movements around the empire.[47] Army commander in AFN Alphonse Juin complained that intelligence supplied to the Italian control commission by a fifth column of Italian settlers made it difficult to secrete troops and weapons in Tunisia and in the Constantinois.[48] In Morocco, the Germans were able to employ Spanish agents to bolster their inspection efforts. From the early autumn of 1940, Berlin had laid plans to invade the *zone libre* and seize the High Seas Fleet in Toulon, plans which Torch would trigger in November 1942. Furthermore, Weygand's alleged goal to nurture a spirit of revenge in *l'armée d'afrique* was incompatible with his hierarchical fealty to the Marshal. His job, along with that of Admirals Jean-Marie Abrial, appointed Governor General for Algeria, and Jean-Pierre Esteva in Tunis, was to enforce Vichy discipline, not flirt with Murphy. For to tinker with regime change would jeopardize the foundations of colonial equilibrium. Nor did Vichy's upper echelons take American power seriously – Germany had won the war and would impose a new order in Europe, *point final!* Vichy must cooperate with Berlin to carve out a role for France in Hitler's "New Europe."

Nevertheless, in Washington, the fact that Leahy arrived in the wake of Pierre Laval's 13 December 1940 dismissal as Vichy Prime Minister suggested that Vichy remained open to persuasion, an impression reinforced by the fact that Germany also launched a "cold shoulder" policy toward France in January 1941 in retaliation for Laval's sacking. And, indeed, Pétain initially reciprocated Washington's desire to maintain good relations, both to pressure London to ease up on a blockade that was 98 percent ineffective in any case, and to counterbalance importunities from Germany and Japan. As Robert Paxton noted, this temporarily made Leahy the most important ambassador at Vichy.[49] The Murphy–Weygand commercial exchange agreement, concluded on 10 March 1941, freed up French assets frozen in North America to purchase much-needed supplies for AFN – coal, liquid combustibles, and "diverse merchandise" that included sugar, cloth, and spare parts. It was only reluctantly accepted by the British, whose official policy was to blockade France, although the Royal Navy lacked the will and the ships fully to implement it. To insure that US supplied Murphy–Weygand commodities did not fall into Axis hands, Vichy agreed to allow twelve US "economic attachés" to take up residence in five AFN ports and harbors under Murphy's supervision.[50] They were given extraterritorial status, allowed to use secret codes and diplomatic pouches so that their reports were not censored, and travel anywhere in AFN. On this level at least, the Murphy–Weygand deal offered a cover for US intelligence operations in AFN. The vice-consuls were meant to map roads and railways, and to gather information on harbors, the strength of garrisons, and so on. This was blatantly obvious to French counter-espionage, who sold the Americans false documents to raise cash for their own operations. Levisse-Touzé cautions that this Murphy–Weygand commerce, hostage to shipping shortages and periodic suspensions for political reasons, only accounted for 8.13 percent of importations into AFN. While the French admiralty did not allow the vice-consuls to inspect ship cargos, the advantage for Weygand was that the presence of the Americans allowed him to counterbalance the influence of the Axis Control Commissions.[51]

"Defense against Whomever" – Defining Vichy "Neutrality"

Maurice Dejean, a member of the Free French delegation to Washington, complained that US policy toward France was "timid and contingent," because the Roosevelt administration failed to accord a high importance to French affairs. Allied propaganda directed at AFN "seemed stuck in a rhetorical rut," while even Gaullist appeals were directed at an administrative elite.[52] In keeping with Dejean's assessment, speculation in Washington that Vichy foreign policy was up for grabs, and that Pétain's new team simply sought the opportune moment to swing to the Allies, proved to be based on a total misreading of Vichy's outlook, which was mired in the traditional prejudices of the French right, and on the fantasy that secretly Weygand harbored pro-Allied inclinations. Far from altering Vichy collaboration, Leahy offered aid for the populations of AFN and France, and a fig leaf of international legitimacy for the Pétain regime, which actually bolstered it.[53] Pétain's new premier, Admiral François Darlan, and his foreign minister, the conservative Pierre Flandin, were no friends of Washington, and even less so of London. Only malicious rumors put about by Laval's supporters, and Berlin's obvious preference for Laval, underpinned the thesis that Darlan might be lured into cooperation. Flandin had been a major thorn in the side of Paul Reynaud during the Phoney War. He blamed the "war party" in London, in cahoots with Jews and Freemasons, for prosecuting a war that France was totally unprepared to fight. Flandin maintained good relations with the German ambassador to France, Otto Abetz, and he and Darlan insisted that they would implement Montoire while pursuing the development of a joint Franco-German fighter. Only grudgingly did Berlin accept Darlan on the basis of his anti-Gaullist and Anglophobic bona fides. Hitler's declaration of war against the United States tested Vichy's policy of "neutrality." Vichy was saved from joining the Axis in part because Hitler had no interest in welcoming France as a co-belligerent, despite the fact that the possibility was discussed with Abetz and that a majority of Vichy cabinet members voted to declare war on Washington on 9 January 1942, in the wake of Hitler's declaration of war on Washington.[54]

This FDR–Weygand courtship via Murphy's intercession was somewhat ironic, when not hypocritical, as a major Roosevelt grumble about de Gaulle was that the leader of *la France libre* was insufficiently democratic. Nor did Washington's wooing of Weygand prove particularly popular, at least in Morocco, where a March 1942 report complained that one result of the Murphy–Weygand accords was to increase support for *la France libre*.[55] This may have been an exaggeration. Weygand's job in North Africa from 1940 until his recall in November 1941 had been to "isolate public opinion," to convince a population not confronted with a German occupation force to cultivate a "double sentiment" of revenge and obedience.[56] But the defeat, combined with wartime shortages, the growth of a black market in which most Muslims were too destitute to participate, as well as discrimination against the Muslim and Jewish populations, and a lack of diplomacy, flexibility, and transparency on the part of Admirals Esteva and Abrial in charge of Tunisia and Algeria, respectively, saw public tensions rise in those two places.[57] However, the scarcely veiled signal that AFN must either rally voluntarily to the Allied camp, or face an Allied invasion, was lost on a Vichy too parochial, too consumed by its own French civil wars, too overawed by its perception of Axis military superiority, too short-sighted to realize that Hitler's bet had been called and raised on the international stage, and as oblivious to the multidimensional transformation of warfare as French generals had been in 1940. This ignorance translated into the assessment that the Allies would prove unable to invade AFN before spring 1943 at the earliest, and a faith in *l'armée d'Afrique*'s ability to defend AFN "against whomever." Weygand's November 1941 recall was rightly viewed as a German victory. Leahy's direct protest to Pétain fell on deaf ears, a strong indication that US influence at Vichy was negligible, and the Vichy government a "lost cause."[58]

Weygand's passage as *Délégué général* and enforcer of Vichy's National Revolution had mixed results. On one hand, he combined unprecedented military and civil powers, bestowed by Vichy as insurance that AFN did not slither into the Allied camp. Weygand's mission was to stabilize AFN and AOF, and secure them against "whomever." He resolutely opposed Axis attempts to gain use of airfields and naval bases in AFN in the wake of Britain's attack on Mers-el-Kébir, insisting that the Armistice must be strictly applied.[59] At his direction, French counter-espionage and the *Deuxième Bureau* worked to thwart the work of the Axis Armistice

Control Commissions, down to executing several of their informers in 1941, as well as shaving the heads of women who frequented its members and exiling them to southern Algeria. Some would argue that Weygand undermined in part Darlan's 28 May 1941 Paris Protocols that in theory facilitated German access to Bizerte, Casablanca, and Dakar, as well as supplying French equipment and war supplies via Tunisia to Rommel in the Western desert.[60] He sought to purge the administration in AFN of "unreliable" elements, develop transportation and commerce to ease the food crisis, and muscle up *l'armée d'Afrique* as much as possible given Control Commission constraints.[61]

On the other hand, while Weygand was anathema to the Germans, and was often at odds with Vichy ultras, he remained loyal to the Marshal, forcing the empire to accept the armistice, while simultaneously squeezing a dollop of aid from the United States. This made Weygand "one of the great success stories of the Vichy government in 1941."[62] A March 1942 report on army and popular morale in Morocco credited Weygand for maintaining AFN loyalty to Vichy, "because everyone wanted revenge and was convinced that he was preparing it." However, while the army in particular retained respect for the "Victor of Verdun," and very few officers were willing to join an active resistance before November 1942, judging by comments made during cinema newsreels – a frequently cited if unscientific gauge of public opinion in French reports – little sympathy existed in Morocco at least for Vichy or its policies. "Among friends, junior officers don't hesitate to criticize [Pétain]," according to a March 1942 report, an attitude that helps to explain why *l'armée d'Afrique* pivoted so quickly into the Allied camp in November. However, criticism of the Marshal was out of bounds in the navy, "the privileged of the regime." Meknès especially was seen as a hotbed of Gaullist sympathies in the civilian population, where even women had been imprisoned for Gaullist activity. "During ten months in the 7e RTM [*Régiment de tirailleurs marocaines*], I never heard a single word against FL [*la France libre*]," read a March 1942 intelligence report. "That's not to say that everyone is for them certainly, but no one opposes them. Although it is not well known, FL owes its general sympathy to the prestige of its leader and its call for resistance to the invader in keeping with French traditions."[63]

Weygand's flip side was that he was also a defeatist and a dyspeptic reactionary who liked no one, including Pétain, although he did nothing to displease the old Marshal. Weygand regarded foreign policy as a strictly military concern. He opposed the Germans insofar as their demands impinged on French sovereignty, not because he was unsympathetic to their policies. Weygand's primary purpose was to quiet dissent in *l'armée d'Afrique* and *l'armée coloniale*, which he viewed as the capstone of Vichy foreign policy, and the foundation of "colonial equilibrium."[64] Weygand shared Vichy's view that collaboration with the Axis was the only way to protect French interests. For this reason, AFN had to be forced to accept the armistice. Weygand worried lest any hint of dissent in *l'armée d'Afrique* serve the Axis as an excuse to occupy the *zone libre*. While Weygand was not responsible for the abrogation of Crémieux, he vigorously enforced laws excluding Jews from schools, much commercial and professional activity, and the civil service. On 14 August 1941, he created a *service spécial pour la question juive*, carried out purges of Jewish civil servants, and installed the *Légion française des combattants* and the *Chantiers de la Jeunesse* in AFN. He did oppose Jacques Doriot's extreme right-wing *Parti populaire français*. But this was mainly because their racist provocations roiled Franco-Muslim relations, not because he disagreed with their political platform.[65] Any excesses that occurred in AFN on Weygand's watch were blamed on the AFN's civil administration that answered to Laval.[66] His anti-Gaullist views had caused him to dispatch reinforcements to Syria in 1941. After 20 percent of the Syria garrison defected to *la France libre* in the wake of the Syrian campaign, on 14 August 1941, Weygand imposed an oath of loyalty to the Marshal on all officers in AFN. This would contribute to the "fatal ambiguity" of French soldiers during Torch when *l'armée d'Afrique* was beckoned to reenter the war on the Allied side. The Gaullist Larminat agreed that *l'armée d'Afrique* was "apolitical," so long as one shared its antisemitic, anti-Masonic, and collaborationist viewpoint. "Weygand imbued *l'armée d'Afrique* with legalism and a wait-and-see attitude incompatible with the spirit of revenge," concludes Levisse-Touzé.[67]

Despite his acquiescence to the armistice in June 1940, Noguès' solidly republican antecedents and his lukewarm support for Vichy's National Revolution would make him a particular target of Weygand's wrath. In Morocco, Noguès tried both to evade German restrictions and allegedly to temper the application of Vichy's antisemitic measures, citing opposition from the Sultan. According to Juin, who had served under Noguès during the Rif War, the Resident General had German agents followed, secreted weapons, and disguised a division's worth of *goums* as "rural gendarmerie" under Colonel Augustin Guillaume, his director of political affairs, who would later lead his *goums* in Italy and, in 1951, and would succeed Raoul Salan as Resident General of Morocco.[68] But none of this spared Noguès criticism at Vichy, where he was begrudged as a Popular Front artifact and Blum appointee censured for his listless enforcement of Vichy edicts. Weygand wanted to replace him as resident general with General Georges. But Georges balked, and the Moroccan Sultan stood solidly behind Noguès, which insulated the Moroccan Resident General from removal until 1943. So, the vindictive Weygand was forced to content himself with gutting Noguès' staff, on the pretext that they were Masons, Anglophiles, and Jews.[69]

The British and SOE correctly pegged Weygand as a lost cause. If he had signed the February 1941 Murphy–Weygand accords, it was only because he was happy to accept American largesse in a spirit of "collaborate with whomever." The tradeoff was that he had to tolerate the presence of Murphy's "Twelve Apostles," espionage amateurs interested only in sex and food, according to the Germans who watched them like hawks. The accords did not stop the export of strategic metals, petrol, or foodstuffs for Rommel from AFN – the Germans and Italians received a million and a half tons of phosphate and half a million tons of iron ore, as well as cobalt, molydbendum, and antimony exported from AFN. Rommel benefited from the importation through Tunisia of 1,100 French lorries, together with artillery, shells, petrol, and foodstuffs.[70] In return, the French were allowed a notional force of roughly 120,000 men in AFN. But this was a small concession by the Axis, who lacked the troops to garrison the Maghreb in any case. While Weygand was able to stabilize *l'armée d'Afrique* at around 111,000 soldiers with 16,000 Moroccan auxiliaries – although the true number of effective troops may have been considerably less – and lay the foundation for mobilization in 1943, *l'armée d'Afrique* remained a "rag-tag force" whose reentry into the war in 1943–1944 was made possible only because of a massive American rearmament and retraining program.[71] While Weygand was rumored to favor the economic modernization of AFN, which remained an under-optimized imperial hinterland, he nevertheless zealously applied the principles of the National Revolution that he had helped to craft, including purging the civil service of Jews, Masons, and Allied or Gaullist sympathizers, acts which Weygand's memoirs fail to mention. Nor did he tolerate "dissidents" in *l'armée d'Afrique*. Suspicion of Gaullist sympathies qualified one for an extended Saharan holiday at government expense, while a misplaced word in the mess brought fortress arrest, as Georges Loustaunau-Lacau, André Beaufre, and Air Force Major Léon Faye discovered, when they were among those arrested and court martialed at Weygand's instigation for passing intelligence to the Allies. While these men counted more as "*maréchalists revanchards*" than Gaullists, and their punishments of a few months in jail were meant to drive home the requirement of loyalty to the Marshal, their lives were put at considerable risk.

Weygand's crackdown was part of a focused Vichy public order campaign in AFN. In the absence of foreign occupation, "resistance" was categorized as "dissidence," a tag more commonly affixed in AFN to revolt against French authority, the implication being that dissent was at once nostalgic, illegitimate, and desperately out of touch, a primitive, racialized, "indigenous" reaction that was destined to be quashed. Circumscribed by networks of informers and the conformism of the mess, "dissidence" enlisted only a minority in AFN. Furthermore, for better or worse, whatever unity the diverse and spontaneous cast of "dissidents" managed to achieve was largely thanks to Murphy, who corralled them into a common purpose. Nevertheless, it was clear from reports that, despite AFN's Maréchalist repute, support there for Pétain and Vichy collaboration fell short of unconditional. While the Gaullists made little headway beyond a small group organized around René Capitant, editor of the journal *Combat*, Murphy estimated that Algiers contained about 500 active Allied sympathizers prepared to act through sabotage or passing on information. Beyond them, a desire for liberation united a motley group of royalists who hoped to bring the Comte de Paris to power, some republicans, Jews stripped of their citizenship and livelihoods, military men like Colonel Germain Josse on the Algiers' general staff, bound by a common desire to avenge 1940 and liberate France from German occupation, and several tens of thousands of refugees.[72] But they lacked coordination and communication, and were thwarted by highly placed officials who wanted to keep AFN aloof from the war.

"It was not always easy for Americans to work with disparate French personalities, whose volatile temperaments were enhanced by their feelings of defeat, humiliation, pride and exile," Murphy recorded.[73] And if he thought that the French were challenging to work with *before* the liberation of AFN, post-Torch that degree of difficulty spiked. Informers alerted the Intelligence Service of false-flagged Italian ships transiting military goods via Tunisian harbors. By revoking French nationality for the large community of Algerian Jews, Vichy created a constituency for liberation that would help to facilitate Torch. Combat was the only metropolitan resistance group with a presence in Algeria. But individual officers like André Beaufre, or Algiers police commissioner André Achiary, believed it to be in French interests to aid the Allies. What would come to be called the "Group of Five" conspirators assembled by Murphy to aid Torch began to coalesce from April 1942. And so on. But in Murphy's view, "most of the civilians in French Africa were complacently neutral. Far from wanting to be liberated, they just wanted to be left alone."[74]

While historical interest often focuses on this "Group of Five," the intelligence and sabotage networks in Vichy North Africa were much more extensive. To deal with this discreet if burgeoning opposition, on 14 August 1941, Vichy had created "*sections spéciales militaires*," military courts made up of line officers designated by their respective division commanders to control what Vichy saw as a growing wave of "resistance." These courts "with considerable powers" could hand down "on the spot death sentences for an even minor infraction of this nature [communism], of which the decision is immediately executed without appeal, and *that are composed of soldiers with no judicial experience*." (italics in original). The complaint was that these tribunals threatened to sour civil–military relations because they assigned the army a "political" mission for which its officers were unprepared. "The most grave mistakes are to be anticipated, and the army will bear the responsibility," asserted the March 1942 report. "The current errors turn part of public opinion against the army which it does not hesitate to accuse of a biased and arbitrary justice. The military special sections have no judicial competence and hand down sentences by order, it is said. The result is to undermine repression, as well as discredit the government that orders it and the army which applies it." The rebuttal was that regular courts martial were overwhelmed by the growing case load. Only 87 military magistrates remained of a judge advocate corps that had numbered 118 before the defeat. These were the magistrates who had famously condemned de Gaulle to death and confiscation of his property on 2 August 1940, and who had presided over 17,126 cases in 1941 in the *zone libre*, a case load that exceeded by two-thirds that of 1938 in an army reduced to a fraction of the size. Attempts to shift these cases to civilian courts provoked howls of protest from civilian magistrates, who complained that 200 judges were POWs in Germany and that their courts were clogged with common criminal cases. Finally, the Germans, engaged in crushing communism in Russia, and who cared not a fig either for justice or for French public opinion, insisted that the *sections spéciales militaires* continue to function. A law introduced in September 1942 to abolish the *sections spéciales militaires* was overtaken by the demobilization of Vichy's Armistice Army.[75]

Like occupied France, on Weygand's watch, Vichy North Africa became a vast open-air slammer. Reaching Gibraltar or joining *la France libre* became virtually impossible. Police numbers swelled and informants kept them up-to-date on popular attitudes and subversive activities. Sail-powered fishing boats could venture out no more than 1 kilometer from shore, while motorboats were forbidden. The frontier with Spanish Morocco was tightly monitored, while, as in AOF, natives were remunerated for turning in deserters and other would-be fugitives. Internment camps populated by foreign refugees, Jews, and dissenters had mushroomed in the Sahara since 1938. "Thus, AFN seemed to be a marginal space, held apart from events and tightly watched," Harymbat concludes.[76]

It was this evolving situation that Murphy was meant to invigilate and manipulate for Washington's benefit. One of Murphy's problems was that he had violated the State Department's first law of diplomacy by "going native." This was totally comprehensible, as this Irish-American Midwesterner and former post office employee turned consular official had suddenly catapulted to the exalted status of Minister and Roosevelt's personal representative, now sipping champagne with *le tout Alger*. Following Torch, Churchill dispatched Macmillan to counterbalance Murphy's predilection for convivial Cagoulards, con men, and collaborators, which he assimilated into *le gratin Algérois*, while adding a touch of pragmatism to his naively optimistic reading of AFN's political landscape.[77] While resistance in AFN spanned the political spectrum, the future British prime minister was particularly critical of Murphy's "Group of Five" contacts that formed the basis of his pre-Torch conspiracy to aid the Anglo-American invasion. Jean Rigault was "a very low type in my opinion. [Rigault] has a doubtful record; is said to be a drug addict; was a Cagoulard; is a mean, shifty, anti-British, shuffling creature, who always reminds me of a sharp solicitor in a second-rate line of business."[78] The remainder of the Murphy-assembled cast of conspirators were at best frustrated Pétainists. Rigault was an employee of Jacques Lemaigre-Dubreuil, a man of the extreme right, rumored to have been a member of the Cagoule, who had married into the Lesieur family, grown rich through the marketing of culinary oils.[79] Following the Fall of France, Lemaigre-Dubreuil had traveled to Algeria looking to expand production after many of the family's fields had been taken out of cultivation by the Germans in the *zone occupée*. Murphy conceded that Lemaigre-Dubreuil was a chatterbox who promised more than he could deliver.[80] Jacques Tarbé de Saint-Hardouin had been a delegate to the Wiesbaden armistice commission and an aide to Weygand before converting to resistance.

In theory, former Belgian Foreign Legionnaire Jean van Hecke controlled thousands of potential resisters in North Africa's *Chantiers de la Jeunesse*, which presumably provided the basis for the claim of one of Murphy's "consuls," William Eddy, that 35,000 Frenchmen in Algeria stood ready to take "offensive action" on the appearance offshore of the US Navy.[81] In practice, most of these politically clueless adolescents were scattered in the Algerian outback far from the centers of action and so unable to assist Torch even had they been so inclined. Henri d'Astier de la Vigerie, a former member of the *Deuxième Bureau* of the Armistice Army, was a royalist also associated with the extreme right, and would become a person of interest in Darlan's subsequent 24 December 1942 murder. Murphy's military contacts – Béthouart, Mast ("rather a 'fusser,'" according to Macmillan),[82] Josse, Monsabert, and Magnan – were interesting, but hardly pivotal players in the military or governance hierarchy. To be fair to Murphy, one recruited resisters where one could find them. The hope was that they might through persuasion gain French military cooperation, or at least confuse or delay the French military reaction long enough to allow the American-led invasion to gain a solid foothold.

Nor did the scheme to import the American-sponsored Henri Giraud to cap this invasion/coup scenario that underpinned Torch prove to be sound. An Alsacien de Paris, 1900 Saint-Cyr graduate, and fervent Catholic, the tall, slender Giraud with his signature moustache and close-cropped hair looked every inch a soldier. As a colonel during maneuvers near Metz in September 1937, de Gaulle had clashed with Giraud over what the future leader of *la France libre* saw as his superior's flawed concept of armored warfare.[83] Although named to command first the Seventh Army, and subsequently the Ninth Army, in 1940, Giraud's nickname among his fellow generals was "the eternal lieutenant," a man whose emotional immaturity and arrested professional development should have placed even a divisional command beyond his reach. Captured in less than dignified circumstances in June 1940, Giraud had been confined in Königstein, the high-security *Oflag* known among French POWs as the "Bastille of Saxony." At Königstein, the irrepressible Giraud had attempted unsuccessfully to persuade a scrum of superannuated French flag officers – eighty generals and six admiral POWs, whose average age was well over sixty, and who, one of their members noted, could hardly prevent their monocles from splashing into their soup – to form a commando to rush the castle's front gate in a collective flag rank breakout. Giraud's daring April 1942 escape from Königstein embellished his reputation among the "*Vichysto-résistants*," and even temporarily with the Gaullists. Yet, news of Giraud's flight had provoked consternation at Vichy. Laval blasted Giraud, claiming that his escape offered a direct affront to the Führer and sabotaged Laval's negotiations for a large-scale POW release. But Vichy could hardly hand Giraud back to the Germans without publicly revealing the depths of its collaboration. News that Giraud was on the loose was greeted nervously by North Africa's military commander, Alphonse Juin, who feared, correctly as it transpired, that Giraud's political naiveté, erratic behavior, strategic fantasies, and unpredictable enthusiasms might further splinter army unity. "Giraud is not your man," Darlan explained to Murphy during the 8 November 1942 invasion. "Politically he is a child. He is just a good division commander, nothing more."[84] In private, the French Admiral pronounced Giraud "un con" (a moron).[85]

To catapult Giraud from Königstein into the leadership of France's military and political revival was to overlook this man's significant deficit of maturity, intellect, and judgment, as well as reshuffle the political deck in France. Murphy admitted that the selection of Giraud was "almost in desperation ... we needed a well-known military leader who would be satisfied to fight the war and postpone political decisions for post-war France." Beyond the fact that he cut a dashing military figure, Giraud's selling points were the negative ones that he neither shared Darlan's Anglophobia, nor was he a Gaullist. His stint as a POW also meant that he was not tainted with Vichy policies, although once in power he embraced many of them enthusiastically. Giraud's dramatic escape from Königstein removed any suspicion that he had given his parole not to take up arms against Germany, as Juin was rumored to have done as a condition for his June 1941 liberation (he vehemently denied it). But Giraud was reported to have given his word to Pétain not to act against his policies.[86] Giraud's timing was impeccable, and his escape had attracted considerable attention in both London and Washington, on the *qui vive* for candidates to replace de Gaulle as head of what seemed to be an extremely factionalized French exile movement, or at least placing men in the leadership of *la France libre* who might "rein him in." British Foreign Secretary Anthony Eden, normally a de Gaulle supporter, was eager to get Giraud to London, "which presumably meant finding a plausible Vichyite alternative to de Gaulle," concludes Julian Jackson.[87] Murphy had liked Giraud's optimism in the early weeks of the war, and insisted that he came highly recommended. "I felt that he possessed at least the right temperament to lead Frenchmen from the Slough of Despond," the American Minister recorded in his memoirs.[88] However, Macmillan, who had frequent contact with Giraud in Algiers in 1943, found the man "stately and stupid," unaware that he was shilling for Roosevelt and American Secretary of State Cordell Hull to isolate de Gaulle. "He is really out of his depth."[89]

Nor was Giraud's grasp of strategic reality readily obvious. In the interval between his Königstein escape and Torch, Giraud concocted an elaborate plan for "mobile units" of the Armistice Army to attack northward from

Lyon into Alsace and Belgium in 1943 to disrupt the German "rear" in conjunction with Allied assaults in southern France and on the Channel coast, which he believed imminent.[90] Unfortunately for Giraud, the Armistice Army had no plan to attack anyone, least of all the *Wehrmacht*. De Gaulle grumbled that Giraud had no clue how to organize a modern military force, how to deploy French forces to achieve maximum influence in coalition warfare, or how to mobilize the empire.[91] American advisors to the French army from 1943 found Giraud's "incomprehension" of the role of supply, maintenance, and communications in modern warfare, as well as his apparent reluctance or inability even to address these issues, offered a significant stumbling block to the modernization of the post-Torch French army in the wake of the January 1943 Anfa Conference.[92] Worse, in de Gaulle's eyes, at Anfa, Giraud signed a rearmament agreement with the United States without any guarantees of French participation in policy formulation and strategic decision-making. This consigned French soldiers to the virtual status of colonial auxiliaries in the Anglo-American forces. For their part, the British, and especially the Foreign Office, were vested in *la France combattante* and correctly believed Giraud incapable of assuming an important leadership role in France's military and political revival. London feared that, given Giraud's proximity to Vichy, he might turn into another Quisling. The fact that Giraud had allegedly sworn allegiance to Pétain in May 1942, before switching his loyalty to the Anglo-Americans, significantly diminished his standing with *l'armée d'Afrique*, and especially with the French navy. Nor did Giraud's arrival in the baggage trains of the Americans constitute a "mandate" for senior French commanders in AFN. "In this French North Africa whose life blood had been sucked out by the mystique of the oath [to Pétain], the escapee of Königstein was viewed as the Antichrist," concludes Juin's biographer Jean-Christophe Notin.[93]

Lemaigre-Dubreuil had put the Americans in contact with Giraud via OSS agent Robert Solberg, who worked out of the Lisbon embassy. Although Murphy had not discovered Giraud, as State's "French expert" and Roosevelt's "personal representative" in AFN, he should have pointed out the implausibility of the plot to wheel in Giraud as a "Deus ex machina" in the wake of the Allied invasion, especially given the rumor rampant in the *armée d'Afrique* that Giraud had sworn to Pétain not to go against his policies.[94] The subsequent and very predictable shambles was an indirect consequence of Murphy's snobbism, his contacts limited to Algiers high society, and his reliance on "a clique of right-wingers" to smooth the Allied path into North Africa. As Buchanan points out, the most important contribution of Murphy's machinations was to provide "actionable intelligence" – not to be confused with "accurate intelligence" – to Roosevelt to support the President's push for Torch with the Joint Chiefs and his Secretary of War.[95] Murphy overestimated the influence of the "Group of Five" and of Giraud, and assured Roosevelt and Eisenhower that throngs of French men and women would welcome American "liberation," and that Torch would be a cakewalk.[96] On the plus side, Murphy's assurances to French officials that the Anglo-Americans would not invade AFN without a French invitation contributed to the surprised and confused response to Torch in Algiers.

L'armée d'Afrique

Murphy insisted that the immediate objective of the Anglo-American invasion was to integrate the significant French military establishment in AFN, known collectively as *l'armée d'Afrique*, as well as the High Seas Fleet in Toulon, into the Allied order of battle.[97] The June 1940 Armistice initially had only permitted 100,000 soldiers both in France and the empire. The September Anglo-Gaullist attack on Dakar had caused the Axis to authorize 40,000 soldiers in Algeria, 45,000 in Morocco, and 15,000 in Tunisia. But to guard against the possibility that *l'armée d'Afrique* might become an "*armée cadre*" on the model of the inter-war German *Reichswehr*, the officer corps was limited to only 4 percent of the total strength, and NCOs to 16 percent. A further 60,000 soldiers were camouflaged as workers, auxiliaries, and tribal police called *goumiers* or *goums*. *Goumiers* had first appeared in Algeria in 1849, and in Morocco from 1908; the term was a French corruption of "*gaum*," which means a troop. They were used for internal security under the direction of a native affairs officer, who supervised a territory. All were allegedly volunteers, although pressures to enlist might be brought to bear on them or their families by the local *caïd*. Each *goumier* furnished his own horse, but harnesses, arms and munitions, camping material, and pack animals were supplied by the army. In Sicily and Italy, *goumiers* were armed by the US Army. Once *l'armée d'Afrique* concluded that *goums* would be a useful accompaniment to larger military operations, they were integrated into the army as *tabors* (battalions), made up of four companies of *goumiers*, which were eventually collected in Morocco as *Groupements de tabors marocains* (GTM) under the command of a native affairs colonel. Each *goum* was led by six NCOs under an adjutant or adjutant-chef, the equivalent of a sergeant-major/chief warrant officer. While *goumiers* were famous for their robust qualities of courage and endurance most useful on the margins of main force action, their numbers were limited by a fairly narrow recruitment base of Berber mountaineers, while their deployment was restricted by the fact that technically they were auxiliaries under contract, not regular soldiers covered by the Geneva Protocols.[98] In April 1941, Wiesbaden permitted Vichy to raise troop numbers to 127,000, plus 16,000 *goumiers*, to which were added 20,000 indigenous "police" in Morocco.[99] Much of this expansion had been overseen by Weygand, who personified the ambiguity of Vichy's North African posture in this period. Vowing to defend AFN "against whomever," he sought to give AFN as robust a military capability as possible given the constraints imposed by the German Armistice Commission (the *Waffenstillstandskommission*) in Wiesbaden, which traveled under its unfortunate acronym WAKO.

L'armée d'Afrique was regarded as an elite military force, whose combat value lay in its rusticity, its ability to adapt to the terrain and to the adversary, and the iron discipline imposed on its overwhelmingly Muslim soldiers, all qualities that would bring it both success and disrepute in Italy, albeit at significant cost. But *l'armée d'Afrique* was a colonial infantry army – proud, primitive, and picturesque – not a modern military force. It was a composite army, a bastion of racialized colonial conservatism, whose prime mission was to maintain the imperial order, and to backstop the metropolitan *levée* in moments of national crisis.[100] Despite its racial, religious, and political divisions, it functioned as a military force through a "cosmopolitan" socialization of its soldiers through ritual, drill, and discipline. But in essential aspects, military service simply mirrored French imperial realities. In its own mind, *l'armée d'Afrique* served a political purpose as a military bond for a fissiparous, multi-ethnic, pluri-religious North African society whose organizing principle was "hierarchy and violence."[101]

"For these men who came from all the corners of the Mediterranean, those of French origin certainly, but also Spaniards or Italians, even of Maltese or Lebanese origins, to be French had an almost mystical significance," wrote the Metropolitan Louis Bacquier, who the hazards of war had slotted into a Moroccan regiment in the Vosges in 1944–1945. "It was to belong to a very exclusive club. It was also an unequaled honor that erased all the differences of class, wealth, or tradition. The little mechanic from Casablanca or the son of the Marrakech bistro owner are, in this world, equals, no: brothers, of the son of the large colonist of the Moroccan plains or the Tangier notary. The only thing that matters is bravery, comradery. Of course, there are ranks. The orders in combat are executed with unfailing discipline. But, behind the lines, we know that all that counts for little. One could be lieutenant, sergeant, or corporal . . . it's of no importance. We are the French. If we salute, if we conduct ourselves better than the artillerymen or those in support services, it's because we desire it, for the honor of the company. First, and above all, we're the French."[102]

In September 1940, Weygand had found *l'armée d'Afrique*, disorganized by mobilization, and with most of its men and weaponry sent to France, hardly more than a military *tromp d'œil*. "Loathsome impression," Weygand wrote to the war secretariat at Vichy after a quick inspection. "Mediocre training and discipline, listless leadership."[103] By May 1941, almost a year after the armistice, France's North Africa garrison numbered 110,967 regular troops, not counting the Moroccan *goums*. A 1941 report noted that, in Morocco at least, the French had managed to conceal an unspecified number of troops, and evacuate some men and weapons to Dakar, even though the German Armistice Commission employed Spanish officials to supplement its inspectors.[104] By October 1942, the number of regular troops had dropped by almost 6,000. While Levisse-Touzé reckons that French forces may have numbered up to 200,000 men including reservists, tribal police, *goums*, and so on stashed here and there, two years of restrictions had left *l'armée d'Afrique* in piteous fighting shape. "The diktat of February 1941 has withdrawn from this army *all modern characteristics* and imposed reduced strength," read a 13 December 1941 report. "It has left it with outmoded arms and equipment, has reduced its mobility by de-motorization of its logistics, and abolished support services." French arms stocks and transport had been pillaged to support Axis operations in Libya. Nor had Axis armistice commissions permitted the replenishment of men and equipment from France, which might have allowed *l'armée d'Afrique* to "recover its equilibrium."[105] Juin conceded that his North Africa command, along with the entire "army of transition had rather the appearance of a police force."[106] Indeed, *l'armée d'Afrique* that Harold Macmillan witnessed on parade in Tunis on 20 May 1943 to mark the conclusion of the Tunisian campaign resembled a scene from Napoleon's 1812 retreat from Moscow minus the snow, rather than a vanguard of France's military grandeur.[107] Georges Elgozy suggested that Macmillan's description may have been overly complimentary. Many in his *Corps franc d'Afrique*, which fought in Tunisia alongside *l'armée d'Afrique*, "resembled clochards rather than soldiers." While the crowd was wildly enthusiastic, the school children who lined the route of march sang "Maréchal, nous voilà!" because it was the only patriotic song they had been taught.[108]

L'armée d'Afrique could potentially be reinforced by the *Chantiers de la Jeunesse*. By 1942, the *Chantiers* were organized into seven groups based near Cherchell (later moved to Blida), Sidi-Ferruch, Nouvion, and

Djidjelli, well away from corrupting urban influences, with an inevitable *école des cadres* (leadership school) installed in the former casino on the Mediterranean shore in the Fort-de-l'Eau district of Algiers. Colonel Alphonse Van Hecke was named *commissaire régional en Afrique du Nord* of the *Chantiers* headquartered in Algiers, with Captain Raymond Côche in charge of the Algerian chapter. In theory, 25,000 youths in Algeria, almost all of European extraction, belonging to the conscript classes of 1940–1942 were to be cycled through these camps for eight months. This was meant to "give to young Frenchmen a moral and virile complement to education," that included physical hardening and indoctrination into the principles of Vichy's National Revolution. By April 1941, an estimated 7,000 young men were savoring their *Chantiers* experience. Two groups, one reserved for Muslims, were located in Tunisia, and one in Morocco. In October 1942, a camp for 350 Muslims opened in Algeria. Jews were excluded from the *Chantiers* because, according to Van Hecke, Jewish pride and sense of superiority made them poor patriots, resistant to Vichy's uplifting nationalist vision. Exclusion from the *Chantiers* must have counted as a meager consolation to Jews for forfeiting French citizenship. Gaullists denounced Van Hecke's *Chantiers* as "discipline" and "slave camps." And indeed, it is hard to imagine a less persuasive vehicle to convey Vichy's inspirational message. Conditions in the *Chantiers* hovered somewhere between rudimentary and primeval, which often taxed the stamina of young men already weakened by a wartime diet that flirted with famine. The inmates suffered from a lack of water, bad food, poor hygiene, dysentery, and malaria. As in France, soldiers led by Weygand complained that the *Chantiers*' "often infantile practices" undermined their mission. Far from becoming "a nursery of [army] volunteers," only a minuscule percentage of *Chantiers* former pupils sought to enlist.[109]

Van Hecke and Henri d'Astier de la Vigerie, both members of the "Group of Five" conspirators of 8 November 1942, and the chaplain of the *Chantiers*, Father Jarraud, were seen as weak links in Vichy's otherwise vice-like headlock on AFN. Van Hecke had seriously considered making his way to England in 1940, only to be dissuaded by the Royal Navy attack on Mers-el-Kébir. Nevertheless, the former Belgian legionnaire failed to display the mawkish devotion to the Marshal that characterized many of his *armée d'Afrique* colleagues. Unlike the overall *Chantiers* commander General de La Porte du Theil, whose vision for the organization in France was essentially bucolic, Van Hecke's ambition for the *Chantiers* in Algeria was to create "a little army on the margins of the regular army," a citizen force that would lead "a sort of revolutionary war." This caused French commander in North Africa Alphonse Juin to shift the *Chantiers* to military jurisdiction on 16 November 1942, after which the inmates were gradually distributed among the various units of *l'armée d'Afrique* and the French air force.[110]

In the view of Roosevelt, an invasion of AFN would prove beneficial both for the Allies and for France. For the Allies, AFN offered an ideal geostrategic base to open the Mediterranean to Allied shipping, in order to attack what Churchill mislabeled as the "soft underbelly of Europe," while reassuring Stalin that the Western Allics did intend to create a serious second front in Europe. It would tug France back into the war, integrate AFN's significant garrison, and, it was hoped, entice the French High Seas Fleet into the Allied order of battle, while keeping French ships out of Axis hands, a particular concern of both Western Allied leaders. Torch also was calculated to deliver a quick and almost effortless win to ease the American President through the mid-term elections. As will be seen, only some of those calculations proved accurate. One of the myths to emerge from the war was that the colonies had liberated France. However, in the opinion of future French General André Beaufre, "in the military domain as in others, French North Africa was poorly adapted to play the role that one expected of it" in France's resurrection.[111] As discussed, there were several reasons for this, beginning with the fact that AFN enfolded a society whose foundational political, racial, and religious fissures had been further expanded by a constellation of quarreling political and military elites. No existential threat existed to bind this diverse North African society, or forge a sense of unity around a common purpose. This would complicate the organization of a *levée* in AFN.[112]

The problem of transforming AFN into a platform to liberate France began with *l'armée d'Afrique*. In November 1942, Alphonse Juin denied that the army was "collaborationist," although it maintained an abiding faith in Pétain's patriotic guidance and never questioned Vichy's definition of French interests. It was also believed that the Marshal's prestige kept the sullen, ungrateful, and latently insurrectionary Muslim population of AFN in line. In his memoirs, Juin even insisted that the news of the heroic FFL defense of Bir Hakeim had been greeted with joy in messes throughout AFN, although Juin and Pétain knew full well that Tunisia had become a transit point for some of the shells and bullets that ultimately reduced that Gaullist stronghold.[113] In fact, the officers of *l'armée d'Afrique* cultivated a mentality that closely mirrored that of the French navy. By electing to serve in North Africa, professional soldiers had turned their backs on materialism, on the garrison comforts of France, to enter a North African monastery where their lives would be dedicated to sustaining France's "military spirit" in keeping with the philosophy of

Lyautey's "social" and "colonial role" of the army. The 1940 defeat had impugned their professional prestige, as well as their political, social, and racial status as France's representatives in the Maghreb. Loyalty to Pétain became a requirement because, according to Julie Le Gac, "Vichy offered salvation for a defeated caste." Weygand's "feudal" requirement to pledge personal loyalty to Pétain insulated the army from outside criticism by shifting blame for 1940 away from military incompetence and professional obsolescence, and onto the shoulders of a decadent Republic and a defeatist population. The oath eliminated the requirement for self-reflection advocated by *la France libre*. Even though some junior officers might grumble about the military gerontocracy that had sold out France, Le Gac insists that "*l'armée d'Afrique* remained *l'armée du Maréchal*."[114] According to General Jean Delmas, in addition to a "certain innocence [and] spirit of discipline, the oath [to Pétain] steered the armistice army into passivity and powerlessness."[115]

The dyspeptic Weygand embodied the contradiction of allegedly preparing for "revenge" while remaining loyal to a collaborationist leadership that supplied the Axis in North Africa and kept the army under Wiesbaden's iron thumb. Despite post-Torch attempts by *l'armée d'Afrique*, and in particular Moroccan Resident General Charles Noguès, to vault onto the resistance bandwagon through cat-and-mouse concealment of antiquated weaponry from Axis armistice commission snoops, it was obvious that one could not simultaneously remain loyal to Pétain while working for an Allied victory – far from it! As Juin noted in his memoirs, it was difficult to champion "a so-called national revolution" when an enemy gripped one by the throat.[116] Squirreling away weapons and matériel was presented as an activity to maintain morale in an army for whom defeat had removed any sense of purpose, professional worth, and a moral compass. "The general atmosphere of defeat, consecutive reductions-in-force in the army, the precarious economic conditions at the time, the isolation of numerous units in distant garrisons," along with a lack of promotion, hurt morale. "Volunteers who arrived full of enthusiasm, were soon disheartened by the precarious training situation, the lack of means, the utilization of personnel in numerous guard duties and fatigues. This state of morale could make them vulnerable to agents who made contact with them." In an AFN awash with significant numbers of foreign refugees, where the "native milieu," impressed by Axis military power, had been made vulnerable to pro-German Muslim nationalism, and that had witnessed a proliferation of enemy agents, the intelligence service had to maintain a close eye on army morale, and keep the command informed. This was largely the task of the intelligence officers in each military district, and the *Bureau des menées antinationales* (BMA), created in September 1940 to replace the 5e Bureau (security and counter-espionage) in each unit. While after the war some of its participants, such as Paul Paillole, insisted that the task of the BMA was to ferret out German infiltration in the Armistice Army to protect the camouflage of arms, Gaullists and communists were also targeted. The names of suspected agents and spies would be furnished to the *Surveillance du Territoire* (ST) for arrest and subsequent court martial by military tribunals.[117]

The BMA was abolished in the army on 21 August 1942 at Laval's insistence, with an order signed by Darlan the following month, although it was resurrected in Algiers. This came on the heels of German pressure following the execution of one of their agents, a former French POW named Henri Devilliers, who had been released from captivity on condition that he would work for the *Abwehr*. Devilliers was unmasked by the BMA after he had infiltrated Frenay's Combat, court martialed in April, and shot in June 1942, after Pétain refused him a pardon. The complaint at Vichy was the well-worn one that, like POW escape attempts, the BMA's hunt for Axis spies was complicating Vichy–German relations. French intelligence operatives feared that the amateurism of the British and Gaullist intelligence services threatened to compromise the more professional work of the Vichy intelligence in particular, and as a consequence the integrity of the empire in general. The Anglo-Gaullists, were "naive," "egotistical," "astray."[118] But no sooner had it been dissolved than the BMA was immediately resurrected as the *Service de sécurité militaire* (SSM), also under Paillole's direction. So concerned was the Commander of the 19th Military Division by the scale of infiltration and subversion in *l'armée d'Afrique* by the summer of 1942 that he ordered each regional command to double down on surveillance. Officers newly arrived in AFN were given a month's orientation, which included instruction in anti-subversion measures. Muslim POWs released by the Germans and repatriated to Algeria were interrogated at length and put under military surveillance in their *douars*. "The number of arrests made after this date [more than 100] indicates how pervasive this activity was," concludes the report.[119]

With all the moral clarity of post-Torch hindsight, the camouflage of weapons was presented as evidence of *l'armée d'Afrique*'s inner conviction that they would one day resume the armed struggle at the side of the Allies. However, in reality, the officers' mental gearbox was at best stuck in neutral, while their capacity to protect the integrity of an empire in obvious peril from internal subversion or invasion was in free fall. While the company-level officers were thought to be competent but too few, many soldiers had grown stale and complacent in their North African postings. Part of the problem was that officers had self-indoctrinated into the catechism that they possessed a unique cultural and linguistic competence that attuned them to the sensibilities and limitations of their Muslim soldiers. This obviated the need to update and modernize their professional military knowledge. Fundamentally, their Arabic boiled down to a few command phrases and pidgin obscenities combined with an inventory of stereotypical bigotries about the "Arab mentality." "He taught me the most useful Berber words," Bacquier wrote of his batman, Aomar. "Thanks to him, after several weeks, I could command my men in Berber for the daily needs of combat or for services in garrison."[120] "In North Africa as in France, there is a serious officer deficit," complained an October 1942 report. Some of it was the result of armistice restrictions. The expulsion of Sephardic officers and NCOs, many of whom spoke Arabic, constituted a French own goal. Officers thought sympathetic to the Allies were classified as "dissidents" by Weygand, and were incarcerated or marginalized. Their replacements, if they arrived at all from France, discovered "a certain lack of conviviality between the old Africans and the newcomers."[121]

On 18 July 1942, at the behest of the War Secretary, General Eugène Bridoux, and right-wing intellectual, journalist, and member of the *Parti populaire français* (PPF) Jacques Benoist-Méchin, Laval ordered the formation of a *Légion tricolore*. This revived an initiative dating from the summer of 1941 to create a French unit for service elsewhere than in Russia, most specifically, according to the Office of Strategic Services, to fight "American imperialism and Anglo-Saxon greed." This ambitious project was financed with a budget of 10 million francs from Vichy, so that recruitment centers for the *Légion tricolore* could be created under PPF auspices in the *zone libre*. Pay and allowances were extremely generous, especially compared with those of the Armistice Army, and the possibility was dangled that, through service in the *Légion tricolore*, one might free a POW brother or father. *Légion tricolore* service also gave special consideration to those who had failed the baccalaureate school leaving exam. The American naval attaché in Tangier reported in July 1942 that "extreme pressure has been put on superior officers" to recruit for the *Légion tricolore*.[122] The Germans insisted that this legion include an Arab battalion, a task assigned to Juin. An initial contingent of 300 mainly Moroccan recruits were sent to France in August 1942. The following month, a Colonel Magnien, *Commissaire général délégué de la Légion tricolore*, appeared in Algiers to recruit a second contingent, all the while complaining that units were using the *Légion tricolore* to offload their problem soldiers. Reluctant to recruit North African Muslims, Juin argued that *l'armée d'Afrique* was understrength and lacked the ability to supply recruits for the *Légion tricolore*. In this, he was backed up by the Germans who also insisted that the *Légion tricolore* was weakening French defense of the colonies, which revealed that the *Légion tricolore* was a French, not a German, initiative. What the Germans needed in AFN was informers, not soldiers, to report on popular morale and military intrigues. Most German agents were not reliable, while the French and Allied services identified them very quickly. In other cases, problem soldiers in metropolitan France or AFN took the extreme step of volunteering for the *Légion tricolore*, often to escape a punishment. But, for the moment, so upset was the Armistice Army command by this "private" initiative, which aimed further to pillage their diminishing inventory of soldiers, that they asked that soldiers transferring to the *Légion tricolore* be treated as deserters.[123] When, on 16 November 1942, Admiral Platon sought to send the *Légion tricolore* to defend Tunisia from the Allies, OKW refused. A November 1942 German initiative sought to use the prestige accrued by Rommel's victories and the support of the Grand Mufti of Jerusalem to recruit Muslim units. This would ease the requirement to strip other fronts for reinforcements for Tunisia, and it was hoped that it might provoke defections among French *tirailleurs*. But this met opposition from Mussolini, who was reluctant to stimulate Arab nationalism and resented the Germans taking the initiative.[124] On 28 December 1942, the *Légion tricolore* was dissolved, and volunteers directed toward the LVF.[125]

Not surprisingly, by 1942, *armée d'Afrique* units that traditionally recruited among "*Français d'Algérie*" and Jews – the *Chasseurs d'Afrique* and *Zouaves* in particular – as well as the Foreign Legion and artillery, were experiencing significant manpower deficits. Cut off from France, restrictions imposed by the armistice commission had disrupted the army's normal conscript cycle.[126] Young men from Alsace-Moselle had been pressured to return home, often by threats against their families. When eighteen- to twenty-two-year-olds from Alsace-Moselle were called up for service in the German army, "it provoked violent reactions; many are surprised that the French government failed to protest more vigorously. Morale remains high among those from Alsace-Lorraine who see this as proof that Germany is running short of men and will be obliged to surrender." Since April 1941, Wiesbaden had demanded the repatriation of Germans, who had made up an estimated 12 percent of Legionnaires, including Jews and anti-Nazi refugees. Rather than protect their right of asylum, the government in AFN feared that these Germans might become a fifth column, and so imprisoned several of them in Casablanca or in the labor camp at la Lègue north of Fréjus in the *zone libre*.[127] "For the [French Foreign] Legion, the departure of the Germans means that it is becoming increasingly Spanish. Now, Spain directs an intense propaganda at its nationals. In aggregate, this elite force is diminished and risks disappearing altogether."[128] In August 1942, Vichy complained that monthly losses exceeded enlistments in the Legion by 100 men. But the Foreign Legion's manpower problems simply reflected, "from a personnel standpoint, serious difficulites" of the entire *armée d'Afrique*: "lack of cadres, worsened by constant turnover, large deficits in French manpower, lack of indigenous recruitment that, in Algeria especially, does not make up for the deficit of Frenchmen." This posed special problems because the Legion was considered vital for the maintenance of internal order.[129]

On 18 September 1942, Juin ordered that Moslem soldiers should replace legionnaires in many support positions in order to maintain fighting strength. The problem was that, while indigenous recruitment remained strong in Morocco, where it was underpinned by *caïds* working with native affairs officers, in Algeria, Muslims increasingly boycotted army ranks. The army put this down to the fact that "the native earns his living too easily," a willful self-deception, as the misery index had rocketed through the roof in Algeria. But it spoke volumes about the military's attitude to the indigenous population.[130] Obstacles to the transformation of *l'armée d'Afrique* into a modern force began with the recruitment base of North African Muslims, many from small *douars* in Algeria's vast outback, whose literacy rate hovered between 6 and 8 percent. In 1938, less than a quarter of Muslim recruits had been able even to speak French, which made them poor candidates to fill a growing number of technical, mechanical, or administrative roles upon which the Americans would insist after Torch as the price to transform *l'armée d'Afrique* into a combat-capable force. Algerian nationalists complained that the French deliberately excluded Muslims from the air force, navy, artillery, armor, signals, and engineers because they did not want to create a Muslim elite, or hand over modern weaponry to a politically unreliable soldiery, lest AFN witness a reprise of the 1857 Indian Mutiny against the British.

As Le Gac notes, 1940 had propelled *l'armée d'Afrique* to seek refuge in habitual clichés and reactive racism. According to Belkacem Recham, in June 1940, *l'armée d'Afrique* had numbered 373,045 men, 206,000 of whom were Muslims. Those who had escaped death or capture were offered unattractive employment as civilian laborers or rural policemen with demotion in rank, or with the army in the Levant. Tens of thousands had been demobilized. Those who remained in uniform or who volunteered to serve faced unattractive conditions of service. Muslim soldiers received a stipend on service days, rather than monthly pay, which amounted to half that of their European counterparts. This meant that many *tirailleurs* went into debt to send money to their families. Only in October 1943 was pay equalized, but family indemnities remained inferior to those for European volunteers. *Tirailleurs* might be served only tea at midday. In Italy, North African units, whose food ration was less than that of either US or French troops, were found to be undernourished. Many felt that North Africans had been dragged into a war that was not theirs, and confronted with racial prejudice.[131]

Each *tirailleur* regiment was allowed no more than two Muslim captains, while each company contained a Muslim lieutenant and second lieutenant. Promotion was slow because Muslim officers invariably had to come up through the ranks, and aged out at lieutenant or captain. Attempts to change this with a March 1943 ordinance that opened military schools to Muslims had little effect because of the persistence of a belief that Muslims could not read maps, nor report information accurately because of an innate indigenous tendency to exaggerate. Most were considerably older than their French counterparts, were given the least prestigious duties, and at equal rank deferred to the French officer. Men "who knew the country" argued that Muslim soldiers only had confidence in European leadership, in whose absence discipline would disintegrate. Similar conditions were the norm for Muslim NCOs, who messed separately from their French counterparts. "The inequality between Algerian and French NCOs was flagrant," in Sergeant Ahmed ben Bella's 6ᵉ RTA in 1943. "I will skip comment on the awkwardness and the humiliations that followed from this segregation. Algerians were becoming less and less tolerant of it."[132] Attempts to open officer schools and other promotion opportunities with the outbreak of war in 1939 were cut short by the armistice. The result was that the four combat divisions of the *Corps expéditionnaire français* (CEF) in Italy in 1943–1944 that would number over 100,000 men would contain only 26 Muslim officers and 1,419 Muslim NCOs, or 22 percent of the NCO ranks, despite the fact that infantry units were on average 66 percent Muslim. Suicides, mutilation, desertion, and psychological casualties were treated as a disciplinary rather than a medical/psychological problem. The prevailing wisdom in *l'armée d'Afrique* was that only iron discipline could overcome "habitual Arab indolence," "oriental fatalism," or "a great intellectual poverty" manifested by shirking and cowardice. Soldiers were frequently slapped by French superiors, who believed that any demonstration of leniency or compassion would be interpreted as weakness and encourage indiscipline. Punishment usually consisted of beatings or the "tombeau," a traditional punishment in *l'armée d'Afrique* that dated from the early days of the conquest.[133] It may be argued that soldiers of color were treated little better by the British and American armies, although this was not necessarily apparent to indigenous soldiers in the French forces. Of course, Jews and women might – and eventually did – fill some technical and administrative roles in the French army from 1943. But even in the immediate aftermath of Torch, these groups were excluded or underutilized because of prejudice, social convention, and legal and administrative barriers.

Muslim economic distress impacted France's military revival. The events of 1940 had collapsed French prestige in Muslim eyes, increased support for nationalist groups like Messali Hadj's *Parti populaire algérien* (PPA), and stirred discontent, all of which required a diversion of "sovereignty" troops to the countryside, rather than to liberate France. Tens of thousands of Muslim soldiers who had escaped captivity, or who simply deserted in the confusion of defeat, had returned to Algeria in the autumn of 1940 to face a rapidly deteriorating economic situation. The winter of 1940–1941 had experienced a shortage of cereals, especially in the mountainous Berber region of the Kabylia east of Algiers. The 1942 cereal harvest was barely half that of 1939. The inevitable result was a price spike, not matched by a rise in agricultural wages or military pay. The typical Muslim worker was forced to toil for twenty days to pay for the food he had been able to purchase with ten days of labor before the war. Rampant inflation and shortages especially hurt families of Muslim POWs, who had to depend on parsimonious indemnities that were frequently in arrears. Unemployment was widespread. To make matters worse, an epidemic of typhus afflicted a rural population that lacked soap and was forced to dress in lice-infested clothes.[134]

Indeed, US authorities landing in AFN in November 1942 were totally unprepared for the pertaining insanitary conditions and endemic diseases, which they feared might contaminate Anglo-American forces. Algeria had a health infrastructure, one that in theory was also responsible for the Muslim population. The Institute Pasteur, focused on the control of malaria and tuberculosis, both endemic to AFN, was considered very professional by the Allies. Nevertheless, French health services were desperately overstretched and understaffed. In 1939, Algeria counted only 1,033 doctors, or roughly one per 5,000 inhabitants. Dentists and pharmacists were even more rare.[135] Meanwhile, venereal diseases, often spread by numerous prostitutes, who were required by the French to register and submit to perfunctory medical inspections, were widespread. So was malaria, typhus carried by lice, and hepatitis, especially among Muslims, "unwilling to develop habits of personal cleanliness and community sanitation … Poverty and filth, together with the native population's suspicions of French motives, prevented any real progress. Low moral standards, combined with the unsanitary surroundings, presented a serious threat to the health of the American troops …" concluded the US official history. The French admitted that, in the countryside especially, doctors were distrusted by Muslims as agents of colonization. Even in the grip of epidemics like cholera, "[The Muslim] world folds in on itself, because mutual confidence doesn't exist." Only the largest cities and towns had functioning sewer systems, which nevertheless polluted the surrounding seas. Mayors were often indifferent to public health issues, and ignored rubbish collection, so that refuse was simply dumped on vacant land. Otherwise, streets became open sewers full of human and animal feces and where dead animals were left to rot. Human excrement was used to fertilize food crops, which made the consumption of fruits and vegetables an invitation to intestinal ailments. Wartime restrictions had made cloth for new clothes virtually impossible to come by, while soap to wash old ones as well as for personal hygiene was a luxury. One result was that restaurants did not use soap or chlorinated water to wash dishes, nor did barbershops sterilize instruments.[136]

But sanitizing AFN to the point that its ailments would not compromise Allied military efficiency was only the beginning of the Allies' problems. Creating a *levée* out of a Maghrebian boil of racial resentment, religious and ethnic apartheid, and political rancor would prove a challenge. *Les français d'Algérie* treated Muslim veterans with racist contempt, discriminated against them in hotels and cafes, and denied them access to basic services. This attitude was reciprocated – French police complained that Arab children threw rocks at them, Muslims applauded whenever Hitler appeared in the cinema newsreels, and, in June 1941, Weygand was shocked – shocked – that "one encounters indiscipline, a lack of politeness, sometimes insolence," among Muslim soldiers. Vichy had no Muslim policy, despite – or perhaps because of – an April 1941 appeal by Algerian nationalist leader Ferhat Abbas directly to Pétain to improve education, freedom of religious teaching, access to civil service jobs, and agriculture reform for Algeria's Muslims.

Not surprisingly, these tensions translated into low morale among Muslim soldiers, a condition that erupted in mutiny on 25 January 1941, in the Maison Carrée, a poor suburb of Algiers, among a draft of slightly over 3,000 soldiers mustered for the Levant. The trigger seemed to be a combination of imminent departure and the trial of Messali Hadj, founder in the 1920s of *Étoile nord-africaine* and later the *Parti du Peuple algérien*, and twenty militants, held in a nearby prison, for "anti-French acts," for which they would be sentenced to sixteen years' hard labor. Hundreds of *tirailleurs* broke into the armory, wrapped their heads in scarfs, and ran out of the barracks crying "Jihad! Jihad! Follow Allah's command!" "*Tirailleurs*, defend our rights!" In the process, they killed a captain, a dozen NCOs, and seven passers-by, and fired at lighted windows, before laying siege to the town hall and a cinema. Repression was rapidly organized by the police, a machinegun detachment, and the *Chasseurs d'Afrique*, a unit normally recruited among *Français d'Algérie*. Although an estimated 570 *tirailleurs* participated in the mutiny, only 33 were eventually court martialed, of whom 27 were found guilty and condemned to death. Others were expelled from the army. The unit, the *Régiment de marche du Levant*, was disbanded. Some of those given prison sentences were released only in the wake of the 1962 Évian agreement that ended the War for Algerian Independence. Messali Hadj was condemned to sixteen years' hard labor, "*dégradation civique*," and confiscation of his property.[137]

Post-mutiny recriminations replicated predictable patterns. Although the mutineers had made no move to free Messali Hadj and other political prisoners in the Maison Carrée, the army noted that the mutineers were from Constantinois, historically the most politically volatile region of Algeria. Military authorities blamed nationalist agitation and faulted the police for failing to nip the mutiny in the bud. Headquarters complained that few Muslims were volunteering for military service, and that those who stepped forward lacked martial qualities. Low French prestige flowing from 1940 was cited, as was the impact of Gaullist dissidence, as well as a dearth of officers practiced in leading Muslim troops. The Prefecture belittled the role of nationalism, and instead shifted responsibility onto uninspiring military leadership, lack of cohesion and low morale in the army, unequal pay, poor career prospects for Muslims, and a disinclination among Algerian soldiers to ship out for the Levant. *L'armée d'Afrique* was overwhelmingly a "sovereignty" force of impoverished mercenary trigger pullers, not a modern *levée*. Officers did not speak Arabic and so were out of touch with their troops. Such was the situation in AFN when the Allies invaded in November 1942.[138] That Muslim troops performed as well as they did, both in opposition to Torch and in subsequent campaigns for the remainder of the war, was due to the fact that French cadres managed to impose a sense of discipline and military routine on their soldiers. But, by 1945, the numbers of rebellions among imperial troops had peaked, although there was little evidence that these revolts were sparked by nationalist sentiments. Nor did they seem to affect the combat performance of colonial soldiers. In most cases, these protests were over poor conditions of service and subsequently the slow pace of demobilization. But a "continuum of indiscipline" among colonial troops, combined with often brutal repression, accumulated evidence of a growing rejection of the colonial order that had become apparent since 1930.[139]

Despite Republican aspirations for *égalité*, AFN was no melting pot. Relations among and within the three broad communities – settlers, Muslims, and Jews – in Algeria remained tense. To reinforce Vichy's control of metropolitan France and of AFN, the *Légion française des combattants* (French Legion of Combatants, or LFC), had been founded in August 1940 under the leadership of the Minister of Veterans Affairs, Xavier Vallat, to unite the constellation of veterans' associations that had troubled the domestic peace of inter-war France, and reinforce Vichy's National Revolution behind a slogan of "With the Legion, or against France." The LFC's charter from Vichy required "the knights of the Marshal" to "assure the collaboration of veterans with the government officials." It was to act as "a group of reliable men . . . in each village" to be Vichy's "eyes and ears," advocate for the values of the National Revolution and hence extirpate the lingering traces of modern mass culture in France, and remove the requirement for political parties. Weygand and Huntzinger had also hoped that the LFC would act as "*une force de camouflage*" around which a *levée* might be organized, a vision resisted by others in the Armistice Army. Initially, its membership had swelled in the *zone libre* to around 600,000 members, who pledged a quasi-mystical devotion to the Marshal, a reflection of early popular support for Vichy. They also espoused the familiar menu of Vichy pathologies – anti-communism, antisemitism, anti-Masonic, and anti-parliamentarianism. The LFC spun off an administrative hierarchy stretching from communal chapters to departmental and even provincial leadership, with a glut of officers, general secretaries, and committees to orchestrate propaganda, civic and social services like aiding POWs and their families, and security. But the LFC's role as a Vichy prop diminished as the organization became embroiled in all sorts of internal quarrels about hierarchy, oaths, whether or not to admit "the vanquished of 1940," and so on. Many of its members took their mandate to collaborate with government officials so seriously that they began to assume quasi-official functions. By 1941, people had become exasperated by the LFC "surveillance agency," "moral prefects," and "pseudo-government" affectations to exercise power on the local level such as by monitoring local markets and acting as "snitches" to authorities. For their part, officials resented the LFC's pretentions to act as a parallel government. The Church, the Boy Scouts, officials, and even other veterans upset at the suppression of their associations to the benefit of the LFC began to shun their ceremonies, which usually featured portly old men parading with flags through the village in their *bérets basques* and decorations, as a prelude to an incendiary speech shouted by some incoherent, wine-soaked *ancien combattant* over a roaring bonfire. Darlan warned Pétain that LFC "pretentions" meant that the organization had outdistanced its usefulness as a buttress for the National Revolution, while Laval denounced the LFC as "irresponsible Maurrasians," which gave them generous credit for being aware of who Maurras actually was. The LFC's unique redeeming quality was that it was stubbornly anti-collaborationist, a critical disqualification for Vichy "ultras" eager for a "moral force" to generate a Gallic knock-off of the Nazi Party. But attempts to revivify the LFC with propaganda, elaborate ceremonies, and membership drives failed to take off. And by 1941 the Legion was sliding into quiet and well-deserved decline.[140]

The history of the LFC in Algeria roughly paralleled that in France. Heavily subsidized by Vichy and backed by Algerian Governor General Admiral Abrial and right-wing politician and journalist Xavier Vallat, the LFC appeared to have superficial success in Algeria. Initially, soldiers were strictly forbidden to join it, although this prohibition seems to have been either unclear, or poorly enforced.[141] The LFC was active especially in the realms of mutual assistance in resolving administrative problems around demobilization, pensions, and aid to families of POWs. The organization also sought to promote social solidarity through charitable events, reunions, and conferences, and by creating summer camps for LFC "cadets." Its monthly newspaper, *Le Légionnaire*, promoted Vichy themes such as anti-Gaullism, praised Pétain, and denounced the authors of defeat, led by Blum's Popular Front. By June 1941, Algeria counted 107,000 Legionnaires, of whom 64,000 were Europeans and 43,000 Muslims. In 1941, spinoff organizations like "*Les Amis de la Légion*," "*Les Volontaires de la Révolution nationale*," which was open to women and non-veterans, that ballooned to 69,000 members in Algeria, and youth groups that incorporated children as young as fourteen also appeared. In November 1941, the organizations were fused under the cumbersome title "*Légion française des combattants et des Volontaires de la Révolution nationale*," which in 1942 claimed a membership of 220,055 in Algeria. Many of these were the same "*français d'Algérie*" who had mobilized against the proposed Blum–Viollette reforms of 1936, that had sought unsuccessfully to allow 25,000 Muslims access to French citizenship without renouncing their religion.[142]

If Torch was to collapse AFN's – especially Algeria and *l'armée d'Afrique*'s – alleged commitment to the Marshal, the LFC offered a harbinger. Size did not necessarily indicate influence or commitment. "Almost all veterans are members of the Legion," declared a March 1942 report. "This affiliation signifies nothing. They do it to defend their rights, indispensable to obtain a favor."[143] To demonstrate regime loyalty, senior civil servants obliged their subordinates to join. Such was the case, for instance, of the head of customs at Bône, and the Director of Algiers' postal service (PTT), who required his letter carriers and switchboard operators to enlist in the Legion, where they joined the phalanx of shop keepers to whom they delivered mail.[144] But union leaders and Vichy officials like Darlan began to push back against an LFC project to "infiltrate the administration," endorse candidates for municipal office, and have a voice in policy decisions. By 1942, tensions between officials and the LFC had grown in intensity. Size and compulsion to enlist also posed problems of cohesion. Many members simply treated the Legion as a social organization. Most Muslim enlistees were army veterans, and not necessarily representative of the political views of the majority of their co-religionists, who were utterly indifferent, when not hostile, to Vichy's National Revolution. Despite claims by Vichy officials that their October 1940 revocation of the Crémieux decree was done to appease Muslim public opinion, in fact, Muslims were not enthusiastic about an action that simply added another layer of exclusion and discrimination to a system of which they, too, were targets. While antisemitism was prominent in North Africa, the origins of these discriminatory exclusions lay in France, not North Africa. Cantier attributes the relatively large Muslim participation in the LFC to solidarity and camaraderie among former servicemen, to respect for military leaders like Pétain and Weygand, or to the hope that their participation might improve the moral and political position of Muslims in Algeria. This proved illusory, because Muslims remained confined to honorific posts in the LFC, window dressing for an essentially proto-racist European organization.[145]

Rather than a Vichy *levée*, the LFC had degenerated into a "*bordel*," an unwieldy aggregation of "family men" too old and diverse to evolve a coherent doctrine, and deficient in the youthful fanaticism required to promote the National Revolution, in the opinion of former soldier, Cagoulard, convicted felon, and right-wing firebrand Joseph Darnand. In the summer of 1941, Darnand founded an organization called the *Service d'Ordre Légionnaire* (SOL) at Nice, which migrated to AFN in December 1941, where it immediately became the center of denunciations and intrigues. General Charles Mast, who commanded the Algiers division, in November 1942 estimated SOL membership at 5,000 in Algiers alone, although Le Gac believes 1,500 a more realistic number.[146] Indeed, inflating membership numbers of these organizations became a tactic to demonstrate a groundswell of support for Vichy, and a way for the leaders of the LFC and SOL to flex their muscles. In fact, these organizations slipped seamlessly into a tradition of self-defense militias, vigilantism, and "Arab hunts" that had characterized the "veiled violence" of settler rule since the beginning of the French conquest. In theory, the SOL was meant to serve as a militia to reinforce the military garrison, and to tattle on traitors. It was denounced for the arrogance and aggressive actions of its membership, who picked fights and quarrels with those believed insufficiently Maréchalist, even if they were soldiers – indeed, especially if they were soldiers. Barely three weeks before Torch, Juin complained that a 13 September 1942 dust-up at Ain-el-Turck, a seaside suburb of Oran, provoked by the local chapter of the SOL, while perhaps a minor incident, was nevertheless symptomatic of a behavior and attitude among some *français d'Algérie* that fostered anti-militarism in the Muslim population, compromised recruitment, and complicated *l'armée d'Afrique*'s internal order mission. He condemned "the rowdy activity of certain parties or offshoots of parties like the S.O. L. who, under the pretext of enforcing the principles of the National Revolution and insuring order, begin by provoking disorder in Oran in particular. Until now, they've done it with impunity in the face of natives and foreigners who are watching us and who only await a favorable opportunity to intervene themselves for their own ends."[147] In November 1942, members of the SOL would escort US soldiers and sailors captured from the H.M.S. *Hartland* and *Walney*, which had penetrated the harbor, through the streets of Oran, where they were pelted with stones, insulted, and spit upon.[148] The SOL would also contribute some members to the *Phalange africaine* in Tunisia. However, in November 1942, the SOL failed to insure Vichy's survival in AFN.

Indeed, how was Juin to defend the Maghreb against an invasion "from whomever," when AFN's various ethno-religious groups seemed to be at each other's throats? The loyalty of the Muslim population might be in doubt, especially if invaders ever set foot ashore. Already in 1941, Tunisian Resident General Admiral Jean-Marie Esteva had warned Weygand that France's loss of prestige, the economic crisis, and rivalries among Tunisia's constellation of communities – French, Maltese, Italian, Greek, Jew, and Arab – combined with the depredations of nomads in the south, had turned the protectorate into a powder keg. Algeria was equally tense. Upon his return to power in April 1942, Laval had intervened to replace many experienced local officials in Algeria held over from the Republic with LFC and SOL zealots. When combined with the presence in AFN of 200,000 refugees, many of them anti-fascists, this threatened the "unstable equilibrium" that Weygand had managed to impose in AFN.[149] In October 1942, Algiers complained that emphasis on Axis military success by the collaborationist French press further eroded

French prestige with the Muslim population. "The consequence of this state of mind is an ever-growing tension between Europeans and indigenous elements of the population."[150] The Jewish community in Algeria, having been deprived of their French nationality and much more, were rightly regarded as a fifth column that would welcome a liberating Allied invasion.

Defeat and shortages had even eroded the historic veneration for the military as the lynchpin of stability in AFN among *les français d'Algérie.* This was important because *l'armée d'Afrique* advertised itself as an "apolitical" force, the symbol of unity that cemented the fragile and quarrelsome constellation of France's North African tribes. Historically, AFN was not a voluntary fellowship of peoples, but an imperial project forged by military conquest. But as Le Gac argues, by embracing the Marshal and the National Revolution, by excluding Jews, Masons, and Gaullists, and discriminating against Muslims in the ranks, by rejecting parliamentarianism and the "party game," and by thrusting responsibility for 1940 onto the shoulders of the Republic, *l'armée d'Afrique* had become a politically divisive symbol, both in North Africa and in France, which would make it a contentious foundation for a *levée.*[151] "*L'armée d'Afrique*, until then considered the flambeau of a certain type of resistance, lost that role in the eyes of the population," Durand wrote.[152] But the corrosion of civil–military relations had begun even before the first shots of Torch were fired. Air force commander in AFN General Jean Achille Mendigal, for one, recognized the changes taking place in AFN, anchored in the hypocrisy of a military force that claimed to be "apolitical" but that operated as a privileged caste and on-site Vichy enforcer. Civil–military separation was expressed in the considerable resentment against a military that evaded rationing restrictions, over-requisitioned civilian properties for military families, and employed military vehicles for personal use, and on account of the political pronouncements of some senior officers.[153] In this way, discrimination rebounded on the discriminators: "In Algeria, there seems to be in the civilian population a certain hostility, against the Jews, the military, the administration, the government that could be appeased with a better distribution of foodstuffs, and repression of abuses," concluded a report on the eve of the Allied invasion.[154] So, the question became, if an invasion came ashore, where would this fissiparous North African society find the cohesion and resolve to come together to resist?

Reports on French military morale remained mixed in 1942. In January, Juin complained that morale had been laid low because of defeat, because of low pay, which led to economic hardship for junior cadres, and because the "Army of Transition" lacked a mission. Poor pay meant that one-third of officers and NCOs were forced to live in hotels without their families. "If one adds that numerous cadres of the Armistice Army [land and air at least] do not hide their Gaullist sentiments, one easily understands the growing divorce between the Army and the Nation."[155] Meanwhile, *l'armée d'Afrique* complained of an officer deficit, especially a shortage of trained staff officers. Of course, this problem could be traced to the practice of restricting the annual intake at the *école de guerre* to a narrow elite, an outcome of a highly selective French educational philosophy that translated into a staff officer shortage even in peacetime. This staff officer deficit was further accentuated in AFN with the failure to nurture a Muslim officer class, followed by Vichy's exclusion of Jews and Masons from the army after 1940, and Weygand's vigorous war on political dissent in *l'armée d'Afrique*, which led to the arrests of Beaufre and others. Finally, careerism played a role when the post-1940 period saw *l'armée d'Afrique* accelerate promotion cycles, which resulted in the ascension of inordinate and unprecedented numbers of senior colonels to flag rank. As a result, troop commands were continually cannibalized for ever-proliferating staffs. While the Armistice Army derided the Gaullists for rewarding officers like Leclerc and Koenig with meteoric promotion, at least *les Forces françaises libres* were a fighting outfit. Despite their idle "neutrality," *l'armée d'Afrique* continued to manufacture general officers at an unjustifiable and unsustainable rate, requiring only eighteen months rather than the normal two-and-a-half to three years between promotions. The result was that *l'armée d'Afrique* had transformed into a force top heavy with senior officers, each of whom required an expansive staff plucked from companies and battalions, which in turn multiplied regulations and "paper," increased centralization, diminished initiative, devalued troop command, and created a shortage of NCOs and "specialists." In fact, *l'armée d'Afrique* faced a systemic crisis when the Anglo-Americans splashed ashore in November 1942. Both it and *l'armée coloniale* in AOF had once showcased their dexterity, spontaneity, responsiveness, rusticity, and mobility. By 1942, both entities were judged to have become "heavy" garrison forces in the image of the metropolitan army, focused on parades and barrack comforts, to the neglect of *métier*. But the basic problem was that the armistice had failed to provide the anticipated foundation for France's military revival. Unfortunately, the glaring contradiction for Weygand, for *l'armée d'Afrique*, and for France in general, was that national and subsequently military renewal required a liberation that Vichy had mobilized the vestiges of its military to oppose tooth and nail. In this way, *l'armée d'Afrique* had embraced as its mission to resist an invasion from "whomever." What it lacked was an "ideal."[156]

"The Most Dangerous Intangible"

In a 2 May 1942 strategic *tour d'horizon*, the commander-in-chief of Vichy forces, Admiral François Darlan, laid out the threat to AFN as he saw it. The armistice had removed the prospect of any conflict with Axis forces. Washington had imposed some restrictions on the French Antilles and tolerated *la France libre*'s takeover of Saint-Pierre and Miquelon "for the benefit of the British." "Although constantly suspending the application of the Franco-American accords on the supply of North Africa, [the United States] does not seem desirous, without an unanticipated change, to carry out acts that would lead to a rupture with France." Darlan had reached this conclusion despite the fact that Roosevelt had recalled his ambassador to Vichy, Admiral William Leahy, in April 1942 to protest Laval's appointment as prime minister, a sure indication that the White House had lost faith in Vichy "neutrality." But Darlan's assessment merely reflected the prevailing opinion at Vichy that, for all of Washington's tough words about not allowing Great Britain to lose the war, the United States would merely tiptoe around decisive intervention in Europe, for the simple reason that Germany was too strong and America too decadent.[157] In Indochina, the Japanese "had come around to our viewpoint," Darlan noted confidently. Meaning, presumably, that for the moment the Japanese were content only to occupy Tonkin so long as the French supplied them with Indochinese rice and gave them access to air bases in Cochinchina. In fact, American diplomats were struck in 1941 by how Vichy brayed like a distressed donkey over British transgressions in Syria, but remained mute about Japanese encroachments in Indochina. They asked themselves if Vichy would be as acquiescent should the Germans take liberties in Dakar or Casablanca, especially in the wake of the May 1941 Protocols of Paris.[158] Talk of reentering the war was folly, Darlan insisted, because 1940 had demonstrated the dangers of going to war unprepared. The most likely threat in the admiral's mind came from Great Britain that, "since the armistice, has not ceased to carry out hostile acts against us." Gibraltar remained a possible launch pad for an attack, its most likely objective being to seize harbors in Tunisia. But in the shadow of an imminent attack on North Africa, with the assumptions upon which those in power in Vichy had based their June 1940 armistice calculations crumbling around them, Darlan's jawdropping strategic focus was on the "neutralization" of Freetown (Sierre Leone) and, "if we have the resources," Gambia.[159] In this way, Vichy might adjourn threats to AOF and disrupt the important "WS" (Winston Special) Convoys ferrying equipment from Britain to Egypt and India via the Cape. So, Darlan's major offensive strategic focus in the early summer of 1942 was on finding the resources to disrupt supplies to the British in the Western Desert and so aid Erwin Rommel's campaign there.

As commander-in-chief of French forces in AFN, General Alphonse Juin remained concerned about the possibility of an invasion, and about his ability to defend the Maghreb. In his memoirs, Juin claims that he believed that an invasion of AFN was a logical next step for Allied strategy: it would offer a "second front"; take Rommel from the rear; clear the slate in Africa, which was Churchill's desire; and economize on shipping. But Juin's strategic insight appears to have been in retrospect, because he conceded that French intelligence – the famous *Deuxième Bureau* – was focused on internal security, where the French believed that the greatest threat to AFN lay. And to be fair, they were dependent largely on Wiesbaden to inform them about the evolution of the wider war. So, Allied intentions remained a subject of speculation in Algiers. Juin did not believe that the Allies would invade. But if they did, his principal worry was what to do if the Axis rushed reinforcements to AFN. In fact, Juin's nightmare scenario was an Axis invasion of Tunisia to preempt a British takeover. And his January 1942 vision of what would occur eleven months later was remarkably prescient – the German attackers would prioritize the seizure of air bases, followed "eventually" by the arrival of panzers through Tripolitania, aided by a fifth column of Italian residents in Tunisia. The plan was to defend in place until help could arrive from Algeria. But, in May, Juin's plans to defend Tunisia were blown up by Darlan, who argued in the wake of the British seizure of Diego-Suarez that the greater threat to AFN and Tunisia in particular came from the Allies, especially the British. Because France had signed an armistice with both Germany and Italy, no reason existed to fight them. The implication was that resistance to an Allied invasion of AFN would require collaboration with the Axis.[160]

AFN offered a considerable territory simultaneously to defend from external attack and to garrison from an internal security perspective. Tunisia was seriously undermanned on Axis orders. Oran's garrison also remained understrength, so that in August 1942, additional battalions of zouaves and some indigenous troops evacuated from the Levant were transferred there.[161] In Morocco especially, units in the interior had been gutted of "sovereignty troops" to reinforce coastal defenses. This meant that the French relied on *goums* to police the interior. While the quality of these indigenous posses was considered uneven in Algeria, the French martial race theory prized the Berber Moroccan *goums* who later were to play a significant role in Italy. The French Air Force had a relatively large inventory in AFN. But a paucity of airfields and aviation fuel, as well as fears stoked by the October 1942 defection of several pilots from Oran to Gibraltar, restricted flying time to six hours a month. The navy was the strongest force, especially in Casablanca and Oran.[162] Elsewhere, however, deficits in heavy weaponry and radios, and lack of petrol, combined with a rudimentary road and rail network, which compromised mobility and maneuverability, also constituted significant weaknesses. This meant that when the Allies landed in widely dispersed locations in AFN on 8 November 1942, French defenses could not be mutually supporting, but were basically left on their own to resist with the limited range of armaments that remained in their inventory. The political divisions, civil–military friction in AFN, and fears among French commanders that subordinates would not follow orders to resist an Anglo-American invasion combined with ethno-religious tensions to suggest that the staying power of resistance to an invasion most likely would be limited.

On 27 September 1942, Juin attempted to draw lessons from the British success in Madagascar, where, in his estimation, the invaders had benefited from surprise and superior intelligence, while the French response had suffered from a lack of unity of command.[163] Darlan, too, was aware that Weygand's departure had left in its wake a Byzantine chain of command in AFN. Authority splintered between the governor/residents general and military commanders, between army and navy, and between Vichy and Casablanca/Algiers/Tunis threatened to sabotage a coordinated response to an Allied invasion. But Darlan was directly responsible for this situation, because he had used Weygand's November 1941 recall to rupture and disperse the former Military Delegate's unprecedented degree of political and military authority, precisely because he feared it might foster the secession of AFN from Vichy, which ironically Darlan was to initiate.[164]

Weygand's departure also revealed that Vichy lacked a deep bench of senior commanders to replace him – Huntzinger had died in a November 1941 air crash, and Dentz, having surrendered Paris in June 1940, followed by Syria barely a year later, had become the French army's in-house capitulator-in-chief. Weygand and everyone else at Vichy distrusted Noguès' loyalty, but Darlan dared not remove him for reasons already mentioned. Neither General Louis Koeltz nor General Jean de Lattre de Tassigny was viewed favorably in Berlin – although their political views fell reliably within Vichy's acceptably reactionary spectrum, they failed to hold *Deutschland* in their hearts. In this way, de Gaulle's contemporary emerged largely by default. In April 1941, Juin had walked out of Königstein's front gate, without having to climb down the fortress' cliff face in the dead of night on a 150-foot rope concocted of bed sheets, twine, and copper wire as the intrepid Giraud was to do a year later.

Instead, Juin's release from German captivity had been part of a package deal of 961 officers with AFN experience negotiated by far-right journalist and politician Jacques Benoist-Méchin. Juin had been given a fourth star and offered the Secretariat of Defense at Vichy. However, as a native of Constantine and a passionate "*français d'Algérie*," Juin passed on the opportunity to return to the ration-gray métropole, in favor of the command of ground forces in AFN, much to the fury of his chief army rival de Lattre, who had coveted that position.[165]

But as a rather junior general attempting to impose his authority in the shadow of Weygand's forced departure, Juin failed to elicit the deference accorded his predecessor. For starters, rumor held that Juin's Königstein exit had required his parole to the Germans not to take up arms against them in future, a charge which he vehemently denied. Second, hardly had Juin assumed his position as commander-in-chief in AFN than Darlan dispatched him to Germany to meet with Göring to discuss "camouflaged" French aid to Rommel via Bizerte, measures to be taken should Rommel be forced by the British to retreat to Tunisia, and cooperation between French and Axis forces to defend Tunisia. Joint defense with the Spanish and Germans to counter a potential Allied invasion of Morocco was also discussed. While Juin pled poverty of men and resources, remained non-committal, and simply forwarded German demands to Darlan, he proved in Göring's presence to be neither a stout advocate of "defense against whomever," nor a defender of Vichy "neutrality," insofar as those policies actually existed. Potential Franco-German cooperation collapsed on the refusal of Göring to accept Vichy's 22 December 1941 conditions for cooperation.[166] Juin's defense scheme for Bizerte against potential Axis encroachment was demolished by Darlan, who nevertheless retained Juin's plan to counter a British invasion from Gibraltar. In the meantime, Protocols of Paris supplies based on a 28 May 1941 agreement signed between Darlan and General Walter Warlimont continued to flow to Rommel through Tunisia until March 1942, on Juin's watch.[167]

The Meknès garrison was deployed on the Moroccan coast from May through September, by which time the surf was considered too high to make a beach landing practicable. However, air reconnaissance over the coast was limited, ostensibly to save fuel, but in reality to curtail pilot defections to Gibraltar.[168] Nor was *l'armée d'Afrique* prepared for combat. In a reprise of Phoney War assessments, on 10 October, Juin voiced the by now familiar complaint that too few NCOs in AFN "have serious military knowledge, and the qualities of command necessary to apply this knowledge on the battlefield." The solution was the by now familiar Vichy reflex of creating "*écoles des cadres*" in AFN, whose basis would be a moral education, rigorous discipline, and inculcating a team spirit as taught at Uriage and other such character-enhancing establishments in France, like the *Chantiers de la Jeunesse*.[169] Troop training remained rudimentary, and, as in 1940, ground–air coordination was non-existent. The artillery was particularly hard hit by officer deficits, which meant that coastal and anti-aircraft batteries were undermanned, and lacked radio communications. Therefore, with the exception of Casablanca, coordinating harbor defenses might prove problematic.[170] As military commander, Juin set priorities that aimed to remedy AFN's defense deficiencies. But he would have neither the leisure nor the resources to realize them. Nevertheless, French leaders in Vichy and AFN felt secure in the knowledge that from the end of September, invasion season was adjourned until spring.[171] A June 1942 German High Command report on the French army concluded that, although the combined strength of French forces in the Armistice Army and the colonies numbered "about 516,000 men. The combat efficiency of the French army is low, on the whole, due to defective training, lack of modern weapons, and the deficiency of basic white personnel in the colored units, and does not meet the requirements of modern warfare. The supply situation is very unfavorable." The Germans concluded that French forces were capable of defending the coasts of southern France and North and West Africa "for only a limited time, because of the difficulty of obtaining supplies. The defense of Morocco is not absolutely assured." The navy formed potentially Vichy's most solid force. Despite some limited success, "the 'Free France' Movement *has passed its peak and is now receding*" (italics in original) in the wake of the Syria expedition, while its opposition to Pétain has "greatly injured it."[172]

Despite these significant tactical and operational weaknesses, the sense of security in AFN remained high, which was in great part the result of the faulty strategic analysis that underpinned Vichy "neutrality." Indeed, Levisse-Touzé opines that Darlan and Juin shared "a lack of analytical ability," a failing that would become glaringly obvious during the events of Torch.[173] This resulted in part from the fact that their observation of modern war from the sidelines had hardly served to make French sailors and soldiers more cognizant of their strategic peril than they had been in 1940. Nor did they seem to take into account the profundity of the French military's operational and tactical backwardness. In May 1942, a French naval report insisted that, "from October to May, any landing is impossible on the Moroccan coast outside the harbors." Even during the four-month invasion season, it predicted that the strong surf on Morocco's Atlantic beaches would allow the landing of only light forces. Tanks and other motorized equipment could only be brought in by landing craft that it would be difficult to tow from England. Presumably, this assessment was informed by the two unsuccessful Allied amphibious operations to date – Operation Jubilee, the 19 August 1942 assault on Dieppe, and the equally botched amphibious raid on Tobruk by British-led forces barely a month later. Both of these attacks, allegedly undertaken against second-class opposition, nevertheless had been repulsed with great loss of life and equipment. Both had demonstrated the importance of defensive coastal batteries, "and reinforced the need for planning, intelligence, training and surprise," writes Vincent O'Hara.[174] However, Dieppe in particular had both Vichy and the Germans worried that opposition to a potential Allied landing in AFN might fall short of stout, an impression that Juin refuted vigorously. Juin's greatest fear was that a Dieppe-like raid on AFN would trigger Axis intervention – the Italians and Rommel to invade Tunisia, while the Germans, with Spanish aid, would invade Morocco and eastern Algeria from Spanish Morocco and across the Strait. For this reason, he was particularly keen to learn from Murphy whether, in this event, he might count on US assistance. Murphy's unwavering reply was that the United States would invade AFN only by invitation. Juin took Murphy at his word because the American Minister reinforced Juin's belief in the improbability of an Allied invasion before the spring of 1943. Nor did Juin seem to be aware of Murphy's plotting with a fifth column of resisters right under his nose.[175] As Notin observes, "Like Weygand, Juin resolved the complexity of the moment by trusting totally in the wisdom of the Marshal."[176]

Confidence came from the fact that, as the French saw it, the most likely invasion scenario would be a *coup de main* by light Allied forces, along the lines of the "Dieppe raid" – grab a harbor as a foothold, and expand from there. In a 9 May 1942 report, the future Admiral André-Georges Lemonnier insisted that the aggressors "would envisage a rapid occupation of ports and air fields close to the coast. As a result, because they would be few in number, it is relatively easy to organize a defense against this eventuality. Our land and air forces, despite their lack of armor, anti-aircraft artillery, and anti-tank guns, are perfectly capable of repulsing these landings ... An attack on Casablanca seems difficult to accomplish ... The attack of one of the secondary ports [Safi, Fedala, Port-Lyautey, Mogador, or Agadir] is obviously easier ... A commando can easily occupy one of these points, but the possibilities of offloading would permit only the landing of light matériel insufficient to fight against our forces in Morocco ... Put another way, an attack on Morocco would require a regular attack backed by substantial means. Obviously, one cannot rule out this hypothesis ... This would require the Germans to give us larger leeway than they accord at present."[177]

It was difficult for the French to envisage the operational, technological, and tactical proficiency, much less the magnitude of Torch, that incorporated Allied advances in amphibious operations by late 1942, and the firepower packed by Allied invasion forces backed by naval artillery and carrier-borne aircraft. These advances included the development of specialized landing craft like the Higgins boat (Landing Craft Assault, or LCA) and its larger versions that could land men, vehicles, and equipment on beaches and so obviate the immediate requirement to seize a harbor; beacon submarines, transporting pilot teams in folding kayaks (folbots) to guide assault waves to shore; and landing ship headquarters (LSH) carrying extensive communications gear developed in the aftermath of Dakar to better coordinate amphibious operations.[178] While not quite on the scale of the Dyle–Breda Plan, this demonstrated that, despite defeat and occupation, the French command had not forfeited its capacity for self-deception and wishful thinking that would once again, as in 1940, cause them to succumb to strategic surprise. The result proved to be wildly inaccurate net assessments of adversarial intentions and capabilities, and of their own ability to react effectively.

On 18 September, Juin ordered the creation of "mobile forces" to operate against paratroops and commandos.[179] Less than two weeks later, on 30 September, he concluded that "meteorological conditions" on the Moroccan coast "will increasingly reduce the chances of an attempt at an invasion in force on the littoral." Therefore, he ordered troops stationed on the coast to regain their winter quarters in the interior by 12 October.[180] Juin's complacency mirrored that of Vichy. "Throughout the world, the press continues to be interested in the possibility of the opening of a second front, but there is no serious indication that such an eventuality will happen soon," read a report prepared by Vichy chief of staff General Georges Revers on 5 November 1942, literally three days before the Allied invasion of French North Africa. This was in accord with the French assessment that Montgomery's attack at El Alamein appeared to have given only "mediocre results" and turned into a "battle of attrition" as the British had made only minimal advances into Rommel's lines around El Alamein. "It seems therefore, that from a strictly military viewpoint, the global conflict had reached a dead end, and it settles, at the beginning of the fourth winter, into a sort of war of position." In other words, even after over two years of combat, at Vichy the war continued to be viewed as deadlocked. Morocco was quiet. The authorities in Algeria remained concerned about the food supply as winter approached. The fear was that shortages might exacerbate Muslim–French violence that seemed to be on the upswing, to the point that some European farmers in eastern Algeria had moved their families into the relative security of the towns. Nationalist agitation was also growing in Tunisia.[181]

On 5 November, however, and not without some irony, Juin penned a report urging the government to prepare to wage guerrilla warfare in AFN should the Allies invade. He envisioned creating "guerrilla zones" in the mountains, where the locals could deploy their "native qualities" to attack invaders. This would "prolong operations of the armies on campaign by guerrilla actions against the flanks and the rear of the enemy. It is possible to weaken the invader and to prevent him from realizing methodically his plans." But he admitted that it would require an "adroit native policy."[182] The key to a reliance on guerrilla warfare to defend the Maghreb, however, as Noguès recognized, was the attitude of the locals: "If we have the natives with us, then anything is possible," he wrote. "If they are against us, then all will be lost."[183] In this way, Noguès called attention to France's fragile grip on the Maghreb, one further weakened by the deficit of native affairs officers in Morocco.[184] In the event, Juin's call for an insurgency on the eve of Torch came rather late in the day. Presumably Murphy's "apostles" interrupted their culinary and erotic pursuits long enough to pass on Juin's strategic ruminations on guerrilla warfare to AFHQ in the month before the invasion. And while G-2 (intelligence) did not consider Juin's memorandum "surprising," given the paucity of military resources in AFN, it hardly kept them awake at night. Guerrilla warfare requires mobility, which French troops in AFN did not have. While Juin had issued a "Memorandum on Guerrilla Warfare" in June 1942, there was no evidence that the French commander had set up arms, munitions, or petrol dumps for use by mobile forces, or instituted any training for mobile warfare beyond small groups of raiders in Morocco and the Oranais. Above all, "Guerrilla tactics require and imply a high state of patriotism and morale, great endurance and unswerving belief in a cause," read the 20 October 1942 assessment. "Generally speaking there is little evidence that these qualities exist in French North Africa to a degree sufficient to ensure the maintenance of organized guerrilla warfare."[185] Given the accelerating deterioration of Muslim–French relations, not to mention endemic antisemitism and exclusion incarnate in the revocation of the Crémieux decree, and an embryonic but expanding Gaullist undercurrent in AFN which had even contaminated the army, especially in Morocco, insurgency would have proven a desperate move, one that might easily have slipped from French army control, and could have been exploited by invaders who promised "liberation" for one or more of AFN's disenfranchised communities. No one understood French vulnerabilities in AFN better than Constantine native Juin. While German assessments agreed that French forces in AFN were robust enough to keep internal order, "Neither their training, armament, and mobility, nor their supply of motor fuel and ammunition, however, suffice to permit them to *resist a well-led enemy of equal strength, equipped with modern arms*" (italics in original).[186]

Conclusion

In 1942, as two years earlier in France, the French in Vichy and in AFN had set themselves up for surprise on the strategic, operational, and tactical levels. While Vichy recognized that the armistice had placed AFN in the cross-hairs of the war, its overall assessment in the wake of US entry into the war was that the conflict had entered a stalemate, so that its collaborationist policies need not be open to reevaluation. In fact, a stalemated war became the mantra of Vichy's strategic assessment. While the Vichy French conceded that US entry into the war might prevent Britain's defeat, the US military was too weak to best that of Germany. In fact, the assumption was that US aid to London aimed merely to acquire British assets in the Western Hemisphere, "without materially improving Britain's parlous military situation," writes Michael S. Neiberg. "This strategy would produce an extended stalemate that would unnecessarily prolong the conclusion of a final peace agreement and, consequently, potentially put Vichy in the advantageous position of mediator between the British and the Germans. *Barbarossa* pushed Vichy deeper into collaboration, as its leadership viewed the war as a struggle against communism."[187] Even as Darlan and Juin speculated that AFN might become a target of invasion, they could not agree on likely invasion scenarios – via Morocco, Bizerte, or southern Tunisia – and hence were in conflict over whether the Allies, the Axis, or both might invade, and what France's response should be. In the view of Vichy's military leadership, an Allied invasion of AFN could not occur before the spring of 1943 at the earliest, both because they underestimated the speed and scope of the American mobilization, and underrated Allied strategic reach, and because they believed weather conditions for an amphibious invasion unfavorable in the winter months. Their strategic miscalculation was matched on the operational level by ignorance of the advances in Allied amphibious capabilities since Dakar. As a consequence, they speculated that, at most, the Allies might attempt to seize a minor harbor as a bridgehead *à la* Dieppe. French intelligence was focused on detecting internal "dissidence," which, in AFN just as in France, they saw as the major threat. Even then, Vichy's ability to react was compromised by the fact that, to checkmate a potential defection of AFN to the Allies, the chain of command had been intentionally fragmented following Weygand's 1941 departure. This guaranteed that any response to an Allied invasion would be muddled and piecemeal. *L'armée d'Afrique* was in a systemic crisis – underarmed, undertrained, top heavy but understaffed on the company level, and lacking in mobility. Fears persisted that Gaullist "dissidence" had infected the officer corps. At the last minute, Juin flirted with the idea of laying the groundwork for a popular insurgency in the event of an invasion. But, given the deep political, religious, racial, and economic divisions in AFN, a strategy of guerrilla warfare could only hasten the demise of AFN, not preserve it. In the end, French policy for the defense of AFN was never directed against "whomever," but prioritized the Allies. Nor, given the weaknesses of French forces, responsibility to secure 2,483 nautical miles of coastline between Dakar and Bizerte, and the deep divisions within North African society, would "defense against whomever" afford much of a defense.

10 Torch

As Robert Paxton noted in 1966, the Anglo-American landings in French North Africa (AFN) on 8 November 1942 on beaches in Morocco, Oran, and Algiers – Operation Torch – were significant on two levels. First, they offered a pivotal step in the evolution of Allied strategy that belongs to the combat history of the Second World War. The 22 July 1942 decision by American President Franklin Roosevelt to commit major US forces to the invasion of AFN marked an important turning point of the war. While Torch did not create a Mediterranean theater, it strengthened and ballooned the Mediterranean into a major "Second Front" with enormous strategic, operational, and even tactical repercussions for the evolution of that conflict. The Anglo-Americans were now on the strategic offensive, a momentum that they would sustain until the war's end, in the process enlisting the French as fitful, sometimes reluctant, and even resentful allies.

But also, Torch marked a significant turning point for France that is often omitted, or at least overlooked and minimized in the Second World War's grand narrative. Torch crystalized the contradictions of Vichy's wartime posture, and dispelled all ambiguity of "the order to defend against whomever." Because French national priorities had become conflated with those of *l'armée d'Afrique*, France experienced what is called political–military fusion as the barriers that separated political, bureaucratic, and military roles progressively dissolved. The goal of Vichy's proconsuls in Africa became to maintain the solidarity of the officer corps, and deflect civilian interference, a factor that in their view had precipitated defeat in 1940. But 8 November 1942 balked that plan. "The collapse of the Vichy formula on which they had staked all: a French Army surviving within a sovereign, neutral France," punctuated by an open invitation to Axis forces to enter Tunisia and Constantine, and the scuttling of the French High Seas Fleet at Toulon, confirmed France's descent to the status of a second-, if not third-tier power. Torch brought the political sentiments of many French soldiers into agonizing conflict with a sclerotic professional concept of military discipline, hierarchy, duty, and obedience.[1] Going forward, it is possible to speak of pre- and post-Torch France. Torch removed any incentive for the Germans further to coddle Vichy, accelerating a trend toward collaboration in metropolitan France that ironically had become more, not less, manifest at Vichy with US entry into the war.

At the same time, Vichy's progressive delegitimization exposed the miscalculation of Roosevelt's "Vichy gamble," which had sought to entice Pétain, and subsequently Weygand, to reenter the war on the Allied side. This would be underscored by the chorus of protests both in Britain and the United States that would accompany the so-called "Darlan deal" of November 1942. Justifying the post-Torch maintenance in AFN of a Vichy-lite regime by invoking Roosevelt's political "pragmatism," combined with Eisenhower's "operational focus" on Tunisia, made Torch appear out of sync with the idealism of the classic American liberation narrative – one of using force for benevolent ends to vanquish evil. For Roosevelt, the liberation and revival of Mediterranean societies was central to his wartime vision of imposing a Pax Americana and reconstructing Western European nations as liberal democracies. "Roosevelt understood that a U.S. victory required defeating the Axis powers while *simultaneously* preparing for a new world order of capitalist nations and free markets structured under the hegemony of the United States," writes Andrew Buchanan. Far from being a "British Theater" as much post-war historiography has asserted, the presence of US forces in the Mediterranean offered an opportunity to shape the emerging post-war configuration of Southern European and Mediterranean peoples.[2]

The Darlan deal was condemned rightly as incompatible with the precepts of the Atlantic Charter and Roosevelt's "Four Freedoms." Roosevelt's goal was to insure France's reentry into the war and its integration into a liberal democratic order that he envisioned to insure post-war stability.[3] The policy contradiction was that a de-Vichyfication of AFN and the application of Atlantic Charter principles to the French empire would have been at odds with a plan to integrate *l'armée d'Afrique* as well as the French fleet into the Allied order of battle. The Darlan deal also scuttled the narrative that a democratic "resistance" had mobilized to invite and assist Allied intervention, and to return France to the path of democracy, when, by confirming Darlan, all that the Americans had done was to keep the collaborators in power.[4] So, while, on the military level, "Anglo-Saxon" intervention in AFN might be considered progress in the war against the Axis, on the political level, Torch embodied the contradiction between the "liberation" of French territory and the continuation of Vichy's iron grip on AFN, with its antisemitic laws, its desert internment camps for refugees and "dissidents," and the repression of colonial peoples that contravened the Atlantic Charter spirit. One result was to tarnish the moral impact of the dramatic entry of US forces into the European theater. Because AFN was "liberated" from without by the Allies, who nevertheless enabled a *de facto* continuation of Vichy, Torch fitted awkwardly into the binary resistance/collaboration Gaullist narrative of the war. As a consequence, facilitators of the Allied landing on 8 November failed to be embraced as heroes by the Gaullist and communist gatekeepers of resistance memory. Furthermore, Torch was extremely embarrassing to the Gaullists, in part because it caught them by surprise, which merely confirmed their outsider status in the Allied coalition. But also, Torch allowed Vichy to reiterate and reinforce its message that the Gaullists were accessories to the Anglo-American plan to dismantle the French empire and hence diminish France's international status and independence. To counter Vichy's narrative of betrayal, de Gaulle would be obliged repeatedly to pick quarrels with "les Anglo-Saxons" over what he saw as bedrock requirements of French sovereignty, independence, and grandeur.

The knock-on effects of Torch within the French camp were also significant. Handed the reins of power in AFN by the Americans on Darlan's demise, General Henri Giraud initially refused to recognize and reward many who had facilitated Torch. This was either because, in his view, they had betrayed their military obligations, or because it would have required him to recognize and reinstate the citizenship rights of Algerian Jews. In the wake of Torch, Muslim nationalists moved further away from assimilationist goals toward independence, a trend that would mature with the 8 May 1945 uprisings at Sétif and Guelma. The political struggles that evolved within the French exile movements, and de Gaulle's seeming ingratitude for Allied efforts to liberate France, reinforced a negative image among the Allies of the French as quarrelsome, intermittently cooperative, and divided – or, in Eisenhower's colloquialism, "not knowing on which side their bread is buttered."[5] It also served to devalue in the minds of the Allied high command, among Allied populations, and in the historical verdict the importance of Torch and the Mediterranean strategy generally as a significant stepping stone to Allied victory.[6]

A further consequence of Torch was that AFN was to become the trampoline for the liberation of the Hexagon. But for that to happen, Charles de Gaulle would first have to gain political control and stamp his moral authority on the notoriously Maréchalist *armée d'Afrique*.[7] This would prove difficult, because if Torch had lifted *l'armée d'Afrique* out of Vichy, it proved much harder to strip Vichy out of *l'armée d'Afrique*. Although Roosevelt's policy of Vichy engagement had failed spectacularly, American entry into the war and Torch in particular threatened further to marginalize de Gaulle and *la France combattante.* However, as Guillaume Piketty notes, Torch would constitute both Fighting France's low point and its finest hour.[8] To the injury of Roosevelt's deliberate exclusion of de Gaulle from Torch was added the insult of the Darlan deal. Unfortunately for the American President, this simply infused new energy and focus into the Gaullist-led campaign to claim leadership of the French exile government. This was because Torch caused de Gaulle to realize that if Fighting France were to survive and triumph, it must expand beyond an emotional community of military adventurers and wounded patriots of diverse origins bonded by their rejection of the armistice, reinforced by their humiliation, suffering, pride, bitterness, and isolation within the Allied coalition. *La France combattante* must embody a vision to reconstruct the French nation on a democratic foundation.[9]

In a moving speech delivered at the Albert Hall on 11 November 1942, as Darlan ordered a ceasefire in Algiers, and Axis troops terminated the fiction of the *zone libre*, the leader of Fighting France announced that the war against the enemy was inseparable from the resurrection of the one and indivisible Republic.[10] This declaration identifying Gaullism with Republicanism was pivotal, because until then, many exiles and resisters feared that de Gaulle was simply another aspiring dictator. He had no democratic legitimacy within a French political tradition. On the contrary, an anti-Vichy opposition compared de Gaulle's "coup" of 18 June 1940 to Pétain's "legal coup" of 10 July. Even to a growing internal resistance, not to mention the Allies, de Gaulle seemed focused more on fighting Vichy than the Axis. For the military who wished to maintain "a free empire and an intact fleet," the requirement for unity and legality was key. Torch forced Gaullism to alloy with Republicanism as a first step to unify resistance in France and make it more difficult for the Allies to quarantine de Gaulle as an autocratic opportunist. In this way, de Gaulle put paid to accusations that he was merely a dictator-in-waiting, and confirmed *la France combattante*'s status as an elite warrior fraternity united in a crusade to restore France's republican traditions.[11]

At the same time, de Gaulle's task would continue to be an uphill struggle because it launched from a position of inferiority, when not desperation against a US-backed Vichy rump in AFN. In the process, Algiers became the venue where *la France combattante* metamorphosed from a diminutive sect into an umbrella movement that assembled an increasingly heterogeneous cast of actors beneath the Cross of Lorraine. This was made possible because, while the internal resistance in France pre-dated Torch, for the first time, the Allied invasion of AFN integrated resistance as a dimension of operational planning, showcasing at once its strategic, operational, and tactical potential as well as its limitations. The Darlan deal inadvertently strengthened de Gaulle's hand because it alerted a growing resistance movement in France that it must forge a precarious unanimity lest, upon liberation, *les Anglo-saxons* merely foist a Vichy remodel upon them. To avoid a Darlan deal reprise, de Gaulle must assemble a heterogeneous cast of leaders and technicians both to restore French fighting power and to impose political unity over a very diverse "resistance in France." On the margins, this made the confirmation of resistance status appear increasingly arbitrary and politically driven.

Finally, while AFN would become the geopolitical "trampoline" to advance the Allies' strategic agenda,[12] it would supply a brittle base for France's resurrection. De Gaulle's legitimacy hinged in part on his ability to preserve the empire, which even the French left acknowledged had kept France from "falling to the level of Portugal."[13] However, as Benjamin Stora notes, Torch coming on the heels of 1940 and Syria in 1941, as well as concessions forced on Vichy by the Japanese in Indochina, handed the French army yet another defeat that "announced the crisis of the French empire."[14] Julie Le Gac agrees that the serial defeats of the French army, combined with the Vichy–Gaullist quarrels, rattled the "colonial equilibrium" upon which the liberation of France was to depend.[15] Torch saw the Allies invade and occupy AFN while failing to "liberate" it. Instead, the Allies left intact its Vichy governance and military structures with their personnel, discriminatory edicts, and desert camps filled with political and "racial" internees. This only served to highlight a looming crisis of legitimacy of French governance, as well as to import French tensions and divisions into the center of the Alliance. In this way, war and defeat threatened both France's grip on North Africa and its power to dictate the conditions of governance upon the Liberation. American power demonstrated at Torch actually served to undermine France's image in the eyes of its colonial population, and gave a boost to Muslim nationalism, as did the French eviction of the Bey of Tunis in May 1943 at the end of the Tunisian campaign. The Anglo-American occupation of AFN would also accentuate the tenuous and conflicted association between *la France métropolitaine* and its North African hinterland, one roiled by the volatility of AFN's demographic makeup, and the peculiar and artificial relationship between AFN – particularly Algeria – and the mainland. At the same time, by invading AFN, the Anglo-Americans became referees of France's smoldering intramural disputes, forced to accommodate its divided political culture while at the same time needing to organize and direct a war against the Axis and lay the foundation for a post-war Europe.

Allied "Jackals" Prowl the French Empire

Despite historical speculation that the presence of Admiral François Darlan in Algiers on 8 November 1942 indicated that he was aware of the imminence of the Anglo-American invasion of AFN, and even offered to cooperate, indications are that with the exception of a handful of officials tipped off by Robert Murphy, perhaps Ciano's intuition, and the deductions of a few *Deuxième Bureau* officials, Vichy French officials and the Axis were almost totally blindsided by Torch. French North Africa buzzed with rumors of an imminent Allied invasion in 1942, to the point that the Free French had opened an office in Gibraltar in July to have someone in proximity should it occur. During the summer of 1942, the Gaullist BCRA had begun to infiltrate agents into North Africa via Tangier to collect intelligence.[16] German speculation about a possible Allied invasion of Morocco fell far short of unanimity.[17] Other explanations were advanced for Allied troop concentrations at Gibraltar, detected as early as 30 October. Focused on the battles shaping up at El Alamein and Stalingrad, the Axis took their eye off AFN.[18]

As in Berlin, the French at Vichy and in AFN believed the Allies incapable of invading AFN in 1942. While, in July, Juin had speculated that France might witness Allied raids against Dakar or Casablanca "*pour les questions de prestige*," he was more concerned by the prospect of an Axis invasion. During the summer, he and Noguès had supervised maneuvers based on the scenario of a German invasion through Spanish Morocco. Between February and September 1942, Juin had reworked defense plans for Algiers, although he seemed reassured by Murphy that the Allies had no reason to invade AFN, *sans invitation*.[19] Unsuccessful attacks on Dieppe in August 1942, and subsequently at Tobruk in September, demonstrated that the Allies had yet to master the complexities of amphibious operations, even on a relatively small scale. The general conclusion of the French general staff had been that the war had reached a stalemate.[20] Although Vichy had warned that an Anglo-American action against AFN could not be ruled out, both Juin and Darlan were skeptical when on 2 November the French naval attaché in Lisbon signaled a significant Allied convoy off the Azores. The next day, reports reached Algiers that large numbers of British warships and planes had converged on Gibraltar. Warnings of Allied ship movements also came through the Germans via the Armistice commission in Wiesbaden, which caused the French to activate air reconnaissance missions over the Mediterranean. By 6 November, everyone, including the Italians, had noticed the Allied convoys steaming into the Mediterranean, to the point that emissaries were dispatched from Vichy to raise the alarm in Algiers.

While Darlan minimized the dangers, by the afternoon of 7 November, Admiral Jacques Moreau, chief of the 4th Maritime Region headquartered in Algiers, noted that the intervals that separated the three convoys steaming east matched the distances between AFN's main ports, and that the lead convoy would arrive at the longitude of Bône on the night of 8–9 November. All they need do was to execute a 90° turn, and all major French harbors from Tunisia to Oran could be assaulted. Yet, when Moreau pointed this out to Darlan on the evening of 7 November, the Admiral replied: "That's not what I was told," a reference to Murphy's assurances that the Allies had no intention of attacking AFN.[21] Darlan ordered no preparatory defensive measures for Oran and Algiers. Instead he alerted Vichy to take measures to repel a possible attack against France's Mediterranean coast. On 7 November, the naval attaché in Lisbon warned of ships off the Moroccan coast. Juin ordered that troops take up their coastal defense positions on 8 November. In Oran, while the navy went on alert on 6 November, the army remained in a "normal" posture.[22]

Darlan's actions during Torch have provoked speculation that the opportunistic admiral had concluded that the Anglo-Saxons were going to win the war, and so traveled to Algiers on 8 November to rally to them.[23] But this would have required imagination, foresight, and a willingness to take risks, none of which counted among Darlan's admittedly slender attributes. Darlan was neither a sentimentalist nor a moralist. Cold, gruff, suspicious, and authoritarian, the charisma fairy had not lingered long over his crib. A vain, vulgar, man with "an embarrassing taste for luxury," for Benoist-Méchin, "[Darlan's] mind was limited, he was short-sighted and not particularly cultivated." Darlan's naval education had left him with the practical intelligence of a good staff officer, "adequate for concocting a military plan, carrying out an order, fulfilling a duty. But beyond that, he had nothing much to offer." This had been fully demonstrated by his period at the summit of the French navy, during which "*la belle flotte de Darlan*" in fact turned out to be an antiquated battleship force, for which the requirement for radar, carriers, and anti-aircraft defenses remained underappreciated. While Darlan enjoyed a reputation as a realist, his Anglophobia and belief in German invincibility had diverted him into brutal and perilous policies.[24]

The American representative to Vichy, William Leahy, had failed to bond with his fellow admiral at Vichy, finding his interlocutor "emotionally unstable, dangerously impulsive, and devious." Darlan was disarmingly open about his desire to collaborate with Germany, while his deep Anglophobia, expressed in periodic "anti-British rants" during which he appeared "unhinged," meant that he "definitely underestimates British

Sea Power." By March 1942, on the eve of Leahy's recall, relations between the two admirals had transitioned from mutual incomprehension into shared contempt.[25] The author of the Paris Protocols had traveled to AFN in October on a tour of *armée d'Afrique* messes to warn the troops that Anglo-American "jackals" prowled the perimeters of the empire, and to cajole them to defend it. Nevertheless, he suspected that warnings of possible Allied action against Casablanca or Dakar from Axis sources were a "provocation" to give them an excuse to occupy AFN.[26] In the process, those in charge at Vichy advertised a strange, even willful, obliviousness to the consequences of their own actions, and to the evolution of the war. This began with the assumption that France might remain on the margins of a world war by posturing as a "neutral" nation primed to defend itself against "whomever," while surreptitiously supporting the Axis war effort. This "neutrality" fiction required that Vichy ignore or diminish the significance of the invasion or defection of large swaths of empire. The failure of the 19 August Anglo-Canadian attack on Dieppe, which was followed by Vichy cooperation with the Germans to track down resistance radio operators, stirred fantasies, at least in Darlan's mind, that Hitler might allow France to assume a greater role in its own defense. With Rommel's victories in the Western Desert, and German armies deep into the Soviet Union, the war in Darlan's view was deadlocked. High autumn surf in the Atlantic meant that Morocco and Dakar were, for the moment, safe from Anglo-Saxon assault, Laval assured his cabinet.[27] In this way, Vichy revealed the detachment, even the incongruity, of its strategic assessment both of the evolution of Allied strategic thinking and of the operational and tactical progress of modern warfare, especially the advances in airpower and amphibious operations. In fact, the alleged symbols of Vichy sovereignty – Hitler's empty armistice guarantees of French territorial integrity, a *zone libre*, empire loyalty, the Armistice Army and the High Seas Fleet – became rapidly wasting assets. Vichy's sham "neutrality" and fragile sovereignty translated into a policy and strategy "schizophrenia," encapsulated in the doctrine of "defense against whomever," which targeted domestic "dissidence" as much as foreign invasion. Vichy, Darlan, and France's North African proconsuls showed their true colors when they opposed the Anglo-Americans in November 1942, but permitted the Axis a resistance-free entry into Tunisia.[28]

Vichy had presided over the transformation of France into a victim nation that, stripped of capacity and initiative, had surrendered control of its destiny, and was forced passively to await its assailants. This outcome should have been apparent from the moment that France signed the armistice. But, as Robert Paxton and others have noted, survival for

Vichy hinged on the restoration of "order," not "liberation." This reality underpinned Pétain's paternalist image, and explains Weygand's authoritarian application of the National Revolution in AFN and his crusade to root out "dissidence" in *l'armée d'Afrique*, which included the imposition of a personal oath of loyalty to the Marshal. It also fueled Laval's campaign to carve out a leading role for France in a German-led European order. As Julie Le Gac notes, the principle of collaboration was especially seductive for the French military, who saw it as the only way to preserve a fragile status quo in AFN. Liberation by the Allies threatened to fling open the floodgates of anarchy narrowly averted by the 1940 armistice, stoke the embers of Muslim nationalism, restore citizenship to scheming Jews, validate Gaullist rebellion, and so unravel the fabric of empire and undermine the very foundations of military obedience. And, in the long run, they were correct – this imperial unstitching proved to be precisely the ongoing process in AFN that Torch would accelerate. But the simple truth was that France could not be restored to great power status – indeed, even intermediate power status – without US assistance, as Jean Monnet and the more prescient French exiles with direct cognizance of the immense population and industrial disparities between the two countries recognized. And in the short run at least, the Atlantic Charter to the contrary, French rearmament would require Washington's unwavering support for French colonial rule in AFN.[29] But even without Torch, AFN was on life support, because the longer the war continued, the more Vichy's police state became contested. Vichy's fundamental dilemma was that, to survive even in the short term, the regime required an Axis victory.[30] But this looked increasingly unlikely as 1942 revealed that the Allies had absorbed the best punches the Axis could throw, and were coiled to counterstrike.

From Gymnast to Torch

David Reynolds calls the decision for Torch a "half-baked political compromise," between the British, who desired to pursue operations in the Mediterranean, and the American chiefs of staff, who looked to launch a cross-Channel invasion in 1943.[31] But the notion that the decision to invade AFN pitted reluctant Americans against ardent British is an exaggeration, as the Fall of France had caused Roosevelt to worry about "Nazi agents penetrating the bulge of Africa and opening the way for Hitler to make a quick strike through the Iberian peninsula into north Africa."[32] Churchill's push for a more muscular approach to Vichy France, launched at the January 1942 Arcadia conference with Gymnast – the code name for the plan for an Allied invasion of northwest Africa – got push-back from the American chiefs of staff and the Secretary of Defense, Cordell Hull. But, by the summer of 1942, American opposition to Mediterranean engagement had mellowed, as the Vichy cave-in to Japanese pressure in Indochina triggered fears in the White House of a repeat performance in AFN. "Now that Vichy has without objection handed Indochina over to Japan it will be difficult to refuse Germany a present of French Africa when a new demand backed by threats is made," Leahy wrote to Roosevelt.[33]

Both Roosevelt and Leahy viewed the large army favored by Army chief of staff George Marshall, with its promise of titanic, casualty-heavy clashes, as an outdated concept. Instead, they favored "an air–sea machinery-based war, with a remarkably small land army, all things considered."[34] For the map-traveling American President Roosevelt, a disciple of the turn-of-the-century naval strategist Alfred Thayer Mahan, an Axis seizure of the great shoulder of Africa could jeopardize a war plan that sought to deploy sea power to give the Allies mobility, and air power to weaken the Axis economy before closing in for the kill. However, one of the requirements of a "machinery-based war" was that the Axis must not be allowed to preempt the occupation of important strategic locations.[35] Roosevelt also found political and tactical reasons to promote his Mediterranean strategy at what is called the Second Washington Conference (19–25 June 1942), after Churchill faced a Parliamentary vote of no confidence following the defeat at Gazala capped by the 21 June fall of Tobruk, hitherto a symbol of British tenacity in the desert war. The two Allied war leaders agreed that Egypt and Suez as the gateways to the Middle East had to be secured.[36] Furthermore, neither leader desired to risk the outcome of the war on a premature invasion of Northern Europe. Rather than Roosevelt being "manipulated" by Churchill to support British interests as American generals complained, on the contrary, the invasion of the Mediterranean bought time for the United States to mobilize its industrial and military assets and so to assert its power in the alliance during the war's concluding stages. But, to win over a skeptical Hull, Stimson, and Marshall to the strategic possibilities of Mediterranean intervention, Andrew Buchanan has convincingly argued that Roosevelt required "actionable intelligence." In early 1942, Leahy had warned the President that Vichy would not resist if Germany moved into AFN, an assessment that FDR had conveyed to Churchill.[37] Intelligence was collected in AFN through Murphy's "Apostles," operating under the cover of the Murphy–Weygand trade accord. Murphy reported enthusiastically that many factions in AFN would welcome, and be prepared to assist, an American invasion. Although much information in Murphy's rosy reports that AFN awaited "liberation" was inaccurate and exaggerated, even fabricated, they proved crucial, Buchanan believes, because they provided the American President with "useable" and "actionable" material to bolster his argument for Gymnast. "Measured by its delivery of the product that Roosevelt wanted, the covert operation in the Maghreb was a resounding success," Buchannan asserts.[38]

Murphy's objective remained to secure an "invitation" from high officials for an Allied invasion of AFN. However, following Weygand's ouster, Murphy had been forced to broaden his contacts and cultivate other actors as well as collect information on the Maghreb that might be useful to invasion planners.[39] Murphy's attention focused on a "Group of Five" well-connected conservatives led by businessman and former *Cagoule* supporter Jacques Lemaigre-Dubreuil, who claimed to have a network of contacts in high places willing to facilitate an Allied invasion.[40] With Murphy's encouragement, OSS agent in the Lisbon embassy, former Czarist officer, and naturalized American Robert Solberg had made contact with Lemaigre-Dubreuil to discuss installing General Henri Giraud as head of a regime in AFN backed by American lend-lease aid. Enlisting Giraud offered just one more half-baked idea in Roosevelt's "indirect approach" to Torch, but one attractive as well to the British, eager to unburden themselves of the truculent de Gaulle. Australian war correspondent Alan Moorehead agreed that while the tall, elegant cavalryman appeared to have strolled out of French army central casting, Giraud was, nevertheless, "a little unsubtle, a little narrow and intransigent, and very vulnerable indeed to designs of the skilled political manipulators who at that moment were flooding into Algiers . . ."[41]

By the summer of 1942, Murphy had managed to forward a plethora of intelligence on French fortifications, troop dispositions, beach gradients, and the like in Morocco and Algeria, as well as concoct a plausible political scenario whereby Giraud would be flown in to captain an insurrectionary movement in AFN. "Cheerful accounts of the progress of the conspiracy and the probability of its success in capturing the allegiance of the French Armed Forces," retailed by Murphy's "Apostles" over the summer, were greeted with "cautious reservations" by American intelligence, that pointed out that none of the major players in AFN – Juin, Noguès, or Michelier – was party to the plot. Nevertheless, the assurance of an active resistance that promised to muster 35,000 Frenchmen prepared to facilitate an Anglo-American invasion of AFN smoothed acceptance of Torch. In this way, Murphy's intelligence and conspiratorial activity, as inaccurate, amateurish, and plagiarized from Polish sources as it frequently was, served Roosevelt's purpose in helping to overcome the objections of his Secretaries of State and War, and Army COS Marshall, to Torch. In any case, Sledgehammer, the plan to capture Brest or Cherbourg, was a non-starter, and concentrating on the Pacific would merely allow Germany further to consolidate its hold on Europe. A target invasion date of 30 October 1942 was set.[42]

The promise of popular support did not only serve to legitimize Torch in the eyes of the Anglo-American public as an exercise in liberation. According to North American scholar Sophie Roberts, the presence of a network of 350–400 young resisters in Algiers, 85 percent of whom were Jews, was vital to the success of Torch: "The Allied troops were able to land in Algiers without serious resistance because insurgents had effectively neutralized the city," concludes Roberts.[43] She is certainly correct that the only successful part of Murphy's conspiracy was its civilian component in Algiers. But while a flash resistance might have played a brief tactical role in Algiers, as a phenomenon it hardly offered the key to Torch's success. The elements of Torch's triumph did not reside in the resistance, which was limited to a handful of second-tier and third-tier players, who acted only on the margins of the invasion. At least five factors contributed to the neutralization of *l'armée d'Afrique*, beginning with Vichy's policy of "defense against whoever," that had failed to define a threat. For Juin and the army, the Axis represented the greater peril to French sovereignty, attacking either through Spanish Morocco or through southern Tunisia. True to his Anglophobic instincts, Darlan and the French navy envisaged a Royal Navy descent on Bizerte. Failure to define a threat contributed to the second factor that worked to Allied benefit – surprise on the strategic, operational, and tactical levels. Strategically, the French command did not believe an Allied attack against AFN possible before the spring of 1943 at the earliest. On the operational level, the French navy and *l'armée d'Afrique* were confident that they could repel a Dieppe-style Allied "raid" against a secondary harbor. AFN was completely unprepared to confront an invasion force of 100,000 men inserted across multiple beachheads, supported by a major Allied naval and air armada. And if that were not enough, the deliberate fragmentation of the French command in AFN out of fears of political disloyalty, as well as inter-service discord, constituted a third factor that sabotaged a unified response to the Allied invasion. A fourth factor was Darlan's presence in Algiers on 8 November 1942. This further disaggregated the military hierarchy left without firm direction as the admiral pursued his own political agenda. It was this, rather than the temporary interruption of a handful of Jewish resisters, that caused command confusion in Algiers. Darlan's presence further undermined Alphonse Juin, who, unlike his predecessor, had failed to inherit the broad civil–military powers that had been accorded Weygand in September 1940 when Vichy feared Africa's defection to the Gaullists. Nor was he even fully in charge of AFN's defenses, as events were to prove.

A final factor that undermined the French response was not what the resistance actually did. Rather, the senior echelons of *l'armée d'Afrique* feared that many of their subordinates would refuse to resist the allies beyond a *pro forma* "*baroud* (skirmish) *d'honneur*." The 1940 armistice had been sold to *l'armée d'Afrique* as a tactic to buy time to prepare *la revanche*. Torch offered French soldiers the opportunity to reenter the war. While organized resistance in AFN did very little directly to disaggregate and delay the French response, what it did accomplish was to trigger fears, especially in Constantine and Tunis, that the command had been infiltrated by "dissident" officers prepared to facilitate an Allied invasion. The knowledge that their own troops might not follow orders produced further hesitation and indecision in a military command whose lines of authority had been intentionally splintered along service lines and between Vichy, Rabat, Algiers, and Tunis. Caught between Vichy orders to resist, indecision in Algiers caused by Darlan's prevarications, and the fear of losing control of their subordinates, the French command failed to muster a coherent response to the Anglo-American invasion.

To reinforce this hesitation, on 8 November the American invaders broadcast that they came as friends, offering the opportunity to liberate France from Axis occupation. Not surprisingly, this appeal worked less well with the navy, with its history of Anglophobia and imperial rivalry, reinforced by Mers-el-Kébir and Dakar. The navy was also a much smaller service, with a tight, centralized chain-of-command better able to enforce homogeneity of outlook among men confined to shipboard, than was the sprawling, socially and racially diverse *armée d'Afrique*. This inter-service friction further scrambled the defense's response. In a confusion of orders and counter-orders issued by Vichy, Algiers, Casablanca, and Tunis, and through the various service hierarchies, officers were left isolated, without information, prey to rumor, and fearful that "dissidence" had contaminated *l'armée d'Afrique*. Indecision at the top of the hierarchy communicated itself downwards, meaning that the predominant reflex among lower cadres was hesitation and prevarication. This vacillation in army ranks in particular worked its way back up the chain of command, to make leaders hesitant to act out of fear that subordinates might disobey their orders, or even defect to the Anglo-American invaders.[44]

The underlying implication here is that France's senior military leadership was unsure that *l'armée d'Afrique*'s undying loyalty to the Marshal could withstand the stress of an Allied invasion. And, while unwilling to slide openly into "dissidence" as had Mast, Béthouart, and Beaufre, a significant number of company- and field-grade officers nonetheless seemed privately to have viewed the Anglo-American invasion as a golden opportunity to reenter the war, redeem their shame over the armistice, and avenge 1940. By excluding the Gaullist FFL, and confining the British to peripheral objectives in Oran and Algiers, while spearheading the main invasion in Bône with the goal of quickly marching to Tunis, the invaders sought to minimize the civil war and Anglophobia dimensions that had goaded Vichy troops into stiff opposition in 1941 Syria. Prolonged confusion in Algiers combined with a muddled command structure to create space for individual initiative, as soldiers reclaimed the freedom to make "moral choices" within an evolving disciplinary concept and hierarchical muddle. Left to make their own decisions in isolation, many officers acquiesced to Allied *force majeure*.[45]

A Fragmented Chain of Command

Traditionally, Algeria's Governor General and the Residents General in Tunisia and Morocco were responsible for the internal and external defense of their territories. In September 1942, a new command scheme was activated that separated the defense of AFN into a "Maritime Theater," a "Terrestrial Theater," and Morocco. Inside the Mediterranean littoral, the Maritime Prefect of the 4th Region, headquartered in Algiers, was responsible for surveillance, naval combat, and the harbor defense. The new regulations specified that, in the case of an external attack, land, air, and "maritime elements dedicated specifically to littoral defense" would comprise the "Terrestrial Theater." This fell under the General Commander-in-chief – who, since 20 November 1941, had been Alphonse Juin. Juin's direct subordinates included the commanders of the 19th Military Region, that incorporated Algeria and Tunis, and their sector commanders headquartered in Oran, Algiers, Constantine, and Tunis. The September 1942 command reorganization had divided Tunisia into the "Bizerte sector" under Vice-Admiral Edmond Derrien, which extended from the Medjerda valley to the Algerian frontier, and the "Tunisia sector" that covered the rest of the country to the border with Tripolitania, commanded by General Georges Barré.[46]

There were at least five problems with this command scheme. First, the regulations stated that, "as soon as a landing attempt occurs, the responsibility for the initial defense falls instantly in each sector, on the commander of that sector who has the means of defense without having to refer to other authorities. He will notify his subordinates immediately that he is taking charge." While military organizations seek to encourage initiative in theory, in practice they are rigidly hierarchical. In the confused situation of 8 November 1942, one fraught with political implications, which saw the breakdown of communications, a paralysis of decision-making, and contradictory orders, rescinded orders, or no orders at all emanating from Algiers and Vichy, local commanders guided only by the vague nostrum of "defense against whomever" understandably hesitated in most cases to react to the invasions of AFN with conviction. This occurred because of a second problem unforeseen by the regulations: "As soon as possible, the commander of the Theater of operations must assume the general direction of the battle." Juin failed to do this. The confusion caused by Murphy and the Algiers resistance was partly responsible. But, more importantly, it was unclear if his authority extended to the invasion beaches.

Third, a unified command structure was not in effect throughout AFN, because, in November 1942, "this system was still being studied and discussed in Morocco." The reason for this delay was that Noguès insisted that political stability in Morocco required that the Resident General maintain complete command authority.[47] In practice, however, Vice-Admiral François-Félix (Frix) Michelier had been assigned the title of "commander-in-chief of the navy in Morocco," responsible for coordinating the defense of the beaches and harbors attacked by the Americans, while the air force in Morocco remained antiquated and undertrained, its reconnaissance and defense role restricted by a lack of aviation fuel and fear of defections to Gibraltar.[48] Furthermore, these regulations, no doubt a compromise between *l'armée d'Afrique* and the navy, offered an invitation to inter- and intra-service friction. Inside the Mediterranean, the Maritime Prefect of the 4th Region at Algiers was responsible for the "Maritime Theater," which was defined as "combat at sea, implying the surveillance of the littoral and the defense of harbor installations." Juin's subordinate commanders in Oran and Bizerte were also vice-admirals, men networked to a separate service hierarchy whose loyalties remained solidly Vichyite.

Inter-service friction would work further to fragment the French response to Torch. The French navy remained a law unto itself, a situation that had prevailed even under Weygand and that Darlan had no intention of changing. This made Tunisia virtually a navy fiefdom, especially after Juin ordered the army commander in Tunisia, General Georges Barré, to withdraw his forces into Algeria. This was also the case with Casablanca, where, during the Allied invasion, Michelier communicated directly with Vichy, not with his immediate superior Noguès in Rabat, nor with Juin in Algiers. This built-in command confusion was sharpened by Darlan's fortuitous presence in Algiers, by the initial disruptions caused by the Algiers resistance, and by the contradictory and ill-defined mandate of "defense against whomever."

But with the Anglo-Americans attacking Morocco and Algeria, while Axis forces piled into Tunisia, local commanders were left to decipher the confusing and contradictory directives coming from Algiers and Vichy.

So, while some historians emphasize the impact of the Algiers resistance in delaying and confusing the French reaction to Torch,[49] in fact, the French command muddle was inbuilt, both organizationally, in the failure to define a threat, and in the fears among commanders that *l'armée d'Afrique* was honeycombed with "dissidence" and might not respond to orders. For these reasons, and because of the improvized and inchoate plans of resistance in AFN, Murphy predicted that the French reaction to Torch would provide the operation's "most dangerous intangible."[50] Both Darlan and Juin realized the potential for confusion, but believed that they had ample time to sort out the problem as any Allied invasion could not materialize before the spring of 1943. The 8 November surprise would cause Juin, Darlan, and Vichy to scramble, would further confuse, complicate, and tangle lines of authority, and brought to the surface all the contradictions and jumbled allegiances, accentuated by Weygand's imposition of loyalty oaths and unquestioned obedience to the Marshal. Torch would also lay bare the conflicting attitudes, insecurities, careerism, and policies of Vichy and its North African proconsuls. Above all, Torch, like its mirror on the mainland – the Axis occupation of the *zone libre* – punctured the myth of Vichy sovereignty wrapped in a mantle of "neutrality," and "defense against whomever."[51]

This fragmentation was exacerbated by Darlan's dithering, which can be explained not because he believed the Allies would win the war, but, in Bernard Costagliola's view, in terms of his pathetic hope that Germany might lighten the conditions of the armistice as a reward for Vichy's vigorous defense of AFN. This virtually guaranteed that the French defense would crumble from below. The absence of information, poor communications, and rumor combined with a chaos of contradictory orders coming out of an overlapping and ill-defined command structure left soldiers and sailors virtually on their own either to make their own decisions to resist or acquiesce, or to choose which leader to follow. The largely Jewish resistance in Algiers initially contributed to the confused command response, but it did not cause it. Finally, the power of the Anglo-American attack against three widely separate and isolated French centers of resistance, manned by sailors and soldiers whose weaponry was inadequate as well as outdated due in large part to restrictions imposed by Axis armistice commissions, virtually guaranteed that French opposition, while tenacious in places, must prove short-winded. Therefore, unlike El Alamein, Torch was never a close-run victory, that hung by the thread of the actions of a handful of Jewish resisters in Algiers.[52] "Defense against whomever" translated into opposition to the Allies from the navy, especially in Morocco and Algeria, mixed with hesitation in the army, especially in the Constantinois and Tunisia, combined with the complicity of French admirals with the Axis in Tunisia.

But the importance of the resistance ultimately did not lie with their tactical success in Algiers. Rather, Murphy's quasi-failure would eventually rebound on Roosevelt with the so-called "Darlan deal" – the compromise struck by Eisenhower and Mark Clark on 13 November 1942, after tortuous negotiations and hundreds of deaths, to allow Darlan to remain in charge in return for ordering a ceasefire throughout AFN. The "Darlan deal" was excused as an impromptu tactical decision, and the promise to allow the French to continue to run their own affairs advertised as a pragmatic response meant to end French resistance and save Allied lives. In fact, the Darlan deal suggested at best a frantic improvization, at worst the foreseeable outcome of Roosevelt's discredited courtship of Vichy and Weygand through Leahy and Murphy. Darlan represented what Crémieux-Brilhac called "Vichy *BIS* " in AFN.[53] The deal was also interpreted as a betrayal of those who had assisted the Allied success in North Africa. Rather than a strategy impelled by a moral "crusade" as per the Atlantic Charter and the Four Freedoms to rescue the world from fascism, in the short run at least, Torch gave a new, if limited, lease on life to Vichy officials and policies in AFN. In the process, Murphy and the American "liberators" would betray those who had aided them, and bring discredit and suspicion on Roosevelt's political agenda, both in the eyes of the Anglo-American public and, more particularly, in de Gaulle's view.[54]

Casablanca or Bône? Planning for Torch

Planning for Torch had begun in London on 31 July 1941. It was clear from the beginning that this would be a hugely ambitious undertaking, especially this early in the war, that would transport 100,000 soldiers in 1,400 ships from harbors in the United States and the UK to converge simultaneously at several points in AFN (Map 10.1), without being detected and possibly intercepted by Axis or French forces. Its size and complexity contrasted with the fact that preparation was very much a seat of the pants affair, organized on relatively short notice, one that was experimental in many aspects. Furthermore, operational planning was handicapped by multiple factors, beginning with the fact that the British were overstretched, so that availability of ocean liners converted into

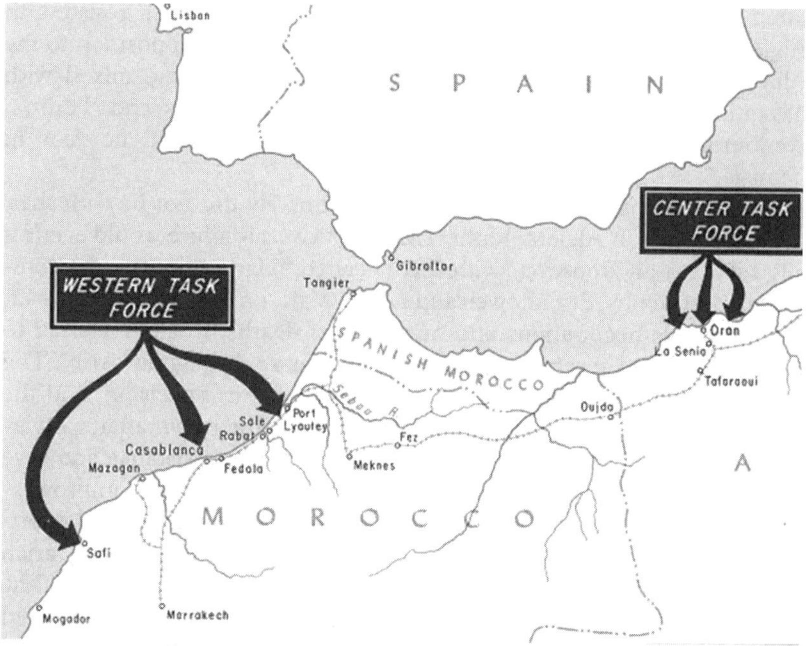

Map 10.1 Map of French North Africa. Center for Military History.

troop transports, naval landing craft, carrier-borne aircraft, and naval fire support would be limited. The Americans were also in a frantic expansion mode, and as yet had little operational experience, especially in amphibious landings.[55] The Allies had first to devise a joint and combined chain of command to direct Torch, and coordinate planning staffs and logistics on both sides of the Atlantic. Two separate national armies, navies, and air forces had to be fused on short notice into a single operational force. Whether the Army or the Navy was actually in command of amphibious operations was an open question. Allied Forces Headquarters (AFHQ) under Eisenhower came into existence only on 12 September 1942, less than two months before GIs and Tommies splashed ashore in AFN. Therefore, a deficit of French opposition, be it through complicity, surprise, disruption, or weak French defensive capabilities, would ease success. Secrecy and deception aimed to eliminate an Axis reaction. The sinking by the *Luftwaffe* or U-boats of a few vital ships in the Allied armada, such as communication ships – added as a "lesson learned" following the failed Dakar expedition – would potentially jeopardize the success of the entire operation.[56]

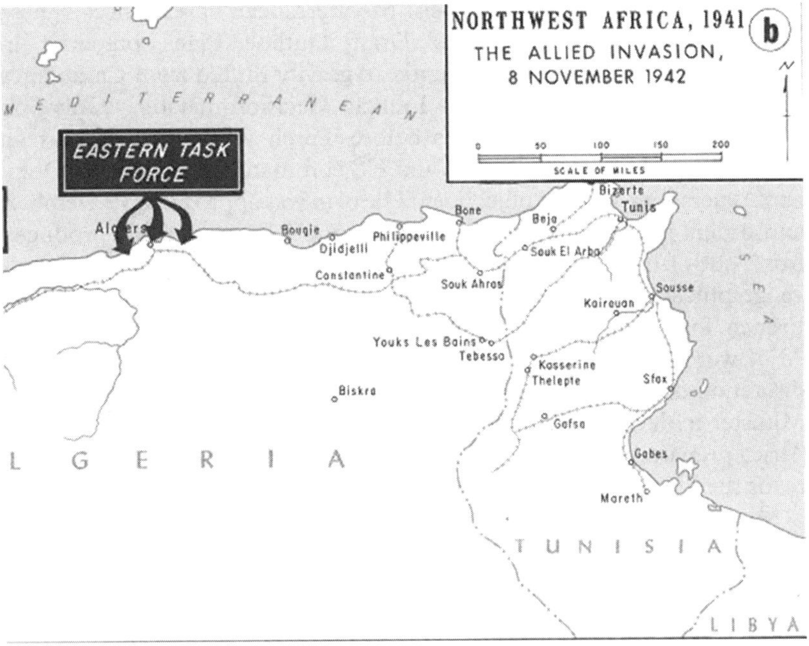

Map 10.1 (Cont.)

Not surprisingly, given that over 2,000 kilometers separate Casablanca and Tunis, the Americans and British debated where the focus of the landings should lie – the British favored Mediterranean beachheads as far east as Bône (Annaba), roughly 300 kilometers west of Tunis, so as to forestall an Axis occupation of Tunisia. They also pointed out that roiling Atlantic surf ruled out amphibious landings on the Moroccan coast "four days out of five." The Americans favored an assault on Casablanca, advancing the argument that, if the goal of Torch were to pry open the Mediterranean, landings well inside that sea risked being cut off by a German thrust through Spain to Gibraltar, whose air and naval base was vital to the success of Torch. Although British intelligence dismissed this scenario as unlikely, an opinion since validated by historians,[57] George Marshall agreed that it was "better to take a chance on the surf at Casablanca than on the closing of the Strait of Gibraltar." British COS Alan Brooke also believed it imprudent to bypass potentially hostile French divisions in Morocco. But he was an outlier in London.[58]

Quite apart from uncertainties about Spain's reaction, the Dieppe fiasco of 19 August 1942 introduced a note of planning caution, as did the American President's "Western Mediterranean" preferences. These influences shaped the various Draft Outline Plans prepared in August 1942 that saw Torch's center of gravity shifted from Casablanca to Algiers, the fulcrum of French decision-making. Only on 20 September, barely six weeks before Torch was launched, was an official plan submitted to British and US commands. Casablanca, Oran, and Algiers were fixed as objectives. The plan was approved on 2 October, and orders issued on 8 October. Maps of AFN were quickly produced from out-of-date, large-scale sketches archived in the British army's geographical section. But some fundamental questions regarding how French forces were to be dealt with and governing arrangements in AFN were not addressed, were left vague, would be entrusted to the discretion of local commanders, or were left to the President and Prime Minister to decide. "The Allies would therefore approach French North Africa prepared to fight but preferring an amicable association in arms," reads the US Army official history.[59]

Murphy's optimistic reports encouraged "best case" assumptions among the planners. Nevertheless, the operational challenges of Torch would be immense: three Allied flotillas, sailing separately from the United States and the UK, must arrive off the coast of AFN without being detected. Neophyte sailors were to launch roughly 100,000 indifferently trained soldiers using largely untested technology along a 1,000-mile coastline, stretching from south of Casablanca to Algiers, and these troops were to seize three major harbors, before hopscotching to Bône to position for an accelerated thrust to Tunis, all before Axis forces could react. Obviously, the success of this venture would require catching the Axis by surprise, a rapid collapse of French opposition, and meteorological cooperation.

The problem for the Allies in planning an attack on Morocco was that the French protectorate had no obvious center of gravity, like Algiers or Tunis. Seizing Casablanca, Morocco's largest city and economic hub, with the only large harbor in the country, was obviously vital. However, Morocco's political capital was Rabat, almost 90 kilometers to the north of Casablanca, where the decision to fight or forfeit would be made. Western Task Force, commanded by Admiral Kent Hewitt, composed of ninety-nine ships, including four carriers and three battleships, set sail from various ports on the east coast of the United States and Bermuda on 23 October. Once off the coast of Morocco, the invasion force of 35,000 men under Major General George Patton would face the challenge of high beach surf, combined with the fact that Casablanca, like Dakar in September 1940, with its array of coastal and anti-aircraft batteries, a significant naval force that included the battleship *Jean Bart* and the cruiser *Primauguet*, and an army garrison that could potentially be reinforced from Meknès and Marrakech, was considered too well defended to storm head on.[60] Therefore, the plan called for seizing shallow anchorages to the north and south of Casablanca to land tanks and artillery, which would allow Patton if necessary to approach Morocco's principal port city from the land side.[61] This scattershot attack hardly constituted a hammer blow, especially as invasion momentum would be sustained initially by supplies and reinforcements brought in over beaches notorious for high surf. The strong French naval squadron at Casablanca required that the battleship *Massachusetts* be included in the "covering force," while a US submarine was posted off Dakar to guard against the possibility that the battleship *Richelieu* might be dispatched north to aid in the defense.

The Central and Eastern Task Forces would sail from the UK in ten separate convoys, the first from 2 October, that grouped in all 240 troop transport ships, cargo ships, and auxiliaries and 94 escorts, including three battleships and six carriers. Although the harbors at Oran and Algiers were considered less well defended than Casablanca, the calculation was that they too could be more easily enveloped from the land side. However, a rugged Mediterranean coastline and the fact that 16,700 French troops were barracked within a day's march of the city presented a challenge for the 37,100 US troops, principally from the US 1st Armored and 1st Infantry Divisions, and 3,600 British soldiers deposited on four beaches along the Bay des Andalouses, 20 kilometers west of the city, and at Arzew 40 kilometers to the East. With the aid of paratroops, these troops would seize the two airfields at Tafaraoui and Sénia, estimated to contain at least 100 combat aircraft, and the promontories to the east and west of Oran to silence their coastal batteries, and then drive into the city. Two small shiploads of US troops were to be landed in the port itself to prevent sabotage. Christened "Operation Reservist," this head-on assault by two small ships and a few dozen infantrymen was decried as suicidal. But so important was Oran deemed to operational logistics that "Reservist" was nevertheless approved. Air cover would fly out of Gibraltar, and then land on captured airfields around Oran.[62]

The all-important Algiers operation was assigned to Eastern Task Force. As at Oran, 23,000 British and 10,000 US soldiers, commanded by US Major General Charles Ryder, would come ashore on beaches to the east and west of the city, with air support provided by five US and four UK carriers. As at Oran, a special forces assault aimed directly at Algiers harbor was folded into the plan. Between Algiers and Constantine, the Allies estimated that the French could muster around 30,000 troops, and a significant number of aircraft from the airfields surrounding the capital. Algiers was assigned the most robust naval force, because the Allies deemed the rapid submission of Algiers critical, so that British and US forces under British General Kenneth Anderson could advance quickly through Bougie, Philippeville, and Bône toward Bizerte and Tunis. It was also meant to shield the invasion force against the intervention of the Italian or French navies, and from U-boats. Stretching to the horizon off the coast of Algiers on the morning of 8 November, this naval array must have been impressive indeed.[63] An intensive bombing campaign against mainland Italy, Sicily, and Sardinia tied down Axis air defenses, while on 8 November, 350 planes parked wingtip-to-wingtip at Gibraltar, and Allied reconnaissance aircraft kept a close watch on the three North African ports, where it was calculated that the French Air Force (FAF) had assembled 500 planes in various states of air worthiness, but with limited aviation fuel. A further concern was that the French fleet in Toulon might sortie to defend AFN. German Mediterranean commander Albert Kesselring was aware of the Allied build-up in Gibraltar, and that a large convoy had left the UK. But was unable to determine Allied objectives with accuracy.[64]

Given the apparently very narrow margin of Allied military superiority, political preparation of the battlefield was deemed essential. Murphy was in charge of an overall campaign of "subversive activities, propaganda, and political warfare" as a member of Eisenhower's staff. In September, he flew to Washington to coordinate plans for Torch. After meeting with Roosevelt in his Hyde Park home, and with Eisenhower in London, Murphy returned to Algiers with instructions that no French leader should be notified of the invasion until it was imminent. The promise was that, upon liberation, French forces would be rearmed by the Allies and would remain under French command. An active program of propaganda was prepared to minimize French resistance. The Allied plan was "to win campaigns in the field while allowing the French to work out their own internal problems, unhampered and unaided," declares the official history. "This policy was avowed by the President and set forth as approved military doctrine ... The basic method would be to supervise the operation of existing civil agencies by the French. The past political sympathies of officeholders were to be treated as of small significance compared with their ability to discharge the technical duties of their respective positions." Murphy would assume the position of chief civil administrator and political advisor to Eisenhower. Given that Washington's grasp of French politics remained "exploratory," Michael Neiberg declares this policy "both politically naïve and strategically misguided."[65]

If the Allies at least managed to achieve surprise, it was because, in the opinion of John Patch, Torch "represents the first actual, operational use of ULTRA and other special intelligence in the planning and execution of large-scale campaigns and the first instance of Allied collaborative strategic deception."[66] French naval cyphers were an open book, as the Vichy Admiralty had only tinkered with them since 1940. French weather reports, sent in a low-grade cypher, were particularly informative for code-crackers. A splintered Axis command system, combined with low priority assigned to AFN, also made it difficult for them to assess and prioritize threats.[67] In any case, as well as El Alamein, German forces were also battling for their lives at Stalingrad and in the Caucasus, and had few assets to spare for AFN. On 5 November, the German commander in the Mediterranean, Albert Kesselring, realized that the Allied convoys passing through the Strait were too large for Malta. But his operational reaction was to set his U-boat ambush west of the Sicilian Channel, which on the night of 7 November allowed the Eastern and Central Task Forces to veer south toward Algiers and Oran unmolested. Only at this point did naval headquarters in Algiers send out a "danger" message and alert Casablanca.[68] Realizing their mistake on the morning of 8 November, the Germans ordered the U-boats to reverse course, by which time it was too late. In the end, three significant convoys reached AFN, with U-boats only managing two attacks, in the process damaging a single ship. "In the final assessment, a combination of detailed planning, aggressive signals intelligence efforts, a viable deception scheme, a high degree of operational security, and fortuitous events produced operational surprise that in turn facilitated an Allied bridgehead into northwest Africa," concludes Patch.[69]

Having avoided Axis interception, everything came down to the reaction of the Vichy command in AFN and the fighting capacities of *l'armée d'Afrique*. Mast was warned on 28 October that the invasion would be launched in a few days. When Mast protested that nothing would be ready, Murphy asked Eisenhower to postpone the invasion by two weeks – an absurd request, as Murphy later acknowledged, as the fleets had sailed.[70] The result was that resistance was stillborn at Casablanca, and a non-starter at Oran. Only at Algiers did it meet with limited success. But even here, Murphy's resistance had almost blown the cover on the invasion.

A Tale of Three Cities

Casablanca

Creating a resistance in Morocco was considered especially important. An expansive coastline, the inadequacy of the harbors other than Casablanca, the requirement to neutralize the air base at Port-Lyautey north of Rabat, and the Atlantic swells that ran especially high from October to May all complicated the prospects of a successful amphibious landing, while making a concentration of assault forces problematic. Casablanca would be the prize. However, it was thought imprudent to tackle it head-on as the city garrison and surrounding barracks could muster around 7,000 mainly Moroccan and Senegalese troops, backed by strong naval coastal defense artillery, a substantial force of warships, and fifty fighters and thirty bombers stationed at two airfields on the outskirts. In case of attack, the Moroccan defenses would be coordinated and commanded by Resident General Noguès.[71] However, in November 1942, the assignment of defense responsibilities in Morocco was still a work in progress. All the places where the Americans elected to land, namely Medhia, Port-Lyautey, Casablanca, Fedala, and Safi, technically fell under Vice-Admiral Michelier's authority.[72]

The task of organizing a resistance to facilitate the American incursion was entrusted to the commander of the Casablanca division, General Antoine Béthouart. Two years had served to convince the Narvik veteran, who in June 1940 in London had declined his Saint-Cyr classmate de Gaulle's invitation to rally to his exile movement, to join Murphy's "Group of Five" conspiracy. On 2 November, Béthouart had received a visit from one of Murphy's contacts, Jean Rigault – the man Macmillan compared to a shady solicitor – to announce the imminence of invasion. When it occurred, Béthouart was to assume command of all troops in Morocco under Giraud's authority, provide guides and liaisons for US forces upon landing, and arrest Noguès and the members of the German and Italian control commissions, as well as occupy all telephone and telegraph exchanges. But, barely three days before the invasion, Murphy set these orders aside, and left all decisions to Béthouart.[73]

This proved to be a serious mistake, the first of several tactical errors by the American Minister. Unfortunately, while Béthouart's battlefield courage was beyond question, among the conspirators, he counted as a trimmer. For starters, Béthouart truly admired Noguès, who, in his view, had reconstituted the army in Morocco, camouflaged equipment, and was a friend of the Sultan, who had kept Morocco relatively stable in comparison with Algeria and Tunisia, where social and political tensions had intensified. Furthermore, Béthouart, his chief of staff, Colonel Eugène Molle, and his G-2 were skeptical that the Allies were capable of mounting a large-scale invasion less than a year after Washington had entered the war. Perhaps the invasion was a hoax? Nor could they come up with a reliable contact in the pro-Vichy navy, responsible for coastal defense. Even the army, that had been whipped back into line by Weygand and reinforced by refugees from the fervently anti-Gaullist

Syrian garrison, was not considered by the conspirators to be trustworthy. Rather than arrest Noguès and Michelier, Béthouart and his co-conspirators hoped that they would acquiesce to an Allied *fait accompli*.[74]

Given the tentative planning and doubts that the invasion would actually happen, not surprisingly the execution of the coup also went off half-cocked. On the evening of 4 November, Rigault returned to say that the invasion convoy had departed the United States, but gave no arrival date. Only two days later did Béthouart learn that the invasion would occur on 8 November at 02:00.[75] Béthouart planned to neutralize Rabat by surrounding the residency with troops, occupying the telephone and telegraph offices, and ordering the mainly Moroccan and Senegalese troops who guarded the beaches to stand down. Inexplicably, given that he had involved his intelligence chief in his conspiracy, Béthouart claimed not to realize that Noguès had a separate communication system that linked him with Michelier, who was responsible for the defense of Casablanca, and the two army divisions headquartered in Meknès and Marrakech. Béthouart dispatched his intelligence chief to coordinate with the Sultan, who denied all knowledge of an invasion. Attempts to contact Gibraltar and conspirators in Algiers for directions were equally unsuccessful. Béthouart complained of feeling abandoned and without direction.[76]

At 17:00 on 7 November, Béthouart ordered his colonels to arrest the German control commission that night, and alert the airfields and units on the beaches. At this point, however, as three USN naval attack groups collected off Safi, Fedala, and Mehdia/Port-Lyautey, these imprecise preparations began to run off the rails. Béthouart contacted one of Juin's staff officers, assuming that the commander was in the know, only to discover that Juin's staff was clueless. At 22:30 in the evening of 7 November, Michelier was tipped off by the French naval liaison to the German commission of the plan to arrest the Axis officers at 04:00 on 8 November. At midnight, Béthouart left Casablanca with the commander of the *Regiment d'infanterie colonial du Maroc* at Rabat, Colonel Pierre Magnan, and drove 50 miles to Moroccan army headquarters at Rabat to set up a command center for the night. The Residency was surrounded by Magnan's troops, who also occupied the telephone exchange. Béthouart sent his aide-de-camp to wake up Noguès at 00:30 on 8 November, inform him of the imminent American attack, tell him that Béthouart was taking command under the authority of General Giraud, and ask for his support. Simultaneously, Lieutenant-colonel Molle, Béthouart's chief of staff, appeared at navy headquarters to present Michelier with a letter from Béthouart as well as copies of the same documents given to Noguès, which Michelier rejected as counterfeit.[77]

In contact at 01:00 on 8 November through their secure phone line, Michelier insisted to Noguès that "It is not possible that there is a convoy off Casablanca." Michelier's stunning miscalculation became obvious when daybreak revealed to the naked eye fifty-eight Allied warships aligned on the horizon.[78] Despite the heavy traffic passing through Gibraltar on the nights of 5–6 and 7–8 November, a warning on the night of 7 November of the threat of an attack on the Moroccan coast, and the meteorological predictions of a lower than normal surf, the Admiralty remained totally unaware of the Western Attack Group's existence, much less that the Americans had arrived off Fedala, 16 miles north of Casablanca, shortly before midnight. However, the American assault was delayed by inexperience, loading problems, poor coordination, and navigation issues, and by high surf that knocked many of the new Higgins boats out of control and drowned their heavily laden soldiers. Only at 05:20 did Michelier sortie four submarines to carry out reconnaissance in front of Casablanca, followed by air surveillance out of Port-Lyautey at 07:00.[79]

Quick phone calls revealed that neither of Morocco's other two divisions, at Marrakech and Meknès, had joined Béthouart's rebellion. No GIs had landed. Roosevelt's personal letter to Noguès had been delivered, but, unrecognized, it was laid aside. Nor had Noguès heard Roosevelt's radio broadcast. Therefore, the Moroccan Resident General concluded that Béthouart's sheaf of documents was a hoax, and so ordered Michelier to take steps to counter any rebellion in the Casablanca division, and to prevent the arrest of the members of the German control commission.[80] General Roger Leyer, cavalry commander in Morocco, dispatched troops to rescue Noguès. When no US troops had appeared by dawn, the opportunistic crowd of officers gathered at Béthouart's headquarters at Rabat began to thin out. Béthouart phoned Noguès, who was beside himself with rage at having been humiliated and betrayed by a subordinate. Béthouart obeyed Noguès' order to report to the residency at 06:00, planning naively to convince Noguès to work with the Americans. Instead, Noguès ordered the arrest of Béthouart and Molle, who were transferred to the military prison in Meknès to be guarded by SOL volunteers until court martialed on 10 November.[81] "Hostilities had come to Morocco in a manner perhaps determined at Vichy but certainly attributable to the resolute French admiral at Casablanca and accepted by the Resident General at Rabat," concluded the US Official History. "The latter assumed command later in the morning and announced that a state of siege prevailed throughout French Morocco."[82]

All that the pro-Allied resistance had managed to accomplish in Morocco was to forfeit, or at least mitigate, the effect of surprise and alert the French defense, concludes Levisse-Touzé.[83] "General Noguès himself confirmed the order to execute the defense plan," concludes the official French Navy history of Torch. "General Béthouart's intervention therefore was to have an effect opposite of that he had sought, by alerting the entire defense." The "Danger" message went out at 02:28, followed by "Alert" at 03:26. The defenders were at their stations at 04:40 when they saw the lights on the landing craft approaching the beaches. At 05:00, an American plane flew over Casablanca to drop tracts with a declaration by President Roosevelt, by which time news of the assaults on Oran and Algiers had reached Casablanca. Nevertheless, when at 04:28 coastal batteries at Safi opened fire on an American destroyer, Noguès concluded that it was a raid, whose purpose might be to incite a Muslim revolt.[84]

The fact that the resistance had been too "soft" was offset by the stunningly but predictably confused reaction of Vichy and its North African chain-of-command. The fundamental problem in Morocco, as in the rest of AFN, was that an insecure command was more focused on the possibility of "*un coup de force intérieur*" than the seemingly remote likelihood of an Anglo-American invasion. Thus, the intentionally fragmented lines of authority between Vichy and AFN, between Governors/Residents General and military commanders, and among services that aimed to balk a wholesale colonial defection from Vichy authority wrong-footed the French defense. When the American consul at Rabat gave Noguès two letters from President Roosevelt, one of which was for the Sultan, presenting Torch as a preemptive strike to prevent Axis intervention, Noguès requested instructions from Juin – an odd reaction from the man who had insisted that he control all decisions in Morocco. The reply was inadvertently sent to Vichy, where Laval ordered Noguès to resist the Americans, and contemplated replacing him with Michelier, who stonewalled all attempts by the Western Task Force commander, George Patton, to contact him.[85] Encouraged by Laval, Noguès had concluded that the attack was a weak one and that the defense was holding. In fact, the US advance was held up not by French resistance, but by high surf that scattered landing craft beyond their designated beaches, in the process swamping and wrecking many of them, which delayed the landing of support weapons, communications equipment, and transportation.[86] This made the invasion a much more equal struggle than it might otherwise have been (Map 10.2). These logistical problems were complicated by French shelling and occasional strafing runs by French aircraft. Nevertheless, O'Hara concludes that "there were far too many troops coming ashore for the invasion to fail."[87]

Allied air cover focused on preventing French reinforcements arriving from Marrakech, whose commander, General Henri Martin, supposedly

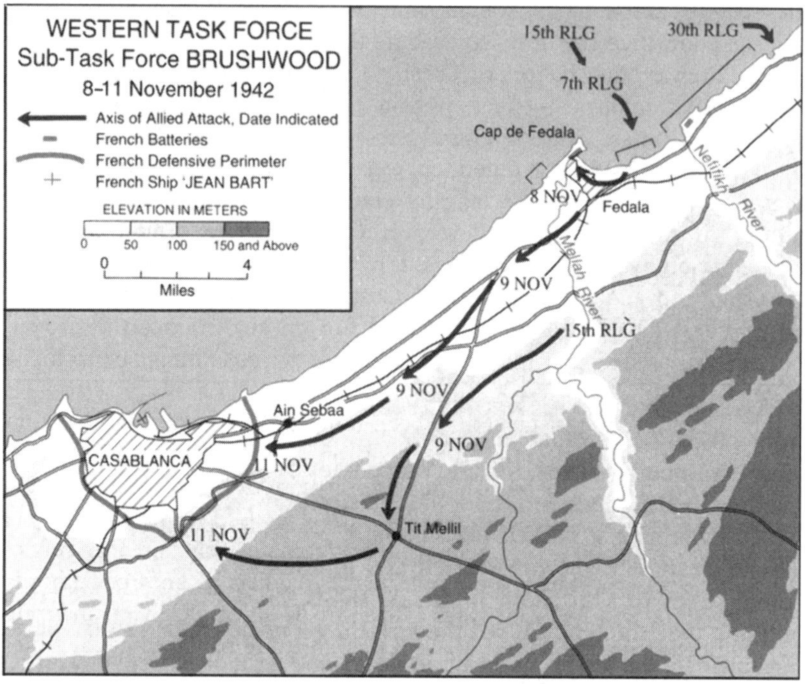

Map 10.2 Map of Casablanca landing. Center for Military History.

part of Béthouart's pro-Allied conspiracy, in the end followed command orders to dispatch reinforcements to Safi.[88] Totally unanticipated by the invaders was the presence of large groups of Moroccan civilian spectators, completely oblivious to the dangers of small arms fire. "Street intersections were crowded with natives turning their heads like a tennis gallery, in trying to watch the exchange of fire," declares the official history. "The wounded were poked and jabbered at. An unfolded map quickly attracted an excited group." If the French had counted on the support of the indigenous population, they were destined to be disappointed. Muslim men and boys flocked to the beach and harbor to offer GIs a hand at offloading equipment in return for cigarettes or a tin of C-rations, in the process pilfering significant amounts of stores. The armored forces landed at Safi were too far away to reach Casablanca before the ceasefire was declared on 11 November.[89]

From 05:20 on the morning of 8 November, Michelier ordered five submarines to engage the invaders. He then ordered the 2nd Light Squadron, consisting of the light cruiser *Primauguet* and seven destroyers under Rear Admiral Gervais de Lafond, who had been decorated for action against the British in the Eastern Mediterranean in 1941, to steam up the coast to attack the vulnerable troop transports of the Allied flotilla. Desperately outgunned by the Allied ships, and harassed by SBD (Scout Bomber Douglas) Dauntless dive-bombers, in a naval battle lasting four hours, the light cruiser *Primauguet* and the destroyer *Milan* were so heavily damaged that they were run aground. Four torpedo boats, a patrol boat, and eight submarines were lost, while the battleship *Jean Bart*, two destroyers, and seven smaller boats were heavily damaged, leaving only one seaworthy ship in the Casablanca squadron. When, on 17 January 1943, Eisenhower arrived in Casablanca for the Anfa conference, his naval aide Harry Butcher found that the *Jean Bart* "had, as advertised, been shot up 'proper,' although ... Patton only permitted the quickest of glances at her ... for fear of offending the pride of the French."[90] While US airpower had proved particularly effective against French ships and shore batteries, the FAF concentrated on the beaches and did virtually nothing to aid the French navy in their unequal struggle against the invaders, during which the French lost eighty planes to forty-four for the Americans.[91]

Surprisingly tough French resistance from the 1er RTM at Mehdia/Port-Lyautey meant that "the situation of General [Lucien] Truscott's force at nightfall, 8 November, was insecure and even precarious," concludes the official history. The Americans had failed to seize the important airfield, and the surf was running too high to unload additional equipment, while French reinforcements under General André Dody had been dispatched from Meknès. So precarious, in fact, that Truscott's appeals to the Commander of the 1er RTM, Colonel Charles Petit, reminding him of the long history of Franco-American fraternity of arms, did nothing to lessen French resistance.[92] On 9 November, the airfield, along with the Kasba, were captured. But the French still held Port-Lyautey when the order to cease fire arrived at 19:30 on that night.[93]

By the end of the day on 8 November the Americans had landed 7,750 men at Fedala, who by 18:00 were only around 15 kilometers north of Casablanca. In part by following the railway behind numerous anti-tank weapons, US forces reached the outskirts of Casablanca late on 10 November, as Patton put the finishing touches on a plan of attack to be launched on Casablanca at 07:00 on the morning of 11 November. But news that a ceasefire had been concluded in Algiers arrived at Noguès' headquarters at 18:10 on the evening of 10 November, which aborted the attack. Nevertheless, Michelier, to whom Darlan's 11:05 order of a ceasefire had been radioed to Casablanca at 14:30, proved more difficult to persuade, insisting at 21:40 that "The order of the Marshal is to continue hostilities as long as possible." This required several phone conversations between Michelier and Noguès before a "ceasefire" order was given out between 01:45 and 02:00 on 11 November.[94]

The subsequent meeting at Fedala's Hotel Miramar at 13:00 on 11 November between Patton, Admirals Hewitt and Hall, and Michelier, who were subsequently joined by Noguès, established no separate agreement for Morocco, beyond facilitating use by US forces of French ports, roads, and railways. The modalities of the Allied occupation of Morocco were to be worked out by Eisenhower and Darlan. That evening, Noguès received a communication from Vichy that designated him as the Marshal's representative in AFN, so that he left the next day, 12 November, for Algiers.[95] On 15 November, Patton was forced to intervene to free Béthouart and Magnan. Others had to wait for months for freedom and even longer for rehabilitation. The two senior French officers were subsequently transported on an American plane to Algiers, where they met a frosty reception from Giraud, who advised the Casablanca conspirators to spend some time in Gibraltar to allow emotions to cool. Béthouart was subsequently dispatched to Washington to negotiate the rearming of the French army decided at the Anfa Conference of January 1943. Once de Gaulle came to power in Algiers from the summer of 1943, Béthouart's ascension would be dazzling.[96] Still, he must have wondered what life might have been like had he accepted de Gaulle's June 1940 offer to join him in London.

Oran

Heavily defended by 13 coastal batteries, significant anti-aircraft emplacements, around 100 aircraft, and a garrison of 10,000 that could balloon within 24 hours to 22,500, according to Allied estimates, Oran (Map 10.3) threatened to become a reprise of the Dakar raid. To avoid this, two landing beaches were designated 34 and 12 miles, respectively, west of Oran, and a third at Arzew, 25 miles east of western Algeria's largest city. The naval support for the Central Task Force was entirely Royal Navy. Teams launched in portable boats by submarine were to guide the landing craft toward the invasion beaches. Operation Reservist called for two cutters, H.M.S. *Hartland* and H.M.S. *Walney*, to convey 71 officers and 367 soldiers from the 1st US Armored Division to seize the harbor to prevent sabotage. An airborne operation was to be mounted from Cornwall to drop 500 paratroops on Latigue and La Sénia airfields, separated by 8 miles, southwest of Oran. The attackers were to be aided by a pro-Allied fifth column organized by Roger Carcassonne, an industrialist friend of Lemaigre-Dubreuil and Colonel Pierre Tostain, chief of staff to Oran division

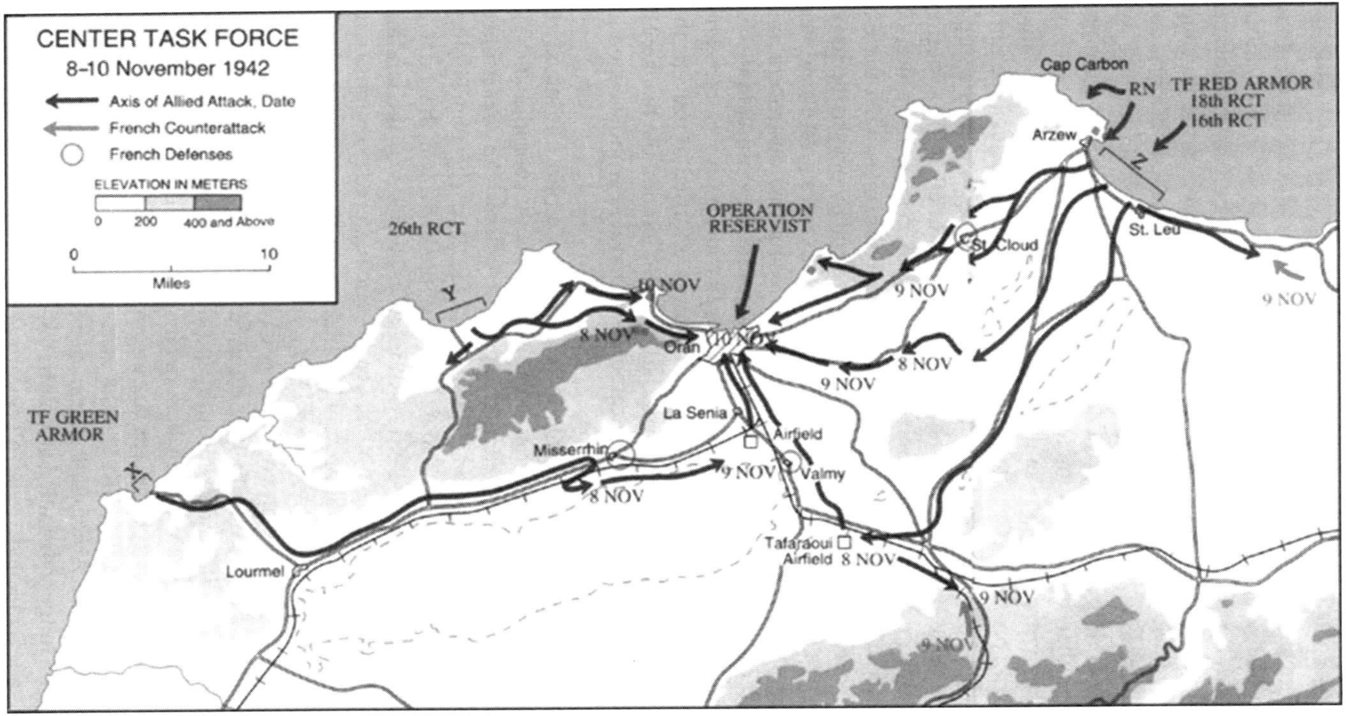

Map 10.3 Map of Oran landing. Center for Military History.

commander General Robert Boisseau. The plan was to have an "uprising" to seize strategic points in the city. However, as in Casablanca, the urge to confess to one's superior proved so overwhelming that, on 6 November, Tostain told Boisseau of the impending invasion.[97] Fortunately for the Allies, Boisseau proved incredulous, and so did not pass on the warning. But Murphy's vice-consul in Oran, Ridgeway Knight, called off a planned civilian insurrection, fearing that the invasion had been compromised.

The invasion fleet arrived 5 miles off Oran at 23:00 on 7 November. Slightly less than four hours later, the attack on Oran began at 02:45 on 8 November with a direct assault on Oran's inner harbor, which failed bloodily, with over 200 GIs killed. Drenched and many shoeless, the three officers and 44 soldiers captured, along with other survivors of the ship's crew, were marched through the street of Oran lined with a jeering crowd.[98] But that proved to be the last victory of the day for a French navy that seemed intent on mass suicide. As at Casablanca, what the US Army official history categorizes as "repeated weak challenges to the naval blockade off Oran and Mers el-Kébir" by French naval vessels proved gallant but sacrificial, the French eventually losing two destroyers and a sub-chaser to British warships. At 16:50, the admiral commanding the navy in Oran ordered the thirty ships in the harbor, both warships and thirteen commercial vessels, as well as dry docks, scuttled to prevent the Allies from using the harbor.[99] Beyond to the west loomed the blackened hulks of Mers-el-Kébir, as Oran became a vast naval necropolis, soon to be joined by Toulon.

Fortunately, the Allies were able to seize Arzew, a port and naval air base 25 miles to the east of Oran, in the face of only sporadic and ill-organized resistance from French troops and sailors who were taken completely by surprise. Likewise, American forces at the two landing beaches west of Oran – Bou Zadar, that saw the arrival of the 1st US Armored Division, and the Baie des Andalouses, which was the landing spot of the 26th Regimental Combat Team – encountered no opposition. In fact, the few French troops present pitched in to help unload the LSTs, as did local Muslims. By the end of D-Day, all three Allied beachheads had been firmly established, with around 15,000 Allied troops ashore.

The second day – 9 November – promised to be more difficult. Allied troops were scattered to the east, south, and west, with inadequate signals equipment. The French established defensive positions on the main approach roads behind Oran, in an attempt to delay the American advance until reinforcements could arrive.[100] By the evening of 9 November, as the Americans began to prepare for the final assault, the French no longer controlled any air bases. Their attempts to break the naval blockade had failed, as had all counterattacks on land, in the process sacrificing what remained of French armored forces. Night marches to put troops of the 1st US Armored Division and 1st US Infantry Division in place for a concentric dawn attack had begun. By first light on 10 November, French troops in Oran realized that they were surrounded. Naval gunfire support massed at sea, and dive-bombers prepared to take out the remaining battery at Fort du Santon. Yet, French artillery fire offered stubborn resistance and the French batteries had to be dealt with one by one. But once two American columns broke into Oran at 10:15 on 10 November, scattered snipers offered the only resistance. Fortunately for the Allies, according to Barjot, pro-Allied resisters in Oran thwarted Vice-Admiral André Georges Rioult's plans to sabotage Oran's harbor infrastructure, blow the tunnel that linked the main port with Mers-el-Kébir, and destroy fuel reserves and the electrical station. Advancing columns encountered only a few roadblocks, which were easily cleared by artillery fire. The streets were deserted so that neither artillery preparation nor strafing was required. The goal was to reach the harbor as soon as possible to prevent further destruction. At 12:15 on 10 November, Boisseau ordered a ceasefire, while pockets of French soldiers still fought tenaciously outside the city. At 12:30, Rioult and General Boissau surrendered. French forces were confined to barracks but retained their arms. French flags continued to fly over the city, surmounted by a white flag of surrender. The US Army official history credits the quick seizure of Oran and the occupation of the harbor by US infantry with preventing sabotage of the harbor infrastructure.[101]

US commander Lloyd Fredendall announced that all French administrators would be retained in their positions. General Boissau remained in charge of the police and responsible for order. This proved unwelcome news to "pro-Allied Frenchmen," who continued to suffer retribution in the days and weeks that followed. Oran had been seized in under three days, without the benefit of Murphy's resistance. French losses had been 347 killed or missing and 353 wounded. Allied casualties numbered 593 killed and 569 wounded, most as a result of Operation Reservist.[102]

Algiers

With its 7,000-man garrison and another 8,000 reinforcements located within hiking distance, backed by 20,000 armed SOL, Algiers might in theory have been considered the most hardened Allied objective (Map 10.4).[103] Algiers also constituted the cockpit of Vichy Africa, a government and military center from which General Alphonse Juin commanded French forces in AFN. Unlike Oran or Morocco, Algiers would also see the muster of a significant civilian resistance, one which

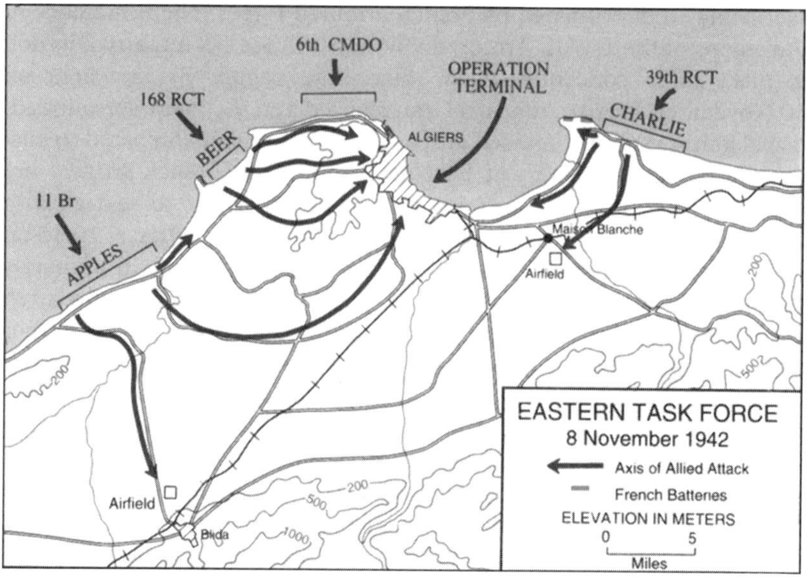

Map 10.4 Map of Eastern Task Force. Center for Military History.

Sophie Roberts laments has been insufficiently acknowledged, either at the time by Murphy, or in most subsequent histories of Torch, a view backed by other historians.[104] While resistance in Algiers combined a diverse group, Jews were prominent among them. They joined other resisters, both Jews and non-Jews, to create a very eclectic collection of what Roberts estimates to be around 800 resisters in Algiers on the eve of the invasion, "neither highly trained nor particularly well-coordinated." Nor was this resistance well-armed, because promised Allied weapons had not been delivered. Their role in Torch would be to disrupt the defense by occupying offices, interrupting communications, and detaining Vichy officials.[105]

Given the presence of numerous ships at Gibraltar, Juin had taken the precaution from 3 November to cancel leave and put his forces on a rolling alert along the Mediterranean littoral from Oran to Tunis. The fortuitous presence in Algiers of Darlan represented a senior symbol of Vichy legitimacy and a direct link to the Marshal. For these reasons, events in Algiers are seen as offering the key to crumbling opposition to the Anglo-American invasion in Casablanca and Oran, although not in Tunisia. Algiers was also the only place where the Murphy-organized resistance created enough confusion temporarily to disrupt the defense.

On Saturday night, 8 November, the BBC broadcast the message meant to trigger a carefully crafted putsch: "*Allo, Robert. Franklin arrive.*" Murphy alerted the rebels, who consisted of Van Hecke, Henri d'Astier, police commissioner André Achiary, and Colonel Germain Josse, operations officer for the Algiers division, who assigned missions, issued false orders to the defense, and provided safe-conduct passes to about 350–400 "*volontaires de place*" – VPs or civil defense volunteers, mostly young Algerine Jews organized by a medical student named José Aboulker. Their job was to seize key installations – the seat of government at the Palais d'Été, the houses of senior generals and admirals, Radio Algiers, the central telephone exchange, the Caserne Pélisser, headquarters of the Algiers division, the central police commissariat and army HQ in the Palais d'Hiver – as well as sequester key figures like Juin and XIX Corps commander Louis Koeltz. This would make General Mast the senior commander in Algiers. Colonel Joseph de Goislard de Monsabert, 5th Brigade commander at Miliana, was tasked with capturing the airfield at Blida. As Tunis would reveal, the airfields offered the key to seizing these objectives. Within a day, both Maison Blanche and Blida were in Allied hands, the latter thanks to Monsabert. The idea was to paralyze the defense without firing a shot, occupy Algiers with GIs, and then fly in Giraud, who would rally the military. The US Army official history insists that this group of "pro-Allied French" managed to "control" Algiers from 01:30 to 07:00 on 8 November.[106]

At first, the plan seemed to go flawlessly. Around 01:00 on 8 November, the duty officer at the Palais d'Hiver, Juin's headquarters, noticed that the phones had gone dead.[107] He alerted Algiers's Maritime Prefect Vice-Admiral Jacques Moreau at the Hôtel Saint-Georges through a direct line. The result was that, when an armed group of VPs arrived at the Hôtel Saint-Georges, the duty officer told them they could guard the streets outside the building. The VPs soon left, abandoning their weapons in the garden. Events followed similar patterns elsewhere: when a group of VPs appeared at the Palais d'Hiver, the guards slammed the gates to keep them out. Juin's residence at the Villa des Oliviers on the western edge of Algiers and that of air force commander Mendigal were surrounded but not occupied. The house of Vice-Admiral Raymond Fenard, the general secretary of the governor general's office where Darlan was staying, had not even been included in the list of VP targets.

However, the plans of the "Group of Five," in Algiers as elsewhere, quickly slipped off the rails. Having more-or-less decapitated the High Command in Algiers, the moment had arrived for General Mast to take charge and issue orders. However, he had traveled to the beach to greet arriving American troops, leaving an order written on 7 November to assist the invasion, to be distributed to a limited number of units in the Algiers division.[108] A second hope was that Juin would join the plotters. However, when Murphy asked Juin to order French forces to stand down and allow the Americans to land, Juin pointed out that Giraud had no legal authority. Furthermore, as commander-in-chief of all Vichy forces, Darlan could countermand any order that Juin might give. Juin's biographer Notin argues that Juin's reaction was entirely consistent both with his pro-Vichy mindset and with his disinclination to take decisive action to aid the invasion.[109]

Pendar was dispatched to fetch Darlan, who arrived at Juin's villa some 20 minutes later. Murphy informed Darlan of the invasion and urged him to issue orders not to resist. When Darlan realized that the phone lines had been cut and the villa was surrounded by VPs, among them a young man named Bonnier de la Chapelle, who burned to execute the admiral on the spot, he exploded with rage.[110] He accused Murphy of having committed a "monumental error," and reaffirmed his loyalty to Pétain. He did agree to send a message to the Marshal informing him of the crisis and ask for a free hand to deal with it. The message was written up and given to Pendar, who was to take it to the Maritime Prefecture to dispatch to Vichy. Instead, he turned it over to Rigault, who archived it.[111]

José Aboulker's plan had been to capture Juin and Darlan, and take them to a secluded villa several kilometers outside of Algiers, thereby removing a vital command node of French reaction. Aboulker subsequently criticized Murphy's "critical mistake" in alerting Juin, and eventually Darlan, of the invasion, and then subsequently attempting to negotiate with them.[112] For when the Prefecture maritime, the Algiers Admiralty, and the XIX Corps headquarters became aware in the early hours of the morning that units were receiving Mast's order to aid the American invasion, they dispatched officers to the residences of Juin and Koeltz, who returned to report them surrounded by VPs. A petty officer dressed in civilian clothes managed to smuggle out a note from Darlan written at 05:15 stating that he and Juin were prisoners: "Until you hear otherwise from me, do everything possible to execute the orders of the Marshal." "A little before 06:00" the *gardes mobiles* appeared at the Villa des Oliviers to disperse Aboulker's VPs and arrest Murphy and Pendar. Juin gave orders to free XIX Corps commander Koeltz, air force chief Mendigal, and the Prefect of Algiers. He promptly relieved Mast of his command. By 07:00, Juin and Darlan were at the Fort l'Empereur to organize resistance to the invasion. All of the sequestered buildings had been cleared of VPs, except the police Commissariat, which was only recaptured after a firefight in the early afternoon. The naval commander at Oran was put on alert and told to arm his batteries.

Darlan requested *Luftwaffe* attacks on Allied naval forces off Algiers from their bases on Sicily and Sardinia, which was passed to the Germans through the Wiesbaden Armistice Commission. To follow up, Navy Secretary of State at Vichy Rear Admiral Gabriel Auphan forwarded a German request to both Darlan and Noguès to send *Luftwaffe* liaison officers to AFN, asking to designate air bases where they might land. Noguès rejected the request outright, while by the time it was received by Darlan, a ceasefire had already been declared in Algiers. At German insistence, at 01:30 on 9 November, Resident General in Tunis Admiral Esteva was informed that German planes had permission to land at El Aouina airbase near Tunis.[113]

Although liberated, Darlan and Juin were under a time constraint. Landings at Algiers by the Eastern Task Force which began at 00:45 were forced to overcome confusion, as some landing craft foundered, and others drifted to the wrong beaches. French troops guarding the beaches suffered from poor communications. Shore batteries were hampered by mist, and those that attempted to fire on the Allied armada were immediately attacked by aircraft, subjected to naval gunfire, or surrounded by GIs, and their garrisons disarmed. Only the Fort d'Estrée on Cape Matifo east of Algiers continued to resist until ordered to cease fire on the morning of 9 November. Nevertheless, events went more smoothly than at Fedala, Port-Lyautey, or Oran. As at Oran, an assault by soldiers of the 135th Infantry Regiment, carried directly into the harbor on two destroyers, failed. But as the French had prepared no sabotage of harbor facilities, it proved immaterial. The first GIs set foot ashore at Sidi-Ferruch (Fredj) just west of Algiers around 03:00, where the local commander, General Ryder, was met by Mast. Unfortunately for the invaders, Mast's orders to aid the Americans had been canceled by General Koeltz, so that American troops advancing into Algiers from the east began to meet resistance as they progressed into town. The news was better at Blida airfield southeast of Algiers, where Monsabert and Lemaigre-Dubreuil had appeared early in the morning at the head of troops who encircled the base. Koeltz and Mendigal ordered the base commander to resist. Some of Monsabert's troops withdrew, but such was the confusion that the first Allied plane landed at 10:34 without opposition. By noon, the base had been secured by British commandos. By 09:30, the first Allied planes began to land at Maison Blanche. Those troops advancing from the west encountered resistance only from coastal batteries, troops under navy command, and a detachment of the *29ᵉ Régiment de tirailleurs algériens* repatriated from Syria. But the advance was running behind schedule. Which meant that the invaders were too slow to profit from resistance-induced disruption in Algiers.[114]

Figure 10.1 In the wake of the Anglo-American landing, Darlan confers with army commander Alphonse Juin, Governor General Yves Châtel, and the Prefect of Algiers, Emmanuel Temple, with the Maritime Prefect Vice-Admiral Jacques Moreau in the background. According to Costagliola, Darlan unsuccessfully sought to buy time for Laval to negotiate a revision of the 1940 Armistice with Hitler.

Although freed from Aboulker's VPs, Darlan nevertheless failed to galvanize the defense (Figure 10.1). Judging that Algiers was about to fall, but eager to cover his bases in France, Darlan resorted to his favorite tactic – redistribute power in an already-splintered French command, by placing Morocco and Oran under Noguès, while he declared Tunisia and Constantine to be under the authority of CSTT General Georges Barré. But as they would have no link with Algiers, this further fragmented the French command chain.[115] The High Seas Fleet was to remain in Toulon. Moreau's chief of staff Captain Robert, prepared by his own admission "to smash the first American head" that showed itself, was "shocked and depressed" that Darlan spent most of the morning standing on the balcony of his HQ at the Hôtel Saint-Georges, collecting information, smoking his pipe, eating sandwiches, but giving no orders, as if he were a mere spectator "as American troops spread like a tide around the town ... One officer below asked for permission to fire ... 'No,' Darlan replied, 'that would be idiotic.'"[116] After conferring with Juin, around noon on 8 November, Darlan informed Pétain that Algiers would probably be in American hands by evening. By that time, Pétain had already rejected a personal appeal from Roosevelt to join the Allies, and severed diplomatic relations with Washington. According to Juin, Darlan had received *carte blanche* from Pétain to "act for the best under the circumstances," which essentially handed him a mandate to represent legal authority.[117] Vichy agreed to a German proposal for air support launched from Sardinia and Sicily.[118] So much for the myth of the "double game," and "defense against whomever." "Vichy had chosen the Axis camp," concludes Levisse-Touzé. "The acquiescing to German assistance was a turning point for AFN and the prelude to the Tunisian campaign that would last no less than five months."[119]

The official French naval history of the invasion concludes that while the resistance in Algiers contributed to the success of the invasion, it was only one of several factors that compromised the French defense at Algiers. Although by 07:00 French troops had regained control of the town from the VPs and other resisters, there had been little fire in the defense – none tried to engage the Americans in a decisive manner. Troops at Sidi-Ferruch and Kolea had obeyed Mast's orders to assist the Americans, which allowed the Western prong of the invasion to progress without opposition. Fog had prevented the takeoff of French planes at Maison Blanche, while Monsabert's troops had neutralized Blida. If there was a critical factor that allowed Torch to succeed, it was Juin's decision to eschew resistance that might seriously have impeded the invasion in Algiers, a view that subsequently Juin vigorously promoted.[120] "After a brief debate with my conscience, I pushed aside with horror the idea of a fratricidal combat that could have been provoked by a professional reflex and also perhaps by the bitter memory of the trap that was set for me [by Murphy]." Still, with only vague information about events in Casablanca and Oran, Juin too refused to commit, for he knew that many of his subordinates would have the reflex to resist, and would not understand his passivity. "Not having the time to explain, much less to convince, I decided on my own that there would not be a battle for Algiers." Juin ordered Mast's replacement, General Jean Roubertie, to maintain "*un contact élastique sans agressivité*." In the interim, he fully expected that the Germans would do something to shift opinion.[121]

The limp reaction by French troops, together with the courageous acts of the resistance, joined with the confused response of the French chain of command to compensate for the mistakes and delays of the assault.

Algiers' two important air bases, Blida and Maison Blanche, were chock-a-block with Allied planes by noon. Predictably, the most tenacious resistance came from the French navy.[122] With American troops closing in on Algiers, Juin sent for Murphy and asked him to find an American commander with whom to negotiate. Just after 16:00, with GIs occupying the high ground around Algiers, Juin met with General Ryder, commander of the US 34th Infantry Division, at Juin's headquarters. "[Ryder] was calm and relaxed, with an open and smiling demeanor," Juin remembered. The two men came to a "gentleman's agreement" to end the fighting in Algiers at 18:40 as darkness fell. French troops returned to barracks with their arms, while abandoning most of their ammunition. The French would retain police powers in the city. Darlan allowed ships from Eastern Task Force to sail into Algiers harbor at first light on 9 November. But Darlan assured Vichy that, while he would report what the Americans had to say, he had no intention of negotiating with them.[123] Also on 9 November, British General Kenneth Anderson arrived at Blida to assume command of Eastern Task Force for a march to Tunisia, where German paratroops had begun to arrive in force at the El Aouina airfield outside of Tunis. Giraud's broadcast from Gibraltar, ordering French troops to cease fire, was completely ignored. In Clark's absence, Ryder proposed that Darlan call a ceasefire throughout all of AFN. In return, French sovereignty would be guaranteed, and all generals would be maintained in their positions.[124]

"*L'accord intime du Maréchal*" – the Darlan Deal

Speed was vital for the success of Torch. Allied planners had bet that the French would rally quickly to the Allied cause, after which Allied forces would hopscotch along the North African coast to preempt the arrival of Axis forces at Tunis and Bizerte. But although AFN's commanding elite had been sequestered in Algiers, and fulsome promises had been made to preserve French sovereignty and independence, while rearming French forces, suddenly and inexplicably, negotiations between the Americans and the French stalled. According to Costagliola, this was because Darlan and Laval sought to deploy the surprise Allied arrival in AFN to revise the restrictive conditions of the 1940 armistice. Darlan's delaying tactics sought to give time for Laval, who had flown to Munich, to renegotiate the armistice as a precondition for French collaboration: "If Germany helps us it is essential that she modifies the armistice situation, and replaces it with another political arrangement that would permit us to recover our possibilities," he had written to Auphan in Vichy on 9 November as he awaited the arrival of Mark Clark. At 17:05 on that day, he wired Admirals Esteva in Tunis and Derrien in Bizerte (with copies to Auphan and Barré): "The Americans having invaded Africa *first* are our adversaries and we must fight them *alone or with assistance.*" The message was clear, according to Costagliola: "The arrival of Axis forces is not inopportune, at least in Tunisia, to repel the Americans who have become our adversaries because they were the *first* to attack the Empire."[125] Not surprisingly, Torch was to create bad blood between the French and the Allies in 1943. The defense of Juin and others was that the Americans had attacked, and that the French had only reacted as was to be expected.

After Torch, Eisenhower sought to play down the "who fired first" controversy in the interest of Franco-American reconciliation.[126] Torch cost the Anglo-Americans 1,469 dead, including 530 Americans.[127] In his memoirs, de Gaulle lamented the huge waste of lives – 999 French soldiers, sailors, and airmen killed, and 1,654 wounded – in the "absurd fighting" during Torch. Torch, followed by the collective suicide of Darlan's High Seas Fleet at Toulon, eliminated any possibility that the French navy might play a significant role in the war going forward. Of 168 French planes based in Algeria and Morocco, 135 had been destroyed, so that the FAF needed to be rebuilt from scratch.[128] More important, however, was the political consequences of Torch, which had yet to play out, both for the Allies and for the French.

Darlan's tactic in suspending resistance in Algiers while encouraging it elsewhere was to convince Hitler to preserve the *zone libre* at a minimum. But his margin of maneuver contracted as Pétain disavowed his action, Oran was surrounded and Patton's tanks prepared to assault Casablanca. Meanwhile, in Munich, Hitler demanded from Laval access to Tunisia. In response, Laval meekly requested a fig leaf of a German ultimatum to hide his acquiescence.[129] Giraud flew into Blida at 14:30 on 9 November. At 17:45, Darlan held a second meeting with Ryder, who handed him an outline armistice proposal.[130] It was in these conditions, made more chaotic by a *Luftwaffe* attack on Algiers, that Mark Clark arrived to negotiate with Darlan in the evening of 9 November. Darlan simply insisted that he could enter into no agreement without the Marshal's authorization. After Clark and Murphy left, Darlan conferred with his command in Algiers, who unanimously urged Darlan to accept the American proposal, which would maintain French sovereignty in AFN, and simply inform Pétain that the invasion was irresistible. But Darlan refused to take any initiative that would put the 1940 armistice at risk, while in Germany Laval authorized the *Luftwaffe* to land in Tunis.[131]

This set up the "crisis of 10 November." Clark and Murphy were under pressure to bring hostilities to a rapid conclusion in all of AFN, not just

Algiers, and focus Allied attention on Tunisia. They also sought to entice the fleet to sail from Toulon to North Africa before Axis forces could seize it. Allied admirals clamored to get their ships standing off Algiers to shelter before U-boats could converge.[132] The fact that Murphy had initiated negotiations with Darlan had sabotaged US plans to declare Giraud commander-in-chief, and forced Clark to intervene in a French political crisis that he neither comprehended nor was authorized to resolve. Throughout the day, Darlan continued to insist that only the Marshal had the authority to order a ceasefire. The other senior officers present resolutely refused to recognize Giraud, although privately they urged Darlan to accept the American conditions. Juin conceded that poor Clark attempted to negotiate with a deflated French chain of command fearful of assuming responsibility for actions for which they would later be held accountable. Juin is given credit for finally persuading a shaken Darlan to acquiesce to Clark's demands, not out of pro-Allied sentiments, but to preserve the already fragile equilibrium in AFN. Darlan's order to cease hostilities with Allied forces and "assume an attitude of complete neutrality vis-à-vis all belligerents" was broadcast "in the name of the Marshal" and dispatched by courier plane at 11:05. He justified the accord with Clark to Vichy as necessary to keep Giraud from taking command, to maintain order in AFN, to save lives in a deteriorating situation, and because it would permit him "to maintain authority in Africa in your name." He asked Pétain to approve his action "because I had no other choice." Darlan even added an addendum for Tunisia that the mission remained unchanged and forces there must resist anyone who tried to invade. At 16:45 on 10 November, Pétain's response arrived in Algiers: "I gave the order to defend against the aggressor. I maintain my order." Darlan concluded that as he now had no mandate to act in Pétain's name, he requested that Clark make him a prisoner.[133] This, in Juin's words, provoked "a violent scene with General Clark, extremely irritated by this delay caused by the subtle conflicts of conscience, the result of internal contradictions, of which the logic totally escaped him."[134] Clark arrested Darlan, and insisted that Giraud would take command. Juin, Koeltz, and Mendigal immediately refused to recognize Giraud's authority.

The tide of contradictory orders and counter-orders had left officers in AFN confused and demoralized, not knowing whether to obey Darlan's order to cease fire, or Pétain's broadcast to continue to resist, or the Darlan–Juin revocation of their ceasefire order. In this way, Darlan's head-spinning prevarications and policy pirouettes became a significant factor in disorganizing French opposition to the Torch landings. Meanwhile, Noguès allowed the members of the Axis control commissions to escape into the Spanish zone, before initiating negotiations with Patton at Fedala.

At 02:30 on 11 November, the ceasefire went into effect in Morocco. Auphan congratulated Michelier, who through the sacrifice of his flotilla had allowed the Marshal to "save France."[135] By then, however, Berlin had exhausted all hope that November 1942 might witness a reprise of Dakar in 1940, and began to operationalize "Anton," the plan to invade the *zone libre*. In these conditions, Pétain announced that he was taking command of French forces and designated Noguès as his representative in AFN, which in theory sidelined Darlan. But from the perspective of the leadership in Algiers, the situation remained in flux, in part because of the intermittent nature of communications with Vichy, and because of back-channel contact between Auphan and the various actors in AFN. On 11 November, Darlan seems to have been reassured by Auphan in a message passed through Moreau that the Marshal had secretly approved of his agreement with Clark, and that "negotiations therefore continue."[136] So was born the famous "*accord intime du Maréchal*" ("The Marshal's secret approval") that allegedly bestowed upon Darlan the Marshal's laying on of hands to rule AFN through apostolic succession. In the long run, it allowed Pétain's post-war defenders to allege that Vichy all along had supported the Allies as part of Pétain's "double game," and was simply awaiting an opportunity to rejoin the war.[137] In the short run, the "*accord intime*" provided cover for French soldiers to abandon "neutrality" and join the Allies. In this way, Darlan became "truly the providential man" who expedited AFN's pivot to the Allies, not some ephemeral "dissidence."[138] A contrary view is that "*l'accord intime*" was a "bad joke," although it is quite possible that Darlan actually believed it. It assured the continuity of French imperial rule and command authority, excluded Giraud and the Gaullists, preserved the position of *l'armée d'Afrique*, thus handing Vichy a new lease on life in North Africa, and vindicated the wisdom of the Marshal. It also helped to convince Boisson and his commanders in Dakar that in his 23 November decision to rally AOF to the Allies, he was merely following the Marshal's secret directive and profound desires. Although Boisson must also have been aware that, in the view of the Navy command in AOF, if the Anglo-Saxons wished to repeat their 1940 assault on Dakar, this time few in the garrison would resist them, while the population was "ready to join the dissidence." In this way, "*l'accord intime*" served to create an image of Pétain as hostage and martyr to France, and to "soothe the consciences of those who hesitated to follow Darlan" that they were remaining faithful to their oath.[139] "For these officers, discipline remained the supreme virtue," concludes Levisse-Touzé. De Gaulle's prediction to Antoine Béthouart as they had dined in London's Hotel Rubens on 26 June 1940 had been vindicated: "You'll see. It's a gang of old wimps."[140]

On the afternoon of 11 November, Clark vigorously insisted that Darlan order the fleet to sail to AFN. Darlan at first refused. But when he learned of the German invasion of the *zone libre*, and of Pétain's protest to Marshal Gerd von Rundstedt, which "made resistance to the Axis legal," he "invited" the commander of the High Seas Fleet, Admiral Jean de Laborde, to sail to North Africa. The next day, de Laborde declined in a very explicit manner. On 11 November also, Juin sent out a message that the policy of neutrality toward the Axis had ceased, and that Axis troops must be opposed, only to rescind his order several hours later on the pretext that he must await Noguès' arrival.[141] In this way, 12 November became another "lost day" as Noguès arrived from Rabat claiming to speak for Pétain, and refusing to acknowledge Darlan's accord with Clark. After greeting Giraud with a cordial "*Bonjour, traître*," Noguès refused to recognize the authority of Girard, "whose conduct he judged severely," an outburst that left bad blood between the two men. "The dilemma for the Americans was Giraud without the army, or the army without Giraud," remarks Levisse-Touzé.[142] Driven by an awareness that AFN was slipping into anarchy, and linked to Giraud by common service in the Rif War and their shared POW incarceration at Königstein castle, Juin agreed to place himself under Giraud's orders, thus cracking the solid front of flag-rank resistance. The final agreement stipulated that Darlan would take over as head of the "civil and military government" in AFN, while Noguès and Châtel would continue as Resident in Morocco and Governor in Algeria, respectively. Michelier would command the navy, or what, thanks to him, was left of it. Eisenhower, newly arrived in Algiers, approved. Proclamations were subsequently broadcast on Radio Algiers from Darlan, Noguès, and Châtel announcing the new arrangement, "in the name of the Marshal," embellished with various patriotic bromides about "honor," "order," and "discipline," and calling for "Every man to his post."[143] All of which must have provoked hilarious audience comments during cinema newsreels.

André Beaufre argued that the American invasion had been "too soft." The French navy was the Vichy heart of AFN, so that the admiralty should have been a center of gravity both in Algiers and Casablanca. Darlan and Juin should have been removed and incarcerated, as José Aboulker had intended. Giraud arrived in the middle of confused negotiations between Clark, Eisenhower, and Darlan, when he should have been able to take charge and impose a plan to take power, although *l'armée d'Afrique* might have failed to obey him. The Darlan deal undercut the resistance in AFN, because it sabotaged the Allies' liberation narrative – in an ideological war, one had to stake out a political position, not excuse compromises with the enemy as "pragmatic" and "realist," as Eisenhower did. This was especially so, as Darlan clearly held a busted flush – the fighting was over in Algiers and Oran by 11 November, and Noguès would have been obliged to throw in the towel two days later at the latest.[144]

When Pétain learned of the accord on 14 November, he disavowed it as incompatible with the instructions of the Vichy government. This caused Juin to issue "General Order No. 7," which stated: "We have to think that at this moment the Marshal is a prisoner. Since 10 November, his official messages have been dictated by the occupier. His heart is with us and to underline it he has abandoned all powers as the Chief of State to which we have not given our oath. The orders of this person, even if presented in the name of the Marshal, are therefore worthless."[145] The problem was that Admirals Laborde in Toulon, Esteva in Tunis, and Derrien in Bizerte believed that Darlan's orders were dictated by the Americans, so that one man's patriot became another man's prisoner. While these negotiations were proceeding, *Luftwaffe* torpedo bombers managed to sink 183,000 tons of Allied shipping, and damage another 234,000 tons between 7 and 13 November. Meanwhile, planeloads of Axis forces were disembarking in Tunis. In this way, Darlan's prevarication not only helped to lose the race to Tunis, but also cost the Allies considerable naval assets.[146] And while this "Darlan deal" ended the debate and aligned *l'armée d'Afrique* at the side of Allies, many remained unhappy with Giraud's defiance of the Marshal. Public rejection by Pétain and Laval of his "treasonous" decision to join the Allies required "the Eternal Lieutenant" Giraud to undertake a *tournée des popotes* (tour of the messes) to convince officers that, as Vichy was now under German occupation, making Pétain in effect a POW, as well as being possibly senile and befuddled, they were released from their oath.[147]

Reaction to the Darlan Deal

The "Darlan deal" would roil Allied–Gaullist relations, as well as throw the cat among the pigeons between Washington and London, which questioned Eisenhower's ability to command in a politically complex Mediterranean environment.[148] To be fair to Eisenhower and Clark, Roosevelt's anti-Gaullist policy, shaped in large part by Leahy and Murphy, had severely hobbled their options.[149] That said, de Gaulle had only a minuscule following in AFN, although, thanks in part to the Darlan deal, that was about to change. A principal danger of the Darlan deal was that Stalin might conclude that the political opportunism of the Western Allies might extend to Rome and Berlin. Hence the obvious need to repair the blunder of the Darlan deal by declaring a policy of "unconditional surrender" at the Anfa Conference in January 1943. An agreement which Darlan insisted had been achieved "in the name of the Marshal" tarnished an Allied "victory" concluded on the cusp of conquest, a betrayal that left Allied populations to question what Torch had actually accomplished.[150] The Darlan deal capped a campaign that compared unfavorably with the other two winter headliners emblazoned on the Allied marquee – Montgomery's punch-out of Rommel at El Alamein and the crushing Soviet victory at Stalingrad in February 1943. The Darlan deal was marketed as a "pragmatic" compromise to secure a strategic Mediterranean foothold. The Allies needed a single authority with whom to negotiate, one capable in the immediate moment of squelching Allied–French hostilities, and blocking Axis forces from Tunisia, able to rope Dakar and AOF into the agreement, and if possible entice the High Seas Fleet to sail from Toulon. But cutting a last-minute agreement to keep a notorious collaborationist in power failed to reinforce the US credo that American military power should be deployed for moral purpose and beneficial ends. Furthermore, Roosevelt's willingness to tolerate continued French rule in AFN so long as they kept the Germans out rather undermined Roosevelt's Atlantic Charter declaration.

Although the "Darlan deal" was eventually blessed by the President, the Prime Minister, and the Combined Chiefs,[151] it met blowback for at least four reasons. First, it proved a "base and squalid" agreement with a turncoat who only hours before had been killing Allied troops, one that betrayed Allied goals and principles.[152] In his memoirs, de Gaulle mocks Roosevelt's hypocrisy in overcoming "his democratic and legal scruples that, for two years, he used to oppose General de Gaulle" to order Clark to recognize Darlan.[153] War correspondent for the National Broadcasting Company John MacVane compared General Mark Clark's press conference to explain and justify the "Darlan deal" to "something out of *Alice in Wonderland* being told, not by a Mad Hatter, but by an apparently sane and collected American general ... We correspondents were dumbfounded."[154]

Second, British Foreign Minister Anthony Eden objected that the Darlan deal proliferated the number of French actors, which complicated Allied diplomacy. One of the ironic consequences was that Darlan became a spent force, even before his assassination. According to Juin, the admiral was crushed by the loss of his precious High Seas Fleet. He was also fully aware that his conduct had made him the object of an "unspoken hostility" in Algiers that caused people to look to Giraud and ultimately de Gaulle for leadership. Juin claimed that he encouraged

Darlan to make contact with de Gaulle, because France could not have two dissident governments plus the "legal" one at Vichy. But Darlan had become totally demoralized and allegedly told Eisenhower that he was ready to exit the political stage, perhaps seek exile with his family in the United States.[155]

A third consequence was that the Darlan deal was ultimately sterile and even counterproductive. Darlan's pro-German actions had been widely reported in the US and British media, so that public opinion received news of the Darlan deal with stunned disbelief. According to Masson, Darlan was also isolated and had no political base in AFN, nor even in "*la belle flotte de Darlan*," as events were to prove. While Darlan was a competent administrator, he "lacked the warmth, the ideological outreach indispensable for a political leader."[156] His indecision and prevarications between 8 and 13 November had hardly enhanced his standing with the Allies, much less with the Vichy-besotted French navy, which compromised his ability to deliver the fleet. For these reasons, Eisenhower's "pragmatism" that allegedly justified the Darlan deal proved a hard sell with the Allied public, not to mention the Gaullists. A fourth and final concern resided in the implications for future Allied policy toward belligerents.

"Why was Darlan in charge? – the professional Britain-hater, the turn coat admiral, the friend of Laval and the German collaborationists," Moorehead claimed that people were asking. "Why were the Gaullists who had helped us land suddenly clapped into prison? Were we going to advance on one place after another in Europe, raising up Quislings as we went? . . . Why not the House of Savoy in Italy? And if it came to that, why not Goering, even Hitler himself?"[157]

Why not the House of Savoy, indeed! American historians Carlo D'Este and Robert Dallek defend Eisenhower's decision as realpolitik. D'Este dismisses much of the fallout over the Darlan deal as "contrived hypocrisy" and "crocodile tears." The Darlan deal "brought a quick halt to French resistance, saved lives, and put Dakar under Allied control," concludes Dallek.[158] Idealism may have had an appeal for Allied and European populations, but it was poor strategy in the Mediterranean's byzantine and complex political environment.[159] Alas, this view is difficult to defend. Even at the time, journalists wondered what Darlan had actually brought to the party. Overall, French resistance to the Allies had been at best uneven, the most tenacious coming predictably from the French navy, which in any case was totally outgunned by the Allied invasion fleets, and for which it had paid a heavy price.[160] Resistance had ceased in Oran and Algiers, and Noguès was on the verge of throwing in the towel in Morocco before Casablanca's inevitable fall to Patton. No insurrection against the Allies had materialized. Nor were dissident French officers likely to initiate a popular insurrection that might easily boomerang against the French empire. Making peace with the invading Allies carried huge advantages for *l'armée d'afrique*, beginning with rearmament and an opportunity to join the war's winning side. If they balked, all the Allies need do was to dangle the promises of the Atlantic Charter, and North Africa's indigenous populations would have rallied behind them. But the Anglo-Americans' goal was to secure a North African base and to incorporate French forces into their inventory as a prelude to the invasion of the European continent, not embark on a crusade of colonial emancipation.

Pétain had already fired Darlan, so he no longer could claim to speak for the Marshal. The Axis invasion of Tunisia, the 11 November occupation of the *zone libre*, and the subsequent abolition of the Armistice Army collapsed Vichy "neutrality," removing any illusion of Vichy's sovereignty, as had ostensibly been guaranteed by the clauses of the 1940 armistice, or that things would soon return to "normal." Pétain no longer had any cards to play. Clark would have done better simply to incarcerate Darlan and Juin and keep them incommunicado as José Aboulker had originally planned to do, rather than persist in his table-pounding theatrics. As it was, Clark left Darlan free to continue his treacherous behavior – he ordered Admiral Jean Esteva to oppose the German entry into Tunis, but then revoked the order on the night of 11–12 November. Nor did Darlan have the clout to order the High Seas Fleet to weigh anchor at Toulon. So, Darlan proved to be a spent force whose delaying tactics wasted time, cost lives, both French and American, divided the Allies, and raised justifiable suspicions about how far Washington's "pragmatism" would shape both its policy toward France and its war termination strategy.[161]

The claim in AFN that Darlan's "legitimacy" sprang from the "intimate accord of the Marshal" for the Darlan–Clark agreement invited skepticism, when not derision. Darlan's power in AFN had been bestowed on him, albeit reluctantly, by Eisenhower. Atkinson voices the majority historical consensus that Eisenhower was "naïve" to sign off on Clark's arrangement with the notorious collaborator and opportunist.[162] Eisenhower biographer Stephen Ambrose argues that, given Darlan's prevarications, his on again/off again resistance to Allied forces, the American general would have been well within his rights to have "dumped" the French admiral, but did not because he feared it might touch off a French civil war. Nor, as has been seen, did Ike wish to govern AFN.[163]

Nevertheless, if Eisenhower's priorities were Tunisia, Dakar, and the French fleet, dithering with Darlan for almost five days delivered only one out of three. In fact, he allowed Noguès and Murphy to divert him by raising fears that failure to reach an accord would push the US Army into the tribal management business, which he was assured would be required should the French administration be decapitated or refuse to cooperate. In fact, it was an empty threat, as the French could not simply declare an administrative and security walkout, thus allowing the natives to run amok, without placing a major cornerstone of empire, and France's geopolitical position in the Mediterranean, at risk, not to mention the lives of a million *français d'Algérie*. But, by invading North Africa, the Anglo-Americans had handed the manipulative Darlan the whip hand. And while for the Allied commander the supervision of North Africa's volatile indigenous population might seem like a piece of cake compared with refereeing the querulous French, upon whom in North Africa could he count for help? Murphy's "resistance" had gone off like a damp squib, while Van Hecke's unarmed, adolescent *Chantiers* inmates on the whole remained in their bleak, rural fastness, too remote and too undernourished to influence events.[164] Rather than rally to the Anglo-Americans, in Eisenhower's opinion, French flag officers in AFN behaved like "selfish, conceited worms."[165] Mark Clark's opinions of his French interlocutors in Algiers are unprintable. Distrust of the French communicated itself to Allied soldiers, especially GIs, and persisted even to the end of the Tunisia campaign. While service relations were described in French reports as, "correct and cordial ... Nevertheless, in a number of cases there is much reticence and distrust. Oran and Casablanca remain unhealed wounds. There have been several cases of French officers and NCOs harassed in Tunis without provocation on their part. 'Français – no comrades– no good.'"[166] So, for the moment, Ike was willing to deal with Darlan in the interest of assuring French cooperation and logistical support, and the stability of AFN.

Unlike Badoglio, who was to see the writing on the wall in September 1943, the Darlan deal also drove Vichy deeper into collaboration, what Paxton calls that "burned boat feeling," confirmed by Pierre Pucheu's arrest in May 1943 when he arrived in North Africa via Spain. Recognition of de Gaulle by the internal resistance, that would be engineered by Jean Moulin in a 27 May 1943 meeting of the newly formed *Conseil national de la résistance*, would challenge the legitimacy not only of Vichy, but also of Giraud.[167] The surging unpopularity of the Vichy regime did the rest. In Vichy's nightmare scenario, liberation threatened to unleash an orgy of retribution and resistance-induced chaos. But the Darlan deal also encouraged the Vichy leadership to hope that they, too, might strike a bargain with the Allies when and if that time came. A knock-on of the Darlan deal found Pétain fantasizing about how he might become a peacemaker, on call should Hitler care to craft a compromise peace with the Western Allies, liberating him to concentrate his energies against the communists. "Mediation" became the phantom strategy of a bankrupt, introverted, and outmaneuvered Vichy regime to restore French prestige and influence. The key was for everyone in France to close ranks behind the Marshal, to display a united front, in this way avoiding the "moral crisis" that an Allied landing had triggered in AFN. But it was too late – the Marshal's last remaining card in November 1942 had been to defect to the Allies, and he had folded.[168]

After Torch, Vichy indulged in a brief spasm of recalibration in an attempt to strike a more neutral posture, that began with a government reshuffle to bring back some of the Third Republic's parliamentary representatives and liberalize the constitution. Pétain also tried to sack Laval, the symbol of collaboration, but was stymied by Hitler. Pétain temporarily reigned in protest, but by 5 December he was stubbornly determined to hold on to power. Berlin had forced him to accept collaborationists like Philippe Henriot as Secretary of State for Information, Joseph Darnand, who on 30 January 1943 founded *la Milice*, to head the police, and Marcel Déat at the Labor Secretariat, with responsibility for implementing STO – forced labor for Frenchmen in Germany and France. In the wake of Torch, Vichy fell hostage to "the most collaborationist team in the regime's history," records Burrin, "urging it on and setting an example." Laval bowed to Fritz Sauckel's demands, expanding labor conscription, while prefects drew up lists of Jews, including French Jews, to be netted in "round-ups" by Germans and French police in cities like Poitiers and Bordeaux, without distinction of nationality.[169]

Torch and the Gaullists

The real beneficiary of the Darlan deal was ironically the man whom it aimed to sideline – Charles de Gaulle. Although the fact that the Anglo-Americans would eventually invade AFN had not surprised him, failure to have included him in Torch planning had left de Gaulle fuming. That the Allies would ultimately leave Darlan in charge after their failure to impose Giraud was to him unconscionable. His instinctive reaction had been to wish that Torch would fail: "I hope that the people at Vichy will throw them back into the sea," he had exclaimed when first hearing the news of the invasion.[170] But he quickly recovered his equilibrium after Churchill assured him over lunch that he had been excluded from Torch on Roosevelt's insistence, and that London recognized only the authority of *la France combattante*. Above all, de Gaulle realized that the

Figure 10.2 In a vibrant speech to a packed Albert Hall in London on 11 November 1942, Charles de Gaulle pledged Fighting France to the restoration of "French liberties ... and the laws of the Republic," thus allaying fears that he nurtured dictatorial ambitions.

liberation of AFN had further discredited Vichy, while opening new opportunities for his exile movement. In a vibrant and emotional 11 November Albert Hall speech, de Gaulle hammered home the message that only those who had rejected the armistice were worthy to lead a revitalized France, that must reclaim its Republican roots (Figure 10.2). By anointing Darlan, the Americans had legitimized the Quisling regime at Vichy, that once already had betrayed France and the Allies. The Darlan deal offered yet another attempt to divide French opinion and perpetuate Vichy in AFN.[171] Despite being passed over, de Gaulle held several trump cards, beginning with the fact that he occupied the moral high ground, while he was becoming a household name not only in France, but also among the Allied populations. Finally, Roosevelt's "Darlan deal," followed by his promotion of Giraud who had no following, basically sabotaged the American President's search for a viable French alternative to de Gaulle, while Axis occupation of the *zone libre* terminated Vichy's phantom sovereignty and hence its authority in the colonies.

Following Darlan's assassination, Gaullist propaganda focused on Giraud's links to Pétain, thus helping the Resistance press to galvanize the internal resistance behind de Gaulle as France's legitimate ruler dedicated to the restoration of the Republic.[172] Writing in *La Marseillaise* on 6 December, French resistance leader and Gaullist consigliere Pierre Brossolette suggested that if Algiers were well worth a Darlan deal, might not Paris merit a pact with Laval? He blasted the American readiness to sacrifice their ideals and the Resistance on the "altar of realism and cynicism." In this way, Torch enfolded a "defeat in the victory."[173] So, in signing off on Eisenhower's "pragmatic" decision in Algiers, Roosevelt ultimately torpedoed his own French policy of Gaullist marginalization. The Darlan deal became exhibit A in the leader of Fighting France's case laid out before the French Resistance that Washington had become the principal threat to French sovereignty, and that the American President might simply catapult another Vichy opportunist to power at the Liberation. Finally, many French people, who had been confused by de Gaulle's hitherto seemingly baffling diatribes against "les Anglo-Saxons," at last began to understand why the Americans might constitute a threat. For these reasons, the Darlan deal in fact made de Gaulle's capture of the French exile government that was to unfold in the course of 1943 virtually a foregone conclusion. The reaction in London was equally shrill. On 13 November, the Gaullist-friendly Eden instructed British Ambassador to Washington Lord Halifax to caution Roosevelt against creating yet another faction among the constellation of anti-German French exiles. "We are fighting for international decency," was the Foreign Office message to Washington, "and Darlan is the antithesis of that." In a reply to Churchill, FDR at least acknowledged that danger – Giraud and Darlan were already squabbling "like rag pickers," and now poor Eisenhower had to manage two French "divas" instead of one.[174] But as George Kennan pointed out, it was Roosevelt's preference for back-channel negotiations out of sight of State and War that had resulted in the dispatch of a third-tier "Vichyite" Murphy and a team of politically neophyte generals to negotiate a deal that risked the Allies' – and Roosevelt's – political credibility.[175]

The former diplomat Harold Nicholson compared the "incredible mistake" of the Darlan deal to Appeasement and Munich.[176] In Parliament, Labour leader Clement Attlee took up de Gaulle's charge of a "Quisling" covenant, while his Labour colleague Aneurin Bevan pointed out that the Darlan deal brought into question the sort of Europe the Allies intended to build.[177] Surprisingly, perhaps, Crémieux-Brilhac excused the Darlan deal as a pragmatic decision on Roosevelt's part, balancing a 120,000-man *armée d'Afrique*, the Maghreb, and AOF against de Gaulle's diminutive movement, of which he was a part. But at dinner in London with his wife, an Englishman at the next table offered a prophetic toast: "*À la crévaison de Darlan.*"[178] In the United States, the liberal press exploded with wrath when the news broke on 14 November, a reaction that completely blindsided the as yet politically unschooled Eisenhower, as his subordinate Omar Bradley noted.[179] *The Nation* likened Darlan to a prostitute, and analogies went downhill from there. The most influential American commentators, among them Walter Lippmann, Drew Pearson, Walter Winchell, and Edward Murrow, condemned a "deal with the Devil," while *Time* denounced a pact with one of "Hitler's stooges." Treasury Secretary Henry Morgenthau lectured Roosevelt for 20 minutes in the Oval Office about how this arrangement had impugned the nation's honor. Above all, Mrs. Roosevelt opposed it.[180] The Office of Psychological Warfare instantly concluded that Ike's betrayal of democratic values would make its job harder.[181] The Darlan deal was denounced as an inevitable outcome of Roosevelt's policy of coddling Vichy "fascists" through Leahy and Murphy, that might presage future compromises with other "Quislings."[182] For many, the Darlan deal betrayed American values, and compromised the mission of the United States to restore liberty to the world. The distressing compromises with the Vichy French deprived the Allies and Roosevelt of a clear military victory to celebrate. Moorehead believed that the adverse public reaction to the Darlan deal was due in part to a poorly managed "propaganda" campaign surrounding Torch.[183] Nevertheless, it was difficult to escape the implication that Roosevelt's attempt to bring France back into the war through collaborators made the goals of the Atlantic Charter appear hollow, and helped to discredit the decision to fight in the Mediterranean, where too many political compromises were required.

For this reason, El Alamein, a climactic battle fought between two colorful protagonists in Montgomery and Rommel, nudged out Torch as the indispensable victory in the Mediterranean theater. El Alamein eclipsed in the public imagination both Torch and its knock-on, the never-should-have-happened-had-Torch-been-better-managed Tunisia campaign, led by anonymous and inexperienced Allied generals seemingly outmaneuvered and outfought by their Axis opposites. The Darlan deal also perpetuated an image among Allied countries of the French as scheming, quarrelsome, and morally compromised allies. It deepened de Gaulle's suspicion of Allied, especially American, intentions toward France, which he communicated to a growing internal resistance to bolster his legitimacy. Going forward, Franco-American cooperation would be compared to a "loveless marriage of convenience," while the Anglo-French condominium in the Levant steamed like boiling lava amid growing unrest. The quickening demand for change among France's imperial subjects had been stimulated in part by Arabic-language broadcasts on Nazi radio, as well as London's "willingness to speak the language of self-determination (selectively) at France's expense." However, tethered to the status quo by Vichy's charge of a colonial sell-out to perfidious Albion, and by de Gaulle's inflexible commitment to French grandeur, the Gaullists' response to nationalist demands was limited to vague platitudes.[184]

This stark public reaction to the Darlan deal gave both Allied leaders pause. "Anything for the battle, but the politics will have to be sorted out later," Churchill had consoled Eisenhower at the time. The Darlan deal further solidified support in the Foreign Office for de Gaulle. Eden dispatched Harold Macmillan as "minister of state" in Algiers, where he established "a relationship of intimate confidence" with Eisenhower that gave London significant influence with the Allied commander.[185] In a defensive mood following mid-term electoral losses for the Democrats, Roosevelt was stung by the outcry over Darlan. In his next, particularly testy press conference on 17 November, the American President was at pains to assert that the Darlan pact was merely a "provisional" expedient that would be revisited after Tunisia was secure. The outcry over the Darlan deal and the fear that it might presage compromises with "fascists" elsewhere – de Gaulle cunningly suggested to the Soviet Ambassador to London, Ivan Maisky, that the Red Army had better reach Berlin before the Americans, lest Roosevelt conclude a "Goering deal" – helped to fuel the equally confusing "unconditional surrender" policy announced at the January 1943 Anfa Conference.[186]

One reason that Roosevelt proved so thin-skinned about Darlan was that he took a lot of heat for a man whom he did not trust, and who would fail to deliver the Toulon fleet, a particular priority for the President.[187] When Bonnier de la Chappelle assassinated the French admiral on Christmas Eve 1942, no one mourned him, least of all Roosevelt and Eisenhower. Nor has the mystery of Darlan's assassination been solved, although theories abound. He had accumulated an impressive array of enemies that ran from collaborators who accused him of betraying Vichy, to the resistance led by the Gaullists, to royalists on the right. The British are also suspected of having a role in Darlan's demise.[188] The assassin Bonnier de la Chapelle was executed with indecent haste following a perfunctory trial. Giraud subsequently opened an enquiry, which pointed to the royalists Henri d'Astier and Henri Pose, who had conspired to hoist the Comte de Paris, France's royalist pretender, into power. The enquiry was adjourned, and the prosecution dossier disappeared and with it all evidence.[189] De Gaulle certainly had a strong motive to eliminate Darlan, for as long as the admiral remained in charge, the leader of *la France combattante* would have no chance to establish himself in AFN. The Gaullist movement certainly contained men who advocated eliminating the French admiral, and in the BCRA had a mechanism to carry out the assassination. However, BCRA historian Sébastien Albertelli could find no conclusive evidence linking the Gaullists to Darlan's assassination.[190] "It shows how wrong you get if once you compromise with evil," Oliver Harvey, Eden's private secretary, wrote in the aftermath of Bonnier de la Chappelle's execution. "You find yourself shooting a good man for doing what you should have done yourself."[191]

During Torch, Roosevelt's emissaries had been at pains to reassure Vichy's proconsuls in AFN that he had no intention of upsetting the colonial status quo. Even the US official history concludes that, by allowing Vichy officials to retain their positions, the invaders made reprisals against "pro-American Frenchmen who had risked their lives or personal freedom before the landings" inevitable. But in the short run, local commanders like Fredendall in Oran proved unwilling to prevent reprisals against those who had assisted the Allies.[192] Nevertheless, this "second defeat" of the French army, this time at the hands of the Anglo-Americans, transmitted a strong message to nationalists of waning French imperial power, that their French "protectors" now had protectors.[193] Above all, through the wide diffusion of the Atlantic Charter of August 1941 and Roosevelt's "Four Freedoms," the United States undermined French prestige and the legitimacy of its racialized imperial order. The 11 December 1942 mobilization of reservists in Algeria found a lack of enthusiasm to liberate France, even within the settler population. Nationalist leader Ferhat Abbas, emboldened by dismissive US attitudes toward the French colonial authorities, including Roosevelt's personal meeting with the Sultan of Morocco in January 1943 without the presence of Noguès, petitioned to create a Muslim assembly and extend Muslim rights based on Atlantic Charter principles. On 10 February 1943, Abbas delivered his *Manifeste algérien* to Eisenhower and any other Ally with an official address, that stressed a lack of Muslim confidence in French leadership. In Morocco, *Istiqlal* (Independence) became a political party in 1943, and in January 1944 proclaimed its goal to separate from France. From the perspective of the North African Muslims, "the war provoked an acceleration of history," in the words of Levisse-Touzé. Torch was a critical moment that hastened the pace of that transition. Nationalism may not have been the only game in town among the very diverse indigenous population of AFN. But the incoherent French response to Torch, typified by "*La 'comédie' politique d'Alger* " of November 1942 and the subsequent quarrels between Gaullists and Giraudists that played out in North Africa from the summer of 1943, helped to make it so. This Franco-French war joined the 1940 defeat, the fratricidal struggle in Syria in 1941, and the presence of a powerful, liberating Anglo-American army to erode French prestige among the colonized. At Constantine in eastern Algeria on 12 December 1943, de Gaulle promised to open positions in the army, the administration, commerce, and banks to Muslims. But by then, some Muslim nationalists led by Messali Hadj were no longer interested in equality, but sought independence. The unpopularity of mobilization, combined with the inequality of the conditions of military service, including pay, only accelerated Muslim discontentment. By May 1945, when rebellion erupted in Sétif and Guelma, nationalism had become a mass movement throughout the Maghreb.[194]

Toulon

The crowning insult of the Darlan deal was that Eisenhower had stuck his neck out for a French admiral and commander-in-chief unable to command his own forces, whose writ ran neither in Toulon nor in Tunis. The pride of the French navy, the High Seas Fleet at Toulon, counted three battleships, four heavy cruisers, three light cruisers, one seaplane transport, several destroyers, and ten submarines. Amounting to more than 300,000 tons, it constituted a potentially formidable weapon that "remained the president's 'paramount' concern."[195] During negotiations at Algiers, Clark repeatedly demanded that Darlan order the fleet to sail to Gibraltar, because the harbors in AFN had become too congested with ships from the three Allied task forces. But Darlan had refused on the pretext that he had been deprived of his command by Clark, and because he did not want to disrupt good order and discipline in the fleet.[196] On 11 November, as German troops surged into the *zone libre*, Darlan wired the fleet commander, stating that with the German violation of the armistice, the French navy had recovered its "liberty of action . . . I invite their commander-in-chief to direct them to French West Africa (e.g. Dakar)." A naval aviator whose well-known antipathy for the "Freemason" Darlan offered Pétain an extra margin of control over his actions, "Count Jean" de Laborde refused to reply, arguing that Darlan's defection to the Allies had removed him from the chain of command. Darlan's "invitation" to Laborde was repeated the next day. This time, Laborde answered with an implied obscenity.[197]

In fact, as Paxton points out, steam was raised in the Toulon fleet on the morning of 8 November, as the Admiralty in Vichy urgently requested permission through Wiesbaden and Turin to weigh anchor "to aid the defense of Algeria." Turin welcomed the request, and by 08:30 on 10 November, two French liaison officers had arrived in Rome to coordinate the use of Italian naval bases and Italian air support from Sardinia and Sicily. However, negotiations quickly bogged down because the Axis had decided to invade the *zone libre* on the following day.[198] The Toulon fleet again raised steam on 12–13 November. But the intention was not to evade German seizure, but to repel potential British attacks on France's south coast, which Vichy's sailors planned to do in conjunction with the Armistice Army and the Germans. The Toulon fleet was perfectly capable of weighing anchor for Gibraltar or Dakar. The *Luftwaffe* was in no position to impede its departure before 25 November. The attitude of Vichy's Chief of the Naval Staff, Rear Admiral Gabriel Auphan, appears equivocal. According to Paxton, Auphan regarded flight to North Africa as an "act of war" against Germany and a breach of Article 8 of the armistice. He asked German Admiral Raeder not to occupy Toulon, a request that Raeder rejected on 12 November. On 14 November, Clark again urged Darlan to order the fleet to sail. Biographers sympathetic to Darlan believe that Auphan did indeed want to join AFN, and encouraged Pétain to flee. He also wanted to wait until the situation clarified in Algiers. Auphan resigned on 16 November after Pétain refused to give him command of the High Seas Fleet, citing the Marshal's desire to do nothing to violate the 1940 armistice. Two commanders thought sympathetic to the Allies were relieved.[199] Masson believes that Auphan was reluctant to order the fleet to sail over the objections of Laborde and the Maritime Prefect at Toulon, André Marquis, who had pledged their word to representatives of the *Kriegsmarine* that they would only fight "the Anglo-Saxons and the French who were enemies of the Marshal's government."[200] Coutau-Bégarie and Huan argue that Laborde and Marquis did not believe that the Germans would move against the fleet. If so, this constituted an extraordinary negligence and dereliction of duty, as their only fallback plan was to scuttle.[201]

By 25 November, eight U-boats lurked before Toulon, while the *Luftwaffe* was positioned to intervene from air bases at Lézignan, Toulouse, Avignon, and Nîmes. The French ships were fueled, and would require three to four hours to build up steam and cast off, for the twelve-hour sail to Algiers. But even had officers of La Royale been so inclined, such was Laborde's smoldering resentment against the British over Mers-el-Kébir and Dakar that it would have taken a direct order from Pétain to force them to sail, an order that, of course, was never issued. What did come was Laborde's directive to scuttle should the Germans invade the Toulon enclave or come aboard French ships. Laborde did not even hold out the option of sailing to a neutral port, or to the French West Indies, that the British had offered during Catapult. On 15 November, two days after the armistice in Algiers was formally concluded between Darlan and the Allies, the Germans, claiming no longer to have confidence in the word of French officers, ordered that all Armistice Army troops evacuate Toulon. The next day, Vice-Admiral Jean-Marie Abrial was named as navy minister. On 22 November, FAF planes were forbidden to overfly Toulon. On 27 November Operation Lila was set in motion, which brought German troops from the 7th and 10th Panzer Divisions and 1,300 men from the Das Reich SS Division to the gates of the Toulon naval base with the mission to disarm the French ships, as the Germans had neither the sailors nor the fuel to operate them. At 04:30, German troops moved to occupy the port. At 05:15, Laborde issued the order to scuttle. With the exception of five of the ten French submarines, the Toulon fleet of ninety ships totaling 250,000 tons settled into the mud of Toulon harbor (Figure 10.3). Those in Algiers learned of the scuttle only in the early afternoon when they intercepted a radio message sent in clear from Pétain to Laborde, ordering him to abandon his flagship *Strasbourg*. The scope of the disaster was confirmed by air reconnaissance. This scuttle represented the loss of one-third of the French fleet as it had existed in 1939, in what Paxton called "Vichy's most determined act of neutrality."[202]

Figure 10.3 The High Seas Fleet in Toulon, 27 November 1942.

"*Le sabordage*" of the High Seas Fleet destroyed Darlan's already damaged prestige with the Allies. While the FNFL, combined with repairable ships or those ceded by the Allies to the French, kept the French navy in the war, the Toulon scuttle, combined with naval losses during Torch, meant that "it was however but a pale reflection of the navy of 1939, or even that of 1940–1942," writes Masson.[203] Nor, even after the occupation of the *zone libre*, "*le sabordage*," the loss of AFN and AOF, which rallied to the Anglo-Americans, and the effective dissolution of the French armed services, was Darlan even able to convince Vice-Admiral René-Émile Godfroy to order the 66,000 tons of Force X ships, consisting of the battleship *Lorraine*, four cruisers, three destroyers, and a submarine, interned at Alexandria since 1940, to reenter the war. This only happened in May 1943. Warships amounting to 33,000 tons in the West Indies were also effectively mothballed until July 1943. The adhesion of Dakar to the Algiers armistice did, however, bring the damaged *Richelieu* and three heavy cruisers back into the war.[204]

By that time, though, the Allies might have wondered if the French navy had been worth the bother. The June 1940 armistice had been justified in part as a requirement to preserve French maritime power. In the event, it proved a desperate miscalculation. Since 1940, the navy had lost 65 percent of its tonnage, while Laborde's naval air arm had been virtually eliminated. The French navy was fourteen times smaller than the United States Navy, and eight times smaller than the Royal Navy. Even the Italian navy was now larger. Furthermore, by bailing out of the war in June 1940, the navy, like the French army and air force, had failed to keep up with the rapid developments in warfare, as had the diminutive but far more feisty *Forces navales françaises libres* (FNFL). Only 55 percent of the French ships remaining in the war could be considered modern. And only after the liberation of Tunisia in May 1943 did the French navy gain access to its unique small overseas shipyard in Bizerte. The Toulon scuttle marked the loss of most of the best ships in the French inventory. Hence the plea to the United States from 1943 to refurbish the battleship *Richelieu* and a handful of light cruisers and destroyers. Nevertheless, at war's end, Darlan's "undefeated navy" of 1940 was one-third of what it had been in September 1939, despite the fact that it had hardly fired a shot in anger except at the Anglo-Americans. Its losses had been largely self-inflicted. And yet, the Vichy navy took a perverse pride in its loyalty to the Marshal, in contrast to what they viewed as the sectarianism and chronic indiscipline of the "rebel" and "émigré" FNFL. And they convinced themselves that the suicide of the Toulon High Seas Fleet represented a victory over the Germans, an act of "resistance" and sacrifice that authenticated their sense of honor and loyalty.[205] In fact, Darlan subsequently tried to take credit for the Toulon scuttle, claiming that it resulted from his standing order that dated from the armistice, an assertion that hardly embellished Darlan's already tarnished credibility.[206]

But the implications of "*le sabordage*" took some time to sink in. In the immediate wake of the event, the Allies breathed a sigh of relief. Churchill confided to Eden that "Darlan has done for us more than de Gaulle" ever did.[207] Even the Gaullists and the Resistance press, including the communists, agreed that naval officers had made a "*sacrifice héroïque*." Invited to dinner with de Gaulle and three naval officers in the wake of *le sabordage*, Crémieux-Brilhac was somewhat surprised to hear the leader of *la France combattante* rationalize the scuttle, against the opinion of the three officers present, as the result of "the navy's nurtured Anglophobia and the oath to the Marshal. But he heaped blame on Pétain."[208] In his memoirs, de Gaulle laments that "France, without a great navy, cannot be France." The problem, in de Gaulle's view, stemmed from the fact that the Republic had allowed the navy to transform into the personal fiefdom of officers like Darlan, who nurtured their own political ambitions. But ultimately, the fate of the fleet remained Pétain's responsibility in November 1942. "The accord of 'neutrality' that Vichy concluded with the enemy diverted our sailors from some ultimate action. It was a step toward oblivion." De Gaulle confessed that he had sent a letter to Laborde, only to have the admiral threaten his personal emissary, Colonel Fourcault. "Also, the Marshal, his ministers, the maritime prefect, the fleet commander-in-chief, paralyzed by the consequences of their own neglect, found nothing better to do than to send these powerful warships to the bottom ... [in] the most lamentable, most sterile suicide that one can imagine ... For my part, sunk in anger and despair, I was reduced to watching from afar disappear what had been one of France's major opportunities." Churchill's phone call of condolences, "nobly expressed but with secret satisfaction," especially rankled. Nevertheless, in his memoirs, de Gaulle insists that the combination of the Darlan deal, the Axis occupation of the *zone libre*, and the scuttling of the French fleet had the silver lining of both demonstrating the bankruptcy of Vichy policy and reinforcing de Gaulle's claim that France could not rely on the Allies to make decisions compatible with French interests.[209]

The Anglo-Americans were relieved that at least the fleet had not fallen into German hands, although Hitler's intention was to disarm the Toulon ships, and perhaps surrender a few of them to the Italians, who might have pressed them into service to supply Tunisia, because the *Kriegsmarine* lacked the manpower, resources, and sailors to man, fuel, and sortie the French vessels. The Gaullists concocted a victorious narrative of "the great Toulon suicide" as a gesture of patriotic French naval officers who wished to avoid the spectacle of seeing French ships pressed into the service of the enemy. Lacouture reminds us that, for de Gaulle, the scuttle took place in the context of his deep humiliation at being excluded from knowledge of Torch, and what he saw as Churchill's insincere "condolences" over the loss of the French fleet. He also railed against "*Vichyisme à la sauce américaine*" in Algiers. So, in this context of another French humiliation, de Gaulle looked to give the "suicide" a "halo of virtue."[210] *Life* magazine's 15 March 1943 opinion that the Toulon scuttle offered perhaps France's most important contribution to the war so far must qualify as irony, or at best damning with faint praise. Such was de Gaulle's low opinion of *La Royale* that he, too, concurred that at least scuttling was preferable to allowing the fleet to fall into Axis hands, although the Axis powers impounded many other ships.[211]

While the French navy's action may be condemned alternately as inopportune, deluded, wasteful, or unpatriotic, what is usually ignored is that it appeared positively heroic when compared with that of the Armistice Army and Air Force. Many French soldiers cheered at the announcement of the dissolution of the Armistice Army, as they had on hearing news of the armistice two years earlier.[212] The Germans helping themselves to French military equipment and much more had been going on since August 1940.[213] The Germans impounded an estimated 1,800 undamaged French tanks in 1940.[214] Overall, Thomas Vaisset and Philippe Vial estimate that the French army supplied the *Wehrmacht* with 800–900 artillery pieces, 6,000 mortars, 9,000–12,000 machine-guns, 150,000–250,000 rifles, and countless munitions as well as other equipment.[215] Not to be outdone, according to Jacques Belle, the *Luftwaffe* appropriated 1,876 planes and the *Regia Aeronautica* 604 from the FAF inventory. While many of these airframes were out of date, the French stock did contain some relatively modern models like the Leo 451 and the Dewoitine 520. The two Axis air forces were above all interested in the 1,271 transport planes, vital to support their operations in Tunisia. Claude d'Abzac-Epezy estimates the Axis bonanza to have been slightly more modest. The occupation of the *zone libre* also allowed the Axis to seize control of French aircraft factories that had been displaced to Toulouse before the war, and to up the French financial contribution to the occupation to 500 million francs a day.[216] All in all, Torch proved very costly for Vichy. Nor were the Allies in a mood to cut their new ally a particularly favorable deal in AFN. French officials may have regretted not being saddled with AMGOT, because they now had to pay the wages of French officials – and their "colonial fourth" salary plus-ups – as well as other normal costs hitherto met by the mainland. And, as they were cut off from the metropole, AFN became dependent on the importation of American products.[217]

To place the Toulon action in a broader context, one must note that the act of scuttling was neither a uniquely Gallic reflex, nor was it necessarily dishonorable *per se*. But previous scuttles had taken place in situations of hopeless defeat and surrender.[218] In November 1942, the obvious option open to the French High Seas Fleet was to sail to Gibraltar, Dakar, or North Africa and continue the fight to liberate France. In early September 1943, the Italian fleet would escape to the Allies from La Spezia in the face of a violent reaction by the *Luftwaffe*. Apologists for the French navy argued that the Italian situation was different, because Italian leader Pietro Badoglio had switched sides with the Allied–Italian armistice negotiated at Cassibile. For certain, Pétain was no Badoglio – Pétain was not *even* Badoglio.[219] Furthermore, on closer inspection, the reaction of the Italian fleet was more ambiguous. In all, the Allies recouped only about half of the Italian fleet.[220]

Nevertheless, with time, opinion began to shift toward the view that the Toulon scuttle offered a sterile and humiliating act in the context of Vichy collaboration that constituted a national disgrace. "*Le sabordage*" typified Vichy's – and the French navy's – opportunism and absence of a patriotic and moral compass. It dishonored the service, because it sealed the French navy's acceptance of defeat in the midst of the "moral meltdown of the Vichy state." It was an insult to those sailors who gave their lives in the Resistance, like Lieutenant Honoré d'Estienne d'Orves, Captain Jacques Trolley de Prévaux, or Chief Engineer Jacques Stosskopf. Whatever other contributions the French navy made to Allied victory in the war, the memory associated with "*la marée bleue*" ("the blue tide") would be "the scuttle" of 27 November 1942. Toulon became the French navy's necropolis, and, in the view of Vaisset and Vial, "the metaphor for Vichy's moral bankruptcy."[221]

The post-Torch amalgamation of the *Barbaresques* – as French sailors associated with the Barbary Coast referred to themselves – and the FNFL in the shadow of "the scuttle" became a predictably tempestuous one. The *Barbaresques* maintained a perverse pride in their discipline as expressed in their unswerving loyalty to Pétain, as opposed to the indiscipline and politicization of the FNFL. They convinced themselves that the Toulon scuttle represented a victory over the Germans, an act of resistance and sacrifice that confirmed their honor and loyalty to their word not to surrender their ships. As in the army, this shotgun marriage witnessed friction over portraits of Pétain that continued to decorate wardrooms, and ignited tensions between the Vichy bridge and the Gaullist lower decks for the remainder of the war. For its part, the collaborationist right denounced the fleet's mass *harakiri* as "treason" because it also scuttled their plans for cooperation with Germany. After initial relief, the left refused to label "the scuttle" as an act of resistance from a nautical service that had refused for two years to fight anyone but the Allies.[222] Moreover, for a nation that nurtured pretentions to global power, Ciano was one of the first to pick up on the fact that, stripped of its navy, France was no longer even a Mediterranean player. France saw its prestige among the Anglo-Americans plummet, and its clout in the Alliance diminished to the status of courtesy power. France would require a hitchhike from the Royal Navy to reestablish its regime in Indochina in 1945. Admirals Michelier at Casablanca and Rioult in Oran were retired in 1943. The "admirals' trial" that opened in the summer of 1946, and continued into the spring of 1947, asked why Laborde and Marquis had not ordered the fleet to sail. Laborde's defense was that he was simply applying the standing orders issued by Darlan even before the Armistice. After initially taking credit for the scuttle, Darlan shifted the blame to Laborde. On the Liberation, the high court agreed, and sentenced de Laborde to death, subsequently commuted to life in prison. The 1951 amnesty saw his release. He died in 1977 at age ninety-eight.[223]

Conclusion

Torch generated at least two myths, beginning with an assertion that the operation's success hinged on the Resistance, especially that in Algiers which sequestered Darlan and Juin in the early hours of 8 November, thereby disrupting and delaying the French reaction to the Anglo-American landings. In fact, by its indiscretions, the Resistance almost compromised Torch. Indeed, it failed to do so only because the French leadership both in Vichy and in Algiers was incredulous that the Anglo-Americans would be capable of pulling together such a substantial and complex operation barely ten months after the United States had entered the war. Nor, they calculated, would the Allies dare launch such an audacious invasion in the late autumn when tides were running high, especially on Morocco's Atlantic coast. Furthermore, with the possible exception of Dakar in 1940, to date Allied amphibious operations had been limited to tactical raids on poorly defended secondary harbors, all of which had been unsuccessful. For these reasons, Resistance leaks and intelligence warnings of the movement of Allied convoys were ignored or misinterpreted, while Michelier and the FAF had failed to patrol aggressively, an action that might at least have detected the approach of Western Task Force and raised the alarm. Whether this might have added Torch to the list of failed Allied amphibious operation is doubtful, however. As the Germans recognized, the French defenders in AFN were undergunned, undertrained, and frequently undermotivated. Furthermore, the surprise invasion catapulted the French command, whose lines of authority had been intentionally muddled upon Weygand's departure to prevent the defection of AFN to the Allies, into utter confusion. Their hesitation was amplified by a fear, stimulated by indications of "dissidence" in *armée d'Afrique* ranks, that pro-Allied subordinates might refuse to follow their orders. The confusion and hesitation at the top of the chain of command scrambled the signal for subordinates, left to choose their own courses of action about whether to resist, fold, or, in Tunisia, cooperate with the Axis.

Berlin's – and Vichy's – fear since Weygand had commanded in Africa was that an upgraded *armée d'Afrique* capable of defending AFN on its own would simply defect to the Allied camp. Yet, in the end, the Axis lacked the forces to garrison AFN. A German counter-thrust through Spain aimed at Gibraltar, that the Americans feared, had been taken off the table due to shifting Spanish politics, inadequate Spanish infrastructure, and Hitler's indifference to the strategic possibilities offered by the Mediterranean generally, and Spain in particular.

Therefore, Berlin's remaining policy option for the defense of the Western Mediterranean was to rely on the frail reed of Vichy's North African commanders, who, to give them their due, did a credible job of confusing Eisenhower and Clark long enough to insure a successful Axis invasion of Tunisia. But to imagine that Hitler would ease up on the conditions of the armistice as did Laval and Darlan constituted the daydream of desperate men who failed to comprehend the Total War mindset of Hitler and the Nazis. In the meantime, Darlan's tedious delaying tactics and contradictory orders confused his own subordinates. Berlin's attention was focused on El Alamein and the growing crisis at Stalingrad; Axis forces in Italy were too far away to intervene immediately, while U-boats had been positioned in the Sicilian Channel to intercept convoys thought destined to relieve Malta or assault Tripoli to cut off Rommel's retreat from Egypt. Juin had earlier concluded that any attempt to spark a popular insurrection against the Allies would put French rule in AFN on a fast track to termination. By dithering in Algiers with Darlan, Eisenhower lost focus on the race to Tunis.

A second misperception was that Torch brought the French back into the war on the Allied side. In fact, such a conclusion proved premature. GIs who expected the French to welcome them as liberators were more than a little annoyed by the surprisingly stiff resistance they often encountered, in Morocco especially, but also when they attempted direct assaults on the harbors of Oran and Algiers. While sold as a "pragmatic" decision to stop the fighting and move Allied forces quickly toward Tunisia to preempt the arrival of Axis armies there, the "Darlan deal" left the loyalties of Vichy French forces, torn between the Marshal and the Allies, uncertain. Torch had revealed a High Command in North Africa fearful of taking any initiative that might displease Pétain. For this reason, Darlan justified the ceasefire with the Anglo-Americans as having "the Marshal's secret accord." This froze AFN and its *armée d'Afrique* in a sort of alliance limbo whose position could be categorized as "to be determined."

Nor did the "Darlan deal" recuperate the High Seas Fleet for Allied benefit, which had been one of Torch's major objectives. While the initial reaction to the Toulon scupper was to praise the patriotic response of the French navy that committed suicide rather than surrender the fleet to the Axis, in fact, the French Admiralty squandered the opportunity to raise steam and sail to safety before U-boats sealed the harbor exits and German soldiers scrambled onto the Toulon docks. The Armistice Army had self-confined to barracks rather than defend the so-called *zone libre*, while, as the following volume will recount, French forces allowed the Axis resistance-free access to Tunisia. So, all in all, given the high expectations – one might even say the illusions – of the Allies, Torch had underdelivered.

Epilogue

For the purposes of a counter-offensive in the secondary phase of the war in Europe, Operation Torch in late 1942 marked a significant advance for the Allies, at crossed purposes whether to strike at Hitler's New Order from the periphery, versus a direct continental assault as favored by the US Army. Torch reinforced alliance cohesion, held the potential to bring France back into the war, and preserved maritime flexibility characteristic of the indirect approach. The success of Torch also assuaged Roosevelt's fear that Gibraltar and "the great shoulder of Africa" with its European imperial realm might be infiltrated and occupied by Axis forces. As abstruse as this idea seems in the twenty-first century, that might have preempted a mortal threat to the American hemisphere where an Axis fifth column lurked in the southern cone.[1] While contemporaries at the cusp of 1942–1943 may not have been instantaneously aware that Axis power had crested, with the defeat at the battle of El Alamein, to be followed in February 1943 by the German surrender at Stalingrad, made a hat trick by "Tunisgrad" in May, the net assessment by potentates in the Vichy government of the year 1942 that the war had achieved "stalemate" proved clearly passé. Operationally, the Torch campaign signaled a huge advance in Allied amphibious operations since Dakar in 1940. By 1942–1943, the Allied war effort, that combined virtually unobstructed maritime mobility and increasing command of the air, had freed the Allies to strike anywhere in the Mediterranean littoral and eventually on the European mainland, although any desire for a swift cross-Channel invasion was held in abeyance by the geopolitical reality of Axis power.

Yet the implications of the unmistakable Allied ascendency the Torch operation represented for France in Axis Europe were willfully ignored at Vichy. When the 1940 defeat ejected France from great power ranks, the Marshal and his entourage had bet on an Axis victory, as had many others at that moment. Through "neutrality," Vichy had hoped to protect the empire and rebuild French military power, to secure a position of influence in the Europe of the Axis New Order, with an immediate payoff calculated in the release of the roughly 1.8 million French POWs. But rather than Vichy receiving compensation for its compliance to Berlin, the majority of French POWs remained hostage to a continued French role in the system of Axis conquest and governance, where France was nevertheless better off than Poland and conquered parts of the USSR. Furthermore, transforming soldiers who personified France's greatest defeat and hence embodied the nation's crisis of confidence and masculine identity into "Vichy's adored children," symbols of France's penitence and contrition, only served further to exile them from the war's narrative, promoted by certain authors of United Nations mass persuasion aligned with London and Washington, of occupation hardship and a growing resistance movement against a Nazi rule of hangmen, madmen, Quislings, Pétains, and Lavals.

Vichy had hoped to escape the most dire consequences of its 1940 defeat through a policy of "neutrality." However, the demobilization of the Armistice Army, the High Seas Fleet scuttle, the loss of control over virtually all its colonies in the aftermath of November 1942, and the subjugation of the former *zone libre* by a German regime that now imported occupation practices from the bloodlands of Eastern Europe eclipsed any fading illusions of Vichy autonomy. As the year 1943 took hold, the character of the New Order transformed into that of Goebbels' Total War in the debris of defeats in North Africa and especially on the Eastern Front. But rather than recognize that nothing now impeded Germany's domination and ruthless exploitation of France, Vichy doubled down on collaboration, explained by Robert Paxton as the result of:

> bureaucratic inertia and blindness to considerations beyond the efficiency of the state. Beyond that was the attraction of the National Revolution for its partisans. At bottom, however, lay a more subtle intellectual culprit: fear of social disorder as the highest evil. Some of France's best skill and talent went into a formidable effort to keep the French state afloat under increasingly questionable circumstances. Who would keep order, they asked, if the state lost authority? By saving the state, however, they were losing the nation.[2]

The naked truth was that, without an Axis victory, Vichy would cease to exist. In these conditions, for Hitler, the Vichy government would be a gift that kept on giving, especially as the requirements of this total war in Nazi Europe vassalized French industry and manpower to support the overdue full mobilization of an increasingly outmatched German war effort.

If Vichy's unequal partnership with Germany contravened over a century of French diplomacy, the France that fought with the Alliance, too, struggled to propel de Gaulle's refugee crusade into relevance amid the enduring problems of alliance cohesion in which varying national interests and the outlook and philosophies of the leaders bulked large in this crucial domain of war. De Gaulle's first problem was to convince the Allies – especially the highly skeptical Americans – that he represented France's interests and embodied its legitimacy because of a legacy of strained Franco-American relations going back at least to 1919, if not before. This challenge would lead to a complex, and frequently adversarial, relationship between FDR's Washington and Fighting France in its successive evolutions. Eisenhower's ad hoc "Darlan deal" in the fall of 1942 has been excused by some historians as a "pragmatic" response "to end the fighting" in the wake of the Torch operation, where the local French commanders had failed to react in the manner naively anticipated by Anglo-Saxon campaign planners. However, with the imposition of Henri Giraud, three authorities now claimed to represent France. Giraud's *deus ex machina* act at Algiers also lent credence to de Gaulle's contention that the Anglo-Americans sought to marginalize France in the Alliance. In de Gaulle's not wholly unfounded telling, Giraud personified Roosevelt's scheme to dictate France's political future by excluding the French from Allied planning for the invasion of the European continent and imposing an illegitimate government on Liberated France, while shouldering France out of the major decisions that would affect its future as a global and European power. To preempt this possibility, "Fighting France" accelerated its transition from a military organization with a political agenda into a political movement with an, albeit constricted and perpetually reconstituting, armed wing. The contradiction was that, while de Gaulle would often be at odds with the Anglo-Americans on policy and strategy for France, he was utterly dependent on the Anglo-Saxon powers to arm, equip, and organize his military forces, as well as transport them to the battlefield in numbers sufficient to accomplish de Gaulle's multiple political goals on Liberation. Foremost among them was to reestablish the supremacy of the French state and its duly constituted armed forces, followed by an occupation zone in Germany, and France's participation in the conferences and commissions that would reconfigure and regulate post-war Europe and the global order. With the Allies poised to invade France in 1943–1944, these issues would guarantee that relations among the Western Allies would grow more complex, and frequently become adversarial.[3]

Initially, much of this conflict of alliance cohesion and competing national interests among allies in wartime would play out in AFN. Seen from London and Washington, where the indirect and maritime strategy of this initial phase of the counter-offensive held sway, the Maghreb had seemed to offer an ideal geostrategic base to open the Mediterranean to Allied shipping, and attack what Churchill mischaracterized as the "soft underbelly of Europe." At the same time, Torch offered a down payment on the Soviet demand for the second front, to reassure a skeptical Stalin that the Western Allies intended to assault the center of gravity of Hitler's Europe sooner rather than later. For Torch planners, AFN also seemed to offer the springboard for a renascent France's return to the war's main flow as part of the Alliance, spearheaded by *l'armée d'Afrique* and France's High Seas Fleet. Yet, the Torch campaign had not immediately suspended France's two-and-a-half-year quarantine from the Second World War. On the contrary, the Western Allies had crashed a complex political, social, and religious milieu in French state and society in North Africa, one whose foundational fissures had been further exacerbated by a constellation of highly conflicted political and military elites typical of the epoch from 1871 until 1940, and by budding anti-imperial unrest among North Africa's indigenous population. And whatever AFN's geographical advantages, the Anglo-Americans were not merely "liberating" a portion of overseas France and its empire, and setting up a base for further Mediterranean operations, whatever their intentions. Rather, if defeat and occupation had exacerbated existing divisions in France, racial, confessional, and economic tensions became more acute in AFN in the wake of Operation Torch. In short, no existential threat existed to unify a profoundly tribalized North African society, or forge a sense of purpose through association with a common crusade.

Nor would AFN's factiousness facilitate de Gaulle's task of establishing a political base there, and then deploying a revivified and up-gunned *armée d'Afrique* to achieve his geopolitical as well as domestic political goals for France. One dimension of military history is to examine how armies adapt and reconstitute themselves in the challenging circumstances of war. On a motivational level, many French officers burned to redeem France's martial reputation forfeited in 1940, a goal partially achieved by the *Corps expéditionnaire français* (CEF) under the command of Alphonse Juin in Italy in 1943–1944. But on a political level, in 1943, loyalty to Pétain had become a political, professional, and even emotional requirement for *l'armée d'Afrique*'s "defeated caste." Furthermore, as in times prior of international violence and domestic upheaval, the professional army had become a politically divisive symbol, both in North Africa and in France, which would make it a contentious foundation for a resistance *levée* on liberation. On the level of military organization and order of battle, even when amalgamated with the remnants of de Gaulle's *Forces françaises libres*, and mobilized for war, first in Italy, and then for France, *l'armée d'Afrique*, like its sub-Saharan confrères in *l'armée coloniale*, remained a "rag-tag force" inexperienced in the techniques and technologies of a swiftly evolving modern conflict. The French army's reentry into the war in 1943–1944 would be made possible only by a massive American rearmament and retraining program. But if this American managerial scale gave real meaning to the idea of total war, a fractured and underresourced AFN struggled to realize it. This infusion of US arms and technology overwhelmed an underdeveloped AFN, that lacked an industrial base. Nor was it able to supply a deep bench of technicians, educated cadres, and replacements, that would impede France's ability to field a modern, technologically capable air–land fighting force. Not surprisingly, given their self-reverential sense of superiority over their fellow citizens, reinforced by the French navy's tight hierarchy, and iron loyalty to Pétain, French admirals chose to abstain from the war at a crucial moment when the French navy might have made an important contribution to the Allied effort, thereby enhancing France's status in the Alliance. In this way, the Toulon scuttle deprived de Gaulle of an important maritime card to play in his game of Texas Hold'em with the Allies.

A growing internal resistance formed a third component of post-Torch France. Historians are divided on the role of the Resistance in the success of Torch. On the other hand, it is certainly possible to argue, as does Andrew Buchanan, that without the prospect of "resistance," Torch might have never proceeded from plan to execution. The principal value of the US diplomat/warrior Murphy-sponsored Resistance on the strategic level had been to bolster the argument in Allied councils that AFN awaited liberation and the opportunity for France to rejoin the Allied crusade, so that its defenders were unlikely to offer serious opposition to an Anglo-American liberation. Unfortunately, the divided, and on the official level recalcitrant, response in AFN to the opportunity to rejoin the war continued to disappoint and frustrate Allied expectations. But, in the larger narrative of the war, the point was that, with the success of the Torch landings, resistance had now entered the vocabulary of France at war. From London and Algiers, the Anglo-American "interface services," always a central part of the psychological offensive as well as self-mass persuasion in Washington and London, organized to mobilize, militarize, operationalize, and integrate into Allied planning a timid resistance *levée* that collected in France. Vichy and Axis repression had combined with labor drafts to push some of France's young male population beyond *attentisme*. Around 20,000 *évadés de France* crossed the Pyrenees to reach AFN, usually in poor condition after spending several months incarcerated in Franco's jails. However, many in flight from forced labor in Germany joined a spontaneous tsunami of internal refugees known collectively as the *maquis*. From early 1943, these young men began to collect in France's more remote regions like the Alps, the Jura, the Massif Central, and the West, where they increasingly became targets of sweeps by German troops and the thuggish Vichy *Milice*, both of which were disinclined to recognize *maquisards* as lawful combatants, but rather treated them as "terrorists" stripped of Geneva Convention protections. This *maquis* was distinct from a more structured and clandestine *résistance organisation* with more defined roles – intelligence collection, sabotage, propaganda, escape and evasion, and so on – also under the loose direction of the interface services. In fact, the *maquis* phenomenon threatened to overwhelm these established resistance groups, and challenged the interface services, taken by surprise in the course of 1943, to evaluate the scope of the *maquis* mobilization, find resources and create the logistical structures to support them, and evolve a military role for them on liberation. Therefore, having gained a kind of continental foothold in Allied perceptions, "resistance" would loom ever larger in the strategic and political calculations of Allied and French planners, and in the mythology of France at war.

However, the growth of internal resistance in France, combined with the intervention of Anglo-American interface services into what was in effect French politics on the local level, would further complicate Franco-Alliance relations by enhancing existing tensions surrounding the issue of France's post-liberation government. Nothing suggested that the demise of the republic had been a source of personal bereavement for French men and women. A common view, certainly one popular at Vichy and in AFN, was the cultural pessimist canard that mirrored Nazi propaganda that democracy had lost the war. As a military man of authoritarian temperament and witness to the domestic chaos of the 1930s, de Gaulle might seem disinclined to return to France's governmental status quo ante – a desire hardly unique to him and part of the war's level of ambition to remake combatant states and societies to achieve vastly more than the disappointments of the epoch 1919–1939. A growing internal resistance, a significant segment of which was loyal to a French communist party whose definition of "democratic" was not universally embraced, sought France's "renewal," not a restoration of *la troisième*. Beyond these military preparations and alerted by the communist clutch for power that accompanied the September 1943 liberation of Corsica, de Gaulle feared with reason that, driven by their own institutional agendas, the interface services were arming and enabling political factionalism that threatened to explode into civil war, as was to be the case in liberated Greece and Yugoslavia.

Therefore, at the top of de Gaulle's priorities upon liberation of the French mainland was a desire to revitalize the French army through the imposition of a citizen *levée*, while simultaneously corralling France's fissiparous resistance movement, impose order, and transition France to post-war stability and security. As a first step to avoid a repetition of Corsica and waylay any attempt by Roosevelt to impose an Allied Military Government of Occupied Territories (AMGOT), or – worse – replicate a "Darlan deal" in Paris with some Murphy-supplied Vichy hack or mothballed admiral, he created a shadow administration that slipped into place as advancing Allied armies liberated French territory. The dual goals of revitalizing the French army while bringing the resistance to heel would be accomplished in three stages. The first step was to expel the Anglo-American interface services from liberated France. And while, at the time, this was interpreted as yet another act of ingratitude toward the Allies by the notoriously brusque French leader, de Gaulle believed the eviction of SOE and OSS operatives an essential first step to curtail the resources, parallel chain of command, and pretentions to independence of some of the more flamboyant resistance leaders who, as in Corsica, had emerged in some provincial cities like Toulouse to dispute power on the local level with the emerging Gaullist state as German forces exited the country.

De Gaulle's second priority was to integrate French resisters into the regular forces. This he sought to accomplish in stages, first by assembling them as *Forces françaises de l'intérieur* (FFI) under the command of Pierre Koenig for the purposes of Allied planning for D-Day. Once Allied armies came ashore, resistance formations might be integrated as complete units into regular forces. However, this proved problematic for several reasons: a lack of uniformity in numbers; disputes over the self-conferred military status of resistance leaders who might refuse to acknowledge the hierarchical authority of military commanders whom they "outranked"; political infighting among resistance leaders who sought to parley their forces into political power; lack of resources; and an incapacity of inexperienced and sparsely armed Resistance units and their leaders to transition from a "war of the shadows" to lead platoons, companies, and battalions in conventional combat in the murderous conditions of warfare in the autumn and winter of 1944. For these reasons, de Gaulle ordered the dissolution of Resistance formations. In the absence of census data as well as the mechanisms on the local level to reestablish conscription, with many potential young recruits deported to Germany as laborers or escaped to the hills to avoid that fate, he obliged those who desired to fight to enlist as individuals, thus placing themselves under the iron thumb of military jurisdiction. While some Resistance leaders led by the communists protested that the measures sought to short-circuit a democratic dialogue in post-Liberation France, de Gaulle's goal was to reestablish the authority of the State, defuse disorder, minimize extra-judicial political retribution, and avoid the civil war that was to erupt in Southeastern Europe.

Unfortunately for de Gaulle, integration of the resistance into the regular forces did not translate into a renaissance of French military power. Washington insisted that the January 1943 Anfa agreement committed the United States to rearm only eleven French divisions to defeat Germany, not reconstruct a post-war French military. Furthermore, the two Allied nations agreed that, as the French were now *chez eux*, they should assume responsibility for training their own troops, thus dismantling the training infrastructure and feedback loop that had been created by the Americans in AFN to modernize *l'armée d'Afrique* and keep it up-to-date with the latest battlefield evolutions. As a result of these manpower, equipment, and training limitations, and because it made for better liberation optics, the French instituted a *blanchiment* or "whitening" of French army ranks, as many imperial levies were switched out for "fifis" – a derisive nickname for members of *les forces françaises de l'intérieur* – in the autumn of 1944. Beyond the Anfa restrictions, the French scratched a few new divisions out of their own meager resources, often arming them with Axis weapons captured in North Africa or France. Needless to say, these units, chronically deficient in leadership, training, armaments, and logistical support, suffered severely in the harsh battlefield conditions in Alsace and in the siege of the German-controlled "Atlantic pockets" in the winter of 1944–1945. Nor, during the invasion of Germany in the spring of 1945, as previously in Italy in 1944, did poor discipline always reflect well on French arms, which among the Germans would earn French soldiers the unflattering sobriquet "the Russians of the West." De Gaulle's insistence that French First Army Commander Jean de Lattre de Tassigny violate operational orders from his American superiors to seize objectives in Germany which the French President deemed essential to French interests would continue to roil Franco-Allied relations to the war's end, and beyond.

Acknowledgments

This study launched as a modest paper on the *levée en masse* delivered in an Oxford University conference in the spring of 2014. A year at Oxford's excellent "Changing Character of War Centre" allowed me to lay the foundation for a book, thanks to a friendship I prize since my Corpus Christi College, Cambridge days with Hew Strachan. I am also grateful to Margaret Macmillan, who as warden kindly hosted me as a visitor at St Antony's College during the 2014–2015 academic year. It remains for me to thank the many people in Britain, France, and the United States who generously shared their research with me, commented on portions of the manuscript, or suggested books and approaches which expanded and enriched my appreciation of the topic, among them: Robert Gildea, Guillaume Piketty, Olivier Wieviorka, Thomas Vaisset, Julie le Gac, Claire Miot, Géraud Létang, Raphaële Balu, Robin Leconte, Morgane Barey, Nicole Cohen-Addad, Ethan Katz, Phillips O'Brien, Peter Jackson, Diego Celaya Gaspar, Rachel Chin, and Jean-Louis Armand, as well as an anonymous reader for Cambridge University Press among others. My colleague at the Naval Postgraduate School Donald Abenheim has been a careful and constructive critic, keeping me focused on the fundamental questions of strategy, alliance politics, and military renewal. I thank Eliane Lenoir and Martine Briens for their generous hospitality in France, as well as my wife Françoise for her encouragement, patience, and support over the months and years of research and writing. I must also thank my editor Michael Watson for inviting me to write this book, and his excellent team at Cambridge University Press for helping to shape and transition a sizable manuscript to publication.

Notes

Introduction

1. Douglas Porch, *Counterinsurgency: Exposing the Myths of the New Way of War* (Cambridge: Cambridge University Press, 2013).

1 France in the Age of Total War

1. 31 December 1999. Quoted in Margaret Macmillan, *Paris 1919: Six Months That Changed the World* (New York: Random House, 2002), 493.
2. Macmillan, *Paris 1919*, 486–494.
3. Klaus-Jürgen Müller, *The Military in Politics and Society in France and Germany in the Twentieth Century* (Oxford and Washington, D.C.: Berg, 1995), 132.
4. Michael Geyer, "German Strategy in the Age of Machine Warfare, 1914–1945," in Peter Paret (ed.), *Makers of Modern Strategy from Machiavelli to the Nuclear Age* (Princeton: Princeton University Press, 1986), 538–539, 545, 548–549, 566; Klaus-Jürgen Müller, *The Army, Politics and Society in Germany, 1933–45: Studies in the Army's Relation to Nazism* (Manchester: Manchester University Press, 1987), 9.
5. Müller, *The Military in Politics and Society in France and Germany*, 132.
6. Brian Bond and Martin Alexander, "Liddell Hart and De Gaulle: The Doctrines of Limited Liability and Mobile Defense," in Paret (ed.), *Makers of Modern Strategy from Machiavelli to the Nuclear Age*, 598.
7. Müller, *The Military in Politics and Society in France and Germany*, 121.
8. Bond and Alexander, "Liddell Hart and De Gaulle," 598.
9. Peter Jackson, "Europe. The Failure of Diplomacy 1933–1940," in Richard J. B. Bosworth and Joseph A. Maiolo, *The Cambridge History of the Second World War*, volume II, *Politics and Ideology* (Cambridge: Cambridge University Press, 2015), 233.
10. Jackson, "Europe. The Failure of Diplomacy 1933–1940," 225–227.
11. Talbot C. Imlay, *Facing the Second World War: Strategy, Politics, and Economics in Britain and France, 1938–1940* (Oxford: Oxford University Press, 2003), 126.
12. Talbot Imlay, "Western Allied Ideology, 1939–1945," in Richard J. B. Bosworth and Joseph A. Maiolo, *The Cambridge History of the Second World War*, volume II, *Politics and Ideology* (Cambridge: Cambridge University Press, 2015), 47–48.

13. Imlay, *Facing the Second World War*, 357.
14. Martin S. Alexander, "French Grand Strategy and Defense Preparations," in John Ferris and Evan Mawdsley (eds.), *The Cambridge History of the Second World War* (Cambridge: Cambridge University Press, 2015), 80.
15. Jackson, "Europe. The Failure of Diplomacy 1933–1940," 249.
16. Jackson, "Europe. The Failure of Diplomacy 1933–1940," 244–245.
17. Jackson, "Europe. The Failure of Diplomacy 1933–1940," 242–243.
18. Daniel Hucker, *Public Opinion and the End of Appeasement in Britain and France* (Farnham: Ashgate, 2011), 2.
19. Mark Mazower, *Dark Continent: Europe's Twentieth Century* (New York: Vintage Books, 1998), 69.
20. Gaines Post, Jr., *Dilemmas of Appeasement: British Deterrence and Defense 1934–1937* (Ithaca and London: Cornell University Press, 1993), 5–6, 17, 26, 158, 168–175, 335.
21. Martin Thomas, "France and the Czechoslovak Crisis," *Diplomacy and Statecraft*, 10/2–3 (1999), 130.
22. Jonathan Kirshner, *Appeasing Bankers: Financial Caution on the Road to War* (Princeton and Oxford: Princeton University Press, 2007), 115; Thomas, "France and the Czechoslovak Crisis," 129–130.
23. Robert J. Young, *In Command of France: French Foreign Policy and Military Planning, 1933–1940* (Cambridge, MA: Harvard University Press, 1978), 211.
24. Georges Vidal, "Le Haut commandement et la crainte de 'l'ennemi intérieur' en juin 1940. Origins et caractéristiques de la peur du complot communiste dans la hiérarchie militaire," in Christine Levisse-Touzé (ed.), *La Campagne de 1940* (Paris: Tallandier, 2001), 358–359, 362.
25. Paul Reynaud, *Mémoires*, tome II, *Envers et contre tous: 7 mars 1936–16 juin 1940* (Paris: Flammarion, 1963), 406.
26. Vidal, "Le Haut commandement et la crainte de 'l'ennemi intérieur' en juin 1940," 357–381.
27. Hucker, *Public Opinion and the End of Appeasement*, 4.
28. Julian Jackson, *The Popular Front in France: Defending Democracy, 1934–1938* (Cambridge: Cambridge University Press, 1988), 199–201.
29. Müller, *The Military in Politics and Society in France and Germany*, 123.
30. Charles de Gaulle, *Vers l'armée de métier* (Paris: Berger-Levrault, 1944), 87.
31. Robert O. Paxton, *Vichy France: Old Guard and New Order, 1940–1944* (London: Barrie & Jenkins, 1972), 57.
32. Olivier Wieviorka, *Histoire de la Résistance 1940–1945* (Paris: Perrin, 2013), 119.
33. Hucker, *Public Opinion and the End of Appeasement*, 3.
34. Mazower, *Dark Continent*, 69–75; Ernest R. May, *Strange Victory: Hitler's Conquest of France* (New York: Hill and Wang, 2000), 151–153.
35. Peter Jackson, *France and the Nazi Menace: Intelligence and Policy Making 1933–1939* (Oxford: Oxford University Press, 2000), 390–391.
36. Daladier had served as vice-premier in Blum's 1936 cabinet as well as minister of war and of national defense. From April 1938, he combined the Premiership with the Ministry of Defense. Edward W. Bennett, *German*

Rearmament and the West, 1932–1933 (Princeton: Princeton University Press, 1979), 85.

37. While Gamelin did not consider Bonnet a traitor, as Foreign Minister Bonnet divulged information in his political milieu or to journalists that within twenty-four hours had found its way to Europe's chancelleries. General Maurice Gamelin, *Servir: Les Armées françaises de 1940* (Paris: Plon, 1946), 24–25.
38. On problems of intelligence reception in France, see Jackson, *France and the Nazi Menace*, 38–44, 392–395.
39. Paxton, *Vichy France*, 25.
40. Jean-Baptiste Duroselle, *Politique étrangère de la France: La décadence 1932–1939* (Paris: Imprimerie nationale, 1979), 125; Paxton, *Vichy France*, 26–28.
41. Mussolini's hand in the assassination of France's Petite Entente partner Alexander I of Yugoslavia during an official October 1934 visit to Marseilles "could easily be traced" because the Italian dictator harbored Balkan ambitions. Laval tried to influence the outcome of the trial in favor of the murders. "His one idea was to earn the despot's [Mussolini's] gratitude." Pertinax (André Géraud), *The Gravediggers of France: Gamelin, Daladier, Reynaud, Pétain, and Laval. Military Defeat, Armistice, Counterrevolution* (Garden City, New York: Doubleday, Doran & Company, 1944), 383–384.
42. Duroselle, *Politique étrangère de la France*, 131; Frederick Brown, *The Embrace of Unreason: France, 1914–1940* (New York: Knopf, 2014), 209; Paxton, *Vichy France*, 63.
43. Imlay, *Facing the Second World War*, 359.
44. Mussolini claimed that the January 1935 Franco-Italian agreement, which Laval had traveled to Rome to negotiate, gave Italy a green light to ingest Abyssinia in return for Rome's agreement to "consult" should Hitler rearm. Laval protested that he had promised only that France would desist from pushing its economic interests in Abyssinia. France was also ceded some territory in the Côte française des Somalis and in Libya; Paris promised progressively to abolish the special status of Italians in Tunisia; agreed to work to create a non-aggression pact among the nations that bordered on Austria; and agreed to consult should Germany rearm. Duroselle, *Politique étrangère de la France*, 134–139.
45. Hoare had been forced to resign after the terms of the secret December 1935 Hoare–Laval agreement to allow Mussolini to occupy most of Abyssinia became public. George F. Melton, *From Versailles to Mers el-Kébir: The Promise of Anglo-French Naval Cooperation, 1919–1940* (Annapolis: Naval Institute Press, 2015), 23–26; Joel Colton, *Léon Blum: Humanist in Politics* (New York: Alfred A. Knopf, 1966), 198–99; Duroselle, *Politique étrangère de la France*, 132–133.
46. Paxton, *Vichy France*, 28; Jackson, "Europe. The Failure of Diplomacy 1933–1940," 226–227, 252; Sean McMeekin, *Stalin's War: A New History of World War II* (New York: Basic Books, 2021), 52, 57–58.
47. Müller, *The Military in Politics and Society in France and Germany*, 133.
48. Duroselle, *Politique étrangère de la France*, 167–168. May argues that Gamelin had almost exclusive access to intelligence. May, *Strange Victory*, 144.

49. Martin S. Alexander, *The Republic in Danger: General Maurice Gamelin and the Politics of French Defence, 1933–1940* (Cambridge: Cambridge University Press, 1992), 259.
50. Jackson, *France and the Nazi Menace*, 177; Kirshner, *Appeasing Bankers*, 117.
51. Alexander, *The Republic in Danger*, 260–261. On the Rhineland remilitarization, see also Christopher Andrew, *Her Majesty's Secret Service: The Making of the British Intelligence Community* (New York: Viking, 1985), 418; Anthony Adamthwaite, "French Military Intelligence and the Coming of War, 1935–1939," in Christopher Andrew and Jeremy Noakes (eds.), *Intelligence and International Relations, 1900–1945* (Liverpool: Liverpool University Press, 1987), 193. The *Deuxième Bureau* warned that ratification of the Franco-Soviet pact would provide a pretext for Hitler's invasion of the Rhineland.
52. Duroselle, *Politique étrangère de la France*, 172; May, *Strange Victory*, 301.
53. Jackson, *France and the Nazi Menace*, 177; Alexander, *The Republic in Danger*, 257–262; Duroselle, *Politique étrangère de la France*, 167–68.
54. Eugen Weber, *The Hollow Years: France in the 1930s* (New York: W. W. Norton, 1994), 145.
55. Duroselle, *Politique étrangère de la France*, 171–172, 179; May, *Strange Victory*, 145–146, 150.
56. Colton, *Léon Blum*, 122–123.
57. Alexander, *The Republic in Danger*, 182.
58. May, *Strange Victory*, 142–144.
59. P. Jackson, *France and the Nazi Menace*, 177; Stephen Schuker, "France and the Remilitarization of the Rhineland, 1936," in Patrick Finney (ed.), *The Origins of the Second World War* (London: Arnold Press, 1997), 206–221; Alexander, *The Republic in Danger*, 258–259; Brown, *The Embrace of Unreason*, 121.
60. Duroselle, *Politique étrangère de la France*, 165–179; Jackson, *The Popular Front*, 190.
61. Anthony Adamthwaite, *France and the Coming of the Second World War 1936–1939* (London: Frank Cass, 1977), 356.
62. Weber, *The Hollow Years*, 145.
63. Julian Jackson, *The Fall of France: The Nazi Invasion of 1940* (Oxford: Oxford University Press, 2003), 213.
64. The term is Pierre Renovin's quoted by Jackson, *The Popular Front*, 190; also by Jean-Baptiste Duroselle, *France and the Nazi Threat: The Collapse of French Diplomacy 1932–1939* (New York: Enigma Books, 2004), 233.
65. Pertinax, *The Gravediggers of France*, 372.
66. Pertinax, *The Gravediggers of France*, 371–372; Weber, *The Hollow Years*, 163.
67. Jean Lacouture, *Léon Blum* (New York and London: Holmes & Meier, 1982), 536, 538.
68. Alexander, *The Republic in Danger*, 30–31, 85.
69. Blum's pacifist rival in the SFIO was Paul Faure. Imlay, *Facing the Second World War*, 140–141, 184.

70. Jackson, *The Popular Front in France*, 212.
71. There was never a question of sending French troops to Spain, but there was a possibility of supporting the Republic with aid. In the famous cabinet meeting of 25 July 1936 where the issue was bitterly argued, Radicals Pierre Cot and Jean Zay, Socialists Vincent Auriol, Marx Dormoy, Jules Moch, and Léo Lagrange, and Republican-Socialist Maurice Violette argued for assistance, against Radicals Camille Chautemps and Minister of Foreign Affairs Yvon Delbos. Daladier seemed to sit on the fence. Jean Lacouture, *Léon Blum* (New York: Holmes & Meier, 1982), 314–315.
72. Pierre Cot later claimed that British threats to distance themselves from France should Paris intervene also played a role in Blum's decision, although there is no evidence of official British pressure for non-intervention. Julian Jackson suggests that Foreign Minister Yvon Delbos may have passed on British objections to pressure Blum to abandon a policy of intervention to which he was opposed. Jackson, *The Popular Front in France*, 199–201.
73. Colton, *Léon Blum*, 259; British conservatives were especially reluctant to intervene. Daladier initially supported intervention, but changed his position because of constituent pressure. There was a strong pro-Franco lobby in the Radical Party led by Louis Malvy. As well as French arms, some Soviet material for the Republic was landed in France and transported over the Pyrenees. Lacouture, *Léon Blum*, 308, 313, 317, 322, 344–345. Air Minister Pierre Cot was put in charge of organizing the flow of clandestine supplies to the Spanish Republicans.
74. Blum's inaction seemed especially pusillanimous when Germany and Italy quite openly dispatched supplies, troops, equipment, and aircraft to the nationalists despite an agreement not to do so. The Foreign Office and the Quai d'Orsay cooperated to limit French intervention in Spain. May, *Strange Victory*, 149.
75. Duroselle, *Politique étrangère de la France*, 314.
76. Blum complained in 1942 that intervention in Spain would have provoked civil war in France, and he probably believed it, according to Julian Jackson, who thinks it unlikely. Nevertheless, the government no doubt would have fallen, as many Radicals, led by Chautemps, opposed French aid to the Spanish Republic. Jackson, *The Popular Front*, 207–209; Colton, *Léon Blum*, 481.
77. Colton, *Léon Blum*, 262–265; Lacouture notes that the three French armed services were uniformly hostile to the Spanish republicans, although some, like French Admiral François Darlan, worried about a Franco victory that would leave three fascist powers on France's borders. French diplomats were heavily pro-nationalist. In Blum's defense, the Spanish Republican army was so poorly trained and led that some argue that the Republic could have been saved only by the early intervention of French troops before Franco's forces had gained momentum. *Léon Blum*, 320–321, 349–358; Darlan believed that the French and Royal navies could together have mounted a successful blockade of Spain. Melton, *From Versailles to Mers el-Kébir*, Chapter 2. While not discounting that Blum may have faced

a military revolt had he intervened in Spain, Duroselle thinks it extremely unlikely. Many on the right feared that a Franco victory would put the Germans on the Pyrenees. This was not a fanciful assessment, given Franco's enthusiasm for Hitler. See Paul Preston, "Spain: Betting on a Nazi Victory," in Richard J. B. Bosworth and Joseph A. Maiolo, *The Cambridge History of the Second World War*, volume II, *Politics and Ideology* (Cambridge: Cambridge University Press, 2015), 324–348. To reinforce his "decadence" verdict, Duroselle fails to see how French intervention in Spain might have triggered a general European War. Duroselle, *Politique étrangère de la France*, 301–305, 316–317.

78. Jackson, *The Popular Front in France*, 190–191.
79. Timothy Snyder, *Bloodlands: Europe between Hitler and Stalin* (New York: Basic Books, 2010), 67–68, 74.
80. Jean-Louis Crémieux-Brilhac, *Les français de l'an 40*, tome I, *La Guerre oui ou non?* (Paris: Gallimard, 1990), 617.
81. J. Jackson, *The Popular Front in France*, 196–197; Anthony Adamthwaite, *France and the Coming of the Second World War 1936–1939* (London: Frank Cass, 1977), 171–172.
82. The December 1934 murder in Leningrad of Stalin's close associate Sergei Kirov triggered the series of purges that went on until the eve of Barbarossa in June 1941. In all, an estimated 50,000 members of the Communist Party, the civil service, and the military were executed. Snyder, *Bloodlands*, 72–75. Robert Frankenstein blamed the Quai as the main culprit. Robert Frankenstein, *Le Prix du réarmament français* (Paris: Publications de la Sorbonne, 1982), 297. French observers of the 1936 maneuvers declared the Red Army "insufficiently prepared for a war against a great European power." J. Jackson, *The Popular Front in France*, 196.
83. Gamelin, *Servir*, 118, 137–138.
84. David E. Kaiser, *Economic Diplomacy and the Origins of the Second World War: Germany, Britain, France, and Eastern Europe, 1930–1939* (Princeton: Princeton University Press, 1980), 313.
85. Kaiser, *Economic Diplomacy and the Origins of the Second World War*, 313–315.
86. Snyder, *Bloodlands*, 68.
87. Martin Thomas, "France and the Czechoslovak Crisis," in Igor Lukes and Erik Goldstein (eds.), *The Munich Crisis, 1938: Prelude to World War II* (London and Portland: Frank Cass, 1999), 148.
88. Jackson, *The Popular Front in France*, 193–198.
89. Kaiser, *Economic Diplomacy and the Origins of the Second World War*, 307.
90. Kaiser, *Economic Diplomacy and the Origins of the Second World War*, 207. The quotation is from Pertinax, *The Gravediggers of France*, 113.
91. The request from Warsaw was for France and Britain to advance cash so that Poland could purchase arms in the United States. Kaiser, *Economic Diplomacy and the Origins of the Second World War*, 198–199, 307–308.
92. Kaiser, *Economic Diplomacy and the Origins of the Second World War*, 200–208, 215–217, 316–317. Romania exported its oil as refined, while France wanted crude. 198 As for London's role in discouraging French initiatives in

the East, there were several attempts to abolish exchange controls in the Danubian basin to reconcile the *petite entente*, most notably in the fall of 1937. But British Prime Minister Neville Chamberlain wished to concede German economic dominance of Central Europe as the basis for a general settlement. Kaiser, *Economic Diplomacy and the Origins of the Second World War*, 205, 287–288.

93. This was especially the view of Camille Chautemps, see Jackson, *The Popular Front in France*, 211.
94. Robert Frankenstein, *Le Prix du réarmament français 1935–1939* (Paris: Publications de la Sorbonne, 1982), 298.
95. Frankenstein, *Le Prix du réarmament français 1935–1939*, 197; Julian Jackson discusses these 1936 strikes as well as conditions in the workplace. Jackson, *The Popular Front in France*, 86–112.
96. Funds for naval modernization were voted almost every year between 1924 and 1934. Philippe Masson, "La 'belle marine' de 1939," in Guy Pedroncini (ed.), *Histoire militaire de la France*, tome 3, *De 1871 à 1940* (Paris: Presses universitaires de France, 1992), 445–454.
97. Alexander, *The Republic in Danger*, 27–28; French government spending was slashed by 20 percent between 1932 and 1934. Kirshner, *Appeasing Bankers*, 98. Defense spending fell from 15.3 to 10.4 billion francs, most of the cuts in appropriations for new weaponry. Kaiser, *Economic Diplomacy and the Origins of the Second World War*, 203.
98. Alexander, "French grand strategy and defence preparations," 80.
99. Weber, *The Hollow Years*, 173.
100. Frankenstein, *Le Prix du réarmament français 1935–1939*, 289–290.
101. Frankenstein, *Le Prix du réarmament français 1935–1939*, 295.
102. François Cochet, *Les soldats de la drôle de guerre: Septembre 1939–mai 1940* (Paris: Hachette, 2004), 35.
103. Frankenstein, *Le Prix du réarmament français 1935–1939*, 295–296; Kirshner, *Appeasing Bankers*, 117.
104. The Bank of France had 40,000 shareholders, of which only 200 were allowed to vote. These appointed fifteen regents and three auditors. To oversee this, the government appointed a governor and two assistant governors from among the shareholders. The loyalties of the governors, Kirshner insists, were with the regents and shareholders, not the government. Kirshner, *Appeasing Bankers*, 96.
105. Kirshner, *Appeasing Bankers*, 120.
106. Jackson, *The Popular Front in France*, 182; Blum replaced the regents with twenty councilors, of whom only two were appointed by the bank's shareholders. The Governor of the Bank of France was no longer a shareholder, but paid directly by the government. But this did not put a stop to Bank of France commitment to financial orthodoxy. Kirshner, *Appeasing Bankers*, 105–106.
107. Colton, *Léon Blum*, 182–184.
108. Kirshner, *Appeasing Bankers*, 107.
109. Between 1929 and 1938, industrial production increased by 20 percent in Great Britain, and 16 percent in Germany, but fell by 24 percent in France.

Kirshner, *Appeasing Bankers*, 89–90, 107, 114–121; Jackson, *The Popular Front*, 160.

110. Kaiser, *Economic Diplomacy and the Origins of the Second World War*, 204.
111. The delay in the appointment of a Minister of Armaments, according to Pertinax, was because of Gamelin's objections. Pertinax, *The Gravediggers of France*, 125.
112. Philip Nord, *France 1940: Defending the Republic* (New Haven: Yale University Press, 2015), 45.
113. Imlay, *Facing the Second World War*, 297–298.
114. Alexander, *The Republic in Danger*, 358.
115. Élisabeth du Réau, *Édouard Daladier 1884–1970* (Paris: Fayard, 1993), 372–373, 379–380; Crémieux-Brilhac, *Les français de l'an 40*, tome I, *La Guerre oui ou non?*, 352.
116. Claude Carlier, "Le Destin manqué de l'aéronautique française," in Guy Pedroncini (ed.), *Histoire militaire de la France*, tome 3, *De 1871 à 1940*, 409–415; Patrick Facon, *L'Armée de l'air dans la tourmente: La bataille de France 1939–1940* (Paris: Economica, 1997), 47–52.
117. Carlier, "Le Destin manqué de l'aéronautique française," 416–417.
118. Robin Higham, *Two Roads to War: the French and British Air Arms from Versailles to Dunkirk* (Annapolis: Naval Institute Press, 2012), 2–6, 32–35, 51–71. Quoted in Alexander, "French Grand Strategy and Defense Preparation," 82; Carlier, "Le Destin manqué de l'aéronautique française," 421.
119. Patrick Facon, *L'Armée de l'air dans la tourmente: La bataille de France, 1939–1940* (Paris: Economica, 2005), 51, 56; Carlier, "Le Destin manqué de l'aéronautique française," 420–421.
120. Facon, *L'Armée de l'air dans la tourmente*, 21–22.
121. Pertinax, *The Gravediggers*, 43. The age of French officers, especially when compared with their younger, more modern, and more energetic German counterparts, was a factor often cited in the 1940 defeat. The commanders of the 55e and 71e DIs which broke at Sedan were subsequently judged to have been too old for the job. Crémieux-Brilhac, *La Guerre oui ou non?*, 501, 571.
122. Claude d'Abzac-Epezy, *L'Armée de l'air des années noires: Vichy 1940–1944* (Paris: Economica, 1998), 78–81, 106; Carlier, "Le Destin manqué de l'aéronautique française," 419–420.
123. P. Jackson, *France and the Nazi Menace*, 221–222.
124. Cot moved to the United States, and spent the early years of the war teaching at Yale, before joining the Provisional Consultative Assembly in Algiers in November 1943. Accusations that Cot was a Soviet agent resurfaced after his death, but have been generally discounted by historians. Jean-Pierre Azéma, *Jean Moulin: Le politique, le rebelle, le résistant* (Paris: Perrin, 2003), 507.
125. Facon, *L'Armée de l'air dans la tourmente*, 20; Carlier, "Le Destin manqué de l'aéronautique française," 421.
126. Pertinax, *The Gravediggers of France*, 113, 125.
127. Sir Edward Spears, *Assignment to Catastrophe*, volume II, *The Fall of France* (New York: A. A. Wyn, 1955), 17, 31.

128. Pertinax, *The Gravediggers of France*, 43.
129. Jackson *France and the Nazi Menace*, 222.
130. Indeed, La Chambre's allegation was that Cot had deliberately sidelined the *Conseil supérieure de l'Air* so that he could act as the *de facto* air force commander. Facon, *L'Armée de l'air dans la tourmente*, 24.
131. Facon, *L'Armée de l'air dans la tourmente*, 150; P. Jackson *France and the Nazi Menace*, 269, 325, 330, 342.
132. Carlier, "Le Destin manqué de l'aéronautique française," 421–425.
133. Facon, *L'Armée de l'air dans la tourmente*, 58–60.
134. Karl-Heinz Frieser, *The Blitzkrieg Legend: The 1940 Campaign in the West* (Annapolis: Naval Institute Press, 2005), 45–55.
135. Cochet, *Les soldats de la drôle de guerre*, 205–206.
136. Facon, *L'Armée de l'air dans la tourmente*, 64–65, 68, 70–92, 142–143, 163–170; Cochet, *Les soldats de la drôle de guerre*, 206–207.
137. Frieser notes that it was fortunate for Berlin that the Polish campaign of September 1939 lasted only eighteen days, because the *Wehrmacht* was fast exhausting its ammunition and the *Luftwaffe* its bombs. Frieser, *The Blitzkrieg Legend*, 11, 21.
138. Crémieux-Brilhac, *La Guerre oui ou non?*, 350.
139. Weber, *The Hollow Years*, 173.
140. Gérard Chauvy, *Le Drame de l'armée française du Front populaire à Vichy* (Paris: Pygmalion, 2010), 291–292, 396.
141. Donald Abenheim and Carolyn Halladay, *Soldiers, War, Knowledge and Citizenship: German–American Essays on Civil–Military Relations* (Berlin: Carola Hartmann Miles-Verlag, 2017), 186.
142. J. Jackson, *The Fall of France*, 13.
143. Robert Alan Doughty, *The Seeds of Disaster: The Development of French Army Doctrine 1919–1939* (Hamden: Archon Books, 1985), 170.
144. J. Jackson, *The Fall of France*, 23–25.
145. Lieutenant-colonel Henry Dutailly, *Les Problèmes de l'armée de terre française (1935–1939)* (Paris: Imprimerie nationale, 1980), 17.
146. Alexander, *The Republic in Danger*, 78–79.
147. One problem was that de Gaulle had insisted that soldiers serving in these tank divisions be professionals, which was unacceptable to most French politicians. Jean-Louis Crémieux-Brilhac, *Les français de l'an 40*, tome I, *La Guerre oui ou non?* (Paris: Gallimard, 1990), 391–393; Cochet, *Les soldats de la drôle de guerre*, 204.
148. Doughty, *The Seeds of Disaster*, 174.
149. SHD-GR, 3P 112, "Analyse – Les chars de combat (Deuxième Partie). Titre I – Emploi des chars," 22 March 1941, 3.
150. Doughty, *The Seeds of Disaster*, 177.
151. SHD-GR, 3P 112, "Analyse," 4–5.
152. Gérard Saint-Martin, *L'arme blindée française*, tome 1, *Mai–juin 1940! Les blindés française dans la tourmente* (Paris: Economica, 1998), 306–308.
153. Crémieux-Brilhac, *Les français de l'an 40*, tome I, 379–392.
154. SHD-GR, 3P 113, Dossier 1.

155. Doughty points out that the basic problem for the French artillery, as with the French army in general, was that new concepts and weapons were grafted onto old organization and doctrines. In the French army's "methodical battle" concept, the artillery was strongly centralized to provide massive fire support for large units, a centralization that often left smaller, undergunned units on their own. Doughty, *The Seeds of Disaster*, 182
156. SHD-GR, 3P 113, Dossier 2, "Remarques sur l'organisation et l'emploi de la batterie anti-chars," Annex nos. IV–VIII.
157. SHD-GR, 3P 111, Dossier 1, Captain Tulous, 19 August 1942.
158. SHD-GR, 3P 113, Dossier 2, "Remarques sur l'organisation et l'emploi de la batterie anti-chars," Annex XIV.
159. SHD-GR, 3P 113, Dossier 2, Captain Paul Gail, "Rapport sur les enseignements à tirer de la guerre," 24 August 1940, 4–5.
160. SHD-GR, 3P 113, Dossier 2, "Remarques sur l'organisation et l'emploi de la batterie anti-chars," Annex no. I, "Matériel de 47 anti-char"; 3P 111, Dossier 1, "Enseignements tirés de la campagne 1939–1940," "Ce qu'il faut remplacer," 7.
161. SHD-GR, 3P 115, Rapport du Captaine Paul . . . Sur le Canon de 25 et son rendement contre les chars," 2 October 1940; 3P 111, Dossier 1, "Enseignements tirés de la campagne 1939–1940," "Ce qu'il faut remplacer," 6; SHD-GR, 3P 111, Dossier 2, "Rapport du Lieutenant Vuchot, sur les enseignements à tirer de la campagne 1939–1940," no date, page numbers not chronological.
162. SHD-GR, 3P 113, Dossier 1. The army calculated that each artillery piece required on average the support of two officers, fifty men, fifty horses, and ten wagons. "Rapport du Colonel Bréveté Baillon concernant l'emploi de l'artillerie dans la campagne 1939–1940," 19 August 1940, 6.
163. SHD-GR, 3P 113, Dossier 2, Captain Paul Gail, "Rapport sur les enseignements à tirer de la guerre," 24 August 1940, 5.
164. SHD-GR, 3P 113, Dossier 1, Colonel M. Morel, 27 August 1940.
165. Michel de Cazotte, "Oflag Adventure," Unpublished manuscript, edited by Louis Denis de Cazotte, summer 1997, Hoover Archives, Stanford University, 26–27, 32.
166. SHD-GR, 3P 113, 21 March 1941 letter from General Marèscaud to General Picquendar.
167. SHD-GR, 3P 115, "Remarques faites au cours des combats de Saint-Omer (20 mai) et de Dunkerque (24 mai–3 juin) relative au matériel," 1, 4; Sous-lieutenant Jean, "Enquête sure les matérials," 13 September 1940. Other reports on the deficiencies of the AAA are to be found in documents prepared for the Riom trials: 3P 113, "Insuffisance de l'A/D.C.A. au cours des années qui ont immédiament précédées la Guerre et au moment de la mobilization." Raugel would have an interesting war: ordered to surrender the arms caches that he had meticulously built up as an officer in the Armistice Army, in 1943, he crossed the Pyrenees as an *évadé de France*, to join French forces in North Africa. At fifty-nine considered too old to participate in the Dragoons as a combatant, and disinclined to serve on

a military tribunal, he resigned and reenlisted as a private in the *2e régiment de dragons* in Oran, with whom he fought the campaigns in Alsace and Germany, "retiring" in 1945 as staff sergeant and *commandeur de la Légion d'honneur*, https://fr.wikipedia.org/wiki/Bernardin_Raugel.

168. Cochet, *Les soldats de la drôle de guerre*, 204–207, 213.
169. SHD-GR, 3P 111, Dossier 1, "Enseignements tirés de la guerre de 1939–1940," "F. – La tactique des petites unités."
170. SHD-GR, 3P 111, Dossier 1, "Enseignements tirés de la guerre de 1939–1940," "F. – La tactique des petites unités."
171. SHD-GR, 3P 111, Dossier 1, "Enseignements tirés de la campagne 1939–1940," "Les moyens de liaison et de transmissions," 8.
172. SHD-GR, 3P 113, Dossier 2, "Remarques sur l'organisation et l'emploi de la batterie anti-chars," Annex XIII.
173. SHD-GR, 3P 113, Dossier 1, "Report of Second lieutenant Chevalier".
174. SHD-GR, 3P 111, Dossier 1, "Enseignements tirés de la campagne 1939–1940," "La tactiques des petites unités."
175. Frieser, *The Blitzkrieg Legend*, 29–31.
176. Crémieux-Brilhac, *Les français de l'an 40*, tome I, 347–355. One problem with Crémieux-Brilhac's argument is that industrial production continued to fall until 1938, while that of the UK increased by 20 percent and that of Germany by 16 percent. Kirshner, *Appeasing Bankers*, 107.
177. de Gaulle, *L'Appel 1940–1942*, 26.
178. Frankenstein, *Le Prix du réarmament français 1935–1939*, 290.
179. SHD-GR, 3P 113, Dossier 2, "Étude sur les causes de notre defaite et les renseignements a en tirer," 16 November 1941, 6.
180. Dutailly, *Les Problèmes de l'armée de terre française*, 33.
181. Alexander, *The Republic in Danger*, 94.
182. Alexander, *The Republic in Danger*, 391.
183. Nord, *France 1940*, 101–104.
184. Pertinax, *The Gravediggers of France*, 42.
185. A. J. Liebling, *World War II Writings: The Road Back to Paris. Mollie and Other War Pieces, Uncollected War Journalism. Normandy Revisited* (New York: Literary Classics of the United States, 2008), 30.
186. On Weygand's antisemitism, see Yves C. Aouate, "La place de l'Algérie dans le projet antijuif de Vichy (octobre 1940–novembre 1942), "*Revue d'histoire d'outre-mer*, 301 (1993), 599–613, www.persee.fr/doc/outre_0300-9513_1993_num_80_301_3150.
187. Cochet, *Les soldats de la drôle de guerre*, 107.
188. Geyer, "German Strategy in the Age of Machine Warfare, 1914–1945," 584–587.
189. Robert O. Paxton, *L'armée de Vichy: Le corps des officiers francais, 1940–1944* (Paris: Tallandier, 2004), 454–456.
190. Alexander, *The Republic in Danger*, 93–94, 390–391; Doughty, *The Seeds of Disaster*, 184–185; Cochet, *Les soldats de la drôle de guerre*, 107, 116, 138, 191, 195–196; Abenheim and Halladay, *Soldiers, War, Knowledge and Citizenship*, 191–192.

191. Harold Macmillan, *War Diaries: Politics and War in the Mediterranean January 1943–May 1945* (London: Macmillan, 1984), 103, 117.
192. Gamelin, *Servir*, 60.
193. Pertinax, *The Gravediggers of France*, 40.
194. Gamelin, *Servir*, 61.
195. Max Schiavon, *Le général Alphonse Georges: Un destin inachevé* (Parçay-sur-vienne: Éditions Anovi, 2009), 562–565; General André Beaufre, *1940: The Fall of France* (New York: Knopf, 1968), 162, 183; Gamelin, *Servir*, 62; on Billiotte's call for heavy armored divisions, see Alexander, *The Republic in Danger*, 344–345.
196. Dutailly, *Les Problèmes de l'armée de terre française*, 9, 290.
197. Alexander, *The Republic in Danger*, 85, 87.
198. Dutailly, *Les Problèmes de l'armée de terre française*, 37.
199. François Fonvieille-Alquier, *The French and the Phoney War 1939–40* (London: Tom Stacey, 1973), 70–71.
200. Crémieux-Brilhac, *Les français de l'an 40*, tome I, 375–376; Duroselle, *Politique étrangère de la France*, 26–27.
201. Roderick Macleod and Denis Kelly (eds.), *The Ironside Diaries, 1937–1940* (London: Constable, 1962), 173–174, 176.
202. Liebling, *World War II Writings*, 36.
203. Beaufre, *1940*, 53, 163.
204. Alexander, *The Republic in Danger*, 397.
205. Alexander, *The Republic in Danger*, 399; Nord, *France 1940*, 104.
206. Douglas Porch, *The March to the Marne: The French Army 1871–1914*, (Cambridge: Cambridge University Press, 1981), especially Chapters 5 and 6.
207. Alexander, *The Republic in Danger*, 14–31, 259, 396–402; May, *Strange Victory*, 346.
208. Alexander, *The Republic in Danger*, 91–93.
209. Williamson Murray and Allan R. Millett, *Military Innovation in the Interwar Period* (Cambridge: Cambridge University Press, 1996), 31.
210. Gamelin, *Servir*, I, 62–63.
211. Quoted in May, *Strange Victory*, 390.
212. Jean-Louis Crémieux-Brilhac, *Les français de l'an 40*, tome I, 376; Pertinax, *The Gravediggers of France*, 39–40.
213. Dutailly, *Les Problèmes de l'armée de terre française*, 35, 37; Schiavon, *Le général Alphonse Georges*, 194–204, 211–218, 244.
214. Pertinax, *The Gravediggers of France*, 40.
215. Pertinax, *The Gravediggers of France*, 41.
216. Alexander, *The Republic in Danger*, 93.
217. Thomas Vaisset, *L'Amiral d'Argenlieu: Le moine-soldat du gaullisme* (Paris: Belin, 2017), 41.
218. Vaisset, *L'amiral d'Argenlieu*, 34, 44, 53.
219. Robert O. Paxton, *Parades and Politics at Vichy: The French Officer Corps under Marshal Pétain* (Princeton: Princeton University Press, 1966), 152.
220. Jean-Baptiste Bruneau, *La Marine de Vichy aux Antilles juin 1940–juillet 1943* (Paris: Les Indes Savantes, 2014), 237–241.

221. In 1932, an Haut comité militaire had been created, replaced in June 1936 by the CPDN, that included the Premier, the service ministers, principal military commanders, and Marshal Pétain. The military direction of the war would be handled by the Comité de guerre that included the President of the Republic, the Premier, the service ministers, the Chief of Staff of National Defense, the Chiefs of Staff, and the Foreign Minister. In June 1936, Blum revived the Defense Ministry, but subordinated it to the War Ministry, both portfolios held by Daladier, who blocked moves to give the Defense Ministry direction of the three services. Adamthwaite, *France and the Coming of the Second World War*, 169–171. See also Dutailly, *Les Problèmes de l'armée de terre française*, 34; Alexander, *The Republic in Danger*, 92–93, 389.
222. Alexander, *The Republic in Danger*, 91, 402.
223. Matthieu, Boisdron, "Le projet de pacte oriental (février 1934–mai 1935)," in *Guerres mondiales et conflits contemporains* 2005/4, no. 220 (2005), 23–43; McMeekin, *Stalin's War*, 82–98.
224. Müller, *The Military in Politics and Society in France and Germany*, 133.
225. Imlay, *Facing the Second World War*, 356.
226. In the 1920s, the high command was split over the value of maneuver versus fixed defenses that would absorb much of the military budget and manpower, cover "a simple slice of a battlefield on the frontier" that could be outflanked, give a false sense of security, discourage innovation, and limit France's strategic options. It was under Paul Painlevé, Minister of War from November 1925, that what would become the Maginot Line began to take shape. The introduction of one-year service and the impending evacuation of the Rhineland in 1930 removed more preemptive options for the French and clinched the argument on the military level. Judith M. Hughes, *To the Maginot Line: The Politics of French Military Preparation in the 1920s* (Cambridge, MA: Harvard University Press, 1971), 200–207. The Maginot Line's major selling point was that "these fortifications enjoyed near-unanimous approbation . . . endorsed by parliamentarians of the left and center as much as they were supported by those of the right." Alexander, *The Republic in Danger*, 180.
227. "Report on French Tactical Doctrine, Organization, and Materiel Based on Observations Made While at the Ecole Superieure de Guerre (1935–1937)" (no accent marks in the original) by Major Ralph C. Smith, Infantry, 1937 August 10, 12–13. NARA, RG 165, Entry 77, Box 873.

2 From Phoney Peace to Phoney War, 1938–1940

1. Talbot C. Imlay, *Facing the Second World War: Strategy, Politics, and Economics in Britain and France 1938–1940* (Oxford: Oxford University Press, 2003), 356. One view is that the failure to intervene in Spain had undermined any urgency to intervene in Austria. France's refusal to react convinced Austrian Chancellor Schuschnigg to resign so that his successor Seyss-Inquart could call in the Germans. Eden's departure from the Foreign Office in February and his replacement by Halifax, who along with Chamberlain counted as one of the great "appeasers" in Britain, also undermined a joint Franco-British response. Jean-Baptiste Duroselle, *Politique*

étrangère de la France: La décadence 1932–1939 (Paris: Imprimerie nationale, 1979), 326–28; see also Jean-Pierre Azéma, "La France de Daladier," in Jean-Pierre Azéma and François Bédarida (eds.), *La France des années noires*, tome 1, *De la défaite à Vichy* (Paris: Éditions du Seuil, 1993), 16, 18.

2. Duroselle, *Politique étrangère de la France*, 329–333.
3. Azéma, "La France de Daladier," 11.
4. Élisabeth du Réau, *Édouard Daladier 1884–1970* (Paris: Fayard, 1993), 455.
5. Pertinax (André Géraud), *The Gravediggers of France: Gamelin, Daladier, Reynaud, Pétain, and Laval. Military Defeat, Armistice, Counterrevolution* (Garden City, New York: Doubleday, Doran & Company, 1944), 88–89.
6. The expression was that of the President of the Senate, Jules Jeanneney. Du Réau, *Édouard Daladier*, 221.
7. Julian Jackson, *The Popular Front in France: Defending Democracy, 1934–1938* (Cambridge: Cambridge University Press, 1988), 70–73; Daniel Hucker, *Public Opinion and the End of Appeasement in Britain and France* (Farnham: Ashgate, 2011), 251.
8. Pertinax, *The Gravediggers of France*, 94, 114; Julian Jackson, *The Fall of France: The Nazi Invasion of 1940* (Oxford: Oxford University Press, 2003), 121; Robert J. Young, *In Command of France: French Foreign Policy and Military Planning, 1933–1940* (Cambridge, MA: Harvard University Press, 1978), 177.
9. Martin S. Alexander, *The Republic in Danger: General Maurice Gamelin and the Politics of French Defence, 1933–1940* (Cambridge: Cambridge University Press, 1992), 83.
10. Peter Jackson, *France and the Nazi Menace: Intelligence and Policy Making 1933–1939* (Oxford: Oxford University Press, 2000), 331; Martin Thomas, "France and the Czechoslovak Crisis," in Igor Lukes and Erik Goldstein (eds.), *The Munich Crisis, 1938: Prelude to World War II* (London and Portland: Frank Cass, 1999), 123–125.
11. Imlay, *Facing the Second World War*, 361.
12. Azéma, "La France de Daladier," 29–30.
13. Du Réau, *Édouard Daladier*, 379–384, 442–443; Jean-Louis Crémieux-Brilhac, *Les français de l'an 40*, tome I, *La Guerre oui ou non?* (Paris: Gallimard, 1990), 352, 380.
14. For instance, Nord argues that "armies ... have internal cultures, not independent of the wider national setting but connected to it in complicated, even oppositional ways. A cadre of first-rate generals is not of necessity proof positive of the high moral caliber or even general efficiency of the surrounding society." Philip Nord, *France 1940: Defending the Republic* (New Haven: Yale University Press, 2015), 101–102.
15. Pertinax, *The Gravediggers of France*, 87.
16. Alexander, *The Republic in Danger*, 89–94.
17. Paul Reynaud, *Mémoires*, tome II, *Envers et contre tous: 7 mars 1936–16 juin 1940* (Paris: Flammarion, 1963), 331.
18. Du Réau, *Édouard Daladier*, 360.

19. Ernest R. May, *Strange Victory: Hitler's Conquest of France* (New York: Hill and Wang, 2000), 321
20. Bonnet argued that the neither the Poles nor the Russians would support action to defend Czechoslovakia. He also judged France's economic and financial situation as too precarious to risk war. Nor did he want to precipitate a rupture with London. Relations between Hitler and Mussolini had been warmed by Hitler's 5–9 May visit to Rome, while Mussolini had spurned an outreach by France. Du Réau, *Édouard Daladier*, 238.
21. The French military wargamed a strike at Cologne. But Gamelin's deputy, General Alphonse Georges, believed that the French lacked the armored units to spearhead a successful attack. This reinforced the conventional military verdict that the *Anschluss*, which had outflanked Czechoslovakia, combined with a large German-speaking minority in the Czech army rendered Czechoslovakia indefensible. Du Réau, *Édouard Daladier*, 235; May, *Strange Victory*, 163–165.
22. Lieutenant-colonel Henry Dutailly, *Les Problèmes de l'armée de terre française (1935–1939)* (Paris: Imprimerie nationale, 1980), 289.
23. Patrick Facon, *L'Armée de l'air dans la tourmente: La bataille de France, 1939–1940* (Paris: Economica, 2005), 25–29.
24. Gamelin emphasized the superiority of German armored divisions, their rapid mobilization capabilities, and their better cadres. Thomas, "France and the Czechoslovak Crisis," 137–138. Peter Jackson argues that French intelligence assessments were not decisive in France's diplomatic retreats of 1936–1938, but contributed to the growing sense of confidence following Munich. Jackson, *France and the Nazi Menace*, 296–297, 310–315, 377–378.
25. Du Réau, *Édouard Daladier*, 239, 249–253, 286–287.
26. Thomas, "France and the Czechoslovak Crisis," 139–140, 152.
27. Duroselle, *Politique étrangère de la France*, 367
28. Stalin told his Politburo that he could "see nothing wrong in their [Germany, France, and Britain] having a good hard fight and weakening each other. It would be fine if at the hands of Germany, the position of the richest capitalist countries (especially Britain) were shaken. Hitler, without understanding it or desiring it, is shaking and undermining the capitalist system ... We can manoeuvre, pit one side against the other to set them fighting as fiercely as possible." In this way, diplomacy became "a tool to help ensure that 'inevitable war' would take place under conditions favourable to the USSR." Peter Jackson, "Europe. The Failure of Diplomacy 1933–1940," in Richard J. B. Bosworth and Joseph A. Maiolo (eds.), *The Cambridge History of the Second World War*, volume II, *Politics and Ideology* (Cambridge: Cambridge University Press, 2015), 227.
29. Jean Lacouture, *Léon Blum* (New York: Holmes & Meier, 1982), 394.
30. Anthony Adamthwaite, *France and the Coming of the Second World War 1936–1939* (London: Frank Cass, 1977), 159.
31. Mark Mazower, *Dark Continent: Europe's Twentieth Century* (New York: Vintage Books, 1998), 68.

32. Quoted in Eugen Weber, *The Hollow Years: France in the 1930s* (New York: W. W. Norton, 1994), 177.
33. Jackson, *The Popular Front in France*, 280–284, 210.
34. Indeed, Hucker's argument was that Daladier was more in sync with British public opinion in 1938–1939 than was Chamberlain, especially regarding their willingness to accept a Soviet alliance. Hucker, *Public Opinion and the End of Appeasement*, 174–175, 252–254.
35. Duroselle, *Politique étrangère de la France*, 493.
36. Imlay, *Facing the Second World War*, 75.
37. Du Réau, *Édouard Daladier*, 354.
38. Crémieux-Brilhac, *Les français de l'an 40*, tome II, 710; Hucker, *Public Opinion and the End of Appeasement*, 250.
39. P. Jackson, *France and the Nazi Menace*, 377–387, 394.
40. Jean-Pierre Azéma, *From Munich to the Liberation 1938–1944* (Cambridge: Cambridge University Press, 1984), 6–7; Duroselle, *Politique étrangère de la France*, 325–66; Mazower, *Dark Continent*, 75; May, *Strange Victory*, 180.
41. Hucker, *Public Opinion and the End of Appeasement*, 250.
42. Richard Vinen, *France, 1934–1970* (New York: St. Martin's Press, 1996), 26.
43. P. Jackson, *France and the Nazi Menace*, 306.
44. Azéma, "La France de Daladier," 30.
45. Du Réau, *Édouard Daladier*, 319–325.
46. Hucker, *Public Opinion and the End of Appeasement*, 250; du Réau, *Édouard Daladier*, 288, 340–347.
47. Hucker, *Public Opinion and the End of Appeasement*, 251.
48. P. Jackson, *France and the Nazi Menace*, 331.
49. Christopher Thorne, *The Approach of War 1938–39* (New York: St. Martin's Press, 1967), 106–109.
50. Imlay, *Facing the Second World War*, 74.
51. Hucker, *Public Opinion and the End of Appeasement*, 252–253.
52. Ian Kershaw, *Fateful Choices: Ten Decisions That Changed the World 1940–1941* (London: Penguin, 2007), 256–257.
53. David E. Kaiser, *Economic Diplomacy and the Origins of the Second World War: Germany, Britain, France, and Eastern Europe, 1930–1939* (Princeton: Princeton University Press, 1980), 314–315. "Germany was the recipient of millions of tons of grain, timber and petroleum products as well as tens of thousands of tons of precious manganese and chromium." Kershaw, *Fateful Choices*, 259.
54. Imlay, *Facing the Second World War*, 75.
55. Azéma, "La France de Daladier," 34–35; Hucker, *Public Opinion and the End of Appeasement*, 182, 253.
56. P. Jackson, *France and the Nazi Menace*, 10, 393.
57. P. Jackson, *France and the Nazi Menace*, 315–78; Azéma, *From Munich to the Liberation*, 15–17.
58. J. Jackson, *The Fall of France*, 120.
59. Imlay, *Facing the Second World War*, 74; Adamthwaite, *France and the Coming of the Second World War*, 353.
60. Du Réau, *Édouard Daladier*, 360, 364.

61. Duroselle, *Politique étrangère de la France*, 472.
62. Gamelin insisted that the question asked by Daladier was "are our measures in place?" "If the military chiefs believed that they could or not accept the eventuality of a war." He took that to mean were the measures in place for mobilization? He was not speaking of matériel or industrial mobilization, which Daladier knew was not "ready." Nor, he claimed, did he want to give an inventory of military weaknesses in front of Bonnet, who would use it to argue against war. General Maurice Gamelin, *Servir: Les Armées française de 1940* (Paris: Plon, 1946), 23–25, 35.
63. P. Jackson, *France and the Nazi Menace*, 379–382.
64. Duroselle, *Politique étrangère de la France*, 483.
65. François Fonvieille-Alquier, *The French and the Phoney War 1939–40* (London: Tom Stacey, 1973), 126.
66. Nord, *France 1940*, 55.
67. Du Réau, *Édouard Daladier*, 367. Du Réau suggests that Daladier's delay sought to give Gamelin time to prepare for mobilization. But he still retained two notorious appeasers, Bonnet and Monzie, in his reshuffled cabinet. Du Réau, *Édouard Daladier*, 368, 371.
68. François Cochet, *Les soldats de la drôle de guerre: Septembre 1939–mai 1940* (Paris: Hachette, 2004), 10.
69. Alexander, *The Republic in Danger*, 390; May, *Strange Victory*, 454–455.
70. Du Réau, *Édouard Daladier*, 364, 388–390; Crémieux-Brilhac, *Les français de l'an 40*, tome I, 400–401.
71. May, *Strange Victory*, 454.
72. Imlay, *Facing the Second World War*, 358.
73. Georges Vidal, "Le Haut commandement et la crainte de 'l'ennemi intérieur' en juin 1940. Origins et caractéristiques de la peur du complot communiste dans la hiérarchie militaire," in Christine Levisse-Touzé (ed.), *La Campagne de 1940* (Paris: Tallandier, 2001), 357–381, 424.
74. Crémieux-Brilhac, *Les français de l'an 40*, tome I, 713–714.
75. J. Jackson, *The Fall of France*, 211; Antoine Capet, "Churchill's view of France and the French on the Eve of War," unpublished paper delivered at *France and Britain in World War II*, conference held at the British Ambassador's Residence, Paris, 16 October 2015.
76. René Rémond, "Des Lendemains qui chantent?," in Jean-Pierre Azéma and François Bédarida (eds.), *La France des années noires*, tome 2, *De l'Occupation à la Libération* (Paris: Éditions du Seuil, 1993), 488. Frank noted that the 1940 defeat "constitue la grande cassure de l'image que les Français avaient d'eux-mêmes," which helps to explain why initially they acquiesced so meekly to Vichy. Robert Frank, "La Mémoire empoisonnée," in Azéma and Bédarida (eds.), *La France des années noires*, tome 2, 503.
77. Cochet, *Les soldats de la drôle de guerre*, 30.
78. SHD-GR, 3P 111, Dossier 2, "Rapport du Lieutenant Vuchot, sur les enseignements à tirer de la campagne 1939–1940," no date, 1.
79. SHD-GR, 3P 115, "Rapport sur l'habillement" par le Lieutenant de la Rocque; "Rapport du Lieutenant Menière. Fusil mod. 1936."

80. SHD-GR, 3P 111, Dossier 2, "Rapport du Lieutenant Vuchot," 2.
81. Michel de Cazotte, "Oflag Adventure," unpublished manuscript, edited by Louis Denis de Cazotte, summer 1997, Hoover Archives, Stanford University, 9, 19.
82. Jean-Paul Sartre, *The War Diaries of Jean-Paul Sartre: November 1939/ March 1940* (New York: Pantheon Books, 1984), 104.
83. SHD-GR, oral archives, Crémieux-Brilhac GR 3K 32–1, Planche 2; Cochet, *Les soldats de la drôle de guerre*, 47.
84. Oscar Fallek, Imperial War Museum Docs 15593; Cochet, *Les soldats de la drôle de guerre*, 99.
85. Georges Sadoul, *Journal de Guerre (2 septembre 1939–20 juillet 1940)* (Paris: Éditions l'Harmattan, 1994), 28, 30.
86. Crémieux-Brilhac, *Les français de l'an 40*, tome I, 429–431; SHD-GR, 3P 111, Dossier 2, "Rapport du Lieutenant Vuchot," 2. Gaston Vuchot was an extraordinarily courageous man. A 1932 graduate of Saint-Cyr, Vuchot was twice wounded on 12 June 1940 and cited in army orders. On recovery, he was transferred to North Africa, and post-Torch in November 1942 became part of a Jedburgh team at le Vercors. He was killed on 1 February 1945 in the liberation of Colmar as a major in the 1re régiment de chasseurs parachutistes (1re RCP).
87. SHD-GR, oral archives, Colonel Dominique Magnant GR 3K 12–1, Planche 5.
88. Laird M. Easton (ed.), *Journey to the Abyss: The Diaries of Count Harry Kessler, 1880–1918* (New York: Vintage Books, 2013), 658.
89. Eugenia C. Kiesling, *Arming against Hitler: France & the Limits of Military Power* (Lawrence: University Press of Kansas, 1996), 174.
90. General André Beaufre, *1940: The Fall of France* (New York: Knopf, 1968), 37–41.
91. Pierre Rocolle, *L'hécatombe des généraux* (Paris: Lavauzelle, 1980), 373; Cochet, *Les soldats de la drôle de guerre*, 138, 192–196, 214; Jacques Sapir, Frank Stora, and Loïc Mahé, *1940: Et si la France avait continué la guerre . . .* (Paris: Tallandier, 2010), 46.
92. Kiesling, *Arming against Hitler*, 174. Future resistance hero Pierre Brossolette also railed against "embusqués" and "planquées." Guillaume Piketty, *Pierre Brossolette: Un héros de la résistance* (Paris: Éditions Odile Jacob, 1998), 144.
93. Du Réau, *Édouard Daladier*, 379–387; Bédarida says four and a half million were in uniform, including 700,000 in the colonies. François Bédarida, "Huit mois d'attente et d'illusion: La 'Drôle de guerre,'" in Jean-Pierre Azéma and François Bédarida, *La France des années noires*, tome 1, *De la défaite à Vichy* (Paris: Éditions du Seuil, 1993), 39. Crémieux-Brilhac's figures are closer to those of du Réau. He points out that most of the colonial troops were "sovereignty troops" to maintain order in the colonies. Few were available for service in France. Crémieux-Brilhac, *Les français de l'an 40*, tome I, 395.
94. Cochet, *Les soldats de la drôle de guerre*, 237–238.
95. Robert O. Paxton, *L'armée de Vichy: Le corps des officiers francais, 1940–1944* (Paris: Tallandier, 2004), 291–293.

96. SHD-GR, oral archives, Colonel Dominique Magnant GR 3K 12–1, Planche 5.
97. Cochet, *Les soldats de la drôle de guerre*, 40–41.
98. Michel de Cazotte, "Oflag Adventure," 11, 14.
99. Teachers had the opportunity to follow "military preparation" courses as part of their normal school curriculum, which reduced their active service time. As a consequence, they made up 15–20 percent of reserve officers in A infantry regiments, and up to 40 percent in B infantry regiments. Teachers also furnished a significant percentage of NCOs. Crémieux-Brilhac, *Les français de l'an 40*, tome I, 508–510.
100. Crémieux-Brilhac GR 3K 32–1, Planche 1.
101. Sartre, *The War Diaries of Jean-Paul Sartre*, 222.
102. Beaufre, *1940*, 43.
103. Cochet, *Les soldats de la drôle de guerre*, 105–107, 237.
104. Sadoul, *Journal de Guerre*,138.
105. Sartre, *The War Diaries of Jean-Paul Sartre*, 203, 206, 222.
106. Cochet, *Les soldats de la drôle de guerre*, 152.
107. Gamelin, *Servir*, 147; SHD-GR, 3P 111, Colonel Desroche, Report 9 January 1941; Dossier 1, Cadre et morale.
108. Cochet, *Les soldats de la drôle de guerre*, 127–128.
109. Sartre, *The War Diaries of Jean-Paul Sartre*, 22–23, 33.
110. Crémieux-Brilhac, *Les français de l'an 40*, tome I, 498–506, 508, 513–514.
111. This included the *Geheime Feldpolizei* (Secret Field Police), whose job was to detect "treason" in German units, and assist prosecutions in the notorious *Kriegsverrat*, a system of courts martial that allegedly ordered 30,000 German soldiers to be executed for disciplinary infractions or cowardice in the course of the Second World War. Charles Hawley, "Germany Considers Rehabilitating Soldiers Executed for 'Treason,'" *Der Spiegel*, 29 June 2007, www.spiegel.de/international/germany/overturning-hitler-s-military-tribunals-germany-considers-rehabilitating-soldiers-executed-for-treason-a-491332.html. The definition of mercy in the *Wehrmacht*'s disciplinary lexicon might mean assignment to a penal battalion (*Strafbataillon*) that in wartime might be ordered to undertake suicide missions.
112. Marc Bloch, *Strange Defeat: A Statement of Evidence Written in 1940* (New York and London: W. W. Norton, 1968), 88–89.
113. Sartre, *The War Diaries of Jean-Paul Sartre*, 143.
114. Michael Howard and Peter Paret (eds.), *Carl von Clausewitz: On War* (Princeton: Princeton University Press, 1976), 613.
115. Henri Dutailly, "Une puissance militaire illusoire, 1930–1939," in Guy Pedroncini (ed.), *Histoire militaire de la France*, tome 3, *De 1871 à 1940* (Paris: Presses universitaires de France, 1992), 357 and "Conclusion," 472.
116. Imlay, *Facing the Second World War*, 358.
117. Michael I. Handel, *Masters of War: Sun Tzu, Clausewitz and Jomini* (London: Frank Cass, 1992), 65.
118. Cochet, *Les soldats de la drôle de guerre*, 132, 217, 219.
119. Romain Gary, *La promesse de l'aube* (Paris: Gallimard, 1980), 278.

120. Crémieux-Brilhac, *Les français de l'an 40*, tome I, 13, 406–408, 711; SHD, oral archives, Crémieux-Brilhac GR 3K 32–1, Planche 1; Fonvieille-Alquier, *The French and the Phoney War*, 78.
121. Sartre, *The War Diaries of Jean-Paul Sartre*, 225.
122. Jérémie Halais, *Saint-Lô et son canton dans la tourmente de la Seconde Guerre mondiale 1939–1945* (Saint-Lô: Société d'archéologie et d'histoire de la Manche, 2007), 17–30; du Réau, *Édouard Daladier*, 376; Crémieux-Brilhac, *Les français de l'an 40*, tome I, 403–404, 412–414; Sadoul, *Journal de Guerre*, 91; Cochet, *Les soldats de la drôle de guerre*, 133–134.
123. Du Réau, *Édouard Daladier*, 353.
124. Jackson, *The Fall of France*, 226.
125. Bédarida, "Huit mois d'attente et d'illusion," 43–44.
126. Cochet, *Les soldats de la drôle de guerre*, 13.
127. Cochet, *Les soldats de la drôle de guerre*, 24–34, 39–40.
128. Martin Thomas writes that 300,000 soldiers were raised in North Africa, almost 200,000 in sub-Saharan Africa, and 116,000 in Indochina, with a further 313,750 to be raised in 1940–1941. Martin Thomas, *The French Empire at War 1940–1945* (New York and Manchester: Manchester University Press, 1998), 12.
129. Julien Fargettas, *Les Tirailleurs sénégalais: Les soldats noirs entre legends et réalités 1939–1945* (Paris: Tallandier, 2012), 44–54, 84; Myron Echenberg, *Les tirailleurs sénégalais en Afrique occidentale française (1857–1960)* (Paris and Dakar: Karthala et Crepos, 2009), 159–160; Alain Fogue Tedom, "Les Indigènes dans les armées françaises, le cas des 'tirailleurs Sénégalais' pendant les guerres de 1914–1918 et de 1935–1945," in Yves Jeanclos (ed.), *La France et les soldats d'infortune au XXe siècle* (Strasbourg: Economica, 2003), 67–84; Armelle Mabon, *Prisonniers de guerre "indigènes": Visages oubliés de la France occupée* (Paris: Éditions La Découverte, 2010), 21–24.
130. David French, "British Military Strategy," in John Ferris and Evan Mawdsley (eds.), *The Cambridge History of the Second World War*, volume I, *Fighting the War* (Cambridge: Cambridge University Press, 2015), 30–34.
131. Du Réau, *Édouard Daladier*, 367.
132. SHD-GR, 3P 111, Dossier 1, "Renseignements tirés de la campagne 1939–1940, 4 – L'infanterie dans l'attaque." See also General Requin, Fourth Army commander, to Commandant le Groupe d'armées no. 2, 7 January 1940, with a list of French ground force tactical and matériel deficiencies revealed by the Saar incursion.
133. Cochet, *Les soldats de la drôle de guerre*, 163–168.
134. Many of these are summed up by du Réau, *Édouard Daladier*, 364–385.
135. Alexander, *The Republic in Danger*, 314–322.
136. Du Réau, *Édouard Daladier*, 360, 364.
137. Du Réau, *Édouard Daladier*, 402.
138. Cochet, *Les soldats de la drôle de guerre*, 121.
139. Adamthwaite, *France and the Coming of the Second World War*, 353.
140. Cochet, *Les soldats de la drôle de guerre*, 121.
141. Bédarida, "Huit mois d'attente et d'illusion," 61.

142. Bédarida, "Huit mois d'attente et d'illusion," 61.
143. Fonvieille-Alquier, *The French and the Phoney War*, 125–127.
144. Bédarida, "Huit mois d'attente et d'illusion," 60–63.
145. Crémieux-Brilhac, *Les français de l'an 40*, tome I, 445.
146. A reference to the unsuccessful April 1917 offensive commanded by General Robert Nivelle. A. J. Liebling, *World War II Writings: The Road Back to Paris. Mollie and Other War Pieces, Uncollected War Journalism. Normandy Revisited* (New York: Literary Classics of the United States, 2008), 39.
147. Sartre, *The War Diaries of Jean-Paul Sartre*, 140.
148. SHD-GR, 3P 111, Dossier 1, "Conseils aux unités de contact."
149. Kaiser, *Economic Diplomacy and the Origins of the Second World War*, 302; May, *Strange Victory*, 455. Richard Toye, *The Roar of the Lion: The Untold Story of Churchill's WWII Speeches* (Oxford: Oxford University Press, 2013), 35.
150. Crémieux-Brilhac, *Les français de l'an 40*, tome I, 535.
151. Imlay, *Facing the Second World War*, 357.
152. Fonvieille-Alquier, *The French and the Phoney War*, 135.
153. Richard Davenport-Hines (ed.), *Letters from Oxford: Hugh Trevor-Roper to Bernard Berenson* (London: Phoenix, 2007), 4 note 12.
154. Weber, *The Hollow Years*, 267, 269.
155. Liebling, *World War II Writings*, 37.
156. Sartre, *The War Diaries of Jean-Paul Sartre*, 140.
157. Crémieux-Brilhac, *Les français de l'an 40*, tome I, 444, 458–461.
158. Cochet, *Les soldats de la drôle de guerre*, 117.
159. Cochet, *Les soldats de la drôle de guerre*, 215, 239.
160. Imlay, *Facing the Second World War*, 358–359.
161. Bédarida, "Huit mois d'attente et d'illusion," 61.
162. At his post-war trial, Ferdonnet claimed that he never broadcasted because his radio delivery was considered substandard. Cochet, *Les soldats de la drôle de guerre*, 117. He was executed for treason nevertheless.
163. J. Jackson, *The Fall of France*, 201.
164. Fonvieille-Alquier, *The French and the Phoney War*, 73–76, 80, 87–88.
165. Crémieux-Brilhac, *Les français de l'an 40*, tome I, 457–462.
166. Nord, *France 1940*, 44–45.
167. Bédarida, "Huit mois d'attente et d'illusion," 59.
168. Despite having to deal with an isolationist American public and a conflict-averse and factious US Congress, Roosevelt managed to increase the USAAF budget in January 1939, which allowed the expansion of the aeronautical industry, and replaced the Neutrality Acts in November 1939 to allow "cash and carry" in an obvious attempt to aid Great Britain. Over the next two years, Roosevelt would take a series of measures designed to support Britain, Free France, and China. Du Réau, *Édouard Daladier*, 385–386.
169. Imlay, *Facing the Second World War*, 311, 318–319.
170. Imlay, *Facing the Second World War*, 345.
171. Frankenstein argues that the managerial class used rearmament as a tool to regain control of the factory floor and reverse the gains of the Popular Front.

Robert Frankenstein, *Le Prix du réarmament français 1935–1939* (Paris: Publications de la Sorbonne, 1982), 299; Hucker, *Public Opinion and the End of Appeasement*, 252–254.

172. Imlay, *Facing the Second World War*, 361.
173. Imlay, *Facing the Second World War*, 351–352.
174. Imlay, *Facing the Second World War*, 361.
175. Kiesling, *Arming against Hitler*, 90.
176. Crémieux-Brilhac, *Les français de l'an 40*, tome I, 444. In reality, workers in defense industries could legally be forced to work seventy-two hours a week in conditions that bordered on penal servitude. And just to show his gratitude for their sacrifices, Finance Minister Reynaud upped the taxes on their pay. Frankenstein, *Le Prix du réarmament français*, 297.
177. Crémieux-Brilhac, *Les français de l'an 40*, tome I, 347–355.
178. Joachim Fest, *Speer: The Final Verdict* (San Diego: Harcourt, 1999), 76, 139–144.
179. Du Réau, *Édouard Daladier*, 381.
180. Imlay, *Facing the Second World War*, 243, 363.
181. Bédarida, "Huit mois d'attente et d'illusion," 58.
182. For a discussion of conditions of the mobilization, Crémieux-Brilhac, *Les français de l'an 40*, tome I, 425–474.
183. Cochet, *Les soldats de la drôle de guerre*, 129–130.
184. Cochet, *Les soldats de la drôle de guerre*, 129–130.
185. Bloch, *Strange Defeat*, 89–90.
186. Cochet, *Les soldats de la drôle de guerre*, 127–129
187. Liebling, *World War II Writings*, 34.
188. Crémieux-Brilhac, *Les français de l'an 40*, tome I, 515; Cochet, *Les soldats de la drôle de guerre*, 17, 237.
189. Sartre, *The War Diaries of Jean-Paul Sartre*, 163.
190. Crémieux-Brilhac, *Les français de l'an 40*, tome I, 523.
191. Sadoul, *Journal de Guerre*, 89–90.
192. Arthur Waldron, "Introduction," in Daniel Moran and Arthur Waldron (eds.), *The People in Arms: Military Myth and National Mobilization since the French Revolution* (Cambridge: Cambridge University Press, 2003), 2.
193. Roderick Macleod and Denis Kelly (eds.), *The Ironside Diaries, 1937–1940* (London: Constable, 1962), 243.
194. SHD-GR, interviews, Cremieux-Brilhac GR 3K 32–1, Planche 1.
195. Cochet, *Les soldats de la drôle de guerre*, 125–126.
196. Cochet, *Les soldats de la drôle de guerre*, 97.
197. Fonvieille-Alquier, *The French and the Phoney War*, 118–123; Crémieux-Brilhac, *Les français de l'an 40*, tome I, 433,438, 463–474.
198. Bloch, *Strange Defeat*, 70, 76.
199. In the Ardennes, for instance, 197 of 503 communes had been evacuated, a total of 152,000 inhabitants out of 294,000 in the department. Cochet, *Les soldats de la drôle de guerre*, 101; Pierre Rigoulot, *L'Alsace-Lorraine pendant la guerre 1939–1945* (Paris: Presses universitaires de France, 1998), 10–11.
200. Sadoul, *Journal de Guerre*, 18–25.

201. Liebling, *World War II Writings*, 60.
202. Macleod and Kelly (eds.), *The Ironside Diaries*, 199.
203. De Cazotte, "Oflag Adventure," 28.
204. Cochet, *Les soldats de la drôle de guerre*, 101.
205. Cochet, *Les soldats de la drôle de guerre*, 130.
206. Cochet, *Les soldats de la drôle de guerre*, 100.
207. Sadoul, *Journal de Guerre*, 135.
208. Sartre, *The War Diaries of Jean-Paul Sartre*, 32–33, 43, 76.
209. Sadoul, *Journal de Guerre*, 58.
210. Rigoulot, *L'Alsace-Lorraine pendant la guerre 1939–1945*, 11–14.
211. Sadoul, *Journal de Guerre*, 93, 101.
212. Rigoulot, *L'Alsace-Lorraine pendant la guerre 1939–1945*, 15.
213. Sartre, *The War Diaries of Jean-Paul Sartre*, 154.
214. Crémieux-Brilhac, *Les français de l'an 40*, tome I, 441–442.
215. Cochet, *Les soldats de la drôle de guerre*, 217.
216. Cochet, *Les soldats de la drôle de guerre*, 141, 143–144.
217. Sadoul, *Journal de Guerre*, 126.
218. Simone de Beauvoir (ed.), *Quiet Moments in a War: The letters of Jean-Paul Sartre to Simone de Beauvoir, 1940–1963* (London: Hamish Hamilton, 1994), 142.
219. SHD-GR, 3P 113, Dossier 2, "Étude sur les causes de notre defaite et les renseignements à en tirer," 16 November 1941.
220. Cochet, *Les soldats de la drôle de guerre*, 75.
221. Macleod and Kelly (eds.), *The Ironside Diaries*, 202.
222. SHD-GR, 3P 114, "Considérations générales sur les travaux et les plans de travaux," Chapter II, "Fortification Permanent," 4. This report lists several defects in the Maginot Line.
223. SHD-GR, 3P 113, Dossier 2, "Remarques sur l'organisation et l'emploi de la batterie anti-chars," Annex XI, "Matériels de R.F."
224. SHD-GR, 3P 114, "Considérations générales sur les travaux et les plans de travaux." For La Ferté, see Chapter II, "Fortification Permanent," 1.
225. Sadoul, *Journal de Guerre*, 115–116; Cochet, *Les soldats de la drôle de guerre*, 75–90; interviews, General Albéric Vaillant SHD-GR 3K 1, Planches 3–11; SHD-GR, 3P 115, Lieutenant R. Weil, "Ouvrage Latiremont"; "Renseignements fournis par l'Adjutant Darchen," 9 October 1940; SHD-GR, 3P 113, Dossier 2, "Remarques sur l'organisation et l'emploi de la batterie anti-chars," Annex XI, "Matériels de R.F."
226. Cochet, *Les soldats de la drôle de guerre*, 148.
227. Simone de Beauvoir (ed.), *Quiet Moments in a War*, 187.
228. SHD-GR, 3P 111, Dossier 2, "Rapport du Lieutenant Vuchot," 3.
229. Cochet, *Les soldats de la drôle de guerre*, 83, 241.
230. SHD-GR, oral archives, General Albéric Vaillant GR 3K 13/4, Planche 5.
231. Fonvieille-Alquier, *The French and the Phoney War*, 124.
232. Liebling, *World War II Writings*, 54–57.
233. Cochet, *Les soldats de la drôle de guerre*, 42, 69.
234. Kiesling, *Arming against Hitler*, 62–71.
235. SHD-GR, 3P 111, Dossier 2, "Rapport du Lieutenant Vuchot," 3.

236. Beaufre, *1940*, 45.
237. Gamelin, *Servir*, 147.
238. Cochet, *Les soldats de la drôle de guerre*, 237.
239. Cochet, *Les soldats de la drôle de guerre*, 148–152.
240. SHD-GR, 7N 2475. "Extraits de fiches de renseignements établis après l'armistice par le commandant Jacquot." Quoted in Porch, *The French Foreign Legion: A Complete History of the Legendary Fighting Force* (New York: Harper Collins, 1991), 457.
241. Piketty, *Pierre Brosolette*, 142, 145.
242. Sadoul, *Journal de Guerre*, 121–123, 138, 142.
243. De Cazotte, "Oflag Adventure," 22, 27–29.
244. "Liasse: 205e RI: Compte-rendu du colonel Furioux, 15 mars 1940," SHD-GR, 14P 13. Cited in Robin Leconte, "Comprendre la défaite. La commission d'enquête sur les repliements suspects 1940–1944," Mémoire de Master 2, Université Paris I Panthéon-Sorbonne – UFR Histoire Centre d'histoire sociale du XXe siècle, 2013, 161–162.
245. Sartre, *The War Diaries of Jean-Paul Sartre*, 117.
246. Leconte, "Comprendre la défaite," 24.
247. Colonel Desroche, Report 9 January 1941, SHD-GR, 3P 111. XIV Tactique.
248. Kiesling, *Arming against Hitler*, 62.
249. David Fraser, *And We Shall Shock Them: The British Army in the Second World War* (London: Hodder and Stoughton, 1983), 8, 19–23; Imlay, *Facing the Second World War*, 335.
250. Fraser, *And We Shall Shock Them*, 9.
251. Fraser, *And We Shall Shock Them*, 26–31.
252. Fraser, *And We Shall Shock Them*, 28–29.
253. General Sir John Kiszely, "The British Campaign in Norway, 1940," unpublished manuscript, 14–15, 166. Subsequently published as John Kiszely, *Anatomy of a Campaign: The British Fiasco in Norway, 1940* (Cambridge: Cambridge University Press, 2017). To be fair to Ironside, the outbreak of war had caught the bluff artilleryman and Boer War veteran on a glide path to retirement, serving in honorific roles as aide-de-camp to the king and Governor General of Gibraltar. Although Ironside's limitations were recognized, he stepped in to replace Lord Gort as CIGS in September 1939, when Gort was named to command the BEF in France. Responsibility for poor training must be shared by Gort, whose advocacy of building a force for continental intervention while CIGS had often found him at odds with Secretary of State for War Hore-Belisha.
254. Crémieux-Brilhac, *Les français de l'an 40*, tome I, 504; Sartre, *The War Diaries of Jean-Paul Sartre*, 143.
255. Sartre, *The War Diaries of Jean-Paul Sartre*, 165.
256. Colonel Desroche, Report 9 January 1941, SHD-GR, 3P 111. Possibly Henri-Paul Desroche who commanded the 45e RI in 1940. Wounded at Dunkirk, he joined the Armistice Army, but was retired by Darlan, allegedly after having been denounced by a subordinate for his Gaullist sentiments, and died in February 1942 as a result of complications from his wound.

257. Macleod and Kelly (eds.), *The Ironside Diaries*, 173–174.
258. Cochet, *Les soldats de la drôle de guerre*, 198–199.
259. Macleod and Kelly (eds.), *The Ironside Diaries*, 203.
260. Crémieux-Brilhac, *Les français de l'an 40*, tome I, 442, 449–453, 571, 589.
261. De Cazotte, "Oflag Adventure," 22.
262. Sartre, *The War Diaries of Jean-Paul Sartre*, 192–194.
263. Sartre, *The War Diaries of Jean-Paul Sartre*, 163, 194–196.
264. Sadoul, *Journal de Guerre*, 106, 108–109, 173.
265. Sartre, *The War Diaries of Jean-Paul Sartre*, 201–202, 220–221.
266. Sadoul, *Journal de Guerre*, 122.
267. Julian Jackson, *France: The Dark Years 1940–1944* (New York: Oxford Universtiy Presss, 2003), 113.
268. Jean-Paul Sartre, *Carnets de la drôle de guerre, septembre 1939–mars 1940* (Paris: Gallimard, 1995), 472. Quoted in Cochet, *Les soldats de la drôle de guerre*, 132.
269. Crémieux-Brilhac, *Les français de l'an 40*, tome I, 514.
270. Sartre, *The War Diaries of Jean-Paul Sartre*, 163–164; Cochet, *Les soldats de la drôle de guerre*, 102–104.
271. Cochet concludes that morale in most units had recovered by March 1940. Cochet, *Les soldats de la drôle de guerre*, 11.
272. Deserters: 0.018 percent in 1914; 0.099 percent in 1939. Cochet, *Les soldats de la drôle de guerre*, 47.
273. This reflects a debate among historians about how much military institutions generate their own culture and make decisions which determine success or failure on the battlefield, a view that reflects the position of historians like Drévillon, Nord, and May. Or, conversely, there is a more "war and society" approach, influenced by Edward Mead Earl's 1943 edition of *Makers of Modern Strategy* and pioneered in the 1960s by Michael Howard, that argues for "the relationship between national policy and the use of force as strategy" and the reciprocal impact of militaries and societies on each other, https://tnsr.org/roundtable/captain-professor-sir-some-lessons-from-michael-howard/#_ftn3. Michael Howard, *Captain Professor: A Life in War and Peace. The Memoirs of Professor Michael Howard* (London and New York: Continuum, 2006), 145.
274. Crémieux-Brilhac, *Les français de l'an 40*, tome I, 518–531.
275. SHD-GR, 3P 113, Dossier 1, Colonel M. Morel, 27 August 1940.
276. Macleod and Kelly (eds.), *The Ironside Diaries*, 192.
277. Crémieux-Brilhac, *Les français de l'an 40*, tome I, 515, 527.
278. Macleod and Kelly (eds.), *The Ironside Diaries*, 189.
279. Imlay, *Facing the Second World War*, 9.
280. George E. Melton, *From Versailles to Mers el-Kébir: The Promise of Anglo-French Naval Cooperation 1919–40* (Annapolis: Naval Institute Press, 2015), 135.
281. Alexander, *The Republic in Danger*, 392
282. Kiszely, "The British Campaign in Norway, 1940," 165.
283. Foreign Office 371/23659. This assessment was based in part on a report by exiled German steel magnate Fritz Thyssen that Swedish iron ore was vital

to Germany's war making potential. Cited in Kiszely, "The British Campaign in Norway, 1940," 14–15. On Ironside, 27–28. I thank Sir John for permission to cite from his work. See also Jack Adams, *The Doomed Expedition: The Campaign in Norway, 1940* (London: Leo Cooper, 1989), 2.

284. P. Jackson, *France and the Nazi Menace*, 382–385.
285. Eleanor M. Gates, *End of the Affair: The Collapse of the Anglo-French Alliance, 1939–40* (Berkeley and Los Angeles: University of California Press, 1981), 38–39.
286. May, *Strange Victory*, 332–333.
287. In an 18 February meeting of the War Cabinet, it was pointed out that if Britain diverted some of its few divisions to Scandinavia, it would have none to reinforce France. The risks of triggering a war with Stalin and reservations from the chiefs of staff about the feasibility of the plan were also voiced. Kiszely, "The British Campaign in Norway, 1940," 29.
288. Kiszely, "The British Campaign in Norway, 1940," 43–47.
289. Gates, *End of the Affair*, 42; du Réau, *Édouard Daladier*, 408–409.
290. Fonvieille-Alquier, *The French and the Phoney War*, 162–168; Frankenstein, *Le Prix du réarmament français*, 297; Alexander, *The Republic in Danger*, 391; Jackson, The Fall of France, 125; Jean Lacouture, *De Gaulle*, tome 1, *Le Rebelle 1890–1944* (Paris: Éditions du Seuil, 1984), 242; May, Strange Victory, 325, 339; Pertinax, *The Gravediggers of France*, 177–179, 185; Sir Edward Spears, *Assignment to Catastrophe,* volume II, *The Fall of France* (New York: A. A. Wyn, 1955), 27.
291. This articulated an ancient narrative in French history that traced the misfortunes of France to the schemes of influential females – Madame de Maintenon who encouraged Louis XIV's slide toward religious intolerance and war in the last quarter of his reign; Madame de Pompadour's influence exercised through the procurement of whores for Louis XV and her role in the forging of the Franco-Austrian alliance of 1757 that drew France into the disastrous Seven Years' War; the scandals and sexual perversion attributed to Marie Antoinette that helped to collapse the *ancien régime*; and Empress Eugenie who catapulted Napoleon III into the ill-fated Mexican expedition constitute familiar episodes.
292. Pertinax, *The Gravediggers of France*, 184.
293. May, *Strange Victory*, 325.
294. Spears, *The Fall of France*, 195, 228.
295. The most balanced treatment of Hélène de Portes' alleged intrigues is Gates, *End of the Affair*, appendix C, 409–412. In 1991, the heirs of Reynaud and de Portes successfully sued the author and journalist Jean-Jacques Servan-Schreiber for printing the spy and gold bars story in a book entitled *Passions*. Susan Heller Anderson, "Chronicle," *New York Times*, 19 July 1991, www.nytimes.com/1991/07/19/style/chronicle-644491.html. One of the arguments of the counterfactual school is that, returned to sanity in the wake of de Portes' death, Reynaud would have been a much more effective leader of a government transferred to North Africa. Sapir, Stora, and Mahé, *1940*, 47.

296. Pertinax, *The Gravediggers of France*, 168, 171.
297. May, *Strange Victory*, 338.
298. Gates, *End of the Affair*, 45.
299. Paul Reynaud, *Mémoires*, tome II, *Envers et contre tous* (Paris: Flammarion, 1963), 296, 316–322.
300. Kiszely, "The British Campaign in Norway, 1940," 55–61.
301. Melton, *From Versailles to Mers el-Kébir*, 149; Kiszely, "The British Campaign in Norway, 1940," 72–73.
302. Winston Churchill, *The Second World War*, volume 1, *The Gathering Storm* (Boston: Houghton Mifflin, 1948), 526.
303. Walter Warlimont, *Inside Hitler's Headquarters, 1939–1945* (San Franscisco: Presido Press, 1991), 69. Cited in Kiszely, "The British Campaign in Norway, 1940," 47.
304. Kiszely, "The British Campaign in Norway, 1940," 125–127.
305. Kiszely, "The British Campaign in Norway, 1940," 106, 110–112.
306. Gates, *End of the Affair*, 50; Melton, *From Versailles to Mers el-Kébir*, 152.
307. Gamelin, *Servir*, 5–6; Reynaud, *Mémoires*, tome II, 323; Alexander, *The Republic in Danger*, 352, 392.
308. Churchill, *The Second World War*, volume 1, 658–659; Toye, *The Roar of the Lion*, 39–41.
309. Sartre, *The War Diaries of Jean-Paul Sartre*, 343.
310. Macleod and Kelly (eds.), *The Ironside Diaries*, 243, 293.
311. Fonvieille-Alquier, *The French and the Phoney War*, 116.
312. Philippe Burrin, *France under the Germans: Collaboration and Compromise* (New York: The New Press, 1996), 33, 43.
313. Beaufre, *1940*, 207.
314. Jackson, *France and the Nazi Menace*, 377–387, 394–395.
315. Cochet, *Les soldats de la drôle de guerre*, 239.
316. Jackson, *The Fall of France*, 226.
317. Cochet, *Les soldats de la drôle de guerre*, 146.
318. This view is most clearly advocated by Ernest May's *Strange Victory* and Philip Nord's *France 1940*.
319. Imlay, *Facing the Second World War*, 185.

3 Case Yellow

1. Michael Howard and Peter Paret (eds.), *Carl von Clausewitz: On War* (Princeton: Princeton University Press, 1976), 186.
2. Michael Handel, "Intelligence and the Problem of Strategic Surprise," *The Journal of Strategic Studies*, 7/3 (September 1984), 229–230.
3. Julian Jackson, *The Fall of France: The Nazi Invasion of 1940* (Oxford: Oxford University Press, 2003), 76.
4. Jean-Louis Crémieux-Brilhac, *Les français de l'an 40*, tome I, *La Guerre oui ou non?* (Paris: Gallimard, 1990), 407–415.
5. Office of the United States Chief of Counsel for Prosecution of Axis Criminality and Aggression, *International Military Trials Nuremburg: Nazi*

Conspiracy and Aggression, Volume VII, Document L-52, 800–814, www.loc.gov/rr/frd/Military_Law/pdf/NT_Nazi_Vol-VII.pdf.

6. Robert Allan Doughty, *The Breaking Point: Sedan and the Fall of France 1940* (Hamden: Archon Books, 1990), 19–23.
7. Crémieux-Brilhac, *Les français de l'an 40*, tome I, 415–422, 568–570.
8. Karl-Heinz Frieser, *The Blitzkrieg Legend: The 1940 Campaign in the West* (Annapolis: Naval Institute Press, 2005), 98.
9. For a discussion of conditions in the German forces and the evolution of the German plan, see Frieser, *The Blitzkrieg Legend*, 23–24, 28, 31–33. On comparative numbers and quality of armaments, 37–44; on air comparisons 44–54; on the evolution of plans 60–102. See also Doughty, *The Breaking Point*, 23–26.
10. Richard J. Evans argues that counterfactual history treats historical actors as free-floating agents, ignoring the factors that constrained their choices. Richard J. Evans, *Altered Past: Counterfactuals in History* (London: Little Brown, 2014), 88.
11. Ernest R. May, *Strange Victory: Hitler's Conquest of France* (New York: Hill and Wang, 2000), 367–370.
12. Douglas Porch, *The French Secret Services: From the Dreyfus Affair to the Gulf War* (Oxford: Oxford University Press, 1997), 159–165.
13. Jackson, *The Fall of France*, 220.
14. May, *Strange Victory*, 458.
15. Philip Nord, *France 1940: Defending the Republic* (New Haven: Yale University Press, 2015), 88. For Seventh Army deficiencies, see Martin S. Alexander, *The Republic in Danger: General Maurice Gamelin and the Politics of French Defence, 1933–1940* (Cambridge: Cambridge University Press, 1992), 367–368.
16. Alexander, *The Republic in Danger*, 397–398; Patrick Facon, *L'Armée de l'air dans la tourmente: La bataille de France, 1939–1940* (Paris: Economica, 2005), 179 note; General Maurice Gamelin, *Servir: Les Armées françaises de 1940* (Paris: Plon, 1946), 81–108; SHD-GR, 3P 111, Dossier 1, "Enseignements tirés de la campagne 1939–1940," "Les tactiques des petites unités."
17. Jackson, *The Fall of France*, 77–85.
18. May, *Strange Victory*, 346.
19. Porch, *The French Secret Services*, 173.
20. Crémieux-Brilhac, *Les français de l'an 40*, tome I, 569, quoting the Taittinger report of March 1939.
21. Crémieux-Brilhac, *Les français de l'an 40*, tome I, 589.
22. Frieser, *The Blitzkrieg Legend*, 119; Andreas Ulrich, "Hitler's Drugged Soldiers," *Der Spiegel*, 6 May 2005, https://freerepublic.com/focus/f-news/1398439/posts.
23. Crémieux-Brilhac, *Les français de l'an 40*, tome I, 542–560; Jackson, *The Fall of France*, 86–87; SHD-GR, 3P 111, Dossier 2, Gérodias to 3e Bureau, 12 April 1941, 13.
24. SHD-GR, 3P 111, report of Guy Maréchal, 5.
25. Simone de Beauvoir (ed.), *Quiet Moments in a War: The Letters of Jean-Paul Sartre to Simone de Beauvoir, 1940–1963* (London: Hamish Hamilton, 1994), 180.

26. Crémieux-Brilhac, *Les français de l'an 40*, tome I, 569.
27. SHD-GR, 3P 111, Dossier 2, Gérodias to 3e Bureau, 12 April 1941, 17.
28. Crémieux-Brilhac, *Les français de l'an 40*, tome I, 565, 569–571.
29. SHD-GR, 3P 111, Dossier 2, Gérodias to 3e Bureau, 12 April 1941, 14–15.
30. SHD-GR, 3P 113, "Le rendement du S.R.A. au cours des opérations." The argument was that the French army was unable to train for counter-battery fire and air reconnaissance during the Phoney War because most counter-battery capabilities had been deployed behind the Maginot Line and German batteries had been inactive. The two batteries in the Ninth Army dedicated to counter-battery fire were too far west to intervene in the battle. One in the Second Army quickly lost two-thirds of its capabilities, while two others around the Montmédy sector managed to find 60 percent of the German batteries, which did not bother to camouflage themselves. In general, counter-battery fire suffered from the same inadequacies that hindered the performance of the French army overall: too many poorly trained reservists; a lack of air reconnaissance; and communications and liaison difficulties. See also "La campagne de 1940. Un rendez-vous manqué," ht tps://artillerie.asso.fr/basart/article.php3?id_article=1419.
31. SHD-GR, 3P 111, Dossier 2, Gérodias to 3e Bureau, 12 April 1941, 25.
32. Robin Leconte, "Comprendre la défaite. La commission d'enquête sur les repliements suspects 1940–1944," Mémoire de Master 2, Université Paris I Panthéon-Sorbonne – UFR Histoire Centre d'histoire sociale du XXe siècle, 2013. 15, 179–180.
33. SHD-GR, 3P 111, Dossier 2, Gérodias to 3e Bureau, 12 April 1941, 14, 20.
34. Major Ralph. G. Smith, "Report on French Tactical Doctrine, Organization, and Materiel Based on Observations Made While at the Ecole Superieur [sic] de Guerre (1935–1937)," 10 August 1937, NARA, RG 165, Entry 77, Box 873.
35. Frieser, *The Blitzkrieg Legend*, 336–337; Leconte, "Comprendre la défaite," 127–128.
36. Frieser, *The Blitzkrieg Legend*, 338.
37. SHD-GR, 3P 111, Dossier 2, Gérodias to 3e Bureau, 12 April 1941, 22–23.
38. SHD-GR, 14P 6, "Liasse: 55e DI: Avis de la commission rendu par le général Doumenc à propos de l'artillerie de la Meuse, 22 décembre 1941." Cited in Leconte, "Comprendre la défaite," 181.
39. SHD-GR, 3P 114, "Considérations générales sur les travaux et les plans de travaux," 4.
40. SHD-GR, 3P 111, Dossier 2, Gérodias to 3e Bureau, 12 April 1941, 29.
41. SHD-GR, 3P 111, Dossier 2, Gérodias to 3e Bureau, 12 April 1941, 30.
42. SHD-GR, 3P 111, Dossier 2, Gérodias to 3e Bureau, 12 April 1941, 25.
43. J. Jackson, *The Fall of France*, 46–47; General André Beaufre, *1940: The Fall of France* (New York: Knopf, 1968), 183.
44. Charles de Gaulle, *Mémoires de guerre*, tome 1, *L'Appel 1940–1942* (Paris: Plon, 1954), 42–43, 47.
45. Smith, "Report on French Tactical Doctrine, Organization, and Materiel," 12.
46. Georges Sadoul, who served in a signals unit, describes French radios as serviceable in "colonial wars or wars of position," but not for a war of

movement. Radios were cumbersome, heavy, short-range, lacked sufficient mobility, and took considerable time to deploy. The operator had to "regulate the net" by signing in with other radios, and establish a table of frequencies for the day. In Sadoul's company, the radios had been stored during the winter. The officer responsible for establishing the table of frequencies, call signs, and check-in times had been assigned other duties from the end of April. When combat broke out on 10 May, his company never managed to "establish the network." Messages were supposed to be encoded. Most radio posts had only one person capable of taking down and transmitting a message "and he was generally mediocre." NCOs were tasked to train radio operators over the winter and rate them as "good," "medium", "weak," and "bad." But these courses seldom took place, and the list of classifications did not change. Georges Sadoul, *Journal de Guerre (2 septembre 1939–20 juillet 1940)* (Paris: Éditions l'Harmattan, 1994), 240–241.

47. Pascal Griset, "Les industries d'armement: L'example des transmissions," in Christine Levisse-Touzé (ed.), *La Campagne de 1940* (Paris: Tallandier, 2001), 331–345.
48. SHD-GR, 3P 113, Dossier 1, "Emploi général de l'artillerie. Moyens de liaison et de transmissions employés devant la carence des moyens nouveaux et dans les décrochages rapides."
49. SHD-GR, 3P 113, Dossier 1, "Rapport du sous lieutenant de Montmarin."
50. SHD-GR, 3P 113, Dossier 1, Lieutenant-colonel Deboulos, "Rapport," 18 September 1940. The Germans too used field telephones. But they were presumably able to recover their wire as they advanced.
51. SHD-GR, 3P 113, "Rapport établi à la suite des operations de la guerre 1939–1940 sur les enseignements à tirer de cette dernière."
52. Crémieux-Brilhac, *Les français de l'an 40*, tome I, 617–618, 624.
53. Sir Edward Spears, *Assignment to Catastrophe*, volume II, *The Fall of France* (New York: A. A. Wyn, 1955), 178.
54. Frieser, *The Blitzkrieg Legend*, 338–341.
55. SHD-GR, 3P 111, Dossier 2, Gérodias to Chief of 3e Bureau, 12 April 1941.
56. Facon, *L'Armée de l'air dans la tourmente*, 1–2, 247.
57. Frieser, *The Blitzkrieg Legend*, 44–54.
58. Facon, *L'Armée de l'air dans la tourmente*, 173; Crémieux-Brilhac, *Les français de l'an 40*, tome I, 654–655.
59. Sadoul, *Journal de Guerre*, 272.
60. Facon, *L'Armée de l'air dans la tourmente*, 191–192.
61. Frieser, *The Blitzkrieg Legend*, 345–346.
62. Marc Bloch, *Strange Defeat: A Statement of Evidence Written in 1940* (New York and London: W. W. Norton, 1968), 54–57.
63. Jean-Jacques Arzalier, "La campagne de mai–juin 1940. Les Pertes?," in Levisse-Touzé (ed.), *La Campagne de 1940*, 432.
64. SHD-GR, 3P 111, Dossier 1, Colonel Desroche, Report, 9 January 1941, XIV Tactique.
65. SHD-GR, 3P111, Dossier 2, Gérodias to 3e Bureau, 12 April 1941, 30.
66. Facon, *L'Armée de l'air dans la tourmente*, 181–185.

67. Facon, *L'Armée de l'air dans la tourmente*, 65, 163–165, 198; Crémieux-Brilhac, *Les français de l'an 40*, tome I, 658.
68. Facon, *L'Armée de l'air dans la tourmente*, 192; Richard Hallion, *Strike from the Sky* (Washington, D.C.: Smithsonian Institution Press, 1989), 144, quoted in Frieser, *The Blitzkrieg Legend*, 42–54; Crémieux-Brilhac, *Les français de l'an 40*, tome I, 653, 654, 658.
69. Crémieux-Brilhac, *Les français de l'an 40*, tome I, 658.
70. Crémieux-Brilhac, *Les français de l'an 40*, tome I, 620–621.
71. Facon, *L'Armée de l'air dans la tourmente*, 187–191.
72. Robert O. Paxton, *Vichy France: Old Guard and New Order, 1940–1944* (London: Barrie & Jenkins, 1972), 4; Alistair Horne, *To Lose a Battle: France 1940* (London: Penguin, 1982), 223–224.
73. Horne, *To Lose a Battle*. Horne devotes but one short chapter to post-Dunkirk operations.
74. Indeed, Leconte notes that the committee's dossier on Sedan is remarkably thin, especially compared with the voluminous dossiers on individual officers, while "L'artillerie de la Meuse" was treated as a separate investigation. Leconte, "Comprendre la défaite," 180–182. Robert Doughty speculates that the order to withdraw was given by a subordinate while Poncelet was on an inspection tour of outlying units. Robert Doughty, *The Breaking Point: Sedan and the Fall of France, 1940* (Mechanicsville: Stackpole Books, 1990), 204.
75. Leconte, "Comprendre la défaite," 183.
76. De Beauvoir (ed.), *Quiet Moments in a War*, 199, 201.
77. Leconte, "Comprendre la défaite," 176.
78. SHD-GR, 3P 113, General Delestraint, "Nos Chars de combat pendant le drame de mai–juin 1940. Les grandes unités blindées. Le groupement cuirassé," Chapter 1, "Les origines," 5, 74.
79. Pierre Billotte, *Le Temps des armes* (Paris: Plon, 1972), 36–45.
80. SHD-GR, 3P 113, Delestraint, "Nos Chars de combat pendant le drame de mai–juin 1940," 5.
81. Crémieux-Brilhac, *Les français de l'an 40*, tome I, 586; J. Jackson, *The Fall of France*, 47–48; Beaufre, *1940*, 186.
82. Leconte, "Comprendre la défaite," 221–222.
83. Robert Merle, *Ahmed ben Bella* (Paris: Gallimard, 1965), 33–34.
84. Crémieux-Brilhac, *Les français de l'an 40*, tome I, 631.
85. Belkacem Recham, *Les Musulmans algériens dans l'armée française (1919–1945)* (Paris: Éditions L'Harmattan, 1996), 48–58.
86. Myron Echenberg, *Les tirailleurs sénégalais en Afrique occidentale française (1857–1960)* (Paris and Dakar: Karthala et Crepos, 2009), 165.
87. SHD-GR, 3P 111, Dossier 2, "Rapport du Lieutenant Vuchot, sur les enseignements à tirer de la campagne 1939–1940," no date, page numbers not chronological.
88. SHD-GR, 3P 111, Dossier 2, "Rapport du Capitaine Filet du 21e Régiment d'infanterie coloniale," 11 September 1940.
89. SHD-GR, 3P 111, Dossier 2, "Citations à l'ordre de l'armée."

90. Armelle Mabon, *Prisonniers de guerre "indigènes": Visages oubliés de la France occupée* (Paris: Éditions La Découverte, 2010), 24.
91. Crémieux-Brilhac, *Les français de l'an 40*, tome I, 587, 628.
92. SHD-GR, 3P 111, Dossier 2, "Rapport du Lieutenant Vuchot," 3–4. On Vuchot's subsequent career, see "Gaston Claude Vuchot (Jedburgh)," http://museedelaresistanceenligne.org/media418-Gaston-Claude-Vuchot-Jedburgh.
93. Bloch, *Strange Defeat*, 55–57.
94. Crémieux-Brilhac, *Les français de l'an 40*, tome I, 633–634.
95. Leconte, "Comprendre la défaite," 165–167.
96. Martin Alexander, "After Dunkirk: The French Army's Performance against 'Case Red,' 25 May to 25 June 1940," *War in History*, 14/2 (2007), 219–264.
97. Anthony King, *The Combat Soldier: Infantry Tactics and Cohesion in the Twentieth and Twenty-First Centuries* (Oxford: Oxford University Press, 2013), 167.
98. King, *The Combat Soldier*, 164–167; J.-L. Crémieux-Brilhac, "L'évolution du moral des troupes," in Levisse-Touzé (ed.), *La Campagne de 1940*, 292.
99. King, *The Combat Soldier*, 78.
100. S. L. A. Marshall, *Men against Fire: The Problem of Battle Command in Future War* (New York: William Morrow, 1947), 158.
101. Leconte, "Comprendre la défaite," 186–194. For an inventory of the French uniform, see http://stalag3b.free.fr/equip_unif.htm.
102. Crémieux-Brilhac, "L'évolution du moral des troupes," 294–296.
103. SHD-GR, 3P 113, "Rapport établi à la suite des operations de la guerre 1939–1940 sur les enseignements à tirer de cette dernière."
104. General Sir John Kiszely, "The British Campaign in Norway, 1940," unpublished manuscript, 106. Since published as John Kiszely, *Anatomy of a Campaign: The British Fiasco in Norway, 1940* (Cambridge: Cambridge University Press, 2017).
105. Alan Moorehead, *Desert War: The North African Campaign 1940–1943* (London and New York: Penguin, 2001), 239–241.
106. King, *The Combat Soldier*, 188–189.
107. John Ellis, *Brute Force: Allied Strategy and Tactics in the Second World War* (London: Viking, 1990), 12–13.
108. Crémieux-Brilhac, *Les français de l'an 40*, tome I, 611–614.
109. Winston S. Churchill, *The Second World War: Their Finest Hour* (Boston: Houghton Mifflin Company, 1949), 42.
110. SHD-GR, 3P 111, Dossier 2, Gérodias to 3e Bureau, 12 April 1941, 26.
111. SHD-GR, 3P 111, Dossier 2, Gérodias to 3e Bureau, 12 April 1941, 26; Frieser, *The Blitzkrieg Legend*, 185–189.
112. Crémieux-Brilhac, *Les français de l'an 40*, tome I, 607–608.
113. Marc Bloch, *The Historian's Craft* (New York: Alfred A. Knopf, 1963), 74.
114. SHD-GR, 3P 111, Dossier 2, Gérodias to 3e Bureau, 12 April 1941, 28.
115. SHD-GR, 3P 111, Dossier 2, Gérodias to 3e Bureau, 12 April 1941, 26–28.
116. SHD-GR, 3P 111, Dossier 2, Gérodias to 3e Bureau, 12 April 1941, 28.
117. Crémieux-Brilhac, *Les français de l'an 40*, tome I, 589–590.
118. De Beauvoir (ed.), *Quiet Moments in a War*, 189.

119. SHD-GR. 3P 113, “Rapport établi à la suite des operations de la guerre 1939–1940 sur les enseigements à tirer de cette dernière.”
120. SHD-GR, 3P 113, “Rapport sur les enseignements à tirer de la guerre.”
121. Crémieux-Brilhac, *Les français de l’an 40*, tome I, 623.
122. Yves Durand, *Prisonniers de guerre dans les Stalags, les Oflags et les Kommandos, 1939–1945* (Paris: Hachette, 1994), 40–41.
123. De Gaulle, *Mémoires de guerre*, tome 1, 39.
124. Jean Lacouture, *De Gaulle*, tome 1, *Le Rebelle 1890–1944* (Paris: Éditions du Seuil, 1984), 311.
125. Gérard Saint-Martin, *L’arme blindée française*, tome 1, *Mai–juin 1940! Les blindés française dans la tourmente* (Paris: Economica, 1998), 214–221.
126. Arzalier, “La campagne de mai-juin 1940,” 433.
127. De Gaulle, *Mémoires de guerre*, tome 1, 39–47.
128. SHD-GR, 3P 112, Capitaine René Ribes, “Rapport concernant le matériel char types B-1 bis,” 6–7.
129. De Gaulle, *Mémoires de guerre*, tome 1, 39–47.
130. SHD-GR, 3P 112, Capitaine René Ribes, “Rapport,” 8.
131. SHD-GR, 3P 112, Capitaine René Ribes, “Rapport,” 9–10; Arzalier, “La campagne de mai–juin 1940, 433.
132. Lacouture, *De Gaulle*, tome 1, 310–313; Saint-Martin, *L’arme blindée française*, tome 1, 224–253; SHD-GR, 3P 113, Delestraint, “Nos Chars de combat pendant le drame de mai–juin 1940,” 7–8, 35–40, 56, 59, 112–113, 116–117.
133. Charles de Gaulle, *Vers l’armée de métier* (Paris: Berger-Levrault, 1944), 102–103.
134. De Gaulle, *Mémoires de guerre*, tome 1, 46.
135. T. C. W. Blanning, *The Culture of Power and the Power of Culture: Old Regime Europe 1660–1789* (Oxford: Oxford University Press, 2002), 192.
136. Bloch, *Strange Defeat*, 88–89.
137. Julian Jackson, *De Gaulle* (Cambridge, MA: Harvard University Press, 2018), 107.
138. Raoul Salan, *Mémoires*, tome 1, *Fin d’un empire: “Le sens d’un engagement” juin 1899–septembre 1946* (Paris: Presses de la Cité, 1970), 79.
139. Lacouture, *De Gaulle*, tome 1, 316–319.
140. J. Jackson, *The Fall of France*, 215.

4 “Stand and Fight . . .”

1. Alistair Horne, *To Lose a Battle: France 1940* (London: Penguin, 1969), 543–544. Although not large, this secret, anti-communist, and antisemitic organization was vicious and well financed, with tentacles allegedly deep into organized crime and sections of the army, especially the intelligence services. Philippe Bourdrel, *La Cagoule: Histoire d’une société secrète du Front populare à la Vᵉ République* (Paris: Albin Michel, 1992), 181–213. Though much discussed at the time and since, the *Cagoule*, whose official name was *Organisation Secrète d’Action Révolutionnaire Nationale*, was composed of perhaps 2,000 conspirators – Édouard Daladier’s biographer Élisabeth du Réau puts their number at

between 3,000 and 5,000. Élisabeth du Réau, *Édouard Daladier 1884–1970* (Paris: Fayard, 1993), 327–328. This group was funded in part by Italy and Nationalist Spain, as well as by industrialists like Eugène Schueller, CEO of L'Oréal, Louis Renault, Lemaigre Dubreuil, owner of both Lesieur oil and Le Printemps, and perhaps members of the Michelin family. The *Cagoule*'s specialty was planting bombs and carrying out contract killings against left-wing émigrés from Spain and Italy, most notoriously the murders of Italian anti-Fascist exiles Carlo and Nello Rosselli in June 1937. The great enemy of the *Cagoule* was Interior Minister Marx Dormoy, who led a crackdown on the organization in 1937–1938 following the discovery of plans to launch a coup. For his troubles, Dormoy was assassinated in 1941, probably by members of the *Cagoule*. Bourdrel, *La Cagoule*, 287–93. A *Corvignolle* network provided the link between the *Cagoule* and the French military. Organized from the autumn of 1936 by Colonel Georges Loustaunau-Lacau, a member of Pétain's staff, the *raison d'être* of *Corvignolle* was to arrest key figures and seize strategic locations in the name of certain generals. The purpose of this action was to thwart what they believed to be a PCF plan to neutralize the military through communist cells allegedly organizing within military units, as a prelude to revolution. Allegedly, a dozen French generals were associated with the *Cagoule/Corvignolle* plot. Édouard Daladier, who was Minister of War under the first Popular Front government, and subsequently Premier from 1938, impeded Dormoy's investigations of the *Cagoule*'s influence in the army because he feared it would implicate too many senior officers, including both Pétain and Weygand, and trigger a purge that would disorganize national defense. François Fonvieille-Alquier, *The French and the Phoney War 1939–1940* (London: Tom Stacey, 1973), 67. Du Réau notes that official records of Daladier's intervention are limited to writing a letter to defend the services of one member of *Corvignolle*. Du Réau 328. According to Lacouture, Loustaunau-Lacau was a friend of de Gaulle, although he never attempted to recruit the future leader of Free France into his network. Jean Lacouture, *De Gaulle*, tome 1, *Le Rebelle 1890–1944* (Paris: Éditions du Seuil, 1984), 223. General Henri Giraud was also rumored to have links to the *Cagoule*. Pierre Péan, *Le mystérieux Docteur Martin* (Paris: Fayard, 1993), 140. See also Joel Blatt, "The Cagoule Plot, 1936–1937," in Kenneth Mouré and Martin Alexander (eds.), *Crisis and Renewal in France, 1918–1962* (New York: Berghahn Books, 2002), 86–104. Frederick Brown believes that whether a dangerous threat or the invention of a feverish left-wing imagination, the *Cagoule* simply added to "the army of hobgoblins undermining confidence in a Republic seemingly unable to govern." Frederick Brown, *The Embrace of Unreason: France, 1914–1940* (New York: Knopf, 2014), 268.

2. Julian Jackson, *The Fall of France: The Nazi Invasion of 1940* (Oxford: Oxford University Press, 2003), 131; Robert O. Paxton, *L'armée de Vichy: Le corps des officiers francais 1940–1944* (Paris: Tallandier, 2004), 188–189.
3. Philip Bankwitz, *Maxime Weygand and Civil–Military Relations in Modern France* (Cambridge, MA: Harvard University Press, 1967), 207, 213–215, 220, 234.

4. Jean-Louis Crémieux-Brilhac, *Les français de l'an 40*, tome I, *La Guerre oui ou non?* (Paris: Gallimard, 1990), 618.
5. General André Beaufre, *1940: The Fall of France* (New York: Knopf, 1968), 189.
6. Edgard de Larminat, *Chroniques irrévérencieuses* (Paris: Plon, 1962), 41.
7. Richard Hofstadter, "The Paranoid Style of American Politics," *Harper's Magazine*, November 1964, 77. Hofstadter's description of a "paranoid" personality type is taken from Norman Cohn.
8. Jackson, *The Fall of France*, 131.
9. Martin S. Alexander, *The Republic in Danger: General Maurice Gamelin and the Politics of French Defence, 1933–1940* (Cambridge: Cambridge University Press, 1992), 21, 28–29, 31–32; Barnett Singer, *Maxime Weygand: A Biography of the French General in Two World Wars* (Jefferson and London: McFarland & Company, 2008), 91, 97.
10. Pertinax (André Géraud), *The Gravediggers of France: Gamelin, Daladier, Reynaud, Pétain, and Laval. Military Defeat, Armistice, Counterrevolution*, (Garden City, New York: Doubleday, Doran & Company, 1944), 511.
11. Sir Edward Spears, *Assignment to Catastrophe*, volume II, *The Fall of France* (New York: A. A. Wyn, 1955), 77–78, 154.
12. Charles de Gaulle, *Mémoires de guerre*, tome 1, *L'Appel 1940–1942* (Paris: Plon, 1984), 48–49.
13. Eleanor M. Gates, *End of the Affair: The Collapse of the Anglo-French Alliance, 1939–40* (Berkeley: University of California Press, 1981), 89–91; Crémieux-Brilhac, *Les français de l'an 40*, tome I, 616–618.
14. Marc Bloch, *Strange Defeat: A Statement of Evidence Written in 1940* (New York: W. W. Norton & Company, 1968), 66–67, 87, 112, 124–125.
15. Crémieux-Brilhac, *Les français de l'an 40*, tome I, 608, 618.
16. Karl-Heinz Frieser, *The Blitzkrieg Legend: The 1940 Campaign in the West* (Annapolis: Naval Institute Press, 2005), 291–300, 312–314.
17. Gates, *End of the Affair*, 89–100.
18. Bloch, *Strange Defeat*, 16–20.
19. Yves Durand, *Prisonniers de guerre dans les Stalags, les Oflags et les Kommandos, 1939–1945* (Paris: Hachette, 1994), 23.
20. Michel de Cazotte, "Oflag Adventure," unpublished manuscript, edited by Louis Denis de Cazotte, summer 1997, Hoover Archives, Stanford University, 39–42.
21. Jean-Jacques Arzalier, "La campagne de mai–juin 1940. Les Pertes?," in Christine Levisse-Touzé (ed.), *La Campagne de 1940* (Paris: Tallandier, 2001), 430.
22. Gates, *End of the Affair*, 117.
23. Gates, *End of the Affair*, 118.
24. Patrick Facon, *L'Armée de l'air dans la tourmente: La bataille de France, 1939–1940* (Paris: Economica, 2005), 200, 202–204, 207; Arzalier estimates that the French air force lost 541 killed, 364 wounded, and 105 missing, of whom 136 were fighter pilots. In all, the air force lost 29 percent of its combat strength. Arzalier, "La campagne de mai–juin 1940," 431–432.
25. Arzalier, "La campagne de mai–juin 1940," 430.

26. Crémieux-Brilhac, *Les français de l'an 40*, tome I, 619.
27. Durand, *Prisonniers de guerre dans les Stalags, les Oflags et les Kommandos*, 42; J.-L. Crémieux-Brilhac, "L'évolution du moral des troupes," in Christine Levisse-Touzé (ed.), *La Campagne de 1940* (Paris: Tallandier, 2001), 297.
28. Jackson, *The Fall of France*, 131.
29. Reynaud also notes that on 20 May, the Swedish ambassador brought a note from Göring proposing an armistice. Paul Reynaud, *Mémoires*, tome II, *Envers et contre tous: 7 mars 1936–16 juin 1940* (Paris: Flammarion, 1963), 351, 357, 363.
30. Spears, *The Fall of France*, 20; Crémieux-Brilhac, *Les français de l'an 40*, tome I, 618.
31. Gates surmises that only from 7 June did Weygand conclude that the military situation was irreparable and forcefully demand that France seek an armistice. Gates, *End of the Affair*, 105, 107, 170. For his part, Crémieux-Brilhac reckons that five days into his command, around 24 May, Weygand realized that the situation was hopeless. Crémieux-Brilhac, *Les français de l'an 40*, tome I, 608.
32. Crémieux-Brilhac, "L'évolution du moral des troupes," 296.
33. Twelve died in combat, five of them in Corap's Ninth Army, while Billote was killed in a car accident. Robin Leconte, "Comprendre la défaite. La commission d'enquête sur les repliements suspects 1940–1944," Mémoire de Master 2, Université Paris I Panthéon-Sorbonne – UFR Histoire Centre d'histoire sociale du XXe siècle, 125.
34. Crémieux-Brilhac, *Les français de l'an 40*, tome I, 635, 647.
35. Martin S. Alexander, "After Dunkirk: The French Army's Performance against 'Case Red', 25 May to 25 June 1940," *War in History*, 14/2 (2007), 220, 251, 253; Jackson, *The Fall of France*, 180.
36. Arzalier, "La campagne de mai–juin 1940," 430.
37. Bloch, *Strange Defeat*, 14–15.
38. Leconte categorizes the Picard saga as illustrative of a quarrel between "the ancients and the moderns" in the 1930s French army over the virtues of mechanization versus the continued relevance of the horse. This was not the first time that Picard had been accused of drunkenness by his underlings, accusations that had been investigated and dismissed. Once the campaign began, several of Picard's subordinates continued to quibble over his orders, insisting that they did not meet standards of "commander's intent." Picard's career-ending dismissal seemed illustrative of an atmosphere of competition and backbiting that characterized the French army, and which was to continue into the Vichy era. Leconte, "Comprendre la défaite," 150–158.
39. SHD-GR, 3P 111, Dossier 2, "Rapport du Chef de bataillon Vallette d'Osia," October 1940.
40. "The enemy surprised us in his advance toward the Aisne," reported Colonel Morel. "We detected no attempt to maneuver, nor use camouflage, nor concealment of his many horse-drawn batteries that were taken apart by our artillery observers. The losses inflicted on the enemy caused him to

rectify his mistakes." SHD-GR, 3P 113, Dossier 1, Colonel M. Morel, 27 August 1940, 5.

41. Alexander, "After Dunkirk," 250.
42. Beaufre, *1940*, 202.
43. De Gaulle, *Mémoires de guerre*, tome 1, 47–48.
44. Spears, *The Fall of France*, 63.
45. Gates, *End of the Affair*, 118.
46. Horne, *To Lose a Battle*, 622.
47. Gates, *End of the Affair*, 118 119; Alexander, "After Dunkirk," 224.
48. Spears, *The Fall of France*, 64.
49. SHD-GR, 3P 111, Dossier 1, 6 July 1940.
50. SHD-GR, 3P 111, Dossier 1, 18 July 1940; 6 August 1940.
51. SHD-GR, oral archives, Crémieux-Brilhac GR 3K 32–1, Planche 2.
52. Georges Sadoul, *Journal de Guerre (2 septembre 1939–20 juillet 1940)* (Paris: Éditions l'Harmattan, 1994), 386, 392. A family friend in Normandy recounted to the author that his father had been awarded a Croix de guerre after Dunkirk, but never wore it because he believed that he had done nothing to earn it.
53. Pierre Pellissier, *De Lattre* (Paris: Perrin, 1998), 186.
54. SHD-GR, 2P 70, Lieutenant colonel Legrez to Darlan, 5 April 1942, Part II, 2.
55. Paxton, *L'armée de Vichy*, 201, 458.
56. Sadoul, *Journal de Guerre*, 273–278.
57. SHD-GR, 3P 113, Dossier 1, Colonel M. Morel, 27 August 1940, 3.
58. SHD-GR, 3P 113, Dossier 1, Colonel M. Morel, 27 August 1940, 5. See also "Rapport sure les enseignements à tirer de la guerre," 19 August 1940; SHD-GR, 3P 113, Dossier 1, Aspirant Louis Aubry, "Rapport sur l'emploie de l'artillerie pendant la guerre de 1939–1940. Period: Mai et Juin 1940," 24 August 1940; SHD-GR, 3P 113, Dossier 2, "Remarques sur l'organisation et l'emploi de la batterie anti-chars," appendix XIV; 3P 111, Dossier 1, "Renseignements tirés de la campagne 1939–1940," "Les moyens de ravitaillement et d'evacuation."
59. SHD-GR, 3P 111, Dossier 2, "Rapport du Chef de bataillon Vallette d'Osia," 1 October 1940.
60. SHD-GR, 3P 113, Dossier 1, Colonel M. Morel, 27 August 1940, 2–3.
61. SHD-GR, 3P 114, Lieutenant-colonel Mathieu, "Le Problème des communications. Le franchissement des rivières et passage des lignes fortifées au cours de la campagne de France 1940," February 1942.
62. SHD-GR, 3P 114, "Enseignements de la campagne 1939–1940 Genie," 13–14; 3P 111, Colonel Desroche, Report, 9 January 1941, "VIII Défense anti-chars"; SHD-GR, 3P 113, Dossier 2, "Remarques sur l'organisation et l'emploi de la batterie anti-chars," 3; SHD-GR, 3P 111, Dossier 2, "Rapport du Chef de bataillon Vallette d'Osia," 1 October 1940.
63. SHD-GR, 2P 70, 16–17.
64. Crémieux-Brilhac, "L'évolution du moral des troupes," 294–295.
65. SHD-GR, 3P 114, "Enseignements de la campagne 1939–1940 Genie," 17.
66. SHD-GR, 3P 111, Dossier 2, "Rapport du Chef de bataillon Vallette d'Osia," 1 October 1940, 31–32, 34.

67. Alexander, "After Dunkirk," 225, 233–234, 238, 240, 242, 245, 254, 256; Crémieux-Brilhac, *Les français de l'an 40*, tome I, 644.
68. Colonel Desroche, Report, 9 January 1941, SHD-GR, 3P 111, IX: Cadres et morale.
69. SHD-GR, 3P 113, "Rapport sur les enseignements à tirer de la guerre," 5.
70. Colonel Desroche, Report, 9 January 1941, SHD-GR, 3P 111, Dossier 1, "Fronts et unités beaucoup trop étendus." See also "Enseignements de la bataille de Champagne," which makes the same point.
71. SHD-GR, 3P 113, Colonel Robert Noirot-Nerin, "Affaires durant lesquelles ces commandements ont été exercés en grandes unités supérieures," 19 August 1940, 13–14.
72. Leconte, "Comprendre la défaite," 163.
73. SHD-GR, 3P 113, "Rapport relative aux missions confiée à la 6ème batterie du 76ème R.A. aux modes d'execution et au résultat constaté."
74. Pellissier, *De Lattre*, 180.
75. SHD-GR, 3P 111, Dossier 2, "Rapport du Chef de bataillon Vallette d'Osia," 1 October 1940.
76. Crémieux-Brilhac, *Les français de l'an 40*, tome I, 648.
77. Colonel Desroche, Report, 9 January 1941, SHD-GR, 3P 111, "Points d'appui fermés."
78. SHD-GR, 3P 113, Dossier 1, "Rapport Sommaire du Capitaine Convert, ex-Commandant de la 6e batterie du 21e R.A.D.," 2 September 1940.
79. Beaufre, *1940*, 203; SHD-GR, 3P 113, Dossier 1, "Rapport sur les enseignements à tirer de la guerre," 3, 7–8.
80. Beaufre, *1940*, 204.
81. Leconte, "Comprendre la défaite," 176.
82. Hanna Diamond, *Fleeing Hitler: France 1940* (Oxford: Oxford University Press, 2007), 42, 72, 76–77.
83. Guillaume Piketty, *Pierre Brossolette: Un héros de la résistance* (Paris: Éditions Odile Jacob, 1998), 147–150; see also SHD-GR, 3P 111, Dossier 2, Gérodias to 3e Bureau, 12 April 1941, 33.
84. SHD-GR, 3P 113, Dossier 2, Le Capitaine Fould, "Rapport," no date, 2.
85. Beaufre, *1940*, 209.
86. Durand, *Prisonniers de guerre dans les Stalags, les Oflags et les Kommandos*, 23.
87. SHD-GR, oral archives, Crémieux-Brilhac GR 3K 32–1, Planche 2.
88. Leconte, "Comprendre la défaite," 175.
89. SHD-GR, 3P 111, Dossier 2, "Rapport de Capitaine Casalta," 27 September 1940.
90. Leconte, "Comprendre la défaite," 164–167.
91. SHD-GR, 2P 70, 51.
92. Pellissier, *De Lattre*, 185. However, the sheer confusion of 1940, the intermixing of civilians and soldiers during the "exode" of May–June, disagreement over what actually constituted a "combat casualty," meant that figures of around 120,000 French killed in action (KIA) were never more than a "best case" estimate, perhaps inflated for political purposes. The disorganization of the French army following the armistice, with most of its units behind barbed wire, and its headquarters transferred to Vichy, which lacked

access to those files and reports that existed, meant that casualty figure estimates contain a high degree of speculation, maybe even double counting. For instance, one report compiled in March 1945 lists combat deaths in May–June 1940 at 81,000, before adding civilian deaths, and subsequent POW deaths and those in Syria in separate categories. SHD-GR, 7P 81, "Situation des pertes françaises au 15 mars 1945." This report lists 128,000 deaths for the entire war up to March 1945, including those who died as POWs. But it does not seem to include Tunisia and Italy in its calculations. An annex estimates 111,348 KIA and 112,495 wounded from September 1939 to 25 June 1940. The report also admits that, with three general staffs during the course of the war split between London, Algiers, and Paris, accurate statistics were difficult to compile. The number of wounded who perished was probably as high as 10 percent, Arzalier believes, because French medical services were no more adapted to a war of movement than was the rest of the French army. One result was that French wounded were often evacuated in haste without being triaged. In the First World War, 12 percent of French wounded died in hospital, compared with a death rate of 4.5 percent achieved by US military medical services in 1941–1945. Arzalier estimates the death rate for French wounded in May–June 1940 at 10 percent. Arzalier, "La campagne de mai–juin 1940," 433–434.

93. Arzalier comes up with a figure of 50,000–90,000, but tends to favor the lower figure. Arzalier, "La campagne de mai–juin 1940," 435–442. France lost 301,000 men between September and the end of December 1914, compared with 349,000 men in the twelve months of 1915, the war's most casualty-heavy year. For a breakdown of French casualties, see Guy Pedroncini (ed.), *Histoire militaire de la France*, tome 3, *De 1871 à 1940* (Paris: Presses universitaires de France, 1992), 288–291.
94. Based on a calculation of 65,000 dead to 1,500,000 POWs. On MIAs as an indicator of demoralization, see Jonathan Fennell, *Combat and Morale in the North African Campaign: The Eighth Army and the Path to El Alamein* (Cambridge: Cambridge University Press, 2011), 40.
95. François Cochet, *Les soldats de la drôle de guerre: Septembre 1939–mai 1940* (Paris: Hachette, 2004), 135.
96. Frieser, *The Blitzkrieg Legend*, 150, 338–339.
97. Leconte, "Comprendre la défaite," 167–170.
98. SHD, oral interviews, Colonel Dominique Magnant, GR 3K 12–1, Planche 6.
99. SHD-GR, 3P 113, Dossier 1. At Sedan in May 1940, heavy batteries of 155 mm pieces without anti-tank guns to defend themselves suddenly found themselves under attack by Panzers. Colonel Bonnet to Direction de l'Artillerie, 10 August 1940, 2. For the inadequacies of land lines and lack of radios, see also, "Rapport Sommaire du Capitaine Convert, ex-Commandant de la 6e batterie du 21e R.A.D.," 2 September 1940.
100. SHD-GR, 3P 113, Dossier 1, Second Lieutenant Joseph Thirant, "Compte Rendu." No date, but probably August 1940.
101. Bloch, *Strange Defeat*, 22.

102. Leconte, "Comprendre la défaite," 172–173.
103. During the "summer battles" on the Gazala Line in May–August 1942, 85 percent of British "casualties" fell into the MIA category. Others argue that these high surrender figures were due to the mobile conditions of warfare in the desert, not morale problems, that in many ways replicated those of France in May–June 1940, where units often found themselves without transport and surrounded by enemy tanks against which they had no defense, and so surrendered. Contemporary studies also showed far lower surrender rates for Australians and New Zealanders, who no doubt had more social cohesion and their own wellsprings of *esprit de corps*. "It is clear that Eighth Army did experience a morale crisis in the desert," in the summer of 1942, writes Jonathon Fennell. This crisis had multiple sources – lack of confidence in their leadership, their weapons, inadequate training, the inconclusive nature of the fighting, a depressing, monochromatic Saharan landscape, and peculiarities of Eighth Army organization like "composite battalions" and a constant turnover of units that militated against the formation of "primary group" solidarity in units and habits of trust and cooperation among them. Jonathan Fennell, *Combat and Morale in the North African Campaign*, 41–49.
104. Sadoul, *Journal de Guerre*, 359.
105. Crémieux-Brilhac, *Les français de l'an 40*, tome I, 628–629, 675–682, 687–691. Crémieux-Brilhac attributes the relatively smaller number of officer POWs – 50 percent compared with 70 percent of soldiers – to the fact that more staff, support, and air force officers without troop responsibilities did succeed in avoiding capture. Julian Jackson, *France: The Dark Years 1940–1944* (New York: Oxford Universtiy Presss, 2003), 126.
106. Durand, *Prisonniers de guerre dans les Stalags, les Oflags et les Kommandos*, 25–27.
107. Myron Echenberg, *Les tirailleurs sénégalais en Afrique occidentale française (1857–1960)* (Paris and Dakar: Karthala et Crepos, 2009), 167.
108. Echenberg, *Les tirailleurs sénégalais en Afrique occidentale française*, 166–167; Armelle Mabon, *Prisonniers de guerre "indigènes": Visages oubliés de la France occupée* (Paris: Éditions La Découverte, 2010), 24–25; Julien Fargettas, *Les Tirailleurs sénégalais: Les soldats noirs entre legends et réalités 1939–1945* (Paris: Tallandier, 2012), 91–102, 142–167.
109. Spears, *Assignment to Catastrophe*, volume II, 237.
110. Colonel Jacques Minart, *P.C. Vincennes* (Paris: Berget Levrault, 1945), 221–222.
111. SHD-GR, 3P 111, "VIII Défense anti-chars."
112. Diamond, *Fleeing Hitler*, 117–118.
113. Crémieux-Brilhac, *Les français de l'an 40*, tome I, 681.
114. Jackson, *France: The Dark Years*, 122.
115. Spears, *Assignment to Catastrophe*, 120.
116. Gates, *End of the Affair*, 173–177.
117. Gates, *End of the Affair*, 168; Horne, *To Lose a Battle*, 623–628.
118. Crémieux-Brilhac, *Les français de l'an 40*, tome I, 618–619.

119. Talbot C. Imlay, *Facing the Second World War: Strategy, Politics, and Economics in Britain and France 1938–1940* (Oxford: Oxford University Press, 2003), 185.
120. François Kersaudy, *Churchill and de Gaulle* (London: Collins, 1981), 74.
121. J. Jackson, *The Fall of France*, 210–211.
122. Gates, *End of the Affair*, 177.
123. Imlay, *Facing the Second World War*, 11, 359–360.
124. Gates, *End of the Affair*, 201–202.
125. De Gaulle, *Mémoires de guerre*, tome 1, 53.
126. Gates, *End of the Affair*, 190.
127. Gates, *End of the Affair*, 214, appendix E. Raoul Dautry argued that Reynaud should have reconstituted his cabinet in June excluding both Weygand and Pétain. Gates, *End of the Affair*, 242; Spears, *Assignment to Catastrophe*, 259.
128. Philippe Burrin, *France under the Germans: Collaboration and Compromise* (New York: The New Press, 1996), 6.
129. Diamond, *Fleeing Hitler*, 96.
130. Pierre Servent, *Le mythe Pétain: Verdun ou les tranchées de la mémoire* (Paris: Éditions CNRS, 2014), 235, 238.
131. The idea had been kicking around since 1939. The argument was that Reynaud should have introduced it earlier for it to look like anything but a last-ditch attempt to avert disaster. Nor was there any guarantee that the British cabinet would go along with it. Gossip attributed its failure to Hélène de Portes' opposition. Gates, *End of the Affair*, 234–236.
132. Burrin, *France under the Germans*, 7–9.
133. Gates, *End of the Affair*, 218, 239–243, appendix H; Jackson, *France: The Dark Years*, 126.
134. Jean-Pierre Azéma and Olivier Wieviorka, *Vichy 1940–1944* (Paris: Perrin, 2004), 30–31.
135. Jackson, *France: The Dark Years*, 126, 130.
136. Spears, *Assignment to Catastrophe*, 310–311.
137. Gates, *End of the Affair*, 188.
138. Diamond, *Fleeing Hitler*, 96.
139. Paxton, *Vichy France*, 9–11, 16.
140. Diamond, *Fleeing Hitler*, 83, 97, 183, 190.
141. Spears, *Assignment to Catastrophe*, 246.
142. Gates, *End of the Affair*, 181–186, 202–205.
143. Gates, *End of the Affair*, 181–186, 202–205.
144. Robert Gildea, *Fighters in the Shadows: A New History of the French Resistance* (Cambridge, MA: Harvard University Press, 2015), 44.
145. Sadoul, *Journal de Guerre*, 274, 278.
146. Beaufre, *1940*, 211.
147. Christine Levisse-Touzé, "La poursuite de la guerre en Afrique du Nord," in Jean Delmas (ed.), Colloque International, *Les armées française pendant la seconde guerre mondiale 1939–1945* (Paris: École nationale supérieure de techniques avancées, 1985), 88–99; Philippe Masson, *La marine française et la guerre 1939–1945* (Paris: Tallandier, 1991), 69–70.

148. Gates, *End of the Affair*, 383–384; Barnett Singer, *Maxime Weygand: A Biography of the French General in Two World Wars* (Jefferson and London: McFarland & Company, 2008), 114–116; Spears, *Assignment to Catastrophe*, 239; Anthony Clayton, *General Maxime Weygand 1867–1965: Fortune and Misfortune* (Bloomington and Indianapolis: Indiana University Press, 2015), 97.
149. Jacques Sapir, Frank Stora, and Loïc Mahé, *1940: Et si la France avait continué la guerre . . .* (Paris: Tallandier, 2010), 30–45.
150. Chantal Metzger, *Le Maghreb dans la guerre 1939–1945* (Paris: Armand Colin, 2018), 75; Christine Levisse-Touzé, "L'Afrique du Nord dans la guerre," paper delivered at the conference "Afrique du Nord: Vichy, Résistance, Alliés," Paris, 12–13 November 2017, 1. I thank Professor Levisse-Touzé for permission to quote from her paper.
151. Levisse-Touzé, *L'Afrique du Nord dans la guerre 1939–1945*, 58.
152. Julie Le Gac, *Vaincre sans gloire: Le corps expéditionnaire français en Italie (novembre 1942–juillet 1944)* (Paris: Les Belles Lettres/Ministère de la défense-DMPA, 2013), 366–367; Metzger, *Le Maghreb dans la guerre 1939–1945*, 85.
153. Richard J. Evans, *Altered Past: Counterfactuals in History* (London: Little Brown, 2014), 85–88, 145, 162, 171.
154. Jackson, *France: The Dark Years*, 93–94. Indeed, critics of the Sapir argument see his political scenario for rebuilding a Republican government in a deeply antisemitic AFN based around Reynaud, Blum, and Mandel as the least plausible, with the incompetent and defeatist Huntzinger replacing Weygand as commander-in-chief, and the evil influence of Hélène de Portes over Reynaud eliminated. Sapir, Stora, and Mahé, *1940*, 46–47. For a review, see Alain Bihr, *Interrogations?* no. 11 (December 2010), www.revue-interrogations.org/Jacques-Sapir-Frank-Stora-et-Loic.
155. Gates, *End of the Affair*, 197–200.
156. Spears, *Assignment to Catastrophe*, 275.
157. Gates, *End of the Affair*, 204.
158. Spears, *Assignment to Catastrophe*, 180.
159. Gates, *End of the Affair*, 181–186, 202–205.
160. Bloch, *Strange Defeat*, 160.
161. Azéma and Wieviorka point out that the charge that the parliament elected with the Popular Front in 1936 assassinated the Third Republic by voting "full powers" to Pétain on 10 July needs to be nuanced. PCF deputies had been forced into hiding or jailed. The twenty-seven deputies keenest to fight on had left on the *Massilia* for Casablanca on 21 June, where several of the most prominent were arrested on arrival. The Senate, a bastion of conservatism, had twice overthrown Blum's governments. Azéma and Wieviorka, *Vichy 1940–1944*, 46. On Pétain seen as "apolitical," see Robert Belot, *La Résistance sans de Gaulle* (Paris: Fayard, 2006), 19.
162. Lacouture, *De Gaulle*, tome 1, 379.
163. Belot, *La Résistance sans de Gaulle*, 42–44.
164. On the situation in AFN in June 1940, see Levisse-Touzé, *L'Afrique du Nord dans la guerre 1939–1945*, 58–64.

165. Frédéric Harymbat, *Les Européens d'Afrique du Nord dans les armées de la libération française (1942–1945)* (Paris: Éditions l'Harmattan, 2014), 17–20; Maréchal Alphonse Pierre Juin, *Mémoires*, tome 1, *Alger, Tunis, Rome* (Paris: Fayard, 1959), 32.
166. Levisse-Touzé, "L'Afrique du Nord dans la guerre," 1–2, 65–77. Stora points out that 65 percent of Oran's European residents in 1936 were of Spanish origin, only 41 percent of whom had been given French nationality, numbers replicated in the towns throughout the Oranie, Algeria's eastern province that bordered Morocco. Benjamin Stora, *Histoire de l'Algérie coloniale (1830–1954)* (Paris: Éditions La Découverte, 2004), 55.
167. Edgard de Larminat, *Chroniques irrévérencieuses* (Paris: Plon, 1962), 49–55; Belot, *La Résistance sans de Gaulle*, 21, 42–44; Lacouture, *De Gaulle*, tome 1, 376–377.
168. Christine Levisse-Touzé, "La poursuite de la guerre en Afrique du nord," 88–99; Levisse-Touzé, *L'Afrique du Nord dans la guerre 1939–1945*, 37–38, 65–87, 151–156; Juin, *Mémoires*, tome 1, 31.
169. Jean-Pierre Azéma, "Le choc armée et les débandades," in Jean-Pierre Azéma and François Bédarida, *La France des années noires*, tome 1, *De la défaite à Vichy* (Paris: Éditions du Seuil, 1993), 99. This view is also supported by Ernest R. May, *Strange Victory: Hitler's Conquest of France* (New York: Hill and Wang, 2000). These general divisions of historical interpretation are admirably summed up by Peter Jackson, *France and the Nazi Menace: Intelligence and Policy Making 1933–1939* (Oxford: Oxford University Press, 2000), 1–2. Jackson puts authors like Jean-Bapiste Duroselle, Anthony Adamthwaite, and François Bédarida in the "Decadence School" which leans toward determinism. More circumscribed but still believing that French policy lacked clear direction are Maurice Vaïsse, Ladislas Mysyrowicz, Henri Dutailly, and Robert Doughty. Among the "structuralists" he lists Robert Frank, Robert Young, Élisabeth du Réau, and Pierre Grosser. The third revisionist group, who reject the "determinism" of the other schools of interpretation, would include scholars like Martin Alexander and Jenny Kiesling. A counterfactual approach to the Fall of France has served to point up some of the weaknesses of those who argue that fighting on from the empire was a non-starter. Sapir, Stora, and Mahé, *1940*.
170. Jackson, *The Fall of France*, 215.
171. Imlay, *Facing the Second World War*, 363.
172. Jackson, *The Fall of France*, 210–211.
173. Imlay, *Facing the Second World War*, 359.
174. Richard Toye, *The Roar of the Lion: The Untold Story of Churchill's WWII Speeches* (Oxford: Oxford University Press, 2013), 55–57, 64.
175. Imlay, *Facing the Second World War*, 363.
176. Richard Evans notes that "counterfactualism" is most often mobilized to attack historical "determinism," which in the case of 1940 would be the "decadence" school represented by Jean-Baptiste Duroselle. It also has a "presentist" agenda, such as separating 1940 from "a verdict on France" and emphasizing the contingency of events. In this way, it tells us more

about the present than the past. Because "determinism" emphasizes structural forces, and is more likely to be used by historians of the left, "counterfactualism" is more popular among conservative historians, who deemphasize institutional inertia, ideas, class friction, and so on. "Most 'what-if' versions of the past posit a powerful individual at the heart of their histories," which comes perilously close to "great man" theories of history. But counterfactual scenarios "tread on thin evidentiary ice," and quickly spin out of control because once alternative scenarios are posited, reasoning is no longer linear, becomes arbitrary, leaves out variables, quickly becomes implausible, and risks degenerating into "virtual history" that represents "conservative wishful thinking with a vengeance" – not only "what if," but "if only." Evans, *Altered Past*, 47–59, 85–88, 153, 162, 170, 176.

5 "The War Is Over for Us"

1. Yves Durand, *Prisonniers de guerre dans les Stalags, les Oflags et les Kommandos, 1939–1945* (Paris: Hachette, 1994), 11. OKW claimed to have captured 1,926,000 French POWs, of whom 29,000 were officers. The *Secrétariat d'État aux Anciens Combattants* recognized 1,850,000 POWs. The Red Cross maintained 1,605,000 French POW files. Michel Boivin, *1939–1945: Les Manchois dans la tourment de la Seconde Guerre mondiale*, tome 2, *De la veille de la guerre à la défaite* (Marigny: Éditions Eurocibles, 2004), 128.
2. Joan Beaumont, "Review Article: Prisoners of War in the Second World War," *Journal of Contemporary History*, 42/3 (2007), 535.
3. Fabrice Virgili, *La France "virile": Des femmes tondues à la libération* (Paris: Payot, 2000), 305–306.
4. Sara Fishman, "Grand Delusions: The Unintended Consequences of Vichy France's Prisoner of War Propaganda," *Journal of Contemporary History*, 26/2 (April 1991), 230, 234, 242, 244–246.
5. Richard Bennaïm, *Le Journal du soldat juif* (Lormont: Le Bord de l'Eau, 2017), 65–66.
6. Michel de Cazotte, "Oflag Adventure," unpublished manuscript, Hoover Institution, Stanford University, 44. Evelyne Gayme makes a similar point, *Les Prisonniers de guerre français: Enjeux militaires et stratégiques (1914–1918 et 1940–1945)* (Paris: Economica, 2010), 71.
7. SHD oral archives, Crémieux-Brilhac GR 3K 32–1, Planche 2; 3P 111, Dossier 1, "Enseignements tirés de la campaign de 1939–1940," " B. Valeur physique. Chargement et equipment du fantassin," 3.
8. Gayme, *Les Prisonniers de guerre français*, 53.
9. De Cazotte, "Oflag Adventure," 44.
10. SHD, oral archive, Colonel Dominique Magnant GR 3K 12–1, Planche 7.
11. Durand, *Prisonniers de guerre dans les Stalags, les Oflags et les Kommandos*, 27–34.
12. SHD interviews, Colonel Dominique Magnant GR 3K 12–1, Planche 7.

13. Thomas Vaisset, *L'Amiral d'Argenlieu: Le moine-soldat du gaullisme* (Paris: Belin, 2017), 177–178.
14. Jérémie Halais, *Saint-Lô et son canton dans la tourmente de la Seconde Guerre mondiale 1939–1945* (Saint-Lô: Société d'archéologie et d'histoire de la Manche, 2007), 36.
15. SHD-GR, 3P 115, "Renseignements fournis par l'Adjutant Darchen," 9 October 1940.
16. Pierre Billotte, *Le Temps des armes* (Paris: Plon, 1972), 47.
17. Alain de Boissieu, *Pour combattre avec de Gaulle: Souvenirs 1940–1946* (Paris: Plon, 1981), 56, 63.
18. De Cazotte, "Oflag Adventure," 49.
19. SHD-GR, oral archives, Colonel Dominique Magnant GR 3K 12–1, Planche 7.
20. Boivin, *1939–1945: Les Manchois dans la tourment de la Seconde Guerre mondiale*, tome 2, 129.
21. Michel Boivin, *1939–1945: Les Manchois dans la tourment de la Seconde Guerre mondiale*, tome 3, *L'Occupation: L'ordre allemande, le régime de Vichy et la collaboration* (Marigny: Éditions Eurocibles, 2004), 48.
22. De Cazotte, "Oflag Adventure," 26.
23. François Boudot, "Pour une histoire de la captivité: Souvenirs de qualité," *Annales. Economies, Sociétés, Civilisations*, 12e année, no. 1 (1957), 134.
24. Durand, *Prisonniers de guerre dans les Stalags, les Oflags et les Kommandos*, 12–13; Jean-Pierre Azéma, *1940: L'année noir* (Paris: Fayard, 2010), 221.
25. Boivin, *1939–1945: Les Manchois dans la tourment de la Seconde Guerre mondiale*, tome 2, 131–132; *1939–1945: Les Manchois dans la tourment de la Seconde Guerre mondiale*, tome 3, 38.
26. Jacques Lechevalier, *1939–1945: Ils furent les témoins de la seconde guerre mondiale dans le Cotentin* (published by the author, no date), 16–17.
27. Armelle Mabon, *Prisonniers de guerre "indigènes": Visages oubliés de la France occupée* (Paris: Éditions La Découverte, 2010), 52.
28. Mabon, *Prisonniers de guerre "indigènes,"* 37.
29. The term is that of François Boudot, "Aspects de l'histoire de la captivité," *L'Actualité de l'histoire*, no. 10 (January 1955), 27.
30. Durand, *Prisonniers de guerre dans les Stalags, les Oflags et les Kommandos*, 35–37, 43; Boivin, *1939–1945: Les Manchois dans la tourment de la Seconde Guerre mondiale*, tome 3, 38–39.
31. Durand, *Prisonniers de guerre dans les Stalags, les Oflags et les Kommandos*, 37. Azéma places the figure at around 20,000. Azéma, *1940: L'année noir*, 220.
32. Robert Gildea, *Marianne in Chains: In Search of the German Occupation of France 1940–45* (London: Macmillan, 2002), 92–93.
33. De Boissieu, *Pour combattre avec de Gaulle*, 64.
34. Georges Sadoul, *Journal de Guerre (2 septembre 1939–20 juillet 1940)* (Paris: Éditions l'Harmattan, 1994), 374.
35. Gayme, *Les Prisonniers de guerre français*, 52.
36. Matthias Reiß, "Des nazis à moitié nus: Masculinité et genre dans les camps de prisonniers de guerre allemands aux États-Unis pendant la Seconde Guerre mondiale," in Anne-Marie Pathé and Fabien Théofilakis (eds.),

La Captivité de guerre au XXe siècle: Des Archives, des histoires, des mémoires (Paris: Armand Colin, 2012), 118–127.

37. Pierre Billotte, *Le Temps des armes* (Paris: Plon, 1972), 174.
38. Gayme, *Les Prisonniers de guerre français*, 88–89.
39. Bennaïm, *Le Journal du soldat juif*, 151–152.
40. Edgar Jones and Simon Wessely, "British Prisoners-of-War: From Resilience to Psychological Vulnerability: Reality or Perception, "*Twentieth Century British History*, 21/2 (2010), 166.
41. Gayme, *Les Prisonniers de guerre français*, 21–33.
42. René Rémond, "Des Lendemains qui chantent?," in Jean-Pierre Azéma and François Bédarida (eds.), *La France des années noires*, tome 2, *De l'Occupation à la Libération* (Paris: Éditions du Seuil, 1993), 487–488.
43. See, for instance, the 12 April 1941 report by General Gérodias, Inspector General of the Infantry, who cited the "mediocre quality" of command leadership in the infantry that failed to manage the "encounter battle" as one of six factors that contributed to defeat. SHD-GR, 3P 111, 2–3.
44. Durand, *Prisonniers de guerre dans les Stalags, les Oflags et les Kommandos*, 37–43.
45. The role of rumor is discussed in Paul Fussell, *The Great War and Modern Memory* (New York and London: Oxford University Press, 1975), 115, 121, 124.
46. Boudot, "Pour une histoire de la captivité," 134–135; Boudot, "Aspects de l'histoire de la captivité," 27.
47. SHD, interviews, Crémieux-Brilhac GR 3K 32–1, Planche 2. On transfer to Germany, see Boivin, *1939–1945: Les Manchois dans la tourment de la Seconde Guerre mondiale*, tome 3, 39–40.
48. SHD-GR, 2P 70, "Rapport du Gendarme Codignon Maurice de la Brigade de Doyet (Allier) rapatrié d'Allemagne sur les conditions de son internment et sur les incidents pénibles dont il a été le témoin pendant sa capitivté," 5 November 1941.
49. Boudot, "Pour une histoire de la captivité," 135.
50. De Cazotte, "Oflag Adventure," 50–51, 65.
51. Durand, *Prisonniers de guerre dans les Stalags, les Oflags et les Kommandos*, 43–48.
52. Durand, *Prisonniers de guerre dans les Stalags, les Oflags et les Kommandos*, 65, 175.
53. Fishman, "Grand Delusions," 235–237.
54. Boudot, "Pour une histoire de la captivité," 138.
55. SHD-GR, 2P 71, "Renseignements fournis par les prisonniers de guerre rapatriés," 19 October 1942, 13; Boudot, "Aspects de l'histoire de la captivité," 32–33.
56. SHD-GR, 2P 79, "Renseignements fournis par les prisonniers de guerre rapatriés," Vichy, 19 March 1942.
57. Bob Moore, "Unruly Allies: British Problems with French Treatment of Axis Prisoners of War, 1943–1945," *War in History*, 7/2 (2000), 183–184, 187.

58. SHD-GR, 2P 71, Pavillon to Vichy, 8 August 1942.
59. John Ferris and Evan Mawdsley (eds.), *The Cambridge History of the Second World War*, volume I, *Fighting the War* (Cambridge: Cambridge University Press, 2015), pictures between pp. 466 and 467. Sean McMeekin estimates that 57.5 percent of Soviet POWs died in German captivity, and attributes the high mortality rate to a variety of causes, beginning with the fact that the Germans were simply overwhelmed by the three to four million Soviet POWs who fell into their hands in 1941. The high mortality rate was also tied up with the nature of the race war in the East, as well as reciprocity, as German POWs in Soviet hands also fared badly in the shadow of Hitler's "Commissar Order," and in keeping with the "self-reinforcing logic to this war of attrition on the eastern front." Stalin had refused to sign the 1929 Geneva convention on POWs, withheld names of captured Axis POWs, and banned International Red Cross representatives from inspecting Soviet-run POW camps. But the fundamental problem was that the Soviets refused to accept the legal concept of a POW. They regarded Red Army soldiers captured on the battlefield as "malicious deserters." whom the NKVD was allowed to execute, and whose families were often arrested under the concept of "collective guilt." In these conditions, large numbers of Soviet POWs perished because their government took no interest in their welfare. Soon, Berlin woke up to the fact that Soviet POWs could be useful as workers and even soldiers – 1.5 million Soviet POWs eventually enlisted in the German forces as *Osttruppen*. Sean McMeekin, *Stalin's War: A New History of World War II* (New York: Basic Books, 2021), 313–322.
60. SHD-GR, 2P 71, Pavillon to Vichy, 15 April 1942, 9–11; 2P 70, 8 April 1942, "Reception d'un évadé."
61. Luc Capdevila, "The Quest for Masculinity in a Defeated France, 1940–1945," *Contemporary European History*, 10/3 (November 2001), 423.
62. Irène Némirovsky, *Suite Française* (Paris: Éditions Denoël, 2004), 344–345.
63. Gildea, *Marianne in Chains*, 73, 77–78, 88. See also Chapter 3, "Separation" in Gildea's book for the strains that incarceration in Germany placed on POW marriages. Philippe Burrin, *France under the Germans: Collaboration and Compromise* (New York: The New Press, 1996), 205–209.
64. Julie Le Gac, "L''étrange défaite' du divorce? (1940–1946)," *Vingtième Siècle. Revue d'histoire* 2005/4, no. 88 (2005), 51.
65. Julian Jackson, *France: The Dark Years 1940–1944* (New York: Oxford University Press, 2003), 34–35, 333–335; Sarah Fishman, *We Will Wait: Wives of French Prisoners of War, 1940–1945* (New Haven and London: Yale University Press, 1990), 49–50; Jean-Pierre Azéma and Olivier Wieviorka, *Vichy 1940–1944* (Paris: Perrin, 2004), 174.
66. Luc Capdevila, François Rouquet, Fabrice Virgili, and Danièle Voldman, *Sexes, genre et guerres (France, 1914–1945)* (Paris: Payot, 2010), 139, 209–211.
67. Camille Fauroux, "'Souvenirs d'une petite amie en captivité': Ouvrières françaises et prisonniers de guerrc à Berlin entre 1940 et 1945," *Guerres mondiales et conflits contemporains*, 294 (April–June 2019), 29–37. An October 1942 report said that special brothels were created for POWs, where a visit cost 7 Marks. SHD-GR, 2P 71, 19 October 1942, 15.

68. SHD-GR, 2P 71, Pavillon to Vichy, 30 October 1942, 25; 5 October 1942, 8, 24.
69. Boudot, "Aspects de l'histoire de la captivité," 31.
70. SHD-GR, 2P 70, "Les prisonniers," October 1941.
71. Gayme, *Les Prisonniers de guerre français*, 112, 114–115, 118, 121–124, 141, 145.
72. SHD-GR, 2P 71, 5 June 1942, 11.
73. SHD, oral archives, Crémieux-Brilhac GR 3K 32–1, Planche 3. Jean-Louis Crémieux-Brilhac, *L'étrange victoire: De la défense de la République à la libération de la France* (Paris: Gaillimard, 2016), 61. De Cazotte disagreed, arguing that these antisemitic measures produced a great wave of sympathy for the Jewish officers among them. De Cazotte, "Oflag Adventure," 128.
74. Aron Shneyer, *Pariahs among Pariahs: Soviet-Jewish POWs in German Captivity, 1941–1945* (Jerusalem: Yad Vashem, 2016), 347.
75. SHD-GR, 2P 72, "Oflag X.C. Lubeck," 30–31; Review of Shneyer, *Pariahs among Pariahs*, in *Journal of Military History*, 81/4 (October 2017), 1203.
76. Bennaïm, *Le Journal du soldat juif*, 56, 67.
77. Rüdiger Overmans, "Le traitement allemand des prisonniers de guerre juifs durant la Seconde Guerre mondiale," in Anne-Marie Pathé and Fabien Théofilakis, *La Captivité de guerre au XXe siècle: Des archives, des histoires, des mémoirs* (Paris: Armand Colin, 2012), 59–68.
78. Durand, *Prisonniers de guerre dans les Stalags, les Oflags et les Kommandos*, 213–215.
79. Olivier Wieviorka, *Une Certaine idée de la Résistance: Défense de France 1940–1949* (Paris: Éditions du Seuil, 1995), 25.
80. Wieviorka, *Une Certaine* idée *de la Résistance*, 13.
81. Gayme, *Les Prisonniers de guerre français*, 35, 39, 60.
82. Bennaïm, *Le Journal du soldat juif*, 108–109.
83. SHD, oral archives, GR 3K 39 Colonel André Perrin GR 3K 39–1, Planche 7. Once Perrin reached France, he escaped across the Pyrenees to Spain, where he was again incarcerated. He eventually reached Casablanca in December 1943, then went to Algiers, where he joined military intelligence and became a liaison with the OSS.
84. SHD, oral archives, Crémieux-Brilhac GR 3K 32–1, Planche 3.
85. Boudot, "Pour une histoire de la captivité," 137.
86. The officers were fined 25,000 Marks for "damages," and punished by being forced to hold up their arms in the air all night. Those with previous escape attempts were transferred to Lübeck or other camps, while listening devices were installed throughout the camp. SHD-GR, 2P 71, du Pavillon to Secrétaire d'état à la guerre, 19 October 1942, 5–6.
87. De Cazotte, "Oflag Adventure," Chapter 13, "Escapes."
88. SHD-GR, 2P 72, "Oflag X.C. Lubeck," 37.
89. SHD-GR, 2P 70, "Note du service," General Lucien, 18 February 1942.
90. In 1942, Robert Blum and Stalin's eldest son Yakov Iosifovich Dzhugashvili were both kept under strict surveillance in Lübeck. An artillery officer captured during Barbarossa, Dzhugashvili was frequently in the punishment cells for refusing to salute German officers. SHD-GR, 2P 72, "Oflag

X.C. Lubeck," 40. Dzhugashvili died in 1943, either killed by a camp guard or by suicide.

91. Pierre Daix, *Braudel* (Paris: Flammarion, 1995),187–201.
92. SHD-GR, 2P 72, "Oflag X.C. Lubeck"; Chief of Staff of the Army Picquendar to Secretary of State Bridoux, 15 May 1942, stating that POWs suspected of subversive behavior should be reported to the *Bureau des menées anti-nationales* (BMA), SHD-GR, 2P 66.
93. Pierre Billotte, *Le Temps des armes* (Paris: Plon, 1972), 90–112; Crémieux-Brilhac GR 3K 32–1 1939, Planches 4 and 5; de Boissieu, *Pour combattre avec de Gaulle*, 70–123.
94. Fishman, "Grand Delusions," 237–238.
95. Boudot, "Pour une histoire de la captivité," 133, 138.
96. SHD-GR, 2P 70, Report of July 1942, 2.
97. Belkacem Recham, *Les Musulmans algériens dans l'armée française (1919–1945)* (Paris: Éditions l'Harmattan, 1996), 227–228.
98. De Cazotte, "Oflag Adventure," 180.
99. SHD-GR, 2P 70, Report of April 1942, 11.
100. SHD-GR, 2P 71, "Renseignements fournis par les prisonniers de guerre rapatriés," 15 April 1942, 12
101. SHD-GR, 2P 71, "Renseignements fournis par les prisonniers de guerre rapatriés," 15 April 1942, 16.
102. SHD-GR, 2P 71, "Renseignements fournis par les prisonniers de guerre rapatriés," 15 April 1942, 23.
103. Fabien Théofilakis, *Les Prisonniers de guerre allemandes: France, 1944–1949* (Paris: Fayard, 2014), 566.
104. Joan Beaumont, "Review Article: Prisoners of War in the Second World War," 535.
105. Boudot, "Pour une histoire de la captivité," 134.
106. S. P. Mackenzie, *The Colditz Phenomenon* (Oxford: Oxford University Press, 2006).
107. Bennaïm, *Le Journal du soldat juif*, 130.
108. SHD-GR, 2P 70, "Rapport de l'Adjutant Ragu Jacques, à son retour de captivité," 6 March 1942, 9.
109. SHD, oral archives, Colonel André Perrin GR 3K 39–1, Planche 6.
110. Boudot, "Aspects de l'histoire de la captivité," 35; de Cazotte, "Oflag Adventure," 92–93; SHD-GR, 2P 70, 12 February 1943, reports on factional divisions in various Stalags.
111. Jones and Wessely, "British Prisoners-of-War," 167.
112. Jones and Wessely, "British Prisoners-of-War," 171–173, 176. Most escapes occurred when Italy surrendered in September 1943. But many British POWs were forced to hide out for almost a year before they could regain contact with British troops after the breakthrough at Monte Cassino in May 1944. The authors note that, ironically, British survivors of Japanese POW camps "showed fewer psychiatric symptoms and a much more stable and satisfactory reaction to their captivity than prisoners of war from German hands … due in large measure to the contempt which British soldiers were able to feel for the Japanese and the absence of any feeling

that the enemy was a man of a similar outlook and cultural background to themselves." Jones and Wessely, "British Prisoners-of-War," 177.

113. De Cazotte, "Oflag Adventure," 54–58; SHD-GR, 2P 72, "Oflag X.C. Lubeck," 24.
114. De Boissieu, *Pour combattre avec de Gaulle*, 74.
115. De Cazotte, "Oflag Adventure," 59–60, 63, 70.
116. De Cazotte, "Oflag Adventure," 58, 90.
117. SHD-GR, 2P 72, "Oflag X.C. Lubeck," 23, 36.
118. De Cazotte, "Oflag Adventure," 76–80, 84; SHD-GR, 2P 72, "Oflag X.C. Lubeck," 28.
119. Boudot, "Aspects de l'histoire de la captivité," 33.
120. SHD-GR, 2P 72, "Oflag X.C. Lubeck," 23.
121. SHD-GR, 2P 72, "Oflag X.C. Lubeck," 22.
122. Raffael Scheck, *French Colonial Soldiers in German Captivity during World War II* (Cambridge: Cambridge University Press, 2014), 24.
123. Boivin, *1939–1945: Les Manchois dans la tourment de la Seconde Guerre mondiale*, tome 3, 268. According to de Cazotte, officers tried to remit as large a percentage of their salaries as possible to their families because camp-issued marks were "useless." Furthermore, the French government refused to exchange camp marks for francs at war's end, which is one reason why he believed that the Gaullists were unpopular among former POWs. De Cazotte, "Oflag Adventure," 59, 121–122.
124. As a result, Churchill contemplated turning over 1,000 Italian POWs captured by the British to the Free French as "working capital." It is unclear if he ever did so, because of fears of retaliation against British POWs. Moore, "Unruly Allies," 183–186.
125. De Cazotte, "Oflag Adventure," 97–98.
126. Peter Schöttler, "Fernand Braudel, prisonnnier en Allemagne: Face à la longue durée et au temps présent," in Pathé and Théofilakis (eds.), *La Captivité de guerre au XXe siècle*, 128–140.
127. Boudot, "Aspects de l'histoire de la captivité," 34.
128. Boudot, "Aspects de l'histoire de la captivité," 35; de Cazotte, "Oflag Adventure," 92–93. De Cazotte estimated that 40–45 percent of the officers were "indifferent" to religion, while 10 percent were "violently hostile to religion, in any form." Protestant POWs remained particularly close knit but cordial, while he attributed Catholic religious renewal behind the wire to the fact that priests earned respect through their shared ordeal, since many refused repatriation when offered, and to the presence of exceptionally gifted clerics led by Benedictine, Dominican, and Jesuit POWs. An empty barracks was transformed into a magnificently decorated camp "cathedral," with parish "chapels" on every barrack block. Religious processions were organized on holy days. De Cazotte, "Oflag Adventure,"127–137.
129. De Cazotte, "Oflag Adventure," 87–119. How POWs came to sing this song is unclear, as "Franklin D. Roosevelt Jones" was made popular by the 1941 film *Babes on Broadway*, where it was sung by then nineteen-year-old Judy Garland as part of the film's "Minstrel Show Sequence." However, the song debuted in 1938 with Ella Fitzgerald. Or perhaps de Cazotte's memory was faulty.

130. For daily life in an *Oflag*, see Durand, *Prisonniers de guerre*, 141–156.
131. Gayme, *Les Prisonniers de guerre français*, 44–46.
132. De Cazotte, "Oflag Adventure," 72, 89–90, 138–140.
133. Fishman, "Grand Delusions," 235.
134. Gayme, *Les Prisonniers de guerre français*, 27–28.
135. Fishman, "Grand Delusions," 243.
136. Henry Rousso, *The Vichy Syndrome: History and Memory in France since 1944* (Cambridge, MA: Harvard University Press, 1991), 303.
137. SHD-GR, 2P 13, "Note sur la situation politique," 21 May 1941.
138. Gayme, *Les Prisonniers de guerre français*, 58, 66.
139. SHD-GR, 2P 70, "Les prisonniers," October 1941.
140. Martin Thomas, "The Vichy Government and French Colonial Prisoners of War, 1940–1944," *French Historical Studies*, 25/4 (Fall 2002), 660.
141. Boivin, *1939–1945: Les Manchois dans la tourment de la Seconde Guerre mondiale*, tome 3, 37, 41; Durand, *Prisonniers de guerre dans les Stalags, les Oflags et les Kommandos*, 211.
142. SHD oral archives, Crémieux-Brilhac GR 3K 32–1, Planche 3; Thomas, "The Vichy Government and French Colonial Prisoners of War," 661.
143. 1,000 francs was about $12. Bennaïm, *Le Journal du soldat juif*, 149–150.
144. Burrin, *France under the Germans*, 184–185; H. R. Kedward, *Resistance in Vichy France: A Study of Ideas and Motivation in the Southern Zone 1940–1942* (Oxford: Oxford University Press, 1978), 256.
145. Thomas, "The Vichy Government and French Colonial Prisoners of War," 675.
146. Gayme, *Les Prisonniers de guerre français*, 97–99.
147. Ministère des affaires étrangères, Centre des Archives Diplomatiques de la Courneuve, Papiers d'agents-Archives privées, 661PAAP, Fonds Georges Scapini, www.diplomatie.gouv.fr/IMG/pdf/461paap_cle05cd9d__papiers_georges_scapini.pdf; Robert O. Paxton, *L'armée de Vichy: Le corps des officiers francais 1940–1944* (Paris: Tallandier, 2004), 283.
148. Du Pavillon to Directeur du Service Civil de Recrutement et de Placement des Militaires SHD-GR, 2P 71, 19.
149. SHD-GR, 2P 71, Pavillon to Secrétaire d'état à la guerre, 19 October 1942, 26.
150. Patrice Arnaud, *Les STO: Histoire des français requis en Allemagne nazi 1942–1945* (Paris: Éditions CNRS, 2014), 55–56.
151. Durand, *Prisonniers de guerre dans les Stalags, les Oflags et les Kommandos*, 199–201, 206–208, 257, 318; Fishman, "Grand Delusions," 239.
152. Durand, *Prisonniers de guerre dans les Stalags, les Oflags et les Kommandos*, 17–18, 212–218; Gayme, *Les Prisonniers de guerre français*, 100–101.
153. Billotte, *Le Temps des armes*, 49
154. SHD oral archives, Colonel André Perrin GR 3K 391, Planche 6.
155. SHD-GR, 2P 71, Pavillon, Chef du service d'accueil et d'information gare de Mâcon to Directeur du service civil de recrutement et de placement des militaires du carrière à Vichy, 27 May 1942.
156. Marie Vassiltchikov, *Berlin Diaries 1940–1945* (New York: Vintage Books, 1988), 93.

157. SHD-GR, 2P 71, "Renseignements fournis par les prisonniers de guerre rapatriés," 19 March 1942, 14
158. SHD-GR, 2P 70, "Réflexions d'un officier supérieur de l'activité rapatrié," 23 October 1941.
159. Gayme, *Les Prisonniers de guerre français*, 148–149, 157. The 1929 Geneva Convention Relative to the Treatment of Prisoners of War, Article 31, https://ihl-databases.icrc.org/customary-ihl/eng/docs/v1_rul_rule95. Durand, *Prisonniers de guerre dans les Stalags, les Oflags et les Kommandos*, 106.
160. SHD-GR, 2P 70, "Rapport du Général A. Lucien," 9 February 1943.
161. Durand, *Prisonniers de guerre dans les Stalags, les Oflags et les Kommandos*, 241–243, 250–253, 258.
162. Burrin, *France under the Germans*, 138–139.
163. SHD-GR, 2P 71, "Renseignements fournis par les prisonniers de guerre rapatriés," 27 May 1942, 3.
164. SHD-GR, 2P 71, Pavillon to Vichy, 19 October 1942, 5.
165. Boudot, "Aspects de l'histoire de la captivité," 29.
166. Crémieux-Brilhac, *L'étrange victoire*, 62.
167. Fishman, "Grand Delusions," 234.
168. Boudot, "Pour une histoire de la captivité," 138.
169. Boudot, "Aspects de l'histoire de la captivité," 31–32; Boudot, "Pour une histoire de la captivité," 135; Bennaïm, *Le Journal du soldat juif*, 97.
170. Durand, *Prisonniers de guerre dans les Stalags, les Oflags et les Kommandos*, 207–209; Boudot, "Aspects de l'histoire de la captivité," 31; Fishman, "Grand Delusions," 239–240.
171. Gayme, *Les Prisonniers de guerre français*, 117–118.
172. Durand, *Prisonniers de guerre dans les Stalags, les Oflags et les Kommandos*, 65–67, 69–98, 195–196.
173. Sarah Fishman, *We Will Wait*, xvii, 49–50, 54, 58–59, 80.
174. Gayme, *Les Prisonniers de guerre français*, 57.
175. Jackson, *France: The Dark Years*, 174.
176. Mabon, *Prisonniers de guerre "indigènes,"* 40–63.
177. Yves Durand, *La Captivité: Histoire des prisonniers de guerre francais 1939–1945* (Paris: FNCPG-CATM, 1980), 34. Discussed in Burrin, *France under the Germans*, 143.
178. Richard Vinen, *The Unfree French* (New Haven: Yale University Press, 2007), 212.
179. Marc Hillel, *L'occupation française en Allemagne 1945–1949* (Paris: Balland, 1983), 64–66. In 1949, Scapini escaped to Switzerland to avoid a trial, which sentenced him to five years' hard labor. He returned to France in 1952, where a military tribunal acquitted him.

6 "The Wisdom of a Great Leader"

1. Philippe Burrin, *France under the Germans: Collaboration and Compromise* (New York: The New Press, 1996), 32–33.
2. Burrin, *France under the Germans*, 73.

3. Pertinax (André Géraud), *The Gravediggers of France: Gamelin, Daladier, Reynaud, Petain, and Laval. Military Defeat, Armistice, Counterrevolution* (Garden City, New York: Doubleday, Doran & Company, 1944), 334.
4. Pertinax, *The Gravediggers of France*, 333.
5. Elizabeth Greenhalgh, *The French Army and the First World War* (Cambridge: Cambridge University Press, 2014), 213.
6. Pertinax, *The Gravediggers of France*, 333–334.
7. Henry Rousso, *The Vichy Syndrome: History and Memory in France since 1944* (Cambridge, MA: Harvard University Press, 1991), 7.
8. Jean-Pierre Azéma, *1940: L'année noir* (Paris: Fayard, 2010), 258–266.
9. William D. Leahy, *I Was There: The Personal Story of the Chief of Staff to Presidents Roosevelt and Truman Based on His Notes and Diaries Made at the Time* (London: Victor Gollancz, 1950), 22, 62, 75.
10. Robert O. Paxton, *L'armée de Vichy: Le corps des officiers français 1940–1944* (Paris: Tallandier, 2004), 151; Leahy, *I Was There*, 43.
11. Charles de Gaulle, *Mémoires de guerre*, tome 1, *L'Appel (1940–1942)* (Paris: Plon, 1994), 68.
12. Robert O. Paxton, *Vichy France: Old Guard and New Order, 1940–1944* (London: Barrie & Jenkins, 1972), 32–35, 44–45.
13. Pierre Servent, *Le mythe Pétain: Verdun ou les tranchées de la mémoire* (Paris: Éditions CNRS, 2014), 231.
14. Guillaume Piketty, *Français en résistance: Carnet de guerre, correspondances, journaux personnels* (Paris: Robert Laffont, 2009), 192.
15. SHD-GR, 3P 113, Dossier 2, Captain Paul Gail, "Rapport sur les enseignements à tirer de la guerre." 24 August 1940, 9.
16. Servent, *Le mythe Pétain*, 239.
17. Paxton, *L'armée de Vichy*, 22–28.
18. Servent, *Le mythe Pétain*, 227–228, 231, 233–234; Burrin, *France under the Germans*, 9, 72–74.
19. Paxton, *Vichy France*, 136–185; Martin Thomas, "The Vichy Government and French Colonial Prisoners of War, 1940–1944," *French Historical Studies*, 25/4 (Fall 2002), 659.
20. Robert Belot, *La Résistance sans de Gaulle* (Paris: Fayard, 2006), 57, 65, 91, 258–259.
21. Burrin, *France under the Germans*, 76.
22. Belot, *La Résistance sans de Gaulle*, 283.
23. Jean-Pierre Azéma and Olivier Wieviorka, *Vichy 1940–1944* (Paris: Perrin, 2004), 39, 42.
24. Evelyne Gayme, *Les Prisonniers de guerre français: Enjeux militaires et stratégiques (1914–1918 et 1940–1945)* (Paris: Economica, 2010), 76.
25. Thomas Vaisset, *L'Amiral d'Argenlieu: Le moine-soldat du gaullisme* (Paris: Belin, 2017), 186.
26. Pierre Péan, *Une jeunesse française: François Mitterand, 1934–1947* (Paris: Fayard, 1994), 188, 197.
27. Phillips Payson O'Brien, *The Second Most Powerful Man in the World: The Life of Admiral William D. Leahy, Roosevelt's Chief of Staff* (New York: Dutton, 2019), 151.

28. On lack of respect for authority, see "Rapport sur mes impressions de la guerre" by Lieutenant Rieffel of the 79th Infantry Regiment, 20 March 1941, SHD-GR, 3P 111; "Note sur la reconstitution de l'armée allemande à partir de novembre 1918," 9 July 1940, SHD-GR, 3P 102; Robert O. Paxton, *Parades and Politics at Vichy: The French Officer Corps under Marshal Pétain* (Princeton: Princeton University Press, 1966), 185.
29. Paxton, *L'armée de Vichy*, 198.
30. Claude d'Abzac-Epezy, *L'Armée de l'air des années noires: Vichy 1940–1944* (Paris: Economica, 1998), 1–2.
31. Paxton, *Vichy France*, 20.
32. Paxton, *L'armée de Vichy*, 72, 79; Burrin, *France under the Germans*, 463; Gérard Saint-Martin, *L'arme blindée française*, tome 2, *1940–1945: Dans le fracas des batailles* (Paris: Economica, 2000), 45.
33. Michael R. Marrus and Robert O. Paxton, *Vichy France and the Jews* (New York: Basic Books, 1981), 7, 126–127.
34. Pierre-André Taguieff, "L'invention du 'complot Judéo-Maçonnique.' Avatars d'un mythe apocalyptique moderne," *Revue d'Histoire de la Shoah*, 2013/1, no. 98 (2013), 28–30.
35. Paxton, *Parades and Politics at Vichy*, 174–176.
36. Alain Bauer and Roger Dachez, *Nouvelle histoire des francs-maçons en France: Des origines à nos jours* (Paris: Tallandier, 2018), 495–510.
37. Robert Belot, *La Résistance sans de Gaulle*, 251. On plans for the Armistice Army to facilitate an Allied invasion of the south coast, see André Martel (ed.), *Histoire militaire de la France*, tome 4, *De 1940 à nos jours* (Paris: Presses universitaires de France, 1994), 26–27.
38. Belot, *La Résistance sans de Gaulle*, 92, 258–259.
39. Paxton, *L'armée de Vichy*, 171–175, 240, 243; Julian Jackson, *France: The Dark Years 1940–1944* (New York: Oxford University Press, 2003), 147. For the turmoil following the 1830 Revolution, see Douglas Porch, *Army and Revolution: The French Army 1815–1848* (London: Routledge and Kegan Paul, 1974).
40. Paxton, *L'armée de Vichy*, 65.
41. Leahy, *I Was There*, 107.
42. "The treatise entitled 'The French Army.' Status on June 20, 1942." OB West. NARA, RG 165, Entry 77, Box 865.
43. Paxton, *L'armée de Vichy*, 81–88, 164–165, 243.
44. Paxton, *L'armée de Vichy*, 55–63, 176–177, 198–199, 225–226.
45. Belot, *La Résistance sans de Gaulle*, 258–263.
46. Belot, *La Résistance sans de Gaulle*, 283.
47. Jackson, *France: The Dark Years*, 141.
48. According to Pierre Pellissier, André Laffargue was the only other Vichy division commander to take defensive action. However, unlike de Lattre, he was not punished. Pierre Pellissier, *De Lattre* (Paris: Perrin, 1998), 238. Presumably, this was because Laffargue was considered to be more reliable by the Vichy elite than was the mercurial de Lattre. Although Laffargue was later to assist de Lattre's First Army on the Liberation, he testified for the defense in Pétain's post-war trial.

49. Belot, *La Résistance sans de Gaulle*, 250.
50. Jacques Cantier, *L'Algérie sous le régime de Vichy* (Paris: Éditions Odile Jacob, 2002), 394.
51. Paxton, *Parades and Politics at Vichy*, 374, 376.
52. Lacouture writes that Colonel Jean de Lattre de Tassigny was "more or less involved" in the 6 February 1934 demonstrations by the right-wing Leagues that degenerated into an anti-parliamentary riot, although he does not elaborate. The left charged that the demonstrations were a harbinger of an attempted right-wing overthrow of the Republic. Lacouture, *De Gaulle*, tome 1, 223.
53. Pertinax, *The Gravediggers of France*, 19. Another version of this incident, recounted by Pierre Pellissier, was that Weygand ordered de Lattre to convey the army chief's objections to de Gaulle's book, which were basically three: France required a citizen army; de Gaulle's proposal was budget busting; and finally, Weygand objected to de Gaulle enlisting Reynaud, or any politician for that matter, to press his ideas. Another of Pertinax's guests, Le Provost de Launay, remembered that de Lattre deployed all the tact and diplomacy for which he was to become famous, to lay out his boss's objections. De Lattre's effort was wasted on de Gaulle, "in his fierce solitude, always wanting to be right in the face of all opposition, even that of his best friends." Pellissier, *De Lattre*, 143–144.
54. Ivan Cadeau, *De Lattre* (Paris: Perrin, 2017), 152–157; Pellissier, *De Lattre*, 230–250; Bernard Destremau, *De Lattre* (Paris: Flammarion, 1999), 257–281; Claire Miot, "Sortir l'armée des ombres. Soldats de l'Empire, combattants de la Libération, armée de la Nation: La Première armée française, du débarquement en Provence à la capitulation allemande (1944–1945)," Thèse du doctorat, Université Paris-Saclay, 2016, 71–75.
55. See, for instance, Marc Olivier Baruch, *Servir l'État français: L'administration en France de 1940 à 1944* (Paris: Fayard, 1997); and Issac Levendel, *Not Germans Alone: A Son's Search for the Truth of Vichy* (Chicago: Northwestern University Press, 2001).
56. Paxton, *L'armée de Vichy*, 134, 308–321; Martel (ed.), *Histoire militaire de la France*, tome 4, 26–27.
57. Belot, *La Résistance sans de Gaulle*, 253–254, 258.
58. Philip Nord, "Vichy et les survivances: Les Compagnons de France," *Revue d'histoire moderne et contemporaine*, 2012/4, no. 59-4 (2012), 125–163.
59. Bernard Comte, "L'école d'Uriage: De la défaite à la résistance armée par l'éducation," in Jean-William Dereymez et al. (ed.), *Les militaires dans la résistance: Ain – Dauphiné – Savoie 1940–1944* (Avon-les-Roches: Éditions Anovi, 2010), 67–69.
60. Olivier Faron, *Les chantiers de jeunesse: Avoir 20 ans sous Pétain* (Paris: Grasset, 2011), 34.
61. Paxton, *L'armée de Vichy*, 221; Pellissier, *De Lattre*, 197.
62. Comte, "L'école d'Uriage," 70–73.
63. Eugen Weber, "France's Downfall," *The Atlantic* (October 2001), www.theatlantic.com/magazine/archive/2001/10/frances-downfall/302317/.
64. Romain Durand, *De Giraud à de Gaulle: Les Corps francs d'Afrique* (Paris: Éditions l'Harmattan, 1999), 17.
65. Charles de Gaulle, *Mémoires de guerre*, tome 1, *L'Appel (1940–1942)* (Paris: Plon, 1994), 53–54.
66. Faron, *Les chantiers de jeunesse*, 12, 31, 33.

67. Faron, *Les chantiers de jeunesse*, 34. De Lattre is believed to have been "probably bi-sexual." Jeffrey Merrick and Michael Sibalis (eds.), *Homosexuality in French History and Culture* (Binghampton, New York: Routledge, 2012), 208.
68. Pellissier insists that de Lattre was never in the running to head the *Chantiers*. Pellissier, *De Lattre*, 202–204; Faron, *Les chantiers de jeunesse*, 35.
69. With the goal of better preparing French youth for the experience of military service, these societies were qualified to issue a *brevet d'aptitude militaire* to those able to pass a physical fitness test. The criticism was that the test was too easy. But when, in 1914, the war ministry raised the score required to secure the *brevet*, the failure rate rocketed to 75 percent. The push to introduce physical education in French schools largely foundered on the lack of qualified PE teachers before 1914. Douglas Porch, *The March to the Marne: The French Army 1871–1914* (Cambridge: Cambridge University Press, 1981), 206–210. At this time, French naval officer Georges Hébert, inspired like Olympic Games impresario Pierre de Coubertin by ancient Greek athletics, pioneered the reform of physical training for the French marines at Lorient, by, among other things, giving it a moral dimension. What became known as Hébertism was eventually adopted by some French educational institutions.
70. Faron, *Les chantiers de jeunesse*, 31.
71. Richard Davenport-Hines (ed.), *Letters from Oxford: Hugh Trevor-Roper to Bernard Berenson* (London: Phoenix, 2007), 88. For a discussion of the scouting movement in America, see David E. Shi, *The Simple Life: Plain Living and High Thinking in American Culture* (Athens and London: University of Georgia Press, 2007), 207–212.
72. Faron, *Les chantiers de jeunesse*, 63, 68, 105–106.
73. Paxton, *L'armée de Vichy*, 227–237.
74. Pellissier, *De Lattre*, 203–204.
75. Henry Rousso, *Pétain et la fin de la collaboration: Sigmaringen, 1944–1945* (Brussels: Complexe, 1984), 338. Quoted in Faron, *Les chantiers de jeunesse*, 15.
76. Jean-Pierre Azéma, "*Statistiques sans conscience n'est que ruine ...*" (Paris: Syndicats CFDT-CGT de l'Insee, 1998), quoted in Johanna Barasz, "De Vichy à la Résistance: Les vichysto-résistants 1940–1944," *Guerres mondiales et conflits contemporains*, 2011/2, no. 242 (2011), 27–50, www.cairn.info/revue-guerres-mondiales-et-conflits-contemporains-2011-2-page-27.htm#no14.
77. Durand, *De Giraud à de Gaulle*, 18, 22; Benjamin Stora, *Histoire de l'Algérie coloniale (1830–1954)* (Paris: Éditions La Découverte, 2004), 37.
78. Frédéric Harymbat, *Les Européens d'Afrique du Nord dans les armées de la libération française (1942–1945)* (Paris: Éditions l'Harmattan, 2014), 100–101.
79. Jean-Louis Crémieux-Brilhac, *La France libre*, tome 1, *De l'appel du 18 juin à la libération* (Paris: Gallimard, 2001), 586–594, 654.
80. Faron, *Les chantiers de jeunesse*, 13–14, 255, 282–286, 311–312; Azéma and Wieviorka, *Vichy 1940–1944*, 172.
81. D'Abzac-Epezy, *L'Armée de l'air des années noires*, 27, 29.
82. D'Abzac-Epezy, *L'Armée de l'air des années noires*, 31, 33–36.
83. François Kersaudy, *Churchill and de Gaulle* (London: Collins, 1981), 83–84.
84. Martin Thomas, "After Mers-el-Kebir: The Armed Neutrality of the Vichy Navy," *English Historical Review*, 112/447 (June 1997), 650–651.
85. Paxton, *L'armée de Vichy*, 131; Thomas, "After Mers-el-Kebir," 652–653.

86. Edgard de Larminat, *Chroniques irrévérencieuses* (Paris: Plon, 1962), 85; Jean-François Muracciole, *Les Français libres: L'autre Résistance* (Paris: Tallandier, 2009), 135.
87. Vaisset, *L'Amiral d'Argenlieu*, 194–198. Paxton agrees that Dakar was the more important event in shaping Anglo-French relations. Paxton, *L'armée de Vichy*, 151.
88. Philippe Masson, *La marine française et la guerre 1939–1945* (Paris: Tallandier, 1991), 181–189.
89. Belot, *La Résistance sans de Gaulle*, 323.
90. Paxton, *L'armée de Vichy*, 89–95, 102–103, 130–131.
91. D'Abzac-Epezy, *L'Armée de l'air des années noires*, 51–53, 57, 59.
92. The ninth occasion occurred during a brief war with Thailand in January 1941, when, encouraged by Tokyo, Bangkok claimed territory in French Indochina. The French ground campaign failed after French indigenous troops disbanded and deserted. Face was saved by the navy, which defeated the Thai navy in the Battle of Ko Chang. Nevertheless, the Japanese intervened to force the French to cede border provinces in Cambodia and Laos to Bangkok. Philippe Franchini, *Les Guerres d'Indochine*, tome 1, *Des origines de la présence française à l'engrenage du conflit international* (Paris: Éditions Pygmalion, 1988), 156; Martel (ed.), *Histoire militaire de la France*, tome 4, 60.
93. D'Abzac-Epezy, *L'Armée de l'air des années noires*, 5, 374, 376.
94. Azéma and Wieviorka, *Vichy 1940–1944*, 31, 37, 54, 65–67. For the text of the Armistice, see http://mjp.univ-perp.fr/france/1940armistice.htm.
95. Barbara Lambauer, "Un engagement pour l'Europe allemande: La collaboration," in Alya Aglan and Robert Frank (eds.), *1937–1947: La guerre-monde* (Paris: Gallimard/Folio, 2015), 1109–1110.
96. Lambauer, "Un engagement pour l'Europe allemande," 1121–1122.
97. Azéma and Wieviorka, *Vichy 1940–1944*, 65–66.
98. Masson, *La marine française et la guerre 1939–1945*, 189.
99. Azéma and Wieviorka, *Vichy 1940–1944*, 73.
100. Paul Sanders, "Anatomie d'une implantation SS – Helmut Knochen et la police nazie en France, 1940–1944," *Revue d'histoire de la Shoah*, 165 (January–April 1999), 121–122.
101. The "zone interdite" was a swath of territory created on 20 July 1940 that ran roughly from the Somme to the Swiss frontier. It ran through the north of the departments of the Somme, Aisne, the Ardennes, part of Lorraine, part of the territory of Belfort, part of the Haute-Marne, Marne, and Côte-d'Or. The departments of the Nord and the Pas-de-Calais were placed under the German military administration in Brussels. Those who had fled were forbidden to return. Hitler intended to use part of this territory for German settlement.
102. The German police were responsible for overseeing the French police and administration, as well as collecting information on French politics, culture, and the economy. They depended on denunciations, often for personal or economic motives, as well as assistance from ideological sympathizers. The amateurism, lack of security consciousness in many resistance networks, and "breakdowns" which occurred when multiple Allied services were operating, but not cooperating, in the same area also benefited the Sipo/SD. Sanders, "Anatomie d'une implantation SS," 130, 139–145.

103. Azéma and Wieviorka, *Vichy 1940–1944*, 54–55.
104. Azéma and Wieviorka, *Vichy 1940–1944*, 53, 81.
105. Servent, *Le mythe Pétain*, 253–255; Burrin, *France under the Germans*, 459.
106. Miot, "Sortir l'armée des ombres," 519–520.
107. Pierre Rigoulot, *L'Alsace-Lorraine pendant la guerre 1939–1945* (Paris: Presses universitaire de France, 1997), 126.
108. Eugène Riedweg, *Les "malgré nous": Histoire de l'incorporation de force des Alsaciens-Mosellans dans l'armée allemande* (Strasbourg: La Nuée Bleue, 2008), 324; Jackson, *France: The Dark Years*, 237, 247–248.
109. Pierre Weisenhorn, "Les Alsaciens-Lorrains enrôlés dans l'armée Allemande," in Yves Jeanclos (ed.), *La France et les soldats d'infortune au XXe siècle* (Strasbourg: Economica, 2003), 25.
110. Rigoulot, *L'Alsace-Lorraine pendant la guerre 1939–1945*, 24.
111. Weisenhorn, "Les Alsaciens-Lorrains enrôlés dans l'armée Allemande," 26–27.
112. Rigoulot, *L'Alsace-Lorraine pendant la guerre 1939–1945*, 29.
113. Nina Barbier, *Malgré-elles: Les Alsaciennes et Mosellanes incorporées de force dans la machine de guerre nazi* (Paris: Tallandier, 2018), 79.
114. Rigoulot, *L'Alsace-Lorraine pendant la guerre 1939–1945*, 24.
115. Riedweg, *Les "malgré nous,"* 54–55, 294.
116. Riedweg, *Les "malgré nous,"* 26–27.
117. Riedweg, *Les "malgré nous,"* 17–22.
118. Philippe Valode and Gérard Chauvy, *La Gestapo française* (Paris: Éditions Acropole, 2018), 64–82.
119. Rigoulot, *L'Alsace-Lorraine pendant la guerre 1939–1945*, 36.
120. Barbier, *Malgré-elles*, 30.
121. Rigoulot, *L'Alsace-Lorraine pendant la guerre 1939–1945*, 43, 49.
122. This included bi-weekly meetings of the *Hitlerjugend* (HJ, Hitler Youth), which grew to 130,000 members, and became increasingly focused on military preparation for boys, which amounted mainly to drill and tossing practice grenades. Also, a *Bund Deutscher Mädel* (BDM, Association of German Girls); a *Nationalsozialistisches Kraftfahrerkorps* (NSFK, National Socialist Drivers Corps); a *Nationalsozialistische Fliegerkorps*, for those with aspirations of being blown out of the sky; the *Sturmabteilung* (SA or Brownshirts); the NS *Frauenschaft* for women; and above all the *Deutsche Arbeitsfront* (DAF), which replaced trades unions, completed the list of new institutions. Apart from the NS *Frauenschaft*, which was basically an apolitical mutual aid organization, and the DAF, which presumably all workers were required to join, collectively these organizations managed to attract only 2.65 percent of the population. Azéma and Wieviorka, *Vichy 1940–1944*, 259.
123. Riedweg, *Les "malgré nous,"* 110–114.
124. Barbier, *Malgré-elles*, 51–52.
125. Barbier, *Malgré-elles*, 42, 43, 51, 68, 84, 88.
126. Riedweg, *Les "malgré nous,"* 29, 63, 143–144; Burrin, *France under the Germans*, 49–51, 362–365; Charles Mitschi, "L'Incorporation de force," in Jeanclos (ed.), *La France et les soldats d'infortune au XXe siècle*, 55.
127. The solution was to bestow German citizenship on those who had German grandparents. Those living in Alsace-Moselle between 1870

and 1918 had been German citizens, and so qualified. Riedweg, *Les "malgré nous,"* 69–75.

128. Barbier, *Malgré-elles*, 36–37; Riedweg, *Les "malgré nous,"* 156.
129. Riedweg, *Les "malgré nous,"* 156–166.
130. Riedweg, *Les "malgré nous,"* 167–172.
131. Barbier, *Malgré-elles*, 148–149, 153.
132. Riedweg, *Les "malgré nous,"*` 124–127.
133. Barbier, *Malgré-elles*, 105–107, 110, 146, 155–156.
134. Barbier, *Malgré-elles*, 188–212.
135. Riedweg, *Les "malgré nous,"* 177–184, 237.
136. Philippe Carrard, *The French Who Fought for Hitler* (Cambridge: Cambridge University Press, 2010), 169–170.
137. Pierre Rostaing, *Le Prix d'un serment: 1941–1945. Des plaines de Russie à l'enfer de Berlin* (Paris: La Table Ronde, 1975), 222.
138. Christian de la Mazière, *Ashes of Honour* (London: Allan Wingate, 1975), 143, 195.
139. Ronald Smelser and Edward J. Davies II, *The Myth of the Eastern Front: The Nazi–Soviet War in American Popular Culture* (Cambridge: Cambridge University Press, 2008), 248–249.
140. Rostaing, *Le Prix d'un serment*, 40, 217, 231. Carrard discusses the myth of "Mongolian" human wave assaults. Carrard, *The French Who Fought for Hitler*, 61. On rapes, see André Bayle, *De Marseille à Novossibirsk* (Sausset-Les-Pins: André Bayle, 1992), 176. Nor was this view necessarily inaccurate, but underpins Sean McMeekin's thesis in *Stalin's War: A New History of World War II* (New York: Basic Books, 2021).
141. Carrard, *The French Who Fought for Hitler*, 170, 192–193.
142. Burrin calculates that 12,000 were serving in German uniform in the summer of 1944, 10,000 in auxiliary service, to which were added 1,800 from *La Milice*. Burrin, *France under the Germans*, 436. Krisztián Bene calculates that 29,360 to 34,360 French people were serving directly in German units or support services. Krisztián Bene, *La collaboration militaire française dans la Seconde Guerre mondiale* (Talmont St Hilaire: Éditions-Codex, 2012), 389–390.
143. Carrard, *The French Who Fought for Hitler*, 178; J. Delperrie de Bayac, *Histoire de la Milice 1918–1945* (Paris: Fayard, 1969), 529.
144. Smelser and Davies, *The Myth of the Eastern Front*, 252, 258–259.
145. Rostaing, *Le Prix d'un serment*, 21.
146. De la Mazière, *Ashes of Honour*, 41.
147. Bayle, *De Marseille à Novossibirsk*, 12.
148. Carrard, *The French Who Fought for Hitler*, 135.
149. Rostaing, *Le Prix d'un serment*, 25.
150. Bayle, *De Marseille à Novossibirsk*, 64.
151. Antoine Béthouart, *Cinq années d'espérance: Mémoires de guerre 1939–1945* (Paris: Plon, 1968), 93.
152. Rostaing, *Le Prix d'un serment*, 23–24.
153. J. G. Shields, "Charlemagne's Crusaders. French Collaborators in Arms," *French Cultural Studies*, 18/1 (February 2007), 101.

154. After time in various prisons, Collette was deported to Mauthausen, where he miraculously survived, to be decorated as a resistance hero after the war, despite a history of involvement in right-wing groups. "Étude sur la légion des volontaires français contre le bolchévisme," 1 June 1942; George Augey, armorer, letter of 20 November 1941 on the political vendettas in the LVF; and "Rapport concernant l'esprit, l'organisation et l'activité de la Légion française antibolchévique," 12 December 1941, SHD-GR, 2P 14.
155. J. G. Shields, "Charlemagne's Crusaders. French Collaborators in Arms," *French Cultural Studies*, 18/1 (February 2007), 102.
156. Burrin, *France under the Germans*, 436; SHD-GR, 2P 14, 24 June 1943.
157. "... it was reliable reported that the figure [of the LVF] in fact never exceeded 3,500. The volunteers included many Italians, Russians, and even Germans resident in France. At first, enlistment was accepted without any examination of the volunteer's antecedents, with the result that 40 percent of the recruits turned out to be habitual criminals and at least 20 percent suspects. From time to time, numerous arrests were carried out at the Borgnes [sic] barracks, and those taken in custody included murders, thieves and pimps. Further, a number of men volunteered not only to escape police who were pursuing them for common law crimes, but to escape political police. Thus, among the recruits were even found a few Jews. The junior officers and some of the N.C.O.s were chosen from the ranks of the M.S.R. and the P.P.F., and there was frequent dissension in the ranks. From a military point of view, therefore, the role of the Legion was never more than negligible." "Recruiting of French Forces against the Soviets," American Consulate General, Algiers, 22 January 1942. NARA, RG 166, Entry 77, Box 866.
158. Memorandum to Consul General H. Earle Russell, "Desertions from French Legion attached to German Army in Russia," Casablanca, March 12 1942. NARA, RG 165, Entry 77, Box 866.
159. Shields, "Charlemagne's Crusaders," 85–88. According to Colonel Roger Labonne, the LVF's first commander, an initial surge of 20,000 volunteers was rapidly reduced because of the uniform issue, and because of political disagreements among the three French right-wing leaders, fomented in his opinion by the Gestapo at the direction of the German embassy with a view of sabotaging the LVF. Doriot attached himself to the regimental staff, and actively sought to eliminate supporters of his two rivals from the regiment. Rapport du Colonel Labonne sur la création et la composition de la L.V. F.," SHD-GR, 7P 133, 15 May 1945.
160. Paxton, *Vichy France*, 315.
161. Chris Bishop, *Hitler's Foreign Divisions: Foreign Volunteers in the Waffen-SS 1940–1945* (Staplehurst: Spellmount, 2005), 38–40.
162. "Le brigade Charlemagne," SHD-GR 7P 133, 28 December 1945.
163. "Au sujet du Recrutement des Volontaires pour la L.V.F. provenant des formations dissoutes de l'Armée d'Armistice," 14 August 1943. Also SHD-GR 2P 14, 4 January, 13 August, and 31 July 1943.
164. Rostaing, *Le Prix d'un serment*, 41–43; letter from Adjutant Albert Rolland, SHD-GR 12P 14, 27 December 1941.
165. Alexander Hill, *The Red Army and the Second World War* (Cambridge: Cambridge University Press, 2019), 270–271.
166. Hill, *The Red Army and the Second World War*, 266–267.

167. Ben H. Shepherd, "Guerrillas and Counterinsurgency," in John Ferris and Evan Mawdsley (eds.), *The Cambridge History of the Second World War*, volume I, *Fighting the War* (Cambridge: Cambridge University Press, 2015), 696–700.
168. Hill, *The Red Army and the Second World War*, 280.
169. Hill, *The Red Army and the Second World War*, 282–287.
170. "Expédition de Dubowoje," 9 February 1943. Battalion commander Simoni denounced these accusations as a partisan calumny. Also SHD-GR 2P 14, 23 April 1943.
171. Rostaing, *Le Prix d'un serment*, 45–84
172. SHD-GR, 2P 14, 26 June 1943.
173. Shepherd, "Guerrillas and Counterinsurgency," 696–700.
174. Rostaing, *Le Prix d'un serment*, 84–106; Giolitto, *Histoire de la milice*, 487.
175. Alexander Hill, *The War behind the Eastern Front: The Soviet Partisan Movement in North-West Russia 1941–1944* (London and New York: Frank Cass, 2005), 5, 132–133, 171–177; Shepherd, "Guerrillas and Counterinsurgency," 703–703, 714.

7 La France libre

1. "Je dis l'honneur! Car la France s'est engagée à ne déposer les armes que d'accord avec les Alliés. Tant que ses Alliés continuent la guerre, son gouvernement n'a pas le droit de se rendre à l'ennemi. Le Gouvernement polonais, le Gouvernement norvégien, le Gouvernement belge, le Gouvernement hollandais, le Gouvernement luxembourgeois, quoique chassés de leur territoire, ont compris ainsi leur devoir." From www.france-libre.net/differents-textes-de-lappel.
2. Jacques Sapir, Frank Stora, and Loïc Mahé, *1940: Et si la France avait continué la guerre . . .* (Paris: Tallandier, 2010), 31–34.
3. Jean-Noël Vincent, *Les forces françaises dans la lutte contre l'Axe en Afrique*, tome I, *Les forces françaises libres en Afrique 1940–1943* (Vincennes: Service historique de l'armée de terre, 1983), 21. Jean-François Muracciole places FFL numbers at 70,000, of whom 63,000 were combat troops; 32,000 of them were French citizens, 3,000 were foreigners, while 33,000 were colonial subjects. Jean-François Muracciole, "Le devenir des officiers Français libres après la guerre," in Claire Miot, Guillaume Piketty, and Thomas Vaisset (eds.), *Militaires en résistances en France et en Europe* (Villeneuve d'Ascq: Presses universitaires du Septentrion, 2020),185.
4. Olivier Wieviorka, *Histoire de la Résistance 1940–1945* (Paris: Perrin, 2013), 19–21.
5. Vincent, *Les forces françaises dans la lutte contre l'Axe en Afrique*, tome I, 15.
6. Charles de Gaulle, *Mémoires de guerre*, tome 1, *L'Appel (1940–1942)* (Paris: Plon, 1994), 57. For text of 18 June 1940, see www.gouvernement.fr/partage/8708-l-appel-du-18-juin-du-general-de-gaulle.
7. Jean-François Muracciole, *Les Français libres: L'autre Résistance* (Paris: Tallandier, 2009), 176. Included in this exclusion were army officers and French women, who were not allowed to vote before 1945, as well as foreign

enlistees, most categories of imperial subjects, and those French male enlistees too young to vote in 1939.

8. De Gaulle, *Mémoires de guerre*, tome 1, 91.
9. A corps of monarchist émigrés organized by Louis XVI's cousin the Prince de Condé and financed by the British, that fought against Revolutionary France between 1792 and 1800 in the ranks of the Austrian and Russian armies.
10. SHD-GR, 3P 102. "Situation en Angleterre à la date du 17 septembre," 17 October 1940.
11. R. Toye, *The Roar of the Lion: The Untold Story of Churchill's World War II Speeches* (Oxford: Oxford University Press, 2013), 62.
12. Rachel Chin, "After the Fall. British Strategy and the Preservation of the Franco-British Alliance in 1940, "*Journal of Contemporary History*, 55/2 (2019), 10–11, https://journals.sagepub.com/doi/abs/10.1177/0022009419846951.
13. Chin, "After the Fall," 12.
14. Chin, "After the Fall," 8–10.
15. Martin Thomas and Richard Toye, *Arguing about Empire: Imperial Rhetoric in Britain and France, 1882–1956* (Oxford: Oxford University Press, 2017), 166–167.
16. Chin, "After the Fall," 18.
17. Muracciole, *Les Français libres*, 92; Philippe Masson, *La marine française et la guerre 1939–1945* (Paris: Tallandier, 1991), 194.
18. Guillaume Piketty, *Français en résistance: Carnet de guerre, correspondances, journaux personnels* (Paris: Robert Laffont, 2009), 467.
19. Romain Gary, *La promesse de l'aube* (Paris: Gallimard, 1980), 37–38. In fact, Kacew made the most of his opportunities – post-war, the highly decorated FAFL veteran was made *compagnon de la libération*, commander of the *légion d'honneur*, twice won the prestigious *Prix Goncourt*, as Romain Gary and Émile Ajar, and was named French consul in Los Angeles, where he unsuccessfully challenged actor and director Clint Eastwood to a duel over the latter's affair with his wife, the actress Jean Seberg.
20. Sir Edward Spears, *Fulfilment of a Mission: The Spears Mission to Syria and Lebanon 1941–1944* (London: Leo Cooper, 1977), 42.
21. Alain de Boissieu, *Pour combattre avec de Gaulle: Souvenirs 1940–1946* (Paris: Plon, 1981), 149.
22. Max Egremont, *Under Two Flags: The Life of Major-General Sir Edward Spears* (London: Weidenfeld & Nicolson, 1997), 317.
23. De Boissieu, *Pour combattre avec de Gaulle*, 149; Antoine Béthouart, *Cinq années d'espérance: Mémoires de guerre 1939–1945* (Paris: Plon, 1968), 95, 97.
24. Bernard Destremau, *De Lattre* (Paris: Flammarion, 1999), 310–311.
25. Winston S. Churchill, *The Second World War*, volume II, *Their Finest Hour* (Boston: Houghton Mifflin, 1949), 215.
26. Piketty, *Français en résistance*, 221, 237.
27. Theodore Zeldin, *France 1848–1945*, volume 2, *Intellect, Taste and Anxiety* (Oxford: Oxford University Press, 1977), 904.
28. Masson, *La marine française et la guerre 1939–1945*, 195.

29. SHD, oral archives, Crémieux-Brilhac GR 3K 32-2, Planche 2; Jean-Louis Crémieux-Brilhac, *L'étrange victoire: De la défense de la République à la libération de la France* (Paris: Gallimard, 2016), 197, 219. Charles X had been the last Bourbon king of France, put to flight by the Revolution of 1830
30. Claude Hettier de Boislambert, *Les fers de l'espoir* (Paris: Plon, 1978), 187.
31. Criticism or contrary opinions were dealt with "as if they resulted from a disability or lack of patriotism. Within the imperious qualities that distinguish your manner and which cause too many of your collaborators to approach you with hesitation, to say the least, there probably lurks a certain grandeur. But rest assured that they also constitute more of a danger. The first is that in your entourage, the less capable will only agree with you, while the worst will toady, and the best will cease voluntarily to interact with you. Therefore, you achieve a situation, calming in the midst of your daily worries, where you encounter nothing but gratifying assent. But you realize as well as I where this track had led others in history, and where it might lead you." Guillaume Piketty, *Pierre Brossolette: Un héros de la résistance* (Paris: Éditions Odile Jacob, 1998), 218.
32. Sadoul records the address as having taken place on 23 June, when it was actually a day earlier. Georges Sadoul, *Journal de Guerre (2 septembre 1939–20 juillet 1940*) (Paris: Éditions l'Harmattan, 1994), 378–379.
33. Louis Bacquier, *Aïwah: Au combat avec les Marocains. Souvenirs d'un officier de tirailleurs 1942–1945* (Paris: Éditions Laville, 2012), 46–47.
34. Vincent, *Les forces françaises dans la lutte contre l'Axe en Afrique*, tome I, 15, 21; Diego Gaspar Celaya, "Portrait d'oubliés. L'engagement des Espagnols dans les Forces françaises libres, 1940–1945," *Revue historique des armées*, 265 (2011), 47–49, https://journals.openedition.org/rha/7345. Muracciole believes that foreigners comprised only 3,000 of 70,000 FFL. Muracciole, "Le devenir des officiers Français libres après la guerre," 185.
35. Thomas Vaisset, *L'Amiral d'Argenlieu: Le moine-soldat du gaullisme* (Paris: Belin, 2017), 182.
36. Robert Gildea, *Fighters in the Shadows: A New History of the French Resistance* (Cambridge, MA: Harvard University Press, 2015), 28–31.
37. Edgard de Larminat, *Chroniques irrévérencieuses* (Paris: Plon, 1962), 208.
38. SHD-GR, 3P 102, "Sitation en Angleterre à la date du 17 septembre," 17 October 1940.
39. Gildea, *Fighters in the Shadows*, 109.
40. Gary, *La promesse de l'aube*, 329–360.
41. Egremont, *Under Two Flags*, 203, 205.
42. Commander of the port of Marseilles, Muselier had been cashiered from the navy in November 1939 by Darlan himself after Muselier had arrested several Marseilles merchants whom he accused of smuggling. However, according to Crémieux-Brilhac, the real reason for Muselier's firing was that he was communicating classified information to parliamentary deputies, presumably those from the Radical Party, with which he had close ties. But, for Darlan, this was probably the last straw. Jean-Louis

Crémieux-Brilhac, *La France libre*, tome 1, *De l'appel du 18 juin à la libération* (Paris: Gallimard, 2001), 119.

43. Masson, *La marine française et la guerre 1939–1945*, 193.
44. According to Spears, he and de Gaulle plotted in August 1940 to send Muselier to Alexandria, "under the pretense of seeing whether he can convert the French sailors still there to the de Gaulle cause and whether he could obtain weapons from the ships there." When Britain's Middle East commander, General Sir Archibald Wavell, nixed the idea, Spears asked facetiously: "Couldn't you make him Colonel-in-Chief of the 'Muselier Marines' and land him somewhere in Africa? . . . The physical effect might not be very great, but as the man is such a crashing bore it would wear down the nerves of even the stoutest Touareg." Egremont, *Under Two Flags*, 217; St. Antony's College, Middle East Library, Spears Collection, GB165-0269, Box 1, file 2, letters of 11, 13, 19, and 21 August 1940.
45. St. Antony's College, Middle East Library, Spears Collection, GB165-0269, Box 1, file 2, Roberts report.
46. Piketty, *Français en résistance*, 170; Hettier de Boislambert, *Les fers de l'espoir*, 181; Vaisset, *L'Amiral d'Argenlieu*, 200–201.
47. Vaisset, *L'Amiral d'Argenlieu*, 212, 321. In his memoirs, de Gaulle incorrectly, or perhaps intentionally, attributes the idea of the Cross of Lorraine to d'Argenlieu, see de Gaulle, *Mémoires de guerre*, tome 1, 87. On Muselier's various intrigues, see Crémieux-Brilhac, *La France libre*, tome 1, 228–230. The idea to control de Gaulle was to create a council on which Muselier would serve as vice-president. François Kersaudy, *Churchill and de Gaulle* (London: Collins, 1981), 162.
48. "Roosevelt's extreme suspicion of de Gaulle has been poorly explained by historians," concludes Philipps O'Brien. The reason was that, coming in the immediate wake of Pearl Harbor and because it supposedly violated the Monroe Doctrine, de Gaulle's initiative irritated a number of American officials, including Secretary of State Cordell Hull, who henceforth prefaced any reference to the Free French with the adjective "so-called." More important in shaping Roosevelt's attitudes, however, was the US ambassador to Vichy, Admiral William Leahy, a close friend and advisor to the American President. Leahy communicated his distrust of de Gaulle to Roosevelt, who "regularly tried to marginalize or even humiliate the French leader, starting with completely excluding him from any knowledge of Torch." Phillips Payson O'Brien, *The Second Most Powerful Man in the World: The Life of Admiral William D. Leahy, Roosevelt's Chief of Staff* (New York: Dutton, 2019), 232; Julian Jackson, *De Gaulle* (Cambridge, MA: Harvard University Press, 2018), 207.
49. Charles-Robert Ageron, "La survivance d'un mythe. La puissance par l'Empire colonial (1944–1947)," in René Girault and Robert Frank (eds.), *La puissance française en question! 1945–1949* (Paris: Publications de la Sorbonne, 1988), 49.
50. Géraud Létang, "La promesse de l'ordre. Rébellion et imaginaires du commandement chez les Français libres du Tchad (1940–1943)," in Claire Miot, Guillaume Piketty, and Thomas Vaisset (eds.), *Militaires en*

résistances en France et en Europe (Villeneuve d'Ascq: Presses universitaires du Septentrion, 2020), 55–59.

51. From 20 June 1940, when it became obvious that the British could no longer overfly France, London began to ship partially assembled planes to Takoradi on the Gold Coast (present-day Ghana), where aircraft mechanics completed their construction. The first contingent of British airmen and mechanics reached Takoradi on 21 August. On 5 September, the first planes began to arrive in crates. Fifteen days later, on 18 September, the first air convoy consisting of a Blenheim bomber and six Hurricane fighters left Takoradi to fly the 3,700 miles via Khartoum to Egypt. Churchill, *The Second World War*, volume II, 453–454; I. S. O. Playfair, *The Mediterranean and the Middle East*, vol. I (London: HMSO, 1954), 195–197, 244–250.
52. On "les trois glorieuses," see de Gaulle, *Mémoires de guerre*, tome 1, 100–104. Olivier Wieviorka suggests that while the term "free French" had been used in a generic sense in Churchill's 28 June recognition of de Gaulle "as leader of all free Frenchmen, wherever they may be, who rallied to you in support of the Allied cause," which was a juridical definition in the 7 August agreement, the movement adopted "*France libre*" on 29 August. Olivier Wieviorka, *Histoire de la Résistance 1940–1945* (Paris: Perrin, 2013), 20–21; Sir Hersch Lauterpacht, *Recognition in International Law* (Cambridge: Cambridge University Press, 1947), Part II, 164.
53. SHD-GR, 4P 3, Moyet to de Gaulle, 18 December 1942.
54. Létang, "La promesse de l'ordre," 60–61.
55. Thomas and Toye, *Arguing about Empire*, 169.
56. Thomas and Toye, *Arguing about Empire*, 168; Martin Thomas, *The French Empire at War, 1940–1945* (Manchester: University of Manchester Press, 2007), 56–60, 70–72; Crémieux-Brilhac, *La France libre*, tome 1, 135–150; Eric Jennings, *La France libre fut africaine* (Paris: Perrin, 2014), 11–15, 26–53, 115–116, 125.
57. Jean-Marc Regnault and Ismet Kurtovich, "Les ralliements du Pacifique en 1940. Entre legend gaulliste, enjeux stratégiques mondiaux et rivalités Londres/Vichy," *Revue d'histoire modern et contemporaine*, 2002/4. no. 49–4 (2002), 71–90. On Les comptoires des Indes, see Philippe Bonichon, Pierre Gény, and Jean Nemo, *Présences françaises outre-mer (XVIe–XXIe siècles)*, tome 1, *Histoire: Périodes et continents* (Paris: Karthala, 2012), 667–668.
58. A. B. Gaunson, *The Anglo-French Clash in Lebanon and Syria, 1940–1945* (London: Macmillan, 1987), 2.
59. Thomas, *The French Empire at War 1940–1945*, 4, 45; Jean-Baptiste Bruneau, *La Marine de Vichy aux Antilles juin 1940–juillet 1943* (Paris: Les Indes Savantes, 2014), 16–17, 23–24, 27–29.
60. The expression "Charles-sans-terre" is Lacouture's: Jean Lacouture, *De Gaulle*, tome 1, *Le Rebelle 1890–1944* (Paris: Éditions du Seuil, 1984), Chapter 21, 444.
61. Harold Macmillan, *War Diaries: Politics and War in the Mediterranean, January 1943–May 1945* (London: Macmillan, 1984), 73–74.
62. Sébastien Albertelli, *Les Services secrets du Général de Gaulle: Le BCRA 1940–1944* (Paris: Perrin, 2009), 31.

63. Henri Lerner, *Catroux* (Paris: Albin Michel, 1990), 150–158.
64. Macmillan, *War Diaries*, 128.
65. Jackson, *De Gaulle*, 179, 217.
66. Spears, *Fulfilment of a Mission*, 7–10; Piketty, *Français en résistance*, 221, 307; Lerner, *Catroux*, 141–165; Crémieux-Brilhac, *La France libre*, tome 1, 36, 166–167, 188–189; Thomas, *The French Empire at War 1940–1945*, 62; Kersaudy, *Churchill and de Gaulle*, 105. On Marguerite Catroux, see Élodie Jauneau, "La feminization de l'armée française pendant les guerres (1938–1962): Enjeux et réalités d'un processus irreversible," Thèse du doctorat, Université Paris Diderot (Paris 7), 2011, 115; Macmillian, *War Diaries*, 74.
67. Thomas and Toye, *Arguing about Empire*, 168.
68. Egremont, *Under Two Flags*, 200–201; St. Antony's College, Middle East Library, Spears Collection, GB165-0269, Box 1, file 2, Memo from Major O. A. Archdale.
69. De Gaulle, *Mémoires de guerre*, tome 1, 104.
70. The Admiralty and the Joint Planning Committee resisted. De Gaulle's intelligence chief, André Dewarvin (Passy), pointed out that, given AFN's loyalty to Vichy, Dakar would be impossible to hold even if it were seized. Lacouture, *De Gaulle*, tome 1, 430.
71. Churchill, *The Second World War*, volume II, 473.
72. In the unlikely event that the garrison did show opposition, it would be quickly broken by a few naval artillery shells, "in the hope that this limited action against recalcitrant shore batteries will permit General de Gaulle's troops to disembark without further opposition." If not, then the shore bombardment would intensify to allow a general landing by British forces. SHD-GR, 4P 2, "Instructions militaires et navales."
73. A naval taskforce left Liverpool between 26 and 31 August. On 13 September, they rendezvoused with Force H out of Gibraltar to make up a significant naval expedition. Force M was made up of two older battleships, HMS *Barham* and HMS *Resolution*, the carrier *Ark Royal*, four cruisers, nine destroyers, three FNFL dispatch boats, and four freighters. Land forces included two battalions of Royal Marines, one of Free French, the 13ème DBLE, some gunners, and service troops – 8,000 soldiers in all, 2,000 of whom were French. The French contingent led by de Gaulle was transported in the former Dutch liners *Pennland* and *Westernland* that would fly the tricolor.
74. Jackson, *De Gaulle*, 149–150.
75. De Gaulle, *Mémoires de guerre*, tome 1, 116. Vaisset, *L'Amiral d'Argenlieu*, 233–236.
76. Dentz was not the first choice, but was named High Commissioner and Commander in Chief in the Levant by Pétain after Jean Chiappe was killed on 27 November 1940 when the airplane carrying him to Beirut was shot down by the Italians. François Broche, Georges Caïtucoli, and Jean-François Muracciole, *Dictionnaire de la France Libre* (Paris: Robert Lafont, 2010), 434–435.
77. Thomas, *The French Empire at War 1940–1945*, 60–65.

78. Jackson, *De Gaulle*, 151.
79. Christine Levisse-Touzé, "L'Afrique du Nord: Un désert pour la France libre?," in Sylvain Cornil-Frerrot and Philippe Oulmont (eds.), *Les Français libres et le monde: Actes du colloque international au musée de l'Armée 22 et 23 novembre 2013* (Paris: Nouveau Monde Éditions, 2015), 67.
80. Thomas and Toye, *Arguing about Empire*, 168.
81. Muracciole, *Les Français libres*, 135.
82. There were multiple reasons for this. London did not seek a showdown with Vichy when the Royal Navy had its hands full escorting convoys in the Atlantic, defending the Home Islands, and fighting for maritime dominance in the Mediterranean, especially at a time when the U-boat menace was growing. London also feared provoking a reaction that could lead to attacks against Gibraltar, possibly even the loss of this vital outpost. Furthermore, the French technically could move ships from Oran to Casablanca without leaving French territorial waters. Bernard Costagliola, *La Marine de Vichy: Blocus et collaboration* (Paris: Tallandier, 2009), 332, 349–350, 357.
83. Hettier de Boislambert, *Les fers de l'espoir*, 235–237, 252, 254, 276 and passim.
84. SHD-GR, 4P 2, "Instructions militaires et navales"; Masson, *La marine française et la guerre 1939–1945*, 197–220.
85. MI5 reported that de Gaulle's indiscretions included buying tropical kit at Simpson's in Piccadilly and discussing the operation over the telephone, along with those of Free French officers who hosted pre-campaign celebrations in prominent London restaurants which featured inebriated toasts "to Dakar!" Egremont, *Under Two Flags*, 214–215; M. R. D. Foot, *SOE in France* (London: Her Majesty's Stationary Office, 1966), 151; Douglas Porch, *The French Secret Services: From the Dreyfus Affair to the Gulf War* (Oxford: Oxford University Press, 1997), 181–182.
86. Masson, *La marine française et la guerre 1939–1945*, 222–224.
87. As it was, the Royal Navy lacked the ships to enforce a blockade of Vichy France and its colonies – despite the strong advocacy of blockade by Hugh Dalton at the Ministry of Economic Warfare, less than 2 percent of goods was intercepted by the Royal Navy. Diplomatic pressure in Latin America and filing lawsuits in the United States proved far more effective weapons than a naval blockade in preventing goods from reaching Vichy. Costagliola, *La Marine de Vichy*, 329–330.
88. Lacouture, *De Gaulle*, tome 1, 447.
89. Kersaudy, *Churchill and de Gaulle*, 103–108, 193; Crémieux-Brilhac, *La France libre*, tome 1, 175–183; Thomas, *The French Empire at War 1940–1945*, 62.
90. Vaisset, *L'Amiral d'Argenlieu*, 244–249; Crémieux-Brilhac, *La France libre*, tome 1, 168–170.
91. The Île de Sein is off the extreme western tip of Brittany. Jean-Mathieu Boris, *Combattant de la France Libre* (Paris: Perrin, 2012), 10.
92. Crémieux-Brilhac, *La France libre*, tome 1, 231. Pierre Tissier, Professor Jean Escarra, General de Larminat, and "many other 'moderates'" numbered among those willing to accommodate themselves to a slightly softer

version of Vichy's anti-Jewish statutes, to the point that Cassin had continually to persuade de Gaulle that France had no "Jewish problem." Crémieux-Brilhac, *L'étrange victoire*, 159, 162.

93. Muracciole, *Les Français libres*, 60–70, 361–362; see also Muracciole's entries on "Français libres" in Broche, Caïtucoli, and Muracciole, *Dictionnaire de la France Libre*, 616–624.
94. Cited by Géraud Létang, "'Une armée de clochards.' Sentiment de déclassement et fabrique d'une identité collective chez les Français libre du Tchad, (1840–1943)," paper delivered at "E Pluribus Unum? Pluralité et identité des français libres," 27–28 November 2019.
95. Charles de Gaulle, *Discours et messages 1940–1946* (Paris: Plon, 1970), 24 March 1942. Cited by Létang, "'Une armée de clochards.'"
96. SHD-GR, 3YD 1529, "Note-Circulaire aux unités des 1ère et 2ème Divisions," no date.
97. Cited by Létang, "'Une armée de clochards.'"
98. Crémieux-Brilhac, *La France libre*, tome 1, 135; Jennings, *La France libre fut africaine*, 11–15; Thomas, *The French Empire at War 1940–1945*, 5.
99. A. B. Gaunson, *The Anglo-French Clash in Lebanon and Syria*, 63; Sudhir Hazareesingh, *In the Shadow of the General: Modern France and the Myth of de Gaulle* (Oxford: Oxford University Press, 2012), 12.
100. Albertelli, *Les Services secrets du Général de Gaulle*, 29–30; Julian Jackson, "General de Gaulle and His Enemies: Anti-Gaullism in France since 1940, "*Transactions of the Royal Historical Society*, 9 (1999), 47.
101. The basis of the arrest was a set of documents brought to the Prime Minister by MI5, the British counter-espionage service, alleging that Muselier had tipped off the French air attaché in London, Colonel Joseph Rozoy, about Dakar just prior to the attaché's repatriation to Vichy. MI5 also charged that Muselier had conspired to hand over the FNFL submarine *Surcouf* to Vichy, and that he had sought to sabotage recruitment to the FNFL. Muselier was stripped, and incarcerated at Pentonville Prison, in a cell with a broken window with only a dirty mattress on the floor. Some others close to Muselier were also arrested. Shown photocopies of the incriminating documents, de Gaulle immediately concluded that they could not have been written by a French flag officer. De Gaulle contacted Eden to say that if there were other reasons for Muselier's detention, he should be informed. Otherwise, grave consequences would follow from Muselier's further detention, as it would impact morale in the FNFL and spread the fear in *la France libre* that any of its officers might be arrested arbitrarily. He added that treating Muselier as a common criminal constituted an insult to the FNFL. As Scotland Yard, as well as Passy, had also concluded that Muselier had been framed, Muselier was freed on 9 January. Four days later, a letter of apology followed stating that the French admiral had been detained "on suspicions which have now proved to be unsubstantiated." That was hardly the end of the episode, however. And it was the tip of the iceberg of a much deeper story. The forgeries were traced to two BCRA agents, Captain Jacques Meffre, also known as Howard, and his assistant, Adjutant Serge Colin. Both men worked in the "*service de renseignement*

intérieur," a counter-espionage section of the BCRA that Passy had created in July 1940 to cooperate with MI5 and the British police to verify the identities of volunteers and to carry out investigations. Meffre had come to the BCRA via the British Ministry of Supply, where his job had been to vet French technicians arriving from France. The British Attorney General investigating the Muselier case, Sir Donald Somervell, concluded that "Meffre himself was strongly supported by Lord Suffolk and Major Golding who apparently had great faith in him." Furthermore, Somervell noted, Suffolk and Golding had speeded his naturalization papers. The fact that Meffre had been working in the office with Suffolk and Golding in the Ministry of Supply was no coincidence. Meffre was a Great War veteran who had worked in French intelligence in Germany in the inter-war years, and had been tasked by Paul Paillole to infiltrate the *Comité France–Allemagne*. On the outbreak of war, he had been posted to the Ministry of Armaments, where he had met Suffolk and Golding, assigned as liaisons between the two British and French ministries. As France collapsed, these men had spirited the French supply of heavy water, as well as atomic physicists Lew Kowarski, Hans von Halban, and Jean-Frédéric Jolio-Curie out of Bordeaux in June 1940. Upon arriving in Britain, Suffolk and Golding took Meffre to work in their Ministry of Supply office. His job is unclear, but a note in the Spears papers states that he was creating difficulties for de Gaulle at the Ministry of Supply, where Meffre may have been directing French technicians and scientists arriving in Britain to the British services rather than to the Gaullists. On 12 September, Meffre became Victor John Edward Howard. This is assumed to be a pseudonym. But as Meffre was also now a British subject, it may be his naturalized name, as Suffolk's real name was Charles Henry George Howard. In October 1940, on the recommendation of Major O. A. Archdale, who had been liaison to the French First Army Group in 1940, Meffre/Howard became head of the BCRA's "*service de renseignement intérieur*," where he, Serge Colin, and a Penelope Lloyd-Thomas were in charge of vetting recruits to *la France libre*. See www.telegraph.co.uk/news/newstopics/world-war-2/7849612/The-scruffy-earl-who-swung-the-war.html. The story inside the BCRA was that the nomination of Meffre/Howard, as well as a Lieutenant Robert Jobez, a former police inspector in the French concession at Shanghai who had reached London and *la France libre* via Canada, and Colin, had initially been supported by the chief of Muselier's *Deuxième Bureau*, Captain Moret. At this early stage, Passy the gullible novice saw no problem in accepting British suggestions for recruitment for a section in the BCRA that worked directly with MI5. De Gaulle had departed for Dakar by then, and on his return did not make the connection between Meffre in the Ministry of Supply and Howard in the BCRA. However, Meffre/Howard "made a point of running down, in a particularly nasty way, different persons working with General de Gaulle," Somervell's investigation revealed, to the point that an exasperated Moret accused Meffre/Howard and Colin of being British spies. For his part, Meffre had become convinced that the FNFL was full of Vichy sympathizers, and Colin began to produce documents to back up Meffre's accusations that Muselier was in direct contact with Vichy. Meffre was exposed. However, the British declined to prosecute, presumably because it would have exposed classified or sensitive material about Dakar, MI5, and the BCRA, and instead interned Meffre on the Isle of Man for the remainder of the war. Jobez, who was deemed to have no part in the conspiracy, was dispatched to Africa, held various security and consular posts, and retired in 1963 after a very honorable consular career in the Quai d'Orsay. He was also the author of several books on China. On Meffre/Howard, see http://discovery.nationalarchives.gov.uk/details/r/C14206419. On Robert Jobez, see www.francaislibres.net/liste/fiche.php?index=75562; and Pierre Accoce, *Les français à Londres, 1940–1941* (Paris: Balland, 1989).

102. Albertelli, *Les Services secrets du Général de Gaulle*, 35–37, 49; Kersaudy, *Churchill and de Gaulle*, 120–123; Porch, *The French Secret Services*, 181–184; Colonel Passy, *Souvenirs*, tome 1, *2e Bureau Londres* (Monte Carlo: Raoul Solar, 1947), 83, 127–133; Lacouture, *De Gaulle*, tome 1, 489–492; Egremont, *Under Two Flags*, 195; St. Antony's College, Oxford, Spears Papers, GB165-0269, Box 1, file 2, correspondence 4 January–13 February 1941.
103. The Intelligence Service (IS) collected intelligence from French agents via Lisbon, and recruited arriving Frenchmen through the Royal Victoria Patriotic School, created in early 1941 to interview and establish the bona fides of everyone arriving into Britain from the Continent. Albertelli, *Les Services secrets du Général de Gaulle*, 29, 32–35, 49–51.
104. Wieviorka, *Histoire de la Résistance 1940–1945*, 28–31, 38–42; Porch, *The French Secret Services*, 174–181; Albertelli, *Les Services secrets du Général de Gaulle*, 38–49.
105. Crémieux-Brilhac, *La France libre*, tome 1, 76–79, 97, 259.
106. Vincent, *Les forces françaises dans la lutte contre l'Axe en Afrique*, tome I, 15.
107. Crémieux-Brilhac, *L'étrange victoire*, 161, 181.
108. Belot, *La Résistance sans de Gaulle*, 646; Patrice Arnaud, *Les STO: Histoire des français requis en Allemagne nazi 1942–1945* (Paris: Éditions CNRS, 2014), 595; Piketty, *Français en résistance*, xxii–xxvi, 164. For the early days in London, see, for example, Lacouture, *De Gaulle*, tome 1, 385–397; Hazareesingh, *In the Shadow of the General*, 17–21; Kersaudy, *Churchill and de Gaulle*, 79; Wieviorka, *Histoire de la résistance 1940–1945*, 185.
109. Vaisset, *L'Amiral d'Argenlieu*, 34.
110. Crémieux-Brilhac, *La France libre*, tome 1, 48, 129–130, 259.
111. Claude Bouchinet-Serreulles, *Nous étions faits pour être libres: La résistance avec De Gaulle et Jean Moulin* (Paris: Grasset, 2000), 196. Quoted in Vaisset, *L'Amiral d'Argenlieu*, 34, 234.
112. Vaisset, *L'Amiral d'Argenlieu*, 274. On de Gaulle's asceticism, see Egremont, *Under Two Flags*, 154.
113. Crémieux-Brilhac, *L'étrange victoire*, 201–202.
114. O'Brien, *The Second Most Powerful Man in the World*, 151–152.
115. François Bédarida, "L'histoire de la résistance. Lectures de hiers, chantiers de demain," *Vingtième siècle. Revue d'histoire*, 1986/11 (1986), 80;

Alan Milward, "The Economic and Strategic Effectiveness of Resistance," in Stephen Hawes and Ralph White (eds.), *Resistance in Europe, 1939–1945* (London: Viking, 1975), 193, 197; M. R. D. Foot, *Resistance* (London: Granada, 1978), 313.

116. Wieviorka, *Histoire de la Résistance 1940–1945*, 106. Much of this section is based on Wieviorka's work.
117. Wieviorka, *Histoire de la Résistance 1940–1945*, 185.
118. Jean-François Muracciole, "La France a contribué à la Victoire des Alliés," in Jean Lopez and Olivier Wieviorka (eds.), *Les Mythes de la seconde guerre mondiale* (Paris: Perrin, 2015), 340.
119. Jean Estèbe, *Toulouse 1940–1944* (Paris: Perrin, 1996), 318.
120. Wieviorka, *Histoire de la Résistance 1940–1945*, 44, 100, 109.
121. "Tu verras, c'est une bande de vieux dégonflés." Béthouart, *Cinq années d'espérance*, 93.
122. Romain Durand, *De Giraud à de Gaulle: Les Corps francs d'Afrique* (Paris: Éditions l'Harmattan, 1999), 21.
123. Wieviorka, *Histoire de la Résistance 1940–1945*, 495.
124. Olivier Wieviorka, *Une Certaine idée de la Résistance: Défense de France* 1940-1949 (Paris: Éditions du Seuil, 1995), 383; Wieviorka, *Histoire de la Résistance 1940–1945*, 14.
125. Belot, *La Résistance sans de Gaulle*, 11.
126. H. R. Kedward, *Resistance in Vichy France: A Study of Ideas and Motivation in the Southern Zone 1940–1942* (Oxford: Oxford University Press, 1978), 229.
127. Gildea, *Fighters in the Shadows*, 2.
128. Rousso drew on earlier utilization of the term. A report probably written in August/September 1944 criticized the "Romantisme Résistencialiste" of strategists in Algiers who sent commandos to support uprisings like that of le Vercors. SHD-GR, 12P 92, "Le détachment special de commandos de France." After the war, the term "resistentialist" was deployed by the communists to excuse resistance excesses committed during the war.
129. Bédarida, "L'histoire de la résistance," 81–89; Henry Rousso, *The Vichy Syndrome: History and Memory in France since 1944* (Cambridge, MA: Harvard University Press, 1991), 11; Robert O. Paxton, "The Truth about the Resistance," *New York Review of Books*, 25 February 2016, www.nybooks.com/articles/2016/02/25/truth-about-french-resistance.
130. Gildea, *Fighters in the Shadows*, 3–7.
131. Bédarida, "L'histoire de la résistance," 81.
132. Belot, *La Résistance sans de Gaulle*, 12–13, 642–643.
133. Rousso, *The Vichy Syndrome*, 17–18.
134. Gaël Eismann, *Hôtel Majestic: Ordre et sécurité en France occupée (1940–1944)* (Paris: Tallandier, 2010), 459. Part of the RSHA or the Reich Main Security Office, the *Sipo/SD* combined the internal and foreign security service which represented the SD with the Gestapo (Secret State Police) and Kripo (criminal police), which made up the Sipo. Philippe Valode and Gérard Chauvy, *La Gestapo française* (Paris: Acropole, 2018), 21.
135. Valode and Chauvy, *La Gestapo française*, 85–87.

136. Denis Peschanski and J.-P. Azéma, "Vichy état policier," in Jean-Pierre Azéma and François Bédarida (eds.), *La France des années noires*, tome 2, *De l'Occupation à la Libération* (Paris: Éditions du Seuil, 1993), 358–360; Anise Postel-Vinay and Jacques Prévotat, "La Déportation," in Azéma and Bédarida (eds.), *La France des années noires*, tome 2, 435.
137. Peschanski and Azéma, "Vichy état policier," 366–367.
138. Postel-Vinay and Prévotat, "La Déportation," in Azéma and Bédarida (eds.), *La France des années noires*, tome 2, 437–439.
139. Eismann, *Hôtel Majestic*, 457–469; Gaël Eismann, "Maintenir l'ordre. Le MBF et la sécurité locale en France occupée," *Vingtième siècle. Revue d'histoire*, no. 98 (April–June 2008), 125–139, www.cairn.info/revue-vingtieme-siecle-revue-d-histoire-2008-2-page-125.htm.
140. Gildea, *Fighters in the Shadows*, 58–59.
141. Bacquier, *Aïwah*, 47.
142. Gildea, *Fighters in the Shadows*, 164–165.
143. Hazareesingh, *In the Shadow of the General*, 24–27.
144. Wieviorka, *Histoire de la Résistance 1940–1945*, 79–82; Gildea, *Fighters in the Shadows*, 62–65; Jean Bezy, *Le S.R. Air* (Paris: Éditions France-Empire, 1979), 27–90.
145. Wieviorka, *Histoire de la Résistance 1940–1945*, 86–87, 101, and passim.
146. Wieviorka, *Histoire de la Résistance 1940–1945*, 39.
147. Gildea, *Fighters in the Shadows*, 62–65, 152, 157–159, 239.
148. Wieviorka, *Histoire de la Résistance 1940–1945*, 247–252.
149. SHD-GR, 4P 2, Chapter V, "L'Afrique française libre."
150. Muselier, Cassin, Larminat, Sicé, Sautot, d'Argenlieu, and Leclerc were on the Conseil de l'Empire. De Gaulle, *Mémoires de guerre*, tome 1, 127; Jennings, *La France libre fut africaine*, 79; Lacouture, *De Gaulle*, tome 1, 447; Gildea, *Fighters in the Shadows*, 478.
151. Crémieux-Brilhac, *La France libre* tome 1, 159, 167, 173–174, 184–186; Vaisset, *L'Amiral d'Argenlieu*, 239; Jennings, *La France libre fut africaine*, 115–116.

8 *"Grandi soldati"*

1. Charles de Gaulle, *Vers l'armée de métier* (Paris: Berger-Levrault, 1944), 102–103.
2. Bernard Costagliola, *La Marine de Vichy: Blocus et collaboration* (Paris: Tallandier, 2009), 356.
3. Eric Jennings, *La France libre fut africaine* (Paris: Perrin, 2014), 125.
4. André Martel, "De Gaulle et la France Libre," in André Martel (ed.), *Histoire militaire de la France*, tome 4, *De 1940 à nos jours* (Paris: Presses universitaires de France, 1994), 105. A brigade normally contained three infantry battalions each composed of three infantry companies and a heavy company, and accompanying artillery, which in the FFL's case was gradually upgraded as French 75 mm canon were replaced with British 25-pounder (87.6 mm) howitzers. Jean-Noël Vincent, *Les forces françaises dans la lutte contre l'Axe en*

Afrique, tome I, *Les forces françaises libres en Afrique 1940–1943* (Vincennes: Service historique de l'armée de terre, 1983), 56.

5. Jennings, *La France libre fut africaine*, 162, 166; www.axl.cefan.ulaval.ca/afrique/indigenat_code.htm.
6. André Martel, *Leclerc* (Paris: Albin Michel, 1998), 165.
7. Vincent, *Les forces françaises dans la lutte contre l'Axe en Afrique*, tome I, 21.
8. Such was the fate of the Bataillon de Marche 4, recruited at Fort-Lamy, and left behind in Somalia at the end of the East Africa campaign as a "representation" force to guard Italian POWs. Vincent, *Les forces françaises dans la lutte contre l'Axe en Afrique*, tome I, 101–102.
9. Jennings, *La France libre fut africaine*, 11–12, 148–167, 285.
10. Sir Edward Spears, *Fulfilment of a Mission: The Spears Mission to Syria and Lebanon 1941–1944* (London: Leo Cooper, 1977), 5–6.
11. Susan Travers, *Tomorrow to Be Brave* (London: Corgi Press, 2001), 23–81, 88, 91–92.
12. Guillaume Piketty, *Français en résistance: Carnet de guerre, correspondances, journaux personnels* (Paris: Robert Laffont, 2009), 484. For a description of French participation in the Ethiopian campagn, see Vincent, *Les forces françaises dans la lutte contre l'Axe en Afrique*, tome I, Chapter 3, 60–102.
13. Travers, *Tomorrow to Be Brave*, 94–106; Douglas Porch, *The French Foreign Legion: A Complete History of the Legendary Fighting Force* (New York: Harper Collins, 1991), 473–474. On the East Africa campaign, see Douglas Porch, *Path to Victory: The Mediterranean Theater in World War II* (New York: Farrar, Straus, Giroux, 2004), 128–138; SHD-GR, 4P 4, Monclar report.
14. SHD-GR, 4P 4, "L'attaque et la prise de Massawa"; and Lieutenant-colonel Reyniers, "Episodes de la campagne d'Erythrée"; 4P 5. On armored forces see 4P 4, "Rapport. La création d'une deuxième compagnie de chars pose plusieurs problèmes importants," 5 September 1940. These problems included not only an absence of experienced French armor officers in FFL ranks but also that the British had no tanks to spare for the FFL.
15. Vincent, *Les forces françaises dans la lutte contre l'Axe en Afrique*, tome I, 103–116.
16. Spears, *Fulfilment of a Mission*, 49.
17. Porch, *Path to Victory*, 116; Martel, "De Gaulle et la France Libre," 107.
18. Vincent, *Les forces françaises dans la lutte contre l'Axe en Afrique*, tome I, 238–248.
19. Vincent, *Les forces françaises dans la lutte contre l'Axe en Afrique*, tome I, 230–238.
20. SHD-GR, 4P 4, "General de Larminat, Brazzaville, 24/2/41."
21. Jean-François Muracciole, *Les Français libres: L'autre Résistance* (Paris: Tallandier, 2009), 274. SHD-GR, 4P 4, "Opération de Koufra," 22 March 1941, lists only one tirailleur killed at Kufra for the Régiment des tirailleurs sénégalais du Tchad, but also three "gravely" wounded. The highest casualties seemed to be among the crews of two aircraft lost in the operation. For a narrative of the operation, see Leclerc, "Rapport concernant l'activités des forces françaises libres du Tchad en janvier et février 1941." For a detailed account of the siege, see Vincent, *Les forces françaises dans la lutte contre l'Axe en Afrique*, tome I, 252–271, 353–357.
22. Martel, "De Gaulle et la France Libre," 108.

23. Spears, *Fulfilment of a Mission*, 50–51.
24. Jennings, *La France libre fut africaine*, 130–138. Various versions of the Kufra episode exist, all of which differ to a degree. Martel, *Leclerc*, 157–167; Jean-Christophe Notin, *Leclerc: Le croisé de la France libre* (Paris: Perrin, 2015), 51–66; Ministère de la défense, "Koufra, début d'une épopée," www.cheminsdememoire.gouv.fr/fr/koufra-debut-dune-epopee.
25. Notin, *Leclerc*, 15.
26. Claire Miot, "Sortir l'armée des ombres. Soldats de l'Empire, combattants de la Libération, armée de la Nation: La Première armée française, du débarquement en Provence à la capitulation allemande (1944–1945)," Thèse du doctorat, Université Paris-Saclay, 2016, 546–547.
27. Max Egremont, *Under Two Flags: The Life of Major-General Sir Edward Spears* (London: Weidenfeld & Nicolson, 1997), 226.
28. The Anglo-Egyptian treaty was decried by Egyptian nationalists, so that resentment over several of the treaty's provisions actually contributed to the overthrow of the Egyptian monarchy in 1951. A. B. Gaunson, *The Anglo-French Clash in Lebanon and Syria, 1940–1945* (London: Macmillan, 1987), 4–19, 24.
29. Bernard Costagliola, *Darlan: La collaboration à tout prix* (Paris: Éditions CNRS, 2015), 123–124.
30. Jean-Louis Crémieux-Brilhac, *La France libre*, tome 1, *De l'appel du 18 juin à la libération* (Paris: Gallimard, 2001), 195–196.
31. Gaunson, *The Anglo-French Clash in Lebanon and Syria*, 29; Spears, *Fulfilment of a Mission*, 62–63.
32. Crémieux-Brilhac, *La France libre*, tome 1, 200.
33. Travers, *Tomorrow to Be Brave*, 123.
34. De Gaulle's conditions were as follows: (1) honorable treatment of armed forces and civil servants; (2) representation of France in the Levant will be assured by *la France libre* within the framework of the independence promised and which Great Britain guaranteed; (3) French troops and civil servants who want to join the Allies will be given the opportunity to remain; (4) all war material to be handed over to the Allies; and (5) *la France libre* would take part in armistice negotiations. François Kersaudy, *Churchill and de Gaulle* (London: Collins, 1981), 137; Charles de Gaulle, *Mémoires de guerre*, tome 1, *L'Appel (1940–1942)* (Paris: Plon, 1994), 169–170.
35. Julian Jackson, *De Gaulle* (Cambridge, MA: Harvard University Press, 2018), 175.
36. De Gaulle, *Mémoires de guerre*, tome 1, 171.
37. Spears, *Fulfilment of a Mission*, 89–90.
38. Martin Thomas, *The French Empire at War, 1940–1945* (Manchester: University of Manchester Press, 2007), 107.
39. Guillaume Piketty, *Français en résistance: Carnet de guerre, correspondances, journaux personnels* (Paris: Robert Laffont, 2009), 208.
40. Piketty, *Français en résistance*, 490.
41. Muracciole, *Les Français libres*, 129. In his memoirs, de Gaulle claimed that 127 officers and 6,000 soldiers and NCOs joined *la France libre*. The discrepancy may come from the fact that many in the Vichy garrison were under pressure from their superiors not to break ranks during the armistice signing

ceremony, but subsequently deserted to *la France libre*. De Gaulle, *Mémoires de guerre*, tome 1, 183; Travers, *Tomorrow to Be Brave*, 126, 155, 157, 159, 166; SHD-GR, 4P 7, "Numerical table of the personnel of the combatant forces"; 4P 5, "Annexe I du chapitre XIII."

42. Jackson, *De Gaulle*, 179–180.
43. Kersaudy, *Churchill and de Gaulle*, 127.
44. Thomas, *The French Empire at War*, 107–118.
45. Egremont, *Under Two Flags*, 228, 231–245; Gaunson, *The Anglo-French Clash in Lebanon and Syria*, 15–19, 29, 27–87, 184–188; Kersaudy, *Churchill and de Gaulle*, 124–160.
46. SHD-GR, 2P 13, "Note relative au conflit dans les états du Levant"; "Notice sur l'utilisation des troupes de l'Armée du Levant," 5 August 1941. See also "Étude sur la manière dont se sont comportées les différentes formations autochtones durant la campagne de Syrie (6 juin–11 julliet 1941)"; Major Loth, deputy chief of staff, commander-in-chief Troupes du Levant, "Rapport sur les événements qui se sont déroulés en Syrie depuis la signature de l'Accord de Saint-Jean d'Acre (14 juillet 1941)," 6, 12, 15.
47. Jean Lacouture, *De Gaulle*, tome 1, *Le Rebelle 1890–1944* (Paris: Éditions du Seuil, 1984), 339.
48. De Gaulle chaired the committee; Pleven held the portfolio of the economy, finances, and the colonies; Maurice Dejean, foreign affairs; Legentilhomme, war; Muselier, the navy and merchant marine; Cassin, justice and education; Diethelm, the interior, labor and information; Valin, air; and Argenlieu was without portfolio. Crémieux-Brilhac, *La France libre*, tome 1, 249, 262–275; François Broche, Georges Caïtucoli, and Jean-François Muracciole, *Dictionnaire de la France Libre* (Paris: Robert Laffont, 2010), 322–324.
49. David Mayers, *FDR's Ambassadors and the Diplomacy of Crisis: From the Rise of Hitler to the End of World War II* (Cambridge: Cambridge University Press, 2012), 149.
50. The Greeks had even lower priority than the French, and so were not equipped to join the Eighth Army until the end of 1942. The British coalition also counted 1,600 Czechs, 1,906 Yugoslavs, and 4,720 Poles. Another 23,483 FFL troops garrisoned the Levant in mid 1942. Steven O'Connor, "Fighting a Coalition War: the Experience of the Free French Soldier in the British 8th Army," in Claire Miot, Guillaume Piketty, and Thomas Vaisset (eds.), *Militaires en résistances en France et en Europe* (Villeneuve d'Ascq: Presses universitaires du Septentrion, 2020), 157, 163.
51. Numbers are difficult to pin down, because the FFL often incorporated auxiliary or labor troops into their strength reports. SHD-GR, 11P 1, 14 July 1941; "Rapport du Camp du 21 Mai 1941"; 4P 7, "Situations approximatives des effectifs de l'armée à la fin de mars 1942"; 4P 13, "Plan de refonte des F.F.L. Unités mobiles offensives" (no date, probably late 1941); 4P 4, "Situations approximatives des effectifs de l'armée à la fin de mars 1942" claims 54,746 troops in the FFL, almost half of them in the Levant, which was by then no longer a combat theater.
52. SHD-GR, 4P 13, 10 April 1942.

53. Alan Moorehead, *The Desert War: The North African Campaign 1940–1943* (London: Penguin, 2002), 579.
54. Jonathan Fennell, *Combat and Morale in the North African Campaign: The Eight Army and the Path to El Alamein* (Cambridge: Cambridge University Press, 2011), 34–49.
55. O'Connor, "Fighting a Coalition War," 153.
56. Caleb Milne, *"I Dream of the Day . . .": Letters from Caleb Milne. Africa, 1942–1943* (Woodstock, New York: privately published, 1944), 99.
57. Milne, *"I Dream of the Day . . .,"* 70.
58. Moorehead, *The Desert War*, 238.
59. Irving argues that it was Rommel's failure to react to the British advance on Gabr Saleh that forced them to push forward, thus splitting their forces. David Irving, *The Trail of the Fox: The Life of Field-Marshal Erwin Rommel* (London: Book Club Associates, 1977), 121.
60. Fennell, *Combat and Morale in the North African Campaign*, 65–66.
61. Milne, *"I Dream of the Day . . .,"* 36–38.
62. Travers, *Tomorrow to Be Brave*, 103–104, 172–173.
63. Fennell, *Combat and Morale in the North African Campaign*, 74–75, 249–250.
64. Fennell, *Combat and Morale in the North African Campaign*, 200, 214–215, 225.
65. O'Connor, "Fighting a Coalition War," 161–162.
66. Milne, *"I Dream of the Day . . .,"* 41.
67. Travers, *Tomorrow to Be Brave*, 178–179; Jean-Mathieu Boris, *Combattant de la France Libre* (Paris: Perrin, 2012), 84–86. An arms inventory and list of units can be found in Vincent, *Les forces françaises dans la lutte contre l'Axe en Afrique*, tome I, 124–126.
68. Egremont, *Under Two Flags*, 233–234.
69. At Bir Hakeim, Koenig organized two Jock columns, each composed of a half-company of infantry, a battery of 75 mm guns, and three Bofors 40 mm guns. The columns usually dispersed to avoid detection, but could come together quickly when summoned by radio. Each column alternated on fifteen-day patrols. Their greatest weakness was a lack of tanks. Vincent, *Les forces françaises dans la lutte contre l'Axe en Afrique*, tome I, 130–131.
70. Broche, Caïtucoli, and Muracciole, *Dictionnaire de la France Libre*, 833–835. The entry on Bir Hakeim says that Koenig did not take command of the 1ère Division légère française libre until April 1942, 166.
71. Travers, *Tomorrow to Be Brave*, 136, 138–139, 173, 181–183.
72. Crémieux-Brilhac, *La France Libre*, tome 1, 457.
73. SHD-GR, 4P 7, Dossier Bir-Hacheim 26–29/5/42. This offers a very succinct log based on signals traffic and orders issued. See also Travers, *Tomorrow to Be Brave*, 191–192; Vincent, *Les forces françaises dans la lutte contre l'Axe en Afrique*, tome I, 140–142.
74. SHD-GR, 4P 7, Dossier Bir-Hacheim 30–31/5/42; 01/6/42; Vincent, *Les forces françaises dans la lutte contre l'Axe en Afrique*, tome I, 143–150.
75. Travers, *Tomorrow to Be Brave*, 193–199.
76. Vincent, *Les forces françaises dans la lutte contre l'Axe en Afrique*, tome I, 154–163.

77. Vincent, *Les forces françaises dans la lutte contre l'Axe en Afrique*, tome I, 164–167.
78. SHD-GR, 4P 7, "Note de service," 8 June 1942.
79. Piketty, *Français en résistance*, 499.
80. For a general account of the breakout, see Vincent, *Les forces françaises dans la lutte contre l'Axe en Afrique*, tome I, 174–183.
81. Travers, *Tomorrow to Be Brave*, 202–237; Boris, *Combattant de la France Libre*, 83–121; de Gaulle, *Mémoires de guerre*, tome 1, 266; I. S. O. Playfair, *The Mediterranean and the Middle East*, volume III, *British Fortunes at Their Lowest Ebb* (London: HMSO, 1960), 235–237; Jackson, *De Gaulle*, 224–225; SHD-GR, 1P 47, "Note de service," 12 June 1942.
82. Vincent, *Les forces françaises dans la lutte contre l'Axe en Afrique*, tome I, 368–372.
83. Muracciole, *Les Français libres*, 275–276. Early reports put the death total at 129 killed, including 13 officers, 190 wounded, and 984 missing. SHD-GR, 1P 47, 16 June 1942. For a description of the battle from a German perspective, see Horst Boog, Werner Rahn, Reinhard Stumpf, and Bernd Wegner, *Germany and the Second World War*, vol. 6 (Oxford: Oxford University Press, 2001), 682–692.
84. The British took 74,300 casualties in this period, of whom 62,900 were either missing or POWs. Fennell, *Combat and Morale in the North African Campaign*, 40–41.
85. Galeazzo Ciano, *Ciano's Diary 1937–1943* (London: Enigma Books, 2002), 497; Boog, Rahn, Stumpf, and Wegner, *Germany and the Second World War*, 692; de Gaulle, *Mémoires de guerre*, tome 1, 266–267.
86. Barry Pitt, *The Crucible of War: Auchinleck's Command. The Definitive History of the Desert War*, vol. 2 (London: Cassell, 2001), 47.
87. SHD-GR, 1P 47, 16 June 1942.
88. O'Connor, "Fighting a coalition war," 159.
89. Broche, Caïtucoli, and Muracciole, *Dictionnaire de la France libre*, 161; Jean-François Muracciole, "La France a contribué à la Victoire des Alliés," in Jean Lopez and Olivier Wieviorka (eds.), *Les Mythes de la seconde guerre mondiale* (Paris: Perrin, 2015), 334–339; de Gaulle, *Mémoires de guerre*, tome 1, 262–269.
90. Lacouture, *De Gaulle*, tome 1, 684. I'm also grateful to Géraud Létang for these observations.
91. Vincent, *Les forces françaises dans la lutte contre l'Axe en Afrique*, tome I, 184–187.
92. Muracciole, "La France a contribué à la victoire des Alliés," 336–337.
93. The Poles were estimated to have contributed 250,000 ground troops to the war in the West by 1945, not to mention Polish forces on the Eastern Front as well as air combat units in the RAF, see www.angelfire.com/ok2/polisharmy/chapter1.html.
94. Leo J. Meyer, "The Decision to Invade North Africa (Torch)," in Kent Roberts Greenfield (ed.), *Command Decisions* (Washington, D.C.: Center for Military History, 1990), 174.
95. Robert O. Paxton, *Vichy France: Old Guard and New Order, 1940–1944* (London: Barrie & Jenkins, 1972), 313.

96. De Gaulle, *Mémoires de guerre*, tome 1, 327–329.
97. Vincent, *Les forces françaises dans la lutte contre l'Axe en Afrique*, tome I, 197–201.
98. Broche, Caïtucoli, and Muracciole, *Dictionnaire de la France Libre*, 513–515; Muracciole, *Les Français libres*, 274. SHD-GR, 4P 9, "Chapitre II. Attaque de l'Himeimat" lists 100 casualties in all, with 11 killed and 10 MIA. Vincent, *Les forces françaises dans la lutte contre l'Axe en Afrique*, tome I, 197–217.
99. Travers, *Tomorrow to Be Brave*, 255–257, 259, 265, 272–273; Milne, *"I Dream of the Day . . .,"* 20.

9 France's North African Hinterland

1. Christine Levisse-Touzé, "La poursuite de la guerre en Afrique du Nord," 99; Pierre Lesouef, "La crise de novembre 1942 en Afrique française du nord et la campagne de Tunisie," in Colloque International, *Les armées française pendant la seconde guerre mondiale 1939–1945* (Paris: École nationale supérieure de techniques avancées, 1985), 306.
2. Frédéric Harymbat, *Les Européens d'Afrique du Nord dans les armées de la libération française (1942–1945)* (Paris: Éditions l'Harmattan, 2014), 13–14.
3. Julie Le Gac, *Vaincre sans gloire: Le corps expéditionnaire français en Italie (novembre 1942–juillet 1944)* (Paris: Les Belles Lettres/Ministère de la défense-DMPA, 2013), 23, 117, 505–506.
4. Benjamin Stora, *Histoire de l'Algérie coloniale (1830–1954)* (Paris: Éditions La Découverte, 2004), 21.
5. Theodore Zeldin, *France 1848–1945*, volume 2, *Intellect, Taste and Anxiety* (Oxford: Oxford University Press, 1977), 929.
6. For a discussion of Algerian society, see: Sophie B. Roberts, *Citizenship and Antisemitism in French Colonial Algeria, 1870–1962* (Cambridge and New York: Cambridge University Press, 2018).
7. Historians object that the term *pied-noir* only became common after Algerian independence, when European refugees from Algeria came to be resented in France, accused, through their racism and obstruction of political reform in Algeria, of provoking the conditions that led to the War of Algerian Independence (1954–1962). Typical of this attitude was Pierre Nora's 1961 book, sometimes accused of offering a compendium of bigotry acquired during his two years as a lycée instructor in Oran. Pierre Nora and Charles-André Julien, *Les français d'Algérie* (Chantenay: Julliard, 1961).
8. Richard Bennaïm, *Le Journal du soldat juif* (Lormont: Le Bord de l'Eau, 2017), 31.
9. Stora, *Histoire de l'Algérie coloniale*, 29, 88.
10. Stora, *Histoire de l'Algérie coloniale*, 55–56, 68; Bennaïm, *Le Journal du soldat juif*, 18; Chantal Metzger, *Le Maghreb dans la guerre 1939–1945* (Paris: Armand Colin, 2018), 36.
11. Alfred Salinas, "L'irredentisme espagnole en Oranie sous le regime de Vichy (juillet 1940–novembre 1942)," paper presented at a conference entitled "Deuxième guerre mondiale en Afrique du nord – Résistance et débarquement allié," Paris, 25–26 November 2018.

12. Le Gac, *Vaincre sans gloire*, 91.
13. Belazzouz Larbi, "Les républicains espagnols en Algérie de 1939 à 1962: Vicissitudes d'une communauté dans la colonie," *Oussour Al Jadida*, 7/26 (Winter–Spring 2016–2017), 102–106.
14. Many towns in the region, such as Guelma, Batna, Tébessa, and Sétif, were military garrisons surrounded by majority-Muslim populations. Muslims constituted 50 percent of the population of the coastal city of Bône, Algeria's third-largest port, with the other half divided between Italians and Maltese. Constantine, a fortress town of eastern Algeria surrounded by the 100-meter deep Gorges du Rummel and a center of the grain trade, counted 56,000 Muslims and 50,000 "Europeans," including 14,000 naturalized Jews, in 1936. Stora, *Histoire de l'Algérie coloniale*, 56–60.
15. Stora, *Histoire de l'Algérie coloniale*, 52–53.
16. Stora, *Histoire de l'Algérie coloniale*, 25, 81.
17. Jacques Cantier, *L'Algérie sous le régime de Vichy* (Paris: Éditions Odile Jacob, 2002), 33. Levisse-Touzé offers a higher estimate of Muslim POWs from North Africa to include 60,000 Algerians, 12,000 Tunisians, and 18,000 Moroccans. Christine Levisse-Touzé, "L'Afrique du Nord dans la guerre," paper delivered at the conference "Afrique du Nord: Vichy, Résistance, Alliés," Paris, 12–13 November 2017, 109.
18. Metzger, *Le Maghreb dans la guerre 1939–1945*, 21.
19. Mohammed Kably, *Histoire du Maroc: Réactualisation et synthèse* (Rabat: Édition de l'Institut Royal, 2012), 597, 603–604, 607, 632, 646–647.
20. Kably, *Histoire du Maroc*, 587; Jean Brignon et al., *Histoire du Maroc* (Paris: Hatier, 1967), 354–356, 365.
21. Metzger, *Le Maghreb dans la guerre 1939–1945*, 35.
22. Protestant and secular scouting groups were founded in France in 1911. Catholic and Jewish scouting and guides organized after the Great War. As in France, scouting in Algeria offered only one of several vehicles for patriotic mobilization associated with the PPA: the Association des femmes musulmanes, sports groups, medersas (Islamic schools), unions, and so on. Mahfoud Kaddache, "'Les soldats de l'avenir'. Les Scoutes musulmans algériens (1930–1962)," in Nicolas Bancel, Daniel Denis, and Youssef Fates, *De l'Indochine à l'Algérie: La jeunesses en mouvements des deux côtés du miroir colonial 1940–1962* (Paris: Éditions la Découvert, 2003), 68–71.
23. Martin Thomas, "France and Its Colonial Civil Wars, 1940–1945," in Richard J. B. Bosworth and Joseph A. Maiolo, *The Cambridge History of the Second World War*, volume II, *Politics and Ideology* (Cambridge: Cambridge University Press, 2015), 587.
24. Charles-Robert Ageron, "La Survivance d'un mythe: La puissance par l'empire colonial (1944–1947)," *Revue française d'Histoire d'Outre-Mer*, LXXII, no. 269 (1985), 388, 392, 394–395; Stora, *Histoire de l'Algérie coloniale*, 35.
25. Stora, *Histoire de l'Algérie coloniale*, 19.
26. Stora, *Histoire de l'Algérie coloniale*, 32–33.
27. Ethan Katz notes that, while Algerian Jews adopted broader French cultural norms and language, Jewish society with its social contacts and institutions

still formed their "primary community." For a discussion of the evolution of Jewish society in Algeria, see Joshua Schreier, *Arabs of the Jewish Faith: The Civilizing Mission in Colonial Algeria* (New Brunswick: Rutgers University Press, 2010). On the interconnection between family and citizenship in modern France, see Mary Louise Roberts, *Civilization without Sexes: Reconstructing Gender in Postwar France 1917–1927* (Chicago: University of Chicago Press, 1994); and Judith Surkis, *Sexing the Citizen: Morality and Masculinity in France, 1870–1920* (Ithaca, NY: Cornell University Press, 2011). I thank Ethan Katz for these references.

28. Stora, *Histoire de l'Algérie coloniale*, 34. Listen also to Benjamin Stora, "Voyage au bout de l'Algérie," France Culture, www.franceculture.fr/emissions/series/benjamin-stora-voyage-au-bout-de-lalgerie.
29. As of 1931, Algiers counted 156,971 Europeans (61 percent), 23,550 Jews (9 percent), and 76,601 Muslims (31 percent). Population census, 1931, detailed in Maurice Eisenbeth, *Les Juifs de l'Afrique du Nord: Démographique et onomastique* (Algiers: Imprimerie du Lycée, 1936), 14. There were around 230,000 Jews in Morocco, and 85,000 in Tunisia. Frédéric Harymbat, *Les Européens d'Afrique du Nord dans les armées de la libération française (1942–1945)* (Paris: Éditions l'Harmattan, 2014), 14.
30. Christine Levisse-Touzé, "L'Afrique du Nord: Un désert pour la France Libre?," in Sylvain Cornil-Ferrot and Philippe Oulmont (eds.), *Les Français libres et le monde: Actes du colloque international au musée de l'Armée 22 et 23 novembre 2013* (Paris: Nouveau Monde Éditions, 2015), 68.
31. Jews decorated in 1914–1918 and 1940 did not lose their citizenship rights, nor did 1,348 Algerian Jewish POWs in Germany. Sophie Roberts, "Jews, Vichy, and the Algiers Insurrection of 1942," *Holocaust Studies: A Journal of Culture and History*, 12/3 (winter 2006), 65.
32. Roberts, "Jews, Vichy, and the Algiers Insurrection of 1942," 63.
33. Yves-Claude Aouate, "La place de l'Algérie dans le projet antijuif de Vichy, "*Revue française d'histoire d'outre-mer*, 80/301 (1993), 601–613.
34. Andrew Buchanan, *American Grand Strategy in the Mediterranean during World War II* (Cambridge: Cambridge University Press, 2014), 7, 9, 11, 270.
35. Buchanan, *American Grand Strategy in the Mediterranean*, 7.
36. David Mayers, *FDR's Ambassadors and the Diplomacy of Crisis: From the Rise of Hitler to the End of World War II* (Cambridge: Cambridge University Press, 2012), 139–142.
37. Antoine Béthouart, *Cinq années d'espérance: Mémoires de guerre 1939–1945* (Paris: Plon, 1968), 283.
38. Julian Jackson, *De Gaulle* (Cambridge, MA: Harvard University Press, 2018), 263.
39. Harold Macmillan, *War Diaries: Politics and War in the Mediterranean January 1943–May 1945* (London: Macmillan, 1984), 151, 256, 393.
40. Maxime Weygand, *Mémoires*, tome III, *Rappelé au service* (Paris: Flammarion, 1950), 351.
41. Metzger, *Le Maghreb dans la guerre 1939–1945*, 110.
42. Robert Murphy, *Diplomat among Warriors* (London: Collins, 1964), 54, 56, 77–78, 94–97, 120–123.

43. Buchanan, *American Grand Strategy in the Mediterranean*, 22, 45.
44. Christine Levisse-Touzé, *L'Afrique du Nord dans la guerre 1939–1945* (Paris: Albin Michel, 1998), 136–139; Metzger, *Le Maghreb dans la guerre 1939–1945*, 91–93.
45. "President Roosevelt to the Appointed Ambassador to France (Leahy), 20 December 1940," US Department of State, Publication 1983, *Peace and War: United States Foreign Policy, 1931–1941* (Washington, D.C.: US Government Printing Office, 1943), 595–599.
46. Levisse-Touzé insists that 85 percent of imports into AFN came from France. Levisse-Touzé, "L'Afrique du Nord dans la guerre," 5.
47. Levisse-Touzé, "L'Afrique du Nord dans la guerre," 3.
48. Maréchal Alphonse Pierre Juin, *Mémoires*, tome 1, *Alger, Tunis, Rome* (Paris: Fayard, 1959), 35.
49. Robert O. Paxton, *Vichy France: Old Guard and New Order, 1940–1944* (London: Barrie & Jenkins, 1972), 90–91.
50. Commercial Exchanges in North Africa (Murphy–Weygand Agreement), www.loc.gov/law/help/us-treaties/bevans/b-fr-ust000007-1059.pdf. The commodities included coal, gasoline and oil, twine, iron wire, spare parts for agricultural machinery, pitch, sugar, and pharmaceuticals. Office of the Historian, US Department of State, "The French Minister for Foreign Affairs (Darlan) to the American Ambassador in France (Leahy)," 10 March 1941; "Memorandum of Conversation, by the Assistant Chief of the Division of Near Eastern Affairs (Villard)," 8 April 1941; "The French Ambassador (Henry-Haye) to the Secretary of State," 3 June 1941. See https://history.state.gov/historicaldocuments/frus1941v02/d192. See also Elliott Burton Litsky, "The Murphy–Weygand Agreement: The United States and French North Africa (1940–1942)," Ph.D. thesis, Fordham University, 1986.
51. Mayers, *FDR's Ambassadors and the Diplomacy of Crisis*, 147; Olivier Lahaie, *Guerre des services spéciaux en Afrique du Nord 1941–1944: Les mémoires du Général Jean Chrétien ancient chef du contre-espionnage à Alger* (Paris: Histoire & Collections, 2015), 99–100. The US concern was to prevent commodities like cobalt and molybdenum used in steel alloys from being exported to Germany. Deliveries were sporadic, depending on objections by the British or the Germans, or suspension of deliveries to pressure Vichy on some policy issue. Levisse-Touzé, *L'Afrique du Nord dans la guerre 1939–1945*, 132–133, 164–167, 187.
52. Martin Thomas and Richard Toye, *Arguing about Empire: Imperial Rhetoric in Britain and France, 1882–1956* (Oxford: Oxford University Press, 2017), 181–182.
53. Phillips Payson O'Brien, *The Second Most Powerful Man in the World: The Life of Admiral William D. Leahy, Roosevelt's Chief of Staff* (New York: Dutton, 2019), 149.
54. Paxton, *Vichy France*, 101–109, 129.
55. These portions of the report had been crossed out, presumably because higher authority would not be happy to read them. SHD-GR, 2H 165. "États d'esprits," March 1942.

56. Pierre Lesouef, "La crise de novembre 1942 en Afrique française du nord et la campagne de Tunisie," 306.
57. Levisse-Touzé, *L'Afrique du Nord dans la guerre 1939–1945*, 141–142.
58. Mayers, *FDR's Ambassadors and the Diplomacy of Crisis*, 147–148; O'Brien, *The Second Most Powerful Man in the World*, 172.
59. Metzger, *Le Maghreb dans la guerre 1939–1945*, 93–96.
60. O'Brien, *The Second Most Powerful Man in the World*, 168; Thomas Laub, *After the Fall: German Policy in Occupied France, 1940–1944* (Oxford: Oxford University Press, 2013), Chapter 2. Weygand ordered that Muslims who informed the Armistice Commission were to be arrested. "Some North African nationalists were sent to the south or convicted because of their relations with the AC [Armistice Commission]. The environs of the Spanish consulates that are frequented by the AC are especially watched by the police." SHD-GR, 2H 165, March 1942.
61. Levisse-Touzé, *L'Afrique du Nord dans la guerre 1939–1945*, 149–150.
62. O'Brien, *The Second Most Powerful Man in the World*, 168.
63. SHD-GR, 2H 165, "États d'esprits."
64. Le Gac, *Vaincre sans gloire*, 97.
65. On 28 September 1942, barely a month before Torch, Juin complained once again to his superiors in Vichy about "the rowdy activity of certain parties or offshoots of parties like the S.O.L. who, under the pretext of enforcing the principles of the National Revolution and insuring order, begin by provoking disorder in Oran in particular. Until now, they've done it with impunity in the face of natives and foreigners who are watching us and who only await a favorable opportunity to intervene themselves for their own ends." SHD-GR, 1P 35, Juin to Vichy, 28 September 1942.
66. Jean-Christophe Notin, *Maréchal Juin* (Paris: Tallandier, 2015), 95–97.
67. Levisse-Touzé, *L'Afrique du Nord dans la guerre 1939–1945*, 159, 175, 207; Le Gac, *Vaincre sans gloire*, 128. Weygand also gives a long self-justification in his memoirs. Weygand, *Mémoires*, tome III, 347–533.
68. Pierre Montagnon, *Dictionnaire de la colonisation française* (Paris: Pygmalion/Flammarion, 2010).
69. Juin also believed that Huntzinger's death in a November 1942 air crash had postponed Noguès' recall. Juin, *Mémoires*, tome 1, 24–26; Notin, *Maréchal Juin*, 107.
70. Levisse-Touzé, *L'Afrique du Nord dans la guerre 1939–1945*, 3, 114–118.
71. Levisse-Touzé, *L'Afrique du Nord dans la guerre 1939–1945*, 196–197, 202; Notin, *Maréchal Juin*, 94–100, 110. Marcel Spivak and Colonel Armand Leoni estimate the permissible size of the AFN garrison in February 1941 at 134,997, depending upon who was counted. "Probably the question [of manpower] was given only a relative importance given the inadequacies of armament, matériel, and equipment left in AFN." Marcel Spivak and Armand Leoni, *Les forces françaises dans la lutte contre l'Axe en Afrique*, tome II, *La campagne de Tunisie 1943–1943* (Vincennes: Ministère de la Defense, État-major de l'armée de terre, Service historique, 1985), 27–29.
72. Levisse-Touzé, "L'Afrique du Nord: Un désert pour la France Libre?", 65–71.

73. Murphy, *Diplomat among Warriors*, 142–143.
74. Levisse-Touzé, *L'Afrique du Nord dans la guerre 1939–1945*, 208–222; Murphy, *Diplomat among Warriors*, 141.
75. SHD-GR, 2P 21, 26 March 1942. See also "Compte-rendu du jugement par contumace du 2 août 1940 dans l'affaire de Gaulle," 17 September 1942, for the bill to disband the *Sections spéciales militaires*.
76. Harymbat, *Les Européens d'Afrique du Nord*, 25, 29–31, 35.
77. Macmillan, *War Diaries*, 27, 45, 69, 256.
78. Macmillan, *War Diaries*, 45.
79. Lemaigre-Dubreuil's motives for cooperating with an Allied invasion are unclear as he appeared to be a supporter of the National Revolution and, in 1944, keen to convince the United States to organize a compromise peace with Nazi Germany to prevent the Soviet Union from overrunning Europe. Paxton, *Vichy France*, 328.
80. Murphy, *Diplomat among Warriors*, 150.
81. Buchanan, *American Grand Strategy in the Mediterranean*, 45.
82. Macmillan, *War Diaries*, 264.
83. Jean Lacouture, *De Gaulle*, tome 1, *Le Rebelle 1890–1944* (Paris: Éditions du Seuil, 1984), 265–266; Jackson, *De Gaulle*, 95.
84. Murphy, *Diplomat among Warriors*, 167.
85. Notin, *Maréchal Juin*, 77–78, 200.
86. Juin, *Mémoires*, tome 1, 23.
87. Giraud's arrival coincided with a crisis in *la France libre* over the retention of Muselier, who some in Britain had seen as a successor to de Gaulle, and a fear that tensions in the movement were acute to the point that it might splinter. Jackson, *De Gaulle*, 208–211.
88. Murphy, *Diplomat among Warriors*, 148–149.
89. Macmillan, *War Diaries*, 68, 136, 166.
90. Robert O. Paxton, *Parades and Politics at Vichy: The French Officer Corps under Marshal Pétain* (Princeton: Princeton University Press, 1966), 298–299.
91. Le Gac, *Vaincre sans gloire*, 42–49, 51, 187.
92. Marcel Vigneras, *United States Army in World War II: Rearming the French* (Washington, D.C.: Center of Military History, United States Army, 1989), 106–107, 123–124.
93. Michèle Cointet, *Nouvelle histoire de Vichy* (Paris: Fayard, 2011), 536–538; Notin, *Maréchal Juin*, 193, 196.
94. Juin, *Mémoires*, tome 1, 23.
95. Buchanan, *American Grand Strategy in the Mediterranean*, 44–45.
96. Notin, *Maréchal Juin*, 159–161.
97. Murphy, *Diplomat among Warriors*, 142.
98. Sophie Quentin, "Les Goums: La Place des soldats marocains dans l'armée française," in Yves Jeanclos (ed.), *La France et les soldats d'infortune au XXe siècle* (Strasbourg: Economica, 2003), 86–90.
99. Le Gac, *Vaincre sans gloire*, 53–54.
100. Le Gac, *Vaincre sans gloire*, 504–505; Claire Miot, "Sortir l'armée des ombres. Soldats de l'Empire, combattants de la Libération, armée de la

Nation: La Première armée française, du débarquement en Provence à la capitulation allemande (1944–1945)," Thèse du doctorat, Université Paris-Saclay, 2016, 740.

101. Zeldin, *France 1848–1945*, volume 2, 905.
102. Louis Bacquier, *Aïwah: Au combat avec les marocains. Souvenirs d'un officier de tirailleurs 1942–1945* (Paris: Éditions Laville, 2012), 201.
103. Weygand, *Mémoires*, tome III, 388.
104. SHD-GR, 2H 165, March 1942. See also a 10 May 1943 report that sums up Noguès' efforts to hide matériel from German armistice commission surveillance: "L'Effort de résistance du Maroc du juin 1940 à novembre 1942 à la preparation à la reprise de la lutte contre l'Allemagne," SHD-GR, 5 P2.
105. SHD-GR, 1P 121, "Note de service," 4 May 1941; "Renforcement de l'Afrique du Nord," 13 December 1941; 1 P 86, "Note sur l'instruction provisoire sur l'emploi des forces mobiles," 18 September 1942; 1P 122, "La situation des effectifs au 25 octobre 1942"; Levisse-Touzé, *L'Afrique du Nord dans la guerre 1939–1945*, 202; Juin, *Mémoires*, tome 1, 63.
106. Juin, *Mémoires*, tome 1, 36.
107. Macmillan, *War Diaries*, 89.
108. Georges Elgozy, *La vérité sur mon Corps Franc d'Afrique 1942–1943* (Monaco: Éditions du Rocher, 1985), 197.
109. Cantier, *L'Algérie sous le régime de Vichy*, 76, 289–296; Harymbat, *Les Européens d'Afrique du Nord*, 28–29; Metzger, *Le Maghreb dans la guerre 1939–1945*, 114–115.
110. Harymbat, *Les Européens d'Afrique du Nord*, 28–29, 100; Romain Durand, *De Giraud à de Gaulle: Les Corps francs d'Afrique* (Paris: Éditions l'Harmattan, 1999), 17–25.
111. Général André Beaufre, *Mémoires 1920–1940–1945* (Paris: Presses de la Cité, 1965), 288–289.
112. Harymbat, *Les Européens d'Afrique du Nord*, 115–116.
113. Juin, *Mémoires*, tome 1, 61.
114. Le Gac, *Vaincre sans gloire*, 123–126.
115. General Jean Delmas, "Syntheses des travaux du colloque," in Colloque International, *Les armées françaises pendant la seconde guerre mondiale*, 449.
116. Juin, *Mémoires*, tome 1, 62–63.
117. Paxton, *Parades and Politics at Vichy*, 303–304; "L'Effort de résistance du Maroc du juin 1940 à novembre 1942 à la preparation à la reprise de la lutte contre l'Allemagne," 24–25, SHD-GR, 5P 2; M. R. D. Foot, *SOE in France* (London: Her Majesty's Stationary Office, 1966), 116–119; Henri Noguères, *La vie quotidienne des résistants de l'Armistice à la Libération* (Paris: Hachette, 1984), 97–105. For Paillole's insistence that the BMA's role had no police function and if some officers turned over information on Resistance networks to the ST, it was the result of a few "errors" or "mistakes" and not the result of BMA policy, see Henri Noguères, *Histoire de la résistance en France*, vol. II (Paris: Laffont, 1969), Annexe VIII, 698–700.
118. Abetz complained that Devilliers' execution was evidence of an anti-German spirit in the Armistice Army. But some in Vichy, led by General

Bridoux, were upset at Devilliers' execution because he had been an important source of information about Gaullist agents, which suggests Vichy's ambiguous attitude toward espionage and its uneven treatment of spies. Simon Kitson, *Vichy et la chasse aux espions Nazis: 1940–1942. Complexités de la politique de collaboration* (Paris: Éditions Autrement, 2005), 72–73, 82–85, 168–169, 182–183.

119. SHD-GR, 5P 2. "L'Effort de résistance du Maroc du juin 1940 à novembre 1942 à la preparation à la reprise de la lutte contre l'Allemagne," 26.
120. Bacquier, *Aïwah*, 111.
121. Durand, *De Giraud à de Gaulle*, 17.
122. For a brief overview of the *Légion tricolore*, see Chantal Metzger, *L'empire colonial français dans la stratégie du troisième Reich (1936–1945)*, vol. I (Paris and Brussels: Direction des Archives, Ministère des Affaires étrangères/P.I.E. Peter Lang, 2002), 469–471. See also "Recruiting of French Forces against the Soviets," American Consulate General Algiers, 22 January 1942; Office of Strategic Services, Foreign Nationalities Branch, "The French Tricolor Legion," 7 July 1942; "Guarantees Given to Members of the Tricolor Legion," Military Attaché Report, 16 September 1942; Intelligence Report, US Naval Attaché, Tangier, 23 July 1942. NARA, RG 165, Entry 77, Box 866.
123. SHD-GR, 2P 14, "Note pour l'état major de l'armée," 25 September 1942. A note of 28 September 1942 argued that many of these men had indeed volunteered for the *Légion tricolore* to avoid punishment for disciplinary infractions. The solution was simply to have these men fail the physical examination at the depot at Guéret, set up in the middle of July 1942, and return them to their units for disciplinary action. But indications are that significant numbers of soldiers in AFN were also volunteering for the *Légion tricolore*. A 30 August 1942 wire from Rabat lists 177 volunteers for a battalion of *tirailleurs marocains* to be raised for the *Légion tricolore*. "Situation numérique des militaires de l'armée d'Armistice volontaires pour la Légion tricolore, et incorporés dans cette Légion à la date du 2 Septembre 1942." See also 10 July 1942, on Guéret; and 15 September 1942, "Fiche au sujet du recrutement pour la Légion tricolore." On that day, an estimated 225 NCOs and soldiers from units in the 19th Army Corps that covered AFN had volunteered for the *Légion tricolore*, of which 138 had been accepted. A 2 September 1942 report put their numbers at 378, of whom 228, including 20 officers, were from the *armée d'Afrique*: "État numérique des sous officiers et hommes de troupe volontaires pour servir à la Légion tricolore à la date du 15 septembre 1942." The numbers on 1 October were 54 officers, 118 NCOs, and 595 soldiers, including 105 Moroccans: "*Effectifs de la Légion tricolore*," 5 October 1942. See a complaint letter about the *Légion tricolore* hurting the readiness of *l'armée d'Afrique*, 30 September 1942. Levisse-Touzé, *L'Afrique du Nord dans la guerre 1939–1945*, 335–337.
124. Metzger, *L'empire colonial français dans la stratégie du troisième Reich*, 668–671.
125. Eric Lefèvre and Jean Mabire, *La Légion perdue face aux partisans 1942* (Paris: Jacques Grancher, 1995), 260.

126. Estimated to be around 4,000 men after the liberation of the class of 1939, with another 4,000 volunteers not yet allowed to exit metropolitan France.
127. Metzger, *Le Maghreb dans la guerre 1939–1945*, 76.
128. SHD-GR, 1P 89, 10 September to 10 October 1942; 1P 35, "Voyage d'information en Afrique du nord . . . Troupes."
129. SHD-GR, 1P 86, "Recrutement de la légion tricolore," 25 August 1942.
130. SHD-GR, 1P 86, 21 October 1942; SHD-GR, 1P 229. Letter from the President of the German Armistice Commission, 9 May 1941. Also other correspondence, including 28 November 1941. 1P 86, 18 September 1942, "Note du service."
131. Part of this may have been due to a monotonous diet of US B rations that were not part of a normal North African diet. Vigneras, *Rearming the French*, 256–257; Jean-François Muracciole, *Les Français libres: L'autre Résistance* (Paris: Tallandier, 2009), 239.
132. Robert Merle, *Ahmed ben Bella* (Paris: Gallimard, 1965), 41.
133. Belkacem Recham, *Les Musulmans algériens dans l'armée française (1919–1945)* (Paris: Éditions l'Harmattan, 1996), 46–56, 72–91, 233, 237–241, 253–255; Le Gac, *Vaincre sans gloire*, 301–306, 324–337. "Dans un camp baraqué, la cellule suit le régime de la régulière; dans un campement, le puni de cellule loge sous ce qu'on appelle le *tombeau* ou le *guignol*, c'est-à-dire la toile de tente pliée en deux en forme de prisme triangulaire. Le puni couche alors à même la terre, gèle la nuit, cuit le jour, ne peut bouger; le moindre mouvement pouvant démolir la tente et étant formellement defendu." htt ps://fr.wikisource.org/wiki/Les_Corps_disciplinaires_(La_Revue_Blanche)/ 15_juillet_1900.
134. Recham, *Les Musulmans algériens dans l'armée française*, 191–195; Harymbat, *Les Européens d'Afrique du Nord*, 137–140.
135. Stora, *Histoire de l'Algérie coloniale (1830–1954)*, 100.
136. Ebbe Curtiss Hoff, *Preventative Medicine in World War II*, volume VIII, *Civil Affairs/Military Government Public Health Activities* (Washington, D.C.: Office of the Surgeon General, Department of the Army, 1976), 258–259, 269–275; Stora, *Histoire de l'Algérie coloniale (1830–1954)*, 100.
137. Stora, *Histoire de l'Algérie coloniale (1830–1954)*, 81–82.
138. Recham, *Les Musulmans algériens dans l'armée française*, 194–204; Levisse-Touzé, *L'Afrique du Nord dans la guerre 1939–1945*, 145; SHD-GR, 1P 35, "Voyage d'information en Afrique du Nord."
139. Miot, "Sortir l'armée des ombres," 688.
140. Pierre Giolitto, *Histoire de la milice* (Paris: Librairie Académique Perrin, 1997), 9–59.
141. SHD-GR, 2P 14, 30 January 1942, "Circulaire," and General Revers' letter of 14 March 1942 reiterating prohibition on membership for officers "on armistice leave."
142. Cantier, *L'Algérie sous le régime de Vichy*, 207–218; Levisse-Touzé, *L'Afrique du Nord dans la guerre 1939–1945*, 156–157; SHD-GR, 2P 14, "Organisation de la Légion française des combattaants et des volontaires

de la Révolution nationale," November 1941; 2P 14, Picquenard letter of 15 December 1940 forbidding soldiers to join the LFC; 2P 14, "Feuille de renseignement" of 4 September 1941 allowing former officers employed by the war commissariat to join the LFC.

143. SHD-GR, 2H 165, "État d'esprit," March 1942.
144. Harymbat, *Les Européens d'Afrique du Nord*, 26–27; SHD-GR 2P 14, for the foundation of the Légion, see Darlan's letter of 15 December 1940; "Organisation de la Légion française des combattants et des volontaircs de la Révolution nationale"; and "Instructions portant règlement de la Légion française des combattants volontaires de la Révolution nationale." for the order forbidding soldiers to join it, see Picquenar, 15 December 1940. For its reversal, see "Note relative à l'opportunité de la création de nouvelles amicales," 17 January 1941.
145. Recham, *Les Musulmans algériens dans l'armée française*, 193; Cantier, *L'Algérie sous le régime de Vichy*, 209–212, 216–218; Le Gac, *Vaincre sans gloire*, 128–131; Levisse-Touzé, *L'Afrique du Nord dans la guerre 1939–1945*, 142.
146. Le Gac, *Vaincre sans gloire*, 134.
147. SHD-GR, 1P 35, 28 September 1942. For more background on the LFC and SOL, see Giolitto, *Histoire de la milice*, 61–62, 102–124.
148. Harymbat, *Les Européens d'Afrique du Nord*, 26, 31.
149. Durand, *De Giraud à de Gaulle*, 16.
150. SHD-GR, 1P 89, "Synthèse hebdomadaire pour l'Afrique du Nord. Période du 2 au 9 Octobre 1942."
151. Le Gac, *Vaincre sans gloire*, 128.
152. Durand, *De Giraud à de Gaulle*, 16.
153. SHD-GR, 1P 89, 29 January 1942; 24 February 1942 "note." Low morale was also reported in a 29 March 1942 report, "Note sur le moral de la troupe et des cadres en A.F.N."
154. SHD-GR, 1P 35, 6 March 1941; 1P 89, 10 September to 10 October 1942.
155. SHD-GR, 1P 121, "Le Morale de l'Armée," letter of Juin, 16 January 1942; 1P 89, Mendigal report.
156. SHD-GR, 1P 89, 29 March 1942, "Note sur le morale de la troupe et des cadres en A.F.N.," 3–7; Durand, *De Giraud à de Gaulle*, 43.
157. Peter Jackson and Simon Kitson, "The Paradoxes of Vichy Foreign Policy," in Jonathan R. Adelman (ed.), *Hitler and His Allies in World War II* (New York: Routledge, 2007), 110.
158. William Leahy, *I Was There: The Memoirs of FDR's Chief of Staff* (New York: Enigma Books, 2017), 47; Sumner Welles, *Seven Major Decisions* (London: Hamish Hamilton, 1951), 66; O'Brien, *The Second Most Powerful Man in the World*, 163.
159. SHD-GR, 1P 35, 13 May 1942, with the 2 May 1942 attached. Bernard Costagliola places this in the context of a riposte in the event that the British attacked Marseilles or Toulon. Bernard Costagliola, *Darlan: La collaboration à tout prix* (Paris: Éditions CNRS, 2015), 237.

160. Juin, *Mémoires*, tome 1, 69–71; Costagliola, *Darlan*, 237; SHD-GR 1P 35, "Instructions personnelles et secrètes pour le général commandant supérieur des troupes de Tunisie pour la défense de Tunisie en cas de l'aggression de l'Axe par surprise," 30 January 1942; "Envoi de la directive N° 1," 13 May 1942.
161. SHD-GR, 1P 34, 14 August 1942.
162. Levisse-Touzé, *L'Afrique du Nord dans la guerre 1939–1945*, 135, 206.
163. SHD-GR, 1P 86, 27 September 1942, "Note du service."
164. Levisse-Touzé, *L'Afrique du Nord dans la guerre 1939–1945*, 176.
165. Notin, *Maréchal Juin*, 106-107.
166. These included the release of more *Armée d'Afrique* officer POWs, rearmament of and freedom of movement for the forces in North Africa, whom the Germans would agree to supply with petrol, the remilitarization of southern Tunisia, and *Luftwaffe* protection for ports and shipping in eastern Algeria and Tunisia. Metzger, *Le Maghreb dans la guerre 1939–1945*, 107.
167. This included roughly 2,000 lorries for the Afrika Korps full of supplies; the use of Bizerte by German merchant ships free of customs control; impressment of French ships to convoy and escort supplies; and use of the Bizerte–Gabès railroad to send supplies to Rommel, who would also have access to matériel from French stocks in AFN. The agreement was never fully applied because of opposition from Weygand, the "apathy" of Darlan, Hitler's hostility to the agreement, fears that the British would blockade AFN and Dakar, and Roosevelt's threats to suspend food aid. Metzger, *Le Maghreb dans la guerre 1939–1945*, 143–144; Levisse-Touzé, *L'Afrique du Nord dans la guerre 1939–1945*, 177–185.
168. SHD-GR, 2H 165, "Défense du territoire," March 1942; Levisse-Touzé, *L'Afrique du Nord dans la guerre 1939–1945*, 135.
169. SHD-GR, 1P 86, "Note du service," 10 October 1942.
170. SHD-GR, 1P 35, "Voyage d'information en Afrique du Nord . . . Troupes." For instance, out of a normal strength of thirty officers, the 65th Artillery Regiment lacked a major, four captains, and twelve lieutenants.
171. SHD-GR, 1P 35, 1942, "Voyage d'information en Afrique du Nord . . . Troupes"; Costagliola, *Darlan*, 240–241.
172. High Command of the Army, Army General Staff/Division of Foreign Armies of the West, "The Treatise Entitled 'The French Army' Status on June 20 1942" (document translated 14 May 1943), Chapter XIII. NARA RG 165, Entry 77, Box 865.
173. Levisse-Touzé, *L'Afrique du Nord dans la guerre 1939–1945*, 186.
174. The two successful Allied amphibious assaults to date at Guadalcanal and Diego-Suarez had succeeded against no opposition. Vincent P. O'Hara, *Torch: North Africa and the Allied Path to Victory* (Annapolis: Naval Institute Press, 2015), 26–27.
175. Levisse-Touzé, *L'Afrique du Nord dans la guerre 1939–1945*, 181–183.
176. Notin, *Maréchal Juin*, 153.

177. SHD-GR, 1P 35, "Possibilités de débarquement sur les côtes du Maroc," 9 May 1942.
178. Other specialized landing craft developed and used in Torch were the landing craft personnel (LCP), with a ramped version (LCPR), landing craft vehicle (LCV), landing craft mechanized (LCM), landing craft support (LCS), and landing ship tank (LST), an adaptation of Lake Maracaibo tankers capable of carrying twenty-one tanks to shore. O'Hara, *Torch*, 27–29.
179. SHD-GR, 1P 86, "Note sur l'Instruction provisoire sur l'emploi des forces mobiles."
180. SHD-GR, 1P 35, "Rentrée des troupes du Maroc dans leurs garnisons normales," 30 September 1942.
181. SHD-GR, 1P 46, General Revers, "Situation générale. 1–31 Octobre 1942," 5 November 1942, 1, 85.
182. SHD-GR, 1P 86, Juin, "Memento général sur la guerilla ou 'combat sur les arrières de l'ennemi' en Afrique du Nord," 5 November 1942, 1, 4–6.
183. SHD-GR, 1P 35, 1942, "Voyage d'information en Afrique du nord."
184. SHD-GR, 1P 35, 1942, "Voyage d'information en Afrique du nord." A further complaint was that native affairs offered a poor career path, especially for staff brevets, because command of an administrative "circle" or territory was not considered a fulfillment of the troop command requirement for promotion.
185. Allied Forces Headquarters, Office of the Assistant Chief of Staff, G-2. G-2 Intelligence Report No. 6, 16 October 1942. NARA RG 165, Entry 77, Box 865.
186. High Command of the Army, Army General Staff/Division of Foreign Armies of the West, "The Treatise Entitled 'The French Army,' Status on June 20, 1942." NARA, RG 165, Entry 77, Box 865.
187. Michael S. Neiberg, *When France Fell: The Vichy Crisis and the Fate of the Anglo-American Alliance* (Cambridge, MA: Harvard University Press, 2021), 61.

10 Torch

1. Robert O. Paxton, *Parades and Politics at Vichy: The French Officer Corps under Marshal Pétain* (Princeton: Princeton University Press, 1966), 344–346; Christine Levisse-Touzé, *L'Afrique du Nord dans la guerre 1939–1945* (Paris: Albin Michel, 1998), 365.
2. Andrew Buchanan, *American Grand Strategy in the Mediterranean during World War II* (Cambridge: Cambridge University Press, 2014), 7. For the US military's role in shaping foreign policy, see Steven L. Rearden, *Council of War: A History of the Joint Chiefs of Staff, 1942–1991* (Washington, D.C.: National Defense University Press, 2012); and Andrew Roberts, *Masters and Commanders: How Four Titans Won the War in the West, 1941–1945* (New York: Harper, 2009).
3. Buchanan, *American Grand Strategy in the Mediterranean*, 87.
4. Robert Belot, *La Résistance sans de Gaulle* (Paris: Fayard, 2006), 330.

5. Dwight David Eisenhower, *The Papers of Dwight David Eisenhower: The War Years* (Baltimore: Johns Hopkins University Press, 1970), 695.
6. For an assessment of the importance of the Mediterranean theater in the Allied victory, see Douglas Porch, *Path to Victory: The Mediterranean Theater in World War II* (New York: Farrar, Straus, Giroux, 2004).
7. Levisse-Touzé, *L'Afrique du Nord dans la guerre 1939–1945*, 237.
8. Guillaume Piketty, "La France combattante au cœur du maelstrom," paper delivered at the conference "8 November 1942. Débarquement allié et Résistance en Afrique du Nord," Hôtel des Invalides, Paris, 12–13 November 2017.
9. SHD-GR, P7 111, Circulaire de Larminat, 15 June 1943.
10. Jean-Louis Crémieux-Brilhac, *La France Libre*, tome I, *De l'appel du 18 juin à la Libération* (Paris: Gallimard, 2013), 547.
11. Summation by Guillaume Piketty, at "E Pluribus Unum? Pluralité et identité des français libres," conference 27–28 November 2019, Château de Vincennes, Paris. See also Belot, *La Résistance sans de Gaulle*, 21–41.
12. Levisse-Touzé, *L'Afrique du Nord dans la guerre 1939–1945*, 237, 365.
13. Akhila Yechury and Emile Chabal, "Introduction," in Robert Tombs and Emile Chabal (eds.), *Britain and France in Two World Wars: Truth, Myth and Memory*, (London: Bloomsbury, 2013), 88–89.
14. Benjamin Stora, *Histoire de l'Algérie coloniale (1830–1954)* (Paris: Éditions La Découverte, 2004), 84.
15. Julie Le Gac, *Vaincre sans gloire: Le corps expéditionnaire français en Italie (novembre 1942–juillet 1944)* (Paris: Les Belles Lettres/Ministère de la défense-DMPA, 2013), 97.
16. Sébastien Albertelli, *Les Services secrets du Général de Gaulle: Le BCRA 1940–1944* (Paris: Perrin, 2009), 235.
17. Presumably totally ignorant of the outcome of the Battle of the Coral Sea in May 1942, followed by the Battle of Midway the following month, and progress on Guadalcanal, which US troops had invaded in August 1942, some in Berlin speculated that the Allies needed a spectacular coup to compensate for their setbacks in the Pacific. Admiral Erich Raeder saw an Allied invasion of AFN as the best way to preempt his ambition to transform Dakar into a U-boat base. The *Abwehr* predicted an Allied landing in Morocco between 15 October and 15 November. But its chief, Admiral Wilhelm Canaris, could convince no one, least of all Hitler, that the Anglo-Americans had the ability to carry out such an ambitious plan. The intelligence prediction did not mention Algeria and Tunisia, considered the province of Italian intelligence. Hitler, whose imperial ambitions remained focused on continental Europe, considered the prognostication to be yet another warmed-over Pan-Germanist fantasy about Morocco as "the California of Africa." Chantal Metzger, *L'empire colonial français dans la stratégie du troisième Reich (1936–1945)*, vol. I (Paris and Brussels: Direction des Archives, Ministère des Affaires étrangères/P.I.E.-Peter Lang, 2002), 473–476.

18. The purpose of the unusual number of Allied ships in Gibraltar was thought to be to support the British effort in Egypt, perhaps by landing troops in the Tripoli–Benghazi region. Malta, Sicily, or Sardinia, even the Aegean, were also considered possible targets. Metzger, *L'empire colonial français dans la stratégie du troisième Reich*, 480–481.
19. Jean-Christophe Notin, *Maréchal Juin* (Paris: Tallandier, 2015), 150–151. Part of the skepticism was based on the calculation by the general staff at Vichy in September 1942 that U-boats were sinking Allied tonnage faster than ships could be constructed. SHD-GR, 1P 46, "Situation générale 1–30 septembre 1942," 5 October 1942, 12.
20. French intelligence, apparently based on Italian sources, reported that, at Tobruk, "the attackers . . . were forced to re-embark, abandoning numerous dead and several hundred prisoners, and suffering significant naval losses [two cruisers, four destroyers, and some small boats, according to the Italians – the British admit two destroyers] . . ." SHD-GR, 1P 42, "Situation générale 1–30 septembre 1942." 5 October 1942, 3, 18.
21. The Americans were aware that Darlan had been in AFN since 23 October. He presided over a military review in Algiers on 29 October, and met with American minister Robert Murphy. Darlan's plan was to return to France. But he remained in Algiers to be close to his son, who had been struck with what seemed to be polio. American historian Arthur Layton Funk speculated that Darlan lingered in Algiers because he knew of the imminent Allied invasion. Arthur Layton Funk, *The Politics of Torch: The Allied Landings and the Algiers Putsch, 1942* (Lawrence: University Press of Kansas, 1974), 178–180. But the majority of historians reject that supposition, among them the doyen of French naval historians, Philippe Masson, *La marine française dans la guerre, 1939–1945* (Paris: Tallandier, 1991), 368–370. French historian Olivier Lahaie counters that, while Darlan and Revers had been warned by French intelligence, which was aware of the activity of Murphy and others, of an imminent Allied invasion, Darlan remained convinced that the Allies were incapable of mounting an invasion of North Africa in the autumn of 1942. Instead, the more likely scenario in the mind of Darlan and Revers was an invasion of southern France in the spring of 1943. Olivier Lahaie, *Guerre des services spéciaux en Afrique du Nord 1941–1944: Les mémoires du Général Jean Chrétien ancient chef du contre-espionnage à Alger* (Paris: Histoire & Collections, 2015), 101–112. The American official history also concluded that "[Darlan] was caught by surprise and was exasperated that he had not been forewarned," as he apparently expected to be by Murphy. George F. Howe, *United States Army in World War II: The Mediterranean Theater of Operations, Northwest Africa: Seizing the Initiative in the West* (Washington, D.C.: Center of Military History, United States Army, 1991), 250. This is also the conclusion of Vincent P. O'Hara, who records that Darlan was warned by Italian intelligence, and by his own subordinates, on 6–7 November 1942 that the Allied convoys passing through the Mediterranean might be headed for Morocco or Algeria, but rejected this in favor of Bizerte as a more likely target. Vincent P. O'Hara, *Torch: North Africa*

and the Allied Path to Victory (Annapolis: Naval Institute Press, 2015), 80–82. Darlan's latest biographer, Bernard Costagliola, agrees that Darlan was taken totally by surprise by Torch. Bernard Costagliola, *Darlan: La collaboration à tout prix* (Paris: Éditions CNRS, 2015), 241.

22. René Pierre Eugène Caroff, *Les débarquements alliés en Afrique du Nord (novembre 1942)*, second edition (Vincennes: Service historique de la marine, 1987), 9–14. Moreau subsequently speculated that Darlan's motive in blocking the ship channel at Bizerte was to prevent Vichy from ordering the High Seas Fleet to sail from Toulon to Bizerte, to avoid a sea battle with the British fleet.
23. This scenario has most recently been laid out by O'Hara, that Darlan was willing to collaborate with the Allies. However, associating Darlan with the conspiracy was rejected because the Allies had already committed themselves to Giraud, and the Group of Five refused to associate with a man with a deeply collaborationist past. O'Hara, *Torch*, 66–68.
24. Philippe Burrin, *France under the Germans: Collaboration and Compromise* (New York: The New Press, 1996), 75.
25. Phillips Payson O'Brien, *The Second Most Powerful Man in the World: The Life of Admiral William D. Leahy, Roosevelt's Chief of Staff* (New York: Dutton, 2019), 152–153, 173.
26. Notin, *Maréchal Juin*, 162; Costagliola, *Darlan*, 240.
27. Costagliola, *Darlan*, 240–241.
28. Notin, *Maréchal Juin*, 93–95, 131; Christine Levisse-Touzé, *L'Afrique du Nord dans la guerre 1939–1945* (Paris: Albin Michel, 1998), 249.
29. Buchanan, *American Grand Strategy*, 87.
30. Robert O. Paxton, *Vichy France: Old Guard and New Order, 1940–1944* (London: Barrie & Jenkins, 1972), 16–17, 34, 286, 291, 321; Notin, *Maréchal Juin*, 100; Le Gac, *Vaincre sans gloire*, 135.
31. David Reynolds, "Afrique du nord et stratégie planétaire," in Nicola Labanca, David Reynolds, and Olivier Wieviorka (eds.), *La Guerre du Désert* (Paris: Perrin, 2019), 75.
32. Ian Kershaw, *Fateful Choices: Ten Decisions That Changed the World 1940–1941* (London: Penguin, 2007), 316.
33. This view was shaped in part by information leaked to the US embassy from a mid-level official in the Vichy Foreign Ministry's Far Eastern Affairs section, Jean Chauvel, whose motivation was to secure US support to resist Japanese pressure to occupy southern Indochina. Chauvel also tipped off the embassy about Barbarossa. O'Brien, *The Second Most Powerful Man in the World*, 155, 159. The operation was also eased by growing criticism both in the British and in the American press of the policy of Vichy appeasement, and by a geopolitical worst-case scenario in which an Axis takeover of French possessions in Africa might compromise US security in the Western Hemisphere. Michael S. Neiberg, *When France Fell: The Vichy Crisis and the Fate of the Anglo-American Alliance* (Cambridge, MA: Harvard University Press, 2021), 162–164.
34. O'Brien, *The Second Most Powerful Man in the World*, 203–209, 227.
35. Buchanan, *American Grand Strategy in the Mediterranean*, 281.

36. Buchanan, *American Grand Strategy in the Mediterranean*, 33–41; Leo J. Meyer, "The Decision to Invade North Africa (Torch)," in Greenfield Kent Roberts (ed.), *Command Decisions* (Washington: Center of Military History, United States Army, 1990), Chapter 7.
37. This was based in part on Vichy's seeming acquiescence to Japanese encroachment in Indochina. O'Brien, *The Second Most Powerful Man in the World*, 158.
38. Buchanan, *American Grand Strategy in the Mediterranean*, 45. O'Brien notes that, while Leahy supported an invasion of AFN "as part of a world-wide maritime strategy and to get US troops acclimated to battle in an area where he thought casualties would be low," he feared that it might open further operations in the Mediterranean that would overstretch US assets. O'Brien, *The Second Most Powerful Man in the World,* 223.
39. Robert Murphy, *Diplomat among Warriors* (London: Collins, 1964), 126. Murphy's agents included Lebanese-born and Arab-speaking US Marine Colonel William Eddy, who acted as naval attaché in Tangier, Kenneth Pendar, J. Rives Childs, and Felix Cole in Algiers. These men were supplemented by reports from the Office of the Coordinator of Information, the forerunner of the OSS, which was also collecting information on AFN. Sophie Roberts, "Jews, Vichy and the Algiers Insurrection of 1942," *Holocaust Studies: A Journal of Culture and History*, 12/3 (Winter 2006), 68.
40. Levisse-Touzé argues that "Group of Five" was a mischaracterization applied in the post-war period that ignores a much larger and more diverse group of resisters. Christine Levisse-Touzé, "L'Afrique du Nord dans la guerre," paper delivered at the symposium on Torch, Hôtel des Invalides, Paris, 12–13 November 2017, 6.
41. Alan Moorehead, *The Desert War: The North African Campaign 1940–1943* (London: Penguin, 2001), 478–479.
42. Michael Howard, *Grand Strategy*, volume IV, *August 1942–September 1943* (London: HMSO, 1970), 148; Buchanan, *American Grand Strategy in the Mediterranean*, 40–45. On the Polish intelligence network in AFN, see Malgosha Gago and Boleslaw Sulik, *Les ombres de Casablanca* (Paris: Arte, 2009); Jean Medrala, *Les Réseaux de renseignements franco-polonais, 1940–1944* (Paris: Éditions l'Harmattan, 2005), Chapter 9; and Nigel Hamilton, *The Mantle of Command: FDR at War, 1941–1942* (New York and Boston: Mariner Books, 2015), 349–362.
43. Roberts, "Jews, Vichy and the Algiers Insurrection of 1942," 63, 82. Of 377 young men who participated in the Algiers plot on the night of 7–8 November 1942, 315 were Jews according to Renée Poznanski, *Propagandes et persecutions: La Résistance et le "problème juif," 1940–1944* (Paris: Fayard, 2008), 394. For a more complete list of Resistance personalities in AFN, see Nicole Cohen-Addad and Tramor Quemeneur, "Analyse sociohistorique des acteurs du 8 novembre 1942," in Nicole Cohen-Addad, Aïssa Kadri, and Tramor Quemeneur (eds.), *8 novembre 1942: Résistance et débarquement allié en Afrique du Nord. Dynamiques historiques, politiques et socio-culturelles* (Vulaines-sur-Seine: Éditions du Croquant, 2021).

44. Robin Leconte, "Face au débarquement allié de novembre 1942: La Division de Marche de Constantine, entre obeisance et résistances aux ordres," in Claire Miot, Guillaume Piketty, and Thomas Vaisset (eds.), *Militaires en résistances en France et en Europe* (Villeneuve d'Ascq: Presses universitaires du Septentrion, 2020), 71–73.
45. I thank Robin Leconte for these observations.
46. Caroff, *Les débarquements alliés en afrique du nord,* 1–2.
47. "As a consequence, [Noguès] does not admit the possible separation between military and political command. In his opinion, the Resident General must play an important role in operations. His view seems to be that, in case of conflict, he alone can command the Moroccan theater of operations ... The ideas concerning the articulation of the naval command during operations have not been made clear. Especially in Morocco ...," where the navy treated Casablanca as its personal fiefdom. Nor had the Air Force commander in AFN, General Mendigal, "abandoned one iota of this air force spirit of independence that he already defends in the HC." On the contrary, he "tends to consider his own responsibilities far beyond that of the command." Senior air commanders clung to their bases on the coast, and refused to shift more of their planes and resources to the interior where they would be more secure from attack. "In sum, all the aviation is a façade, and will be bombed before they give the alert. No one takes remedial action, counting on a warning of several days, or at least several hours. That's a delusion. One must immediately study the relocation of air squadrons to the interior with the creation of housing and corresponding infrastructure." SHD-GR, 1P 35, "Voyage d'information en Afrique du Nord," no date.
48. When the Americans attacked on 8 November 1942, Noguès declared that the French must operate under the new command structure, and not that of 1941, which was still in place. In effect, responsibility for coastal defense in November 1942 fell to Rear Admiral Pierre-Jean Ronarc'h, who totally lost touch with Safi and Port-Lyautey when the Americans attacked. Caroff, *Les débarquements alliés en afrique du nord,* 103–104.
49. See, for instance, Roberts, "Jews, Vichy, and the Algiers Insurrection of 1942." See also Pierre Barjot, *Le Débarquement du 8 novembre 1942 en Afrique du Nord* (Paris: J. de Gigord, 1946), appendices.
50. Murphy, *Diplomat among Warriors*, 143, 159.
51. Notin, *Maréchal Juin*, 149–150; Jacques Belle, *L'Opération* Torch et la *Tunisie: De Casablanca à Tunis et au-delà (novembre 1942–septembre 1943)* (Paris: Economica, 2011), 56.
52. Glyn Harper, *The Battle for North Africa: El Alamein and the Turning Point for World War II* (Bloomington: Indiana University Press, 2017).
53. Jean-Louis Crémieux-Brilhac, *La France libre*, tome I, *De l'appel du 18 juin à la Libération* (Paris: Gallimard, 2013), 541.
54. Buchanan, *American Grand Strategy in the Mediterranean*, 74–75.
55. Howe, *Northwest Africa*, 60–67.
56. John Patch, "Fortuitous Endeavor. Intelligence and Deception in Operation TORCH," *Naval War College Review*, 61/4 (Autumn 2008), 82.

57. Although Admiral Erich Raeder identified Gibraltar as the Achilles heel of Britain's Mediterranean presence, he found no support in OKW. Operation Felix, a plan to seize Gibraltar with a two-corps attack through Spain, had been abandoned after German generals argued that Spain would prove "a useless political partner," whose army was primitive, its infrastructure underdeveloped, and its food situation so precarious that the dispatch of the *Wehrmacht* would require a huge logistical effort. Nor did Hitler want to defend Spanish beaches against an Allied invasion. In the end, Franco was kept out of the war by a fortuitous combination of circumstances that included the skill of Anglo-American diplomacy backed by commercial and financial inducements to Spain. Paul Preston, "Spain. Betting on a Nazi Victory," in Richard J. B. Bosworth and Joseph A. Maiolo, *The Cambridge History of the Second World War*, volume II, *Politics and Ideology* (Cambridge: Cambridge University Press, 2015), 324–348.
58. Quoted in O'Hara, *Torch*, 50. Brooke also believed that not enough fighter cover would be available for Bône, which was thus vulnerable to Axis air attack from Sicily and Sardinia.
59. Howe, *Northwest Africa*, 25–39; O'Hara, *Torch*, 48–57.
60. Caroff, *Les débarquements alliés en Afrique du Nord*, 105–106.
61. The problem was that the small ports close to Casablanca were too shallow to dock transports, while other more suitable harbors like Agadir and Mogodor were too distant from Casablanca to play a supporting role. Planners finally settled on Safi, a phosphate port 200 kilometers south of Casablanca, and the Bay of Fedala, 25 kilometers or 18 miles north of Casablanca, as the principal landing beaches. A third assault would enter the mouth of the Wadi Sebou at Méhédia, roughly 50 kilometers north of Rabat, with its target the airfield at Port-Lyautey (Kénitra). Howe, *Northwest Africa*, 39–46.
62. Howe, *Northwest Africa*, 46–50.
63. In addition to the three cruisers, two carriers, thirteen destroyers, and other odds and ends, the Eastern Task Force was covered by the Royal Navy's Force H under Admiral Andrew Cunningham, composed of three battleships, a battle cruiser, two carriers, four light cruisers, and seventeen destroyers. Samuel Elliot Morrison, *History of U.S. Naval Operations in World War II*, volume 2, *Operations in North African Waters* (Boston: Little Brown, 1950), 189–190.
64. Robert S. Ehlers, Jr., *The Mediterranean Air War: Airpower and Allied Victory in World War II* (Lawrence: University Press of Kansas, 2015), 251–252.
65. Howe, *Northwest Africa*, 50–58; Neiberg, *When France Fell*, 182.
66. Patch, "Fortuitous Endeavor," 74.
67. The Allies could also read some *Luftwaffe* cyphers, which included reconnaissance aircraft convoy sightings and the locations and deployment of Axis aircraft in Sicily and Sardinia. Intelligence revealed that, while the *Luftwaffe* had detected the buildup of ships at Gibraltar – mainly slow colliers and tankers sent ahead of the troopships and fire support escorts – they interpreted it as intended for Malta, reinforcements destined for Tripolitania, or simply routine ship rotations. Other decrypts suggested that Berlin believed that an Allied invasion of AFN fell within the realm of

possibility. Indeed, Grand Admiral Erich Raeder had expressed his concerns to Hitler in August about AFN as a potential target. But this seemed to be based more on distrust of the French than on hard intelligence about Allied intentions. Rome was certainly concerned about AFN as a potential Allied invasion objective. But these anxieties were crowded out by other potential Allied targets in Norway, Northwestern Europe, or the Aegean, especially Crete, perceptions reinforced by false agent reports sent through the London Controlling Station (LCS), the British strategic deception center, false radio transmissions, and deceptive convoy courses. Patch, "Fortuitous Endeavor," 88–90. On convoy organization and German concerns, see Howe, *Northwest Africa*, 67–77.

68. Costagliola, *Darlan*, 241.
69. F. H. Hinsley, *British Intelligence in the Second World War: Its Influence on Strategy and Operations*, vol. 2 (New York: Cambridge University Press, 1981), 479, 482; O'Hara, *Torch*, 75–79; Patch, "Fortuitous Endeavor," 78–81, 83, 85, 93.
70. Howard, *Grand Strategy*, volume IV, 154–155.
71. Under Noguès' orders were Vice-Admiral François Michelier, as naval commander in Morocco, and ground forces commander General Georges Lascrou, while the air force answered to General Auguste Lahoulle. A new defense structure designed in September 1942 envisioned the division of Morocco into four sectors based on Meknès in the north that covered Port-Lyautey, Casablanca under Michelier in the center, Marrakech, which was responsible for the Safi–Mogador sector where the Americans would also land, and Agadir in the far south. Coastal defense would be bolstered by a system of "mobile reserves" to be coordinated from Casablanca.
72. Howe, *Northwest Africa*, 93, 118–119. A more detailed description of the French command arrangements and order of battle is offered in Caroff, *Les débarquements alliés en Afrique du Nord*, 103–104 and passim, esp. 219.
73. Howe, *Northwest Africa*, 92.
74. Levisse-Touzé, *L'Afrique du Nord dans la guerre 1939–1945*, 245–246; Caroff, *Les débarquements alliés en Afrique du Nord*, 113.
75. According to Barjot, Rigault's warning came too late to alert the civilian resistance. Rigault subsequently claimed that he had told Béthouart the invasion date on 4 November, which Béthouart denied. As has been seen, the Official History insists that it was Murphy who stood down the civilian resistance in Morocco, placing the entire burden of resistance onto Béthouart's shoulders. Béthouart says that he was never given the list of resisters by Rigault. So, Béthouart convened Colonel Dewinck, chief of staff of the Meknès division, and told him to implement a "protection plan" to disperse the division so that it could not intervene against the Americans around Casablanca. Barjot, *Le Débarquement du 8 novembre 1942 en Afrique du Nord*, 113; Howe, *Northwest Africa*, 92; Antoine Béthouart, *Cinq années d'espérance: Mémoires de guerre 1939–1945* (Paris: Plon, 1968), 132; Caroff, *Les débarquements alliés en Afrique du Nord*, 113–114.

76. Béthouart, *Cinq années d'espérance*, 128–145. The invaders and Béthouart's conspirators appeared to have miscommunicated about what each was expected to do. Caroff, *Les débarquements alliés en Afrique du Nord*, 114.
77. The sheaf of documents included a proclamation that Giraud was to read on Radio Algiers; a 2 November letter from Murphy declaring that Giraud's views were compatible with those of the US government; a letter from Murphy promising to include France in lend-lease and to continue to supply AFN; a letter that stipulated the conditions for financial support; a letter from Murphy to Giraud promising that the United States would restore France as a power; and a note laying out the parameters of US intervention in AFN. None of them was signed. Furthermore, the statement that "Tunisia has just been attacked by German–Italian forces," and the fact that the navy in Morocco had as yet not detected the Allied attack, caused Michelier to reject them. Caroff, *Les débarquements alliés en Afrique du Nord*, 114–116. Béthouart, *Cinq années d'espérance*, 147–149.
78. Barjot, *Le Débarquement du 8 novembre 1942 en Afrique du Nord*, 115. Without radar, Michelier might have sortied over 200 aircraft in Morocco, as well as submarines and destroyers in Casablanca in vigorous patrolling. However, FAF sorties had been restricted in the wake of defections of pilots to Gibraltar, while submarines and destroyers were largely confined to port for repairs, but also due to a lack of fuel, which was prioritized for convoy escorts between Casablanca and Dakar. O'Hara, *Torch*, 143–145. The citation is from Charles Moran, *The Landings in North Africa, November 1942* (Washington, D.C.: Naval Historical Center, 1992), 41fn.
79. Caroff, *Les débarquements alliés en Afrique du Nord*, 159–161.
80. Béthouart considered the control commission to be spies capable of informing Berlin on the Allied invasion, while Noguès and Michelier saw them as a diplomatic mission, who, if arrested, might bring reprisals on the French representatives in Weisbaden. Caroff, *Les débarquements alliés en Afrique du Nord*, 116.
81. Caroff, *Les débarquements alliés en Afrique du Nord*, 117.
82. Howe, *Northwest Africa*, 96.
83. Levisse-Touzé, *L'Afrique du Nord dans la guerre 1939–1945*, 248.
84. Paxton, *Parades and Politics at Vichy*, 350–358; Howe, *Northwest Africa*, 94–95. Caroff makes the same point for Port-Lyautey, Caroff, *Les débarquements alliés en Afrique du Nord*, 134–135, 160.
85. Levisse-Touzé, *L'Afrique du Nord dans la guerre 1939–1945*, 247; Caroff, *Les débarquements alliés en Afrique du Nord*, 116–117.
86. Howe, *Northwest Africa*, 132, 139.
87. Vincent P. O'Hara, "Operation Torch November 1942," in *Revue algérienne de prospective & d'études stratégiques* (2017), 46–48; Howe, *Northwest Africa*, 123–127, 134–137.
88. Béthouart, *Cinq années d'espérance*, 146; Howe, *Northwest Africa*, 111–112.
89. Howe, *Northwest Africa*, 108–109.

90. Captain Harry C. Butcher, *My Three Years with Eisenhower* (London and Toronto: William Heinemann, 1946), 204. For a list of French ships lost in Torch, see O'Hara, *Torch*, 323–324.
91. Furthermore, seventeen ships were sunk at anchor or irreparably damaged, as well as a number of commercial ships. Although the French had managed to sink a US destroyer and a few landing craft, and to fire torpedoes at the US battleship *Massachusetts*, as well as the cruisers *Tuscaloosa* and *Brooklyn*, they failed to hit them. The transports were obscured by smoke from oil fires at Fedala. Although it was moored in the harbor, the guns of the unfinished battleship *Jean Bart* also managed to get off seven main battery rounds, before US naval gunfire put it out of action. O'Hara, *Torch*, 195–218.
92. Caroff, *Les débarquements alliés en Afrique du Nord*, 145–146.
93. One of the emissaries was killed when a Moroccan sergeant opened fire on the jeep. There was also a copy of Truscott's letter in French. Caroff, *Les débarquements alliés en Afrique du Nord*, 139–146.
94. Howe, *Northwest Africa*, 147–171. Other versions hold that Sultan Mohammed V summoned Noguès to the palace and ordered him to cease combat. Bernard Lugan, *Histoire du Maroc: Des origines à nos jours* (Paris: Criterion, 1992), 263. Caroff gives an account of an emissary sent to Vichy, where Pétain accorded his powers in AFN to Noguès. Caroff, *Les débarquements alliés en Afrique du Nord*, 224–229.
95. Caroff, *Les débarquements alliés en Afrique du Nord*, 229–230.
96. Howe, *Northwest Africa*, 174. Named secretary of the *Comité de libération nationale* in April 1944, he became chief of staff in April 1944 and eventually a corps commander in de Lattre's French First Army for the liberation of France and the invasion of Germany. From 1945, he would command French troops in Austria, and he served as French High Commissioner in that country until 1950. Béthouart, *Cinq années d'espérance*, 145–177.
97. Barjot, *Le Débarquement du 8 novembre 1942 en Afrique du Nord*, 118.
98. Howe, *Northwest Africa*, 202–204; O'Hara, *Torch*, 119–123; Caroff, *Les débarquements alliés en Afrique du Nord*, 40–42.
99. Howe, *Northwest Africa*, 213. The warships lost included a destroyer, five minesweepers, three sloops (sub-chasers), and four submarines. Lists of lost vessels are given in O'Hara, *Torch*, 323. The term destroyer is confusing, as the French navy has employed various terms to describe destroyers over the decades. From 1922 until the 1950s, destroyers were most commonly called *contre-torpilleurs*, but also *croiseur-torpilleurs*, *torpilleurs d'escort*, *croiseurs légers*, and so on.
100. Howe, *Northwest Africa*, 220.
101. Barjot, *Le Débarquement du 8 novembre 1942 en Afrique du Nord*, 119–120; Howe, *Northwest Africa*, 223–225.
102. Howe, *Northwest Africa*, 192–228; O'Hara, *Torch*, 123–136.
103. A dozen strong shore batteries protected the harbor, and an estimated fifty-two fighters and thirty-nine bombers idled on the airfields of Blida and

Maison Blanche. It offered a port and railway center, as well as the two airfields vital to support a move into Tunisia. Howe, *Northwest Africa*, 229.

104. "Most accounts of Operation Torch agree that the Allied landings in and around Algiers would not have succeeded without the aid of the resistance," asserts Roberts. Roberts, "Jews, Vichy and the Algiers Insurrection of 1942," 63, 69. In 1946, Barjot concurred with Roberts that, because of landing difficulties, "without French assistance, the Algiers expedition would have turned into a disaster." Barjot, *Le Débarquement du 8 novembre 1942 en Afrique du Nord*, Appendix. More recently, Jacques Belle affirms that the resistance "greatly contributed to the paralysis of the local defense." Resistance-induced paralysis facilitated the taking of Algiers and led directly to a local ceasefire on the same day in recognition of the facts on the ground. Jacques Belle, *L'Opération* Torch *et la Tunisie: De Casablanca à Tunis et au-delà (novembre 1942–septembre 1943)* (Paris: Economica, 2011), 102.
105. The Géo Gras Group (GGG), created in 1940 to respond to attacks on Jews, collected weapons, forged identity papers, and distributed pro-Allied propaganda. According to Roberts, by 1942 the GGG numbered around 250 young Jewish men organized into five-man cells. Roberts, "Jews, Vichy and the Algiers Insurrection of 1942," 74–75.
106. Howe, *Northwest Africa*, 249.
107. The command centers had their own direct lines independent of the municipal system, not only with each other, but which also connected with Casablanca, Oran, Bône, Bizerte, and Vichy via Marseilles. Each headquarters also had radio transmitters, as well as a communications ship anchored in Algiers harbor. However, this system was not linked to the residences of the commanders, who, sequestered by the VPs, were temporarily out of action. Caroff, *Les débarquements alliés en Afrique du Nord*, 19.
108. Mast's order presents Torch as a preemptive action to head off an imminent Axis takeover of the zone libre and AFN. While it acknowledges that the Royal Navy will form part of the naval flotilla, "it is understood that neither an Englishman nor a Gaullist will set foot in the territory of AFN." Because of secrecy, not all units are included in this order – in fact, only eight units are on the distribution list. As a consequence, "Every effort will be made at the different echelons to cease resistance if it is offered and avoid any misunderstanding." French troops were to occupy the harbors and airfields, remain in small groups, and wave a French flag as Americans approached. Caroff, *Les débarquements alliés en Afrique du Nord*, 21–22.
109. To encourage the Algiers garrison not to oppose the invasion, the diplomat Jacques Tarbé de Saint Hardouin, one of Murphy's "five," had convinced the Algiers intelligence chief Colonel Jean Chrétien to accompany Murphy to the Villa des Oliviers. At 00:30 on Sunday 8 November, Chrétien had phoned Juin to tell him that Murphy wanted to speak to him. At 01:30, Murphy, Chrétien, and US Vice-council Kenneth Pendar arrived at Juin's residence in the Villa des Oliviers. Murphy announced that the invasion was imminent and that Giraud would soon launch an appeal. Notin, *Maréchal*

Juin, 183; Maréchal Alphonse Pierre Juin, *Mémoires*, tome 1, *Alger, Tunis, Rome* (Paris: Fayard, 1959), 74–76.

110. According to Costagliola, Bonnier de la Chapelle was talked out of it with the assurance that the admiral would subsequently be tried. Costagliola, *Darlan*, 241.
111. Caroff, *Les débarquements alliés en Afrique du Nord*, 16–17.
112. Notin, *Maréchal Juin*, 178.
113. Howe, *Northwest Africa*, 249–250; Rick Atkinson, *An Army at Dawn: The War in North Africa, 1942–1943* (New York: Henry Holt & Co., 2002), 93–96; Kenneth S. Davis, *FDR: The War President, 1940–1943. A History* (New York: Random House, 1999), 681–684; Juin, *Mémoires*, tome 1, 77–78; Costagliola, *Darlan*, 243; Caroff, *Les débarquements alliés en Afrique du Nord*, 75–76.
114. Caroff, *Les débarquements alliés en Afrique du Nord*, 24–28.
115. Notin, *Maréchal Juin*, 187.
116. Costagliola, *Darlan*, 242.
117. Juin, *Mémoires*, tome 1, 82.
118. Costagliola, *Darlan*, 243.
119. Levisse-Touzé, *L'Afrique du Nord dans la guerre 1939–1945*, 241–243.
120. Caroff, *Les débarquements alliés en Afrique du Nord*, 20.
121. Juin, *Mémoires*, tome 1, 80–81; Caroff, *Les débarquements alliés en Afrique du Nord*, 32.
122. Paxton, *Parades and Politics at Vichy*, 348; Belle, *L'Opération* Torch *et la Tunisie*, 103.
123. Costagliola, *Darlan*, 244.
124. Howe, *Northwest Africa*, 239–240, 249–252; Davis, *FDR*, 684; Juin, *Mémoires*, tome 1, 85–86.
125. Costagliola, *Darlan*, 245.
126. Notin, *Maréchal Juin*, 190–191.
127. Howe, *Northwest Africa*, 173; Atkinson, *An Army at Dawn*, 97–100.
128. The battleship *Jean Bart*, the cruiser *Primauguet*, ten destroyers, ten submarines, and a number of smaller vessels were sunk or severely damaged in Torch. Two submarines escaped to Toulon, where they would scuttle. Overall, Torch would cost the Allies twenty transports and thirteen warships, including a carrier, to combined French and Axis forces. Charles de Gaulle, *Mémoires de guerre*, tome 2, *L'Unité 1942–1944* (Paris: Plon, 1994), 317. For French losses in Morocco, see Caroff, *Les débarquements alliés en Afrique du Nord*, 233–235. O'Hara lists both French and Allied ships "sunk" during Torch. His list includes neither the *Jean Bart* nor the light cruiser *Primauguet*, presumably because, although *hors de combat*, they were not technically "sunk." O'Hara, *Torch*, Appendix IV, 321–324. Masson lists the inventory of ships and boats in the French navy and what became of them during the war. Masson, *La marine française dans la guerre*, Annex VIII.
129. Burrin, *France under the Germans*, 162–163.
130. The principal points were as follows: cessation of all resistance to the Allied invasion throughout AFN; the maintenance of French sovereignty; French troops would keep their arms and would be responsible for internal security;

partial disarmament of warships; and commercial shipping would be put at the disposition of the Allies. Caroff, *Les débarquements alliés en Afrique du Nord*, 81–82.

131. This included Juin, Koeltz, Mendigal, and Vice-Admiral Hubert Moreau, commander-in-chief of the French Navy in the Mediterranean and Prefect of the 4th Maritime Region in Algiers. Costagliola, *Darlan*, 246.
132. Ryder became worried as negotiations dragged on that the French might reopen hostilities. Therefore, he began discretely collecting French ammunition and placing it under armed guard. Howe, *Northwest Africa*, 254.
133. Caroff, *Les débarquements alliés en Afrique du Nord*, 83–85; Costagliola, *Darlan*, 247–248.
134. Juin, *Mémoires*, tome 1, 103.
135. Costagliola, *Darlan*, 248.
136. Costagliola speculates that this might mean that the admiral still hoped that a deal might be struck by Laval in Berchtesgaden to revise the 1940 armistice and liberate the POWs. And this would help to explain why Darlan was reluctant to order de Laborde to have the High Seas Fleet put to sea. Costagliola, *Darlan*, 249.
137. Not surprisingly, this thesis was pushed by Rear Admiral Auphan, the author of the telegram, which he subsequently cited as conclusive evidence that Pétain supported the American invasion of AFN. Paul Auphan and Jacques Mordal, *La Marine française pendant la guerre* (Paris: Hachette, 1958), 302. It also allowed the *Vichysto-résistants* to shift the blame for collaboration to Laval. André Martel (ed.), *Histoire militaire de la France*, tome 4, *De 1940 à nos jours* (Paris: Presses universitaires de France, 1994), 26.
138. Hervé Coutau-Bégarie and Claude Huan, *Darlan* (Paris: Fayard, 1989), 622–623.
139. Costagliola, *Darlan*, 252–253, 259–260. Costagliola considers the Auphan telegram at best a misunderstanding, at worst a deliberate deception. For starters, it stated that the notorious collaborator Laval was on board with AFN's defection to the Allies, which was nonsense. The most likely possibility is that Auphan picked up on Noguès' lead to sideline Giraud, perpetuate Vichy "neutrality," especially in Tunisia, and to maintain in power those loyal to Vichy. Auphan's actual message was sent on 13 November. But, according to Costagliola, Auphan had been making assurances of the Marshal's acquiescence since 11 November. Caroff, *Les débarquements alliés en Afrique du Nord*, 87, 301–303; Davis, *FDR*, 687–688; Levisse-Touzé, *L'Afrique du Nord dans la guerre 1939–1945*, 250–253; Juin, *Mémoires*, tome 1, 96–103.
140. Levisse-Touzé, *L'Afrique du Nord dans la guerre 1939–1945*, 259. "Tu verras, c'est une bande de vieux dégonflés." Béthouart, *Cinq années d'espérance*, 93.
141. Costagliola, *Darlan*, 250; Caroff, *Les débarquements alliés en Afrique du Nord*, 85–86.
142. Levisse-Touzé, *L'Afrique du Nord dans la guerre 1939–1945*, 257.
143. Caroff, *Les débarquements alliés en Afrique du Nord*, 87–89. On *l'accord intime*, see Marcel Spivak and Armand Leoni, *Les forces françaises dans la lutte contre*

l'Axe en Afrique, tome II, *La campagne de Tunisie, 1942–1943* (Vincennes: Service historique de l'armée de terre, 1985), 395–397, 471.

144. Général André Beaufre, *Mémoires 1920–1940–1945* (Paris: Presses de la Cité, 1965), 382–384.
145. SHD-GR, 5P 50, 20 November 1942.
146. Allied naval losses included three cruisers and four destroyers sunk, and another twenty-five warships damaged, including three carriers and a battleship. Juin, *Mémoires*, tome 1, 91–96; Ehlers, *The Mediterranean Air War*, 254–255; Costagliola, *Darlan*, 247. O'Hara lists Allied ships lost to hostile action during November 1942. Apart from the three destroyers lost in the failed attacks on the harbors of Algiers and Oran on 8 November, the remaining losses were due to Axis submarine and air attacks. O'Hara, *Torch*, 321–322.
147. Paxton, *Parades and Politics at Vichy*, 358–362; Howe, *Northwest Africa*, 262–267; SHD-GR, 1P 110, 14 November 1942; Levisse-Touzé, *L'Afrique du Nord dans la guerre 1939–1945*, 238–259; Juin, *Mémoires*, tome 1, 107–109; Costagliola, *Darlan*, 256–258.
148. Davis, *FDR*, 696–697.
149. Leahy viewed de Gaulle "as an egoist and violent nationalist who 'thirsted for power!'" O'Brien, *The Second Most Powerful Man in the World*, 437.
150. Martin Thomas and Richard Toye, *Arguing about Empire: Imperial Rhetoric in Britain and France, 1882–1956* (Oxford: Oxford University Press, 2017), 184–185.
151. Howe, *Northwest Africa*, 269–273.
152. Robert Dallek, *Franklin D. Roosevelt and American Foreign Policy, 1932–1945* (Oxford: Oxford University Press, 1995), 364.
153. De Gaulle, *Mémoires de guerre*, tome 2, 320.
154. John MacVane, *War and Diplomacy in North Africa* (London: Robert Hale, 1944), 63.
155. Juin, *Mémoires*, tome 1, 112–113.
156. Masson, *La marine française et la guerre*, 403.
157. Moorehead, *The Desert War*, 455.
158. D'Este, *Eisenhower*, 354, 356; Dallek, *Franklin D. Roosevelt and American Foreign Policy*, 365.
159. Matthew Jones, *Britain, the United States and the Mediterranean War* (New York: St. Martin's, 1996), 95.
160. Belle, *L'Opération* Torch *et la Tunisie*, 103–104.
161. Davis, *FDR*, 688–689.
162. Atkinson, *An Army at Dawn*, 159.
163. Stephen E. Ambrose, *The Supreme Commander: The War Years of General Dwight D. Eisenhower* (Jackson: University Press of Mississippi, 1999), 125
164. Buchanan, *American Grand Strategy in the Mediterranean*, 72. According to one of Eisenhower's biographers, Stephen Ambrose, the attitude of the State Department's chief "French expert," who had resided in AFN for almost two years and in Paris for the previous four years, and who knew the French players well, particularly frustrated the Allied Commander. Murphy simply slipped into a translator role, insisting that the political compromise

to be achieved in AFN was an operational, not a political decision, to be arrived at by the generals. Not surprisingly, Murphy's ploy was viewed as an attempt to absolve himself of any responsibility for the ensuring uproar over the Darlan deal. Ambrose, *The Supreme Commander*, 126–128. If so, it failed because, according to Eisenhower's naval aide, Harry C. Butcher, "Murphy seems to be the main target of criticism, on the ground that he is a Vichyite and has been giving bum advice to the 'brilliant' General," all of which was true. Butcher, *My Three Years with Eisenhower*, 211.

165. D'Este, *Eisenhower*, 354, 356.
166. SHD-GR, 2H 194, Synthèse de renseignements, 30 April 1943, 4.
167. Olivier Wieviorka, *Histoire de la Résistance 1940–1945* (Paris: Perrin, 2013), 286.
168. Paxton, *Vichy France*, 285–291.
169. Burrin, *France under the Germans*, 172–174.
170. Lacouture, *De Gaulle*, tome 1, *Le Rebelle, 1890–1944* (Paris: Éditions du Seuil, 1984), 607.
171. Charles de Gaulle, *Discours et Messages*, vol. I (Paris: Plon, 1970), 235–240.
172. Jackson, *De Gaulle*, 245–250; Thomas and Toye, *Arguing about Empire*, 186–187.
173. Wieviorka, *Histoire de la Résistance 1940–1945*, 194; Albertelli, *Les Services secrets du Général de Gaulle*, 246.
174. National Archives (Kew Gardens) PREM 3/442/9, Eden to Halifax, 13 November 1942; NA PREM 3/442/11, Churchill to Roosevelt, 13 November 1942, Roosevelt to Churchill, 12 November 1942. This and following points on the impact of the Darlan deal in Britain are taken from a paper delivered by Robert Gildea at a conference on Torch at Les Invalides in Paris in November 2015, generously communicated to the author by Professor Gildea. See also Dallek, *Franklin D. Roosevelt and American Foreign Policy*, 364.
175. Dallek, *Franklin D. Roosevelt and American Foreign Policy*, 364–365; John Lamberton Harper, *American Visions of Europe* (Cambridge: Cambridge University Press, 1996), 193.
176. Harold Nicolson, *Diaries and Letters, 1939–1945* (London: Collins, 1967), 262–263.
177. Parliamentary Debates (Hansard), Fifth Series, vol. 385, 17 November 1942, 271; Michael Foot, *Aneurin Bevan: A Biography I. 1887–1945* (London: MacGibbon & Lee, 1962), 404.
178. "To Darlan's kicking the bucket." Jean-Louis Crémieux-Brilhac, *L'étrange victoire: De la défense de la République à la libération de la France* (Paris: Gaillimard, 2016), 132.
179. Omar Bradley, *A Soldier's Story* (New York: Henry Holt, 1951), 32.
180. Thomas Flemming, *The New Dealer's War: F.D.R. and the War within World War II* (New York: Basic Books, 2001), unpaginated.
181. Stanley Sandler, *"Cease Resistance; It's Good For You": A History of U.S. Army Combat Psychological Operations* (self-published, 1999), 50.
182. Buchanan, *American Grand Strategy in the Mediterranean*, 30, 74.
183. Moorehead, *The Desert War*, 455.

184. Thomas and Toye, *Arguing about Empire*, 189–194.
185. Howard, *Grand Strategy*, volume IV, 178–179.
186. NA PREM 3/442/9, Churchill to Roosevelt, 17 November 1942; NA PREM 3/442/9, Roosevelt to Churchill, 17 November 1942; D'Este, *Eisenhower*, 357; Buchanan, *American Grand Strategy in the Mediterranean*, 75; Jackson, *De Gaulle*, 249.
187. Dallek, *Franklin D. Roosevelt and American Foreign Policy*, 365.
188. David Reynolds believes it to have been a plot cooked up between local Gaullists and SOE agents in Algiers. Nicola Labanca, David Reynolds, and Olivier Wieviorka (eds.), *La Guerre du Désert* (Paris: Perrin, 2019), 82.
189. Levisse-Touzé, *L'Afrique du Nord dans la guerre 1939–1945*, 276–277.
190. According to Albertelli, in 1941, Pierre Fourcaud, founder of the Brutus network, and Rémy, the Resistance *nom de guerre* of Gilbert Renault, considered eliminating Darlan, but did not follow through. Only one document in the OSS archives implicates the BCRA in the assassination – the testimony in June 1943 by a Frenchman named Prémorel. But much of his testimony was not credible, and after he subsequently vanished, the OSS concluded that Prémorel was a German agent. Albertelli, *Les Services secrets du Général de Gaulle*, 247–248. Suspicion of Gaullist complicity in the assassination focused on Air Force General François d'Astier de la Vigerie, who had been sent to Algiers from London on 19–22 December 1942, to explore the possibility of establishing a Gaullist presence in AFN. He had numerous interviews with Giraud and Darlan, but also with his brother Henri d'Astier and the Comte de Paris.
191. Max Hastings, *Finest Years: Churchill as Warlord 1940–45* (London: Harper Press, 2009), 349.
192. Howe, *Northwest Africa*, 227.
193. Lugan, *Histoire du Maroc*, 264.
194. Levisse-Touzé, *L'Afrique du Nord dans la guerre 1939–1945*, 343–354, 368–369; Le Gac, *Vaincre sans gloire*, 105–106, 108.
195. O'Brien, *The Second Most Powerful Man in the World*, 148.
196. Costagliola, *Darlan*, 249.
197. Laborde did not actually use an obscenity, but rather referred to an example in 1940 well known in the French navy when an officer used an obscenity in reply to Muselier's request that he join *la France libre*. According to Darlan's biographers, the admiral sent a third message on the 13 November saying that Italian ships were approaching, in an attempt to get the Toulon fleet to sortie. But the wireless operators failed to decipher it. Coutau-Bégarie and Huan, *Darlan*, 640–643.
198. Caroff, *Les débarquements alliés en Afrique du Nord*, 76–78.
199. Coutau-Bégarie and Huan, *Darlan*, 605, 645.
200. Paxton, *Vichy France*, 307; Masson, *La marine française et la guerre*, 392–394; Lacouture, *De Gaulle*, tome 1, 618.
201. Coutau-Bégarie and Huan, *Darlan*, 646.
202. Paxton, *Vichy France*, 307; Coutau-Bégarie and Huan, *Darlan*, 646–647.
203. Masson, *La marine française dans la guerre*, 404.

204. Paxton, *Parades and Politics*, 381–390; Coutau-Bégarie and Huan, *Darlan*, 643–650; Bernard Costagliola, *La Marine de Vichy: Blocus et collaboration* (Paris: Éditions CNRS, 2009), 311–312. Of the five submarines that escaped, three went to Algeria, one interned itself in neutral Spain, and one scuttled in the open sea. Masson, *La marine française et la guerre*, 397–400.
205. Thomas Vasset and Philippe Vial, "Toulon 27 novembre 1942. Rien qu'une défaite, ou plus qu'une défaite?," 2. Unpublished manuscript communicated by the authors.
206. Coutau-Bégarie and Huan, *Darlan*, 647–648.
207. John Harvey (ed.), *The War Diaries of Oliver Harvey* (London: Collins, 1978), 192–193. Quoted in Labanca, Reynolds, and Wieviorka (eds.), *La Guerre du Désert*, 92.
208. Crémieux-Brilhac, *L'étrange victoire*, 130.
209. De Gaulle, *Mémoires de guerre*, tome 2, 321–322.
210. Lacouture, *De Gaulle*, tome 1, 618–619.
211. The Germans seized 111 freighters, as well as some submarines and torpedo boats in the southern French ports, plus naval stores at Toulon and Marseilles, while the Italians confiscated another 90 freighters. Belle, *L'Opération* Torch *et la Tunisie*, 127.
212. Belle, *L'Opération* Torch *et la Tunisie*, 127.
213. Paxton estimates that 949 lorries were confiscated by the *Wehrmacht* in the *zone libre* following November 1942. The German armistice commission reported finding 45,000 hidden rifles, almost 6,000 machineguns, 3,193 mortars, 17 75 mm cannons, and a number of anti-tank guns, already out of date in 1940. The Italians discovered another 130 clandestine arms depots east of the Rhône containing enough small arms and munitions to equip a division. Paxton, *Vichy France*, 53.
214. Most of these *Beutepanzers*, literally "captured tanks," were transformed into observation tanks, ammunition transports, artillery tractors, and self-propelled guns, or were allocated to anti-partisan units or passed on to the armies of Germany's Axis allies, including Italian tank units in Sicily, who deployed the Renault R35 against the Allied landing in July 1943. Nicola Pignato and Filippo Cappellano, *Gli autoveicoli da combattimento dell'Esercito Italiano*, volume secondo, *1940–1945* (Rome: Ufficio Storico dello Stato Maggiore dell'Esercito, 2002), 630–632. See also Philippe Garraud, "Le rôle de la 'doctrine défensive' dans la défaite de 1940: Une explication trop simple et partielle," *Guerres Mondiales et Conflits Contemporains*, no. 214 (April 2004), 119, note 55.
215. Paxton, *Parades and Politics at Vichy*, 389–390. On weapons caches in the zone libre, see Paxton, *Parades and Politics at Vichy*, 393–396. Paxton, *L'armée de Vichy: Le corps des officiers français 1940–1944* (Paris: Tallandier, 2004), 307–315; Vasset and Vial, "Toulon 27 novembre 1942," 4.
216. Belle, *L'Opération* Torch *et la Tunisie*, 127–128. The booty amounted to 540 French planes to the *Luftwaffe*, and 167 for the *Regia Aeronautica*. Claude d'Abzac-Epezy, *L'armée de l'Air des années noires: Vichy 1940–1944* (Paris: Economica, 1998), 264.

217. The exchange rate in AFN was set at 75 francs to the dollar, about double the going amount. Nor were the Allies to pay direct or indirect taxes. Their troops were accorded extraterritorial status, and had the option of insuring order if the need arose, a real blow at French sovereignty, as was the fact that the French lost their monopoly on cinema, press, and postal censorship. Levisse-Touzé, *L'Afrique du Nord dans la guerre 1939–1945*, 262–267.
218. The largest maritime mass suicide in history had been that of the German *Hochseeflotte* whose 52 warships totaling over 400,000 tons went to the bottom at Scapa Flow in June 1919, rather than allow the ships to be divvied up among the victorious Allies at Versailles. The *Admiral Graf Spee* scuttled in Montevideo harbor in December 1939 to avoid falling into British hands. The small Danish fleet was to scuttle at Copenhagen on 29 August 1943 rather than be seized by the Germans. Likewise, in April 1945, German Admiral Dönitz ordered over 200 U-boats sunk to keep them from falling into Allied hands. The French navy had previously scuttled around 15,000 tons of ships in June 1940, or 20 percent of the navy's inventory at the time, rather than allow the Germans to seize them. This included two large capital ships under construction, the battleship *Clemenceau* and what would have been the French navy's first true carrier, the *Joffre*.
219. At his trial, Pétain argued that he failed to give the order to sail out of fear of German reprisals. He refused to promote Auphan and appoint him commander of the Hight Seas Fleet so that he could sail to AFN. This provoked Auphan's resignation. Masson, *La marine française et la guerre*, 395–396.
220. Many Italian naval officers were shocked and shamed by the announcement of the Cassibile armistice because, as one Italian admiral testified, "the Royal Italian Navy was subjected to much less interference from the fascist political authorities and the German commands than the other armed services," while Great Britain "had always been the traditional enemy." The Italian fleet was to rendezvous in Malta. Discipline was mostly maintained by the fact that the Navy Minister stayed in contact, reiterating that the fleet would remain intact and continue to fly the Italian flag, and after it was realized that the battleship *Roma* had been sunk by a German glider bomb, and not by the British as initially thought. Most officers also imagined that Rome would soon be in Allied hands. A handful of Italian captains scuttled, and were executed by the Germans. A few captains preferred to be interned with their ships in the Balearic Islands. Elena Agarossi, *A Nation Collapses: The Italian Surrender of September 1943* (Cambridge: Cambridge University Press, 2000), 100–101.
221. Jean-Baptiste Bruneau and Thomas Vaisset, "Déchirements, déclassment et relèvement (1939–1945)," in Philippe Vial (ed.), "L'histoire d'une revolution. La Marine depuis 1870," *Études marines*, no. 4 (March 2013), 76; Vasset and Vial, "Toulon 27 novembre 1942," 8, 11.
222. This did not prevent some post-war apologists from offering the five submarines that had fled Toulon as "the resistentialist trees that hid the forest of scuttled ships." Vaisset and Vial, "Toulon 27 novembre 1942," 10.
223. Thomas Vaisset and Philippe Vial, "Louis Jacquinot Ministre de la Marine, le 'Colbert de la Libération'?," in Olivier Dard, Julie Bour, Lydiane Gueit-

Montchal, and Gilles Richard (eds.), *Louis Jacquinot, un indépendant en politique*(Paris: Presses de l'université Paris-Sorbonne, 2013), 113–114, 121, 124; Vial, "L'histoire d'une révolution," 74–78; Vaisset and Vial, "Toulon 27 novembre 1942," 6.

Epilogue

1. Mary Jo McConahay, *The Tango War: The Struggle for Hearts, Minds, and Riches of Latin America during World War II* (New York: St. Martin's Press, 2018).
2. Robert O. Paxton, *Vichy France: Old Guard and New Order, 1940–1944* (London: Barrie & Jenkins, 1972), 382.
3. Jean-Louis Crémieux-Brilhac, *La France libre*, tome 1, *De l'appel du 18 juin à la libération* (Paris: Gallimard, 2013), 159, 167, 173–174, 184–186; Thomas Vaisset, *L'Amiral d'Argenlieu: Le moine-soldat du gaullisme* (Paris: Belin, 2017), 239; Eric Jennings, *La France libre fut africaine* (Paris: Perrin, 2015), 115–116.

Bibliography

Archival Sources

Service Historique de la Défense, Château de Vincennes

GR-N: Troisième République
Direction et services du ministre. Gouvernement de Paris – GR 9 N

GR-P: Deuxième guerre mondiale (1940–1946)
Vichy: instance de défense nationale – GR 1P
Vichy: cabinet du ministre et organismes en dependant directement – GR 2P
Vichy: état-major de l'armée puis organe liquidateur de l'armée – GR 3P
Londres: état-major du Gal de Gaulle et commissariat national à la guerre – GR 4P
Alger: état-major particulier du Gal Giraud, état-major du Gal Juin – GR 5P
Alger puis Paris: état-major général de guerre puis état-major de l'armée – GR 7P.
Alger puis Paris: missions de liaison auprès des alliés – GR 8P
Armées et corps d'armée – GR 10P
Divisions et brigades – GR 11P
Petites unités – GR 12P
Comission d'enquêtes sur les repliements suspects de 1940 – GR 14P
Généraux de division et de brigade – GR 13 YD

SHD-GR, oral archives
Colonel Dominique Magnant, GR 3K 12-1, Planches 6, 7
Jean-Louis Crémieux-Brilhac GR 3K 32-1, Planche 2
Colonel André Perrin GR 3K 39-1 (Planches 6, 7)

Hoover Institution, Stanford University
René de Chambrun Papers, 1919–1946
Cazotte, Michel de, "Oflag Adventure." Unpublished manuscript, edited by Louis Denis de Cazotte, summer 1997

Papers of Paul Van der Stricht (OSS section chief "Western Europe" 1943–1944)

National Archives and Records Administration (NARA) Washington, D.C.

Record Group (RG) 165, Records of the War Department:
Entry 77, Box 861 service de renseignements; 862 conditions in occupied France; 863 Allied bombing and French morale; 865, Armistice Army, armée d'Afrique, conditions in North Africa, etc.; 866 la Milice, SOL, LVF; 869 Conditions of Armistice; 873 French tactical doctrine, organization, materiel 1930s; 925 Fighting French 1942; 926–927 general French matters, occupation zone in Germany, etc.
RG 218, Records of the Joint Chiefs of Staff:
Boxes 54–58 relations with Vichy, Fighting France, etc.
RG 319, Free French Army World War II:
Entry A1 145A, Boxes 1–48.
RG 331, Records of Allied Operational and Occupation Headquarters World War II:
Entry 2, Box 109
Entry 3C, Box 190
Entry 30, Box 192, 193, 194, 195
Entry 30A, Box 145, 147 French Resistance
Entry 30C, Box 186 Operation Wallace–Hardy, 189 resistance in Brittany, 190 Poches Atlantiques, 196–197 First French Army
Entry 240A, Box 1
Entry 240D, Boxes 8, 9, 10, 31, 206
Entry 272, Box 110 French air force
RG 407, The Adjutant General's Office: World War II Operational Report:
Entry 427, Box 1622 French Action, Rapido–Cassino Operations January–February 1944; 1777, 1783, 1784 French Operations Italy, 1786 Training lessons from the Tunisian Campaign; 1787–1791 Italy
RG 0498, French Army Military Government:
Entry UD578, Box 3904, 3905, 3908

National Archives Kew Gardens

FO 660: Foreign Office and War Cabinet: Offices of Various Political Representatives

Second World War

16 Political situation: France. 1943 July 18–Dec. 20.

188 French Army: re-entry into active operations against German Forces. Parts I and II. 1943 Nov. 19–1944 Mar. 12.
253 Army: French. Parts I and II. 1944 September 26–1945 January 4.
FO 892 Armaments for the Free French Forces 1
FO 1055/10 Reports on various visits to the Free French forces at Camberley 1941–1943

CAB 106: War Cabinet and Cabinet Office: Historical Section
361

HW 40: Government Communications Headquarters (GCHQ)
137 Reports revealing enemy successes against French Army high grade communications and related correspondence 1942 Jun. 12–1945 Apr. 02. L11 (A).
138 Reports revealing enemy successes against French Army high grade communications and related correspondence 1943 Oct. 21–1945 Apr. 05. L11 (B).

WO 204: War Office, Armed Forces, Judge Advocate General, and Related Bodies
1917 Free French Forces: operations 1944 Mar.–May
ADM 199/614
Free French Forces 1941–1943

Saint Antony's College, Oxford University

Middle East Library, Speers Collection.
GB165-0269, Box 1A-B-C, Box 2.

Film

Gago, Malgosha and Sulik, Boleslaw, *Les ombres de Casablanca* (Paris: Arte, 2009).
"Mystères d'archives 1944 dans le maquis du Vercors," www.youtube.com/watch?v=zoq7QREIgB8&t=1393s

Books, Theses, and Documents

Abbas, Ferhat et al., "10 février 1943, Le Manifest du peuple algérien," https://texturesdutemps.hypotheses.org/1458.
Abenheim, Donald and Halladay, Carolyn, *Soldiers, War, Knowledge and Citizenship: German–American Essays on Civil–Military Relations* (Berlin: Carola Hartmann Miles-Verlag, 2017).
Abzac-Epezy, Claude d ', *L'Armée de l'air des années noires, Vichy 1940–1944* (Paris: Economica, 1998).

Adamthwaite, Anthony, *France and the Coming of the Second World War 1936–1939* (London: Frank Cass, 1977).
Adelman, Jonathan R., *Hitler and His Allies in World War II* (New York: Routledge, 2007).
Agarossi, Elena, *A Nation Collapses: The Italian Surrender of September 1943* (Cambridge: Cambridge University Press, 2000).
Aglan, Alya and Frank, Robert (eds.), *1937–1947: La guerre-monde*, II (Paris: Gallimard, 2015).
Alary, Eric, *La Ligne de démarcation* (Paris: Perrin, 2003).
Albertelli, Sébastien, *Les Services secrets du Général de Gaulle: Le BCRA 1940–1944* (Paris: Perrin, 2009).
Albertelli, Sébastien, *Atlas de la France Libre: De Gaulle et la France Libre, une aventure politique* (Paris: Éditions Autrement, 2010).
Alexander, Martin S., *The Republic in Danger: General Maurice Gamelin and the Politics of French Defence, 1933–1940* (Cambridge: Cambridge University Press, 1992).
Allport, Alan, *Browned Off and Bloody Minded: The British Soldier Goes to War 1939–1945* (New Haven: Yale University Press, 2015).
Ambrose, Stephen E., *Eisenhower: Soldier, General of the Army, President Elect, 1890–1952* (New York: Simon & Schuster, 1983).
Ambrose, Stephen E., *The Supreme Commander: The War Years of General Dwight D. Eisenhower* (Jackson: University Press of Mississippi, 1999).
Andrew, Christopher, *Her Majesty's Secret Service: The Making of the British Intelligence Community* (New York: Viking, 1985).
Andrew, Christopher and Noakes, Jeremy (eds.), *Intelligence and International Relations, 1900–1945* (Liverpool: Liverpool University Press, 1987).
Army Service Forces, *Legal Work of the War Department. 1 July 1940–31 March 1945. A History of the Judge Advocate General's Department* (Washington, D.C.: Office of the Judge Advocate General, no date), www.loc.gov/rr/frd/Military_Law/pdf/Legal-Work_War-Department.pdf.
Arnaud, Patrice, *Les STO: Histoire des français requis en Allemagne nazi 1942–1945* (Paris: Éditions CNRS, 2014).
Ashdown, Paddy, *The Cruel Victory: The French Resistance, D-Day and the Battle for Vercors 1944* (London: William Collins, 2014).
Atkinson, Rick, *An Army at Dawn: The War in North Africa, 1942–1943* (New York: Henry Holt & Co., 2002).
Auphan, Paul and Mordel, Jacques, *The French Navy in World War II* (Annapolis: United States Naval Institute Press, 1959).
Azéma, Jean-Pierre, *From Munich to the Liberation 1938–1944* (Cambridge: Cambridge University Press, 1984).
Azéma, Jean-Pierre, *Jean Moulin: Le politique, le rebelle, le résistant* (Paris: Perrin, 2003).
Azéma, Jean-Pierre, *1940: L'année noir* (Paris: Fayard, 2010).
Azéma, Jean-Pierre and Bédarida, François, *La France des années noires* (Paris: Seuil, 1993).
Azéma, Jean-Pierre and Wieviorka, Olivier, *Vichy 1940–1944* (Paris: Perrin, 2004).

Bacquier, Louis, *Aïwah: Au combat avec les Marocains. Souvenirs d'un officier de tirailleurs 1942–1945* (Paris: Éditions Laville, 2012).
Ball, Simon, *The Bitter Sea: The Struggle for Mastery in the Mediterranean, 1935–1945* (New York: HarperPress, 2009).
Balu, Raphaële, "Les maquis de France, la France libre et les Alliés (1943–1945): retrouver la coopération," Thèse du doctorat, Université de Caen Normandie, 2018.
Bancel, Nicolas, Denis, Daniel, and Fates, Youssef, *De l'Indochine à l'Algérie: La jeunesses en mouvements des deux côtés du miroir colonial 1940–1962* (Paris: Éditions la Découvert, 2003).
Bankwitz, Philip, *Maxime Weygand and Civil–Military Relations in Modern France* (Cambridge, MA: Harvard University Press, 1967).
Barbier, Nina, *Malgré-elles: Les Alsaciennes et Mosellanes incorporées de force dans la machine de guerre nazi* (Paris: Tallandier, 2018).
Barjot, Pierre, *Le Débarquement du 8 novembre 1942 en Afrique du Nord* (Paris: J. de Gigord, 1946).
Barnes, Julian, *England, England* (New York: Vintage Books, 1996).
Baruch, Marc Olivier, *Servir l'État français: L'administration en France de 1940 à 1944* (Paris: Fayard, 1997).
Baruch, Marc Olivier, *Une poignée de misérables: L'épuration de la société française après la Seconde Guerre mondiale* (Paris: Fayard, 2003).
Bauer, Alain and Dachez, Roger, *Nouvelle histoire des francs-maçons en France: Des origines à nos jours* (Paris: Tallandier, 2018).
Bayle, André, *De Marseille à Novossibirsk* (Sausset-Les-Pins: André Bayle, 1992). Republished in 2008 as *Des Jeux Olympiques à la Waffen-SS* (Chevaigne: Éditions du Lore, 2008).
Beaufre, Général André, *Mémoires 1920–1940–1945* (Paris: Presses de la Cité, 1965).
Beaufre, General André, *1940: The Fall of France* (New York: Knopf, 1968).
Beauvoir, Simone de (ed.), *Quiet Moments in a War: The Letters of Jean-Paul Sartre to Simone de Beauvoir (1940–1963)* (New York: Scribners, 1993).
Beevor, Antony and Cooper, Artemis, *Paris after the Liberation* (London: Penguin, 1994).
Belle, Jacques, *L'Opération* Torch *et la Tunisie: De Casablanca à Tunis et au-delà (novembre 1942–septembre 1943)* (Paris: Economica, 2011).
Belot, Robert, *Aux frontières de la liberté: Vichy–Madrid–Alger–Londres: S'évader de la France sous l'Occupation* (Paris: Fayard, 1998).
Belot, Robert, *La Résistance sans de Gaulle* (Paris: Fayard, 2006).
Benbassa, Esther and Attias, Jean-Christophe, *Dictionnaire de Civilisation juive* (Paris: Larousse, 1997).
Bene, Krisztián, *La collaboration militaire française dans la Seconde Guerre mondiale* (Talmont St Hilaire: Éditions-Codex, 2012).
Bennaïm, Richard, *Le Journal du soldat juif* (Lormont: Le Bord de l'Eau, 2017).
Bergère, Marc, *L'Épuration en France* (Paris: Que sais-je?, 2018).
Berlière, Jean-Marc and Chabrun, Laurent, *Les Policiers français sous l'occupation* (Paris: Perrin, 2001).

Béthouart, Antoine, *Cinq années d'espérance: Mémoires de guerre 1939–1945* (Paris: Plon, 1968).
Bezy, Jean, *Le S.R. Air* (Paris: Éditions France-Empire, 1979).
Billotte, Pierre, *Le Temps des armes* (Paris: Plon, 1972).
Billotte, Pierre, *Trente ans d'humour avec de Gaulle* (Paris: Éditions Mengès, 1978).
Bimberg, Edward L., *The Morocan Goums: Tribal Warriors in a Modern War* (Westport and London: Greenwood Press, 1999).
Bishop, Chris, *Hitler's Foreign Divisions: Foreign Volunteers in the Waffen-SS 1940–1945* (Staplehurst: Spellmount, 2005).
Blanning, T. C. W., *The Culture of Power and the Power of Culture: Old Regime Europe 1660–1789* (Oxford: Oxford University Press, 2002).
Bloch, Jean-Richard, *De la France trahie à la France en armes: Commentaires à Radio Moscou, 1941–1944* (Paris: Éditions Sociales, 1949).
Bloch, Marc, *The Historian's Craft* (New York: Alfred A. Knopf, 1963).
Bloch, Marc, *Strange Defeat: A Statement of Evidence Written in 1940* (New York: W. W. Norton & Company, 1968).
Boissieu, Alain de, *Pour combattre avec de Gaulle: Souvenirs 1940–1946* (Paris: Plon, 1981).
Boivin, Michel, *1939–1945: Les Manchois dans la tourment de la Seconde Guerre mondiale*, 6 volumes (Marigny: Éditions Eurocibles, 2004).
Bonichon, Philippe, Gény, Pierre, and Nemo, Jean, *Présences françaises outre-mer (XVIe–XXIe siècles)*, tome 1, *Histoire: Périodes et continents* (Paris: Karthala, 2012).
Boog, Horst, Rahn, Werner, Stumpf, Reinhard, and Wegner, Bernd, *Germany and the Second World War*, vol. 6 (Oxford: Oxford University Press, 2001).
Boris, Jean-Mathieu, *Combattant de la France Libre* (Paris: Perrin, 2012).
Bosworth, Richard J. B. and Maiolo, Joseph A., *The Cambridge History of the Second World War*, volume II, *Politics and Ideology* (Cambridge: Cambridge University Press, 2015).
Bouchinet-Serreulles, Claude, *Nous étions faits pour être libres: La résistance avec De Gaulle et Jean Moulin* (Paris: Grasset, 2000).
Bourderon, Roger, *Rol-Tanguy: Des Brigades internationales à la libération de Paris* (Paris: Tallandier, 2013).
Bourdrel, Philippe, *La Cagoule: Histoire d'une société secrète du Front populare à la Ve République* (Paris: Albin Michel, 1992).
Boulle, Lieutenant-Colonel Georges, *Le Corps expéditionnaire français en Italy (1943–1944)* (Paris: Imprimerie nationale, 1971).
Bourke, Joanna, *An Intimate History of Killing* (London: Granta, 1999).
Boyce, Robert and Maiolo, Joseph A. (eds.), *The Origins of World War II* (London: Palgrave Macmillan, 2003).
Bradley, Omar, *A Soldier's Story* (New York: Henry Holt, 1951).
Brignon, Jean et al., *Histoire du Maroc* (Paris: Hatier, 1967).
Broch, Ludivine, *Ordinary Workers, Vichy and the Holocaust: French Railwaymen and the Second World War* (Cambridge: Cambridge University Press, 2016).
Broche, François, Caïtucoli, Georges, and Muracciole, Jean-François, *Dictionnaire de la France Libre* (Paris: Robert Lafont, 2010).

Broche, François, Caïtucoli, Georges, Muracciole, Jean-François, and Gallo, Max, *La France au combat: De l'appel du 18 juin à la victoire* (Paris: Perrin, 2007).
Brousse, Vincent and Grandcoing, Philippe, *Un siècle militant: Engagement(s), resistance(s), et memoire(s) au XXe siècle en Limousin* (Limoges: Presses universitaires de Limoges, 2005).
Brown, Frederick, *The Embrace of Unreason: France, 1914–1940* (New York: Knopf, 2014).
Bruneau, Jean-Baptiste, *La Marine de Vichy aux Antilles juin 1940–juillet 1943* (Paris: Les Indes Savantes, 2014).
Buchanan, Andrew, *American Grand Strategy in the Mediterranean during World War II* (Cambridge: Cambridge University Press, 2014).
Buchanan, Andrew, *World War II in Global Perspective, 1931–1953: A Short History* (London: Wiley-Blackwell, 2019).
Burdick, Charles B., *Germany's Military Strategy and Spain in World War II* (Syracuse: Syracuse University Press, 1968).
Burrin, Philippe, *France under the Germans: Collaboration and Compromise* (New York: The New Press, 1996).
Butcher, Captain Harry C., *My Three Years with Eisenhower* (London and Toronto: William Heinemann, 1946).
Buton, Philippe, *Les lendemains qui déchantent: Le Parti communiste français à la Libération* (Paris: Presses de la Foundation Nationale des Sciences Politiques, 1993).
Caddick-Adams, Peter, *Monte Cassino: Ten Armies in Hell* (London: Arrow Books, 2013).
Cadeau, Ivan, *De Lattre* (Paris: Perrin, 2017).
Campo, Joseph, "Desert Fox or Hitler Favorite? Myths and Memories of Erwin Rommel: 1941–1970," Ph.D. Thesis, University of California Santa Barbara, 2019.
Cantier, Jacques, *L'Algérie sous le régime de Vichy* (Paris: Éditions Odile Jacob, 2002).
Capdevila, Luc, Rouquet, François, Virgili, Fabrice, and Voldman, Danièle, *Sexes, genre et guerres (France, 1914–1945)* (Paris: Payot, 2010).
Caroff, René Pierre Eugène, *Les débarquements alliés en Afrique du Nord (novembre 1942)*, second edition (Vincennes: Service historique de la marine, 1987).
Carrard, Philippe, *The French Who Fought for Hitler* (Cambridge: Cambridge University Press, 2010).
Carswell, Richard, *The Fall of France in the Second World War: History and Memory* (London: Palgrave Macmillan, 2019).
Catala, Michel (ed.), *Les poches de l'Atlantique 1944–1945: Le dernier acte de la Seconde Guerre mondiale en France* (Rennes: Presses universitaires de Rennes, 2019).
Cazals, Claude, *La Gendarmerie sous l'occupation* (Paris: Les Éditions La Musse, 1995).
Chaubin, Hélène, *La Corse à l'épreuve de la guerre 1939–1943* (Paris: Vendémiaire Éditions, 2012).
Churchill, Winston S., *The Second World War*, 6 volumes (Boston: Houghton Mifflin Company, 1951).
Ciano, Galeazzo, *Ciano's Diary 1937–1943* (London: Enigma Books, 2002).

Clark, Jeffrey J. and Smith, Robert Ross, *United States Army in World War II: European Theater of Operations. Riviera to the Rhine* (Washington, D.C.: Center of Military History, United States Army, 1993).
Clark, Mark W., *Calculated Risk* (New York: Harper, 1950).
Clayton, Anthony, *Three Marshals of France: Leadership after Trauma* (London: Brassey's, 1992).
Clayton, Anthony, *General Maxime Weygand 1867–1967: Fortune and Misfortune* (Bloomington: Indiana University Press, 2015).
Cochet, François, *Les soldats de la drôle de guerre: Septembre 1939–mai 1940* (Paris: Hachette Littératures, 2004).
Cohen-Addad, Nicole, Kadri, Aïssa, and Quemeneur, Tramor (eds.), *8 novembre 1942: Résistance et débarquement allié en Afrique du Nord. Dynamiques historiques, politiques et socio-culturelles* (Vulaines-sur-Seine: Éditions du Croquant, 2021).
Cointet, Michèle, *Nouvelle histoire de Vichy* (Paris: Fayard, 2011).
Cointet, Michèle, *La milice française* (Paris: Fayard, 2013).
Colton, Joel, *Léon Blum: Humanist in Politics* (New York: Alfred A. Knopf, 1966).
Comor, André-Paul, *L'Épopée de la 13ème Demi-brigade de Légion Étrangère, 1940–1945* (Paris: Nouvelles Éditions Latines, 1989).
Conan, Éric and Rousso, Henry, *Vichy, un passé qui ne passe pas* (Paris: Fayard, 1994).
Cornil-Frerrot, Sylvain and Oulmont, Philippe (eds.), *Les Français libres et le monde: Actes du colloque international au musée de l'Armée 22 et 23 novembre 2013* (Paris: Nouveau Monde Éditions, 2015).
Costagliola, Bernard, *La Marine de Vichy: Blocus et collaboration* (Paris: Tallandier, 2009).
Costagliola, Bernard, *Darlan: La collaboration à tout prix* (Paris: CNRS Éditions, 2015).
Coutau-Bégarie, Hervé and Huan, Claude, *Darlan* (Paris: Fayard, 1989).
Crémieux-Brilhac, Jean-Louis, *Les français de l'an 40*, 3 volumes (Paris: Gallimard, 1990).
Crémieux-Brilhac, Jean-Louis, *La France libre*, 2 volumes (Paris: Gallimard, 2013).
Crémieux-Brilhac, Jean-Louis, *De Gaulle, la République et la France libre, 1940–1945* (Paris: Perrin, 2014).
Crémieux-Brilhac, Jean-Louis, *L'étrange victoire: De la défense de la République à la libération de la France* (Paris: Gaillimard, 2016).
Cuvillier, Solange, *Tribulations d'une femme dans l'armée française, ou Le Patriotisme Écorché* (Paris: Éditions Lettres du Monde, 1991).
Dard, Olivier, Bour, Julie, Gueit-Montchal, Lydiane, and Richard, Gilles (eds.), *Louis Jacquinot, un indépendant en politique* (Paris: Presses de l'université Paris-Sorbonne, 2013).
Daeffler, Michel, Leleu, Jean-Luc, Passera, Françoise, and Quellien, Jean (eds.), *La France pendant la Seconde Guerre mondiale: Atlas historique* (Paris: Fayard, 2010).
Daix, Pierre, *Braudel* (Paris: *Flammarion*, 1995).
Dallek, Robert, *Franklin Roosevelt and American Foreign Policy, 1932–1945* (New York and Oxford: Oxford University Press, 1995).

Davenport-Hines, Richard (ed.), *Letters from Oxford: Hugh Trevor-Roper to Bernard Berenson* (London: Phoenix, 2007).

Davis, Kenneth S., *FDR: The War President, 1940–1943. A History* (New York: Random House, 2000).

Deakin, F. W. *The Brutal Friendship: Mussolini, Hitler and the Fall of Italian Fascism* (New York: Harper and Row, 1962).

Dear, I. C. B. and Foot, M. R. D., *The Oxford Companion to World War II* (Oxford: Oxford University Press, 1995).

de Gaulle, Charles, *Vers l'armée de métier* (Paris: Berger-Levrault, 1944).

de Gaulle, Charles, *Mémoires de guerre*, 3 volumes (Paris: Plon, 1984).

de Gaulle, Charles, *Discours et messages 1940–1946* (Paris: Plon, 1970).

Delperrie de Bayac, J., *Histoire de la Milice 1918–1945* (Paris: Fayard, 1969).

Dereymez, Jean-William (ed.), *Les militaires dans la résistance: Ain – Dauphiné – Savoie, 1940–1944* (Avon-les-Roches: Éditions Anovi, 2010).

Desquesnes, Rémy, *Les poches de résistance allemandes: Août 1944–mai 1945* (Rennes: Éditions ouest-France, 2013).

D'Este, Carlo *World War II in the Mediterranean, 1942–1945* (Chapel Hill: Algonquin Books, 1990).

D'Este, Carlo, *Patton: A Genius for War* (New York: Harper Collins, 1995).

D'Este, Carlo, *Eisenhower: A Soldier's Life* (New York: Henry Holt, 2002).

Destremau, Bernard, *De Lattre* (Paris: Flammarion, 1999).

Diamond, Hanna, *Fleeing Hitler: France 1940* (Oxford: Oxford University Press, 2007).

Dominé, Jean-François, *Les Femmes au combat: L'arme féminine de la France pendant la Seconde Guerre mondiale* (Vincennes: Service historique de la défense, 2008).

Doughty, Robert Allan, *The Seeds of Disaster: The Development of French Army Doctrine 1919–1939* (Hamden: Archon Books, 1985).

Doughty, Robert Allan, *The Breaking Point: Sedan and the Fall of France 1940* (Hamden: Archon Books, 1990).

Durand, Romain, *De Giraud à de Gaulle: Les Corps francs d'Afrique* (Paris: Éditions l'Harmattan, 1999).

Durand, Yves, *Prisonniers de guerre dans les Stalags, les Oflags et les Kommandos, 1939–1945* (Paris: Hachette, 1994).

Duroselle, Jean-Baptiste, *Politique étrangère de la France: La décadence 1932–1939* (Paris: Imprimerie nationale, 1979).

Dutailly, Lieutenant-colonel Henry, *Les Problèmes de l'armée de terre française (1935–1939)* (Paris: Imprimerie nationale, 1980).

Echenberg, Myron, *Les tirailleurs sénégalais en Afrique occidentale française (1857–1960)* (Paris and Dakar: Karthala et Crepos, 2009).

Egremont, Max, *Under Two Flags: The Life of Major-General Sir Edward Spears* (London: Weidenfeld & Nicolson, 1997).

Ehlers, Robert S. Jr., *The Mediterranean Air War: Airpower and Allied Victory in World War II* (Lawrence: University Press of Kansas, 2015).

Eisenbeth, Maurice, *Les Juifs de l'Afrique du Nord: Démographique et onomastique* (Algiers: Imprimerie du Lycée, 1936).

Eisenhower, Dwight D., *Crusade in Europe* (Garden City, NY: Doubleday & Company Inc., 1950).

Eisenhower, Dwight David, *The Papers of Dwight David Eisenhower: The War Years* (Baltimore: Johns Hopkins University Press, 1970).
Eismann, Gaël, *Hôtel Majestic: Ordre et sécurité en France occupée (1940–1944)* (Paris: Tallandier, 2010).
Eismann, Gaël and Martens, Stefan, *Occupation et repression militaire allemandes: La politique de "maintien de l'ordre" en Europe occupée, 1939–1945* (Paris: Éditions Autrement, 2007).
Ellis, John, *Cassino: The Hollow Victory. The Battle for Rome, January–June 1944* (New York: McGraw-Hill, 1984).
Ellis, John, *Brute Force: Allied Strategy and Tactics in the Second World War* (London: Viking, 1990).
Estèbe, Jean, *Toulouse 1940–1944* (Paris: Perrin, 1996).
Evans, Martin, *Algeria: France's Undeclared War* (Oxford: Oxford University Press, 2012).
Evans, Richard J., *Altered Past: Counterfactuals in History* (London: Little Brown, 2014).
Evans, Richard J., *The Third Reich in Memory and History* (Oxford: Oxford University Press, 2015).
Facon, Patrick, *L'Armée de l'air dans la tourmente: La bataille de France, 1939–1940* (Paris: Economica, 2005).
Fargettas, Julien, *Les Tirailleurs sénégalais: Les soldats noirs entre legends et réalités 1939–1945* (Paris: Tallandier, 2012).
Faron, Olivier, *Les chantiers de jeunesse: Avoir 20 ans sous Pétain* (Paris: Grasset, 2011).
Fennell, Jonathan, *Combat and Morale in the North African Campaign: The Eighth Army and the Path to El Alamein* (Cambridge: Cambridge University Press, 2011).
Fennell, Jonathan, *Fighting the People's War: The British and Commonwealth Armies and the Second World War* (Cambridge: Cambridge University Press, 2019).
Ferris, John and Mawdsley, Evan (eds.), *The Cambridge History of the Second World War* (Cambridge: Cambridge University Press, 2015).
Finney, Patrick (ed.), *The Origins of the Second World War* (London: Arnold Press, 1997).
Finney, Patrick, *Remembering the Road to World War II: International History, National Identity, Collective Memory* (London: Routledge, 2011).
Fisher, Ernest F. Jr., *The Mediterranean Theater of Operations: Cassino to the Alps* (Washington, D.C.: Government Printing Office, 1977).
Fishman, Sarah, *We Will Wait: Wives of French Prisoners of War, 1940–1945* (New Haven and London: Yale University Press, 1990).
FitzGibbon, Constantine, *Denazification* (New York: W. W. Norton & Co., 1969).
Fleming, Thomas, *The New Dealer's War: F.D.R. and the War within World War II* (New York: Basic Books, 2001).
Florentin, Eddy, *Quand les Alliés bombardaient la France 1940–1945* (Paris: Perrin, 2008).
Fondation pour les études de défense nationale, Institut d'histoire des conflits contemporains, Service historique de l'Armée de terre, Service historique de la

Marine, and Service historique de l'Armée de l'air, *Les armées française pendant la seconde guerre mondiale 1939–1945* (Paris: École nationale supérieure de techniques avancées, 1986).
Fonvieille-Alquier, François, *The French and the Phoney War 1939–1940* (London: Tom Stacey, 1973).
Foot, M. R. D., *SOE in France* (London: Her Majesty's Stationary Office, 1966).
Foot, M. R. D., *Resistance* (London: Granada, 1978)
Foot, Michael, *Aneurin Bevan: A Biography I. 1887–1945* (London: MacGibbon & Lee, 1962).
Footitt, Hilary, *War and Liberation in France: Living with the Liberators* (New York: Palgrave Macmillan, 2004).
Footitt, Hilary and Simmonds, John, *France 1943–1945* (Leicester: Leicester University Press, 1988).
Franchini, Philippe, *Les Guerres d'Indochine*, tome 1, *Des origines de la présence française à l'engrenage du conflit international* (Paris: Éditions Pygmalion, 1988).
Frankenstein, Robert, *Le Prix du réarmament français 1935–1939* (Paris: Publications de la Sorbonne, 1982).
French, David, *Raising Churchill's Army: The British Army and the War against Germany 1919–1945* (New York: Oxford University Press, 2000).
Frieser, Karl-Heinz, *The Blitzkrieg Legend: The 1940 Campaign in the West* (Annapolis: Naval Institute Press, 2005).
Funk, Arthur Layton, *The Politics of Torch: The Allied Landings and the Algiers Putsch, 1942* (Lawrence: University Press of Kansas, 1974).
Funk, Arthur Layton, *Hidden Ally: The French Resistance, Special Operations, and the Landings in Southern France, 1944* (Westport: Greenwood Press, 1992).
Fussell, Paul, *The Great War and Modern Memory* (New York and London: Oxford University Press, 1975).
Fussell, Paul, *Doing Battle: The Making of a Skeptic* (Boston, New York, Toronto, and London: Little, Brown and Company, 1996).
Gallois, William, *A History of Violence in the Early Algerian Colony* (London: Palgrave Macmillan, 2013).
Gamelin, General Maurice, *Servir: Les Armées françaises de 1940* (Paris: Plon, 1946).
Gary, Romain, *La promesse de l'aube* (Paris: Gallimard, 1980).
Gaujac, Paul, *Le Corps expédionnaire français en Italie* (Paris: Histoire & Collections, 2003).
Gaunson, A. B., *The Anglo-French Clash in Lebanon and Syria, 1940–1945* (London: Macmillan, 1987).
Gayme, Evelyne, *Les Prisonniers de guerre français: Enjeux militaires et stratégiques (1914–1918 et 1940–1945)* (Paris: Economica, 2010).
Genet-Rouffiac, Natalie (ed.), *Des prisonniers de guerre aux personnes capturées* (Paris: Service Historique de la Défense, 2010).
Gildea, Robert, *Marianne in Chains: In Search of the German Occupation of France 1940–45* (London: Macmillan, 2002).
Gildea, Robert, *Fighters in the Shadows: A New History of the French Resistance* (Cambridge, MA: Harvard University Press, 2015).

Gillis, John R., *Commemorations: The Politics of National Identity* (Princeton: Princeton University Press, 1994).
Gimbel, John, *A German Community under American Occupation: Marburg 1945–1952* (Stanford: Stanford University Press, 1961).
Gimbel, John, *The American Occupation of Germany: Politics and the Military, 1945–1949* (Stanford: Stanford University Press, 1968).
Giolitto, Pierre, *Histoire de la milice* (Paris: Librairie Académique Perrin, 1997).
Giolitto, Pierre, *Volontaires français sous uniform allemand* (Paris: Tempus Perrin, 2007).
Girardet, Raoul, *La crise militaire française 1945–1962: Aspects sociologiques et idéologiques* (Paris: Armand Colin, 1964).
Giraud, Henri, *Mes évasions* (Paris: Juillard, 1946).
Giraud, Henri, *Un seul but – la victoire: Alger 1942–1944* (Paris: Juillard, 1949).
Girault, René and Frank, Robert, *La puissance française en question! 1945–1949* (Paris: Publications de la Sorbonne, 1988).
Graham, Dominique and Bidwell, Shelford, *Tug of War: The Battle for Italy, 1943–1945* (New York: St. Martin's Press, 1986).
Gras, Yves, *La 1ère D.F.L.: Les Français libres au combat* (Paris: Presses de la Cité, 1983).
Greenfield, Kent Roberts, *Command Decisions* (Washington, D.C.: Center for Military History, 1990).
Greenhalgh, Elizabeth, *The French Army and the First World War* (Cambridge: Cambridge University Press, 2014).
Grémillon, Hélène, *Le Confident* (Paris: Plon, 2010).
Grey, Colin S., *Strategy for Chaos: Revolutions in Military Affairs and the Evidence of History* (London: Frank Cass, 2002).
Halais, Jérémie, *Saint-Lô et son canton dans la tourmente de la Seconde Guerre mondiale 1939–1945* (Saint-Lô: Société d'archéologie et d'histoire de la Manche, 2007).
Hallion, Richard, *Strike from the Sky* (Washington, D.C.: Smithsonian Institution Press, 1989).
Hamilton, Nigel, *Monty: The Making of a General, 1887–1942* (New York: McGraw Hill, 1981).
Hamilton, Nigel, *Master of the Battlefield: Monty's War Years, 1942–1944* (New York: McGraw-Hill, 1983).
Hamilton, Nigel, *The Mantle of Command: FDR at War, 1941–1942* (New York and Boston: Mariner Books, 2015).
Hampel, August, *J'occupais Royan 1943–1945* (Rioux-Martin: Le Croît Vif, 2011).
Hampton, Ellen, *Women of Valor: The Rochambelles on the WWII Front* (New York: Palgrave Macmillan, 2006).
Hargreaves, Andrew L., *Special Operations in World War II: British and American Irregular Warfare* (Norman: University of Oklahoma Press, 2013).
Harper, Glyn, *The Battle for North Africa: El Alamein and the Turning Point for World War II* (Bloomington: Indiana University Press, 2017).
Harper, John Lamberton, *American Visions of Europe* (New York: Cambridge University Press, 1994).

Harymbat, Frédéric, *Les Européens d'Afrique du Nord dans les armées de la libération française (1942–1945)* (Paris: Éditions l'Harmattan, 2014).

Hastings, Max, *Finest Years: Churchill as Warlord 1940–45* (London: Harper Press, 2009).

Hastings, Max, *Das Reich: The March of the 2nd SS Panzer Division through France, June 1944* (Saint Paul, MN: Zenith Press, 2013).

Hawes, Stephen and White, Ralph (eds.), *Resistance in Europe, 1939–1945* (London: Viking, 1975).

Hazareesingh, Sudhir, *In the Shadow of the General: Modern France and the Myth of de Gaulle* (Oxford: Oxford University Press, 2012).

Hettier de Boislambert, Claude, *Les fers de l'espoir* (Paris: Plon, 1978).

Higham, Robin, *Two Roads to War: The French and British Air Arms from Versailles to Dunkirk* (Annapolis: Naval Institute Press, 2012).

Hill, Alexander, *The Red Army and the Second World War* (Cambridge: Cambridge University Press, 2019).

Hillel, Marc, *L'occupation française en Allemagne 1945–1949* (Paris: Balland, 1983).

Hinsley, F. H., *British Intelligence in the Second World War: Its Influence on Strategy and Operations*, 5 volumes (New York: Cambridge University Press, 1981).

Hirshon, Stanley P., *General Patton: A Soldier's Life* (New York: Harper Collins, 2002).

Hitchcock, William I., *Liberation: The Bitter Road to Freedom, Europe 1944–1945* (London: Faber and Faber, 2009).

Hoff, Ebbe Curtiss, *Preventative Medicine in World War II*, volume VIII, *Civil Affairs/Military Government Public Health Activities* (Washington, D.C.: Office of the Surgeon General, Department of the Army, 1976).

Horne, Alistair, *To Lose a Battle: France 1940* (London: Penguin, 1982).

Howard, Michael, *Grand Strategy*, volume IV, *August 1942–September 1943* (London: HMSO, 1970).

Howard, Michael, *Captain Professor: A Life in War and Peace. The Memoirs of Professor Michael Howard* (London and New York: Continuum, 2006).

Howard, Michael and Paret, Peter (eds.), *Carl von Clausewitz: On War* (Princeton: Princeton University Press, 1976).

Howe, George F., *United States Army in World War II: The Mediterranean Theater of Operations, Northwest Africa. Seizing the Initiative in the West* (Washington, D. C.: Center of Military History, United States Army, 1991).

Hucker, Daniel, *Public Opinion and the End of Appeasement in Britain and France* (Farnham: Ashgate, 2011).

Hughes, Judith M., *To the Maginot Line: The Politics of French Military Preparation in the 1920s* (Cambridge, MA: Harvard University Press, 1971).

Hull, Cordell, *Memoirs*, 2 volumes (New York: Macmillan, 1948).

Hull, Elizabeth, *Absolute Destruction: Military Culture and the Practices of War in Imperial Germany* (Ithaca and London: Cornell University Press, 2005).

Imlay, Talbot C., *Facing the Second World War: Strategy, Politics, and Economics in Britain and France, 1938–1940* (Oxford: Oxford University Press, 2003).

Irving, David, *The Trail of the Fox: The Life of Field-Marshal Erwin Rommel* (London: Book Club Associates, 1977).

Jackson, Julian, *The Popular Front in France: Defending Democracy, 1934–1938* (Cambridge: Cambridge University Press, 1988).
Jackson, Julian, *The Fall of France: The Nazi Invasion of 1940* (Oxford: Oxford University Press, 2003).
Jackson, Julian, *A Certain Idea of France: The Life of Charles de Gaulle* (Cambridge, MA: Harvard University Press, 2018).
Jackson, Peter, *France and the Nazi Menace: Intelligence and Policy Making 1933–1939* (Oxford: Oxford University Press, 2000).
Jauneau, Élodie, "La feminization de l'armée française pendant les guerres (1938–1962): Enjeux et réalités d'un processus irreversible," Thèse du doctorat, Université Paris Diderot (Paris 7), 2011.
Jaurès, Jean, *L'Armée nouvelle: L'organisation socialiste de la France* (Paris: Publications Jules Rouff, 1911).
Jeanclos, Yves (ed.), *La France et les soldats d'infortune au XXe siècle* (Strasbourg: Economica, 2003).
Jennings, Eric, *La France libre fut africaine* (Paris: Perrin, 2014).
Jennings, Eric T., *Free French Africa in World War II: The African Resistance* (Cambridge: Cambridge University Press, 2015).
Jones, Benjamin F., *Eisenhower's Guerrillas: The Jedburghs, the Maquis, and the Liberation of France* (Oxford: Oxford University Press, 2016).
Jones, Matthew, *Britain, the United States and the Mediterranean War* (New York: St. Martin's Press, 1996).
Jordan, Nicole *The Popular Front and Central Europe: The Dilemmas of French Impotence, 1918–1940* (Cambridge: Cambridge University Press, 1992).
Judge Advocate General, *Digest of Opinions of the Branch of the Judge Advocate General with the European Theater of Operations*, no date, volume II, 435–480, www.loc.gov/rr/frd/Military_Law/pdf/ETO-Index-Digest-Vol-II.pdf.
Judt, Tony, *Past Imperfect: French Intellectuals 1944–56* (Berkeley: University of California Press, 1997).
Judt, Tony, *Postwar: A History of Europe since 1945* (New York: Penguin, 2005).
Juin, Maréchal Alphonse Pierre, *Mémoires*, tome 1, *Alger, Tunis, Rome* (Paris: Fayard, 1959).
Kably, Mohammed, *Histoire du Maroc: Réactualisation et synthèse* (Rabat: Édition de l'Institut Royal, 2012).
Kaiser, David E., *Economic Diplomacy and the Origins of the Second World War: Germany, Britain, France, and Eastern Europe, 1930–1939* (Princeton: Princeton University Press, 1980).
Kaiser, David E., *No End Save Victory: How FDR Led the Nation into War* (New York: Basic Books, 2014).
Kaspi, André, *La Libération de la France juin 1944–janvier 1946* (Paris: Perrin, 2004).
Katz, Robert, *The Battle for Rome: The Germans, the Allies, the Partisans, and the Pope, September 1943–June 1944* (New York: Simon & Schuster, 2003).
Kedward, H. R., *Resistance in Vichy France: A Study of Ideas and Motivation in the Southern Zone 1940–1942* (Oxford: Oxford University Press, 1978).
Kedward, H. R., *In Search of the Maquis: Rural Resistance in Southern France 1942–1944* (Oxford: Oxford University Press, 1993).

Kedward, H. R. and Wood, Nancy, *The Liberation of France: Image and Event* (Washington and Oxford: Berge Publishers, 1995).

Kennett, Lee, *G.I.: The American Soldier in World War II* (New York: Scribner, 1987).

Kersaudy, François, *Churchill and de Gaulle* (London: Collins, 1981).

Kershaw, Ian, *Fateful Choices: Ten Decisions That Changed the World 1940–1941* (London: Penguin, 2007).

Kesselring, Albert, *Kesselring: A Soldier's Record* (New York: William Morrow, 1954).

Kiesling, Eugenia C., *Arming against Hitler: France & the Limits of Military Power* (Lawrence: University Press of Kansas, 1996).

King, Anthony, *The Combat Soldier: Infantry Tactics and Cohesion in the Twentieth and Twenty-First Centuries* (Oxford: Oxford University Press, 2013).

Kirshner, Jonathan, *Appeasing Bankers: Financial Caution on the Road to War* (Princeton and Oxford: Princeton University Press, 2007).

Kiszely, Sir John, *Anatomy of a Campaign: The British Fiasco in Norway, 1940* (Cambridge: Cambridge University Press, 2017).

Kitson, Simon, *Vichy et la chasse aux espions Nazis, 1940–1942: Complexités de la politique de collaboration* (Paris: Éditions Autrement, 2005).

Knapp, Andrew, *Les français sous les bombes alliées, 1940–1945* (Paris: Tallandier, 2014).

Kundahl, George G., *The Riviera at War: World War II on the Côte d'Azure* (London and New York: I. B. Tauris, 2017).

Kupferman, Fred, *Le Procès de Vichy – Pucheu, Pétain, Laval* (Paris: Éditions Complexe, 2006).

Labanca, Nicola, Reynolds, David, and Wieviorka, Olivier, *La Guerre du Désert* (Paris: Perrin, 2019).

Lacouture, Jean, *De Gaulle*, tome 1, *Le Rebelle 1890–1944* (Paris: Éditions du Seuil, 1984).

Lacouture, Jean, *De Gaulle: The Ruler 1945–1970* (New York: W. W. Norton, 1993).

Lahaie, Olivier, *Guerre des services spéciaux en Afrique du Nord 1941–1944: Les mémoires du Général Jean Chrétien ancient chef du contre-espionnage à Alger* (Paris: Histoire & Collections, 2015).

Lanquetot, André, *Un Hiver dans les Abruzzes: Le 8e Régiment de tirailleurs Marocains et le 3e Groupe du 63e Régiment d'Artillerie d'Afrique* (Vincennes: SHAT, 1990).

Lapouge, Jean, *De Sétif à Marseille, par Cassino: Carnet de guerre de Jean Lapouge, sous-lieutenant au 7e RTA. Campagnes de Tunisie, Italie et Provence, 1942–1944* (Parçay-sur-Vienne: Éditions Anovi, 2007).

Larminat, Edgard de, *Chroniques irrévérencieuses* (Paris: Plon, 1962).

Lattre de Tassigny, Jean de, *Histoire de la première armée française: Rhin et Danube* (Paris: Presses de la Cité, 1971).

Laub, Thomas, *After the Fall: German Policy in Occupied France, 1940–1944* (Oxford: Oxford University Press, 2013).

Lauterpacht, Sir Hersch, *Recognition in International Law* (Cambridge: Cambridge University Press, 1947).

Leahy, William D., *I Was There: The Personal Story of the Chief of Staff to Presidents Roosevelt and Truman Based on His Notes and Diaries Made at the Time* (London: Victor Gollancz, 1950).
Leconte, Robin, "Comprendre la défaite: La commission d'enquête sur les repliements suspects 1940–1944," Mémoire de Master 2, Université Paris I Panthéon-Sorbonne – UFR Histoire Centre d'histoire sociale du XXe siècle, 2013.
Lee, Ulysses, *The Employment of Negro Troops* (Washington, D.C.: Center of Military History, United States Army, 1965).
Lefèvre, Eric and Mabire, Jean, *La Légion perdue face aux partisans 1942* (Paris: Jacques Grancher, 1995).
Lefort-Rouquette, Suzanne, *Des Ambulancières dans les combats de la Libération: Avec les soldats de la 9e division d'infanterie coloniale* (Paris: Éditions l'Harmattan, 2005).
Le Gac, Julie, *Vaincre sans gloire: Le corps expéditionnaire français en Italie (novembre 1942–juillet 1944)* (Paris: Les Belles Lettres/Ministère de la défense-DMPA, 2013).
Leleu, Jean-Luc, *La Waffen-SS: Soldats politiques en guerre* (Paris: Perrin, 2007).
Lerner, Henri, *Catroux* (Paris: Albin Michel, 1990).
Levendel, Issac, *Not Germans Alone: A Son's Search for the Truth of Vichy* (Chicago: Northwestern University Press, 2001).
Levine, Alan J., *The War against Rommel's Supply Lines, 1942–1943* (Westport and London: Praeger, 1999).
Levisse-Touzé, Christine, *L'Afrique du Nord dans la guerre 1939–1945* (Paris: Albin Michel, 1998).
Levisse-Touzé, Christine (ed.), *La Campagne de 1940* (Paris: Tallandier, 2001).
Liddell Hart, B. H., *The Rommel Papers* (New York: Harcourt, Brace, 1953).
Lieb, Peter, *Vercors 1944: Resistance in the French Alps* (London: Osprey Publishing, 2012).
Liebling, A. J., *World War II Writings: The Road Back to Paris. Mollie and Other War Pieces, Uncollected War Journalism. Normandy Revisited* (New York: Literary Classics of the United States, 2008).
Litsky, Elliott Burton, "The Murphy–Weygand Agreement: The United States and French North Africa (1940–1942)," Ph.D. thesis, Fordham University, 1986.
Loisy, Philibert de, *1944, les FFI deviennent soldats: L'amalgame: de la résistance à l'armée régulière* (Paris: Histoire & Collections, 2014).
Lopez, Jean and Wieviorka, Olivier (eds.), *Les mythes de la seconde guerre mondiale* (Paris: Perrin, 2015).
Ludewig, Joachim, *Rückzug: The German Retreat from France, 1944* (Lexington: University Press of Kentucky, 2012).
Lugan, Bernard, *Histoire du Maroc des origines à nos jours* (Paris: Critérion, 1992).
Lukes, Igor and Goldstein, Erik (eds.), *The Munich Crisis, 1938: Prelude to World War II* (London and Portland: Frank Cass, 1999).
Lynn, John, *Women, Armies and Warfare in Early Modern Europe* (Cambridge: Cambridge University Press, 2008).
Mabon, Armelle, *Prisonniers de guerre "indigènes": Visages oubliés de la France occupée* (Paris: Éditions La Découverte, 2010).

Mackenzie, S. P. *The Colditz Phenomenon* (Oxford: Oxford University Press, 2006).

MacKenzie, S. P., *Flying against Fate: Superstition and Allied Aircrews in World War II* (Lawrence: University of Kansas Press, 2018).

Macleod, Roderick and Kelly, Denis (eds.), *The Ironside Diaries, 1937–1940* (London: Constable, 1962).

Macmillan, Harold, *War Diaries: Politics and War in the Mediterranean, January 1943–May 1945* (London: Macmillan, 1984).

MacVane, John, *War and Diplomacy in North Africa* (London: Robert Hale, 1944).

Marcus, Sheldon, *Father Coughlin: The Tumultuous Life of the Priest of the Little Flower* (Boston: Little, Brown and Co, 1972).

Marrus, Michael R. and Paxton, Robert O., *Vichy France and the Jews* (New York: Basic Books, 1981).

Marshall, S. L. A., *Men against Fire: The Problem of Battle Command in Future War* (New York: William Morrow, 1947).

Martel, André (ed.), *Histoire militaire de la France*, tome 4, *De 1940 à nos jours* (Paris: Presses universitaires de France, 1994).

Martel, André, *Leclerc: Le soldat et la politique* (Paris: Albin Michel, 1998).

Masson, Philippe, *La marine française et la guerre 1939–1945* (Paris: Tallandier, 1991).

Massu, Suzanne, *Quand j'étais Rochambelle* (Paris: Grasset, 1969).

Mathieu, Yves, *Policiers perdus: Les GMR dans la Seconde Guerre mondiale* (Toulouse: self-published, 2009).

Mauraic, Claude, *Un autre de Gaulle: Journal, 1944–1954* (Paris: Hachette, 1971).

May, Ernest R., *Strange Victory: Hitler's Conquest of France* (New York: Hill and Wang, 2000).

Mayers, David, *FDR's Ambassadors and the Diplomacy of Crisis: From the Rise of Hitler to the End of World War II* (Cambridge: Cambridge University Press, 2012).

Mazière, Christian de la, *Ashes of Honour* (London: Allan Wingate, 1975).

Mazower, Mark, *Inside Hitler's Greece: The Experience of Occupation, 1941–1944* (New Haven: Yale University Press, 1993).

Mazower, Mark, *Dark Continent: Europe's Twentieth Century* (New York: Vintage Books, 1998).

McConahay, Mary Jo, *The Tango War: The Struggle for Hearts, Minds, and Riches of Latin America during World War II* (New York: St. Martin's Press, 2018).

McMeekin, Sean, *Stalin's War: A New History of World War II* (New York: Basic Books, 2021).

Medrala, Jean, *Les Réseaux de renseignements franco-polonais, 1940–1944* (Paris: Éditions l'Harmattan, 2005).

Melton, George E., *From Versailles to Mers el-Kébir: The Promise of Anglo-French Naval Cooperation, 1919–40* (Annapolis: Naval Institute Press, 2015).

Merle, Robert, *Ahmed ben Bella* (Paris: Gallimard, 1965).

Metzger, Chantal, *L'empire colonial français dans la stratégie du troisième Reich (1936–1945)*, 2 volumes (Paris and Brussels: Direction des Archives, Ministère des Affaires étrangères/P.I.E.-Peter Lang, 2002).

Metzger, Chantal, *Le Maghreb dans la guerre 1939–1945* (Paris: Armand Colin, 2018).

Micaud, Charles, *The French Right and Nazi Germany, 1933–1939* (Durham: Duke University Press, 1943).

Milne, Caleb, *"I Dream of the Day . . .": Letters from Caleb Milne. Africa, 1942–1943* (Woodstock, New York: privately published, 1944).

Miot, Claire, "Sortir l'armée des ombres. Soldats de l'Empire, combattants de la Libération, armée de la Nation: La Première armée française, du débarquement en Provence à la capitulation allemande (1944–1945)," Thèse du doctorat, Université Paris-Saclay, 2016.

Miot, Claire, *La première armée française* (Paris: Perrin, 2021).

Miot, Claire, Piketty, Guillaume, and Vaisset, Thomas, *Militaires en résistances en France et en Europe* (Villeneuve d'Ascq: Presses universitaires du Septentrion, 2020).

Miquel, Pierre, *La Grande guerre* (Paris: Fayard, 1983).

Monsabert, General Joseph Goislard de, *Notes de Guerre* (Hélette: Éditions Jean Curutchet, 1999).

Montagnon, Pierre, *Dictionnaire de la colonisation française* (Paris: Pygmalion/ Flammarion, 2010).

Montgomery, Bernard, *The Memoirs of Field Marshal Montgomery* (London: Collins, 1958).

Moore, William Mortimer, *The Life of Philippe Leclerc, de Gaulle's Greatest General* (Philadelphia and Newbury: Casemate Publishers, 2011).

Moorehead, Alan, *Desert War: The North African Campaign 1940–1943* (London and New York: Penguin, 2001).

Moran, Charles, *The Landings in North Africa, November 1942* (Washington, D. C., Naval Historical Center, 1992).

Moran, Daniel and Waldron, Arthur (eds.), *The People in Arms: Military Myth and National Mobilization since the French Revolution* (Cambridge: Cambridge University Press, 2003).

Morrison, Samuel Elliot, *History of U.S. Naval Operations in World War II*, volume 2, *Operations in North African Waters* (Boston: Little Brown, 1950).

Mouré, Kenneth and Alexander, Martin (eds.), *Crisis and Renewal in France, 1918–1962* (New York: Berghahn Books, 2002).

Muracciole, Jean-François, *Les Français libres: L'autre Résistance* (Paris: Tallandier, 2009).

Mysyrowicz, Ladislas, *Autopsie d'une défaite: Origines de l'effondrement militaire française de 1940* (Lausanne: L'Age d'homme, 1973).

Naimark, Norman M., *The Russians in Germany: A History of the Soviet Zone of Occupation, 1945–1949* (Cambridge, MA: Harvard University Press, 1995).

Neal, Colonel John J., "The Shared Burden: United States–French Coalition Operations in the European Theater of World War II," Master's thesis, School of Advanced Studies, U.S. Army Command and Staff College, Ft. Leavenworth, KS, 2013.

Neiberg, Michael S., *When France Fell: The Vichy Crisis and the Fate of the Anglo-American Alliance* (Cambridge, MA: Harvard University Press, 2021).

Némirovsky, Irène, *Suite Française* (Paris: Éditions Denoël, 2004).

Nicolaïdis, Dimitri, *Oublier nos crimes: L'amnestie national, une specificité française* (Paris: Autrement, 2002).

Nicolson, Harold, *Diaries and Letters, 1939–1945* (London: Collins, 1967).

Nora, Pierre and Julien, Charles-André, *Les français d'Algérie* (Chantenay: Julliard, 1961).

Nord, Philip, *France 1940: Defending the Republic* (New Haven: Yale University Press, 2015).

Notin, Jean-Christophe, *La Campagne d'Italie 1943–1945: Les victoires oubliées de la France* (Paris: Perrin, 2007).

Notin, Jean-Christophe, *Maréchal Juin* (Paris: Tallandier, 2015).

Notin, Jean-Christophe, *Leclerc: Le croisé de la France libre* (Paris: Perrin, 2015).

Noguères, Henri, *Histoire de la résistance en France*, 10 volumes (Paris: Laffont, 1969).

Noguères, Henri, *La vie quotidienne des résistants de l'Armistice à la Libération* (Paris: Hachette, 1984).

Novick, Peter, *The Resistance versus Vichy: The Purge of Collaborators in Liberated France* (London: Chatto and Windus, 1968).

Novick, Peter, *L'épuration française 1944–1949* (Paris: Éditions Balland, 1985).

O'Brien, Phillips Payson, *The Second Most Powerful Man in the World: The Life of Admiral William D. Leahy, Roosevelt's Chief of Staff* (New York: Dutton, 2019).

Office of the Historian, *Foreign Relations of the United States: Diplomatic Papers, 1945, Europe*, vol. IV, https://history.state.gov/historicaldocuments/frus1945v04/d664.

O'Hara, Vincent P., *Torch: North Africa and the Allied Path to Victory* (Annapolis: Naval Institute Press, 2015).

Olson, Lynne, *Last Hope Island: Britain, Occupied Europe, and the Brotherhood That Helped Turn the Tide of War* (New York: Random House, 2017).

Orr, Andrew, *Women and the French Army during the World Wars, 1914–1940* (Bloomington: Indiana University Press, 2017).

Paret, Peter, *French Irregular Warfare from Indochina to Algeria: An Analysis of a Political and Military Doctrine* (New York: Praeger, 1964).

Passy, Colonel, *Souvenirs*, 2 volumes (Monte Carlo: Raoul Solar, 1947).

Pathé, Anne-Marie and Théofilakis, Fabien, *La Captivité de guerre au XXe siècle: Des Archives, des histoires, des mémoires* (Paris: Armand Colin, 2012).

Paxton, Robert O., *Parades and Politics at Vichy: The French Officer Corps under Marshal Pétain* (Princeton: Princeton University Press, 1966).

Paxton, Robert O., *Vichy France: Old Guard and New Order, 1940–1944* (London: Barrie & Jenkins, 1972).

Paxton, Robert O., *L'armée de Vichy: Le corps des officiers francais, 1940–1944* (Paris: Tallandier, 2004).

Payne, Stanley G., *Franco and Hitler: Spain, Germany, and World War II* (New Haven and London: Yale University Press, 2008).

Péan, Pierre, *Le mystérieux Docteur Martin, 1895–1969* (Paris: Fayard, 1993).

Péan, Pierre, *Une jeunesse française: François Mitterand, 1934–1947* (Paris: Fayard, 1994).

Pedroncini, Guy (ed.), *Histoire militaire de la France*, tome 3, *De 1871 à 1940* (Paris: Presses universitaires de France, 1992).

Pellissier, Pierre, *De Lattre* (Paris: Perrin, 1998).
Pertinax (Henri Géraud), *The Gravediggers of France: Gamelin, Daladier, Reynaud, Pétain, and Laval. Military Defeat, Armistice, Counterrevolution* (Garden City, New York: Doubleday, Doran & Company, 1942).
Pesquer, Michel, "L'emploi des blindés français sur le front occidental d'août 1944 à mai 1945," Thèse du doctorat, Université de Lorraine, 2018.
Pigenet, Michel, *Les "Fabiens" des barricades au front (septembre 1944–mai 1945)* (Paris: Éditions l'Harmattan, 1995).
Pignato, Nicola and Cappellano, Filippo, *Gli autoveicoli da combattimento dell'Esercito Italiano*, volume secondo, *1940–1945* (Rome: Ufficio Storico dello Stato Maggiore dell'Esercito, 2002).
Piketty, Guillaume, *Pierre Brossolette: Un héros de la résistance* (Paris: Éditions Odile Jacob, 1998).
Piketty, Guillaume, *Français en résistance: Carnet de guerre, correspondances, journaux personnels* (Paris: Robert Laffont, 2009).
Pineau, Frédéric, *Femmes en guerre, 1940–1946* (Antony: ETAI, 2013).
Pitt, Barry, *The Crucible of War: Auchinleck's Command. The Definitive History of the Desert War*, vol. 2 (London: Cassell, 2001).
Planchais, Jean, *Une histoire politique de l'armée*, tome 2, *1940–1967: De de Gaulle à de Gaulle* (Paris: Éditions du Seuil, 1967).
Playfair, I. S. O., *The Mediterranean and the Middle East*, 5 volumes (London: HMSO, 1954).
Porch, Douglas, *Army and Revolution: The French Army 1815–1848* (London: Routledge and Kegan Paul, 1974).
Porch, Douglas, *The March to the Marne: The French Army 1871–1914* (Cambridge: Cambridge University Press, 1981).
Porch, Douglas, *The French Foreign Legion: A Complete History of the Legendary Fighting Force* (New York: Harper Collins, 1991).
Porch, Douglas, *The French Secret Services: From the Dreyfus Affair to the Gulf War* (Oxford: Oxford University Press, 1997).
Porch, Douglas, *Path to Victory: The Mediterranean Theater in World War II* (New York: Farrar, Straus, Giroux, 2004).
Porch, Douglas, *Counterinsurgency: Exposing the Myths of the New Way of War* (Cambridge: Cambridge University Press, 2013).
Post, Gaines Jr., *Dilemmas of Appeasement: British Deterrence and Defense 1934–1937* (Ithaca and London: Cornell University Press, 1993).
Poznanski, Renée, *Propagandes et Persécutions: La Résistance et le "problème juif" 1940–1944* (Paris: Fayard, 2008).
Queloz, Dimitry, *De la manœuvre napoléonienne à l'offensive à outrance: La tactique générale de l'armée française, 1871–1914* (Paris: Economica, 2009).
Rahn, Rudolf, *Un diplomat dans la tourmente* (Paris: France Empire, 1980).
Réau, Élisabeth du, *Édouard Daladier 1884–1970* (Paris: Fayard, 1993).
Recham, Belkacem, *Les Musulmans algériens dans l'armée française (1919–1945)* (Paris: Éditions l'Harmattan, 1996).
Reynaud, Paul, *Mémoires*, tome II, *Envers et contre tous: 7 mars 1936–16 juin 1940* (Paris: Flammarion, 1963).

Riedweg, Eugène, *Les "malgré nous": Histoire de l'incorporation de force des Alsaciens-Mosellans dans l'armée allemande* (Strasbourg: La Nuée Bleue, 2008).

Rigoulot, Pierre, *L'Alsace-Lorraine pendant la guerre 1939–1945* (Paris: Presses universitaires de France, 1997).

Roberts, Mary Louise, *Civilization without Sexes: Reconstructing Gender in Postwar France 1917–1927* (Chicago: University of Chicago Press, 1994).

Roberts, Mary Louise, *What Soldiers Do: Sex and the American GI in World War II France* (Chicago: University of Chicago Press, 2013).

Roberts, Sophie B., *Citizenship and Antisemitism in French Colonial Algeria, 1870–1962* (Cambridge and New York: Cambridge University Press, 2018).

Robertson, Charles L., *When Roosevelt Planned to Govern France* (Amherst and Boston: University of Massachusetts Press, 2011).

Rocolle, Pierre, *L'hécatombe des généraux* (Paris: Lavauzelle, 1980).

Rolf, David, *The Bloody Road to Tunis: Destruction of the Axis Forces in North Africa, November 1942–May 1943* (London: Greenhill Books and Pennsylvania Stackpole Books, 2001).

Rosner, Elliott J., "The Jedburghs: Combat Operations in the Finisterre Region of Brittany, France from July–September, 1944," Master's thesis, U.S. Army Command and Staff College, Fort Leavenworth, Kansas, 1990, https://apps.dtic.mil/dtic/tr/fulltext/u2/b148370.pdf.

Rostaing, Pierre, *Le Prix d'un serment, 1941–1945: Des plaines de Russie à l'enfer de Berlin* (Paris: La Table Ronde, 1975).

Rouquet, François, *Une Épuration ordinaire (1944–1949): Petits et grands collaborateurs de l'administration française* (Paris: CNRS Éditions, 2011).

Rouquet, François and Virgili, Fabrice, *Les françaises, les français et l'épuration (1940 à nos jours)* (Paris: Gallimard, 2018).

Rousso, Henry, *The Vichy Syndrome: History and Memory in France since 1944* (Cambridge, MA: Harvard University Press, 1991).

Sadoul, Georges, *Journal de Guerre (2 septembre 1939–20 juillet 1940)* (Paris: Éditions l'Harmattan, 1994).

Sainclivier, Jacqueline and Bougeard, Christian (eds.), *La Résistance et les Français: Enjeux stratégiques et environnement social* (Rennes: Presses universitaires de Rennes, 1995).

Saint-Martin, Gérard, *L'arme blindée française*, tome 2, *1940–1945: Dans le fracas des batailles* (Paris: Economica, 2000).

Sajer, Guy, *Le soldat oublié* (Paris: Robert Laffont, 1967).

Salan, Raoul, *Mémoires*, tome 1, *Fin d'un empire: "Le sens d'un engagement," juin1899–septembre 1946* (Paris: Presses de la Cité, 1970).

Sandler, Stanley, *Glad to See Them Come and Sorry to See Them Go: A History of the U.S. Army Tactical Civil Affairs/Military Government, 1775–1991* (self-published, 1994).

Sandler, Stanley, *"Cease Resistance: It's Good For You": A History of U.S. Army Combat Psychological Operations* (self-published, 1999).

Sapir, Jacques, Stora, Frank, and Mahé, Loïc, *1940: Et si la France avait continué la guerre . . .* (Paris: Tallandier, 2010).

Sartre, Jean-Paul, *The War Diaries of Jean-Paul Sartre: November 1939/March 1940* (New York: Pantheon Books, 1984).

Scheck, Raffael, *French Colonial Soldiers in German Captivity during World War II* (Cambridge: Cambridge University Press, 2014).

Scheipers, Sibylle, *Unlawful Combatants: A Genealogy of the Irregular Fighter* (Oxford: Oxford University Press, 2015).

Schiavon, Max, *Le général Alphonse Georges: Un destin inachevé* (Parçay-sur-Vienne: Éditions Anovi, 2009).

Schmitt, Jacques, *Journal d'un officier de tirailleurs 1944* (Paris: Bernard Giovannangeli éditeur, 1944).

Schreier, Joshua, *Arabs of the Jewish Faith: The Civilizing Mission in Colonial Algeria* (New Brunswick: Rutgers University Press, 2010).

Schrijvers, Peter, *The Crash of Ruin: American Combat Soldiers in Europe during WWII* (New York: New York University Press, 1998).

Servent, Pierre, *Le mythe Pétain: Verdun ou les tranchées de la mémoire* (Paris: Éditions CNRS, 2014).

Shneyer, Aron, *Pariahs among Pariahs: Soviet-Jewish POWs in German Captivity, 1941–1945* (Jerusalem: Yad Vashem, 2016).

Singer, Barnett, *Maxime Weygand: A Biography of the French General in Two World Wars* (Jefferson and London: McFarland & Company, 2008).

Smelser, Ronald and Davies, Edward J. II, *The Myth of the Eastern Front: The Nazi–Soviet War in American Popular Culture* (Cambridge: Cambridge University Press, 2008).

Smith, Denis Mack, *Mussolini* (New York: Knopf, 1986).

Smith, Jean Edward, *Lucius D. Clay: An American Life* (New York: Henry Holt, 1990).

Smith, Leonard V., *Between Mutiny and Obedience: The French Fifth Infantry Division in World War I* (Princeton: Princeton University Press, 1994).

Snyder, Timothy, *Bloodlands: Europe between Hitler and Stalin* (New York: Basic Books, 2010).

Soustelle, Jacques, *Envers et contre tout: Souvenirs et documents sur la France Libre*, tome 2, *D'Alger à Paris, 1942–1944* (Paris: Robert Laffont, 1950).

Spears, Sir Edward, *Assignment to Catastrophe*, volume II, *The Fall of France* (New York: A. A. Wyn, 1955).

Spears, Sir Edward, *Fulfilment of a Mission: The Spears Mission to Syria and Lebanon 1941–1944* (London: Leo Cooper, 1977).

Spivak, Marcel and Leoni, Armand, *Les forces françaises dans la lutte contre l'Axe en Afrique*, tome II, *La campagne de Tunisie, 1942–1943* (Vincennes: Service historique de l'armée de terre, 1985).

Stoler, Mark A., *Allies and Adversaries: The Joint Chiefs of Staff, the Grand Alliance, and U.S. Strategy in World War II* (Chapel Hill and London: University of North Carolina Press, 2000).

Stora, Benjamin, *Histoire de l'Algérie coloniale (1830–1954)* (Paris: Éditions La Découverte, 2004).

Strachan, Hew and Harris, Ruth, *The Utility of Military Force and Public Understanding in Today's Britain* (Santa Monica and Cambridge: RAND Corporation, 2020).

Surkis, Judith, *Sexing the Citizen: Morality and Masculinity in France, 1870–1920* (Ithaca: Cornell University Press, 2011).

Tenenbaum, Elie, *Partisans et centurions: Une histoire de la guerre irrégulière au XXe siècle* (Paris: Perrin, 2018).
Thomas, Martin, *The French Empire at War, 1940–1945* (Manchester: University of Manchester Press, 2007).
Thomas, Martin and Toye, Richard, *Arguing about Empire: Imperial Rhetoric in Britain and France, 1882–1956* (Oxford: Oxford University Press, 2017).
Thorne, Christopher, *The Approach of War 1938–39* (New York: St. Martin's Press, 1967).
Tombs, Robert and Chabal, Emile (eds.), *Britain and France in Two World Wars: Truth, Myth and Memory* (London: Bloomsbury, 2013).
Torrie, Julie S., *German Soldiers and the Occupation of France* (Cambridge: Cambridge University Press, 2018).
Toye, Richard, *The Roar of the Lion: The Untold Story of Churchill's World War II Speeches* (Oxford: Oxford University Press, 2013).
Travers, Susan, *Tomorrow to Be Brave* (London: Corgi Press, 2001).
Truscott, Lucien, *Command Missions: A Personal Story* (New York: Dutton, 1954).
Tucker, Spencer C. (ed.), *The Definitive Encyclopedia of World War II* (Santa Barbara and Denver: ABC-CLIO, 2016).
Turpin, Frédéric, *De Gaulle, les gaullistes et l'Indochine* (Paris: Les Indes Savantes, 2005).
United States, Department of State, *Peace and War: United States Foreign Policy, 1931–1941* (Washington, D.C.: US Government Printing Office, 1943).
Vaisset, Thomas, *L'Amiral d'Argenlieu: Le moine-soldat du gaullisme* (Paris: Belin, 2017).
Valode, Philippe and Chauvy, Gérard, *La Gestapo française* (Paris: Acropole, 2018).
Vergez-Chaignon, Bénédicte, *Histoire de l'épuration* (Paris: Larousse, 2010).
Vergez-Chaignon, Bénédicte, *Pétain* (Paris: Perrin, 2014).
Vergnon, Gilles, *Le Vercors: Histoire et mémoire d'un maquis* (Paris: Les éditions de l'Atelier/Éditions Ouvrières, 2002).
Verity, Hugh, *We Landed by Moonlight: Secret RAF Landings in France, 1940–1944* (Manchester: AirData Publications Limited, 1995).
Vernejoul, Henri de and Durlewanger, Armand, *Autopsie d'une Victoire morte* (Colmar: Saep, 1970).
Vernet, J., *Le réarmament et la réorganization de l'armée de terre française, (1943–1946)* (Vincennes: Ministère de la défense, État-major de l'armée de terre, Service historique, 1980).
Vigneras, Marcel, *United States Army in World War II: Rearming the French* (Washington, D.C.: Center of Military History, United States Army, 1989).
Vincent, Jean-Noël, *Les forces françaises dans la lutte contre l'Axe en Afrique*, tome I, *Les forces françaises libres en Afrique 1940–1943* (Vincennes: Service historique de l'armée de terre, 1983).
Vinen, Richard, *France, 1934–1970* (New York: St. Martin's Press, 1996).
Vinen, Richard, *The Unfree French* (New Haven: Yale University Press, 2007).
Virgili, Fabrice, *La France "virile": Des femmes tondues à la libération* (Paris: Payot, 2000).

Wall, Irwin M., *The United States and the Making of Postwar France, 1945–1954* (Cambridge: Cambridge University Press, 1991).
Weathersby, Major Russell A., "The Field Artillery Group in Support of Corps and Field Army, 1942–1953," Master of Arts, Command and General Staff College, Fort Leavenworth, Kansas, 1965.
Weber, Eugen, *The Hollow Years: France in the 1930s* (New York: W. W. Norton, 1994).
Weber, Thomas, *Hitler's First War: Adolf Hitler, the Men of the List Regiment, and the First World War* (Oxford: Oxford University Press, 2010).
Weiss, Stéphan, *Les forces françaises de l'Ouest: Forces françaises oubliées? 1944–1945* (Paris: Les Indes Savantes, 2019).
Weygand, Maxime, *Mémoires*, tome III, *Rappelé au service* (Paris: Flammarion, 1950).
Wheeler, James Scott and Atkinson, Rick, *Jacob L. Devers: A General's Life* (Lexington: University Press of Kentucky, 2015).
Wieviorka, Annette, *The Era of the Witness* (Ithaca: Cornell University Press, 2006).
Wieviorka, Olivier, *Une Certaine idée de la Résistance: Défense de France 1940–1949* (Paris: Éditions du Seuil, 1995).
Wieviorka, Olivier, *Normandy: The Landings to the Liberation of Paris* (Cambridge, MA: Harvard University Press, 2008).
Wieviorka, Olivier, *Histoire de la Résistance 1940–1945* (Paris: Perrin, 2013).
Wieviorka, Olivier, *Une histoire de la résistance en Europe occidentale* (Paris: Perrin, 2017).
Wilkinson, Peter and Astley, Joan Bright, *Gubbins & SOE* (London: Leo Cooper, 1993).
Willis, Frank Roy, *The French in Germany 1945–1949* (Stanford: Stanford University Press, 1962).
Wolfe, Robert (ed.), *Americans as Proconsuls: United States Military Government in Germany and Japan, 1944–1952* (Carbondale and Edwardsville: Southern Illinois University Press, 1977).
Young, Robert J., *In Command of France: French Foreign Policy and Military Planning, 1933–1940* (Cambridge, MA: Harvard University Press, 1978).
Young, Robert J., *France and the Origins of the Second World War* (New York: St. Martin's Press, 1996).
Zahner, Armand, *Le Soldat Honteux: J'était un "Malgré-Nous"* (Mulhouse: Éditions Salvator, 1972).
Earl Ziemke, The *U.S. Army in the Occupation of Germany*, Part I (Grandview Heights: Bibliogov, 2013).
Zeldin, Theodore, *France 1848–1945*, 2 vols. (Oxford: Oxford University Press, 1977).

Articles

Abzac-Epezy, Claude d', "Épuration, dégagements, exclusions. Les réductions d'éffectifs dans l'armée française (1940–1947)," *Vingtième Siècle, Revue d'histoire*, 59 (1998), 62–75.
Abzac-Epezy, Claude d', "La pensée militaire de Camille Rougeron: Innovations et marginalité," *Revue française de science politique*, 54/5 (2004), 761–779.

Abzac-Epezy, Claude d', "La France face au rapatriement des prisonniers de guerre allemands," *Guerres mondiales et conflits contemporains*, 2009/1, no. 233 (2009), 93–108.

Abzac-Epezy, Claude d', "L'armée française et les prisonniers de guerre de l'Axe," in Natalie Genet-Rouffiac (ed.), *Les prisonniers de guerre aux personnes capturées*, Actes de la journée d'études organisée par le service de la Défense en mai 2007, SHD collection d'études 2010, 39–54.

Ageron, Charles-Robert, "La Survivance d'un mythe: La puissance par l'empire colonial (1944–1947)," *Revue française d'Histoire d'Outre-Mer*, LXXII, no. 269 (1985), 387–403.

Alexander, Martin, "After Dunkirk: The French Army's Performance against 'Case Red,' 25 May to 25 June 1940," *War in History*, 14/2 (2007), 219–264.

Aouate, Yves-Claude, "La place de l'Algérie dans le projet antijuif de Vichy," *Revue française d'histoire d'outre-mer*, 80/301 (1993), 599–613.

Barasz, Johanna, "De Vichy à la Résistance: Les vichysto-résistants 1940–1944," *Guerres mondiales et conflits contemporains*, 2011/2, no. 242 (2011), 27–50, www.cairn.info/revue-guerres-mondiales-et-conflits-contemporains-2011-2-page-27.htm#no14.

Baris, Tommaso, "Le corps expéditionnnaire français en Italie. Violence des 'libérateurs' durant l'été 1944," *Vingtième Siècle. Revue d'histoire*, 93 (January–March 2007), 47–61.

Bédarida, François, "L'histoire de la résistance. Lectures de hiers, chantiers de demain," *Vingtième Siècle. Revue d'histoire*, 1986/11 (1986), 75–90.

Belazzouz, Larbi, "Les Républicains Espagnols en Algérie de 1939 à 1962. Vicissitudes d'une communauté dans la colonie," *Oussour Al Jadida*, 7/26 (Winter–Spring 2016–2017), 102–114.

Boudot, François, "Aspects de l'histoire de la captivité," *L'Actualité de l'histoire*, no. 10 (January 1955), 22–35.

Boudot, François, "Pour une histoire de la captivité: Souvenirs de qualité," *Annales. Economies, Sociétés, Civilisations*, 12e année, no. 1 (1957), 132–140.

Bruneau, Jean-Baptiste and Vaisset, Thomas, "Déchirements, déclassment et relèvement (1939–1945)," in Philippe Vial (ed.), "L'histoire d'une révolution. La Marine depuis 1870," *Études marines*, no. 4 (March 2013), 82–104.

Burgess, Greg, "The Repatriation of Soviet Prisoners and Displaced Persons from the Auvergne after the Second World War," 169–181, https://h-france.net/rude/wp-content/uploads/2017/08/vol7_Burgess.pdf.

Burgess, Greg, "Remaking Asylum in Post-war France, 1944–52," *Journal of Contemporary History* 46/3 (2014), 556–576.

Callender, Harold, "Derrien on Trial at Secret Session," *New York Times*, 11 May 1944, www.nytimes.com/1944/05/11/archives/derrien-on-trial-at-secret-session-defense-protests-that-admiral.html.

Campbell, D'Ann, "Women in Combat: The World War II Experience in the United States, Great Britain, Germany, and the Soviet Union," *Journal of Military History*, 57/2 (April 1993), 301–323.

Capdevila, Luc, "La mobilisation des femmes dans la France combattante (1940–1945)," *Clio. Histoire, femmes et sociétés*, 12/2000 (2000), unpaginated, https://journals.openedition.org/clio/187.

Capdevila, Luc, "The Quest for Masculinity in a Defeated France, 1940–1945," *Contemporary European History*, 10/3 (November 2001), 423–445.

Capdevila, Luc, "L'identité masculine et les fatigues de la guerre (1914–1945)," *Vingtième Siècle. Revue d'histoire*, 2002/3, no. 75 (2002), 97–108, www.cairn.info/revue-vingtieme-siecle-revue-d-histoire-2002-3-page-97.htm.

Capps-Tunwell, David, Passmore, David G., and Harrison, Stephan, "An Evaluation of Allied Intelligence in the Tactical Bombing of German Supply Depots during the Normandy Campaign, 1944," *The Journal of Military History*, 84/3 (July 2020), 825–842.

Celaya, Diego Gaspar, "Portrait d'oubliés. L'engagement des Espagnols dans les Forces françaises libres, 1940–1945," *Revue historique des armées*, 265 (2011), 46–55, https://journals.openedition.org/rha/7345.

Celaya, Diego Gaspar, "De l'oubli, des mythes, de l'histoire. Histoire et mémoire des volontaires espagnols dans Résistance française," *Historiografías*, 12 (July–December 2016), 70–86.

Chin, Rachel, "After the Fall. British Strategy and the Preservation of the Franco-British Alliance in 1940," *Journal of Contemporary History*, 55/2 (2019), 1–19, https://journals.sagepub.com/doi/abs/10.1177/0022009419846951.

Crang, Jeremy, "'Come into the Army, Maud': Women, Military Conscription, and the Markham Inquiry," *Defence Studies*, 8 (2008), 381–395.

Crémieux-Brilhac, Jean-Louis, "Les Glières," *Vingtième Siècle. Revue d'histoire*, no. 45 (January–March 1995), 54–66.

Crémieux-Brilhac, Jean-Louis, "Une stratégie militaire pour la Résistance: Le Bloc Planning et l'insurrection nationale," *Espoir*, no. 139 (2004), www.charles-de-gaulle.org/wp-content/uploads/2017/10/Une-strategie-militaire-pour-la-Resistance.pdf.

Creswell, Michael and Trachtenberg, Marc, "France and the German Question, 1945–1955," *Journal of Cold War Studies*, 5/3 (Summer 2003), 5–28.

Daddis, Gregory A., "Mansplaining Vietnam: Male Veterans and America's Popular Image of the Vietnam War," *The Journal of Military History*, 82/1 (January 2018), 181–207.

Eismann, Gaël, "Maintenir l'ordre. Le MBF et la sécurité locale en France occupée," *Vingtième Siècle. Revue d'histoire*, no. 98 (April–June 2008), 125–139, www.cairn.info/revue-vingtieme-siecle-revue-d-histoire-2008-2-page-125.htm.

Fauroux, Camille, "'Souvenirs d'une petite amie en captivité': Ouvrières françaises et prisonniers de guerre à Berlin entre 1940 et 1945," *Guerres mondiales et conflits contemporains* (April–June 2019), 27–46.

Fieseler, Beate, Hampf, M. Michaela, and Schwarzkopf, Jutta, "Gendering Combat: Military Women's Status in Britain, the United States, and the Soviet Union during the Second World War," *Women's Studies International Forum*, 47 (2014), 115–126.

Fishman, Sarah, "Grand Delusions: The Unintended Consequences of Vichy France's Prisoner of War Propaganda," *Journal of Contemporary History*, 26/2 (April 1991), 229–254.

Fitzpatrick, Sheila, "The Motherland Calls: "Soft" Repatriation of Soviet Citizens from Europe, 1945–1953," *The Journal of Modern History* 90/2 (June 2018), 323–350.

Funk, Arthur Layton, "Les Américains et les britanniques dans la libération de la Corse," *Guerres mondiales et conflits contemporaines*, 174 (1994), 7–21.

Garraud, Philippe, "Le rôle de la 'doctrine défensive' dans la défaite de 1940: Une explication trop simple et partielle," *Guerres Mondiales et Conflits Contemporains*, no. 214 (April 2004), 97–123.

Gildea, Robert, "Resistance, Reprisals, and Community in Occupied France," *Transactions of the Royal Historical Society*, 13 (2003), 163–185.

Gras, Général Yves, "18 juin 1945. Le défilé de la victoire," http://ekladata.com/kdhGQ1qYOiIRpJvO1UgGm5QiYJs/1eredfl-n-51-8-Mai-18-Juin-1945-La-France-Libre-fete-sa-Victoire.pdf.

Gurley, Franklin L., "Politique contre stratégie: La défense de Strasbourg en décembre 1944," *Guerres mondiales et conflits contemporains*, no. 166 (April 1992), 89–114.

Hagemann, Karen, "Mobilizing Women for War: The History, Historiography, and Memory of German Women's War Service in Two World Wars," *Journal of Military History*, 75/4 (2011), 1055–1094.

Handel, Michael, "Intelligence and the Problem of Strategic Surprise," *The Journal of Strategic Studies*, 7/3 (September 1984), 229–281.

Hofstadter, Richard, "The Paranoid Style of American Politics," *Harper's Magazine* (November 1964), 77–86.

Humbert, Laure, "French Politics of Relief and International Aid: France, UNRRA and Rescue of European Displaced Persons in Postwar Germany, 1945–47," *Journal of Contemporary History*, 51/3 (July 2016), 606–634.

Jackson, Julian, "General de Gaulle and His Enemies: Anti-Gaullism in France since 1940," *Transactions of the Royal Historical Society*, 9 (1999), 43–65.

Jackson, Peter, "Post-war Politics and the Historiography of French Strategy and Diplomacy before the Second World War," *History Compass*, 4/5 (2006), 870–905.

Jancar, Barbara, "Women in the Yugoslav National Liberation Movement: An Overview," *Studies in Comparative Communism*, 14/2 (1981), 143–164.

Jauneau, Élodie, "Des femmes dans la France combattante pendant la deuxième guerre mondiale: Le corps des volontaires françaises et le groupe Rochambeau," *Genre et histoire*, 3 (Autumn 2008), https://journals.openedition.org/genrehistoire/373.

Jones, Edgar and Wessely, Simon, "British Prisoners-of-War: From Resilience to Psychological Vulnerability: Reality or Perception," *Twentieth Century British History*, 21/2 (2010), 163–183.

Lambauer, Barbara, "Un engagement pour l'Europe allemande: La collaboration," in Aglan, Alya and Frank, Robert (eds.), *1937–1947: La guerre-monde* (Paris: Gallimard/Folio, 2015), pp. 1109–1178.

Leconte, Robin, "La Division de Marche de Constantine face au débarquement allié en novembre 1942: Entre obéissance et résistances aux ordres, la mécanique du basculement," Militaires en résistance pendant la deuxième guerre mondiale, Colloque internationale, Château de Vincennes, 13–14 June 2018.

Le Gac, Julie, "L''étrange défaite' du divorce? (1940–1946)," *Vingtième Siècle. Revue d'histoire* 2005/4, no. 88 (2005), 49–62.

Le Gac, Julie, "Le corps expéditionnaire français et l'armée américaine en Italie (1943–1944): Une alliance asymétrique," *Revue historique des armées*, 258 (2010), 57–66, https://journals.openedition.org/rha/6923.

Le Gac, Julie, "'Le Mal Napolitain': Les Alliés et la prostitution à Naples (1943–1944)," *Genre et Histoire*, 15 (Autumn 2014–Spring 2015), https://journals.openedition.org/genrehistoire/2154.

Lesouef, Pierre, "La crise de novembre 1942 en Afrique française du nord et la campagne du Tunisie," in Colloque International, *Les armées française pendant la seconde guerre mondiale 1939–1945* (Paris: École nationale supérieure de techniques avancées, 1985), 305–315.

Lieb, Peter, "Wehrmacht, Waffen-SS et Sipo/SD: La répression allemande en France 1943–1944," in *La répression en France à l'été 1944*, Actes du colloque organisé par la Foundation de la Résistance et la ville de Saint-Amand-Montrond, Saint-Amand-Montrond le mercredi 8 juin 2005, www.fondationresistance.org/documents/ee/Doc00004-002.pdf.

Lieb, Peter and Paxton, Robert O., "Maintenir l'ordre en France occupée. Combien de divisions?," *Vingtième Siècle. Revue d'histoire* 2011/4, no. 112 (2011), 115–126.

Lilly, J. and Le Roy, François, "L'armée américaine et les viols en France: Juin 1944–mai 1945," *Vingtième Siècle. Revue d'histoire*, 2002/3, no. 75 (2002), 109–121.

Lyautey, Hubert, "Du rôle social de l'officier," *Revue des deux mondes*, 3e période, 104 (1891), 443–459.

Major, Patrick, "'Our Friend Rommel': The *Wehrmacht* as 'Worthy Enemy' in Postwar British Popular Culture," *German History*, 26/4 (2008), 520–535.

Matsunuma Miho, "La politique du gouvernement de Vichy vis-à-vis des militaires coloniaux rapatriables," *Outre-mers*, 96/362–363 (2009), 227–240.

McNab, Chris, "Cheap Shot: How the Sten Gun Saved Britain," *HistoryNet* (Autumn 2019), www.historynet.com/cheap-shot-how-the-sten-gun-saved-britain.htm.

Michalon, Lieutenant-colonel Roger, "L'amalgame F.F.I.–1ère Armée et 2ème D.B.," in *Colloque international d'histoire de la 2ème guerre mondiale, 28–31 octobre 1974* (Paris: Ministère de la guerre, État-major de l'armée de terre, Service historique, 1974), 1–55.

Miot, Claire, "Combattantes sans combattre? Le cas des ambulancières dans la première armée française (1944–1945)," *Revue historique des armées* 272 (2013), 25–35.

Miot, Claire, "La retrait des tirailleurs sénégalais de la première armée française en 1944. Hérésie stratégique, bricolage politique ou conservatism coloniale?," *Vingtième Siècle. Revue d'histoire*, no. 125 (2015), 77–89.

Monsuez, Jean-Jacques, "Les sections sanitaires automobiles féminines," *Revue historique des armées*, 247 (2007), 98–113.

Moore, Bob, "Unruly Allies: British Problems with French Treatment of Axis Prisoners of War 1943–1945," *War in History*, 7/2 (April 2000), 180–198.

Morley, Neville, "Decadence as a Theory of History," *New Literary History*, 35/4 (Autumn 2004), 573–585.

Morris, Madeline, "By Force of Arms: Rape, War, and Military Culture," *Duke Law Journal*, 4/45 (February 1996), 651–781, https://scholarship.law.duke.edu/dlj/vol45/iss4/1.

Moullec, Gaël, "Alliés ou ennemis? Le GUPVI-NKVD, le Komintern et les 'Malgré-nous'. Le destin des prisonniers de guerre français en URSS (1942–1955)," *Cahiers du Monde russe*, 42/2–4 (April–December 2001), 667–678.

Nord, Philip, "Vichy et les survivances: Les Compagnons de France," *Revue d'histoire moderne et contemporaine*, 2012/4, no. 59-4 (2012), 125–163.

Nye, Robert A., "Neurasthenia and the Culture of Sport in Belle Epoque France," *Journal of Contemporary History*, 17/1 (January 1982), 51–68.

Offen, Karen, "Depopulation, Nationalism, and Feminism in Fin-de-Siècle France," *The American Historical Review*, 89/3 (June 1984), 648–676.

O'Hara, Vincent, "Operation Torch November 1942," in *Revue algérienne de prospective & d'études stratégiques* (2017), 27–54.

Oliel, Jacob, "Les camps de Vichy en Afrique du Nord (1940–1944)," *Revue d'histoire de la Shoah*, 2013/1, no. 198 (2013), 227–244.

Patch, John, "Fortuitous Endeavor. Intelligence and Deception in Operation TORCH," *Naval War College Review*, 61/4 (Autumn 2008), 73–97.

Piketty, Guillaume, "Héros de la France libre – héros de la Résistance," *Revue de la France Libre*, no. 285 (1994), www.france-libre.net/sacrifice-brossolette/.

Piketty, Guillaume, "Français libre à l'épreuve de la libération," *Revue historique des armées*, 245 (2006), 27–35.

Piketty, Guillaume, "Souffances et ambiguïtes de la défaite," *Hypothèses* 2008/1, no. 11 (2008), 341–348.

Piketty, Guillaume, "From the Capitoline Hill to the Tarpeian Rock? Free French Coming out of War," *European Review of History*, 25/2 (2018), 354–373.

Regnault, Jean-Marc and Kurtovich, Ismet, "Les ralliements du Pacifique en 1940. Entre legend gaulliste, enjeux stratégiques mondiaux et rivalités Londres/Vichy," *Revue d'histoire modern et contemporaine*, 2002/4, no. 49-4 (2002), 71–90.

Roberts, Sophie, "Jews, Vichy, and the Algiers Insurrection of 1942," *Holocaust Studies: A Journal of Culture and History*, 12/3 (Winter 2006), 63–88.

Sanders, Paul, "Anatomie d'une implantation SS – Helmut Knochen et la police nazie en France, 1940–1944," *Revue d'histoire de la Shoah*, 165 (January–April 1999), 111–145.

Schöttler, Peter, "Trois formes de collaboration: L'Europe et la réconciliation franco-allemande – à travers la carrière de Gustav Krukenberg, chef de la 'Division Charlemagne,'" *Allemagne d'aujourd'hui*, 207 (2014), 225–246.

Scianna, Bastian Matteo, "Rommel Almighty? Italian Assessments of the 'Desert Fox' during and after the Second World War," *The Journal of Military History*, 83/1 (January 2018), 125–145.

Shields, J. G., "Charlemagne's Crusaders. French Collaborators in Arms," *French Cultural Studies*, 18/1 (February 2007), 83–105.

Soucy, Robert J., "The Nature of Fascism in France," *Journal of Contemporary History*, 1/1 (1966), 27–55.

Storer, Mrs. Bellamy and Storer, Maria Longworth, "The Decadence of France," *The North American Review*, 191/651 (February 1910), 168–184.
Strachan, Hew, "Strategy and Democracy," *Survival*, 62/2(2020), 51–82.
Taguieff, Pierre-André, "L'invention du 'complot Judéo-Maçonnique'. Avatars d'un mythe apocalyptique moderne," *Revue d'Histoire de la Shoah*, 2013/1, no. 98 (2013), 23–97.
Tenenbaum, Elie, "French Exception or Western Variation? A Historical Look at the French Irregular Way of War," *Journal of Strategic Studies*, 40/4 (2017), 554–576.
Thomas, Martin, "After Mers-el-Kebir: The Armed Neutrality of the Vichy Navy," *English Historical Review*, 112/447 (June 1997), 643–670.
Thomas, Martin, "France and the Czechoslovak Crisis," *Diplomacy and Statecraft*, 10 (1999), 122–159.
Thomas, Martin, "The Vichy Government and French Colonial Prisoners of War, 1940–1944," *French Historical Studies*, 25/4 (Fall 2002), 657–692.
Trevor-Roper, H. R., "Fernand Braudel, the *Annales*, and the Mediterranean," *The Journal of Modern History*, 44/4 (December 1972), 468–479.
Varley, Karine, "'Laboratory of Liberation.' Lessons for France from the Liberation of Corsica," https://francehistory.wordpress.com/2014/05/31/laboratory-of-liberation-lessons-for-france-from-the-liberation-of-corsica/.
Varley, Karine, "Defending Sovereignty without Collaboration: Vichy and the Italian Fascist Threats of 1940–1942," *French History*, 33/3 (2019), 422–443.
Vial, Philippe (ed.), "L'histoire d'une révolution. La Marine depuis 1870," *Études marines*, no. 4 (March 2013).
Virgili, Fabrice, "Les viols commis par l'armée allemande en France (1940–1944)," *Vingtième Siècle. Revue d'histoire*, 2016/2, no. 130 (2016), 103–120.
Weber, Eugen, "Gymnastics and Sports in *Fin-de-Siècle* France: Opium of the Classes?," *American Historical Review*, 76/1 (February 1971), 70–98.
Weber, Eugen, "France's Downfall," *The Atlantic* (October 2001), www.theatlantic.com/magazine/archive/2001/10/frances-downfall/302317/.
Weiss, Stéphane, "Quotidien et moral des combattants volontaires des sièges de la Pointe de Grave, de Royan et de La Rochelle en 1944–1945," *Écrits d'Ouest*, no. 19 (2011), 127–146.
Weiss, Stéphane, "La régularisation des formations combattantes FFI engagés lors des sièges de la Pointe de Grave, de Royan et de La Rochelle en 1944–1945," *Ecrits d'Ouest*, no. 20 (2012), 175–192.
Weiss, Stéphane, "Recréer une artillerie française en 1945: La part belle à la récupération," *Révue historique des armées*, 274 (2014), 95–107.
Wood, Elisabeth, "Rape as a Practice of War: Toward a Typology of Political Violence," *Politics & Society* 46/4 (2018), 523–537.
Xueref, Louis, "Mémoires d'outre-mer. 1942–1943 (Autour de la campagne de Tunisie) Souvenirs d'une tranche de vie" (1999), http://tunisie-france.pagesperso-orange.fr/souvenirs_souvenirs.htm.

Index